THE PRACTICAL GUIDE TO PRACTICALLY EVERYTHING

THE PRACTICAL GUIDE TO PRACTICALLY EVERYTHING

PETER BERNSTEIN & CHRISTOPHER MA
EDITORS

RANDOM HOUSE NEW YORK

In the preparation of this book, every effort has been made to offer current, correct, and clearly expressed information. Nonetheless, inadvertent errors can occur and information can change. The information in the text is intended to afford general guidelines on matters of interest. Accordingly, the information in this book is not intended to serve as legal, accounting, tax, or medical advice. Readers are encouraged to consult with professional advisers concerning specific matters before making any decision, and the editors and publisher disclaim any responsibility for positions taken by readers in individual cases or for any misunderstanding on the part of readers.

 Published in the United States by Random House, Inc., New York, and simultaneously in Canada by Random House of Canada Limited, Toronto.

Library of Congress Cataloguing-in-Publication Data is available.

ISBN# 0-679-75491-1

Manufactured in the United States of America on acid-free paper.

98765432

First Edition

To our families

Amy, Elisabeth, Alexander, and Nicky

Nathalie, Olivia, and Rohan

"He that lives well is learned enough."

Ben Franklin
Poor Richard's Almanac

TABLE OF CONTENTS

THE PRACTICAL GUIDE

TABLE OF CONTENTS

THE PRACTICAL GUIDE

TABLE OF CONTENTS

THE PRACTICAL GUIDE

TABLE OF CONTENTS

THE PRACTICAL GUIDE

CONTRIBUTORS

Editors: Peter Bernstein and Christopher Ma

Editorial Design: Janice Olson
Managing Editor: Luke Mitchell
Staff Editors: Anna Mulrine and Jill Hockman
Design: Rob Covey
Maps and Illustrations: Steve McCracken
Charts and Graphs: David Merrill

Reporters: Sasha Abramsky, Julia Angwin, Darcy Bacon, Sarah Bacon, Alison Bishop, Colleen Brennan, Eva Canoutas, Andrea Chipman, Rachel Englehart, Lavinia Edmunds, Susannah Zak Figura, Arti Finn, Sarah Halsted, Maureen Heffernan, Sarah Hodder, Anna Isgro, Jason Kaplan, Ben Klasky, Doug Lederman, Christina Lowery, Jeremy Milk, Booth Moore, Tim Noonan, Mark Pener, Rick Phipps, Jennifer Pitts, Galt Niederhofer, Rachel A. Schwartz, Sara Shay, Annie Silberman, Molly Tschida, Susan Gregory Thomas, Josh Tyrangiel, Alex Ulam, Leonard Wiener, Ruth Yodaiken, Ronald Zizmor

Copy Editors: Vicky Macintyre, Patricia Abdale, Michael Burke, Eva Young
Production: Mary Yee

INTRODUCTION

From the editors

DEAR READER,

In the current age of information overload and racing clocks, when vitamins are heralded one day and discounted the next and shopping for a mortgage can be affected by the falling dollar and the federal deficit, it's no wonder that you may be confused by all the conflicting stories in the media that appear to apply to you. What's needed once a year is a practical, expert, no-nonsense guide to the most important developments in everything from health and nutrition to money management and career planning, travel, entertainment, and consumer technology. That's why we decided to create *The Practical Guide to Practically Everything*—to provide you with authoritative information and expert views on all the subjects that could really make a difference in your daily life. Our Expert Picks, Tips, Lists, Q & As, and Sources will cut through all the smoke and give you the bottom line on what you need to know to navigate the '90s with peace of mind and money in your pocket.

In doing so, we take as our inspiration Benjamin Franklin and the many other almanac makers who made this form a must-read for earlier American generations. In those early years, the historian Marion Barber Stowell has written, "the almanac had no substitute. From its pages the farmer and his family could learn what to plant, when and how to tend the sick, and how to care for their stock. For the man of affairs, it was an indispensable aid, a protection, a measure of security, a help meet, a crutch, a veritable companion."

For all the change since then, the roads we travel now are even less well-marked and full of far more forks than in Ben Franklin's heyday. We hope this book will be a compass that will help you find your way.

Peter Bernstein and Christopher Ma

CHAPTER ONE

MONEY

EXPERT QUOTES

"What makes sense in business also makes sense in stocks."

—Warren Buffett, the second richest man in America

Page 18

"Planets affect the market through electromagnetic fields."

—Arch Crawford, Wall Street's best-known astrologer

Page 21

"Finally, there's been a value established for Elvis."

—Jimmy Velvet, former lounge singer and collector of Presley memorabilia

Page 92

THE YEAR AHEAD: **EXPECT** prosperous times and a bull market through 1996... **WATCH** emerging stock markets in China, India, and South Africa... **BET** that investment clubs will continue to blossom... **BEWARE** newsletters that say they beat the market... **KEEP AN EYE ON** mutual funds fees... **FORGET** about an '80s-style housing boom... **ANTICIPATE** rising prices for vacation homes, especially in mountain areas... **GET READY** for the great flat tax debate...

INVESTING

A GET-RICH SLOWLY SCHEME

Consider the case of Louie the Loser; stocks made him a winner

Buy low, sell high—it's the dream of all investors hoping to strike gold in the stock market. The strategy sounds simple enough, but, as most investors know, timing the market is elusive at best. Now it turns out that timing may not matter much after all. Analysts at Capital Research and Management Co., a mutual fund company, created Louie the Loser, an investor with the world's worst timing. Every year for 20 years, Louie pumped $5,000 into Investment Co. of America, an actual fund managed by Capital Research. Each year Louie invested at the worst possible time—the day that the Dow Jones average hit its peak for the year.

How did Louie fare? He was hardly a loser. After 20 years, Louie's $100,000 grew to $441,000—a respectable average annual return of 13.3 percent. By comparison, if a Willie the Winner had invested $5,000 a year on the day the market hit its annual low, he would have shown a 14.9 percent return, only slightly better than Louie's. Small wonder that shrewd investors, like Warren Buffett (see page 18), advise ignoring the day-to-day gyrations of the market, preferring a simple buy-and-hold strategy for stock investing.

When devising your overall investment strategy, the best approach is to allocate your money among different investments, based on factors like your age, income and when you'll need the money. To manage the risk of stock market ups and downs, a basic buy-and-hold strategy known as dollar cost averaging can help. By investing a set dollar amount regularly, say, $200 once a month, you get more shares when stock prices are low and fewer when prices are high. Over time, the strategy reduces your average cost per share, improving your chances of becoming a slow but steady winner.

History shows that stocks are sturdy. Measure stocks against bonds, cash, diamonds, you name it, and in the long run, stocks win. Stashing your cash in houses, gold, oil, or in collectibles like stamps and diamonds, for example, is considered smart during times of high inflation, which can hurt stocks and bonds. But not over the long haul, says R. S. Salomon Jr., founder of the Stamford, Conn. investment management firm STI Management. After tracking the returns of different assets since the late 1970s, Salomon found that returns on tangible assets fluctuate wildly from year to year(see table, page 4). Silver may be hot

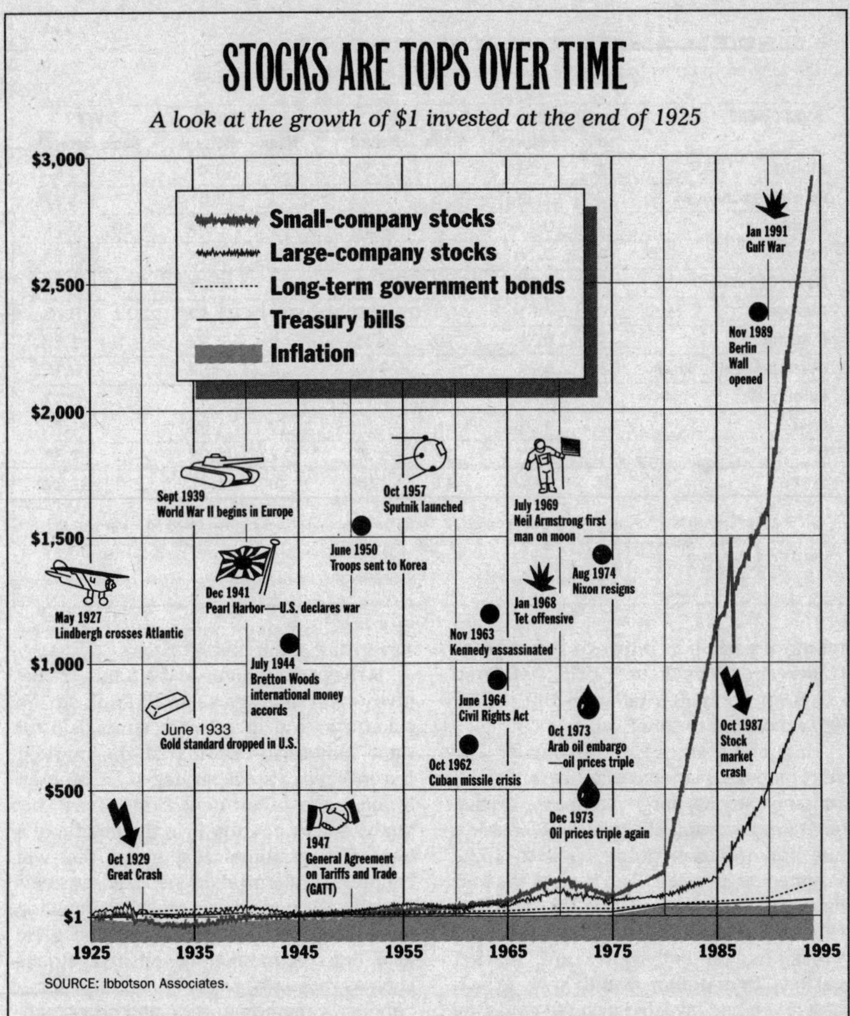

one year, farmland the next. But in the long run, financial assets—stocks, bonds, and even plain old cash—beat out collectibles and hard assets. This exercise, says Salomon, proves that how you allocate your portfolio among broad categories is important, probably more so than which stocks or bonds or hard assets you buy.

What happens if you pit stocks against cash over the long term? Again, stocks are tops. A cash investment is money invested in three-month Treasuries or a first-rate money market fund, not the emergency reserve you keep on hand for a rainy day. Looking back 50 years, cash has beat out stocks only 10 times, according to Ibbotson Associates. One of those rare periods was between August 1993 and the end of 1994, when the returns on the 30-day Treasury bill outperformed the Standard & Poor 500 stock index by three percentage points and the 20-year Treasury bond by 15 percentage points. Usually, though, periods when cash is king have not lasted longer than 24 months. Over the long term, cash has been a loser. After accounting for

TANGIBLE ASSETS VS. STOCKS AND BONDS

How long do you plan to invest? For long-term stability, stocks are the champ.

INVESTMENT	20 YEARS		10 YEARS		5 YEARS		1 YEAR	
	Rank	Return[1]	Rank	Return[1]	Rank	Return[1]	Rank	Return[1]
Stocks	1	13.1%	1	15.5%	2	10.4%	6	2.6%
Foreign exchange[2]	2	11.9%	3	13.0%	1	10.6%	5	3.3%
Bonds	3	10.2%	2	14.1%	3	9.9%	10	0.7%
Stamps	4	9.1%	10	–0.9%	11	1.1%	8	1.9%
3-month T-bills	5	8.3%	4	6.7%	4	5.6%	4	4.3%
Diamonds	6	7.9%	5	5.9%	9	1.4%	11	0.0%
Housing	7	6.3%	6	4.1%	6	2.9%	9	1.8%
Consumer Price Index	8	5.7%	7	3.6%	5	3.5%	7	2.1%
Farmland[3]	9	4.6%	9	–0.7%	7	2.4%	2	6.4%
Gold	10	4.5%	8	–0.2%	10	1.3%	3	4.7%
Oil	11	2.9%	12	–5.2%	12	–1.9%	12	–9.8%
Silver	12	1.0%	11	–4.9%	8	1.9%	1	31.1%

NOTES: 1. Average annual return as of the end of June 1994. 2. Combines money market returns with change in exchange rates. 3. Excludes farming income. SOURCE: R.S. Salomon, Jr. STI Management, Stamford, Conn. Reprinted by permission of *Forbes* magazine. © Forbes, Inc., 1994.

inflation, cash has returned an average 0.5 percent per year since 1926, compared with 6.9 percent after inflation for the S&P 500, according to Ibbotson.

How about stocks versus bonds? The chart on page 3 compares returns of small company stocks, large company stocks, long-term government bonds, U.S. Treasury bills and inflation going back to 1926. Assume you invested $1 in each of the four instruments at the end of 1925. Through wars, depressions, bouts of high inflation, recessions, oil embargoes and market crashes, that dollar would have grown most if you had invested in small-company stocks. It would have ballooned to $2,757.15 by 1993. By comparison, a $1 investment in ultra-safe Treasury bills would have returned a mere $11.73. (The figures assume income from the investments is reinvested and do not consider commission costs or taxes.)

Together, returns on large and small-company stocks averaged 11.3 percent a year. Long-term Treasury bonds did less well, yielding an average 5.02 percent. Bond yields generally don't match stock returns in the long race, but then again, bond investors experience fewer hairpin turns than stock market riders.

Is the past prologue to the future? Many investment analysts seem to think so. We asked two top investment strategists for their long-term reading of the market. Byron Wien, a stock strategist for Morgan Stanley, the investment firm, offers this analysis: The country is in the middle of a long, slow economic expansion that will continue through 1996. Wien advises steering clear of consumer stocks and moving toward bank and other financial stocks. He also likes economically-sensitive stocks such as railroads, paper companies, semiconductor manufacturers, and other technology stocks.

David Jones, chief economist at Aubrey G. Lanston & Co., a firm that specializes in bond investment, and author of *The Buck Stops Here* (Prentice-Hall, 1995), expects the global economy to perk up in the coming years, boosting the prices of assets like timber, oil, gold, and real estate. Jones strikes a cautious note, however: Stocks and bonds were overachievers during the past decade, he says, and odds are they will underperform their historical showing in the 1990's. If so, the Louies and Willies may have to muster a bit more patience.

STOCKS

HOW TO BEFRIEND A BEAR MARKET

Fight the instinct to run away. You may be better off feeding it money

Nobody likes a bear market. The Dow dips more than 30 percent on average, downdrafts usually last over a year, and it often takes the market another year to recover. But bear markets aren't all bad. In fact, they can be great buying opportunities.

Consider, for example, a 1994 study by Ibbotson Associates for the *Wall Street Journal* of the bruising bear market of 1973 and 1974, the worst the country had experienced since the 1930s. The Standard & Poor's 500 stock index lost 43 percent, even with dividends reinvested, and didn't rebound to its 1972 level until mid-1976.

Nevertheless, people who steadily invested in stocks would have done pretty well. By January 1976, in fact, they would have come out ahead of someone who had put the same amount into Treasury bills, even though T-bills were paying a respectable 6 to 7 percent a year at the time.

The analysis assumed that an investor put $100 a month into stocks beginning in January 1973. When the market hit bottom in September 1974, the investor would have invested a total of $2,100 and held stocks worth less than $1,500. But seven months later, the investor would have been about even with the $2,800 that he or she had invested. And by the first quarter of 1976, as the stock market was just returning to its previous high, the investor would have had more money than if he or she had instead invested $100 a month in T-bills.

Despite a brief dip in 1979, the long-term outlook remained bright. By the end of 1992, the investor's $24,000 stake would have been worth $124,000—more than twice the $54,000 it would have earned in Treasuries.

RIDING WALL STREET'S ROLLER COASTER

The average bear this century lasted 410 days, during which the Dow Jones Industrial Average dropped some 31 perecent. On the upside, there have been 31 bull markets in the same period. On average, they lasted about two years with a near 85 percent increase in the Dow. The last 10 bulls haven't run quite as strong, however.

BEAR MARKETS

Beginning date	Ending date	Number of days	Loss in Dow	Mos. to recover
2/9/66	10/7/66	240	–25.2%	6
12/3/68	5/26/70	539	–35.9%	22
4/28/71	11/23/71	209	–16.1%	64
1/11/73	12/6/74	694	–45.1%	4
9/21/76	2/28/78	525	–26.9%	6
9/8/78	4/21/80	591	–16.4%	10
4/27/81	8/12/82	472	–24.1%	4
11/29/83	7/24/84	238	–15.6%	3
8/25/87	10/19/87	55	–36.1%	23
7/16/90	10/11/90	87	–21.2%	5

BULL MARKETS

Beginning date	Ending date	Number of days	Gain in Dow
10/7/66	12/3/68	788	32.4%
5/26/70	4/28/71	337	50.6%
11/23/71	1/11/73	415	31.8%
12/6/74	9/21/76	655	75.7%
2/28/78	9/8/78	192	22.3%
4/21/80	4/27/81	371	34.9%
8/12/82	11/29/83	474	65.7%
7/24/82	8/25/87	1127	150.6%
10/19/87	7/16/90	1001	72.5%
10/11/90	1/31/94	1208	68.2%

SOURCE: *The Chartist*, June 1994.

RIDING OUT A RECESSION

Like a bear market, recessions reward those with patience

There are investors who would sooner plunge into the Arctic than the stock market during a recession, which often coincides with a bear market (see story, page 5). But many pros say investing when the environment looks bleak could turn out to be a boon. Stock prices—like the price of clothing, cars, and condos—also plunge during an economic slowdown. Investors buying stocks for the long run then could end up with solid returns.

Recessions generally last about 11 months, with the market turning up 6 months before the economy picks up. Returns vary, depending on when you invest—before, during, or after a recession. The most lucrative time: at the midpoint of a recession, according to data compiled by Twentieth Century Mutual Funds.

■ Those who bought at a recession's start made an average 12.6 percent a year later:

Holding period	S&P 500 annualized return
11/30/73 to 3/31/76	7.8%
1/30/80 to 7/31/81	14.6%
7/31/81 to 11/30/83	16.5%
7/31/90 to 3/31/92	11.6%

■ Those who bought at a recession's midpoint and held for 12 months after the recession raked in an average 30.5 percent:

Holding period	S&P 500 annualized return
7/31/74 to 7/31/75	17.5%
3/31/80 to 3/31/81	39.9%
3/31/82 to 3/31/83	44.1%
11/30/90 to 11/30/91	20.4%

■ Even those who waited until the tail end of a recession to buy were richer by an average 19.4 percent one year later:

Holding period	S&P 500 annualized return
3/31/75 to 3/31/76	28.2%
7/31/80 to 7/31/81	12.9%
11/30/82 to 11/30/83	25.6%
3/31/91 to 3/31/92	10.9%

SOURCE: Twentieth Century Mutual Funds.

EXPERT PICKS

PICKING STOCKS IN A DOWNDRAFT

Look at industry groups that led the way out of past recessions, advises Elaine M. Garzarelli, one of Wall Street's most respected analysts. Here is Garzarelli's list of industry groups that have historically scored big gains in the first 12 months after the stock market has bottomed out and their average percent gain.

Industry group	Average gain
Leisure time	**111.9%**
Retail drug stores	**97.1%**
Pollution control	**94.8%**
Newspaper publishing	**86.6%**
Homebuilding	**75.5%**
Airlines	**65.8%**
Electronic instrumentation	**64.5%**
Trucking	**64.1%**
Semiconductors	**60.8%**
Broadcast media	**58.2%**
Publishing	**57.8%**
Textile, apparel manufacturing	**51.8%**

SOURCE: Elaine M. Garzarelli.

WHEN INTEREST RATES RISE

Share prices can increase as long as rates go up gradually

To ward off inflation during times of a growing economy, the Federal Reserve Board, the nation's central bank, typically raises interest rates. The Fed can push up the federal funds rate—what banks pay to borrow from each other—and the discount rate—what banks pay to borrow money from the Fed. As interest rates rise, money becomes tighter, keeping inflation in check. Low inflation, economists believe, paves the way for sustained economic growth.

What happens to stock prices when the Fed hikes interest rates? The common belief is that higher rates ultimately produce lower stock prices as investors pull out of the stock market and put their money into other investments. Studies show that a sell-off of stocks usually follows an announcement of a hike in interest rates.

But research by the Kidder, Peabody brokerage firm also shows that stocks bounce back after investors realize that the increase will do little harm to the economy. Often the rate hike helps the economy because consumers speed up interest-rate dependent purchases of goods such as cars and houses.

Easton Ragsdale, formerly with Kidder, Peabody and now at State Street Research and Management Co., has studied the 13 periods during which the Fed has raised interest rates since World War II. He found that in the 12 months after the federal funds rate began to rise, the total return for the Standard & Poor's 500 was 11.6 percent, a respectable increase.

True, stocks had a better showing in the 12 months before the Fed's tightening, when the S&P total return was 18.7 percent. But the historical average gain of 11.6 percent, says Ragsdale, argues for sticking with the stock market even after rates start rising. As long as increases in the federal funds rate are small and gradual—no larger than a quarter of a point at a time, for example—the stock market continues to push higher.

A rising discount rate, however, can spell trouble for stocks. Ragsdale's research shows that prices took a downturn in the months immediately following a discount-rate increase. Total performance after 12 months was a weak 1.5 percent gain. The good news: Discount rate increases are fairly infrequent and generally don't come for some time after the Fed's initial tightening, giving stock market investors the chance to rack up gains.

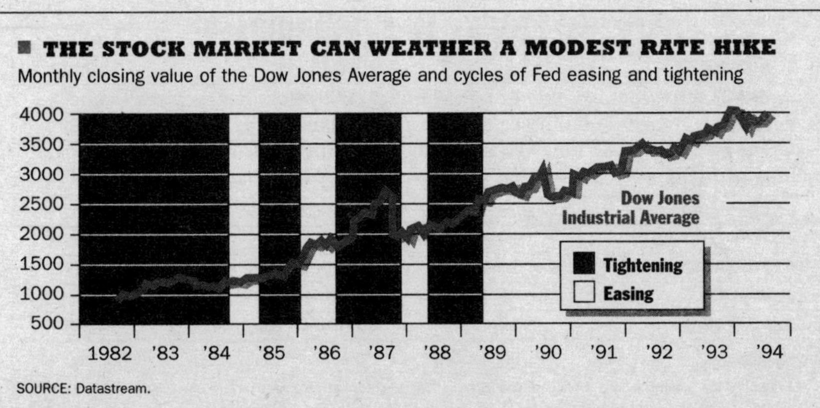

EMERGING MARKETS

THINK CAREFULLY, INVEST GLOBALLY

Risky emerging markets offer big returns. Here are the ones to watch

The United States isn't the only place to invest your hard-earned cash. In fact, it may not even be the best place. Consider: In 1993, all 24 emerging stock markets then open to foreign investors and tracked by the World Bank's International Finance Corporation showed greater returns than the Standard & Poor's 500. And that was no one-year fluke: The IFC's composite index of emerging stock markets for the five-year period ending December 1993 showed a mean annual return of 30 percent, twice the S&P 500 return over the same period.

The catch: Emerging stock markets lack the regulatory safeguards that protect U.S. shareholders, and many are dominated by just a few stocks or are rife with speculation. Such instability can feed on itself. For example, the horrific devaluation of the Mexican peso—35 percent in the final 11 days of 1994 alone—sent Latin American markets into a tailspin. The IFC's Latin American index dropped over 21 percent in the fourth quarter. Overall, only 5 of the now 26 emerging markets tracked by IFC indexes posted fourth-quarter 1994 gains. Even so, almost half of the 26 emerging markets tracked by the IFC in 1994 outperformed the S&P 500.

You can buy foreign stocks directly, but an emerging market mutual fund may be a better bet. Professional managers examine a country's political stability, work ethic, education, family structure, and other factors before investing. Mark Mobius, president of the Templeton Emerging Markets Funds, also pays special attention to a country's productivity rate. For Mobius, at least, such consideration has paid off; his emerging markets fund earned actual returns of more than 97 percent in 1993. Below, Mobius shares his top picks for emerging markets to watch. Some have taken heavy hits in the recent past, but Mobius believes all appear to be poised for big growth in the long term.

■ **CHINA:** The world's most populous nation has doubled its aggregate output since 1978. An evolving market economy and abundant, cheap labor makes it a standout.

■ 1994'S BEST AND WORST PERFORMING STOCK MARKETS

The World Bank's International Finance Corporation Price Index rates markets in a manner similar to the Standard & Poor's 500. Here are the winners and losers in 1994.

■ BEST	Change in IFC index
1. NIGERIA	168.79%
2. BRAZIL	67.59%
3. PERU	52.10%
4. CHILE	41.19%
5. SOUTH AFRICA	28.50%
6. COLOMBIA	26.80%
7. JAPAN, NIKKEI*	26.30%
8. ZIMBABWE	22.50%
9. TAIWAN	21.48%
10. PORTUGAL	16.47%

■ WORST	Change in IFC index
1. THAILAND	–13.14%
2. HUNGARY	–17.46%
3. INDONESIA	–20.58%
4. MALAYSIA	–22.82%
5. ARGENTINA	–25.11%
6. VENEZUELA	–27.18%
7. CHINA	–34.45%
8. MEXICO	–41.60%
9. POLAND	–42.61%
10. TURKEY	–43.30%

*Developed market.

SOURCES: Central Intelligence Agency; International Finance Corporation; Morgan Stanley Capital International.

MARK MOBIUS'S TOP 10 MARKETS TO WATCH

In addition to the usual measures of a market's health, emerging markets expert Mark Mobius recommends that you look at the number of televisions a country has. People see how others live and want the same for themselves. Here are Mobius's picks for long-term investment.

Country	TVs per 1,000 inhabitants	Share of market capitalization held by 10 largest stocks[1]	Return in U.S. dollars[2]	Total return, 5-year annualized mean[3]	1994 change in IFC index
CHINA	31	17.3%	–33.31%	6.60%	–34.74%
INDIA	32	19.4%	7.44%	22.92%	6.50%
INDONESIA	60	29.8%	–19.32%	5.40%	–20.58%
SOUTH AFRICA	105	48.6%	31.32%	46.92%	28.50%
BRAZIL	213	34.5%	69.18%	46.32%	66.96%
MEXICO	139	33.8%	–40.79%	26.88%	–41.72%
ARGENTINA	222	41.7%	–23.14%	42.12%	–25.00%
PHILIPPINES	48	44.3%	–0.60%	20.16%	–1.05%
RUSSIA	329	NA[4]	NA[4]	NA[4]	NA[4]
HONG KONG	274	44.4%	–29.90%	23.67%	–29.90%
UNITED STATES	815	14.9%	1.31%	9.12%	–2.00%

NOTES: 1. Largest and most active stocks as a percentage of total market. 2. Percentage change for 12-month period. 3. Percentage change from 1990 to 1994. 4. Russian stock exchanges are not unified and many are private.
SOURCES: Central Intelligence Agency; International Finance Corporation; Morgan Stanley Capital International.

INDIA: Policy reforms since 1991 have slashed government controls on production, trade, and investment. The world's second most populous country has great potential, but also sporadic problems with religious opposition.

INDONESIA: It will benefit from abundant natural resources as central planning gives way to private enterprise. Beware of continued corruption and inflation, however.

SOUTH AFRICA: Apartheid's fall has sparked massive economic restructuring in the world's largest producer of gold and platinum. Many previously untraded stocks will become available to foreign investors.

BRAZIL: South America's largest nation and the world's largest producer of coffee and orange juice concentrate is dealing with past problems, such as inflation and deficit spending, but beware continued inflation.

MEXICO: Passage of the 1993 North American Free Trade Agreement may increase wealth over the long term. U.S. Treasury officials say the peso, which plummeted in value in late 1994, should be recovering by the end of 1995. Now that Mexico has gone through the test of fire, it is a good time to look at Mexican investments.

ARGENTINA: The government's successful economic restructuring since 1991 has pushed the once-enormous inflation rate to the lowest level in 20 years. A good sign: Stable stock prices have boosted Argentines' investment in their own industrial stocks.

PHILIPPINES: Since a new government took power in 1992, exports have continued to rise, led by earnings from electronics and garment industries.

RUSSIA: Its enormous market potential is tempered by doubts about whether it will move toward full privatization and fear of political and exchange rate volatility.

HONG KONG: China has promised to respect Hong Kong's bustling free-market economy when it takes over in 1997, but watch out: The market there has crashed four times in the past 30 years.

GLOBAL STOCKS

GOING ON A FOREIGN FLING

American depository receipts make it easier than you think

Americans used to be innocents abroad when it came to foreign investing. Today, however, it's getting easier and easier for Americans to invest overseas; even novices are joining in. The easiest way to invest abroad is to buy shares in a mutual fund that specializes in overseas companies. But increasingly investors are purchasing shares of individual companies in the form of American depository receipts, or ADRs.

More than 1,300 foreign companies now trade on U.S. stock exchanges in the form of ADRs, dollar-denominated securities that represent a given number of company shares. In 1994, trading volume topped $265 billion, more than six times what it was in 1988. That's in addition to the almost $50 billion U.S. investors poured into international equity funds.

It's easy to understand the enthusiasm. Merrill Lynch's ADR Composite Index has been chalking up impressive gains compared to the Standard & Poor's 500 stock index, though no one knows whether that will continue to be the case. For some time now, however, many investment pros have felt that U.S. stocks are pricey compared to bargains that can be found overseas.

You don't have to leave home to buy an ADR. They are issued by U.S. banks that hold the underlying foreign shares in custody, and ADRs are sold in U.S. dollars through brokers, just like stocks. All you have to do to buy one is pick up the phone.

Getting timely information about the company whose stock you're buying can be more difficult. About two-thirds of ADRs are listed on the "pink sheets," a thinly traded part of the over-the-counter market that is exempt from the rules of the bigger exchanges. These companies do not have to file financial statements with the Securities and Exchange Commission nor are they required to send income reports to shareholders.

Pros generally counsel that average investors stick with the 220 or so companies trading on the big exchanges that meet U.S. standards of accounting and disclosure. In 1994, however, Chicago-based Morningstar Inc., a publisher of mutual fund reports, started Morningstar American Depository Receipts (☎ 800-876-5005), which is issued bi-weekly. The report tracks more than 700 ADRs, with up to 10 years of data, business summaries, and market snapshots.

Accurate financial information doesn't always shield investors from some of the risks inherent in ADR investing. Because the underlying stock is denominated in local currency, a strengthening dollar hurts an ADR's value. (The reverse is also true.) Also, faraway economic and political developments can jolt an ADR's price. Investors in STET, one of Italy's leading telecommunications companies, for instance, may now find that they take more than a passing interest when the next Italian government falls, as it inevitably will.

EXPERT SOURCE

Consumer online services such as America Online, CompuServe, and Prodigy offer at least rudimentary financial data about companies abroad—including the prices of listed American depository receipts. But, according to *Business Week*, the premier information service remains Dow Jones News/Retrival, ☎ 800-815-5100.

BONDS

STAYING AHEAD OF THE CURVE

Want to know where bonds are headed? Consult the yield curve

Should you buy a three-month T-bill, a 30-year bond, or something in between? A look at the yield curve, which can be found daily in the *Wall Street Journal* or *Investor's Business Daily,* may provide the answer.

A yield curve is simply a line that plots the interest rate paid by similar bonds with different maturities. The X-axis plots the length of time until the bonds mature. The Y-axis plots the yield of each bond. The average spread between the shortest-term and longest-term Treasuries is usually about two percentage points.

Reading the yield curve can be especially useful for long-term investing. If you have a shorter time frame—say, you'll need to cash in your bond in three years for a child's tuition—you should probably buy a bond that matures within that time period. Keep in mind, also, that interest rates and bond prices move in opposite directions: Higher rates mean lower bond prices. Rising interest rates can play havoc on the bond market. This was the case in 1994, when even the highest-quality bond portfolio lost value as interest rates climbed. When rates start heading down, on the other hand, it's usually a good time to buy long-term bonds as a way to lock in current high yields.

A common misconception is that if a bond's yield is going up, the investment is worth more. It's just the opposite; when a bond's yield rises, its price has fallen because the increase in yield comes at the expense of the bond's market value. Conversely, if a bond's yield falls, its market value rises. Another risk: rising inflation, which can cut the worth of a bond's coupon payments and its eventual redemption value.

The yield curve usually slopes upward. That's because longer-term investments carry more of the aforementioned risks and must pay higher interest rates to compensate. When short and long-term interest rates are roughly the same, the curve is flat. A thin spread means the market sees little difference between the short-term and long-term risks of inflation. So buying longer-term bonds gives you only a slight premium.

When short-term yields exceed long-term yields, the curve turns downward or inverts. An inverted curve usually means that a recession is coming. The last time the curve inverted was 1989, signaling the slowdown that led to the 1990–91 recession. An inverted curve has predicted all eight recessions since 1950.

Some analysts say that inverted curves also signal a buying opportunity for long-term bonds. In other words, when the economy softens and interest rates come down, you want to be in long-term bonds because eventually the curve will normalize and the value of long-term bonds will rise.

READING THE YIELD CURVE

Yield curves show how interest rates and time to maturity relate in otherwise similar bonds. A normal, or positive, yield curve moves upward, showing that interest rates rise as maturities increase. When the curve inverts, or bends downward, short-term rates are higher than long-term rates, a sign of a recession to come.

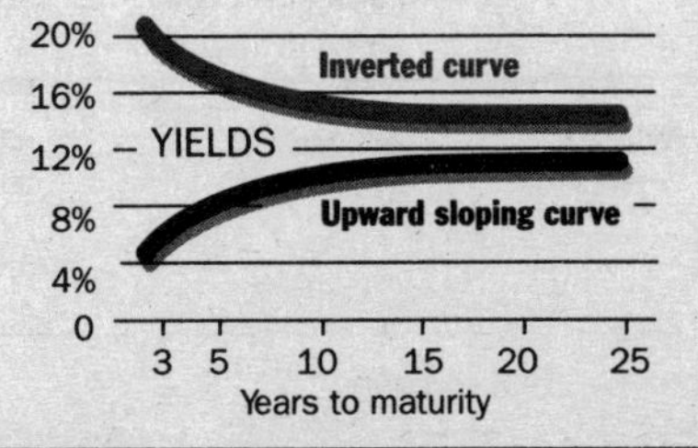

WHERE TO GET GOOD PAPER

Brokers, funds, and Uncle Sam all offer an on-ramp to investing

Once you've selected from the variety of available bonds—government bonds, U.S. Savings bonds, Treasury bills, Treasury notes, municipal bonds, and corporate bonds—how do you go about buying them? Depending on the type, you have a few choices.

Municipals and corporate bonds are bought through brokers. You can buy Treasuries through a bank, a broker, a mutual fund, or through a government program called Treasury Direct, ☎ 202-874-4000. The advantage of buying through the government is that there is no commission. For more information, write: Department of the Treasury, Bureau of the Public Debt, Washington, D.C. 20239.

You also can open an account and learn about scheduled bond auctions. Two- and three-year bonds are available for a minimum $5,000 investment. Five- and 10-year notes require a minimum $10,000 investment.

For greater diversification, you can turn to bond funds (see table, below). They are convenient—you can invest in small amounts and a professional manager runs the show. A drawback: Bond funds constantly trade bonds and don't hold them to maturity, so you lose the guarantee that you'll get a bond's face value at a certain date.

When investing in bond funds, also be sure to scrutinize fees and other expenses. After all, the return on bond funds is so low, why dish out 4 percent or 5 percent? To find the true return, find out the yield and subtract the fund's annual expense ratio.

CHOOSING A BOND STRATEGY

The determining factor is when you expect to cash in

Time frame	Type of bond	Comments
Less than 1 year	**Any**	You may want to consider a money market fund for stability of principal.
1–2 years	**Short-term bond**	If interest rates are stable or fall, you could get higher than money market fund yields as well as potential capital appreciation. If interest rates rise, this fund could still be a good choice. Unless rates rise substantially, the income you get may make up some of the losses to principal and may still put you ahead of where you'd be in a money market fund.
2–4 years	**Federal or state tax-free bond, mortgage bond, government bond, investment grade bond**	If you're counting on the fund to supply you a stream of income, keep in mind that higher yields can help compensate for some of the drop in the value of your account. If you invested to diversify a stock portfolio, keep in mind that the long-term price volatility of bonds is typically lower than that of stocks.
More than 4 years	**Aggressive bond**	Although interest rates can affect these funds, they tend to benefit from a healthy economy. Over the long term, income provides the bulk of total return in bond funds. If you are comfortable with the quality risk, aggressive funds provide the highest income.

SOURCE: Fidelity Investments.

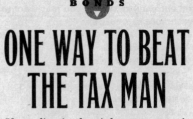

ONE WAY TO BEAT THE TAX MAN

If you live in the right state, munis can triple your tax exemption

For investors grappling with high tax rates, municipal bonds may be a way to make tax time less painful. Municipal bonds, or munis, are debt obligations issued by city, state, and local governments. The appeal of munis is that interest income is exempt from federal taxes, making them one of the few tax shelters around. Better yet, taxpayers in some localities can get even more tax breaks from buying munis issued by their home states.

Tax rules vary from state to state, so it's wise to find out about local laws. Residents of high-tax states, such as California, Massachusetts, and New York, may do well to allocate a good portion of their municipal investments to munis sold by their home state. The benefits of doing so include a double and sometimes triple tax exemption. For residents of states such as Illinois, Oklahoma, Wisconsin, and Iowa, it's a wash, since most in-state bonds are taxed the same as out-of-state bonds. In Indiana, Utah, and the District of Columbia, municipal-bond interest is tax-free, regardless of where the bonds were issued. And residents of low or no-tax states like Texas, would be better off putting their money into a more diversified portfolio of quality bonds.

Municipal bonds are sold by brokers and require a $5,000 minimum investment. One way to get around this is to invest in a municipal bond mutual fund. There are nearly 800 muni funds, including 600 or so single-state funds, according to Morningstar Inc., a Chicago research firm that tracks mutual funds. Muni bond funds carry another important plus: They are less risky because they offer geographic diversity.

A few caveats: Munis often have higher transaction costs than Treasuries, driving down their effective yields. When shopping for muni bonds, check the credit quality, that is, the strength of the cash flow used to meet principal and interest payments. Your fund's bonds should have an average credit quality of A or better from one of the major rating agencies. High-quality bonds hold up better during bad times.

SHINING A LIGHT ON MUNIS

Two new ways to find out more about mysterious municipal bonds

Municipal bonds have long worn a veil of obscurity. But they are becoming friendlier to small investors, thanks in part to recent rule changes by the Securities and Exchange Commission.

The new rules require muni bond underwriters to keep small investors well informed about financial factors that might affect the issuers' credit rating by providing them with annual financial reports and disclosing all important information regarding muni bonds.

At the same time, the Public Securities Association, a trade group in New York, is working with the Standard & Poor's Corp. to make it easier for small investors to get the best muni's bond prices available with two new services.

The first is the PSA/Bloomberg National Municipal Bond Yields, a new yield scale that will be published in newspapers across the country. The second is the Standard & Poor's/PSA Municipal Bond Service, a toll-free hotline that provides the transaction prices (or an evaluation of the prices from Standard & Poor's Corp.) and the yields of muni bonds. ☎ 800-266-3463.

THE PERFECT PORTFOLIO

A twelve-step program to get your investments to meet your goals

Deciding to invest for your future is the easy part. Picking the right mix of stocks, bonds, and short-term money market accounts is more taxing. Fidelity Investments, the huge mutual-fund company based in Boston, has come up with a simple quiz to help you find that mix. Called FundMatch, the test asks 12 questions about your finances, your needs for the future, and how aggressive an investor you are. The total will suggest the mix of stocks, bonds, and short-term instruments right for you. Note that the test is designed for those who plan to invest for more than two years. If you are investing for less than two years, Fidelity suggests you consider only short-term bond or money market funds, regardless of your score.

1. What portion of your total "investable assets"—the dollar amount of the investments you currently have—will this investment represent? The percentage of your portfolio that this investment represents can make a difference in how conservative or aggressive you may want to be. Do not include your home or vacation house in calculating investable assets.

ANSWER	POINTS
Less than 25%	8
25% to 50%	7
51% to 75%	3
More than 75%	2

2. Which one of the following describes your expected future earnings over the next five years? Assume inflation will average 4 percent. If you are expecting significant earnings increases, you may want to invest more aggressively.

ANSWER	POINTS
I expect my earnings will far outpace inflation (due to promotions or a new job.)	5
I expect my earnings increases to stay somewhat ahead of inflation	3
I expect my earnings to keep pace with inflation	2
I expect my earnings to decrease (due to retirement, part-time work, or some other reason)	1

3. Approximately what portion of your monthly take-home income goes toward paying off installment debt, such as auto loans, credit cards, etc., but not including a home mortgage? If a large portion of your income goes toward paying debt, you may want to have cash available for emergencies.

ANSWER	POINTS
Less than 10%	8
10% to 25%	6
25% to 50%	3
More than 50%	1

4. How many dependents do you have? Include children and parents you support. If you have ongoing family obligations, you may need to be more conservative.

ANSWER	POINTS
None	4
1	3
2 or 3	2
More than 3	1

5. Do you have an emergency fund, that is, savings from three to six months' after-tax income? Such a fund helps protect against the unexpected, such as a job loss. Without this reserve to tap, you may want to invest more conservatively.

ANSWER	POINTS
No	2
Yes, but less than six months of after-tax income	6
Yes, I have an adequate emergency fund	8

6. Do you have a separate savings plan to cover major expenses, such as college tuition, home downpayment, repairs, etc.?

Yes, I have a separate savings plan for these expenses	8
I do not expect to have any such expenses	6
I intend to withdraw a portion of this new investment for these expenses (Answer question 12 accordingly)	5
I have no separate savings plan for these expenses	2

7. Have you ever invested in individual bonds or bond mutual funds? How comfortable you are with different risks can help you determine how aggressive or conservative you want to be.

No, I would be uncomfortable with the risk	1
No, but I would be comfortable with the risk	9
Yes, but I was uncomfortable with the risk	2
Yes, and I felt comfortable with the risk	10

8. Have you ever invested in individual stocks or stock mutual funds?

No, I would be uncomfortable with the risk	1
No, but I would be comfortable with the risk	15
Yes, but I was uncomfortable with the risk	3
Yes, and I felt comfortable with the risk	16

9. Which one of the following statements describes your feelings toward choosing an investment? You should balance the comfort level you choose with your desire to attain your investment goals.

I would only select investments that have a low degree of risk associated with them (i.e., it is unlikely I will lose my original investment)	2
I prefer to select a mix of investments with emphasis on those with a low degree of risk and a small portion in others that have a higher degree of risk that may yield greater returns	5
I prefer to select a balanced mix of investments—some that have a low degree of risk, others that have a higher degree of risk that my yield greater returns	9
I prefer to select an aggressive mix of investments—some that have a low degree of risk, but with emphasis on others that have a higher degree of risk that may yield greater returns	12
I would only select an investment that has a higher degree of risk and a potential for higher returns	16

10. If you could increase your chances of improving your returns by taking more risk, would you:

Be willing to take a lot more risk with all your money	16
Be willing to take a lot more risk with some of your money	12
Be willing to take a little more risk with all your money	10
Be willing to take a little more risk with some of your money	5
Be unlikely to take much more risk	2

11. How long can you tie up this money? Your time frame is critical to your investment strategy. Stocks outperform bonds and short-term investments over long periods. The longer your money can sit and take advantage of market cycles, the more aggressive you may want to be. In approximately how many years do you expect to need the money you are investing?

2–3 years	5
4–6 years	25
7–10 years	40
10–15 years	45
More than 15 years	50

12. Do you expect to withdraw more than one-third of the money within 10 years? (For a home purchase, college tuition, or other major need?)

No	50
If yes, when do you expect to withdraw from the account?	
Within 3 years	5
4–6 years	30
7–10 years	50

TOTAL SCORE FOR ALL 12 QUESTIONS

(See the bottom of the next page for investment strategies.)

SAFE BETS FOR THE RISK-AVERSE

Certificates of deposit aren't the only alternative for conservative investors

You can always stash your money in the proverbial mattress, where it will not earn any interest at all. But for millions of risk-averse investors, certificates of deposit, or CDs, have seemed a preferable choice. Conservative by nature, CD investors tend to be attracted by the promise that they can't lose their principal, which is covered by federal deposit insurance, to $100,000 per account.

Until interest rates tumbled in 1993, CDs were a respectable way to go. Yields, while never robust, were at least decent by conservative standards. By the fall of 1993, however, the average yield on six-month CDs, among the most popular with individual investors, had fallen to 2.81 percent, about par with the then inflation rate. Once taxes were taken out, the return was a negative number. Rates have since climbed up a bit.

CDs are not, however, the only alternative for the risk-averse. Of course, other investments carry additional risks. For example, even when sold by banks, mutual funds don't carry federal deposit insurance. And the values of stocks and bonds rise and fall with market conditions, which can cut into your investment principal. If interest rates rise just one percentage point in a year, the price of a 30-year bond will fall more than 11 percent. On a bond with a 7 percent coupon, an investor's annual return would be a negative 4 percent.

If you stick with CDs, you may be able to find better yields by looking beyond your local bank. Otherwise, here's a quick look at some things to consider before rolling over another CD:

- **SHORT-TERM BOND FUNDS:** The net asset value of the shares vary with the underlying value of the bonds, and the total return falls if interest rates rise. But the variation is much smaller than with longer-term bonds.

- **TAX-EXEMPT SECURITIES:** If the yield on a short-term municipal bond fund is 4 percent, it's equivalent to a taxable yield of 6.25 percent for an investor in the 36 percent tax bracket. Again, the shorter the term, the lower the risk.

- **CONSERVATIVE STOCK FUNDS:** Funds that invest in utilities are generally stable and pay decent dividends. Yield-conscious investors tend to like them. In addition, several fund companies now offer asset-allocation funds, in which the fund manager decides how much of the portfolio to put into stocks, bonds, cash, and other investments. Another choice: equity-income funds, which invest in stocks that pay chunky dividends.

- **MONEY MARKET MUTUAL FUNDS:** Money funds sometimes yield even less than six-month CDs, but they're completely liquid.

THE RIGHT MIX FOR YOU

SCORE: 0–75 
CAPITAL PRESERVATION PORTFOLIO

Short-term	50%
Bonds	30%
Stocks	20%

SCORE: 76–132 
MODERATE PORTFOLIO

Short-term	20%
Bonds	40%
Stocks	40%

SCORE: 133–179 
WEALTH-BUILDING PORTFOLIO

Short-term	5%
Bonds	30%
Stocks	65%

SCORE: 180 or more
AGGRESSIVE GROWTH PORTFOLIO

Stocks	100%

SOURCE: Fidelity Investments.

STRATEGIES

AS JANUARY GOES, SO GOES THE YEAR

This indicator is almost always right. Here's why

Yale Hirsch's theory about the stock market is simple enough. If the Standard & Poor's composite index is up in the month of January, the market average for the rest of the year also will be up. And if the S&P index is down in January, it also will be down over the rest of the year. Since 1950, the indicator has predicted the annual course of the market with astonishing accuracy. According to Hirsch, a publisher of three financial newsletters, his indicator has been right 39 of the last 44 years, or 89 percent of the time.

There's no great mystery, Hirsch believes, about why January is such an accurate barometer of the year. As he explains in his book, *Hirsch's 1995 Stock Trader's Almanac* (Hirsch Organization, 1994), January is the month that many major economic and national policy decisions are announced by the government to kick off the new year. Congress convenes on January 3 and, every four years, a president is inaugurated less than three weeks later. More often than not, the president delivers his State of the Union message before the end of the month, laying out the year's national goals. And the government's budget also is released early in the year. "Switch these events to any other month and chances are the January Barometer would become a memory," Hirsch says.

Here are some of Hirsch's conclusions after studying a lot of Januarys:

■ The top 23 Januarys launched the best market years. Except in 1987, they had gains of 1 percent.

■ Twenty Januarys were losers or had very small gains. All bear markets were preceded or accompanied by downbeat Januarys. Only one good year, 1992, followed a January loss.

■ There were only three major errors in 44 years. They were in 1966, 1968, and 1982. Hirsch can account for the first two, citing the Vietnam War. He doesn't have an explanation for 1982.

What can we expect in the next couple of years? "1995 is a good, positive year," says Hirsch because there has not been a losing pre-election year for the stock market in 56 years. New presidents generally get rid of the tough jobs in the first year or two, then pull out all the stops to make things look good for the election. According to Hirsch, this has been going on for at least 150 years. As for 1996, Hirsch sees prosperous times and bull markets ahead.

■ JANUARY BAROMETER

In 7 of the past 10 years, gains logged in January on the Standard & Poor's 500 stock index roughly telegraphed a good year ahead. And, in 1990, January losses suggested the slow year to come. On the other hand, 1992 saw a bad January but a good year, and 1994 just the reverse.

Year	January change	12-month change
1985	7.4%	26.3%
1986	0.2%	14.6%
1987	13.2%	2.0%
1988	4.0%	12.4%
1989	7.1%	27.3%
1990	–6.9%	–6.6%
1991	4.2%	26.3%
1992	–2.0%	4.5%
1993	0.7%	7.1%
1994	3.3%	–1.5%

SOURCE: *Hirsch's 1995 Stock Trader's Almanac*, Hirsch Organization, 1994.

EXPERT TIPS

THE ORACLE OF OMAHA SPEAKS

A guru expounds on stocks, fortune tellers, and other secrets of success

Warren Buffett, the chairman of the Omaha-based holding company Berkshire Hathaway, Inc., is famous both for his spectacular investment acumen and his folksy, common-sense approach to choosing stocks. He also is, according to *Forbes* magazine, the second richest person in the nation, with an estimated fortune of some $9.2 billion. (Microsoft chairman Bill Gates is the richest.) With an initial investment of $100,000 at the age of 25, Buffett built a business empire worth nearly $20 billion today that includes major holdings in Coca-Cola, the insurance giant GEICO, the *Washington Post,* and General Dynamics.

Buffett enjoys a reputation as a maverick outsider, preferring small-town Omaha to Wall Street canyons. But, as *Forbes* said in 1994, "Don't bet he's lost his touch."

We asked Buffett if we could print his gems of investment wisdom gleaned from his letters to shareholders in recent Berkshire Hathaway annual reports. He agreed.

✔ "What makes sense in business also makes sense in stocks: An investor should ordinarily hold a small piece of an outstanding business with the same tenacity that an owner would exhibit if he owned all of that business."

✔ "I am quite content to hold a security indefinitely, so long as the prospective return on equity capital of the underlying business is satisfactory, management is competent and honest, and the market does not overvalue the business."

✔ "Beware of past performance proofs in finance. If history books were the key to riches, the Forbes 400 would consist of librarians."

✔ "The only value of stock forecasters is to make fortune tellers look good. Even now, Charlie [Charles Munger, Berkshire's vice chairman] and I continue to believe that short-term market forecasts are poison and should be kept locked up in a safe place, away from children and also from grown-ups who behave in the market like children."

✔ "The most common cause of low prices is pessimism—sometimes pervasive, sometimes specific to a company or industry. We want to do business in such an environment, not because we like pessimism but because we like the prices it produces. It's optimism that is the enemy of the rational buyer."

✔ "When a management with a reputation for brilliance tackles a business with a reputation for poor fundamental economics, it is the reputation of the business that stays intact."

✔ "Just as you should be suspicious of managers who pump up short-term earnings by accounting maneuvers, asset sales and the like, so also should you be suspicious of those managers who fail to deliver for extended periods and blame it on their long-term focus. (Even Alice, after listening to the Queen lecture her about 'jam tomorrow,' finally insisted, 'It must come sometimes to jam today.')"

✔ "We think the very term 'value investing' is redundant. What is 'investing' if it is not the act of seeking value at least sufficient to justify the amount paid? Consciously paying more for a stock than its calculated value—in the hope that it can soon be sold for a still-higher price—should be labeled speculation (which is neither illegal, immoral nor—in our view—financially fattening)."

WHAT IS THE WARREN BUFFETT WAY?

How the world's champion stockpicker makes his picks

Robert G. Hagstrom, Jr., in his bestseller *The Warren Buffett Way* (John Wiley & Sons, 1994), synthesizes the formula that made Warren Buffett the world's greatest investor. We asked Hagstrom, who manages the Focus Trust in Philadelphia, to explain how Buffett does it:

■ **Turn off the stock market.** Warren Buffett doesn't have a stock quote machine in his office and he seems to get by fine without it. If you plan on owning shares in an outstanding business for a number of years, what happens in the market on a day-to-day basis is inconsequential.

■ **Don't worry about the economy.** If you find yourself discussing and debating whether the economy is poised for growth or tilting toward a recession, STOP! Except for his preconceived notions that the economy inherently has an inflation bias, Buffett dedicates no time or energy to analyzing the economy.

■ **Buy a business, not a stock**. Consider first if the business is easy to understand. Then determine if the business has a consistent operating history and favorable long-term prospects. What about its management? Is it rational, candid with shareholders, and able to avoid the herd mentality? Look at the financials, focusing on return, on equity, not earnings per share. Buffet seeks out companies that generate cash in excess of their needs and companies with high profit margins, which reflect not only a strong business but a management with a tenacious spirit for controlling costs. Other financials to look at: retained earnings, estimated cash flows, and the value of a business. Once you have determined the value of a business, the next step is to look at the stock price. Buffett's rule is to buy the business only when the stock price is at a significant discount to its value. Note that only at this final step does Buffet look at the stock market price.

■ **Manage a portfolio of businesses.** Buffett does not believe that wide diversification is required, so long as you understand business economics and can find 5 to 10 sensibly priced companies that have long-term competitive potential. In Buffett's mind, it is too difficult to make hundreds of smart decisions in a lifetime. He would rather position his portfolio so he only has to make a few smart decisions.

✔ "We try to stick to businesses we believe we understand. That means they must be relatively simple and stable in character. If a business is complex or subject to constant change, we're not smart enough to predict future cash flows. Incidentally, that shortcoming doesn't bother us. What counts for most people in investing is not how much they know, but rather how realistically they define what they don't know. An investor needs to do very few things right as long as he or she avoids big mistakes."

✔ "Tax-paying investors will realize a far, far greater sum from a single investment that compounds internally at a given rate than from a succession of investments compounding at the same rate."

✔ "An investor who does not understand the economics of specific businesses and nevertheless believes it in his interest to be a long-term owner of American industry, should both own a large number of equities and space out his purchases. By periodically investing in an index fund, for

ONE EXPERT'S WAY TO BEAT THE DOW

This strategy outperforms the market almost every year

There may be no sure-fire way to beat the market, but there is a strategy that comes convincingly close. John Downes, author with Michael B. O'Higgins of *Beating the Dow* (HarperPerennial, 1992), suggests this system: At the beginning of the year, buy the 10 stocks out of the 30 Dow Jones industrials with the highest yields, often an indication that they've been labeled losers. (Calculate the yield by dividing the annual dividend by the stock price.) Hold the stocks for one year and then repeat the process.

Sounds simple, but over the past 20 years, the strategy would have netted a handsome average annual 19 percent return, including dividends, compared to 14.3 percent for the Dow 30-stock average. The strategy has outperformed the Dow Jones Industrials for 17 of the past 22 years.

Downes suggests you budget at least $1,000 for each stock. By buying the individual stocks on your own, you can save the $450 or so it would cost to set up a $10,000 portfolio with a discount broker. Adjusting stock picks at the end of the year usually is not costly because typically more than half the stocks will remain on the list from year to year.

You also can buy the bargain 10 through unit trusts, which are sold through brokers such as Merrill Lynch, Smith Barney, and Prudential Securities. The units are called the Select 10 portfolio and typically come with a 1 percent initial sales charge and a 1.75 percent annual fee. The minimum purchase: $1,000 ($250 for individual retirement accounts). The trusts are liquidated each year, so to avoid capital gains taxes, you may want to hold on to them in an IRA.

A final tip: Investing in the cheapest 5 stocks of the 10 highest yielders gives you an extra kicker. Why? Because lower-priced stocks tend to move in greater percentage increments than higher-priced stocks and get better returns—even in grit-your-teeth years like 1994.

■ HIGH YIELDS VS. THE DOW

	RETURNS*		
	Bargain ten	Cheapest five	Dow Jones Ind. Avg.
1991	39.3%	61.9%	23.9%
1992	7.9%	23.1%	7.4%
1993	27.3%	34.3%	16.8%
1994	4.1%	8.6%	4.9%
5 years	13.0%	19.7%	10.2%
10 years	18.2%	20.5%	16.0%
20 years	18.8%	22.1%	14.3%

*Appreciation plus dividends.
SOURCE: *Beating the Dow*, newsletter, 800-477-3400.

example, the know-nothing investor can actually outperform most investment professionals. Paradoxically, when 'dumb' money acknowledges its limitations, it ceases to be dumb."

✔ "If you are a know-something investor, able to understand business economics and to find five to ten sensibly priced companies that possess important long-term competitive advantages, conventional diversification makes no sense for you. It is apt simply to hurt your results and increase your risk. I cannot understand why an investor of that sort elects to put money into a business that is his 20th favorite rather than simply adding that money to his top choices—the businesses he understands best and that present the least risk, along with the greatest profit potential."

SOURCE: Reprinted with permission from Warren E. Buffett's letters to shareholders in Berkshire Hathaway annual reports.

EXPERT Q&A

A NEW READING ON ASTRO-INVESTING

Wall Street's best-known astrologer on how planets affect markets

Does astrology affect the stock market? Arch Crawford, called "Wall Street's best-known astrologer" by *Barron's*, is convinced it does. In his much-read newsletter, *Crawford Perspectives*, Crawford uses astrology and a variety of financial indicators to forecast favorable times to trade stocks, bonds, and gold. Skeptics should note that the newsletter is often among the top market timers in the popular rating services. Here Crawford explains what astro-investing is all about.

■ What's the connection between the planets and the stock market?

Planets affect the market through electromagnetic fields. The planets stir the sun's surface and the resultant particle flows affect the earth's magnetic field and weather. Nearly 30 years of astronomical research have proven to me beyond any doubt that planetary movements exert an important influence on people, just as they do on the ocean tides, and that the changes they cause in behavior are reflected in the stock and commodities markets.

In the mid-1970s, I made what I believe is a quantum leap in market prediction by correlating numerous planetary cycles with the movements of the Dow from 1897 through 1970. I found that the reliability factor in catching the course of the stock market runs very high.

■ How did you get interested in astrology?

In the early 1960s, I was struck by a front-page article in the *Wall Street Journal* about David Williams, who had developed a way to predict the direction of the stock market by using the relative position of the planets. That stirred my interest.

I was also influenced by John Nelson, who was a radio propagation specialist for the RCA Corporation during the '40s and '50s. He showed that the alignment of the planets in relation to the sun helped him time sunspots and solar flares, helping his company reroute radio transmission efficiently. Later, when Nelson retired, he would call me and tell me that a flare was in progress, for example, and that radio communications across the Atlantic were totally blocked. I would then call a broker and find that, typically, the stock market was dropping sharply and that gold was rising during the geomagnetically disturbed period.

■ Why did you begin to introduce astrology into your forecasts?

When I was a technical market analyst at Merrill Lynch, I started to sense that there was something lacking in traditional econometric models. I observed, for example, that there is often little relation between news reports about a stock and the price of that stock. Around that time, I became interested

■ STAR-CROSSED MARKET

Overlaying the Dow Industrial averages are the movements of Jupiter and Pluto, as the planets spin away from each other and then align again—a cycle that takes about 12 ½ years. Astro-investors say the strongest down period will come in late '95, bottoming out in '96.

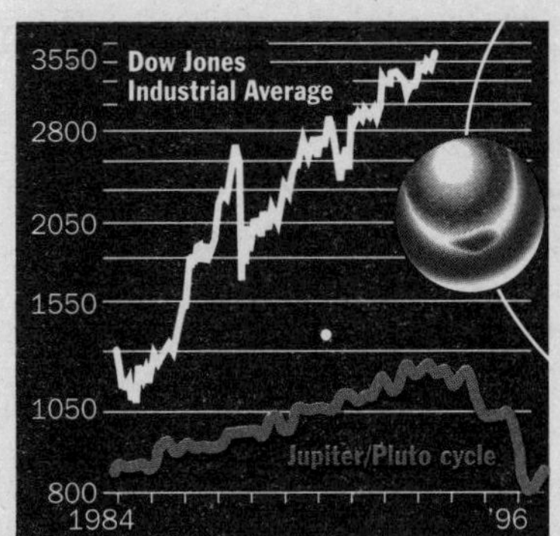

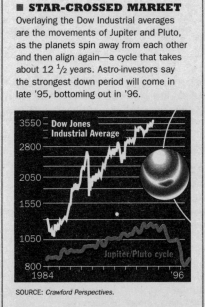

SOURCE: *Crawford Perspectives.*

EXPERT SOURCES

WHERE TO HEAR ABOUT STARS AND STOCKS

Untold numbers of Wall Streeters are quietly subscribing to an expanding universe of astro-investing newsletters. Among the best known:

ASTRO GEOMETRICS JOURNAL
$282 per year (12 issues)
■ Uses geometric techniques to cruise market, astrology as timing tool.
☎ **312-559-5500**

ASTRO INVESTOR
$45 per year (12 issues)
■ Uses planetary configurations and market wave patterns.
☎ **317-357-6855**

ASTRO TREND NEWSLETTER
$7,000 per year (12 issues)
■ Personal consultations, specific buy-sell recommendations. Uses technical research, astrology.
☎ **813-261-7261**

CAROLAN SPIRAL CALENDAR RESEARCH
$279 per year (12 issues)
■ Links lunar timing and market peaks, crashes.
☎ **404-718-0032**

CASH IN ON CHAOS
$250 per year (12 issues)
■ Studies effect of planetary movements and changes in electromagnetic fields on humans.
☎ **303-452-5566**

CRAWFORD PERSPECTIVES
$250 per year (12 issues)
■ Often rated among top 100 newsletters in the business. Uses astrology and technical research.
☎ **212-535-6202**

FUTURE NEWS NETWORK
$260 per year (52 issues)
■ Weekly summary of trends in leading astro-economic newsletters.
☎ **310-395-5309**

MARKET SYSTEMS
$366 per year (10 issues)
■ Stock market timing using technical analysis, cycles, and scientific methods.
☎ **818-509-1133**

WHOLE EARTH FORECASTER
$195 per year (12 issues)
■ Studies solar activity and its effect on weather, markets, and other business indicators.
☎ **402-894-2138**

in astronomy and began to use sunspot activity and astrology to chart the stock and commodities market. By using astrology, along with a lot of technical analysis, I have an edge over people who simply rely on numbers.

■ What factors other than astrology do you consider in making your forecasts?

Astrological events may signify a turning point, but they don't always indicate in which direction.

As a former technical analyst at Merrill Lynch, I also maintain 28 technical market indicators, including the volatility of the most active Big Board stocks, the number of new highs and lows, and advances versus declines.

■ What happens if the astronomical readings and the technical findings don't agree?

As technical data become more available, I would move more heavily on that side. But some types of planetary configurations, such as eclipses or multi-planet alignments, override such considerations.

■ What's your advice for the long term?

Stay extremely negative on the long term—through 1996. Even those bearish people who believe in a good correction cannot conceive of a long-lasting bear market similar to 1972 to 1974 or the period from 1966 to 1982, where the Dow Jones industrials languished under the impenetrable 1000 level. We are afraid of the long-term market and atmosphere.

INVESTMENT CLUBS

HOW AMATEURS BEAT THE PROS

You and your friends have a good chance of beating the market

Afraid to dip into the stock market alone? Try an investment club, a group of like-minded people who pool their time, skills, and money to research and invest in stocks. There are nearly 13,000 investment clubs in the United States, with 270,000 members holding an estimated $50 billion of stocks. The average club has a portfolio of $95,000, although the average member's portfolio is $200,000.

Small wonder. In 1994, 45 percent of investment clubs performed as well as or better than the Standard & Poor's 500 stock index, according to the National Association of Investors Corp., the parent organization of Investment Clubs of America. Fewer than 25 percent of Wall Street's heaviest hitters beat the S&P during the same period.

The stock-picking credo of NAIC members is simple. First, look for companies with five-year growth rates in earnings and revenues of about 15 percent a year or more. Try to buy stocks when the price earnings ratio (share price divided by the company's earnings per share), is at or below their average price/earnings ratio over the past five years.

Once you've picked a stock, stick with it. Reinvest dividends and earnings and don't sell unless the company really sours. One or two down quarters isn't enough to trigger a sell. So long as the company's underlying financials are still healthy, it may be a good time to buy. Finally, diversify your portfolio to spread the risk.

HOW TO START AN INVESTMENT CLUB

Want to launch your own investment club? Here are some tips on how to get it off the ground.

■ Invite interested family, friends, and co-workers to a meeting. Ask each of them to bring someone else but limit the total number to fewer than 30. Your goal is to have 10 to 15 members of varied ages and interests. Be sure all prospective members know they are expected to investigate and analyze securities and make periodic reports. Screen out those who are joining as a way to get rich quick. NAIC officials have found that 40 percent of clubs break up within two years.

■ At the first meeting, discuss how much money each member will invest. Most groups set a monthly figure of $10 to $100 per person, although many allow members to occasionally invest larger sums.

Choose an investment strategy. Will the club buy stock for long-term gain or current income? Pick a broker or a discount brokerage. In many cases, you can buy stock directly from companies through dividend reinvestment plans, sidestepping commissions and management fees.

FACT FILE:

INVESTMENT CLUB HITS

■ *The 10 most popular stocks held by members of the nation's investment clubs, ranked by dollar value of the holdings as of December 31, 1994. Most have made the list for many years.*

STOCK	VALUE OF HOLDINGS
AFLAC, Inc.	$149.5 million
McDonald's	$133 million
Sara Lee	$81 million
Merck & Co.	$70.8 million
PepsiCo	$58 million
Wal-Mart Stores	$57.9 million
AT&T	$50.5 million
General Electric	$47.4 million
Abbott Laboratories	$47.1 million
Coca-Cola Co.	$45 million

SOURCE: National Association of Investors Corp.

AMATEUR'S LIST

THE BEARDSTOWN LADIES' TOP 10 PLUS A RECIPE

In the past decade, the 16 women who make up the Beardstown Ladies Investment Club of Illinois have enjoyed an impressive 23.4 percent average annual return on a portfolio of fewer than 20 stocks. In their bestseller, The Beardstown Ladies' Common Sense Investment Guide *(Hyperion, 1994), they reveal their top 10 reasons for choosing a stock, as adapted below:*

1. The company is ranked in the top third of its industry by Value Line.

2. The Value Line timeliness rating (how fast it will grow relative to other stocks) is one (highest) or two (above average).

3. The Value Line safety rating is one (highest) or two (above average).

4. Its total debt is no more than a third of total assets.

5. Its beta falls between 0.90 and 1.10. (Beta compares the volatility of a stock's price relative to the total market.)

6. The company has had five years of growth in sales and earnings, and is projected to grow 12 to 15 percent in the next several years.

7. Its price per share is $25 or less.

8. The price-earnings ratio is below the company's average p/e ratio for the last five years.

9. Its upside-down ratio is at least 3 to 1. (The upside-down ratio evaluates the relative odds of potential gain versus the risk of loss for a given price per share.)

10. The company has competent and experienced management.

SHIRLEY'S STOCK MARKET MUFFINS

(Guaranteed to Rise)

7 1/2 oz. (4 cups) Raisin Bran
1 1/2 cups sugar
2 1/2 cups flour
2 1/2 tsp. baking soda
1 tsp. salt
1 stick melted margarine
2 eggs
2 cups buttermilk

1. Mix Raisin Bran, sugar, flour, baking soda, and salt by hand.
2. Add the margarine, eggs, and buttermilk.
2. Refrigerate a few days before baking.
4. Bake in muffin tins at 400 degrees for 15 to 20 minutes.

SOURCE: From *Beardstown Ladies' Common Sense Investment Guide.* ©1994 The Beardstown Ladies Investment Group. Reprinted by arrangement with Hyperion.

■ Join the National Association of Investors, which provides a wealth of educational materials, including step-by-step guidelines and a sample partnership agreement. For information, write NAIC, PO Box 220, Royal Oak, MI 48068. ☎ 810-583-6242.

An investor's manual helps you get your club together, tells you how to conduct meetings, find and pick stocks, maintain tax records, and other basics. Annual membership in the NAIC is $35 for the club, plus $11 per member. (The $18 cost of the manual is deducted from the membership fee.)

■ If you'd rather join an existing investment club, you'll have to do some digging to locate one in your area. Most investment clubs are also social groups and members save openings for other friends. The NAIC doesn't release names and addresses of clubs in your area, but its magazine, *Better Investing*, carries a list of regional contacts who may be able to steer you. Once you've found a club in your area, try to attend at least one meeting as an observer. See if the personalities and investment goals fit your own before you sign on.

NEWSLETTERS

TIP SHEETS YOU CAN USE

Top newsletters beat the market, but the worst could lose you lots

It used to be that only Wall Street gnomes looked at stock-tip sheets, and an editor's call to sell could send a ripple through the market. Today, more than two million people read investment newsletters. Hundreds of advisory publications are published, many of which carry one or more sample stock or mutual fund portfolios for subscribers to follow.

Financial newsletters are founded on the idea that you can beat the market, if you're just smart enough or fast enough. "If you don't believe in market timing, you're wasting your time with a newsletter," says Peter Eliades, editor and publisher of the Santa Rosa, California-based *Stockmarket Cycles*, one of the top-ranked mutual fund newsletters of the past five years.

"Most people subscribe because they think there are geniuses out there who are going to make them rich quickly," Eliades says. "But they really should examine the past track record of these newsletters first."

The Hulbert Financial Digest, based in Alexandria, Va., and edited by Mark Hulbert, does just that. It monitors and rates the performance of 160 investment newsletters, examining a portfolio's total return as well as its return on a "risk-adjusted" basis. If a newsletter recommends more than one portfolio, its ranking is based on an average of its portfolios. Hulbert's risk-adjusted ratings are based on a ratio of return to risk to measure net profit. A five-issue trial subscription is $37.50. ☎ 703-683-5905.

Newsletters with the best-performing portfolios significantly outpace the stock market averages. For example, newsletters at the top of Hulbert's rankings over the past five years—such as the *Turnaround Letter*, *OTC Insight*, and the *Oberweis Report*—had compound annualized returns of more than 20 percent in their portfolios. That's one to one-third times the S&P 500 return. Over the same time, the Wilshire 5000 Value Weighted Total Return Index, a broadly based index of 5,000 companies, showed a compound annualized return of over 8.8 percent.

Beating the market on a risk-adjusted basis—the comparison is performance per unit of risk—is more difficult. Only 6 out of 48 stock letters followed by the *Hulbert Financial Digest* did it over the last 10 years. The lowest-risk market-beating strategy came from Gerald Appel's *Systems & Forecast*. Hulbert says that Appel's approach is more statistical and sophisticated than the strategies of many of his competitors, and he has made good use of index options.

One of the highest risk-takers to beat the market was *The Chartist*, edited by Dan Sullivan, which is the rare newsletter with a real account—a $500,000 portfolio. Sullivan, who errs on the side of caution, says he makes his mark by buying when the market is declining.

Two other market-beating timers, *Zweig Forecast* and *Zweig Performance Ratings Report*, both published by Martin Zweig, took on average risk, according to Hulbert. Zweig's Ph.D. in finance provides a clue to his rigorous investing, Hulbert says, but most of his overall success rate can be traced to a hedge he bought smartly just before the October 1987 crash.

Overall, however, most newsletters' real or sample portfolios have only turned in so-so performances. Hulbert notes: "Thirty percent of the 72 letters followed by HFD since the high just before the October 1987 crash have beaten the market over these last two market cycles." That means, of course, that 70 percent of the newsletters didn't make the grade. In the last five years, the percentage of letters that outperformed the Wilshire 5000 remained the same, but now the pool has swelled to 160 letters.

Most readers, of course, don't slavishly follow the investment advice dished out. Yet, some investors who already know what they want may still rely on an editor's talent for market timing to flash a red or green light when it's time to climb in or out of the market altogether. Many newsletters record daily messages on telephone hotlines for their subscribers. Because newsletter editors don't earn a commission on your stock transactions, they may be more objective than a traditional stockbroker. After all, it's their insights that convince subscribers to pay, on average, $100 to $300 a year.

But in their efforts to lure subscribers, newsletters often make exaggerated advertising claims and routinely cherry-pick statistics. "Recent investment letter advertising is making outrageous claims that strain the business' already high tolerance for hype," Hulbert warns. He cites a well-known newsletter whose editor advertised that he was "considered by many to be America's foremost stock market analyst." In fact, 11 years of performance data for his newsletter showed that it was second from the bottom in Hulbert's rankings.

EXPERT LIST

THE TOP-PERFORMING INVESTMENT NEWSLETTERS

So which newsletters offer the most lucrative advice? For the rankings below, the Hulbert Financial Digest *examined dozens of newsletters over 5-year and 10-year periods ending December 30, 1994 and ranked the performance of the portfolios those newsletters recommended on both a total-return and risk-adjusted basis. If a newsletter recommended more than one portfolio, its ranking was based on an average of all of its portfolios. The risk-adjusted ratings are based on average monthly gain per unit of risk. The Wilshire 5000 Value-Weighted Total-Return Index is included below as a benchmark. The Wilshire 5000 is equal to 100, so the higher a newsletter's number, the better. The best mutual fund newsletters are ranked similarly.*

TEN YEARS, 49 NEWSLETTERS MONITORED

TOTAL RETURN	10 year total ret.	Average ann. ret.
1. MPT Review	+1,086.1%	28.1%
2. The Chartist	+364.5%	16.6%
3. BI Research	+360.3%	16.5%
4. Zweig Forecast	+330.2%	15.7%
5. Value Line Investment Survey	+302.8%	15.0%
Wilshire 5000 Total Return	+265.9%	14.0%
T-Bill Portfolio	+76.6%	5.9%

RISK ADJUSTED (100-market)	Rating
1. MPT Review	149.1
2. Zweig Performance Ratings Rep.	142.9
3. Zweig Forecast	142.3
4. Systems & Forecasts	126.4
5. The Chartist	110.4
Wilshire 5000 Total Return	100.0

FIVE YEARS, 93 NEWSLETTERS MONITORED:

TOTAL RETURN	5 year total ret.	Average ann. ret.
1. OTC Insight	+185.0%	23.3%
2. Oberweis Report	+176.2%	22.5%
3. Turnaround Letter	+161.0%	21.2%
4. New Issues	+138.5%	19.0%
5. MPT Review	+133.6%	18.5%
Wilshire 5000 Total Return	+52.6%	8.8%
T-Bill Portfolio	+26.4%	4.8%

RISK ADJUSTED (100-market)	Rating
1. Professional Timing Service	272.1
2. Fidelity Monitor	245.2
3. InvesTech Mutual Fund Advisor	214.4
4. New Issues	202.9
5. Oberweis Report	191.3
Wilshire 5000 Total Return	100.0

EXPERT LIST

TOP-PERFORMING MUTUAL FUND LETTERS: FIVE YEARS, 40 NEWSLETTERS MONITORED:

TOTAL RETURN	5 year total ret.	Average ann. ret.
1. Stockmarket Cycles[1]	+186.0%	23.4%
2. Timer Digest[1]	+124.5%	17.6%
3. Fidelity Monitor[2]	+113.0%	16.3%
4. Fundline[2]	+93.9%	14.2%
5. Professional Timing Service[1]	+85.7%	13.2%
Wilshire 5000 Total Return	+52.6%	8.8%
T-Bill Portfolio	+26.4%	4.8%

RISK ADJUSTED (100-market)	Rating
1. Stockmarket Cycles[1]	348.1
2. Professional Timing Service[1]	301.0
3. Fidelity Monitor[2]	245.2
4. InvesTech Mutual Fund Advisor	214.4
5. Timer Digest[1]	191.4
Wilshire 5000 Total Return	100.0

NOTES: 1. Fund portfolio. 2. Average. SOURCE: *Hulbert Financial Digest*, 316 Commerce St., Alexandria, VA 22314, 703-683-5905.

WHERE TO GET THE TOP NEWSLETTERS

BI RESEARCH
Tom Bishop, ed., $90
PO Box 133
Redding, CT 06875
No phone calls

THE CHARTIST
Dan Sullivan, ed., $150
PO Box 758
Seal Beach, CA 90740
☎ 310-596-2385

FIDELITY MONITOR
Jack Bowers, ed., $96
PO Box 1294
Rocklin, CA 95677
☎ 800-397-3094

FUNDLINE
David Menashe, ed., $127
PO Box 663
Woodland Hills, CA 91365
☎ 818-346-5637

INVESTECH MUTUAL FUND ADVISOR
James B. Stack, ed., $175
2472 Birch Glen
Whitefish, MT 59937
☎ 406-862-7777

MPT REVIEW
Louis Navellier, ed., $245
PO Box 5695
Incline Village, NV 89450
☎ 702-831-1396

NEW ISSUES
Norman Fosback and Glen King Parker, eds., $95
3471 N. Federal Hwy.
Ft. Lauderdale, FL 33306
☎ 800-327-6720

OBERWEIS REPORT
James D. Oberweis, ed., $249
841 N. Lake
Aurora, IL 60506
☎ 708-801-4766

OTC INSIGHT
James Collins, ed., $195
PO Box 127
Moraga, CA 94556
☎ 800-955-9566

PROFESSIONAL TIMING SERVICE
Curtis J. Hesler, ed., $185
PO Box 7483
Missoula, MT 59807
☎ 406-543-4131

STOCKMARKET CYCLES
Peter Eliades, ed., $198
PO Box 6873
Santa Rosa, CA 95406
☎ 707-579-8444

SYSTEMS & FORECASTS
Gerald Appel, ed., $195
150 Great Neck Rd.
Great Neck, NY 11021
☎ 516-829-6444,

TIMER DIGEST
Jim Schmidt, ed., $225
PO Box 1688
Greenwich, CT 06836
☎ 800-356-2527

TURNAROUND LETTER
George Putnam III, ed., $195
225 Friend St., Suite 801
Boston, MA 02114
☎ 617-573-9550

VALUE LINE INVESTMENT SURVEY
Value Line, Inc., ed., $525
711 Third Ave., NY, NY 10017
☎ 800-634-3583,

ZWEIG FORECAST
Martin Zweig, ed., $265
PO Box 2900
Wantagh, NY 11793
☎ 516-785-1300

ZWEIG PERFORMANCE RATINGS
Timothy Clark, ed., $205
PO Box 2900
Wantagh, NY 11793
☎ 516-785-1300

STOCKS ONLINE

USING YOUR PC TO PICK YOUR STOCKS

Computers can't choose stocks, but they can give you a lot more choices

Your personal computer can be a window into the stock exchanges. You can examine current stock quotes and analysts' reports and screen tremendous databases for any number of stock characteristics. You can even buy stock on a PC.

You don't have to be a computer expert to use the screening techniques of Wall Street pros, but you do have to invest some time and money. The better screening programs are as easy to use as a spreadsheet or database program. Most disk-based programs cost between $100 and $800 a year. If you plan to purchase a computer for stock screening, the American Association of Individual Investors (AAII), an independent nonprofit group, suggests you chose an IBM- compatible PC. Investing software for the Apple Macintosh is not as widely available and what little there is, is rapidly disappearing.

Stock screening online can be pricier, since online services, such as CompuServe, generally charge users for the time their computer is hooked up. You'd be well-advised to study your manual closely before logging on and become familiar with abbreviations for certain financial ratios.

The big advantage of the online screening services is timeliness. These services generally update stock prices nightly and corporate data weekly. Subscribers to disk services, however, receive financial data by mail. But users can generally get more detail from disk-based services. Besides, disk-based services can offer more flexibility and depth. Typically, online users can compare stocks in just a few dozen categories. On disk, you have greater freedom to manipulate data.

Of course, says AAII president John Markese, "screening stocks won't make you a better investor."

It will, however, make it easier to sift through data. A subscription to AAII's 28-page bi-monthly newsletter on screening techniques and the latest investment-related computer developments, *The Individual Investor's Guide to Computerized Investing,* costs $40 per year and includes a year-end 500-page guide by the same name. Members pay $30. Membership costs $49 annually. ☎ 800-428-2244.

CHOOSING A STOCK-SCREENING SERVICE

Stock-screening services vary widely. Some only provide raw data, while others offer complete analysis systems. In selecting which service works best for you, the American Association of Individual Investors, an independent, nonprofit group, suggests that you pay attention to how the service provides data, what information is provided, which computer systems can use the data, the cost, and even how the service determines what to charge for the data. Some items on the AAII checklist:

■ **Take a close look at the features the service offers.** Obviously the service should supply the information you are searching for, but a quick look through the grids or product descriptions will show that services vary greatly in breadth and depth. If you are a technician, then you should probably seek a service that specializes only in providing historical data for the markets you analyze. You do not want to pay for features that you will never use.

■ **Charges for access and data can vary greatly between services.** The best way to compare two services is to determine the type of data that you are going to need and compute how much it is going to cost to obtain it.

■ **If you are looking for real-time data, watch out for exchange fees.** Stock and securities exchanges charge individuals for access to real-time data. All real-time vendors must collect this fee, but may not mention it in their pricing lists.

SCREENING THE STOCK-SCREENING SERVICES

Online or on disk, here's what the leading services have to offer

SERVICE	COST[1]	SECURITIES	CRITERIA	COMMENTS
■ ONLINE SCREENS				
CompuServe ☎ 800-848-8199	$8.95/mo., $5–$10/hr. extended use	90,000	40	*Money* magazine's Fund, E*Trade, Quick & Reilly brokerage.
GEnie ☎ 800-638-9636	$8.95/mo., $3–$13 for extended use	67,000	50	Dow Jones News/Retrieval, Charles Schwab.
Prodigy CANSLIM ☎ 800-776-3449	$29.90/mo.	20,000	50	Includes a popular preset screen of seven criteria.
Reuters Money to set Network ☎ 800-346-2024	$19.95/mo., $50 for extended use	18,500	121	Allows user to set price-limit triggers at which system will sound an alert.
Telescan ProSearch 4.0 ☎ 800-324-8246	$295/software, $99/mo., $10/hr. peak	50,000	207	Access to 500 single stocks traded worldwide.
■ DISK-BASED SCREENS				
AAII Criteria Stock Investor ☎ 312-280-0170	Member, $99/yr.; nonmember $150/yr.	8,000	250	Requires 30 MB on hard-drive, twice what others require.
Morningstar's U.S. Equities OnFloppy ☎ 800-876-5005	From $59 for trial issue to $2,300/yr.	6,100	100	Allows you to customize database to create your own rankings.
Value/Screen III ☎ 800-654-0508	$325–$1,995/yr.	1,600	52	Database of widely traded stocks, good tool for conservative investor.
■ MUTUAL FUND ONLY SCREENS				
Morningstar ☎ 800-876-5005	CD-ROM $295-$795/yr.; Floppy, $45–$185/yr.	4,600	94	CD-ROM offers 20 times the data on same funds as floppy.
Alexander Steele's Mutual Fund Expert ☎ 800-237-8400	$199–$499/yr.	4,940	68	Fast and easy to use.

NOTES: 1. Prices indicated are as of March 1995; may vary depending on speed of transmission.
SOURCE: Individual services.

■ **Check to see if there is a monthly minimum.** If you are an infrequent user, you might be paying for data that you never use.

■ **If it is a dial-up service, ask where the closest access number is.** The difference in cost between two services may change if you take the cost of a long-distance phone call into account.

■ **Ask about off-line options.** Programs that allow you to construct your data request off-line and then automatically connect, retrieve data, and log off will keep online charges to a minimum.

■ **Make sure data are transferrable.** Check to see if the data can be exported for use in other programs. Some systems are closed.

EXPERT TIPS

BROKERS YOU CAN TRUST

Where to look before you leap into the market

You've carefully considered your financial goals. You've talked with brokers at several investment firms. You've quizzed them about their investment experience and double-checked their professional and educational backgrounds. Now, you're ready to pick the broker who will take your money and make it grow. Before you leap, though, remember that hundreds of brokers are either barred from doing business or suspended for cheating, stealing, forging paperwork, borrowing money against customers' accounts, and other assorted rules violations every year.

That's the exception, of course, but before hiring a broker, you should consider these tips from the National Association of Securities Dealers (NASD). The advice could spare you trouble later on.

■ **Check on the broker's disciplinary history.** State securities regulators can tell you if a broker is licensed to do business in your state. And the NASD operates a hotline, ☎ 800-289-9999, that can also get you information on disciplinary actions taken against a broker by securities regulators and criminal authorities. The NASD often

HOW TO GRADE YOUR BROKER...

Is your broker doing a good job with your money? Give him a report card by asking yourself the following questions from the editors of Stand Up to Your Stockbroker *(©1991 Consumers Union of U.S., Inc.).*

■ **Have your investments kept pace with market averages?**
If the S&P 500 average has grown 15 percent over the past six months, have you done about as well? If not, investigate the situation.

■ **Are you paying too much in commissions for what you are earning?**
If you would have had an 18 percent return but your commission costs were 15 percent, you actually earned only 3 percent. If so, your broker may be recommending too many short-term trades.

■ **Does your broker recommend you buy only proprietary products?**
If so, find out why and ask if there are other products that are just as suitable. Overdependence on in-house products could mean the broker is more interested in winning in-house contests than in earning money for you.

■ **Does your broker advise you only to buy and rarely to sell?**
That may be fine if you own nothing but blue-chip securities. In any case, you should discuss this with your broker.

■ **Has your broker tried to assume full control of all investment decisions without your permission?**
If so, he is acting dishonestly, even if you have made money. Complain immediately.

■ **Is your broker difficult or impossible to reach when things are going badly?**
A broker should be in touch with you in good times and bad. That doesn't mean your broker should hold your hand through every transaction, but he or she should be available when you have to make tough decisions.

will not disclose information on pending lawsuits or complaints, however.

■ **Ask for a copy of the brokerage firm's commission schedule.** This will tell you how the broker is paid. Firms usually pay sales staff based on the amount of money invested by a customer and the number of transactions done in a customer's account. The broker may be paid more for selling the firm's own investment products. Ask what fees or charges you will be required to pay when opening, maintaining, or closing an account.

■ **Decide whether you need a full-service firm or a discount brokerage firm.** A full-service firm recommends stocks, fills orders, and offers research support. Discount brokerage firms take orders but do not offer recommendations. The charges you pay differ depending on the services provided.

■ **Ask if the brokerage firm is a member of the Securities Investor Protection Corporation.** The SIPC provides some customer protection if a member firm becomes insolvent. Also, ask if the firm has other insurance beyond the SIPC limits. For instance, the SIPC does not insure against losses attributable to a decline in the market value of your securities. For more information, call the SIPC, ☎ 202-371-8300.

■ **Do not rush into a decision.** Investigate the firm and broker thoroughly. Resist salespeople who urge you to open an account with them immediately. Never send money to buy an investment based simply on an effective telephone sales pitch. And never make a check out to a sales representative or send checks to an address different from the business address of the brokerage firm.

...AND WHAT TO DO IF HE FLUNKS

The SEC is the top securities regulator, but it has only about 50 inspectors to police the nation's 20,000 brokers and investment advisers, so the settlement of disputes is left largely to industry groups. The steps you can take:

■ **CONTACT YOUR BROKER FOR AN EXPLANATION.** If you are not satisfied, contact the broker's manager. Explain your position and ask if the matter can be resolved without resorting to law suits. If you get no satisfaction from the branch manager, file a complaint with SEC, NASD, or your local state securities regulator. These agencies can take disciplinary action against a broker but usually will not resolve a dispute or help you get your money back.

■ **FILE FOR ARBITRATION.** Arbitration has become the main route for settling disputes between investors and brokers because most investors sign an arbitration clause when they sign a customer agreement with a brokerage firm. You pay a small fee to have your claim reviewed and a decision made by an impartial arbitrator. You can file for arbitration with the NASD, ☎ 202-728-8000, or the New York Stock Exchange, ☎ 212-656-3000, among other exchanges. The American Arbitration Association, ☎ 202-296-8510, also provides securities arbitrators. If the amount in dispute is less than $10,000, your case will be assigned one public arbitrator. If the amount is over $10,000, two public arbitrators and one industry arbitrator will be used. It's a quick and fairly inexpensive process—unless you choose to have a lawyer represent you. Recent figures show that investors who enter arbitration win their cases and recover some damages more than half the time. Once a decision is made, however, you have almost no recourse to appeal.

■ **GO TO COURT.** If you did not sign an arbitration agreement, you can take your dispute to court. Though expensive and time-consuming, going to court offers the advantage of being judged by a jury of your peers, and you can appeal to a higher court if you lose the first round.

DISCOUNT BROKERS

BUYING STOCK ON THE CHEAP

If you know what you want, there's no need to pay full commission

Discount brokers now account for about a third of individual stock trades. No wonder. While full-service brokerages provide customers with investment advice and other services, discount brokers stick to making trades and offer fewer services, passing the savings on to you. Cost-conscious investors can take a huge chunk out of the commissions they pay on stock trades by using a discount brokerage firm. But you have to know what you want and you have to be comfortable making your own investment decisions.

There's no question you can save a bundle using a discount stockbroker to execute your trades. According to the 1995 Discount Brokerage Survey, published by Mercer, Inc., in New York, ☎ 800-582-9854, the average commission among the 10 cheapest discount brokers to trade 100 shares at $50 per share was $29.60. The Big Three regular discounters—Charles Schwab, Fidelity, and Quick & Reilly—have an average commission of $52.70 for this trade, while full-service brokers typically charge $103.

It's difficult to say which discount brokerage firm offers the best deal, because they set their prices differently. Rates often are based on the total dollar value of a

EXPERT LIST

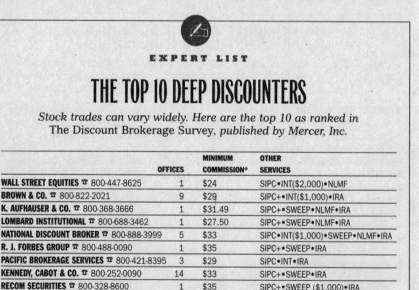

THE TOP 10 DEEP DISCOUNTERS

Stock trades can vary widely. Here are the top 10 as ranked in The Discount Brokerage Survey, *published by Mercer, Inc.*

	OFFICES	MINIMUM COMMISSION*	OTHER SERVICES
WALL STREET EQUITIES ☎ 800-447-8625	1	$24	SIPC•INT($2,000)•NLMF
BROWN & CO. ☎ 800-822-2021	9	$29	SIPC+•INT($1,000)•IRA
K. AUFHAUSER & CO. ☎ 800-368-3666	1	$31.49	SIPC+•SWEEP•NLMF•IRA
LOMBARD INSTITUTIONAL ☎ 800-688-3462	1	$27.50	SIPC+•SWEEP•NLMF•IRA
NATIONAL DISCOUNT BROKER ☎ 800-888-3999	5	$33	SIPC•INT($1,000)•SWEEP•NLMF•IRA
R. J. FORBES GROUP ☎ 800-488-0090	1	$35	SIPC+•SWEEP•IRA
PACIFIC BROKERAGE SERVICES ☎ 800-421-8395	3	$29	SIPC•INT•IRA
KENNEDY, CABOT & CO. ☎ 800-252-0090	14	$33	SIPC+•SWEEP•IRA
RECOM SECURITIES ☎ 800-328-8600	1	$35	SIPC+•SWEEP ($1,000)•IRA
BARRY MURPHY & CO. ☎ 800-221-2111	2	$32.50	SIPC+•SWEEP ($1,000)•NLMF•IRA

SIPC: Securities Investor Protection Corp. insures securities and cash up to $500,000. Plus sign indicates coverage beyond $500,000 at no extra charge.
SWEEP: Automatically invests cash balances in interest-bearing money market fund until those funds are reinvested. (Money market funds usually offer better interest than cash balance accounts.)

INT: Pays interest on customers' cash balances Amounts in parentheses, if any, indicate minimum amount above which interest is paid. If a discount firm offers a sweep account, we do not include information on cash balance interest.
NLMF: No-load mutual funds can be purchased through the firm. Charges may apply, and available funds vary.
IRA: Self-directed IRAs can be set up. Charges may vary.

SOURCE: *The Discount Brokerage Survey,* Mercer, Inc., 1994.

transaction, the number of shares purchased or simply a flat fee for each type of transaction. Sometimes, small commissions and fees for non-routine trades are added on. Large dollar volume trades or trades ordered using a computer or Touch-Tone phone get further discounts at some firms.

What all this means is that some firms will be cheaper for some trades, and more expensive for others. The American Association of Individual Investors, ☎ 312-280-0170, advises that you choose a broker by first comparing the commissions they charge for the kinds of trades you are most likely to make. Call several discounters directly, or use one of the annual surveys published by Mercer or the AAII. Mercer's is easier to use, because it lists the 30 cheapest discounters in descending order by cost for each of 22 typical trades, while the AAII lists them alphabetically, and for only three sample trades. But AAII's list is much more inclusive, covering all 88 discount brokerage firms. Mercer also ranks 110 bank brokers by state and all the independent brokers.

After you have chosen several candidate firms, AAII recommends that you ask for a commission schedule and description of services, fees, and bonus discounts. Keep in mind that some firms charge a flat fee to open a new account and charge high fees to wire funds and for copies of reports and bounced checks.

The Big Three discounters, and some of the others, try to compete with the full-service firms by offering research information, investment recommendations, 24-hour Touch-Tone service, asset management accounts (with check-writing privileges and ATM cards), and margin accounts for trading other instruments, such as options, bonds, and certificates of deposit, as well as extensive branch networks.

That said, you shouldn't expect a lot of hand-holding. Andre Scheluchin, managing editor of Mercer's survey, warns investors to keep in mind that discounters have set rates and offer little maintenance of your account. If you want more attention, and more control over the price you pay, then you're better off with a full-service broker. And, Scheluchin notes, it is not impossible to negotiate a cut in commission with a full-service broker, so you may only pay a little more than with a discounter.

If you want to check out a brokerage firm before doing business, background information is available from the National Association of Securities Dealers, ☎ 800-289-9999, or from the Central Registration Depository of your state securities agency, listed in the blue pages of the phone book.

FACT FILE:

NO BROKER REQUIRED

■ *If you make an initial purchase directly from the company offering the stock, you can do away with brokerage commissions altogether. The American Association of Individual Investors reports that 17 companies sell stock directly to investors, at commissions of only a few cents a share. Most of these are sold nationwide.*

Arrow Financial Corp.
Atlantic Energy Inc.
Barnett Banks Inc.
Central Vermont Public Service*
COMSAT Corporation
Dial Corp
DQE Co.*
Exxon Corp.
First Alabama Bancshares Inc.
Johnson Controls Inc.
Kellwood Co.
Kerr-McGee Corp.
Mobil Corp.
SCANA Corp.
Summit Bancorp (N.J.)
Texaco Inc.
U.S. West Inc.

*Not available to residents in certain states.
SOURCE: American Association of Individual Investors.

EXPERT TIP

READING A BALANCE SHEET

A guided tour from a noted investment authority

John Train is well known as the author of *The New Money Masters* (HarperCollins, 1989) and *Most Remarkable Occurances* (HarperCollins, 1978), and founder of Train, Smith Investment Counsel in New York. The following article, which originally appeared in *Harvard Magazine*, outlines Train's basic approach to understanding a financial statement:

The most important single truth to grasp about investing is that when you buy a share of stock you become a partner in a business. The essence of investing is thus understanding businesses, companies.

Company events are reported in dollar terms. To invest sensibly you therefore need to understand what the company is trying to tell you in its financial statement, which is published in a conveniently stylized form, like a sonnet. Though the elements are fairly simple, I observe that many of my clients have trouble reading one. So here is a simple guide to help get started. A company's financial statement comes in four parts: the balance sheet, the income statement, the cash flow statement, and the statement of shareholders' equity.

The first of these, the balance sheet, is in essence a financial snapshot of the company at one moment in time, the end of its fiscal year. It is generally brought up to date each quarter thereafter.

The income (or profit and loss) statement shows how the business did during the period: that is, sales minus costs.

The cash flow statement shows where cash came from and what it was used for. The amounts don't quite match those on the income statement, which includes, for example, purchases or sales on credit, where cash has not yet changed hands.

The statement of shareholders' equity tells how much the company's book value rose or fell during the period, whether because it made or lost money or took in new capital by selling stock. If the company made money, this statement will show how much of the profit was put back into the business and how much was paid out to shareholders.

A company's financial statement ordinarily includes an auditor's opinion. A "qualified" opinion often indicates trouble.

The balance sheet is called that because it is set up to balance, like an equation: There's an implied equal sign between the two parts. On the left (or "asset") side you show all the assets in the company at that moment — what it owns—and on the right (or "liability") side you show all the company's debt—what it owes—plus the money that has been put up by the owners and kept in the business: the "shareholders' equity." If you think about it, the money you have invested in a house—your equity—plus the mortgage—a debt—perforce corresponds to the physical structure: the asset.

Here is an example. Let's suppose the shareholders of a company put up $1 million, which goes to buy $1 million worth of gold. A simplified balance sheet would look like this:

Assets
Gold: $1,000,000

Liabilities + Shareholders' Equity
Shareholders' Equity: $1,000,000

Suppose we now borrow a million dollars from the bank and buy an additional million dollars worth of gold. Our simplified balance sheet would then look like this:

Assets	
Gold	$2,000,000
	$2,000,000
Liabilities + Shareholders' Equity	
Bank debt	$1,000,000
Shareholders Eq.	$1,000,000
	$2,000,000

In other words, the two sides of the equation still balance.

Good. Now suppose that during our first year of business the price of gold doubles, and we happily sell half our hoard for the original cost of the entire amount. Our simplified income statement now looks like this:

Revenues	$2,000,000
Less: costs of goods sold*	$1,000,000
Profit before tax	$1,000,000
Less: Provision for taxes	$250,000
Net income	$750,000

* Sales are ordinarily shown on an accrual basis—that is, what you are committed to—rather than a cash basis (when you actually take in the money).

We can use this $750,000 of free cash to pay down the bank loan, pay ourselves a dividend, build up our shareholders' equity or buy back our own stock. Let's look at the first case. After paying taxes, we pay down the bank loan:

Assets	
Cash	$1,000,000
Gold (at cost)*	$1,000,000
	$2,000,000

Liabilities + Shareholders' Equity	
Bank Debt	$250,000
Shareholders' Equity:	
Common stock	$1,000,000
Retained earnings	$750,000
	$2,000,000

*At market: $2,000,000. Accounting principles require that you show the lower of cost or market value.

"Retained earnings" on the balance sheet is where you put money the company has earned and left in the business, not paid out in dividends.

An interesting question arises when we add to our inventory at various prices. For instance, suppose that in our gold-trading activities we bought at different prices and sold at different prices. The two major systems of showing these transactions are called "First In-First Out" or FIFO, and "Last In-First Out" or LIFO. When the costs of raw materials are rising, FIFO makes the profits look higher, since sales are taken against the earlier, low-cost, purchases. LIFO makes the profit look lower. Why might you want to do this? (1) To improve the bottom line of the balance sheet; (2) to lower taxes.

Footnotes to the financial statements may include information that does not show up in any of the numerical tables, such as pending litigation, company restructuring, or prospective mergers. So always read the footnotes.

Perhaps the biggest difference between the way business professionals and non-professionals examine financial statements is that if you have actually been in business, you tend to look at the cash and equivalents, and at the cash flow section of the report. If a business is doing well, cash will be building up and can be put to work in useful ways: paying off debt, adding to plant, buying back the company's own shares in the market. If things are going badly, the company will be short of cash, bank and other debt will be rising, and management will be run ragged coping with creditors instead of improving its products. (A hot growth company may also want cash because it has so many opportunities, but that's a more agreeable problem.)

After you have worked with financial statements for a while, you get in the habit of calculating the return on equity, how fast the inventory turns over, the operating profit margin, and a hundred other things.

So much for the Shortest Possible Course. To continue on your own, send to Merrill Lynch for their excellent 28-page pamphlet called *How to Read a Financial Report.* (It may be that sooner or later their "financial consultant" will call.) After that, try Benjamin Graham's admirable *Interpretation of Financial Statements* (HarperCollins, 1987). It's out of print, but should be available at your library.

The whole thing is a lot more fun than you might think. And consider this: Even if you've only got this far, you're already well ahead of the mass of investors!

EXPERT LIST

STOCKING UP ON INVESTOR FREEBIES

There's a gold mine of freebies, perks, and giveaways awaiting investors in many companies, says Charles Carlson, author of Free Lunch on Wall Street *(McGraw-Hill, 1993). Carlson drew up the following list of companies that lavish goodies on investors. Most offer dividend reinvestment programs as well.*

AMERICAN RECREATION CENTERS, INC.
11171 Sun Center Dr. #120
Rancho Cordova, CA 95670

■ Shareholders of 500 or more shares join the Distinguished Shareholder Club, which entitles them to five free games of bowling per day at any of the firm's bowling centers.
☎ **916-852-8005**

ANHEUSER-BUSCH CO.
One Busch Place
St. Louis, MO 63118

■ Shareholders get a 15 percent discount at the company's amusement and theme parks, including Busch Gardens and Sea World. The company also gives free tours of its main brewery to shareholders and non-shareholders alike.
☎ **314-577-3342**

BROWN-FOREMAN CORP.
850 Dixie Highway
Louisville, KY 40210

■ The company has traditionally provided shareholders with a 50 percent discount on certain Lenox holiday china and ornaments, as well as a 50 percent discount on its Hartmann-brand luggage.
☎ **502-585-1100**

CHALONE WINE GROUP
621 Airpark Rd.
Napa, CA 94558

■ Shareholders of 100 or more shares get up to 25 percent off on wine, including older vintages and special reserve bottles, and VIP tours of vineyards.
☎ **707-254-4200**

CML GROUP
524 Main St.
Acton, MA 01720

■ Shareholders get discounts of 10 to 15 percent on certain NordicTrack equipment.
☎ **508-264-4155**

CSX CORP.
901 East Cary St.
Richmond, VA 23219

■ CSX is best known for its railroad operations, but it also operates a prestigious resort, the Greenbrier, in White Sulphur Springs, WV. Shareholders receive discounts on stays at the resort.
☎ **804-782-1400**

GENERAL MILLS
One General Mills Blvd.
Minneapolis, MN 55426

■ The company offers a holiday package of products and coupons with a retail value of $50 for just $19.95. Packages include a range of products from Cheerios to Gold Medal muffin mix to Gushers fruit snacks.
☎ **612-540-2311**

TANDY CORP.
1800 One Tandy Center
Fort Worth, TX 76102

■ Around the holidays, Tandy shareholders receive a 10 percent discount on purchases of up to $10,000 at Radio Shack home electronics stores.
☎ **817-390-3700**

WALT DISNEY CO.
500 South Buena Vista St.
Burbank, CA 91521

■ Shareholders may join Disney's Magic Kingdom Gold Card Program at a reduced rate to receive reduced prices on hotel accommodations and tickets to theme parks and discounts on Disney store merchandise.
☎ **818-505-7040**

WILLIAM WRIGLEY, JR., CO.
410 North Michigan Ave.
Chicago, IL 60611

■ Shareholders are sent a box of 20 packs (100 sticks) of the company's chewing gum each year.
☎ **312-644-2121**

MUTUAL FUNDS

LONG-TERM INVESTING

MAKING THE MOST OF MUTUAL FUNDS

There are now more funds than stocks. Here's our annual ranking

Hardly a week passes that some publication isn't coming out with its "exclusive rankings" of the best mutual funds ever. Most of the rankings are perfectly legitimate and loaded with useful information. But if you're the average investor, you needn't watch your mutual funds as closely as a three-minute egg. On the other hand, neither should your mutual funds be stored untended for years, like fine wines in a cellar. An annual check-up seems about right.

With that perspective very much in mind, we asked Morningstar, Inc., to rank the performance of the top mutual funds for the long-term investor. The funds are ranked based on their annualized three-year return, as of December 31, 1994—though returns for one year and five years are also provided. We settled on ranking funds by their three-year performance mainly because that seemed the most appropriate time horizon for the buy-and-hold investor.

The top 10 funds in each of 14 categories are included in Morningstar's rankings, which start on page 39. The categories themselves are worth some explanation. Different kinds of funds have different investment objectives; that's generally how funds are grouped so that investors can compare apples with apples. But, in truth, the dividing line between categories can be somewhat squishy. Typically, the funds themselves decide what category they belong in—not some independent authority or government agency. And different publications often classify funds in different categories. What exactly, for example, is the difference between a "growth" fund and an "aggressive growth" fund? How different will the investment strategy of one fund be from another? A careful investor will want to understand the fund classification categories. Following is a brief explanation of the categories Morningstar used to compile its rankings.

■ **AGGRESSIVE FUNDS:** They seek the rapid growth of capital, often through investment in smaller companies and with investment techniques involving greater-than-average risk, such as frequent trading, leveraging, and short-selling. This category also includes Small Company funds, a type of fund that seeks capital appreciation by investing primarily in stocks of small companies, as determined by market capitalization.

■ **GROWTH FUNDS:** They invest primarily in equity securities. Current income, if it is considered at all, is a secondary objective.

■ **TOTAL RETURN FUNDS:** They include Equity Income funds that invest at least 65 percent of assets in equity securities with above-average yields, and Growth and Income funds that seek growth of capital and current income as near-equal objectives, primarily by investing in equity securities with above-average yield for appreciation.

■ **INTERNATIONAL FUNDS:** Among the international funds are European stock funds, which generally invest at least 65 percent of assets in equity securities of European issuers; Foreign Stock funds, which invest primarily in equity securities of issuers located outside the United States; Pacific stock funds, which invest primarily in issuers located in countries in the Pacific Basin, including Japan, Hong Kong, Malaysia, Singapore, and Australia; and World Stock funds , with holdings in equity securities of issuers located throughout the world, maintaining a percentage of assets (normally 25 to 50 percent) in the United States.

■ **SPECIALTY FUNDS:** This type of fund seeks capital appreciation by investing in equity securities in a single industry or sector, like health, technology, utilities, or natural resources.

■ **HYBRID FUNDS:** These have substantial holdings in both stocks and bonds, or hold securities that have characteristics of both stocks and bonds.

■ **CONVERTIBLE BOND FUNDS:** They invest primarily in bonds and preferred stocks that can be converted into common stocks.

■ **CORPORATE BOND HIGH-YIELD FUNDS:** This type of fund will generally invest 65 percent or more of its assets in bonds rated below investment grade. The price of these issues generally is affected more by the condition of the issuing company (similar to a stock) than by the interest-rate fluctuation that usually causes bond prices to move up and down.

■ **CORPORATE BOND FUNDS:** These funds invest in fixed-income securities, primarily corporate bonds of various quality ratings. This category also includes High-Quality Corporate Bonds funds that have at least 65 percent of their holdings in securities rated A or higher.

■ **GOVERNMENT BOND GENERAL FUNDS:** This type of fund invests in a blend of mortgage-backed securities, Treasuries, and agency securities.

■ **GOVERNMENT BOND TREASURY FUNDS:** These funds invest at least 80 percent of their assets in U.S. Treasury securities.

■ **GOVERNMENT BOND MORTGAGE FUNDS:** These funds generally invest 65 percent of their assets in securities that are backed by mortgages.

■ **INTERNATIONAL BOND FUNDS:** These funds seek current income with capital appreciation as a secondary objective by investing primarily in bonds denominated in currencies other than the U.S. dollar. These bonds are frequently issued by foreign governments. Also includes Short-Term World Income funds that seek income and a stable net asset value by investing primarily in a portfolio of various non-U.S.-currency-denominated bonds, usually with maturities of three years or less. Short-term world income funds seek higher yields than a money market fund and less fluctuation of their net asset value (NAV) than a world bond fund.

■ **MUNICIPAL BOND FUNDS:** These funds seek income that is exempt from federal income tax by investing primarily in bonds issued by any state or municipality.

EXPERT LIST

THE TOP 140 MUTUAL FUNDS

Here Morningstar, Inc., the Chicago-based investment information publisher, ranks the top 10 mutual funds in 14 different categories. The funds are ranked based on their three-year annualized return as of December 31, 1994. The rating column refers to Morningstar's exclusive five-star rating system. Notes explaining the rating system and other various terms used throughout the tables can be found on pages 40 and 41.

Rank	Fund	Style	Return 1 yr.	Return 3 yr.	Return 5 yr.	Rating	Expense ratio	Max. sales charge	Net assets ($mm)
	AGGRESSIVE								
1.	**PBHG GROWTH** ☎ 800-433-0051	SG	4.75	**25.42**	21.98	5★	1.40	—	746
2.	**AIM AGGRESSIVE GROWTH** ☎ 800-347-1919	SB	17.18	**23.37**	23.54	4★	1.00	5.50	715
3.	**20TH CENTURY GIFTRUST INVESTORS** ☎ 800-345-2021	SG	13.49	**20.74**	22.00	5★	1.00	—	274
4.	**SKYLINE SPECIAL EQUITIES** ☎ 800-458-5222	SV	–1.17	**20.03**	18.25	5★	1.50	—	203
5.	**HEARTLAND VALUE** ☎ 800-432-7856	SV	1.71	**19.84**	16.35	5★	1.49	—	339
6.	**PIMCO ADVISORS OPPORTUNITY C** ☎ 800-426-0107	SG	–4.73	**18.56**	21.01	5★	1.90	1.00D	551
7.	**ROYCE MICRO-CAP** ☎ 800-221-4268	SV	3.55	**18.34**	NA	5★	1.99	—	27
8.	**G.T. GLOBAL AMERICA GROWTH A** ☎ 800-824-1580	SB	15.69	**18.20**	12.77	4★	1.66	4.75	200
9.	**FIDELITY LOW-PRICED STOCK** ☎ 800-544-8888	SV	4.81	**17.56**	18.88	5★	1.13	3.00	2,355
10.	**JOHN HANCOCK SPECIAL EQUITIES A** ☎ 800-225-5291	SG	2.02	**16.79**	21.83	5★	1.63	5.00	311
	GROWTH								
1.	**OAKMARK** ☎ 800-625-6275	MB	3.31	**26.15**	NA	5★	1.25	—	1,627
2.	**CRABBE HUSON SPECIAL** ☎ 800-541-9732	SV	11.72	**26.10**	19.48	5★	1.48	—	377
3.	**PARNASSUS** ☎ 800-999-3505	SV	11.98	**21.58**	16.63	4★	1.26	3.50	161
4.	**PIONEER CAPITAL GROWTH A** ☎ 800-225-6292	SB	14.83	**20.02**	NA	5★	1.29	5.75	438
5.	**PUTNAM NEW OPPORTUNITIES A** ☎ 800-225-1581	SG	3.35	**19.85**	NA	5★	1.23	5.75	920
6.	**LONGLEAF PARTNERS** ☎ 800-445-9469	MB	8.96	**17.08**	13.25	5★	1.21	—	754
7.	**FIDELITY VALUE** ☎ 800-544-8888	MB	7.63	**17.03**	12.02	4★	0.77	—	3,720
8.	**GABELLI VALUE** ☎ 800-422-3554	MB	0.00	**16.26**	11.34	4★	1.52	5.50	438
9.	**FRANKLIN BALANCE SHEET INVESTMENT** ☎ 800-342-5236	SV	1.50	**15.87**	NA	5★	1.19	1.50	144
10.	**FIDELITY DESTINY II** ☎ 800-752-2347	LB	4.48	**15.23**	16.10	5★	0.80	8.24	1,468

■ EXPERT LIST

Rank	Fund	Style	Return 1 yr.	Return 3 yr.	Return 5 yr.	Rating	Expense ratio	Max. sales charge	Net assets ($mm)
	TOTAL RETURN								
1.	**OPPENHEIMER MAIN ST. INCOME/ GRTH. A** ☎ 800-525-7048	MB	–1.53	**20.45**	22.23	5★	1.28	5.75	1,269
2.	**WARBURG PINCUS GROWTH & INCOME** ☎ 800-257-5614	MB HL	7.57	**17.18**	13.60	5★	1.28	—	628
3.	**MUTUAL BEACON** ☎ 800-553-3014	MV	5.61	**16.86**	11.50	5★	0.72	—	2,056
4.	**MUTUAL QUALIFIED** ☎ 800-553-3014	MV	5.73	**16.76**	11.62	5★	0.76	—	1,789
5.	**SAFECO EQUITY** ☎ 800-426-6730	SB	9.93	**16.29**	12.96	5★	0.85	—	449
6.	**MUTUAL SHARES** ☎ 800-553-3014	MV	4.53	**15.35**	10.86	5★	0.73	—	3,745
7.	**FIDELITY EQUITY-INCOME II** ☎ 800-544-8888	LV	3.16	**13.45**	NA	5★	0.84	—	7,698
8.	**BABSON VALUE** ☎ 800-422-2766	MV LL	2.51	**13.28**	10.68	4★	1.00	—	122
9.	**FPA PARAMOUNT** ☎ 800-982-4372	MB	9.40	**13.17**	12.85	4★	0.90	6.50	490
10.	**MAXUS EQUITY** ☎ 800-446-2987	MV	0.62	**12.47**	11.60	4★	2.61	—	17
	INTERNATIONAL								
1.	**NEWPORT TIGER** ☎ 800-776-5455	LG	–11.99	**23.49**	15.03	5★	1.56	5.00	456
2.	**PUTNAM ASIA PACIFIC GROWTH A** ☎ 800-225-1581	MB	–0.48	**18.85**	NA	5★	1.53	5.75	155
3.	**DEAN WITTER PACIFIC GROWTH** ☎ 800-869-3863	MG	–17.52	**18.82**	NA	5★	2.41	5.00D	1,418
4.	**GAM INTERNATIONAL** ☎ 800-426-4685	LG	–10.22	**18.53**	12.27	5★	1.58	5.00	159
5.	**GAM PACIFIC BASIN** ☎ 800-426-4685	LB	7.46	**17.28**	11.58	5★	2.06	5.00	49
6.	**T. ROWE PRICE NEW ASIA** ☎ 800-638-5660	MG	–19.15	**17.15**	NA	5★	1.22	—	1,988
7.	**FIDELITY EMERGING MARKETS** ☎ 800-544-8888	MG	–17.93	**16.45**	NA	4★	1.52	3.00	1,508
8.	**JOHN HANCOCK PACIFIC BASIN EQUITIES A** ☎ 800-225-5291	LB	–9.28	**16.41**	6.40	4★	2.43	5.00	42
9.	**IVY INTERNATIONAL A** ☎ 800-456-5111	LV	3.85	**15.50**	9.41	4★	1.64	5.75	222
10.	**HARBOR INTERNATIONAL** ☎ 800-422-1050	LV	5.43	**15.23**	10.89	4★	1.10	—	2,953

EXPLANATION OF TERMS

STYLE/SIZE
Growth-oriented funds (G), generally include companies with the potential to increase earnings faster than the rest of the market. Value-oriented funds (V) focus on stocks that are undervalued by the market. A blend of the two (B) may contain growth and value stocks, or stocks that exhibit both characteristics. Funds with median-market capitalizations of less than $1 billion are labeled small-company funds (S). Funds with median market capitalizations between $1 billion and $5 billion are labeled medium (M) offerings, and funds with median market capitalizations exceeding $5 billion qualify for the large (L) label. Fixed-income funds are split into three maturity groups—short (S), intermediate (I), and long (L)—and three credit quality groups—high (H), medium (M), and low (L). Funds with an average effective maturity of less than four years qualify as short-term bond funds; those with maturity longer than 10 years are long term.

TOTAL RETURN
Total return is calculated by taking the change in investment value, assuming the reinvestment of all income and capital-gains distributions during the period, and dividing by the initial investment value. Total returns for peri-

EXPERT LIST

Rank	Fund	Style	Return 1 yr.	Return 3 yr.	Return 5 yr.	Rating	Expense ratio	Max. sales charge	Net assets ($mm)
	SPECIALTY								
1.	SELIGMAN COMM. & INFORMATION A ☎ 800-221-2783	SG	35.30	**28.96**	24.22	5★	1.58	4.75	308
2.	FIDELITY SELECT HOME FINANCE ☎ 800-544-8888	SV	2.67	**27.30**	23.59	5★	1.39	3.00	130
3.	FIDELITY SELECT ELECTRONICS ☎ 800-544-8888	MB	17.17	**25.41**	23.07	5★	1.71	3.00	157
4.	FIDELITY SELECT COMPUTERS ☎ 800-544-8888	MB	20.45	**23.71**	23.99	5★	1.70	3.00	175
5.	FIDELITY SELECT SOFTWARE & COMP. ☎ 800-544-8888	MG	0.39	**21.78**	21.58	5★	1.50	3.00	212
6.	ALLIANCE TECHNOLOGY A ☎ 800-227-4618	MG	28.51	**21.77**	21.97	4★	1.66	4.25	216
7.	FIDELITY SELECT DEVELOPING COMM. ☎ 800-544-8888	MG	15.13	**21.15**	NA	5★	1.57	3.00	276
8.	JOHN HANCOCK REGIONAL BANK B ☎ 800-225-5291	MV	–0.20	**21.03**	18.19	5★	2.01	5.00D	477
9.	FIDELITY SELECT MULTIMEDIA ☎ 800-544-8888	MG	4.00	**20.37**	12.15	4★	1.88	3.00	27
10.	T. ROWE PRICE SCIENCE & TECH. ☎ 800-638-5660	MG	15.79	**19.55**	21.98	5★	1.21	—	915
	HYBRID								
1.	FIDELITY PURITAN ☎ 800-544-8888	MB ML	1.78	**12.58**	10.71	5★	0.79	2.00	11,769
2.	BERWYN INCOME ☎ 800-824-2249	SV LL	–1.10	**12.08**	11.74	5★	1.00	—	56
3.	SOGEN INTERNATIONAL ☎ 800-628-0252	SB	2.52	**12.07**	10.54	5★	1.26	3.75	1,823
4.	FIDELITY ASSET MANAGER: GROWTH ☎ 800-544-8888	LB	–7.39	**11.98**	NA	5★	1.15	—	2,853
5.	KEMPER DIVERSIFIED INCOME A ☎ 800-621-1048	MI	–3.72	**11.09**	12.70	3★	1.12	4.50	461
6.	LINDNER DIVIDEND ☎ 314-727-5305	MB	–3.31	**10.40**	9.89	4★	0.64	—	1,605
7.	QUEST FOR VALUE OPPORTUNITY A ☎ 800-232-3863	MB	4.92	**10.23**	12.72	4★	1.78	5.50	166
8.	CRABBE HUSON ASSET ALLOCATION ☎ 800-541-9732	MB	–0.84	**9.56**	9.60	4★	1.47	—	107
9.	FRANKLIN INCOME ☎ 800-342-5236	LV LI	–6.37	**9.47**	11.05	4★	0.64	4.25	4,789
10.	DODGE & COX BALANCED ☎ 800-621-3979	LV HL	2.05	**9.39**	9.79	5★	0.58	—	725

ods over a year are expressed in terms of compounded average annual returns.

RATING
Morningstar rates a funds' return performance relative to its class based on total returns adjusted for maximum front-end and applicable deferred loads and redemption fees. It then calculates the fund risk, mindful that most investors' biggest fear is losing money (defined as underperforming the risk-free rate of return an investor can earn from the three-month Treasury bill). The fund's comparative Risk score is then subtracted from its Return score. The result is plotted along a bell curve to determine the fund's rating. The top 10 percent of the class receives five stars (Highest); the next 22.5 percent receives four stars (Above Average); the middle 35 percent earns three stars (Neutral or Average); those lower still in the next 22.5 percent receive two stars (Below Average); and the bottom 10 percent get one star (Lowest).

EXPENSE RATIO
The annual expense ratio expresses the percentage of assets deducted each fiscal year for fund operating expenses.

SALES CHARGE
Maximum level of various fees and sales charges imposed by fund. A deferred sales charge (D) is paid when you sell a fund.

NET ASSETS
The mutual fund's year-end net assets, recorded in millions of dollars.

■ EXPERT LIST

Rank	Fund	Style	Return 1 yr.	Return 3 yr.	Return 5 yr.	Rating	Expense ratio	Max. sales charge	Net assets ($mm)
	CONVERTIBLE BOND								
1.	**BOND FUND FOR GROWTH** ☎ 716-383-1300	LV	–2.51	**15.74**	12.85	5★	1.57	3.25	124
2.	**FIDELITY CONVERTIBLE SECURITIES** ☎ 800-544-8888	LG	–1.76	**12.19**	13.72	5★	0.87	—	891
3.	**PACIFIC HORIZON CAPITAL INCOME** ☎ 800-332-3863	MB	–5.85	**11.91**	13.14	5★	1.09	4.50	201
4.	**PUTNAM CONVERTIBLE INCOME GRTH. A** ☎ 800-225-1581	LV	–1.92	**11.60**	10.11	4★	0.99	5.75	667
5.	**MAINSTAY CONVERTIBLE B** ☎ 800-522-4202	SV	–1.34	**11.57**	13.98	5★	1.90	5.00D	180
6.	**FRANKLIN CONVERTIBLE SECURITIES** ☎ 800-342-5236	SV	–1.64	**11.25**	11.63	4★	0.84	4.50	64
7.	**GABELLI CONVERTIBLE SECURITIES** ☎ 800-422-3554	MG	–0.17	**8.44**	8.79	4★	1.36	—	112
8.	**VANGUARD CONVERTIBLE SECURITIES** ☎ 800-662-7447	SG	–5.68	**8.42**	9.47	4★	0.73	—	171
9.	**SBSF CONVERTIBLE SECURITIES** ☎ 800-422-7273	MV	–6.45	**7.73**	8.80	4★	1.32	—	58
10.	**VALUE LINE CONVERTIBLE** ☎ 800-223-0818	NA	–5.28	**7.38**	8.94	4★	1.07	—	45
	CORPORATE BOND—HIGH YIELD								
1.	**DEAN WITTER HIGH-YIELD SECURITIES** ☎ 800-869-3863	LI	–7.15	**14.89**	8.71	3★	0.69	5.50	432
2.	**FIDELITY SPARTAN HIGH-INCOME** ☎ 800-544-8888	NA	2.61	**14.73**	NA	5★	0.80	—	618
3.	**FIDELITY CAPITAL & INCOME** ☎ 800-544-8888	SB	–5.09	**14.71**	13.51	5★	0.95	—	2,040
4.	**MAINSTAY HIGH-YIELD CORP. BOND B** ☎ 800-522-4202	SV LI	1.50	**14.52**	12.86	5★	1.60	5.00D	1,122
5.	**NORTHEAST INVESTORS** ☎ 800-225-6704	MV LI	2.20	**14.07**	11.24	5★	1.06	—	555
6.	**ADVANTAGE HIGH-YIELD BOND** ☎ 800-241-2039	LL	–2.18	**14.05**	13.17	5★	1.35	4.00D	136
7.	**VENTURE INCOME (+) PLUS A** ☎ 800-279-0279	LI	1.63	**13.76**	5.96	3★	1.48	4.75	57
8.	**COLONIAL HIGH-YIELD SECURITIES A** ☎ 800-248-2828	SV LI	–0.34	**13.06**	12.11	4★	1.23	4.75	390
9.	**FIDELITY ADVISOR HIGH-YIELD A** ☎ 800-522-7297	SG LI	–2.08	**13.05**	15.91	5★	1.22	4.75	683
10.	**SELIGMAN HIGH-YIELD BOND A** ☎ 800-221-2783	LI	0.78	**12.99**	11.82	5★	1.23	4.75	59
	CORPORATE BOND								
1.	**LOOMIS SAYLES BOND** ☎ 800-633-3330	ML	–4.07	**10.25**	NA	5★	0.88	—	83
2.	**FORTRESS BOND** ☎ 800-245-5051	MI	–3.36	**9.23**	11.25	5★	1.05	1.00	142
3.	**ALLIANCE BOND CORPORATE BOND A** ☎ 800-227-4618	ML	–12.75	**9.01**	10.04	3★	1.30	4.25	213
4.	**STRONG INCOME** ☎ 800-368-1030	ML	–1.31	**8.04**	6.31	3★	1.10	—	123
5.	**FPA NEW INCOME** ☎ 800-982-4372	HI	1.46	**7.50**	9.85	5★	0.74	4.50	130
6.	**HAWTHORNE BOND** ☎ 800-272-4548	NA	1.77	**7.16**	NA	5★	0.95	—	0
7.	**IDS BOND** ☎ 800-328-8300	ML	–4.32	**6.91**	9.07	5★	0.68	5.00	2,136

■ EXPERT LIST

Rank	Fund	Style	Return 1 yr.	Return 3 yr.	Return 5 yr.	Rating	Expense ratio	Max. sales charge	Net assets ($mm)
8.	**INVESCO SELECT INCOME** ☎ 800-525-8085	ML	–1.20	**6.70**	8.62	5★	1.11	—	137
9.	**STRONG ADVANTAGE** ☎ 800-368-1030	MS	3.55	**6.68**	7.43	5★	0.80	—	911
10.	**BOND FUND OF AMERICA** ☎ 800-421-4120	MI	–5.02	**6.48**	8.58	4★	0.71	4.75	4,941
	GOVERNMENT BOND-GENERAL								
1.	**STRONG GOVERNMENT SECURITIES** ☎ 800-368-1030	HI	–3.37	**5.97**	8.58	5★	0.90	—	277
2.	**LOOMIS SAYLES U.S. GOVT SECS.** ☎ 800-633-3330	NA	–6.25	**5.68**	NA	3★	1.00	—	17
3.	**ADVANTAGE GOVERNMENT SECURITIES** ☎ 800-241-2039		–9.82	**5.47**	7.88	3★	1.30	4.00D	153
4.	**HEARTLAND U.S. GOVT SECURITIES** ☎ 800-432-7856	HI	–9.64	**5.45**	8.57	3★	1.02	—	65
5.	**WILLIAM PENN U.S. GOVT SECS. INCOME** ☎ 800-523-8440	HL	–3.82	**5.32**	7.39	3★	1.00	4.75	44
6.	**RIGHTIME GOVERNMENT SECURITIES** ☎ 800-242-1421		–0.44	**5.32**	3.29	2★	1.90	4.75	25
7.	**CALIFORNIA INVEST. U.S. GOVT. SECS.** ☎ 800-225-8778		–6.99	**5.28**	8.25	3★	0.62	—	27
8.	**SIT U.S. GOVERNMENT SECURITIES** ☎ 800-332-5580	HS	1.79	**4.84**	7.61	5★	0.80	—	36
9.	**FIDELITY GOVERNMENT SECURITIES** ☎ 800-544-8888	HL	–5.21	**4.74**	7.86	3★	0.69	—	611
10.	**DREYFUS SHORT-INTERMEDIATE GOVT.** ☎ 800-645-6561	HS	–0.75	**4.46**	7.32	5★	0.42	—	472
	GOVERNMENT BOND-TREASURY								
1.	**BENHAM TARGET MATURITIES 2010** ☎ 800-331-8331	HL	–11.97	**5.76**	7.12	1★	0.68	—	56
2.	**VANGUARD F/I LONG-TERM U.S.TREASURY** ☎ 800-662-7447	NA	–7.04	**5.26**	7.69	2★	0.29	—	644
3.	**SCUDDER ZERO COUPON 2000** ☎ 800-225-2470	HI	–7.92	**4.92**	7.71	2★	1.00	—	25
4.	**VANGUARD F/I INTERM-TERM U.S. TREAS.** ☎ 800-662-7447	HI	–4.33	**4.74**	NA	3★	0.29	—	844
5.	**BENHAM TARGET MATURITIES 2005** ☎ 800-331-8331	HL	–9.43	**4.73**	7.23	1★	0.64	—	102
6.	**STAGECOACH U.S. GOVT. ALLOC. A** ☎ 800-222-8222		–6.99	**4.59**	7.14	2★	1.00	4.50	140
7.	**DREYFUS 100% U.S. TREAS. INTRM.-TERM** ☎ 800-648-9048	HI	–3.96	**4.56**	7.42	4★	0.88	—	185
8.	**BENHAM TARGET MATURITIES 2000** ☎ 800-331-8331	HI	–7.16	**4.56**	7.75	1★	0.59	—	255
9.	**DREYFUS 100% U.S.TREAS. SHORT-TERM** ☎ 800-648-9048	HS	–0.29	**4.55**	6.51	4★	0.29	—	172
10.	**ISI TOTAL RETURN U.S. TREASURY** ☎ 800-955-7175	HI	–3.98	**4.48**	7.11	2★	0.77	4.45	195
	GOVERNMENT BOND-MORTGAGE								
1.	**DREYFUS INVESTORS GNMA** ☎ 800-645-6561	NA	–1.06	**4.82**	7.21	5★	0.00	—	45
2.	**FIDELITY MORTGAGE SECURITIES** ☎ 800-544-8888	HI	1.94	**4.46**	7.41	5★	0.79	—	349
3.	**USAA INVESTMENT FEDERAL SECS. GNMA** ☎ 800-382-8722	HI	–0.03	**4.35**	NA	4★	0.31	—	245

■ EXPERT LIST

Rank	Fund	Style	Return 1 yr.	Return 3 yr.	Return 5 yr.	Rating	Expense ratio	Max. sales charge	Net assets ($mm)
4.	**SMITH BARNEY MANAGED GOVTS. A** ☎ 800-451-2010a		−1.98	**4.32**	7.92	3★	1.22	4.50	550
5.	**ASSET MGMT INTERM MORTGAGE SECS.** ☎ 800-527-3713	HL	−1.76	**4.29**	6.96	4★	0.37	—	211
6.	**NORTH AMERICAN U.S. GOVT. SECS. A** ☎ 800-872-8037	HI	−1.66	**4.26**	6.81	3★	1.25	4.75	91
7.	**OPPENHEIMER LIMITED-TERM GOVT. A** ☎ 800-525-7048	NA	0.50	**4.20**	7.60	4★	0.99	3.50	248
8.	**BENHAM GNMA INCOME** ☎ 800-331-8331	HI	−1.51	**4.19**	7.56	5★	0.57	—	952
9.	**VICTORY GOVERNMENT MORTGAGE** ☎ 800-539-3863	NA	−2.07	**4.02**	NA	3★	0.73	4.75	154
10.	**IDS FEDERAL INCOME** ☎ 800-328-8300	HI	−0.31	**3.96**	6.53	4★	0.76	5.00	1,010
	INTERNATIONAL BOND								
1.	**FIDELITY YEN PERFORMANCE** ☎ 800-544-8888	NA	12.64	**9.29**	10.97	4★	1.50	0.40	4
2.	**FRANKLIN/TEMPLETON HARD CURRENCY** ☎ 800-342-5236	NA	15.10	**7.19**	9.89	4★	1.47	3.00	59
3.	**BULL & BEAR GLOBAL INCOME** ☎ 800-847-4200	ML	−13.46	**6.94**	6.94	3★	1.98	—	41
4.	**T. ROWE PRICE INTERNATIONAL BOND** ☎ 800-638-5660	HI	−1.84	**6.46**	10.52	4★	0.99	—	738
5.	**IDS GLOBAL BOND** ☎ 800-328-8300	LG HL	−6.26	**6.10**	9.25	4★	1.26	5.00	450
6.	**INTERNATIONAL INCOME A** ☎ 800-245-5051	HI	−4.64	**6.07**	NA	3★	1.30	4.50	199
7.	**FRANKLIN/TEMPLETON GLOBAL CURRENCY** ☎ 800-342-5236		8.08	**5.90**	7.90	4★	1.41	3.00	55
8.	**FIDELITY DEUTSCHEMARK PERF** ☎ 800-544-8888	NA	16.39	**5.14**	8.34	3★	1.50	0.40	9
9.	**CAPITAL WORLD BOND** ☎ 800-421-4120	HL	−1.43	**5.07**	8.35	4★	1.11	4.75	563
10.	**WARBURG PINCUS GLOBAL FIXED-INCOME** ☎ 800-257-5614	HI	−5.48	**5.04**	NA	3★	0.95	—	85
	MUNICIPAL BOND								
1.	**SMITH BARNEY MANAGED MUNICIPALS A** ☎ 800-451-2010	ML	−4.53	**6.59**	7.81	4★	0.72	4.00	1,607
2.	**UNITED MUNICIPAL HIGH-INCOME** ☎ 800-366-5465	NA	−3.11	**6.50**	7.70	5★	0.76	4.25	339
3.	**AMERICAN CAPITALTAX-EXEMPT H/Y MUNIA** ☎ 800-421-5666	NA	0.19	**6.37**	7.14	5★	1.02	4.75	418
4.	**FRANKLIN HIGH-YIELD TAX-FREE INCOME** ☎ 800-342-5236	ML	−2.58	**6.37**	7.29	5★	0.58	4.25	3,124
5.	**THORNBURG INTERMEDIATE MUNICIPAL A** ☎ 800-847-0200	MI	−2.48	**6.34**	NA	5★	0.90	3.50	209
6.	**VENTURE MUNI (+) PLUS B** ☎ 800-279-0279	ML	2.29	**6.28**	6.64	5★	2.08	4.00D	143
7.	**VISTA TAX-FREE INCOME A** ☎ 800-648-4782	HL	7.64	**6.23**	7.95	3★	0.48	4.50	82
8.	**UST MASTER LONG-TERM TAX-EXEMPT** ☎ 800-233-1136	HL	−5.83	**6.22**	7.65	2★	0.85	4.50	73
9.	**STRONG MUNICIPAL BOND** ☎ 800-368-1030	ML	−4.55	**6.16**	7.25	4★	0.80	—	280
10.	**FORUM TAXSAVER BOND** ☎ 207-879-8900	ML	−0.86	**6.06**	7.11	5★	0.60	3.75	16

SOURCE: Morningstar, Inc.

WORDS TO WATCH ON WALL STREET

Here's your guide to the terms you need to know before you invest

Do you know the difference between a "load" and a "no-load" fund? What does it mean when a fund labels itself a "growth and income fund?" Even within the mutual funds industry, there is disagreement about what some terms mean. Definitions for different types of mutual funds (described below) are from the Investment Company Institute, the trade association for the mutual fund industry. However, interpretations of terms, such as "aggressive growth," may vary from fund to fund. Morningstar Mutual Fund's definitions of different categories of funds are explained on pages 37 and 38. Before picking a mutual fund, read the prospectus for a precise explanation of the fund's strategy and investment objective. Included below are definitions of some of the other terms that you're likely to stumble across when reading a prospectus.

Aggressive growth fund—A fund that seeks maximum capital gains. Current income is not a significant factor. Some may invest in businesses somewhat out of the mainstream, such as fledgling companies, new industries, companies fallen on hard times, or industries temporarily out of favor. Some may also use specialized investment techniques such as option writing or short-term trading.

Back-end Load—A sales commission charged when you sell your shares in a mutual fund. Usually ranges from 0.5 to 6.0 percent.

Balanced fund—Generally has a three-part investment objective: to conserve investors' initial principal; to pay current income; and to promote long-term growth of both principal and income. Balanced funds mix bonds, preferred stocks, and common stocks.

Convertible securities fund—Invests primarily in debt securities that can be converted into equity securities of the issuing corporation.

Corporate bond fund—Purchases bonds of corporations for the majority of portfolio. The rest of the portfolio may be in U.S. Treasury bonds or bonds issued by a federal agency.

Derivatives—Financial instruments with values linked to some underlying asset, such as a bond, stock, or index.

Emerging markets fund—Invests primarily in the equity securities of companies in, or doing business in, emerging countries and markets.

Energy stock fund—Invests in the energy sector, which may include companies developing new energy-efficient technologies.

Environmental securities fund—Generally invests in environment-related firms. May include companies involved in hazardous waste treatment, waste recycling, and other related areas. Such funds may or may not screen companies to determine whether they also meet specific social objectives.

Flexible portfolio fund—A fund that may be 100 percent invested in stocks, bonds, or money market instruments, depending on market conditions. These funds give the money managers the greatest flexibility in anticipating or responding to economic changes.

Front-end Load—A sales commission charged when you buy your shares. Some funds charge up to 8.5 percent. Usual range: 1 to 3 percent of your investment.

Ginnie Mae or GNMA Fund—Invests in mortgage securities backed by the Government National Mortgage Association (GNMA). To qualify for this category, the majority of the portfolio must always be invested in mortgage-backed securities.

Global bond fund—Invests in bonds of companies and countries worldwide.

HOW TO PICK LOW-COST FUNDS

When funds do poorly, fees can worsen your return

There are some 4,000 mutual funds out there, more than 30 times the number available in 1980. Yet the annual cost of running the funds hasn't fallen much. For some stock funds, fees actually have increased. Fund expenses matter: Fees charged by mutual funds get taken out of the investor's pocket before any returns are paid out. When funds do poorly, expenses worsen a fund's losses. Studies show that, although investors sometimes do well even with high-expense funds, your odds of gaining better returns improve when you invest in lower-cost funds.

How do you pick funds with low fees? The table at right provides some guidelines. It shows the average annual expenses shareholders can expect from the major types of stock funds and three types of bond funds. The expenses are shown as a percentage of the fund's assets. For example, a 0.77 percent expense ratio for municipal bonds means that the average fund of this type costs 77 cents per $100 in assets to run.

The table's annual fund expenses include: fees paid to the fund's adviser, costs of accounting, shareholder and annual reports, phone representatives, advertising, and payments to custodians, or the institutions that hold the fund's securities.

Should low-cost fees be the main reason you choose a mutual fund? Hardly. Fund advisers say the most important factor is to decide what type of fund—aggressive growth, diversified foreign, corporate bond, etc.—you want to invest in and the degree of risk involved. Only after deciding on funds that reflect your goals should you compare fund costs.

■ WHAT TO AIM FOR

Average annual expenses as a percentage of assets for various stock types.

DIVERSIFIED U.S. STOCK FUNDS	**1.29%**
Aggressive growth	1.72%
Equity income	1.25%
Growth	1.28%
Growth and income	1.18%
Small company	1.37%
INTERNATIONAL STOCK FUNDS	**1.77%**
Diversified foreign	1.62%
Europe	1.90%
Pacific	1.84%
BOND FUNDS	
Corporate bonds	.84%
Government bonds	.91%
Municipal bonds	.77%

SOURCE: Morningstar Inc.

Global equity fund—Invests in securities traded worldwide, including the United States. Compared to direct investments, global funds offer investors an easier avenue to investing abroad. Professional money managers handle trading and record-keeping details and deal with differences in currencies, languages, time zones, regulations, and business customs. In addition to another layer of diversification, global funds add another layer of risk—the exchange rate factor.

Growth and income fund—Invests mainly in the common stock of companies that have had increasing share value as well as a solid record of paying dividends. Attempts to combine long-term capital growth with a steady stream of income.

Health and biotechnology securities fund—Invests in stocks of companies in the medical industry. Individual funds may emphasize a limited portion of the broad health care and biotechnology field, which ranges from large pharmaceutical companies, to service companies supplying laundry to hospitals, to start-up medical research firms.

High-yield bond fund—Maintains at least two-thirds of its portfolio in lower-rated corpo-

HOW TO ESTIMATE TOTAL RETURN

A simple way to figure out how much money you're really making

Just following your mutual fund in the newspaper won't tell you how you're really doing. To find out a fund's total return, you need to know not only the fund's net asset value over a given period of time, but also the distributions per share of dividends and capital gains during that period.

The quickest—and certainly the easiest—way to learn your fund's total return may be to simply ask the fund via its toll-free number. Before you can estimate a fund's one-year total return yourself, you need to know three things:

1. The fund's net-asset value per share a year ago.
2. Its NAV now.
3. Distributions per share of dividends and capital gains in the interim.

You should be able to find all this information on your account statement. You can look up distributions per share in an issue of *Barron's* newspaper.

Here's how to perform the calculation: As of January 31, 1995, Zebra Fund's net asset value was $64.67 per share. A year later, its NAV was $73.65. During the year, it distributed $7.25 per share in income and capital gains. Therefore, subtract the beginning NAV from the ending NAV:

$73.65 – $64.67 = $8.98

And add to that all the distributions:

$8.98 + $7.25 = $16.23

The result gives you the total return in dollars. Now convert this dollar amount to a percentage by dividing the total return by the starting NAV and multiplying by 100.

$16.23 ÷ $64.67 x 100 = 25.1%

Other, more complex, formulas that are figured by computer may produce a slightly different answer, but this estimate is close enough.

SOURCE: Adapted from *Kiplinger's Personal Finance* magazine, April 1994.

rate bonds (Baa or lower by Moody's rating service and BBB or lower by Standard and Poor's rating service). In return for generally higher yield, investors bear a greater degree of risk than for higher-rated bonds.

Income-bond fund—Seeks a high level of current income by investing at all times in a mix of corporate and government bonds.

Income-equity fund—Invests primarily in equity securities of companies with good dividend-paying records.

Income-mixed fund—Invests in income-producing securities, including both equities and debt instruments.

Index funds—Construct portfolios to mirror a specific market index. They are expected to provide a rate of return that will approximate or match, but not exceed, that of the market they are mirroring. Index funds offer a number of investment choices that include various stock market indexes or indexes of international or bond portfolios.

International fund—Invests in equity securities of companies outside the United States. Two-thirds of its portfolio must be so invested at all times to be categorized as international.

Load—A fee or commission imposed by a mutual fund. Some loads are a flat percentage, others are based on the amount you invest or how long you remain in the fund. A load can be as high as 8.5 percent. Low loads run between 1 and 3 percent.

Management fee—A yearly charge for managing the fund. Ranges from 0.2 to 1.6 percent of fund assets.

MANAGERS WHO REALLY MANAGE

A new system grades the folks who make the big decisions

When super investor Peter Lynch left as manager of Fidelity's Magellan Fund, many investors wondered whether to ditch the fund or take a chance with a new manager. After all, there was no way to test a mutual fund manager's record. But a new rating system devised by Value Line, the New York-based mutual fund research firm, does just that. It helps investors figure out which fund managers stand out and which don't.

Unlike other systems that analyze what happened at a fund no matter who is in charge, Value Line correlates funds' results specifically to their managers. The ranking compares the record of every manager who has been running a fund for at least two years against the records of other funds that invest in the same kinds of securities—corporate bond funds or growth funds, for example. The ratings are described as a percentage of total return the manager has achieved above or below other managers in his basket of securities.

As for Magellan investors who stayed put: Jeff Vinik has fared pretty well, earning a rating above many managers in his group.

HOW THEY'RE DOING

The overall fund rank is Value Line's evaluation of the fund, with one being the highest score. Manager rating refers to the percentage points the manager rates above or below his peers.

FUND	MANAGER	FUND RANK	MANAGER RATING
BERGER 100	Rodney Linafelter	3	5.1%
FIDELITY MAGELLAN	Jeff Vinik	2	2.0%
FOUNDER'S SPECIAL	Charles Hooper	3	–2.5%
JANUS	James Craig	2	3.1%
LINDNER DIVIDEND	Eric Ryback	2	3.6%
NICHOLAS INCOME FUNDS	Albert Nicholas	1	–1.4%
SCUDDER SHORT-TERM GLOBAL BOND	Margaret Craddock	2	1.8%
STEIN ROE CAPITAL OPPORTUNITIES	Gloria Santella	3	–2.5%
T.ROWE PRICE NEW HORIZON	John Laporte	3	–0.9%
WINDSOR FUND	John Neff	2	3.5%

SOURCE: Value Line Mutual Fund Survey.

Mutual fund—Pools shareholder cash to invest in a variety of securities, including stocks, bonds, and money market instruments.

NAV or net asset value—The market value of one share of a mutual fund, calculated at the close of each business day.

No load fund—Mutual fund that doesn't charge a fee or commission to buy or sell its shares.

Redemption fee—One to 2 percent charge when you sell your shares. Often waived if you hold shares for given number of years.

Small company growth fund—Seeks aggressive growth of capital by investing primarily in equity securities of small companies—usually in the developing stages of their life cycle—with rapid-growth potential. Shares of such companies are often thinly traded and may be subject to more abrupt market movements than those of larger firms.

Specific social objectives fund—Screens companies for compliance with certain social or ethical criteria, in addition to using traditional measures of financial value when choosing securities for their portfolios.

FUNDS THAT SERVE WITH A SMILE

Some treat your money with the respect it deserves

Service is now the name of the game in the crowded field of mutual funds. Many funds are looking to grab market share by bending over backwards to cater to investors. Which funds provide the best service? DALBAR, Inc., a Boston-based mutual fund research firm, tests about two dozen mutual fund groups each year before selecting a handful that provide kid-glove service to investors.

For the 1994 awards, DALBAR looked at more than 10,000 transactions designed to test 55 different aspects of service, ranging from routine matters, like opening an account and checking fund share prices, to whether dividends, annual reports, and tax statements were received on time. DALBAR invested about $125,000 of its own money in the funds and conducted more than 80,000 evaluations throughout the year before awarding its excellence-in-service seal.

What should you do to get the best service from your funds? After many years of conducting its surveys, DALBAR has gleaned the following advice for investors:

■ **Ask how you can get your money out efficiently.** Ask the company if you can get a checkbook and check-writing privileges so that if you want cash from your account, you can simply write yourself a check.

■ **Know how your money flows.** Find out beforehand what you must do to transfer money between funds or switch from reinvesting dividends to taking them in cash, or vice versa.

■ **Ask who to call for advice or help.** For example, funds should be able to tell you how to use your investment as collateral for a loan. Some will issue a certificate acceptable to the lender; a stockbroker, if you use one, should be able to put your account on margin.

■ **AND THE WINNERS ARE:**

DALBAR doesn't reveal the losers, but here's the list of winners of the 1994 DALBAR's Quality Tested Service Seal.

	Assets
AMERICAN CAPITAL ☎ 800-421-5666	$13 billion
FRANKLIN ☎ 800-632-2180	$75 billion
PUTNAM ☎ 800-225-2465	$101 billion
PASADENA GROUP ☎ 800-648-8050	$600 million
TWENTIETH CENTURY ☎ 800-345-2021	$29 billion

Taxable money market fund—Invests in the short-term, high-grade securities sold in the money market. Generally the safest, most stable securities available, including Treasury bills, certificates of deposit of large banks and commercial paper (the short-term IOUs of large U.S. corporations.) Money market funds limit the average maturity of their portfolio to 90 days or less.

Tax-exempt money market fund—Invests in municipal securities with relatively short maturities. Investors who use them seek tax-free investments with minimum risk.

U.S. Government income fund—Invests in variety of government securities, including U.S. Treasury bonds, federally guaranteed mortgage-backed securities, and other government notes.

Utilities fund—Generally invests about two-thirds of its portfolios in securities issued by companies in the utilities industry.

Variable annuities—Insurance products, mainly used for retirement income, that offer investors some advantages of mutual funds, in addition to tax-deferred earnings.

RISK ASSESSMENT

WHEN BIGGER IS BETTER

Small funds are more likely to soar—and more likely to flop

When it comes to safety, big stock funds, such as Scudder, Vanguard, or T. Rowe Price, are often better. Smaller stock funds may carry bigger rewards, but they also carry bigger risks. "You're more likely to find a smaller fund that soars, but you're also more likely to get a fund that flops," says Catherine Voss Sanders, associate editor of *Morningstar Mutual Funds*, a publication of Morningstar, Inc., of Chicago.

Morningstar studied stock funds over the 10 years from 1983 to 1993, dividing them into four groups based on their assets. (Average assets among diversified stock funds are $500 million or so.) The results: The very smallest funds—those ranking in the bottom 25 percent in assets—didn't necessarily generate poorer results each year. In fact, on average the smallest funds came out on top in 1984, 1991, and 1992. But a look at the three worst-performing funds in each year for the four different size groups shows a different picture. In 9 of the 10 years, the biggest losers came from the smallest 25 percent of all funds, a group that today would include funds with less than $12 million in assets.

Small funds have a lot of pluses, including an ability to move quickly to gain investing advantages. But, smaller funds also generally carry huge annual fund expenses that cut into investors' returns. Big funds, though lumbering, have other advantages, including deep research capabilities and more consistent performance.

MIXING PRINCIPLES AND PROFIT

Funds that put their money where their ethics are

Investors who want to put their money where their ethics are can now choose from about 30 funds. Socially responsible investing, or SRI, involves screening out companies heavily involved in activities like gambling or weapons production, for example, and picking companies with good records on the environment, treatment of minorities, and other social issues. Do socially responsible investors sacrifice monetary rewards? Hardly. As this chart from the newsletter *Investing for a Better World*, ☎ 617-423-6655, shows, many of the largest have turned in fairly respectable returns over the past three years. The newsletter awards an "A" to funds with strict criteria for choosing companies with above-average social profiles. "B" goes to funds that invest in firms with some shareholder activism and that may emphasize avoiding bad companies rather than finding good ones. "C" is given to funds with minimal or no shareholder activism.

SOCIALLY RESPONSIBLE MUTUAL FUNDS

Fund	Phone	Assets	Objective	Return*	Grade
ARIEL APPRECIATION	☎ 800-292-7435	$140 million	Growth	5.5	B–
DOMINI SOCIAL EQUITY	☎ 800-762-6814	$40 million	Growth	10.2	B
DREYFUS THIRD CENTURY	☎ 800-645-6561	$348 million	Growth	3.9	C–
NEW ALTERNATIVES	☎ 800-423-8383	$29 million	Environmental	4.1	B+
PARNASSUS FUND	☎ 800-999-3505	$183 million	Growth	18.8	A–
PAX WORLD FUND	☎ 800-767-1729	$404 million	Balanced	3.4	B+

* Three-year average annual percentage. SOURCE: *Investing for a Better World*, Franklin Research & Development Corp.

INVESTOR'S GUIDE

HOW THE TOP MUTUAL FUND FAMILIES STACK UP

How do you choose a fund family? The table below compares the biggest families,[1] including both no-load funds, which charge no fees or commissions when you buy or sell fund shares, and load funds, which do levy them. Front-end loads are sales charges paid before an investor's money goes into the mutual fund. With back-end loads, sales charges are paid when an investor redeems or sells shares. The average expense ratio is the annual expenses shareholders can expect shown as a percentage of the funds' assets. For example, Vanguard's 0.40 percent average expense ratio means that the group's average stock fund costs 40 cents per $100 in assets to run. The industry average is 1.34 percent.

FUND FAMILY ☎ Business hours[2]	Assets in $billions and type[3]	Number of funds	Best fund *Worst fund*[4]	Exp. ratio front (F) back (B)	Initial min. investment	Minimum check-writing
CAPITAL RESEARCH & MGT. ☎ 800-421-9900 8 a.m.-8 p.m., M-F	$110 Load	14 stk 11 bnd 3 mm	American High Income *Tx. Exmt. Mo. Fnd. of America*	0.78% F	$250- $2,500	$250
DEAN WITTER INTERCAPITAL ☎ 800-869-3863 8 a.m.-8 p.m., M-F	$59 Load	19 stk 27 bnd 9 mm	Dean Witter American Value *Dean Witter NY Muni*	1.75% B	$1,000- $10,000	$500
DREYFUS CORP. ☎ 800-782-6620 24 hours, 7 days	$65 No-load	36 stk 70 bnd 33 mm	Dreyfus New Leaders *Dreyfus Cap Value: A*	0.92%	$2,500- $25,000	$500
FIDELITY MGT. & RESEARCH ☎ 800-544-8888 24 hours, 7 days	$340 No-load	83 stk 43 bnd 23 mm	Fidelity Select Home Fin *Fidelity Select Environment*	0.91%	$2,500- $10,000	$500
FRANKLIN ADVISORS, INC. ☎ 800-632-2180 9 a.m.-11 p.m, M-F	$118 Load	29 stk 55 bnd 6 mm	Franklin Age HI Inc. *Franklin NY TF; Mf.*	0.65% F	$100	$100- $500
MERRIL LYNCH ASSET MGT. ☎ 800-637-3863 9 a.m.-5 p.m., M-F	$150 Load	22 stk 27 bnd 28 mm	Merrill Lynch Gr. Inv. & Ret: A *Merrill Global Resources: B*	1.07% F 2.09% B	$250- $5,000	$500
PRUDENTIAL ☎ 800-225-1852 8 a.m.-6 p.m., M-F	$53 Load	15 stk 29 bnd 5 mm	Prudential Gr. Oppty: A *Prudential Muni: NY MM*	1.27% F 2.04% B	$1,000- $5,000	$500
PUTNAM MGT. CO. ☎ 800-225-1581 8:30 a.m.-8 p.m., M-F	$101 Load	28 stk 28 bnd 5 mm	Putnam Voyager: A *Putnam CA Txex MM*	1.16% F	$500	$500
SMITH BARNEY INC. ☎ 800-221-8806 8:30 a.m.-5:30 p.m., M-F	$58 Load	28 stk 21 bnd 12 mm	SB Fdmntl Val: A *SB Global Opp: A*	0.86% F	$1,000- $10,000	None
VANGUARD GROUP ☎ 800-635-1511 8 a.m.-9 p.m, M-F	$146 No-load	33 stk 24 bnd 9 mm	Vanguard Spl: Health *Vanguard CA-TX-Fr: MM*	0.40%	$500- $50,000	$250

NOTES: 1. Federated Investors is ommitted from this list because it sells heavily through bank trust departments. 2. Eastern Standard Time. 3. Assets as of March 1995. 4. Based on growth rates from March 31, 1990, to March 31, 1995.

SOURCES: Lipper Analytical Serices, Inc., Investment Company Institute; company reports.

GLOBAL INVESTING

NAVIGATING FOREIGN WATERS

Can you do better overseas? It depends on the economic weather

Some $160 billion crosses the oceans every year in search of better mutual fund returns. The rewards from overseas mutual funds can be sizable but the risks are also huge. Wild swings from year to year are not unheard of. International stock funds gained 38.3 percent on average in 1993, for example, compared with 12.6 percent for domestic stock funds. In 1994, international stock funds fell an average 17.8 percent, compared with a 1.6 percent decline for general equity funds, according to Lipper Analytical Services, Inc.

Still want to swim in foreign waters? Your options include investing in domestic funds with big overseas stock holdings, or in one of two types of international mutual funds: conventional open-end mutual funds, and closed-end, single-country or single-region funds. You can also buy shares directly in a foreign company (see "Think Carefully, Invest Globally," page 8).

A closed-end fund is not as esoteric as it sounds. It's like an investment company, of which a certain number of shares are sold to the public. Its shares trade on major stock markets like those of any other company. The reason for such funds is simple: They allow countries or regions to open up markets to U.S. investors without the risk of floods of new capital washing in and out and destabilizing their markets.

Most financial advisers agree that individuals who invest overseas should be willing to make a commitment of at least three years, and preferably five. Foreign markets, funds, and stocks are generally more volatile than those in the United States. Investors who pull out at the first sign of trouble are most likely to get walloped. Experts generally suggest that you allocate 10 to 30 percent of your portfolio overseas—some counsel as much as half. Despite the risks, a lot of big investors have been looking abroad, and small investors are following in their wake.

One possible solution for small investors edgy about foreign adventures but tempted by potential high returns is to sink some money into the handful of international mutual funds that go practically anywhere on the planet (see "Tracking International Funds," right). These funds put most of their money into well-developed foreign markets, which tend to be safer and less volatile, but funnel 20 percent or more into wilder markets such as China and Chile.

MIXED-UP CRAZY WORLD

A look at the following graph comparing general U.S. equity funds and world equity funds over the last 10 years shows that U.S. and world markets seem to be moving in tandem.

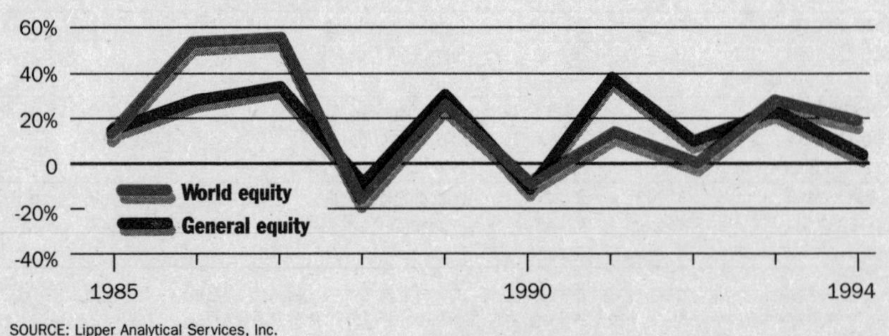

SOURCE: Lipper Analytical Services, Inc.

BEST OF THE CLOSED-END FUNDS

Country-fund fever started spreading in late 1989, with lots of investors paying premium prices for the funds. Here are the top 10 performing closed-end stock funds for 1994. Most are selling at sizable discounts, a reflection of low investor demand. Closed-end funds had a tough '94, with only 5 percent ending the year on a positive note.

FUND	STOCK PRICE[1]	PREMIUM/DISCOUNT[2]	TOTAL RETURN[3]
1. Brazil Fund	$25.37	10.00%	58.04%
2. Brazilian Equity	$15.37	12.70%	51.69%
3. Chile Fund	$39.87	–19.30%	33.05%
4. Japan Equity	$13.25	5.70%	29.45%
5. Korea Fund	$21.37	3.40%	24.96%
6. ROC Taiwan	$10.62	–15.40%	23.45%
7. Taiwan Fund	$21.00	–16.40%	22.87%
8. Korean Invest.	$12.12	–8.40%	22.83%
9. India Growth	$18.87	7.30%	21.23%
10. Gemini II Fund	$10.87	15.30%	20.21%

NOTES: 1. As of Dec. 1994. 2. Current percentage by which fund's share price exceeds or falls below its portfolio value per share. 3. Includes reinvested dividends. SOURCE: Lipper Analytical Services, Inc.

TRACKING INTERNATIONAL FUNDS

The best and worst of the conventional international stock mutual funds over the five years ending in December 1994 and their five-year annualized return.

TEN BEST	
1. GAM International	12.27%
2. Merrill Lynch Dev CapMkts A	12.19%
3. Smith Barney Intl Equity A	11.19%
4. Harbor International	10.89%
5. Warburg Pincus Intl.	10.75%
6. EuroPacific Growth	10.69%
7. Morgan Stanley Instl Intl Equity	10.42%
8. Templeton Foreign	9.53%
9. Managers Intl Equity	9.42%
10. Ivy International A	9.41%

TEN WORST	
1. Ivy Canada A	–1.63%
2. Quantitative Intl Equity	–0.31%
3. Dreyfus/Laurel Intl Inv	0.09%
4. Invesco International Growth	0.59%
5. Flag Inv International	0.80%
6. WPG International	0.88%
7. Alliance International A	1.55%
8. Keystone International	1.69%
9. Rodney Square Intl Equity	1.94%
10. G.T. Global Intl. Growth A	2.49%

SOURCE: Morningstar, Inc.

HOME-GROWN FUNDS WITH THE MOST FOREIGN INTERESTS

The five domestic funds that had the highest percentage of overseas holdings at the end of 1994.

FUND	FIVE-YEAR ANNUALIZED	'94 RETURN	PERCENT FOREIGN
1. Aetna Growth Sel	NA	5.63%	93.0%
2. Excel Value	–10.19%	–25.11%	44.4%
3. Fidelity Capital Appreciation	8.10%	2.52%	35.8%
4. Capital Income Builder	10.11%	–2.26%	35.4%
5. Prudential Multi-Sector A	NA	3.48%	34.7%

SOURCE: Morningstar, Inc.

DISCOUNT BROKERS

SCHWAB OR FIDELITY?

That is the question when you're looking for a discount broker

Discount brokerage firms Charles Schwab and Fidelity Investments have battled for years to lure investors to their no-fee mutual funds. The winners are the investors, who stand to save on fees and tap into a bounty of services. Both fund programs, Schwab's OneSource and Fidelity's FundsNetwork, have several conveniences in common, such as 24-hour, toll-free phone service. And both allow investors to manage a portfolio of funds from different families, get one statement, and switch among funds and cash-management accounts. In both programs, to switch funds, you simply fill out a transfer form and the brokerages consolidate the funds you own.

Which one's the better deal? Fidelity has the edge when it comes to sheer numbers of funds. OneSource offers 254 funds at no transaction fee, although nearly 500 more funds are available for a sales charge. Fidelity's FundsNetwork is huge with 327 no-fee funds, plus 1,600 funds for fees. Another plus for Fidelity: The company won't allow Schwab to offer Fidelity funds for no transaction fee, so OneSource doesn't include Fidelity funds in its lineup of no-fee funds. However, FundsNetwork offers 86 of Fidelity's 202 funds without a transaction fee. To buy one of its low-loads, you still pay a 3 percent or so sales charge.

Beware of too much hopping around from one fund to another in both programs. Schwab allows an unlimited number of free switches among funds held for more than three months within a calendar year. But, switches made before three months are subject to a $39 fee. Fidelity's policy is more onerous, though the company says it is reviewing it. Investors get five free redemptions in a 12-month period for a fund held in their account fewer than six months. Then fees kick in, which are determined by the amount of the transaction and can run about $50 for a $5,000 investment.

If it's face-to-face contact you're looking for, Schwab is the clear winner: Schwab has 202 branches, compared to Fidelity's 77.

DISCOUNT BROKERS, MANO A MANO

Charles Schwab's OneSource vs. Fidelity's FundsNetwork

CHARLES SCHWAB'S ONESOURCE	FIDELITY'S FUNDSNETWORK
202 branches	77 branches
No minimum investment	No minimum investment
254 no-fee funds from 27 families	350 funds, 32 families, including Fidelity
Charges a fee of 0.6 percent of assets to buy less than $15,000 of funds not in program $29 minimum fee	Fee for investing less than $10,000 in outside fund is $17.50 plus 0.8 percent of assets $28 minimum fee
Annual fee of $22 is waived for all mutual fund IRAs of more than $10,000	$20 annual fee is waived for brokerage account IRAs of more than $5,000
Unlimited free switches among funds held more than three months; $39 fee for switches before three months	Transaction fees charged after the fifth redemption from a fund held less than 6 months within 12 months; fees vary
Free quarterly mutual fund performance guide and list of top performers	Software about retirement planning, fund performance directory, and other guides
☎ 800-266-5623	☎ 800-544-9697

SOURCE: Charles Schwab and Fidelity Investments reports.

A TWO-FOR-ONE INVESTMENT

Variable annuities are hot, but are they the right choice for you?

Money has been gushing into variable annuities, which are essentially tax-advantaged mutual funds in a life insurance wrapper. Some $50 billion was poured into variable annuities in 1994, up from just $8 billion in 1991, according to the Georgia-based research firm VARDS Report.

Variable annuities are retirement accounts that allow you to invest in a menu of mutual funds, stocks, bonds, and money markets. Unlike regular annuities, the amount you get when you start withdrawing depends on the performance of the funds you choose.

One big attraction of variable annuities is that earnings within the annuity are tax deferred until you start withdrawing the money. Another lure: If you die before age 59-and-a-half your heirs will get back at least what you put in. Even if the funds you pick do poorly, your heirs won't suffer. The guarantee doesn't apply if you live past 59-and-a-half, however.

Annuities come in several varieties. Younger people who are saving for retirement often choose deferred annuities, which allow you to pick a future date for income payments to start. Older folks prefer immediate annuities, often purchased with a lump-sum payment, which provide a stream of income payments at once or soon after you buy them. Variable annuities give you the option of investing in different mutual funds, so that monthly payments fluctuate with the markets. Fixed annuities are invested in bonds and mortgages with fixed return rates, so you are guaranteed at least a specified minimum payment.

For all their allure, variable annuities have some big drawbacks. For one, most of them have surrender fees—fees that you pay if you decide to withdraw funds before

BEST AND WORST OF THE BUNCH

Morningstar, Inc. rates variable-rate annuities based on performance and risk in one comprehensive evaluation. Morningstar gives five stars to annuities, or subaccounts, as they are called, with the most attractive risk/reward profile. The least attractive get one star.

Subaccount	Objective	Five-year ann. return[1]	Rating
BEST PERFORMERS			
1. Manulife Account 2 Lifestyle Emerging Growth Equity	Aggressive	18.61 %	4★
2. Manulife Account 2 Annuity Emerging Growth Equity	Aggressive	18.61 %	4★
3. Aetna Marathon Plus Alger Growth	Growth	18.38 %	5★
4. Amer Skandia Advisors Choice/Alger Growth	Growth	18.14 %	5★
5. Amer Skandia Advisors Design/Alger Growth	Growth	18.14 %	5★
WORST PERFORMERS			
1. Guardian Investor/ Guardian Real Estate Account	Specialty	–4.77 %	1★
2. Anchor National ICAP II Foreign Securities	International	–1.10 %	1★
3. PaineWebber Advantage Annuity Global Growth	International	2.17 %	1★
4. Prudential Discovery Plus Real Property Account	Specialty	2.39 %	2★
5. Prudential VIP-86 Real Property Account	Specialty	2.38 %	2★

1. As of April 1995. SOURCE: Morningstar, Inc.

EXPERT SOURCES

ALL ABOUT ANNUITIES

Need information about annuities sources or immediate annuity payout rates and data? Try the following

REPORTS

COMPARATIVE ANNUITY REPORTS
$10 per issue, $80 per year (12 issues)
■ First-year rates for fixed annuities.
☎ **916-487-7863**

LIFE INSURANCE AND ANNUITY SHOPPER
$24 per issue, $45 per year (four issues)
■ Immediate-annuity payout rates and other statistics on fixed and variable deferred annuities.
☎ **800-872-6684**

MORNINGSTAR VARIABLE ANNUITY/LIFE PERFORMANCE REPORT
$45 per issue, $95 per year (quarterly updates), $195 per year (monthly updates)
■ Performance rankings and various other statistics for variable annuity subaccounts.
☎ **800-876-5005**

BASIC INFORMATION

NATIONAL INSURANCE CONSUMER HELPLINE
■ This hotline is sponsored by the insurance industry trade associations. Trained personnel and licensed agents will answer questions about insurance sources and send consumer brochures. They also will give advice on other insurance issues.
☎ **800-942-4242**

the end of the term—that start as high as 9 percent. As with other retirement accounts, the IRS will hit you with a 10 percent tax penalty on earnings if you withdraw your money before you turn 59-and-a-half.

Another downside: hefty ongoing expenses. The average expense ratio or variable annuities is 2.1 percent, but it can run as high as 3 percent, compared with 1.3 percent for the typical diversified stock mutual fund.

The high costs come from running the account, for compensating the broker or financial planner who sells you the annuity, and for providing insurance protection. Expenses are paid directly out of earnings, reducing both yield and total return.

Still, if you've exhausted other tax-deferred plans and are in a high-income tax bracket, variable annuities may be for you. Steven B. Weinstein, editor of the *Arthur Andersen Personal Financial Planning Newsletter,* suggests asking the following questions before investing in variable annuities:

Have you already made the maximum contributions available to other tax advantaged investment plans? Do you plan to hold your investment at least until you reach age 59-and-a-half? If you are in the 28 percent or 31 percent federal tax bracket, do you intend to hold your investment for 10 years or more? If you are in the 36 percent or higher tax bracket, do you expect to hold your investment for at least 15 years for bonds and at least 20 years for stocks? Do you expect to be in a lower tax bracket when you retire and annuity withdrawals begin?

If you can answer "yes" to any of these, variable annuities may fit the bill.

One further bit of advice from financial advisers: Pick solid, aggressive funds with low fees, and then stick with them for the long haul.

REAL ESTATE

DON'T BET YOUR HOUSE

The value of your largest single investment won't soar—or slump

Forget about another '80s-style housing boom. Housing prices, which broke through the roof in the late '80s and then crashed at least back down to the living room in the early '90s, are settling back into a more comfortable and more familiar pattern until at least the turn of the century.

More homes were sold in 1994 than at any time since 1978, but that's likely to be the best year for some time to come. In 1995, sales of existing homes are expected to fall 7 percent, according to Regional Financial Associates, a West Chester, Pa., economic consulting firm. The falloff in new home sales is expected to be even sharper.

The pace is not expected to pick back up again any time soon. RFA forecasts that the bottom should be felt in early 1997, with sales of existing homes down about 10 percent from 1994's peak.

The sales slowdown doesn't mean, however, that prices will drop. On the contrary, most experts predict it will rise 3 to 3.5 percent in 1995, about the same as the expected inflation rate. Price increases should pretty much keep pace with inflation through 1997. In that respect, the late '80s were an aberration. Historically, housing prices have for the most part tracked the inflation rate.

The further south and west you go, the brighter the long-term outlook. While most of the South will grow on a par with the national average, prospects are better in North Carolina, Georgia, Florida, and Texas, which is booming again. Five of the 10 fastest-growing states in 1995 should be in the Mountain States. Computer-related manufacturing and software growth will continue to buoy the Pacific Northwest. Meanwhile, in New England, house prices will only creep upward.

Baby boomers will continue to work their special magic on the housing market. Many boomers are now old enough and rich enough to pine for a second home. Expect vacation home sales to boom with the boomers (see "A House in the Country," page 72). Those that aren't in the market for another place—and some that are—will be trading up. WEFA, an economic consulting firm, estimates that there will be 24 million households in the 35 to 44 age group by the year 2000, some 20 percent more such households than there were at the end of the '80s. That, WEFA says, means that the trade-up market will be "very active" over the next six years.

HOMEBUYER'S GUIDE

THE TOP 132 HOUSING MARKETS

Spurred by low mortgage rates, the median price of existing homes nationwide is expected to reach $112,703 in 1995, up from $109,208 in 1994. Homeowners who live west of the Rockies were more likely to see the value of their homestead rise in 1994 than those who resided back East. The market rankings cover median prices for single-family detached and attached existing homes.

Metropolitan area	1994	% chng. from '93
1. Salt Lake City-Ogden, Utah	$98,000	15.4
2. Eugene-Springfield, Ore.	$96,200	14.0
3. Denver, Colo.	$116,800	11.6
4. Colorado Springs, Colo.	$104,200	11.2
5. Madison, Wis.	$116,000	10.9
6. Spokane, Wash.	$94,600	10.6
7. Portland, Ore.	$116,900	10.3
8. Albuquerque, N.M.	$110,000	9.6
9. Richland/Kennewick, Pasco, Wash.	$111,300	9.2
10. Boise, Idaho	$99,000	8.3
11. Tucson, Ariz.	$95,400	8.2
12. Louisville, Ky.	$80,500	8.1
13. Peoria, Ill.	$67,900	7.4
14. Sioux Falls, S.D.	$80,100	7.1
15. Appleton, Wis.	$80,600	6.9
16. Nashville, Tenn.	$96,500	6.7
17. Champaign, Ill.	$74,100	6.3
18. Pensacola, Fla.	$76,400	6.3
19. Green Bay, Wis.	$86,600	6.3
20. Jacksonville, Fla.	$81,900	6.2
21. Cedar Rapids, Iowa	$82,800	6.2
22. Lexington-Fayetteville, Ky.	$87,500	6.1
23. Davenport/Moline, Iowa	$61,800	6.0
24. Reno, Nev.	$133,600	5.8
25. Tallahassee, Fla.	$97,800	5.7
26. Norfolk/Va. Beach, Va.	$103,800	5.7
27. Lincoln, Neb.	$76,600	5.7
28. Cincinnati, Ohio	$96,500	5.6
29. Biloxi-Gulfport, Miss.	$70,900	5.5
30. Raleigh-Durham, N.C.	$115,200	5.5
31. Austin/San Marcos, Texas	$96,200	5.4
32. Gary-Hammond, Ind.	$87,200	5.3
33. Chattanooga, Tenn.	$77,500	5.3
34. Kalamazoo, Mich.	$74,800	5.2
35. Waterloo/Cedar Falls, Iowa	$53,100	5.1
36. Corpus Christi, Texas	$74,100	5.1
37. Charleston, W.V.	$78,600	5.1
38. El Paso, Texas	$75,300	4.9
39. Tacoma, Wash.	$118,900	4.8
40. Indianapolis, Ind.	$90,700	4.7
41. Milwaukee, Wis.	$109,000	4.7
42. Knoxville, Tenn.	$89,200	4.6
43. Miami, Fla.	$103,200	4.5
44. Rockford, Ill.	$84,900	4.4
45. Springfield, Ill.	$84,900	4.4
46. Kansas City, Mo.	$87,100	4.2
47. Omaha, Neb.	$75,600	4.0
48. Tulsa, Okla.	$74,100	3.9
49. Birmingham, Ala.	$100,200	3.8
50. Seattle, Wash.	$155,900	3.8
51. Cleveland, Ohio	$98,500	3.7
52. Des Moines, Iowa	$81,700	3.7
53. Boston, Mass.	$179,300	3.5
54. Minneapolis-St. Paul, Minn.	$101,500	3.4
55. Columbus, Ohio	$94,800	3.3
56. Wichita, Kan.	$73,700	3.2
57. Lansing, Mich.	$75,500	3.1
58. Youngstown-Warren, Ohio	$63,100	3.1
59. Sarasota, Fla.	$97,000	3.1
60. Greenville-Spartanburg, S.C.	$87,400	2.9
61. Ocala, Fla.	$59,500	2.9
62. Beaumont, Texas	$65,000	2.8
63. Canton, Ohio	$77,500	2.8
64. Fargo, N.D.	$77,600	2.8
65. Oklahoma City, Okla.	$66,700	2.8
66. W. Palm Beach-Boca Raton, Fla.	$117,600	2.6
67. Phoenix, Ariz.	$91,400	2.6
68. Dayton-Springfield, Ohio	$84,200	2.6
69. Mobile, Ala.	$69,900	2.5
70. Bergen-Passaic, N.Y.-N.J.	$192,700	2.3
71. Aurora-Elgin, Ill.	$124,400	2.2
72. Las Vegas, Nev.	$110,500	2.1
73. Bradenton, Fla.	$88,300	2.1
74. Toledo, Ohio	$73,800	2.1
75. Amarillo, Texas	$64,500	2.1
76. Gainesville, Fla.	$84,600	2.1

HOMEBUYER'S GUIDE

77. Akron, Ohio	$84,900	2.0
78. Greensboro/Winston Salem, N.C.	$96,600	2.0
79. Baton Rouge, La.	$77,400	2.0
80. Atlanta, Ga.	$93,600	2.0
81. Charleston, S.C.	$91,600	1.9
82. Melbourne-Titusville, Fla.	$76,700	1.9
83. Daytona Beach, Fla.	$69,000	1.8
84. Columbia, S.C.	$86,600	1.8
85. Shreveport, La.	$70,200	1.7
86. South Bend-Mishawaka, Ind.	$64,700	1.7
87. Tampa-St. Petersburg, Fla.	$76,200	1.6
88. San Antonio, Texas	$76,200	1.6
89. Chicago, Ill.	$144,100	1.5
90. Richmond-Petersburg, Va.	$95,400	1.4
91. Philadelphia, Pa.	$119,500	1.3
92. Worcester, Mass.	$130,600	1.2
93. N.Y.: Newark, N.J.	$187,300	1.2
94. Detroit, Mich.	$87,000	1.2
95. Middlesex-Somerset, N.Y.-N.J.	$170,700	1.1
96. Saginaw-Bay City-Midland, R.I.	$58,900	1.0
97. Rochester, N.Y.	$85,600	.9
98. Ft. Myers-Cape Coral, Fla.	$77,800	.9
99. Atlantic City, N.J.	$107,600	.8
101. Orlando, Fla.	$90,700	.7
102. Lake County, Ill.	$130,800	.5
103. Dallas, Texas	$95,000	.5
104. Grand Rapids, Mich.	$76,900	.5
105. San Francisco, Calif.	$255,600	.5
106. Honolulu, Hawai'i	$360,000	.4
107. Charlotte-Gastonia, N.C.-S.C.	$360,000	.4
108. Saint Louis, Mo.	$85,000	.2
109. New Orleans, La.	$76,900	.1
110. Providence, R.I.	$116,400	.1
111. Nassau-Suffolk, N.Y.	$159,300	.1
112. N.Y.:-North NJ-Long Island, N.Y.	$173,200	0.0
113. Ft. Lauderdale-Hollywood, Fla.	$103,100	0.0
114. Monmouth-Ocean, N.Y.-N.J.	$137,000	-0.1
115. Washington, D.C.-Md.-Va.	$157,900	-0.3
116. Baltimore, Md.	$115,400	-0.3
117. Albany-Schenectady-Troy, N.Y.	$112,000	-0.3
118. Ft. Worth-Arlington, Texas	$82,500	-0.5
119. Houston, Texas	$80,500	-0.5
120. San Diego, Calif.	$176,000	-0.5
121. Memphis, Tenn.	$86,300	-0.8
122. Montgomery, Ala.	$82,200	-1.2
123. Hartford, Conn.	$133,400	-1.4
124. Buffalo-Niagara Falls, N.Y.	$82,300	-1.4
125. Trenton, N.J.	$131,300	-1.6
126. Pittsburgh, Pa.	$80,700	-1.8
127. Syracuse, N.Y.	$83,100	-1.9
128. New Haven-Meriden, Conn.	$139,600	-2.0
129. Anaheim-Santa Ana, Calif.	$211,000	-2.9
130. Los Angeles-Long Beach, Calif.	$189,100	-3.2
131. Sacramento, Calif.	$124,500	-3.6
132. Riverside-San Bernadino, Calif.	$129,100	-3.9

SOURCE: Reprinted with permission from *Real Estate Outlook: Market Trends and Insights*, ©National Association of Realtors®, Washington, D.C.

A DECADE-LONG LOOK AT HOUSING PRICES

In the last two years, the price gap between new homes and existing homes has widened as new construction has become more costly while the prices of existing homes has eased.

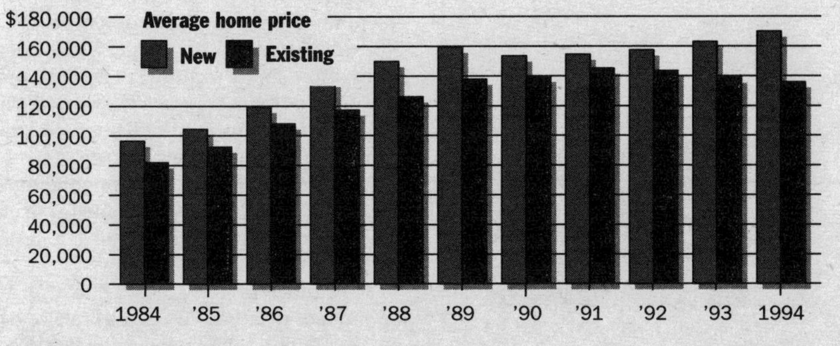

SOURCE: Lomas USA.

■ HOW MUCH A MONTH?

Homebuying costs 1984–94

The average monthly payment (including taxes and insurance)

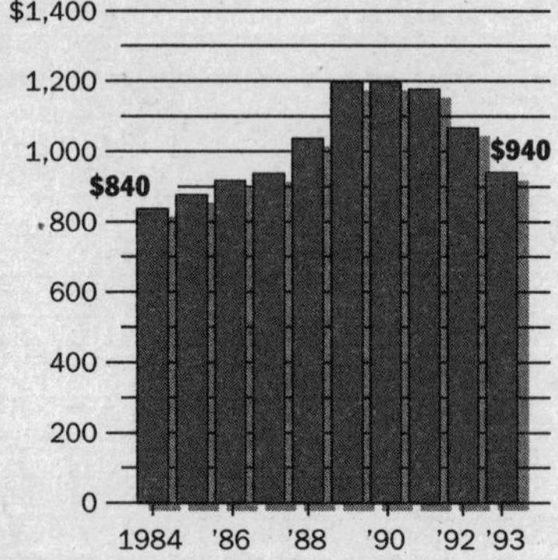

■ HOW MUCH DOWN?

Initial outlay for a house

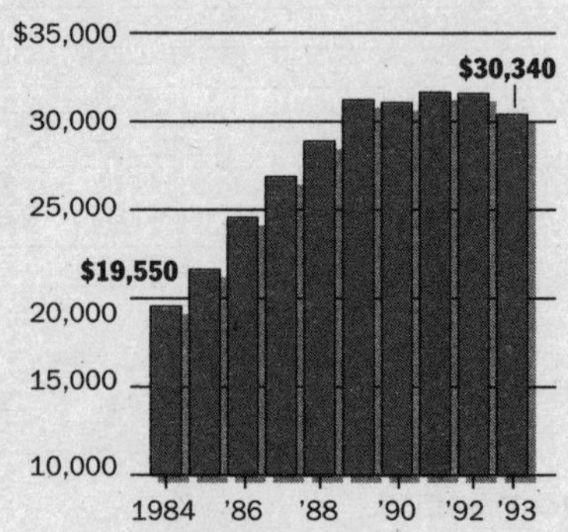

■ ROLLER-COASTER RATES

Average mortgage interest rates

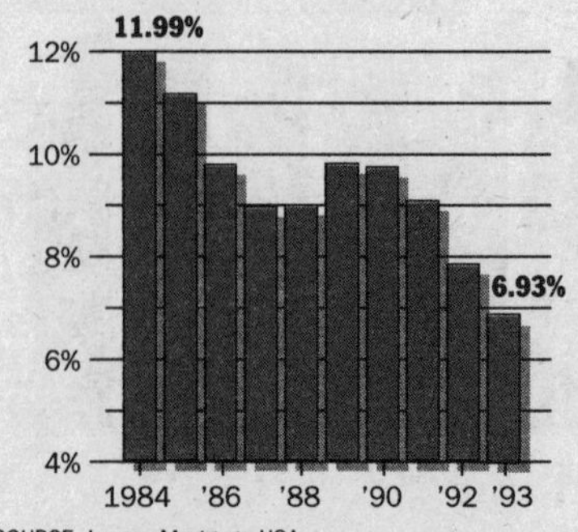

SOURCE: Lomas Mortgage USA.

CAN YOU AFFORD TO BUY A HOME?

In the '90s, more Americans can own a home of their own

Forty acres and a mule were the American entitlement in the nineteenth century. In the twentieth century, it's a home of one's own. But can you afford one? As home prices soared in the '70s and '80s, fewer and fewer Americans could afford to purchase a home. In 1989, 64 percent of U.S. households owned their homes, down from 66 percent in 1980.

Young adults trying to scrape together enough for their first down payment had a hard time. Only 39 percent of households headed by people under the age of 35 owned their residences in 1989, down from 41 percent in 1982. The drop-off in home ownership was sharper among households headed by people aged 35 to 39. Home ownership fell to 63 percent from 68 percent in 1982. The housing affordability crunch affected older people as well.

Things seem to be taking a turn for the better in the '90s. Lower interest rates mean smaller monthly mortgage payments for all buyers, and the purchasing power of home buyers reached its highest point in two decades in February 1994, according to the National Association of Realtors Housing Affordability Index, which measures affordability factors. But the index for first-time purchasers wasn't as rosy. A typical first-time buyer still fell short of qualifying for a conventional mortgage on a $90,900 starter home. But someone earning $24,098—the median income for prime first-time buyers—could afford a home costing $83,500.

How much of a house you can afford—or, indeed, whether you can afford one at all—depends a lot on where you live. Each year, Lomas Mortgage USA ranks the 50 states by the percentage of household income that goes to monthly payments on a conventionally financed purchase. The most affordable states, according to Lomas's 1994 survey: Wyoming, where on average only 14.5 percent of household income goes to pay the mortgage; Nebraska (15.5 percent), and Idaho (15.6 percent). At the other end of the scale is California (26.6 percent), Hawai'i (25.7 percent), and Virginia (23.6 percent). Generally, you'll spend more of your household income meeting the mortgage if you live on the East Coast, less in the Western and Southern states.

Housing in a big city can be just as affordable as a place in the boonies—if you pick your city carefully. The most affordable metro markets, according to the Lomas survey, are Tampa (14.3 percent of household income should be enough to cover monthly mortgage payments, taxes, and insurance), Houston (16.4 percent), and St. Louis.

The least affordable included Los Angeles (26.6 percent), San Francisco (26 percent) and, of course, New York (24.1 percent). Housing costs in some of the country's boom towns are, well—booming. Expect to pay around a quarter of your household income to cover the mortgage in Salt Lake City and around Puget Sound, the area that surrounds Seattle.

Whatever the median household income (which the Lomas survey factors into its considerations), some cities are just plain expensive. The priciest market in the country in 1994, as it has been for some time now, was Honolulu, Hawai'i, where the median price of a house was an eye-popping $357,000. But price increases in the top markets have been leveling off in recent years. In Honolulu, for example, the median price dropped almost 1 percent in 1994. The biggest bargain in 1994 was in Cedar Falls, Iowa. The median price was $55,000. But you better hurry—the median price jumped almost 5 percent last year.

MORE HOUSE, SMALLER PAYMENTS

As price increases have moderated, mortgage rates dropped, and median family income increased, housing has become more affordable for many Americans. The National Association of Realtors composite Housing Affordability Index measures affordability for all home buyers. When the index measures 100, a family earning the median income has exactly the amount needed to purchase a median-priced resale home, using conventional finacing and a 20 percent down payment. Thus in 1994, the composite index shows that half the families in the nation had at least 134.3 percent of the income needed to qualify for the purchase of a home with a median price of $109,400. The typical family could afford a home costing $147,000.

COMPOSITE AFFORDABILITY INDEX

YEAR	Median-priced home	Mortgage rate	Monthly principle and interest payment	Payment as % of income	Median family income	Qualifying income	Composite affordability index
1989	$93,100	10.11	$660	23.1	$34,213	$31,665	108.0
1990	$95,500	10.04	$673	22.8	$35,353	$31,291	109.5
1991	$100,300	9.30	$663	22.1	$35,939	$31,825	112.9
1992	$103,000	8.11	$615	20.0	$36,837	$29,525	124.8
1993	$106,800	7.16	$578	18.26	$37,970	$27,727	136.9
1994	$109,400	7.47	$610	18.62	$39,332	$29,287	134.3

SOURCE: National Association of Realtors.

EXPERT TIP

SHOULD YOU RENT OR BUY A HOME?

A formula for the biggest investment decision you're likely to make

It's often hard to remember that buying a home is an investment fraught with some of the risks of Wall Street. And much as you might wish to own a place of your own, you might feel a bit better about parting with your down payment if you were convinced that you were making a savvy investment. A quick rule of thumb: You can assume you're probably better off renting if you do not itemize deductions on your tax returns or if you plan to move in a few years.

Gaylon Greer, professor of real estate at the University of Memphis, has devised a more sophisticated formula by adapting for potential homeowners a calculation used to decide whether to rent or buy. Keep in mind that Greer's calculation only considers the financial aspects of the decision. Here's how it works:

Consider the hypothetical predicament of Tracy and Jeff Summers, who are renting an apartment in Chicago for $1,200 a month. They are considering buying a similar-sized home for $200,000 and plan to live in the house for seven years.

■ **STEP 1:** Figure out the yearly financial cost for each scenario. For renting, that would be the Summers's annual rent of $14,400. For buying, it would be the after-tax costs of mortgage payments, property taxes, and maintenance.

IT'S HARDER THE FIRST TIME

With lower mortgage rates, first-time homebuyers can afford more expensive houses. The National Association of Realtors' first-time home buyer index shows the ablity of renters who are prime potential first-time buyers to qualify for a mortgage on a starter home. When the index equals 100, the typical first-time buyer can afford the typical starter home under existing financial conditions with a 10 percent down payment. The first-time buyer median income represents the typical income of a renter family with wage earners between the ages of 25 and 44 years. The 1994 first-time buyer index shows that the qualifying income needed for conventional financing covering 90 percent of a $93,000 starter home was $28,699. Yet the median income of prime first-time buyers was $24,998, a difference of $3,701. Even so, a typical first-time buyer could afford a home costing $78,300.

FIRST-TIME BUYERS AFFORDABILITY INDEX

YEAR	Starter home price	Loan	Mortgage rate	Monthly payment	Payment as % of income	Prime first time median income	Qualifying income	Index
1989	$79,100	$71,190	10.11%	$644	34.5%	$22,405	$30,901	72.5
1990	$81,200	$73,080	10.04%	$657	34.5%	$22,842	$31,538	72.4
1991	$85,300	$76,770	9.30%	$648	33.3%	$23,345	$31,120	75.0
1992	$88,100	$79,290	8.11%	$602	30.6%	$23,625	$28,887	81.8
1993	$90,800	$81,720	7.16%	$566	28.0%	$24,249	$27,186	89.2
1994	$93,000	$83,700	7.47%	$598	28.7%	$24,998	$28,699	87.1

SOURCE: National Association of Realtors.

Greer suggests estimating annual maintenance costs at about 1 percent of the house's value for a new home and up to 3 or 4 percent for an older house. The local tax assessor can give you property tax rates.

The Summers estimated spending about $2,000 a year on maintenance and paying $8,000 in property taxes. Their yearly mortgage payments come to approximately $16,000, assuming a $180,000 mortgage at 8.1 percent. However, the total yearly cost of buying is brought down substantially once you factor in the fact that property tax and mortgage payments are mostly tax-deductible. Since the Chicago couple falls into the 39.6 percent income tax bracket, they can roughly estimate that the government pays that percentage of their costs. Therefore their total yearly costs for buying would be $16,000.

■ STEP 2: Figure how much you will recoup when you sell your house. You should expect about 8 to 10 percent of the final value to be consumed by transaction costs, such as brokerage and legal fees. After subtracting their transactions costs, the Summers estimate getting $290,000 for their house after living there for seven years. And they will still owe about $165,000 on their mortgage, so after taxes their net gain will be roughly $90,000.

■ STEP 3: Estimate how much you might make if you had invested your money in something other than a home. You can use the table on this page to give you the value today of a dollar available at various points in the future. The table is based on an 8 percent rate of return on high-grade corporate bonds. This number can change—if it does you can use a present value table found in any finance book.

Each number corresponds to a year, so for year one, the factor will be .9259. Multiply that number by the annual cost of $16,000 to get a "present value equivalent" for the first year cost of ownership. Continue with similar calculations for each year you plan to live in the house. At the end you will add what you expect to recoup from selling the house and the down payment. You should end up with something like this. Parentheses indicate negative numbers, or costs.

Year	(Cost) or benefit	Factor	Present value equivalent
1	($16,000)	.9259	($14,814.40)
2	($16,000)	.8573	($13,716.80)
3	($16,000)	.7983	($12,772.80)
4	($16,000)	.7350	($11,760.00)
5	($16,000)	.6806	($10,889.60)
6	($16,000)	.6502	($10,403.20)
7	($16,000)	.5835	($9,336.00)
7*	$90,000	.5835	$52,515.00
Present value equivalent (Total)			**($31,177.80)**
Include:			
Down payment to buy			**($20,000.00)**
Net present value equivalent			**($51,177.80)**

* Sold in seventh year.

■ STEP 4. Go through the same calculation for renting—minus the down payment and net gain from selling. The lower cost is the best financial option.

Year	(Cost) or benefit	Factor	Present value equivalent
1	($14,400)	.9259	($13,332.96)
2	($14,400)	.8573	($12,345.12)
3	($14,400)	.7983	($11,495.52)
4	($14,400)	.7350	($10,584.00)
5	($14,400)	.6806	($9,800.64)
6	($14,400)	.6502	($9,362.88)
7	($14,400)	.5835	($8,402.40)
Present value equivalent (Total)			**($75,323.52)**

The bottom line for the Summers: They should buy the house. Figuring the present value of their money, they will come out ahead by over $20,000 if they purchase the home.

Of course, even if the result favors renting, you might decide to buy the house you saw because it has such a lovely view from the kitchen window. That's simply a different definition of present value.

CHOOSING THE BEST MORTGAGE

Some old rules of thumb can help you figure how much you can afford

Choosing a mortgage used to be simple—a one-kind fits all proposition. No longer. New choices are continually being introduced. Deciding which one will work best requires that you make some guesses—how long you will live in the house or what your income will be in future years, for example.

The old rule of thumb was that you could qualify for a mortgage if you had a "housing ratio" of 28 percent or lower. Your housing ratio is the percentage of your gross monthly income that you'll need to spend on housing expenses like taxes, insurance, and the mortgage itself. Your "total-obligation ratio" should come in below 36 percent. It is the portion of your income that goes to both housing expenses and any other obligations like credit card debt, car loans, and child support.

The catch is, these ratios are no longer inviolable. Some lenders have more lenient standards—a housing ratio of 33 percent, say, and a total obligation ratio of 38 percent. To find out what different lenders' ratios are, all you have to do is ask. If you come in over the 28 percent threshold in some years but not others, you might look for a "non-income verfication" loan. These are designed for self-employed people, who often have a hard time showing a steady income. Bankers generally require 25 percent of the purchase price—on other loans 20 percent or even less is acceptable. Typically, non-income verification loans also have a slightly higher interest rate. You can sometimes get around the total-obligation ratio simply by shifting your finances around. You might stretch out a car loan so that you have lower monthly payments.

The reason lenders are so particular about the 28 percent and 36 percent ratios is that they sell most of their loans into the secondary markets. Fannie Mae and Freddie Mac, two quasi-governmental organizations, are two of the biggest marketers of mortgages and they set the standards. A local bank or S&L might be willing to make an exception for clients who don't conform.

HOW MUCH INCOME YOU NEED TO GET A MORTGAGE

Figures based on a 30-year loan and assume a down payment of 20 percent of purchase price.

Interest rate	$50,000 loan	$75,000 loan	$100,000 loan	$150,000 loan	$200,000 loan	$250,000 loan
6%	$16,754	$25,131	$33,508	$50,261	$67,015	$83,769
6.5%	$17,451	$26,176	$34,901	$52,352	$69,802	$87,253
7%	$18,163	$27,244	$36,325	$54,488	$72,651	$90,814
7.5%	$18,889	$28,334	$37,779	$56,668	$75,558	$94,447
8%	$19,630	$29,445	$39,260	$58,889	$78,519	$98,149
8.5%	$20,383	$30,574	$40,766	$61,149	$81,532	$101,915
9%	$21,148	$31,722	$42,296	$63,444	$84,593	$105,741
9.5%	$21,925	$32,887	$43,849	$65,774	$87,698	$109,623
10%	$22,711	$34,067	$45,423	$68,134	$90,845	$113,557
10.5%	$23,508	$35,262	$47,016	$70,523	$94,031	$117,539
11%	$24,313	$36,470	$48,626	$72,940	$97,253	$121,566
11.5%	$25,127	$37,690	$50,254	$75,380	$100,507	$125,634

NOTE: Calculations assume property taxes equal 1.5 percent of purchase price and hazard insurance costs 0.25 percent of purchase price. SOURCE: Fannie Mae.

HOMEBUYER'S GUIDE

WHICH MORTGAGE IS FOR YOU?

It's hard to keep track of all the different kinds of mortgages currently being offered, much less choose the one that's the best deal for you. Here's an explanation of some of the most popular varieties, adapted from The Mortgage Money Guide, *published by the Federal Trade Commission, along with the pros and cons of each and some expert tips.*

FIXED-RATE MORTGAGE

Fixed interest rate, usually long term; equal monthly payments of principal and interest until debt is paid in full.

■ **PROS:** Offers some stability and long-term tax advantages.

■ **CONS:** Interest rates may be higher than other types of financing. New fixed rates are rarely assumable.

■ **EXPERT TIP:** Can be a good financing method, if you are in a high tax bracket and need the interest deductions.

FIFTEEN-YEAR MORTGAGE

Fixed interest rate. Requires down payment or monthly payments higher than 30-year loan. Loan is fully repaid over 15-year term.

■ **PROS:** Frequently offered at slightly reduced interest rate. Offers faster accumulation of equity than traditional fixed rate mortgage.

■ **CONS:** Has higher monthly payments. Involves paying less interest but this may result in fewer tax deductions

■ **EXPERT TIP:** If you can afford the higher payments, this plan will save you interest and help you build equity and own your home faster.

ADJUSTABLE RATE MORTGAGE

Interest rate changes over the life of the loan, resulting in possible changes in your monthly payments, loan term, and/or principal. Some plans have rate or payment caps.

■ **PROS:** Starting interest rate is slightly below market. Payment caps prevent wide fluctuations in payments. Rate caps limit amount total debt can expand.

■ **CONS:** Payments can increase sharply and frequently if index increases. Payment caps can result in negative amortization.

■ **EXPERT TIP:** Remember that if your payment-capped loan results in monthly payments that are lower than your interest rate would require, you still owe the difference.

RENEGOTIABLE RATE MORTGAGE

Interest rate and monthly payments are constant for several years; changes possible thereafter. Long-term mortgage.

■ **PROS:** Less frequent changes in interest rates offer some stability.

■ **CONS:** May have to renegotiate when rates are higher.

BALLOON MORTGAGE

Monthly payments based on fixed interest rate; usually short term; payments may cover interest only with principal due in full at term end.

■ **PROS:** Offers low monthly payments.

■ **CONS:** Possibly no equity until loan is fully paid. When due, loan must be paid off or refinanced. Refinancing poses high risk if rates climb.

■ **EXPERT TIP:** Some lenders guarantee refinancing when the balloon payment is due, although they do not guarantee a certain interest rate.

GRADUATED PAYMENT MORTGAGE

Lower monthly payments rise gradually (usually over 5 or 10 years), then level off for duration of term. With adjustable interest rate, additional payment changes possible if index changes.

■ EXPERT LIST

■ **PROS:** They are easier to qualify for.
■ **CONS:** Buyer's income must be able to keep pace with scheduled payment increases. With an adjustable rate, payment increases beyond the graduated payments can result in additional negative amortization.

SHARED APPRECIATION MORTGAGE

Below-market interest rate and lower monthly payments, in exchange for a share of profits when property is sold or on a specified date. There are many variations.
■ **PROS:** Low interest rate and low payments.
■ **CONS:** If home appreciates greatly, total cost of loan jumps. If home fails to appreciate, projected increase in value may still be due, requiring refinancing at possibly higher rates.
■ **EXPERT TIP:** You may be liable for the dollar amount of the property's appreciation even if you do not wish to sell at the agreed-upon date. Unless, you have the cash available, this could force an early sale of the property.

ASSUMABLE MORTGAGE

Buyer takes over seller's original, below-market rate mortgage.
■ **PROS:** Lower monthly payments.
■ **CONS:** May be prohibited if "due on sale" clause is in original mortgage. Not permitted on most new fixed-rate mortgages.
■ **EXPERT TIP:** Many mortgages are no longer legally assumable. Be especially careful if you are considering a mortgage represented as "assumable."

SELLER TAKE-BACK

Seller provides all or part of financing with a first or second mortgage.
■ **PROS:** May offer a below-market interest rate.
■ **CONS:** May have a balloon payment requiring full payment in a few years or refinancing at market rates, which could sharply increase debt.
■ **EXPERT TIP:** If an institutional lender arranges the loan, uses standardized forms, and meets certain other requirements, the owner take-back can be sold immediately to Fannie Mae. This enables seller to obtain equity promptly.

WRAPAROUND

Seller keeps original low rate mortgage. Buyer makes payments to seller, who forwards a portion to the lender holding original mortgage.
■ **PROS:** Offers lower effective interest rate on total transaction.
■ **CONS:** Lender may call in old mortgage and require higher rate. If buyer defaults, seller must take legal action to collect debt.
■ **EXPERT TIP:** Wraparounds may cause problems if the original lender or the holder of the original mortgage is not aware of the new mortgage. Some lenders or holders may have the right to insist that the old mortgage be paid off immediately.

GROWING EQUITY MORTGAGE

Rapid payoff mortgage. Fixed interest rate but monthly payments may vary according to agreed-upon schedule or index.
■ **PROS:** Permits rapid payoff of debt because payment increases reduce principal.
■ **CONS:** Buyer's income must be able to keep up with payment increases. Does not offer long-term tax deductions.

LAND CONTRACT

Seller retains original mortgage. No transfer of title until loan is fully paid. Equal monthly payments based on below-market interest rate with unpaid principal due at loan end.
■ **PROS:** Payments figured on below-market interest rate.
■ **CONS:** May offer no equity until loan is fully paid. Buyer has little protection if conflict arises during loan.
■ **EXPERT TIP:** Land contracts are being used to avoid the "due on sale" clause. The buyer and seller may assert to the lender who provided the original mortgage that the

■ EXPERT LIST

clause does not apply because the property will not be sold to the end of the contract. Therefore, the low interest rate continues.

BUY-DOWN

Developer (or other party) provides an interest subsidy that lowers monthly payments during the first few years of the loan. Can have fixed or adjustable interest rate.

■ **PROS:** Offers a break from higher payments during early years. Enables buyer with lower income to qualify.

■ **CONS:** With adjustable rate mortgage, payments may jump substantially at end of subsidy. Developer may increase selling price.

■ **EXPERT TIP:** Consider what your payments will be after the first few years. They could jump considerably. Also check to see whether the subsidy is part of your contract with the lender or with the builder. If it's provided separately with the builder, the lender can still hold you liable for the full interest rate.

RENT WITH OPTION

Renter pays "option fee" for right to purchase property at specified time and agreed-upon price. Rent may or may not be applied to sales price.

■ **PROS:** Enables renter to buy time to obtain down payment and decide whether to purchase. Locks in price during inflationary times.

■ **CONS:** Payment of option fee. Failure to take option means loss of option fee and rental payments.

REVERSE ANNUITY MORTGAGE

Equity conversion. Borrower owns mortgage-free property and needs income. Lender makes monthly payments to borrower, using property as collateral.

■ **PROS:** Can provide homeowners with needed cash.

■ **CONS:** At end of term, borrower must have money available to avoid selling property or refinancing.

■ **EXPERT TIP:** You can't obtain a RAM until you have paid off your original mortgage.

SOURCE: *The Mortgage Money Guide*, Federal Trade Commission.

■ PAYMENTS MONTH-BY-MONTH

The following chart shows the maximum monthly amount you could spend for home payments and total monthly credit obligatons at a variety of income levels and meet the guidelines required by most lenders. As a rule of thumb, no more than 28 percent of your gross monthly income should be used for your mortgage payment (principal, interest, taxes, insurance, condo fees, owners association fee, mortgage insurance premium) and no more than 36 percent of your gross monthly income should be going toward your mortgage payment plus all other monthly credit obligations (car loans, credit cards, utility payments).

Your gross annual income	Monthly mortgage payments	Maximum monthly credit obligations
$20,000	$467	$600
$30,000	$700	$900
$40,000	$933	$1,200
$50,000	$1,167	$1,500
$60,000	$1,400	$1,800
$70,000	$1,633	$2,100
$80,000	$1,867	$2,400
$90,000	$2,100	$2,700
$100,000	$2,333	$3,000
$130,000	$3,033	$3,900
$150,000	$3,500	$4,500
$200,000	$4,667	$6,000

SOURCE: *Unraveling the Mortgage Loan Mystery*, Federal National Mortgage Association.

EXPERT TIP

WHAT LENDERS WANT TO KNOW

If you want to get your loan approved, be ready with answers

You can speed up the loan application process by having the right information with you when you meet with your mortgage lender. Here—from the Federal National Mortgage Association, the government-chartered company otherwise known as Fannie Mae that buys mortgages from 3,000 lenders nationwide—are some of the things lenders look for:

■ **PURCHASE AGREEMENT/SALES CONTRACT:** Outlines terms and conditions of the sale.

■ **YOUR ADDRESSES:** All from last seven years.

■ **EMPLOYMENT INFORMATION:** Name, address, and phone number of all employers for the past seven years.

■ **SOURCES OF INCOME:** Two recent pay stubs and your W-2 forms for the previous two years. Verification of income from social security, pension, interest or dividends, rental income, child support, and alimony may also be needed.

■ **CURRENT ASSETS:**. Balance, account number, name and address of financial institutions for your savings, checking, and investment accounts. Recent statements should suffice. Real estate and personal property can also be listed on your application as assets. Bring an estimate of market value.

■ **CURRENT DEBTS:** Names and addresses of all creditors plus account numbers, current balances, and monthly payments. Recent bank statements may be required.

■ **SOURCE OF DOWN PAYMENT.** May be savings, stocks, investments, sale of other property, or life insurance policies. May be from relatives if it doesn't have to be repaid.

FOLLOW THE BOUNCING RATE

What to look for in an adjustable rate mortgage

As interest rates dropped in the early '90s, the race to ARMs (adjustable rate mortgages) slowed dramatically. But, in 1994, interest rates started rising again, and so did ARM applications, accounting for some 40 percent of all mortgages.

Lenders use indexes—such as the rate on six-month Treasury bills or three-year Treasury notes—to decide when to raise or lower the interest rate on an adjustable rate mortgage. For example, when the financial index your lender uses rises, the interest rate on your mortgage may also increase—it depends on how the index is applied. Fluctuations in the interest rate can change your monthly payments, mortgage length, or principal balance. Some indexes reflect what the market will bear across the country; others reflect local trends. Other money indexes are controlled solely by individual lenders. The index you select should be one that is verified easily.

Its past performance may give you an indication of how stable it is. Have someone with expertise translate past and potential changes into dollars and cents. Also, find out how the index is used. For example, if the index changes monthly, is the lender also changing the rate on your loan monthly, or are there limits on the number of times and/or the amount your rate can fluctuate? Finally, check how much advance warning the lender will give you before new rates or payments go into effect.

HOMEBUYER'S GUIDE

MAKING SENSE OF YOUR MORTGAGE PAYMENTS

These tables show what your monthly payments (principal and interest) will be assuming different interest rates and loan terms. For example, monthly payments for a $90,000, 30-year fixed mortgage at 8 percent would be $660.39. For amounts over $100,000, add the numbers for the amount equal to the amount of mortgage.

AMOUNT	MONTHLY PAYMENTS (principal and interest)					
FINANCED	5 years	10 years	15 years	20 years	25 years	30 years
6% ANNUAL PERCENTAGE RATE						
$25,000	$483.33	$277.56	$210.97	$179.11	$161.08	$149.89
$30,000	$579.99	$333.07	$253.16	$214.93	$193.30	$179.87
$35,000	$676.65	$388.58	$295.35	$250.76	$225.51	$209.85
$40,000	$773.32	$444.09	$337.55	$286.58	$257.73	$239.83
$45,000	$869.98	$499.60	$379.74	$322.40	$289.94	$269.80
$50,000	$966.65	$555.11	$421.93	$358.22	$322.16	$299.78
$60,000	$1,159.97	$666.13	$506.32	$429.86	$386.59	$359.74
$70,000	$1,353.30	$777.15	$590.70	$501.51	$451.02	$419.69
$80,000	$1,546.63	$888.17	$675.09	$573.15	$515.45	$479.65
$90,000	$1,739.96	$999.19	$759.48	$644.79	$579.88	$539.60
$100,000	$1,933.29	$1,110.21	$843.86	$716.44	$644.31	$599.56
7% ANNUAL PERCENTAGE RATE						
$25,000	$493.03	$290.28	$224.71	$193.83	$176.70	$166.33
$30,000	$594.04	$348.33	$269.65	$232.59	$212.04	$199.60
$35,000	$693.05	$406.38	$314.59	$271.36	$247.38	$232.86
$40,000	$792.05	$464.44	$359.54	$310.12	$282.72	$266.13
$45,000	$891.06	$522.49	$404.48	$348.89	$318.06	$299.39
$50,000	$990.06	$580.55	$449.42	$387.65	$353.39	$332.66
$60,000	$1,188.08	$696.66	$539.30	$465.18	$424.07	$399.19
$70,000	$1,386.09	$812.76	$629.18	$542.71	$494.75	$465.72
$80,000	$1,584.10	$928.87	$719.07	$620.24	$565.43	$532.25
$90,000	$1,782.11	$1,044.98	$808.95	$697.77	$636.11	$598.78
$100,000	$1,980.12	$1,161.09	$898.83	$775.30	$706.78	$665.31
8% ANNUAL PERCENTAGE RATE						
$25,000	$506.91	$303.32	$238.91	$209.11	$192.95	$183.44
$30,000	$608.29	$363.98	$286.70	$250.93	$231.54	$220.13
$35,000	$709.67	$424.65	$334.48	$292.75	$270.14	$256.82
$40,000	$811.06	$485.31	$382.26	$334.58	$308.73	$293.51
$45,000	$912.44	$545.97	$430.04	$376.40	$347.32	$330.19
$50,000	$1,013.82	$606.64	$477.83	$418.22	$385.91	$366.88
$60,000	$1,216.58	$727.97	$573.39	$501.86	$463.09	$440.26
$70,000	$1,419.35	$849.29	$668.96	$585.51	$540.27	$513.64
$80,000	$1,622.11	$970.62	$764.52	$669.15	$617.45	$587.01
$90,000	$1,824.88	$1,091.95	$860.09	$752.80	$694.63	$660.39
$100,000	$2,027.64	$1,213.28	$955.65	$836.44	$771.82	$733.76

HOMEBUYER'S GUIDE

AMOUNT FINANCED	MONTHLY PAYMENTS (principal and interest) 5 years	10 years	15 years	20 years	25 years	30 years
9% ANNUAL PERCENTAGE RATE						
$25,000	$518.96	$316.69	$253.57	$224.93	$209.80	$201.16
$30,000	$622.75	$380.03	$304.28	$269.92	$251.76	$241.39
$35,000	$726.54	$443.36	$354.99	$314.90	$293.72	$281.62
$40,000	$830.33	$506.70	$405.71	$359.89	$335.68	$321.85
$45,000	$934.13	$570.04	$456.42	$404.88	$377.64	$362.08
$50,000	$1,037.92	$633.38	$507.13	$449.86	$419.60	$402.31
$60,000	$1,245.50	$760.05	$608.56	$539.84	$503.52	$482.77
$70,000	$1,453.08	$886.73	$709.99	$629.81	$587.44	$563.24
$80,000	$1,660.67	$1,013.41	$811.41	$719.78	$671.36	$643.70
$90,000	$1,868.25	$1,140.08	$912.84	$803.75	$755.28	$724.16
$100,000	$2,075.84	$1,266.76	$1,014.27	$899.73	$839.20	$804.62
10% ANNUAL PERCENTAGE RATE						
$25,000	$531.18	$330.38	$268.65	$241.26	$227.18	$219.39
$30,000	$637.41	$396.45	$322.38	$289.51	$272.61	$263.27
$35,000	$743.65	$462.53	$376.11	$337.76	$318.05	$307.15
$40,000	$849.88	$528.60	$429.84	$386.01	$363.48	$351.03
$45,000	$956.12	$594.68	$483.57	$434.26	$408.92	$394.91
$50,000	$1,062.35	$660.75	$537.30	$482.51	$454.35	$438.79
$60,000	$1,274.82	$792.90	$644.76	$579.01	$545.22	$526.54
$70,000	$1,487.29	$925.06	$752.22	$675.52	$636.09	$614.30
$80,000	$1,699.76	$1,057.20	$859.68	$772.02	$726.96	$702.06
$90,000	$1,912.23	$1,189.36	$967.14	$868.52	$817.83	$789.81
$100,000	$2,124.70	$1,321.51	$1,074.61	$965.02	$908.70	$877.57
11% ANNUAL PERCENTAGE RATE						
$25,000	$543.56	$344.38	$284.15	v258.05	$245.03	$238.08
$30,000	$652.27	$413.25	$340.98	$309.66	$294.03	$285.70
$35,000	$760.98	$482.13	$397.81	$361.27	$343.04	$333.31
$40,000	$869.70	$551.00	$454.64	$412.88	$392.05	$380.93
$45,000	$978.41	$619.88	$511.47	$464.48	$441.05	$428.55
$50,000	$1,087.12	$688.75	$568.30	$516.09	$490.06	$476.16
$60,000	$1,304.54	$826.50	$681.96	$619.31	$588.07	$571.39
$70,000	$1,521.97	$964.25	$795.62	$722.53	$686.08	$666.63
$80,000	$1,739.39	$1,102.00	$909.28	$825.75	$784.09	$761.86
$90,000	$1,956.81	$1,239.75	$1,022.94	$928.97	$882.10	$857.09
$100,000	$2,174.24	$1,377.50	$1,136.60	$1,032.19	$980.11	$952.32

SOURCE: *The Mortgage Money Guide*, Federal Trade Commission.

REFINANCING

WHEN TO TRADE IN YOUR MORTGAGE

The right answer may be a lot sooner than you think. Here's why

The conventional wisdom is that interest rates have to drop 2 percent to make refinancing attractive. The conventional wisdom may be wrong. In fact, if you're planning to live in your house for many years, refinancing to a lower rate by as little as 1 percent can be profitable.

For a typical mortgage that involves refinancing costs of 1 percent of the total loan, the accounting firm of Ernst & Young figures that, if you can lower your interest rate by a single percentage point, the new loan will put you ahead after just 18 months.

Refinancing can give you other opportunities, like switching from a 30-year fixed mortgage to 15 years. The switch usually will bump up your monthly payments, but it will also reduce the overall cost of your loan, and the interest rate you pay will generally be about a half percentage point lower than a 30-year mortgage. Another advantage: You build up more equity in your home that you can tap into later. Recent figures show that a third of the holders of 30-year mortgages choose 15-year loans when they refinance.

They may not neccesarily be making the right choice, though. Consider the following example: If you get a $150,000, 30-year mortgage at 7.3 percent, you will pay $229,208 in interest over the life of the loan. A 15-year mortgage at 6.8 percent would cost less than half that—$89,612. The difference in monthly payments is $304—$1,028 for the 30-year mortgage versus $1,332 for the 15-year mortgage.

But suppose you opt for the 30-year loan and invest the $304 difference in the stock market, where it earns 7 percent after tax. (The historic return on stocks is about 10 percent before taxes.) And suppose you also invest the extra tax savings generated by the longer-term loan.

Since the loan amortizes more slowly than a 15-year mortgage, more of your monthly payment is tax-deductible interest. After 10 years, the 30-year loan looks like a better and better deal. By the end of 15 years, the holder of the 30-year loan would have earned enough on his investment to pay off the remaining debt on the house and still have some $10,000 left.

Once you choose a mortgage, you'll have to decide about refinancing costs. You'll have the choice of covering them at the outset by paying points or spreading them over the life of the loan by accepting a somewhat higher interest rate. In most cases, you should opt for not paying points. By investing the money you would have paid in points, you can build up a tidy nest egg over the life of your mortgage, which should amount to more than you'd save if you paid the points and invested the amount you saved in lower interest costs on your loan.

The bottom line, everything considered: the best mortgage for you will be the one whose term most closely matches the time you expect to keep your house.

MONEY IN THE BANK?

Payments and savings on a $100,000 mortgage refinanced to 8 percent.

Current rate	Current monthly payment	Monthly saving at 8%	Annual saving at 8%
9.0%	$805	$71	$852
9.5%	$841	$107	$1,284
10.0%	$878	$144	$1,728
10.5%	$915	$181	$2,172
11.0%	$952	$218	$2,616
11.5%	$990	$256	$3,072
12.0%	$1,029	$295	$3,540
12.5%	$1,067	$333	$3,996
13.0%	$1,106	$372	$4,464

VACATION HOMES

A HOUSE IN THE COUNTRY

The neighbors don't come to call and prices are reasonable

Ah, the vacation villa. "I enjoy here a cozier, more profound and undisturbed retirement," wrote Pliny the Younger of his Tuscan retreat. "I am at a greater distance from the business of the town and the interruption of troublesome clients. All is calm and composed."

Tuscany still beckons, but so do a lot of other spots in newer worlds. Recent surveys show that Americans' interest in owning a vacation home has tripled, but prices, which crashed in 1988, still have not recovered. The *New York Times* reports that prices in some places in the Northeast are still 30 percent lower than they were in 1987. Mortgage bankers note that while prices in Florida are starting to come back and California prices are stabilizing, prices in much of the West are still down. John Tuccillo, chief economist of the National Association of Realtors, notes that "although there was a brief rebound in 1994, prices are still going down on both coasts, as well as the South and West." Only in the Midwest, Tuccillo says, have prices remained stable.

As baby boomers move into their prime earning years, prices could nudge upward. According to Mediamark Research, Inc. in New York, the median household income of families owning vacation homes is just $54,000. And another survey found that almost half of all respondents believed they had "some chance" of purchasing recreational property within the next decade. But the supply of homes is also growing and most experts doubt prices will climb above the levels of the late '80s anytime soon.

Suburban sprawl is making it harder to find a perfect spot nearby. Already the average American travels over 300 miles to reach his vacation destination, and one-third of Americans travel over 500 miles. Besides, buyers are eschewing traditional summer homes for ones that can be used all year. That's created something of a boom in mountain areas like Taos, New Mexico, and the counties outside of Denver as action-oriented vacationers seek outdoor activities and more privacy.

EXPERT TIPS

UNCLE SAM LENDS A HAND

Second-home owners can take advantage of several tax breaks

■ If you rent out your vacation house 15 days or less per year, mortgage interest payments are deductible, as they are for your primary home. The rent doesn't have to be declared as income and is tax-free.

■ A vacation home is classified as rental property if you rent it out for 15 or more days per year and stay in it yourself no more than 14 days or 10 percent of the total days it's rented. All rent must be declared as income, but some of the utilities and maintenance costs can be deducted, as can losses on the building.

■ If you rent out your home for over 15 days but also stay in it yourself over 14 days or 10 percent of the total days it's rented, it's considered "mixed-use property." You can deduct expenses that don't exceed your income on the property. But losses in excess of expenses aren't deductible.

BUYER'S GUIDE

THE TOP VACATION HOME MARKETS

Nearly 140 second-home markets around the country were evaluated in May and June 1994, through a nationwide opinion survey of residential real estate brokers affiliated with Century 21. The selection of the top markets was based on home price appreciation between 1992 and 1993 and availability of the widest range of recreational opportunities—including beach access, boating, fishing, snow skiing, golfing, hiking, camping, and proximity to population centers. An increasing number of vacation home shoppers purchase with present or future plans for retirement (see "Plan to retire" in the table below). Indeed, in some areas such as Key Biscayne, Fla., 90 percent of buyers select properties for retirement purposes.

Location	Average price	1992–94 increase	Plan to retire	Nearest city	Distance from nearest city
WEST					
SEDONA, Ariz.	$215,000	16%	60%	Flagstaff, Ariz.	35 miles
				Phoenix, Ariz.	100 miles
VAIL, Colo.	$350,000	17%	20%	Denver, Colo.	100 miles
MCCALL, Idaho[1]	$150,000[1]	18%	30%	Boise, Idaho	100 miles
KALISPEL, Mont.	$93,300	24%	10%	Billings, Mont.	500 miles
BEND, Ore.	$117,000	4%	10%	Portland, Ore.	160 miles
OGDEN, Utah	$98,000[2]	44%	40%	Salt Lake City, Utah	40 miles
JACKSON HOLE, Wyo.	$250,000	25%	0%	Idaho Falls, Wyo.	85 miles
MIDWEST					
BOYNE CITY, Mich.	$220,000[1]	19%	50%	Detroit, Mich.	300 miles
GRAND RAPIDS, Mich.	$42,000	9%	20%	Minneapolis-St. Paul, Minn.	140 miles
LAKE OF THE OZARKS, Mo.	$78,500	14%	55%	Kansas City, Kan.	160 miles
				St. Louis, Mo.	160 miles
SIREN, Wisc.	$79,700	39%	35%	EauClaire, Wis.	100 miles
				Milwaukee, Wis.	350 miles
SOUTH					
HOT SPRINGS, Ark.	$128,800	21%	30%	Little Rock, Ariz.	65 miles
AMELIA ISLAND, Fla	$170,000	13%	75%	Jacksonville, Fla.	40 miles
KEY BISCAYNE, Fla.	$300,000	20%	90%	Miami, Fla.	5 miles
ST. SIMONS, Ga.	$172,500	5%	20%	Jacksonville, Fla.	75 miles
				Savanah, Ga.	70 miles
EMERALD ISLE, N.C.	$150,000	15%	30%	Raleigh-Durham, N.C	150 miles
MT. VERNON, Texas	$110,000	22%	60%	Dallas-Ft. Worth, Texas	100 miles
NORTHEAST					
McHENRY, Md.	$187,900	20%	40%	Baltimore, Md.	170 miles
				Pittsburgh, Pa.	80 miles
NANTUCKET, Mass.	$375,000	15%	10%	Boston, Mass.	100 miles
LAKE PLACID, N.Y.	$135,000	13%	30%	Albany, N.Y.	150 miles
PENN-YAN, N.Y.	$176,000	10%	72%	Syracuse, N.Y.	60 miles
				Rochester, N.Y.	60 miles

1. Price for cabin or chalet. 2. Price for condominium.
SOURCE: Century 21 Realtors.

COLLECTING

HOT TRENDS

WHAT COLLECTORS COVET MOST

The latest trends in collecting, from folk art to PEZ dispensers

Collecting is a social pursuit. Different people may collect different things—beer cans, fine art, barbed wire, cars—but even the most solitary of stamp collectors likely derives pleasure from knowing that other collectors covet the same stamps he does. Trends in collecting covetry sometimes are based on investment value alone, the classic example being that when an artist dies, the value of his work will skyrocket because the supply has become finite. But trends often are generated by less obvious social forces. Black memorabilia, for instance, is becoming popular as America comes to grips with issues of racial identity. Below is a survey of the trends in objects that America desires. It is also, not incidentally, a portrait of the nation.

■ **FOLK ART:** Prices for weather vanes, embroideries, and ships' mastheads are commanding almost as much as Old Master paintings. At a Sotheby's auction in early 1994, a Pilgrim-period blanket chest sold for $354,500. For portraits, prices are based more on prettiness than on quality or rarity: cute children and young women might go for $100,000, but a dour old man brings less than $2,000.

Outsider art, primitive work done during any period by painters with little formal training, is especially sought after. But the field has seen a small post-recession slump—prices are down, so bargains are out there for the persistent.

■ **VICTORIAN DECORATIVE ARTS:** Victorian items—particularly wicker and glass—have seen a resurgence of interest. Terry Kovel, author with her husband Ralph of *Kovels' Antiques & Collections Price List 1995*, notes that Victorian furniture from the Aesthetic Revival of the 1870s is commanding top dollar. A single chair recently sold to a museum for $125,000.

■ **MODERN COLLECTIBLES:** Anticipating Andy Warhol by half a decade, Campbell's Soup in 1905 produced a tin sign that showed a waving American flag made up of soup tins. In 1981, one went for $5,000; it was resold in 1992 for $93,500. Other popular collectibles include Hawai'ian shirts, mechanical toys and Pez candy dispensers (first produced in 1952, and now going for up to $2,000). A caveat from *Maine Antiques Digest* editor Sam Pennington about mass-produced toys, baseball cards, and other

PAINTING BY THE NUMBERS

A poll discovers what Americans like in their paintings

Animals frolic among the vibrantly hued trees and shrubs as festive folk in old-fashioned garb wander along the shore. Such a scene, according to a recent survey of 1,001 Americans, is the pinnacle of beauty in art. Russian émigré artist Alex Melamid, who conducted the survey with Vitaly Komar and support from the Nation Institute, was surprised by the consensus on what looks good in paintings. The paint-by-consensus breakdown:

■ **The style should be realistic, with visible brushstrokes, pale and vibrant colors, and thick, textured surfaces.**

■ **The painting should be simple and relaxing to look at. Please leave out the black, gold, and turquoise as well as the bold designs and sharp angles. And no nudes.**

■ **The favored size for a painting is that of a dishwasher or of a 19-inch TV set.**

■ **We like our scenes outdoors, our figures historical and our subjects secular.**

■ **When all is said and done, 57 percent would still rather take the money a painting is worth in cash than the art itself.**

collectibles: "Usually the first one comes out of the attic and it brings a big price. But there were more made—somebody else will see that and others will come out."

■ **BLACK MEMORABILIA:** Dealers are still getting used to hawking items with potentially negative connotations like ceramic mammies with ingratiating smiles and minstrel-figure mechanical banks that dance for pennies, but with an annual trade show, a magazine (*Black Ethnic Collectibles*), and an estimated 35,000 collectors in the U.S. alone, black memorabilia has taken off in the last few years.

Recently, some sheet music went for $88, a Dapper Dan mechanical toy brought $522, and African prince and princess dolls made in France sold for $115,000 and $112,000 each. Watch out, though: Increased popularity has inspired a run on reproductions.

■ **PRINTS:** John James Audubon painted all 435 species of birds known in the United States in the early 19th century. A complete set of prints of his paintings ran about $1,000 in the 1830s and has been appreciating ever since, probably since only five sets are now in existence. All birds aren't equal: A turkey cock could fetch as much as $50,000 today, while $600 might get you a small songbird like the red-breasted nuthatch. Maps are hot, too. Particularly popular are 18th-century maps of America and historical prints, especially Old West scenes.

■ **'50S FURNITURE:** High-style furniture by well-known designers like Charles Eames is hot *because* it's less expensive. The pieces are "one of the few things you can find at a bargain because people are still living with them," Kovel says. Bargains can be found for several hundred dollars or even less.

THE ART MARKET

AN ARTFUL GUIDE FOR THE ARTLESS

Starting an art collection means dealing with dealers. Here's how

The art world can be a confusing place for even the most experienced of art buyers. Squishy factors such as "historical interest" or "artistic integrity," will determine whether your purchase is the bargain of a lifetime or just expensive wallpaper. And if you're just starting out, you're at the mercy of the judgement of experts.

To even the odds, we asked veteran collector Alan S. Bamberger, author of the syndicated column "Art Talk" and the book *Buy Art Smart* (Wallace-Homestead, 1990), to advise the beginning art collector. Here's what he suggested:

■ **Make sure that what you want is there to collect, and then collect the best in the field.** If you want to collect Vincent Van Gogh paintings, you have to have a lot of money, or you will get the worst of the worst of what Van Gogh ever did, because that's what's on the market. To find out what's out there, talk to dealers about finding other dealers in the same field, turn to international directories of dealers, or place ads in trade papers.

■ **Establish as wide of a range of resources as possible.** Not only will you see and learn more, but you'll also be able to play the market for the best price and make intelligent price comparisons. There's a difference between purposely playing dealers off one another—you shouldn't do that—and asking intelligent questions. It's

INVESTING IN OILS

A study shows that investing in paintings can be unpredictable indeed

Oil paintings can be a good investment—problem is, they can also be a rotten investment. Knowing the difference means knowing a lot about what makes buyers, critics, and auction houses tick. And even then, the market can be unpredictable.

In *Art Auction Trends*, James Coleman compared the investment value of selected artists' works to the consumer price index and the Standard & Poor's 500. Between 1971 and 1991, 68 percent of the artists studied by Coleman kept pace with inflation and 54 percent outperformed the S&P 500. Sounds good—but how do you tell if your favorite artist is in the winner's circle?

It's hard. Consider the work of the highly regarded American impressionist Mary Cassatt. Her work was a good investment over the long run, but its value declined steadily throughout the 70s. Despite a brief spike in 1981, the median price for Cassatt's watercolors and drawings by 1984 had dropped well below the increase in the consumer price index and the stock market, and almost below the median price for her work sold in 1971.

Nonetheless, those who stuck to their guns made a killing when the median price for her work skyrocketed four years later, surpassing the increase in the CPI and nearly tripling the rate for the S&P 500.

How does one find stability in such a market? A painting's ability to survive in a recession without a big price drop is a good sign of stability.

Better yet, just collect what you like. That way, you can ride out the bad times in good company.

like comparing cars at auto dealerships. You should ask dealers to explain why you saw something similar somewhere else for a different price.

■ **Start by collecting an artist's typical works.** It's a question of salability down the road—if you want things that will be liquid, you'd be well advised to go with the mainstream. At first you'll want to find out what the artist is most famous for. Or if you like landscapes of Cape Cod, say, find out what people who collect them like to have in them, and then you look for that in your pictures.

■ **Don't confuse the work with the environment.** Properly lit and displayed, even a sack of trash can look great. You can take anything—a tape measure, a can of soup—and put it up on a pedestal, light it, put it in an art gallery and you're going to have people walk by and say, "Wow that's fantastic." But when you get it home, all it is, is a can of soup. Take it out of the gallery environment, take it home on approval for a week. Usually you leave some sort of deposit, with no commitment to buy. On the other hand, unless you're really experienced, it can be hard to see how beautiful something can be. At a garage sale it may look like a piece of junk, but a collector who knows what he's doing will clean it up and display it properly and it'll look like a million dollars.

■ **Don't take bullying.** If you've got an art dealer who's giving you a hard time, leave. When you get stuff like "The artist is almost dead" or "We sold six of these last month for X dollars," just get out. If you feel pressure in any sense to do something, that's a warning sign that you're in the wrong place.

■ **Start by working with the experts.** Avoid galleries without direction or focus. These are good places to go for experienced collectors because chances are something's going

RENT-A-MASTERPIECE

How about a limited edition, worth $300, for $22 for three months?

A Picasso in your living room. A Degas in the music room. A Henry Moore sculpture in the garden? Not quite, but a slew of national art museums—including the Los Angeles County Museum of Art, the Philadelphia Museum of Art, and the Indianapolis Museum of Art—and local galleries are making it possible for shallow-pocketed connoisseurs to hang museum quality art on their walls. For the cost of a museum membership and charges depending on the value of the piece, a culture vulture can walk away with works of up-and-coming local artists as well as artists with well-established reputations. The individual renter can't, as cool as it might be and as much as you promise to treat it well, rent from the permanent exhibitions. But how about a limited-edition Charles Cuniff photograph from the Seattle Art Museum, worth $300, for $22 for three months? Or a David Hockney lithograph from Art Dimension in Santa Monica, Calif., selling price $8,000, for $200 a month.

Museums differ in the number of months they'll rent a piece for and whether they'll renew. But all allow the satisfied customer to buy the pieces he or she rents, minus a percentage of the rental fee or of the money already spent renting. "It's a win-win situation," says Andrea Voinot, Gallery Coordinator for the San Francisco Museum Rental/Sales Gallery. "We make money, the artist gets exposure and income, the public gets access to affordable artwork."

So far, the only hitches have been nasty little natural disasters like earthquakes. Please, the museums plead, along with your real fine taste, have real fine-art insurance.

to slip through. But galleries like that are repositories for whatever people who are running around the area happen to find at flea markets and estate sales—the only focus they have is getting things they can mark up and sell for more. Those galleries have their place, and if you have experience, you can find bargains there.

■ **Don't ask, don't tell.** Forgeries are a touchy area, because you don't want to call in one dealer to comment on another's painting—that would be a conflict of interest—he would rather sell you one of his paintings. As you spend more time collecting, try to meet people—museum people or scholarly types, real true collectors who are not overly concerned about the money and who will give you the straight dope. If you recognize a forgery, don't point it out. You can get involved in legal problems and you can make enemies fast.

■ **Don't let investment factors weigh too heavily.** Art is immediately liquid only if you want to take a severe hit. If you buy and sell stocks and bonds and the like, you normally pay a 1 to 2 percent commission. If you pay a 20 percent commission to buy a work of art and then pay a 20 percent commission when you sell it—and those are very modest commissions in the art world—the art has to increase in value 40 percent before you see your first penny of profit.

■ **Don't try to chisel on prices, unless you have a really good argument.** You shouldn't worry about letting on that you really like a painting. A poker face won't work anyway. If you're the type of person who likes getting a deal, dealers will bump their price up a bit when they see you coming, and then drop it down to what they wanted to sell it for in the first place. Or, worse, they'll just sell you medium-quality art that they would rather have out the door anyway. Sure they'll flex on the price a little bit, but you're not going to get the good stuff. You have to work for that—there's a lot of competition.

THE SMALL PRINT ON PRINTS

They decorate a wall, but stocks do a better job of decorating a portfolio

Most art forms defy financial analysis because each work is highly individual. Prints are a different case because they generally are created in batches of 50 or 100. A 1993 study by University of Toronto economist James Pesando took advantage of this uniformity by analyzing the sales between 1977 and 1992 of 27,961 prints by 28 modern artists, including Picasso and Matisse.

The results were not encouraging. The mean return for the prints was 1.51 percent annually, whereas a low-risk government bond would have gotten you a 2.54 percent return. Wily investors can still make a killing—annual returns on the prints ranged from a disastrous –35.34 percent to a healthy 47.18 percent. The method? Similar prints sold within a few weeks of each other varied in price by as much as 30 percent.

■ **COMPARING INVESTMENTS**

The real annual rate of return from 1977 to 1992

INVESTMENT VEHICLE	RETURN Worst	Average	Best
Modern Prints	–35.34%	1.51%	47.18%
Stocks	–28.58%	8.14%	65.50%
Government Bonds	–38.35%	2.54%	76.09%

SOURCE: James E. Pesando, University of Toronto.

PHOTOGRAPHY

SO YOU WANT TO BE IN PICTURES!

Photography is great art and a good investment to boot

Until recently, few serious collectors thought photographs were worthy of their attention. Photos were bought and sold mostly through antiquarian book dealers, and though Sotheby's in London held its first photography auction in 1971, it was not until 1975 that photo sales become an annual event there. As the price of contemporary paintings skyrocketed in the early '80s, though, collectors began to turn to the sleepy photography market for bargains, and critics paid more attention to the art form.

Nobody would call the photography market sleepy now. In 1993 Sotheby's photography department established a new world record for a single photograph at auction when Man Ray's "Glass Tears," a 9-by-12-inch work from about 1930, sold for $190,100.

And there's still room for persistent new collectors. Prices for prized photographs are still a pittance compared to those for modern paintings. Be aware, though, that although a major show or a new publication about a photographer will almost certainly increase the artist's cachet and keep his work in demand, it won't likely have much of an immediate effect on the price of his work.

An auction may be more important. That was the case when the Museum of Modern Art in New York City recently decided to auction off 12 photographs by Dorothea Lange, an American well known for her depression-era photos. The works commanded high prices and may appreciate in the future.

Here, Susan Arthur Whitson, director of

EXPERT LIST

HOW MUCH IS THAT PHOTO IN THE WINDOW?

An Edward Steichen portrait of George F. Watts sold in 1989 for a record-breaking $110,000, but many outstanding works can be had for under $10,000. Here, culled from auction and gallery reports, is a sampler of less expensive works by popular photographers.

UNDER $1,500

- **W. E. SMITH:** *13x19 unposed shot of doctors, circa 1950.* **$550**
- **WILLIAM WEGMAN:** *11x14 portrait from ongoing dog series.* **$1,200**
- **WEEGEE:** *7x9 unposed jazz club scene circa 1950.* **$1,210**

UNDER $5,000

- **GARY WINOGRAND:** *16x11 publicity still of Marilyn Monroe.* **$2,420**
- **HARRY CALLAHAN:** *8x10 gelatin silver print from 1952 titled "Eleanor Chicago."* **$3,000**
- **ROBERT JACKSON:** *8x10 shooting of Lee Harvey Oswald. (Won Pulitzer Prize.)* **$3,520**

UNDER $10,000

- **JOHN DIVOLA:** *60x48 smoke against abstract backdrop.* **$5,500**
- **ROBERT FRANK:** *11x14 gelatin silver print of Interstate 91.* **$7,500**
- **CINDY SHERMAN:** *7x10 self-portrait taken with a mirror.* **$8,250**

the Houk Friedman Gallery in New York City, which represents many respected photographers, offers some other pointers for beginning photo collectors.

■ **A photographer's most typical works are also the most valuable.** If you're building a collection, you want to get something that speaks to you about the artist. Of course, you don't want to buy a picture just because it's the most famous thing the artist did. Just remember that the typical image will sell best.

■ **Photography is a two-stage process:** Shooting of the negative, then making the print. A print may not have been printed by the photographer, but by his or her assistant, which will reduce its value. You can get a Berenice Abbot vintage for $9,000; you can also get a later print for $3,000. If you have the money, get the original artifact instead of a late knockoff.

■ **Watch the number of prints in a limited edition.** Prices rise as the prints are sold. It is important to know how many have been made and whether the artist has reserved the right to make more later on. A photographer may offer an edition of 25 large prints and 25 less expensive smaller prints. If the artist, as is common, also reserves the right to make 25 additional prints, the gallery should sell each print as one of a limited edition of 75.

■ **Print quality is important.** Collecting photographs is like collecting etchings— surface quality is very important. Nonetheless, technique is undervalued in the current market. The hottest works are blurry images and torn photographs inspired by modernist photographers like Man Ray and László Moholy-Nagy. Works by their less popular contemporaries can be had for more moderate prices.

■ **Know your materials.** The paper most photographs are printed on is extremely susceptible to chemicals and ultraviolet light. Some processes like color printing on Ektacolor paper are especially prone to fading. You can buy glass with a special UV filter, but your best bet is to simply make sure that your pictures are hung away from direct sunlight.

EXPERT SOURCES

PHOTOS THROUGH THE AGES

Want to learn more? Photo expert Susan Arthur Whitson recommends her favorite resources

BOOKS

THE HISTORY OF PHOTOGRAPHY
Beaumont Newhall, The Museum of Modern Art with Little, Brown and Co., 1993, $29.95
■ Emphasizes big names and social impact.

A WORLD HISTORY OF PHOTOGRAPHY
Naomi Rosenblum, Abbeville, 1989, $60
■ An overview of photo history—popular in college classes for its clarity and depth.

LOOKING AT PHOTOGRAPHS
John Szarkowski, The Museum of Modern Art with Little, Brown and Co., 1988, $27.50
■ Compiled by the photo curator of New York's Museum of Modern Art from their collection.

MAGAZINES

PHOTOGRAPHY IN NEW YORK
$2.95 per issue, $18 per year (6 issues)
■ A publication of the Association of International Photography Art Dealers that lists shows and upcoming auctions in New York City, as well as around the country.
☎ **212-787-0401**

ANTIQUES

IS IT OLD, OR JUST A LITTLE BEAT UP?

Telling an imitation from an antique requires more than a good eye

Techniques for roughing up a sculpture to make it look older than it actually is have been around ever since an inspired ancient Roman sculptor made a copy of an ancient Greek statue. Like art forgeries, subtle restorations in the style of even the finest antiques can challenge the eye of discriminating collectors. Even repairs and replaced parts can substantially reduce a piece's value.

But how can you tell? An educated eye and a knowledge of history help. George Read, who once oversaw Sotheby's English furniture department in New York and now leads workshops on buying antique furniture, says he can tell whether a mahogany chair is old from across the room. When Europeans first began gathering mahogany from the forests of the new world, he explains, they harvested the easy-to-reach trees near the shore. Those trees, subjected to harsher weather from the ocean, grew slowly, giving the wood a complex, close grain. Decades later, after the seaside trees were depleted, sailors were forced to collect faster-growing trees from up-river, trees with a wide and less pleasing grain.

Read never leaves home without a postage stamp-sized magnifying glass with its own light to check for the tiny flaws that can give away a forgery. He offers some tips below for fledgling furniture sleuths on how to spot them as well.

■ **SHRINKAGE:** Wood shrinks across the grain. If a round tabletop is actually round when measured in two dimensions, it's new. If the table is old, there should be a difference of about 1/8 inch per foot. Marquetry, too, tends to contract irregularly, usually sinking below the rest of the surface. If a piece with marquetry has a perfectly smooth surface, the marquetry was probably added much later to add flash or "tart up" the object, as dealers like to say.

■ **UPHOLSTERY:** Always lift the edge of the fabric underneath upholstered pieces to see whether there are several sets of nail holes—you should figure a change of fabric every 50 years or so. You might have to pry up a nail or two, but in an auction, it's likely that a previous viewer has already done so for you. If the fabric is in good condition and you don't see any nail holes, be especially wary—you may be looking at a fake.

■ **SURFACES:** "A really good patina might account for 50 percent of the value of a piece," Read says. Though you might be disappointed to find dents or bleached spots on a beautiful piece, however, they do have an upside. Bleaching on one side of an object—indicating that the piece sat for years with a window to one

FACT FILE:

A TOTALLY FAKE ANTIQUE

■ *Pseudo-antiques are especially common among country pine furniture. Furniture makers get that handsome worn look by using old wood, often from 18th-century barns or houses. To make a table, for instance, they will take four posts from a banister for legs, the top of the banister for rails, and floorboards or wall paneling for the top. "They're very nice pieces, I like them myself," says antique expert George Read. "But they are not antiques."*

side—is very hard to fake convincingly, and it's a good sign of age. So are the hairline cracks in the surface and the irregular, slight buckling from underneath that come only from true age.

For pieces of furniture that sell for less than $5,000, Read says, fakers cannot afford to take the time to create a convincing patina. Instead they either simply paint the piece and rub off the paint in sections, or else, before painting, they treat the wood with a chemical that makes a uniform "alligator" crackle over the entire object. As for the surface of a table or chest, when you shine a flashlight over it, it should look like a pond blown by the wind—a perfectly smooth surface means either a replaced top or sloppy, destructive restoration.

■ **HARDWARE:** To tell whether brass handles or keyhole covers have been changed, take them off and look at the fade outline—if the hardware is original, the line will be cookie-cutter sharp. Also look inside to see whether there are extra screw holes from previous hardware.

If the piece is American, good hardware is critical to collectors. American furniture made in the 18th century was valued very highly at the time it was made, and it got little wear and tear compared with European works of the same vintage. Dealers in American furniture value original hardware highly. While replaced hardware might not affect the value of a European antique, it is significant in an American one.

Also, look at the screw heads. Screws were not made with a tapered edge before 1840. Parallel edges on the screws of an object aren't definitive, but they serve as another useful clue about an object's age. Beware of using old screws and hardware as proof of age, however. Fakers keep large stores of antique hardware to dress up new pieces.

■ **MIRRORS AND GILDING:** Original mirrors are extremely rare, so a replaced mirror won't hurt the value much, as long as it looks attractive. Likewise, re-gilding was common and shouldn't reduce a frame's value much if it was done well. To tell if a mirror is genuinely old, though, there is an easy test: touch a pencil tip or business card to the surface in several places, and note the distance between the tip and its reflected image. In old glass, the distance should vary visibly across the mirror because the glass has become less flat. Also, in old glass you may see a beveled edge, but you will just barely feel it. With glass made in the Victorian era or later, you can feel a very sharp bevel.

■ **DOVETAILS:** Dovetailing is the tongue-in-groove technique carpenters use to join boards at an angle. The grooves used in 18th-century dovetails were particularly wide, as much as three-eighths of an inch. Although they continued to be made by hand through the middle of the 19th century, tools and skills grew finer, and dovetails made in 1830 may be as small as one-eighth of an inch.

■ **CHANDELIERS:** Chandeliers made before about 1860 have solid arms. After that, they began to have hollow arms so as to allow gas to be pumped into them from ducts in the ceiling. As for telling whether those shiny teardrops hanging from the chandelier's arms are really crystal or are just cut glass, Read says there is a fail-safe test: "If you hold one of the teardrops in your hand and it gets colder as you hold it, you will know it's crystal. But if it's glass, it will get warmer."

EXPERT QUOTE

"People are not buying a liquid investment when they buy antiques. It's like good real estate; it takes time to liquidate. You're not going to call a broker tomorrow and sell the highboy to put a kid through college."

—Harold Sack, New York antique dealer

SIZING UP A CHEST OF DRAWERS

"When you're trying to decide whether a chest has been repaired or altered, there are three things you automatically look for: top, feet, and hardware," says antique expert George Read. "Ninety-five percent of the restorations on a chest of drawers will be in those places, so you can save a whole lot of time if you start there."

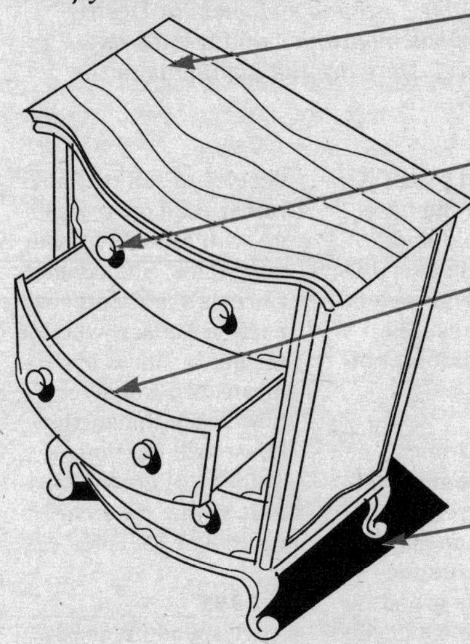

■ Watch how the light rakes across the top—if the surface is mirror-smooth, or if the top's back edge doesn't look as old as the rest of the back, it's probably new.

■ Remove the hardware to look at the fading. If the hardware is original, it will leave a sharp fade line.

■ Look at the drawers. Do they look as though they've been altered? Do the dovetails look new or machine-made? Large, hard-to-sell pieces are sometimes reduced. One change often made to a chest is to reduce its depth by cutting off part of the back and reattaching it closer to the front.

■ Tip the piece back to see whether the feet look as old as the rest of the chest, and notice if there are any spare marks or holes to indicate that something's been replaced.

■ REPAIRS: MINOR OR MAJOR?

Although it's impossible to put a general dollar value on the effect of a given repair, George Read says some typical repairs are minor—maybe reducing the value of a piece by 10 percent—while major changes might cause a piece to lose as much as 75 percent of its value.

MINOR:

- ■ Any changes that are reversible.
- ■ Replaced hardware, on European furniture.
- ■ Hardware added for embellishment (usually is reversible).
- ■ New feet on a chest, or on any European furniture.
- ■ Replaced mirror.
- ■ New gilding.
- ■ A damaged or stripped patina.
- ■ Missing casters on chair legs of French furniture.
- ■ Small alterations to the cornice of a bookshelf.

MAJOR:

- ■ Replaced hardware, on American furniture.
- ■ New feet on a chest, or on American furniture.
- ■ A damaged or stripped patina, on American furniture.
- ■ A new top on a chest.
- ■ Marriage of pieces that don't belong, such as a bookshelf on top of a slant-front desk.
- ■ Reduction in the depth of a chest.
- ■ Replaced chair rails.
- ■ Spliced or repaired chair legs using all of the original parts.
- ■ Even worse—legs with newly carved pieces.

ONE ANTIQUE'S FANTASTIC JOURNEY

When the "Garvan carver" created an exquisite card table 200 years ago in Philadelphia, he had no idea it would be worth nearly $1 million today. "This table was an extraordinary thing. Lush vines dripped down its legs and the claws of its feet clung tightly to wooden balls," begins author Thatcher Freund's description of the Willing card table. "If you stared at it for a while, the table almost sprang to life." Freund's Objects of Desire *(Pantheon, 1994, $24) is the Willing table's biography, and it ends as triumphantly as any Horatio Alger novel. Here are the highlights of the Willing card table's picaresque journey:*

■ 1759

Still in his 30s, flush with profits from his insurance firm, and looking to plug a tiny corner of his Georgian mansion, Thomas Willing commissions a card table from one of Philadelphia's dozen or so professional carvers. The Garvan carver, so called because his work today features prominently in the Mabel Brady Garvan collection at Yale University, charges about **£10** for his labors.

■ 1821

On Thomas Willing's death, the executors of his will take inventory of his estate and value the table at **50¢**. A bottle of Madeira is valued at $1. No longer fashionable, the table is packed away by Willing's son George—perhaps to the servants' quarters.

■ 1898

Phebe Barron Willing, granddaughter of George, carefully wraps the table and places it in storage in the basement of an old and prominent Philadelphia bank along with several other treasures. The cache is soon forgotten.

■ 1964

Seeking maritime antiques, Thomas Willing's great-great-great grandson, Tom Hughes, stumbles across the crate with his grandmother's name stenciled on it. Hughes shares the treasures with other Willing heirs and, taken with its beauty, keeps the table for himself.

■ 1990

Eight years after his death, Hughes's widow decides to sell the table rather than try to keep up with mounting insurance rates. She contacts Christie's and Sotheby's auction houses, who bid for her business by means of reserve, or how much the auction house will guarantee. Sotheby's gets the business with a guaranteed reserve of **$850,000**.

■ 1991

After spending nearly $30,000 to promote the sale with advertisements in antique magazines and the wining and dining of the ten or so buyers that could afford to spend upwards of $1 million for a single item of furniture, Sotheby's sends the table to the block. The final bid of **$950,000** is well over the reserve bid and is made by an anonymous buyer for the Chipstone Foundation, a museum in Milwaukee. The Willing card table is taken to its new home to rest finally among other treasures and admiring visitors.

EXPERT TIPS

GOING, GOING, GONE!

Some advice for when the bidding gets going fast and furious

It's easy to lose big at an auction, especially if you don't know some of the tricks of the trade. Here, expert auctiongoers from around the country offer some advice to bear in mind before you raise your paddle.

✔ "If there is a catalog, read it carefully. Most people gloss over the introductory material that lists the terms and conditions, and that's a mistake, because often you're given clues about what the auction house actually thinks about an object by the way they phrase attributions and dates. If the book says 'in the Chippendale style,' that means they don't think it was made in the Chippendale period [mid- to late-18th century]."

—Charles Hummel, Deputy director for the Collection at Winterthur in Wilmington, Del.

✔ "You should write your bid down on the catalog, and remember when you set your limit that on top of the hammer price you'll pay a 10 percent fee—15 percent at Sotheby's and Christie's—as well as sales tax. I stick to my game sheet. Auctions are exciting, and all of a sudden things are moving along and you can find yourself bidding $200 when you meant to spend $100."

—Kenneth Newman, Owner of The Old Print Shop in New York City

✔ "Don't bid on anything you haven't personally examined or anything you feel uneasy about—the bad feelings you get about an object at an auction will only increase with time and eat away at you over the years. During the preview, stand near what interests you. If you like a table, look at a chair next to it as other people—maybe people who know a lot more than you do—examine the table. Listen to what they say about it."

—Chuck Muller, Editor of Antique Review

✔ "You might consider commissioning a dealer to bid for you—a typical charge would be 10 percent. Read the magazines and look at the ads for dealers, or go to antique shows and size up the dealers. See what they're selling. At antique shows, you're on neutral territory—you both paid to be there, so you've both got a stake in the thing. Collecting and buying antiques and art is one place that really rewards knowledge, so go to the best dealers in the field."

—Sam Pennington, Editor of Maine Antique Digest

✔ "I believe in material that has a proven track record—things that have survived bad economic times well: Chinese export porcelain, Delftware, early metalwork, Old Master paintings and drawings. These things very rarely ever take a downturn. Representative pieces by outstanding craftsmen—those will always hold their value."

—Mark Allen, Antique dealer in Putnam Valley, NY

✔ "It's a good idea to note who the dealers are and how they're bidding, but you need to take what you hear from them with a grain of salt. Remember that they're stopping their bidding at close to wholesale prices, so that even if you go above what the dealers are bidding, you can still get a fair price—probably something closer to retail. On the whole, the published estimates are a good guide; the pieces that sell for more than the estimate are very often the finest pieces."

—Karen Keane, Managing director of Skinner auction house in Boston, Mass.

EXPERT SOURCES

FINDING THE AUCTION ACTION

Here are the leading journals in the world of antiques, art, and auctions. Richard and Sabine Yanul, owners of the Franz Bader Bookstore in Washington, D.C., also recommend their favorite books.

MAGAZINES

ART & AUCTION
$5 per issue; $42 for one year (11 issues).
■ A classy glossy that covers the international art scene with good gossip and features on collecting. Calendars cover auctions, fairs, museums, events, and galleries in the United States and abroad.
☎ **800-777-8718**

MAINE ANTIQUE DIGEST
$2.50 per issue; $29 for one year (12 issues).
■ The bible for antique dealers. 300 quirky pages each month with listings of auctions all over the country, and reports on many of them, both famous and obscure. This is the one magazine to get.
☎ **800-752-8521**

ANTIQUE REVIEW
$2 per issue; $19.95 for one year (12 issues).
■ A 100-page tabloid focused on pre-1900 antiques. It's best for news about the auction action in the Midwest and features great coverage of the artists and makers.
☎ **800-992-9757**

ART & ANTIQUES
$4.95 per issue; $20 for one year (10 issues).
■ More of a tony coffee-table mag, less market-oriented than the others. A good read, with a column on collecting in different cities and features on artists and trends.
☎ **800-274-7594**

BOOKS

THE NEW FINE POINTS OF FURNITURE
Albert Sack, Crown, 1993, $50.
■ The classic, first published in 1950 by a son of Israel Sack, one of New York City's most respected antique dealers. Lives up to subtitle *Early American—Good, Better, Best, Superior or Masterpiece* with exhaustive, definitive rankings of about 200 different furniture types, including hundreds of photos.

THE COLLECTORS' ENCYCLOPEDIA OF ANTIQUES
Phoebe Phillips, ed., World Publications, 1986, $12.95.
■ Includes sections on types of furniture, porcelain, tapestries, a glossary, tips on repairs and maintenance, hints about fakes and forgeries, lists of good museum collections, and recommended reading. 2,000 (mostly small) illustrations.

FIELD GUIDE TO AMERICAN ANTIQUE FURNITURE
Joseph T. Butler, Henry Holt & Co., 1985, $18.95.
■ Provides an anatomy of furniture types, with easy-to-read line drawings labeled with the relevant terms. Includes an overall history and chapters on different periods, with 1,700 drawings.

SOTHEBY'S ART AT AUCTION: THE ART MARKET REVIEW
Conran-Octopus, published yearly, $65.
■ Gorgeous color photos of the works on every page, but more useful for window shopping than serious research.

ART AT AUCTION IN AMERICA
Krexpress, published yearly, $39.50
■ The most affordable price guide available—and one of the best that can be found anywhere.

STAMPS & COINS

MINTING A NEW COLLECTION

From rodeo stars to Buffalo Nickels, the latest trends in stamps and coins

Considering collecting coins? Want to start a stamp collection? If you're in it for the money, think again. "We never encourage it because it's such a risky business," says stamp expert Kathleen Wunderly of the American Philatelic Society. "If you want to make money, invest in real estate."

Of course, that hasn't stopped America's four million philatelists, and similar warnings from numismatic mavens haven't slowed America's two million coin collectors, either. Both groups are drawn to the beauty and historic value of what are essentially high-grade government documents. Moreover, stamps and coins are often issued in the form of commemoratives with the sole and honest intention of enticing collectors.

No matter what your motivation is, though, bragging rights depend on knowing what's hot. To fill you in, we've put together this primer of the latest trends.

STAMPS

Celebrities stamps are doing boffo box office as philatelists snap up the $7 Schwarzenegger from Mali, the $1 Madonna from St. Vincent, and the ever-popular Elvis from St. Vincent, Tanzania, and, of course, the United States.

A new hit: Marilyn Monroe. Tanzania was first in 1991, with an oversized $7 stamp. Then came Gambia in 1993, which was soon followed by the tiny island nation of St. Vincent and, a little while later, Mali.

Cash-strapped governments like to issue commemoratives of this sort because they are rarely used for postage, which makes them a painless way of raising revenue. So far, these governments—with the help of private, multinational stamp distributors—have predicted well what philatelists will desire. All of the Marilyn stamps have been sold and are now available only through dealers and other collectors.

Not wanting to miss out on a good thing, the U.S. Postal Service in 1995 introduced its own Marilyn stamp, and expects to sell the entire 400 million run within a year.

The Postal Service generated another popular stamp somewhat less intentionally when it decided to commemorate rodeo star Bill "The Bulldogger" Pickett in 1994.

Pickett, one of America's first black rodeo stars, got his nickname in the 1930s because he could stun an enraged steer by pinching a lip nerve with a well-placed chomp. Sadly, that sort of precision was nowhere evident when the Postal Service decided to include Pickett in its "Heroes of the American West" series. Instead of portraying Pickett's famous teeth (as well as the rest of his face), the Postal Service mistakenly based its por-

FACT FILE:

SOME STAMPS COST 32¢, OTHERS...A LITTLE MORE

■ *The highest price paid at auction for a U.S. stamp collection was $8.2 million in 1993, and despite the price tag, the Japanese seller didn't come close to recovering his initial investment. The highest price paid at auction for a single stamp was $1.35 million in 1990 for a rare Swedish stamp, the first to break the $1 million mark. The Swiss industrialist who bought it had coveted the stamp ever since he saw it at an exhibition as a child.*

trait on a photo of Pickett's brother and manager Ben.

In all of its 147-year existence, the Postal Service had not once put the wrong face on a stamp. This was the sort of rarity that stamp collectors could really sink their teeth into, especially since a mortified Postal Service had stopped the presses and recalled the 5.2 million panes that already had been released. A meager 183 panes were leaked out to a lucky few collectors.

Corrected versions of the panes were released within months, but no one cared about them. The new stamps were plentiful, accurate, and easy to obtain. The remaining Ben Pickett stamps, on the other hand, were under lock and key in a warehouse in Kansas City. Collectors wanted them, the Pickett family wanted them destroyed, and the Postal Service wanted to forget about the whole thing.

Eventually, two stamp distributors filed suit against the Postal Service, saying that collectors deserved access to the stamps and that Postal Service regulations forbade it from intentionally creating rarities. The dealers lost the suit, but with the permission of Pickett's relatives, the Postal Service decided to sell 150,000 of the panes by lottery for a mere $14.50 (face value plus "postage and handling").

Stamp experts estimated at the time that a single pane would fetch over $100 in the private market because, like any good performer, Pickett had left his audience wanting more.

COINS

Numismatists trying to nickel-and-dime their way into a new collection should forget the dimes and double-check their nickels. Today's Jefferson nickel hasn't been through a design change since 1938, so it is possible to collect almost every mint since then just by checking out your pocket change.

The precursor to the Jefferson nickel was the Indian head buffalo nickel, which was minted from 1913 to 1938. "They're a beautiful coin, and they've seen some gains recently," says Kari Stone, Managing Editor of *COINage* magazine. She attributes their popularity to their relatively

FACE VALUE: WHO'S WHO ON A $100 BILL

The U.S. Treasury ceased printing bills over $100 in 1969, but many remain in circulation. $364,568,111,464 worth of paper was in circulation in August 1994 and $21,402,174,638 worth of coins. The total: $386,050,286,102.

AMOUNT	FRONT	BACK	CIRCULATION (AUGUST 1994)
$1	GEORGE WASHINGTON	U.S. Seal	$5,772,813,662
$2	THOMAS JEFFERSON	Signers of Declaration	$976,023,972
$5	ABRAHAM LINCOLN	Lincoln Memorial	$6,022,128,480
$10	ALEXANDER HAMILTON	U.S. Treasury	$13,066,968,420
$20	ANDREW JACKSON	White House	$76,376,592,100
$50	ULYSSES GRANT	U.S. Capitol	$42,022,616,050
$100	BENJAMIN FRANKLIN	Independence Hall	219,236,790,200
$500	WILLIAM MCKINLEY	Ornate Denomination	145,832,000
$1,000	GROVER CLEVELAND	Ornate Denomination	$169,062,000
$5,000	JAMES MADISON	Ornate Denomination	$1,775,000
$10,000	SALMON CHASE*	Ornate Denomination	$3,450,000

* U.S. Supreme Court Justice 1864–73.

SOURCE: U.S. Bureau of Engraving and Printing.

low prices, especially since excitement from a big investment peak year of 1989 is now past and the market is now settling into the lower end of the business cycle. Although some U.S. coins run into five and six figures, a good buffalo nickel (i.e., one in "extremely fine condition") will cost you about $100.

Lincoln cents also are popular. A 1909-S VDB—that is, a penny designed by Victor D. Brenner and minted in San Francisco in 1909—would be worth $700 today if it were in mint condition.

Commemoratives, on the other hand, are not doing so well. The U.S. Treasury stopped issuing them in the '50s because the constant creation of new commemoratives as a source of painless funds glutted the market and alienated collectors. They gave it another shot in 1982, and many commemoratives since then have been popular. But Stone warns that so many coins are now being minted that collectors will again lose interest, citing the 1994 World Cup commemorative—a coin that collectors ignored in droves.

FACT FILE:

COIN COLLECTORS, PHONE HOME

■ *Colorful, prepaid telephone cards are catching on as a subset of the field of numismatics. A trend in Europe since Italy released the first debit card in 1976, COINage magazine reports that collectors here are snapping up the cards, which are printed in about 150 countries. The U.S. alone creates 25 million cards a year, and some now are worth up to $1,000. A card depicting a Big Mac that was given free with McDonald's purchases in 1993, for instance, is now worth $125.*

EXPERT SOURCES

WHERE TO GO TO GET STARTED

Associations, catalogs and magazines for stamp and coin collectors

STAMPS

AMERICAN PHILATELIC SOCIETY
Annual membership dues, $25
■ Oldest and largest, services include insurance and certification.
☎ **814-237-3803**

THE SCOTT CATALOG
Scott Publishing Co., Annual, $34 per volume
■ Six volumes of definitive numbers and prices.
☎ **800-572-6885**

LINN'S STAMP NEWS
$1.75 per issue, $34 per year (52 issues)
■ All the stamp news that's fit to print.
☎ **800-448-7293**

COINS

AMERICAN NUMISMATIC ASSOCIATION
Annual membership dues, $32
■ Like APS, it is the oldest, the largest, and the best.
☎ **800-367-9723**

THE STANDARD CATALOG OF WORLD COINS
Krause Publications, annual, $49.95
■ Definitive prices for coins minted from 1801 to the present.
☎ **800-258-0929**

COIN WORLD
$1.95 per issue, $28 per year (52 issues)
■ Lives up to its motto: "Enriching coin collecting through knowledge."
☎ **800-253-4555**

GEMSTONES

WHAT'S IN A ROCK?

Using the "Four C's" to size up a gemstone

If you've considered following in the footsteps of Bluebeard or the Queen Mother by sinking your assets into gemstones, you probably already know that not all gems of a certain type are equal, or even particularly valuable.

Dealers may use different grading systems to determine those values, but they are all based on the four C's: the stone's carat weight, its degree of clarity, its color, and the skill with which it was cut. Richard Drucker, publisher of an international wholesale price list called *The Guide,* here explains the various factors that go into determining a gem's worth.

■ **CUT:** This is the only factor determined by the cutter and not by nature. A gemstone is like a tiny prism—the slightest change in the angle of a cut will affect how it refracts light—thus the "fire" in a ruby can only be released by a skilled cutter. A well-polished gem will be far more radiant and, therefore, far more valuable.

■ **COLOR:** Color quality is determined by the gem's actual color (hue), how rich the color is (saturation), and how light or dark it is (tone). This is "by far, the most important factor affecting price," Drucker says. "Slight differences in color may mean great differences in price." Unfortunately for the beginner, judging color is a highly subjective process, and one that requires a practiced eye to find the perfect saturation of green in an emerald.

■ **CARAT WEIGHT:** Gemstone weight traditionally was measured with carob seeds, which weigh about one-fifth of a gram. Today's standard measure, the carat, sprouted from the carob seed both etymologically and physically—one carat equals 200 milligrams, or one-fifth of a gram.

Remember that the increase in a gemstone's value is not linear. A half-carat ruby might cost $55, but a one-carat ruby of the same quality might be $150, simply because larger rubies are harder to come by or, as Drucker says, "because it has more intrinsic value to say you own one carat of something."

■ **CLARITY:** Nothing is perfect, but the closer to flawless a gemstone is, the more valuable. In this case, a flaw refers either to tiny mineral deposits, which are called inclusions, or to fractures in the stone, which are called cleavages. Some gems, like emeralds, are more likely to be fractured and are thus graded more leniently.

FACT FILE:

WHAT'S YOUR STONE?

■ *The origins of ancient birthstone designations are lost to history, but we know modern birthstones were designated not by a poet or some other qualified stone interpreter, but by a jeweler's association. They may have been concerned about the limited availability of some gems.*

	Ancient	Modern
JAN.	Garnet	Garnet
FEB.	Amethyst	Amethyst
MAR.	Jasper	Bloodstone, aquamarine
APR.	Sapphire	Diamond
MAY	Agate	Emerald
JUNE	Emerald	Pearl, Moonstone, Alexandrite
JULY	Onyx	Ruby
AUG.	Carnelian	Carnelian, Peridot
SEPT.	Chrysolite	Sapphire
OCT.	Aquamarine	Opal, Pink Tourmaline
NOV.	Topaz	Topaz, Citrine
DEC.	Ruby	Turquoise, Zircon

SOURCE: Jewelers of America.

PUTTING A LITTLE SPARKLE IN YOUR LIFE

■ **GEMSTONES.** *The value of most gemstones is pretty steady compared to commodities like coffee and gold, changing no more than 10 or 15 percent in a given year. But like any commodity, their value is tied to the vagaries of the global marketplace—a mine strike can send prices up as suddenly as a glut can send prices down. Keeping that in mind, these numbers were compiled by Richard Drucker, who publishes a guide to wholesale gem values, to give you a feel for how gems are priced across a wide spectrum of quality. They are accurate as of the quarter ending April of 1995 and have been modified to reflect retail prices.*

STONE	WEIGHT	GRADE			
		COMMERCIAL	GOOD	FINE	EXTRA FINE
RUBY	1/2 carat	$55	$550	$1,500	$3,000–$5,000
	1 carat	$150	$2,200	$6,000	$9,600–$16,000
SAPPHIRE	1/2 carat	$30	$125	$250	$600–$1,400
	1 carat	$100	$600	$1,600	$4,000–$7,200
EMERALD	1/2 Carat	$35	$350	$1,300	$2,700–$5,000
	1 carat	$80	$1,500	$3,500	$6,400–$15,000
AMETHYST	1 carat	$2	$6	$16	$36–$50
	3 carats	$6	$24	$60	$120–$210
PINK TOURMALINE	1 carat	$30	$40	$100	$200–$300
	3 carats	$120	$210	$420	$810–$1,080
GREEN TOURMALINE	1 carat	$20	$40	$80	$150–$200
	3 carats	$90	$150	$360	$600–$900
PERIDOT	1 carat	$8	$24	$50	$80–$120
	3 carats	$24	$72	$150	$240–$360
AQUAMARINE	1 carat	$20	$50	$150	$380–$600
	3 carats	$90	$300	$900	$1,650–$2,550
RHODOLITE GARNET	1 carat	$4	$20	$40	$60–$120
	3 carats	$24	$120	$180	$270–$540
TANZANITE	1 carat	$80	$120	$230	$370–$540
	3 carats	$480	$900	$1,380	$2,070–$2,700

■ **DIAMONDS.** *The Gemological Institute of America has developed a grading system for diamonds. The best diamond would be an "ideally cut DIF"*

Color is graded from D (the best) to Z. (D to M is the general range, though.)

Clarity ranges from best to worst as follows: "internally flawless" (IF), "Very, very slightly included" (VVS1), VVS2, "Very slightly included" (VS1), VS2, "Slightly included" (SI1), SI2, "Imperfect" (I), I2, and I3.

Cut can range from ideal cut to poorly cut. (Well-cut is a good standard.)

GIA Standard		COLOR / CLARITY			
		J / SI2	I / SI1	H / VS2	G / VS1
DIAMOND (well-cut)	1/2 carat	$1,500	$2,100	$2,600	$3,050
	1 carat	$5,800	$7,100	$8,100	$9,600

SOURCE: Richard Drucker, Publisher, *The Guide.*

MEMORABILIA

THE MARKET FOR PRESLEYANA

Collectors pay a king's ransom for rock 'n' roll memorabilia

Almost everything Elvis Presley ever touched has since turned to gold. At a 1994 auction, his sunglasses went for $26,450. His rhinestone jumpsuit garnered $68,500. Even his American Express Card pulled in $36,000.

The items in the auction were from the collection of Jimmy Velvet, a former lounge singer and friend of Presley's. "Finally, there's been a value established for Elvis," Velvet said after the sale, which brought in $2.5 million—considerably more than he expected.

Some experts think the success of the Elvis auction has big implications for the broader, million-dollar Hollywood and music memorabilia market, one of the few sectors that, at least so far, has defied the art market's recession.

Historically, however, the liquidation of a major collection often turns out to be the peak of the market. Indeed, it already may be too late for amateurs to dive into the pricey King's collectible market. Those who started buying Elvis items after 1977 will have a hard time selling their stuff, according to Steve Templeton, co-author of *Elvis Collectibles*. The market boomed in the '80s, Templeton says, and has now leveled off. The price of Elvis records and toys has fallen. But, Templeton adds, Elvis movie memorabilia is still hot.

Other experts recommend investing in rock bands like U2, Pearl Jam, and especially Nirvana since their lead singer, Kurt Cobain, committed suicide. As for Velvet, he is taking his auction proceeds and pouring the money into memorabilia owned by Dolly Parton, Liberace, and Madonna, all, he says, "good bets" for future price appreciation.

TOYS WORTH THEIR WEIGHT IN GOLD

TOY	PRICE	COMMENTS
Howdy Doody Puppets	$300 to $500	The tin wind-up toy featuring Buffalo Bob at the piano can bring as much as $1,000.
Beatles Ceramic Figurines	$500 to $600	Figures of the heavy metal heroes of Kiss are also popular.
Japanese Toy Cars	$300 to $600	The highly detailed tin lithograph versions from the'50s and '60s are particularly popular.
PEZ Candy Dispensers	$200 to $300	Loo k for limited editions like Santa Claus. Also big: vintage Flintstones.
Battery-operated Robby the Robot	$3,000 to $5,000	From the sci-fi classic "Forbidden Planet." Other Robby figures are collected as well.
Star Trek Memorabilia	$100 to $300	Trekkers love just about anything to do with the original cast.
1959 Barbie	$3,000 to $5,000	Costumes and accessories are also hot.
1967 GI Joe Nurse	$3,000	Other original one-foot-tall GI Joe dolls bring in about $150.

SOURCE: *Family Life* magazine.

BASEBALL CARDS

WHAT CARDS ARE COLLECTIBLE?

Our expert tells you his favorites and why cards become popular

A child collects a complete set of 1951 Topps cards and keeps them in a shoe box under the bed. Years later, mom pitches them in the trash. "$21,000 down the drain!" the collector cries.

Theo Chen says the story is mostly apocryphal. But Chen, an analyst for the authoritative price guide that makes up the bulk of *Beckett Baseball Card Monthly*, admits cards can be valuable, "otherwise, our publication wouldn't be built around a price guide."

But the value of a baseball card is as hard to predict as a player's batting average. Here are some tips from Chen on how to guess which cards will be batting .500 in the years to come.

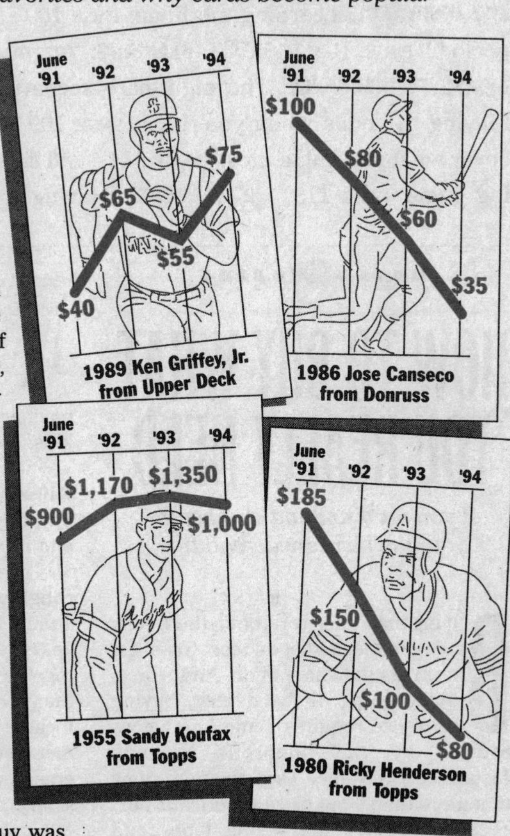

■ **Put your money on popularity.** The first thing is the player—his popularity, his accomplishments, his place in sports history. There are cases of players with better stats whose cards are much less valuable than other players. It really just comes down to popularity, whether the guy was a flashy player, whether he did a lot of endorsements that made him larger than life, whether he played during the right era. Dwight Gooden, for instance, was seen as the potential greatest pitcher of the era. Now he's gotten into off-field problems and his cards are almost unsellable.

■ **Condition is important.** Old cards in good shape are worth so much because so many people didn't take care of their cards. They kept them in shoe boxes, put them in bike spokes, flipped them, whatever. Ones that survived are tough to find.

■ **Get these cards.** Seattle Mariners outfielder Ken Griffey, Jr., and White Sox slugger Frank Thomas are the twin titans of baseball cards. They're young; they're seen as friendly, nice guys; they are dominant offensive forces in the sport; and they are creating incredible early numbers that put them well on track toward the hall of fame. Also, keep an eye on Jeff Bagwell of the Houston Astros. If he keeps up the pace he's been going, he might be seen as the National League's version of Frank Thomas.

INSURANCE

BUYER'S GUIDE

HOW TO BUY WHAT YOU REALLY NEED

If you read nothing else before you buy insurance, read this

Buying insurance is right up there with going to the dentist on most folks' list of things they hate to do. And worse, unlike going to the dentist, buying insurance requires some know-how. Studies by the nonprofit National Insurance Consumer Organization show that more than 9 out of 10 Americans purchase and carry the wrong types and amounts of insurance coverage.

The insurance industry doesn't make it any easier. Sorting through all the policies offered requires the patience of a crossword puzzle addict and the mathematical skills of an astrophysicist.

Some simple guidelines can help, though. Find a strong, healthy company that tailors policies to the coverage you need, and then focus on getting the best value for your dollar. Here's how to figure out what kind and just how much coverage you really need for the most common varieties of insurance.

LIFE INSURANCE: Your life insurance needs will vary over the course of your life, peaking as you cope with hefty mortgage payments and big tuition bills for your kids, and falling after you've retired.

■ **How much you need:** Whatever policy you buy, the most important thing is that you end up with enough coverage.

The amount of life insurance you need roughly correlates with your family's annual living expenses for the number of years you'll need the insurance. Add together all of your family's expenses for the years you'll need insurance. You should include future college costs, mortgage payments, costs to settle your estate, and an emergency fund (typically, three months salary). Then subtract all family income other than your salary. Be sure to include Social Security and pension payments as well as any income you may receive from your investments. Adjust both your future expenses and income to take account of inflation. The result of this calculation is how much life insurance you need. Some experts suggest an even simpler formula: multiply your annual take-home pay by five.

■ **What your options are:** Term insurance will pay your survivors a death benefit if you die while the contract is in force. It is often called "pure" insurance because it offers a death benefit without a savings

WHAT SOCIAL SECURITY PAYS SURVIVORS

Your survivors may be able to count on more than life insurance proceeds in the event of your death. This table shows the approximate monthly benefits they would receive if you were to die in 1995 and had steady earnings during your working life:

Age of worker	Worker's family	DECEASED WORKER'S EARNINGS IN 1995				
		$20,000	$30,000	$40,000	$50,000	$57,600[1] or more
35	Spouse and 1 child[2]	$1,152	$1,542	$1,758	$1,940	$2,088
	Spouse and 2 children[3]	$1,426	$1,800	$2,051	$2,264	$2,435
	1 child only	$576	$771	$879	$970	$1,044
	Spouse at age 60[4]	$549	$735	$838	$925	$995
45	Spouse and 1 child[2]	$1,150	$1,540	$1,750	$1,914	$2,086
	Spouse and 2 children[3]	$1,423	$1,797	$2,049	$2,235	$2,342
	1 child only	$575	$770	$875	$957	$1,003
	Spouse at age 60[4]	$548	$734	$837	$913	$957
55	Spouse and 1 child[2]	$1,150	$1,540	$1,714	$1,816	$1,876
	Spouse and 2 children[3]	$1,422	$1,797	$2,001	$2,120	$2,189
	1 child only	$575	$770	$857	$908	$938
	Spouse at age 60[4]	$548	$734	$817	$866	$894

NOTES: 1. Use this column if the worker earned more than the maximum Social Security earnings base.
2. Amount also equals benefits paid to two children if no parent survives or surviving parent has substantial earnings.
3. Equals the maximum family benefits.
4. Amounts payable in 1995. Spouses turning 60 in the future would receive higher benefits.

SOURCE: Social Security Administration.

component. A term life insurance policy can be locked in for 1 to 20 years. It is often the best—and cheapest—bet for families who want to provide for the future in the event of the loss of a breadwinner and who want to target the years when their insurance needs will be greatest.

A term insurance policy can often be rolled into a whole life policy later. "Whole life" (also called guaranteed-permanent) insurance provides a death benefit until you reach the age of 90 or 100, as long as you pay fixed premiums—premiums that cannot have unscheduled increases. Whole life insurance premiums are substantially higher at first than the same amount of term insurance, but term insurance premiums skyrocket as you get older. With whole life, you are betting that you will be around awhile, paying the higher premium at first and then averaging the cost out over a lifetime.

If you are older, the kids have graduated from college, and the mortgage is paid off, the fixed premiums of a whole life policy might be more attractive. These policies also offer an investment opportunity. Here, part of your premium payment is invested into a plan where earnings are tax deferred, so that the policy builds "cash value" over the years. At some point, the cash value of the policy should be enough to pay your premiums. "Cash-value" policies can help build wealth for you, and possibly your heirs—life insurance proceeds are not subject to income tax, or, for the most part, estate tax. However, they still need to be carefully evaluated. You should weigh each policy's returns against those you're getting from your other investments.

■ **What to watch out for:** Remember, the agent's computer models showing the projected returns are estimates, and are by no means guaranteed.

Not all policies that appear to provide fixed premiums and cash values are guaranteed-permanent insurance. Universal life, for example, is a form of cash-value insurance that combines term insurance with a "side fund" that is credited with earnings. Instead of making fixed premium payments, you have the flexibility to decide the size and frequency of your payments to the side fund, which accumulates interest on a tax-deferred basis. You get death-benefit protection as long as the side fund can cover the cost of the insurance.

If you make low payments to the side fund early on, you will have to make sharply higher payments later to maintain death-benefit protection. This flexibility means that universal life can function more like term or guaranteed-permanent insurance, depending on how you fund it.

Variable life insurance products can be even riskier. You choose among the investment options offered by the insurance company—stocks, bonds, fixed-rate funds, etc. Depending upon how the investments perform, you either build up cash value in the policy or not.

FACT FILE:

HOW LONG WE LIVE

■ *The average American born in 1990 can expect to live more than 25 years longer than his ancestor born in 1900.*

LIFE EXPECTANCY IN YEARS

Year born	Male	Female
1900	46.3	48.3
1910	48.4	51.8
1920	53.6	54.6
1930	58.1	61.6
1940	60.8	65.2
1950	65.6	71.1
1960	66.6	73.1
1970	67.1	74.7
1980	70.0	77.4
1990	71.8	78.8

SOURCE: *Life Insurance Fact Book*, American Council of Life Insurance.

DISABILITY:

Disability insurance may be the most important kind of insurance to have. Indeed, during the peak-earning years of your career, the possibility of suffering a long-term disability is considerably greater than the possibility of death. The Society of Actuaries says that a 35-year-old is three times likelier to become disabled for three months before reaching 65 than he is to die younger than 65.

■ **How much you need:** You can figure out how much disability insurance you need in the same way that you calculated your life insurance needs. Take your annual expenses and subtract your family's annual income without your salary. Buy as much disability insurance up to that level as you can. Generally, insurers will sell you only enough insurance to replace 60 percent of your income, so that, they say, you will have an incentive to return to work.

■ **What your options are:** The cost of disability income insurance depends on factors like your age, your profession, the amount of time you've worked or owned your business, whether you smoke and, more recently, whether you're a man or a woman. Since women file for disability benefits more often than men, many insurance companies have recently begun to raise women's rates, while at the same time lowering the rates for men.

■ **What to watch out for:** Look for a policy that can't be canceled and has no increase in premium until you are 65. Get a cost-of-living adjustment provision, so that your benefits increase once a year for as long as you are disabled. You should also insist on a provision allowing you to boost your coverage as your income increases.

Pay particular attention to the definition of disability. Some insurers say you qualify for benefits if you are unable to do your job, others only if you are unable to do any job. Residual or partial disability benefits can be tacked on to provide a percentage of lost income if you take a lower-paying job because of your disability. Set as long a waiting period as you can afford before the benefits kick in—delaying payments for three months to a year can substantially reduce premiums. A final tip: You can usually earn substantial premium discounts from insurers simply by doing things such as supplying a copy of your tax return at application time or pre-paying a few years' premium up front.

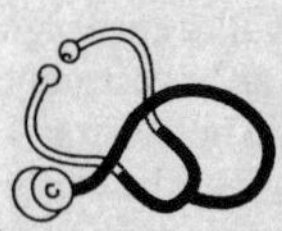

HEALTH:
You're probably covered by group health insurance by your employer, but if you're not, you can buy individual coverage that will meet your needs—at a higher cost.

■ **How much you need:** At a minimum, you should buy a catastrophic policy that protects you from serious and financially disastrous losses that can result from an illness or injury. You need to factor in how much you must absorb in deductibles and co-payments.

■ **What your options are:** Even if you buy a comprehensive policy that covers most medical, hospital, surgical, and pharmaceutical bills, it won't cover everything. You may need additional single-purpose coverage. You may want a Medicare supplement policy to fill in the gaps in your Medicare coverage if you are over 65. Private insurers offer "MedSup" specifically to cover Medicare co-payments and deductibles. Some also cover outpatient prescription drugs. Hospital indemnity insurance pays you cash benefits for each day you are hospitalized, up to a designated number of days. The money can be used to meet out-of-pocket medical co-payments or any other need. Specified disease policies—usually for cancer—are not available in every state. Even so, benefits are limited.

Depending on your age and circumstances, a long-term care policy might be a good idea. This type of policy covers the cost of custodial care either in a nursing home or in your own home. The Health Insurance Association of America estimates that nursing home care costs $30,000 to $50,000 per year or more, depending on where you live. Having someone in your home three days a week to care for you can cost almost $7,500 a year. If those kinds of expenses make you shudder, a long-term care policy can offer some relief. But remember this: If you are 65, there's slightly more than a 60 percent chance you'll never collect anything from a long-term care policy.

■ **What to watch out for:** You can reduce your premiums by opting for a large deductible—you will pay the entire amount due up to a certain limit. You may be able to save more by enrolling in a managed care plan, such as a health maintenance organization (HMO).

If you have a problem getting insurance because of a pre-existing condition, find out if your state is one of the growing number that have risk

FACT FILE:

HOW WE DIE

■ *More than half the deaths in the U.S. stem from heart disease or cancer.*

CAUSES OF DEATH IN THE U.S.

Heart disease	34.0%
Cancer	23.5%
Cerebrovascular disease	6.7%
Influenza and Pneumonia	3.7%
Diabetes	2.2%
Diseases of arteries, arteriole	2.0%
Chronic liver disease/cirrhosis	1.2%
Other diseases	19.7%
Total natural causes	**93.0%**
Motor vehicle accidents	2.2%
Suicide	1.4%
Homicide	1.2%
Other accidents	2.2%
Total external causes	**7.0%**

SOURCE: *Life Insurance Fact Book*, American Council of Life Insurance.

pools, which provide insurance for people who can't get it elsewhere.

HOMEOWNER'S:

It doesn't matter what you paid for your house. What you need to insure is the cost to rebuild it. The two figures can be wildly different.

■ **How much you need:** The conventional formula for gauging how much insurance you need on your home is to figure out how much it would actually cost to rebuild it, then tack on the extras, such as the cost of central air conditioning or a new furnace. If you can't afford insurance for 100 percent of the house's value, make sure you're covered for at least 80 percent. That way, if you suffer a partial loss—say, a fire destroys your bedroom—an insurer will likely cover the entire cost. If you're less than 80 percent insured, your insurer will only pay that percentage of partial damages.

■ **What your options are:** There are three types of homeowner's policies: cash-value, replacement cost and guaranteed replacement cost. Cash-value insurance is the least expensive. It will pay you whatever your valuables would sell for today, which is unlikely to buy you a similar new item. Replacement cost insurance will replace the item that was lost or damaged with something new, but not necessarily the same as the one you lost, because this type of insurance usually comes with a price cap. You'll be able to replace, say, your furnace, but not necessarily with the best model. Guaranteed replacement cost insurance has no cap and offers the best coverage. The only thing it generally will not cover is the cost of upgrading your house to meet building codes that may have changed since the policy was issued.

Homeowner's insurance also includes liability coverage. Most policies come with up to $300,000 worth of coverage. Unless your total assets are less than that, you should probably pay a little more and get more coverage. For example, experts counsel that if you have $200,000 to $500,000 in assets, you need about $1 million in liability coverage. The best way to do this is to buy an "umbrella policy" that covers both your home and car. Liability coverage comes fairly cheap. It's unlikely that a claim against you will exceed $300,000, so underwriters can afford to give you a price break. A $300,000 to $1 million umbrella liability policy will cost anywhere from $80 to $300 annually, the average being about $150. For another $1 million in coverage, double the price.

■ **What to watch out for:** Cash-value coverage may be a little risky, since an investment you made years ago that is still holding up—such as a good furnace—may now be worth just a fraction of its cost. Replacement-cost coverage, which usually costs 10 percent to 20 percent more, is preferable—and worth it. You should be sure to find out if there are any caps on what will be reimbursed for individual items, such as jewelry. For example, the amount you can recover if all of your jewelry is stolen may be, say, $1,000, if that is the amount of the cap for jewelry. If you have valuables that are worth more, you may want to buy more insurance by adding riders to your policy. This generally costs about $1.50 per $100 of insurance.

AUTO:

In most states, drivers are required to have liability insurance for each driver, for accidents, and for the other person's car in case of an accident.

■ **How much you need:** Generally, insurance experts counsel that you buy as much liability coverage as you're worth. You should also consider an "umbrella policy," described above, that covers both your home and car.

■ **What your options are:** Collision and comprehensive coverage accounts for 30 percent to 45 percent of your premium. If the cost of your collision and comprehensive insurance is more than 10 percent of your car's Blue Book value, it probably makes sense to drop it. Remember, though, that if you get into an accident, you'll have to decide if it's worth getting your car fixed.

EXPERT LIST

INSURANCE COVERAGE NOT TO BUY

The Consumer Federation of America's Insurance Group is a nonprofit, public interest organization that promotes the interests of insurance buyers. Here are some of its recommendations of insurance coverage not worth buying.

- **Air travel insurance:** It costs too much and pays back only about 10 cents for each dollar of premiums. It is not comprehensive. You're more likely to die from a heart attack.

- **Life insurance if you're single:** If you have no dependents, there is no economic reason to buy life insurance since there is no economic catastrophe associated with your death.

- **Life insurance if you're married with children and your spouse has a good job:** If one of you dies, can the other get along on one income? If so, perhaps no life insurance is necessary beyond that which you have at work.

- **Mortgage insurance:** You should use annual renewable term insurance to protect you and your family against all economic consequences of your death.

- **Insurance that pays only if you're hurt or killed in a mugging:** A classic example of "junk" insurance. This risk is covered by good life and health policies.

- **Contact lens insurance:** The cost of a premium is about equal to the cost of a lens at a discount eyeglass store.

- **Cancer insurance:** What good is a cancer insurance policy if you have a heart attack? To buy only specific illness coverage is like buying toothpaste one squeeze at a time.

- **Rental car insurance:** Your own auto insurance policy probably covers you if you do damage to a rental car. Also, many credit cards cover this.

- **Life or health insurance sold to cover a car loan or other loan.**

- **Rain insurance:** It pays if it rains a lot on your vacations.

- **Health insurance that pays $100 a day while you are in the hospital in lieu of comprehensive coverage.**

- **Health insurance on your pet.**

SOURCE: Consumer Federation of America's.

Uninsured or underinsured motorist coverage also is sometimes desirable, but it is probably cheaper to purchase it in your home or life policy. You may be able to slash the price of your car insurance by adding safety or anti-theft features to your car, maintaining a safe driving record or simply by driving a low number of miles each year.

What to watch out for: For an old jalopy, the insurance cost may not be worth the amount you'd receive in the event of an accident. The most you'll receive if your car is damaged is the Blue Book value of the vehicle—not that much if your car is more than five years old.

A last tip: Medical payment, income replacement, and rental car insurance can add substantially to your premiums and may be covered elsewhere. Some credit card companies, for example, offer rental car insurance.

LEARNING THE LINGO OF LIFE

The terms you need to know before you sign up

There's no shortage of books and other references to consult if you want to learn more about life insurance. But you won't get very far unless you know some of the terms of the trade. This glossary is adapted from *A Consumer's Guide to Life Insurance*, published by the American Council of Life Insurance, an industry group. We also consulted other insurance primers and publications put out by various insurance and business groups.

Accelerated death benefits—The benefits available in some life insurance policies before policyholder's death.

Accidental death benefit—A provision added to a life insurance policy for payment of an additional benefit in case of death as a result of an accident. This provision is often called "double indemnity."

EXPERT QUOTE

There are two basic types of life insurance policies: term insurance and whole life insurance. All other types of policies are variations of these two types.

—The American Council of Life Insurance, Washington, D.C.

Annuity—A life insurance product that provides an income either for a specified period of time or for a person's lifetime.

Beneficiary—The person or financial instrument (a trust fund, for example) named in the policy as a recipient of insurance money in the event of the policyholder's death.

Cash value (cash surrender value)—The amount available in cash upon surrender of a policy before it becomes payable upon death or maturity.

Cash-value insurance—"Cash-value" insurance is any life insurance product that offers some opportunity to accumulate cash value, in addition to ensuring a death benefit.

Convertible term insurance—Term insurance that offers the policyholder the option of exchanging it for a permanent plan of insurance without evidence of insurability.

Cost index—A way to compare the costs of similar life insurance plans. A policy with a smaller index number is generally a better buy than a comparable policy with a larger index number.

Dividend—Dividends are a partial or full refund of premiums paid to owners of certain kinds of participating life insurance contracts.

Face amount—The amount stated on the face of the policy that will be paid in case of death or at maturity. It does not include dividend additions or additional amounts payable under accidental death or other special provisions.

Group-term insurance—Group-term insurance typically is provided by or through your employer. It has several potential advantages. It can be inexpensive if your employer pays the premiums or subsidizes it. And the only thing you have to do to join is sign the application—you do not have to pass a medical exam. The downside: If you lose your job, you generally lose your insurance.

TAKING OUT A LIFETIME CONTRACT

	Yearly renewable term	Re-entry term	Group-term	Universal life	Term/ guaranteed permanent	Guaranteed permanent
Are premiums guaranteed not to increase?	No, they will increase*	No, they will increase*	No, they will increase but employer may pay cost	There is no fixed premium	Yes, for guaranteed-permanent, but not for term	Yes
Can I continue the coverage if I get sick?	Yes, for the period of renewability	Yes, prior to re-entry; thereafter at a high cost	Yes, while you remain employed; thereafter at a high cost	Yes	Yes	Yes
Is there an asset accumulation element?	No	No	No	Yes	Yes	Yes
Does the insurance company guarantee my coverage will last?	No, generally not available after age 70 and usually too costly after age 60	No, generally not available after age 70 and usually too costly after age 60	Yes, but employer may provide reductions beyond a certain age	As long as the "side fund" is not exhausted	Yes, for the guaranteed-permanent portion, but no for the term	Yes

* Certain level term contracts have premiums that are fixed for a given period, such as 10 years.

Guaranteed insurability—An option that permits the policyholder to buy additional stated amounts of life insurance at stated times in the future without evidence of insurability.

Guaranteed-permanent life insurance—Sometimes called "whole-life," guaranteed-permanent insurance provides a death benefit until the age of 90 to 100 as long as you pay fixed premiums that cannot have unscheduled increases. Guaranteed-permanent products can build substantial cash values over time.

Joint life insurance—Joint life insurance—also called survivorship life or "second-to-die" insurance—covers two lives (typically a husband and wife) and pays a benefit only after the second death.

Level premium insurance—Insurance for which the cost is distributed evenly over the premium payment period. The premium remains the same from year to year and is more than the actual cost of protection in the earlier years of the policy and less than the actual cost in later years.

Load—The amount of your premium that is taken out to cover administrative costs, commission and premium taxes in a lump sum. The load generally is taken at the beginning of a policy, but sometimes in the middle or even at the ending of the policy. Depending on the company, the load is either a percentage of the worth of the policy or a percentage of the cost.

Paid-up additions—Paid-up additions are increments of guaranteed-permanent insurance on which all premiums are paid in one lump sum.

Policy riders—Riders are optional features you may add to your policy, for an increase in premium.

Re-entry term insurance—"Re-entry" term insurance products appear to be guaranteed renewable, but require steep premium increases at specified intervals, such as every five years, unless you pass a medical examination.

Renewable term insurance—Term insurance providing the right to renew at the end of the term for another term or terms, without evidence of insurability. The premium rates increase at each renewal as the age of the insured increases.

Term insurance—Term insurance pays your survivors a death benefit if you die while the contract is in force. It is often called "pure" insurance because it offers only a death benefit with no savings component.

Universal life insurance—Universal life is a form of cash-value insurance that combines term insurance with a "side fund" that is credited with earnings.

Variable life insurance—"Variable life" encompasses a variety of cash-value products that allow you to decide how to invest your policy's cash values. You can choose among options offered by the insurance company—typically stocks, bonds, fixed-rate funds, or money market funds—and participate directly in the investment results.

Waiver-of-premium benefit—A waiver-of-premium rider keeps your life insurance protection in place by paying the policy premiums if you became disabled.

EXPERT QUOTE

"If you forget everything else about buying life insurance, remember to ask how much you'd get if you cashed in your policy after one year—the so-called cash surrender value."

—Glenn Daily, insurance expert

WHAT'S YOUR AGENT'S CUT?

The answer can be the difference between a good policy and a rip-off

If you want to rein in your insurance costs, start by finding out how much of your premium goes directly into your insurance agent's pocket. It is not unusual for the commission to be as much as 100 percent of the first year's premium on a universal or whole life cash-value life insurance policy.

Consider, for example, a typical $350,000 whole life policy on a 38-year-old male, paying a $4,600 premium annually. If he paid full commission to purchase the policy, the cash surrender value—the amount available in cash—after a year would be zero. That means if he, for whatever reason, decided to abandon the policy after a year, he would not get any of his money back.

However, if he bought the same policy without paying any commission, the policy would have a cash surrender value of $3,800. By the fifth year, the policy bought on full commission could be cashed in for $14,700. The policy bought without any commission would pay $20,500.

After 10 years, if the projections on both policies pan out, things become a little confusing: the policy on which full commission was paid would pay $46,700; but the policy bought without paying commission would pay just $44,500. That's because the projections assume that the cash invested in the policies will earn interest at a certain rate, and full commission products often offer higher interest rates that may eventually compensate for their higher costs. But that is only after about 10 years, and those projections cannot be guaranteed. The National Association of Insurance Commissioners is considering banning long-term projections because they can be misleading.

The lower the agent's commission you can negotiate, the greater the savings that will be building up value in your insurance policy. The National Insurance Consumer Organization recommends that consumers buy only cash-value policies with first-year surrender values of no less than 50 percent of the annual premium. In other words, you should be able to get out of a policy after a year and still be able to recoup at least half of what you put into it.

Although your agent is not required by law to tell you how much he'll earn on your business, he might at least be persuaded to tell you about other insurance packages the company has to offer—the same policy, but with lower commission rates. You can also cut out the agent altogether and buy no-commission—often called low-load—cash-value insurance directly from Ameritas or USAA Life, or through a fee-based financial planner.

Another alternative: term insurance. The policy itself does not build up any cash-value, and it pays a benefit only when you die, but agents' commissions on term insurance are usually lower than on other insurance products.

EXPERT TIPS

DO I HAVE A DEAL FOR YOU!

In Hollywood, everyone from the parking attendant to the prima donna has an agent. But buying insurance isn't like inking a pact with a movie mogul. You might do better without an agent. The Buyer's Guide to Insurance *from Consumer Federation of America's Insurance Group offers some guidance:*

■ **The best way to use an agent:** Agents almost always sell insurance on a commission basis. The more money you pay them, the more money they make. Agents representing only one company usually receive a lower commission, so that their prices can be lower than "independent agents who sell for several companies. Companies that don't use agents usually have the lowest rates. Furthermore, consumer satisfaction tends to be higher for the lowest-priced companies. The best way to use an agent is to get a good low price from a company that doesn't use agents and then ask the agent if he or she can beat that deal. According to CFA, USAA (which only sells insurance to active or retired armed forces commissioned officers) and Ameritas are "the best companies" that don't use agents.

■ **When more means less:** Premiums tend to be proportional to policy limits; a $120,000 homeowner's policy costs about 20 percent more than a $100,000 policy, even though the extra risk for insurance companies (because most claims are for partial losses) is far less than 20 percent more. So don't automatically go along with agent or company suggestions of higher limits. Beware of inflation-guard automatic increases in coverage or premiums. The percentage insurers select may be too high (or, sometimes, too low) for your house. Check it out against recent sales in your neighborhood.

■ **Why not to drop an old policy:** Don't let an agent talk you into dropping an old life insurance policy, if it pays dividends. Replacement of such policies has reached scandalous proportions in recent years as agents churn such policies for commissions.

LIFE INSURANCE

PLAYING THE RATING GAME

How you can tell which insurance companies have staying power

The financial strength of your insurance company is all the assurance you have that the firm will be around when it's time for you to collect on a policy. But how can you tell if any one company is financially strong or weak?

Fortunately, you don't need to spend hours poring over financial statements. Several independent organizations specialize in issuing "ratings" of life insurance companies. The five best-known rating agencies are A. M. Best in Oldwick, N.J., ☎ 908-439-2200; Standard & Poor's, ☎ 212-208-1527, and Moody's Investor Service, ☎ 212-553-0300, in New York City; Duff & Phelps in Chicago, ☎ 312-368-3157; and Weiss Research in West Palm Beach, Fla., ☎ 800-289-9222.

Best's, for example, analyzes a company's financial strength and overall operations considering factors such as control of expenses, investment performance, claims experience, and management philosophy. Moody's and Standard & Poor's focus primarily on the company's financial strength and claims-paying ability. All publish a great deal of data, some of which can be difficult to interpret. They also issue a simpler overall rating for each company.

According to a study by *Consumer Reports,* A. M. Best is the easiest grader. Weiss Research is considered by most experts to be the stingiest with A grades, particularly for the biggest companies. A 1994 report by the U.S. General Accounting Office concluded that Weiss had the best record of identifying weak insurance companies from mid-1989 through mid-1992. The report chiefly compared Weiss with A. M. Best and largely ignored the other three rating agencies because they covered fewer insurers. (The GAO report itself came under fire from actuaries, academics, and others outside the industry who considered its methodology flawed.)

It's often difficult to compare the results of different companys' ratings. The A category alone may include several gradations. Here's the top grade for each: Best, A++; D&P, AAA; Moody's Aaa; S&P, AAA; and Weiss, A+.

What's a smart consumer to do? One clue that trouble's brewing is a drop of two or more ratings over a short period of time. And some experts recommend choosing an insurer that gets A or top B grades from four of the five raters. That's pretty good insurance that your insurer will be around when needed.

EXPERT PICKS

TOP-RATED INSURANCE COMPANIES

Peter C. Katt, a fee-only life insurance adviser in West Bloomfield, Mich., writes frequently in the American Association of Individual Investors Journal. Here are his top four picks:

- **GUARDIAN:** Targets small-business owners.
- **NORTHWESTERN MUTUAL:** They provide exceptional and fair service to policyholders through their own salespersons.
- **MASS MUTUAL:** One-stop shopping for diversified financial services.
- **STATE FARM:** Agents cater to homeowner and auto insurance needs in their own communities.

LIFE INSURANCE

THE RIGHT TERM POLICY FOR YOU

You can renew every year or you can lock in for two decades

When in doubt about which life insurance policy is best for you, opt for a no-frills term life policy that covers you for the life of the policy and pays only upon death. It gives you the most coverage at the cheapest price for short-term needs, and can protect you anywhere from 1 to 20 years. You can take out a term policy to span the years when you're worried about your home mortgage, college costs, car payments, or other pressing monthly commitments. When that's behind you, you can downsize to a policy with lower premiums and benefits to complement Social Security and pension payments.

WHAT YOUR OPTIONS ARE

If you're not sure what your insurance needs will be a few years from now, annual renewable term lets you reconsider your coverage each year. Term policies are renewable each year, or can be locked in for 5, 10, or even 20 years. The catch is, your premium rate will rise each year as you get older. The initial rate may be low, but it can more than double by the tenth year.

You also can opt for a product called guaranteed level-premium term, which locks in a flat premium for up to 20 years. The benefit of a long-term policy commitment is that your premiums stay flat for at least five years and you don't face a medical exam until the term of the entire policy expires.

There are other term options, as well. Term insurance offers protection up until you're 65. At the end of the term, the coverage stops, but it can be picked up for another term if you have a "renewable" policy. Renewable policies are easy to extend, but your premiums will be higher because you are older. Or you might choose "convertible" term life, which allows you to trade in your old term policy for a whole life policy—which includes a savings component and a death benefit—without a medical examination. Whole life policies command higher premiums, but those premiums won't ever change.

WHAT THE EXPERTS SAY

In the short run, annual renewable term is cheaper, but level-premium term usually wins out over five years or longer. A 40-year-old man who needs $200,000 of coverage, for example, can purchase an annual renewable term policy from USAA Life with a first-year premium of only $282 per year. By year 15, the annual premium would reach $860. The projected cost over 15 years: $8,102. (Of course, the actual cost might be higher, since rates could rise.) A 15-year term policy from First Colony Life Insurance Co., a major seller of level-premium term, has a guaranteed premium of $368 annually for a total of $5,520 over 15 years. That's a savings of $2,582.

A warning: New insurance regulations are in the works that, if enacted, might cause insurers to guarantee rates only for the first five years.

■ UNBEATABLE RATES

These rates may not be the lowest you can get for a term life policy, but they represent a good value. The rates are first-year premiums for a $100,000 annual renewable term insurance policy from USAA Life, ☎ 800-531-8000, which sells life insurance products by phone. A preferred risk usually is a healthy nonsmoker.

Age	PREFERRED		STANDARD	
	Female	Male	Female	Male
25	$119	$128	$150	$153
35	$130	$132	$178	$191
45	$206	$221	$303	$381
55	$401	$474	$704	$889

SOURCE: USAA Life Insurance, 1995.

LOW-LOAD POLICIES

TWO FOR THE PRICE OF ONE

Your agent may not tell you about this life insurance option

Ever heard of a low-load policy? Probably not from your agent. Here's what *Consumer Reports* said about it in a 1993 report: "Low-load policies may not be in the best interest of agents, but they are in the best interest of consumers." That's because these policies aren't sold by agents. Instead they are sold by phone and through fee-based financial planners. They charge an overall fee but receive no commission on the products they recommend.

Low-load policies are a variety of the "universal-life" policy, which is really two products in one: simple term insurance, which pays off if the policyholder dies, and an investment account that earns interest and can be used to pay for the term-insurance. *Consumer Reports* says a 45-year-old man who needs $250,000 in coverage will pay about $3,700 a year for a good universal-life policy.

Your insurance agent typically earns 50 percent of your first-year premium, but low-load policies cut out the middleman. They also keep other costs lower and impose no, or very low, surrender charges on policyholders who eventually drop their coverage. That makes them a particularly good deal in the early years and, *Consumer Reports* says, a good deal in later years, too.

Ameritas, John Alden, USAA Life, Southland, and Peoples Security/Commonwealth offer low-load policies. USAA sells directly, ☎ 800-531-8000, as does Ameritas, ☎ 800-552-3553. Fee For Service, represents nine companies and gives free quotes over the phone, ☎ 800-874-5662. For a $250 fee, they will take applications for policies and arrange for necessary medical exams. Planners typically charge $100 to $150 an hour for their services.

EXPERT TIPS

SHOPPING ADVICE FROM A PRO

Insurance consultant Glenn S. Daily's tips for shopping for life insurance

- **Find out the financial strength of the insurance company you're considering.** Although rating scales differ, you are probably safe if you stay above an AA on all five rating companies' charts.

- **Use policy illustrations only to screen out inferior products.** They aren't reliable in comparing policies because they don't show premiums, interest rates, or guarantees.

- **Focus on the costs.** You can't predict earnings, but you can better the odds for a good return by avoiding companies with a lot of overhead expenses, such as high commissions, broad expense account allowances, and large administrative costs.

- **Don't equate premiums with price.** Low premiums can hide high commissions spread over years.

- **Don't switch policies unless your current policy is not performing well.** Though something newer may look better, you will pay a second commission while your existing policy was probably earning a return.

ESTATE PLANNING

ATTENTION, HEIRS APPARENT

Ways to escape estate taxes and die happily ever after

There's no getting around death and taxes. Even after death, there can be taxes—and lots of them. Sure, if all of your assets go to your spouse, there won't be any estate taxes. And you get a break on the first $600,000 of your estate, which is tax-free. But after that, estate tax rates start at 37 percent and rise to 55 percent. For estates of $10 million to $21 million, there's an extra 5 percent surcharge, which brings the top rate to 60 percent. What's a rich guy to do?

Well, buy life insurance for one. Financial planners generally urge couples with estates of $2 million or more to look into using life insurance to pay estate taxes. When you die, your life insurance proceeds are not subject to income tax. If the policy is owned by someone else, such as a child or an irrevocable trust, it will not be part of your estate and will not be subject to estate taxes either.

Your first estate-planning step is to calculate the approximate value of your estate, including all the property you own and life insurance in your name. You then could buy a life insurance policy to cover the federal estate tax owed—or as much as you chose to cover with insurance. And remember, there may also be state taxes due on your estate.

Whether using life insurance to cover your estate taxes is a smart move or not depends chiefly on what kind of policy you buy and, of course, when you die. A 65-year-old man and 62-year-old woman, for example, could buy a $1 million policy for a premium of $24,420 for nine years and a final premium of $12,643, or a total of $232,423. The policy is a second-to-die, or survivorship, policy, which means that it does not pay off until the second person dies. This makes premiums significantly lower than they would be on a policy covering only one individual since, from the insurer's perspective, it is more likely that at least one of the two people covered will live a while and the death benefit won't have to be paid. If both die during the first year after they bought the policy, their heirs would get a fantastic return of 3,995 percent. If, however, either one lives for 20 years, the return is reduced to 10.36 percent. If either one lives 30 years, the return is 7.72 percent.

There's another catch: taxable gifts. You can give gifts of up to $10,000 per person per year without affecting the status of your estate, but if you give a single person more than $10,000 in a year, the difference will reduce the taxable threshold of your estate. If you give one of your children a gift of $50,000 in a given year, for instance, the taxable threshold of your estate will be $560,000.

THE ESTATE TAX BITE

Your heirs only pay the top rate on the top end of your estate.*

If estate is above this base	Your tax is this...	Plus this % over base
$600,000	$0	37%
$750,000	$55,500	39%
$1,000,000	$153,000	41%
$1,250,000	$255,500	43%
$1,500,000	$363,000	45%
$2,000,000	$588,000	49%
$2,500,000	$833,000	53%
$3,000,000	$1,098,000	55%
$10,000,000	$4,948,000	60%
$21,040,000	$11,572,000	55%

* Table does not account for taxable gifts.
SOURCE: Internal Revenue Service.

DISABILITY INSURANCE

THE NIGHTMARE SCENARIO

Rates are zooming, but you can't afford not to have a policy

Here's a frightening fact: Insurance companies report that if a disability keeps you out of work more than 90 days, you're not likely to work again for about three years.

The usual source of long-term disability coverage is your employer. But if you ever need it, this coverage will probably not be sufficient. For starters, only 60 percent of your present earnings are covered. Disability insurance payments paid under your employer's policy are taxable. Pension and retirement funds, bonuses, overtime, or special pay may not be covered by your group disability plan.

An individual disability insurance policy is a good idea but it will cost you—especially now. Disability insurers chalked up huge losses in 1992 and 1993 in part because their policies didn't charge enough to cover the benefits offered. As a result, some big insurers are scaling back policies and raising prices. Disablitiy policies used to be noncancelable—meaning if you pay your premiums, the insurer must continue covering you without lowering benefits or raising premiums. No longer. It will also be tougher to find a policy with an "own occupation" rider, which provides benefits if you can't work in your chosen occupation. In early '95, Provident Life & Accident, the nation's second largest individual disability insurer, stopped offering noncancelable, own-occupation policies in all but 13 states. Other insurers are doing the same, or charging up to 20 percent more.

Women are likely to pay more than men. Insurance companies have recently discovered that women are more likely than men to claim disability benefits. Therefore, women are higher risks and premiums are accordingly steeper. Your premiums will also depend on your profession. Ministers and editors are higher risks than lawyers, architects, coporate executives, and accountants.

Disability policies consider all forms of income in figuring how much of a benefit you'll receive in case of a mishap. The policies are portable, so you'll still be insured should you change jobs. Premiums don't increase. You can find policies that you can carry for the rest of your life.

If you're self-employed or a so-called fee-for-service provider—insurance jargon for a doctor, lawyer, etc.—you should look for a policy with recovery benefits. Recovery benefits will supplement your income while you build up your client base after a long absence. Recovery benefits kick in when you're back working full-time.

You'll also need residual benefits to cover you while you're working part-time. Doctors, lawyers, and other self-employed individuals, especially, will also want their policy to include "own-occupation benefits."

THE HIGH COST OF DISABILITY INSURANCE

The annual cost of a non-cancelable individual disability income policy for a 40-year-old nonsmoker earning $60,000 to replace 60 percent of lost income to age 65:

TOP-OF-THE-LINE PROFESSIONAL COVERAGE (includes own-occupation and residual benefits)

	FEMALE	MALE	MULTI-LIFE[1]
Architect, attorney, CPA, corp. exec.[2]	$1,882	$1,376	$1,021
Actuary, pharmacist, optometrist	$2,042	$1,492	$1,218

NOTES: 1. Multi-life policies are individual plans purchased by groups in a corporate or association setting.
2. Corporate executives receiving this rate must be in firm of 25 or more and have office or consulting duties only.
SOURCE: Paul Revere Life Insurance Company, Worcester, Mass.

LONG-TERM CARE

PLAYING THE ODDS WHEN YOU'RE 65

Premiums are expensive, and benefits could be a long way away

If you're 65, there's slightly more than a 60 percent chance you'll never collect anything from a long-term care policy. There's a 75 percent chance that you'll need care for less than a year, and chances are, you will have the resources to pay for it. On the other hand, there's a 1-in-10 chance that you or your spouse will need nursing care for five years or more. That bill could wipe you out.

Even so, long-term care coverage is expensive, and policies are often full of loopholes that allow insurers to avoid paying claims. No wonder few people over 65 have ponied up. Long-term care insurance isn't for everybody. In fact, it isn't for most people. This kind of insurance only makes sense for people who have assets to protect, specifically those whose net worth, excluding their house, is roughly between $100,000 and $1 million. With less, you're denying yourself Medicaid assistance that you would be entitled to if you had no insurance. If your assets are above that range, you'd probably be better off saving the money you would pay in premiums and being prepared to pay for any care out of your savings.

The best time to buy a long-term care policy is probably when you're in your 60s, before premiums skyrocket. But you've got to be prepared for the long haul. The average age for nursing home admittance is 81 for men and 84 for women. Former United Seniors Heath Cooperative director Susan Polniaszek here cites factors to consider when buying a policy.

■ **WHAT'S COVERED:** Some companies will only dole out money for medical problems. Polniaszek recommends a company that provides more than medical attention, such as assistance with bathing, dressing, eating, moving, going to the

■ **AVERAGE AGE OF ADMISSION TO A NURSING HOME**

Men	81 years old
Women	84 years old

■ **WHO WILL CARE FOR YOU IF AGE DISABLES YOU?**

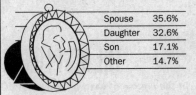

Spouse	35.6%
Daughter	32.6%
Son	17.1%
Other	14.7%

■ **WHAT ARE YOUR CHANCES OF A NURSING HOME STAY?**

LENGTH OF STAY	MEN	WOMEN
At least one day	33%	52%
3 months or more	22%	41%
1 year or more	14%	31%
More than 5 years	4%	13%

■ **WHO PAYS FOR NURSING HOME CARE?**

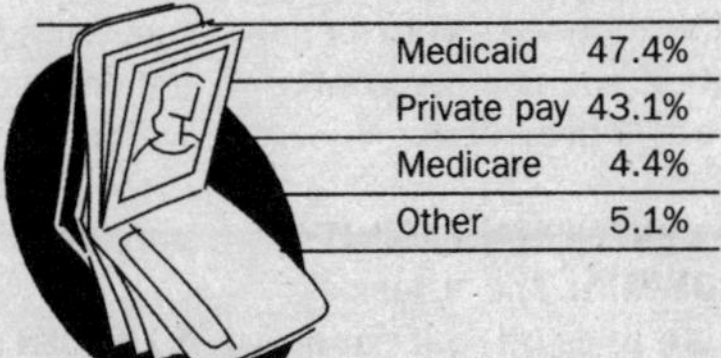

Medicaid	47.4%
Private pay	43.1%
Medicare	4.4%
Other	5.1%

SOURCE: *Long-Term Care: A Dollar and Sense Guide*, Susan Polniaszek, United Seniors Health Cooperative, 1993.

bathroom, or in the case of Alzheimer's, constant supervision.

■ **HOME CARE:** Many people would prefer to avoid nursing homes. Insurance companies have begun offering limited care outside of institutions. However, most policies only pay a flat dollar amount per day, which may only cover a few hours of care.

■ **BENEFIT AMOUNT:** Check out the costs of nursing homes in your area to determine the appropriate daily benefits. For example, if they charge $125 a day, you might want to insure yourself for $110 a day and cover the remainder from your own income.

■ **BENEFIT PERIOD:** The majority of nursing home stays are less than three or four years, so you may want to pare your premium by choosing a shorter time period.

■ **ELIMINATION PERIOD:** This is your deductible, measured in the number of days of care you pay for before the insurance company kicks in its share. Polniaszek recommends 20 to 100 days.

■ **INFLATION PROTECTION:** For buyers under age 70, experts recommend purchasing a policy that increases your benefit amount by 5 percent each year. Otherwise your fixed daily benefit could shrink in proportion to the real cost of care over the years.

EXPERT PICKS

THE BEST LONG-TERM CARE POLICIES

In the course of writing Long-Term Care: A Dollar and Sense Guide, *Susan Polniaszek examined nearly 1,000 policies. Here are her favorites:*

■ **AMEX:** The former Fireman's Fund offers a traditional policy focusing on nursing home care with an option for home health care. It also offers an "integrated" policy, which means you can buy four years of care and apply it to either nursing home or home health care, with a managed care option that increases your benefits if you use the company's providers.

■ **CONTINENTAL CASUALTY COMPANY:** The "Classic" plan lives up to its name as a traditional nursing home plan. A second, "Premium" plan allows you to buy a "pool of days" instead of the usual "pool of money." Your benefits are limited by the number of days you need care instead of the care's cost.

■ **JOHN HANCOCK:** A higher standard of admittance than most. You need to have help with two of the five activities of daily living before receiving benefits. A policy debuting in late 1995 will allow spouses to draw on each other's pool of funds.

■ **LINCOLN NATIONAL:** This life insurance company offers a traditional policy as well as a policy that allows you to combine your life insurance and long-term care policies. It is expensive, but guarantees you or your family will see some return on your investment.

■ **THE TRAVELERS INSURANCE COMPANY:** Their "pool of funds" policy mostly follows the traditional model.

■ **UNUM:** This life insurance company markets an expensive benefit that allows your family members to be paid for home health care. Most plans require a licensed professional to receive the benefits, but UNUM allows spouses or children to be compensated.

HOME INSURANCE

HOME SWEET HOME INSURANCE

You may be able to cut your premiums as much as 50 percent

Experts estimate that over a third of the some 59 million people who pay homeowner premiums could cut their home insurance bills significantly—in many cases by 50 percent or more. Yet many are unaware that they qualify for various discounts. Slimming down your bill needn't be time-consuming. Nor does it require much expertise about the fine print in insurance policies. In fact, your research may amount to no more than a few well-placed telephone calls.

Insurance companies sell in different ways. Big companies, such as State Farm and Allstate, employ their own sales force to sell their policies. "Agency writers," such as Aetna, ITT Hartford, and Chubb, are represented by independent agents. The so-called "direct writers," such as American Express, Amica, and USAA, sell over the phone. As you might guess, they have the lowest selling costs and the best deals—if you qualify.

Not everyone does. USAA, ☎ 800-531-8100, limits its pool of potential customers to people who have served in or have some connection to the armed forces. And Amica, ☎ 800-242-6422, gets most of its new business from referrals from existing customers. American Express, ☎ 800-535-2001, taps its cardholders—first for auto-insurance customers, then for homeowners insurance. Generally, it looks for cardholders in areas with a history of low loss ratios, such as Arizona, Connecticut, and Illinois.

Allstate and State Farm can almost compete on price with the direct writers because they keep sales commissions low, usually no more than 8 percent. An agency writer, like Aetna, is more likely to pay 13 percent or even 20 percent. What keeps the agency writers in business is that the other insurers either won't cover some applicants, or will do so only at much higher rates. Also, a good insurance agent

DISCOUNTS FOR HOME INSURANCE

A new home security system combined with a $1,000 deductible can cut your premium in half.

TYPE OF DISCOUNT[1]	STATE FARM	ALLSTATE	AMEX	AMICA	AETNA	USAA[3]
New Home	20%	25%	15%	20%	20%	20%
Less than 7 years old	3%	6%	2%	10%	12%	8%–18%
Less than 10 years old	NONE	NONE	NONE	4%	9%	2%–6%
Less than 12 years old	NONE	NONE	NONE	NONE	3%	NONE
Central alarm	15%	10%	15%	5%	20%	15%
Fire/smoke alarm	4%	3%	15%	2%	7%	2%
Sprinklers	10%	10%	NONE	13%	7%	8%
Slow-burning materials	NONE	NONE	NONE	NONE	NONE	NONE
Home/auto combination	NONE	5%	15%	NONE	5%	NONE
Renovations	NONE	25%	15%	NONE	NONE	NONE
Retirees	NONE	10%	NONE	NONE	NONE	NONE
Customer for 3+ years	5%	NONE	NONE	NONE	5%	NONE
Customer for 6+ years	10%	NONE	NONE	NONE	NONE	NONE
$1,000 deductible[2]	24%–33%	21%	25%	19%	22%	30%–32%

NOTES: 1. Type and amount of discount may vary from state to state. 2. Standard deductible ranges from $100 to $250. 3. Eligibility restricted to present and former U.S. military officers and their families. SOURCE: Company reports, April 1995.

can be a useful source of advice and counsel, a service many are willing to pay for.

No matter what firm you buy your insurance from, you can shave your annual premium by taking advantage of the discounts insurers offer. Your existing policy should list the discounts you already have, but that doesn't mean they are the only ones for which you are eligible. For instance, you should inform your insurance company if you install or upgrade a home security system or if you have a live-in housekeeper, all of which may reduce your premium because they reduce the chance of a break-in. You also may qualify for a discount simply because you live in an area in which the company is trying to increase its market share. If you combine your homeowner's policy with your auto policy, you may get another break. And raising your deductible is always a sure way to lower your premium.

All discounts are not available from all insurance carriers in every state. And discounts vary from one company to another. Some are far more generous than others. But finding out exactly what you qualify for is easy enough. All you have to do is ask.

PICKING UP AN EXTRA RIDER

Standard policies often don't cover the things you value the most

A rider is an extra piece of insurance that covers special property in special circumstances. For example, if you read the fine print of your policy, you may discover that jewelry is covered up to a specified amount against certain named "perils." But what if your necklace is stolen and "theft" isn't one of the named perils? You're out of luck—unless you have a rider. Some circumstances in which you might consider adding a rider to your policy:

■ **You own jewelry:** Many basic insurance policies exclude theft from named perils when it comes to jewelry and limit coverage to a maximum payout of $1,500. A jewelry rider—also known as a "personal articles policy" generally costs about $1.20 per $100 of coverage. The policy should itemize each piece of jewelry insured, including its appraised value. If the piece is lost or stolen, you and your insurance company have already agreed on its worth. The rider will cover replacement of the insured items wherever or however, they're lost.

■ **You own silverware:** Silverware generally is covered for everything but theft and usually limited to $2,500 worth of coverage. The cost of a rider is usually less than $1 per $100 of coverage.

■ **You own Oriental rugs:** Standard homeowner policies limit the reimbursement for damage to Oriental rugs to $5,000 on any one rug and $10,000 total. You can buy an Oriental rug rider for about the same price as a silverware rider.

■ **You own art or antiques:** Basic policies usually limit contents coverage to 50 percent to 75 percent of the face value of your homeowner's policy. That may not be enough if you have a lot of expensive antiques. "Fine arts" riders come surprisingly cheap, costing about 25 cents per $100 of coverage.

■ **You own computer gear:** Your homeowner's policy may not cover the full cost of your tech stuff—particularly if you have a home office. Rates vary, but it should cost about $50 to $100 a year to increase coverage to $10,000 from the standard $2,500 coverage for office equipment and furniture.

CAR INSURANCE

THE AUTOMOTIVE GUESSING GAME

Reading your insurer's mind can save you money

If you're a 22-year-old male driving a souped-up Porsche, you may want to think about getting married. There's nothing cheap about a high performance sports car, including insurance premiums, but insurers do give a discount to married sports car enthusiasts under the assumption—based on hard data—that they will get into fewer accidents.

That doesn't mean you should get married just to get a lower rate, of course, just that auto insurers know more about you than you think. Like anyone that makes a living by gambling, insurance companies make it a point to know the odds. Years of accumulating data on the kinds of people who will get into accidents have allowed them to play the percentages with increasing accuracy.

You can't change who you are, but it helps to know how insurers make their calculations—that way, you can make a few calculations yourself about how to save on your bill when you, say, buy your next car. Here are some of the basics that insurance companies consider when setting rates.

■ **PRIOR ACCIDENT AND CONVICTION RATE:** Most insurers will give a break of 20 percent to 40 percent for maintaining a clean driving record. In California, a 20 percent "good driver" discount is even mandatory.

■ **YOUR AGE:** According to insurers' bell curves, drivers between 50 and 64 have the fewest accidents. The peak accident rates are after 75 and (no surprise) at about 16. Marriage, of course, can throw you into an entirely different part of the bell curve.

■ **CHOICE OF CAR:** Insurers tend to charge more for pricey, high-performance vehicles. State Farm and Allstate both publish rankings of cars by their risk category. The Acura Legend, the Ford Explorer SPW, and the GMC Safari van are included on both lists as vehicles with lower-than-standard collision and comprehensive premiums. The BMW 325 and Camaro Z-28, on the other hand, are ranked by Allstate as "much worse than average risks" and rates are set higher.

■ **WHERE YOU LIVE:** The higher the density of vehicles, the more likely you are to have an accident, so cities can be more expensive than suburbs.

■ **SAFETY DEVICES:** Air bags and anti-lock brakes can bring down the cost of insurance by more than 10 percent. Some states, like Florida and New York, require discounts on collision coverage for cars equipped with anti-lock brakes or other safety devices.

■ **MULTI-CAR DISCOUNTS:** When you insure more than one car with the same company, you can sometimes qualify for a 10 percent to 25 percent discount.

■ **ANNUAL MILEAGE:** Less time on the road and shorter commutes mean less of a chance of getting into accident.

■ **GOOD GRADES:** Students who keep a "B" average can win themselves or their parents a 10 percent to 20 percent discount.

■ **ANTI-THEFT DEVICES:** Devices that set themselves automatically are likely to win bigger discounts since insurers know that people sometimes forget to set car alarms. (Do your neighbors a favor, though: don't set the sensitivity too high. Heavy trucks passing by often can set off the device.)

■ **DEFENSIVE-DRIVING COURSES:** Most insurance companies will give you a discount for taking a state-approved defensive driving course. Check first; sometimes the discount only applies to drivers over 55.

SETTLEMENTS

HAVING TROUBLE WITH A CLAIM?

Just when you thought things couldn't get any worse...

It's bad enough that your car's been smashed, your house broken into, or you've suffered some other unfortunate calamity. Now, you have to face your insurance company. The good ones make it almost painless. But, if you're having difficulty getting a fair claim settlement, the Consumer Federation of America's Insurance Group suggests the following:

EXPERT TIP

If you have an accident:

- **Call medical help for anyone who may be injured, call the police, and don't leave the accident scene before they arrive.**
- **Get the name, address, phone number, insurance company, and driver's license number of anyone who was involved. Get the names and addresses of anyone who saw the accident.**
- **Notify your insurance agent or company immediately.**
- **Write down details of the accident and get a copy of the police report. Save copies of everything.**

—National Consumers League and Insurance Information Institute

■ **Keep good records.** When you have a claim, keep a file on what happens. Write down who said what and when. It could mean thousands of dollars later because the company, the state insurance department, and any attorney you might go to will need clear facts to work with.

■ **Contact your insurance company.** It is best to do this in writing and to insist that your company reply in writing so that you have documentation of the course of events. Ask for your company's position on the situation. Do not send your original policy or any original policy materials. Send copies. If you find that your company is not responding in a fair manner, then go to the next step.

■ **Don't give up.** One important thing to know is that since the company writes the insurance policy language, if it is unclear to you if they are correct in denying your claim, you probably will win in court. Courts hold that any ambiguity in the policy language is held against the insurance company. If you're reasonable in reading the clause the company says it is relying upon to deny your claim, and you don't agree with them, hang in there; you should win.

■ **Contact your state insurance department.** Each state's insurance department has a section to address consumer complaints. They may not take your side in every dispute, but they can make sure the company is responsive to your complaint. When you write to them, send copies of all correspondence between you and your company. Give the name of the company and the policy number. Do not send your policy; send a copy if the insurance department needs it. If you are not receiving a satisfactory response, you have a third option.

■ **Go to small claims court or to a lawyer.** If your claim is small, a small claims court, where you can be your own lawyer, may be your best bet. For major claims, it may pay to use a lawyer. In some states, if insurer behavior is particularly abusive, you may be able to collect additional money if a court finds the insurer acted improperly.

EXPERT SOURCES

HELP IS JUST A PHONE CALL AWAY

Some sources for insurance advice, discounts, and information

BASIC INFORMATION

NATIONAL INSURANCE CONSUMER HELPLINE
■ Sponsored by the insurance industry. Offers general information and advice about choosing the right policy, though it will not offer advice on specific products. It can help with life, health, home, and auto insurance.
☎ **800-942-4242**

THE INSURANCE INFORMATION INSTITUTE
■ A nonprofit trade group for property and casualty insurers, answers questions on homeowners and car insurance.
☎ **212-669-9200**
For information about fee-only insurance alliances in your area:
☎ **800-874-5662**

THE HEALTH INSURANCE ASSOCIATION OF AMERICA
■ Provides information on health insurance.
☎ **202-223-7780**

THE AMERICAN COUNCIL OF LIFE INSURANCE
■ The industry's trade organization.
☎ **202-624-2416**
☎ **212-245-4198**

YOUR STATE INSURANCE DEPARTMENT
■ Can tell you what products and companies are available in your area. Usually able to assist consumers with complaints. Check directory assistance for toll-free number.

INDEPENDENT APPRAISERS

Unlike insurance agents, who get a commission, independent appraisers do not have a vested interest in the kind of insurance you buy.

CONSUMER FEDERATION OF AMERICA'S INSURANCE GROUP
■ A nonprofit public interest group. Provides general tips on buying insurance. An actuary will evaluate your computer illustrations of cash-value policies you're thinking of buying or currently own for a flat $40 fee for the first one, $30 for each additional assessment, and $75 for second-to-die policies.
☎ **202-547-6426**

THE LIFE INSURANCE ADVISERS ASSOCIATION
■ Charges $150 to $200 an hour to analyze a policy and help you identify exactly what you need.
☎ **800-521-4578**

PRICE QUOTES

To shop rates by phone without an agent:

INSURANCE QUOTE
■ Free quotes over the phone for term and whole life.
☎ **800-972-1104**

SELECTQUOTE
■ Identifies companies that give you the best rates for term and sells policies by mail.
☎ **800-343-1985**

QUOTESMITH
■ Will search pool of policies sold by independent agents and provide quotes for $15.
☎ **800-556-9393**

INSURANCE INFORMATION
■ Will find cheapest policies for $50. Full refund if it doesn't save $50 over current policy.
☎ **800-472-5800**

WHOLESALE INSURANCE NETWORK
■ Prices for low-load policies.
☎ **800-808-5810**

YOUR TAXES

CHANGES

GETTING READY FOR TAX DAY '96

Knowing about some recent changes could save you big money

The current tax rules? What day of the week is it? After more than a decade of almost nonstop rearranging of the tax code there's no end in sight. In 1995, Congress was once again considering some major revisions in the tax law. (As this book was going to press in early summer, none had passed.) Chances are that 1996 will bring a gaggle of fresh proposals. There have already been changes aplenty to confuse even the most diligent student of the tax code. Here are 18 recent changes that you need to know about and some tips that could save you money:

■ **TAX RATES:** Back in 1981, the top tax rate was 70 percent; then it was cut to 50 percent in 1982 and to 28 percent in 1988; now it's back to 39.6 percent. Adding new insult: People whose income exceeds certain levels—$114,700 in 1995—are allowed to claim only part of their deductions. High-income families—over $172,050 for couples, over $143,350 for people filing as a head of household—can deduct only a part of the amount normally allowed for personal and dependent exemptions.

■ **SOCIAL SECURITY BENEFITS:** Before 1984, Social Security benefits were tax-free. Then up to half became subject to tax. Starting in 1994, up to 85 percent of benefits became taxable. A retiree's vulnerability to tax varies with income. The first step: Add to adjusted gross income (generally, income before personal deductions and exemptions) the amount of any tax-free interest and one-half of your Social Security benefits. When the total is less than $25,000 for a single person or $32,000 for a couple, there's no tax on the benefits.

Up to half the benefits are taxable above those limits until a second threshold is passed—$34,000 for a single person and $44,000 for a couple. After that point, up to 85 percent of benefits get taxed.

■ **NANNY TAX:** After public attention focused on the so-called nanny tax following the troubles that some early Clinton appointees faced because they hadn't paid Social Security tax on household employees, Congress finally refurbished the levy. People who employ domestic workers now don't owe Social Security tax unless the worker's wages hit $1,000 a year, up from just $50 a quarter previously. And there's now no Social Security tax due at all on household workers under 18 who don't do the work

HOW TAX RATES BITE HARDER AS INCOME RISES

A look at 1995 taxable income by filing status

Tax rate	Married filing jointly	Head of household	Single	Married filing separately
15%	$0–$39,000	$0–$31,250	$0–$23,350	$0–$19,500
28%	$39,000–$94,250	$31,250–$80,750	$23,350–$56,550	$19,500–$47,125
31%	$94,250–$143,600	$80,750–$130,800	$56,550–$117,950	$47,125–$71,800
36%	$143,600–$256,500	$130,800–$256,500	$117,950–$256,500	$71,800–$128,250
39.6%	$256,500 +	$256,500 +	$256,500 +	$128,250 +

NOTE: Taxable income is gross income after subtracting exemptions, deductions and other allowances. A tax rate applies only to the portion of overall income that falls within that specific bracket.
SOURCE: Internal Revenue Service.

as a principal occupation—a youngster, for example, who babysits or mows lawns.

Those who do owe the tax may find compliance easier. Instead of quarterly filings, they will now generally include the tax and paperwork with their income tax returns. (You may, however, want to increase withholding from your paychecks or make quarterly estimated tax payments to avoid owing a bundle at tax filing time.)

MORTGAGE POINTS: In a significant switch of policy, the IRS now says that people who buy homes can deduct not only the points they pay to obtain a mortgage but can also deduct any points paid on their behalf by the seller. Points are a lump-sum interest charge often required up front by mortgage lenders. The IRS ruling is retroactive to sales in 1991 or later, so many people who missed the break when they bought a home on which the seller paid points can now file an amended return to claim a deduction for those points. You have three years from the due date of a return in which to amend it.

EXPERT SOURCE

The IRS publishes over 100 free taxpayer information publications. One of these, Publication 910, Guide to Free Tax Services, is a catalog of the free services the IRS offers. You can order these publications and any tax forms or other instructions that you need by calling the IRS toll-free at: ☎ 800-829-3676.

CHARITIABLE DONATIONS: Your word may be as good as gold, but the IRS is demanding more hard proof these days when sizable charitable deductions are claimed. When a charitable donation totals $250 or more, a canceled check is no longer sufficient to back up a deduction. You need written acknowledgement of the gift from the charity, and the receipt must be in your hands before you file your tax return. The IRS is also ordering charities to give more information about how much of a donation is deductible when a gift or premium is given to donors as an incentive. That's to enforce a rule that you can't deduct the part of a donation that covers the cost of a treat—say, a meal or performance at a charitable benefit—that's more than nominal.

MOVING EXPENSES: These benefits have been narrowed. To be deductible, a move must now be necessitated by a job change that would extend your daily commute by at least 50 miles. Before 1994, the requirement was 35 miles. The cost of a mover and travel to your new home remains deductible (including lodging along the way, but no longer meals). Househunting trips? Temporary living expenses? They're no longer allowed. A new break: People who do not itemize deductions can claim the moving deduction in addition to the standard deduction. And for people who are reimbursed by their employers there's less paperwork. You no longer must go through the exercise of reporting reimbursements as income and then claiming deductions to offset that income.

■ **HOME OFFICE:** More people than ever are working out of their homes, but Uncle Sam is not very avuncular about tax breaks for doing so. You generally can't depreciate the part of a home used as an office, claim a share of rent or deduct a portion of utility bills, taxes, and upkeep unless you spend most of your business hours at home engaging in the activity that generates income. Performing vital administrative chores isn't enough. A handyman using the office to set up jobs and send out bills probably does not qualify for a deduction; a sales representative doing business by phone probably does. Someone who regularly meets with clients at home may qualify for an exception that allows a deduction in such cases. Proposals in Congress would allow easier office deductions, but the resulting tax loss to the federal treasury is a barrier to enactment.

FACT FILE:

MARK YOUR CALENDAR

■ *An extension is granted for filing your return, not for paying any tax due. Interest and a possible penalty will be charged on tax not paid by the April deadline. A penalty may apply on returns filed late without an extension.*

TAX FILING DEADLINES

For filing 1995 income tax returns:
April 15, 1996

With extension, using Form 4868:
August 15, 1996

With second extension, using Form 2688:
October 15, 1996

■ **BUSINESS MEALS:** No one can argue that eating while on a business trip isn't a necessity, but how well you eat is a matter of debate. Before 1987, you could deduct 100 percent of business meals—when traveling or entertaining clients locally. To raise revenue and cut down on dining at taxpayers' expense, the law was changed to allow a deduction for only 80 percent of a business meal. The latest change, begun in 1994, cuts the deduction to 50 percent.

■ **DUES:** Don't enjoy yourself too much. That seems to be the new test to qualify to deduct club dues as a business expense. Generally deductible, according to a 1994 rule change, are civic clubs such as Kiwanis and Rotary, as well as professional and business organizations such as chambers of commerce. No longer deductible: Athletic, luncheon, and country clubs, as well as airline clubs.

■ **BUSINESS EQUIPMENT**: Small entrepreneurs who buy new equipment in 1995 can sidestep depreciation deductions that are spread over several years and deduct all at once up to $17,500 in such spending. This break—known as "first-year expensing" or a "Section 179 deduction"—has been a favored tax incentive. Congress doubled it from $5,000 to $10,000 in 1987 and then raised it to $17,500 starting in 1993. There's support in both Congress and the White House to lift the ceiling higher.

■ **LUXURY TAX:** A 10 percent luxury tax imposed in 1991 on fancy furs and jewelry, boats and planes was repealed in 1993, but a levy on costly cars continues. For 1995, there's a 10 percent tax on the portion of a car's price exceeding $32,000. But that may seem palatable when compared with the insurance premiums.

SELF-EMPLOYED HEALTH INSURANCE: A special tax provision that allowed self-employed people to deduct 25 percent of their health-insurance premiums was left to die at the end of 1993, but it now has been reenacted retroactive to the start of 1994. The deduction also was made permanent and increased to 30 percent for 1995 and later. People who filed returns for 1994 before the reinstatement can file an amended return to claim the deduction.

A recent IRS ruling opens a bigger break for some. The IRS says it is permissible for a self-employed person to hire a spouse and deduct 100 percent of the cost of the spouse-employee's health coverage as a business expense. Since it's OK to provide family coverage to a spouse-employee, this tactic can provide a self-employed person with fully deductible medical protection.

EMPLOYEE COMMUTING: Free parking at work is an untaxed fringe benefit for most workers, but employees in areas where the value of parking is high may have to treat part of the perk as taxable income. When the monthly value of employer-paid parking tops $160 in 1995, the excess is counted as taxable income. Employers who encourage mass transit for commuting can provide up to $60 of transit passes or reimbursement a month before any of the benefit is taxable.

EDUCATIONAL ASSISTANCE: Payments by an employer for tuition, fees, and books so that an employee can earn a degree, say, at night school, are no longer considered a tax-free fringe benefit. Those payments must be considered taxable income since Congress didn't extend the exemption for such educational aid. But payments by an employer to help you improve or maintain the skills you use in your current job—not to prepare for a new one—may still be tax-free.

MEDICARE TAX: After wages and self-employment income top a certain amount—$61,200 in 1995—the Social Security tax ends. (Employees and employers each pay 6.2 percent on a worker's wages.) But Medicare tax now continues without limit—at 1.45 percent for both employee and employer. Self-employed people pay both the employee and employer shares of Social Security and Medicare tax, but the double bite is eased by special deductions that a self-employed person can claim when completing his or her tax return.

WHO MUST FILE

Your tax rate depends on your personal or family status as of the last day of 1995.

Filing status	Age	Gross income at least
SINGLE (including legally separated)		
	Under 65	$6,400
	65 or older	$7,350
MARRIED filing joint return (living together)		
	Both spouses under 65	$11,550
	One spouse 65 or older	$12,300
	Both spouses 65 or older	$13,050
MARRIED filing joint return (not living together)		
	Any age	$2,500
MARRIED filing separate return		
	Any age	$2,500
HEAD OF HOUSEHOLD		
	Under 65	$8,250
	65 or older	$9,200
QUALIFYING WIDOW or widower with dep. child		
	Under 65	$9,050
	65 or older	$9,800
DEPENDENT CHILD (any investment income)		
	Any age	$651
DEPENDENT CHILD (job income only)		
	Any age	$3,901

NOTE: Figures are for 1995 returns to be filed in 1996. The income levels are the thresholds for having to file a return, not necessarily for having to pay tax. Head of household status applies to single people and separated married people who care for a child or relative. A qualifying widow or widower is one whose spouse died in one of the three most recent tax years. People with income from self-employment must file a return if their net income from self-employment (after business deductions) totals $433.13 or more.

SOURCE: Based on IRS rules and inflation-adjusted allowances for 1995.

RETIREMENT DISTRIBUTIONS: The Treasury has set a trap for people who receive a lump-sum payout from a retirement plan after they quit a firm to change jobs or to retire. You could end up paying tax when none will be owed, and then have to wait for a refund. There's generally no tax on a retirement plan payout if it is rolled over within 60 days into another retirement plan—such as another employer's plan or an individual retirement account.

The catch is that 20 percent of a lump-sum payout will be withheld for possible tax when an employee takes the cash rather than telling his or her ex-employer where to directly reinvest it. So if you complete a rollover on your own after taking the cash—and want to avoid any tax—you'll have to tap other savings to make up for the portion of the distribution withheld. You won't get back the withheld amount until you file your tax return.

ESTIMATED TAX: The IRS expects you to pay tax on your income throughout the year, not wait until tax filing time to settle up. Congress complicated the rules on making timely payments for 1992 and 1993, but recently recanted and made them easier. The basic rule remains: You're subject to a penalty if more than 10 percent of your 1995 tax liability is outstanding at the filing deadline in April 1996. (Owing less than $500 usually is OK.) But there is a newly simplified way to escape punishment. As long as the total of 1995's withholding and required quarterly estimated tax payments at least equals your total tax for 1994, you can generally avoid a penalty next April no matter what you owe. One exception: Someone whose adjusted gross income for 1994 was more than $150,000, won't escape a penalty unless the tax collected during 1995 adds up to at least 110 percent of 1994's liability.

EARNED-INCOME CREDIT: A special tax break for lower-income people who hold jobs and have children has been greatly expanded—and can mean a bigger tax refund or a boost in weekly take-home pay. For 1995, single or married people get a tax credit of up to $2,094 when they care for one child and $3,110 when they care for more. The credit is subtracted from tax owed; if the tax falls to zero with credit left over, the taxpayer collects the difference from the government. The credit, designed to reward working, generally rises at first as job income grows then gradually phases out. For 1995, the credit doesn't end until total income is $24,396 when there's one child and $26,673 when there are more. People eligible for the credit can claim part of it in advance—lifting take-home pay up to $105 a month—by giving their employers a Form W-5. A new twist: Workers without children can get a credit of up to $314 for 1995 when their income is below $9,230.

HOW YOUR ITEMIZED DEDUCTIONS STACK UP

The amounts shown are estimates for 1993 returns filed in 1994 and are the averages claimed by taxpayers who deducted those specific expenses. People with incomes over a certain ceiling ($114,700 for couples and single people in 1995) may be prohibited from deducting 100 percent of what they claim. The medical deduction is the amount claimed that exceeds 7.5 percent of adjusted gross income; the miscellaneous total is the amount exceeding 2 percent of adjusted gross income.

Adjusted gross income	Interest on home mortgage	Taxes	Medical expenses	Contributions	Misc.
$20,000–$30,000	$5,048	$2,274	$3,797	$1,308	$2,675
$30,000–$50,000	$5,517	$3,033	$3,559	$1,455	$2,900
$50,000–$75,000	$6,481	$4,411	$5,081	$1,676	$3,245
$75,000–$100,000	$8,177	$5,980	$2,510	$2,571	$4,314
$100,000–$200,000	$10,965	$10,196	$10,522	$3,833	$5,697

SOURCE: *Statistics of Income Bulletin*, Internal Revenue Service.

EXPERT LIST

FORTY EASILY OVERLOOKED DEDUCTIONS

Expenses for everything from contact lenses to dry cleaning could help you lower your tax bill. IRS regulations allow many personal and business expenses to be deducted from your gross income before you figure your tax liability. The more you can subtract, the more you reduce the amount of your taxable income. Here's a list from Ernst & Young, one of the nation's largest accounting firms, of 40 deductions that are easily overlooked:

1. APPRAISAL FEES: When paid to determine value of a charitable gift or extent of a casualty loss.

2. BREACH OF EMPLOYMENT: An employee who paid damages because he or she broke a contract can deduct the damages.

3. BUSINESS GIFTS: No more than $25 to any one person per year.

4. CASUALTY LOSS: An unreimbursed loss exceeding $100 is deductible when the loss exceeds 10 percent of your adjusted gross income. This also applies to losses from theft.

5. CELLULAR TELEPHONE: When used in your business, or required by your employer, the cost of the phone may be deductible, plus phone calls made.

6. CHARITABLE EXPENSES FOR VOLUNTEER WORK: Twelve cents a mile for use of your car, plus out-of-pocket spending for such items as uniforms and supplies; but the value of your time is not deductible.

7. COMMISSIONS ON SALE OF ASSETS: Brokerage or other fees to complete a sale are taken into account when you figure your profit or loss, generally by being added to your cost for the asset.

8. CONTACT LENSES: You can also include the cost of eyeglasses or cleaning solution.

9. CONTRACEPTIVES: Prescriptions, including birth control pills, are legitimate medical items. So, too, are abortions.

10. CONTRIBUTIONS TO PUBLIC PARKS: Help funding a park or recreation site can qualify as a charitable gift.

11. DISABLED PERSON'S JOB EXPENSES: A normal commute isn't deductible, but getting to a job for occupational therapy is deductible as medically related transportation.

12. DRUG AND ALCOHOL ABUSE TREATMENT: Includes meals and lodging when staying at a treatment center, but not programs to quit smoking.

13. EDUCATIONAL EXPENSES: To improve or keep up your skills at your current job, but not to prepare for a new occupation.

14. EMPLOYMENT AGENCY FEES: Whether you get a new job or not; but not if you're looking for your first job or switching occupations. Résumé and travel costs also are deductible.

15. FOREIGN TAX: If you pay tax to another country on income from foreign investments, you can get a deduction or credit for those payments when figuring your U.S. tax.

16. GAMBLING LOSSES: Only up to the amount of reported winnings.

17. GUIDE DOG: For the blind or severely impaired. Include dog's food, care.

18. HEARING AIDS: Includes batteries.

19. HOME COMPUTER DEPRECIATION: If it's used in your business or to manage investments, or if your employer requires you to have it.

■ EXPERT LIST

20. IRA TRUSTEE'S FEES: Administrative charges (but not brokerage commissions) when billed and paid separately. But not when taken from the IRA balance.

21. LABOR UNION DUES: Deductible by members and by workers required to pay dues though not union members.

22. LAUNDRY SERVICE ON A BUSINESS TRIP: You needn't pack for an entire trip.

23. MOVING EXPENSES: When changing jobs or starting work for the first time. To be eligible, new job must mean a 50-mile or longer extra commute if you don't move.

24. PREMIUM ON TAXABLE BONDS: Investors who buy taxable bonds for more than face value can gradually deduct the excess each year they own the bond.

25. MEDICAL TRANSPORTATION: If driving, you can claim nine cents per mile plus tolls and parking.

26. MORTGAGE PREPAYMENT PENALTY: Charge for early mortgage payoff is deductible.

27. ORTHOPEDIC SHOES: The extra amount over the cost of normal shoes.

28. PENALTY FOR EARLY WITHDRAWAL OF SAVINGS: When a certificate of deposit is cashed in before maturity, a penalty is deductible as an adjustment to income.

29. PERSONAL PROPERTY TAX ON CARS: Include licensing fees when based on the value of the car.

30. POINTS ON A HOME MORTGAGE: Deductible as a lump sum when paid on a loan to buy or remodel a main residence; deductible gradually over the life of the loan when paid to refinance a mortgage.

31. PROPERTY TAX AFTER REAL ESTATE IS SOLD: Buyers and sellers must allocate a year's tax, so a buyer can get a deduction for the part of the year after a sale even though the seller paid the property tax.

32. SAFE-DEPOSIT RENTAL: When box stores stock certificates or other taxable investment documents.

33. SELF-EMPLOYMENT TAX: Adjustment allows those who work for themselves to reduce taxable income by half their self-employment Social Security and Medicare tax.

34. SPECIAL SCHOOLING: For the mentally or physically impaired when the school is primarily to help them deal with their disability, even though the day includes regular education. Meals and lodging may also be deductible.

35. STATE DISABILITY FUND PAYMENTS: California, New Jersey, New York, Rhode Island, Washington State, Alabama, and West Virginia workers can deduct mandatory payments to disability and unemployment funds as state income tax.

36. SUPPORT FOR A VISITING STUDENT: Up to $50 per month in housing, food, and support for live-in exchange student is deductible, as long as you receive no reimbursement.

37. TAX PREPARATION: Accountant's fees, legal expenses, tax guides, and computer programs.

38. UNIFORMS AND WORK CLOTHES: When required for work, but not suitable for ordinary wear.

39. WIG: When one is essential to mental health, but not when used only to enhance appearance.

40. WORTHLESS STOCK: Claimed as a capital loss in the year it first has no value. (Less than one cent per share generally is considered worthless.)

NOTE: Some deductions are limited. For example, only the portion of total medical expenses exceeding 7.5 percent of your adjusted gross income is deductible. "Miscellaneous" deductions, including most employment-related and investment expenses, are deductible only to the extent they exceed 2 percent of adjusted gross income.

SOURCE: Adapted from *The Ernst & Young Tax Guide 1995*, Peter W. Bernstein, ed., John Wiley & Sons, 1994.

WHAT TO BRING YOUR ACCOUNTANT

The better prepared you are, the more efficient the process will be

Whether you prepare your own tax return or let an accountant do all the work, the task of gathering your tax information together is unavoidable. In general, you should have documentation that supports all income, deductions, and credits that will appear on your return, but supporting documentation can come in many forms, as this listing, adapted from *The Ernst & Young Tax Guide 1995* (John Wiley & Sons, 1994) makes apparent.

■ **WAGES AND SALARIES:** W-2 forms, usually provided by your employer.

■ **DIVIDENDS AND INTEREST:** Form 1099-Div and Form 1099-Int, usually provided by the bank or company paying the dividend or interest.

■ **CAPITAL GAINS AND LOSSES:** Broker's statements for purchase and sale of assets disposed of during the year and Form 1099-B, usually provided by the broker who sold the assets.

■ **BUSINESS INCOME FROM SOLE PROPRIETORSHIPS, RENTS, AND ROYALTIES:** Books and records. Form 1099-MISC may also be provided by the payor of the income.

■ **BUSINESS INCOME FROM PARTNERSHIPS, ESTATES, TRUSTS, AND S CORPORATIONS:** Form K-1, usually provided by the partnership.

■ **UNEMPLOYMENT COMPENSATION:** Form 1099-G, usually provided by the governmental agency paying the unemployment compensation.

■ **SOCIAL SECURITY BENEFITS:** Form SSA-1099, usually provided by the federal government.

■ **STATE AND LOCAL INCOME TAX REFUNDS:** Form 1099-G; usually provided by the state or city that refunded the taxes.

■ **ORIGINAL ISSUE DISCOUNT:** Form 1099-OID, usually provided by the issuer of the long-term debt obligation.

■ **ALL DISTRIBUTIONS, BOTH TOTAL AND PARTIAL, FROM PENSIONS, ANNUITIES, INSURANCE CONTRACTS, RETIREMENT OR PROFIT-SHARING PLANS, AND INDIVIDUAL RETIREMENT ARRANGEMENTS (IRA):** Form 1099-R, usually provided by the trustee for the plan making the distribution.

■ **BARTER INCOME:** Form 1099-B, usually provided by the barter exchange through which the property or services were exchanged.

■ **SALE OF YOUR HOME:** Form 1099-S, should be provided by the person that is responsible for the closing of the real estate transaction.

■ **IRA CONTRIBUTIONS:** Form 5498; provided by the trustee or custodian of the IRA.

■ **MOVING AND EMPLOYEE BUSINESS EXPENSES:** Receipts and canceled checks and Form 4782, if moving expenses are paid or reimbursed by your employer.

■ **MEDICAL EXPENSES:** Receipts and canceled checks.

■ **MORTGAGE INTEREST AND POINTS PAID ON THE PURCHASE OF A PRINCIPAL RESIDENCE:** Form 1098 or mortgage company statement, usually provided by the mortgage company.

■ **BUSINESS AND INVESTMENT INTEREST:** Canceled checks and brokers' statements.

■ **REAL ESTATE TAXES:** Canceled checks and mortgage company statements (if they are applicable).

■ **OTHER TAXES:** Receipts and canceled checks.

■ **CONTRIBUTIONS:** Receipts and canceled checks; written acknowledgment from the charitable organization is generally required for contributions of $250 or more.

■ **WHAT NOT TO BRING TO YOUR ACCOUNTANT:** You need not bring all of your documentation to your accountant. For example, if you provide a summary of your dividends or charitable contributions, just provide your accountant with the summary. If you do give your accountant all of your documentation, he or she will probably feel obligated to verify the accuracy of your summaries, which, as you probably well know, can be a time-consuming process. Your fee increases accordingly. However, you should be able to provide full documentation on request.

COMMON TAX ERRORS TO AVOID

Some things to remember before you sign the check

■ Include your Social Security number on each page of your tax return so that, if a page is misplaced by the IRS, it can be reattached.

■ Check that you have claimed all of your dependents, such as elderly parents who may not live with you.

■ Recheck your cost basis in the shares you sold this year, particularly shares of a mutual fund. Income and capital gains dividends that were automatically reinvested in the fund over the years increase your basis in the mutual fund and thus reduce a gain or increase a loss that you have to report.

■ Fill out Form 8606, Nondeductible IRA Contributions, for your contributions to an IRA account, even if you don't claim any deduction for the contribution.

■ Be sure that your W-2s and 1099s are correct. If they're wrong, have them corrected as soon as possible so IRS records agree with the amount shown on your return.

■ If you are married, check to see if filing separate returns rather than a joint return is more beneficial.

■ If you are single and have a dependent who lives with you, check to see if you qualify for the lower tax rates available to a head of household or surviving spouse with a dependent child.

■ If you worked for more than one employer, be sure to claim the credit for any overpaid Social Security taxes withheld.

■ Check last year's return to see if there are any items that carry over to this year, such as charitable contributions or capital losses that exceeded the amount you were previously able to deduct.

■ If you did not pay enough taxes during the year, complete form 2210, Underpayment of Estimated Tax, to calculate the underpayment penalty. You may come up with a lower penalty than the IRS would.

■ Don't miss deadlines: December 31, 1995, to set up a Keogh plan; April 15, 1996, to make your IRA contribution, file your return, or request an extension.

■ If you regularly get large refunds, you're having too much withheld and, in effect, giving an interest-free loan to the IRS. Changing the number of allowances you claim on a W-4 form will increase your take-home pay.

TAX FORMS

SHOULD YOU FILE ELECTRONICALLY?

Chances are you'll get a refund faster and avoid IRS clerical errors

Seven out of ten taxpayers get refunds after they file their returns. To speed the process, you can bypass the Post Office and file your return electronically. Refunds on paper returns often take about six weeks to arrive, but people filing electronic returns typically get theirs in half that time, or even faster if they ask the IRS to deposit the refund directly into their bank account.

Tax-preperation firms often offer to file electronically for an extra charge. And tax programs for home computers often include procedures to let you transmit a completed return via modem to an IRS-approved processor who will forward it to the IRS. But there's still paperwork. You must complete Form 8453 to authorize electronic filing and attach your W-2.

The fastest "refunds"—generally just a few days—go to people who file electronically and arrange for an immediate short-term loan in the amount of their coming refund. Banks make these refund anticipation loans through tax preparers and get repaid directly from the refund. The charge varies, but the loans have never been much of a bargain, and loan rates went up earlier this year after the IRS began new procedures to check returns for fraudulent refund claims. Banks said the loans became riskier after the IRS stopped providing credit information about taxpayers to the lenders and delayed some refund claims for authenticating.

The IRS hopes to encourage widespread use of electronic filing since electronic returns have fewer math and other errors that the agency must fix. Electronic filing also saves the IRS embarrassment. Many errors that crop up on paper returns are caused by IRS personnel themselves as they copy data from the returns.

EXPERT TIPS

FIVE SMART PLANNING MOVES

Planning ideas that make a difference, from the experts at Ernst & Young

1. Make your contributions to an IRA or Keogh plan early in the year. The combination of making contributions early in the year and compounding will make your money grow faster.

2. Contribute the maximum to your 401(k) plan early in the year. If you wait too long, you may not be able to contribute the full amount because of limitations.

3. Focus on the after-tax yield when comparing the returns on different investments.

4. Replace personal debt with mortgage debt to the extent possible. Interest expense on mortgage loans is—subject to some limitations—deductible; personal or consumer interest is not.

5. If you roll over a pension distribution to an IRA account, be sure you do it in a timely fashion. You must complete the transfer within 60 days of a payout.

SOURCE: Adapted from *The Ernst & Young Tax Saving Strategies Guide 1995*, Peter W. Bernstein, ed., John Wiley & Sons, 1994.

TAX AUDITS

IF THE IRS COMES KNOCKING

Odds are you'll end up paying more in tax but there's no reason to panic

If you get audited, odds are you'll end up paying more taxes. Thanks to computer-aided selection of targets, about 80 percent of audits pull in extra tax. And starting in 1995 there's going to be more sniffing around as the agency plans to audit some 2.5 million individual returns, or about 2.2 percent of the total filed. That's double the auditing the IRS has been accustomed to doing and the most probing since the 1970s. Upper-income professionals, self-employed people, investors claiming big losses, and people with considerable income from tips are the top targets—but no group is immune.

Audits come in three flavors. Least intimidating is a correspondence audit, which usually involves a letter asking for documentation to back up a single item on a return—perhaps a charitable donation. More fearsome are office audits in which you are asked to come to an IRS office for a more detailed probe that may cover a number of topics. At the top tier are field audits, which most often involve business-related returns, may cover more than one year, and are conducted by highly trained revenue agents at a taxpayer's home or office. Self-employed people may be selected for a field audit at their place of business since that's where records are usually kept.

When the IRS contacts you, it has usually found something suspicious and may propose an increase to your tax up front. Virginia CPA Richard Greene, who specializes in helping taxpayers under attack, warns:

- **The IRS has the presumption of correctness.** You have to show why their proposed changes are wrong.

- **Be wary of a wolf in sheep's clothing.** The examiner you meet is likely to be friendly, professional, and even sympathetic, but his or her goal is to extract more tax from you.

- **Don't volunteer information or stray when answering questions.** Taxpayers can paint themselves into a corner by failing to understand the tax implications of their answers. Being laconic but responsive reduces the danger.

Correspondence audits can often be handled on your own, but if you face an office audit, you may want to turn to an accountant for guidance. When the extra tax involved is small, it may not be economic to hire a professional. But if you paid someone to prepare your return, that person should be willing to give you some guidance—his or her fee may already have included representing you.

And you can always hope for a surprise. In recent years, about one out of 15 taxpayers who have been audited ended up getting money back from the government.

WHO GETS CHECKED THE MOST BY THE IRS

A look at individual tax returns audited in 1993 shows that estates are the most likely to attract Uncle Sam's attention:

Type of return	Percentage audited
PERSONAL	
Income under $100,000	0.70%
Income over $100,000	4.03%
SELF-EMPLOYED	
Gross revenue under $100,000	2.34%
Gross revenue over $100,000	3.91%
FARMERS	
Gross revenue under $100,000	1.06%
Gross revenue over $100,000	2.06%
ESTATES	
Assets under $1 million	9.42%
Assets $1 million to $5 million	24.87%
Assets over $5 million	53.08%

SOURCE: Internal Revenue Service.

DOLLARS & SENSE

WHERE THE LIVING IS EASY

Everyday necessities cost less in the Midwest and the South

Residents of New York City pay twice as much for movie tickets as their counterparts in Sioux City, Iowa. A visit to the doctor costs more in Los Angeles than in Montgomery, Ala. Prices for a range of items differ from city to city and state to state, sometime dramatically. As a rule, the cost of basic items—from food to housing to entertainment—tends to be higher in a large metropolis than in smaller cities or towns. The cost of living is cheaper in the South and Midwest than it is on either the East or West Coast.

Nationwide, there isn't much of a difference in the cost of basic consumer items, largely because of national brands and efficient interstate transportation. But there are significant regional differences in the prices of some services—notably health care and child care. Together, goods and services account for 35 to 40 percent of annual family spending.

The biggest cost differentials are in housing and taxes, which account for the lion's share of most family budgets. According to figures compiled by Runzheimer International, a management consulting firm that determines relocation for businesses, the annual cost of a three- to four-bedroom house or apartment in Little Rock, Ark., for example, is a third the cost of a similarly sized place in Washington, D.C.

Of course, everything's relative. Even the most expensive cities in the United States are bargains compared with many cities abroad. Runzheimer, in fact, touts the United States to its foreign clients as an attractive relocation destination because of its comparatively low living costs.

FACT FILE:

THE COST OF LIVING

■ *The top and bottom five states. A figure of 100 represents the U.S. average.*

HIGHEST		LOWEST	
D.C.	133.8	Mississippi	86.7
Alaska	132.9	W. Virginia	86.7
Hawai'i	132.5	Arkansas	87.2
New Jersey	120.0	Oklahoma	87.3
Massachusetts	115.7	Louisiana	87.7
California	112.3	Kentucky	87.9

SOURCE: American Federation of Teachers.

CITY DWELLER'S GUIDE

WHERE QUARTERS ARE CRAMPED AND PRICES HIGH

Any large metropolitan area is going to be more expensive than a small town, but some big cities are a lot more expensive than others. Here's the good news: New York looks like a bargain compared to Hong Kong.

CITY	HOME OR APT. RENTAL[1]	DOCTOR'S VISIT[2]	HOSPITAL ROOM[3]	BABY-SITTER[4]	MOVIE[5]	FAST-FOOD MEAL[6]	DINNER OUT FOR TWO[7]	DRY CLEAN MAN'S SUIT	MICROWAVE OVEN	COMPACT DISC
AMERICA'S 10 LARGEST METROPOLITAN AREAS										
New York, N.Y.[8]	$56,853	$68.33	$1,187.50	$8.00	$7.83	$5.45	$70.62	$6.92	$244.50	$14.66
Los Angeles, Calif.	$22,025	$54.10	$601.25	$4.97	$6.15	$3.96	$51.58	$5.82	$219.66	$16.10
Chicago, Ill.	$29,168	$46.33	$521.67	$3.27	$5.31	$4.04	$54.60	$5.36	$163.96	$14.54
Houston, Texas	$18,505	$41.17	$352.38	$3.75	$4.88	$3.83	$46.71	$6.65	$169.97	$17.19
Philadelphia, Pa.	$16,731	$43.33	$903.00	$4.79	$5.71	$4.32	$40.76	$6.98	$176.38	$16.82
Dallas, Texas	$21,801	$48.83	$364.75	$3.22	$5.03	$3.76	$42.31	$7.20	$186.97	$16.66
Detroit, Mich.	$21,134	$38.17	$538.50	$2.31	$5.31	$3.84	$50.34	$6.94	$162.00	$16.53
Boston, Mass.	$29,565	$46.67	$549.25	$4.63	$5.34	$4.27	$53.10	$6.49	$192.46	$16.65
Washington, D.C.	$35,146	$59.83	$767.50	$4.67	$5.88	$4.14	$55.09	$7.50	$179.00	$14.29
San Francisco, Calif.	$26,461	$45.50	$889.00	$4.68	$6.07	$4.17	$53.31	$7.91	$205.67	$15.32
FIVE SMALLER CITIES										
Montgomery, Ala.	$11,567	$39.63	$217.29	$4.34	$4.68	$3.69	$35.67	$5.97	$183.99	$14.58
Corpus Christi, Texas	$12,425	$38.50	$329.54	$3.51	$4.45	$3.25	$39.69	$6.58	$169.15	$15.69
Lincoln, Neb.	$12,292	$39.58	$327.83	$2.34	$4.17	$3.81	$35.46	$6.92	$162.46	$15.29
Little Rock, Ark.	$12,169	$41.00	$280.00	$4.00	$4.50	$4.20	$36.23	$6.22	$169.95	$15.78
Sioux City, Iowa	$12,852	$37.45	$356.64	$2.05	$4.32	$4.04	$34.87	$7.45	$213.51	$15.98
AND 10 CITIES AROUND THE WORLD										
Toronto, Canada	$19,987	NA	NA	$3.70	$5.17	$6.78	$40.52	$6.78	$222.72	$13.76
London, England	$45,447	$58.60	$482.34	$4.24	$8.67	$5.69	$63.73	$10.19	$232.85	$20.49
Paris, France	$49,756	$34.26	$524.62	$5.84	$8.22	$6.67	$70.98	$14.39	$329.65	$25.23
Milan, Italy	$32,813	$41.03	$368.21	$7.89	$7.57	$6.31	$62.07	$15.78	$294.56	$19.34
Moscow, Russia	$41,152	$35.00	$64.00	$5.00	$0.94	$3.29	$69.34	$15.00	$644.07	$17.28
Tokyo, Japan	$123,060	$37.39	$248.14	$9.47	$17.95	$7.20	$152.93	$19.65	$40.69	$24.39
Sydney, Australia	$24,891	$24.56	$228.44	$3.72	$8.56	$4.84	$50.67	$10.92	$262.17	$20.29
Buenos Aires, Arg.	$48,850	$65.00	$243.33	$7.00	$6.00	$6.90	$60.28	$15.00	$359.00	$15.00
Mexico City, Mexico	$49,177	$58.81	$101.46	$2.94	$3.92	$4.82	$42.83	$5.68	$324.36	$18.62
Hong Kong	$127,435	$36.74	$118.24	$6.47	$5.98	$2.69	$83.15	$8.02	$267.07	$14.43

NOTES: 1. Yearly rental cost of a three- to four-bedroom house or apartment; cost is representative of yearly mortgage on residence of similar size. 2. Cost of a standard office visit, excluding diagnostic tests, prescriptions, etc. 3. Cost per day of standard hospital room. 4. Hourly cost of in-home sitter. 5. One adult ticket, standard price. 6. Cost of 1/4-pound hamburger, fries, and medium drink. 7. Sit-down meal at above-average restaurant. 8. Manhattan.

SOURCE: Runzheimer International, Rochester, Wisc.

CHILDREN

TEACHING KIDS ABOUT MONEY

Start young, give allowance early in the week, and stress savings

Of the many required tasks parents confront raising their children, educating them about money and sound personal finance is on any list. Should you give your child an allowance? At what age? How much? What should kids pay for? Should you pay your children for doing jobs around the house? Here's what the experts advise.

TO GIVE OR NOT TO GIVE?

Not all experts agree that children should get an allowance. Proponents say an allowance is a good way to teach kids how to handle money responsibly and to show them that they are working members of the family. Critics argue that an allowance creates a welfare system in which parents provide spending money. Most experts agree, though, that parents who choose to give their kids allowances should not offer it as payment for chores or withhold it as a punishment. Chores should be part of the child's family duty, they say. And parents who want to discipline a child should take away privileges other than an allowance.

As the age-old debate rages on, about one-half of the kids in the United States get an allowance. Patricia Schiff Estess and Irving Barocas, authors of *Kids, Money & Values* (Betterway Books, 1994), offer these tips for parents who give their kids an allowance:

- **Start an allowance when a child starts elementary school.** School signals the beginning of important responsibilities for children.

- **Set a specific time when money is distributed and stick to it.** Being late implies it's OK to be irresponsible.

- **Distribute allowance at the beginning of or in the middle of the week.** Most kids spend most of their money on the weekend. Giving early in the week forces them to think about how they'll spend it later.

HOW MUCH DOES IT COST TO RAISE A CHILD TO AGE 18?

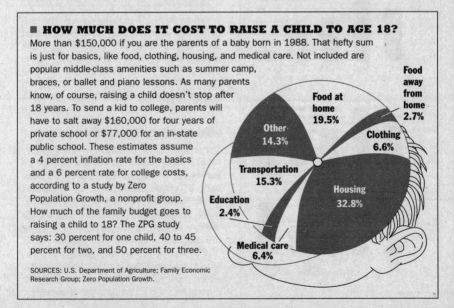

More than $150,000 if you are the parents of a baby born in 1988. That hefty sum is just for basics, like food, clothing, housing, and medical care. Not included are popular middle-class amenities such as summer camp, braces, or ballet and piano lessons. As many parents know, of course, raising a child doesn't stop after 18 years. To send a kid to college, parents will have to salt away $160,000 for four years of private school or $77,000 for an in-state public school. These estimates assume a 4 percent inflation rate for the basics and a 6 percent rate for college costs, according to a study by Zero Population Growth, a nonprofit group. How much of the family budget goes to raising a child to 18? The ZPG study says: 30 percent for one child, 40 to 45 percent for two, and 50 percent for three.

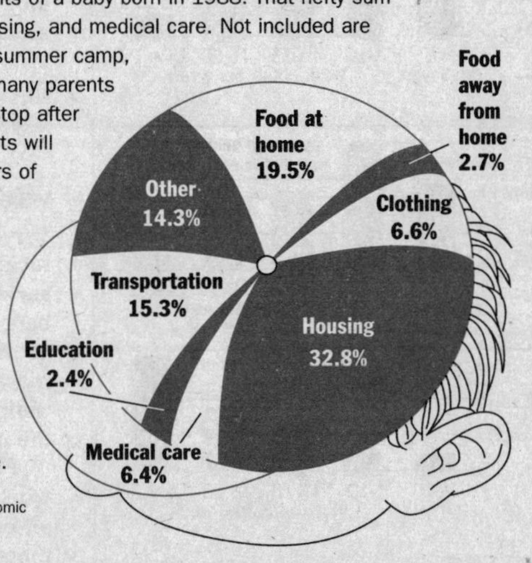

SOURCES: U.S. Department of Agriculture; Family Economic Research Group; Zero Population Growth.

SHOULD KIDS WORK?

Parents have long suspected that teenagers who work long hours outside the home do poorly in school. A 1991 study by professors of psychology Laurence Steinberg of Temple University and Sanford Dornbush of Stanford University, confirms that suspicion. Steinberg and Dornbush found that teens who worked 20 hours or more a week after school got grades half a letter lower than youngsters who worked fewer than 10 hours a week.

Kids who spent more than 20 hours at work compensated for shorter hours spent on school work by cheating, copying assignments, and cutting classes more frequently. More alarming are the results of another Steinberg study: Teens who worked more than 20 hours a week used drugs and alcohol 33 percent more often than those who didn't work at all.

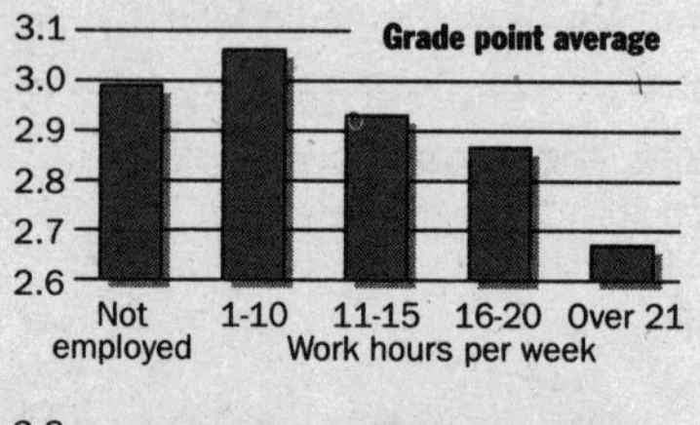

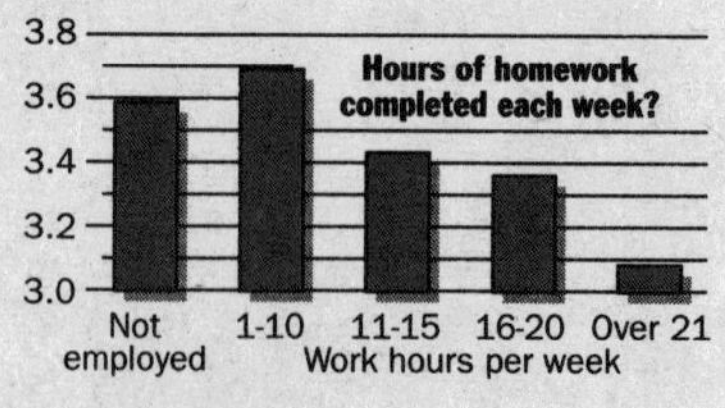

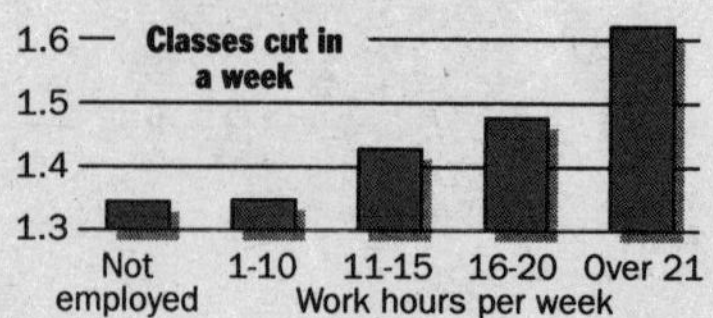

- **Make the allowance large enough so that some of it can be saved.** If a kindergartner gets $1 a week and every penny is accounted for, he or she will lose the opportunity to develop the planning-ahead and saving skills of money management.

- **As children get older, increase their allowance and what it should cover.** This gives them more experience managing larger sums of money and more opportunity to make choices about how to spend it.

HOW MUCH IS TOO MUCH?

What's too little? What's too much? The amount of allowance to give depends mostly on whether you live in an expensive metropolis or a less costly suburb. It also reflects which costs the child is expected to absorb, such as bus or lunch money, for example.

Here's what parents across the country have been giving their kids in weekly allowances, according to a 1993 survey by Youth Monitor, a syndicated service of Nickelodeon, and the market research firm of Yankelovich Partners, Inc.:

AGE:	6–8	9–11	12–13	14–15	16–17
AMOUNT:	$2	$4	$6	$10	$11

Many kids are making money the old-fashioned way: working for it. Here's what kids are earning per week from work around the house or outside jobs:

AGE:	6–8	9–11	12–13	14–15
AMOUNT:	$15	$21	$35	$78

WHAT DO TEENS SPEND THEIR MONEY ON?

Very little of a teenager's money gets tucked away for the future, according to a survey of teenagers by Laurence Steinberg of Temple University. Only 11 percent of the students he surveyed were saving most or all of their monthly income for tuition, and a mere 3 percent were using the money to help out their families.

Perhaps not surprisingly, the overwhelming majority of the youngsters spent all or most of their monthly earnings on themselves for immediate purchases.

EXPERT SOURCES

TEACHING KIDS HOW TO SAVE

Several studies show that today's kids know less about financial matters than did children 30 years ago. What's the best way for parents to teach their kids money skills? By being good role models and discussing family finances on a regular basis, say experts. Some teaching aids:

PUBLICATIONS

Much of the information provided by the groups below is available free of charge. Some charge a nominal fee.

NATIONAL CENTER FOR FINANCIAL EDUCATION
PO Box 34070
San Diego, CA 92163
■ A variety of kids' books about money.
☎ **619-232-8811**

CONSUMER FEDERATION OF AMERICA
PO Box 12099
Washington, DC 20005
■ Send SASE for brochures about saving and spending.

FEDERAL RESERVE BANK OF NEW YORK
Public Information Dept.
33 Liberty St.
New York, NY 10045
■ Comic books about inflation, trade, etc.
☎ **212-720-6130**

SECURITIES INDUSTRY ASSOCIATION
120 Broadway, 35th Fl.
New York, NY 10271
■ Offers a game for kids called the Stock Electronic Market game.
☎ **212-608-1500**

NATIONAL ASSOCIATION OF INVESTMENT CLUBS
1515 East Eleven Mile Rd.
Royal Oak, MI 48062
■ Information about forming or joining a stock investment club.
☎ **313-543-0612**

LIBERTY FINANCIAL COMPANIES, INC.
Federal Reserve Plaza
600 Atlantic Ave.
Boston, MA 02210
■ The *Young Investor Parent's Guide* helps parents introduce their kids to the basics of investing.
☎ **617-722-6000**

SOFTWARE

Many parents are enlisting computers to help kids hone their math and money skills. Patricia Schiff Estess, co-author with Irving Barocas of Kids, Money & Values *(Betterway Books, 1994), offers the following list of programs to help make your kids money-smart:*

LITTLE SHOPPERS KIT
Tom Snyder Productions, $99.95
■ Basic math skills such as making change, for 5- to 9-year-olds. Available for Apple only.
☎ **800-342-0236**

MONEY! MONEY!
Hartley, $49.95
■ Counting and change-making skills for 7- to 9-year-olds. Available for Apple only.
☎ **800-247-1380**

MATH SHOP
Scholastic, Inc., $29.95
■ Math functions and the value of coins for 9- to 14-year-olds. Available for Apple only.
☎ **800-541-5513**

BE A SMART SHOPPER
Queue, Inc., $39.95
■ How to work with a budget, comparison shopping for 11- to 17-year-olds. Available for Apple or TRS-80.
☎ **800-232-2224**

THE WHATSIT CORPORATION SURVIVAL MATH SKILLS
Sunburst Communications, $65
■ Simulates a real business with all the extras: the hiring, the firing, and the taxes. Available for Apple, DOS, and TRS-80.
☎ **800-321-7511**

CREDIT CARDS

PICKING YOUR PLASTIC

Pay closest attention to the financial terms—not the perks or the hype

If your mailbox seems to fill up with new credit card offers every time you turn your back, you are not alone. Fueled by a growth in consumer spending over the past few years, the credit card market is booming. Yet while bargains abound, you need to be aware of your own spending patterns to pick the best card for you.

About two-thirds of all Americans regularly carry a monthly credit card balance, according to Robert McKinley, president of RAM Research and publisher of *CardTrak*, an industry newsletter. The average unpaid balance now hovers around $1,700. For many people, attempting to control their credit card spending is a constant battle. A zero balance for a month or two is frequently followed by a longer period of debt that is carried over at substantial interest rates.

If that's your pattern, credit cards promising no annual fee probably are not your best option. No-fee cards tend to carry higher interest rates, making them more costly to cardholders who maintain a balance. As a rule, McKinley says, consumers should look for cards with an interest rate calculated at no more than six or seven percentage points above the prime rate.

On the other hand, if you're among the one-third of cardholders who pay off their balance each month, a no-fee card could be just the ticket. More than half of all bankcards charge no annual fee. In case you come up short one month, you should look for no-fee cards with the lowest rate on unpaid balances.

You may also be tempted by a card that offers perks (say, frequent flier miles) or rebates. Most of these cards have annual fees and high interest rates and you have to be a pretty big spender to accumulate a free ticket or a sizable rebate. But credit card experts generally steer people away from cards with lots of bells and whistles. You're better off just keeping the money in your pocket.

In all cases, consumers who are considering transferring their credit card balance to a bank that offers better terms should contact their own card issuer first. Banks spend upwards of $100 per customer to attract a new account, says *Card Industry Directory* editor Kevin Higgins, and in this increasingly competitive market they are usually willing to negotiate more attractive terms to retain your business.

Above all, cardholders should be skeptical of pre-approved offers with "teaser" interest rates and fees or fancy perk promotions. The proof is usually in the "fine print" found in the disclosure box printed on the back of most credit card applications. Read it carefully.

Nor is collecting credit cards a smart idea. Two cards are more than enough for most consumers' needs.

FACT FILE:

YOUR CREDIT REPORT

- *One in four people who reviewed their credit report in 1994 found an error, according to the National Center for Financial Education. If you've been denied credit within the past 60 days, you can check on your report at no cost. Send a copy of the denial letter to the credit agency along with your request. One of the four big credit-rating agencies can tell you how:*

CSC Credit Serv.	☎ 800-392-7816
Equifax	☎ 800-685-1111
Trans Union Corp.	☎ 800-851-2674
TRW Information Syst.	☎ 800-392-1122

SHOPPER'S GUIDE

THE MOST POPULAR AND BEST CREDIT CARDS

We've listed the largest credit card issuers as well as the top low-interest, no-fee, rebate, frequent flyer, and secured credit cards in the following guide. The interest rate charged can, of course, vary. (The rates shown are as of April 21, 1995.) You'd be wise to check before signing up. We've listed the rates for standard cards in all cases; fees and perks for gold cards tend to be higher. Diner's Club and American Express green, gold, and platinum cards are excluded from the tables since they are charge cards and must be paid in full each month.

THE 10 BIGGEST CREDIT CARD ISSUERS

The 10 biggest credit card companies are ranked by numbers of card holders. While both Visa and MasterCard are widely accepted in the United States, cardholders who travel abroad should be aware that Visa is more frequently recognized overseas.

Issuer	No. of accounts	Interest rate (standard card APR)[1]	Annual fee	Grace period	Annual cost on $1,500 balance[2]	Card choices
1. **DISCOVER**[3] ☎ 800-347-2683	29,300,000	19.8% VARIABLE	$0	25 DAYS	$297.00	Discover
2. **CITICORP** ☎ 800-462-4642	23,600,000	18.4% VARIABLE	$0	30 DAYS	$276.00	Visa, MasterCard
3. **MBNA AMERICA** ☎ 800-421-2110	12,000,000	18.9% (PRIME +9.9%)	$20/FEE WAIVER POLICY	25 DAYS	$303.50	Visa, MasterCard
4. **AT&T UNIVERSAL** ☎ 800-662-7759	11,700,000	18.9% (PRIME +9.9%)	$20/FEE WAIVER POLICY	25 DAYS	$303.50	Visa, MasterCard
5. **FIRST CHICAGO CORP.** ☎ 800-368-4535	10,275,137	18.9% (PRIME +9.9%)	VARIES/FEE WAIVER POLICY	25 DAYS	$283.50	Visa, MasterCard
6. **HOUSEHOLD** ☎ 800-477-6000	10,064,811	15.9% VARIABLE	$0	25 DAYS	$238.50	Visa, MasterCard
7. **CHASE MANHATTAN** ☎ 800-282-4273	8,000,000 APPROX.	7.9% VARIABLE	$0	30 DAYS	$118.50	Visa, MasterCard
8. **FIRST USA** ☎ 800-537-6954	8,000,000 APPROX.	5.9% VARIABLE	$0	25 DAYS	$88.50	Visa, MasterCard
9. **CHEMICAL BANK** ☎ 800-356-5555	5,200,000	17.8% VARIABLE	$20/FEE WAIVER POLICY	25 DAYS	$287.00	Visa, MasterCard
10. **SIGNET BANK** ☎ 800-952-3388	3,406,691	8.9% VARIABLE	$20	25 DAYS	$153.50	Visa, MasterCard

THE FIVE BEST LOW-RATE CARDS

Banks usually offer a range of interest rates that depend on the cardholder's perceived credit risk. Arkansas rates are among the most attractive because of the state's strict usury laws.

Issuer	Interest rate (standard card APR)	Annual fee	Grace period	Annual cost on $1,500 balance[2]	Card choices
1. **WACHOVIA BANK** (Ga.) ☎ 800-842-3262	9% (PRIME FIRST YEAR, THEN PRIME +3.9%)	$18	25 DAYS	$153.00	Visa, MasterCard
2. **ARKANSAS FEDERAL CREDIT CARD** ☎ 800 477-3348	10.75% VARIABLE	$35	25 DAYS	$196.25	Visa, MasterCard

■ SHOPPER'S GUIDE

LOW RATE CARDS Issuer	Interest rate (standard card APR)	Annual fee	Grace period	Annual cost on $1,500 balance[2]	Card choices
3. **CENTRAL CAROLINA BANK** (N.C.) ☎ 800-577-1680	11.5% VARIABLE	$29	25 DAYS	$201.50	Visa, MasterCard
4. **AFBA INDUSTRIAL BANK** (Colo.) ☎ 800-776-2265	11.5% VARIABLE	$35	25 DAYS	$207.50	Visa, MasterCard
5. **CRESTAR BANK** (Va.) ☎ 800-368-7700	9.9% VARIABLE	$20	25 DAYS	$168.50	Visa, MasterCard

■ THE FIVE BEST CARDS WITH NO ANNUAL FEE

The number of credit card issuers that wave their fees continues to increase. However, since no fee frequently means a higher interest rate, consumers who run a monthly balance should beware.

Issuer	Interest rate (standard card APR)	Grace period	Annual cost on $1,500 balance[2]	Card choices	Additional perks
1. **PRIMECARD FIRST OF AMERICA** ☎ 800-676-7746	16.15% VAR. (PRIME +8.9%)	25 DAYS	$247.50	Visa	A 25% discounts on meals at restaurants. Up to 50% rebate on hotels and theaters.
2. **CHASE MANHATTAN CASH BUILDER** ☎ 800-282-4273	13% VAR. FIRST 6 MOS., THEN 18.4% VAR.	30 DAYS	$195.00/ $276.00	Visa, MasterCard	Refund of 1% on total sales of at least $200; 10% back on finance charges.
3. **MELLON CORPORATE** ☎ 800-468-2225	20.9% VAR. (PRIME +11.9%)	25 DAYS	$313.50	MasterCard	After account is 2 years old, interest rate payments start to be partly refunded.
4. **AMERICAN EXPRESS/ OPTIMA** ☎ 800-467-8462	7.9% FIX FIRST 6 MS., THEN 17.75% VAR.	25 DAYS	$118.50		Optima "True Grace" offers grace period for interest on new purchases.
5. **FIRST VIRGINIA BANK** ☎ 800-634-8803	14.7% FIXED	25 DAYS	$220.50	Visa, MasterCard	No fee if 3 or more purchases per year.

■ THE FIVE LARGEST REBATE PROGRAMS

Consumers can now charge their way to rebates on everything from Rolling Stone's merchandise to investments in Fidelity money markets. To get the greatest benefit, however, cardholders should plan to make use of the rebates and charge all of their purchases to their cards.

Issuer	Interest rate (standard card APR)	Annual fee	Annual cost on $1500 balance[2]	Card choices	Rebates
1. **AT&T UNIVERSAL** ☎ 800-786-3131	18.9% VAR. (PRIME +9.9%)	$20 FEE/WAIVER POLICY	$303.50	Visa, Master card	One point for every dollar on monthly statements, incl. both purchases and balances carried over on point per dollar spent on calling card.
2. **GM/HOUSEHOLD BANK** ☎ 800-846-2273	19.4% VAR. (PRIME +10.4%)	$0	$291.00	Master Card	A 5% rebate on every dollar up to $500 per year or $3,500 over 7 years. Redeemable on GM autos.
3. **FORD/CITIBANK** ☎ 800-934-2788	18.9% VAR. (PRIME +10.4%)	$0	$283.50	Visa, Master Card	Each purchase earns 5% rebate toward purchase/lease of new Ford. Maximum of $3,500 in 5 yrs.
4. **SMARTRATE/ DISCOVER** ☎ 800-347-2683	19.8% VAR.	$0	$297.00	Discover	Cash back bonus up to 1% paid yearly, based on amount of annual purchases, calculated monthly.

■ SHOPPER'S GUIDE

REBATE PROGRAMS Issuer	Interest rate (standard card APR)	Annual fee	Annual cost on $1,500 balance[2]	Card choices	Rebates
5. **GE REWARDS/ CAPITAL CONSUMER CARD CO.** ☎ 800-437-3927	16% to 18% (DIFFERENT RATES APPLY)	$0	$240.00/ $270.00	Master Card	Tiered rebate structure; up to 2% cash back on annual purchases up to $10,000 (up to $140 annually).

■ THE FIVE LARGEST FREQUENT FLYER CARDS

All major U.S. airlines except Delta now offer a credit card, and the programs listed here all have generous tie-in programs. In addition, both American Express and Diner's Club offer mileage plans that can be applied to a number of airlines, although it takes longer to qualify for rewards.

Issuer	Interest rate (standard card APR)	Annual fee	Grace prd. (mileage exp. prd.)	Annual cost on $1,500	Rebate
1. **AMERICAN AIRLINES AADVANTAGE/ CITIBANK** ☎ 800-359-4444	18.4% VAR. (PRIME +9.4%)	$50	20-25 DAYS (3 yrs.)	$326.00	1 mile for each dollar charged; 60,000 miles cap per calendar year.
2. **UNITED AIRLINES/ FIRST CHICAGO** ☎ 800-247-3927	18.9% VAR. (PRIME +9.9%)	$60	25 DAYS (VARIES)	$343.50	1 mile for each dollar charged, excl. cash advances. Certificates issued each 5,000 miles earned.
3. **TWA/EUROPEAN AMERICAN BANK** ☎ 800-322-8921	17.9% VAR. (PRIME +8.9%)	$50 (FEE WAIVED FIRST 6 MS.)	25 DAYS (NONE)	$318.50	1 mile for each net dollar charged.
4. **USAIR/ NATIONS BANK** ☎ 800-759-6262	18.4% VAR.	$35	20 DAYS (NONE)	$311.00	1 mile for each dollar in purchase volume, plus 2,500 miles for initial purchase.
5. **NORTHWEST WORLDPERKS/ FIRST BANK** ☎ 800-285-8585	18.75% VAR.	$55	25 DAYS (3 YRS.)	$336.25	1 mile for each dollar charged.

■ THE FIVE BEST-SECURED CREDIT CARDS

For many, including students and those with bad or nonexistent credit histories, getting a credit card is a hurdle. "Secured" cards require cardholders to make a deposit to be held as collateral on which interest is paid. Interest rates tend to be high and credit limits low, but there are deals to be had.

Issuer	Interest rate (standard card APR)	Annual fee	Grace period	Card choices	Minimum deposit/ interest paid on deposit
1. **CITIBANK** (S.D.) ☎ 800-933-2484	18.4%	$20	25 DAYS	Visa, MasterCard	$300/4%
2. **FEDERAL SAVINGS BANK** (Ariz.) ☎ 800-285-9090	9.75%	$39	25 DAYS	Visa	$250/2.5%
3. **ORCHARD BANK** (Ore.) ☎ 800-873-7307	18.9%	$0	25 DAYS	Visa	$400/4%
4. **KEY FEDERAL** (Md.) ☎ 800-228-2230	18.9%	$35	25 DAYS	Visa, MasterCard	$300/4% to 4.5%
5. **SIGNET BANK** (Va.) ☎ 800-333-7116	20.8%	$20	25 DAYS	Visa	$200/5%

NOTES: 1. Fixed rates can be changed with 15 days' notice.
2. Annual cost on $1,500 balance includes annual fee where applicable.
3. The Discover Card also offers rebates. (See "The 10 Biggest Credit Cards.")

Complete updated listings of these and other cards are available for $4 to $5 from Bankcard Holders of America, 524 Branch Drive, Salem, VA, 24153, ☎ 703-389-5445, or from RAM Research Corp., PO Box 1700, Frederick, MD 21702, ☎ 301-695-4660.

SOURCE: All tables, RAM Research Corp; "Best Cards with No Annual Fee," Bankcard Holders of America.

EXPERT TIPS

THE QUICKEST WAYS TO PAY YOUR BILLS

You can pay your bills electronically even if the most sophisticated equipment you own is a touch-tone phone. As the technology gets more complex, the costs tend to go up. The cost of paying with pen and checkbook is comparable to paying electronically, but the amount of time you spend at least triples.

TOUCH-TONE PHONE

It's the cheapest and most basic way to pay your bills electronically. All you need is a touch-tone phone.

TIME TO PAY 20 BILLS: 30 minutes.

COST: Payline, $4 per month for up to 99 bills; CheckFree, $9.95 per month for up to 20 bills.

MAJOR PLAYERS: Payline, ☎ **800-572-95446;** CheckFree, ☎ **800-882-5280.**

SCREEN PHONE

Your bank will provide you with the phone. You can also check account balances, make transfers, and buy securities. As of 1995, the service is available only at Citibank in Chicago, New York, and Washington, D.C.

TIME TO PAY 20 BILLS: 30 minutes.

COST: $10 per month phone-rental fee for unlimited bill-paying (if you have $10,000 in deposits and/or loans).

MAJOR PLAYERS: Citibank (call your local branch). Others, such as Bank of Boston, Chemical Bank, and Crestar, are gearing up, too.

SOFTWARE

You'll need a PC capable of running Windows 3.1 or DOS 3.1, and at least a 1200-baud-rate modem. Onscreen checkbooks are linked to bill-paying applications.

TIME TO PAY 20 BILLS: 30 to 40 minutes.

COST: $9.95 per month for up to 20 bills through a check-processing firm and about $15 to $99 for the program.

MAJOR PLAYERS: Microsoft Bob and Microsoft Money, retail only; Kiplinger's Simply Money, ☎ **800-773-5445;** Managing Your Money, ☎ **800-537-9993**; Quicken, ☎ **800-624-8742.**

ONLINE SERVICES

You'll need a PC capable of running Windows 3.1 or DOS 3.1, and at least a 1200-baud-rate modem. Prodigy also offers home banking for 18 major banks via BillPay USA.

TIME TO PAY 20 BILLS: 30 to 40 minutes.

COST: $9.95 per month for up to 30 payments on BillPay or 20 payments on CheckFree, plus approximately $9.95 per month plus user fees for online service.

MAJOR PLAYERS: BillPay USA via Prodigy, ☎ **800-776-3449**; CheckFree via CompuServe, ☎ **800-848-8199**.

CHECKBOOK

You already know what you need. Plus, you have to find a mailbox.

TIME TO PAY 20 BILLS: One and a half to two hours.

COST: $3.60 to $4.80 for 20 checks, and $6.40 for postage.

SOURCE: Adapted from *Kiplinger's Personal Finance Magazine,* April 1995.

ATTENTION TV SHOPPERS!

There's a bazaar of goods for sale on the tube. Not all are bargains

Those 24-hour shopping shows are luring more than chronic TV browsers. Viewers are shelling out billions to buy a vast array of goods. The variety touted by the shows is immense: autographed baseballs, kitchen storage containers, exercise bikes, floating cordless phones, you name it. The quality ranges from phony gems to genuine diamonds, from trendy fashions to fine silk suits.

The two big players in the business, the Home Shopping Network (HSN) and QVC Network, each sell about $1 billion a year. Catalog 1, the cable shopping channel developed by Time Warner and Spiegel in early 1994, pitches more upscale goods from the likes of Williams-Sonoma, Neiman Marcus, and the Bombay Company.

There are a few bargains to be found on TV sales shows. An 18-karat gold bracelet, for example, recently sold on QVC for $278.00. An independent appraiser later valued it at more than $600. But recent research by *Consumer Reports* found that a number of goods selling on QVC and HSN could be bought for less in local stores. An Arch-brand quilt selling for $147.72 on QVC, for example, was going for $99 at a department store.

Clothing is tough to buy from television. Getting those form-fitting jeans to fit your form is hard to do without trying them on. As a result, TV shoppers return an average 20 percent of items they buy, compared with only 3 percent for store shoppers. Jewelry is an easier buy. The networks will send callers sizing kits to help determine ring sizes and necklace lengths.

QVC and HSN use different styles to hawk their goods. Hosts at HSN sell in a high-pressure frenzy. They add to the pressure by putting deadlines on prices—"Buy now or cry later." Hosts at QVC, which stands for quality, value, and convenience, use a softer sell.

All the TV shopping shows have mastered some form of celebrity sales, though. Celebrities entertain viewers as they pitch their wares, often taking on-air calls from the audience. Even the non-famous hosts are becoming mini-celebrities. At QVC hosts receive an average 500 letters every week. At HSN, the average is 1,000. Meanwhile, the stars are striking gold. Joan Rivers has raked in more than $30 million in two years peddling her line of jewelry on QVC. Vanna White has sold more than $25 million in pumps, clothes, and jewelry on the HSN. Ivana Trump's initial appearance on HSN drew such huge clothing sales that the network ran out of Ivana fashions to sell.

■ HOW THE TV SHOPPING NETWORKS STACK UP

Every smart consumer knows that you've got to do some comparison shopping before you put your money down.

QVC NETWORK		HOME SHOPPING NETWORK
47 million	**AUDIENCE**	60 million
About 30 percent off retail	**DISCOUNTS**	About 50 percent off retail
30-day money-back guarantee	**RETURN POLICY**	30-day money-back guarantee
Low-key	**SALES PITCH**	Huckster-style
Gold	**BESTSELLER**	Gold
Novels	**WORST SELLER**	Blue jeans
800-345-1515	☎	800-284-3100

SOURCES: QVC Network; Home Shopping Network

EXPERT Q&A

A TIGHTWAD TELLS ALL

Some penny-pinching advice we've included at no extra charge

Tightwads believe you can reach financial goals by saving more, not earning more. Amy Dacyczyn has made a personal crusade of finding ways to recycle milk jugs, bread tabs, brown paper bags, egg cartons, you name it. Dacyczyn, editor of *The Tightwad Gazette II* (Villard Books, 1995), says recycling aluminum foil won't cut it, but attention to the thousands of ways we spend money can make a huge difference. Here, Dacyczyn offers her philosophy of tightwaddery and some dollar-saving tips.

■ What is a tightwad?

A tightwad uses unconventional methods to save money. We push the normal limits to make things last longer. We reuse things in unusual ways. We experiment to find new, cheaper ways to do almost anything.

■ What's the first step toward becoming a tightwad?

Record your spending habits for three months. Write down everything from the mortgage payment to the candy bar at the checkout counter. The expenses will be either essential or optional, like coffee, candy, and soda. The point of the list is to give a clear picture of where your money is going and where you can best cut back.

■ What's next?

Keep what I call a price book. It helps me save more time and money than anything else I do. My price book is a small loose-leaf binder. Each page contains prices for one item, in alphabetical order—apple juice, bananas, etc. Include the store name, the brand, the item size, the price, and the unit price. You can get prices from sale flyers, from grocery slips, and from comparison shopping trips. The time investment will pay off because you will get a feeling of control over your budget.

■ Does it pay to clip coupons?

There's been a lot of misleading information in the media that leads people to believe coupons are more useful than they truly are. But you *can* save some money by using coupons correctly. Compare the price you pay after the coupons with alternative products, and with other options such as making the same item from scratch or not buying it at all, if it's not essential. To slash your grocery bill further eliminate convenience foods, especially those packaged in single-serving containers. Eat fewer expensive-meat meals; casseroles, stews, and stir-fry meals are more economical. Start a garden and preserve garden surplus by home canning and freezing.

■ Does bulk-buying really save money?

The average family can save at least $50 a month by buying in bulk. But bulk buying isn't just for big families. Simply put, buy enough to get you to the next sale or enough until it's convenient for you to shop there again. Know your prices. Generally, the leader sale items on the cover and the back of sale flyers beat wholesale prices.

■ What are some frugal gifts you can give the kids and still keep them happy?

Kids generally don't appreciate only homemade presents, but I like to give at least one to each of my children at Christmas. You can easily make bean bags with pieces of durable fabric and dried beans. Then decorate them with bric-a-brac. For the young child who likes to empty Mom's purse, fill a thrift-shop purse with a ring of old keys, wallet with play paper money, old credit cards, an empty compact, etc.

■ Are there ways to save on pet care?

A good dry pet food is generally nutritionally the same as a good canned food. Dry food is the tightwad choice, because it is cheaper. Don't attempt to economize by buying low-quality food, though. Treating a common ailment like pancreatitis, caused by feeding your dog too many fatty table scraps, can cost at least $150, not to mention the discomfort to your dog.

■ How can a tightwad save on utility bills?

Use small appliances, if possible. In one recipe I tried, a slow cooker used about one-fourth the energy of the oven. The microwave uses less than one-tenth the energy of a conventional oven. Low-flow shower heads are great energy savers. They use less water and they have an on/off switch so that you can turn off the water when lathering.

■ How do thrift shops compare to garage sales?

You'll pay more for clothes at thrift shops than garage sales, but the selection is better. Consignment shops have the best selection, although you'll pay double the thrift shop prices. When you look at used clothing, just think of it as a new item that's been washed 10 times.

■ What are your thoughts on trash picking?

We call it treasure hunting. We've found that many usable items are discarded for want of a screw.

■ What are a few of your favorite tips?

To reuse wrapping paper, put a bow on a the spot where the old tape left a hole. Alternative wrapping can be made from Sunday paper comics, wallpaper, old maps, or department store bags. It's been five years since we last bought wrapping paper.

Hold a smorgasbord night. Thaw a variety of leftovers, line up the family and have them choose. Our kids love this chance to escape my you-get-what-you-get philosophy.

For urban families, a rooftop, fire escape, balcony, or a patio are all good places to garden. Almost any vegetable can be grown in a container. Apple boxes, bushel baskets—even laundry baskets with trash-bag liners make good containers. You can often get a good five-gallon plastic bucket for free from a health food store or Dunkin' Donuts, for example.

EXPERT TIPS

10 PAINLESS WAYS TO SAVE $100 THIS YEAR

Here are Amy Dacyczyn's penny-pinching suggestions, good all year-round:

1. Purchase 10 articles of clothing at thrift shops and yard sales this year instead of paying department store prices.

2. Hang four loads of laundry per week instead of using your dryer.

3. Once a month make a pizza from scratch instead of having one delivered.

4. Write a good letter instead of making a monthly long-distance phone call.

5. Reduce your soda consumption by four cans per week.

6. Bake one batch of bread (two loaves) per week.

7. Save $50 each on two children's birthday parties by making homemade decorations, cake, wrapping paper, and one present.

8. Reduce your smoking by three cigarettes per day (or give up smoking altogether and save even more).

9. Reduce your whole milk consumption by four gallons per week, substituting dry milk in cooking, homemade cocoa mix, and in half-and-half for drinking.

10. Pack four inexpensive school lunches per week.

TELEPHONES

LONG-DISTANCE, CALLING

It's not as confusing as you think. Rule 1: sign up for a discount plan

There's no place to hide from the marketing blitz by long-distance phone carriers trying to lure new customers. Some 25 million phone users switched in 1994 alone, but half of all phone users stuck with basic long-distance rates. To switch or not to switch? That's the question.

The answer is that you will save by choosing a discount calling plan over the basic rate, no matter what the company. Prices among the big three companies—AT&T, MCI, and Sprint, which have a nearly 90 percent share of the $61 billion market—are very close. AT&T is only marginally more expensive than the other two. Certain programs may fit your calling pattern more effectively than others, however.

In searching for a carrier, don't overlook the smaller long-distance phone companies or the resellers, some 400 companies that buy long-distance capacity from the majors at special rates and then resell the time cheaply. The smaller guys usually charge a flat per-minute rate. Some require a $50 or so monthly minimum. If your long-distance bills are less than $10 a month, you can probably get a better deal with cut-rate carriers. (The average long distance bill for an AT&T customer is $17 a month.)

To locate a local reseller, call VanTek Communications, ☎ 800-826-8351. The service, which is funded by resellers, is offered free to consumers.

Keeping up with frequent rate changes in the industry is neither difficult nor time-consuming, once you know your calling habits and can easily see which increases affect you. One way to do so is by picking up a copy of Teletips *Residential Long-distance Comparison Chart*. The $3 chart is put out by the Telecommunications Research & Action Center, ☎ 202-462-2520, a nonprofit group in Washington, D.C. Another way is to take advantage of company programs such as MCI's Proof of Savings, ☎ 800-624-7766. You provide them with the numbers you call most often and they'll give you a comparison of costs between MCI and AT&T rates.

COMPARING THE BIG THREE

Base rates at AT&T and MCI are nearly identical.* Daytime rates are between 27 and 28 cents a minute. Evening rates are 16 to 17 cents and late-night and weekend rates are 14 to 15 cents. Sprint has a flat rate policy. Some popular discount plans:

AT&T — **True USA and True Savings** — ☎ **800-878-3872**

True USA gives a 30 percent discount on domestic long-distance calls if you spend $75 or more per month. Charges of $25 to $74.99 are cut by 20 percent; $10 to $24.99 gets a 10 percent discount. True Savings offers 25 percent off $10 to $49.99 and 30 percent off $50 or more. No monthly charge or sign-up fee.

MCI — **New Friends & Family** — ☎ **800-444-3333**

Make $10 or more of domestic calls and get a 25 percent discount from MCI's basic rates, more than $50 a month gets 30 percent off. No fees. A further 50 percent off if you call other plan members.

SPRINT — **Sprint Sense** — ☎ **800-746-3767**

Flat rate fee of 10 cents per minute from 7 p.m. to 7 a.m., and weekends for domestic calls. Daytime: 22 cents. No minimum.

*Rates are as of April 17, 1995.

CHARITY

FOR GOODNESS' SAKE

There's no shortage of good causes. These do the most with your dollars

In days of yore, the clang of a coin or the drop of a dollar satisfied the conscience of most donors. Signing a check meant helping the have-nots. But charitable giving isn't as straightforward anymore. A new provision of the tax law requires that donors have written acknowledgment for every gift over $250 if they intend to claim a deduction on their income tax form (see "Getting Ready for Tax Day '96," page 116). Furthermore, you can't be sure that your dollars are being put to good use—or, at least, the use that you intended. In recent years, numerous press and government reports exposing the scandalous practices of a few charities' top dogs have left some almsgivers disillusioned.

The philanthropic fabric of the country remains strong, but knee-jerk donations are a thing of the past. Wary donors are demanding more information before pulling out their checkbooks. To make sure that your donations don't end up lining the pockets of your favorite charity's board of directors, you'll need to do a little homework.

A good way to check up on the effectiveness of a charity is to zero in on how they are handling your funds. Managerial and fund-raising expenses invariably guzzle a good portion of charitable dollars. To feel confident that your offering is not consumed by high overhead costs, look to see if at least 60 percent of the revenues goes to programs. Although this yardstick may vary with the charity's services, generally the higher the percentage of funds going to programs, the more efficient the charity and the more likely your offering reaches the intended recipients.

Unfortunately, deciphering a charity's financial documents can be painfully tedious (if you can even get a hold of them). And if you do take the time to examine an annual report or IRS form, neither one is likely to reveal potential skullduggery. Fortunately, there are watchdog groups out there evaluating the performance of charities for you (see "Put Your Money Where the Need Is," page 142).

CHARITY BEGINS WITH YOUR BUDGET

How much can you afford to give? Claude Rosenberg, author of *Wealthy and Wise* (Little Brown, 1994), finds that most Americans can afford to give more than they do, especially when they factor in investment earnings. The following chart gives an estimate of what percentage of discretionary income (net income minus average annual expenses) Americans dole out to charity.

WHAT OTHERS ARE DONATING

Adjusted gross income	Average estimated discretionary income	Average contribution	Percentage of disc. income donated
$25,000 to $50,000	$1,500	$500	33%
$50,001 to $75,000	$8,000	$1,200	15%
$75,001 to $100,000	$18,000	$2,000	11%
$100,001 to $200,000	$30,000	$3,200	11%
$200,001 to $500,000	$79,000	$7,000	9%
$500,001 to $1,000,000	$211,000	$18,000	9%
Over $1,000,000	$790,000	$87,000	11%

PHILANTHROPIST'S GUIDE

PUT YOUR MONEY WHERE THE NEED IS

Each year, The NonProfit Times, *a leading publication for nonprofit management, conducts an in-depth study of America's leading charities to help people avoid giving in a willy-nilly manner. They are ranked according to how much of funding received is dedicated to programs. A look at a few stellar charities:*

CHARITY	LOCATION	INCOME ($MM)	SHARE FOR PROGRAMS	TELEPHONE
■ HUMAN SERVICES: Revenues to these agencies grew at a rate of 8.5% in the past 2 years.				
ASSOC. FOR RETARDED CITIZENS	Arlington, Texas	$478.1	87.9%	☎ **817-261-6003**
AMERICAN RED CROSS	Washington, D.C.	$1,795.9	86.5%	☎ **202-639-3286**
SALVATION ARMY	Alexandria, Va.	$1,297.1	85.7%	☎ **703-684-5500**
GOODWILL INDUSTRIES INTL.	Bethesda, Md.	$848.6	84.1%	☎ **301-530-6500**
CATHOLIC CHARITIES, USA	Alexandria, Va.	$1,934.1	82.8%	☎ **703-549-1390**
■ RELIEF AND DEVELOPMENT: Donations to relief organizations tend to correlate with the occurrence of natural disasters and world crises.				
INTL. RESCUE COMMITTEE	New York, N.Y.	$78.7	92.3%	☎ **212-551-3000**
HABITAT FOR HUMANITY INTL.	Americus, Ga.	$126.2	81.4%	☎ **912-924-6935**
CHRISTIAN CHILDREN'S FUND	Richmond, Va.	$112.5	81.3%	☎ **804-756-2700**
COMPASSION INTERNATIONAL	Colorado Springs, Colo.	$55.1	80.8%	☎ **719-594-9900**
SAVE THE CHILDREN	Westport, Conn.	$84.1	78.5%	☎ **203-221-4000**
■ CONSERVATION: After incredibly high levels of public support in the '80s, environmental organizations have witnessed a decline in funding over the past three years.				
NATIONAL WILDLIFE FEDERATION	Washington, D.C.	$91.7	86.1%	☎ **202-797-6800**
DUCKS UNLIMITED	Memphis, Tenn.	$58.7	80.4%	☎ **901-758-3825**
THE NATURE CONSERVANCY	Arlington, Va.	$278.5	79.3%	☎ **703-841-5300**
WORLD WILDLIFE FUND	Washington, D.C.	$60.8	78.8%	☎ **202-778-9753**
NATIONAL AUDUBON SOCIETY	New York, N.Y.	$36.6	71.8%	☎ **212-979-3160**
■ HEALTH: Revenues for 1993 were up only 3 percent over 1992, less than half of the previous year's rise. This category consistently reports the highest program expenses.				
UNITED CEREBRAL PALSY ASSN.	Washington, D.C.	$462.0	85.4%	☎ **800-872-5827**
CITY OF HOPE	Los Angeles, Calif.	$203.9	84.8%	☎ **213-892-7157**
MUSCULAR DYSTROPHY ASSN.	Tucson, Ariz.	$100.0	81.5%	☎ **602-529-2000**
NATIONAL EASTER SEAL SOCIETY	Chicago, Ill.	$351.8	81.8%	☎ **312-726-6200**
AMERICAN HEART ASSN.	Dallas, Texas	$289.0	78.4%	☎ **214-373-6300**
■ RELIGION: Support for organizations dedicated to transmitting spiritual values remains high.				
WYCLIFFE BIBLE TRANSLATORS	Huntington Beach, Calif.	$76.0	84.8%	☎ **714-969-4600**
THE NAVIGATORS	Colorado Springs, Colo.	$57.1	83.6%	☎ **719-598-1212**
CAMPUS CRUSADE FOR CHRIST	Orlando, Fla.	$174.8	82.7%	☎ **407-826-2200**
FOCUS ON THE FAMILY	Colorado Springs, Colo.	$86.3	79.6%	☎ **719-531-3400**
BILLY GRAHAM EVANGELISTIC ASSN.	Minneapolis, Minn.	$89.4	70.5%	☎ **612-338-0500**

SOURCE: *The NonProfit Times*, November 1994.

RETIREMENT

CAN YOU AFFORD TO QUIT?

More and more, the burden for funding the golden years is on you

Where does the average retiree's income come from? For those pulling in more than $20,000 a year in retirement income, the largest chunk of the pie, 39 percent, comes from personal savings and investments. Employer pensions contribute 15 percent and continued employment by one or both spouses provides 26 percent. Only 20 percent comes from Social Security benefits, according to the Treasury Department.

Most workers use a combination of pension, Social Security, and personal savings to get them through their retirement years. But both Social Security and pensions are undergoing changes. Social Security is being taxed and has a ceiling. And employers also are cutting back on traditional pensions and moving toward 401(k) plans, which workers fund through their own salaries. It's clear that the onus is increasingly on workers to fund their own retirement.

The simple fact that Americans are living longer and more active lives means you'll probably need more than your parents did to finance retirement. What's more, research shows that most baby boomers will retire at living standards below those enjoyed by their parents, who have been able to count on generous government benefits, company pensions, and booming securities and real estate markets.

Just how much will you need to retire comfortably? A good rule of thumb is that you'll need 60 to 80 percent of your pre-retirement annual income to maintain the same standard of living during retirement. Once you've calculated that number, you can figure out if your retirement nest egg, including 401(k)s and other pension plans, will generate enough income for you to retire. The table on page 144, developed by Westbrook Financial Advisers, Inc., a New Jersey retirement planning firm, will tell you if you're putting enough aside to retire.

If you find you're not saving enough, how you face up to that shortfall depends on many factors, including your age, of course, and how you are allocating your assets. You may need to shift investments into more aggressive growth funds, if you have a long way to go before you retire, for example. Retirement experts also suggest the following:

■ **Take full advantage of your 401(k) plan.** Contribute the top allowable amount.

■ **Consider an Individual Retirement Account, if you are younger than 70-and-a-half and have earned income.** You can sock away up to $2,000 into an IRA every year. Your money grows tax-deferred and the contributions

FACT FILE:

FUNDING A LONGER LIFESPAN

■ *Those looking toward retirement should keep in mind that age 65 is not the finish line. Better to focus on how long you are likely to live, say retirement experts, then build in lots of flexibility and contingency plans. Here's a table of how many golden years you can expect to enjoy—and to fund.*

RETIRE AT AGE:	LIFE SPAN	
	SINGLE	COUPLE
55	28	34
60	24	30
65	20	25
70	16	21
75	12	16

■ ARE YOU SAVING ENOUGH?

This table, developed by Westbrook Financial Advisers, will tell you if you have enough put aside to live well during your golden years. Find your approximate savings figure, then look at the number below the age when you want to call it quits. That's the amount you would receive in 1995 dollars for the rest of your life, including Social Security benefits, assuming a 3 percent annual inflation rate, a life expectancy of 92, and that the money is invested at 6.5 percent.

SAVINGS	AGE 50	AGE 55	AGE 62	AGE 65
$50,000	$8,875	$10,701	$14,428	$17,332
$100,000	$11,195	$13,168	$17,192	$20,276
$200,000	$15,836	$18,100	$22,721	$26,165
$300,000	$20,476	$23,033	$28,250	$32,054
$400,000	$25,116	$27,965	$33,779	$37,943
$500,000	$29,757	$32,898	$39,308	$43,832
$600,000	$34,397	$37,830	$44,837	$49,721
$700,000	$39,037	$42,763	$50,366	$55,610
$800,000	$43,678	$47,696	$55,895	$61,499
$900,000	$48,318	$52,628	$61,424	$67,388
$1,000,000	$52,958	$57,561	$66,953	$73,277

SOURCE: Westbrook Financial Advisers, Ridgewood, N.J. and New Canaan, Conn.

often are fully or at least partly tax-deductible.

■ **If you are self-employed, you may be able to save as much as 25 percent of your earned income, up to $30,000 a year, in an SEP-IRA or a Keogh.** You can deduct contributions from your taxable income. And again, earnings are tax-deferred until you take the money out.

■ **A smart and painless way to save:** Have your investment deposited automatically from your paycheck, checking account, or money market fund.

■ **Set realistic goals.** Stick to them and monitor your progress regularly.

Don't think it is going to be easy—especially if you're already 40-something. According to Merrill Lynch, the investment firm, the average baby-boomer household saves at only one-third the rate needed to finance a comfortable retirement.

STAYING ON TRACK

It's never too soon to start planning retirement, nor is it ever too late. Here are the financial and legal mileposts you'll encounter as you look down the road and at what age you should expect them:

■ **Age 55:** Minimum age for many senior communities. If you retire or lose your job, you can withdraw from your Keogh, 401(k), and profit sharing without tax penalty or having to annuitize. You can sell your house tax-free on a capital gain of up to $125,000.

■ **Age 59-and-a-half:** You can withdraw a lump sum from certain pension plans—IRA, Keogh, 401(k), without a tax penalty.

■ **Age 60:** You qualify for senior discounts from stores, hotels, movies, etc.

■ **Age 62:** You qualify for Social Security, but you'll get more if you wait until age 65.

■ **Age 65:** If you're getting Social Security benefits, you are automatically enrolled in the Medicare hospital insurance program. If you're not on Social Security, you must apply for Medicare coverage.

■ **Age 70:** Social Security benefits rise, if you're just starting; personal income—regardless of how much—doesn't reduce Social Security benefits.

■ **Age 70-and-a-half:** You must start withdrawing from private plans, like IRA and Keogh, by April 1 or face tax penalties.

WHAT TO EXPECT FROM UNCLE SAM

In the future, you'll have to work longer before you collect

A retiree would have a tough time surviving on Social Security benefits alone. The average annual Social Security benefit paid in 1994 was a meager $8,088. You can start taking Social Security benefits at age 62 but you'll suffer a permanent 20 percent cut in benefits. If you wait until 65 or beyond, you could get up to several thousand dollars more a year.

Keep in mind that legal changes have extended the age at which people will start getting Social Security payments in the future. The full retirement age will be increased in gradual steps. For example, benefits start at age 65 and two months for those born in 1938, at 65 and four months for those born in 1939, 65-and-a-half for those born in 1940, 65 and 8 months for those born in 1941, and 65 and 10 months for those born in 1942. Those born between 1943 and 1954, will have to wait until they reach 66. The steps increase until those born in 1960 reach full retirement at age 67.

Working beyond your full retirement age can help you get higher Social Security payments because you'll presumably be adding relatively high earnings to your Social Security records. Higher lifetime earnings mean higher benefits. On the other hand, working while you're getting Social Security could lower your benefits. If you are 62 to 64 and earn more than $8,040, you could reduce your payments by $1 for every $2 you earn over the limit. If you are 65 to 69 and earn more than $11,160, your Social Security benefits are cut by $1 for every $3 you earn over the limit. Once you hit 70, your benefits can't be cut, though, no matter how much you earn.

The table below estimates your annual Social Security benefits if you retire at 65. But, benefits depend on your earnings history and that of your spouse's, so you may want to call the Social Security Administration, ☎ 800-772-1213, for a more accurate estimate. And who knows how Congress will tamper with your benefits? Under current law, if you receive income in addition to your Social Security benefits up to 85 percent of your benefits could be included in your taxable income. Congress has been tinkering with the amount subject to tax, and inevitably will do so again.

■ WHAT SOCIAL SECURITY OWES YOU

The projected benefits below assume that you work steadily over the years and do not reflect the automatic cost-of-living adjustments.

TOTAL ANNUAL WORKING INCOME	ANNUAL BENEFITS		
	Single worker	Worker and nonworking spouse	Worker and working spouse
$0 to $25,000	$8,500	$12,750	$12,000
$25,001 to $35,000	$11,000	$16,500	$14,500
$35,001 to $45,000	$12,500	$18,750	$17,000
$45,001 to $62,500	$13,500	$20,250	$20,500
$62,501 or more	$14,500	$21,750	$24,000

SOURCE: Social Security Administration.

RETIREMENT

PAY ATTENTION TO YOUR 401(K)

Fund your do-it-yourself pension plan now or regret it later

For many people, 401(k) plans will be their largest retirement asset. Yet many employees are contributing below levels allowed by law, and fewer than 35 percent of 401(k) plan participants set aside enough money to the plan to earn the maximum company match, according to Hewitt Associates, an employee-benefits firm in Illinois. When you figure in compounding over time, that could mean a loss of hundreds of thousands of dollars.

The plans, which get their awkward name from the section of the 1978 tax code that created them, are available mostly to corporate employees. They are retirement savings plans that allow you to make voluntary pretax contributions of as much as 15 percent of your salary, or up to a sliding limit ($9,240 in 1995), whichever comes first. Employers make contributions on behalf of employees, in most cases matching about half what the employee contributes, up to 6 percent of one's salary. Another attraction: a 401(k) helps cut current taxable income and defer taxes on earnings until they are withdrawn on retirement.

Most plans offer several investment choices, including stock and bond funds, and low-risk options like a money market fund or a guaranteed investment contract (GIC) sold by insurance companies. Despite the varied menus, a whopping 30 percent of 401(k) money went into conservative money market funds or GIC funds, according to Ibbotson Associates of Chicago. The annual yields of GICs have averaged only 9.6 percent since 1985, according to Ibbotson, compared to 14.4 percent return rates for equities and 11.9 percent for bonds.

Nearly all financial advisers agree that investors saving for retirement should allot money for stocks. Just how much depends on the risk level you're comfortable with, but T. Rowe Price, the mutual fund company, suggests that for someone 25 years away from retirement about 80 percent should be invested in stocks. Those closer to retirement, may want to shift some money out of stocks into less volatile investments. If you're five years away from retiring, you may want to allocate 40 percent to stocks, split evenly between an equity income fund and a growth fund. Another 40 percent would go into a balanced fund, which combines stocks and bonds and the remaining 20 percent would go into a low-risk GIC.

SIZING UP THE BIG BOYS' PLANS

Not all 401(k) plans are created equal, even among the nation's largest companies. The maximum percentage of salary that an employee can contribute and the amount that an employer will match vary from company to company. So do the number and type of investment choices. Here's a scorecard comparing the plans of some of the nation's largest companies.

Company	Max. employee pretax contribution	Employer match	INVESTMENT OPTIONS: Money market	Stocks	Bonds
AT&T (management)	16%	67%	1 fund	5 funds	2 funds
EXXON	14%	100%		2 funds	1 fund
GENERAL ELECTRIC	17%	50%	1 fund	1 fund	3 funds
GENERAL MOTORS (salaried employees)	15%	25%	1 fund	35 funds	4 funds
IBM	12%	50%	1 fund	4 funds	2 funds

SOURCE: Company reports.

RETIREMENT

SOCKING AWAY AS MUCH AS YOU CAN

Savings plans that every entrepreneur should consider

As many self-employed workers have found, simplified employee pension plans, or SEP-IRAs are simple and flexible. The plans allow anyone who made at least $400 in self-employment to make tax-deductible contributions of up to 15 percent of earned income each year, with a maximum of $30,000. And you can change the amount you contribute each year—or skip a year if you need to.

Like regular IRAs, SEP-IRAs generally require no complicated tax filings; you just deduct the amount you contributed on your income tax form. Yet you can contribute much more to a SEP-IRA than to a regular IRA, and SEP-IRA contributions are fully tax deductible. If you put $2,000 a year for 20 years in an IRA earning 8 percent, for example, you'd get $98,846. But, if you put away $5,000 annually in a SEP at the same rate, you'd have $247,115. If you have employees, you must contribute the same percentage as you contribute for yourself for each employee's earned income.

Keoghs are geared to small business owners such as engineers, attorneys, or accountants. They require more paperwork than SEP-IRAs to administrate but they also allow you to contribute a higher percentage of earned income.

Keoghs come in three different types: Profit Sharing, Money Purchase, and Paired Plan. Profit-Sharing plans are flexible but, like SEP-IRAs, offer the lowest annual contribution percentage—up to 15 percent of earned income each year up to $30,000 per participant. They vary the percentage of earned income you contribute each year and let you skip a year if necessary.

Money Purchase plans allow contributions of up to 25 percent of earned income, up to $30,000 per year per participant. You specify a fixed annual contribution percentage when you set up the plan and must contribute each year. Paired plans are attractive if you want the maximum annual tax deduction and can afford to make the maximum contribution.

Whatever plan you choose, be sure you choose one.

■ HOW SELF-EMPLOYED RETIREMENT PLANS STACK UP:

SEP-IRA		KEOGH
Up to 15 percent of net earnings yearly, or $22,500, whichever is less.	**CONTRIBUTION**	Up to 25 percent of earned income, with a maximum of $30,000 per year per participant.
Contributions fully deductible. Earnings are tax deferred until withdrawal.	**TAX DEDUCTIBLE**	Contributions fully deductible. Earnings are tax deferred until withdrawal.
10 percent penalty, plus taxes if withdrawn before 59-and-a-half.	**GETTING OUT**	No distributions allowed before 59-and-a-half, unless you lose job.
Banks and financial service companies offer readymade SEPs.	**HOW TO SET UP**	Banks and financial service companies offer many Keogh options.
Set up and contribution: April 15.	**DEADLINES**	Set up: company's fiscal year end, usually Dec 31. Contribution: April 15.
Minimal.	**PAPERWORK**	Considerable.

RETIREMENT

NAVIGATING THE WATERS OF IRAS

Here's how to avoid a minefield of penalties

When tax laws limited the tax benefits of Individual Retirement Accounts in 1986, investors abandoned IRAs by the droves. Contributions tumbled from nearly $40 billion in 1986 to around $10 billion in 1994. Investors may have bailed out too soon, though. Even though some IRA contributions are not deductible, tax deferral on the account's earnings still make IRAs a pretty good deal over the years.

According to Scudder, Stevens & Clark Inc., a global investment management firm, an investor who put $2,000 in an IRA from 1982 to 1986 would have savings worth $16,888 today. By comparison, another saver who continued to pump money into the IRA, would have a cache worth more than $32,000 today, even without the tax deduction.

EXPERT TIP

Putting municipal bonds or other tax-free funds in your IRA makes little sense, say investment advisers. Because such funds give tax breaks they usually have lower returns. But investments in an IRA already grow tax-deferred, so why give up any extra return? It may seem an obvious point; then again, some $51 million in municipal bond funds is parked in IRAs.

Many mutual fund companies lure IRA funds by setting low minimum initial investments and by allowing free automatic withdrawals every month or so. But first, you need to get past the deduction requirements. Well-heeled taxpayers who are covered by an employer-sponsored pension plan or whose spouses are covered by one can contribute to an IRA but cannot deduct the contributions from their taxes. If neither you nor your spouse is covered by a retirement plan at work and if you each earned at least $2,000, you can contribute and deduct as much as $2,000 each. If only one of you works, you can contribute and deduct a total of $2,250.

If you or your spouse are covered by an employer's pension plan, your IRA contribution is fully deductible, as long as your modified adjusted gross income is $40,000 or less. The amount is $25,000 or less for a single taxpayer. You get a partial deduction if you are married and your joint income is between $40,000 and $50,000, or if you are single and your income falls between $25,000 and $35,000. You can calculate modified adjusted gross income by adding your salary and other taxable income, and subtracting any adjustments made on your 1040 income tax forms. Then turn to the worksheet included in your Form 1040 instructions to figure your modified adjusted gross income.

Once your money is in an IRA, you'll have to tread gently to get it out without triggering huge penalties. Some rules to keep in mind:

■ **BREAKING OUT EARLY:** If you're younger than 59-and-a-half and want to pull out money for a non-medical reason, the IRS gets 10 percent off the top. There is an exception. You can make penalty-free withdrawals if they are part of a series of roughly equal annual payments linked to your life expectancy and expected rates of return. To take advantage of this exception, you must take withdrawals for at least five years or until you are 59-and-a-half, whichever comes first. You can then take out as much or as

EXPERT SOURCES

PLANNING FOR YOUR GOLDEN YEARS

These books, pamphlets, and retirement kits can help you make wise decisions as you devise a retirement strategy. Many are free.

■ **THE DREYFUS PERSONAL RETIREMENT PLANNER**
Dreyfus Investments
☎ 800-443-9794

■ **RETIREMENT PLANNING GUIDE**
Fidelity Investments
☎ 800-544-4774

■ **CAN YOU AFFORD TO RETIRE?**
Insurance Marketing and Research Association
☎ 800-235-4672

■ **RETIREMENT PLANNING GUIDE KIT**
(Retirement Planning software kit costs $15.)
T. Rowe Price
☎ 800-541-6066

■ **SHAPING YOUR FINANCIAL FITNESS**
National Association of Life Underwriters
☎ 202-331-6000

■ **A SINGLE PERSON'S GUIDE TO RETIREMENT PLANNING**
American Association of Retired Persons
☎ 202-434-2277

■ **VANGUARD RETIREMENT PLANNER**
(A software kit that costs $15 plus $2.50 shipping)
Vanguard Group
☎ 800-933-1970

■ **THE CONSUMER'S GUIDE TO MEDICARE SUPPLEMENT INSURANCE and THE CONSUMER'S GUIDE TO LONG-TERM CARE INSURANCE**
The Health Insurance Association of America
☎ 202-223-7780

■ **UNDERSTANDING SOCIAL SECURITY**
Social Security Administration
☎ 800-772-1213

little as you like without paying a penalty.

There's some leeway in calculating your equal payment schedule. One method is to divide your account total by your life expectancy and estimate the expected return on your account. If you want to take out as much money as possible early, use the highest interest rate that the IRS will consider reasonable. The IRS has accepted rates between 5 percent and 9 percent lately but not more than 120 percent of the long-term federal rate published monthly by the IRS. The faster your account is projected to grow, the more you can withdraw annually.

■ **SWITCHING IRA FUNDS:** You can move from one IRA to another without paying taxes with either a direct transfer or a rollover. In a direct transfer, your IRA holder transfers funds directly to the new custodian without releasing the money to you. You can make an unlimited number of transfers and don't need to report the switch to the IRS, but you do face costly transaction fees.

In a rollover, your IRA holder sends you the funds, which you reinvest into an existing or new account.You are allowed one rollover every 12 months and must complete it within 60 days, or you'll trigger taxes and the 10 percent early withdrawal penalty. You must report rollovers to the IRS. If you intend to switch the funds to a future employer's retirement plan, don't add more money to the IRA. Otherwise, the IRA will be tainted and you won't be able to roll it over again.

■ **TAPPING TOO LITTLE TOO LATE:** If you withdraw from your IRA after age 70-and-a-half and you take out too little based on your life expectancy, you face a 50 percent penalty. If you should have withdrawn $1,000 but you took out only $600, for example, you'll pay $200 in penalty taxes.

EXPERT Q&A

DO YOU NEED A WILL?

The answer is probably yes. Here's why and what it should include

More than half of American adults do not have wills, according to the American Association of Retired Persons. True, if your estate is under $600,000—and that's the case for most Americans—your heirs may be exempt from paying estate taxes, but that doesn't mean that you don't need a will. What are the potential consequences of not planning for the disposition of your estate? We spoke with Boston attorney Alexander Bove, the author of *The Complete Book of Wills & Estates* (Henry Holt, 1989).

■ What happens if I don't have a will?

If you have no will, your estate will end up in probate court and many important decisions will be out of your hands. Normally, you name an executor, a trusted friend or family member who is responsible for determining taxes, assets, bills, and debts to be paid on your estate. Without a will, the court becomes the executor and your estate is divided under state laws.

■ What are the most important components of a will?

As a rule, wills are broken up into two parts. Specific bequests include specified property, such as specific amounts of money, real estate, and stocks that are left to a designated beneficiary. The residue is everything else, or everything not specifically defined, and will normally go to the primary beneficiary of the estate, usually a spouse, children, or both. Only property in your name at the time of your death can be passed on to your heirs.

■ What are living wills, health care proxies, and durable power of attorney, and why are they important?

A living will is a declaration that indicates whether you would want to be kept alive by artificial means in the event that you are diagnosed with a terminal illness.

A health care proxy allows you to appoint someone to make medical decisions for you.

A durable power of attorney names someone to make financial transactions for you. If you don't have a durable power of attorney, and if your assets or property need to be transferred, your beneficiaries would have to go to probate court in order to appoint a conservator or guardian.

■ How often should I update my will?

Whenever there is a major change in the tax laws, or if there is a change in your family or your family's finances.

■ How can I provide for minor children?

If you have minor children, you should be sure to name a trusted relative or friend as the guardian who will be responsible for the "person and property" of the minor child.

■ What is the difference between a will and a living trust?

A living trust is a legal document that you create while you are alive; you can transfer assets to the trust while you are alive, and the trust governs the assets. You may be your own trustee. Whatever is in the trust does not have to pass through probate. Whatever you do not put into the trust goes into a will. A living trust—including a will, a durable power of attorney, and health care proxy—and a living will are the typical documents in a modern estate plan.

■ How much should I pay to have a will drawn?

It depends on the complexity of the estate. The process of drawing up a will can range between $50 and $5,000, depending on how complicated it is. Often the amount of property is not as important as the family circumstances.

CHAPTER TWO

HEALTH

EXPERT QUOTES

"Just walking requires strong abdominal muscles, so make them strong."

—Florence Griffith-Joyner, Co-chair, President's Council on Physical Fitness and Sports

Page 166

"Fettucini Alfredo has as much saturated fat as three pints of Breyer's ice cream."

—Bonnie Liebman, Nutritionist, Center for Science in the Public Interest

Page 194

"The time when Phoenix, Arizona, was an allergy haven is history."

—Ben Chaiken, Director, Arizona Lung Association

Page 278

THE YEAR AHEAD: EXPECT American exercise habits to impress no one...**APPRECIATE** what the new food labels required by the Food and Drug Administration can tell you...**ANTICIPATE** major new discoveries about the role of antioxidants in fighting disease...**PAY ATTENTION** to the skin problems that can be caused by too much sun ...**BEWARE** the increase in asthma among young children...**FORGET** comprehensive health care reform from Washington...

GETTING FIT

YOU DON'T HAVE TO KILL YOURSELF

It may not up longevity, but workouts will boost life-long health

The medical community has for decades trumpeted the message that even moderate amounts of exercise pay big returns on health. The importance of cutting back on dietary fat has been repeatedly advised as well. Yet, according to a recent study, the average body weight of Americans rose 8 pounds between 1980 and 1991, and a third of all adult Americans are now seriously overweight. That was an increase in the obesity rate of adult Americans of 8 percent in just 11 years.

Amidst this weight gain, exercise participation in several important demographic groups has dropped. Over 58 percent of all adults reported irregular or no leisure time physical activity in a 1991 federal government study. An analysis by the federal Centers for Disease Control and Prevention shows that the pattern is established for many by the time they reach high school.

Don't be one of those statistics. One recent study suggests that women who exercise an average of four hours a week have nearly a 60 percent lower risk of breast cancer, and that even one to three hours of exercise a week cuts a woman's risk by approximately 30 percent. Other research has found that regular exercise helps protect women against a variety of other diseases, including diabetes, heart disease, hypertension, and osteoporosis.

Upping the level of exercise intensity should not only benefit physical and emotional health but also may increase one's likely longevity. In the latest installment of a long-running study of Harvard men in middle age, researchers found that men who reported burning at least 1,500 calories in vigorous exercise each week had a 25 percent lower death rate on average than those whose exercise consumed no more than 150 calories a week. To reach the exercise levels measured in the Harvard study, a person would have to do one or a blend of the following each week: walk at 4 to 5 mph for 45 minutes five times; jog at 6 to 7 mph for 3 hours; play 1 hour of singles tennis three times; swim laps for 3 hours; cycle for 1 hour four times; rollerblade for 2½ hours.

By the way, don't expect to improve your odds of living longer if you slack off your workouts. Previous research on the Harvard group showed that death rates were higher for former varsity athletes who sat out exercise in later life than for bookish grads who began or kept up exercise programs after they left college, whatever their athletic prowess.

EXPERT LIST

PICKING YOUR PASSION

Bowling may be terrific fun, but as exercise it's of limited value. Not so bicycling, jogging, and rowing, which rank near the top of the following exercise analysis by Dr. David R. Stutz, author of 40+ Guide to Fitness.

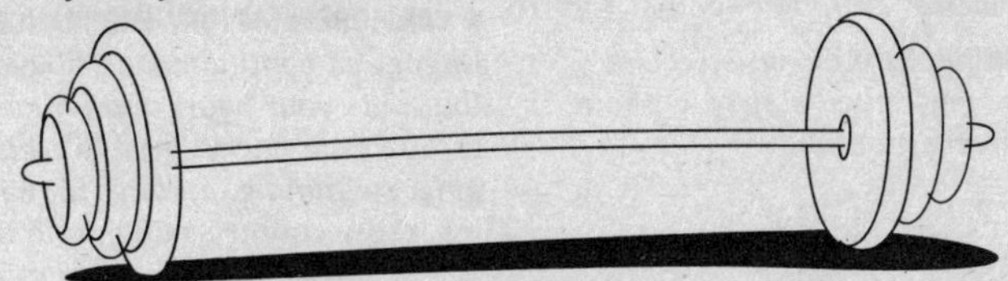

ACTIVITY	AEROBIC TRAINING	WEIGHT CONTROL[1]	MUSCLE TRAINING [2]	STRESS REDUCTION
Aerobic dance	Very good	Very good	Poor	Very good
Alpine skiing	Fair	Poor	Good	Good
Baseball	Fair	Poor	Fair	Fair
Basketball	Very good	Good	Fair	Good
Bicycling	**Excellent**	**Excellent**	Good	**Excellent**
Bowling	Poor	Poor	Fair	Good
Cross-country skiing	**Excellent**	**Excellent**	Fair	**Excellent**
Fishing	Poor	Poor	Fair	Very good
Football	Good	Fair	Fair	Good
Golf	Poor	Poor	Poor	Good
Hiking and climbing	Very good	Very good	Fair	Very good
Horseback riding	Fair	Fair	Fair	Good
Ice skating	Good	Fair	Fair	Good
Jogging and running	**Excellent**	**Excellent**	Fair	**Excellent**
Martial arts	Very good	Very good	Very good	Good
Racquetball and squash	Very good	Very good	Fair	Good
Roller skating	Good	Fair	Fair	Good
Rowing and canoeing	**Excellent**	**Excellent**	Very good	**Excellent**
Sailing	Poor	Poor	Fair	**Excellent**
Soccer	Very good	Very good	Fair	Good
Swimming	**Excellent**	Very good	Good	Very good
Tennis	Good	Good	Poor	Good
Volleyball	Good	Good	Fair	Good
Walking	Good	Very good	Poor	**Excellent**
Weight training	Fair	Good	**Excellent**	Good

1. Largely dependent on the duration of activity. 2. Largely dependent on the intensity of effort.

SOURCE: *40+ Guide to Fitness,* Dr. David R. Stutz, Consumer Reports Books, 1994.

THIRTY MINUTES A DAY KEEPS THE DOCTOR AWAY

Are you a daily jogger, a weekend warrior, or an inveterate couch potato? For minimum physical fitness, the President's Council on Physical Fitness and Sports recommends the following schedule.

DAILY

10-12 minutes

■ **STRETCHING.** *Stretching exercises should be performed slowly, without any bouncing motion.*

TWICE WEEKLY

20-minute sessions

■ **MUSCULAR STRENGTH.** *Exercise all of the major muscle groups. Lifting weights is the most effective means of doing so.*

THREE TIMES OR MORE PER WEEK

30-minute workouts

■ **MUSCULAR ENDURANCE.** *Exercise all of the major muscle groups. Calisthenics, push-ups, sit-ups, pull-ups, and weight training are most effective.*

20-minute programs

■ **CARDIORESPIRATORY ENDURANCE.** *Engage in continuous aerobic activity that puts your heart and lungs through the paces. Brisk walking, jogging, swimming, cycling, rope-jumping, cross-country skiing, and continuous-action games like racquetball and handball fit the bill.*

EVERY WORKOUT

5-10 minutes

■ **WARMUP.** *Exercises such as walking, slow jogging, knee lifts, arm circles, or trunk rotations are effective.*

■ **COOL DOWN.** *Slow walking, or other low-level exercise, and stretching keep muscles loose.*

EXERCISING TO YOUR HEART'S CONTENT

Checking your pulse rate is one of the best ways to gauge whether you're exercising hard enough to improve your heart and lungs. The American Heart Association advises that you push your heart beat during exercise to between 50 percent and 70 percent of your maximum heart rate (calculated by subtracting your age from 220). Anything lower than 50 percent does little for your heart's conditioning; anything higher than 75 percent can cause problems unless you're in superb shape. When you're just starting an exercise program, cardiologists recommend aiming for the lower part of the target heart zone and gradually stepping up your pace.

AGE	Target heart rate beats per minute	Maximum heart rate
20	100–150	200
25	98–146	195
30	95–142	190
35	93–138	185
40	90–135	180
45	88–131	175
50	85–127	170
55	83–123	165
60	80–120	160
65	78–116	155
70	75–113	150

IMPORTANT NOTE: A few high blood pressure medicines lower the maximum heart rate and thus the target zone rate. If you are taking high blood pressure medications, call your physician to find out if your exercise program needs to be adjusted.

THE BODY POLITIC

THE ENDOMORPH

■ *Grover Cleveland was the heaviest: His bull neck and barrel chest rank him as a rare endomorph among presidents.*

THE MESOMORPH

■ *George Washington had a powerful physique with broad sloping shoulders, making him a classic mesomorph.*

THE ECTOMORPH

■ *Abraham Lincoln was tall and thin at 6 feet, 4 inches, and weighed only 180 pounds, making him an ectomorph.*

DO YOU WEIGH WHAT YOU SHOULD?

For decades, medical guidelines on how to figure the "ideal" weight for your height have been based on life insurance industry tables, like those provided below, showing the heights and weights at which their customers have had the greatest longevity. The U.S. Government, citing the results of recent research, has published a height/weight table blessing slightly higher weights for people over the age of 35. But other authorities are questioning the wisdom of that message.

MEN

Height (in shoes)	Small frame	Medium frame	Large frame
5'2"	128–134	131–141	138–150
5'3"	130–136	133–143	140–153
5'4"	132–138	135–145	142–156
5'5"	134–140	137–148	144–160
5'6"	136–142	139–151	146–164
5'7"	138–145	142–154	149–168
5'8"	140–148	145–157	152–172
5'9"	142–151	148–160	155–176
5'10"	144–154	151–163	158–180
5'11"	146–157	154–166	161–184
6'	149–160	157–170	164–188
6'1"	152–164	160–174	168–192
6'2"	155–168	164–178	172–197
6'3"	158–172	167–182	176–202
6'4"	162–176	171–187	181–207

WOMEN

Height (in shoes)	Small frame	Medium frame	Large frame
4'10"	102–111	109–121	118–131
4'11"	103–113	111–123	120–134
5'	104–115	113–126	122–137
5'1"	106–118	115–129	125–140
5'2"	108–121	118–132	128–143
5'3"	111–124	121–135	131–147
5'4"	114–127	124–138	134–151
5'5"	117–130	127–141	137–155
5'6"	120–133	130–144	140–159
5'7"	123–136	133–147	143–163
5'8"	126–139	136–150	146–167
5'9"	129–142	139–153	149–170
5'10"	132–145	142–156	152–173
5'11"	135–148	145–159	155–176
6'	138–151	148–162	158–179

SOURCE: *Build Study, 1979,* Society of Actuaries and Associations of Life Insurance Medical Directors of America, Copyright 1983, Metropolitan Life Insurance Company.

BODY TYPES

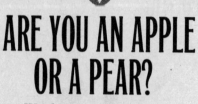

ARE YOU AN APPLE OR A PEAR?

Weight around the hips is healthier than around the belly

How your weight is distributed may be even more important than how much weight you have in the first place, at least when it comes to determining risks to your health. If you are carrying around too much weight in your upper body, your health is at far greater risk than if you are carrying extra weight around your hips, buttocks, and thighs.

All of that excessive fat above the hips, around the belly and in the upper torso has been found by researchers to be associated with an increased risk of breast and uterine cancer, heart disease, and diabetes, as well as a host of other ailments.

To assess whether your weight distribution puts you at higher risk, ask yourself whether your body more closely resembles the shape of an apple or the shape of a pear. "Apples" carry extra weight in the upper body and are often bigger at the waist than in the hips—traits found more often in men than in women. "Pears," on the other hand, carry their weight low. Their waists are smaller than their hips. They are usually women.

A more precise assessment can be obtained by measuring your hips and waist, and then dividing your waist measurement by your hip measurement. If the result is 0.75 or less, you are pear-shaped. If the result is 0.75 to 0.80, you are mildly apple-shaped. And a result greater than 0.80 puts you squarely in the apple category. If that's the case, you'd benefit from directing some of your energy toward taking off some pounds in the right places.

That may be easier said than done, however. According to a team of researchers at Rockefeller University, humans have a gene that tips the brain off when the body has stored all the fat it needs to get by and it is best to stop eating. But mutations in that gene can prevent it from signaling when it's time to push away from the table, the researchers have suggested, resulting in chronic overeating for some.

If you are unlucky enough to have inherited such an "obesity gene," proper exercise will behoove you all the more.

FACT FILE:

LOOKING INTO THE FUNHOUSE MIRROR

- *About one in four American adults has a serious weight problem, but a lot more than that wish they were svelter. Consider the results of this poll by the Los Angeles Times.*

Consider their weight	Male	Female
More than 30 pounds over	5%	9%
21–30 pounds over	5%	8%
10-20 pounds over	16%	20%
Less than 10 pounds over	13%	12%
Proper weight	54%	45%
Less than 10 pounds under	3%	3%
10–20 pounds under	3%	1%
21–30 pounds under	1%	1%
More than 30 pounds under	0%	1%

SOURCE: *Los Angeles Times*, National Center for Health Statistics.

ATHLETE'S GUIDE

BURN, BLUBBER, BURN

The estimated amount of calories burned after 20 minutes of activity

ACTIVITY	WEIGHT						
	105	120	135	150	165	180	195
DAILY ACTIVITIES							
Sleeping	16	20	22	24	26	28	32
Sitting, eating	22	24	28	30	34	36	40
Conversing	26	28	32	36	40	44	46
Office work	36	42	46	52	58	62	68
AEROBIC DANCE							
Low-impact	106	120	136	150	166	180	196
High-impact	154	176	198	220	242	264	286
ALPINE SKIING							
Moderate	112	128	144	160	176	192	208
Steep	168	192	216	240	264	288	312
BASEBALL	66	76	84	94	104	112	122
BASKETBALL							
Half-court	84	96	108	120	132	144	156
Full-court	126	144	162	180	198	216	234
BICYCLING							
8 mph	84	96	108	120	132	144	156
10 mph	98	112	126	140	154	168	182
12 mph	136	154	174	194	212	232	252
15 mph	168	192	216	240	264	288	312
BOWLING (ACTIVE)	98	112	126	140	154	168	182
CALISTHENICS							
Light	52	60	66	74	82	88	96
Heavy	140	160	180	200	220	240	260
CLIMBING							
Casual	84	96	108	120	112	144	156
Vigorous	168	192	216	240	264	288	312
CROSS-COUNTRY SKIING							
3 mph	126	144	162	180	198	216	234
5 mph	172	198	222	246	272	296	320
8 mph	238	272	306	340	374	408	442
FISHING							
Bank, boat, ice	42	48	54	60	66	72	78
Standing-waders	64	72	82	90	100	108	118
Walking-waders	92	104	118	130	144	156	170
FOOTBALL (WHILE ACTIVE)							
Touch, casual	106	120	136	150	166	180	196
Touch, competitive	168	192	216	240	264	288	312
GOLF							
Power cart	42	48	54	60	66	72	78
Pulling cart	66	74	84	94	102	112	122
Carrying clubs	94	106	120	134	146	160	174

■ ATHLETE'S GUIDE

ACTIVITY	WEIGHT						
	105	120	135	150	165	180	195
HIKING							
3.5 mph over field	98	112	126	140	154	168	182
3 mph, 40-lb. pack	96	108	122	136	150	164	176
ICE OR ROLLER SKATING							
Recreational	70	80	90	100	110	120	130
Vigorous	140	160	180	200	220	240	260
JOGGING AND RUNNING							
12 min./mile pace	140	160	180	200	220	240	260
10 min./mile pace	168	192	216	240	264	288	312
8 min./mile pace	210	240	270	300	330	360	390
7 min./mile pace	238	272	306	340	374	408	442
6 min./mile pace	274	314	352	392	432	470	510
MARTIAL ARTS	182	208	234	260	286	312	338
RACQUETBALL AND SQUASH							
Social	140	160	180	200	220	240	260
Competitive	210	240	270	300	330	360	390
ROWING AND CANOEING							
Pleasure/casual	70	80	90	100	110	120	130
Vigorous canoeing	98	112	126	140	154	168	182
Vigorous rowing	210	240	270	300	330	360	390
SAILING	64	72	82	90	100	108	118
SOCCER							
Casual	86	96	108	120	132	144	156
Competitive	210	240	270	300	330	360	390
SWIMMING							
25 yds./min.	84	96	108	120	132	144	156
50 yds./min.	176	200	226	250	276	300	326
TENNIS							
Singles, social	106	120	136	150	166	180	196
Singles, competitive	154	176	198	220	242	264	286
Doubles, social	80	90	102	114	124	136	148
Doubles, competitive	114	130	148	164	180	196	212
VOLLEYBALL	50	56	64	70	78	84	92
WALKING							
24 min./mile pace	42	48	54	60	66	72	78
20 min./mile pace	52	60	66	74	82	88	96
17 min./mile pace	58	68	76	84	92	100	110
5% uphill grade	106	120	136	150	166	180	196
10% uphill grade	140	160	180	200	220	240	260
15% uphill grade	182	208	234	260	286	312	338
15 min./mile pace	79	88	100	110	122	132	144
12 min./mile pace	116	132	150	166	182	200	216
WEIGHT TRAINING (CIRCUIT)	140	160	180	200	220	240	260

SOURCE: *40+ Guide to Fitness,* Dr. David R. Stutz, Consumer Reports Books, 1994.

EXERCISE

THE STRENGTH OF A SIMPLE IDEA

Weight training can trim you down and help prevent health problems

To many people who don't get to the gym frequently, weight lifting may seem like a sweaty version of cosmetic surgery. They may admire the results, but the process by which they were achieved is often thought to be a little too vain and messy to be approved in polite company.

A wealth of recent research has underscored just how outdated that view of strength training has become. The American College of Sports Medicine recently recommended that both aerobic and anaerobic exercise—that is, strength training—be included in any balanced fitness program.

Scientists have found that many people, even those who get regular aerobic exercise, suffer rapid erosion of muscle mass after age 45 or so. With the loss of muscle mass comes a decline in strength, which is reflected by a significant drop in a person's resting metabolic rate. Not only do tasks like lifting become more difficult, but the fall-off in metabolism encourages weight gain that might not have been a problem before.

This muscle drain can be greatly reduced by engaging in a regular program of strength training. A basic program involves lifting small free weights, or lifting weights or stretching large elastic bands on stationary universal exercise machines.

All of these approaches fall under the rubric of "resistance training" and help to replace muscle mass that has been lost to aging. Resistance training can also raise a person's metabolic rate—making it easier to lose weight—and help to prevent osteoporosis, back and joint problems, diabetes, and the kind of high cholesterol counts that can eventually lead to heart disease.

Women may benefit in particular from a program of weight training. According to a recent report in the *American Journal of Health Promotion,* strength training not only improved the muscle strength of women in their 40s, it also boosted their body image and self-esteem far more than walking for exercise. Studies at Ohio State University and Stanford University found that women engaging in regular strength training after menopause also experienced significant gains in the bone mass of the spine and in overall muscle strength.

The elderly have much to gain as well. Another report recently published in the *New England Journal of Medicine* found that, after 10 weeks of strength training, a group of men and women in their 80s and 90s upped their weight-lifting capacity by 118 percent and improved their walking speed and stair-climbing by 12 percent and 28 percent, respectively.

FACT FILE:

FEATS OF FANCY

■ *Tired of the gym? Some slightly more exotic workouts:*

SWIM ACROSS...		Equiv. laps
Atlantic Ocean	4,150 miles	365,200
Lake Michigan	101 miles	8,888
English Channel	21 miles	1,848
Mississippi River	1 mile	88

CLIMB...		Equiv. stairs
Mt. Everest	29,028 ft.	49,762
Mt. Ranier	14,410 ft.	24,703
Empire State Bldg.	1,250 ft.	2,143
Eiffel Tower	984 ft.	1,687

NOTE: One lap equals 60 feet. One stair equals approximately 7 inches.
SOURCE: *A Year of Health Hints,* Dr. Don R. Powell, American Institute for Preventive Medicine, 1992.

BUILDING STRENGTH AND ENDURANCE

The American College of Sports Medicine recommends these exercises to build strength. Be sure to exhale on exertion and to inhale when returning to start.

■ ARMS, SHOULDERS, AND CHEST

SINGLE-ARM ROW: Pull weight to shoulders, then ease to floor. Don't lift with your back.

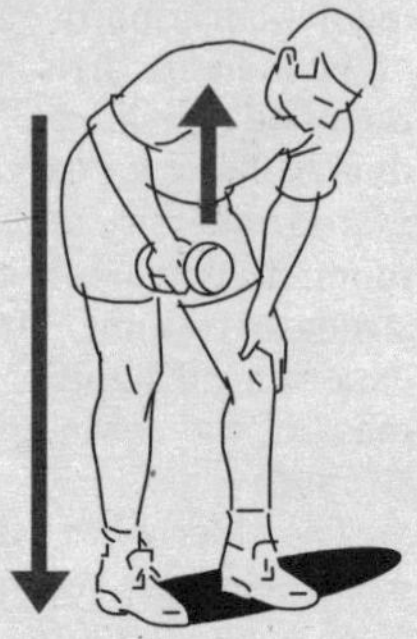

CHAIR PUSH-UP: Keep your hands below your shoulders, and position the chair so that it doesn't slide.

■ ABDOMINALS

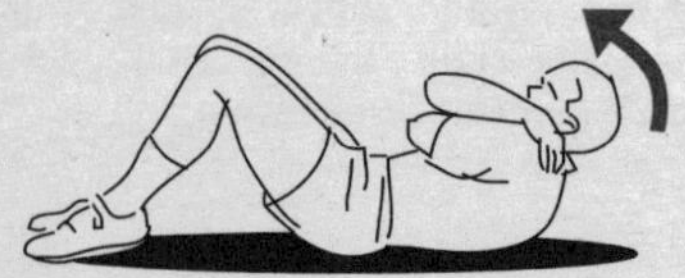

SHOULDER CURL-UP: Lift your back off the floor. But don't sit all the way up; it may strain your back. Use a pad if possible.

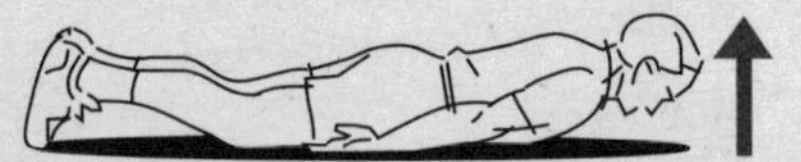

PRONE NECK LIFT: Keep hands up and lift neck. But avoid arching it backward.

■ LOWER BODY

SEATED STRAIGHT-LEG LIFT: Raise your entire leg off the chair by keeping the knee locked. Good for the quadriceps, the muscle that extends the leg.

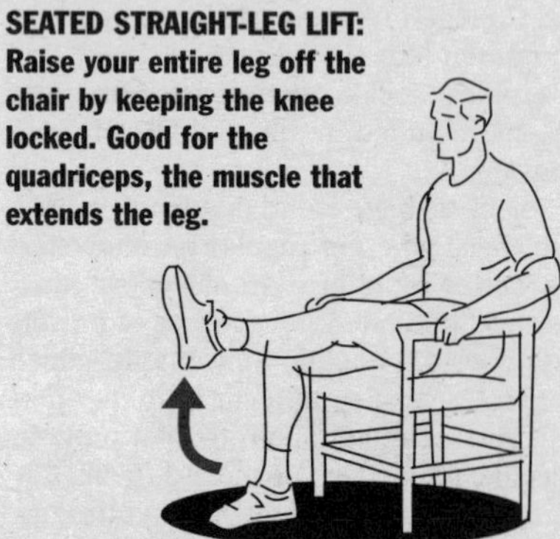

SOURCE: *American College of Sports Medicine Fitness Book*, Human Kinetics, 1992.

■ LESS EFFECTIVE TRADITIONAL EXERCISES

BICYCLES **DONKEY KICKS**

KNEE BENDS

JUMPING JACKS

STAY FLEXIBLE IN WHAT YOU DO

Stretching is important before and after workouts. Limber up with this routine from the American College of Sports Medicine.

NECK

SIDE-TO-SIDE LOOK: Turn head slowly, without jerking motions.

SHOULDER, CHEST, AND BACK

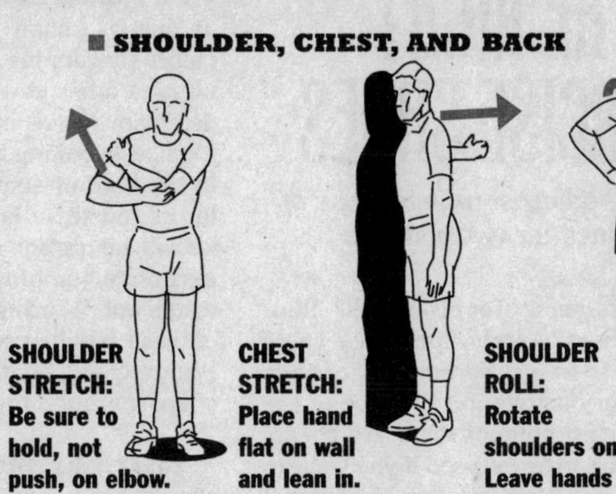

SHOULDER STRETCH: Be sure to hold, not push, on elbow.

CHEST STRETCH: Place hand flat on wall and lean in.

SHOULDER ROLL: Rotate shoulders only. Leave hands on hips.

ABDOMINALS AND LOWER BACK

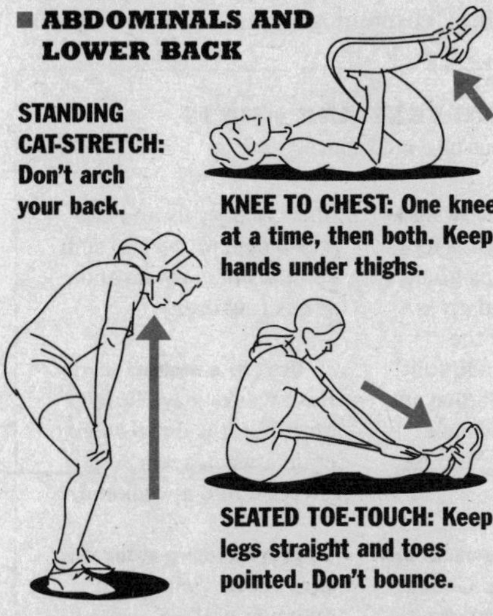

STANDING CAT-STRETCH: Don't arch your back.

KNEE TO CHEST: One knee at a time, then both. Keep hands under thighs.

SEATED TOE-TOUCH: Keep legs straight and toes pointed. Don't bounce.

LOWER BODY

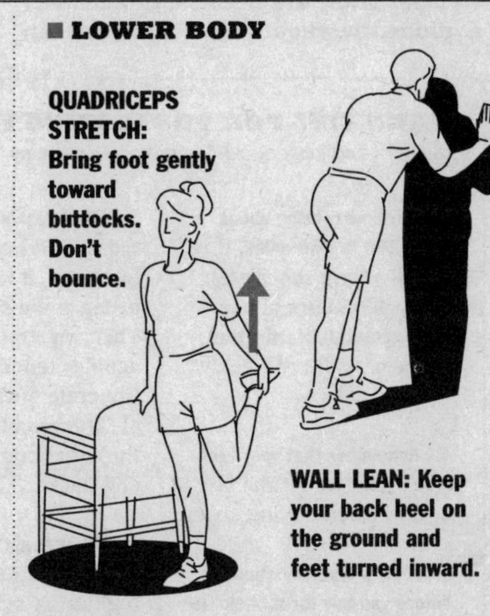

QUADRICEPS STRETCH: Bring foot gently toward buttocks. Don't bounce.

WALL LEAN: Keep your back heel on the ground and feet turned inward.

LESS EFFECTIVE TRADITIONAL EXERCISES

STANDING TOE-TOUCH

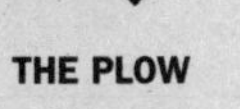

THE PLOW

BACK BENDS

HURDLER STRETCH

EXPERT TIPS

THE RIGHT EXERCISE SHOES

A sports podiatrist makes sense of the sneaker sweepstakes

Cross-trainers? Tennis shoes? Running shoes? Aerobic footwear? There seems to be a different kind of shoe for every activity on the face of the earth, and none of them are cheap, either. You are to be excused if you've been wondering whether all those different varieties really are necessary to conduct a proper workout. Here Dr. Stephen Pribut, a leading Washington, D.C., podiatrist, helps separate the facts from the fiction.

■ **THE RUNNING SHOE:** This top-selling style of exercise shoe is not only a suitable choice for running, but also good for walking and other lower-impact activities that do not involve repetitive lateral motion. But if you are looking for a shoe to participate in the kind of activities that do involve a lot of repetitive lateral motion, like basketball, tennis, and squash, or activities with excessive jumping, such as aerobics—watch out. Wearing running shoes for any of these activities practically invites injury, Pribut warns, because they lack adequate support around the ankles.

■ **BASKETBALL AND TENNIS SHOES:** They should be judged on whether they offer good traction, good ankle support, and firm cushioning. "The extra money you

■ TEN TIPS FOR PROTECTING YOUR FEET AND JOINTS

Runners and joggers can keep their feet happy by using a little common sense.

1. **Buy new running shoes every 250 to 450 miles.** Buy new walking shoes after every 400 hours of use. That translates into ten hours of walking weekly for 40 weeks.

2. **Remember that your feet aren't identical.** Fit the larger one when buying shoes.

3. **Always test new shoes before you buy them.** Ask the sales person if you can jog around the block first. Good shoes should feel comfortable right away, not just when they've been "broken in."

4. **Wear clean dry socks.** You can get blisters otherwise.

5. **Avoid running on sidewalks and sand.** When your foot hits sand, it keeps going because the sand gives. This can stretch the achilles tendon painfully. Concrete doesn't give at all. It transmits shock through your legs, knees and back.

6. **Never begin a workout without first stretching.** Gentle, regular stretching greatly reduces the risk of injury.

7. **Follow the 10 percent rule.**. Runners should increase their mileage by 10 percent a week, but level off every third week. Working out in excess of three to five days a week strains limbs and joints and can cause heel problems, shin splints, ankle twists and stress fractures.

8. **Don't be a weekend warrior.** Busy weeks leave little time, but it is dangerous to cram a week's worth of exercise into a weekend.

9. **Stop exercising at the first signs of pain.** Follow the mnemonic, RICE—which stands for Rest, Ice, Compression, and Elevation—to ease the discomfort.

10. **See a doctor if the pain persists.** It is difficult to tell if a foot bone is broken.

SOURCE: Dr. Stephen Pribut, Washington, D.C.

spend for shoes that fit these criteria will pay off in the medical bills good shoes help you avoid," says Pribut. Some new models that boast flared soles to enhance ankle support also help to prevent the kind of ankle roll-overs that result in painful torn ligaments and sprained or broken ankles.

■ **THE CROSS-TRAINER:** A more recent addition to the athletic shoe panoply, cross-trainers are an economical alternative to purchasing different shoes for every sport. Designed for maximum versatility, cross-trainers can be worn for running, walking, racquet sports, and aerobics, as well as some indoor-court sports such as basketball and volleyball.

Though cross-trainers are versatile, Pribut advises that serious runners are best off wearing real running shoes, because cross-trainers lack the sufficient amount of cushioning and ankle support required for regular jogging.

■ **THE WALKING SHOE:** These are designed for the serious race-walker. They are a needless and expensive investment for those who jog as well as walk for exercise, though. The majority of running shoes are better for your feet than most walking shoes anyway, Pribut says, because running shoes provide more wiggle room for your toes.

■ **SHOES WITH AIR-CUSHIONED SOLES:** Air-cushioning sounds high-tech and therefore helpful, but it can cause more problems than it can prevent. Although air-cushioned athletic shoes provide helpful shock absorption, they lack a firm shank below the back of the foot, Pribut warns. A firm shank and a slight heel lift prevent the arch of the foot from dropping down too far when the foot moves. If the foot drops too far, it can cause a shift of bones and the development of a variety of podiatric deformities.

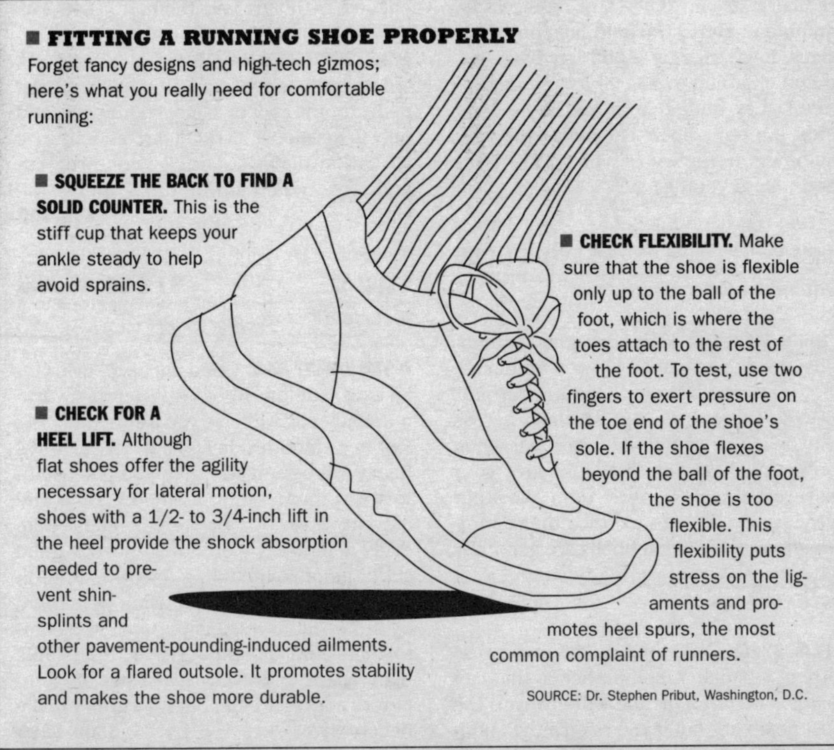

■ FITTING A RUNNING SHOE PROPERLY
Forget fancy designs and high-tech gizmos; here's what you really need for comfortable running:
■ SQUEEZE THE BACK TO FIND A SOLID COUNTER. This is the stiff cup that keeps your ankle steady to help avoid sprains.
■ CHECK FLEXIBILITY. Make sure that the shoe is flexible only up to the ball of the foot, which is where the toes attach to the rest of the foot. To test, use two fingers to exert pressure on the toe end of the shoe's sole. If the shoe flexes beyond the ball of the foot, the shoe is too flexible. This flexibility puts stress on the ligaments and promotes heel spurs, the most common complaint of runners.
■ CHECK FOR A HEEL LIFT. Although flat shoes offer the agility necessary for lateral motion, shoes with a 1/2- to 3/4-inch lift in the heel provide the shock absorption needed to prevent shin-splints and other pavement-pounding-induced ailments. Look for a flared outsole. It promotes stability and makes the shoe more durable.
SOURCE: Dr. Stephen Pribut, Washington, D.C.

EQUIPMENT

BUILDING A GYM AT HOME

Start small and work your way up to your own workout center

Maybe the local health club isn't really all that local. Or maybe you're tired of paying dues to stand in line to pump iron. For about the cost of a one-year club membership, you can buy the basic equipment for a good workout in the privacy of your own home. Doug Garfield, who heads Motioneering Inc., a company that develops high-end exercise equipment for professional athletes, says that your best bet is to build gradually so you don't buy unnecessary equipment. Here, Garfield lays out three stages, beginning at $500 for a basic setup and climbing to $5,000 for a complete circuit. Let budget and space be your guide, but remember: The most expensive equipment in the world won't do you any good unless you use it.

STAGE I $500–$1,000

Requirements for a basic gym:

■ **HAND WEIGHTS:** Hand weights (dumbbells) are the only weights you will need. They are less dangerous than barbells because there is no bar to slash across your throat or to fall on your back when you're doing squats. They also give your postural muscles more of a workout because you have to balance them. Individually weighted dumbbells are generally better than the adjustable type, and a lot more convenient. **$50–$200**

■ **FLAT BENCH:** You can't do a bench press without a bench. A combo-bench that can be adjusted to an incline will give you the most flexibility, but if you're on a tight budget, a plain old flat bench is fine. You will be putting a lot of stress on it, though, so make sure it is solidly built. **$50–$150**

■ **EXERCISE MAT:** Floor exercise can be particularly hard on the hips, so you will want to use some kind of pad. The most useful one will be flexible so that you can scrunch it up to form a pad for your neck or lower back. **$20–$50**

■ **ANKLE WEIGHTS**: These help strengthen one of the most underdeveloped muscle groups: the abductors, or hip muscles. Working them increases overall leg strength and strengthens the joints at the hips, knees, and ankles. All of this will help to prevent painful injuries. **$20–$30**

■ **MINI-TRAMPOLINE:** They're out of fashion today, but mini-trampolines provide a great lower-body workout. They give in all directions, so they're the safest way to exercise the stabilizers in the body to develop good balance. Athletes love them. **$40–$60**

■ **INSTRUCTIONAL MATERIAL:** Get a book or a video that shows you the basic lifting patterns, the proper safety techniques, and how to develop a workout circuit. Software is also available to track your progress and give you helpful hints along the way. **$15–$50**

STAGE II $1,000–$5,000

Include all of the above, plus:

■ **STATIONARY BIKE:** Good ones will give you an excellent lower body and aerobic workout. Bad ones will give you a sore butt. The key to a smooth ride is the flywheel. If it's heavy enough, it will give you a sense of forward momentum, a smooth ride, and a good sense of balance. To repeat bike drills accurately, you'll also need a good set of gauges, including a workload indicator that measures the watts generated by the workout. Also important are a comfortable and adjustable seat, adjustable handlebars, and secure pedal straps. Computer gadgets are fun but they aren't really necessary. **$300–$600**

■ **CROSS-COUNTRY SKI SIMULATOR:** If you're willing to deal with a bit more complexity, these are an even better alternative because they work out the lower and upper body. This lowers the perception of effort by spreading the work between your arms and legs. Watch out for inexpensive systems that use levers for the upper body workout, though. They don't allow your arms to swing through their natural arc, which is both uncomfortable and ineffective. You want a mini-flywheel with good heft that operates smoothly and quietly. You will also want a workload indicator and to be able to select individually adjustable workloads for the upper and lower body. Finally, make sure the hip pad fits comfortably and is adjustable if need be. **$300–$600**

STAGE III — $5,000 and up

Include all of the above, plus:

■ **POWERED TREADMILL:** This will eat up your budget, but it's worth it because the motion fools your inner ear and other balance sensors into really believing that you're moving forward. The proprioceptors, or balance sensors, in your joints send similar signals to your brain, making the whole workout far more involved. Make sure that the motor is at least 1.5 hp and that the tread mechanism has self-adjusting concave rollers to prevent drifting of the belt. The platform should be wide enough for your body and long enough for your natural stride. Some controls are critical: a "dead switch" key that automatically turns the treadmill off, big switches that you can operate while you are in motion, and wheels on the bottom so you can roll it around (these things weigh a lot). The best machine will go at least 10 miles per hour and will allow you to adjust the grade to at least 10 percent. Make sure that it has enough load-bearing capacity to handle the brunt of your weight easily. Finally, buy a machine that operates quietly and smoothly. On a device this expensive, it doesn't pay to stint on quality.
$2,000–$2,500

■ **ROWING MACHINE:** Like the ski trainers, these work out the whole body, so you get more exercise with less perception of effort. If you don't know how to row properly, though, the workout will be close to useless—watch somebody who knows what they're doing before you buy one. Make sure it has a flywheel system, a full-range sliding seat, adjustable angles, and comfortable foot straps. Also important is an indicator that tells you how hard you are working. **$600–$800**

■ **"TOTAL GYM":** So far, only one manufacturer offers this, but there will be others on the market soon because it's such a good idea: a multi-station home gym where you yourself are the weight. Basically, it's a sled that slides up and down an adjustable incline. Through a system of pulleys you can pull yourself up and down the incline. The higher the ramp, the more the load. The advantage: You have a tremendous range of motion with no back discomfort. This makes it popular with physical therapists. **$800–$1,000**

FACT FILE:

STEP RIGHT UP...

■ *Consumers bought $2.5 billion worth of home gym equipment in 1993. The most popular big-ticket items and how many of each were sold:*

Stair climbers	1,869,000
Aerobic step-up boxes	1,659,000
Stationary bikes	1,659,000
Cross-country ski simulators	1,463,000
Treadmills	1,456,000
Multipurpose home gyms	1,086,000
Weight benches	789,000
Rowing machines	159,000

SOURCE: National Sporting Goods Association.

EXPERT Q&A

ENJOYING THE CHILDREN'S HOUR

Getting your kids started early down the fitness track

Olympic track champion Florence Griffith-Joyner, now co-chair of the President's Council on Physical Fitness and Sports, began getting in shape as a child by tussling with her six boisterous brothers. By age 7, she had entered her first competitive race. Here Griffith-Joyner advises on developing the exercise habit in children early.

■ What's a good exercise routine for parents to try with their kids at home?

Let the kids pick out some of their favorite songs to exercise to, even if you don't like them, and make it a family thing. Gather around after a family walk, or walk in place in the living room with the music on for 5 or 10 minutes so you get a good cardiovascular workout. After you cool down, you want to do some light stretching for about 10 minutes.

Make it fun. Do it to music in the living room or wherever there's room. Then you can do a series of sit-ups and push-ups, and you can even do jump roping. A lot of kids like to jump rope, and it's a really good cardiovascular workout.

Sit-ups are also good because they help develop the abdominal muscles that enable you to bend down and lift things. Just walking requires strong abdominal muscles, so it's important that you make them as strong as you can—without overdoing it. Everything should be fun for the kids, so don't push them and make them too sore. Also, let them think of some type of exercise that they want to do so that they feel important and involved.

■ How do you know where to draw the line?

You want to start out really easy with kids, maybe three sets of 5 or 10 sit-ups. If they start doing 5 sit-ups and say, "Oh, mom, my stomach is killing me," just let them stop and tell them: That's great, you're working that muscle and whenever you feel soreness that means you're working a muscle that hasn't been worked, and that soreness means it's working now. Let it rest, come back,and do it again. Remember, everything should be fun for the kids, so don't push them and make them too sore. If you let them suggest the kind of exercise that they want to try, it will make them feel important and engaged.

■ At what age would you start a child on an exercise program?

The younger you start, the longer your child will be able to stay with the program, because the interest will be there. As soon as your child starts walking, walk them down the street and back—you may want to take a stroller—and as the child gets older, walk them further and further. By the age of three, the child should know what good eating habits are and what exercising is all about and why it's important. From the age of five, you may want to start them in some sort of sporting activity. It doesn't have to be in a sport at the park like baseball or soccer. You can start them at home.

■ Would you advise anything different for girls than for boys?

No. I would never put any restraints or limitations on my daughter just because she's a girl. My mom never put them on me, and that way I never said, "Well, I can't do that." The minute you say don't participate in something because it's a boy's sport, you're telling a child that she can't do something and she's going to shy away from it. I learned from experience with six brothers that I could do anything they could do. I challenged them. Sure, I got knocked down and beaten up a lot, but I stayed right there with them and it taught me how to be very competitive while at the same time enjoying what I was doing.

A KID'S CHALLENGE

During the Kennedy administration, the man in the Oval Office exhorted his fellow Americans to test their fitness in a 50-mile walk. Now, the President's Council on Physical Fitness and Sports has issued a new challenge to children ages 6 to 17. Children who score at or above the following scores for their age and sex on all five of the suggested events qualify for the President's Physical Fitness Award and are eligible for both a presidential commendation and a badge.

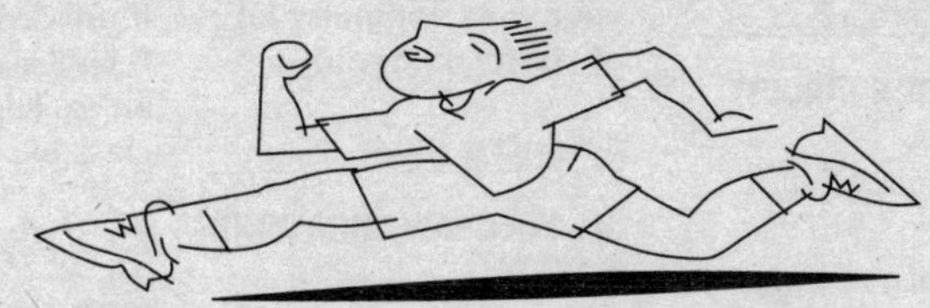

AGE	Curl-ups (per minute)	Shuttle run (seconds)	V-sit reach (inches)	Sit and reach (centimeters)	1-mile run (minutes)	Pull-ups
BOYS						
6	33	12.1	3.5	31	10:15	2
7	36	11.5	3.5	30	9:22	4
8	40	11.1	3.0	31	8:48	5
9	41	10.9	3.0	31	8:31	5
10	45	10.3	4.0	30	7:57	6
11	47	10.0	4.0	31	7:32	6
12	50	9.8	4.0	31	7:11	7
13	53	9.5	3.5	33	6:50	7
14	56	9.1	4.5	36	6:26	10
15	57	9.0	5.0	37	6:20	11
16	56	8.7	6.0	38	6:08	11
17	55	8.7	7.0	41	6:06	13
GIRLS						
6	32	12.4	5.5	32	11:20	2
7	34	12.1	5.0	32	10:36	2
8	38	11.8	4.5	33	10:02	2
9	39	11.1	5.5	33	9:30	2
10	40	10.8	6.0	33	9:19	3
11	42	10.5	6.5	34	9:02	3
12	45	10.4	7.0	36	8:23	2
13	46	10.2	7.0	38	8:13	2
14	47	10.1	8.0	40	7:59	2
15	48	10.0	8.0	43	8:08	2
16	45	10.1	9.0	42	8:23	1
17	44	10.0	8.0	42	8:15	1

SOURCE: President's Council on Physical Fitness and Sports.

EXPERT PICKS

THE BEST FITNESS VIDEOS

Daryn Eller, a writer specializing in health and fitness, along with Self *magazine contributing editor and exercise physiologist Risa Friedman, screened 90 videos to come up with the recent best.*

CIRCUIT TRAINING

STEP REEBOK CIRCUIT CHALLENGE

Reebok International Ltd., 55 min., $19.95

Little chance of boredom during this MTV-style production. Instructor Gin Miller alternates from stepping to resistance training at a rapid-fire pace. Tons of arm work. Beginners will have to watch closely to keep up, since not all levels can be seen at the same time.

■ **Nice touches:** Live music beats the canned tunes of most videos.

■ **You'll like it if**: You need motivation. Miller's energy is infectious.

BEGINNING YOGA

KATHY SMITH NEW YOGA

BodyVision, 60 min., $19.95

Excellent combination of styles, stunning futuristic backgrounds, and explicit instructions. May put hard-core yoga buffs to sleep, though.

■ **Nice touches:** The standing exercises come first, then floor work, so no jumping back and forth.

■ **You'll like it if**: You like your yoga without a lot of spiritual jargon.

ADVANCED YOGA

ALI MacGRAW YOGA MIND & BODY

Warner Home Video, 55 min., $19.98

Instructor Erich Schiffmann offers a good mix of postures, while MacGraw and others demonstrate them. Meditative and relaxing, but even yoga veterans may find some of the postures to be a challenge.

■ **Nice touches:** Exquisite video images shot in a white-sand desert.

■ **You'll like it if**: You're experienced and up for a rigorous workout.

AEROBICS PLUS TONING

DONNA RICHARDSON BACK TO BASICS

Video Treasures, 65 min., $19.98

Few production frills, but Richardson's choreography is easy to follow and fun. The toning portion, composed of traditional calisthenics, covers both high- and low-impact variations.

■ **Nice touches:** You can do two of the four segments if pressed for time.

■ **You'll like it if**: You seek an excellent aerobics class experience.

STEP AEROBICS

DONNA RICHARDSON STEP & AWESOME ABS

Video Treasures, 60 min., $19.98

Easy to medium-hard variation on classic stepping with serious ab-crunching at the end.

■ **Nice touches:** Filmed outdoors overlooking majestic Mexican ruins.

■ **You'll like it if**: You want to learn basics or prefer simple choreography.

BEST ABDOMINAL WORKOUT

TAMILEE WEBB ABS ABS ABS

BodyVision, 45 min., $14.95

Three-part program ranges from easy to hard. Webb concisely provides unusual variations on abdominals theme.

■ **Nice touches:** Modifications for all fitness levels—even ab aficionados won't be bored.

■ **You'll like it if**: You are looking for the secret to washboard abs.

HEALTHY EATING

NUTRITION

THE ABC'S OF ALPHABET SOUP

How to read the new food labels and the rules that go with them

The government says its new food labeling regulations were established to cut consumer confusion about nutrition. But all of those coded abbreviations and numbers on the new labels can add up to aggravation for many consumers who are just trying to figure out what they should be eating.

Don't despair. Decoding the nutritional information on your cereal box or soup can is simple once you understand the logic behind the label. Let these tips be your guide.

First, forget about Recommended Daily Allowances and U.S. Recommended Daily Allowances. (Who really knew the difference, anyway?) They are still considered sound guidelines for a healthy diet, but they are no longer listed on the labels required by the federal government.

The new version of the Recommended Daily Allowance is the Daily Value, or DV. There are two kinds of DVs, although you can't tell by looking. The difference is that the first group is a recommended maximum, and the second group is a recommended minimum. The first group includes things that most people have no trouble finding in their diets: worrisome things like saturated fat, cholesterol, and sodium, as well as good things like fiber, protein, and carbohydrates. The second group includes the vitamins and minerals that many Americans just don't seem to get in their diets in sufficient quantities.

For the first group, the label might indicate that one serving of canned macaroni and cheese contains 300 milligrams of sodium. The next column—the DV—puts that serving into nutritional context. In this case, one serving equals 13 percent of the DV for sodium. Eat eight cans and you've had your sodium for the day.

Daily Values for cholesterol, sodium, and potassium are the same for everyone, regardless of individual calorie needs, but in some cases the DV may not be entirely accurate. That's because the DVs in this first group assume a diet of 2,000 calories a day—about the amount needed by a woman in her 20s. But differences in age and activity require different caloric intakes. To get a more specific reading, you have to figure out how many calories you need every day and do the math in the store (see "The Food Label at a Glance," page 170).

The second group of Daily Values does not change at all. Everybody needs vitamins and minerals. The amounts are based on

THE FOOD LABEL AT A GLANCE

The FDA's new food label, established in 1994, contains an up-to-date, easy-to-use nutrition information guide and is required on almost all packaged foods. It serves as an aid in planning a healthy diet for you and your family.

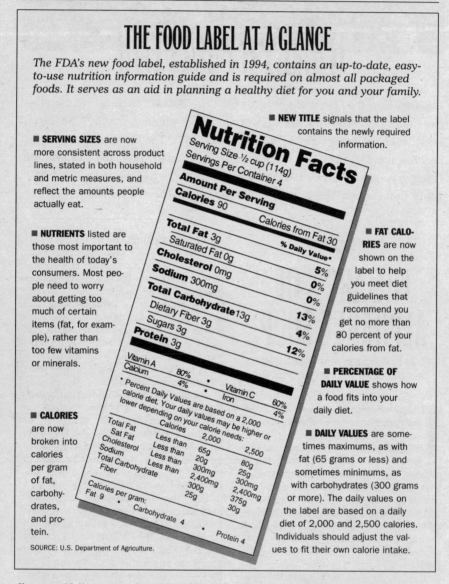

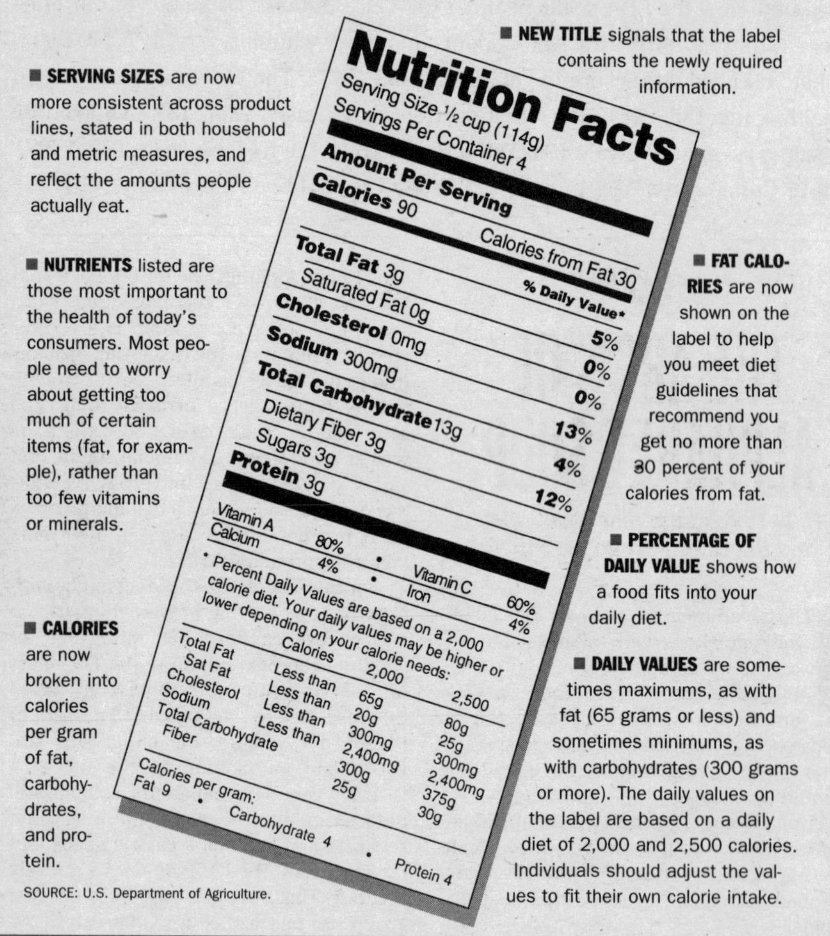

■ SERVING SIZES are now more consistent across product lines, stated in both household and metric measures, and reflect the amounts people actually eat.
■ NUTRIENTS listed are those most important to the health of today's consumers. Most people need to worry about getting too much of certain items (fat, for example), rather than too few vitamins or minerals.
■ CALORIES are now broken into calories per gram of fat, carbohydrates, and protein.
■ NEW TITLE signals that the label contains the newly required information.
■ FAT CALORIES are now shown on the label to help you meet diet guidelines that recommend you get no more than 30 percent of your calories from fat.
■ PERCENTAGE OF DAILY VALUE shows how a food fits into your daily diet.
■ DAILY VALUES are sometimes maximums, as with fat (65 grams or less) and sometimes minimums, as with carbohydrates (300 grams or more). The daily values on the label are based on a daily diet of 2,000 and 2,500 calories. Individuals should adjust the values to fit their own calorie intake.
Nutrition Facts
Serving Size ½ cup (114g)
Servings Per Container 4
Amount Per Serving
Calories 90
Calories from Fat 30
% Daily Value*
Total Fat 3g 5%
Saturated Fat 0g 0%
Cholesterol 0mg 0%
Sodium 300mg 13%
Total Carbohydrate 13g 4%
Dietary Fiber 3g 12%
Sugars 3g
Protein 3g
Vitamin A 80% • Vitamin C 60%
Calcium 4% • Iron 4%
* Percent Daily Values are based on a 2,000 calorie diet. Your daily values may be higher or lower depending on your calorie needs:
Calories 2,000 2,500
Total Fat Less than 65g 80g
Sat Fat Less than 20g 25g
Cholesterol Less than 300mg 300mg
Sodium Less than 2,400mg 2,400mg
Total Carbohydrate 300g 375g
Fiber 25g 30g
Calories per gram:
Fat 9 • Carbohydrate 4 • Protein 4

SOURCE: U.S. Department of Agriculture.

dietary guidelines set up by the U.S. Food and Drug Administration in the 1970s. Although Daily Values have been established for all vitamins, only calcium, iron, vitamin A, and vitamin C are listed, because those are the vitamins and minerals most lacking in the American diet. Of course, manufacturers can voluntarily list other vitamins if they want to, and they usually do. Pages 178 and 183 list Daily Values for vitamins and minerals.

As you peruse food labels, remember this: FDA officials stress that the new Daily Values are not intended to be taken as rigid nutritional requirements for a daily diet. Instead, consumers should use them as reference points to help them evaluate their dietary needs.

PACKAGING

WHEN THE ROAST IS EXTRA-LEAN

The FDA spells out what qualities a food must have to be healthy

"Healthy" no longer is in the eye of the beholder, at least when it comes to the nutritional claims trumpeted across the labels of so-called health foods. As part of the nutrition labeling law recently passed by Congress, the U.S. Food and Drug Administration has actually defined what different foods must contain if food manufacturers wish to claim that their products are high in fiber, low in fat, or just plain healthy. For food manufacturers to simply label a product as "healthy," they must show that the food:

- Meets FDA standards for being low in fat, saturated fat, sodium, and cholesterol.

- Contains at least 10 percent of the FDA's recommended daily value of either vitamin A, vitamin C, iron, calcium, protein, or fiber.

- In the case of frozen dinners, meets the FDA's standards for being low in fat, saturated fat, sodium, and cholesterol, and contains at least 10 percent of the recommended daily value of three of the nutrients specified above.

- Meets the FDA's definition of extra-lean in the case of fresh meat, game meat, or seafood (see definitions below).

The FDA gets even more precise when it comes to specific claims such as "no added sugar" and "fat-free." A food labeled "low-fat food" must not be just low in fat, for instance, but 25 percent lower in fat than the "reference" food to which it is being compared.

VITAL INGREDIENTS

How much is too much? How little is too little? The FDA recommends the following for a healthy diet, assuming a daily intake of 2,000 calories—about the amount required by a young woman.

FOOD COMPONENT	MAXIMUM DAILY VALUE
Fat	65 g
Saturated fatty acids	20 g
Cholesterol	300 mg
Total carbohydrate	300 g
Fiber	25 g
Sodium	2,400 mg
Potassium	3,500 mg
Protein*	50 g

*The DV for protein does not apply to certain populations; for these groups, FDA nutrition experts recommend the following:

Children 1 to 4 years:	16 g
Infants less than 1 year:	14 g
Pregnant women:	60 g
Nursing mothers:	65 g

NUTRIENT	MINIMUM DAILY VALUE
Vitamin A	5,000 International Units (IU)
Vitamin C	60 mg
Thiamin	1.5 mg
Riboflavin	1.7 mg
Niacin	20 mg
Calcium	1.0 g
Iron	18 mg
Vitamin D	400 IU
Vitamin E	30 IU
Vitamin B 6	2 mg
Folic acid	0.4 mg
Vitamin B 12	6 micrograms (mcg)
Phosphorus	1 g
Iodine	150 mcg
Magnesium	400 mg
Zinc	15 mg
Copper	2 mg
Biotin	0.3 mg
Pantothenic acid	10 mg

SOURCE: U.S. Food and Drug Administration.

FIGURING YOUR ENERGY NEEDS

Sometimes you can eat your cake and have it, too

Food is fuel. When your body breaks it down, it creates the energy that your body uses to walk to the fridge for a snack, run a marathon, or hold this book in your hands.

Calories are what nutritionists use to measure how much energy is stored in that food in your fridge. To be exact, 1 calorie equals the amount of energy it would take to raise the temperature of 1 kilogram (2.2 pounds) of water 1 degree Celsius (1.8 degrees Fahrenheit). Fats yield 9 calories per gram, for instance, and carbohydrates provide about 4.

Why, you may wonder, are we told to stay away from fatty food? Couldn't we all use a little more pep? Unfortunately, it doesn't quite work that way. If you are a moderately active person, you probably require about 15 calories for every pound you weigh to give you all the energy you need to get through your daily routine. Your body, marvel of efficiency that it is, will store any caloric intake above that amount for a rainy day.

The problem is, your body stores those calories in the form of fat—a lumpy but efficient sort of battery system. To make matters worse, a major new study has shown that when you do lose weight, your metabolism adjusts by burning calories more slowly, making it even harder not to regain that lost weight.

The bottom line: If you store an extra 3,500 calories of energy somewhere, that somewhere is going to gain about a pound of body fat.

WHO NEEDS WHAT CALORIES?

The energy you expend regulates how much energy you should take in. Light activity like housecleaning, carpentry, restaurant work, or golfing requires fewer calories than moderate activity like weeding, tennis, and dancing, or heavy activity like manual digging and football.

CATEGORY	AGE	CALORIES PER DAY		
		Light activity	Moderate activity	Heavy activity
CHILDREN	4–6		1,800	
	7–10		2,000	
MALES	11–14		2,500	
	15–18		3,000	
	19–24	2,700	3,000	3,600
	25–50	3,000	3,200	4,000
	51+		2,300 [2]	
FEMALES [1]	11–18		2,200	
	19–24	2,000	2,100	2,600
	25–50	2,200	2,300	2,800
	51+		1,900 [2]	

1. Pregnant women in second or third trimesters should add 300 calories; nursing mothers, 500.
2. Based on light to moderate activity.

SOURCE: National Academy of Sciences.

EXPERT Q&A

A CHOLESTEROL PRIMER

Keep an eye on the lipoproteins and you'll keep your arteries clear

If you're confused about the difference between "good" and "bad" cholesterol, you have lots of company. Here, Dr. Dearing Johns, a cardiologist at the University of Virginia School of Medicine, explains how the biochemistry of cholesterol works and what the tests mean.

■ What is cholesterol?

Cholesterol is a pearly-white, waxy substance found in animal fats and oils. It is found throughout the body but is produced primarily by the liver. Cholesterol circulates in the blood, commonly in association with other saturated and unsaturated fats, and can be either beneficial or harmful. For instance, it is necessary for making cell membranes and many important hormones. However, cholesterol may also form gallstones and harmful deposits in blood vessels.

■ Why is it dangerous?

Too much cholesterol in the bloodstream leads to atherosclerosis, which is the build-up of cholesterol and fats in the walls of blood vessels, causing permanent blood vessel damage and blockage of blood flow. Blocked blood flow to the heart will cause a heart attack and death of heart muscle. Lack of blood flow to the brain will cause a stroke and permanent brain damage. Similarly, obstruction of the blood supply to any vital organ will lead to impairment of its normal function. For instance, poor circulation to the kidney may result in the need for dialysis or kidney transplantation, and reduction in blood flow to the eye can lead to blindness.

Just as important as the cholesterol content of the body is whether or not cholesterol is oxidized. Oxidation is an energy-consuming process in which hydrogen ions are removed from a substance. During this process, high-energy molecules, known as free radicals, may damage blood vessels and other tissue. The oxidation of cholesterol in the body increases the likelihood of tissue injury and damage to blood vessel walls.

■ Is there a difference between dietary cholesterol and blood cholesterol?

Most of the cholesterol in the body is formed by the liver, which is capable of producing (and degrading) all the cholesterol the body needs. Usually, about two-thirds of the body cholesterol is produced by the liver and only one-third is derived from the diet. Reducing dietary cholesterol will lower blood cholesterol.

However, blood cholesterol is reduced more efficiently if the intake of saturated fat is decreased. That's because saturated fat slows elimination of cholesterol. Unsaturated fats signal the liver to speed up its elimination of cholesterol. By judiciously altering the proportion of unsaturated fat to saturated fat in your diet, you can protect the body from atherosclerosis

FACT FILE:

LEAN VS. FAT

■ *Cholesterol and fat are not the same thing. In fact, fatty meat and lean meat contain about the same amount of cholesterol. That's because cholesterol is found primarily in the tissue. But before you start back on a diet of greasy burgers, remember this: Studies show that the high saturated fat content in fatty meat can still increase cholesterol levels once it is in your system.*

(blood vessel damage from cholesterol and fats) very effectively.

What makes fats saturated or unsaturated?

Fats in the body are usually in the form of long chains of carbon atoms connected by double or single bonds. A single-bond connection is considered a "saturated" bond (there is no room for additional binding). A double bond connection is an "unsaturated" bond that is potentially able to bond other molecules. Unsaturated fats can be polyunsaturated (multiple double-bond connections) or monounsaturated (mostly single bonds with one double bond).

Saturated fats, such as butter and lard, tend to be solid at room temperature. Saturated fats come from animal products and are seen on the outside or form the "marbling" of meats. Coconut and palm oil are also heavy in saturated fats.

Unsaturated fats are usually liquid at room temperature and are derived from plant sources such as safflower oil, sunflower seed oil, and corn oil. Olive oil and cannola oil are monounsaturated oils.

How can some cholesterol be harmful and some good for you?

Cholesterol does not dissolve in water-based fluids such as blood. In order to circulate in the blood stream, cholesterol and fats are surrounded by protein, thus forming larger cholesterol-rich particles called lipoproteins. Most of the circulating cholesterol is packaged in particles called low-density lipoproteins, or LDL-cholesterol

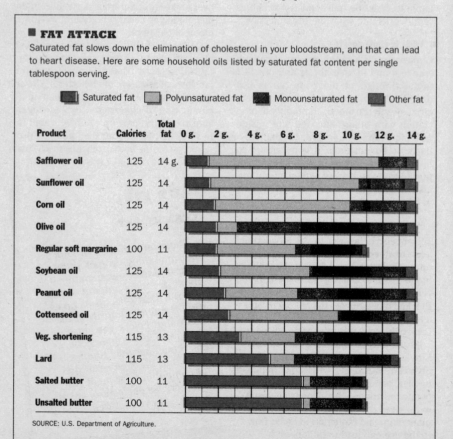

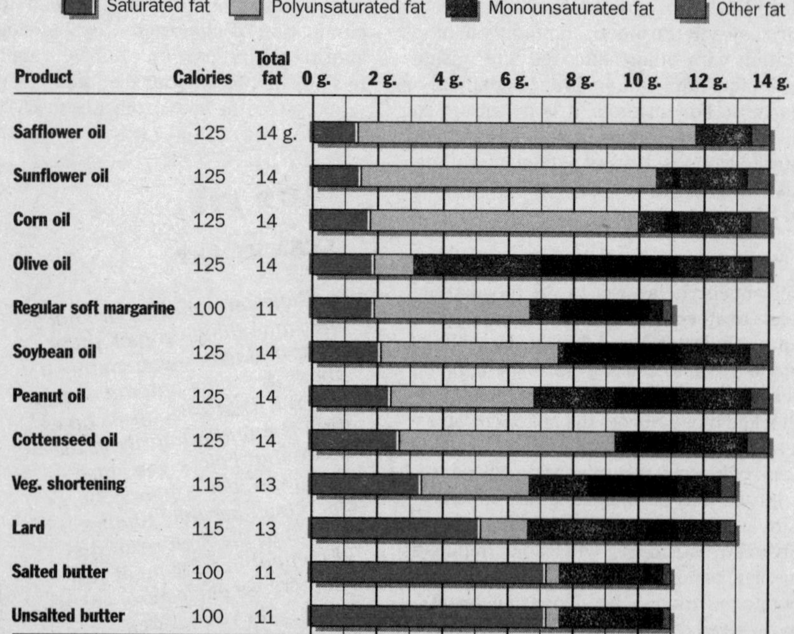

particles. LDL-cholesterol is often called "bad" cholesterol because it leads to clogged arteries and impaired circulation. High-density lipoprotein, or HDL-cholesterol, is often called "good" or "cardioprotective" cholesterol because it is the cholesterol particle that is destined for elimination by the liver.

The more the HDL-cholesterol, the less the chance for cholesterol deposits in the blood vessel walls and the lower the risk of impaired circulation due to blood vessel blockage. Measurement of total cholesterol includes LDL-cholesterol and HDL-cholesterol. Thus it is important, when measuring blood cholesterol, to break down the total cholesterol value into LDL-cholesterol values and HDL-cholesterol values.

How much cholesterol is unhealthy?

That is a difficult question because it depends on a person's innate (genetic) ability to handle cholesterol and fats as well as on other factors that place a person at high risk for heart disease, such as the presence of cigarette smoking, high blood pressure, or family members with heart disease at a young age. If there are no such adverse risk factors, a total cholesterol of less than 200 mg/dl is considered desirable. A total cholesterol between 200 and 239 mg/dl is considered borderline high and greater than 240 mg/dl is definitely too high.

Also important is how high the HDL-cholesterol is. An HDL-cholesterol of less than 35 mg/dl is associated with increased risk of heart disease, especially in women. An HDL-cholesterol above 60 mg/dl confers a protective effect. The lower the LDL-cholesterol, the better. With no risk factors, an LDL-cholesterol less than 160 mg/dl is adequate, but below 130 mg/dl is desirable. If a person already has coronary artery disease (e.g., if they have had a heart attack), then the LDL-cholesterol goal should be less than 100 mg/dl.

The best way to limit high cholesterol is to reduce the total fat intake and to aim to have most dietary fat in the form of monounsaturated or polyunsaturated fats. The American Heart Association recom-

BUTTER VS. MARGARINE

Margarine is marginally better than butter—but it isn't great

Nutrition researcher Martijn Katan calls butter "the cow's revenge." Made from animal fat, its high saturated fat content raises blood cholesterol levels and increases the risk of heart disease. It should only be used occasionally.

Margarine is better, but only relatively. Although it comes from vegetable oils rather than animal fats, the hydrogenation process used to turn it into a solid creates trans-fatty acids, a hybrid that has been found in recent tests to elevate low-density lipoprotein cholesterol (the so-called "bad" cholesterol) to the same extent as saturated fats. What's more, trans-fatty acids appear to lower high-density lipoprotein cholesterol ("good" cholesterol), thereby limiting one of the body's best natural defenses against heart disease.

Even so, margarine remains healthier than butter because it contains no dietary cholesterol and has a lower overall percentage of cholesterol-raising fats. Tub or squeeze varieties are the healthiest because they are the least hydrogenated and so have the least trans-fatty acids.

Healthiest may not seem so desirable if you're using soft margarine to bake cookies. To keep fat content down, these spreads substitute water for fat. But cookie makers have discovered that the more watery spreads make cookies spread while baking and give them a flabby texture and bland taste. To avoid such untoward results, the fat content should be 60 percent or higher, say baking experts. Check the package for percentage fat.

DO-IT-YOURSELF CHOLESTEROL TESTING

Home test kits provide results but following the directions is essential

Home test kits for diabetes, pregnancy, and ovulation have been joined on the market by do-it-yourself kits for testing blood cholesterol levels. The first cholesterol self-test kit was introduced by Johnson & Johnson under the trade name Advanced Care Cholesterol Test and is available off-the-shelf in most pharmacies at a suggested retail price of $15 to $20.

About one-fifth of all adult Americans have cholesterol levels that are considered medically worrisome, according to the National Center for Health Statistics. Yet only one-third know what their cholesterol count actually is. The new home test provides a relatively convenient way to determine when a person's cholesterol level is elevated enough to warrant consulting a physician.

The test, which uses a simple push-button device to prick the finger and draw a drop or two of blood, takes 12 to 15 minutes to complete. When the directions are followed, the manufacturer says, it is 97 percent accurate, which is comparable in accuracy to the readings of total cholesterol made by doctors and laboratories.

The Johnson & Johnson self-test has one major drawback, however. Although it provides a quick overall cholesterol count, it lacks the sophistication to break down a person's cholesterol composition into "good" and "bad" cholesterol.

High-density lipoproteins (HDL) are known as "good" cholesterol because they draw fatty deposits away from the arteries, while low-density lipoproteins (LDL) contribute to the development of plaque along artery walls. A total cholesterol reading of 200 mg/dl is high enough to warrant a follow-up consultation with a doctor, but until a doctor has established what your HDL and LDL levels are, it is difficult to determine your true cardiovascular health.

mends no more than 30 percent of total daily calories be derived from fats (the average American diet is 40 percent to 50 percent fat). Of these fats, only 10 percent should be saturated fats.

■ How effective are cholesterol-lowering drugs?

Cholesterol-lowering drugs will reduce cholesterol in most people. LDL-cholesterol can be cut between 15 percent and 40 percent, depending on which drug is selected. Many of these drugs also will raise the HDL-cholesterol by 5 percent to 25 percent. Your doctor will use your cholesterol profile to guide selection of the most appropriate cholesterol-lowering drug.

Newer cholesterol-lowering drugs, called HMG-CoA reductase inhibitors, actually prevent cholesterol production in the liver. These drugs lower LDL-cholesterol by 20 percent to 40 percent and raise HDL-cholesterol up to 15 percent in some people. These drugs (Mevacor, Zocor, Pravachol, and Lescol) are very effective, but close monitoring is necessary to prevent serious muscle and liver damage.

Several studies have shown that these agents can reduce death from heart disease. More recent studies also show that they slow progression of atherosclerosis and blockages of coronary arteries, and in some cases, actually seem to reverse blockages previously seen in blood vessels.

Overall, it is estimated that for every 1 percent reduction in LDL-cholesterol, the risk of coronary heart disease is reduced 2 percent.

NUTRIENTS

VEGETABLE VIM AND VIGOR

The potency of antioxidants is only just becoming appreciated

Imagine what life would be like without color. Sports cars wouldn't be red, denim wouldn't be blue, and spinach wouldn't be green. And if the chemicals that make most vegetables green weren't around, you'd be likely to find yourself a lot more susceptible to several serious diseases, including heart disease and a common form of blindness.

The chemicals are called carotenoids, and like vitamins, they belong to a category of compounds known as antioxidants. Antioxidants have been widely credited with having amazing effects when it comes to fighting off chronic disease and aging. They are said to squelch the body's production of free radicals, which are oxygen molecules missing an electron.

Scientists have long suspected that chronic diseases like heart disease and cancer may be triggered when free radicals try to replace "AWOL" electrons by stealing from neighboring molecules, resulting in cell breakdown and the onset of disease.

A 1994 study in the *New England Journal of Medicine* unexpectedly questioned these assumptions, however. When supplied as dietary supplements, neither beta-carotene, which is the best-known of the carotenoids, nor Vitamin E appeared to protect heavy smokers from lung cancer. The results of the study even suggested that beta-carotene might contribute to higher rates of lung cancer in heavy smokers.

But a more recent study by researchers at the University of North Carolina and University of Tennessee and published in the *Journal of the American Medical Association* has provided new evidence that carotenoids do cut the risk of heart disease.

Unlike the earlier Harvard study, which measured only the effects of beta-carotene and Vitamin E taken as supplements in pill form, the North Carolina–Tennessee study measured the presence of all carotenoids in the bloodstream and found that among nonsmokers, those with the highest carotenoid levels were 70 percent less likely to suffer a heart attack than those with the lowest carotenoid levels. Among those who smoke, the benefits were less dramatic but still significant.

A third recent Harvard study found that consuming vegetables rich in carotenoids seemed to lower substantially the risk of developing a form of blindness common among the elderly.

Scientists remain uncertain which carotenoids or antioxidants in vegetables may supply the protective effects. They do know enough, however, to urge that your diet should include hearty daily servings of vegetables and fruits.

FACT FILE:

SELECTED SOURCES:

Beta-Carotene

Apricots	Asparagus
Broccoli	Cantaloupe
Carrots	Cherries
Mangoes	Peaches
Peas	Spinach
Tomatoes	Tangerines

Vitamin E

Broccoli	Cabbage
Corn oil	Egg yolk
Fish	Meats
Nuts	Olive oil
Soybean oil	Spinach
Sunflower oil	Wheat germ

EXPERT LIST

THE VITAMIN SHELF

Your body needs vitamins to form blood cells, build strong bones, and regulate the nervous system, but it can't generate them on its own. Here are the FDA's daily values for essential vitamins and the foods that contain them.

VITAMIN A

DAILY VALUE: 5,000 international units	
1 oz. cheddar cheese:	300 IU
1 scrambled egg:	420 IU
1 cup nonfat milk:	500 IU
1 nectarine:	1,000 IU
1 piece watermelon:	1,760 IU

■ **What it does:** Aids in good vision; helps build and maintain skin, teeth, bones, and mucous membranes. Deficiency can increase susceptibility to infectious disease.

■ **What it may do:** May inhibit the development of breast cancer; may increase resistance to infection in children.

■ **Food sources:** Milk, eggs, liver, cheese, fish oil. Plus fruits and vegetables that contain beta-carotene. You need not consume preformed vitamin A if you eat foods rich in beta-carotene.

■ **Supplementation:** Not recommended, since toxic in high doses.

VITAMIN B1 (THIAMIN)

DAILY VALUE:	1.5 milligrams
1 slice enriched white bread:	0.12 mg
3 oz. fried liver:	0.18 mg
1 cup black beans:	0.43 mg
1 packet instant oatmeal:	0.53 mg
1 oz. dry-hull sunflower seeds:	0.65 mg

■ **What it does::** Helps convert carbohydrates into energy. Necessary for healthy brain, nerve cells, and heart function.

■ **Food sources:** Whole grains, enriched grain products, beans, meats, liver, wheat germ, nuts, fish, brewer's yeast.

■ **Supplementation:** Not necessary, not recommended.

VITAMIN B2 (RIBOFLAVIN)

DAILY VALUE:	1.7 milligrams
1 oz. chicken:	0.2 mg
1 bagel:	0.2 mg
1 cup milk:	0.4 mg
1 cup cooked spinach:	0.42 mg

■ **What it does:** Helps cells convert carbohydrates into energy. Essential for growth, production of red blood cells, and health of skin and eyes.

■ **Food sources:** Dairy products, liver, meat, chicken, fish, enriched grain products, leafy greens, beans, nuts, eggs, almonds.

■ **Supplementation:** Not necessary and not recommended.

VITAMIN B3 (NIACIN)

DAILY VALUE:	20 milligrams
1 slice enriched bread:	1.0 mg
3 oz. baked flounder or sole:	1.7 mg
1 oz. roasted peanuts:	4.2 mg
1/2 chicken breast:	14.7 mg

■ **What it does:** Aids in release of energy from foods. Helps maintain healthy skin, nerves, and digestive system.

■ **What it may do:** Megadoses lower high blood cholesterol.

■ **Food sources:** Nuts, meat, fish, chicken, liver, enriched grain products, dairy products, peanut butter, brewer's yeast.

■ **Supplementation:** Large doses may be prescribed by doctor to lower blood cholesterol. May cause flushing, liver damage, and irregular heart beat.

VITAMIN B5 (PANTOTHENIC ACID)

DAILY VALUE:	7 milligrams
8 oz. nonfat milk:	0.81 mg

■ EXPERT LIST

1 large egg:	0.86 mg
8 oz. low-fat fruit-flavored yogurt:	1.0 mg
3 1/2 oz. liver:	4.57 mg

■ **What it does:** Vital for metabolism, production of essential body chemicals.
■ **Food sources:** Whole grains, beans, milk, eggs, liver.
■ **Supplementation:** Not necessary, not recommended. May cause diarrhea.

VITAMIN B6 (PYROXIDINE)

DAILY VALUE:	**2.0 milligrams**
1 bran muffin:	0.11 mg
1 cup lima beans:	0.3 mg
3 oz. cooked bluefin tuna:	0.45 mg
1 banana:	0.7 mg

■ **What it does:** Vital in chemical reactions of proteins, amino acids. Helps maintain brain function and form red blood cells.
■ **What it may do:** May help to boost immunity in the elderly.
■ **Food sources:** Whole grains, bananas, meat, beans, nuts, wheat germ, brewer's yeast, chicken, fish, liver.
■ **Supplementation:** Large doses can cause numbness and other neurological disorders.

VITAMIN B12

DAILY VALUE:	**6.0 micrograms**
1/2 chicken breast:	0.29 mcg
1 large egg:	0.77 mcg
1 cup nonfat milk:	0.93 mcg
3 1/2 oz. lean beef flank:	3.05 mcg

■ **What it does:** Necessary for development of red blood cells. Maintains normal functioning of nervous system.
■ **Food sources:** Liver, beef, pork, poultry, eggs, milk, cheese, yogurt, shellfish, fortified cereals, and fortified soy products.
■ **Supplementation:** Strict vegetarians may need supplements.

EXPERT TIPS

FIVE MYTHS THAT IT'S TIME TO BURY

Though their benefits are substantial, vitamins aren't elixirs. The U.S. Public Health Service advises that you beware of these vitamin myths.

Myth: *Vitamins give you "pep" and "energy."*
Fact: Vitamins yield no calories. They, of themselves, provide no extra pep or vitality beyond normal expectations, nor do they provide unusual levels of well-being.

Myth: *Timing of vitamin intake is crucial.*
Fact: There is no medical or scientific basis for this contention.

Myth: *Vitamin C "protects" against the common cold.*
Fact: Extensive clinical research fails to support this.

Myth: *The more vitamins the better.*
Fact: Taking excessive vitamins is a complete waste, both in money and effect. In fact, excess amounts of any of several different vitamins can even be harmful.

Myth: *You cannot get enough vitamins from the usual foods you eat.*
Fact: Anyone who eats a reasonably varied diet should normally never need supplemental vitamins.

■ EXPERT LIST

VITAMIN C (ASCORBIC ACID)

DAILY VALUE:	**60 micrograms**
1 orange:	70 mcg
1 green pepper:	95 mcg
1 cup cooked broccoli:	97 mcg
1 cup fresh orange juice:	124 mcg

■ **What it does:** Helps promote healthy gums and teeth; aids in iron absorption; maintains normal connective tissue; helps in the healing of wounds. As an antioxidant, it combats the adverse effects of free radicals.
■ **What it may do:** May reduce the risk of lung, esophagus, stomach, and bladder cancers, as well as coronary artery disease; may prevent or delay cataracts and slow the aging process.
■ **Food sources:** Citrus fruits and juices, strawberries, tomatoes, peppers, broccoli, potatoes, kale, cauliflower, cantaloupe, brussels sprouts.
■ **Supplementation:** 250–500 mgs a day for smokers and anyone not consuming several fruits or vegetables rich in C daily. Larger doses may cause diarrhea.

VITAMIN D

DAILY VALUE:	**400 international units**
1 oz. cheddar cheese:	3 IU
1 large egg:	27 IU
1 cup nonfat milk:	100 IU

■ **What it does:** Strengthens bones and teeth by aiding the absorption of calcium. Helps maintain phosphorus in the blood.
■ **What it may do:** May reduce risk of osteoporosis, forestall breast and colon cancers.
■ **Food sources:** Milk, fish oil, fortified margarine; also produced by the body in response to sunlight.
■ **Supplementation:** 400 IU for vegetarians, the elderly, those who don't drink milk or get sun exposure. Toxic in high doses.

VITAMIN E

DAILY VALUE:	**30 international units**
1/2 cup boiled brussel sprouts:	1.02 IU
1/2 cup boiled spinach:	2.7 IU
1 oz. almonds:	8.5 IU

■ **What it does:** Helps form red blood cells. Combats adverse effects of free radicals.
■ **What it may do:** May cut the risk of esophageal or stomach cancers and coronary artery disease; may prevent or delay cataracts; may boost immunity in elderly.
■ **Food sources:** Vegetable oil, nuts, margarine, wheat germ, leafy greens, seeds, almonds, olives, asparagus.
■ **Supplementation:** 200–800 IU advised for everybody; you can't get that much from food, especially on a low-fat diet.

BIOTIN (VITAMIN B)

DAILY VALUE:	**300 micrograms**
1 cup cooked enriched noodles:	4 mcg
1 large egg:	11 mcg
1 oz. almonds:	23 mcg

■ **What it does:** Important in metabolism of protein, carbohydrates, and fats.
■ **Food sources:** Eggs, milk, liver, mushrooms, bananas, tomatoes, whole grains.
■ **Supplementation:** Not recommended.

FOLATE (VITAMIN B)

(Also called Folacin or folic acid)

DAILY VALUE:	**400 micrograms**
1 orange:	47 mcg
1 cup raw spinach:	108 mcg
1 cup baked beans:	122 mcg
1 cup asparagus:	176 mcg

■ **What it does:** Important in synthesis of DNA, in normal growth, protein metabolism. Reduces risk of certain birth defects, notably spina bifida and encephaly.
■ **What it may do:** May reduce the risk of cervical cancer.
■ **Food sources:** Leafy greens, wheat germ, liver, beans, whole grains, broccoli, asparagus, citrus fruit, and juices.
■ **Supplementation:** 400 mcg, from food or pills, for all women who may become pregnant, to help prevent birth defects.

SOURCE: U.S. Food and Drug Administration; *Food Values of Portions Commonly Used*, Jean A. P. Pennington, Harper & Row, 1980.

MINERALS

THE IMPORTANCE OF CALCIUM

You probably need a lot more than you're getting

Most Americans don't meet the recommended dietary allowances for calcium intake set by the National Research Council. What's more, the NRC's calcium standards are themselves too low and are likely to be revised in the next three years, experts believe. In fact, an advisory panel of the National Institutes of Health recently urged that the RDA for calcium be increased to as much as 1,200 milligrams a day for children from 1 to 10 years old to as much as 1,500 milligrams a day for adolescents, young adults, and post-menopausal women, and to 1,000 milligrams a day for women from 25 to 50 years old. That represents increases of 25 to 50 percent over the standards established by the NRC in the past.

Such boosts are necessary, the panel of experts said, to lower the risk of osteoporosis, the brittle bone disease that is crippling 25 million Americans, especially postmenopausal women. The new recommendations are based on research showing that raising calcium levels to build greater bone mass, particularly in adolescents and older women, plays a critical role in fighting osteoporosis.

For both men and women, peak bone density is achieved during late adolescence. Around 35 years of age, bones begin to thin for both sexes. This process accelerates for women when estrogen levels drop at menopause. During their lifetimes, women lose about one-third of their bone mass while men lose about one-fifth. The more bone mass one develops as an adolescent, the more protected one will be from the inevitable loss that occurs with age. In

THE NUTRITIONAL POWER OF BANANAS

Potassium shows its promise in fighting osteoporosis

Calcium isn't the only mineral that helps fight osteoporosis. A recent study in the *New England Journal of Medicine* suggests that potassium bicarbonate, found in many fruits and vegetables, may greatly enhance the body's ability to retain bone mass and stave off osteoporosis. You should "stock up" on potassium bicarbonate because it's robbed from the bones when you eat meat, says Dr. Anthony Sebastian, leader of the University of California San Francisco study.

The findings, however, are preliminary. Potassium bicarbonate supplements are neither suggested nor readily available. It's also not yet clear which foods are the best sources of the substance. But Dr. Sebastian's recommendations are in line with those of many other nutrition experts: eat more fruits and vegetables and less meat.

Researchers are finding other potential potassium benefits as well. Potassium has long been known for the role it plays in muscle, nerve, heart, and kidney functions, but several recent studies suggest that it may also help reduce blood pressure by relaxing blood-vessel linings so that blood can flow more easily. No cause-and-effect relationship has been clearly established, but researchers are impressed enough with their findings to urge that you include plenty of bananas and other potassium-rich foods in your diet.

one recent study of adolescent girls, raising calcium intake with supplements from 80 percent of the current recommended dietary allowance to 110 percent increased bone mass by more than 1 percent per year during adolescent growth. In another study, this time of men and women ages 50 to 79, those in the top third in terms of calcium consumption suffered 60 percent fewer hip fractures over the next 14 years than did the others.

Estrogen replacement therapy can be of great help to older women at a high risk of developing osteoporosis (see related story, page 329). So can raising an older woman's intake of calcium significantly, through either diet or supplements.

Moreover, there is much evidence to suggest that calcium may reduce the risk of high blood pressure and high cholesterol levels as well as cut the chances of colon cancer. Colon cancer risk appears even lower when high calcium consumption is accompanied by high intake of vitamin D. Previous medical concern that too much calcium leads to kidney stones now appears unfounded except in the cases of a few men whose bodies overabsorb the mineral.

Meeting the higher calcium requirements now being advanced by experts will take effort. For adolescents and older women, who are being urged to eat 1,500 milligrams of calcium per day, it will take a cup of nonfat yogurt, two glasses of skim milk, two ounces of cheese, and one-third of a cup of fresh, cooked broccoli to reach the threshold.

Relying on natural food sources is preferable because the body absorbs calcium from foods more easily than from supplements, and the effectiveness of the mineral appears to be enhanced by being ingested along with other nutrients in the food, such as vitamin D, potassium, and magnesium.

"Calcium supplements are a viable option," says John P. Bilezikian, chief of endocrinology at Columbia University College of Physicians and Surgeons and chairman of the National Institutes of Health panel that is urging higher calcium standards, "but so are calcium-fortified foods."

WHEN TO PASS THE SALT SHAKER

Sodium in moderation is no problem unless you have high blood pressure

Yes, sodium contributes to high blood pressure—but without sodium, you would die. Your blood is a saline solution that requires sodium to regulate the pressure in your veins and help your body to retain water. Sodium also plays an important role in transporting nerve impulses to the brain.

Nonetheless, several studies have linked high sodium intake to hypertension, and 5 to 10 percent of Americans are classified as "sodium sensitive," meaning that their blood pressure responds directly to changes in sodium intake.

Moderation is the key. The FDA recommends that you consume at least 500 milligrams of sodium a day, but no more than 2,400 milligrams. Most Americans far exceed this limit, however, consuming from 3,000 to 6,000 milligrams daily.

That's not hard to do: Eat three ounces of ham or a cup of chicken noodle soup alone and you ingest about 1,000 milligrams of sodium. And a single cup of Manhattan clam chowder is brimming with about 2,000 milligrams of sodium.

Ironically, common table salt is only 40 percent sodium. The rest is chloride, which also aids in transmitting neural impulses. Still, it only takes seven grams of table salt to max out on your sodium intake for the day, so go easy on the Morton's.

EXPERT LIST

THE MINERAL MINDER

Minerals help your body form bones, regulate the heart, and synthesize enzymes, but experts say too many, or too few, can lead to heart disease, diabetes, or even cancer. Here are the FDA's daily values and where to get them.

CALCIUM

DAILY VALUE:	1 gram
1 cup hard ice cream:	0.18 g
1 cup nonfat milk:	0.3 g
2 oz. cheddar cheese:	0.41 g
8 oz. nonfat yogurt:	0.45 g

■ **What it does:** Helps form strong bones and teeth. Helps regulate heartbeat, muscle contractions, nerve function, and blood clotting.

■ **What it may do:** May reduce the risk of high blood pressure, high cholesterol, and colon cancer.

■ **Food sources:** Milk, cheese, butter and margarine, green vegetables, legumes, nuts, soybean products, hard water.

■ **Supplementation:** Most Americans don't consume enough calcium, but megadoses are not recommended. High intakes may cause constipation and increase some men's risk of urinary stones.

IRON

DAILY VALUE:	18 milligrams
1 slice whole wheat bread:	1 mg
3 scrambled eggs:	2.1 mg
3 oz. lean sirloin steak, broiled:	2.6 mg
3 oz. fried liver:	5.3 mg
1 packet instant oatmeal:	6.7 mg

■ **What it does:** Vital in forming hemoglobin (which carries oxygen in blood) and myoglobin (in muscle).

■ **Food sources:** Red meat, poultry, liver, eggs, fish, whole-grain cereals, and breads.

■ **Supplementation:** Often (but not always) recommended for dieters, endurance athletes, strict vegetarians, menstruating women, pregnant women, infants, and children. Large doses may damage the heart, liver, and pancreas.

PHOSPHORUS

DAILY VALUE:	1 gram
6 scallops:	0.2 g
1 cup nonfat milk:	0.25 g
3 oz. broiled trout:	0.26 g
1 cup tuna salad:	0.28 g
1 cup low-fat cottage cheese:	0.34 g

■ **What it does:** Helps form bones, teeth, cell membranes, and genetic material. Essential for energy production.

■ **Food sources:** Nearly all foods, including red meat, poultry, liver, milk, cheese, butter and margarine, eggs, fish, whole-grain cereals and breads, green and root vegetables, legumes, nuts, and fruit.

■ **Supplementation:** Not recommended. Deficiencies in Americans are virtually unknown. Excessive intake may lower blood calcium level.

POTASSIUM

DAILY VALUE:	3,500 milligrams
1 cup nonfat milk:	406 mg
1 banana:	451 mg
1 baked potato, with skin:	844 mg
1 cup cooked spinach:	839 mg

■ **What it does:** Needed for muscle contraction, nerve impulses, and function of heart and kidneys. Aids in regulation of water balance in cells and blood.

■ EXPERT LIST

■ **What it may do:** May fight osteoporosis and help lower blood pressure.
■ **Food sources:** Unprocessed foods such as fruits, vegetables, and fresh meats.
■ **Supplementation:** Not usually recommended. Take only under a doctor's supervision.

IODINE

DAILY VALUE:	150 micrograms
1 oz. cheddar cheese:	12 mcg
1 tsp. iodized salt:	400 mcg

■ **What it does:** Necessary for thyroid gland function and thus normal cell metabolism. Prevents goiter (enlargement of thyroid).
■ **Food sources:** Milk, cheese, butter and margarine, fish, whole-grain cereals and breads, iodized table salt.
■ **Supplementation:** Not recommended. Widely dispersed in the food supply, so even if you eat little iodized salt, you probably get enough iodine.

MAGNESIUM

DAILY VALUE:	400 milligrams
1 slice pumpernickel bread:	22 mg
1 tbsp. peanut butter:	28 mg
1/2 cup peas:	31 mg
1 baked potato:	55 mg
1/2 cup cooked spinach:	79 mg

■ **What it does:** Aids in bone growth, basic metabolic functions and the functioning of nerves and muscles, including the regulation of normal heart rhythm.
■ **Food sources:** Milk, fish, whole-grain cereals and breads, green vegetables, legumes, nuts, and hard water.
■ **Supplementation:** Not usually recommended. Deficiency is rare.

ZINC

DAILY VALUE:	15 miligrams
8 oz. lowfat fruit yogurt:	1.52 mg
1 cup boiled lentils:	2.5 mg
3.5 oz. roast turkey, dark:	4.4 mg

■ **What it does:** Stimulates enzymes needed for cell division, growth, and repair (wound healing). Helps immune system function properly. Also plays a role in acuity of taste and smell.
■ **Food sources:** Red meat, fish, seafood, eggs, milk, whole-grain cereals and breads, legumes.
■ **Supplementation:** Not recommended, except by a doctor for the few Americans who have low zinc levels.

COPPER

DAILY VALUE:	2 milligrams
2/3 cup seedless raisins:	0.31 mg
1 oz. dry roasted pistachios:	0.34 mg
1/2 cup boiled mushrooms:	0.39 mg

■ **What it does:** Helps in formation of red blood cells. Helps keep the bones, blood vessels, nerves, and immune system healthy.
■ **Food sources:** Red meat, poultry, liver, fish, seafood, whole-grain cereals and breads, green vegetables, legumes, nuts, raisins, mushrooms.
■ **Supplementation:** Not recommended. A balanced diet includes enough copper.

SOURCE: U.S. Food and Drug Administration; *Food Values of Portions Commonly Used,* Jean A. P. Pennington, Harper & Row, 1980.

EXPERT QUOTE

When a person makes a practice of eating whole grains instead of refined foods, and vegetables and fruits in season, they can feel confident that the next time a new nutrient is discovered, they will discover they've been getting it all along.

–Laurel Robinson, author of the cookbook The New Laurel's Kitchen

FOLLOWING THE APPIAN WAY

Pasta, olive oil, and some vino aren't a bad way to keep your heart happy

The Greeks and the Romans have long been celebrated for the genius they displayed in creating everything from temples, arches, and statuary to poetry, drama, and the foundations of democracy. Now, researchers are discovering that these ancient innovators also bequeathed their countrymen a diet that may be as close to nutritionally perfect as the world has ever seen.

The Mediterranean diet, as it is being referred to by both nutritionists and cookbook writers, is long on pastas, breads, and other grains as well as fruits, vegetables, and generous servings of olive oil. It frowns on eating red meat more than a few times per month and urges that poultry, fish, and eggs be limited to no more than a few times per week. It also advocates, controversially, that adults drink a glass or two of wine daily.

Follow such a diet, say researchers at the Harvard School of Public Health, and you are likely to cut substantially your risk of heart disease and cancer, especially of the colon and prostate.

To make the Mediterranean diet easy to understand, the Harvard researchers recently joined with two other prominent groups, the European office of the World Health Organization, and Oldways Preservation & Exchange Trust, a Boston-based nutrition foundation, to issue a revised version of the USDA food pyramid (see graphic below) that highlights the Mediterranean diet's nutritional priorities.

Unlike the USDA pyramid, which places

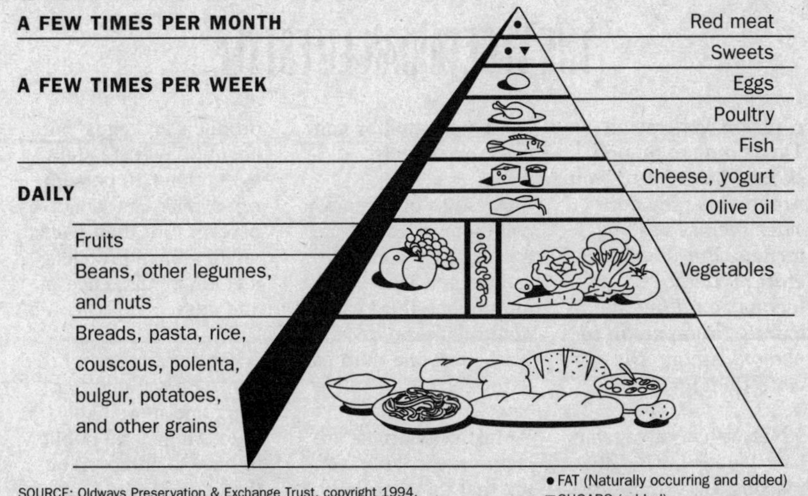

fats, oils, and sweets at its apex to indicate that they are to be used only sparingly, the Mediterranean diet reserves its most disapproving spot at the top of the pyramid for red meat, leaving fat unmentioned. That's because the Mediterranean diet is not low-fat. Under the Med diet's guidelines, in fact, up to 35 percent of calories are allowed to come from fat, although no more than 7 or 8 percent of that may be saturated fat; the USDA pyramid allows only 30 percent fat, but fails to distinguish between saturated and unsaturated fat.

The Mediterranean diet's relatively fat-friendly attitude is explained by the fact that much of its fat comes from olive oil, which means it is mostly monounsaturated. Monounsaturated fat has been repeatedly shown to increase high-density lipoproteins—the "good cholesterol" in the blood—while reducing the body's total cholesterol level. Saturated fat, however, raises the body's blood cholesterol count and boosts the risk of heart disease, yet the USDA pyramid fails to distinguish between saturated and unsaturated fat, a serious flaw as far as Mediterranean diet proponents are concerned.

The Mediterranean diet is not without its critics, to be sure. Its relatively generous fat allowance loads on calories, making obesity more likely, some charge. But the Harvard researchers point out that the body needs some fat for energy and say that regular exercise makes more sense than worrying about an extra splash or two of olive oil.

By far the most controversial aspect of the Mediterranean diet is its recommendation that adults drink a glass or two of wine daily. The dispute pits researchers who have found that having a drink or two a day raises "good cholesterol" and significantly lowers the risk of heart attacks against public health officials who are worried about encouraging alcohol abuse.

As these officials point out, heavy drinkers substantially raise their risks of cirrhosis of the liver, and of mouth, throat, stomach, and colorectal cancer, and heart failure, not to mention the mental impairment of alcoholism. These experts worry that once started on a drinking habit, some drinkers will find it difficult to remain in the "moderate" range, especially those with heavy drinkers in their family histories.

That is a risk, no doubt. But even if you skip that part of the Mediterranean diet menu, there's a lot to be savored in the nutritional choices of the ancient chefs of the Greek Isles and Southern Italy.

THE VEGETARIAN LIFESTYLE

A recent Vegetarian Times *magazine poll shows that 12.4 million Americans now consider themselves vegetarians. But what "vegetarian" actually means can differ significantly from person to person. Among the survey's findings:*

- Nearly half of vegetarians say it's for health reasons. Only 15 percent were motivated by concern for animals.
- One-fifth of those who call themselves vegetarians say they consume red meat at least once a month, one-third eat poultry at least once a week, and one-third eat fish weekly.
- Most vegetarians are lacto-vegetarian, meaning that they eat dairy products and eggs, but about 30 percent shun eggs, about 10 percent reject milk, and about 4 percent turn their backs on all animal products, including milk, cheese, and eggs.
- Vegetarians are more apt to be women than men, and more likely than the general public to have children under the age of 18.

SEAFOOD

A FISH STORY NOT TO IGNORE

Tread carefully when it comes to the catch of the day

Because fish are basically swimming filters, they soak up pesticides, industrial waste, and chemicals that have been dumped into waterways for decades. With more polluted waters than ever, the risk is rising that you'll find a contaminated fish on your dinner plate. Salmonella and scombroid poisoning, which is caused by a histamine produced by bacteria on fish, can also make certain fish unsavory.

Part of the reason that inedible fish are ending up in the grocery store is that there's no government-run process to inspect fish. In fact, fish and shellfish are the only major sources of protein that do not receive comprehensive government inspections for potential contaminations. The $9 billion industry is overseen by a piecemeal system led by the Food and Drug Administration, whose inspectors visit processing plants an average of once every four years.

In a 1991 report issued by the National Academy of Sciences, current safety regulations were deemed "insufficient" and "too limited in frequency and direction to ensure enhanced safety of seafoods." While some efforts to improve seafood handling have been made since then, substantial problems remain.

Freshwater fish are more likely to contain toxic chemicals than fish that spend their lives in the ocean. Because of industrial dumping and air pollution, the Great Lakes have been found to be swimming with polychlorinated biphenyls (PCBs), which are suspected of raising the risk of cancer and birth defects. Residues of DDT, the cancer-causing pesticide banned two decades ago, have been found in Great Lakes whitefish being sold in southern California.

Fish that live in deep, offshore waters, such as cod and haddock, are considered low in chemicals because the areas they live in aren't easily contaminated. But chemicals can be found in saltwater fish that live close to polluted urban shores, or in fish that commute to freshwater. Puget Sound, the Chesapeake Bay, and Santa Monica Bay are all considered risky sources, according to the National Academy of Sciences.

Among ocean-swimming fish, fin fish from tropical or subtropical areas have the most problems. Barracuda, grouper, amerjack, and certain tropical snappers have been linked to scombroid as well as ciguatera—a sometimes-severe disease that affects the nervous system and can cause vomiting and nausea. Neither bacteria is destroyed in the cooking process.

Methyl mercury poisoning from swordfish is a great enough risk that the National Academy of Sciences

FACT FILE:

ONES THAT CAN GET AWAY

■ *The National Academy of Sciences report, Seafood Safety, judged the following seafood to be unsafe at times:*

- Amerjack
- Barracuda
- Raw clams
- The pasty "mustard" in crabs
- Finfish from subtropical waters
- Finfish from tropical waters
- Grouper
- Green-colored tomalley in lobsters
- Mahi-mahi
- Salmon caught in the Great Lakes
- Shellfish (especially raw oysters, mussels, scallops)

recommended that couples who intend to have children in the near future should avoid the fish. Tuna and mahi mahi can also contain methyl mercury in small amounts, but the danger in swordfish is much greater.

The riskiest seafood of all is molluskan shellfish such as oysters, clams, and mussels. The intestines and internal organs of these mollusks are fertile ground for contaminants. The problem is worsened by fishermen who illegally harvest shellfish in polluted waters. Many mollusks get contaminated because they live where rivers and seas meet and, because of nearby cities, these waters often are contaminated.

Oysters, clams, and mussels are also vulnerable to Norwalk viruses, which can cause severe diarrhea unless the shellfish is fully cooked. Another source of contamination is the algae called "Red Tides." The FDA and the coastal states all test for these blooms, and when they appear the waters are closed to all fishing.

Even oysters taken from clean waters occasionally harbor a naturally occurring, unfriendly bacteria known as *Viro vulnificus*, according to a recent report from the National Centers for Disease Control and Prevention. If contaminated mollusks are eaten raw and the bacteria remains alive, it can make a person very sick. Healthy people will probably just get a bout of indigestion. But for those with liver ailments and depressed immune systems, *Viro vulnificus* can be deadly. Symptoms can include sudden chills, indigestion, fever, nausea, vomiting, and stomach pain.

So what is safe? According to the National Academy of Sciences report, catfish, trout, salmon, and other farmed species are generally reliable as long as they are cooked immediately before serving. Processed fish such as fish sticks and fish nuggets are also safe bets because they are made from white-fleshed fish such as cod, haddock, and pollack. And canned tuna is not only the safest of all seafoods, but it is also the most popular.

No matter what the fish, there are some

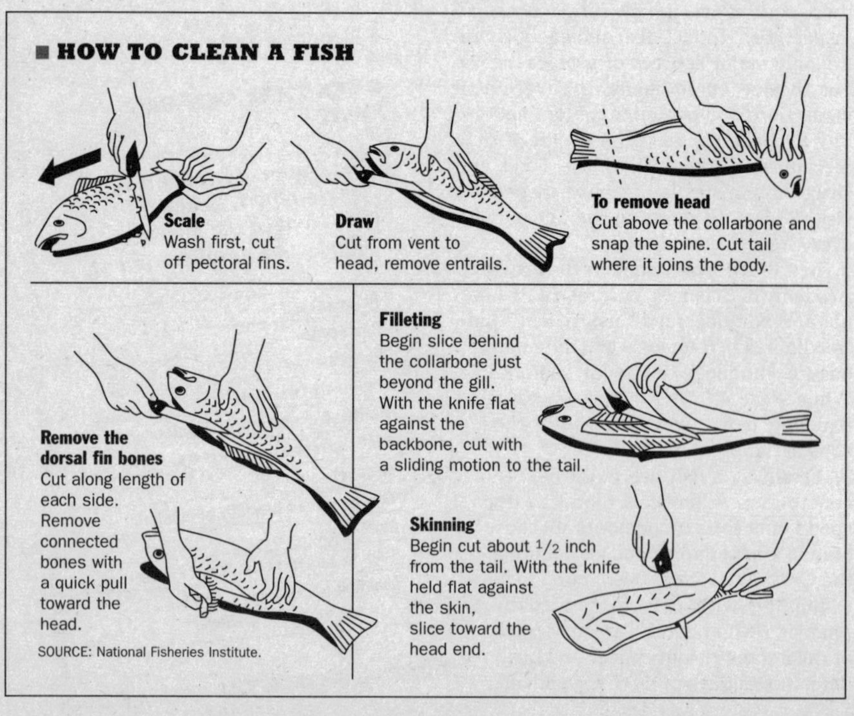
■ HOW TO CLEAN A FISH
Scale
Wash first, cut off pectoral fins.
Draw
Cut from vent to head, remove entrails.
To remove head
Cut above the collarbone and snap the spine. Cut tail where it joins the body.
Remove the dorsal fin bones
Cut along length of each side. Remove connected bones with a quick pull toward the head.
Filleting
Begin slice behind the collarbone just beyond the gill. With the knife flat against the backbone, cut with a sliding motion to the tail.
Skinning
Begin cut about 1/2 inch from the tail. With the knife held flat against the skin, slice toward the head end.
SOURCE: National Fisheries Institute.

simple precautions you can take when shopping for and storing seafood, though. Here are some tips from *Get Hooked on Seafood Safety,* which is published by the U.S. Food and Drug Administration:

■ **Select seafood with a fresh, mild odor.** It should not smell unpleasantly fishy. Fish fillets should be moist, without any traces of browning or drying around the edges.

■ **Check the gills, scales, and eyes.** The gills should be bright pink or red. And the eyes should be bright and clear, not cloudy or sunken. Scales should cling tightly to the skin, and they shouldn't be slimy.

■ **Mollusks in the shell should be alive when you buy them.** When a clam, oyster, scallop, or mussel is alive, its shell is tightly closed or closes when it is lightly tapped.

■ **Test shellfish for freshness.** Hold the shell between your thumb and forefinger and depress it, as though sliding two parts of the shell across one another. If the shells move, the shellfish is not fresh. Throw away any mollusks whose shells aren't closed tightly.

■ **Unless you freeze it, cook fish within two days of purchase.** Smoked fish, pickled fish, and vacuum-packed fish should always be refrigerated. Whatever the fish, keep it in its original wrapper and store in the coldest part of your refrigerator, which is usually under the freezer or in the meat drawer, until it is ready to be cooked.

■ **If you did freeze it, allow one day to thaw.** Thaw frozen seafood in its own container in the refrigerator. Do not thaw seafood at room temperature or under warm running water.

■ **Store mollusks live.** Keep mollusks in your refrigerator in a container covered loosely with a clean, damp cloth. Do not store live shellfish in an airtight container or in water.

■ A TASTER'S GUIDE TO ORDERING FISH

Consult this list and you'll never need to ask the waiter again to describe the fish entrees. If you're cooking at home, you can substitute one fish from the same list for another in a recipe.

WHITE MEAT

■ *Very light, delicate*

Cod
Dover Sole
Haddock
Lake Whitefish
Orange Roughy
Pacific Halibut
Pacific Sanddab
Southern Flounder
Witch Flounder
Yellowtail Flounder
Yellowtail Snapper

■ *Light to moderate*

Butterfish
Catfish
Cobia
English Sole
Mahi Mahi
Pacific Whiting
Red Snapper
Rock Sole
Snook
White King Salmon
White Sea Trout
Whiting
Winter Flounder

LIGHT MEAT

■ *Very light, delicate*

Alaska Pollock
Brook Trout
Giant Sea Bass
Grouper
Pacific Ocean Perch
Rainbow Trout
Smelt
Walleye
White Crappie
White Sea Bass

■ *Light to moderate*

Atlantic Ocean Perch
Atlantic Salmon
Black Drum
Carp
Chum Salmon
Croaker
Jewfish
King Salmon (Chinook)
Lake Herring
Lake Sturgeon
Lake Trout
Monkfish
Mullet
Northern Pike
Perch
Pink Salmon
Pollock
Sand Shark
Striped Bass
Swordfish

■ *Pronounced flavor*

Atlantic Mackerel
King Mackerel
Spanish Mackerel

DARK MEAT

■ *Light to moderate*

Black Seabass
Bluefish
Sockeye (Red) Salmon
Tuna

SOURCE: National Fisheries Institute.

RECIPES

A PERFECTLY PERFECT DINNER

Dr. Dean Ornish's recipes for a healthy heart

On learning they have coronary heart disease, many triple-bypass candidates probably wish they could go back in time to change their eating, exercise, or smoking habits. Time travel, of course, isn't an alternative to heart surgery. But researchers have found that making immediate lifestyle changes just might reverse even the most severe case of heart disease.

Since 1977, Dr. Dean Ornish has been researching ways to prevent and actually reverse heart disease. In several studies since then, Ornish and his colleagues have shown that the progress of heart disease can sometimes be reversed without surgery or cholesterol-lowering drugs. Their prescription: a diet low in fat and cholesterol, moderate exercise, more effective stress management, and quitting smoking. A bonus: patients who followed Ornish's regimen lost an average of 22 pounds during the first year.

Ornish's eating program for reducing heart blockage and losing weight focuses on the type of food you eat instead of the amount. Because the dishes he suggests are very low in fat, you get full before downing too many calories.

Many of his recipes, created with the help of some of the country's most famous chefs, have been printed in Ornish's two latest books: *Dr. Dean Ornish's Program for Reversing Heart Disease* (Random House, 1990), and *Eat More, Weigh Less* (HarperCollins, 1993). First Lady Hillary Rodham Clinton has even asked Ornish to help introduce his heart-healthy menus at the White House.

So which low-fat, low-cholesterol dishes does Ornish consider tasty enough to serve his own dinner guests?

Below is the menu for one of Ornish's favorite meals. All of the following recipes were created by chef Jean-Marc Fullsak at the California Culinary Academy in San Francisco.

■ CHINESE DIM SUM

Do not stack these dumplings while forming or steaming or they will stick together. Serve them with a small bowl of Manchurian Sauce, Chinese barbecue (hoisin) sauce, and/or mustard.

Makes 32 dumplings — serves 8

1/4 cup mung beans, peeled and soaked for 4 hours
3/4 cup vegetable stock
1/2 cup blanched frozen or fresh peas
1/2 cup sliced and blanched napa cabbage leaves
1/2 cup chopped green onion
1/2 cup oven-roasted and chopped onion
1/4 cup egg whites
1 tablespoon soy sauce
1 tablespoon minced lemongrass salt
32 potsticker skins (rounds)

In a small saucepan, combine the mung beans and stock. Bring to a boil and simmer, tightly covered, for 30 minutes, or until the beans are soft.

Transfer the beans to a food processor or blender and puree until smooth. Transfer the beans to a medium-size bowl and add the peas, cabbage, green onion, roasted onion, egg whites, soy sauce, and lemongrass. Stir to combine. Season to taste with salt.

To form the dumplings, moisten the edge of a potsticker skin with water. Place a scant tablespoon of filling slightly off center on a skin, fold the dough over to form a half moon, and pinch the edges to seal. Place in a bamboo steamer and steam for 10 minutes. Should be served immediately.

The filling can be prepared and refrigerated up to six hours ahead of time.

Serving size = 4 dumplings
Includes: 139 calories
1.7 grams fat
0 milligrams cholesterol
555.4 milligrams sodium without added salt

BLACK-EYED PEA SALAD

This very colorful and extremely tasty salad would also serve well as an entrée. Prepare and refrigerate it up to 24 hours ahead of time.

Makes 6 cups — **Serves 6 to 8**

2 1/2 cups frozen black-eyed peas
1 large ear of corn to yield 1 cup fresh corn kernels
1 cup finely diced carrots
1 cup finely diced celery
1 cup finely diced red bell pepper
1 1/2 teaspoons minced red onion
1/4 cup seasoned rice vinegar
1/2 cup whole cilantro leaves
Freshly ground black pepper
Salt

Bring six cups of water to a boil. Add the black-eyed peas. Let the water return to a boil and cook for 20 minutes, or until just tender. Drain and refresh under cold running water. Drain well and set aside.

In another pot, bring six cups of water to a boil. Add the corn, carrots, and celery. Blanch for approximately one minute, or until just tender. Drain and refresh under cold water. Drain well.

In a large bowl, combine the peas, corn, carrots, celery, red bell pepper, and onion. Pour the vinegar over and toss well. Allow to stand for at least 30 minutes at room temperature.

Thirty minutes before serving, add the cilantro and toss well. Season to taste with pepper and salt. Serve.

Serving size = 1 cup
Includes: 145 calories
1 gram fat
0 milligrams cholesterol
342.1 milligrams sodium without added salt

TOMATO CONSOMMÉ

This might look intimidating at first glance, but it is actually quite easy and a lot of fun to make. For an interesting flavor, try one tablespoon pepper vodka stirred into each serving. This consommé can also be used as a soup stock or braising liquid. Prepare it and refrigerate for up to one week or freeze for up to six months.

Makes 4 cups — **Serves 3 to 4**

1 pound tomatoes, peeled, seeded, and quartered
3 cups tomato juice or vegetable juice cocktail
3/4 cup chopped celery
3/4 cup chopped leeks
1/2 cup chopped fresh parsley
2 whole cloves
1 clove garlic
1/2 bay leaf
1 1/2 tablespoons tomato paste
1 teaspoon dried thyme
1 teaspoon coriander seeds
2 cups vegetable stock
6 egg whites with their shells
Cayenne
Salt
1 small tomato, peeled, seeded, and cut in 1/4-inch dice
1 tablespoon chiffonaded basil or chopped tarragon leaves

In a food processor or blender, combine the tomatoes, tomato juice, celery, leeks, parsley, cloves, garlic, bay leaf, tomato paste, thyme, and coriander seeds. Puree thoroughly.

Pour the pureed mixture into a large nonreactive pot. Warm the vegetable stock and add it to the puree. Bring to a boil, then simmer, covered on low heat for 12 to 15 minutes. Turn off the heat and allow the soup to cool for 30 minutes.

Add the eggshells and whites to a large stainless steel bowl. Crush the eggshells and beat the egg whites just enough to break them down. Slowly pour small amounts of the shells and whites into the warm soup, whisking continually to prevent the eggs from cooking.

Place the pot over medium-high heat and continue to whisk the mixture as it comes to a boil.

When the soup reaches a boil, stop whisking and simmer, uncovered, for 5 to 10 minutes. Stir periodically so that the eggshells have contact with the soup.

As a white foam rises to the surface, ladle it into a cheesecloth-lined strainer or a large coffee filter. After all or most of the foam has been removed, strain the hot soup through the foam into another clean bowl.

Season to taste with the cayenne and salt. Pour into individual serving bowls and garnish with the chopped tomato and herbs. Serve hot.

Serving size = 1 cup
Includes: 66 calories
0.5 gram fat
0 milligrams cholesterol
557.8 milligrams sodium without added salt

VEGETARIAN CHILI

This is very spicy and flavorful. Try it with fresh corn tortillas and rice with a generous helping of a cool vegetable salad. Or serve it with a green salad for a complete dinner.

You can prepare and refrigerate this two to three days ahead of time. You can also freeze it for up to three months, although the corn may darken somewhat over time.

Makes 7 cups — Serves 4 to 7

1 cup plus 2 tablespoons vegetable stock
3/4 cup diced carrots
1 cup diced onions
1 cup diced green bell peppers
1 cup diced red bell peppers
1 cup diced celery
1 tablespoon minced garlic
1 teaspoon dried oregano
1 teaspoon dried thyme
1/2 teaspoon ground coriander
1 teaspoon ground cumin
1 1/2 teaspoons chili powder
4 ounces minced canned jalapeño peppers, or to taste
2 cups chopped tomatoes
3 cups cooked pinto beans
1 cup fresh corn kernels
1 1/2 tablespoons red miso paste
1 tablespoon lemon juice
1 teaspoon red wine vinegar
1 teaspoon salt
Freshly ground black pepper
1/2 cup chopped fresh cilantro
Additional chopped cilantro

In a large nonstick pan in two tablespoons vegetable stock, "sweat" the carrots, onions, green and red bell peppers, and celery for four to five minutes. Add the garlic, oregano, thyme, coriander, cumin, chili powder, jalapeños, tomatoes, pinto beans, and remaining vegetable stock.

Bring to a boil, reduce the heat, and simmer for 20 minutes. Add a little extra vegetable or bean liquid if a "saucier" chili is desired. Add the corn kernels and simmer for seven minutes.

In a small bowl, combine the red miso, lemon juice, and vinegar until dissolved. Stir into the chili with 1/2 cup of cilantro. Season to taste with the salt and pepper. Serve hot, with the additional chopped cilantro.

Serving size = 1 cup
Includes: 203 calories
1.4 grams fat
0 milligrams cholesterol
622 milligrams sodium

PEAR RICE PUDDING WITH KIWI SAUCE

This delicious dessert could also be served warm as a tasty breakfast. The brown rice gives a chewy, nutty flavor that nicely complements the fruit. For a softer texture, cook the rice for 10 to 15 minutes longer. The sauce is very tasty, but this pudding could be served without it.

Makes 6 cups — Serves 6 to 8

1 cup uncooked brown rice
2 cups nonfat milk
1 large apple, peeled, cored, and cut

in 1/2-inch dice
4 pears, peeled, cored, and cut in 1/2-inch dice
1/4 cup water
4 tablespoons honey
1 teaspoon pure vanilla extract
1/8 teaspoon ground cinnamon
1 pound kiwis, peeled and roughly chopped
1 teaspoon sugar

In a medium-size saucepan, combine the rice and milk. Bring to a boil. Reduce the heat and simmer for one hour. Set aside.

In the meantime, in a second medium saucepan, combine the apples, pears, water, honey, vanilla, and cinnamon. Bring to a boil, reduce the heat, and simmer for 10 minutes, or until quite tender but not mushy.

In a food processor bowl or blender, combine the kiwis and sugar. Puree until smooth. Strain to remove the seeds if desired.

Combine the rice and fruit mixtures thoroughly. Serve warm or at room temperature with or without the kiwi sauce.

Serving size = 3/4 cup
Includes: 160 calories
0.8 gram fat
1.1 milligrams cholesterol
34.8 milligrams sodium

SOURCE: Recipes from *Eat More, Weigh Less,* Dr. Dean Ornish.

EXPERT TIPS

SOME SUBSTITUTES TO SAVE FAMILY RECIPES

These substitutes keep the comfort in comfort food, not the cholesterol

Switching to a diet low in fat and cholesterol does not mean you'll have to pitch your favorite family recipes. Many recipes can be adapted by replacing fat and cholesterol-laden ingredients with healthier ones, says Helen Roe, a registered dietician and director of nutrition at Ornish's Preventive Medicine Research Institute. But keep in mind that a recipe makeover may require some experimentation, because switching ingredients can change the dish's character. Here are Roe's tips for reducing fat and cholesterol:

- **Instead of sautéing in butter or oil, use vegetable stock or water.** Steaming can also be used to bring out an ingredient's flavor and tenderize it.

- **Try nonfat yogurt or cream cheese instead of heavy cream.** For a dessert topping, chill canned nonfat evaporated milk until it's almost frozen, then whip it to the right consistency.

- **Instead of eggs, use egg whites or an egg substitute product.** Many egg-based recipes—even omelets—taste great without the yolks. Be sure to check the label for fat and cholesterol content.

- **Hold the mayo.** When building a sandwich, forgo the mayonnaise and instead use mustard (yellow, dijon, or honey) to add desired moisture and flavor.

- **Use fat-free products.** Cheeses (regular, cream, and cottage), salad dressings, sour cream, mayonnaise, and a variety of snack foods are all available in fat-free versions. But be warned: Foods labeled fat-free can contain almost half a gram of fat per serving. So when you eat more than one serving, the amount of fat you consume can add up quite quickly.

LASAGNA VS. EGGROLLS

What Marco Polo didn't know about what restaurants are serving

You're in the mood for some tasty dining out but you want it to be healthy. You're not into salad bars, they remind you of rabbit food. Aren't Chinese and Italian foods supposed to be healthy?

According to a recent survey by the Food Marketing Institute and *Prevention* magazine, a majority of Americans believe that Chinese food is healthier than their normal diet and 25 percent view Italian food other than pizza the same way. Olive oil and pasta have long been praised by nutritionists, and a landmark study of Chinese eating patterns by Dr. T. Colin Campbell of Cornell University recently found that in rural China a person is far less likely to suffer from "diseases of affluence" like heart disease or cancer than a typical American diner.

But before you stop at your favorite trattoria or order up a Chinese banquet, consider what the Center for Science in the Public Interest, a respected Washington, D.C., consumer research group, found when it analyzed the nutritional content of many popular Chinese and Italian

DINING ITALIAN

Order Fettuccini Alfredo at your local trattoria and you stuff your arteries with as much saturated fat as three pints of Breyer's butter almond ice cream.

DISH	Calories	Fat (g)	Fat cals. (g)	Sat. fat cals. (g)	Cholesterol (mg)	Sodium (mg)
Spaghetti w/Tomato Sauce (3 1/2 cups)	849	17	18	4	29	1,449
Linguine w/Red Clam Sauce (3 cups)	892	23	23	4	64	1,182
Spaghetti w/Meat Sauce (3 cups)	918	25	25	7	108	1,792
Linguine w/White Clam Sauce (3 cups)	907	29	29	5	110	1,881
Spaghetti w/Meatballs (3 1/2 cups)	1,155	39	30	8	163	2,208
Chicken Marsala (10 oz.), spaghetti	867	33	34	10	175	1,484
Spaghetti w/Sausage (2 1/2 cups)	1,043	39	34	9	114	2,437
Veal Parmigiana (1 1/2 cups), spaghetti	1,064	44	37	12	226	2,043
Cheese Ravioli (1 1/2 cups)	623	26	38	16	117	1,289
Cheese Manicotti (1 1/2 cups)	695	38	49	21	178	1,475
Lasagna (2 cups)	958	53	50	20	217	2,055
Fettuccini Alfredo (2 1/2 cups)	1,498	97	58	29	420	1,029
SIDE ORDERS						
Garlic Bread (8 oz.)	822	40	44	11	38	1,083
Fried Calamari (3 cups)	1,037	70	61	8	924	651
Antipasto (1 1/2 tbsp.)	629	47	67	21	131	2,961

SOURCE: Copyright 1994. *Nutrition Action Health Letter*/Center for Science in the Public Interest.

dishes like Kung Pao chicken and eggplant parmigiana.

The center's staff bought dinner-sized takeout portions of 15 Chinese and 15 Italian dishes at mid-priced restaurants in several U.S. cities. The dishes were then chemically tested under procedures recommended by government nutrition experts. The findings: If the Italians or Chinese ate at home what is served up in their names in American restaurants, they'd be courting nutritional disaster, too.

Instead of the pasta, bread, vegetables, and olive oil that have long been staples of Italian cooking, especially in the south, or the rice, wheat, and vegetables that are the mainstay of most rural Chinese menus, the Italian and Chinese food in most American restaurants is loaded with fat, saturated fat, cholesterol, and sodium. Making things worse is the tendency of American diners to ladle on heaping portions of sodium-laden soy sauce or fatty parmesan cheese.

Though they were by no means nutritional all-stars, Chinese dishes did score better than restaurant Italian in the saturated fat department. The biggest overall loser was Fettuccini Alfredo, which contained a whopping 97 grams of fat. As the CSPI described it, "the Fettuccini quadrupled Kung Pau chicken's saturated fat—as it may quadruple your next bypass."

All is not lost though. You can improve your nutritional risks without sacrificing your palate by taking the CSPI's advice and mixing a cup or so of rice or pasta into every heavy-duty dish you order, and then splitting the meal with one or two dinner companions.

DINING CHINESE

Chinese food generally is lower in saturated fats than Italian food, but Kung Pau chicken still packs a mean wallop when it comes to calories.

DISH	Calories	Fat (g)	Fat cals. (g)	Sat. fat cals. (g)	Cholesterol (mg)	Sodium (mg)
Szechuan Shrimp (4 cups)	927	19	18	2	336	2,457
Stir-fried Vegetables (4 cups)	746	19	22	4	0	2,153
Shrimp w/Garlic Sauce (3 cups)	945	27	25	4	307	2,951
Hunan Tofu (4 cups)	907	28	27	4	0	2,316
Chicken Chow Mein (5 cups)	1,005	32	28	9	205	2,446
House Fried Rice (4 cups)	1.484	50	30	6	346	2,682
Hot and Sour Soup (1 cups)	112	4	32	8	129	1,088
Beef w/Broccoli (4 cups)	1,175	46	35	7	228	3,146
Sweet and Sour Pork (4 cups)	1,163	71	39	7	118	818
Kung Pau Chicken (5 cups)	1,620	76	42	7	277	2,608
Moo Shu Pork (4 cups)	1,228	64	47	10	465	2,593
Egg Roll (1 roll)	190	11	52	2	7	463
SIDE ORDERS						
Soy Sauce (1 Tbsp.)	11	0	0	0	0	1,029
Fortune Cookie (1 cookie)	30	0	6	0	0	22
Chow Mein Noodles (1/2 cup)	119	7	53	1	0	99

SOURCE: Copyright 1994. *Nutrition Action Health Letter*/Center for Science in the Public Interest.

JUNK FOOD

WHY CHOCOLATE ISN'T VERBOTEN

The answer lies in the cocoa butter, which soothes like olive oil

We have Christopher Columbus to thank for introducing cocoa beans to the European palate in the 15th century. But it fell to several American medical researchers recently to reveal that indulging a chocolate habit may be a reasonably healthy thing to do. Not that anyone is recommending that you substitute chocolate for fruits and vegetables, but when it comes to your heart's health, certain types of chocolate seem to have the same salutary effect as olive oil.

This is surprising since chocolate is high in saturated fatty acids, which normally boost blood cholesterol levels sharply, clogging arteries and paving the way for heart attacks. But chocolate is made of cocoa butter, a saturated fatty acid unusual for its large amounts of stearic acid. When stearic acid enters the digestive system, it is converted by the liver to oleic acid, a substance that is also found in olive and canola oils and that has no ill effects on blood cholesterol levels.

In a recent study by Dr. Penny Kris-Etherton of Pennsylvania State University, subjects who followed a diet rich in cocoa butter saw no rise in their blood cholesterol levels; the same results were observed in participants on a diet heavy with olive oil. But a group with a diet rich in dairy butter experienced clear increases in its cholesterol readings.

Dark chocolate is healthier than milk chocolate because milk chocolate includes not only cocoa butter but also milk-based butterfat. Some chocolate products like cocoa mixes and candy bar coatings may also use tropical oils like coconut and palm oil, which also boost cholesterol counts. But if you're eating dark chocolate, two or three chocolate bars a week pose no real heart risk, according to researcher Scott Grundy of the University of Texas Southwestern Medical Center, where much of the chocolate study is taking place.

CANDY'S DIRTY DOZEN

Even the smallest of these sweets contained 14 grams of saturated fats.

CANDY (one box or bar)	Amount	Calories	Saturated Fat	Fat	Sugar
KitKat	3.4 oz.	500	18 g	26 g	40 g
Almond Joy, king size	3.2 oz.	460	16 g	26 g	34 g
Nestle's Crunch	3.5 oz.	500	14 g	26 g	52 g
Reese's Pieces	2.7 oz.	370	14 g	16 g	40 g
Whoppers	2.8 oz.	368	13 g	16 g	45 g
Goobers	3.5 oz.	528	12 g	34 g	41 g
Butterfinger Bite Size	4.0 oz.	532	11 g	20 g	76 g
Sno-Caps	3.1 oz.	418	11 g	18 g	51 g
Raisinets	3.5 oz.	440	10 g	18 g	62 g
Milk Duds	3.0 oz.	368	10 g	13 g	30 g
M & M's Plain	2.6 oz.	360	9 g	15 g	48 g
Reese's Peanut Butter Cups	1.6 oz.	240	6 g	14 g	19 g

Source: Individual manufacturers.

RIPE FOR THE PICKING

A grocery shopper's guide to choosing fresh fruits

For many consumers, buying fresh produce is like a game of roulette. There's no telling whether their fruits and vegetables will be fresh and ripe at home because they don't know how to choose produce at the grocery store.

Even some shoppers who consider themselves knowledgeable produce pickers are merely misinformed victims of old wives' tales. Contrary to popular belief, watermelon thumping, cantaloupe shaking, and pineapple plucking are not valid tests for determining ripeness, according to the Produce Marketing Association.

Experts there offer these tips for choosing the ripest of the most popular fresh fruits:

APPLES

Should have no bruises or broken skin.

AVOCADOS

Should yield to gentle pressure and have no bruises or hard and soft spots.

BANANAS

Fully ripe when skin turns yellow with brown and black flecks. Can be purchased when green and stored at room temperature to ripen.

Only refrigerate ripe bananas. Refrigeration will turn skins black, but will not affect fruit quality.

CANTALOUPES

Will have a cantaloupe smell, yield to pressure on the blossom end, and have a yellowish cast under the netting when ready.

Leave cantaloupes at room temperature to soften and become juicier.

CHERRIES

Should be plump with firm, smooth, and brightly colored skins and intact stems. Avoid cherries with blemished, rotted, or mushy skins or those that appear either hard and light-colored or soft, shriveled, and dull.

GRAPEFRUIT

Should be firm, springy to the touch, heavy for size, well shaped, and thin-skinned.

Grapefruit may show russeting (browning of the peel) or regreening, which do not affect fruit quality.

GRAPES

Bunches should be well colored with plump berries firmly attached to green, pliable stems.

HONEYDEWS

Will have a creamy yellow skin and a slightly soft blossom end. An unripe honeydew has white skin with a green tint and a hard blossom end, and will ripen at room temperature.

Choose melons that are heavy for their size and are well shaped. Unlike can-

FACT FILE:

FRUITS THAT DO NOT RIPEN AFTER HARVEST:

- *Apples*
- *Grapefruit*
- *Lemons*
- *Oranges*
- *Strawberries*
- *Tangelos*
- *Cherries*
- *Grapes*
- *Limes*
- *Pineapples*
- *Tangerines*
- *Watermelons*

taloupe, honeydew does not have a distinctive aroma.

■ KIWIFRUIT
Choose firm, plump, light brown kiwi that gives slightly to the touch.

■ LEMONS
Should have a pleasant citrus fragrance. Should be firm, heavy for size, and have thin smooth skins.

To release more juice, microwave for 10 seconds or apply slight pressure while rolling it on a table or countertop.

■ LIMES
Should be plump and heavy for their size. The same methods used to release more juice from lemons can be applied to limes.

■ NECTARINES
Choose nectarines with a creamy yellow background color without any green at the stem end. Firm fruits can be ripened at home. When they yield slightly to pressure, they're ready to eat.

■ ORANGES
May regreen after harvest, but this is natural and does not indicate unripeness. To get the juiciest fruit, choose oranges that feel heavy for their size.

EXPERT TIP

To speed the ripening of soft fruits such as avocados, bananas, kiwis, nectarines, peaches, pears, plums, and tomatoes, store them in a paper bag with an apple. The apple will boost the partly ripe fruit's exposure to ethylene, a gas required for ripening.

—The Produce Marketing Association

■ PEACHES
Should smell peachy and have no tinge of green in the background color of the skin. The amount of red blush does not indicate ripeness. Choose peaches that are fairly firm and a little soft. They should give a bit when squeezed in the palm of the hand. Stored in a paper bag, they will soften and get juicier, but not sweeter.

■ PEARS
Will yield to gentle pressure near the stem end and side when it's ready to eat. Ripen at home at room temperature.

■ PINEAPPLES
Will have a distinctive pineapple aroma. Should be heavy for their size, well shaped and fresh-looking with dark green crown leaves and a dry, crisp shell. Ripeness is not indicated by shell color or pulling crown leaves.

■ PLUMS
Choose plump fruit that is not excessively soft. To ripen at home, store in a paper bag.

■ STRAWBERRIES
Should be plump, firm, well rounded, and have an even bright red color with natural shine. Caps should be fresh-looking, green, and in place. When possible, avoid fruit that is white near the caps. This is called white shoulders, and it can mean two things: either the fruit was picked too soon, or the berries are fully ripe but missing some color due to a lack of sunshine.

■ TANGERINES
Look for fruit with deep, rich color and "puffy" appearance. Good-quality fruit should be heavy for its size. Avoid fruit with soft or water-soaked spots or mold.

■ WATERMELONS
Should have a dull (as opposed to shiny) rind, a dried stem, and a yellowish underside where the watermelon has touched the ground. Immature watermelons have a shiny rind and a white, pale green, or light yellow underside. Thumping does not indicate ripeness.

APPLES FOR EVERY TASTE

The old saw about an apple a day notwithstanding, an apple only gives you about 10 percent of your daily requirement for vitamin C and a little bit of calcium. But unpeeled apples are high in fiber, low in calories, and delicious—a healthy dessert choice. Grocery stores used to stock just a few apple varieties, but in recent years, tasty hybrids and imports have invaded the apple aisle. The International Apple Institute offers these suggestions:

VARIETY	APPEARANCE	TASTE	BEST USES	AVAILABILITY
AKANE	bright red	**crispy, juicy, sweet-tart**	all-purpose	*late Aug.–Sept., primarily in Northwest*
CORTLAND	red w/green highlights	**tart, tender**	snack, salad, baking	*fall to spring, East to Midwest*
CRISPIN/MUTSU	yellow-green	**sweet, crisp**	all purpose	*year-round, primarily in the East*
CRITERION	yellow	**sweet, mild**	snack, salad	*Oct.–Dec. nationwide*
ELSTAR	bright red, orange, and yellow	**sweet-tart**	snack, salad, baking	*Oct.–Dec. nationwide*
EMPIRE	dark red w/red blush	**crispy, juicy, mildly tart**	snack, salad	*fall to spring, East to Midwest*
GALA	orange-yellow	**sweet**	snacks, salads	*mid-Aug.–Dec., nationwide*
GINGERGOLD	yellow, smooth finish	**sweet, crisp**	all-purpose	*late July to early Sept. in Virginia*
GRAVENSTEIN	red-striped	**moderately tart**	snacks, salad, baking	*late summer, early fall, West Coast*
IDARED	red	**mildly tart, firm, juicy**	salads, baking, cooking	*Sept. to early spring, mainly East to Midwest*
JERSEYMAC	bright red	**juicy, medium-firm**	all-purpose	*late summer to early Sept. nationwide*
JONAGOLD	bright red over gold	**sweet, tangy, juicy**	snacks, salads	*end Sept.–Oct. nationwide*
JONAMAC	deep red	**tart**	snacks, cooking	*Sept., primarily Northeast*
JONATHAN	light red w/yellow or purple highlights	**rich, tartish**	all-purpose	*fall to spring, Midwest*
LODI (old-time apple)	yellowish-green	**tart**	all-purpose	*July to early Aug. nationwide*
MACOUN	red-green	**crisp, semisweet**	snacks, salads, applesauce	*Sept.–Nov. nationwide*
NEWTOWN PIPPIN	green	**mildly tart**	snacks, salads, cooking	*Sept.–Feb., mainly West Coast*
PAULARED	mostly red with green highlights	**mildly tart, firm**	snacks, salads, cooking	*early fall, East*
QUINTE	red	**medium tart to sweet**	snacks, salads	*late summer to early Sept. nationwide*
ROME BEAUTY	red w/smatter of green	**tartish to sweet**	cooking	*Oct.–July nationwide*
SPARTAN	like McIntosh	**crispy, tartish, aromatic**	best for snacks and salads	*fall to winter, Northeast*
STAYMAN	purplish-red	**rich, mildly tart**	snacks, salads, cooking	*fall to spring, Midwest and Southeast*
TWENTY-OUNCE	large, greenish yellow	**slightly tart, crisp**	cooking, baking	*Fall, Western New York*
TYDEMAN EARLY	bright scarlet, fairly large	**firm, mildly tart**	dessert	*summer nationwide*
WEALTHY	bright red	**slightly tart**	cooking, baking	*mid-Sept.–Nov., primarily in Northeast and Michigan*
WINESAP	deep purplish-red	**tangy, juicy, wine-like flavor**	all-purpose	*Oct.–July nationwide*
		OLD STANDBYS		
GOLDEN DELICIOUS	yellow	**tangy, sweet, juicy**	all-purpose	*year-round nationwide*
GRANNY SMITH	green	**tart**	all purpose	*yearround nationwide*
MCINTOSH	red and green	**tart, tender, juicy**	snacks, salads	*Sept. through spring, East to Midwest*
RED DELICIOUS	striped to solid red	**rich, sweet, mellow**	snacks, salads	*late summer to early Sept.*

SOURCE: International Apple Institute.

STIMULANTS

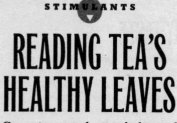

READING TEA'S HEALTHY LEAVES

Green tea may lower cholesterol and even help fight cancer

In the never-ending rivalry between coffee and tea drinkers over whose beverage is superior, the tea drinkers seem to hold the current edge. Not only is tea the second most popular drink in the world after water, but researchers are now investigating whether one variety of tea has properties that can lower cholesterol levels and blood pressure and even inhibit the development of several forms of tumors.

Several preliminary studies of the chemical makeup of green tea have suggested that the leaves may contain powerful cancer-fighting agents. In one study involving laboratory animals, green tea extracts not only seemed to help prevent skin cancer but also to protect arteries from getting clogged by fatty foods. Other laboratory studies of green tea have suggested potential benefits in combating esophogeal and lung cancer.

Green tea is Japan's tea of choice and is popular, too, in China. But it accounts for only about a fifth of all tea consumed around the world; nearly 80 percent is black tea.

Whether black tea has the same intriguing characteristics as green tea is still unclear. When black tea is harvested, its leaves are rolled and exposed to air to stimulate oxidation of its main biological ingredients. Green tea leaves, however, are steamed and heated to remove the enzyme that promotes oxidation, a potentially crucial difference.

Until human trials are conducted under rigorous scientific conditions, the medicinal powers of both will remain uncertain. But as far as some tea researchers are concerned, tea should prevail over coffee under any circumstances. That's because lab tests show that a typical cup of tea has far less caffeine than the average cup of coffee.

STIMULANTS

ANOTHER CUP OF COFFEE, PLEASE

Studies show that a little caffeine in the morning poses no offense

Coffee may not have the medicinal power of green tea, but for most people it gets a relatively clean bill of health. A recent study by researchers at the Harvard University School of Public Health found no significant increase in the risk of heart disease or stroke among men who drank up to four cups of coffee a day.

Since coffee is high in caffeine, and caffeine boosts heart rates and raises blood pressure, scientists had worried that coffee drinking might contribute to higher rates of heart disease. A smaller, earlier study had suggested just that, but the concern now seems alleviated, both by the Harvard research and a second study by the Kaiser Permanente health care organization in California.

This is not to say that there aren't physical effects to coffee drinking. Small amounts of caffeine spur brain cells, helping to improve concentration and reaction time and to relieve drowsiness and fatigue. But too much caffeine can often lead to irritability and restlessness and the inability to sleep. Caffeine also stimulates more frequent urination, as any coffee drinker knows. But earlier suspicions that coffee might be linked to bladder cancer have been dispelled by recent research.

Still, not everyone can drink coffee with impunity. Pregnant women raise their risk of miscarriage 22 percent with just one eight-ounce cup of coffee daily. Caffeine also is likely to cause various "withdrawal" effects, such as headaches or depression, among those attempting to break their coffee habit. But figure this one: According to a 1989 survey of women over 60 in Washtenaw County, Mich., 62 percent of those who drank at least one cup of coffee a day reported being sexually active, compared with only 37.5 percent of the coffee teetotalers.

TODAY'S JIVE ABOUT JAVA

In a recent survey conducted by the National Coffee Association, the following percentage of Americans agreed with these statements:

- **The amount of coffee I am drinking now is about right for me.** 86%
- **Coffee is an affordable luxury.** 60%
- **Drinking coffee is a good a way to relax.** 57%
- **Compared to other beverages you buy and drink away from home, coffee is a better value.** 56%
- **Coffee is becoming more popular among people like me.** 55%
- **I feel better about drinking coffee than I used to.** 53%
- **I feel decaffeinated coffee is a better choice for health-conscious people like me.** 52%
- **The variety of coffees now has really added excitement to drinking coffee.** 50%
- **Coffee helps me get things done.** 39%
- **I am likely to drink more decaffeinated coffee in the coming year.** 30%
- **I am concerned about the amount of coffee I currently drink.** 24%

SOURCE: National Coffee Association, New York City.

BEVERAGES

WHY BOTHER WITH BOTTLED WATER?

What you're getting for your money

Bottled water has become a major presence in the United States. Sales have shot up over 400 percent in the last 15 years to over $2.2 billion annually. There are 700 different regional brands and 75 imported brands available around the country, and Americans now guzzle two billion gallons of the stuff each year. Why do so many spend so much for something they can get from the tap for pennies?

It's mostly a matter of taste. A majority of those surveyed by the International Bottled Water Association in 1993 said that they consumed bottled water because it tastes better then tap water, a difference mostly attributable to different disinfecting agents. Most tap water is purified with chlorine, but the majority of bottled water is disinfected with ozone, which leaves no aftertaste or smell. Differing levels of minerals and sodium also affect the taste.

Others in the poll cited concerns about the quality of tap water, a legitimate fear in areas where municipal water purification is primitive or mismanaged and may have suffered contamination. Doctors also sometimes recommend bottled water to pregnant women and children when the local water supply has high nitrate levels.

Otherwise, bottled water is no healthier than tap water. Most health claims by bottled water distributors are really claims for the healthiness of bottled water as an alternative to soft drinks. So if water is your flavor, remember this: A recent study by the American Water Works Association says if you drink the recommended eight glasses of water a day, 1,000 gallons will provide an adequate supply for the next five years. The cost: $1.65.

EXPERT LIST

A CLEAR DEFINITION OF WATER

It used to be that, depending on where you were, "spring water" could mean anything from water imported from the Swiss Alps to purified tap water. The Food and Drug Administration in 1994 whittled that definition down to one meaning in a set of regulations that defined standards for most types of bottled water. Carbonated water, soda water, tonic water, and seltzer water are considered soft drinks and so are regulated separately.

- **ARTESIAN WELL WATER**: Water drawn from a well where the aquifer (a water-bearing rock formation) is above the level of the natural water table.

- **DISTILLED WATER**: Water that has been vaporized and then condensed to remove minerals.

- **MINERAL WATER**: Water collected at a borehole or spring originating from a geologically and physically protected underground water source.

- **PURIFIED WATER**: Water that has been either distilled, deionized, or passed through membrane filters to remove particles in a process called "reverse osmosis."

- **SPRING WATER**: Water collected as it flows naturally to the surface from a spring or from a borehole to the underground source of the spring.

- **WELL WATER**: Water collected from a hole drilled to tap an aquifer.

MEAT EATER'S GUIDE

COOKING BY THE BOOK

Intimidated by that rack of lamb? Here's how your mom would tell you to cook it

■ TO ROAST BEEF (325° F)

Cut/Weight in pounds	Minutes per pound	Internal temp. (F)
STANDING RIB/4 to 8		
rare	20 to 25	140°
medium	25 to 30	160°
well-done	30 to 35	170°
ROLLED RIB/5 to 7		
rare	30 to 35	140°
medium	35 to 40	160°
well-done	40 to 45	170°
RIB EYE/4 to 6		
rare	20	140°
medium	22	160°
well-done	24	170°
Sirloin tip	5 to 40	160°
TENDERLOIN (roast at 425°)		
whole/4 to 6	10	140°
half/2 to 3	20	140°

■ TO BROIL STEAK 1-inch thick, 2 inches from preheated oven broiler

SIRLOIN, PORTERHOUSE, T-BONE, OR RIB	
rare	5 minutes each side
medium	7 minutes each side
well-done	10 minutes each side

For **FILET MIGNON**, cook 1 minute less per side. If grilling steak, grill 3 inches from fire and cook 1 minute less per side.

■ TO ROAST VEAL (325° F)

Cut/Weight in pounds	Minutes per pound	Internal temp. (F)
LEG/5 to 8	25 to 30	170°
LOIN/4 to 6	30 to 35	170°
RIB (rack)/3 to 5	35 to 40	170°

■ TO ROAST LAMB (325° F)

LEG/5 to 8	30 to 35	175° to 180°
SHOULDER/4 to 6	30 to 35	175° to 180°
RIB (rack)/4 to 5	40 to 45	175° to 180°
CROWN ROAST/4 to 6	40 to 45	175° to 180°

■ TO ROAST PORK (350° F)

Cut/Weight in pounds	Minutes per pound	Internal temp. (F)
LOIN, center/3 to 5	40	185°
half/5 to 7	45	185°
rolled/3 to 5	50	185°
SIRLOIN/3 to 4	50	185°
CROWN/4 to 6	45	185°
PICNIC shoulder/5 to 8	40	185°
ROLLED shoulder/3 to 5	45	185°
SPARERIBS/3	40	185°
FRESH HAM (LEG)		
whole/10 to 14	30	185°
half/5 to 7	40	185°

To roast **HAM** and other **CURED PORK,** temperature should be 325° F. For all boneless meat, allow 1/3 to 1/2 pound per serving; if the meat contains bone, estimate 1/2 to 3/4 pound per serving.

WHOLE HAM/10 to 14		
uncooked	20	160°
fully cooked	15	130°
PICNIC SHOULDER/5 to 8	30	170°
ROLLED SHOULDER/2 to 4	40	170°

■ TO BROIL PORK

CHOPS (3/4-to 1-inch thick), **SHOULDER STEAKS** (1/2- to 3/4-inch thick), and **PATTIES** (1-inch thick) should be broiled about 11 minutes on each side.

■ TO ROAST DUCK OR GOOSE (325° F)

Roast duck or goose about 30 minutes per pound.

■ TO ROAST CHICKEN (375° F)

Chicken weighing between 2 and 4 pounds should be roasted about 30 minutes per pound. Add 15 minutes to the total roasting time if the chicken is stuffed. With bones, estimate about 1/2 pound per serving.

MEAT EATER'S GUIDE

TO ROAST TURKEY (325° F)

Ready-to-cook weight in pounds	Total number of hours
4 to 8	3 to 4
8 to 12	4 to 4 1/2
12 to 16	4 1/2 to 5
16 to 20	6 to 7 1/2
20 to 24	7 1/2 to 9

TO COOK FISH

Method	Time	Temp. (F)
Baked	10 minutes	500°
Broiled	15 minutes	
Deep-fried	2 minutes	370°
Pan-fried	10 minutes	
Poached or steamed:	10 minutes per pound	

Cook fish thoroughly or to an internal temperature of 140 degrees Fahrenheit. For **FIN FISH**, allow 10 minutes of cooking time for each inch of thickness. Turn the fish over halfway through the cooking time unless it is less than a half-inch thick. Add 5 minutes to the total cooking time if the fish is wrapped in foil or cooked in sauce.

TO COOK SHELLFISH

Simmer in boiling water:

SHRIMP	5 minutes
CRAB	20 minutes
LOBSTER	30 to 40 minutes

Cooking shellfish thoroughly or to an internal temperature of 140° F is required to help avoid the threat of food poisoning. **SHRIMP, SCALLOPS, CLAMS,** and **OYSTERS** can be deep-fried at 370° F for about three minutes. **SHRIMP** and **SCALLOPS** can also be sauteed. Other shellfish are best boiled or steamed. Boil for three to five minutes after the shells have opened. Steam shellfish four to nine minutes from the start of steaming. Use small pots for boiling or steaming. If too many shells are cooking in the same pot, it's possible that the ones in the middle won't be thoroughly cooked. Discard any clams, mussels, or oysters that do not open during cooking. If the shells remain closed, it may mean they have not received adequate heat.

GERM WARFARE

Use temperature to kill bacteria before they make you sick

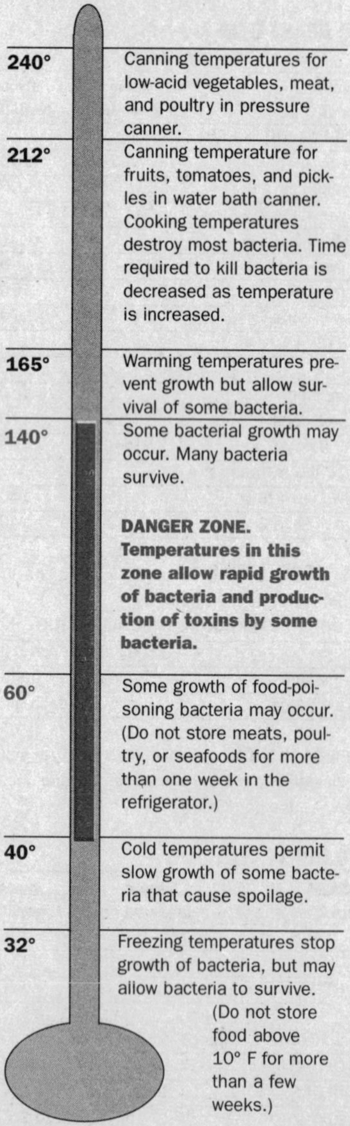

240° Canning temperatures for low-acid vegetables, meat, and poultry in pressure canner.

212° Canning temperature for fruits, tomatoes, and pickles in water bath canner. Cooking temperatures destroy most bacteria. Time required to kill bacteria is decreased as temperature is increased.

165° Warming temperatures prevent growth but allow survival of some bacteria.

140° Some bacterial growth may occur. Many bacteria survive.

DANGER ZONE. Temperatures in this zone allow rapid growth of bacteria and production of toxins by some bacteria.

60° Some growth of food-poisoning bacteria may occur. (Do not store meats, poultry, or seafoods for more than one week in the refrigerator.)

40° Cold temperatures permit slow growth of some bacteria that cause spoilage.

32° Freezing temperatures stop growth of bacteria, but may allow bacteria to survive. (Do not store food above 10° F for more than a few weeks.)

SOURCE: U.S. Department of Agriculture

EXPERT SOURCES

THE JAMES BEARD COOKBOOK HALL OF FAME

The Cookbook Hall of Fame recognizes books that have significantly influenced the way we think about food and honored authors who possess an exceptional ability to communicate their gastronomic vision via the printed page. The first cookbook was inducted into the Hall of Fame in 1977.

1994 GREENE ON GREENS, *Bert Greene, Workman Press, 1989, $15.95*

1993 ALICE LET'S EAT, AMERICAN FRIED AND THIRD HELPINGS (THE TUMMY TRILOGY), *Calvin Trillin, FS&G, 1994, $16*

1992 SIMPLE FRENCH FOOD, *Richard Olney, Macmillan, 1992, $13*

1991 THE SILVER PALATE COOKBOOK, *Julee Rosso and Sheila Lukins with Michael McLaughlin, Workman Press, 1982, $12*

1990 THE FOOD OF FRANCE and **THE FOOD OF ITALY,** *Waverley Root, Random House, 1992, $13*

1989 THE ART OF EATING, *M.F.K. Fisher, Macmillan, 1990, $16*

1988 No award given

1987 FOODS OF THE WORLD *(18 volumes, 1969–1972), Time-Life Books, $19.95–$25*

1986 MASTERING THE ART OF FRENCH COOKING, VOLUMES ONE AND TWO, *Volume One by Julia Child with Simone Beck and Louisette Betholle; Volume Two by Julia Child with Simone Beck, Knopf, 1970, $25 each*

1985 THE AMERICAN WOMAN'S COOKBOOK, *edited by Ruth Berolzheimer, Culinary Arts Institute, 1948, out of print, roughly $35*

1984 GEORGE AUGUSTE ESCOFFIER COOKBOOK COLLECTION, *George Auguste Escoffier, Van Nostrand Reinhold, 1979, $64.95*

1983 THE JAMES BEARD COOKBOOK, *James Beard, Dutton, 1970, out of print, roughly $30*

1982 THE BETTY CROCKER COOKBOOK, *edited by Marjorie Child Hustad, Bentham, 1987, $7.99*

1981 THE NEW YORK TIMES COOKBOOK, *Craig Claiborne, HarperCollins, 1990, $30*

1980 THE CORDON BLEU COOKBOOK, *Dione Lucas, Little Brown, 1947, $25*

1979 THE FANNIE FARMER COOKBOOK, *Fannie Merritt Farmer, 1983, $6.95*

1978 THE JOY OF COOKING, *Irma Rombauer, Dutton, 1991, $9.98*

1977 THE SETTLEMENT COOKBOOK, *Mrs. Simon (Lillian) Kander, Simon & Schuster, 1976, $25*

SELECTED JAMES BEARD FOUNDATION 1995 COOKBOOK AWARD WINNERS

COOKBOOK OF THE YEAR

CHOCOLATE AND THE ART OF LOW FAT DESSERTS
Alice Medrich, Warner Books, 1995, $35

INTERNATIONAL

THE COOKING OF THE EASTERN MEDITERRANEAN
Paula Wolfert, HarperCollins, 1995, $30

VEGETARIAN

MOOSEWOOD RESTAURANT COOKS AT HOME
Moosewood Collective, Simon & Schuster/Fireside, 1995, $15

LOOKING GREAT

A WARNING TO SUNBATHERS

Being "sun smart" means knowing your SPFs

It's hard to pinpoint when America went around the bend in worshipping the bronzed god, but Hollywood no doubt bears a large measure of blame. Even before the movies went Technicolor and George Hamilton and Annette Funicello could prove by their antics that the suntanned really had more fun, moviegoers had already been subjected to years of glamorous Hollywood palm-tree and fun-in-the-sun imagery.

That cinematic fantasy, happily perpetuated by suntan lotion advertising, remains very alive today. According to a recent survey for the American Academy of Dermatology, 59 percent of Americans view a tan as a sign of health and find that it enhances appearances.

Nothing could be further from the truth. In fact, a tan is your skin's way of showing that it's been damaged by the sun's ultraviolet rays. Over the years, that damage will not only "age" your skin visibly—causing wrinkles, sags, and the kind of pigmentation changes associated with growing old—but it may even lead to skin cancer.

The key to being "sun smart" is to use a sunscreen on exposed skin whenever you're outside. To help you choose the appropriate level of protection, the U.S. Food and Drug Administration now requires all sunscreen makers to rate the protective power of each of their products. A sunscreen with a sun-protection factor, or SPF, of two, allows you to stay in the sun without getting burned for twice as long as would otherwise be possible without a screen. An SPF of eight gives you eight times the protection.

In choosing a sunscreen, keep in mind the answers to the following questions:

■ **Is there any difference between a sunscreen and a sunblock?**

Yes, there is. Sunscreens are chemically based and allow some ultraviolet light to penetrate the skin no matter what their SPF. True sunblocks use minerals like zinc oxide or titanium dioxide in an opaque cream or paste. They do not carry SPFs because their reflective powers are so complete that they do not allow any light to reach the skin.

Unfortunately, such products leave an unattractive chalky film on your skin. A few manufacturers now market hybrid products that add titanium dioxide to chemically based screens to give them

SUNBATHER'S GUIDE

HOW SUNSCREENS STACK UP

These leading brands of sunscreen are all waterproof

Product	Type	Protection provided	Contains PABA?	Other features
Bain de Soleil Tropical Deluxe	SUNTAN LOTION	UV-A	NO	Retains its sun protection for at least 80 minutes in the water.
Coppertone Suntan lotion	SUNTAN LOTION	UV-A, UV-B	NO	Contains aloe and vitamin E.
Hawai'ian Tropic Sport	SUNBLOCK	UV-A, UV-B	NO	Waterproof and sweatproof, lasts 8 hours in the water.
Johnson & Johnson Sundown	SUNBLOCK	UV-A, UV-B	NO	Waterproof, lasts 80 minutes in the water.
Schering Plough Shade	SUNSCREEN	UV-A, UV-B	NO	Contains Parsol 1789; company claims it gives extra UVA protection.
Solar Suncare No-Ad	SUNCREEN	UV-A, UV-B	NO	Contains aloe, cocoa butter, and vitamin E.

SOURCE: Individual manufacturers.

reflective properties that they would not otherwise possess.

■ How high an SPF should I choose?

Dermatologists advise that you use a sunscreen with an SPF of at least 15. This will ensure the filtering out of most UV-B rays, the part of the ultraviolet light spectrum most responsible for sunburn and skin cancer.

■ Is a sunscreen's SPF all that I need to worry about?

No. SPF only addresses a sunscreen's ability to guard against UV-B radiation. Researchers have recently discovered that another kind of ultraviolet radiation, known as UV-A radiation, harms the skin's connective tissue, resulting in visible aging and contributing to skin cancer in some cases.

■ What can be done to protect against UV-A radiation?

The best protection comes from sunscreens containing a chemical compound known as avobenzone. Some protection can also be gotten from products that contain oxybenzone, a common ingredient in many sunscreens.

■ Do I need sunscreen if I'm swimming?

Sunscreen is *especially* important if you're swimming. Water magnifies the power of ultraviolet rays, Ensuring that you will burn even more quickly in the water than on the beach unless the sunscreen you use is water-resistant. Even if it is, it's a good idea to reapply it after leaving the water to ensure full protection.

■ What if I have an allergic reaction to sunscreens?

You should avoid sunscreens that contain PABA (para-aminobenzoic acid). Many people are allergic to PABA, and many sunscreens now state on their package that they're PABA-free (see "How Sunscreens Stack Up," above). If you continue to get an allergic reaction, try the new titanium dioxide-based hybrid screens.They are the least likely to cause irritation.

EXPERT Q&A

THE MANY USES OF RETIN-A

It helps fight acne, but the returns aren't in on cancer treatment

Unlike Dorian Gray's temporarily flattering yet ultimately gruesome portrait, Retin-A has been shown in many tests to offset the effects of aging without causing diabolic side effects. Here, Dr. Wilma Bergfeld, who heads the Clinical Research Department of Dermatology of the Cleveland Clinic Foundation and is a past president of the American Academy of Dermatologists, answers questions about the currently accepted uses of tretinoin in the medical community.

■ What is Retin-A?

Based on a vitamin A derivative known generically as tretinoin, the drug was originally developed as a treatment for acne in the late 1960s. It has yet to be approved by the Food and Drug Administration for any other purpose. But doctors can prescribe it at their discretion, and many dermatologists have put people on tretinoin-based programs to treat light wrinkles, liver spots, freckles, and pre-cancerous skin lesions.

■ How effective is Retin-A in treating acne?

Tretinoin is most effective in treating acne when it is combined with a topical antibiotic. The antibiotic works in tandem with the tretinoin to reduce the blackheads, whiteheads, and pimples that are the primary lesions of acne by reducing inflammation and killing yeast and bacteria microorganisms. Cream-based tretinoin applications moisturize, while gels and the lotions dry out skin, which can lead to scaling. Both vehicles, however, aid in the healing process. Tretinoin itself may produce some redness and scaling, but that is a sign of the agent at work.

■ Can it help with warts?

Warts are viral skin tumors, and it appears that tretinoin may have the ability to kill the wart virus, basically by destroying its cell walls. It has also been used to promote the healing of blisters and scars with some success.

■ Does Retin-A really make wrinkles "disappear"?

Actually, the best way to get rid of wrinkles is to not get them in the first place.

■ A SKINCARE WATCH LIST

The aging process brings a variety of changes in one's skin. Some are natural, unavoidable, and harmless. Others are serious and should receive immediate medical attention. Some trouble signs from the American Academy of Dermatology:

- **DERMATITIS or PSORIASIS:** Both may be indicated by excessive dryness and itching that doesn't respond to moisturizers.
- **SHINGLES:** Usually indicated by a vague or sharp local pain or headache followed by itching and the formation of groups of blisters.
- **SKIN CANCER:** Look for a scaly red spot or any new skin growth. Also, watch for change in the color, shape, or size of any mole, as well as bleeding in a mole or other growth. Another warning sign is a cut that fails to heal.

SOURCE: Reprinted by permission, American Academy of Dermatology.

You should always keep your skin well hydrated and as pale as possible. In fact, simply hydrating the skin with simple over-the-counter moisturizers can reduce wrinkles up to 30 percent. What makes tretinoin more effective from a cosmetic perspective, however, is that it not only removes light wrinkles, but it also bleaches some of the yellow in the skin to a more youthful pink by thickening the epidermis and peeling away the layers of skin in which small wrinkles and irregular pigmentation reside.

Who can prescribe it?
Any physician can prescribe tretinoin, but a dermatologist will be better able to help you because he or she will be more aware of some of the adverse effects of the drug such as blotchiness and scaling. The treatment should extend two years for maximum effectiveness, and follow-up treatments can last indefinitely.

Can Retin-A help treat cancer?
Though some research has shown promise for the use of a vitamin A derivative similar to tretinoin in the treatment of cervical cancer and melanoma (a potentially deadly form of skin cancer), these conditions are far too serious to be dealt with by an unproven treatment. Tretinoin can help prevent melanoma, however, if it is used to bleach very flat lesions like freckles.

WRINKLE CREAMS

PEELING AWAY THE MARKS OF AGE

Alpha-hydroxies help smooth aging skin, but they leave you red-faced

As aging baby boomers continue the battle against laugh lines and crow's feet, sales of the latest product to offset the effects of aging have grown to $300 million annually. Known as Alpha-hydroxy acids, or AHAs, the new wrinkle-fighters are classified by the U.S. Food and Drug Administration as cosmetics rather than drugs. But the long-term safety of AHAs has yet to be established by medical testing. The FDA is currently studying the matter and has asked the American Academy of Dermatology to draft clinical guidelines on the use of AHA products, which are available both from dermatologists and in weaker, over-the-counter drugstore versions.

AHAs work by stripping off the top layer of skin and causing cell turnover, which uncovers fresher-looking skin. The skin underneath retains water better, which helps to fill in fine lines and give the skin

OVER-THE-COUNTER WRINKLE FIGHTERS

There are a host of skin creams containing alpha-hydroxy acids now on the market. Their acid concentration is usually no higher than 15 percent. Here are some popular brands and their acid strengths:

Product	Company	Acid conentration
Alpha Ceramide Time Complex System	Elizabeth Arden	3% to 7.5% hydroxy acids
Alpha Hydrox Cream	Neoteric Cosmetics	8% glycolic acid
Anew Intensive	Avon	8% glycolic acid
Eucerin Moisturizing Lotion Plus	Beiersdorf, Inc.	5% sodium lactate
Murad Skin Smoothing Cream	Murad	12% glycolic acid
NeoStrata-15 AHA Face Cream	NeoStrata Company	15% glycolic acid
Almay Time-Off Age Smoothing Eye Cream	Almay	5% alpha-hydroxy acid

SOURCE: Individual manufacturers.

a more youthful appearance. The new skin also sheds dead cells faster for a cleaner look. AHAs also are reported to remove superficial wrinkles, acne, blemishes, and blackheads, and to soften some of the effects of sun damage on the face.

AHAs come in a variety of forms, including moisturizers, facial soaps, gels, toners, astringents, and hand and body products. Some contain salicylic acid, which tightens skin but doesn't slough off dead skin or surface blemishes. Fruit acids are widely used, but they don't penetrate the skin as well as other formulae.

Dermatologists have generally used glycolic acids, which are derived from sugarcane, at 10 percent strength. They apply the formula to the face for a few minutes and then peel it off, taking blackheads, blemishes, and the surface of the skin with it. A neutralizing cream is then applied. The patient will have a reddish face for days until another layer of skin peels off.

Performed by a doctor, the process may cost from $100 to $500; by a beauty salon, anywhere from $50 to $300, depending on how many treatments are required.

Adverse side effects often depend on the strength of the acid being used, as well as the sensitivity of the person's skin. When cosmetic versions of AHAs were first marketed in the early 1990s, the acid concentrations were no more than 4 percent. Today, several cosmetic products such as MD Formulations, Decleor, and Clinique's Turnaround Creme boast concentrations of up to 10 percent. That is no higher than the strengths long applied in doctors' offices, but a patient receiving a peel under medical supervision is much more likely to get prompt attention should there be an adverse skin reaction. At concentrations of 10 percent, even people who follow the directions for a cosmetic product carefully may find that their skin turns red and flaky and remains so for days.

Unless the FDA finds more at fault with AHAs, or a better antiwrinkle treatment is found, the popularity of AHAs is not likely to fade. Legend has it, in fact, that Cleopatra was a believer in alpha-hydroxies, bathing in sour milk because of the benefits lactic acid had on her fabled skin.

THE TEN BIGGEST MAKEUP MISTAKES

Today's most celebrated makeup artist explains where women err

Thanks to his work for leading fashion magazines, makeup artist Kevyn Aucoin has been described by *Mirabella* magazine as a key influence in shaping "the look of women in the Nineties." In his recent best-selling book, *The Art of Makeup,* which he cowrote with Tina Gaudoin, Aucoin reveals his techniques for making-up such well-known beauties as Claudia Schiffer, Christy Turlington, Cindy Crawford, and Liza Minelli. Here's what Aucoin says in his book are the 10 most common mistakes women make when applying their makeup:

■ **TIMIDITY:** "Allowing fear of what other people will think affect the way one thinks about oneself, and therefore the way one presents oneself to others," is a big mistake, says Aucoin. For too many women, he adds, "The big thing is to look good, but not *too* good. We need to break through this attitude and not be afraid."

■ **NOT BLENDING:** "The art of makeup is blending," Aucoin says. When colors aren't merged properly with one another, makeup can end up looking "like a paint-by-numbers painting."

■ **MISUSE OF BRIGHT COLORS:** "Bright colors can look great, but they draw attention to the features they're applied to and run the risk of looking like they are just sitting on top of the face." When that happens, Aucoin warns, other facial features may appear to be weak.

"A lot of women put bright shadow on for the sake of putting on makeup," Aucoin says. "Neutral tones take longer to work with. Bright-colored lipsticks tend to float on the face."

NOT ADAPTING MAKEUP TO ONE'S AGE AND STYLE: "The same makeup cannot be worn at 60 as 16." A woman can be beautiful at any age, Aucoin says, but a face does change over time. "The choice of colors, haircut, and the choice of makeup should change, too. The same clothes aren't often worn 20 years later, and the same should be true of makeup."

INCORRECT FOUNDATION CHOICE: "Most people have predominantly yellow undertones in the skin, not pink as many people think. It's safest, when choosing a foundation to err on the yellow or golden side, not the blue-pink side." Aucoin says that the most effective approach is "to match the color of the neck, not that of the cheek, because the neck and jawline are ultimately the areas that foundation has to blend into." If you don't do this, you can get a "tide line" showing where the foundation ends and the skin's natural hue shows through.

"Women who have freckles might want to skip foundation," recommends Aucoin, "since freckle-faced women might have a hard time finding the right foundation. Women with freckles tend to have good skin and small pores, so they can get away with it."

NOT WAXING FACIAL HAIR OR TWEEZING THE BROW: "The idea that hair will grow back thicker is a myth. Tweezing or waxing regularly will eventually dissuade the hairs from growing so quickly." If you don't like waxing, Aucoin recommends trying facing hair bleach as a gentle and effective alternative.

NOT CURLING YOUR EYELASHES: "Many people think this isn't necessary." But putting on mascara without also curling the lashes "actually closes up the eye, rather than opening it up, as intended," Aucoin says.

APPLYING A POWDER EYESHADOW OR POWDER BLUSH WITHOUT MAKEUP OR JUST FOUNDATION: "The natural oils of the skin and the oil in the foundation will 'grab' the color in blush or eyeshadow, thereby darkening it in places and creating a blotchy look." Always apply face powder before putting on makeup such as eyeshadow and blush, Aucoin advises.

CHOOSING THE WRONG TONES: "For people of color, using makeup with blue tones creates a very ashy look to the skin," Aucoin says. "I recommend using golden-orange colors, which tend to brighten and warm up the face."

CIGARETTE SMOKING: "Aside from the long-term damage to the body," Aucoin says, "cigarette smoke also can constrict blood vessels, deprive the skin of oxygen, and dry the top layers the way the sun can."

SOURCE: Reprinted by permission from *The Art of Makeup,* Kevyn Aucoin with Tina Gaudoin, HarperCollins, 1994.

EXPERT PICKS

Celebrated makeup artist and author Kevyn Aucoin has his own cosmetics line, Inoui, which is marketed by Shiseido only in Japan. In a recent interview in *Mirabella* magazine, he named some of the other makeup products he favors in his work:

- **Jolen bleach to lighten eyebrows**
- **Christian Dior's Mascara Parfait in Black Onyx**
- **Chanel's Translucent Light Loose Powder**
- **Kiehl's Ultra Facial Moisturizer**

EYECARE

EYESIGHT BY A THOUSAND CUTS

A cure for nearsightedness may leave you farsighted

The technique was discovered by a Russian doctor by accident in 1971. Treating a man whose cornea had been cut when his glasses were smashed in a fight, the surgeon Svjatoslav Fyodorov discovered that the patient's sight had improved.

Fyodorov hypothesized that the scoring of the man's eye by the shattered glass had flattened the cornea, which is the transparent dome about the thickness of a credit card that covers the front of the eyeball. When a person is nearsighted, or myopic, the eyeball becomes too long, which causes light rays to focus short of the retina, resulting in blurred distant vision.

By flattening the cornea, Fyodorov realized, an eyeball could be restored to a rounder shape, thereby altering its focal length so that light focused on the retina itself, eliminating the myopia.

Over the next several years, Fyodorov carefully developed the surgical technique now known as radial keratotomy, in which a series of tiny but deliberate incisions are made in the surface of a patient's cornea to flatten the eyeball and reduce the nearsightedness.

American surgeons trained by Fyodorov performed the first radial keratotomies here in 1978, and today more than 250,000 such operations are performed in the United States annually, at a typical cost of $1,500 per eye. According to a study sponsored by the National Institutes of Health over a 10-year period, the technique successfully eliminated nearsightedness in 70 percent of patients, "with a reasonable level of safety."

BEWARE EXTENDED-WEAR CONTACTS

Sleeping with your lenses in can lead to corneal damage

Extended-wear contact lenses, touted for their ability to be worn as long as a week without removal or cleaning, aren't so carefree, after all, according to several recent studies. Researchers have found that the risks of an infection known as ulcerative keratitis, which causes severe inflammation of the cornea and can lead to permanent vision loss, were twice as great for conventional soft extended-wear users as for daily-wear users. Wearers of disposable lenses, which are designed to be worn without removal for up to two weeks and then thrown out before dirt and debris build up, were 13 times as likely to develop a corneal infection as those who regularly removed their contacts for cleaning.

Researchers writing in *Archives of Ophthalmology* found that most of the increased risk was the result of extended-wear users keeping their lenses in overnight and not following proper cleaning procedures. From a half to three-quarters of the corneal infections that now develop could be stopped by not wearing disposable lenses overnight, the group argued.

"Even adequate lens care, although recommended, does not protect against the excess risk of overnight wear," says Dr. Oliver Schein, an opthamologist at Johns Hopkins University and co-author of the study. The message for the four million Americans who now favor the convenience of extended-wear lenses: Remove your lenses and disinfect them while you give your eyes a rest each night.

Of the several hundred patients followed for a decade, about 70 percent had no need for eyeglasses or contact lenses to correct for nearsightedness, 53 percent of the eyes studied had uncorrected vision of 20/20 or better, and 85 percent of the patients could see at 20/40 or better, which is what is required for a driver's license in most places. Vision-threatening complications occurred in only 3 percent of the cases, and in all but three cases, the eyes could be corrected to 20/25 vision with glasses.

Farsightedness was another matter, however. Ten years after surgery, 43 percent of those whose eyes were studied had become farsighted by 1.00 D or more. ("D" stands for diopter, a measure of lens power indicating the need for a new prescription.) In many cases, the study found, the onset of symptomatic presbyopia—a condition where the eye loses natural flexibility—appear to have been accelerated by radial keratotomy, often leading to the need for reading glasses.

One way to offset this drift toward farsightedness is to shorten the length of the incisions made in the cornea, the study group concluded. Most of the vision gain from radial keratotomy comes from the incision's middle portion and not from the edge, and the longer the incisions, the more pronounced the farsightedness is, according to the NIH study.

The shift to farsightedness can be at least partly compensated for by intentionally undercorrecting for myopia in the initial radial keratotomy operation. Over time, the shift toward farsightedness and the undercorrecting for nearsightedness sometimes balance one another out, resulting in virtually normal vision.

Before deciding to get a vision overhaul with radial keratotomy, consider this, however. Once your corneas are slit in the procedure, wearing contact lenses comfortably can be very difficult. That means that if your nearsightedness is not adequately corrected or if you develop complications from the surgery, you are likely to be stuck wearing eyeglasses all the time.

A new treatment also is on the horizon for the nearsighted that leaps into the world of laser surgery. The process, known as photorefractive keratectomy, uses an excimer laser to flatten the cornea's contours and erase nearsightedness, the same way radial keratotomy does. The procedure takes 15 to 30 seconds and is appealing because it removes very little tissue—typically less than 10 percent of the cornea's thickness—and relies more on automation than on the skill of individual surgeons. Approved for use in 35 countries, photorefractive keratectomy was recommended for approval in the United States by an FDA advisory panel late in 1994. The use of laser surgery to treat mild to moderate nearsightedness is expected to be approved in 1995.

A SHIFT TO FARSIGHTED

A diopter is the unit of measurement of change in one's vision. A one-diopter change indicates the need for a new eyewear prescription in the immediate future. The chart tracks the percentage of eyes that have shifted one diopter or more toward farsightedness between a certain amount of years after radial keratotomy.

FROM...	TO... 1 yr.	2 yr.	3 yr.	4 yr.	5 yr.	10 yr.
6 ms.	5%	13%	16%	23%	26%	43%
1 yr.		6%	9%	14%	20%	37%
2 yr.			4%	6%	11%	30%
3 yr.				4%	9%	25%
4 yr.					6%	24%
5 yr.						21%

TEN YEARS AFTER

This chart shows the ability of radial keratotomy patients to read an eye chart (visual acuity) without corrective lenses (uncorrected) 10 years after the procedure.

Uncorrected visual acuity	Percentage of eyes
20/20 or better[1]	53%
20/40 or better[2]	85%
20/160 or better	98%
20/200 or better	100%

NOTES: 1. Normal vision. 2. Required for driver's license.
SOURCE: *Archives of Ophthalmology*, October, 1994.

EXPERT LIST

TINKERING WITH MOTHER NATURE

Facial implants and chemical peels have joined tummy tucks and nose jobs in the panoply of cosmetic procedures that appearance-conscious Americans are resorting to in increasing numbers. The American Society of Plastic and Reconstructive Surgeons provides this guide to today's most-elected interventions with nature.

BREAST ENLARGEMENT

Augmentation Mammoplasty

Enhances the size and shape of breasts using artificial implants.

- **Procedure:** Lasts 1 to 2 hours. Local anesthesia with sedation, or general. Usually outpatient.
- **Side effects:** Temporary pain. Swelling, soreness, numbness of abdominal skin, bruising, tiredness for several weeks or months.
- **Recovery:** Back to work in 2 to 4 weeks. More strenuous activity after 4 to 6 weeks or more. Fading and flattening of scars: 3 months to 2 years.
- **Risks:** Blood clots. Infection. Bleeding under the skin flap. Poor healing resulting in conspicuous scarring or skin loss. Need for a second operation.
- **Duration:** Permanent.

BREAST LIFT

Mastopexy

Raises and reshapes sagging breasts by removing excess skin and repositioning remaining tissue and nipples.

- **Procedure:** Lasts 1½ to 3½ hours. Local anesthesia with sedation, or general. Usually outpatient. Sometimes inpatient 1 to 2 days.
- **Side effects:** Temporary bruising, swelling, discomfort, numbness, dry breast skin. Permanent scars.
- **Recovery:** Feeling better, back to work in a week.
- **Risks:** Thick, wide scars; skin loss; infection. Unevenly positioned nipples. Permanent loss of feeling in nipples or breast.
- **Duration:** Variable; gravity, pregnancy, aging, and weight changes may cause new sagging. May last longer when combined with implants.

CHEMICAL PEEL

Phenol, trichloracetic acid (TCA)

Restore wrinkled, blemished, unevenly pigmented or sun-damaged facial skin, using a chemical solution to peel away skin's top layers. Works best on fair, thin skin with superficial wrinkles.

- **Procedure:** Takes 1 to 2 hours for full face. No anesthesia—sedation and EKG monitoring may be used. Usually outpatient. Full-face phenol peel may require admission for 1 to 2 days.
- **Side effects:** Both: Temporary throbbing, tingling, swelling redness; acute sensitivity to sun. Phenol: Permanent lightening of treated skin; permanent loss of ability to tan.
- **Recovery:** Phenol: Formation of new skin in 7 to 21 days. Normal activities in 2 to 4 weeks. Full healing and fading of redness in 3

SEX DISTRIBUTION

Eyelid surgery is most popular among women, but men prefer to have their noses altered.

Sex distribution of aesthetic procedures, 1992

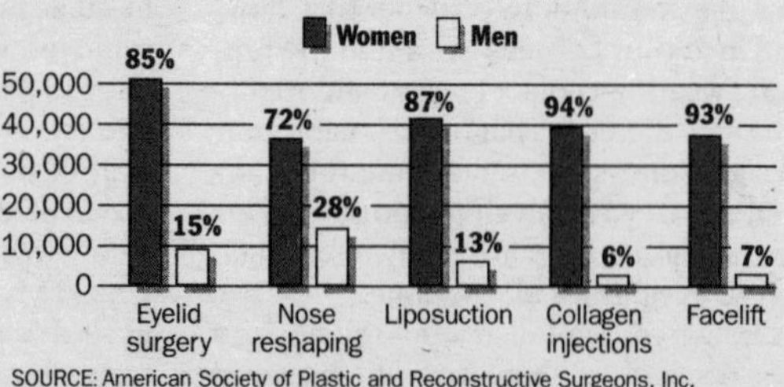

SOURCE: American Society of Plastic and Reconstructive Surgeons, Inc.

■ EXPERT LIST

to 6 months. TCA: New skin within 5 to 10 days.

■ **Risks:** Both: Tiny whiteheads (temporary); infection; scarring; flare-up of skin allergies, fever blisters, cold sores. Phenol: Abnormal color changes (permanent); heart irregularities (rare).

■ **Duration:** Phenol is permanent, although new wrinkles may form as skin ages. TCA is variable (temporary).

COLLAGEN/FAT INJECTIONS

Plump up creased, furrowed, or sunken facial skin; add fullness to lips and backs of hands. Works best on thin, dry, light-colored skin.

■ **Procedure:** Lasts 15 minutes to 1 hour per session. Collagen: usually no anesthesia; local may be included with the injection. Fat requires local anesthesia. Outpatient.

■ **Side effects:** Temporary stinging, throbbing, or burning sensation. Faint redness, swelling, excess fullness.

■ **Risks:** Collagen: allergic reactions including rash, hives, swelling, or flu-like symptoms; possible triggering of connective-tissue or autoimmune diseases. Both: contour irregularities; infection.

■ **Duration:** Variable, from a few months to as long as a year.

DERMABRASION

Mechanical scraping of the top layers of skin using a high-speed rotary wheel. Softens sharp edges of surface irregularities, including acne and other scars and fine wrinkles, especially around mouth.

■ **Procedure:** Lasts a few minutes to 1½ hours. May require more sessions. Anesthesia: Local, numbing spray, or general. Usually outpatient.

■ **Side effects:** Temporary tingling, burning, itching, swelling, redness. Lightening of treated skin, acute sensitivity to sun; loss of ability to tan.

■ **Recovery:** Back to work in 2 weeks. More strenuous activities in 4 to 6 weeks. Fading of redness in about 3 months. Return of pigmentation/sun exposure in 6 to 12 months.

■ **Risks:** Abnormal color changes (permanent). Tiny whiteheads (temporary). Infection. Scarring. Flare-up of skin allergies, fever blisters, cold sores.

■ **Duration:** Permanent, but new wrinkles may form as skin ages.

EYELID SURGERY

Blepharoplasty

Corrects drooping upper eyelids and puffy bags below the eyes by removing excess fat, skin, and muscle. (May be covered by insurance if used to improve vision.)

■ **Procedure:** Lasts 1 to 3 hours. Usually, local anesthesia with sedation, occasionally general. Usually outpatient.

■ **Side effects:** Temporary discomfort, tightness of lids, swelling, bruising. Temporary dryness, burning, itching of eyes. Excessive tearing, sensitivity to light for first few weeks.

■ **Risks:** Temporary blurred or double vision; blindness (extremely rare). Infection. Swelling at corners of eyelids; tiny whiteheads: Slight asymmetry in healing or scarring. Difficulty in closing eyes completely (rarely

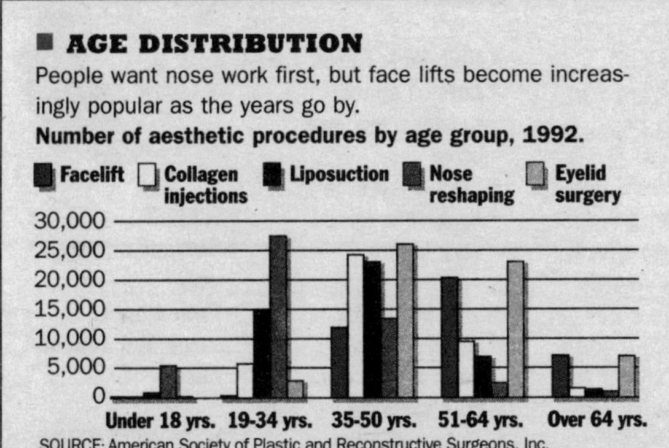

■ EXPERT LIST

permanent). Pulling down of the lower lids (may require further surgery).

■ **Recovery:** Reading in 2 or 3 days. Back to work in 7 to 10 days. Contact lenses in 2 weeks or more. Strenuous activities, alcohol in about 3 weeks. Bruising and swelling gone in several weeks.

■ **Duration:** Several years to permanent.

FACELIFT

Rhytidectomy

Improve sagging facial skin, jowls, and loose neck skin by removing excess, tightening muscles, redraping skin. Most often done on men and women over 40.

■ **Procedure:** Lasts several hours. Anesthesia: Local with sedation, or general. Usually outpatient. Some patients may require short inpatient stay.

■ **Side Effects:** Temporary bruising, swelling, numbness, and tenderness of skin; tight feeling, dry skin. For men, permanent need to shave behind ears, where beard-growing skin is repositioned.

■ **Recovery:** Back to work in 10 to 14 days. More strenuous activity in 2 weeks or more. Bruising gone in 2 to 3 weeks. Must limit exposure to sun for several months.

■ **Risks:** Injury to the nerves that control facial muscles, loss of feeling (usually temporary but may be permanent). Infection. Poor healing, excessive scarring. Change in hairline.

■ **Duration:** Usually about 5 to 10 years.

FACIAL IMPLANTS

Change the basic shape and balance of the face using carefully styled implants to build up a receding chin, add prominence to cheekbones, or reshape the jawline. Implants may be natural or artificial.

■ **Procedure:** Lasts 30 minutes to 2 hours. Anesthesia: Local with sedation, or general. Usually outpatient. Occasionally requires overnight stay.

■ **Side effects:** Temporary discomfort, swelling, bruising, numbness and/or stiffness. In jaw surgery, inability to open mouth fully for several weeks.

■ **Recovery:** Back to work in about a week. Normal appearance in 2 to 4 weeks. Activity that could jar or bump face after 6 weeks or more.

■ **Risks:** Shifting or imprecise positioning of

THE FASHIONABLE FACE THROUGH THE AGES

From the "Rubenesque" beauties of ages past to the "Twiggy Look" of the '60s, culture has always had a profound effect on how one perceives beauty. Never before, however, have people had the range of opportunities to physically reinvent themselves to reflect those shifting ideals, particularly in the the area that most influences one's perception of oneself, the face. Here's a look at some of those perceived ideals and the techniques that emerged to allow people to realize them.

1950s & 1960s

EYEBROW & EYELID SURGERY

- **High-lidded eyes**
- **Lots of space between eye and brow**
- **Wide-eyed look**
- **Eyebrows raised very high**

NOSE SURGERY

- **Turned up, ski-jump angle, nostrils showing**
- **Cute, childlike**
- **Highly sculpted tip**

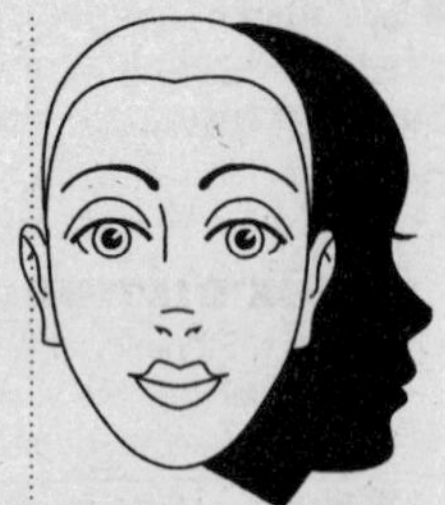

FACELIFT

- **Surface changes only**
- **Pulled-back, stretched appearance**

FACIAL SCULPTING

- **Did not exist**

■ EXPERT LIST

implant, or infection around it, requiring a second operation or removal. Excess tightening and hardening of scar tissue around an artificial implant ("capsular contracture"), causing an unnatural shape.
■ **Duration:** Permanent.

FOREHEAD LIFT

Browlift
Minimize forehead creases, drooping eyebrows, hooding over eyes, furrowed forehead, and frown lines by removing excess tissue and redraping skin. Most often done on people over 40.
■ **Procedure:** Length: 1 to 2 hours. Anesthesia: Local with sedation, or general. Usually outpatient.
■ **Side effects:** Temporary swelling, numbness, headaches, bruising. Possible itching and hair loss for several months. Change in hairline.
■ **Recovery:** Back to work in 7 to 10 days. More strenuous activity after several weeks. Bruising gone after 2 to 3 weeks. Limited exposure to sun for several months.
■ **Risks:** Injury to facial nerve, causing loss of motion, muscle weakness, or asymmetrical look. Infection. Broad or excessive scarring.
■ **Duration:** Usually about 5 to 10 years.

HAIR REPLACEMENT SURGERY

Fill in balding areas with the patient's own hair using a variety of techniques including scalp reduction, tissue expansion, strip grafts, scalp flaps, or clusters of punch grafts (plugs, miniplugs, and microplugs). Works best on men with male pattern baldness after hair loss has stopped.
■ **Procedure:** Lasts 1 to 3 hours. Some techniques may require multiple procedures over 18 months or more. Anesthesia: Usually local with sedation. Flaps and tissue expansion may be done with general anesthesia. Usually outpatient.
■ **Side effects:** Temporary aching, tight scalp. An unnatural look in early stages.
■ **Recovery:** Back to work: usually in 2 to 5 days. More strenuous activities after 10 days to 3 weeks. Final look: may be 18 months or more, depending on procedure.
■ **Risks:** Unnatural look. Infection. Excessive scar-

1970s

EYEBROW & EYELID SURGERY

- Lid width narrows, brow still slightly high
- Entire eyelid sculpted, rather than lifted, for more natural look

NOSE SURGERY

- Transition from stylized, uniform result to more aggressive nose

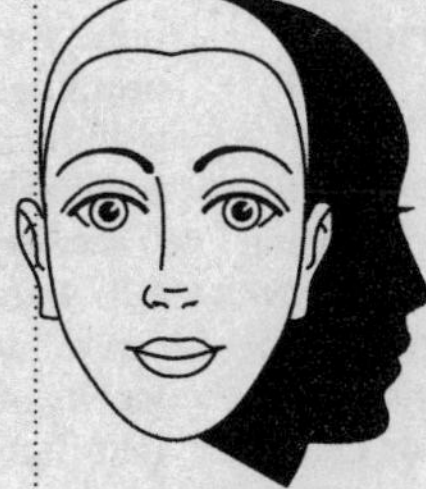

FACELIFT

- Underlying musculature tightened

FACIAL SCULPTING

- Did not exist

TODAY

EYEBROW & EYELID SURGERY

- Narrower lid
- 5 to 6 millimeters of space between brow for eye
- Natural appearance

NOSE SURGERY

- Longer, stronger nose
- Wider bridge
- Fuller, gently refined tip
- Individualized nose
- Natural, nonsurgical look

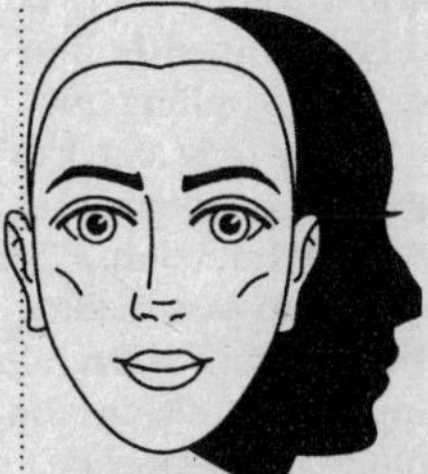

FACELIFT

- Very natural, nonsurgical look

FACIAL SCULPTING

- Bone reshape improves facelift
- Solves facial balance problems not addressed before

SOURCE: The American Academy of Facial Plastic and Reconstructive Surgery.

■ EXPERT LIST

ring. Failure to "take." Loss of scalp tissue and/or transplanted hair.
■ **Duration:** Permanent.

LIPOSUCTION

Suction-assisted lipectomy

Improve body shape using tube and vacuum device to remove unwanted fat deposits that don't respond to dieting and exercise. Locations include chin, cheeks, neck, upper arms, above breasts, abdomen, buttocks, hips, thighs, knees, calves, ankles.
■ **Procedure:** Lasts 1 to 2 hours or more, depending on extent of surgery. Anesthesia: Local, epidural, or general. Usually outpatient. Extensive procedures may require short inpatient stay.
■ **Side effects:** Temporary bruising, swelling, numbness, burning sensation.
■ **Recovery:** Back to work in 1 to 2 weeks. More strenuous activity after 2 to 4 weeks. Swelling and bruising may last 1 to 6 months or more.
■ **Risks:** Infection. Excessive fluid loss leading to shock. Fluid accumulation. Injury to the skin. Rippling or bagginess of skin. Pigmentation changes (may become permanent if exposed to sun).
■ **Duration:** Permanent, with sensible diet and exercise.

MALE BREAST REDUCTION

Gynecomastia

Reduce enlarged, female-like breasts in men using liposuction and/or cutting out excess glandular tissue. (Sometimes covered by medical insurance.)
■ **Procedure:** Lasts 1½ hours or more. Anesthesia: general or local. Usually outpatient.
■ **Side effects:** Temporary bruising, swelling, numbness, soreness, burning sensation.
■ **Recovery:** Back to work in 3 to 7 days. More strenuous activity after 2 to 3 weeks. Swelling and bruising subsides in 3 to 6 months.
■ **Risks:** Infection. Excessive fluid loss leading to shock. Fluid accumulation. Injury to the skin. Rippling or bagginess of skin. Pigmentation changes (may become permanent if exposed to sun). Excessive scarring if tissue was cut away. Need for second procedure to remove additional tissue.
■ **Duration:** Permanent.

NOSE SURGERY

Rhinoplasty

Reshape nose by reducing or increasing size, removing hump, changing shape of tip or bridge, narrowing span of nostrils, or changing angle between nose and upper lip. May relieve some breathing problems .
■ **Procedure:** Length: 1 to 2 hours or more. Anesthesia: Local with sedation, or general. Usually outpatient.
■ **Side effects:** Temporary swelling, bruising around eyes and nose, and headaches. Some bleeding and stuffiness.
■ **Recovery:** Back to work or school in 1 to 2 weeks. More strenuous activities after 2 to 3 weeks. Avoid hitting nose or sunburn for 8 weeks. Final appearance after a year or more.
■ **Risks:** Infection. Small burst blood vessels resulting in tiny, permanent red spots. Incomplete improvement, requiring additional surgery.
■ **Duration:** Permanent.

TUMMY TUCK

Abdominoplasty

Flatten abdomen by removing excess fat and skin and tightening muscles of abdominal wall.
■ **Procedure:** Lasts 2 to 5 hours. Anesthesia: General, or local with sedation. In- or outpatient, depending on individual circumstances.
■ **Side effects:** Temporary pain. Swelling, soreness, numbness of abdominal skin, bruising, tiredness for weeks or months.
■ **Recovery:** Back to work in 2 to 4 weeks. More strenuous activity after 4 to 6 weeks or more. Fading and flattening of scars in 3 months to 2 years.
■ **Risks:** Blood clots. Infection. Bleeding under the skin flap. Poor healing resulting in conspicuous scarring or skin loss. Need for a second operation.
■ **Duration:** Permanent.

SOURCE: American Society of Plastic and Reconstructive Surgeons, Inc.

THE OTHER SIDE OF THE COIN

From Manhattan to Hollywood, what plastic surgery costs

Procedure	Nat'l Average	CA	NY	FL	TX
Breast augmentation	$2,754	$3,141	$3,522	$2,756	$2,718
Breast lift	$3,063	$3,385	$4,010	$3,113	$2,970
Breast reconstruction					
Implant alone	$2,340	$2,719	$2,885	$2,468	$2,444
Tissue expander	$2,846	$2,881	$3,561	$3,204	$2,999
Latissimus dorsi	$4,509	$4,536	$5,395	$5,147	$5,031
TRAM (pedicle) flap	$6,143	$5,187	$7,483	$6,489	$6,209
Microsurgical free flap	$6,758	$5,685	$6,692	$7,262	$6,711
Breast reduction	$4,525	$4,929	$5,432	$5,293	$4,515
Breast reduction in men	$2,325	$2,687	$3,061	$2,470	$2,026
Buttock lift	$3,084	$2,798	$5,120	$3,175	$3,566
Cheek implants	$1,895	$1,870	$2,654	$1,701	$1,530
Chemical peel					
Full face	$1,634	$1,849	$2,217	$1,668	$1,454
Regional	$682	$762	$869	$711	$626
Chin augmentation					
Implant	$1,221	$1,380	$1,907	$1,153	$901
Osteotomy	$2,077	$2,342	$2,990	$2,133	$1,413
Collagen injections per 1 cc	$266	$296	$328	$278	$259
Dermabrasion	$1,551	$1,840	$2,267	$1,486	$1,344
Eyelid surgery					
Both uppers	$1,514	$1,601	$1,939	$1,469	$1,524
Both lowers	$1,519	$1,633	$2,151	$1,447	$1,478
Combination of both	$2,625	$2,784	$3,594	$2,564	$2,593
Facelift	$4,156	$4,448	$5,410	$4,026	$4,148
Fat injection					
Head/neck	$636	$702	$695	$717	$695
Trunk	$622	$571	$794	$645	$300
Extremities	$663	$572	$794	$644	$689
Forehead lift	$2,164	$2,484	$3,207	$2,002	$1,852
Liposuction—any single site	$1,622	$2,028	$2,346	$1,603	$1,563
Male-pattern baldness					
Plug grafts-per plug	$101	$162	$152	$297	$23
Strip grafts-per strip	$1,096	$869	$1,500	$1,150	$1,200
Scalp reduction-all stages	$1,720	$2,549	$2,357	$2,084	$1,350
Pedicle flap-all stages	$2,699	$5,308	$2,525	$3,067	$1,600
Tissue expansion-all stages	$3,081	$3,609	$4,175	$3,244	$2,000
Nose reshaping (primary)					
Fee for open rhinoplasty	$2,997	$3,390	$4,371	$2,947	$3,019
Fee for closed rhinoplasty	$2,825	$3,131	$4,160	$2,705	$2,689
Nose reshaping (secondary)					
Fee for open rhinoplasty	$2,615	$3,130	$3,426	$2,806	$2,662
Fee for closed rhinoplasty	$2,649	$2,958	$3,841	$2,819	$2,525
Retin-A treatment per visit	$92	$56	$83	$58	$39
Thigh lift	$3,090	$3,093	$4,723	$3,115	$3,098
Tummy tuck	$3,618	$4,085	$4,774	$3,754	$3,581

SOURCE: American Society of Plastic and Reconstructive Surgeons, Inc., 1994.

EXPERT Q&A

STRAIGHT TALK ABOUT BRACES

An early trip to the orthodontist can spare you a fearsome dental bill

Dr. Tom Graber has been in the forefront of orthodontic research since he began practicing in 1945. He's authored several textbooks on the subject and has edited *The American Journal of Orthodontics and Dentofacial Orthopedics* since 1985. Though he's never worn braces himself, three of his children have.

■ What does an orthodontist do?

Just as an orthopedic surgeon guides the growth of an abnormally forming leg or arm, an orthodontist guides the growth of the jaw and face, particularly for children with underdeveloped jaws or when the upper and lower jaw don't fit together.

■ What are the tip-offs that preventative measures like an appliance might be needed?

The most obvious problems are the inherited ones, such as when a child inherits a small jaw from one parent and large teeth from another, leading to jaw disorders. Also, the upper jaw can be deformed by finger sucking or, more likely, compensatory tongue-swallowing habits. This happens when kids continue natural back and forth tongue-thrusting when they stop nursing, which pushes the front teeth out. Kids whose front teeth stick out tend to get their lower lip under them every time they swallow, which pushes the teeth even further out. Mouth-breathing or enlarged adenoids and tonsils can also cause compensatory problems.

■ What can be done to prevent such problems?

Children should be seen by a qualified orthodontist by the time they are six. A pediatric dentist may not have the training to recognize the early developmental problems that can be solved with simple interceptive orthodontics, and recognizing these problems can save a lot of trouble down the road. By the time your girl hits 11 or 12 or your boy hits 13 or 14, all you can really do is shove teeth around. Better to start with simple appliance procedures than to go in there later with an expensive long-term procedure.

A simple appliance, for instance, can be used to expand a narrow jaw or to prevent the deleterious effects of bad habits. You probably will want to use a simple fixed appliance which is cemented to the child's upper teeth. A removable appliance relies too much on patient cooperation, which is hard to come by with very young children.

■ What about braces? What are some of the reasons one would get them?

Mostly for cosmetic reasons, but braces also help to correct abnormal jaw growth and function. The cause of real dental health problems is not necessarily crooked teeth but the way the teeth fit together, so you use braces to get a handle on the jaw. When the jaws are not in the right relationship, it places abnormal stress on the jaw joint, and that may cause pain and improper function.

■ Are there any new technologies that can make wearing braces a less traumatic experience for a self-conscious young person?

Lingual braces, which are hidden behind the teeth, are fine for purely cosmetic reasons, but they are much harder to adjust and make eating and talking difficult. And they aren't as effective because you can't get the same kind of control over them.

The alternative is ceramic braces. The brackets are made out of the same sort of material as coffee cups and are nearly invisible against the teeth. Ceramic brackets are bonded to the tooth instead of being glued around it like the old metal bands were. They make very cosmetically acceptable brackets for the wires, which have also come a long way. The new thin nickel titanium wires are light and they need less adjustment. They work so well that you don't need them as long.

In some specialized cases, small magnets can be used to speed up and simplify treatment, for example with growth guidance appliances and the eruption of teeth embedded in the jaw, but this is very unusual.

■ How can a parent know if a price quoted by an orthodontist is reasonable?

Early interceptive work with appliances may run you $300 or $400, but if it's a difficult case that requires braces and a lot of treatment, it may be as much as $4,000. Of course, prices vary geographically, but in most cases, braces will run from $1,800 to around $2,800 for involved programs.

In a lot of cases you have to rely on the integrity of your orthodontist. Make sure he is board certified, which only about 25 percent of orthodontists are. You can also call one of the dental schools in your town to get an idea of what the going rate for a specific procedure is. And, of course, you should always get a second opinion.

■ When does it make sense for adults to undergo an orthodontic procedure?

About 25 percent of the orthodontic work done today is on adults, mostly for cosmetic reasons. There is also a relationship between some gum problems and jaw problems that braces can help. You put up to 350 pounds of pressure on your jaw when you chew, and that can really affect your gums. A lot of adults tend to grind or clench their teeth at night, which, if your bite is wrong, can lead to a popped disc in the jaw joint. Orthodontists can make a splint that will help relieve that pressure.

A DIM REPORT ABOUT TEETH BRIGHTENERS

Using hydrogen peroxide to whiten teeth raises a host of questions

When you brush with teeth brighteners, you may be getting more than just a flashy smile. Teeth brightener sales topped $51 million in 1993, up 25 percent over 1992. But the American Dental Association has raised serious concerns about the safety of teeth brighteners. Prompted by the ADA, the U.S. Food and Drug Administration is now investigating whether the over-the-counter products should be regulated as cosmetics or drugs. None of the products currently on the market are accepted by the ADA.

Although dentists have used hydrogen peroxide as bleaching agents for years, the ADA worries that commercially available at-home kits involve hours of unsupervised exposure to hydrogen peroxide and that users may leave the product on their teeth longer than directed, thinking their teeth will be made even whiter the longer the product is applied. The brighteners often contain acids that can damage enamel, they say, and overuse can also cause tooth sensitivity, gum irritation, and throat and stomach problems. In some cases, oxygenating agents can damage mouth tissues, delay healing, harm the interior of teeth, cause cell changes, and enhance the effects of other carcinogens, they claim. One recent study published in the *Journal of Periodontology* found that hamsters given hydrogen peroxide orally developed precancerous growths. When hydrogen peroxide was combined with cancer-causing products, such as cigarettes, the likelihood of cancer increased greatly.

FDA safety regulations are more stringent for drugs than for cosmetics. According to the FDA, a drug is intended to affect the structure and function of the body while a cosmetic is defined as anything "introduced into or otherwise applied to the human body for promoting attractiveness or altering appearances."

At prices that can be twice as high as regular toothpaste, teeth brighteners carry a healthy profit margin. The FDA will have to determine if they are also as safe.

HAVING CHILDREN

SEQUELS TO THE BABY BOOM

Birth rates are off for women in their twenties, but not for older women

Thinking about having a baby? For most women the decision has never been more complicated. The social, medical, and economic trends that have led to later marriages, greater job opportunities, and career pressures for women, easier contraception and abortion, and new techniques for treating infertility have all contributed to pronounced shifts in the demographic profile of child-bearing women over the last decade.

Although women in their 20s continue to bear the most children, the sharpest increases in birth rates since the late 1970s have been among women aged 30 or older. According to the National Center for Health Statistics, the rate for women aged 30 to 34 increased 31 percent during the 1980s before dipping slightly in 1992, which is the year with the most recent data.

Even sharper increases occurred among women aged 35 to 39 (up 60 percent during the 1980s) and among women in their 40s (up 50 percent for the decade). While the birth rate for women in their mid to late 30s nearly leveled off in the early 1990s, the rate among older Baby Boomer

■ **THE BIOLOGICAL CLOCK**

Recent data shows that 4,065,014 babies were born in the United States in 1992. More than three-fourths were to women in their 20s and early 30s, but the biggest increases were for older women.

SOURCE: National Center for Health Statistics

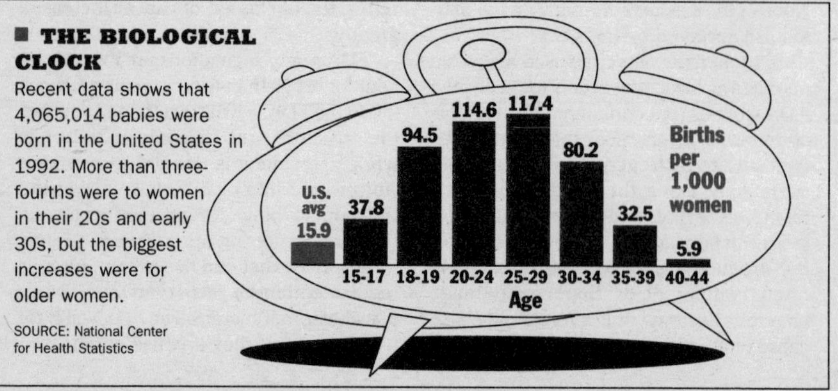

women, aged 40 to 44, continues to rise.

Meanwhile, teen birth rates, which grew at rates of 20 percent or more in the late 1980s, were flat, or in the case of girls aged 15 to 17 even slightly down in the early 1990s. According to the National Center for Health Statistics, "The leveling off of the sharp rate of increase in teenage childbearing during the 1980s may reflect a similar leveling off since 1988 in the proportion of teenagers who are sexually active, especially among the youngest teenagers." Among teenagers who are sexually active, contraceptive use seems to be on the rise, the government researchers reported.

Despite the rise in birth rates among older women, far more women in their 30s remain childless than was true two decades ago. In 1975 about one in nine women aged 35 were childless; it is now about one in five. The group tends to be far better educated than the general population. The National Center for Health Statistics reports that in 1992, 49 percent of first-time mothers aged 30 to 45 were college graduates; that was double what it was for other women that were in this age group.

Infertility problems may affect many older women who still plan to have children. According to one major government survey, a third of childless wives aged 35 to 44 were found to have fertility problems in 1988. Yet many previously untreatable fertility problems (see "If a Couple Can't Conceive," page 232) can now be addressed, even among older women.

The combination of more women in the workforce with later marriages and childbearing has also meant smaller families. During the era of the Kennedy presidency, it was not at all uncommon to have as many as four children. Today the average is two. In 1980 the proportion of families with four or more children under the age of 18 was 7.8 percent. In 1990 it was only 5.7 percent, and over 4 in ten families had only one child.

When it comes to birth trends today, "less is more" and "better late than never" appear to be the watchwords.

DO-IT-YOURSELF PREGNANCY EXAMS

Home test kits that enable a woman to determine for herself if she is pregnant are becoming the messenger of choice for many American women. Not only do the kits allow women to conduct an initial pregnancy test in the privacy of their own homes, but at prices of about $12 to $16 a kit, the home tests cost considerably less than the blood tests, for which physicians normally charge $50 to $100 to determine pregnancy. No prescription is required.

New technology has made the tests highly reliable and easy to use. Results take only five minutes to obtain, and the test can be given as early as the first day of a missed period. The tests detect a hormone in the urine called human chorionic gonadotropin, which is produced by the placenta. Since the hormone is most easily detected in the morning, some kits require that the test be done in the early morning.

Most tests have the user urinate on a plastic indicator stick about the size of a nail file. If the hormone is detected, a chemical reaction registers on a gauge built into the indicator stick. If the woman is pregnant, a colored circle, bar, or plus sign appears on the gauge on the indicator stick. If the results are negative, the window remains unchanged. When test results are positive, the test is 99 percent accurate. They are 80 percent accurate if the results are negative. If the results are negative and a woman's period is still late, the test should be redone in a week. Anytime the results are positive or menstruation is delayed and the test remains inconclusive, a gynecologist should be consulted promptly.

STORK'S GUIDE

FIGURING YOUR DUE DATE

While the average pregnancy is 280 days from the last menstrual period, it is normal to give birth anywhere from 37 to 42 weeks after your last period. To use this chart to determine your estimated delivery date, locate the bold-faced number that represents the first day of your last menstrual period. The light-faced number below it represents the expected delivery date.

JAN	**1**	**2**	**3**	**4**	**5**	**6**	**7**	**8**	**9**	**10**	**11**	**12**	**13**	**14**	**15**		**JAN**
OCT	8	9	10	11	12	13	14	15	16	17	18	19	20	21	22		OCT
JAN	**16**	**17**	**18**	**19**	**20**	**21**	**22**	**23**	**24**	**25**	**26**	**27**	**28**	**29**	**30**	**31**	**JAN**
OCT	23	24	25	26	27	28	29	30	31	1	2	3	4	5	6	7	NOV

FEB	**1**	**2**	**3**	**4**	**5**	**6**	**7**	**8**	**9**	**10**	**11**	**12**	**13**	**14**	**15**		**FEB**
NOV	8	9	10	11	12	13	14	15	16	17	18	19	20	21	22		NOV
FEB	**16**	**17**	**18**	**19**	**20**	**21**	**22**	**23**	**24**	**25**	**26**	**27**	**28**				**FEB**
NOV	23	24	25	26	27	28	29	30	1	2	3	4	5				DEC

MAR	**1**	**2**	**3**	**4**	**5**	**6**	**7**	**8**	**9**	**10**	**11**	**12**	**13**	**14**	**15**		**MAR**
DEC	6	7	8	9	10	11	12	13	14	15	16	17	18	19	20		DEC
MAR	**16**	**17**	**18**	**19**	**20**	**21**	**22**	**23**	**24**	**25**	**26**	**27**	**28**	**29**	**30**	**31**	**MAR**
DEC	21	22	23	24	25	26	27	28	29	30	31	1	2	3	4	5	JAN

APR	**1**	**2**	**3**	**4**	**5**	**6**	**7**	**8**	**9**	**10**	**11**	**12**	**13**	**14**	**15**	**APR**
JAN	6	7	8	9	10	11	12	13	14	15	16	17	18	19	20	JAN
APR	**16**	**17**	**18**	**19**	**20**	**21**	**22**	**23**	**24**	**25**	**26**	**27**	**28**	**29**	**30**	**APR**
JAN	21	22	23	24	25	26	27	28	29	30	31	1	2	3	4	FEB

MAY	**1**	**2**	**3**	**4**	**5**	**6**	**7**	**8**	**9**	**10**	**11**	**12**	**13**	**14**	**15**		**MAY**
FEB	5	6	7	8	9	10	11	12	13	14	15	16	17	18	19		FEB
MAY	**16**	**17**	**18**	**19**	**20**	**21**	**22**	**23**	**24**	**25**	**26**	**27**	**28**	**29**	**30**	**31**	**MAY**
FEB	20	21	22	23	24	25	26	27	28	1	2	3	4	5	6	7	MAR

JUN	**1**	**2**	**3**	**4**	**5**	**6**	**7**	**8**	**9**	**10**	**11**	**12**	**13**	**14**	**15**	**JUN**
MAR	8	9	10	11	12	13	14	15	16	17	18	19	20	21	22	MAR
JUN	**16**	**17**	**18**	**19**	**20**	**21**	**22**	**23**	**24**	**25**	**26**	**27**	**28**	**29**	**30**	**JUN**
MAR	23	24	25	26	27	28	29	30	31	1	2	3	4	5	6	APR

SOURCE: *Planning for Pregnancy, Birth, and Beyond,* American College of Obstetricians and Gynecologists, 1993.

STORK'S GUIDE

JUL	**1**	**2**	**3**	**4**	**5**	**6**	**7**	**8**	**9**	**10**	**11**	**12**	**13**	**14**	**15**		**JUL**
APR	7	8	9	10	11	12	13	14	15	16	17	18	19	20	21		APR
JUL	**16**	**17**	**18**	**19**	**20**	**21**	**22**	**23**	**24**	**25**	**26**	**27**	**28**	**29**	**30**	**31**	**JUL**
APR	22	23	24	25	26	27	28	29	30	1	2	3	4	5	6	7	MAY
AUG	**1**	**2**	**3**	**4**	**5**	**6**	**7**	**8**	**9**	**10**	**11**	**12**	**13**	**14**	**15**		**AUG**
MAY	8	9	10	11	12	13	14	15	16	17	18	19	20	21	22		MAY
AUG	**16**	**17**	**18**	**19**	**20**	**21**	**22**	**23**	**24**	**25**	**26**	**27**	**28**	**29**	**30**	**31**	**AUG**
MAY	23	24	25	26	27	28	29	30	31	1	2	3	4	5	6	7	JUN
SEP	**1**	**2**	**3**	**4**	**5**	**6**	**7**	**8**	**9**	**10**	**11**	**12**	**13**	**14**	**15**		**SEP**
JUN	8	9	10	11	12	13	14	15	16	17	18	19	20	21	22		JUN
SEP	**16**	**17**	**18**	**19**	**20**	**21**	**22**	**23**	**24**	**25**	**26**	**27**	**28**	**29**	**30**		**SEP**
JUN	23	24	25	26	27	28	29	30	1	2	3	4	5	6	7		JUL
OCT	**1**	**2**	**3**	**4**	**5**	**6**	**7**	**8**	**9**	**10**	**11**	**12**	**13**	**14**	**15**		**OCT**
JUL	8	9	10	11	12	13	14	15	16	17	18	19	20	21	22		JUL
OCT	**16**	**17**	**18**	**19**	**20**	**21**	**22**	**23**	**24**	**25**	**26**	**27**	**28**	**29**	**30**	**31**	**OCT**
JUL	23	24	25	26	27	28	29	30	31	1	2	3	4	5	6	7	AUG
NOV	**1**	**2**	**3**	**4**	**5**	**6**	**7**	**8**	**9**	**10**	**11**	**12**	**13**	**14**	**15**		**NOV**
AUG	8	9	10	11	12	13	14	15	16	17	18	19	20	21	22		AUG
NOV	**16**	**17**	**18**	**19**	**20**	**21**	**22**	**23**	**24**	**25**	**26**	**27**	**28**	**29**	**30**		**NOV**
AUG	23	24	25	26	27	28	29	30	31	1	2	3	4	5	6		SEP
DEC	**1**	**2**	**3**	**4**	**5**	**6**	**7**	**8**	**9**	**10**	**11**	**12**	**13**	**14**	**15**		**DEC**
SEP	7	8	9	10	11	12	13	14	15	16	17	18	19	20	21		SEP
DEC	**16**	**17**	**18**	**19**	**20**	**21**	**22**	**23**	**24**	**25**	**26**	**27**	**28**	**29**	**30**	**31**	**DEC**
SEP	22	23	24	25	26	27	28	29	30	1	2	3	4	5	6	7	OCT

GROWTH OF THE FETUS FROM 8 TO 40 WEEKS

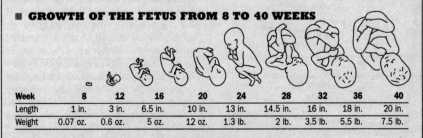

Week	**8**	**12**	**16**	**20**	**24**	**28**	**32**	**36**	**40**
Length	1 in.	3 in.	6.5 in.	10 in.	13 in.	14.5 in.	16 in.	18 in.	20 in.
Weight	0.07 oz.	0.6 oz.	5 oz.	12 oz.	1.3 lb.	2 lb.	3.5 lb.	5.5 lb.	7.5 lb.

SOURCE: *American Medical Association Encyclopedia of Medicine*, Random House, 1989.

EXPERT Q&A

WHEN MORNING SICKNESS HITS

An expert explains the nausea that often goes with pregnancy

Up to 70 percent of pregnant women suffer nausea from morning sickness, and not always in the morning. Dr. Donald Coustan, Chairman of the Obstetrics and Gynecology Department at Brown University School of Medicine, advises how to relieve the discomfort.

■ What is morning sickness and what are its symptoms?

Morning sickness is nausea, with and without vomiting, during pregnancy. It may occur at any time of day, especially when the stomach is empty. While it is most common during the first three months of pregnancy, it may continue beyond that time and may recur toward the end of pregnancy. But the problem usually goes away by 13 to 20 weeks of gestation.

■ What causes morning sickness?

It is not well understood, but many doctors believe that hormonal changes may be involved. Women prone to morning sickness often report that particular odors, sights, or tastes may trigger an episode.

■ Are some more susceptible than others?

Yes, although one study estimated that nausea and vomiting occur in up to 70 percent of pregnancies.

■ What treatment is recommended?

We usually recommend that women prone to morning sickness eat five or six small meals each day in order to avoid an empty stomach as much as possible. Some women are helped by eating dry soda crackers, a peeled apple or a plain potato (peeled and cooked). They are also advised to avoid unpleasant odors and foods that trigger an attack. Women who experience nausea and vomiting so severe that they cannot even keep down frequent small meals, and whose urinary output fails, should consult their obstetrician. In such cases, it may be necessary to provide intravenous fluids and injections of medications to break the cycle and treat dehydration. Otherwise, there could be liver or kidney damage to the mother and even starvation.

■ Are there any drugs that can help?

No. There previously was a medication known as Bendectine, which consisted of vitamin B6 and doxylamine, an antihistamine, which appeared to be effective. It was removed from the market, however, because of lawsuits alleging that it caused birth defects. Although it was never demonstrated that the medication caused birth defects, and most of the lawsuits were won by the defense, the company spent so much money defending the suits that they were unable to continue making the drug. The components of this drug may be useful, but they are not as well-studied as the combination.

FACT FILE:

A MOTHER'S BURDEN

■ *The typical pregnant woman gains about 30 pounds during the 40 weeks of pregnancy:*

7 lbs.	Maternal stores (fat, protein, and other nutrients)
4 lbs.	Increased fluid volume
4 lbs.	Increased blood volume
2 lbs.	Breast enlargement
2 lbs.	Uterus
7½ lbs.	Baby
2 lbs.	Amniotic fluid
1½ lbs.	Placenta

SOURCE: *Planning for Pregnancy, Birth, and Beyond,* American College of Obstetricians and Gynecologists.

KEEPING YOUR BABY FROM HARM'S WAY

Beware of what these agents could do to the fetus

AGENT	REASONS USED	EFFECTS
ALCOHOL	Part of regular diet, social reasons, dependency.	Growth and mental retardation.
ANDROGENS	To treat endometriosis.	Genital abnormalities.
ANTICOAGULANTS Warfarin (Coumadin, Panwarfin) and dicumatrol	To prevent blood clotting; used to prevent or treat thromboembolisms (clots blocking blood vessels).	Abnormalities in bones, cartilage, and eyes; central nervous system defects.
ANTITHYROID DRUGS Propylthiouracil, iodide, and methimazole (Tapazole)	To treat an overactive thyroid gland.	Underactive or enlarged thyroid.
ANTICONVULSANTS Phentoin (Dilantin), trimethadione (Tridione), paramethadione (Paradione), valproic acid (Depakene)	To treat epilepsy and irregular heartbeat.	Growth and mental retardation, developmental abnormalities, neural tube defects.
CHEMOTHERAPEUTIC DRUGS Methotrexate (Mexate) and aminopterin	To treat cancer and psoriasis.	Increased rate of miscarriage, varous abnormalities.
DIETHYLSIBESTROL (DES)	To treat problems with menstruation, symptoms of menopause and breast cancer, and to stop milk production; previously used to prevent preterm labor and miscarriage.	Abnormalities of cervix and uterus in females, possible infertility in males and females.
LEAD	Industries involving lead smelting, paint manufacture and use, printing, ceramics, glass manufacturing, and pottery glazing.	Increased rate of miscarriage and stillbirths.
LITHIUM	To treat the manic part of manic-depressive disorders.	Congenital heart disease.
ORGANIC MERCURY	Exposure through eating contaminated food.	Brain disorders.
ISOTRETINOIN (Accutane)	Treatment for cystic acne.	Increased rate of miscarriage, developmental abnormalities.
STREPTOMYCIN	An antibiotic used to treat tuberculosis.	Hearing loss.
TETRACYCLINE	An antibiotic used to treat a wide variety of infections.	Underdevelopment of tooth enamel, incorporation of tetracycline into bone.
THALIDOMIDE	Previously used as a sedative and a sleep aid.	Growth deficiencies, other abnormalities.
X-RAY THERAPY	Medical treatment of disorders such as cancer.	Growth and mental retardation.

SOURCE: *Planning for Pregnancy, Birth, and Beyond*, American College of Obstetricians and Gynecologists, 1993.

EXAMINING BABIES BEFORE BIRTH

Ultrasound is under fire, but there are other important new tests

For years, ultrasound testing has been as much a part of a pregnant woman's experience as stepping on the scale at the ob-gyn's. The test to diagnose birth defects is routinely given to over two-thirds of all mothers-to-be. But a recent study shows that the benefits of ultrasound may have been oversold.

Along with detecting anatomical abnormalities such as heart defects in the fetus, ultrasound has been used to determine a fetus's age, rate of growth, heart and breathing rate, and position of the fetus and placenta within the womb. It is also a way of establishing the sex of the fetus, gauging the amount of amniotic fluid in the uterus, and determining whether there is more than one child on the way.

The new study by researchers at the University of Missouri at Columbia divided 15,500 women with low-risk pregnancies into two groups—those who had two ultrasound tests during their pregnancies, at four months and at seven months, and those who either didn't have the test or had it only when there was a specific medical need.

The six-year study, the largest ever to examine prenatal testing, found that there was no difference between the two groups in the incidence of premature babies, lung failure, spinal chord injury, infection, probllem deliveries, or prolonged hospital stays. What's more, both groups had the same rate

■ WHEN THERE'S A FAMILY HISTORY

Some defects are more likely to recur if parents already have one child with the same defect.

DISORDER	RISK OF HAVING A FETUS WITH THE DISORDER		
	Overall		**With one affected child**
DOMINANT GENE			
Polydactyly	1 in 300 to 1 in 100		50%
Achondroplasia	1 in 23,000		50%
Huntington disease	1 in 15,000 to 1 in 5,000		50%
RECESSIVE GENE			
Cystic fibrosis	1 in 2,500	White persons	25%
Sickle-cell anemia	1 in 625	Black persons	25%
Tay-Sachs disease	1 in 3,600	Ashkenazi Jews	25%
Beta-thalassemia	1 in 2,500-1 in 800	Persons of Mediterranean descent	25%
X-LINKED			
Hemophilia	1 in 2,500	Men	50% for boy, 0% for girl
CHROMOSOMAL			
Down syndrome	1 in 800	Average risk increases with mother's age	1–2%
Klinefelter syndrome	1 in 800	Men	No significant increase
Turner syndrome	1 in 3,000	Women	No significant increase
MULTIFACTORAL			
Congenital heart disease	1 in 125		2–4%
Neural tube defects	1 in 1,000 to 1 in 500		2–5%
Cleft lip/cleft palate	1 in 1,000 to 1 in 500		2–4%

SOURCE: *Planning for Pregnancy, Birth, and Beyond,* American College of Obstetricians and Gynecologists, 1993.

of birth defects—5 percent. The study's conclusion: Although ultrasound testing, or a sonogram as it is also known, detects more fetal abnormalities, getting the test doesn't change the odds of delivering a baby with birth defects because most birth defects aren't detected within 24 weeks of the onset of pregnancy, which is the cutoff time for an abortion in most states. "Our study shows that most normal pregnant women will have a healthy baby regardless of ultrasound screening," says the study's lead investigator, Dr. Bernard G. Ewigman.

While the routine use of ultrasound is being called into question, other prenatal tests for birth defects and genetic disorders have never shown more potential. They include amniocentesis, alpha-fetoprotein testing, and the latest procedure—percutaneous umbilical blood sampling, or PUBS.

The tests are regularly recommended for: women 35 and over; women with a family history of genetic disorders; women who have had a previous child with a birth defect; women who have been exposed to a virus known to cause birth defects; women who ingest substances such as alcohol or certain medicines during pregnancy or at the time of conception; and women who were insulin-dependent prior to pregnancy. A breakdown of the procedures:

THE RISKS OF WAITING

Birth defect probabilities rise with the mother's age.

Mother's age	Chance of Down Syndrome	Chance of any chromosomal disease
20	1 in 1,667	1 in 526
21	1 in 1,667	1 in 526
22	1 in 1,429	1 in 500
23	1 in 1,429	1 in 500
24	1 in 1,250	1 in 476
25	1 in 1,250	1 in 476
26	1 in 1,176	1 in 476
27	1 in 1,111	1 in 455
28	1 in 1,053	1 in 435
29	1 in 1,000	1 in 417
30	1 in 952	1 in 385
31	1 in 909	1 in 385
32	1 in 769	1 in 322
33	1 in 602	1 in 286
34	1 in 485	1 in 238
35	1 in 378	1 in 192
36	1 in 289	1 in 156
37	1 in 224	1 in 127
38	1 in 173	1 in 102
39	1 in 136	1 in 83
40	1 in 106	1 in 66
41	1 in 82	1 in 53
42	1 in 63	1 in 42
43	1 in 49	1 in 33
44	1 in 38	1 in 26
45	1 in 30	1 in 21
46	1 in 23	1 in 16
47	1 in 18	1 in 13
48	1 in 14	1 in 10
49	1 in 11	1 in 8

SOURCE: *Planning for Pregnancy, Birth, and Beyond,* American College of Obstetricians and Gynecologists, 1993.

AMNIOCENTESIS: The procedure can be done as early as the 12th and as late as the 18th week of pregnancy. The process requires that a needle be inserted into the woman's abdomen and amniotic fluid withdrawn so that it can be tested. Since the genetic makeup of the cells in the amniotic fluid are the same as those of the fetus, the cells can be tested for several chromosonal abnormalities, including those indicating the presence of Down syndrome, a form of severe mental retardation, and spina bifida, a central nervous system disorder that prevents the spinal column from developing fully.

With amniocentesis, there is a 1 in 200 chance of miscarriage. Some women have cramps after the test, and, in rare cases, there is a chance that the fetus will be injured, according to the American College of Obstetricians and Gynecologists. And test results, which take two to four weeks, may show an innacurate "abnormal" reading if the fetus is older or younger than had been estimated.

ALPHA-FETOPROTEIN: This involves a simple blood test given to women who are 15 to 18 weeks pregnant. Also known as maternal serum screening, the simple test uses blood taken from a woman's arm to measure the amount of alpha-fetoprotein—a protein produced by the fetus—in the mother's blood. Unusually low levels of the chemical are linked to chromosome dis-

PRENATAL SCREENING PROCEDURES

In an uncomplicated pregnancy, expect about a dozen doctor visits

FIRST VISIT	■ **Blood tests:** To check the woman's blood group and sometimes, to check for presence of hepatitis B virus, which might be transmitted to the baby.
	■ **Cervical smear test:** To test for an early cancer of the cervix (if a test has not been performed recently). Also called a Pap smear.
FIRST VISIT AND THROUGHOUT THE PREGNANCY	■ **Blood tests:** To check for anemia in the woman, and in women with Rh-negative blood groups, to look for the presence of Rhesus antibodies.
	■ **Urine test:** To check for proteinuria, which could indicate a urinary tract infection or preeclampsia.
	■ **Blood and urine test**: To check for diabetes mellitus.
	■ **Blood pressure check:** To screen for hypertension, which interferes with blood supply to the placenta and is a sign of preeclampsia.
FIRST VISIT AND AFTER ANY INFECTION	■ **Blood tests:** To screen for rubella, which can cause defects in the baby, and for syphilis and HIV (the AIDS virus) which can also be passed on.
FIRST 12 WEEKS	■ **Chorionic villus sampling:** May be performed if there is a risk of certain genetic (inherited) disorders being passed on.
16 TO 18 WEEKS	■ **Ultrasound scanning:** Is carried out to date the pregnancy accurately and to detect any abnormalities present in the fetus.
	■ **Amniocentesis:** Carried out on older women and those with spina bifida or Down's syndrome to detect possible abnormalities in the fetus.
	■ **Blood test:** In some cases, the amount of alpha-fetoprotein in the blood is tested to determine whether the baby has spina bifida.
	■ **Fetoscopy and fetal blood sampling:** In some cases, these are carried out if there is doubt about the normality of the baby.
HIGH-RISK OR OVERDUE PREGNANCIES	■ **Blood and urine tests:** To assess placental function and fetus health.
	■ **Electronic fetal monitoring:** To check on the fetal heart beat.
	■ **Ultrasound scanning:** Extra scans may be recommended to assess fetal growth and development, location of placenta, amount of amniotic fluid.

SOURCE: *Encyclopedia of Medicine*, American Medical Association, Random House, 1989.

orders. When levels of the chemical are higher than normal, it can mean that the fetus has a neural tube defect such as spina bifida. But alpha-fetoprotein levels can also be elevated if the fetus is merely older than originally thought, or if there are twins. When alpha-fetoprotein levels are suspicious, the test is usually followed by a second test such as amniocentesis.

■ **PUBS:** The percutaneous umbilical blood sampling procedure, introduced in 1983, uses blood drawn from the fetus to determine if it has chicken pox, anemia, a form of pneumonia known as cytomegalovirus, or toxoplasma gondii, a potentially fatal parasite. The test can also be used to identify several genetic defects, including Down syndrome and spina bifida. The process takes about five minutes, unless a blood problem is found in the fetus and a transfusion is required. Test results can be processed quickly—2 days as opposed to at least 10 for amniocentesis, although the risk of fetal death from the test is slightly higher for PUBS—1 to 1.5 percent as opposed to a half of 1 percent for amnio. Since amnio can be done as early as the twelfth week of pregnancy, and PUBS can't be done until the 17th or 18th week, amnio remains the primary test for identifying potential genetic abnormalities.

PREECLAMPSIA

ANOTHER REASON TO MAKE LOVE

Your partner's sperm may protect you against severe complications

Even women with no history of hypertension can find the physical and emotional demands of pregnancy to be a recipe for high blood pressure. Untreated, this hypertension can lead to severe complications for both the mother and fetus. And in roughly 1 in 10 pregnancies, a dangerous condition called preeclampsia can develop during the last trimester.

Symptoms include not only hypertension, but blurred vision, swelling in the face and hands as a result of fluid retention, and protein in the urine. Headaches, nausea, vomiting, and abdominal pains may also arise, and, if neglected, this toxemia can lead to full-blown eclampsia, a condition that can produce seizures that are potentially fatal to both the mother and the child.

Now a study published in the respected medical journal, the *Lancet,* has put forth a possible explanation for preeclampsia. Following up on earlier research suggesting that the condition occurs more frequently in women who have never before been pregnant or are pregnant by a new partner if they have been pregnant previously, researchers studied a group of women in Guadeloupe, where it is not unusual for women to have children by many partners. Because of the prevailing social attitude there about having children

TREATING RH SENSITIZATION

What to do when a fetus is allergic to its mother's blood

When a pregnant woman's blood lacks a protein called the Rh factor which helps trigger certain of the body's immune responses, and the father's blood contains that protein, the fetus's blood can end up being incompatible with the mother's blood. When that happens, the mother's body may act as if it were allergic to the fetus and produce antibodies that attack the fetus's red blood cells, resulting in anemia. Known as hemolytic or Rh disease, the condition can be serious enough to cause death in the fetus or newborn. The condition occurs in about 1 in 20 pregnancies.

The best way to prevent this reaction is to inject the mother with a blood product called Rh immunoglubulin (Rhlg) before her body has had an allergic reaction to the fetus's blood. Such a reaction, which is also known as sensitization, can occur any time the mother's and fetus's blood mix. (One prime chance for this to happen is during amniocentesis.) The protection from Rhlg usually lasts about 12 weeks, which means that the treatment may need to be repeated several times during a pregnancy.

Should sensitization occur and antibodies from the mother begin to attack the fetus's blood, there is nothing Rhlg injections can do to remove these antibodies. The doctor will have to monitor the level of antibodies closely, and to conduct special tests on the fetus if too many antibodies are detected.

If anemia is found, the fetus may require a blood transfusion in the uterus, or if the mother is close enough to term, early delivery and treatment in an intensive-care nursery.

with multiple partners, the investigators were able to gather unusually detailed information about their subjects' sexual history for the study.

Among women pregnant for the first time, the authors of the Guadeloupe study found preeclampsia 12 percent of the time, compared with only 5 percent for those who were pregnant by the same man for a second time. Even more striking, the researchers discovered preeclampsia in 24 percent of the women who had had children before, but were pregnant this time by a new partner.

Delving further, the scientists found that the longer a woman had been sexually intimate with the man who had made her pregnant, the less her risk of preeclampsia.

While little is known about the biological mechanisms that trigger preeclampsia, scientists have established that the placenta fails to attach properly to the uterine lining in such instances. The authors of the new study, led by French physician Pierre-Yves Robillard, suspect that preeclampsia may be an adverse immunological reaction by the mother against certain genetic material implanted in the embryo by her partner's sperm.

This could explain why the placenta does not fully attach to the uterine lining in cases of preeclampsia, resulting in heightened blood pressure in the woman late in pregnancy, as her body seeks a way to supply nourishment to the fetus. Based on the Guadeloupe data, the Robillard team hypothesizes that the more exposure a woman has to a partner's semen before becoming pregnant, the more likely she is to develop an immunity to the man's genes, thereby reducing her chances of developing preeclampsia.

Not everyone in the medical community agrees with this scientific hunch. Some researchers suggest that the condition is a largely inherited disease, and others say that it may be a response to a lack of protein or too much salt in the mother's diet. But in any case, the Guadeloupe study offers intriguing support for the maxim, "You dance with the one who brung you."

INFERTILITY

IF A COUPLE CAN'T CONCEIVE

New technologies are making a difference for thousands

Late marriages and biological clocks are frequent factors. Environmental toxins and previous surgery may also play a role at times, but about 1 out of every 12 prospective mothers in the United States has been reported unable to conceive in at least a year of trying. This is despite the fact that more than half those women already had at least one child. For couples frustrated by such fortunes, “every menstrual period is like a funeral,” in the words of one disappointed woman. While the *New England Journal of Medicine* reports that medically assisted reproduction can succeed in more than 80 percent of the cases where it is attempted, few couples in fertility programs succeed because of financial strain and emotional fatigue from the process.

In some cases the causes of the infertility are clear-cut. Certain women do not release enough eggs and can be treated with a fertility drug such as Clomid. (A recent scare linking Clomid to ovarian cancer turned out to be a false alarm, according to the American Society for Reproductive Medicine, but several ongoing studies are looking into its safety.) At other times couples simply need to adjust their schedules to conceive.

But many of the tests and treatments are much more expensive and demanding. For example, a post-coital test is commonly given to test the sperm's ability to make its way to the fallopian tube, where fertilization usually occurs, and requires a couple to have sex just before the woman ovulates, which may be in the middle of the work week. Before washing, the woman must quickly have a pelvic exam at her doctor's, wherever that happens to be. "When it is all over, neither you nor your doctor really has a very good idea whether or not your eggs can be fertilized by your husband's sperm," writes fertility expert Dr. Sherman Silber in his book, *How to Get Pregnant with the New Technology*.

A good rule of thumb in judging a treatment's efficacy, according to Joyce Zeitz of the Fertility Institute in Birmingham, Ala., is, after following a procedure for six full cycles without success—try something else.

The last resort for many couples is medically assisted fertilization procedures, which have only a one-in-seven chance of producing a baby on one try, but have success rates of over 80 percent when six or seven attempts are made. Women over 40 typically experience the most difficulty.

The techniques include in vitro fertilization (IVF), gamete intrafallopian transfer (GIFT), and zygote intrafallopian transfer (ZIFT). With GIFT, the sperm and egg are placed in the fallopian tubes, where fertilization occurs normally. For IVF and ZIFT, the fertilization of the eggs by the sperm takes place in the laboratory and the fertilized egg is placed directly into the woman's uterus for IVF, or her fallopian tubes for ZIFT.

In all cases the woman must have daily hormone injections to control her body's reaction by stimulating egg production, prompting the movement of the eggs out of the fallopian tubes and others to supply normal pregnancy hormones so that a miscarriage does not occur.

Only ten states* require insurance companies to cover such procedures, which can cost anywhere from $6,000 to $10,000 a try. Most successful treatments occur by the fourth attempt, and most clinics limit patients to a total of eight tries. Often patients only try once, however.

* Arkansas, California, Connecticut, Hawai'i, Illinois, Maryland, Massachusetts, New York, Rhode Island, and Texas.

EXPERT SOURCES

FINDING A FERTILITY DOCTOR

What once seemed like simple body chemistry can become an overwhelming technical nightmare for millions of couples faced with infertility. When looking for a doctor to guide you through this maze, consider the following:

RESOLVE
1310 Broadway
Somerville, MA 02144
■ A nonprofit infertility organization with member chapters and support groups around the country. RESOLVE collects data on doctors, including a physician referral list of those certified in reproductive endocrinology. The organization also surveys doctors about their area of expertise and type of patient treated. A warning: The national helpline is often busy.
☎ **617-623-0744**

AMERICAN SOCIETY FOR REPRODUCTIVE MEDICINE
1209 Montgomery Highway
Birmingham, AL 35216
■ A professional organization for fertility doctors and clinics. Serves as a clearinghouse for information on most U.S. fertility treatment programs. Publishes annual reports of both the number of pregnancies in each program and the number of live births recorded in these programs. The ASRM recommends that before you select a fertility specialist or program, it is always a good idea to consult with other couples who have participated in the program to see what concerns they might have.
☎ **205-978-5000**

CHILDBIRTH COURSES

HELPING NATURE DO HER THING

The Lamaze and Bradley methods rely on relaxation techniques

Among most expectant parents today, the name Lamaze has become synonymous with natural childbirth techniques. The Lamaze organization estimates that 2.2 million deliveries each year employ relaxation and breathing methods popularized in Lamaze classes. A second childbirth program, the Bradley method, resembles Lamaze in its premise that much of the pain of childbirth can be alleviated by easing fear and tension. Here is a guide to the two leading approaches:

THE LAMAZE METHOD

Obstetrician Fernand Lamaze developed his birthing philosophy after observing techniques for "painless childbirth" on a 1951 trip to Russia. These techniques were based on the work of Ivan Pavlov, the Russian psychologist who argued that the brain plays a major part in the perception of pain.

The Lamaze method assumes that birth is a natural and healthy process that can run its course with very little need for medical intervention. It teaches women to make informed choices in their health care and then to trust their inner wisdom to guide them through birth. In the typical course, which begins in the seventh month of pregnancy and runs two hours a week for six weeks, expectant couples learn different strategies for helping the pregnant woman cope with the stress of childbirth. At the heart of the course are three techniques: relaxation methods, breathing exercises, and pushing during contractions. For instance, the woman and her partner in the birthing process are taught that by massaging and stroking the mother-to-be and learning to tense single muscle groups while relaxing the rest of the body, the woman can diffuse stress. Parents are also coached in how to relax the body using meditation and other mental imagery. For example, a woman might imagine a blossoming flower, symbolic of her cervix opening. She might envision her baby moving down the birth canal, or she might focus on a certain color or mental picture to help her relax. Walking during labor or changing positions— from the woman lying down on her side to squatting or kneeling on all fours, for instance—can also help relaxation. Many of the Lamaze positions take advantage of gravity and keep the pelvis tilted so that the baby can pass more easily through the birth canal.

The Lamaze system also stresses breathing techniques for each of the three stages of labor. During the first phase, in which contractions begin and the cervix becomes fully dilated, Lamaze emphasizes slow breathing, in which the mother exhales slowly and keeps her stomach muscles tight as she inhales. In the second stage, also known as transition, when the contractions come fast and furious, the woman takes a breath and holds it for 6 to 10 seconds, exerting downward pressure on her stomach muscles as she does so. After no more than ten seconds, she exhales and repeats the pattern until the contractions stop and the third phase begins. During the third phase, the baby's head makes contact with the pelvic floor, stimulating an expulsive reflex which brings the baby through the birth canal. Lamaze teaches the mother to push until the baby is born.

For more information on the Lamaze method, contact the American Society for Psychoprophylaxis in Obstetrics /Lamaze, ☎ 800-368-4404.

THE BRADLEY METHOD

An alternative to Lamaze is the Bradley method, which is used by 30,000 to 40,000 women each year. Developed by Denver obstetrician Robert Bradley in the late 1940s, the method differs from Lamaze in that it doesn't teach breathing techniques; it relies solely on relaxation exercises to control pain during labor. "The whole philosophy is that you can give birth without drugs," says Marjie Hathaway, a leading spokeswoman for the Bradley method. Hathaway became a convert herself after she and her husband first heard Bradley explain his approach in a speech while she was pregnant in California in the mid-1960s. When her own doctor refused to allow her to deliver her baby without using drugs, she arranged to fly to Colorado once she entered labor so that she could have her baby delivered by Bradley.

In the typical Bradley class, which begins when the woman is five-and-a-half months pregnant, expectant couples learn 12 different relaxation techniques to help the woman cope with pain during labor. Classes meet in weekly two-hour sessions.

Many of the relaxation techniques involve the husband either touching or stroking the mother-to-be or offering reassurance to boost her confidence. In another technique, called "warmth," the woman imagines standing in a warm shower.

The Bradley method also teaches women that changing positions during childbirth helps manage pain. "During labor women are encouraged to walk, to take a shower, to change positions, to do anything but lie on her back," says Hathaway. "Lying on your back casues a tremendous amount of pain."

For more information on the Bradley method, contact the Bradley Method Pregnancy Hotline, ☎ 800-422-4784.

ON THE EARLY SIDE OF THE STREET

When a baby ignores the due date and surprises you

By the 30th week or so of pregnancy, most mothers-to-be probably wonder whether their babies will *ever* arrive. They usually will be kept waiting seven or eight more weeks, since term is defined as being from the 37th to the 42nd month of pregnancy. But between 6 and 8 percent of babies in the United States are premies, which means that they are born somewhere between the 20th and 37th week of pregnancy. According to the American College of Obstetricians and Gynecologists, preterm delivery is "the single most important problem of pregnancy."

Thanks to advances in medical technology, even babies born as early as 25 weeks can sometimes be nurtured in a hospital incubator while the infant's body systems develop outside the womb, but breathing problems, brain damage, infection, and intestinal difficulties can all befall a preterm newborn.

The cause of preterm delivery is poorly understood, but the threat appears higher in women with poor prenatal care. Women are also at heightened risk if they have: a history of preterm birth in prior pregnancies; a history of having several induced abortions; multiple pregnancy; uterine abnormalities such as a poorly formed cervix or fibroids; abdominal surgery; an infection; bleeding in the second trimester; an underweight condition; placenta previa (the placenta lies low in the uterus, partly or completely blocking the baby's exit through the cervix); early rupturing of membranes; high blood pressure or a chronic illness.

Rupturing of the membranes is an obvious sign that preterm labor may soon begin, but the signals are often much more difficult to discern. A change in vaginal discharge, pelvic or lower abdominal pressure, a low-grade backache, and abdominal cramps and contractions can often disguise preterm labor.

To stave off preterm birth, doctors may recommend bedrest, the consumption of extra fluids by mouth or intravenously, and in some cases drugs to inhibit uterine contractions. Before doing so, however, the doctor must conclude that delaying labor will pose no harm to either mother or fetus, which, in some cases, it might.

C-SECTIONS AS A LAST RESORT

Fewer cesareans are being performed, even fewer are necessary

The most common surgery in the United States is the cesarean section, so named because Julius Caesar is said to have been born this way. It may also be the nation's most overperformed operation, say many experts. Approximately 1 in 4 babies in the United States are delivered by cesarean birth; in Canada the rate is about 1 in 5, and in Great Britain it is 1 in 10. And while the rate of C-sections has leveled off in the United States since 1989, the incidence remains almost five times higher than it was in 1969.

The reason for the high volume of cesareans may be as much legal as medical. The American College of Obstetricians and Gynecologists (ACOG) has suggested that physicians' fears of being sued for their handling of difficult deliveries may be much to blame for the medical profession's propensity to elect C-sections over vaginal deliveries in many cases. The widespread use of electronic fetal monitoring, a technique that makes it easier for the doctor to detect potential problems in the delivery early, only adds to this jumpiness.

According to ACOG, a self-fulfilling prophecy may also be at work to some extent; once a woman has had one C-section, obstetricians have often fallen into a habit of assuming that a cesarean would be required should the woman ever give birth again.

Other critics have argued that the medical establishment's fondness for cesareans is inspired by a more cynical factor: insurance reimbursement rules that provide substantially higher fees for doctors and hospitals performing C-sections than for those delivering without the need for surgery. These critics point to studies showing that cesareans are more likely to be performed in profit-making hospitals and on women with private health insurance.

Whatever the reasons, most experts agree that in the absence of medical complications, women should be encouraged to attempt vaginal labor rather than undergo a cesarean. Successful vaginal delivery significantly reduces the risk of complications, both during and after the surgery, as well as cuts down the stay required in the hospital from nearly five days to about half of that, with all the financial savings that that entails.

Even women who have had a prior C-section can deliver vaginally the next time around in 60 to 80 percent of cases, says ACOG. Vaginal deliveries are strongly discouraged, however, if a woman's previous cesarean involved either a classical uterine incision, in which the cut was made in an up-and-down direction in the upper part of the uterus, or if warning signs such as an abrupt change in the fetal heart rate appear. Nevertheless, in most cases "the relative safety of vaginal delivery after cesarean birth is compelling," says ACOG, and "women should be counseled and encouraged to undertake a trial of labor."

FACT FILE:

RISK OF MISCARRYING

■ *Miscarriage is nature's way of ending a pregnancy that is not proceeding normally. About a fifth of all pregnancies end this way, mostly during the first trimester, but in some cases as late as the first half of a pregnancy. Heavy bleeding from the uterine lining is the most common warning sign. Cramping pain, usually more severe than menstrual cramps, can also be a symptom.*

EXPERT Q&A

WHEN THE STORK IS A MIDWIFE

Nurse-midwives are better-trained and increasingly common today

The image of the midwife from medieval and pioneer times was not one to inspire confidence. But much has happened in recent years to professionalize the role of midwives in assisting childbirth, and today almost 1 in 20 births are attended by a registered nurse trained as a midwife. Kimberly Pool of the American College of Nurse-Midwives explains what a certified nurse-midwife can—and can't—do.

■ What types of midwives are there?

The two basic categories are nurse-midwives and lay midwives. Lay midwives are people who help women deliver their babies but are not necessarily nurses and differ widely in their level of education and experience.

Nurse-midwives are registered nurses who have completed additional training in obstetrics and gynecology. Often they are certified by passing a national exam administered by the American College of Nurse-Midwives. To qualify for the exam, they must spend a minimum of 18 months learning clinical midwifery skills and advanced obstetrics and gynecology for normal women, as well as newborn care and family planning.

■ What do nurse-midwives do?

By education and experience, a nurse-midwife is qualified to be the main caregiver for healthy women throughout pregnancy and childbirth, and to provide gynecological and family planning care throughout a woman's childbearing years. In 32 states they have the authority to write medical prescriptions.

The nurse-midwifery policy is to consult with a doctor when a condition arises in pregnancy or labor that is considered to be medically dangerous. In most cases, this means that the mother is not healthy, has high blood pressure, gestational diabetes, an abnormal metabolism, infections, or an improperly developed fetus or placenta.

■ Where do nurse-midwives deliver babies?

Many people envision a birth at home when they hear the word "midwife." But the vast majority of nurse-midwives work in hospitals—about 85 percent. Another 11 percent work in birth centers, and the remaining 4 percent attend home births.

■ What kind of backup do nurse-midwives have if something goes wrong?

Whether a problem is apparent during the first prenatal visit or does not arise until the final hour of labor, a nurse-midwife is taught to call in a doctor as soon as the woman's condition strays outside the boundaries of a nurse-midwife's expertise. The mother may be referred to the consulting doctor for medical care, or the physician and the nurse-midwife may co-manage the care, depending on what the complication is.

■ Are doctors always willing to work with nurse-midwives?

Not all doctors think highly of nurse-midwives, but as the number of certified nurse-midwives increases, this attitude is decreasing. A policy statement issued by the American College of Obstetrics and Gynecology and the American College of Nurse-Midwives states that the maternity care team should be directed by a qualified ob/gyn with written medical guidelines that define the individual and shared responsibilities of the doctor and nurse-midwife. These procedures include periodic and joint evaluation of services performed, including chart review, case review, patient evaluation, and review of data on the health of babies over time.

How do nurse-midwives differ from doctors?

Nurse-midwives are trained to treat normal, healthy women, and in that capacity they celebrate the normal. Doctors are trained to handle the emergency situation and because they have spent much more of their training on what to do if something goes wrong, they [may be] more likely to treat a normal pregnancy as if it were a high-risk situation waiting to happen.

Do nurse-midwives only deliver babies "naturally"?

Nurse-midwives use technology when it is needed to learn something about the pregnancy that they otherwise would not know. During labor, nurse-midwives induce labor, break waters, start intravenous lines, use fetal monitoring equipment, and prescribe analgesics when it is medically necessary, thereby minimizing side effects and often ensuring that labor progresses more quickly.

What is the record for nurse-midwives delivering babies?

Over the years nurse-midwives have maintained a superb safety record. Research shows that pregnancy, labor, and delivery for a healthy woman is as safe with a nurse-midwife as with a physician. Studies have also shown that the rate of Cesarean sections, episiotomies, infant and maternal mortality, and low birth weight are often much lower than average among women being cared for by a nurse-midwife.

In fact, government reports have called for an increased use of nurse-midwives as a safe way to improve maternity care.

How does the cost of using a nurse-midwife compare with using a doctor?

Having your baby with a nurse-midwife usually costs less than obstetrical care with a physician in a hospital. The cost of midwifery care usually varies with the setting; most costly is a nurse-midwife in private practice with a hospital birth.

The least expensive is usually a home birth, which may cost a fraction of the price of a hospital birth. Birth centers fall somewhere in the middle. These differences may be significant or minimal; it all depends on the community.

Are nurse-midwives' fees covered by insurance?

All 50 states provide Medicaid reimbursement for nurse-midwifery care, regardless of whether the birth ocurs in a hospital, birth center, or home.

In 26 states, insurers are required to reimburse for nurse-midwifery care, although not necessarily in all possible birth settings.

EXPERT SOURCES

THEY STAND AND DELIVER

A resource guide for those who are considering childbirth options

For more information on certified nurse-midwives:

AMERICAN COLLEGE OF NURSE-MIDWIVES
818 Connecticut Ave., NW,
Suite #900
Washington, D.C. 20006
☎ **202-728-9860**

For information on lay midwives:

INFORMED HOMEBIRTH/ INFORMED BIRTH AND PARENTING
P.O. Box 3675
Ann Arbor, MI 48106
☎ **313-662-6857**

NATIONAL ASSOCIATION OF CHILDBEARING CENTERS
3123 Gottschall Rd.
Perkiomenville, PA 18074
☎ **215-234-8068**

MIDWIFE ALLIANCE OF NORTH AMERICA
☎ **316-283-4543**

SIZING UP THE NEW ARRIVAL

A newborn's weight cannot be used to predict a child's future size

Ask any parent what she or he remembers from the birth of a first child and one of the first details likely to be recalled is the baby's birth weight and height. What is to be made of these vital statistics that are so proudly reported? 80 percent of all infants born in the United States fall between 5 pounds 11½ ounces and 8 pounds 5¾ ounces at birth. About 1 in 10 newborns weighs in above this range; an equivalent number is below the low end of this zone.

Where your child is on this continuum may depend on a number of factors. For instance, the longer a pregnancy goes on, the larger the infant is likely to be, while an unborn baby's growth may be limited by poor nutrition or other complications during pregnancy. Smoking, drinking, or drug use by the mother during pregnancy can also stunt development.

Heredity also plays a part, though it's no guarantee of how large an infant will grow up to be. While babies whose parents are unusually large or small may reflect their parents' size at birth, an infant's birth size should not be taken as a predictor of a child's eventual size, according to the American Academy of Pediatrics.

Babies whose birth size is larger or smaller than average may find life beyond the womb difficult at first. Large babies sometimes experience trouble with their blood-sugar levels and need extra feedings to avoid hypoglycemia Small babies may find feeding difficult or have trouble maintaining proper body temperature.

A newborn's birth size can be a tip-off to doctors and nurses that a baby will require special attention for a few days. But more often than not, these stats will be used mainly as benchmarks by parents and pediatricians in following an infant's advance through childhood.

■ RATING A NEWBORN'S HEALTH

Within a minute of delivering a baby, the obstetrics team will check the newborn's heart rate, respiration, muscle tone, reflexes, and coloration and record a score designed to reflect how that baby came through the delivery process. That rating, known as an Apgar score, is compiled by issuing a ranking between zero and two for each of the vital signs and indicators listed above, and then adding each of the numbers together to arrive at a single score. The process is then repeated five minutes after birth and the two sets of observations are compared to gauge the baby's progress in adjusting to his or her new environment. But Apgar scores are not intended as a reliable predictor of a baby's long-term health prospects, only of how the newborn is adapting to life outside a mother's womb.

COMPONENT	APGAR SCORE		
	0	1	2
HEART RATE	Absent	Slow (< 100 beats/min.)	>100 beats/min.
RESPIRATIONS	Absent	Weak; hypoventilation	Good, strong cry
MUSCLE TONE	Limp	Some flexion	Active motion
REFLEX IRRITABILITY	No response	Grimace	Cough or sneeze
COLOR	Blue or pale	Body pink; extremeties blue	Complete pink

SOURCE: *Planning for Pregnancy, Birth, and Beyond*, American College of Obstetricians and Gynecologists, 1993.

BABY NAMES

JENNIFER, MEET JULIETTE

The names favored for the '90s are sturdy and family-oriented

The philosopher Henry David Thoreau once said. "He who can pronounce my name alright, he can call me, and is entitled to my love and service." The name David means "the beloved one," and is a perennial favorite. Thoreau had little to complain about.

Comedian Jim Carrey's middle name, on the other hand, is Eugene, a designation rife with nerdy implications. Carrey says, "I figured my parents called me that to keep me humble. You can never get too cool with a name like Eugene."

The importance of a name is not lost on the image-makers in hollywood. Would John Wayne have made it as Marion Morrison? John Denver as John Deutschendorf, Jr.? The oddly named (by Hollywood standards) Keir Dullea seemed destined for fame after his star turn in *2001: A Space Odyssey*—and then went nowhere.

Mindful that oddly named children might not do well in a world where names have a powerful hold on how one is judged, parents have always selected names with great deliberation, ever mindful of the bounds of the times. In the '80s, waspy monikers such as Courtney, Brooke, and Tyler held sway. And in the '90s, the pendulum is swinging back to names with sturdy roots in the family tree or the Bible.

Linda Rosenkrantz and Pamela Redmond Satran, authors of the best-selling book, *Beyond Jennifer and Jason* (St. Martin's Press, 1994), have deemed traditional names like Michael or Elizabeth "Volvo Names." Like the car, they are durable and weather the passage of time well. Many of the names are family-oriented, with parents naming their children after their Aunt Julia, Uncle Patrick, or Grandmother Alice.

This trend may have its roots in hard-nosed practicality, as a recent study by Albert Mehrabian and Marlena Piercy of the University of California at Los Angeles shows. When the two researchers asked interview subjects for their impressions of persons with conventionally spelled names like Diane and Joan, and compared those responses to those with less traditionally spelled versions of the same names (e.g., Dyan and Jone), they found that those with conventionally spelled names were viewed as more popular, cheerful, successful, and caring than their more exotically spelled namesakes. Men and women with conventionally spelled names were also considered more masculine and feminine than their more alphabetically challenged counterparts.

FACT FILE:

FAVORITES IN ANY AGE

- *For the first time since Dwight Eisenhower was president, Rose has passed Ann, Marie, and Lynn to be the most popular middle name for girls in America. Below are some of the first names that have stayed popular over the last century:*

For girls:	For boys:
Amanda	Alexander
Elizabeth	Andrew
Emily	David
Jennie	Jacob
Rebecca	John
Rachel	William

SOURCE *Beyond Jennifer and Jason*, Linda Rosenkrantz and Pamela Redmond Satran, St. Martin's Press, 1994.

EXPERT LIST

THE MOST POPULAR NAMES TODAY

Using statistics from government sources, Linda Rosenkrantz and Pamela Redmond Satran in Beyond Jennifer and Jason (St. Martin's Press, 1994), *found that the following names, ranked in order, are among today's most frequently favored.*

FOR GIRLS TODAY:

1. **Ashley** – *Old English, ash tree meadow*
2. **Jessica** – *Hebrew, the rich one*
3. **Amanda** – *Latin, worthy of being loved*
4. **Brittany** – *Latin, Britain*
5. **Sarah** – *Hebrew, princess, royal status*
6. **Samantha** – *Aramaic, a listener*
7. **Megan** – *Celtic, the strong*
8. **Emily** – *Teutonic, industrious, striving*
9. **Kayla** – *Arabic, beloved*
10. **Elizabeth** – *Hebrew, consecrated to God*
11. **Stephanie** – *Greek, crown or garland*
12. **Nicole** – *Greek, the people's victory*
13. **Jennifer** – *French, pure white wave*
14. **Lauren** – *Latin, laurel wreath*
15. **Amber** – *Arabic, jewel*
16. **Rachel** – *Hebrew, innocent as a lamb*
17. **Chelsea** – *From the town of Chelsea*
18. **Danielle** – *Hebrew, God is my judge*
19. **Courtney** – *Old English, from the court*
20. **Kelsey** – *Scandinavian, from ship island*
21. **Rebecca** – *Hebrew, the captivator*
22. **Shelby** – *Old English, from ledge estate*
23. **Heather** – *Anglo-Saxon, flower of moors*
24. **Hannah** – *Hebrew, full of grace*
25. **Melissa** – *Greek, honeybee*

FOR BOYS TODAY:

1. **Michael** – *Hebrew, "Like unto the Lord"*
2. **Christopher** – *Greek, the Christ carrier*
3. **Joshua** – *Hebrew, salvation in the Lord*
4. **Matthew** – *Hebrew, gift of God*
5. **Andrew** – *Greek, strong and manly*
6. **Ryan** – *Gaelic, small king*
7. **Jacob** – *Hebrew, the supplanter*
8. **Nicholas** – *Greek, leader of the people*
9. **Tyler** – *Anglo-Saxon, brick, tile maker*
10. **James** – *Hebrew, see Jacob*
11. **Daniel** – *Hebrew, "The Lord is my judge"*
12. **Joseph** – *Hebrew, "He shall add"*
13. **Justin** – *Latin, the just one*
14. **David** – *Hebrew, beloved one*
15. **John** – *Hebrew, God's gracious gift*
16. **Brandon** – *Anglo-Saxon, beacon on hill*
17. **Robert** – *Teutonic, bright, shining fame*
18. **Zachary** – *Hebrew, Lord has remembered*
19. **Kyle** – *Gaelic, from the strait*
20. **William** – *Teutonic, the strong guardian*
21. **Cody** – *Old English, a cushion*
22. **Anthony** – *Latin, of inestimable worth*
23. **Jordan** – *Hebrew, the descending river*
24. **Jonathan** – *Hebrew, gift of the Lord*
25. **Alexander** – *Greek, protector of man*

IF THIS SURVEY HAD BEEN DONE A HUNDRED YEARS AGO...

FOR GIRLS

Amanda
Annie
Carrie
Christina
Charlotte
Claire
Daisy
Elizabeth
Emily
Jennie
Julia
Katherine
Laura
Leah
Lillie
Louise
Lucy
Madeline
Maggie
Olivia
Polly
Rebecca
Rachel
Sara(h)
Sophia

FOR BOYS

Aaron
Adam
Alexander
Andrew
Anthony
Benjamin
Ben
Charles
David
Edward
Eric
Gregory
Harry
Henry
Jacob
Jesse
John
Jonah
Jonathan
Joshua
Luke
Max
Nathan
Noah
Patrick
Samuel
Seth
Timothy
William

VACCINATIONS

A NEW CALENDAR FOR KIDS' SHOTS

The experts finally agree on an immunization schedule

For years, federal health officials at the Centers for Disease Control recommended a childhood immunization schedule that was followed in public health clinics, while the American Academy of Pediatrics put out a different one that was used widely by private practitioners. Now the two groups have finally issued a uniform timetable for vaccinating children (see below). The new schedule clears up discrepancies over when to administer oral polio, diphtheria, pertussis, and tetanus (DPT); measles, mumps, and rubella (MMR); and infant hepatitis B vaccines.

Since the late 1980s the number of vaccine doses recommended for children has increased from 9 to 15. What's more, federal health officials recently approved a vaccine for chicken pox. While the chicken pox vaccine has not yet been added to the new uniform immunization schedule, such a move is expected shortly. The vaccine is reported to be only 70 to 90 percent effective in preventing the childhood disease, but in nearly every case, says Food and Drug Administration Commissioner David A. Kessler, "almost all of the vaccinated patients who got chicken pox had a milder form of the disease."

The vaccine is expected to cost physicians approximately $39 per dose and to be administered to children 12 to 15 months old and to people over 13 years old who have not had the disease already.

To promote universal childhood vaccination, the Clinton administration recently persuaded the Congress to pay for immunizing children who are uninsured, poor, or of Native American or Native Alaskan ancestry. As of early 1995, about half the states had elected to make vaccines available free through public health clinics while the other half were working through private physicians and reimbursing them. State Medicaid programs remain responsible for supplying vaccines to children enrolled in Medicaid. For the situation in your state, contact your state health department's immunization program.

RECOMMENDED CHILDHOOD IMMUNIZATION SCHEDULE

The Centers for Disease Control and the American Academy of Pediatrics are America's leading authorities on childhood immunization, but, until recently, they disagreed about when children should be immunized. Below is their unified immunization schedule, released in January 1995.

Vaccine	First dose	Second dose	Third dose	Fourth dose	Fifth dose	Sixth dose
Hepatitis B	Before 2 mos.	1–4 mos.[1]	6–18 mos.			
Diphtheria, Pertussis, Tetanus (DPT)	2 mos.	4 mos.	6 mos.	12–18 mos.[1]	4–6 yrs. (booster)[2]	11–16 yrs.
H. influenza type B	2 mos.	4 mos.	6 mos.	12–15 mos. (booster)[3]		
Polio	2 mos.	4 mos.	6–8 mos.	4–6 yrs.		
MMR	12–15 mos.	4–6 yrs. or 11–12 yrs.[4]				

NOTES: 1. Allow at least one month after previous dose before administering next. 2. Allow at least five years after previous dose before administering next. 3. Children who get an H. influenza vaccine known as PRP-OMP do not require a dose at 6 months, but still require the booster. 4. Depends on state school requirements.
SOURCE: Centers for Disease Control and the American Academy of Pediatrics, 1995.

CHECK-UPS

WHEN TO TEST CHILDREN'S EYES

A baby's vision at age one is a good predictor of eyesight later in life

Does the fact that you wear eyeglasses doom your child to the same fate? Not necessarily. But when it comes to vision, poor parental eyesight does up the odds that a child will also need glasses, too. A recent Massachusetts Institute of Technology study found that in families where neither parent is nearsighted, the chances of a child being myopic is less than 1 in 10; if one parent is nearsighted, the odds increase to more than 1 in 5, and if both parents share the condition, the odds rise to over 2 in 5.

What's more, the M.I.T. researchers found that when a baby is nearsighted at age one, that's often a good predictor of whether the child is likely to be nearsighted at a later age. Infants who are nearsighted usually develop normal eyesight between 1 and 5 years of age, but between 6 and 12, their vision often weakens, particularly if the parents are nearsighted.

While there is no known way to improve the odds that a nearsighted infant can escape nearsightedness at an older age, the American Academy of Pediatrics nevertheless recommends that infants be checked for visual problems during their first half-year of life and that eye tests be done at least once a year during their preschool years.

Such examinations not only allow doctors to diagnose rare problems (e.g., cataracts) but also help them identify muscle problems that might cause a child to use only one eye. Early testing can also enable doctors to fit children suffering from extreme cases of nearsightedness with corrective lenses. Early intervention can spare such children frustration, ensuring a smooth transition to school.

Waiting until a child starts school to have his or her eyes tested is too late, experts say, because certain eye problems, such as strabismus or anisemetropia, if left undetected till the the age of five or six, can become permanent. If they are detected earlier, however, they are easily remedied.

FITTING THE YOUNG WITH CONTACT LENSES

A 12-year-old should be able to handle it

Medically speaking, contact lenses are an option no matter what your age. Babies can—and do—wear contact lenses after congenital cataract surgery. Today, even an infant as young as one week old can wear silicone extended-wear lenses, which are permeable and malleable yet hold their shape. Such lenses cost about $110 a pair and can be kept in the baby's eyes for months. Parents can remove them when they need to be cleaned.

Older children are ready for contacts when they're old enough for the responsibility of taking care of them. "If a child can't pick up his room yet, he's not a good candidate," says Dr. James Sprague, an ophthalmologist who also teaches at Georgetown University in Washington, D.C. Sprague recommends that children get daily-wear soft or rigid lenses, which require nightly cleanings but are less likely to pose trouble than disposable or extended-wear lenses that are kept in the eyes longer.

The young contact lens-wearer needs to realize the importance of proper lens care, Sprague says. If eyes look red or hurt, for instance, a doctor should be consulted.

THE BANE OF CHILDHOOD

Earaches are the most common health complaint among children

Measles, mumps, and whooping cough are considered childhood rites of passage, but the most recurring of all children's ailments is the middle ear infection. Indeed, a recent study by the National Center for Health Statistics shows that earaches among children are soaring. Between 1975 and 1990 the number of doctors' visits for ear infections climbed 150 percent. In four out of five cases, the patient was a child under age 15. For children under 2, the proportion of doctors' visits prompted by earaches jumped 225 percent.

The reasons for the sharp increase are unclear. Susan Schäppert, author of the NCHS study, believes that day care programs may be partly to blame. "More kids are in day care," she says, "so that increased contact could cause more ear infections."

Young children are especially susceptible, experts say, because of the shortness of their eustachian tubes, which is the canal leading from the middle ear to the mouth, nasal passages, and esophagus. The shorter tubes make it much easier for infection to reach the middle ear when a small child comes down with a cold.

Improvements in diagnostic equipment could also help explain the rise in reported cases. Thanks to a new instrument called a tympanometer, doctors are able to detect middle ear infections that might have gone undiagnosed in the past.

Along with the climb in ear infections has been a steep increase in middle ear surgeries on children. But a 1994 study suggests that the surgical approach may have been overdone. Published in the *Journal of the American Medical Association*, the study found that of 6,429 proposed surgeries to place small, plastic tubes in the ears to drain fluids, only 42 percent were "appropriate." Another 35 percent were "equivocal," and 23 percent were deemed "inappropriate." The researchers said that, in many cases a simple antibiotic treatment may have been just as effective.

CHILDHOOD DISEASE SCHEDULE

Some of the symptoms of childhood infectious diseases and when to look for them

Disease	Incubation period (days)	Fever	Rash	Swollen glands	Cough
MEASLES	7 to 14	Days 1 to 5	Day 4, dull red blotches	Neck	Day 1
RUBELLA (German measles)	14 to 21	Days 1 to 2	Day 2 or 3, flat, light red spots	Neck, back of the neck	None
CHICKEN POX	7 to 21	Variable	Day 1, groups of itchy, red spots, become blisters	None	None
MUMPS	14 to 28	Day 1	None	One or both sides of the face	None
WHOOPING COUGH	7 to 14	Week 1	None	None	Week 1, gets worse; week 2, severe bouts, characteristic whoop

SOURCE: *American Medical Association Family Medical Guide*, Random House, 1994.

EXPERT Q&A

BEYOND JUST FIDGETY

Identifying and coping with a child's hyperactivity

Mental health experts estimate that as many as one in 33 school-age children has Attention Deficit Hyperactivity Disorder, or ADHD. Early diagnosis and treatment are crucial in preventing a child from struggling both academically and socially. Here, Dr. Larry Silver, director of training in child and adolescent psychiatry at Georgetown University School of Medicine and author of *Dr. Larry Silver's Advice to Parents on Attention Deficit Hyperactivity Disorder* (American Psychiatric Press, 1994), suggests what to do if you suspect your child has ADHD.

■ What are the signs of ADHD?

Children with ADHD have one or more of three behavioral problems. Some are fidgety or hyperactive. Some are very distractible and have short attention spans. And some are impulsive, meaning they interrupt or act before they think. These symptoms must be chronic and pervasive; that is, they must have existed throughout the child's life. If present, these behaviors can frustrate families and most commonly cause the child to do poorly in school.

■ Is there a danger that normal active behavior can be misread as ADHD?

Misdiagnosis of the disorder does occur. At present, about 50 percent of the children with ADHD are being diagnosed properly. However, misdiagnosis of the disorder frequently occurs with children who exhibit the symptom of distractibility. They are perceived as being unmotivated daydreamers or lazy rather than as having ADHD.

There are many causes of fidgeting, distractibility and impulsiveness, only one of which is ADHD. If these behavioral problems have only recently begun to manifest themselves or are related to a particular event, your child may not have ADHD. For instance, a child who becomes distractable in the fourth grade may be suffering from emotional problems caused by a divorce. Or if the child starts having trouble in math, a learning disability, which affects 10 percent of school-age children, could be the cause.

■ Can untreated ADHD be outgrown?

Untreated ADHD can lead to more problems. Children who don't receive treatment fall behind in school. The constant academic failure can result in depression and anxiety. Moreover, the disorder can lead to classroom misbehavior or to getting into trouble in the community. Teachers are often the first to alert parents that their child may have ADHD. Parents must also trust their intuition if they suspect that their child has a problem. Parents should talk to teachers to validate their concerns and then consult a family physician or a mental health professional.

■ How should ADHD be treated?

ADHD is a neurologically based disorder, so the principal part of treatment involves medication. Correctly managed medication can minimize or eliminate these behaviors in about 85 percent of the kids. Doctors prescribe a variety of drugs, but ritalin is used 85 percent of the time.

Psychological and educational intervention is also valuable. Since ADHD often goes undetected until third or fourth grade, a child will need counseling and extra educational accommodations. Many children need help addressing problems of self-esteem because of years of failure in school. Others have developed additional behavioral problems, such as being aggressive to get attention, or have learned that throwing tantrums helps them get their way. Families who have had to live with a disruptive child may also need some support. Most children require extra tutoring or special education to help fill deficiencies in their knowledge. Schools are required by law to provide these extra educational services.

THE BODY'S WONDER YEARS

Most teens will probably tell you that "normal adolescent development" is an oxymoron. But despite the awkwardness that goes with the change from child to adult, the transition is usually a predictable one.

PHYSICAL DEVELOPMENT IN ADOLESCENT GIRLS

	AGE NOTICEABLE CHANGE USUALLY		REMARKS
	BEGINS	STOPS	
INCREASE IN RATE OF GROWTH	10 to 11	15 to 16	If noticeable growth fails to begin by 15, see your doctor.
BREAST DEVELOPMENT	10 to 11	13 to 14	Noticeable development of breasts (one of which may begin to grow before the other) is usually the first sign of puberty. If change doesn't begin by 16, see your doctor.
EMERGENCE OF BODY HAIR	Pubic: 10 to 11 Underarm: 2 to 13	13 to 14 15 to 16	Development of body hair is extremely variable and largely dependent on heredity. Pubic hair usually darkens and thickens as puberty progresses.
DEVELOPMENT OF SWEAT GLANDS UNDER ARMS AND IN GROIN	12 to 13	15 to 16	Sweat glands are responsible for increased sweating, which causes underarm odor, a type of body odor not present in younger children.
MENSTRUATION	11 to 14	15 to 17	Menstruation often begins with extremely irregular periods but by age 17, a regular cycle (3 to 7 days every 28 days) usually becomes evident. If menstruation begins before 10 or has not begun by 17, talk to your physician.

PHYSICAL DEVELOPMENT IN ADOLESCENT BOYS

	AGE NOTICEABLE CHANGE USUALLY		REMARKS
	BEGINS	STOPS	
INCREASE IN RATE OF GROWTH	12 to 13	17 to 18	If noticeable growth fails to begin by 15, see your doctor.
ENLARGEMENT OF GENITALS	Testicles and scrotum: 11 to 12 Penis: 12 to 13	 16 to 17 15 to 16	As testicles grow, the skin of the scrotum darkens. The penis usually lengthens before it broadens. Ability to ejaculate seminal fluid usually begins about a year after the penis starts to lengthen.
EMERGENCE OF BODY HAIR	Pubic: 11 to 12 Underarm: 13 to 15	15 to 16 16 to 18	Development of body hair is extremely variable and largely dependent on heredity. Development of hair on the abdomen and chest usually continues into adulthood.
DEVELOPMENT OF SWEAT GLANDS UNDER ARMS AND IN GROIN	13 to 15	17 to 18	Sweat glands are responsible for increased sweating, which causes underarm odor, a type of body odor not present in younger children.
VOICE CHANGE	13 to 14	16 to 17	Enlargement of the larynx, or voice box, may make the "Adam's apple" more prominent. The voice deepens at 14 to 15, and may change rapidly or gradually. If childlike voice persists after 16, see your doctor.

SOURCE: *American Medical Association Family Medical Guide*, 3rd edition, Random House, 1993.

EXPERT Q&A

WHEN KIDS DON'T LIKE MEAT

Vegetarianism poses a special nutritional challenge in the young

Of the 12 million Americans who consider themselves vegetarians, no one knows how many have yet to celebrate their 21st birthday. Experts say, however, that adolescents make up the fastest-growing group of people who shun meat. But the nutritional needs of young people, particularly during growth spurts, may not be adequately addressed by some vegetarian diets. Dr. Johanna T. Dwyer, Director of the Frances Stern Nutrition Center at the New England Medical Center, explains what's appropriate nutritionally and what's not.

■ **Is vegetarianism safe for children?**

Well-planned vegetarian diets *can* be healthful for children over the age of two *if* they are carefully planned. These diets tend to be low in saturated fat, total fat, and cholesterol and tend to be high in fiber and complex carbohydrates, as well as high in fruits and vegetables for iron.

■ **What precautions are needed for primary school-aged children who are vegetarians?**

Preschool-age vegetarian children on lacto-ovo (eggs and dairy products are allowed) diets, lacto-vegetarian (dairy products are allowed) diets, and semi-vegetarian (no red meat) diets rarely have problems, except occasionally for a lack of iron. The children more likely to have problems are vegans; they don't eat any animal products at all, including milk and eggs. Nutrient supplements can help prevent these problems, though.

■ **What about teen vegetarians?**

Vegetarian adolescents who drink milk and/or eat eggs have few problems if they follow basic nutrition guidelines. Vegetarian diets also seem to have little effect on age of menarche. There may be some effect on the menstrual cycle of female vegans, although these findings have not be substantiated. A vegetarian adolescent may benefit from iron and, possibly, zinc and calcium supplements. All adolescents should keep their ascorbic acid and iron intakes high via whole-grain and fortified cereals to prevent iron-deficiency anemia.

■ **Do teenage girls who are vegetarians need to take special precautions?**

Once again, there may be problems with iron or calcium. When weights are very low, menstrual cycling may be abnormal or absent. Calcium needs are very high, and they are very difficult to meet on vegan diets. It is also very difficult to plan vegan diets that meet the RDA for zinc.

FACT FILE:

CAN, LIKE, GREASY FOOD CAUSE ACNE?

■ *Recent medical research has refuted years of received adolescent wisdom that a diet rich in chocolate and other greasy foods guaranteed a horrific acne eruption. The research shows no evidence to support a link between diet and pimples, except in people allergic to certain foods. The true cause is increased production of sebum (an oily secretion) by the skin—a natural response to increased hormone levels during puberty. But doctors caution that even though candy bars and other greasy foods won't cause acne, they are still high in fat and shouldn't be eaten in excess.*

EATING DISORDERS

WHEN FOOD IS AN AGONY

Understanding anorexia nervosa and bulimia and overcoming them

Perusing the pages of any fashion magazine, a reader is reminded that, more than ever, "thin is in." These magazines echo the values of popular culture, speaking to women loud and clear: It is not enough to strive toward a physical ideal whose proportions defy the laws of nature and gravity. The successful modern woman is, at once, a sex symbol, a mother, and a CEO.

These expectations make many women feel inadequate. In some cases it can lead to anorexia nervosa and bulimia, two serious psychiatric disorders characterized by a preoccupation with food and an obsession with being thin. Anorexia is most prevalent in women in their early 20s, while bulimia tends to afflict a somewhat older group. As many as half of all anorectics become bulimic at some point, according to Dr. William Davis, executive director of Philadelphia's Renfrew Center for Eating Disorders.

Because the symptoms of these sometimes fatal disorders are often easy to hide, it is important to know their characteristics and warning signs:

■ **ANOREXIA NERVOSA:** The woman who is most prone to anorexia nervosa is typically a perfectionist. She demands much of herself, whether as a student, athlete, dancer, or all of the above. Like many high achievers, the anorectic suffers from low self-esteem. By depriving herself of food, she gains some measure of self-worth.

Gradually, she loses touch with reality. As her body fat disappears, her self-perception and value system distort. In her eyes, she is perpetually fat. Motivated by this skewed body image, she uses "willpower" to restrain herself and thus derives a feeling of mastery over her life.

The severe anorectic does not stop at refusing foods she craves. Eventually, she denies herself nourishment she needs. Failing to consume a minimum amount of protein, the anorectic becomes deficient in the amino acids necessary for healthy bones and simple bodily processes. In turn, she becomes increasingly listless, depressed, and energy-deficient. Many stop menstruating due to insufficient amounts of body fat, a condition that endangers fertility later in life. Some 15 to 20 percent of those who suffer from the disorder die.

■ **BULIMIA:** An equally self-destructive disorder, bulimia is often coupled with other problem behaviors such as sexual promiscuity and substance abuse. Another type of bulimia is characterized by a compulsive need to exercise. Like anorectics, bulimics are tormented by unrealistic perceptions and expectations of themselves. Unlike the acetic anorectic, the bulimic binges on large quantities of food, comforted by the knowledge that she will purge herself shortly thereafter by inducing vomiting or using laxatives.

As in anorexia, the victim attains a false sense of control over her life and respite from feelings of worthlessness and desperation by repeating this process.

Depending on the severity of the disease, a victim may binge and purge as often as 20 times a day. Rapid weight fluctuation is an important warning sign, but because many bulimics become adept at hiding their ritual, it is often hard to detect. Bulimics spend long periods of time in bathrooms and most commonly mask their actions by running water. The effects of bulimia include dehydration, hormone imbalance, swelling of internal organs, and the depletion of necessary bodily minerals and electrolytes.

Judith Asner, director of the Eating Disorders Foundation of Washington, D.C., attributes the increase of the two disorders to both media and marketing trends. It is hard for anyone to ignore the proliferation of the "waif" look in magazines, movies, and television. And the "fat-free" claims that assault grocery shoppers reinforce the American obsession with losing weight.

This worshipping of thinness has not always held sway in America. "A society idealizes that which is most difficult to attain," says Asner. "When food and money was scarce, as was the case during World War II, the media enshrined the plumpened housekeeper and mother. Now that times are relatively prosperous, food is abundant, and leisure time is hard to come by, the media puts on a pedestal those women who laugh in the face of excess and spend their few free minutes trimming down to skin and bones." In such times, more voluptuous ideals, such as Guess jeans model Anna Nicole Smith are the exception rather than the rule.

Others see anorexia and bulimia as the result of more insidious societal trends. According to a study in the *Journal of the American Medical Association,* overweight people, especially women, are discriminated against in the workplace. Not only are overweight women hired much less frequently than overweight men, but they earn considerably less pay, the study found.

To blame sociological factors alone for anorexia and bulimia is inaccurate and futile, however. Only those predisposed to the disease will actually transfer these pressures into a disorder. A woman with a healthy self-image will not react to a photograph of an emaciated super-model with an urgent desire to lose 30 pounds.

EXPERT SOURCES

HELP FOR THE TORMENTED EATER

Both anorexia and bulimia are curable. Recent attention has made treatment more accessible and full recovery more probable, and those who lack financial resources can get help by calling a hotline. Usually, hotlines will assess, then recommend a treatment that suits needs and resources of the victim. Treatment options range from psychiatrists to guidance counselors to eating awareness groups, which most schools provide free of charge.

AMERICAN DIETIC ASSOC.
NCND, Suite 800
216 West Jackson Blvd
Chicago, IL 60606
■ Answers nutrition questions and refers callers to dieticians.
☎ **800-366-1655**

EATING DISORDERS AWARENESS & PREVENTION
Lloyd Building, Suite 803,
603 Stewart St.
Seattle, WA 98101
■ Sponsers eating disorders awareness week and other events nationwide.
☎ **206-382-3587**

EATING DISORDERS HOTLINE
Florida Inst. of Technology
150 West University
Melbourne, FL 32901
■ Sends free written information, refers callers to help in their area. Can forward calls to an eating disorders counselor.
☎ **800-872-0088**

NATIONAL ASSOCIATION OF ANOREXIA NERVOSA & ASSOCIATED DISORDERS
PO Box 7
Highland Park, IL 60035
■ Also known as ANAD, the association refers callers to help throughout the United States and in some foreign countries.
☎ **708-831-3438**

NATIONAL EATING DISORDERS ORGANIZATION
445 East Granville Road
Worthington, OH 43085
■ Refers callers to professional help near their homes. Will also send a packet of information about eating disorders for $5.
☎ **614-436-1112**

DOCTORS & MEDICINE

HEALTH CARE IN A NEW AGE

Expect more information, more choices, and more tough decisions

Efforts to remake the health care system may seem to have faltered in Washington, but beyond the Beltway there is a fundamental shift occurring in the way in which Americans get their health care. For the average consumer the financial pressures to enroll in a health management organization or other managed-care plan will continue to intensify, but the employers and insurers most affected by the tab will hold health care providers to much greater accountability for cost increases and the quality of care.

"Report cards" prepared by large health care buyers such as companies, pension funds, and the government, as well as studies by public interest groups, universities, and foundations will provide consumers with far more information with which to compare fee structures and quality of care at hundreds of managed-care organizations nationwide. The report cards are likely to include data on everything from waiting times to get an appointment to what the success rates have been for procedures such as open-heart surgery to how a particular plan is judged by its patients on overall "customer satisfaction."

One study, commissioned by the federal Office of Personnel Management to help government employees choose a health care plan wisely, gathered extensive data on the experience of federal workers at over 250 prepaid health plans or options across the country. The plans involved enroll approximately 65 percent of all persons currently covered by HMOs in the United States. The data should make it easier for both federal employees and other consumers to compare the quality of health care options available to them.

One major corporation, American Express, has not only asked employees to rate their health plans, but, after using this information to develop a consumer satisfaction index for 52 HMOs around the country, offered discounts to workers who enrolled in the top-ranked plans—and charged higher rates to those who chose the low-scoring programs.

Some states, such as California, New York, and Pennsylvania, are even beginning to require that hospitals publish statistics on the medical outcomes and expense of particular surgeries. One of the most important efforts to provide accountability has been launched by the National Committee for Quality Assurance, a nonprofit group established by a consortium of managed-care companies to develop reporting stan-

■ THE NEW HEALTH CARE LANDSCAPE

Fewer than half of all Americans still see doctors on a fee-for-service basis.

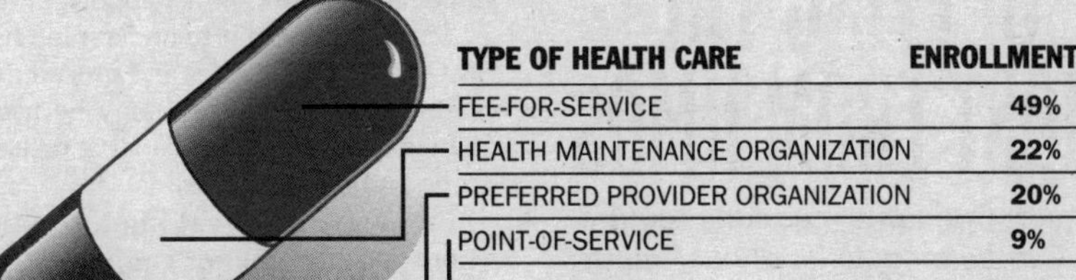

TYPE OF HEALTH CARE	ENROLLMENT
FEE-FOR-SERVICE	49%
HEALTH MAINTENANCE ORGANIZATION	22%
PREFERRED PROVIDER ORGANIZATION	20%
POINT-OF-SERVICE	9%

■ **FEE-FOR-SERVICE**
Private care where the patient chooses any doctor he or she wants to see. The patient pays according to the service rendered.

■ **HEALTH MAINTENANCE ORGANIZATION (HMO)**
Managed care where the patient is limited to seeing doctors employed by the HMO, and there is a set fee for the visit, no matter what service is performed.

■ **PREFERRED PROVIDER ORGANIZATION (PPO)**
Managed care where the patient chooses from a list of specific doctors in his or her area and pays a set fee for the consultation, no matter what service is performed.

■ **POINT-OF-SERVICE**
Managed care where the patient chooses from a list of doctors a primary care physician who coordinates all of his or her care. Patients who want to see a specialist must obtain the primary care physician's approval first.

SOURCE: *Source Book*, Health Insurance Association of America, 1994.

dards and oversee accreditation of plans within their industry.

The organization has been devising report cards that it hopes will enable health care consumers to reliably compare the performance of managed-care plans nationwide on such things as enrollee satisfaction with access to and quality of care; the plan's record in providing preventive services such as childhood immunizations, cholesterol screenings, and mammograms; the frequency with which the plan performed certain medical procedures such as bypass surgeries and angioplasties; the extent of the plan's physician turnover; and its overall financial health. Twenty-one major managed-care plans recently participated in a pilot test of the report card's effectiveness, and the committee hopes to make such report cards an industry standard within the next several years.

The accountability movement is sure to boost the dramatic growth that has occurred in HMOs and managed-care plans in recent years. According to the newsletter *Health Trends*, 36 million people were enrolled in traditional HMO plans in 1990. By 1995, that number shot up to 47 million, and the newsletter predicts that as many as 80 million people may be enrolled by 2000.

HMOs deserve much of the credit for the gradual easing of health care cost increases over the last several years. While those cost increases still exceed the general rate of inflation, for several years now the Labor Department's index of medical price inflation has been declining. The Congressional Budget Office recently estimated that the best-run HMOs can reduce a patient's use of services by 12 percent over what would have occurred in nonmanaged-care programs. Much of this savings comes from reducing the length of hospital stays. Because of such efficiencies, insurance premiums for managed-care plans can sometimes be as much as 15 to 20 percent lower than traditional fee-for-service plans.

MANAGED CARE

GETTING THE MOST FROM HMOs

Health maintenance plans require you to be an activist about health

The age of the health maintenance organization, or HMO, is well upon us, but savvy information on how to use one is hard to come by. Alan Raymond, vice-president of the Harvard Community Health Plan, a large HMO based in Boston, and the author of *The HMO Health Care Companion* (Harper Perennial, a division of HarperCollins, 1994), answers some critical questions for consumers:

■ How should one go about picking an HMO?

The first step is to understand your needs and expectations. What is it that you want from your health care and health insurance plan? Whether it's physician choice, benefits, access to specific doctors, hospitals, or specialists, or the cost, you need to know what's important to you.

The second step is to understand how an HMO works. What rules and procedures are different from what you may be used to? Then you have to find a plan that meets your needs and expectations.

Finally, you have to find a physician whom you trust. As with any other type of health care, it's the personal relationship of the physician or physicians that will likely determine how you feel about your HMO.

■ What questions should I ask of an HMO before I join?

How do you get care on a routine basis, how do you get care in an emergency, how do you get a referral when you need specialty care, how do you get hospitalized if you need it, and what should you do when you're away from home and need care? These are the fundamental issues that most people have to deal with.

■ Is an HMO suitable for someone with special medical needs or problems?

If there are specific types of benefits that are important to you, make sure you know what is covered, and perhaps more important, what is not. Usually the benefits are pretty similar. But there are some areas such as mental health, chronic care, substance abuse, and home care where there may be important differences between HMOs.

It's important, too, to know what hospitals the HMO is affiliated with. If you have a specific hospital in mind, you have to make sure you'll be able to go to that hospital if you want. If you have a special language need, or want a physician of a particular race or sex, you should consider those factors also.

■ Should my HMO be accredited?

There are only a limited number of HMOs that have gone through an accreditation process so far. A couple of years from now, when all health plans have gone through the process, you'll be able to make a better comparison. But it's certainly a useful piece

FACT FILE:

WHAT'S WRONG, DOC?

■ *According to a study by the National Center for Health Statistics, here's what sends people to the doctor the most:*

REASON FOR VISIT	FREQUENCY (%)
1. Hypertension	3.9
2. Middle ear infection	3.5
3. Pregnancy checkup	3.3
4. General exam	3.0
5. Acute upper respiratory infection	2.9
6. Health checkup of infant or child	2.7
7. Diabetes	2.2
8. Allergies	1.7
9. Bronchitis	1.7
10. Sore throat	1.8

SOURCE: National Center for Health Statistics.

of information. So is some of the information being published in health plan report cards by employers and consumer groups. They compare health plans based on the performance in preventive care—Pap smears, prenatal care, immunization. Those types of measures are a good indication of whether the health plan has an organized approach to prevention and improving quality.

■ What is the difference between a high-option or low-option plan?

There are usually two types of HMOs. One that requires you to stay within a network of HMO physicians, hospitals, and specialists in order to be covered. And then there's the point-of-service plan that allows you to choose a physician or hospital or practice outside the HMO network, but requires you to pay more out of pocket and has higher premiums.

■ How much more do point-of-service plans usually cost?

It's very difficult to say. Generally, the difference is that most HMOs only charge 5 or 10 dollars per doctor visit. If you go to a physician outside the HMO network, you might have to pay a deductible, which might be several hundred dollars, and then a co-insurance payment similar to what you have in traditional insurance. So your out-of-pocket expense can be significantly higher, although there is usually a limit on how much you have to pay out of pocket on an annual basis.

Premiums vary a good deal, from 5 to 10 percent or more. A lot depends on whether your employer contributes to the premium, and if so, by how much.

■ Will high-option plans always allow me to go outside an HMO network?

Not necessarily if you're joining through an employer. Your employer may have the choice of a traditional HMO or a point-of-service HMO available but may not always make that option available to you. Most people who join point-of-service plans get 80 to 90 percent of their care inside the network. So people see the point-of-service plans as a kind of safety valve. It may be a way of making a transition into an HMO from fees-for-service health care. It gives people that added assurance that they will be able to choose outside the network, even though most people who belong to those plans use the HMO network with very few exceptions.

■ Once I've picked an HMO, how can I make sure that I'm getting the most out of it?

There are some fundamental questions people need to ask. The first is, how do you choose a primary care doctor and what role will he or she play in your care? You may find that your current doctor participates in one or more HMOs. If so, ask if he or she will have to treat you differently if you're in an HMO. Is there going to be anything about the benefits or rules of coverage that will affect the way in which you'll be treated?

If you're required to choose a new doctor, find out how the HMO chooses its doctors and who is available to you within a convenient distance to where you work or live. If you require specialty care or have an ongoing illness, find out when a primary care doctor will take care of you and when you would be referred to a specialist. Most HMOs have member service or consumer relations departments that can answer such questions. If you're joining through an employer, your employer can often inform you. And in some cases there is comparative information that might be available from state regulators or employer coalitions or consumer magazines.

■ What drawbacks are there to HMOs?

You are more limited in your choice of physicians and hospitals than in a traditional insurance plan. The way to compensate is to establish a strong trusting relationship with your HMO physician. Most HMOs have ample resources available to them, but if you're used to making all of your own decisions about your health care, you are going to have to adjust to a situation where you're making your decisions in concert with your HMO doctor or HMO. Some people end up feeling that the HMO is putting up barriers and standing in the way of getting the care they feel they need.

HOSPITALS

WHEN YOUR LIFE DEPENDS ON IT

Where you are treated is often critical to recovery from an illness

Whether it's fine clothes or a new car, a great kitchen or where your child attends college, "only the best" is a standard that many aspire to but few can afford. Fortunately, there are plenty of perfectly fine alternatives to driving a new Mercedes or eating from a set of Belleek china that won't bankrupt you. But what if the consumer decision you are confronted with is where to get open-heart surgery or have an injured hip repaired? Considering how high the stakes might be then, "only the best" might not seem such an unreasonable standard to apply.

Indeed, recent research supports what many will have figured out on their own: When it comes to specialized medical procedures requiring hospitalization, where you go for treatment is often critical to whether you are treated successfully. In one recent study published in the *Journal of the American Medical Association,* for instance, researchers Harold S. Luft and Patrick S. Romano of the University of California found that death rates from high-risk heart bypass operations could be significantly reduced if the procedures were done at hospitals with consistently low death rates for the surgery.

Using the records of 115 California hospitals that had performed five or more coronary artery bypass operations annually in any year between 1983 and 1989, the researchers developed a methodology for determining when a hospital's death rates for the procedure were higher—or lower—than would ordinarily be expected, given the severity of the disease.

If death rates were merely a function of chance or the difficulty of measuring differences in the seriousness of the patients' conditions, then a hospital that performed well one year would not necessarily excel in a later period, the researchers reasoned.

What they discovered, however, was that hospitals that had significantly lower death rates for the first period tended to maintain that record two years later, while hospitals that compared poorly the first time around continued to do poorly two years later.

The researcher's general thrust was bolstered by a second study published recently in the journal *Annals of Surgery.* There, researchers found that patients were six times more likely to die of a complex pancreatic cancer surgery at hospitals that only attempt the operation a few times a year than at a large regional medical center that performs the procedure on a regular basis.

This is not to say that you need to seek out treatment at a major regional medical center in all cases. There are many conditions that a local hospital or doctor is likely to be fully capable of handling and where postoperative care may be more effectively handled. The quality of a hospital's nursing staff is often critical to the success of the patient's recovery, for instance.

Some community hospitals are comparable to regional medical centers with major teaching programs in their expertise in performing certain procedures and are able to deliver their care at significantly lower prices. But if you or a family member needs treatment for a condition that could jeopardize your long-term health—or even your life—it might well be a good idea to explore with your doctor treatment alternatives by a team that is more specialized and experienced than what is available closer to home.

One excellent source of information about specialty medical centers in the United States is the annual survey, *America's Best Hospitals,* published by the magazine *U.S. News & World Report.* The study assesses the quality of care at major medical centers for 16 specialty fields, from AIDS to urology. Highlights of that survey for the year 1994 appear on the pages that follow.

EXPERT LIST

THE BEST HOSPITALS IN AMERICA

Each year, the magazine U.S. News & World Report *publishes a special report ranking America's best hospitals in 16 different categories. The magazine's rating system was designed by the National Opinion Research Center, a social science research group at the University of Chicago. The model combines three years' worth of reputational surveys conducted by the magazine with nine categories of statistics bearing on quality of care. The reputational ratings were compiled by asking board-certified physicians from around the country to identify the hospitals they deemed to be the five best in their specialty, without regard to cost or location. Only major academic hospitals providing comprehensive, state-of-the-art care were eligible for consideration. Among the objective measures also factored in were everything from the ratio of nurses and board-certified specialists to hospital beds to the availability of advanced technology in various specialties, to death rates in fields where that is relevant. In the 1994 survey, the top-ranked hospital overall was Johns Hopkins Hospital, which ranked in the top 10 in 15 specialities.*

AIDS: Doctors who specialize in AIDS care must keep up with new therapeutic developments because some patients no longer benefit from or cannot tolerate some of the older drugs used to stave off AIDS. The availability of technologies such as X-ray radiation therapy and magnetic resonance imaging is also factored in in evaluating the strength of AIDS treatment. Outpatient care and comprehensive treatment programs are now common at hospitals specializing in AIDS.

Rank Hospital	Overall score	Rep. score	Ratio of staff to beds: Residents	R.N.s	Brd.-cert. M.D.s	Mortality rate	Tech. score	Dischg. plan
1. **San Francisco General Hospital Medical Center**	100.0	40.1%	0.55	1.52	0.40	1.24	6	2
2. **Johns Hopkins Hospital,** Baltimore*	71.9	20.3%	0.45	1.43	0.66	0.78	9	2
3. **Massachusetts General Hospital,** Boston*	62.0	15.6%	0.47	1.14	0.66	0.77	9	2
4. **U. of California San Francisco Medical Center***	55.9	12.0%	0.32	1.82	1.55	0.76	8	2
5. **Memorial Sloan-Kettering Cancer Center,** N.Y.*	50.0	8.4%	0.32	1.37	0.55	0.67	5	2
6. **UCLA Medical Center,** Los Angeles*	49.7	9.1%	0.71	1.20	0.82	0.77	9	2
7. **New York U. Medical Center,** New York*	46.3	5.3%	0.20	1.15	1.25	0.62	6	2
8. **U. of Miami Hospital and Clinics***	45.9	9.0%	0.30	1.42	0.27	0.79	6	2
9. **New York Hospital-Cornell Medical Center***	45.2	7.0%	0.38	1.00	0.99	0.72	8	2
10. **Mayo Clinic,** Rochester, Minn.*	38.3	2.3%	0.37	0.73	1.49	0.64	5	2
11. **Columbia-Presbyterian Medical Center,** N.Y.*	37.4	4.4%	0.31	1.05	0.81	0.78	9	2
12. **U. of Washington Medical Center,** Seattle*	37.0	2.6%	0.30	2.06	1.90	0.73	5	2
13. **Deaconess Hospital,** Boston*	36.8	1.8%	0.63	1.33	0.93	0.69	7	2
14. **Mount Sinai Medical Center,** New York*	36.5	3.6%	0.50	1.50	1.11	0.79	7	2
15. **Beth Israel Hospital,** Boston*	36.4	2.0%	0.54	1.93	2.08	0.75	6	2
16. **Duke U. Medical Center,** Durham, N.C.*	36.4	4.8%	0.43	1.60	0.66	0.86	8	2

TERMS:
REPUTATIONAL SCORE: Percentage of doctors surveyed who named the hospital.
RESIDENTS TO BEDS: Ratio of interns and residents to beds.
R.N.S TO BEDS: Ratio of registered nurses to beds.
BOARD-CERTIFIED M.D.S TO BEDS: Ratio of doctors certified in a specialty to the number of beds.
MORTALITY RATE: Ratio of actual to expected deaths (lower is better).
TECHNOLOGY SCORE: Specialty-specific index from 0 to 9 (AIDS).
DISCHARGE PLANNING: Number of post-discharge services available, from 0 to 2.
* Indicates member of Council of Teaching Hospitals.

■ EXPERT LIST

AIDS Rank Hospital	Overall score	Rep. score	Ratio of staff to beds: Residents	R.N.s	Brd.-cert. M.D.s	Mortality rate	Tech. score	Dischg. plan
17. **Barnes Hospital,** St. Louis*	35.9	3.5%	0.47	0.81	0.90	0.76	7	2
18. **Rush-Presbyterian-St. Luke's Med. Ctr.,** Chicago*	35.3	2.3%	0.63	1.23	0.85	0.75	8	2
19. **Stanford U. Medical Center,** Palo Alto, Calif.*	35.1	4.7%	0.79	0.86	1.81	0.95	8	2
20. **Indiana U. Medical Center,** Indianapolis*	34.4	0.0%	0.37	1.86	0.90	0.69	9	2
21. **U. of Illinois Hospital and Clinics,** Chicago*	34.3	0.0%	1.22	1.95	0.60	0.73	6	2
22. **Northwestern Memorial Hospital,** Chicago*	34.0	4.9%	0.41	1.03	1.14	0.92	7	2
23. **Georgetown U. Medical Center,** Washington, D.C.*	33.7	1.7%	0.34	1.59	1.28	0.75	7	2
24. **Roswell Park Cancer Institute,** Buffalo	33.7	0.0%	0.37	2.58	0.49	0.65	5	2
25. **Thomas Jefferson U. Hospital,** Philadelphia*	33.6	0.0%	0.68	1.44	1.12	0.70	7	2

■ **CANCER:** Cancer is a group of diseases in which cells grow uncontrollably and spread throughout the body. About 1.9 million individuals will learn in 1995 that they have cancer, including 700,000 cases of skin cancer. The death toll in 1994 is expected to number some 340,000. But over 8 million cancer patients are alive today, including 5 million who were diagnosed five or more years ago. Surgery, radiation, chemicals, and hormones all are standard weapons in oncology departments.

Rank Hospital	Overall score	Rep. score	Ratio of staff to beds: Residents	R.N.s	Brd.-cert. M.D.s	Mortality rate	Tech. score	Inpatient op. to beds
1. **Memorial Sloan-Kettering Cancer Center,** New York*	100.0	50.4%	0.32	1.37	0.55	0.67	8	17.9
2. **U. of Texas M. D. Anderson Cancer Center,** Houston*	81.5	40.9%	0.10	1.88	0.61	0.78	10	12.4
3. **Dana-Farber Cancer Institute,** Boston	57.1	27.3%	0.63	1.58	2.17	0.88	2	0.0
4. **Mayo Clinic,** Rochester, Minn.*	56.9	16.4%	0.37	0.73	1.49	0.64	7	21.5
5. **Roswell Park Cancer Institute,** Buffalo	50.6	7.4%	0.37	2.58	0.49	0.65	8	37.7
6. **Fred Hutchinson Cancer Research Center,** Seattle	50.2	10.4%	0.00	0.95	1.13	0.50	1	6.8
7. **Johns Hopkins Hospital,** Baltimore*	49.7	15.7%	0.45	1.43	0.66	0.78	10	15.5
8. **U. of Washington Medical Center,** Seattle*	43.4	8.8%	0.30	2.06	1.90	0.73	8	14.8
9. **Stanford U. Medical Center,** Palo Alto, Calif.*	38.5	10.3%	0.79	0.86	1.81	0.95	9	13.9
10. **Duke U. Medical Center,** Durham, N.C.*	36.6	7.6%	0.43	1.60	0.66	0.86	11	15.3
11. **Indiana U. Medical Center,** Indianapolis*	35.1	0.9%	0.37	1.86	0.90	0.69	10	17.3
12. **Massachusetts General Hospital,** Boston*	34.9	4.1%	0.47	1.14	0.66	0.77	11	17.5
13. **U. of California San Francisco Medical Center***	34.4	2.2%	0.32	1.82	1.55	0.76	10	18.3
14. **U. of Wisconsin Hospital and Clinics,** Madison*	34.1	1.0%	0.65	1.24	0.74	0.71	10	18.9
15. **New York U. Medical Center,** New York*	34.1	0.0%	0.20	1.15	1.25	0.62	8	13.6
16. **UCLA Medical Center,** Los Angeles*	34.0	3.5%	0.71	1.20	0.82	0.77	10	14.6
17. **Cleveland Clinic,** Ohio*	33.8	2.0%	0.59	1.47	0.38	0.76	10	19.9
18. **Thomas Jefferson U. Hospital,** Philadelphia*	33.2	0.0%	0.68	1.44	1.12	0.70	9	16.3
19. **U. of Illinois Hospital and Clinics,** Chicago*	33.0	0.0%	1.22	1.95	0.60	0.73	8	13.7

TERMS:
REPUTATIONAL SCORE: Percentage of doctors surveyed who named the hospital.
RESIDENTS TO BEDS: Ratio of interns and residents to beds.
R.N.S TO BEDS: Ratio of registered nurses to beds.
BOARD-CERTIFIED M.D.S TO BEDS: Ratio of doctors certified in a specialty to the number of beds.
MORTALITY RATE: Ratio of actual to expected deaths (lower is better).
TECHNOLOGY SCORE: Specialty-specific index from 0 to 11 (cancer).
INPATIENT OPERATIONS TO BEDS: Ratio of annual inpatient operations to beds.
* Indicates member of Council of Teaching Hospitals.

■ EXPERT LIST

CANCER Rank Hospital	Overall score	Rep. score	Ratio of staff to beds: Residents	R.N.s	Brd.-cert. M.D.s	Mortality rate	Tech. score	Inpatient op. to beds
20. Deaconess Hospital, Boston*	32.9	0.0%	0.63	1.33	0.93	0.69	9	16.9
21. Green Hospital of Scripps Clinic, La Jolla, Calif.	32.9	0.6%	0.00	1.99	0.51	0.69	5	23.1
22. Lahey Clinic, Burlington, Mass.	32.6	0.5%	0.28	1.22	0.80	0.70	8	22.4
23. Brigham and Women's Hospital, Boston*	32.4	1.0%	0.64	0.79	1.24	0.75	9	20.0
24. Virginia Mason Medical Center, Seattle	32.3	0.0%	0.37	0.43	1.20	0.76	1	37.7
25. Mount Sinai Medical Center, Cleveland*	32.0	1.6%	0.40	0.86	1.09	0.72	7	15.2

■ **CARDIOLOGY:** At cardiology departments, doctors treat a wide variety of heart and circulatory disorders from arrhythmia, or abnormal rhythm of the heart, to congestive heart failure. Most hospitals' cardiac units can perform routine procedures, such as angiography—X-ray pictures of blood vessels—and coronary bypass surgery. For complex cases that may involve valve problems or congenital heart disease—the most common deformity in newborns—a large medical center is often best.

Rank Hospital	Overall score	Rep. score	Ratio of staff to beds: Residents	R.N.s	Brd.-cert. M.D.s	Mortality rate	Tech. score	Inpatient op. to beds
1. Mayo Clinic, Rochester, Minn.*	100.0	32.5%	0.37	0.73	1.49	0.64	8	21.5
2. Cleveland Clinic, Ohio*	95.6	32.7%	0.59	1.47	0.38	0.76	9	19.9
3. Massachusetts General Hospital, Boston*	68.9	19.8%	0.47	1.14	0.66	0.77	9	17.5
4. Stanford U. Medical Center, Palo Alto, Calif.*	56.0	15.5%	0.79	0.86	1.81	0.95	8	13.9
5. Duke U. Medical Center, Durham, N.C.*	54.8	14.1%	0.43	1.60	0.66	0.86	9	15.3
6. Brigham and Women's Hospital, Boston*	54.2	11.7%	0.64	0.79	1.24	0.75	8	20.0
7. Emory U. Hospital, Atlanta*	51.1	12.5%	0.31	1.28	0.68	0.84	7	17.2
8. Johns Hopkins Hospital, Baltimore*	47.4	8.9%	0.45	1.43	0.66	0.78	9	15.5
9. U. of California San Francisco Medical Center*	45.5	6.8%	0.32	1.82	1.55	0.76	8	18.3
10. Texas Heart Inst. (St. Luke's), Houston*	43.4	12.7%	0.19	1.36	0.62	1.16	8	19.3
11. New York U. Medical Center, New York*	41.5	2.2%	0.20	1.15	1.25	0.62	8	13.6
12. Barnes Hospital, St. Louis*	39.9	5.3%	0.47	0.81	0.90	0.76	9	11.1
13. Indiana U. Medical Center, Indianapolis*	39.6	2.1%	0.37	1.86	0.90	0.69	9	17.3
14. Columbia-Presbyterian Medical Center, New York*	39.2	5.4%	0.31	1.05	0.81	0.78	9	12.0
15. Cedars-Sinai Medical Center, Los Angeles*	39.1	6.2%	0.26	0.83	1.19	0.81	8	13.4
16. Beth Israel Hospital, Boston*	37.0	1.5%	0.54	1.93	2.08	0.75	8	14.5
17. New York Hospital-Cornell Medical Center, N.Y.*	36.5	2.7%	0.38	1.00	0.99	0.72	8	11.5
18. UCLA Medical Center, Los Angeles*	35.3	2.2%	0.71	1.20	0.82	0.77	9	14.6
19. U. of Illinois Hospital and Clinics, Chicago*	35.2	0.0%	1.22	1.95	0.60	0.73	7	13.7
20. Thomas Jefferson U. Hospital, Philadelphia*	35.0	0.0%	0.68	1.44	1.12	0.70	8	16.3
21. Deaconess Hospital, Boston*	34.7	0.0%	0.63	1.33	0.93	0.69	9	16.9
22. Green Hospital of Scripps Clinic, La Jolla, Calif.	34.6	1.1%	0.00	1.99	0.51	0.69	8	23.1
23. U. of Washington Medical Center, Seattle*	34.0	0.0%	0.30	2.06	1.90	0.73	8	14.8
24. U. of Wisconsin Hospital and Clinics, Madison*	33.7	0.0%	0.65	1.24	0.74	0.71	9	18.9
25. Mount Sinai Medical Center, Cleveland*	33.6	1.0%	0.40	0.86	1.09	0.72	7	15.2

SOURCE: Reprinted from *U.S. News & World Report,* July 18, 1994. © 1994.

EXPERT LIST

ENDOCRINOLOGY: Clinical endocrinologists are internists who diagnose and treat patients with problems involving the hormone-secreting endocrine glands. Over- or underreproduction of those hormones affects a person's rate of growth, metabolism, and sexual development. At top hospitals, clinical endocrinologists consult with other specialists on such wide-ranging problems as diabetes, osteoporosis, thyroid disorders, infertility, high cholesterol, and hormone-producing tumors.

Rank	Hospital	Overall score	Rep. score	Ratio of staff to beds: Residents	R.N.s	Bd.-cert. M.D.s	Mortality rate	Tech. score
1.	**Mayo Clinic,** Rochester, Minn.*	100.0	42.5%	0.37	0.73	1.49	0.64	8
2.	**Massachusetts General Hospital,** Boston*	84.3	35.8%	0.47	1.14	0.66	0.77	11
3.	**U. of California San Francisco Medical Center***	49.4	12.8%	0.32	1.82	1.55	0.76	10
4.	**UCLA Medical Center,** Los Angeles*	43.7	9.7%	0.71	1.20	0.82	0.77	11
5.	**U. of Washington Medical Center,** Seattle*	43.1	7.7%	0.30	2.06	1.90	0.73	10
6.	**Barnes Hospital,** St. Louis*	42.6	9.9%	0.47	0.81	0.90	0.76	11
7.	**Johns Hopkins Hospital,** Baltimore*	42.4	9.6%	0.45	1.43	0.66	0.78	11
8.	**U. of Chicago Hospitals***	41.5	10.9%	0.75	1.38	0.73	0.91	11
9.	**Deaconess Hospital,** Boston*	41.2	6.3%	0.63	1.33	0.93	0.69	10
10.	**U. of Michigan Medical Center,** Ann Arbor*	40.3	10.2%	0.41	1.29	0.66	0.85	10
11.	**Brigham and Women's Hospital,** Boston*	38.5	6.6%	0.64	0.79	1.24	0.75	10
12.	**Clinical Center, Nat. Inst. of Health,** Bethesda, Md.*	37.1	18.1%	0.00	1.76	1.51	NA	11
13.	**Beth Israel Hospital,** Boston*	35.4	2.8%	0.54	1.93	2.08	0.75	9
14.	**New York U. Medical Center,** New York*	33.9	0.5%	0.20	1.15	1.25	0.62	9
15.	**U. of Minnesota Hospital and Clinic,** Minneapolis*	33.4	3.4%	0.72	0.86	0.89	0.75	10
16.	**Columbia-Presbyterian Medical Center,** New York*	33.4	4.9%	0.31	1.05	0.81	0.78	10
17.	**U. of Illinois Hospital and Clinics,** Chicago*	32.8	0.0%	1.22	1.95	0.60	0.73	8
18.	**Cleveland Clinic,** Ohio*	32.2	2.6%	0.59	1.47	0.38	0.76	11
19.	**Vanderbilt U. Medical Center,** Nashville*	31.8	5.6%	0.45	1.29	0.73	0.91	11
20.	**Thomas Jefferson U. Hospital,** Philadelphia*	31.7	0.0%	0.68	1.44	1.12	0.70	10
21.	**Duke U. Medical Center, Durham,** N.C.*	31.7	4.6%	0.43	1.60	0.66	0.86	11
22.	**Indiana U. Medical Center,** Indianapolis*	31.6	0.0%	0.37	1.86	0.90	0.69	10
23.	**Presbyterian U. Hospital,** Pittsburgh*	31.3	1.7%	0.72	2.10	1.27	0.82	9
24.	**U. of Wisconsin Hospital and Clinics,** Madison*	30.2	0.0%	0.65	1.24	0.74	0.71	11
25.	**Stanford U. Medical Center,** Palo Alto, Calif.*	30.1	4.0%	0.79	0.86	1.81	0.95	11

GYNECOLOGY: Usually linked with obstetrics and the care of routine and high-risk pregnancies, gynecology departments also run the gamut of medical specialties. For example, cancers of the reproductive tract demand doctors trained in oncology as well as gynecology.

Rank	Hospital	Overall score	Rep. score	Ratio of staff to beds: Residents	R.N.s	Brd.-cert. M.D.s	Mortality rate	Tech. score	Inpatient op. to beds
1.	**Johns Hopkins Hospital,** Baltimore	100.0	19.2%	0.45	1.43	0.66	0.78	9	15.5
2.	**Mayo Clinic,** Rochester, Minn.	96.9	18.7%	0.37	0.73	1.49	0.64	5	21.5
3.	**U. of Texas M. D. Anderson Cancer Center,** Houston	81.3	15.3%	0.10	1.88	0.61	0.78	8	12.4
4.	**Brigham and Women's Hospital,** Boston	71.5	12.6%	0.64	0.79	1.24	0.75	8	20.0

■ EXPERT LIST

GYNECOLOGY Rank Hospital	Overall score	Rep. score	Ratio of staff to beds: Residents	R.N.s	Brd.-cert. M.D.s	Mortality rate	Tech. score	Inpatient op. to beds
5. **Massachusetts General Hospital,** Boston	59.8	10.3%	0.47	1.14	0.66	0.77	9	17.5
6. **Duke U. Medical Center,** Durham, N.C.	53.7	8.6%	0.43	1.60	0.66	0.86	9	15.3
7. **Memorial Sloan-Kettering Cancer Center,** N.Y.	52.8	9.0%	0.32	1.37	0.55	0.67	6	17.9
8. **Los Angeles County-USC Medical Center**	45.7	7.7%	0.00	1.30	0.27	0.99	6	28.7
9. **U. of Chicago Hospitals**	41.0	5.4%	0.75	1.38	0.73	0.91	9	17.3
10. **UCLA Medical Center,** Los Angeles	40.1	5.5%	0.71	1.20	0.82	0.77	9	14.6
11. **Cleveland Clinic,** Ohio	39.1	5.2%	0.59	1.47	0.38	0.76	9	19.9
12. **U. of California San Francisco Medical Center**	35.1	3.8%	0.32	1.82	1.55	0.76	8	18.3
13. **Stanford U. Medical Center,** Palo Alto, Calif.	34.7	3.8%	0.79	0.86	1.81	0.95	9	13.9
14. **Yale-New Haven Hospital,** New Haven, Conn.	33.9	4.0%	0.47	1.23	1.67	0.94	8	13.0
15. **Northwestern Memorial Hospital,** Chicago	32.8	4.3%	0.41	1.03	1.14	0.92	8	14.4
16. **U. of North Carolina Hospitals,** Chapel Hill	30.8	3.2%	0.52	1.71	0.98	0.94	8	13.6
17. **New York Hospital-Cornell Medical Center,** N.Y.	30.2	4.1%	0.38	1.00	0.99	0.72	7	11.5
18. **Beth Israel Hospital,** Boston	29.9	2.1%	0.54	1.93	2.08	0.75	7	14.5
19. **Roswell Park Cancer Institute,** Buffalo	28.8	1.5%	0.37	2.58	0.49	0.65	7	37.7
20. **U. of Virg. Health Sciences Center,** Charlottesville	28.6	2.2%	0.84	1.92	0.40	0.88	8	18.8
21. **Hospital of the U. of Pennsylvania,** Philadelphia	28.3	2.6%	0.73	1.33	0.94	0.84	9	15.5
22. **U. of Washington Medical Center,** Seattle	27.5	1.9%	0.30	2.06	1.90	0.73	7	14.8
23. **Cedars-Sinai Medical Center,** Los Angeles	26.3	3.3%	0.26	0.83	1.19	0.81	7	13.4
24. **Parkland Memorial Hospital,** Dallas	26.0	3.4%	0.51	0.93	0.46	1.24	8	10.0
25. **F. G. McGaw Hosp., Loyola Med. Ctr.,** Maywood, Ill.	25.4	1.9%	0.60	1.58	0.88	0.90	8	18.3

■ **NEUROLOGY:** Neurology delves into disorders of the central nervous systems and muscles and has recently been marked by promising experimental therapies, such as the drug Betaseron for multiple sclerosis. Hospitals with outstanding neurology departments often have centers dedicated to epilepsy or other specific diseases.

Rank Hospital	Overall score	Rep. score	Ratio of staff to beds: Residents	R.N.s	Bd.-cert. M.D.s	Mortality rate	Tech. score
1. **Mayo Clinic,** Rochester, Minn.*	100.0	35.9%	0.37	0.73	1.49	0.64	6
2. **Massachusetts General Hospital,** Boston*	83.8	30.1%	0.47	1.14	0.66	0.77	9
3. **Johns Hopkins Hospital,** Baltimore*	78.0	26.8%	0.45	1.43	0.66	0.78	9
4. **Columbia-Presbyterian Medical Center,** New York*	67.5	21.8%	0.31	1.05	0.81	0.78	9
5. **U. of California San Francisco Medical Center***	66.7	19.3%	0.32	1.82	1.55	0.76	8
6. **New York Hospital-Cornell Medical Center,** New York*	53.4	12.7%	0.38	1.00	0.99	0.72	7
7. **Cleveland Clinic,** Ohio*	47.7	9.2%	0.59	1.47	0.38	0.76	9
8. **Barnes Hospital,** St. Louis*	46.8	9.8%	0.47	0.81	0.90	0.76	9
9. **Hospital of the U. of Pennsylvania,** Philadelphia*	44.3	8.6%	0.73	1.33	0.94	0.84	9
10. **UCLA Medical Center,** Los Angeles*	40.2	5.2%	0.71	1.20	0.82	0.77	9
11. **New York U. Medical Center,** New York*	39.5	1.7%	0.20	1.15	1.25	0.62	7

SOURCE: Reprinted from *U.S. News & World Report*, July 18, 1994. © 1994.

■ EXPERT LIST

NEUROLOGY Rank Hospital	Overall score	Rep. score	Ratio of staff to beds: Residents	R.N.s	Bd.-cert. M.D.s	Mortality rate	Tech. score
12. **Duke U. Medical Center,** Durham, N.C.*	37.9	6.1%	0.43	1.60	0.66	0.86	9
13. **U. of Illinois Hospital and Clinics,** Chicago*	36.1	0.5%	1.22	1.95	0.60	0.73	6
14. **Thomas Jefferson U. Hospital,** Philadelphia*	36.1	0.7%	0.68	1.44	1.12	0.70	8
15. **Beth Israel Hospital,** Boston*	36.0	1.3%	0.54	1.93	2.08	0.75	7
16. **Brigham and Women's Hospital,** Boston*	35.5	2.5%	0.64	0.79	1.24	0.75	8
17. **U. of Washington Medical Center**, Seattle*	35.3	0.9%	0.30	2.06	1.90	0.73	8
18. **U. of Wisconsin Hospital and Clinics,** Madison*	35.1	0.9%	0.65	1.24	0.74	0.71	9
19. **Indiana U. Medical Center,** Indianapolis*	35.0	0.0%	0.37	1.86	0.90	0.69	8
20. **New England Medical Center,** Boston*	34.5	1.9%	0.53	1.65	0.66	0.74	6
21. **Deaconess Hospital,** Boston*	34.2	0.0%	0.63	1.33	0.93	0.69	8
22. **Memorial Sloan-Kettering Cancer Center,** New York*	34.0	0.0%	0.32	1.37	0.55	0.67	7
23. **Rush-Presbyterian-St. Luke's Medical Center,** Chicago*	33.3	1.3%	0.63	1.23	0.85	0.75	8
24. **U. of Michigan Medical Center,** Ann Arbor*	33.3	3.8%	0.41	1.29	0.66	0.85	8
25. **Georgetown U. Medical Center,** Washington, D.C.*	32.4	0.7%	0.34	1.59	1.28	0.75	8

■ **ORTHOPEDICS:** The branch of surgery dealing with problems of bones, joints, and muscles covers patients from children born with skeletal defects to seniors crippled by osteoporosis. Injured athletes of all ages also receive care from professionals in this specialty, a major player in the field of sports medicine. Once an orthopedic problem is corrected, intensive rehabilitation is often needed for a full recovery of function, so physical therapists play a key role in the department.

Rank Hospital	Overall score	Rep. score	Ratio of staff to beds: Residents	R.N.'s	Brd.-cert. M.D.'s	Mortality Rate	Tech. score	Inpatient op. to beds
1. **Hospital for Special Surgery,** New York*	100.0	28.5%	0.18	0.78	0.77	0.16	4	27.8
2. **Mayo Clinic,** Rochester, Minn.*	57.9	28.6%	0.37	0.73	1.49	0.64	4	21.5
3. **Massachusetts General Hospital,** Boston*	42.5	19.2%	0.47	1.14	0.66	0.77	5	17.5
4. **Johns Hopkins Hospital**, Baltimore*	26.5	7.6%	0.45	1.43	0.66	0.78	5	15.5
5. **Duke U. Medical Center**, Durham, N.C.*	25.2	7.4%	0.43	1.60	0.66	0.86	5	15.3
6. **U. of Washington Medical Center,** Seattle*	25.0	5.3%	0.30	2.06	1.90	0.73	4	14.8
7. **Cleveland Clinic,** Ohio	23.9	5.3%	0.59	1.47	0.38	0.76	5	19.9
8. **UCLA Medical Center,** Los Angeles*	22.7	4.6%	0.71	1.20	0.82	0.77	5	14.6
9. **Hosp. for Joint Diseases-Orthopedic Inst.**, New York	22.5	5.2%	0.22	1.26	0.81	0.85	4	23.5
10. **U. of Iowa Hospitals and Clinics,** Iowa City*	22.3	5.2%	0.78	1.34	0.54	0.92	5	25.5
11. **U. of Tennessee Medical Center,** Memphis	21.7	5.5%	0.24	0.72	2.28	0.77	2	14.6
12. **Brigham and Women's Hospital,** Boston*	20.7	3.2%	0.64	0.79	1.24	0.75	4	20.0
13. **Presbyterian U. Hospital,** Pittsburgh*	20.0	2.3%	0.72	2.10	1.27	0.82	3	17.2
14. **Hospital of the U. of Pennsylvania,** Philadelphia*	19.6	2.8%	0.73	1.33	0.94	0.84	5	15.5
15. **James Lawrence Kernan Hospital**, Baltimore	19.3	0.0%	0.00	0.67	1.83	0.53	1	16.1
16. **U. of Michigan Medical Center,** Ann Arbor*	19.1	3.2%	0.41	1.29	0.66	0.85	5	16.8
17. **New York U. Medical Center,** New York	18.5	0.5%	0.20	1.15	1.25	0.62	4	13.6
18. **Thomas Jefferson U. Hospital,** Philadelphia*	18.4	0.4%	0.68	1.44	1.12	0.70	4	16.3

■ EXPERT LIST

ORTHOPEDICS Rank Hospital	Overall score	Rep. score	Ratio of staff to beds: Residents	R.N.s	Brd.-cert. M.D.s	Mortality rate	Tech. score	Inpatient op. to beds
19. **Beth Israel Hospital,** Boston*	18.4	0.3%	0.54	1.93	2.08	0.75	4	14.5
20. **Columbia-Presbyterian Medical Center,** N.Y.*	18.3	2.4%	0.31	1.05	0.81	0.78	5	12.0
21. **U. of Illinois Hospital and Clinics,** Chicago*	18.3	0.0%	1.22	1.95	0.60	0.73	3	13.7
22. **U. of Miami Hospital and Clinics***	18.2	2.9%	0.30	1.42	0.27	0.79	3	6.9
23. **Rush-Presbyterian-St. Luke's Med. Ctr.,** Chicago*	18.2	1.5%	0.63	1.23	0.85	0.75	4	13.2
24. **Georgetown U. Medical Center,** Washington, D.C.*	18.2	1.4%	0.34	1.59	1.28	0.75	4	15.4
25. **New England Baptist Hospital,** Boston	18.2	2.4%	0.04	0.75	0.59	0.65	2	26.3

■ **UROLOGY:** Urology departments treat problems of the female urinary tract and the male urinary and reproductive systems. Much of the focus of urologists is on the prostate, and these specialists help men sort out difficult options when faced with cancer. Prostate surgery and radiation can induce incontinence or impotence.

Rank Hospital	Overall score	Rep. score	Ratio of staff to beds: Residents	R.N.s	Brd.-cert. M.D.s	Mortality rate	Tech. score	Inpatient op. to beds
1. **Mayo Clinic,** Rochester, Minn.*	100.0	30.5%	0.37	0.73	1.49	0.64	8	21.5
2. **Johns Hopkins Hospital,** Baltimore*	95.6	31.5%	0.45	1.43	0.66	0.78	11	15.5
3. **Cleveland Clinic,** Ohio*	73.5	19.9%	0.59	1.47	0.38	0.76	10	19.9
4. **UCLA Medical Center,** Los Angeles*	65.5	16.2%	0.71	1.20	0.82	0.77	11	14.6
5. **Memorial Sloan-Kettering Cancer Center,** New York*	58.2	10.8%	0.32	1.37	0.55	0.67	8	17.9
6. **Stanford U. Medical Center,** Palo Alto, Calif.*	55.9	14.3%	0.79	0.86	1.81	0.95	11	13.9
7. **Barnes Hospital,** St. Louis*	54.7	11.7%	0.47	0.81	0.90	0.76	11	11.1
8. **U. of Texas M. D. Anderson Center,** Houston*	49.9	9.8%	0.10	1.88	0.61	0.78	10	12.4
9. **Massachusetts General Hospital,** Boston*	47.2	7.8%	0.47	1.14	0.66	0.77	11	17.5
10. **Duke U. Medical Center,** Durham, N.C.*	44.5	8.0%	0.43	1.60	0.66	0.86	11	15.3
11. **Indiana U. Medical Center,** Indianapolis*	42.1	2.5%	0.37	1.86	0.90	0.69	10	17.3
12. **U. of Washington Medical Center,** Seattle*	41.7	3.1%	0.30	2.06	1.90	0.73	10	14.8
13. **U. of California San Francisco Medical Center***	40.4	3.4%	0.32	1.82	1.55	0.76	10	18.3
14. **Roswell Park Cancer Institute,** Buffalo	40.3	0.4%	0.37	2.58	0.49	0.65	9	37.7
15. **Lahey Clinic,** Burlington, Mass.	40.2	3.4%	0.28	1.22	0.80	0.70	10	22.4
16. **New York U. Medical Center,** New York*	39.7	0.5%	0.20	1.15	1.25	0.62	8	13.6
17. **New York Hospital-Cornell Medical Center,** N.Y.	39.6	3.6%	0.38	1.00	0.99	0.72	9	11.5
18. **Thomas Jefferson U. Hospital,** Philadelphia*	38.7	0.9%	0.68	1.44	1.12	0.70	10	16.3
19. **Brigham and Women's Hospital,** Boston*	38.0	2.5%	0.64	0.79	1.24	0.75	10	20.0
20. **U. of Illinois Hospital and Clinics,** Chicago*	37.1	0.0%	1.22	1.95	0.60	0.73	7	13.7
21. **Columbia-Presbyterian Medical Center,** New York*	36.8	3.6%	0.31	1.05	0.81	0.78	10	12.0
22. **Deaconess Hospital,** Boston*	36.1	0.0%	0.63	1.33	0.93	0.69	9	16.9
23. **Beth Israel Hospital,** Boston*	35.4	0.0%	0.54	1.93	2.08	0.75	9	14.5
24. **U. of Wisconsin Hospital and Clinics,** Madison*	35.4	0.0%	0.65	1.24	0.74	0.71	11	18.9
25. **U. of Minnesota Hospital and Clinic,** Minneapolis*	35.1	1.2%	0.72	0.86	0.89	0.75	10	17.1

SOURCE: Reprinted from *U.S. News & World Report,* July 18, 1994. ©1994.

EXPERT LIST

THE FOLLOWING FOUR FIELDS WERE BASED ON REPUTATIONAL SCORES ONLY BECAUSE DEATH RATES HAVE LITTLE OR NO RELATION TO TREATMENT IN THESE AREAS.

OPHTHALMOLOGY: Ophthalmology procedures, including surgery for cataracts, glaucoma, and detached retina, are generally done on an outpatient basis.

Rank Hospital	Reputational score	Board-cert. M.D.s to beds	Technology score	Inpatient ops. to beds
1. **Bascom Palmer Eye Institute,** U. of Miami	40.0%	2.13	2	37.8
2. **Wilmer Eye Institute,** Johns Hopkins Hospital, Baltimore*	37.7%	0.66	17	15.5
3. **Wills Eye Hospital,** Philadelphia	35.4%	1.10	3	44.5
4. **Massachusetts Ear and Eye Infirmary,** Boston	29.8%	0.39	3	78.4
5. **Jules Stein Eye Institute,** UCLA Medical Center, L.A.*	22.3%	0.82	17	14.6
6. **U. of Iowa Hospitals and Clinics,** Iowa City*	16.1%	0.54	18	25.5
7. **Doheny Eye Hospital,** Los Angeles	8.7%	1.08	0	31.3
8. **Barnes Hospital,** St. Louis*	7.3%	0.90	17	11.1
9. **Duke U. Medical Center,** Durham, N.C.*	5.0%	0.66	19	15.3
10. **U. of California San Francisco Medical Center***	4.6%	1.55	17	18.3
11. **Mayo Clinic,** Rochester, Minn.*	4.3%	0.93	13	20.5
12. **Manhattan Eye, Ear and Throat Hospital,** New York	4.3%	4.21	1	95.9
13. **New York Eye and Ear Infirmary,** New York	3.9%	4.54	3	52.2
14. **Emory U. Hospital,** Atlanta*	3.2%	0.68	11	17.2
15. **U. of Michigan Medical Center,** Ann Arbor*	3.0%	0.66	17	16.8

PEDIATRICS Desperately or chronically ill children can benefit from the range of specialists and level of counseling at a children's hospital or at the pediatric ward of a teaching hospital.

Rank Hospital	Reputational score	Board-cert. M.D.s to beds	Technology score	R.N.s to beds
1. **Children's Hospital,** Boston*	36.1%	1.25	10	1.60
2. **Children's Hospital of Philadelphia***	26.5%	1.13	10	1.89
3. **Johns Hopkins Hospital,** Baltimore*	21.0%	0.66	17	1.43
4. **U. Hospitals of Cleveland** (Rainbow babies and Children's Hospital)	10.3%	1.26	18	1.73
5. **Children's Hospital of Los Angeles**	9.8%	0.62	12	1.45
6. **Children's Hospital of Pittsburgh***	8.1%	1.96	4	2.06
7. **Children's National Medical Center,** Washington, D.C.*	7.6%	1.02	8	1.82
8. **Children's Hospital Medical Center,** Cincinnati*	6.9%	2.10	8	2.18
9. **Children's Hospital,** Denver	6.6%	1.38	8	1.74
10. **Children's Memorial Hospital,** Chicago*	6.3%	0.95	9	1.99
11. **Stanford U. Medical Center,** Stanford, Calif.*	5.7%	1.81	14	0.86
12. **Columbia-Presbyterian Medical Center,** New York*	4.5%	0.81	16	1.05
13. **Children's Hospital and Medical Center,** Seattle*	4.1%	2.19	6	2.23
14. **Miami Children's Hospital**	3.7%	1.02	7	1.68
15. **Texas Children's Hospital,** Houston*	3.6%	1.06	9	1.97
16. **U. of California San Francisco Medical Center***	3.5%	1.55	17	1.82
17. **St. Jude Children's Research Hospital,** Memphis	3.5%	1.06	8	3.63
18. **St. Louis Children's Hospital***	3.3%	1.77	10	1.70
19. **UCLA Medical Center,** Los Angeles*	3.1%	0.82	17	1.20

EXPERT LIST

PSYCHIATRY: Despite the increasing number of drugs for treating mental illness—Prozac for depression, for example—psychotherapy still goes hand in hand with psychopharmacology. A good hospital employs drugs and talk therapy—as well as follow-up care after a patient is discharged.

Rank Hospital	Reputational score	Board-cert. M.D.s to beds	R.N.s to beds	R.N.s to L.P.N.s	Discharge planning	Tech. score
1. **Mclean Hospital,** Belmont, Mass.	14.2%	0.48	0.66	5.0	2	3
2. **Menninger Clinic,** Topeka, Kan.	14.0%	0.19	0.48	NA	2	0
3. **Johns Hopkins Hospital,** Baltimore*	9.1%	0.66	1.43	42.9	2	17
4. **New York Hospital-Cornell Medical Center,** New York*	9.0%	0.99	1.00	30.5	2	16
5. **UCLA Medical Center,** Los Angeles	6.3%	0.51	0.52	4.7	2	0
6. **Sheppard and Enoch Pratt Hospital,** Baltimore	8.0%	0.08	0.28	NA	2	0
7. **Massachusetts General Hospital,** Boston*	7.7%	0.66	1.14	27.9	2	19
8. **Institute of Living,** Hartford, Conn.	6.1%	0.16	0.45	NA	2	0
9. **Columbia-Presbyterian Medical Center,** New York*	5.0%	0.81	1.05	23.5	2	16
10. **Mayo Clinic,** Rochester, Minn.*	4.0%	0.93	0.86	5.3	2	13
11. **Yale-New Haven Hospital,** New Haven, Conn.*	3.7%	1.67	1.23	18.8	2	14
12. **Duke U. Medical Center,** Durham, N.C.*	3.3%	0.66	1.60	6.2	2	19
13. **Chestnut Lodge Hospital,** Rockville, Md.	3.2%	0.05	0.34	3.8	0	0
14. **Timberlawn Mental Health System,** Dallas	3.0%	0.11	0.23	NA	1	0

REHABILITATION: Rehabilitation units specialize in helping patients return to lives as normal as possible following strokes, head and spinal injuries, falls, and sports injuries. The team of specialists includes physical, speech, and occupational therapists; psychologists; social workers; doctors and nurses.

Rank Hospital	Reputational score	Board-cert. M.D.s to beds	R.N.s to beds	Discharge planning	Geriatric services	Tech. score
1. **Rehabilitation Institute of Chicago**	34.7%	0.14	0.52	1	1	1
2. **U. of Washington Medical Center,** Seattle	24.9%	1.90	2.06	2	4	15
3. **Craig Hospital,** Englewood, Colo.	17.0%	0.11	0.41	2	0	1
4. **Institute for Rehabilitation and Research,** Houston	15.2%	0.34	0.35	1	0	1
5. **Rusk Inst. for Rehabilitation Medicine,** New York U. Medical Center	14.5%	1.25	1.15	2	0	13
6. **Mayo Clinic,** Rochester, Minn.	12.8%	0.93	0.86	2	5	13
7. **L.A. County-Rancho Los Amigos Medical Center,** Calif.	10.4%	0.15	1.01	2	5	5
8. **Ohio State U. Medical Center,** Columbus	8.1%	0.68	1.11	2	5	11
9. **Thomas Jefferson U. Hospital,** Philadelphia	7.3%	1.12	1.44	2	3	16
10. **Baylor U. Medical Center,** Dallas	7.0%	0.40	1.38	2	3	14
11. **Kessler Institute for Rehabilitation,** West Orange, N.J.	6.4%	0.11	0.50	2	0	0
12. **U. of Michigan Medical Center,** Ann Arbor	5.8%	0.66	1.29	2	8	17
13. **Moss Rehabilitation Hospital,** Philadelphia	5.0%	0.33	0.28	2	0	2

TERMS:
REPUTATIONAL SCORE: Percentage of doctors surveyed who named the hospital.
BOARD CERTIFIED M.D.S TO BEDS: Ratio of doctors certified in a specialty to the number of beds.
R.N.S TO BEDS: Ratio of registered nurses to beds.
TECHNOLOGY SCORE: Specialty-specific index from 0 to 5 (orthopedics); 0 to 9 (cardiology, gynecology, and neurology); 0 to 11 (endocrinology and urology); 0 to 19 (ophthalmology, pediatrics, psychiatry, and rehabiliation).
INPATIENT OPERATIONS TO BEDS: Ratio of annual inpatient operations to beds.
DISCHARGE PLANNING: Number of post-discharge services available, from 0 to 2.
GERIATRIC SERVICES: Number of geriatric services available, from 0 to 9.
* Indicates member of Council of Teaching Hospitals.
SOURCE: Reprinted from *U.S. News & World Report*, July 18, 1994. © 1994.

PATIENT'S GUIDE

THE DOCTOR'S BILL TODAY WILL BE...

Each year, the publication Medical Economics *compiles data on medical charges by physicians in private, office-based practices across the country. The figures below represent median fees for a variety of medical procedures in 1994. The survey sample was designed to be representative by type of practice, age, geographic region, and gender. Overall, the survey found that fees for medical services and procedures increased less than 5 percent over the previous year.*

PEDIATRICIANS

History, examination of normal newborn	$110
Immunization, DPT	$25
MMR virus vaccine	$40
Circumcision, clamp procedure, newborn	$103

OBG SPECIALISTS

Circumcision, clamp procedure, newborn	$129
Total hysterectomy, abdominal	$2,342
Complete OB care, routine delivery	$2,000
Routine delivery by family physicians	$1,544
Complete OB care, cesarean section	$2,499
Dilation and curettage (for abortion)	$670
Dilation and curettage (diagnostic)	$600
Leparascopy with fulguration of oviducts	$1,180

GENERAL SURGEONS

Total hysterectomy, abdominal	$1,800
Appendectomy	$1,000
Laparoscopy, surgical; appendectomy	$1,250
Cholesystectomy	$1,616
Laparoscopy, surgical; cholecystectomy	$2,049
Inguinal hernia repair, age five and over	$996

OFFICE VISIT FEES FOR A NEW PATIENT

Consider the AMA's evaluation of a new patient in which the physician must: 1. compile a comprehensive history; 2. undertake a comprehensive exam; 3. perform medical decision making of moderate complexity. In a case whose description is adapted here from the journal *Medical Economics*, the problems are of moderate to high severity, typically requiring 45 minutes of physician time. Examples might include a patient in his mid-60s experiencing chest pains possibly related to cardiologic difficulty, or a woman in her mid-30s with an infertility problem.

	East	South	Midwest	West	Urban	Suburban	Rural
Cardiologists	$125	$118	$115	$125	$125	$122	$100
Family physicians	$80	$84	$78	$110	$85	$90	$80
Gastroenterologists	$125	$113	$100	$149	$122	$125	$110
General practitioners	$75	$75	$75	$87	$80	$80	$69
General surgeons	$100	$90	$88	$110	$100	$100	$88
Internists	$100	$100	$95	$125	$105	$100	$100
OBG specialists	$95	$95	$90	$125	$105	$100	$100
Orthopedic surgeons	$122	$110	$100	$139	$120	$123	$100
Pediatricians	$68	$75	$75	$92	$75	$75	$80
All surgical specialists	$100	$95	$90	$125	$100	$100	$90
All non-surgeons*	$90	$90	$85	$114	$100	$95	$81
All doctors	$95	$90	$88	$117	$100	$98	$85

*Includes family physicians and general practitioners. SOURCE: *Medical Economics*, continuing survey, 1994.

■ PATIENT'S GUIDE

Gastrectomy with gastroduodenostomy (partial stomach removal for ulcers)	$2,367
Modified radical mastectomy	$1,915
Excision of cyst fibroadenoma from breast tissue, one or more lesions	$535

ORTHOPEDIC SURGEONS

Colles fracture, closed manipulation (wrist injury common in those over 40)	$576
Open treatment of hip fracture	$2,435
Knee arthroscopy with meniscectomy (Removal of cartilage in knee)	$1,974
Total hip arthroplasty	$4,170
Diagnostic knee arthroscopy (Fiber-optic examination of knee interior)	$912
Total knee arthroplasty	$4,117

CARDIO SURGEONS*

Replacement of aortic valve with cardiopulmonary bypass	$5,000
Insertion of permanent pacemaker with transvenous electrodes, ventricular	$1,550
Coronary artery bypass, with three coronary grafts	$5,486

CARDIOLOGISTS (1993)

Cardiac catheterization	$1,200
Echocardiography	$553

NEUROSURGEONS (1993)

Cranioplasty	$2,847
Carniotomy for evacuation of hematoma (Removal of part of skull to remove potentially fatal blood clot)	$3,615
Neuroplasty (median nerve)	$1,000
Discectomy, anterior and osteophytetomy, cervical, single interspace	$3,275

PSYCHIATRISTS (1993)

Individual psychotherapy, in office, 45–50 minutes	$115
Individual psychotherapy, in hospital, 45–50 minutes	$120
Family psychotherapy, conjoint	$125
Psychiatric diagnostic interview	$150

SOURCE: *Medical Economics*, continuing survey. 1993, 1994. Reprinted by permission.

■ OFFICE VISIT FEES FOR AN ESTABLISHED PATIENT

Doctors' fees tend to be higher in the East and West than in the Midwest and South. In one situation whose AMA description is adapted from the publication *Medical Economics*, the doctor seeing an established patient for an office or other outpatient visit must deal with at least two of three components: 1. an expanded problem-focused history; 2. an expanded problem-focused examination; 3. medical decision making of low complexity. Usually, the problems presented are of low to moderate severity (e.g., an office visit for a patient in his mid-50s, for managing hypertension).

	East	South	Midwest	West	Urban	Suburban	Rural
Cardiologists	$50	$50	$45	$50	$50	$45	$40
Family physicians	$41	$40	$40	$50	$42	$45	$37
General practitioner	$35	$35	$35	$40	$40	$40	$33
Gastroenterologists	$50	$46	$43	$49	$49	$50	$41
General surgeons	$50	$45	$44	$50	$50	$47	$40
Internists	$49	$45	$41	$50	$45	$45	$44
OBG specialists	$60	$50	$45	$59	$53	$53	$45
Orthopedic surgeons	$60	$50	$47	$55	$50	$53	$45
Pediatricians	$45	$40	$39	$45	$43	$43	$38
All surgical specialists	$53	$48	$45	$53	$50	$50	$42
All non-surgeons*	$45	$41	$40	$50	$45	$45	$39
All doctors	$50	$45	$40	$50	$48	$46	$40

*Includes family physicians and general practitioners. SOURCE: *Medical Economics*, continuing survey, 1994.

EXPERT Q&A

BREAST CANCER'S FACTS OF LIFE

Mammography remains a key to defending against the disease

Breast cancer is the most common form of cancer among American women. According to the American Cancer Society, 180,000 American women develop breast cancer each year, and 46,000 die of the disease annually. Although more women now die of lung cancer, one in every nine women in the United States will develop breast cancer over her lifetime. Dr. Mark Brenner, director of the Radiation Oncology Center at Sinai Hospital in Baltimore, Md., explains the risks, the precautions that should be followed, and the treatment options that are available.

■What are the symptoms of breast cancer?

There are rarely symptoms of early breast cancer. The most common sign is a painless lump or thickening that does not go away or change with the menstrual cycle. The upper outer quadrant of the breast is the most common area to find a cancer. Some 80 percent or more of cancers begin in the milk ducts. Cancer that starts in the glands that produce milk is less common.

All lumps should be checked by a doctor. Other signs are swelling, puckering or dimpling in the skin, skin irritation, pain or tenderness in the nipple and discharge from the nipple, and lymph nodes under the armpits that are hard. Any pain or tenderness that persists throughout the menstrual cycle should be reported to a physician.

■Who is at risk of developing breast cancer?

Every woman is at risk for breast cancer. About 75 percent of all breast cancers diagnosed each year are among women without any known risk factors.

■But aren't there certain factors that predispose a woman to breast cancer?

Yes. Risk factors to breast cancer include being older than 50; having a personal family history of breast cancer, especially on the maternal side; never giving birth; giving birth to the first child after age 30; being on birth control pills for 15 or 20 years; getting your first period at an early age; and having late menopause. There is also some data that if you've had endometrial cancer or ovarian cancer, you're at a greater risk of getting breast cancer.

In spite of all this, unless you have a very strong family history of the disease—for example, your sisters, mother, aunt, and grandmother all have it—these factors just slighly increase your risk. If you have one of these risk factors, it doesn't mean you're doomed, it just means you have to be more careful.

■If a woman has one or more of these risk factors, what can she do to protect herself?

Be very fastidious about self-exams, have mammograms when recommended, and see the doctor regularly. Women with one or more of the risk factors should be especially alert to the warning signs of breast cancer and make sure to perform breast self-examination monthly. These women should also have breast exams by a health professional more often and start having exams at an earlier age.

■What should women with no risk factors do?

They should ask their doctor, nurse, or mammography technician to teach them the proper method of performing a monthly breast exam. Women over age 20 should examine their breasts once a month. The best time for a menstruating woman to do a breast self-exam is right after her period when the breast swelling and tenderness is over. Women who are past menopause should perform breast exams at the same time of the month, every month, so that it's not forgotten.

Although the recommendations about when regular mammograms should start are somewhat controversial and may change, at present the American Cancer Society, the American College of Radiology and the American College of Surgeons recommend that a woman get a baseline mammogram beginning at age 35 to 40. This mammogram will be compared to future mammograms.

Between the ages of 40 and 50 a woman should get a mammogram every two years. After age 50 a woman should get a mammogram every year. See your doctor for regular breast exams at least every three years between the ages of 20 and 40 and every year over 40.

■ What good are mammograms?

A mammogram is an X-ray picture of the breast. Mammography can find masses before they can be felt. In some cases, mammograms can find masses several years before they can be felt. There are two major studies that show that early detection significantly increases the chances of beating cancer.

■ Are mammograms safe?

Modern mammography equipment will only expose women to a minimal amount of radiation. A trained radiologic technologist positions your breast between two plastic plates that compress it, spreading the breast out so that the X-ray can produce as precise an image as possible. If a mammography facility is accredited by the American College of Radiology, the mammography machines and the facility staff have met special quality standards and tests. To find out where to get a quality mammogram, call your local American Cancer Society office.

■ How much does a mammogram cost?

A screening mammogram costs about $100 to $150 and is usually covered by insurance.

■ What if the doctor finds breast cancer?

There will be a number of diagnostic studies done on the tumor to find out how advanced it is, to find out what treatments are appropriate, and to make recommendations. The tumor itself is removed from the breast, and usually lymph nodes are taken from the armpit area. The physician needs to know the size of the tumor and whether it has spread to any of the lymph nodes. DNA analysis is done on the tumor to get a feeling for how aggressive the tumor seems to be, and "receptor status" is analyzed to see if the tumor would respond to hormonal therapy.

■ What are the treatment options?

There are two main lines of decision. One

■ PERFORMING A BREAST SELF-EXAMINATION

1. Once a month, after your period, examine your breasts. Get to know their shape and texture, and be alert to changes. Raise each arm above your head and turn from side to side, looking for changes in appearance.

2. Squeeze the nipple to check for discharge. Check surface for peculiarities. Orange-peel texture could indicate a lump.

3. Lie on your back with your arm by your side. Using the flat of your hand, work around the outer parts of the breast in a clockwise direction.

4. Raise arm over head. Check inner parts of the breast, along collarbone and into armpit. Stretching the skin makes detection easier.

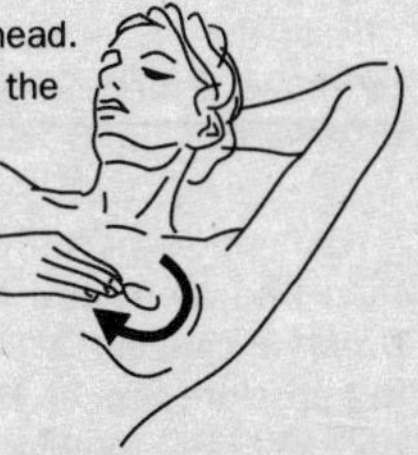

SOURCE: *American Medical Association Encyclopedia of Medicine*, Random House, 1989.

is to ask whether this patient is at risk for the tumor to spread outside the breast to the rest of the body, and whether systemic therapy is therefore appropriate. This can be done through chemotherapy and/or hormonal therapy. Chemotherapy is used more often with premenopausal women, and hormonal therapy is more often used with postmenopausal women.

The second approach is to treat the breast locally. If the doctor simply removes the cancerous lump from the breast and does nothing else locally, there is at least a 40 percent chance that the tumor will regrow within the breast. The two treatment options are either mastectomy, which is removing the entire breast, or treating the remaining breast with radiation. In seven randomized studies worldwide, both mastectomy and lumpectomy with radiation have equal results. The decision whether to undergo a mastectomy or preserve the breast should be made jointly with a surgeon and a radiation oncologist.

■ **What are the chances of beating the disease through treatment?**

According to the American Cancer Society, the 5-year survival rate is 92 percent if the cancer has not spread to the lymph nodes. After 10 years the survival rate for someone who had breast cancer that didn't spread to the lymph nodes is more like 80 percent. If the cancer has spread to the lymph nodes, the chance of survival in 5 years is 70 percent. After 10 years it's 50 to 60 percent. Early detection leaves you with the most options and the best chance of survival.

IF YOU'RE A MAN OVER 40, LISTEN UP

Detecting prostate cancer is becoming easier, thanks to the PSA test

Nearly a quarter-million men develop prostate cancer each year, making it one of the most common cancers in men. The disease claims 40,000 lives annually because of difficulties in detecting the illness early. But that could change thanks to a blood test, known as the PSA test. It measures the amount of a protein in the blood called prostatic specific antigen, which is produced exclusively by the prostate.

The PSA test has been available for about eight years, but it is only now being widely recommended. Dr. William Catalona, Chief of Urology at Washington University School of Medicine and one of the PSA test's developers, highlights what men need to know about the disease and the test:

■ All men—especially African American men and men with a family history of prostate cancer—are at risk of developing prostate cancer. Having a vasectomy does not raise the risk. It is uncertain why the disease develops, but a high-fat diet may be a contributing factor.

■ There are no symptoms in men who are in the early stages of the disease when it is curable. But there will be urinary difficulties and bone pain as the disease progresses.

■ All men aged 40 and above should have an annual digital rectal exam as a safeguard against prostate cancer. African American men and those with a family history should also have an annual PSA test beginning at age 40. After age 50 all men should have an annual digital rectal exam and PSA test.

■ The PSA test is available in most doctors' offices and in hospital labs. It costs about $50 and takes a few days to a week for results to be reported. It is better in detecting prostate cancer than a mammography is in detecting breast cancer.

TRANSFUSIONS

PLAYING IT SAFE AT BLOOD BANKS

The risk has some doctors advising patients to be their own donors

For those who need a blood transfusion during surgery, it can be very reassuring to bank and use your own blood or have a family member with a compatible blood type be your donor. In fact, some doctors now are recommending the procedure, known as an autologous blood transfusion, to their patients. Of the approximately four million blood transfusions that take place in the United States each year, the American Red Cross estimates that the percentage of people collecting blood for personal use has grown from 2 to 5 percent recently, and the organization expects the upward trend to continue.

Although most of the 2,400 blood banks around the country are safer than they have ever been, worrisome problems remain. Improved tests have reduced the risk of contracting the AIDS virus from blood transfusions from between 1 in 30,000 to 1 in 225,000. More disconcerting, however, is the risk of getting hepatitis C, which can cause chronic liver disease. According to data gathered by the Food and Drug Administration, the risk of getting contaminated by hepatitis C is about 1 in 3,300 for one unit of blood. (The average-sized transfusion typically requires four units).

With over 12 million units of blood donated in the United States annually, clerical errors in tracking blood samples are not uncommon. According to a recent investigation by *U.S. News & World Report*, the FDA compiled evidence of about 1,000 errors and accidents at blood banks in 1989. The number increased tenfold in 1992 and has remained at similar magnitudes ever since.

To donate your own blood, you must make arrangements with a blood bank at least a week before surgery. First your doctor writes you a "prescription" to donate your own blood, which you then take to the blood bank. Because your blood has to go through a separate tracking system to make sure it gets to the surgery site on time, the cost is somewhat higher—$65 to $180 to donate your own blood, compared to $75 or so to use blood from a blood bank.

"Doctors prescribe using your own blood more and more," says Liz Hall, a spokesperson for the American Red Cross. "Hospitals agree, it's the safest transfusion."

Not everyone applauds this trend, however. A recent study in the *New England Journal of Medicine* argued that the added expense of an autologous transfusion often is not justified by the small risk of transfusion-associated infection. The study also found that in the majority of cases more blood is collected than used and that the excess blood is usually discarded.

As an editorial in the same issue pointed out, however, cost should not be the only factor in determining a procedure's worth—peace of mind is an unquantifiable, but important, consideration in any medical undertaking.

■ BLOOD YOU CAN USE

In your first months of life, your red blood cells build antibodies that determine what other red blood cells they will associate with. Group-O people (universal donors) can donate red cells to anyone but can receive only from other Os. Group-AB people (universal recipients) can receive red cells from anyone but can donate only to other ABs.

RECIPIENT	DONOR GROUP			
GROUP	A	B	AB	O
A	yes	no	no	yes
B	no	yes	no	yes
AB	yes	yes	yes	yes
O	no	no	no	yes

SOURCE: *American Medical Association Encyclopedia of Medicine*, Random House, 1989.

EXPERIMENTS

A PRIMER ON CLINICAL TRIALS

How to join one, and how to keep their purpose in perspective

Participating in a medical experiment isn't for everyone. Hopefully, you'll never need to join one. But if you or a family member is sick with a life-threatening disease, a clinical trial program may be well worth considering. As experimental programs, the approaches being tested may not work and may even cause further medical problems. But agreeing to be a guinea pig for the latest medical techniques or medications could also add many good years to your life.

Clinical trial research is generally federally funded and federally regulated, but conducted by private researchers at medical schools, drug companies, and hospitals, as well as by government scientists.

Research runs the disease gamut. To fight cancer, for instance, a new form of treatment called biological therapy is being studied in clinical trials sponsored by the National Institutes of Health. This technique uses substances produced by the body's own cells and substances that affect the body's immune system to induce the body to fight the disease. In the AIDS area, one closely watched trial currently under way involves testing two experimental drugs to see if they can prevent the HIV virus from reproducing itself by interfering with the enzymes that reproduce the virus.

Other trials deal with chronic diseases that are not necessarily life-threatening. The NIH is currently conducting a clinical trial on herpes vaccines to determine if a person who is already infected with herpes can stave off further outbreaks by taking the vaccine. The vaccine is also being studied to see, if by taking it, a person who has been exposed to the virus can still be immunized.

Since the purpose of such trials is to answer a set of research questions, you have to fit the guidelines in order to be eligible. Be sure to discuss the suitability of a clinical trial with your personal physician, comparing the case for joining a trial with the arguments for following a more standard treatment. If you do decide to pursue an experimental program, be sure to ask:

- **What is the study's scientific purpose?**
- **What does the treatment involve?**
- **Who will oversee your treatment?**
- **What, if anything, will it cost you?**
- **Does participation require relocation?**
- **What type of follow-up care is involved?**
- **How will the study's results be used?**

Participating in a trial means that you will probably be examined and tested more frequently than usual. If, during the study, it turns out that the trial is not in your best interest, you will be asked to drop out. If you decide not to continue, that, too, is fine.

The cost of trials varies from program to program. Virtually all NIH-sponsored experiments are free of charge to participants. Other clinical trials generally provide drugs for free, but in some cases patients may be charged for lab tests or doctor's visits. Health insurance usually covers such expenses. In some cases, especially those involving an invasive procedure such as a spinal tap, patients may even receive minimal fees.

EXPERT SOURCE

The National Institutes of Health patient referral line can provide information about recent clinical trials, ☎ 301-496-4891.

THE OUTLOOK FOR PRESCRIPTIONS

Mail-order suppliers are one of the few ways to fight rising costs

Political power, declared Chairman Mao, comes from the barrel of a gun. Political clout has even been known to keep prescription drug prices down temporarily. But as the Clinton administration discovered when it recently tried to jawbone down drug prices, moral suasion only works so long as people fear your political might.

According to the Bureau of Labor Statistics, inflation rose 134 percent between 1975 and 1990. In that same period, drug prices increased 255 percent. In 1991 alone, prices jumped 9.4 percent, which was over three times that year's inflation rate. That upward spiral slowed to only 3.3 percent in 1993, however, as First Lady Hillary Rodham Clinton led an all-out drive to overhaul the health care system and to curtail costs.

"Politics was a factor in early 1993," says David Kanudsen, an economist who tracks drug prices for the Bureau of Labor Statistics. Feeling the heat of the Clinton initiative, "pharmaceutical companies made a pledge to restrain prices to overall inflation," Kanudsen says. As a result, wholesale drug prices rose just 1.9 percent in 1993, which was the lowest increase in 20 years, according to a Pharmaceutical Manufacturers Association spokesman. Yet a year later, when the Clinton administration had to abandon its health care reform plan in the face of overwhelming political opposition, medical prices jumped 0.6 percent in a single month. On an annualized basis, that was the equivalent of a 7.5 percent inflation rate.

Though drug price rises have moderated some since then, most experts believe the increases will continue to outstrip inflation. "It's expensive to do research on new drugs—someone has to pay. There's no free

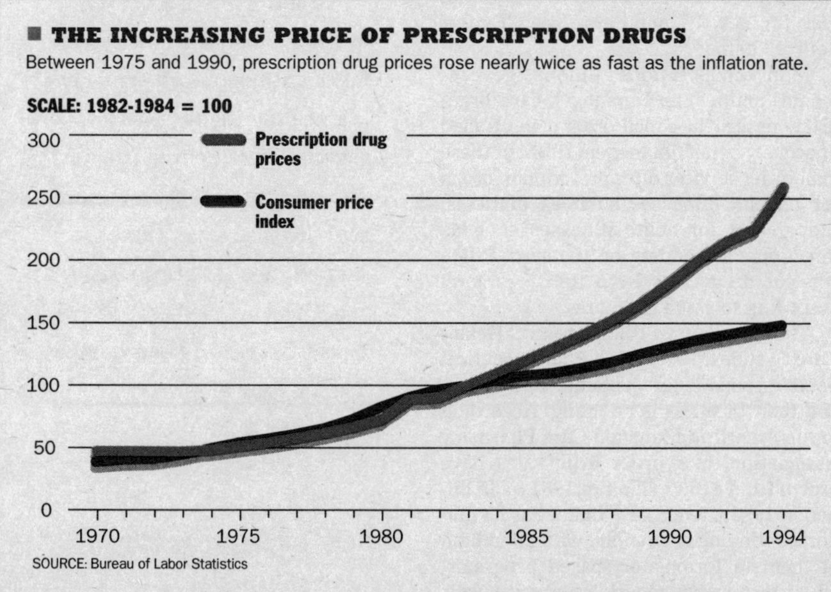

lunch," says Warren Greenberg, a professor of health economics at George Washington University.

Managed-care companies have had some effect on moderating price increases because of the bargaining strength these providers have with the drug makers who supply them. But even managed-care plans are having difficulty keeping drug prices affordable. According to the trade publication, *Drug Topics*, the cost of ingredients in the average drug prescription for HMO participants went from $19.20 in 1992 to $20.39 in 1993, an increase of 6.2 percent. Total annual prescription drug costs for HMO members reached $109.43 in 1993, an increase of 17 percent in just one year.

One restraining force on price hikes today are mail-order drug distributors. Beginning after World War II, the federal government began a program that allowed veterans to buy prescription drugs through the mail. Now the largest distributor of mail-order drugs, the Department of Veterans Affairs fills 40 million prescriptions a year. After the DVA launched its mail-order service, the American Association of Retired Persons followed suit. Today AARP fills some 10 million prescriptions annually. Anyone can use the service, it's not just for AARP members (see "Expert Source" below).

Many corporations, unions, governmental entities, and managed-care organizations also have mail-order plans. Called pharmacy benefit managers (PBMs), these mail-order services offer prescription drugs for chronic illnesses such as diabetes, though not for acute illnesses such as infections. Depending on the case, PBMs can cut drug costs by a third or more, according to some estimates.

The three largest PBMs are PCS Health Care Systems, Diversified Pharmaceutical Services, and Medco Containment Services, and their business is booming. According to the American Managed Care Pharmacy Association, mail-order drug sales have grown from $100 million in 1981 to $5 billion in 1993. Medco says that it has 38 million continuing customers, with 29 million of them in formulatory-based programs, which means that generic brands are used. Their customers' needs are handled through National Rx, a mail-order pharmacy network with 11 centers, and Medco's retail pharmacy chain, which includes over 48,000 pharmacies nationwide.

Some PMBs have disease management programs, which help cut costs further by educating patients on the most effective treatments for their conditions. Medco has a database, for instance, that identifies high-risk or high-cost patients.

Someone with asthma would be considered a high-risk patient, for instance, because asthma sufferers often fail to use their inhalers properly, leading to needless medical problems and needless expense. In a disease management program, a pharmacist would provide asthma patients with instruction in the way to use inhalers to forestall asthma attacks.

If that doesn't help, the pharmacist can also consult with the patient's doctor on whether a different prescription might be in order. The result: The patient receives better treatment and it costs less to boot.

EXPERT SOURCE

To get a mail-order precription filled, customers nationwide can call or write the American Association of Retired People. If you are writing, include the prescription along with your name, address, Social Security number, phone number, and date of birth. Expect the prescription to take 7 to 10 days to fill.

Virginia AARP
Pharmacy Service
PO Box 13671
Richmond, VA 23225
☎ 800-456-2277

ASPIRIN

THE POWER OF A PILL

Scientists keep discovering new benefits of this common painkiller

"Take two aspirin and call me in the morning" has long been doctors' advice for headaches and minor pains. But a profusion of recent research shows that the painkiller that's been used for more than 80 years may be good for more than headaches. The new findings suggest that aspirin may also help prevent heart attacks, certain types of cancers, and pregnancy-induced hypertension.

In its regular form, aspirin is an analgesic—a painkilling drug—available without a prescription to treat headaches, menstrual cramps, and muscle aches. It works by reducing the production of certain hormone-like chemicals, called prostaglandins, that can be responsible for inflammation, pain, fever, or clumping of blood platelets. Because of its anti-inflammatory effects, aspirin is also effective in treating joint pain and muscle stiffness caused by certain types of arthritis. The non-narcotic drug can be used as well to reduce fever, so it is often an ingredient in cold medicines.

Of all of aspirin's prophylactic powers, its role in combating heart attacks has received the most attention. By preventing platelets in the blood from sticking together, aspirin has been shown to decrease the chance of having a heart attack. And, by preventing clots from forming in the bloodstream, it can reduce the severity of a heart attack once it's under way. Indeed, in a recent Harvard University study, healthy middle-aged male doctors who took an aspirin every other day on a continuing basis were 44 percent less likely to have a first heart attack than doctors who took a sugar pill as a placebo. But the aspirin takers showed no decline in overall cardiovascular deaths and only a slight increase in the risk of hemorrhagic strokes. The benefits of low-dose aspirin for women's cardiovascular health are not yet known.

When taken within hours after a heart attack, aspirin can be a life-saving treatment. Heart attack sufferers who took aspirin within 24 hours after the attack began decreased their chance of dying in the following weeks by nearly 25 percent, a recent study found. Based on these findings, a group of doctors recently petitioned the Food and Drug Administration to approve aspirin as standard treatment for patients suffering from the acute stages of a heart attack. The FDA's Office of Drug Evaluation has recommended approval, but a final decision is pending.

When aspirin is taken in small doses on a daily basis, it has also been shown to reduce a pregnant woman's risk of suffering from high blood pressure and of delivering a premature baby of low birth weight. However, there is no evidence that aspirin can reduce high blood pressure among people who aren't pregnant. For reasons not yet understood, it is only when a woman is pregnant that the drug appears to help keep blood pressure down. All these findings are still preliminary, however, and no pregnant woman should take aspirin without consulting her doctor first.

Migraine sufferers not only use aspirin to relieve headaches, but according to a large-scale study of middle-aged men who took aspirin every other day, aspirin can also reduce the frequency of migraines. That study found the men who took the aspirin reduced by 20 percent their chances of getting a migraine episode. When blood platelets clump together in the brain, they may release serotonin, a neurochemical linked to triggering migraines. Aspirin may stop the clumping, and, in turn, diminish the frequency of migraines.

Researchers have also found that those who take an aspirin tablet daily are less likely to contract colon, rectum and possibly stomach cancer. Some tumors produce prostaglandins, which scientists believe are required for a cancer to grow. Aspirin works by stopping the production of prostaglandins, preventing tumors from growing.

WHAT TO TAKE WHEN ASPIRIN IS OFF-LIMITS

Why acetaminophen, ibuprofen, and Aleve may be the painkillers for you

■ **ACETAMINOPHIN:** Tylenol is the most common brand name for this organic compound. The drug reduces pain and fever without the stomach irritation, bleeding, indigestion, and nausea that can occur with aspirin. It is also a more effective fever-fighter than aspirin for children. Since it doesn't slow blood clotting, acetaminophen is also the best nonprescription painkiller for patients before and after surgery, women who are pregnant, and people who have an allergy to aspirin. Acetaminophen does not, however, reduce inflammation or possess any of the powers of aspirin to fight heart attacks and strokes. Keep in mind also that it is dangerous to mix acetaminophen with alcohol and that high doses can cause liver damage.

■ **ALEVE:** Also called naproxen sodium, Aleve is an anti-inflammatory effective in reducing pain and fever. Gentler on the stomach than aspirin, it is becoming popular as a treatment for menstrual cramps. Because Aleve provides relief for 8 to 12 hours, longer than most over-the-counter painkillers, it may be a good choice for arthritis sufferers. Precautions are the same as for aspirin and ibuprofen.

■ **IBUPROFEN:** Found in over-the-counter medicines such as Advil and Motrin, it is stronger than aspirin and acetaminophen, yet easier on the stomach than aspirin. It relieves pain, fever, and inflammation, and is often taken to relieve the discomfort of menstrual cramps. It lacks aspirin's bloodclot-fighting cardiovascular benefits, however, and should be avoided by people susceptible to asthma, high blood pressure, heart or kidney disease, and cirrhosis, as well as those taking lithium or diuretics. If you have a cold, take ibuprofen with a decongestant instead of an over-the-counter cold medicine, which generally contains fewer pain relief ingredients and costs more.

■ **BUFFERED PILLS:** Many pain relievers come in buffered form. The coating makes pills easier to swallow and easier on the stomach than tablets, but it slows down the absorption of the painkiller, so relief takes longer. Time-released capsules or Aleve are the best suited for low-level continuing pain, such as muscle soreness. Never take more than one type of pain reliever at a time unless instructed by your doctor.

Where tumors do exist, aspirin may cause them to bleed, leading to earlier diagnoses.

For those who suffer from certain types of senility, such as senile dementia, doctors sometimes prescribe daily doses of aspirin because it helps prevent blockage of blood vessels in the brain. When aspirin is given to those suffering from dementia, it appears to reduce the chances of having ministrokes, which in turn can cause dementia. This research is very preliminary, however.

Always consult a doctor before taking aspirin as a preventive measure; aspirin's benefits may be many, but there are side effects to take into account. Hearing impairment, stomach problems, excessive bleeding, and complications of pregnancy may occur in those who take aspirin too heavily. Aspirin may also increase the risk of stroke caused by bleeding in the brain.

When a sick child is involved, never give aspirin except under close medical supervision, because there is a slight risk of contracting Reye's Syndrome, a rare brain and liver disorder. Instead, children should be given aspirin alternatives such as Tylenol.

ALLERGIES

NEW WEAPONS AGAINST SNEEZES

Good news for those who sniffle through the pollen season

Spring is when young hearts turn to love, goes the adage, but for as many as 1 in 10 Americans, spring marks the start of the dreaded hay fever season. The airborne pollens that wreak all the havoc are less than the width of an average human hair, yet allergy patients spend some $663 million annually on doctors' fees, allergy shots, and prescription medicines to battle them.

No area is completely pollen-free, though dry areas and those at high altitudes or near a large body of water may provide some relief. Consult an allergist if you are considering a permanent change in residence, however. A doctor may instead be able to prescribe a series of injections that can greatly reduce your sensitivity to pollens without requiring a move to the desert.

Several new drugs may also help bring relief. Such relief is typically found in two ways—antihistamines, which prevent the symptoms from occurring, and decongestants, which work after the symptoms have begun. The negative side effect, particularly with antihistamines, has been drowsiness.

Here's what the American Academy of Allergy and Immunology says about some of the newer drug and treatment options:

■ **CROMOLYN SODIUM (INTAL):** This asthma medication has recently become available as a nasal spray (Nasalcrom) or an eye drop (Opticrom, Vistacrom) and could help nearly a third of the nation's hay fever victims. It is used to prevent the severe symptoms of allergies and often reduces or eliminates the use of antihistamines, decongestants, or steroids.

■ **TERFENADINE:** Usually found under the brand name Seldane or Seldane caplets, this new antihistamine is equal in effectiveness to many other antihistamines but is unique in that it does not cause drowsiness. The medication is designed to stop the hay fever symptoms from occurring by preventing the release of histamine in the body. Histamine is what makes your eyes tear and itch and your nose run and causes swelling of nasal passages and sneezing.

■ **ASTEMIZOLE:** Usually found under the brand name Hismanal, astemizole is a new, nonsedating prescription antihistamine. Its once-daily dosing schedule is enough to help relieve allergic rhinitis, or hay fever, symptoms.

■ **BECLOMETHASONE AND FLUNISOLIDE:** Neither are new, but both of these these cortisone-based drugs are being more widely prescribed now because of their success in fighting inflammation better than many other medications. Beclomethasone can be found under the brand names Vancenase, Beclovent, and Vanceril; flunisolide under the names Nasalide and AeroBid.

FACT FILE:

AVOIDANCE: ANOTHER SOURCE OF RELIEF

■ *For ragweed sufferers, the most hospitable areas include:*

- **Florida's extreme southern tip.**
- **Regions west of the Cascades in Oregon and Washington.**
- **The central Adirondacks.**
- **The wooded areas of Maine, New Hampshire, northern Minnesota, extreme northern Michigan, and California.**
- **The desert regions and forests of the Rocky Mountains.**
- **Hawai'i, Alaska, and the Caribbean.**

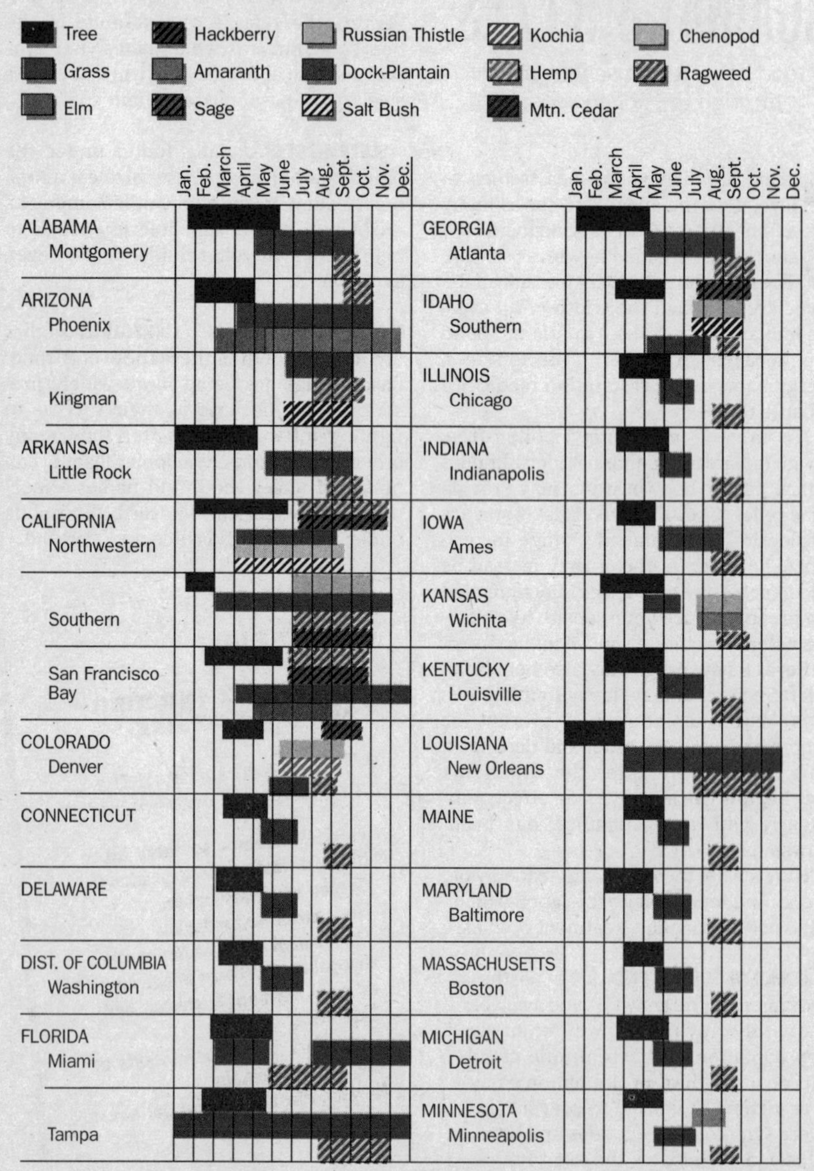
STEELING YOURSELF FOR THE SNEEZE SEASON
Depending on where you are, the pollen season runs from February or March until October. The farther north you live, the later the season's start. Trees pollinate first, then grasses and weeds.
Tree
Grass
Elm
Hackberry
Amaranth
Sage
Russian Thistle
Dock-Plantain
Salt Bush
Kochia
Hemp
Mtn. Cedar
Chenopod
Ragweed
Jan.
Feb.
March
April
May
June
July
Aug.
Sept.
Oct.
Nov.
Dec.
ALABAMA
Montgomery
ARIZONA
Phoenix
Kingman
ARKANSAS
Little Rock
CALIFORNIA
Northwestern
Southern
San Francisco Bay
COLORADO
Denver
CONNECTICUT
DELAWARE
DIST. OF COLUMBIA
Washington
FLORIDA
Miami
Tampa
GEORGIA
Atlanta
IDAHO
Southern
ILLINOIS
Chicago
INDIANA
Indianapolis
IOWA
Ames
KANSAS
Wichita
KENTUCKY
Louisville
LOUISIANA
New Orleans
MAINE
MARYLAND
Baltimore
MASSACHUSETTS
Boston
MICHIGAN
Detroit
MINNESOTA
Minneapolis

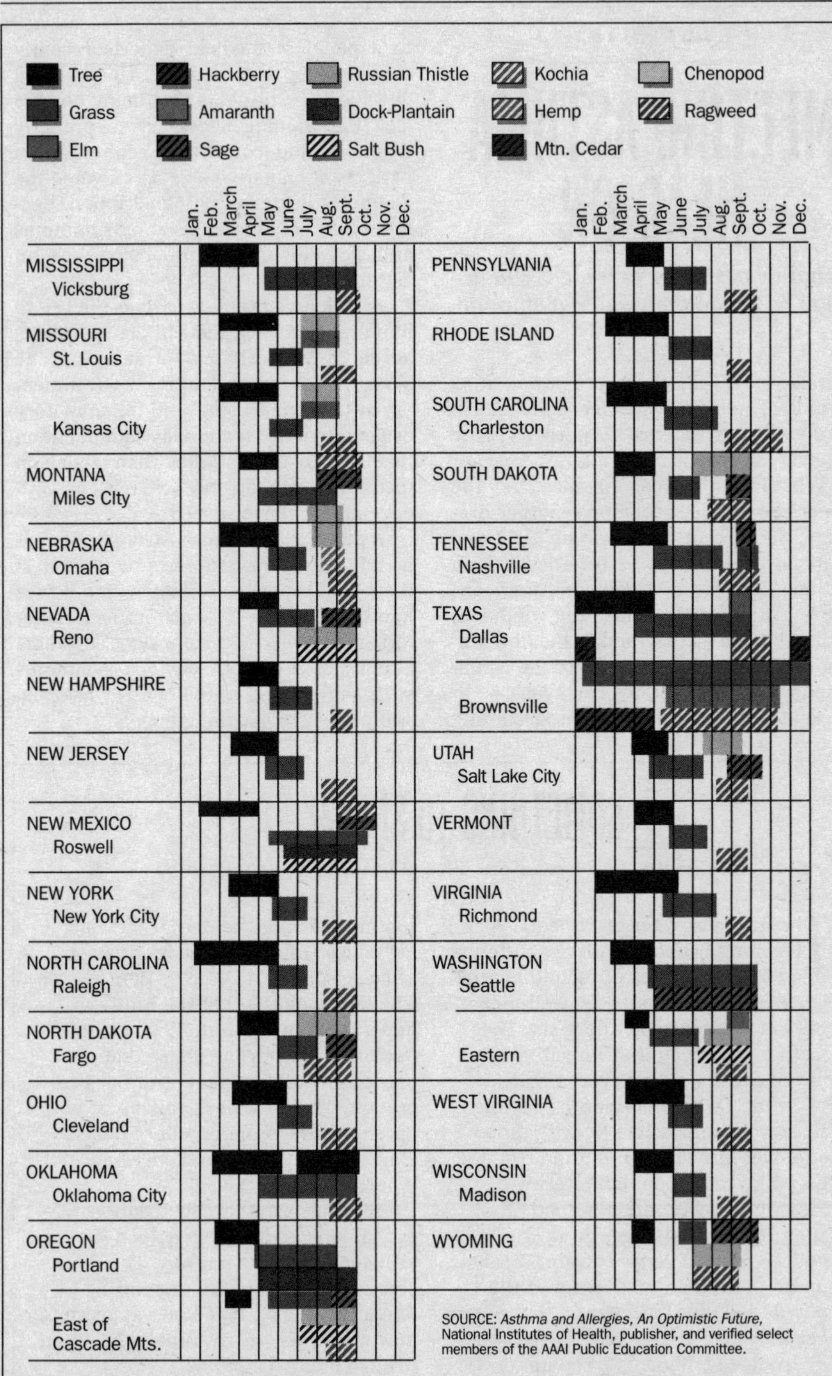

SOURCE: *Asthma and Allergies, An Optimistic Future,* National Institutes of Health, publisher, and verified select members of the AAAI Public Education Committee.

ALLERGIES

MEETING ASTHMA HEAD-ON

That wheezing or persistent cough may be a sign that you're asthmatic

It may be that there are more dust, pollen, mold, and chemical pollutants in the air to irritate us. Or perhaps we're evolving into a more allergic species. Whatever the reasons may be, the American Lung Association reports a dramatic 36 percent rise between 1982 and 1991 in the number of Americans with asthma. As many as 12 million Americans currently suffer from this lung condition, which blocks airflow and makes breathing difficult. Over 5,000 die of the condition in the United States each year.

One of the biggest problems, according to a panel of medical experts recently convened by the National Heart, Lung and Blood Institute, is that many doctors lack the training necessary to properly diagnose and control the condition in patients at an early stage. Even when the diagnosis is made, the panel found, doctors often err by only treating symptoms and not the underlying causes of an asthma attack.

Attacking a problem early is the key to limiting its impact, the asthma specialists agree. Severe asthma attacks can be sharply reduced by limiting environmental irritants and using anti-inflammatory drugs to control the airway inflammation that leads to attacks rather than relying on medication that can only help relax airways once attacks have started.

Asthma experts also strongly recommend that asthma sufferers regularly test their lung capacity at home with a device known as a peak flow meter. Such monitoring can help detect early signs of asthma attacks before more obvious symptoms such as tightness in the chest, wheezing, and persistent coughing appear.

SOMETHING TO SNEEZE AT

Phoenix is no longer the allergy haven it's reputed to be

The arid desert air of Phoenix, Ariz. has long beckoned allergy sufferers and other victims of fecund humidity, a call often echoed by well-meaning but misinformed allergists. The truth is, however, that Phoenix is no haven for the bleary-eyed masses.

In fact, with a 10-month growing season made possible by irrigation and ever-increasing pollution triggered by rapid population growth, Phoenix has become a hotbed of sneezing and sniffling. In most metropolitan areas, allergy sufferers make up no more than 15 percent of the population, but in Phoenix, that number may run as high as 25 percent.

Ironically, Phoenix's reputation for soothing air may be one of the leading causes of this anomaly. Arizona Lung Association Director Ben Chaiken suggests that the influx of hopeful allergy sufferers has created a pool of allergy-prone genes that are passed down from generation to generation. The odds back this up; if both parents suffer from an allergy, their child has a 50 to 75 percent chance of inheriting it.

As it turns out, a new location probably wouldn't have helped the afflicted breathers anyway. Though a change of environment may bring temporary relief, repeated exposure to new materials will eventually bring on the same old symptoms.

GASPER'S GUIDE

ASTHMA TROUBLEMAKERS TO KEEP IN CHECK

Among the most common triggers of asthma attacks, according to the American Lung Association, are allergies to foods and other household products. Here are some of the most likely culprits.

AIR POLLUTION

- Weather inversions.
- Traffic jams.
- Parking jams.
- Smoke-filled rooms.

ALLERGIES

- Foods such as nuts, chocolate, eggs, orange juice, fish, milk, or peanut butter.
- Pollens from flowers, trees, grasses, hay, or ragweed. Mold spores.
- Animals such as rabbits, cats, dogs, hamsters, gerbils, chickens, or birds.
- Feather pillows, down comforters.
- Insect parts, as from dead cockroaches.
- Sensitivity to sulfites, a food preservative, or to aspirin.

DUSTS

- Cloth-upholstered furniture, carpets, or draperies that gather dust.
- Brooms and dusters that raise dust.
- Dirty filters on hot air furnaces and air conditioners that put dust into the air.

EMOTIONAL STRESSES

- Fear.
- Anger.
- Frustration.
- Laughing too hard, crying, coughing.

EXERCISE

- Wheezing from overexertion, especially in cold weather.

HOUSEHOLD PRODUCTS

- Vapors from cleaning solvents, paint, paint thinner, liquid chlorine, or bleach.
- Sprays from furniture polish, starch, cleaners, or room deodorizers.
- Spray deodorants, perfumes, hair sprays, talcum powder, or scented cosmetics.

INFECTIONS

- Colds, other viruses.
- Bronchitis.
- Tonsillitis.
- Sore throat.

IRRITANTS AT WORK

- Dusts, vapors.
- Fumes from wood products (western red cedar, some pine and birch woods, and mahogany).
- Flour, cereals, grains, coffee, tea, papain.
- Metals (platinum, chromium, nickel sulfate, soldering fumes).
- Cotton, flax, hemp.
- Mold from decaying hay.

NIGHTTIME

- Lying down.
- Fatigue.
- Accumulating mucus.

SMOKE

- From cigarettes, cigars, pipes—either yours or someone else's.

WEATHER

- Exercise in cold air.
- Changes in seasons.

SOURCE: *The Asthma Handbook*, American Lung Association, 1992.

ASTHMA'S DISTURBING CLIMB

The incidence of asthma has doubled among the young in the last decade, up to 6 in every 100 kids in 1991.

	1982	1986	1991	Total growth
Under 18	4.01%	5.11%	6.25%	Up 55.9%
18–44	2.90%	3.64%	4.34%	Up 49.7%
45–64	3.63%	3.63%	4.07%	Up 12.1%
85 and up	4.08%	4.26%	3.72%	Down 8.8%
All ages	3.48%	4.10%	4.72%	Up 35.6%

SOURCE: National Center for Health Statistics.

EXPERT Q&A

PROZAC'S CAN AND CAN'T-DO POWERS

The drug of the 1990s doesn't alter personality, it relieves depression

So many claims have been made for Prozac's powers that its reputation as a wonder drug is hardly surprising. Dr. Randolph Catlin, Chief of Mental Health at Harvard University Mental Health Services, puts some of those claims into perspective here.

■ What does Prozac do?

In medical terms, it increases the level of a neurotransmitter called serotonin at the interspace between neurons at the midbrain—in the center of the brain underneath the cortex. What you see clinically is an improvement in a depressed mood. It increases one's sense of well-being, counteracting tendencies to depression.

■ When should a doctor prescribe Prozac?

It should be prescribed when there are indications that one is significantly depressed.

■ What are the advantages of Prozac over other antidepressants?

Prozac has two advantages over the many other kinds of antidepressants. It seems to have fewer side effects, and it is more of a true antidepressant. Many find that others just put a floor on depression—make it more tolerable—whereas Prozac seems to relieve the depression. That is also true for the other serotonin enhancers, which slow down the reabsorption of serotonin.

■ Is Prozac the wonder drug it has been described as being?

Prozac is not a wonder drug. People on Prozac do not have unusual or sensational results, but they do have good antidepressant effects. It's a very useful antidepressant.

■ The drug has been said to alleviate several other conditions, from bulemia to attention deficit disorder. Are those reports accurate?

Prozac has been approved by the FDA for treatment of bulemia and for obsessive compulsive disorders. It is occasionally used for panic disorders and more infrequently for attention deficit hyperactivity disorder. It has also recently been identified as a useful treatment for PMS.

■ Does Prozac alter the personality?

No. There is no way to create something that wasn't there. Doctors do find that a great number of people who are chronically depressed, after taking the drug, say they suddenly feel as if they were a different person. But it does not change their underlying personality.

■ Is it overprescribed?

It may be overprescribed. It is used widely by general practitioners. A doctor may conclude that his patient's chronic backache is related to depression and prescribe Prozac, especially

FACT FILE:

THE GREAT DEPRESSION

■ *A 1993 U.S. Public Health Service review found that depression affects one in eight people in a lifetime and 11 million Americans each year. But most people who could benefit from treatment never get it. A limited course of psychotherapy works for over half of those with mild to moderate depression, but if therapy produces no effect by 6 weeks or nearly full remission by 12 weeks, the agency strongly recommends medication treatment.*

THE SIDE EFFECTS OF ANTIDEPRESSANTS

The side effects of the following drugs are ranked on a scale from zero to four. Zero indicates that a side effect is absent or rare. Four indicates that it is relatively common.

DRUG	DRY MOUTH, BLURRED VISION, URINARY HESITATION, CONSTIPATION	DROWSINESS	INSOMNIA, AGITATION	EXCESSIVE FALL IN BLOOD PRESSURE WHEN STANDING UP	CARDIAC ARRHYTHMIA (HEARTBEAT IRREGULARITY)	GASTRO-INTESTINAL DISTRESS	WEIGHT GAIN (OVER 6 KG)
Amitriptyline	4+	4+	0	4+	3+	0	4+
Desipramine	1+	1+	1+	2+	2+	0	1+
Doxepin	3+	4+	0	2+	2+	0	3+
Imipramine	3+	3+	1+	4+	3+	1+	3+
Nortiptyline	1+	1+	0	2+	2+	0	1+
Proptriptyline	2+	1+	1+	2+	2+	0	0
Trimipramine	1+	4+	0	2+	2+	0	3+
Amoxapine	2+	2+	2+	2+	3+	0	1+
Maprotiline	2+	4+	0	0	1+	0	2+
Trazodone	0	4+	0	1+	1+	1+	1+
Bupropion	0	0	2+	0	1+	1+	0
Fluoxetine	0	0	2+	0	0	3+	0
Paroxetine	0	0	2+	0	0	3+	0
Sertraline	0	0	2+	0	0	3+	0
Monoamine Oxidase Inhibitors (MAOIs)	1+	1+	2+	2+	0	1+	2+

SOURCE: *Depression in Primary Care*, U.S. Department of Health and Human Services, 1994.

since there is no risk involved. A doctor may prescribe Prozac for anything associated with depressed mood, even without a diagnostic work-up. It is important for anyone to get a thorough work-up before being prescribed Prozac, or any antidepressant.

What are the drug's side effects?

It can cause increased agitation, similar to caffeine jitters. Some complain of headaches or nausea. And there are reports of decreased sexual function, delayed or, eventually, complete inhibition of orgasm in women; and, in men, prolonged ejaculation or decreased or no ability to have a penile erection. In addition, there are some people, possibly quite a few, who complain that when on the drug they don't care very much about things that used to matter quite a bit. They sometimes get detached.

What risks are associated with Prozac?

The only real risk is for someone with a fairly serious liver disease. Prozac is metabolized in the liver. There is also a very small risk for someone with diabetes or a seizure disorder.

What about the claims that Prozac causes aggressive behavior or even suicides.

The people who become more aggressive on Prozac are probably those who have been suppressing aggressive tendencies. And there have been extremely few cases of suicide.

How long should one stay on Prozac?

One should stay on Prozac at least 6 months, and possibly up to 10 to 12 months. If, at that point, everything is stable in their lives, they can taper off and see how they do. Some people, however, may need to be off and on the drug for quite a while. It is not yet known if being on the drug for a longer period of time causes damage.

EXPERT Q&A

AN UNVARNISHED LOOK AT STEROIDS

Testosterone boosters have a place, but it's not on the playing fields

Taking steroids to build muscle and improve athletic performance is a dangerous habit for hundreds of thousands of young people. Charles Yesalis, Professor of Exercise and Sport Science at Penn State University and one of the nation's leading experts on the subject, explains the risks.

■ What are steroids?

They are synthetic derivatives of the primary male sex hormone, testosterone. Correctly called anabolic-androgenic steroids, they have both an anabolic (tissue-building) effect and an androgenic (masculinizing) effect. The primary use of steroids is in replacement therapy for men whose testes are not producing normal levels of testosterone and for kids who suffer delayed onset of puberty. Some physicians are giving them to AIDS patients to help maintain body weight and appetite. Other uses currently under evaluation include treatment for men over 50 to maintain strength, and as a male contraceptive.

■ Why do athletes take steroids?

To increase muscle mass and to increase strength—and to train longer, more frequently, and with more intensity. Although no study has demonstrated this last purported effect, most athletes who have used or are using steroids have reported this.

■ So what's wrong with taking steroids?

First of all, it's cheating. When you go into a contest, there is a commitment to play by the rules; every sport federation prohibits the use of these drugs. It's against federal law, and every state bars using them for nonmedical purposes. Distributing is a felony and possession can get you into jail.

In addition, tests show that if you administer testosterone to mice, it increases their aggressive behavior. Aggression among steroid users is not consistently demonstrated in all studies, but 90 percent of the steroid users I have interviewed report feelings of increased aggression. Whether steroids cause fits of rage, known as "roid rage," is yet to be determined.

■ What about physical dangers?

The long-term effects aren't clear. A handful of cases associate steroids with cardiomyopathy, which is when the heart muscle stops functioning and requires a heart transplant. Steroids have also been found to have a deleterious, but temporary, effect on liver function; when you go off the drug, the liver returns to normal. Anabolic steroids, taken orally, have also been associated with nonmalignant liver tumors.

Steroid use affects the reproductive tract as well. When the hypothalamus gland detects high levels of testosterone, it shuts off the portion of the endocrine system that produces testosterone and sperm. In males that have a predisposition to baldness, balding will be accelerated. Some users may have scarring acne, and males can grow fibrous tissue under the nipple, causing the appearance of small breasts.

In addition, the drugs have been tentatively linked to an increased risk of strokes or heart attacks during use, not later. And finally, based on clinical experience, it is believed that young adolescents taking these drugs could permanently and prematurely close their growth plates.

■ How are women affected by steroids?

About 55,000 women have used steroids in the past year. Among high school seniors, between a 1/2 and 2 percent of girls have reported using steroids at some time. Small amounts will have a profound effect on women. Use will shrink the breast tissue, cause male-pattern hair growth and baldness, deepening of the voice, clitoral enlargement, and cessation of the menses. Many of these effects are irreversible.

EXTINGUISHING YOUR HABIT

Are nicotine patches and nicotine gum an easy way to quit smoking?

The "patch" may offer hope to the four out of five American smokers who would like to extinguish their habit. Some one billion dollars' worth of the bandage-like transdermal patches have been sold since they were approved by the Food and Drug Administration in 1991. They work by releasing nicotine into the body through the skin, which alleviates some of the withdrawal symptoms, such as irritability, that are associated with quitting smoking.

The patch is obtained by prescription at about $3.50 to $4 each, significantly more than the pack or so of cigarettes that it replaces. (The patches are changed every 24 hours.) Usually, a doctor will start a patient with the largest, strongest patch, and then taper off to smaller patches within a couple of weeks. Currently, four nicotine patches are on the market—Habitrol, Nicoderm, PROSTEP, and Nicotrol.

A recent study in the *Journal of the American Medical Association* showed that smokers who used the transdermal patch and had counseling were able to stop smoking more easily than those who had counseling without the patch. In the study, two groups of smokers were taken through a 12-week regimen. Half had counseling and used a nicotine patch and the other half had counseling and no patch. After six months, 26 percent of those who used the patch and counseling were not smoking, while only 12 percent of those who were patchless stopped.

Some skeptics argue, however, that the patch's effectiveness depends less on the patch than on the smoker. The more motivated a smoker is to stop smoking, the more likely he will stop for good. A recent report in the *Medical Letter* found that patches were effective in relieving initial withdrawal symptoms, but that their long-term effectiveness was "unimpressive."

There can also be serious side effects for backsliders who smoke while using the patch, including headaches, dizziness, diarrhea, weakness, blurred vision, nightmares, and accentuated dreams. And some people have burning or itching in the area where the patch is placed on the skin.

One alternative to the patch is nicotine gum. Prescribed by a dentist, nicotine gum helps smokers quit the same way the nicotine patch does, by curbing the physical withdrawal symptoms. As with the patch, those who decide to use nicotine gum must first stop smoking.

Patients should chew the gum very slowly until they feel a tingling sensation in the mouth, which is caused by the release of nicotine. The gum should be chewed for 30 minutes at a time; patients should chew enough of it to stave off withdrawal symptoms. Typically, patients chew 10 to 15 pieces a day, but they should never chew more than 30 pieces a day. The gum should be chewed every day for a month or so, while the patient gradually reduces the number of pieces chewed. In three to six months, the patient should no longer need the gum. The effectiveness is the same as it is for patches, and it sometimes gives people an upset stomach.

Whether smokers choose gum, a patch, or sheer will power, the American Cancer Society recommends that they set a specific day, a "Quit Date," to stop smoking. The day should be during a time when the smoker will be under little stress, such as during a vacation.

A week before the Quit Date, the American Cancer Society suggests that smokers begin a diary of their smoking habits by writing down in detail every time they reach for a cigarette, including the time, place, how the smoker felt, and why he or she decided to light up.

When the big day arrives, the smoker should tell as many people as possible that he or she is trying to kick the habit so they can give support when needed.

TROUBLESHOOTER'S GUIDE

DRUGS OF ABUSE AND WHAT THEY DO

Cocaine use is down since the mid-1980s. Marijuana use is off, too, although millions still smoke it.

AMPHETAMINES

Often called speed or uppers

■ **WHAT IT DOES:** Speeds up physical and mental processes.

■ **VISIBLE SIGNS OF USE:** Weight loss, dilated pupils, insomnia, irritability, and trembling.

■ **LONG-TERM EFFECTS:** Paranoia, extreme weight loss, violent behavior.

BARBITURATES

Often called downers

■ **WHAT IT DOES:** Produces extreme lethargy and drowsiness.

■ **VISIBLE SIGNS OF USE:** Blurred and confused speech, lack of coordination and balance.

■ **LONG-TERM EFFECTS:** Disruption of sleeping pattern, double vision, risk of death from overdose, especially when used in conjunction with alcohol.

CANNABIS

Includes marijuana and hashish, often called chronic, dope, pot, grass, or hash

■ **WHAT IT DOES:** Relaxes mind and body, heightens perception, and causes mood swings.

■ **VISIBLE SIGNS OF USE:** Red eyes, dilated pupils, increased appetite, lack of physical coordination, and lethargy.

■ **LONG-TERM EFFECTS:** Unknown. Possible brain, heart, lung, or reproductive system damage.

COCAINE

Often called candy, coke, blow, or crack

■ **WHAT IT DOES:** Stimulates nervous system and produces heightened sensations and sometimes hallucination.

■ **VISIBLE SIGNS OF USE:** Dilated pupils, trembling, apparent intoxication, agitation, rapid breathing, and elevated blood pressure.

■ **LONG-TERM EFFECTS:** Ulceration of nasal passages and perforated septum (area separating the nostrils) if drug is snorted. Generalized itching, which can produce open sores. Possible heart failure.

OPIATES

Including opium, morphine, heroin, and methadone, as well as synthetic painkillers

■ **WHAT IT DOES:** Relieves physical and mental pain and produces temporary euphoria.

■ **VISIBLE SIGNS OF USE:** Weight loss, lethargy, mood swings, sweating, slurred speech, sore eyes, and drowsiness.

■ **LONG-TERM EFFECTS:** Constipation, extreme risk of infection, including hepatitis and HIV, if drug is injected and needles are shared. Absence of periods in women. Possibility of death from overdose.

PSYCHEDELIC DRUGS

Including lysergic acid (LSD) and mescaline, as well as "designer drugs" such as ecstasy (MDMA)

■ **WHAT IT DOES:** Unpredictable. Usually produces hallucinations and intense introspection, which may be pleasant or extremely frightening.

■ **VISIBLE SIGNS OF USE:** Dilated pupils, sweating, trembling, sometimes fever and chills.

■ **LONG-TERM EFFECTS:** Possibly irresponsible behavior.

VOLATILE SUBSTANCES

Includes the inhaled fumes of glue or cleaning fluids

■ **WHAT IT DOES:** Produces hallucinations, giddiness, euphoria, and unconsciousness.

■ **VISIBLE SIGNS OF USE:** Obvious confusion, dilated pupils, flushed face.

■ **LONG-TERM EFFECTS:** Risk of brain, liver, or kidney damage, possible suffocation from inhalation.

SOURCE: *American Medical Association Family Medical Guide*, 3rd ed., Random House, 1993.

FIRST AID

ACCIDENTS

WHEN YOU'RE THE GOOD SAMARITAN

Emergencies require quick action. The worst mistake is to do nothing

Accidents are the leading cause of death among children and young adults in the United States. Heart attacks and strokes claim almost half of all deaths in this country each year, and about two million Americans end up in the hospital with injuries annually. Although the odds of having to cope with a first aid crisis are slim, the consequences of not knowing how to deal with one can be fatal.

One common reaction to happening upon an accident scene is to hold back out of uncertainty over what to do, over fear of contracting a disease, or even of being blamed for making a mistake and being sued. The fact that AIDS can be transmitted through infected blood has only added to the reluctance of many to get involved.

The worst mistake is to do nothing, say experts at the American Red Cross. At a minimum, you should call the rescue squad or 911. The risks of catching a disease from helping are also not very great. Usually you will know the accident victims that need your help because they are likely to be family members or friends. That increases the likelihood that you will know their health condition and can take precautions to guard against any special risks of infection. Whether you know the victim or not, it is best to avoid direct contact with blood, which is the most likely transmitter of infectious disease, including the AIDS virus. Wear gloves, if available, when treating a bleeding victim and wash your hands before and after giving first aid, if possible.

Most states have "Good Samaritan" laws, which protect rescuers who assist accident victims from being sued, provided the samaritan acts in a reasonable manner. That means moving a victim only if his life is imperiled or if another person's will be if you don't move the first. Ask permission of a victim who is conscious before giving first aid, calling the rescue squad or 911 as soon as possible.

To obtain permission to provide assistance, you must tell a conscious victim who you are, what training you have, and what first aid you intend. If permission is refused, stop immediately. If the victim is an infant or child and there is a responsible adult available, ask permission of that adult. If no such adult is present, permission is implied. Permission is also assumed if a victim is unconscious or cannot reply.

For detailed instructions on vital first aid techniques, see the following material from the American Red Cross.

CHECKING AN UNCONSCIOUS VICTIM

When a victim does not respond to you, assume he or she is unconscious. Call for an ambulance at once, if possible. Then check to see if the victim is breathing, has a pulse, or is bleeding severely.

■ **To check for breathing, look, listen, and feel for breathing for about five seconds. Watch the chest to see if it rises.**

■ **To find out if the heart is beating, check the victim's pulse. Check the pulse of an adult or a child at the side of the neck. Check the pulse of an infant at the inside of the arm between the shoulder and the elbow.**

■ **Check for bleeding by looking over the victim's body from head to foot. Bleeding is severe when blood spurts out of a wound. Often the situation may look worse than it is.**

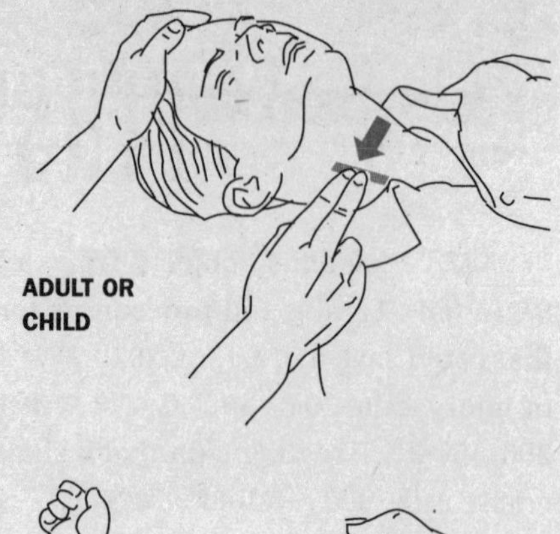

ADULT OR CHILD

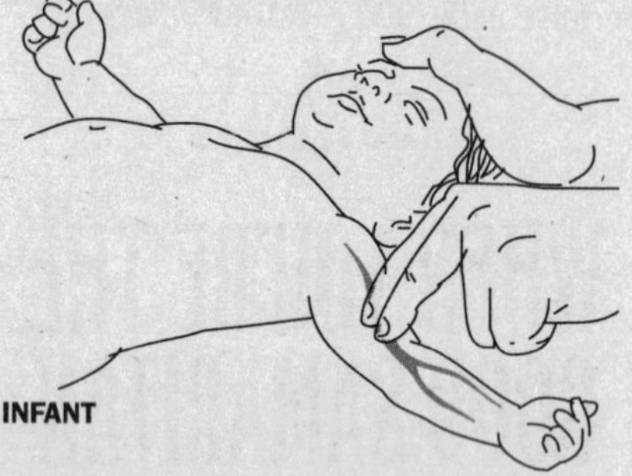

INFANT

ABDOMINAL THRUSTS FOR CHOKING ADULTS

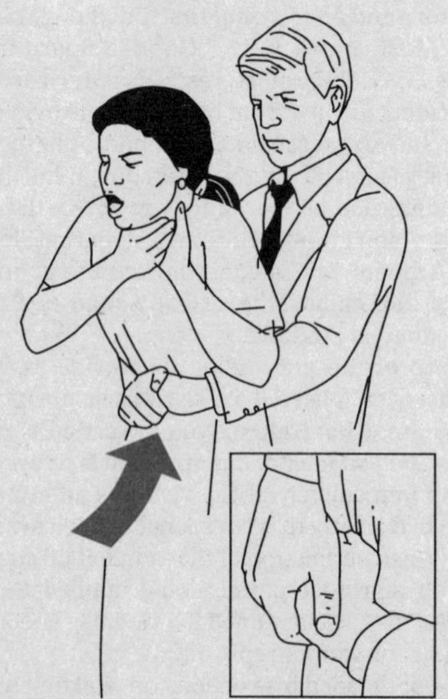

SOURCE: Courtesy of the American Red Cross.

Choking is a common breathing emergency. A conscious person who is choking has the airway blocked by a piece of food or another object. The airway may be partly or completely blocked. If a choking person is coughing forcefully, encourage him or her to cough up the object.

IF THE PERSON IS UNABLE TO COUGH, SPEAK, OR BREATHE...

STEP 1. **Place thumb side of fist against middle of abdomen just above the navel. Grasp fist with other hand.**

STEP 2. **Give quick upward thrusts.**

REPEAT **until object is coughed up or person becomes unconscious.**

Give chest thrusts when choking person is too big to reach around or is noticeably pregnant.

GIVE BACK BLOWS AND CHEST THRUSTS TO BABIES WHO ARE CHOKING

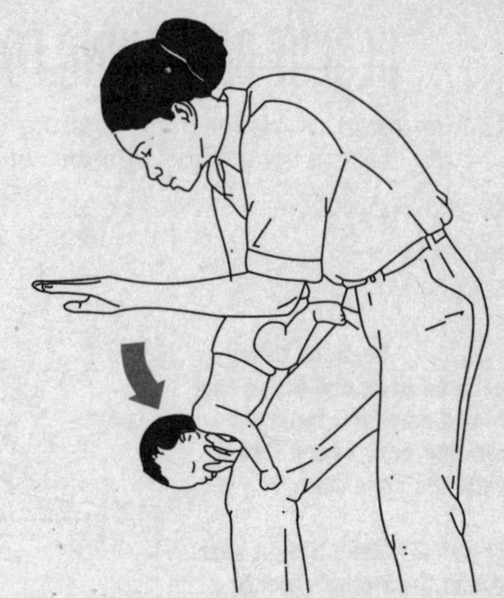

Choking is a leading cause of death and injury in infants, who love to put small objects such as pebbles, coins, beads, and parts of toys, in their mouth. Babies also choke often while eating because they have not yet fully mastered chewing and swallowing. Foods like grapes and nuts are particularly risky. Never let an infant eat or drink alone, the American Red Cross advises.

IF AN INFANT IS UNABLE TO CRY, COUGH, OR BREATHE...

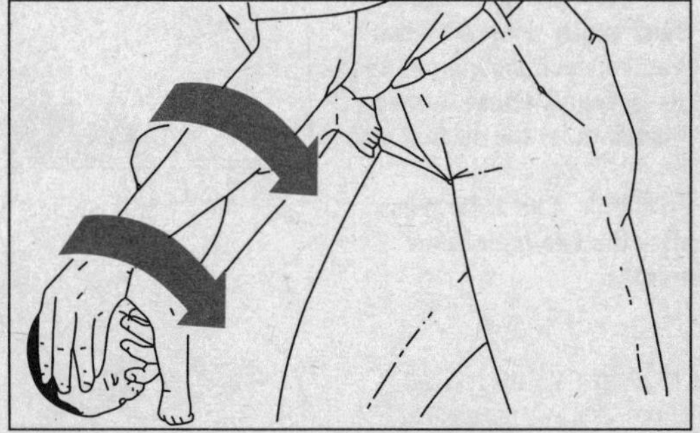

STEP 1. With infant facedown on forearm so that the head is lower than the chest, give five back blows with heel of hand between the infant's shoulder blades.

STEP 2. Holding the infant firmly between both forearms, turn the infant to a faceup position on forearm.

STEP 3. Using two fingers, give five chest thrusts on about the center of the breastbone.

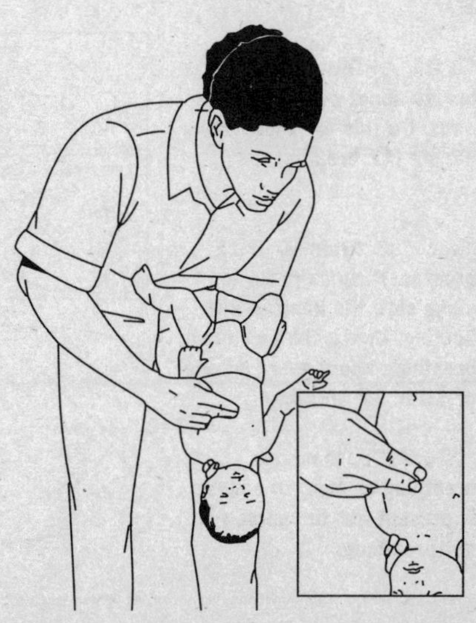

REPEAT the sequence of five back blows and five chest thrusts alternately until the object is coughed up, the infant begins to breathe on his own, or the infant becomes unconscious.

Stop as soon as the object is coughed up or the infant starts to breathe or cough. Watch the infant and make sure that he or she is breathing freely again.

Call the local emergency number if you haven't already done so. The infant should be taken to the local emergency department to be checked, even if the infant seems to be breathing well.

RESCUE BREATHING FOR ADULTS AND CHILDREN

The timing intervals for administering artificial respiration to adults and children are somewhat different, but the mechanics are the same

IF AN ADULT IS UNABLE TO BREATHE...

STEP 1. Begin by tilting the head back and lifting the chin to move the tongue away from the back of the throat. Pinch the nose shut.

STEP 2. Make a tight seal around the victim's mouth with your mouth. Breathe slowly into the victim until chest gently rises. Give two breaths, each lasting one to two seconds. Pause between breaths to let the air flow out.

STEP 3. Check for pulse after the two initial slow breaths.

IF PULSE IS PRESENT BUT PERSON IS STILL NOT BREATHING...

STEP 4. Give one slow breath about every five seconds. Do this for about one minute (12 breaths).

STEP 5. After 10 or 12 breaths, recheck pulse to make sure the heart is still beating. Check the pulse and breathing about every minute or 10 to 12 breaths.

CONTINUE rescue breathing as long as a pulse is present but the person is not breathing.

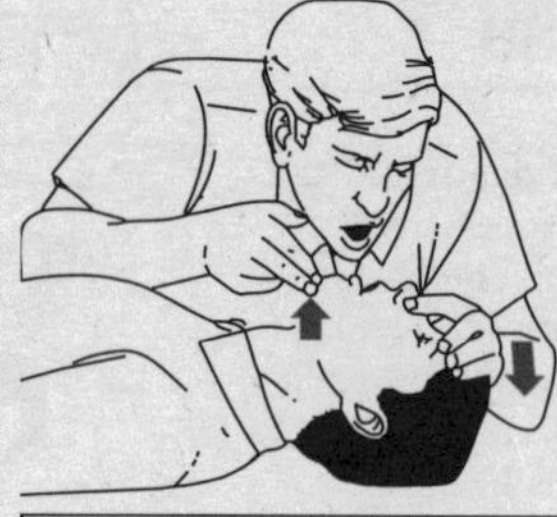

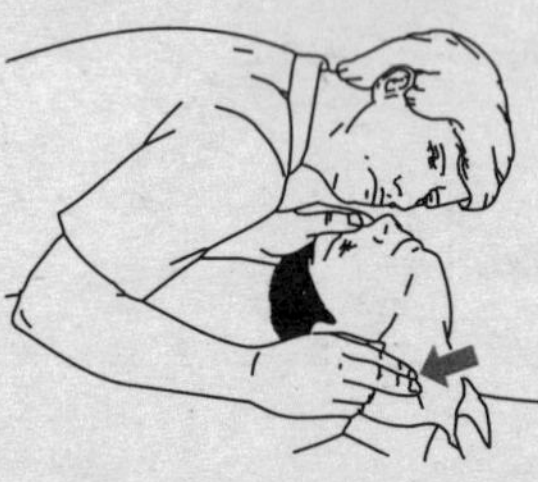

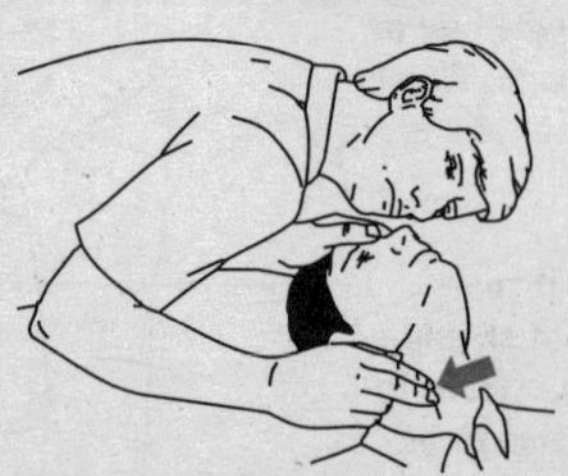

IF A CHILD IS UNABLE TO BREATHE...

STEP 1. Begin by tilting the head back and lifting the chin to move the tongue away from the back of the throat. Pinch the nose shut.

STEP 2. Make a tight seal around the victim's mouth with your mouth. Breathe slowly into the victim until chest gently rises. Give two breaths, each lasting one to two seconds. Pause between breaths to let the air flow out.

STEP 3. Check for pulse after the two initial slow breaths.

IF PULSE IS PRESENT BUT PERSON IS STILL NOT BREATHING...

STEP 4. Give one slow breath about every three seconds. Do this for about one minute (20 breaths).

STEP 5. Recheck pulse and breathing about every minute, or 20 breaths.

CALL the local emergency number if you have not already done so. Then, continue rescue breathing as long as a pulse is present but the child is not breathing.

SOURCE: Courtesy of the American Red Cross.

RESCUE BREATHING FOR INFANTS

Because a baby's mouth is very small, you need to seal your mouth over both the infant's mouth and nose

IF AN INFANT IS NOT BREATHING...

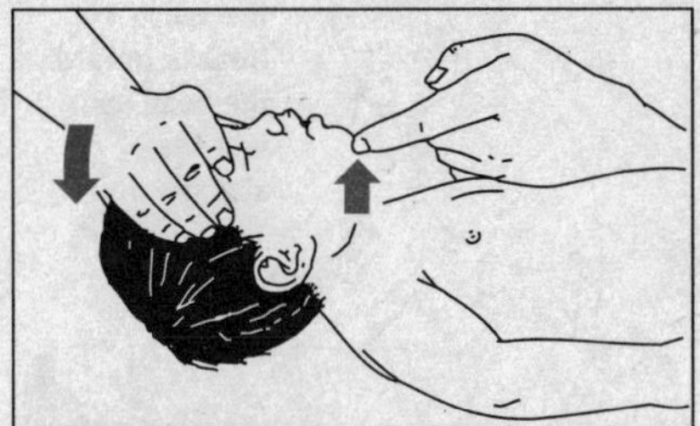

STEP 1. Begin by tilting the head back and lifting the chin to move the tongue away from the back of the throat.

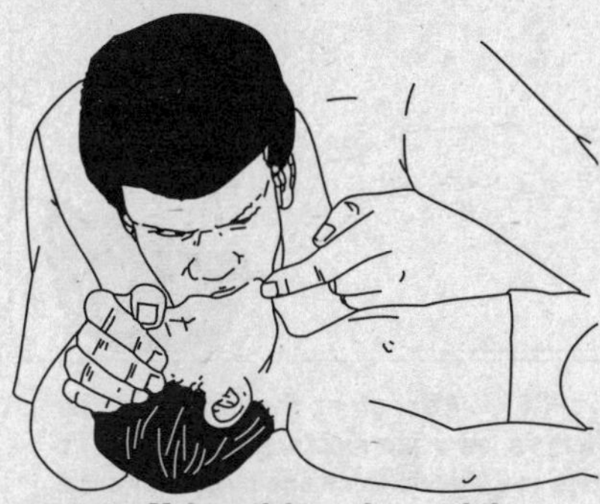

STEP 2. Make a tight seal around the infant's nose and mouth with your mouth.

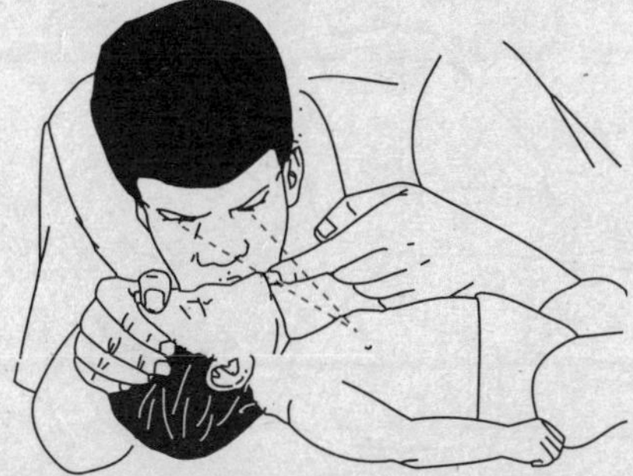

STEP 3. Breathe slowly into the victim until chest gently rises. Give two breaths, each lasting one to two seconds. Pause between breaths to let the air flow out.

STEP 4. Check for pulse after the two initial slow breaths.

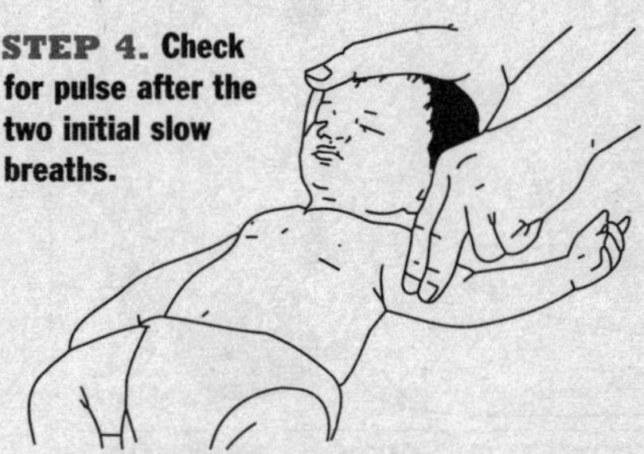

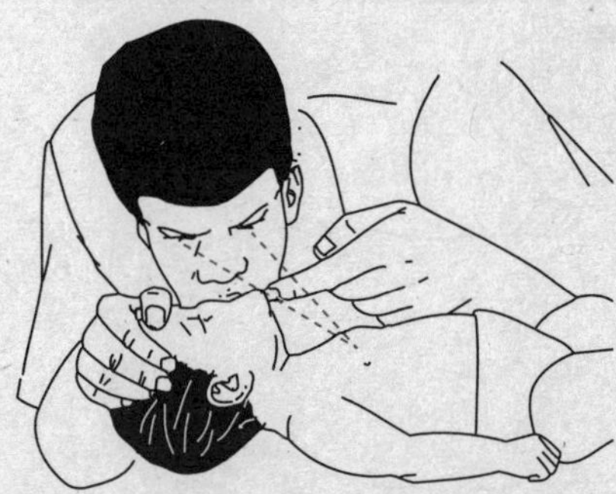

STEP 5. Give one slow breath about every three seconds. Do this for about one minute (20 breaths).

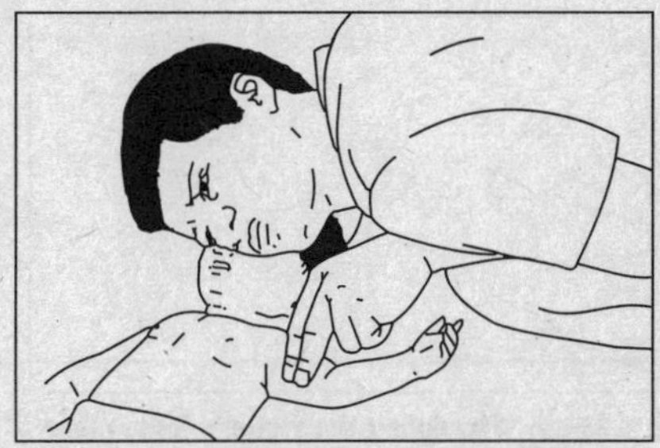

STEP 6. Recheck pulse and breathing about every minute. Call the local emergency number if you haven't already done so. Continue rescue breathing as long as a pulse is present but the child is not breathing.

CLEARING AN OBSTRUCTION WITH ABDOMINAL THRUSTS

When an unconscious person's airway is obstructed, getting air in is more important than removing the object

IF AIR DOES NOT GO IN...

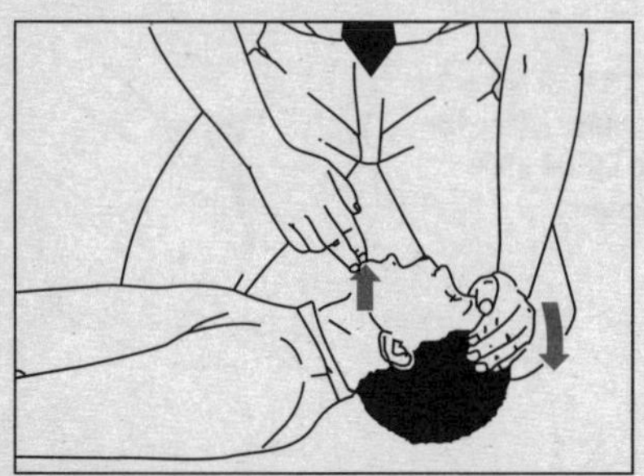

STEP 1. If you don't see the chest rise as you give rescue breathing, retilt the person's head.

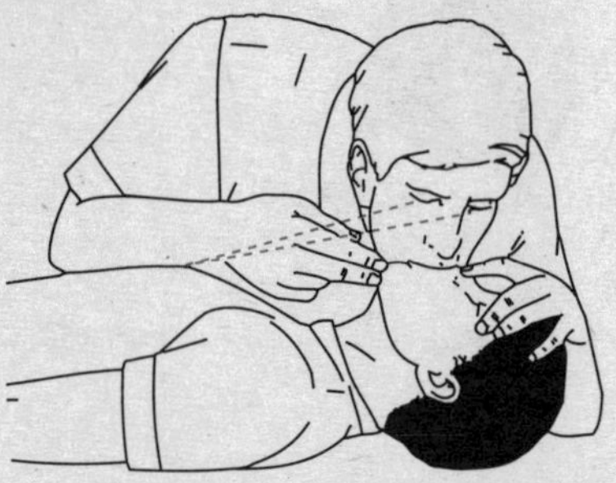

STEP 2. Give two breaths, each lasting one to two seconds. Pause between breaths to let the air flow out. If air still won't go in...

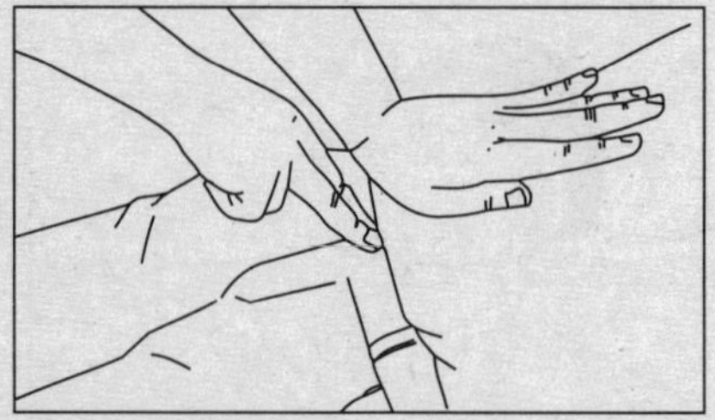

STEP 3. Straddling the victim's legs, place the heel of one hand just above the navel. Place your other hand on top of the first. Point the fingers of both hands toward the victim's head.

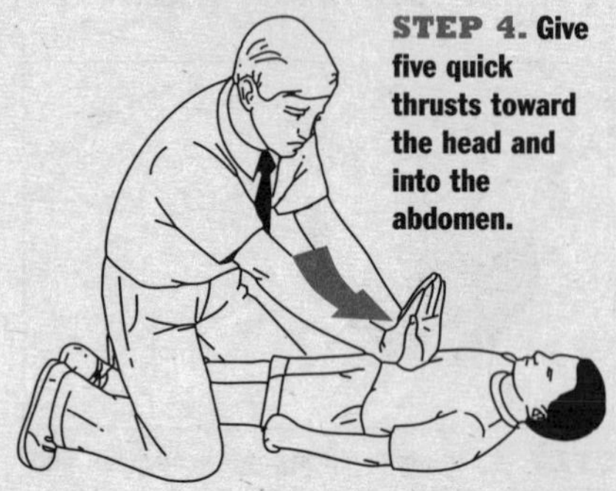

STEP 4. Give five quick thrusts toward the head and into the abdomen.

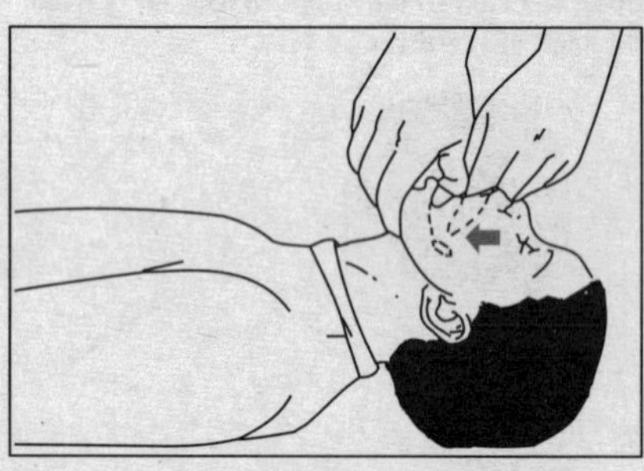

STEP 5. After giving five thrusts, lift the victim's lower jaw and tongue with your fingers and thumb. Slide one finger down the inside of the cheek and try to hook the object out.

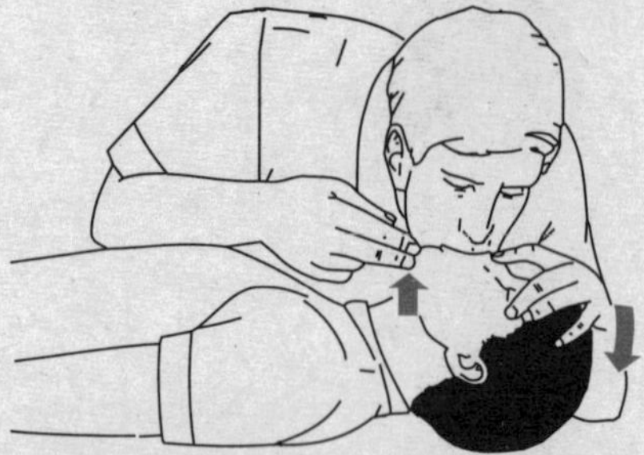

STEP 6. Tilt head back, lift chin, and give two slow breaths again. Repeat breaths, thrusts, and sweeps until breaths go in.

SOURCE: Courtesy of the American Red Cross.

WHEN IT'S AN INFANT WITH THE BLOCKAGE

The technique for clearing an unconscious baby's airway is the same as for one who is choking

IF YOU ARE UNABLE TO BREATHE INTO AN INFANT...

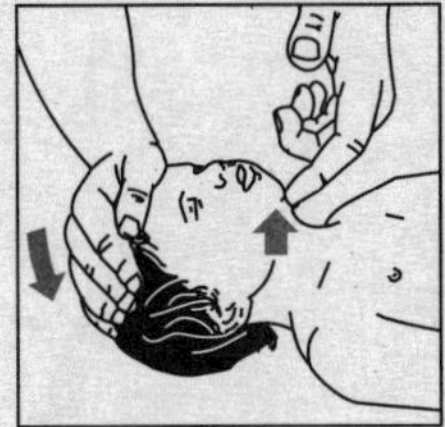

STEP 1. Retilt the infant's head, lifting the chin.

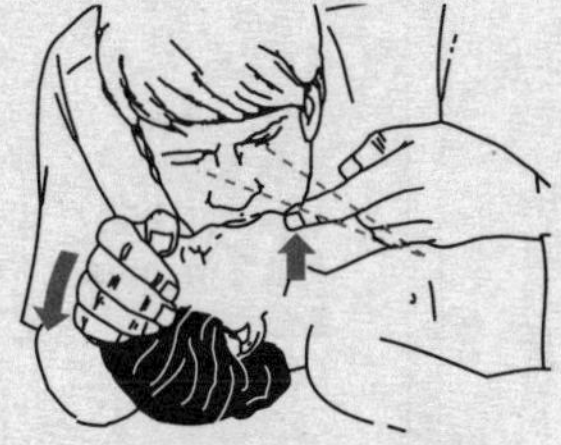

STEP 2. Give two breaths again. If air still won't go in...

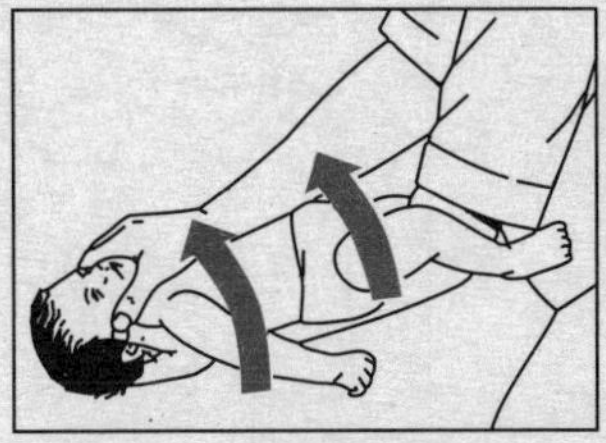

STEP 3. Position infant on forearm, then turn him face-down.

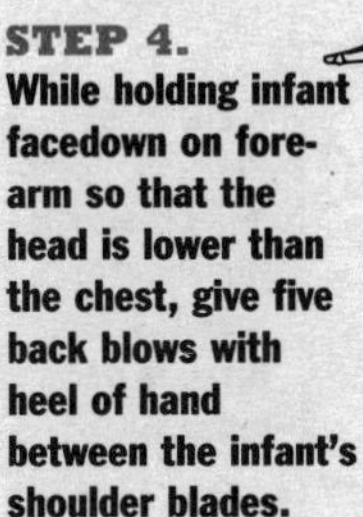

STEP 4. While holding infant facedown on fore-arm so that the head is lower than the chest, give five back blows with heel of hand between the infant's shoulder blades.

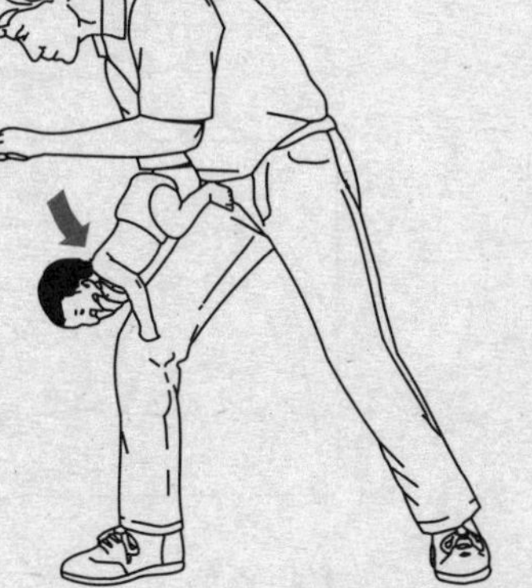

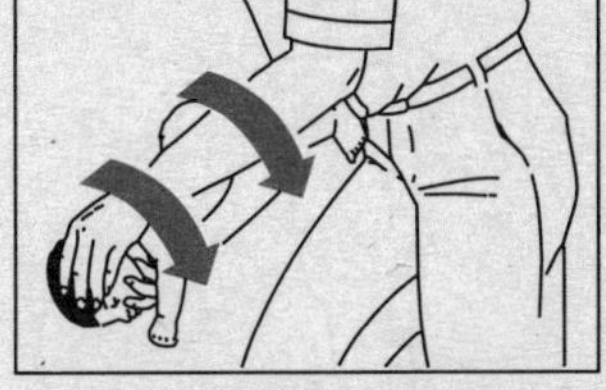

STEP 5. Holding the infant firmly between both forearms, turn the infant to a faceup position on forearm.

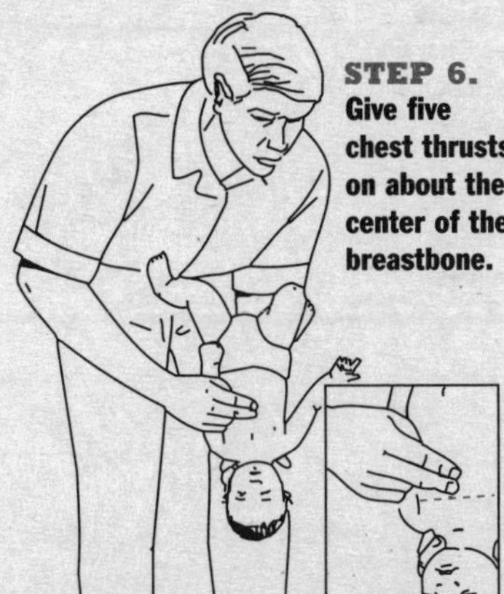

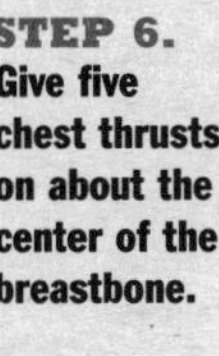

STEP 6. Give five chest thrusts on about the center of the breastbone.

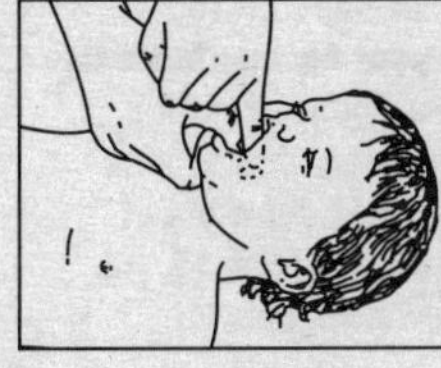

STEP 7. Lift the infant's lower jaw and tongue and check for object. Sweep one finger inside the mouth to hook the object out.

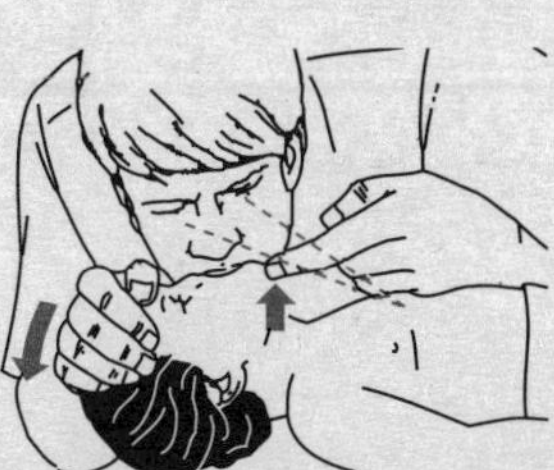

STEP 8. Tilt head back and give two breaths again. Repeat back blows, chest thrusts, sweeps, and breaths until breaths go in.

BASIC CPR FOR ADULTS AND CHILDREN

Give CPR when there is no breathing and no pulse. Without CPR, brain damage can set in within four minutes.

IF A PERSON IS NOT BREATHING AND HAS NO PULSE...

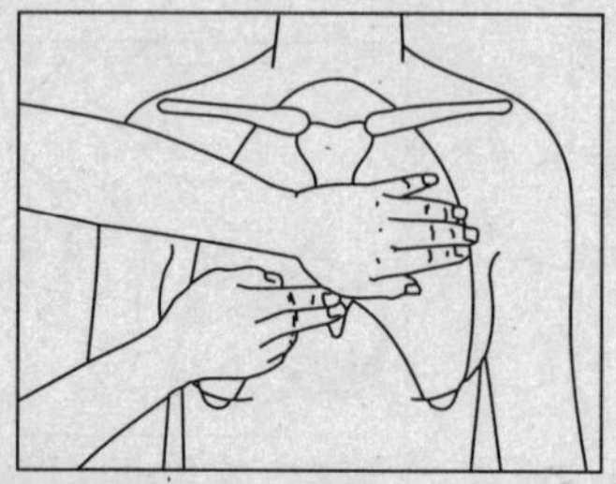

STEP 1. Find hand position–the notch where the ribs meet the lower breastbone. Place the heel of your hand on the breastbone just above your index finger.

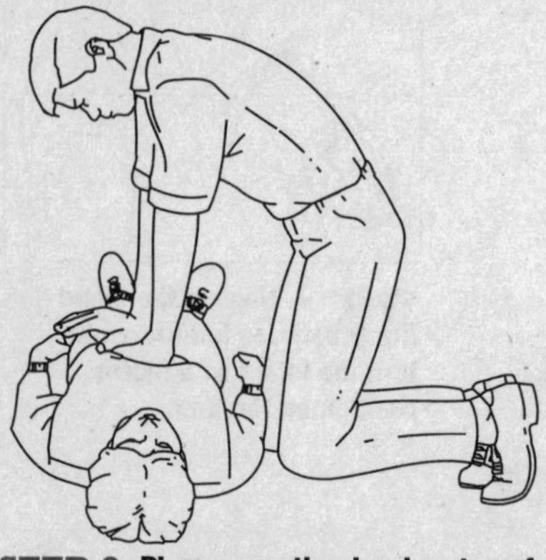

STEP 2. Place your other hand on top of the first. Use the heel of your bottom hand to apply pressure on the breastbone. Position your shoulders directly over your hands with elbows locked. Press the chest down about two inches, and then release. Repeat 15 times keeping a smooth even rhythm.

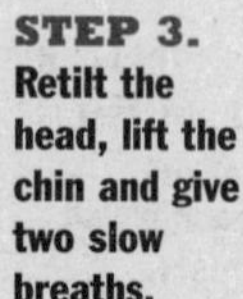

STEP 3. Retilt the head, lift the chin and give two slow breaths.

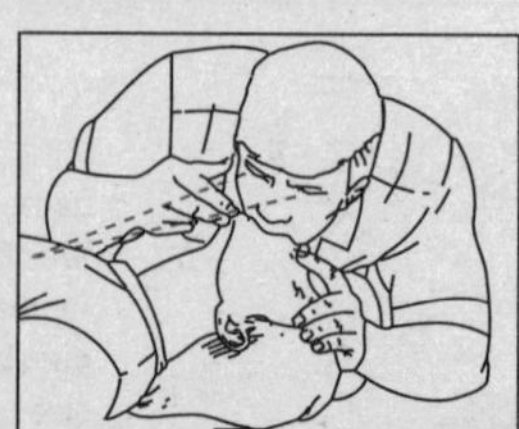

STEP 4. Do three more sets of 15 compressions and 2 breaths. Each cycle takes about 15 seconds.

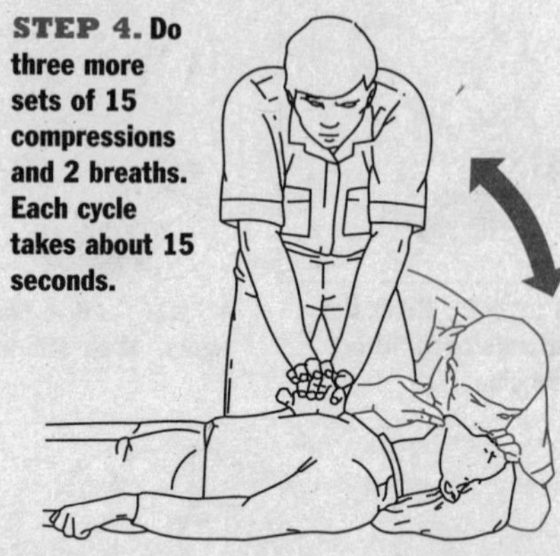

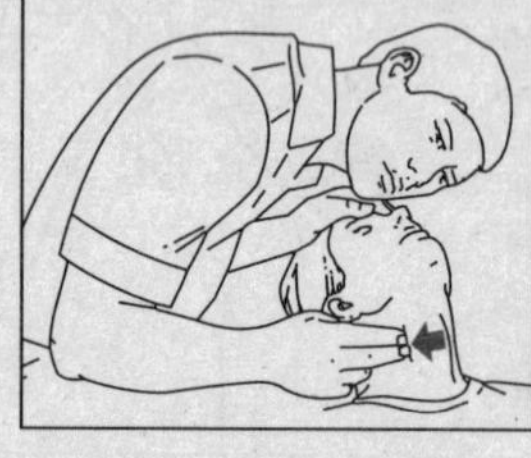

STEP 5. Recheck pulse and breathing for about five seconds. If there is no pulse...

STEP 6. Continue sets of 15 compressions and two breaths, pausing to check for pulse every few minutes. If you find a pulse, check breathing and give rescue breathing if necessary.

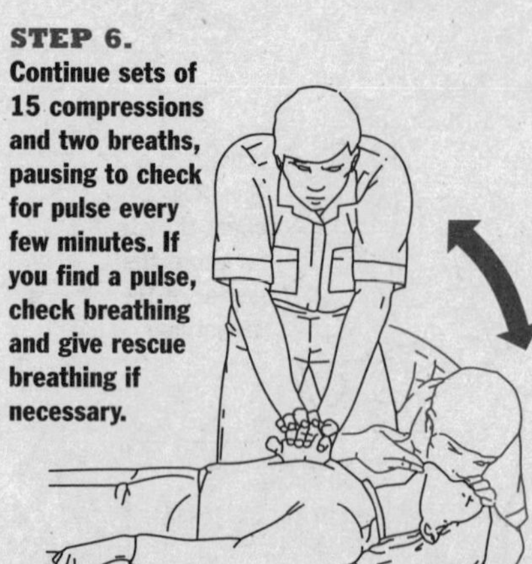

SOURCE: Courtesy of the American Red Cross.

CPR FOR INFANTS HAS IMPORTANT DIFFERENCES

Babies require lighter chest pressure delivered in shorter, more frequent cycles than do older children and adults.

IF AN INFANT IS NOT BREATHING AND HAS NO PULSE...

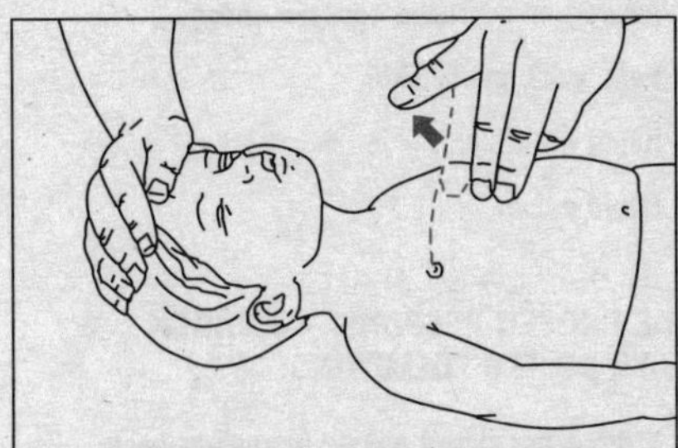

STEP 1. Place the infant on his or her back on a hard surface such as the floor or table. Place two fingers on the breastbone just below an imaginary line between the nipples.

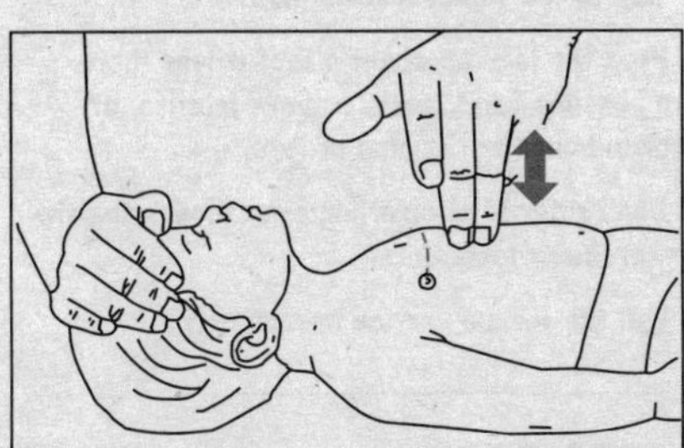

STEP 2. Give five compressions, about 3 seconds each. Count to help keep a regular, even rhythm.

STEP 3. Placing your mouth over the infant's mouth and nose, give one slow breath, about 1.5 seconds.

STEP 4. Begin compressions again. Do 12 cycles of five compressions and one breath, about one minute. Call the local emergency number if you haven't already, carrying the infant to the phone so you can continue giving CPR. Then...

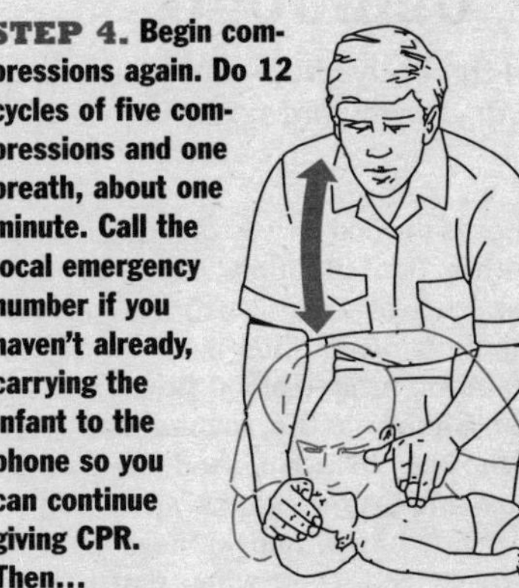

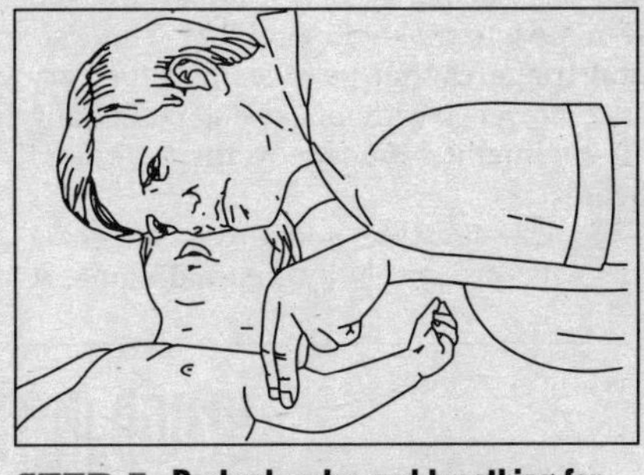

STEP 5. Recheck pulse and breathing for about five seconds. If there is still no pulse...

STEP 6. Continue sets of five compressions and one breath. Recheck pulse and breathing every few minutes. Continue CPR until help arrives.

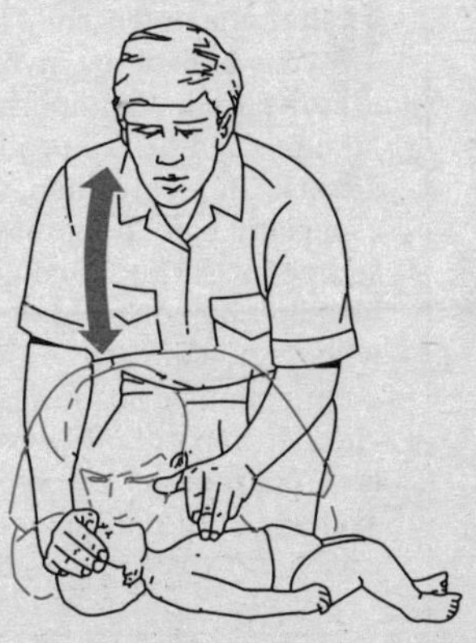

TAKING SHOCK SERIOUSLY

When the body shuts down because of injury, immediate care is critical

Shock is the body's way of trying to deal with a bad situation. When a body experiences trauma from a serious injury, it often finds itself unable to maintain proper blood flow to all its organs. Shock is the mechanism that allows the body to ration blood flow so that the most important organs such as the brain, heart, lungs, and kidneys get the blood they need, even when that means that less vital parts, such as arms, legs, and skin have to make do with less. This natural triage cannot be sustained for very long, however, without causing potentially life-threatening damage to the brain and heart.

Shock, says the Red Cross, "can't be managed effectively by first aid alone. A victim of shock requires advanced medical care as soon as possible."

THE EARLY SIGNS OF SHOCK INCLUDE:

- **Restlessness or irritability.**
- **Altered or confused consciousness.**
- **Pale, cool, moist skin.**
- **Rapid breathing.**
- **Rapid pulse.**

THE PROPER RESPONSE TO SHOCK IS TO DO THE FOLLOWING:

- **Stretch the victim out on his or her back.**
- **Treat any open bleeding.**
- **Help the injured restore normal body temperature, covering him or her if there is chilling.**
- **Talk to the victim reassuringly.**
- **Prop the legs up about a foot unless there are possible head, neck, or back injuries, or broken bones in the hips or legs.**
- **Don't offer food or drink. even though the victim probably feels thirsty.**
- **Call the rescue service immediately.**

BLOOD IN THE AIDS ERA

Some precautions from the American Red Cross

When the emergency that requires your assistance involves heavy bleeding, it's important that you take precautions to protect yourself against the risk of infection. That's especially true if you have a cut, scrape, or sore that could allow a bleeding person's blood to mix directly with yours.One of the easiest ways for an infectious disease such as the AIDS virus or hepatitis B to be transmitted is through direct blood-to-blood exchange. To minimize risk, the American Red Cross advises the following.

- **Avoid blood splashes.**
- **Keep and use disposable latex gloves in emergencies involving bleeding.**
- **If gloves are unavailable, cover the wound with a dressing or other available barrier such as plastic wrap.**
- **Avoid any contact in which the victim's blood touches any cuts, scrapes, or skin irritations you may have.**
- **Always wash your hands as soon as possible, whether or not you wore gloves.**

CONTROL BLEEDING FROM A MAJOR OPEN WOUND

Pressure is the key to stopping blood loss from a serious injury. Bearing down on arterial pressure points may be necessary.

IF A PERSON IS BLEEDING...

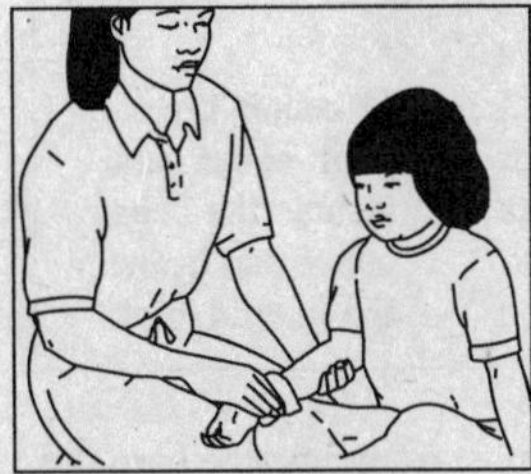

STEP 1. Do not waste time washing wound. Cover it with sterile dressing or clean cloth and press firmly against the wound with hand.

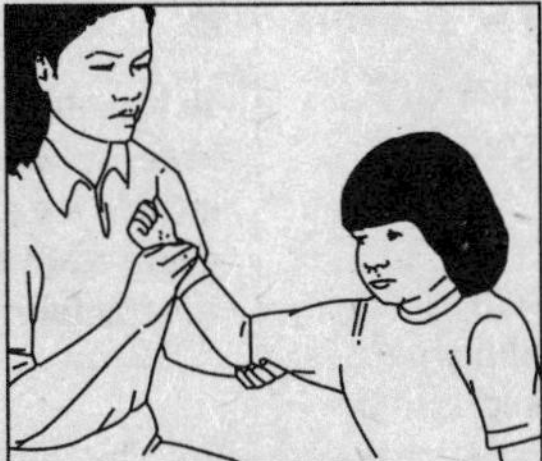

STEP 2. Elevate the wound, if possible, above the level of the heart.

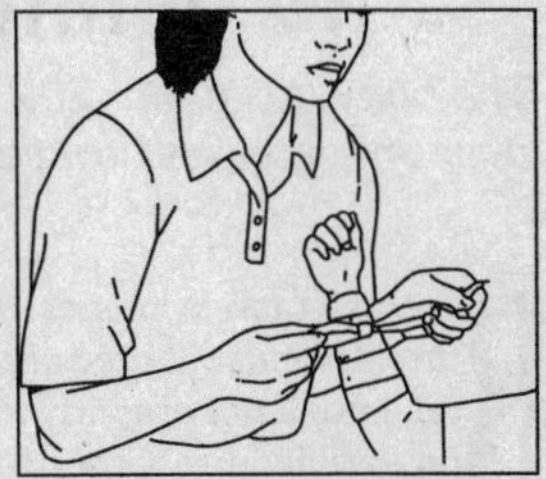

STEP 3. Apply a roller bandage snugly over the dressing to keep pressure on the wound. If bleeding doesn't stop...

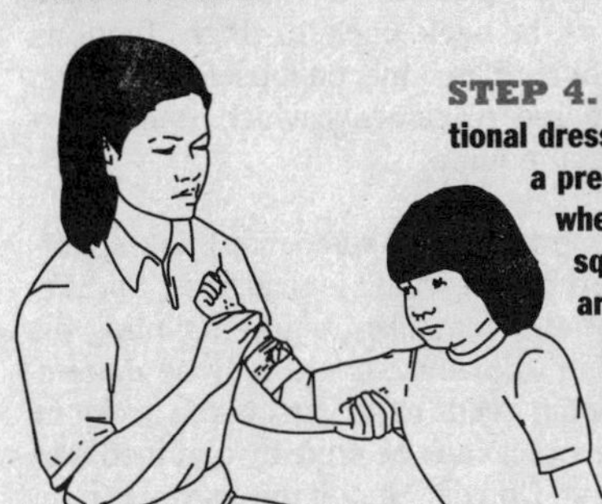

STEP 4. Apply additional dressings. Find a pressure point where you can squeeze the artery against the bone.

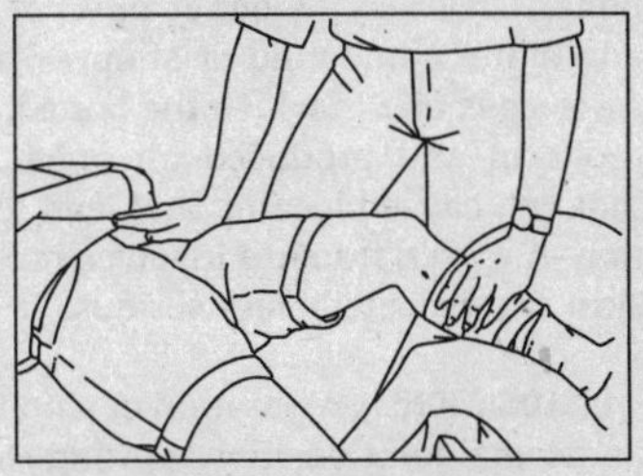

If bleeding is from the leg, press with the heel of your hand where the leg bends at the hip.

■ A ROLLER BANDAGE USED TO CONTROL BLEEDING

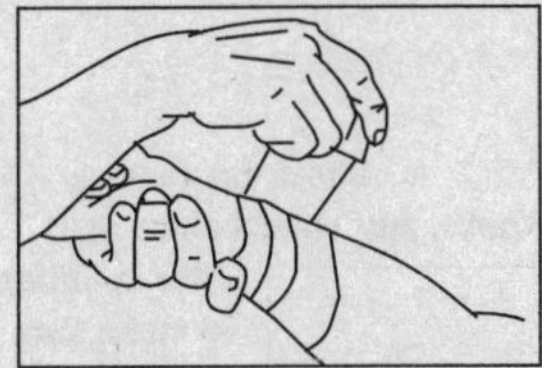

To apply a pressure bandage, start by securing the bandage over the dressing. Use overlapping turns to cover the dressing completely.

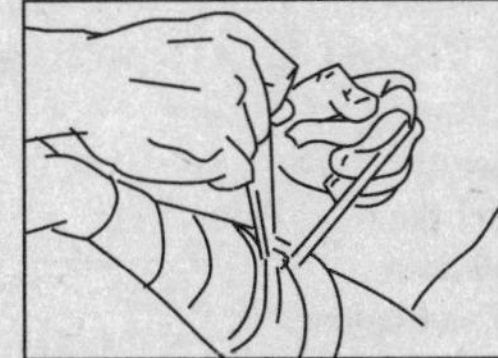

Tie or tape the bandage in place. If blood soaks through, put on more dressings and bandages. Do not remove bloodsoaked ones.

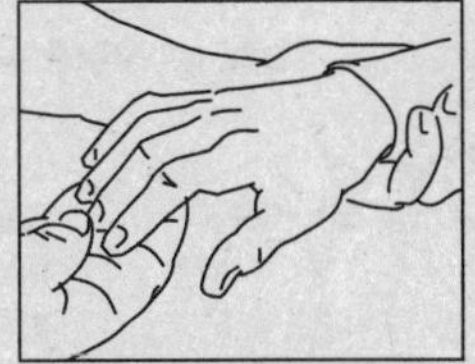

Check fingers or toes for warmth, color, and feeling. If they are pale and cold, bandage is too tight. Loosen it.

SOURCE: Courtesy of the American Red Cross.

INJURIES

ABOUT BREAKS AND SPRAINS

The body has about 200 bones and over 600 muscles that can get hurt

Bone and muscle injuries are seldom life-threatening, but they are usually painful, and, if not properly treated, can be potentially disabling. Here's a breakdown of the things that can go wrong with all those bones, joints, ligaments, and tendons that hold our frames together.

■ **FRACTURE:** Breaks, chips, or cracks in a bone. They may be either open or closed and either compound or simple. An open fracture is one in which the bone has torn the skin and produced an open wound that can cause bleeding and lead to infection. A closed fracture involves no broken skin and is usually less serious.

■ **DISLOCATION:** A separation of a bone from its normal joint position, putting the joint out of commission. The displacement often leaves a bump, ridge, or hollow where the bone and joint should fit naturally.

■ **SPRAIN:** Occurs when there is a tear in the ligaments that hold bones together at a joint. The joints most often involved are the ankle, knee, wrist, and fingers. In serious sprains, there may also be a fracture or dislocation at the joint in question.

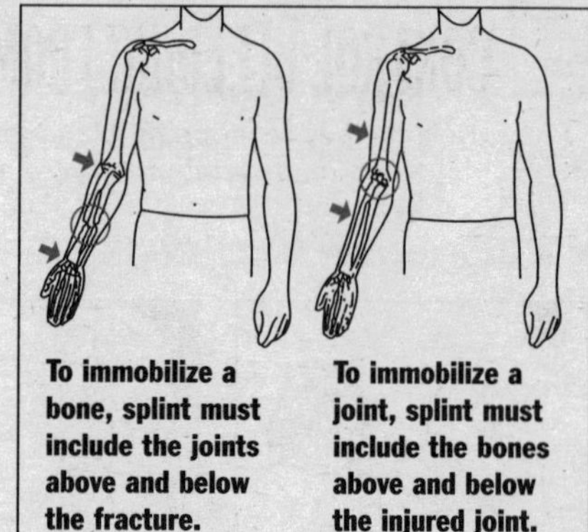

To immobilize a bone, splint must include the joints above and below the fracture.

To immobilize a joint, splint must include the bones above and below the injured joint.

■ **STRAIN:** Results from the stretching and tearing of muscles or tendons in areas such as the neck, back, or thigh. Tendons are fibers that connect a muscle to a bone, as opposed to ligaments, which connect two bones at a joint.

Contrary to what some may think, splinting isn't only reserved for fractures. Sprains and strains may also require splinting on occasion. But this should only be done if the victim needs moving from the accident scene and it can't be done by a trained rescue unit. Don't attempt it unless you can do it without putting the victim in more pain than he already feels. Detailed instructions from the American Red Cross follow.

IF A PERSON IS UNABLE TO MOVE OR USE AN INJURED LEG...

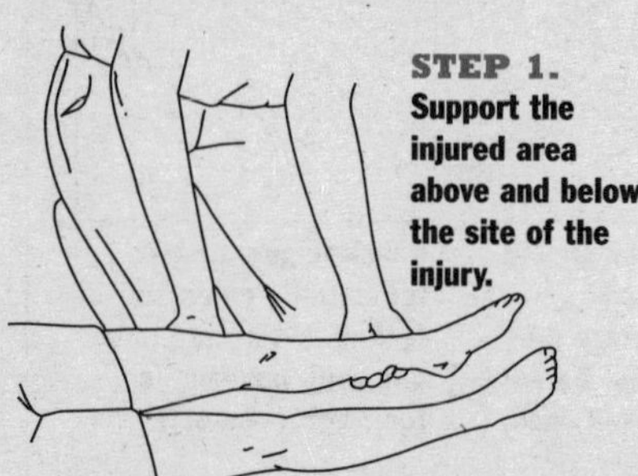

STEP 1. Support the injured area above and below the site of the injury.

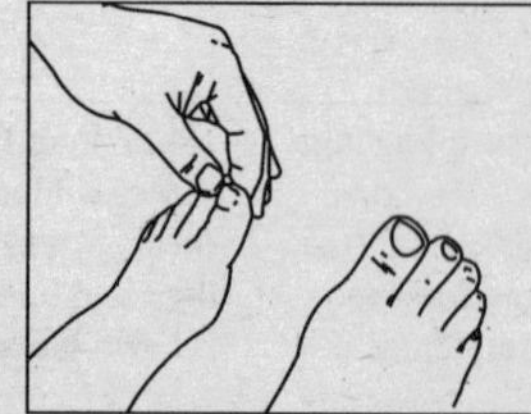

STEP 2. Check for feeling, warmth, and color before and after splinting to make sure the splint is not too tight. Then...

SOURCE: Courtesy of the American Red Cross.

■ TO APPLY ANATOMIC SPLINT TO INJURED THIGH OR FORELEG

First follow steps one and two (see previous page, below), and then...

STEP 3. Place several folded bandages above and below the injured area.

STEP 4. Place injured limb next to uninjured area. You can splint an arm to the chest or an injured leg to the other one.

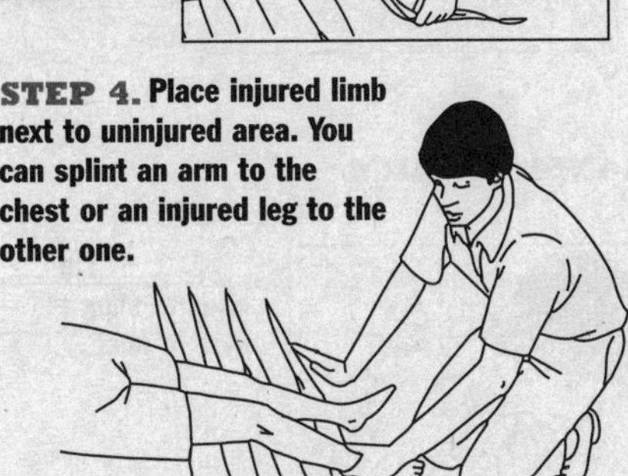

STEP 5. Tie triangular bandages securely.

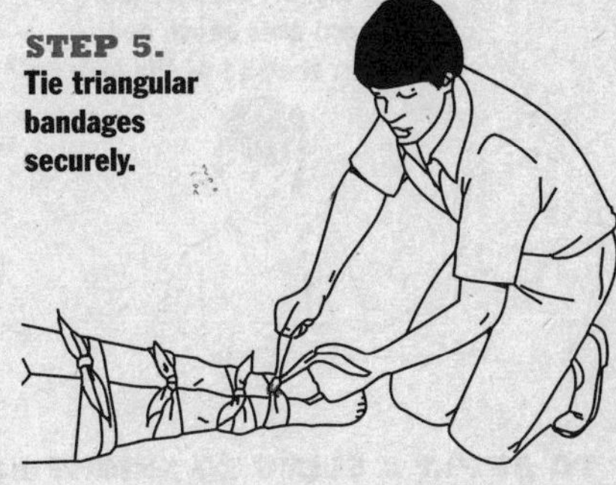

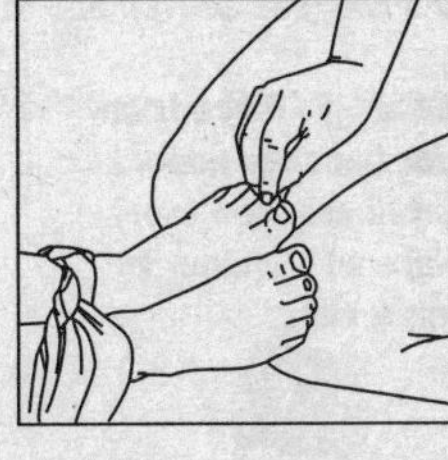

STEP 6. Recheck for feeling, warmth, and color. If cold or pale, loosen the splint a little bit. Apply ice and raise injured limb.

■ TO APPLY SOFT SPLINT TO AN INJURED ANKLE

First follow steps one and two (see previous page, below), and then...

STEP 3. Place several folded bandages above and below the injured area.

STEP 4. Gently wrap a soft object (a folded blanket or a pillow) around the injured area.

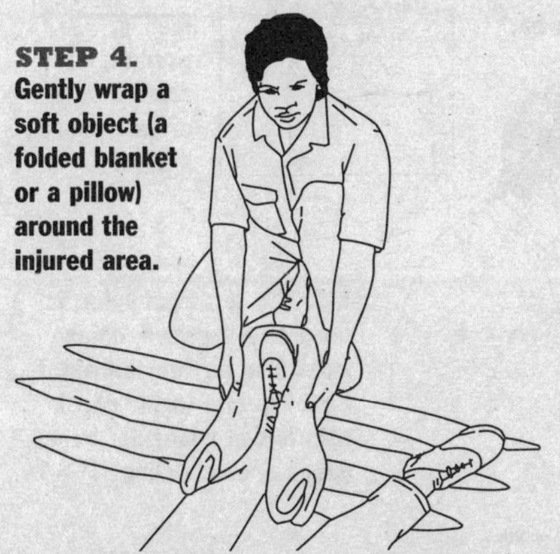

STEP 5. Tie triangular bandages securely.

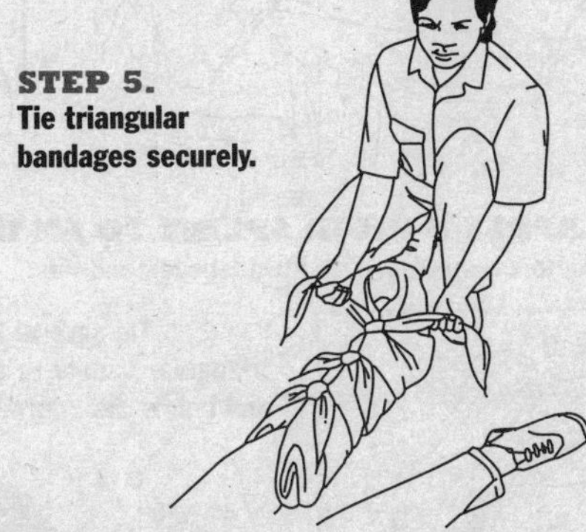

STEP 6. Recheck for feeling, warmth, and color. If you are not able to check warmth and color because a sock or shoe is in place, check for feeling.

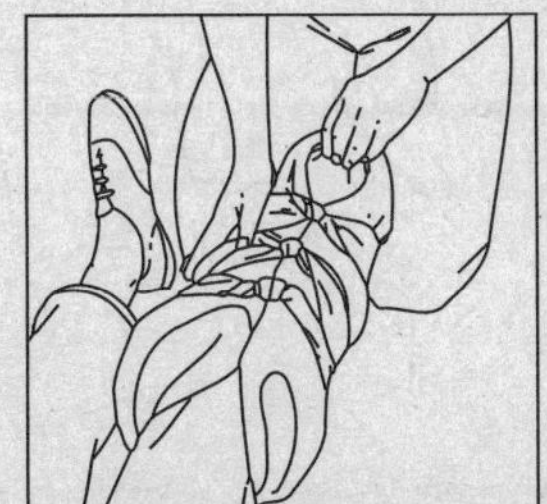

IF A PERSON IS UNABLE TO MOVE OR USE AN INJURED ARM...

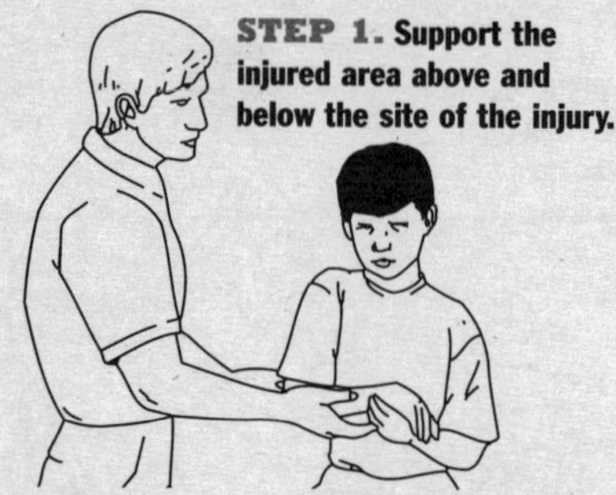

STEP 1. Support the injured area above and below the site of the injury.

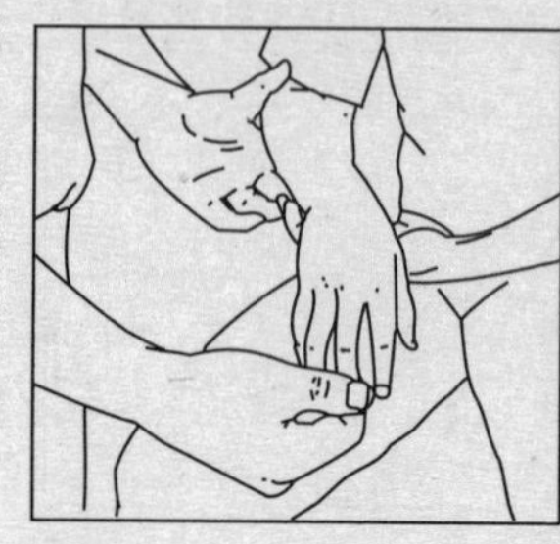

STEP 2. Check for feeling, warmth, and color before splinting to make sure the splint is not too tight. Then...

TO APPLY A SLING TO SPLINT AN INJURED ARM

First follow steps one and two (see above), and then...

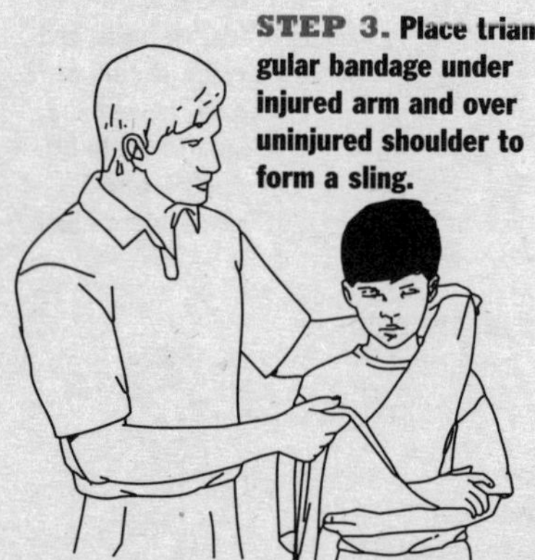

STEP 3. Place triangular bandage under injured arm and over uninjured shoulder to form a sling.

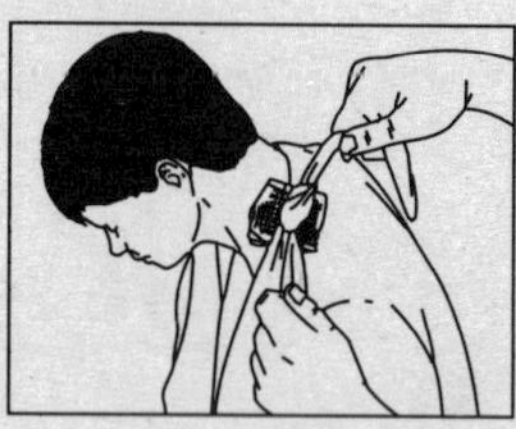

STEP 4. Tie ends of sling at side of neck.

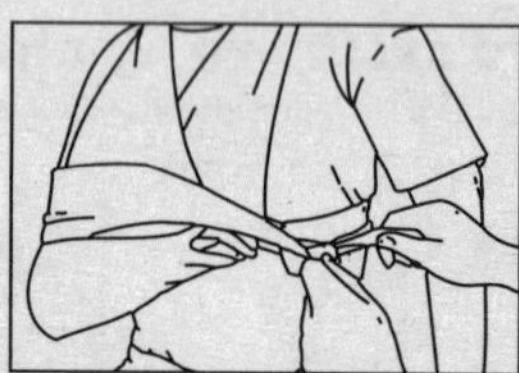

STEP 5. Bind injured area to chest with folded triangular bandage. Recheck for feeling, warmth, and color.

APPLY A RIGID SPLINT TO AN INJURED FOREARM OR WRIST

First follow steps one and two (above), and then...

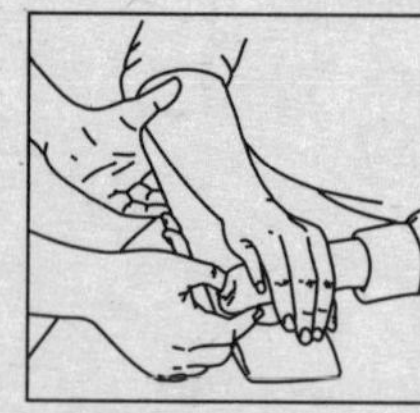

STEP 3. Place the rigid splint (board, magazine, etc.) under the injured area and the joints that are above and below it.

STEP 4. Tie several folded triangular bandages above and below the injured area.

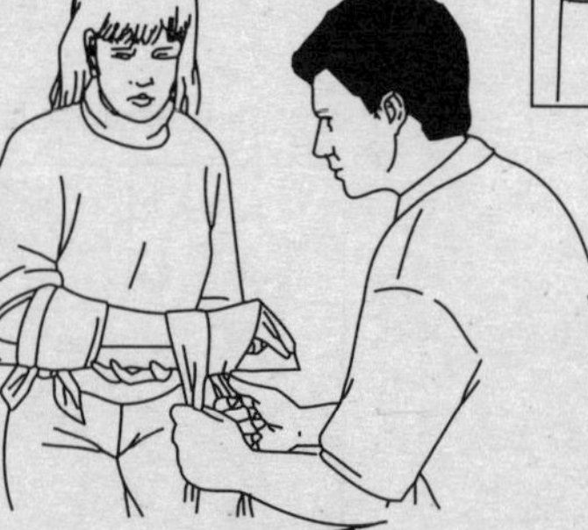

STEP 5. Recheck for feeling, warmth, and color. If cold or pale, loosen a little.

NOTE: If a rigid splint is used on a forearm, elbow must also be immobilized. Bind the arm to the chest with folded triangular bandages or use a sling.

SOURCE: Courtesy of the American Red Cross.

TREATING SKIN THAT'S SINGED

Bring temperature down, but don't use ice unless the injury is slight

Burns are classified as first, second, or third degree by how deeply the skin is damaged. It's not always easy to tell how serious a burn is at first inspection. Electrical burns frequently look small, for instance, but they may be much deeper than suspected. You can't always tell how bad a burn is from the pain, either, because really serious burns may destroy tissue nerve endings, leaving a victim with no feeling in the burn area. And burns whose severity is underestimated may end up needlessly infected. Here are the rules of the road when it comes to burns, from the American Red Cross.

■ **FIRST-DEGREE BURN:** A first-degree burn is on the skin's surface. It turns the skin red and dry, may cause a swell, and can be quite painful. The damage should heal within a week without leaving permanent scars.

■ **SECOND-DEGREE BURN:** A second-degree burn affects several top layers of skin, and not only reddens the skin, but leaves blisters that may pop and leak clear fluid, making the skin look wet. Pain and swelling are common with such burns, and the burned skin sometimes appears blotchy. Healing usually takes three to four weeks.

■ **THIRD-DEGREE BURN:** A third-degree burn not only destroys every skin layer but goes deep enough to destroy other underlying tissue such as fat, muscles, nerves, and even bones sometimes. The pain can range from very intense to relatively minor if nerve endings are destroyed. Unless quickly treated, the risk of infection not only soars, but fluid loss can destroy the body's thermostat and impair a victim's breathing, making the situation potentially life-threatening.

DO'S AND DON'TS FOR BURNS

To help you make the right first aid decisions when dealing with burns, the American Red Cross recommends the following:

DO'S

■ **Do cool a burn by flushing it with water.**

■ **Do cover the burn with a dry, clean covering, such as a sterile dressing.**

■ **Do keep the victim comfortable and keep him or her from getting chilled or overheated.**

DON'TS

■ **Don't apply ice directly to any burn unless it is very minor.**

■ **Don't touch a burn with anything except a clean covering.**

■ **Don't remove pieces of cloth that stick to the burned area.**

■ **Don't try to clean a severe burn.**

■ **Don't break blisters.**

■ **Don't use ointment on a severe burn. Although an antibiotic ointment can be used on a minor burn, ointments may exacerbate more severe burns by sealing in heat without providing pain relief.**

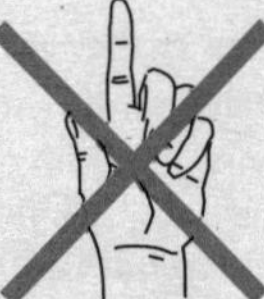

COPING WITH POISONING

Most cases involve children, but most deaths occur among adults

Ninety percent of all poisonings happen in the home. Most cases involve young children swallowing household or garden products or medications that are inappropriate. But most fatalities involve adults and are frequently suicides or drug-related. Here are the American Red Cross's suggestions as to what to do in most cases:

■ How can I tell if someone's been poisoned?

The physical clues to poisoning include nausea, vomiting, diarrhea, pain in the chest or abdomen, difficulty breathing, sweating, seizures, and shifts in consciousness. When the victim is conscious and old enough to communicate, ask him or her what happened. When this is not possible, carefully inspect the scene for clues. Do you see any open or overturned containers, any plants that don't look right, or any medicine cabinet that is opened? Are there any flames, smoke, or unusual smells?

■ What if I strongly suspect a poisoning?

Move the victim away from the poison source if necessary. Check his or her level of consciousness, breathing condition, and pulse. Treat any life-threatening factors. Then call a poison control center or emergency hotline with any information on what the victim may have been exposed to or swallowed.

■ What if the poison has been swallowed?

Never have a victim eat or drink unless medical professionals advise it. If you can't locate the poison source and the victim throws up, save some of the vomit for the hospital to test.

If you do know the poison, contact a poison control center for precise instructions on administering an antidote. If vomiting must be induced, using syrup of ipecac is generally recommended. For someone over 12 years of age, the normal dosage is two tablespoons of syrup, followed by two glasses of water. For children under 12, the dosage normally is one tablespoon followed by two glasses of water. The intended result should come within 20 minutes.

■ When is inducing vomiting a bad idea?

Never induce vomiting when the victim has taken an acid or alkali, which can burn the esophagus, throat, and mouth tissues. The same is true for petroleum products such as gasoline or kerosene.

■ What is the role of activated charcoal in treating poisoning?

A solution made from activated charcoal is often used to help neutralize poison that remains in the stomach even after vomiting. The charcoal comes in both liquid and powder forms and is sold in pharmacies over the counter. The powder form needs mixing with water so that it becomes milk shake–like in its consistency. Young children have a hard time swallowing the mixture and often need it dispensed to them at a hospital.

■ How should toxic fumes be handled?

When the victim's skin is pale or bluish, it's a tip-off that toxic fumes may have been inhaled. The most common toxic fumes are carbon monoxide from car exhaust, carbon dioxide from wells or sewers, and chlorine from swimming pools. Glues, cleaning solvents, and paints also give off fumes, as do drugs such as crack cocaine. The most important thing you can do for a toxic fume victim is to get the person to fresh air as soon as possible. If the victim has lost consciousness, start rescue breathing.

■ How should chemicals on skin be handled?

Flush the area in question with continuously running water and call the rescue service. When the chemical is dry and there's no running water, brush off the chemical and see a doctor as soon as possible.

NATURAL THREATS

THE TRUTH ABOUT INSECT STINGS

A wasp or yellow jacket at a picnic could send you to the hospital

Insect stings are responsible for inducing severe allergic reactions in one to two million people in the United States every year. An estimated 3 percent of the population is susceptible to such a reaction, and about 50 deaths occur each year, many involving adults.

The usual reaction to an insect sting is a mild degree of redness and pain, which normally disappears within one to two hours. As a rule, no treatment is required. But some people have an immune system that produces too much of an antibody called IgE (Immunoglobulin E), which, in combination with the venom, triggers an allergic reaction that can lead to extensive swelling that does not peak for 48 to 72 hours and may last as long as a full week.

A severe allergic reaction can involve the entire body, producing symptoms that include dizziness, weakness, and nausea. Stomach cramps and diarrhea may occur, as well as generalized hives (urticaria), itching, wheezing, difficulty in breathing, mental confusion, a sharp drop in blood pressure, shock, and, finally, unconsciousness. If medical treatment is not obtained immediately, the reaction may be fatal.

The common stinging insects can be divided into two families: the apids, which include honeybees and bumblebees; and the vespids, which include yellow jackets, hornets, and wasps. Of the two, apids are less aggressive than vespids but will sting when provoked. There are also several stinging ants. The fire ant is a major cause of allergic reactions in the Southeast, and the harvester ant is responsible for similar problems in the Southwest.

In the past, the only products available for treatment were processed from the whole body of the insect, termed "whole body extracts." It was found, however, that these extracts did not contain enough pure insect venom and were pronounced unreliable for both diagnosis and treatment.

Pure venoms, highly potent, are now available and are given in gradually stronger doses to stimulate the patient's immune system until it is able to become more resistant to the insect sting. Venoms are taken from honeybees, yellow jackets, yellow hornets, bald-faced hornets, and polistes wasps. Whole-body extracts are still utilized for ant hypersensitivity because ant venoms are not yet available.

For those subject to severe reactions, a physician may recommend a self-treatment kit, containing a syringe with epinephrine (adrenaline), which works within minutes to tighten the blood vessels and keep the airways open. Those who are susceptible should follow a physician's instructions for self-injection in the event of an insect sting.

Scientific studies have shown that a person who has had a previous reaction to an insect sting has a 60 percent chance of another reaction if he or she does not undergo desensitization. But you can reduce the likelihood of reactions to less than 5 percent after desensitization.

EXPERT TIP

Only the honeybee leaves a stinger and an attached venom sac in the skin of its victim. Removal of the stinger within two to three minutes may prevent some harmful effects. Remove the stinger with one quick scrape of the fingernail, but don't compress the sac—it might inject more venom.

—American Academy of Allergy and Immunology

EXPERT LIST

SNAKES, SPIDERS, AND OTHER BITERS

The American Red Cross outlines the different creatures that can bite you and what to do when they strike

ANIMAL BITES

In addition to obvious wounding, animal bites often pose the threat of rabies. Some signs of a rabid animal: a nocturnal animal that is active during day, an animal that normally avoids people that doesn't run away, an animal that seems partly paralyzed, or an animal that acts unusually ill-tempered or quiet.

■ **Physical signs:** Bite mark, bleeding.

■ **Care:** If bleeding is minor, wash wound. Control bleeding. Apply antibiotic ointment and cover. Seek immediate medical attention if wound bleeds severely or if animal seems rabid.

INSECT BITES

Bites can lead to allergic reaction and potentially life-threatening breathing emergency. Persons allergic to insect stings should always carry adrenaline pills and an injection kit containing epinephrine. Painful but rarely fatal in others.

■ **Physical signs:** Pain and swelling at the bite's location. Allergic reaction may cause swelling to spread to entire body and affect breathing.

■ **Care:** Remove stinger by scraping it away or using tweezers. Wash wound and cover. Apply cold pack. Watch for signs of allergic reaction.

MARINE LIFE STINGS

Possible allergic reaction resulting in potentially life-threatening breathing emergency. May make others ill at times. Occur in saltwater.

■ **Physical signs:** Possible marks, pain, swelling at sting's location. Allergic reaction may manifest more general swelling, difficulty in breathing.

■ **Care:** Soak area initially in saltwater. Apply cold-pack or paste of baking soda or meat tenderizer. Call local emergency service if necessary.

SNAKE BITES

There are two groups of poisonous snakes in the United States. Coral snakes can be found from North Carolina to southwestern New Mexico. Pit vipers are found all over, and include the copperhead, water moccasin, and rattlesnake. Most bites take place in inhabited areas, not the wilderness, but those living in remote, snake-infested areas should keep a snakebite kit with them and know how to use it.

■ **Physical signs:** Bite mark, pain, numbness.

■ **Care:** Wash wound and immobilize wounded area, keeping it below heart level. Call local emergency number. Do not apply ice. Do not use electric shock. Do not cut the wound or apply a tourniquet unless medical attention is impossible within 30 minutes.

SPIDER BITES

The black widow and the brown recluse can make you very sick or, in rare cases, kill you. Both are found in dark, out-of-the-way places such as wood piles. The black widow is black with a reddish hourglass shape on its underside. The brown recluse is light brown with a darker brown, violin-shaped marking on its back.

■ **Physical signs:** Bite mark, swelling, pain. Nausea and vomiting. Difficulty breathing or swallowing.

■ **Care:** Wash wound and apply a cold pack. Call medical professionals.

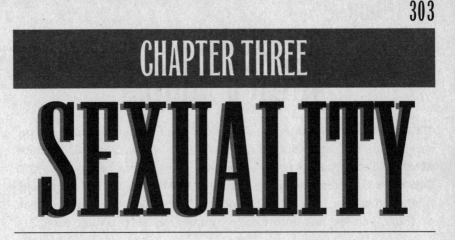

CHAPTER THREE

SEXUALITY

EXPERT QUOTES

"The flirtatious, not the attractive, get the attention."

—Dr. Helen Fisher, author of *The Anatomy of Love: The Mysteries of Mating, Marriage and Why We Stray*

Page 311

"Most co-working couples with successful relationships lead separate lives at work as much as possible."

—Lisa Mainiero, management professor and author of *Office Romance: Love, Power, and Sex in the Workplace*

Page 313

"Social pressure tends to be negative toward sexuality and aging. But the desire for intimacy goes through the end of life."

—Dr. Robert N. Butler, co-author of *Love and Sex After 60*

Page 330

THE YEAR AHEAD: **WATCH** married couples become the new sex symbols... **EXPECT** new research on the roots of homosexuality... **ANTICIPATE** legal fights over the safety of the contraceptive implant Norplant... **GET READY** for the approval of RU-486 as an abortion pill in America... **LOOK FOR** FDA approval for new drug treatments for impotence... **PAY ATTENTION** to the debate over the use of estrogen in relieving menopause's discomforts...

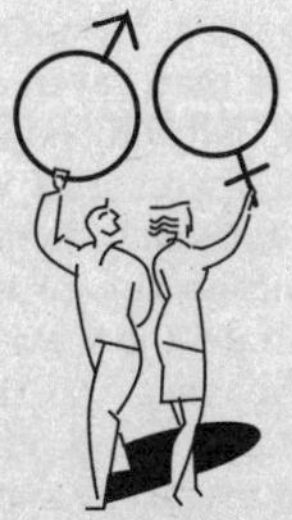

WAYS & MORES

BEHAVIOR

THE AMERICAN WAY OF SEX

The revelations of the most reliable study of sexual practices ever done

Birds do it, bees do it, and until recently it has been assumed that Americans do it more than virtually any other people on the face of the earth. But the sexual revolution may be mostly a sea change in what Americans are willing to say, hear, or watch about sex in the media rather than in what they're actually willing to do behind bedroom doors.

According to an extensive survey of American sexual behavior organized by researchers at the University of Chicago, more than 80 percent of adults had only one sexual partner, or none, in the last year; nearly 75 percent of American adults have sex no more than several times a month; and among married people, 75 percent of men and 85 percent of women say they have been faithful to their spouses.

The Chicago survey is considered far more accurate than earlier sex studies such as the ones by Alfred C. Kinsey, William Masters and Virginia Johnson, and popular magazines such as *Playboy* and *Redbook*. That's because the Chicago survey is the only one to select its pool of study subjects by true random sampling techniques rather than by relying on volunteers or identifying participants through means such as finding participants by searching at sex therapy clinics that cast doubt on the representative nature of the sample.

The Chicago survey dispels many myths about American sexual behavior. For instance, it reveals:

- Americans are not particularly adventuresome when it comes to picking sexual partners. People tend to pair up with those of the same race, approximate age, socioeconomic background, religion, and education. Most partners meet through common social networks, and half of all couples who end up marrying are introduced by friends or family members.

- Young, unmarried couples living together are the most sexually active group in America. But despite their staid reputation, married couples report being the most physically pleased and emotionally content with life.

The Chicago survey not only provides Americans with the first scientifically reliable gauge to what's typical sexual behavior and what's not, but it also helps to explain why Americans do what they do in the bedroom. The following three pages highlight some of the survey's findings.

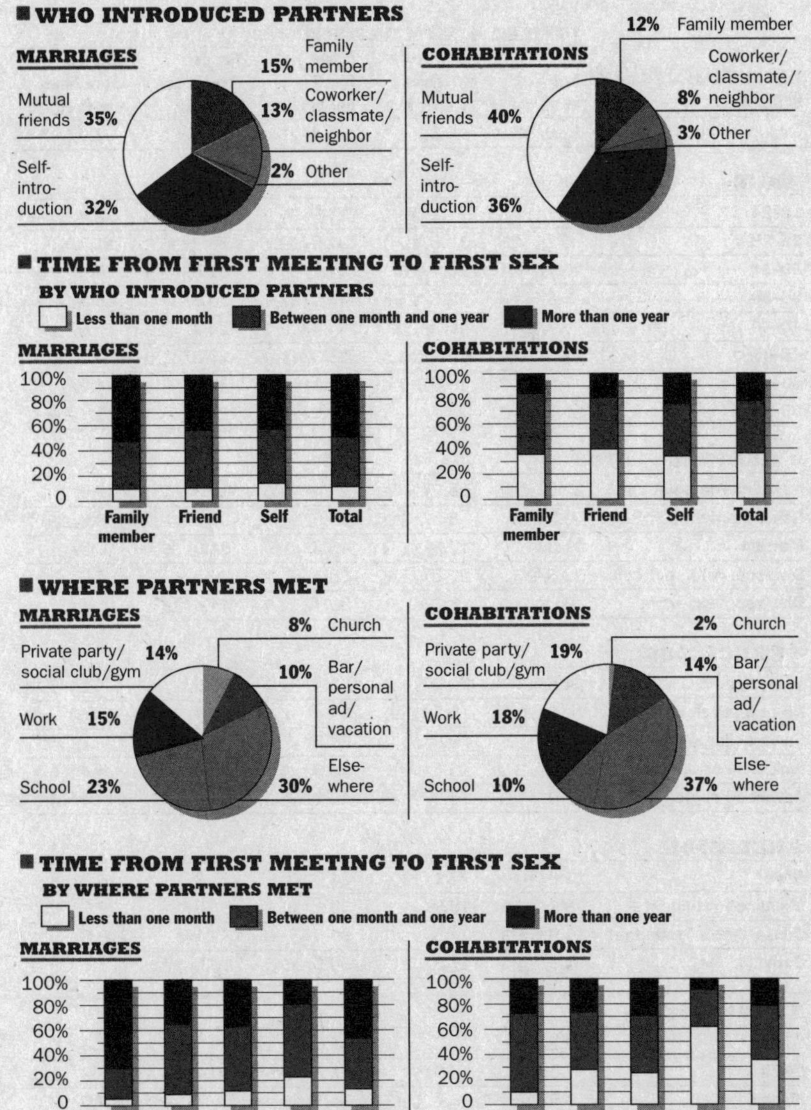

SOURCE: *The Social Organization of Sexuality: Sexual Practices in the United States,* by Edward O. Laumann, John H. Gagnon, Robert T. Michael, and Stuart Michaels, University of Chicago Press, 1994.

LIFE BETWEEN THE SHEETS

About a third of American adults have sex with someone else at least twice a week. Another third engage in sex with a partner no more than a few times a month, and the remainder are largely inactive sexually.

VARIABLES	FREQUENCY OF SEX IN THE PAST YEAR (%) MEN / WOMEN Not at all	A few times per year	A few times per month	Two to three times per week	Four or more times per week
Total population	22.0/30.2	26.2/23.5	25.4/26.0	18.8/13.3	27.6/7.0
AGE					
18–24	14.7/11.2	21.1/16.1	23.9/31.5	28.0/28.8	12.4/12.4
25–29	6.7/ 4.5	14.8/10.3	31.0/38.1	36.2/36.8	11.4/10.3
30–34	9.7/ 8.1	16.7/16.6	34.7/34.6	31.5/32.9	7.4/ 7.8
35–39	6.8/10.8	12.6/15.7	40.0/37.8	35.3/32.5	5.3/ 3.2
40–44	6.7/14.6	16.9/15.5	44.4/46.1	26.4/16.9	5.6/ 6.8
45–49	12.7/16.1	19.8/16.1	33.3/41.0	27.8/41.0	6.3/ 3.1
50–54	7.8/19.3	19.6/20.7	45.1/40.0	22.5/17.8	4.9/ 2.2
55–59	15.7/40.8	24.7/22.4	41.6/29.6	16.9/ 4.8	1.1/ 2.4
MARITAL STATUS					
Never married, not coh.	22.0/30.2	26.2/23.5	25.4/26.0	18.8/13.3	7.6/ 7.0
Never married, coh.	0.0/ 1.4	8.5/ 6.9	35.6/31.9	37.3/43.1	18.6/16.7
Married	1.3/ 3.0	12.8/11.9	46.5/42.5	31.9/36.1	6.6/ 7.3
Div./sep./wid., not coh.	23.8/34.3	22.5/23.2	28.5/21.9	20.5/16.8	4.6/ 3.7
Div./sep./wid., coh.	0.0/ 0.0	8.3/ 9.4	36.1/39.6	44.4/39.6	11.1/11.3
EDUCATION					
Less than HS	14.8/18.7	20.2/14.5	28.4/36.2	29.5/22.6	7.1/ 8.1
HS or equivalent	10.1/10.8	15.1/15.9	34.4/37.7	31.7/29.6	8.7/ 6.0
Some college/voc.	8.7/13.5	19.9/15.9	33.5/37.7	28.8/25.2	7.7/ 9.1
Finished college	9.0/12.5	15.8/18.3	43.9/33.5	25.8/29.7	5.4/ 6.1
Advanced degree	7.0/17.8	15.8/15.8	42.1/44.6	30.7/17.8	4.4/ 4.0
RELIGION					
None	12.6/10.1	25.1/18.9	24.6/36.5	26.8/25.7	10.9/ 8.8
Mainline Protestant	8.1/12.9	18.9/17.4	38.1/39.8	27.0/25.1	7.8/ 4.7
Conservative Protestant	10.9/14.8	14.5/14.3	35.6/36.0	32.1/26.0	6.9/ 8.9
Catholic	7.9/14.4	17.3/15.6	36.5/37.0	30.6/27.5	7.6/ 5.4
ETHNICITY					
White	9.7/12.8	17.3/16.4	35.6/38.1	29.6/26.2	7.8/ 6.7
Black	8.3/17.0	16.5/17.0	37.6/32.5	30.4/26.2	7.2/ 7.1
Hispanic	8.5/11.4	14.7/10.2	34.1/35.2	28.7/33.0	14.0/10.2

SOURCE: *The Social Organization of Sexuality: Sexual Practices in the United States*, University of Chicago Press, 1994.

INTIMATE EXPERIENCES

Most Americans—over 80 percent of all adults under age 60—have one or no sex partners in any given year. Over a lifetime, men tend to have more sex partners than women.

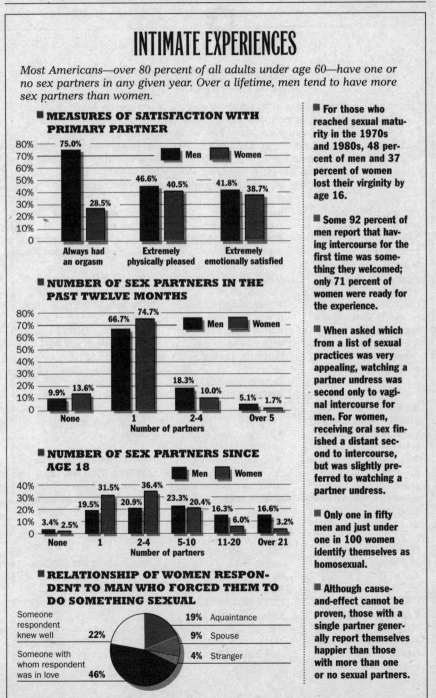

MEASURES OF SATISFACTION WITH PRIMARY PARTNER

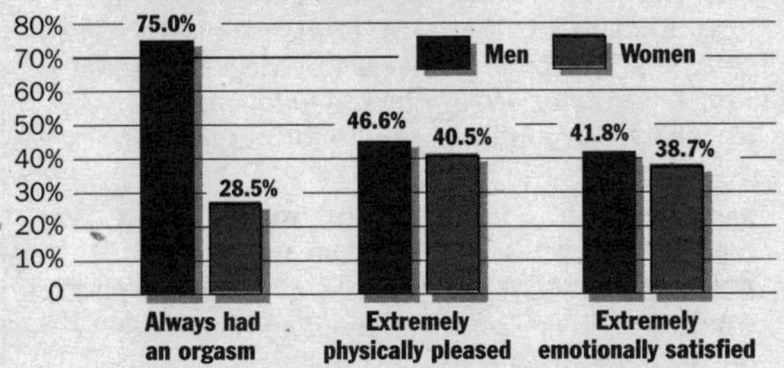

NUMBER OF SEX PARTNERS IN THE PAST TWELVE MONTHS

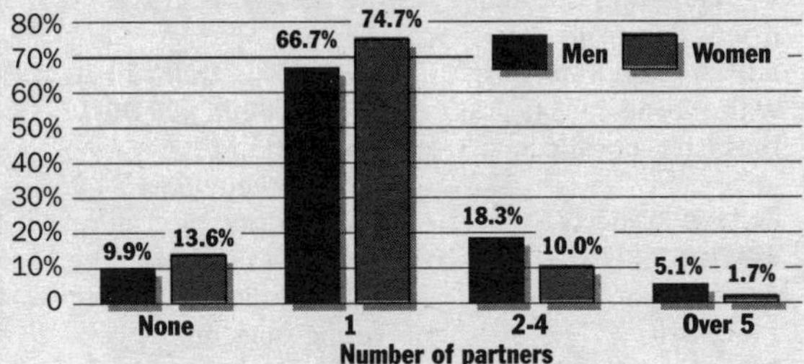

NUMBER OF SEX PARTNERS SINCE AGE 18

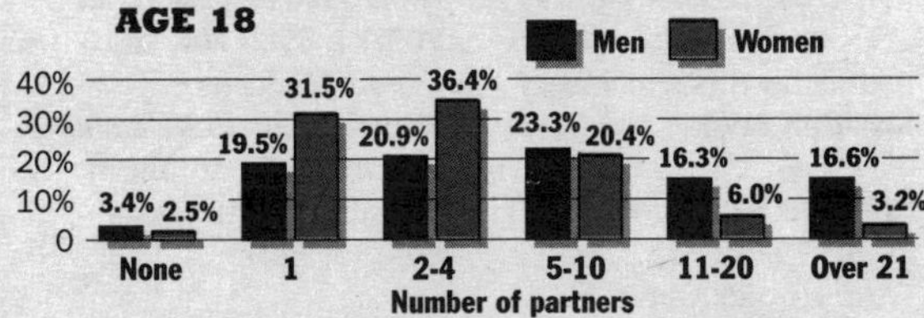

RELATIONSHIP OF WOMEN RESPONDENT TO MAN WHO FORCED THEM TO DO SOMETHING SEXUAL

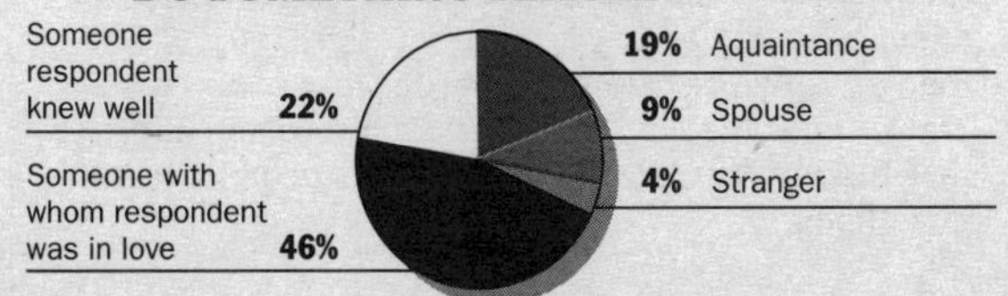

- For those who reached sexual maturity in the 1970s and 1980s, 48 percent of men and 37 percent of women lost their virginity by age 16.

- Some 92 percent of men report that having intercourse for the first time was something they welcomed; only 71 percent of women were ready for the experience.

- When asked which from a list of sexual practices was very appealing, watching a partner undress was second only to vaginal intercourse for men. For women, receiving oral sex finished a distant second to intercourse, but was slightly preferred to watching a partner undress.

- Only one in fifty men and just under one in 100 women identify themselves as homosexual.

- Although cause-and-effect cannot be proven, those with a single partner generally report themselves happier than those with more than one or no sexual partners.

EXPERT PICKS

SEXUALITY 101 FOR KIDS

Knowing what to think of sex is difficult enough if you are an adult. To a child the physical and emotional changes that accompany puberty can be not only bewildering, but even scary. For books that may aid the educational process, Dr. Marty Klein, a sex therapist, family counselor, and author of Ask Me Anything: A Sex Therapist Answers the Most Important Questions for the '90s *(Simon & Schuster, 1993) has the following recommendations. Some are written for children, others for parents:*

ARE YOU THERE GOD? IT'S ME, MARGARET
Judy Blume, Dell, 1970, $3.99
■ A classic from the perennially popular writer for teens, this is a charming, humorous novelette about junior high school girls who are dealing with the changes brought on by puberty.

DID THE SUN SHINE BEFORE YOU WERE BORN?
Sol & Judith Gordon, Prometheus, 1982, $3.95
■ For parents to read to their three- to seven-year-olds. The book answers the basic questions that a child has about sexuality.

THE NEW TEENAGE BODY BOOK
Kathy McCoy & Charles Wibblesman, W. Morrow & Co., 1975, $14.95
■ Answers questions about self-esteem, safe sex, and many of the other issues faced by adolescents.

RAISING A CHILD CONSERVATIVELY IN A SEXUALLY PERMISSIVE WORLD
Sol & Judith Gordon, Simon & Schuster, 1983, $7.95
■ A calm and rational discussion from the authors about dealing with morals in a fashion that isn't moralistic.

RAISING SEXUALLY HEALTHY CHILDREN
Lynn Leight, Avon, 1990, $10
■ The subtitle, *A Loving Guide for Parents, Teachers and Caregivers*, effectively sums up this sensitively written book.

TALKING WITH YOUR CHILD ABOUT SEX
Mary Calderone & James Ramey, Ballantine, 1984, $3.95
■ Full of the questions that kids inevitably ask about sexuality and many positive, sensitive, and responsible answers that their parents can give them.

WHAT YOU CAN DO TO AVOID AIDS
Earvin "Magic" Johnson, Random House, 1992, $3.99
■ A sports legend talks directly to teens about the facts of AIDS.

WHAT'S HAPPENING TO MY BODY? A BOOK FOR BOYS
Lynda Madaras, Newmarket, 1988, $9.95
■ With drawings, stories, and a bit of humor, the author talks straight to young boys about puberty.

WHAT'S HAPPENING TO MY BODY? A BOOK FOR GIRLS
Lynda Madaras, Newmarket, 1988, $9.95
■ More straight talk in the same format, this time for girls.

WHEN SEX IS THE SUBJECT: ATTITUDES AND ANSWERS FOR YOUNG PEOPLE
Pamela Wilson, ETR Associates, 1991, $17.95
■ For parents and teachers, a discussion about how kids actually learn about sex.

EXPERT Q&A

A TIME FOR STRAIGHT TALK

Nothing helps a gay child more than being able to communicate

Parents who learn that they have a gay or lesbian child often are unsure how to handle the news. Ritch Savin-Williams, a professor of development and clinical psychology at Cornell University and co-editor of *The Lives of Lesbians, Gays and Bisexuals: Children to Adults* (with Kenneth M. Cohen, Harcourt Brace, 1995), addresses some of their most common concerns.

■ How should a parent respond when a child confides that he or she is homosexual?

What parents should do, first and foremost, is offer unconditional love. They should tell the child that no matter what your sexual orientation is, the love I have for you is still there. It has always been there, and it will continue to be there. They also have to be prepared to talk openly. They may be shocked, they may be disappointed, they may be hurt, but that should not close down the lines of communication. Parents ought to be willing and able to talk about safer sex, for example. Of course, that's true for parents of any child, but if they haven't discussed it before this point, certainly this is an appropriate time.

■ Is there any advice a parent should give a child in this situation?

They need to be very realistic about the consequences of coming out at school, to prepare the child for the possibility of peer harassment. And although many parents might not be able to do this, I also recommend asking about the child's perspective on the process of self-recognition: How long have you been aware of these feelings? What kinds of struggles have you had? Then the parents will understand better what their child has been through, and the child has an opportunity to talk about the emotions and feelings and reservations he or she has experienced.

■ Should a parent have noticed early signs of a child's homosexuality?

Gays and lesbians have a diversity of childhood experiences. However, I think in most cases when you have an extreme expression of gender atypical behavior, then you're likely to have a gay, lesbian, or bisexual child.

What I've found from talking to parents is that many of them knew on some level before their child told them. They picked up on something, though maybe not consciously. Possibly they wondered why their adolescent child didn't put up posters of the opposite sex on the walls, for example, or show any interest in dating. A mother once asked me about her son who enjoyed playing with dolls and didn't seem to like more masculine toys. She wondered if she should enforce playing with the typical masculine toys and games, and I think her real concern was that he not grow up to be gay.

Other parents have absolutely no idea until the child tells them. Recently I talked to a guy who had played football and baseball and been on the track and wrestling teams in high school, and he realized early that he was attracted to his teammates. His homosexuality came as a surprise to his family because he didn't fit their stereotypes.

■ What does the research reveal about the kind of child who turns out to be gay?

Research has shown that the most extreme gender atypical kids do grow up to be gay, lesbian, or bisexual, but that doesn't account for all gay, lesbian, and bisexual youths, and certainly there are heterosexual kids who engage in those behaviors, too. If I were a parent and I saw my child being very gender atypical, I would prepare myself to accept that my child may not be heterosexual, and that it's fine. My advice to the mother whose son played with dolls was that there was nothing she could do. If you force your child not to play with the toys he likes, what kind of message are you giving and what kind of rapport will you have with the child? Furthermore, you will never change his sexual orientation by changing his toy preference.

■ Are the parents responsible for the child's sexual orientation?

I think that is probably parents' number one concern. They often suffer from self-blame, and wonder what they did wrong: Did I not pay enough attention to my child or did I pay too much attention? Did I smother him or her, or was I too distant? Should I have made my son play football? Did I let my kids play with the wrong friends? They may think their marriage set a bad example of heterosexuality, or blame the other parent.

But the support group Parents, Families, and Friends of Lesbians and Gays (PFFLAG, ☎ 202-638-4200) has three critical central tenets for parents to remember. First of all, researchers and scientists agree that it's natural to be attracted to members of the same sex. That is, homosexuality is a natural variation on the biology of the species. Not all children are right-handed or have brown eyes, and not all of them are attracted to members of the opposite sex. Second, sexual orientation is not a choice. Regardless of what actually causes homosexuality, the child certainly did not go out one day and decide to be gay or lesbian. Finally, PFFLAG emphasizes that no particular pattern of child-rearing characteristically produces homosexual children. They come from families of all economic, racial, and social groups; families with aloof mothers and strong fathers; strong mothers and absent fathers—none of these variations determines sexual orientation.

■ Whom can parents talk to about how they feel?

Often parents' initial reaction is fear—fear for the child's future, for what the neighbors or their own families will think. They may feel alone, that no one else has this kind of experience. They may feel angry at the other parent, at themselves, or at the child for causing this kind of turmoil in the family. But it's very important for parents to grow from this hurt and pain, and it is absolutely critical that they have outlets. Sometimes it's not appropriate for them to talk with their child about all of their concerns—if the child is still young, for example, the parent may need an adult forum. A spouse can provide support, and so can a counselor, rabbi, or priest, and organizations like PFFLAG are especially helpful. Parents also should educate themselves through books, videos, and other sources that can dispel some of their fears and myths about gays and lesbians.

■ How might my child's sexual orientation affect the other children in the family?

Parents sometimes fear that their other children's sexuality may be influenced by a gay or lesbian sibling, but again, sexual orientation is not a choice. Actually, it's not unusual for some kids to tell a brother or a sister first, for support, or to get advice about approaching the parents. Then it becomes a family issue.

■ How should I handle friends or family members who are unaccepting?

Ultimately the parent has to stand firmly behind his or her child, and other family members will come around eventually. They may never be totally comfortable or as open as they should be, but the parent can tackle the problem with continuous support for the child.

■ What can I do to make the coming-out process easier for my child?

It's important to avoid denial, telling the child that it's just a phase, for example, or a kind of rebellion. It shouldn't be boxed away as a family secret. It's also a bad idea to have a counselor or a psychiatrist try to get the child "converted." No evidence exists that you can change sexual orientation.

Most important, parents need to understand that their child is the same person after disclosing as he or she was before. In many ways, disclosure is a gift. It means the child respected them enough, or wanted to maintain a strong relationship enough that they chose to bring out this potential explosive device. Rather than feel as if they have a new child, parents should realize that they now know their child better.

COURTSHIP

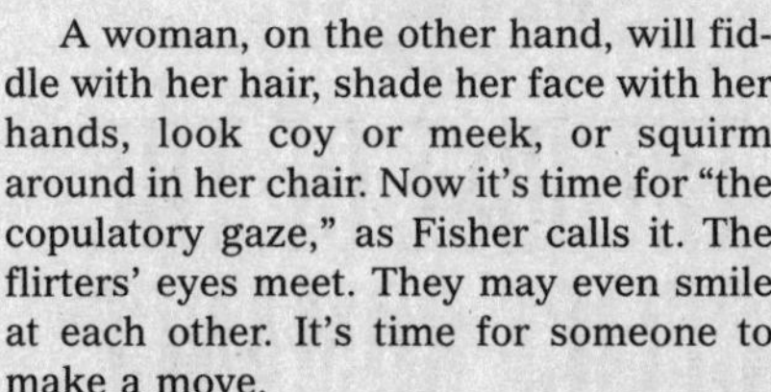

THE FINE ART OF FLIRTING

It's not how gorgeous you are, but how you play the game

She bats her eyelashes and smiles coyly. He throws back his head as he laughs loudly. Their eyes meet. A pattern as old as the story of Adam and Eve has commenced. It's the flirting game.

Scientists who have studied courtship in animals are now turning their attention to humans. And they're finding that we're a lot like our feathered or four-legged friends. "A man may arch his back while he's sitting at a bar stool," says Dr. Helen Fisher, a Rutgers University anthropologist and author of *The Anatomy of Love: The Mysteries of Mating, Marriage and Why We Stray* (Fawcett, 1993). "A lobster does the same thing. A woman will swing her hips; a dog will almost swagger. A woman will look coy; an antelope will turn itself sideways. A man will show off; a peacock will too."

"There's a great deal of non-verbal behavior to flirting," Fisher says. First, men and women both set up shop. "In a bar, a man will throw his coat over the chair to set up a space for himself. A woman will sit in a highly visible place," she says.

Next, they spot each other across a smoky room. At this point in the game, a man will tend to gesture boldly, by using his whole arm to pick up his drink, for example. A man will also tend to laugh very loudly during this stage, and, "like all kinds of male animals, they arch their backs," Fisher says.

A woman, on the other hand, will fiddle with her hair, shade her face with her hands, look coy or meek, or squirm around in her chair. Now it's time for "the copulatory gaze," as Fisher calls it. The flirters' eyes meet. They may even smile at each other. It's time for someone to make a move.

"A lot of flirting ends with talking," says Fisher. Once someone opens his or her mouth, it gives away education, intelligence, and intentions. As a pick-up line, the anthropologist suggests saying something that requires some feedback. "It's best to ask questions or give a compliment because they require a response."

If the couple makes it past the talking stage, then it's time to move on to the next level: touching. The woman is almost always the first to touch, Fisher says. A woman will graze the man's shoulder, or touch his arm. "If he winces, she'll never try again," says Fisher. "If he touches back, she will."

At this point, the two start mirroring each other's body language. He picks up his beer, she picks up her beer, he takes a swig, she takes a swig, he burps....

But what exactly do men and women want? Fisher says that because men once hunted on the plains, they are much more visual than women. A man looks for a healthy woman who can bear children, with clear skin, bright eyes, and a buoyant personality. "The flirtatious, not the attractive, get the attention," she says.

Because of all those years of being cooped up in a cave with the kids, women want a man who is verbal. "Women want to be courted with words. Women want face-to-face contact," says Fisher.

And despite progress for women in the workplace, she is also looking for a man who can support her and her children financially, Fisher says. "More regularly women pick the rich banker instead of the sensitive poet."

WORKPLACE

THE RISE OF THE OFFICE ROMANCE

Old rules about dating co-workers are giving way to new realities

Ask a couple of the '90s where they were when Cupid's arrow struck and chances are they'll say the office. "We've become very work-centered, so the reality is that the workplace is now one of our primary meeting places," says Richard Levin, a clinical psychologist and chairman of Work/Life Enterprises, a Brookline, Mass., consulting firm that helps companies become more family-friendly.

Long workdays that leave little time or energy for the social circuit and the increasing presence of women in formerly male-dominated spheres have made the office a viable, even attractive, alternative to cruising the club scene or scanning the personal ads. People in the same line of work can be sure they have at least one major interest in common. And co-workers who date each other avoid fear of the unknown, as Lisa Mainiero, a professor of management at Fairfield University, points out in Office *Romance: Love, Power and Sex in the Workplace*.

"With the difficulties involved in meeting people of kindred spirit, and the rampant fear of sexually transmitted diseases, we are more comfortable establishing relationships with those whom we already know well," she writes.

It also helps that companies are updating their attitudes toward office lovebirds. The fraternization policies that pervaded corporate culture in the past almost always required one member of a soon-to-be-married office couple to leave the company.

"The woman usually ended up looking elsewhere for work," Mainiero says. "In the past decade, corporations have realized that those policies were somewhat neanderthal."

In fact, a recent *Fortune* magazine survey of 200 corporate chief executives found that 70 percent of them believe office romance is "none of the company's business." And the Society for Human Resource Management reports that in a survey of its members, who are personnel managers in industries from construction to finance, nearly 72 percent don't think employers should be allowed to require a member of a co-working couple to resign if they marry.

Though companies' approaches to office romance are changing, a slight generation gap is still noticeable in the opinions of their employees. According to a 1993 Gallup poll, working men and women under 40 are more likely than their older counterparts to say they would consider dating a co-worker.

No surprise there, says Levin. "The younger workforce has a totally different attitude about work anyway," he explains. "For example, they're not motivated as much by power and money and success. They tend to look more for a balance between work and family."

Office romances can be wonderful, but they require careful planning and maintenance. Mainiero says the most successful relationships she has come across in her research involve people who work in different departments, have different business contacts, and follow different career paths.

Levin sees the same tendency among couples he counsels in his private practice. "As long as people aren't working together too closely, there doesn't seem to be any negative impact on the relationship," he says. He reports that one executive actually saw increased productivity when two employees became romantically involved—they spent more time at the office because they weren't always rushing off to see each other.

Though the office may be a good place to meet a potential mate, the pick-up tactics tolerated at a singles bar are unacceptable at the water cooler. Companies are responding to the increasing awareness of sexual harassment by creating strict policies to deal with the issue. But sexual harassment guidelines shouldn't be extended to outlaw consensual office romances, insists David Weis, a professor of human development and family studies

EXPERT TIPS

IN THE COMPANY OF A COLLEAGUE

Some important do's and don'ts of an office love affair

Office romantics who want to keep their careers and their love lives out of the circular file should heed the advice of Lisa Mainiero, a professor of management at Fairfield University in Fairfield, Conn., and the author of *Office Romance: Love, Power and Sex in the Workplace* (Macmillan, 1989):

■ **Don't fall in love with your boss.** While peer relationships can be manageable in the workplace, research shows very clearly that "hierarchical romance" brings up concerns about favoritism, exploitation, and low morale among employees. The lower-level person struggles (usually without success) to live down the stigma of sleeping his or her way to the top, while the higher-level person's business judgment suddenly looks questionable. People can end up committing career suicide.

■ **Be clear about your intentions, but don't force the issue.** If you sense that your interest in a coworker is not reciprocated, back off immediately. The office is not the place to be persistent. At the first indication that the other person is not interested, drop your pursuit because if you don't, it can be considered harassment.

■ **Be professional at all times.** Don't have lunch with your lover every day, hang out in his or her office, or hold hands in the hallway. When you're at work, act as you would around any other colleague. Most co-working couples with successful relationships lead separate lives at work as much as possible. Some married couples drive in separately, for example, or use different last names. There should be clear boundaries between work and after-hours relationships.

■ **Keep up the professionalism when it's over.** Though breaking up is hard to do, couples who successfully maintain their work relationship after the romance has died have an easier time. It's a good idea to set up a kind of "psychic contract" at the beginning of the relationship, outlining ground rules for making the office a romance-free zone and talking about the best way to handle a possible breakup.

at Bowling Green State University in Ohio.

"Policies will fail that forbid all relationships," he says. "When people find each other attractive, they will act on that. And people who work together can have very satisfying relationships."

"Sexual harassment policies have made people a little more cautious, but I don't think they're putting a lid on the number of office romances," adds Levin. "Though people sometimes try to lump them together, the two issues are separate. Trying to control one is not necessarily going to prevent the other."

The benefits of an office relationship can extend even beyond the couple involved. Mainiero's observations of couples in the workplace have convinced her that their influence can motivate other employees, minimize personality conflicts, and increase communication among departments.

"Attraction and romance at work bring out the best in all of us," she writes, "as long as it is handled properly by the couple."

EXPERT PICKS

SHOW-AND-TELL FOR ADULTS

Most so-called "adult" videos actually appeal to a fairly adolescent mind-set. Some are intended for a more mature audience, however—couples looking for frank and explicit information to understand and improve their sex lives. This sub-genre includes commentary by qualified sex educators and demonstrations that emphasize verbal communication and foreplay rather than extreme close-ups and bizarre physical attributes. Here are some of the best available videos for adults as selected by Dr. Robert Birch, the audiovisual review editor of the Journal of Sex Education and Therapy *and a licensed sex therapist.*

GENERAL KNOWLEDGE

THE BETTER SEX VIDEO SERIES: VOLS. 1–3
Townsend Institute, 1992, $29.95 each
■ "Better Sexual Techniques," "Advanced Sexual Techniques," and "Making Sex Fun with Games and Toys."
☎ **800-888-1900**

EROTIC MASSAGE
Secret Garden, 1989, $29.95
■ Features a male and a female massage therapist who both discuss erotic massage techniques as they demonstrate on partners.
☎ **800-843-0305**

SEX: A LIFELONG PLEASURE
NTV Entertainment Ltd., 1991. $29.95 each
■ A five-tape series. The first two, "Harmony" and "Enjoying Sex," are recommended for their emphasis on non-coital sexuality.
☎ **800-843-0305**

SEXUAL POSITIONS FOR LOVERS: BEYOND THE MISSIONARY POSITION
Sinclair Institute, 1993, $29.95
■ Demonstrations include ideas for dealing with pregnancy or back problems.
☎ **800-955-0888**

SPEAKING OF SEX
Sinclair Institute, 1994, $29.95
■ Five internationally known sex therapists answer common questions as five couples demonstrate methods for intercourse and foreplay.
☎ **800-955-0888**

SPECIAL SITUATIONS

BECOMING ORGASMIC
Sinclair Institute, 1993, $29.95
■ Originally distributed only to therapists, this video for women who have trouble reaching orgasm has been updated and released to the public.
☎ **800-955-0888**

THE BETTER SEX VIDEO SERIES: VOL. 8
Townsend Institute, 1992, $29.95
■ "You Can Last Longer" info for men with ejaculatory control problems.
☎ **800-888-1900**

GETTING IT RIGHT: A GAY YOUNG MALE'S GUIDE TO SAFER SEX
Greenwood/Cooper, 1994, $39.95
■ Includes alternatives to sexual positions in which bodily fluid is exchanged.
☎ **800-959-9843**

SEXUALITY REBORN
Kessler Institute for Rehabilitation, 1994, $40
■ Physically disabled couples demonstrate alternative techniques.
☎ **800-435-8866**

WELL SEXY WOMEN: A LESBIAN'S GUIDE TO SAFER SEX
Greenwood/Cooper, 1993, $24.95
■ Demonstration of positions and techniques.
☎ **800-959-9843**

BIRTH CONTROL

CONTRACEPTIVES THAT DON'T QUIT

Norplant protects for five years, yet Depo-Provera is winning more fans

In 1990, when the Food and Drug Administration approved a new contraceptive known as Norplant for use in the United States, many assumed that the new product would join birth control pills and condoms as one of the dominant forms of contraception in America.

Similar to birth control pills in its chemical makeup, the Norplant device provides highly reliable, reversible contraceptive protection for up to five years. But reported difficulties with the removal of Norplant, which is a contraceptive implant that goes into the underside of a woman's upper arm, and controversy about potential side effects have quieted much of the early enthusiasm for the drug. Instead, another recently approved hormonal contraceptive, Depo-Provera, which is taken by injection and provides about 14 weeks of protection per treatment, is winning wider approval from American women.

Both Norplant and Depo-Provera are based on progestin, a synthetic version of the hormone progesterone that the body produces during menstruation. Progestin protects against pregnancy by inhibiting ovulation, impeding fertilization, and thinning the endometrium (the lining of the uterus), making implantation of a fertilized egg very difficult.

Both Norplant and Depo-Provera are considered over 99 percent effective in preventing pregnancy when administered correctly, but the way they work is very different. Norplant delivers its dosage by employing a series of six matchstick-sized time-release capsules that must be surgically implanted into a woman's upper arm using local anesthesia. If inserted during the first seven days of the menstrual cycle, it becomes effective within 24 hours.

Depo-Provera is injected, rather than implanted, into the muscle of a woman's buttock or an upper arm. The treatment is administered every 12 weeks to ensure that protection from the previous injection has not yet worn off. Fertility may take several months to return for a woman discontinuing Depo-Provera, but more than three-quarters of women who stop in order to conceive become pregnant within 12 months, and more than 90 percent succeed within two years.

The side effects of both Norplant and Depo-Provera are similar to those of women taking the pill. They can include irregular menstrual bleeding and spotting, weight fluctuations both up and down, breast tenderness, headaches, hair loss, and dizziness at times. But unlike Norplant, whose effects can be quickly reversed at any time by removing the implants, Depo-Provera's effects can't be reversed in a woman experiencing side effects until the shot's 14-week cycle has run its course.

Norplant's greatest appeal may be for women who have finished their childbearing but do not wish to undergo sterilization, and for those whose health conditions preclude the use of the Pill or other birth control measures. It is inappropriate for women who are breast-feeding during their first six weeks after delivery or have unexplained vaginal bleeding, blood clots, inflammation of the veins, or a serious liver disease. It is also off-limits to women with a history of breast cancer.

Depo-Provera is not recommended for pregnant women because of a possible link to premature birth. But, unlike Norplant, there is no restriction on use by women who are breast-feeding.

FACT FILE:

BIRTH CONTROL BY THE NUMBERS

■ *Sterilization is the most frequently used contraceptive technique in the U.S.*

Method	Percent who use it
■ **FOR WOMEN**	
Pill	25%
Spermicides (foams, creams, gels)	6%
Diaphragm/cervical cap	5.7%
Sponge	1.1%
Implants (Norplant)	1%
IUD	1%
■ **FOR MEN AND WOMEN**	
Sterilization/tubal ligation	27%
Condoms	19%
Withdrawal/rhythm	7%

SOURCE: Ortho Annual Birth Control Study, 1993.

Both techniques may appeal to women who seek a highly reliable—and highly private—contraceptive method. Depo-Provera requires more frequent visits to a doctor or clinic for treatment, but at about $35 per shot and usually no more than $47 to $80 for a pre-shot examination, it is less of a financial burden than Norplant, which costs between $500 and $750 for insertion by a trained practitioner and another $50 to $150 for removal.

Norplant has been plagued by two other major complaints by users as well. One has been charges, unsubstantiated by scientific studies, that Norplant contributes to everything from strokes to cancer to autoimmune diseases. The drug's manufacturer, Wyeth-Ayerst, revised its labeling to acknowledge that adverse reactions have been reported since the product went on the market, but noted, with the FDA's approval, that health problems such as stroke, thrombosis, and heart attack that have stricken Norplant users on occasion could be entirely coincidental and have nothing to do with the fact that the woman may have been a Norplant user.

Even more controversial has been the difficulties that some women have experienced during the removal of their implants from just below the skin. Because of problems in some physicians' training and techniques for inserting and removing the hormonal rods, some patients report the procedure proved unexpectedly painful and resulted in unsightly scarring. A number of class-action lawsuits have been filed and are being vigorously contested by the manufacturer, but the adverse publicity appears to have slowed the product's acceptance markedly.

Still, properly implanted and removed by trained medical personnel, Norplant has much to recommend for women seeking reliable, long-term, reversible birth control that demands very little involvement on their part from month-to-month. For women wanting something less than five years' protection from a single implant, Norplant's manufacturer is also developing Norplant II, which would use just two rods to provide up to three years' protection.

LOVER'S GUIDE

PROTECTION FOR EVERY OCCASION

Birth control techniques don't work unless they're used regularly

The following efficacy rates, provided by the U.S. Public Health Service, are yearly estimates based on several studies. Methods that are dependent on conscientious use are subject to a greater chance of human error and reduced effectiveness. Without contraception, some 60 to 85 percent of sexually active women would likely become pregnant within a year.

MALE CONDOM

About 85 percent effective

■ **Use:** Applied immediately before intercourse; used only once and discarded. Nonprescription.
■ **Risks:** Rare irritation and allergic reactions.
■ **STD protection:** Latex condoms help protect against sexually transmitted diseases, including herpes and HIV.

FEMALE CONDOM

74 to 79 percent effective

■ **Use:** Applied immediately before intercourse; used only once and discarded. Nonprescription.
■ **Risks:** Rare irritation and allergic reactions.
■ **STD protection:** May give some protection against sexually transmitted disease, including herpes and HIV; but not as effective as male latex condom.

SPERMICIDES USED ALONE

70 to 80 percent effective

■ **Use:** Applied no more than an hour before intercourse. Nonprescription.
■ **Risks:** Rare irritation and allergic reactions.
■ **STD Protection:** Unknown.

SPONGE

72 to 82 percent effective

■ **Use:** Can insert hours before intercourse and be left in place up to 24 hours; used once and discarded. Nonprescription.
■ **Risks:** Rare irritation and allergic reactions; difficult removal; very rarely, toxic shock syndrome.
■ **STD protection:** None.

DIAPHRAGM WITH SPERMICIDE

82 to 94 percent effective

■ **Use:** Inserted before intercourse; can be left in place 24 hours, but additional spermicide must be inserted if intercourse is repeated. Prescription.
■ **Risks:** Rare irritation and allergic reactions; bladder infection; very rarely, toxic shock syndrome.
■ **STD protection:** None.

CERVICAL CAP WITH SPERMICIDE

At least 82 percent effective

■ **Use:** Can remain in place for 48 hours, not necessary to reapply spermicide upon repeated intercourse; may be difficult to insert. Prescription.
■ **Risks:** Abnormal Pap test; vaginal or cervical infections; very rarely, toxic shock syndrome.
■ **STD protection:** None.

PILLS

97 to 99 percent effective

■ **Use:** Pill must be taken on daily schedule, regardless of the frequency of intercourse. Prescription.
■ **Risks:** Blood clots, heart attacks, strokes, gallbladder disease, liver tumors, water retention, hypertension, mood change, nausea; not for smokers.
■ **STD protection:** None.

IMPLANT (NORPLANT)

99 percent effective

■ **Use:** Effective 24 hours after implantation for approximately five years; can be removed by physician at any time. Requires prescription, minor outpatient surgical procedure.
■ **Risks:** Menstrual cycle irregularity; headaches, nervousness, depression, nausea and dizziness, change of appetite, breast tenderness, weight gain, enlargement of ovaries and/or fallopian tubes, excessive growth of body hair; may subside after first year.
■ **STD protection:** None.

■ LOVER'S GUIDE

INJECTION (DEPO-PROVERA)
99 percent effective
■ **Use:** One injection every three months. Prescription.
■ **Risks:** Amenorrhea, weight gain, other side effects similar to Norplant.
■ **STD protection:** None.

IUD
95 to 96 percent effective
■ **Use:** After insertion, stays in until physician removes it. Prescription.
■ **Risks:** Cramps, bleeding, pelvic inflammatory disease, infertility; rarely, perforation of the uterus.
■ **STD protection:** None.

PERIODIC ABSTINENCE
53 to 86 percent effective
■ **Use:** Requires frequent monitoring of the body's functions and periods of abstinence. Instruction from a physician or clinic.
■ **Risks:** None.
■ **STD protection:** None.

SURGICAL STERILIZATION
Over 99 percent effective
■ **Use:** Vasectomy is a one-time procedure usually performed in a doctor's office; tubal ligation is a one-time procedure performed in operating room.
■ **Risks:** Pain, infection, and, for female tubal ligation, possible surgical complications.
■ **STD Protection:** None.

SOURCE: *FDA Consumer* magazine, December 1993.

THE VASECTOMY OPTION

Reversing the process is sometimes possible, but you better not count on it

When it comes to birth control techniques, most of the options belong to women. But when it comes to sterilization, the man takes center stage. That's because vasectomy has long been regarded as both simpler and safer than its female equivalent, tubal ligation. For couples ready to conclude their childbearing, vasectomy is the better course, say doctors. More than half a million men elect this option each year.

Not that vasectomy carries no worries. Two recent studies have raised the possibility that men with vasectomies may have some higher risk of developing prostate cancer. While the research is considered too preliminary to require revising current medical practice, further investigation of the question is warranted.

In a vasectomy, the tube that carries sperm to the penis is cut. The procedure can be done on an outpatient basis for about $450 and requires only 15 to 20 minutes. The doctor injects a local anesthetic in the scrotum and around each of the two vas deferens, the tubes that carry sperm from the testicles to the penis. After making a small incision in the scrotum, the doctor cuts and closes the tube with ties. After the operation, a man will still produce sperm, but the sperm can't enter the penis. Seminal fluid continues to be produced, nevertheless, and erection and ejaculation still take place.

Post-operative complications are relatively rare, and minor in most cases. They can include bleeding, infection, and the development of painful lumps in the scrotum. Risks can be greatly minimized by having the operation done by a doctor who performs it frequently.

Reversal of a vasectomy is often possible, but success is by no means a certainty. Advances in microsurgery techniques make the chances of successfully reconnecting the vas 98 percent, but even if the vas is reconnected, there is only a 50 to 70 percent chance that the man will be able to fertilize an egg. That's because men who have had vasectomies often form antibodies against their own sperm. The antibodies don't appear to harm the man's health, but they can destroy fertility.

RU-486

COMING TO AMERICA

The abortion pill will soon be approved for use in this country

The controversial drug RU-486, known in America as mifepristone, has been available in France since 1989, but opposition by right-to-life groups has deterred its introduction into the United States. Just after taking office in January 1992, however, the Clinton administration pushed the U.S. Food and Drug Administration to reconsider the ban on the drug's import.

Two years later, after much behind-the-scenes discussion, the administration announced that Roussel-Uclaf, the pharmaceutical firm that markets the drug in France, would donate U.S. rights to the drug to the Population Council, a New York–based research firm. In October 1994, the Population Council began clinical trials of the drug at more than a dozen clinics around the country. The trials are designed to determine the safety of mifepristone and to gather data for the FDA as part of the approval process.

The abortion drug is given in different doses, depending on where it's being administered. In France, mifepristone is given as a 600-milligram pill, followed by the synthetic hormone prostaglandin administered orally, two days later. In Great Britain, mifepristone is given orally, and two days later prostaglandin is given in the form of a vaginal suppository. The mifepristone/prostaglandin regimen is used up to 49 days from the last menstrual period in France, and 63 days from the last menstrual period in Britain and Sweden.

The abortion drug works by interrupting pregnancy in its early stages. It does this by blocking the action of a natural hormone called progesterone. Normally, progesterone prepares the lining of the uterus for a fertilized egg. Without progesterone the lining of the uterus breaks down and menstruation begins, resulting in the expulsion of any fertilized egg.

Mifepristone is effective only in the earliest weeks of pregnancy, when the ovaries produce progesterone. By the ninth or tenth week, however, large amounts of progesterone are also produced by the placenta. The amounts involved are too great for the antiprogestins, or mifepristone, to block the pregnancy from progressing.

In Europe, an estimated 150,000 women have used mifepristone. Not only can it be used earlier in the pregnancy than a surgical abortion—with a surgical procedure, women have to wait up to six weeks after a missed period before they can have an abortion—but it requires no invasive surgery or anesthesia, and it doesn't carry the risk of uterine perforation or injury to the cervix.

Many women prefer the technique to surgical abortion because it gives them more privacy and more control over their bodies. But some women opt for surgical abortion because it is over faster and requires fewer office visits.

Surgical abortions are also slightly more effective than medical abortions. Mifepristone is 96 to 99 percent effective in inducing a complete abortion. It fails in one in 100 cases and causes an incomplete abortion in three in 100 cases, and if it causes an incomplete abortion, a surgical procedure is required. With a surgical abortion, the woman notices less blood loss and is unaware of the passing of the fertilized egg.

Either way, there will be some side effects. Mifepristone usually causes light bleeding. Some women experience cramps, abdominal pain, heavy bleeding that can last up to three weeks, and, in rare cases, severe hemorrhaging. In France, about 1 in 1,000 women require a blood transfusion because of severe hemorrhaging.

When and if it does make its way to the United States, mifepristone will be provided in private physician's offices, abortion clinics, and hospitals. The cost has not yet been determined, but experts say that it will probably cost the same as a surgical abortion, about $300.

SPEAKING OF ABORTION

Defining limits to a woman's right to terminate pregnancy

A woman's right to elect an abortion remains the law of the land under *Roe* v. *Wade* and subsequent Supreme Court decisions. But that web of judicial rulings has left the states free to legislate numerous restrictions on the exercise of that right. A glossary of the different types of restrictions is adapted below from information supplied by the National Abortion Rights Action League. The table that begins on page 321 outlines which of the 50 states have enacted which of those laws.

ABORTION BAN—The state prohibits virtually all abortions, but the ban is unconstitutional and therefore unenforceable. In "Pre-*Roe*" states, the ban in question pre-dates *Roe* v. *Wade*. In "Post-*Roe*" states, the state has amended and reenacted its pre-*Roe* ban. Either way, the ban has no legal force.

INFORMED CONSENT—No abortion is allowed unless a woman receives state-prepared materials and counseling on adoptions and abortion alternatives, is told the doctor's qualifications, and has the risks of the procedure explained to her.

MINOR'S ACCESS—Requires one parent's written consent for a minor under 18. Permits abortion without parental consent if court order indicates woman is well informed and sufficiently mature.

PHYSICIAN-ONLY REQUIREMENT—Only a state-licensed physician may perform abortion procedures.

PUBLIC FUNDING—Regulation that a woman eligible for state medical care can't use such funds for abortion unless her life is at risk.

VIABILITY TESTING—Bars physician from performing abortion from 18th week on.

CONSCIENCE-BASED EXEMPTION—Spares any person or hospital from performing a role in an abortion.

POST-VIABILITY RESTRICTIONS—No abortion is allowed after viability unless necessary to preserve woman's health. In event of such, a second physician is required to provide medical attention to the fetus.

CLINIC VIOLENCE AND HARASSMENT—Provides criminal penalties for anyone physically preventing an individual from entering or exiting a health care facility.

HUSBAND CONSENT/HUSBAND NOTICE—No abortion for a married woman living with her husband without his consent.

INSURANCE—No abortion coverage under group health insurance for state workers.

WAITING PERIOD—No abortion unless a woman has waited 24 hours after hearing a state-mandated lecture about fetal development, abortion alternatives, and possible effects on future pregnancies.

LEGISLATIVE DECLARATION (PRO-CHOICE)—A law indicating legislative intent to protect a woman's right to choose abortion.

LEGISLATIVE DECLARATION (ANTI-CHOICE)—A law indicating intent to ban abortion.

MEDICAL ABORTION—State resolutions in favor of research and trials of RU-486 and other non-surgical abortion.

PUBLIC FACILITIES—No use of public facilities to perform abortion services.

COUNSELING BAN—A state "gag rule" that bars state-funded abortion counseling or referrals.

SOURCE: National Abortion Rights Action League.

CITIZEN'S GUIDE

THE ABORTION RULES, THE ABORTION CHOICES

A state-by-state guide to what's required

	ABORTION BAN	ABORTION BAN (POST-ROE)	ABORTION BAN (PRE-ROE)	INFORMED CONSENT	MINOR'S ACCESS	PHYSICIAN-ONLY REQUIREMENT	PUBLIC FUNDING	VIABILITY TESTING	CONSCIENCE-BASED EXEMPTION	POST-VIABILITY RESTRICTIONS	CLINIC VIOLENCE AND HARASSMENT	HUSBAND CONSENT/ NOTICE	INSURANCE	WAITING PERIOD	LEGISLATIVE DECLARATION (PRO)	LEGISLATIVE DECLARATION (ANTI)	MEDICAL ABORTION	PUBLIC FACILITIES	COUNSELING BAN
ALABAMA		✔		✔		✔	✔	✔		✔									
ALASKA				✔	✔	✔	✔		✔										
ARIZONA		✔			✔		✔		✔	✔									
ARKANSAS		✔			✔	✔	✔		✔	✔					✔				
CALIFORNIA		✔		✔	✔	✔	✔		✔	✔	✔						✔		
COLORADO	✔	✔			✔	✔	✔		✔		✔	✔	✔		✔				
CONNECTICUT				✔	✔	✔	✔		✔	✔									
DELAWARE		✔		✔	✔	✔	✔		✔	✔				✔					
DISTRICT OF COLUMBIA		✔				✔	✔												
FLORIDA				✔		✔	✔		✔	✔		✔							
GEORGIA					✔	✔	✔		✔								✔		
HAWAI'I						✔	✔		✔								✔		
IDAHO				✔	✔	✔	✔		✔	✔			✔	✔					
ILLINOIS					✔	✔	✔		✔	✔		✔	✔			✔			
INDIANA				✔	✔	✔	✔		✔	✔				✔					
IOWA						✔	✔		✔	✔									
KANSAS				✔	✔		✔		✔	✔	✔			✔					
KENTUCKY				✔	✔	✔	✔		✔	✔		✔	✔	✔		✔		✔	
LOUISIANA	✔			✔	✔	✔	✔	✔	✔	✔		✔				✔			✔
MAINE				✔	✔	✔	✔		✔	✔					✔		✔		
MARYLAND					✔	✔	✔		✔	✔	✔				✔				
MASSACHUSETTS	✔		✔	✔	✔	✔	✔		✔	✔	✔		✔	✔					
MICHIGAN			✔	✔	✔	✔	✔		✔	✔				✔					
MINNESOTA				✔	✔	✔	✔		✔	✔	✔		✔						
MISSISSIPPI			✔	✔	✔	✔	✔							✔					
MISSOURI				✔	✔	✔	✔	✔	✔	✔			✔			✔		✔	✔
MONTANA				✔	✔	✔	✔		✔	✔		✔				✔			
NEBRASKA				✔	✔	✔	✔		✔	✔			✔	✔		✔			
NEVADA				✔	✔	✔	✔		✔	✔	✔				✔				

■ CITIZEN'S GUIDE

	ABORTION BAN	ABORTION BAN (POST-ROE)	ABORTION BAN (PRE-ROE)	INFORMED CONSENT	MINOR'S ACCESS	PHYSICIAN-ONLY REQUIREMENT	PUBLIC FUNDING	VIABILITY TESTING	CONSCIENCE-BASED EXEMPTION	POST-VIABILITY RESTRICTIONS	CLINIC VIOLENCE AND HARASSMENT	HUSBAND CONSENT/ NOTICE	INSURANCE	WAITING PERIOD	LEGISLATIVE DECLARATION (PRO)	LEGISLATIVE DECLARATION (ANTI)	MEDICAL ABORTION	PUBLIC FACILITIES	COUNSELING BAN
NEW HAMPSHIRE			✔				✔			✔							✔		
NEW JERSEY						✔	✔		✔										
NEW MEXICO			✔		✔	✔	✔		✔										
NEW YORK						✔	✔		✔	✔									
NORTH CAROLINA						✔	✔		✔	✔	✔								
NORTH DAKOTA				✔	✔	✔	✔		✔	✔		✔	✔	✔		✔		✔	✔
OHIO				✔	✔	✔	✔		✔					✔					
OKLAHOMA			✔			✔	✔		✔	✔									
OREGON							✔		✔		✔								
PENNSYLVANIA				✔	✔	✔	✔		✔	✔		✔	✔	✔		✔			
RHODE ISLAND				✔	✔	✔	✔		✔	✔		✔	✔				✔		
SOUTH CAROLINA				✔	✔	✔	✔		✔	✔		✔							
SOUTH DAKOTA				✔	✔	✔	✔		✔	✔				✔		✔			
TENNESSEE				✔	✔	✔	✔		✔	✔				✔			✔		
TEXAS			✔	✔		✔	✔		✔	✔									
UTAH		✔		✔	✔	✔	✔		✔	✔		✔		✔		✔			
VERMONT			✔				✔												
VIRGINIA				✔		✔	✔		✔	✔									
WASHINGTON						✔	✔		✔	✔	✔				✔				
WEST VIRGINIA			✔		✔		✔		✔							✔			
WISCONSIN			✔	✔	✔	✔	✔		✔	✔	✔								
WYOMING					✔	✔	✔		✔	✔									

NOTES:

CALIFORNIA
Ban: Unless the pregnancy is a result of rape or incest or woman's life is in grave danger.

COLORADO
Ban: Unless the mother's life is in danger, the child is likely to be gravely deformed, the pregnancy resulted from rape or incest, and less than 16 weeks of gestation have passed.

DELAWARE
Ban: Unless the pregnancy resulted from rape or incest, or poses a serious health risk to the mother, or the fetus is likely to be deformed.

DISTRICT OF COLUMBIA
Ban: Unless to preserve the life of the mother.

LOUISIANA
Ban: Unless it is to preserve the woman's life or unless the pregnancy is a result of rape or incest. If the pregnancy is a result of rape, the woman must report the rape to law enforcement officials within 10 days; have an abortion within 13 weeks of conception; obtain treatment within 5 days of the rape to make sure she wasn't pregnant prior to the rape. Incest victim must report the crime and have an abortion within 13 weeks of conception.

SOURCE: National Abortion Rights Action League.

RISKS & REMEDIES

WHEN THE PUMP WON'T WORK

There's encouraging news for men who have experienced impotence

Impotence is a treatable condition in more situations today than ever before. For those experiencing difficulties, the stock advice that psychological counseling should be sought may still apply at times, but doctors now have a far better understanding of the physiological conditions that can cause what is known technically as erectile dysfunction. Factors can include everything from high cholesterol intake to prescription drug side effects. Dr. Irwin Goldstein, a professor of urology at the Boston University School of Medicine and a leader in erectile dysfunction research, compares the penis to a hydraulic system: "All hydraulic systems have to be activated or initiated, they have to have a high pressure hose to bring the fluid in, and they have to store the fluid. Failure of any of those systems means impotence."

Here, Dr. Goldstein explains the risk factors and what to do about them:

CAUSES

■ **AGING:** There is a direct correlation between aging and impotence. Studies show that 40 percent of men at age 40 suffer from impotence, 50 percent of men at 50, 60 percent at 60, and so on. Like any other plumbing system that receives constant use, the vascular system simply begins to wear down.

■ **PSYCHOLOGICAL FACTORS:** To attain an erection, your brain has to tell the system to start the flow of blood to the penis. Its failure to do so is the classic psychological basis of impotence. Part of being potent is being in control, so stress, anger, fear, and something called "the inverse of dominance"—which is just what impotence, also a synonym for powerless, means—can all affect performance.

■ **HORMONAL IMBALANCES:** A testosterone imbalance or thyroid condition can also lead to problems with initiation. The hydraulic mechanism is fine, but the desire to have intercourse is simply not there.

■ **MEDICATION:** Make your doctor aware of any and all medications prescribed to you. Many of them can cause impotence: medications to treat high blood pressure, diabetes, heart disease, and depression.

■ **DIABETES AND HEART DISEASE:** Erectile dysfunction stemming from diabetes or heart disease can be a symptom of the illness or of the treatment, as noted before. Both illnesses can cause nerve damage, blood vessel damage, or tissue damage, thus leading to a complete breakdown of the hydraulic system's ability to initiate an erection because the nerves are out; fill the penis with blood because the vessels are shot; or retain the blood because the tissue has lost its holding power.

■ **HYPERTENSION:** Raising blood pressure raises erections, but chronic exposure to high blood pressure can injure the lining of the blood vessels, which leads to blocked arteries and impotence.

■ **CIGARETTES:** Though cigarette smoking doesn't appear to be a significant factor in and of itself, there is evidence that it is a secondary risk factor among people with heart disease or hypertension. Cigarettes tend to aggravate damage to the lining of blood vessels, which is always a problem.

■ **HIGH CHOLESTEROL INTAKE:** If you eat a lot of fatty food, it will clog the circulation to the heart, it will clog the circulation to the legs—and it will clog the circulation to the penis. Without that blood flow, an erection is difficult or impossible to maintain.

■ **PHYSICAL TRAUMA:** Performance-affecting injuries can occur not only to the exposed penile shaft, but to the internal part of the penis in the pelvis and the perineum (the area between the scrotum and the anus). Trauma can also occur when the erect penis is bent during intercourse or masturbation, which can actually fracture it. This causes the tunica (the lining material of the penis) to develop holes and prevents the penis from storing blood, a condition called Peyronie's disease.

TREATMENTS

■ **PROPHYLACTIC CARE:** Theoretically, preventive measures are the most effective. Don't smoke. Watch what you eat. If you need psychological treatment, seek it. Avoid trauma—recognize that your penis is not made of concrete. It can be fractured, so use lubrication during intercourse and if you are in an unusual position with your partner that causes pain, stop.

■ **HORMONAL TREATMENT:** This treatment is reserved exclusively for those who have hormonal problems. It should not be used indiscriminately to boost your libido, because it can cause your prostate to grow, which can lead to prostate cancer. Moreover, if the problem is with your plumbing, hormonal treatment will simply be ineffective and add frustration to an already serious problem.

■ **ORAL MEDICATIONS:** There are no FDA-approved oral treatments for erectile dysfunction. But several drugs are recognized

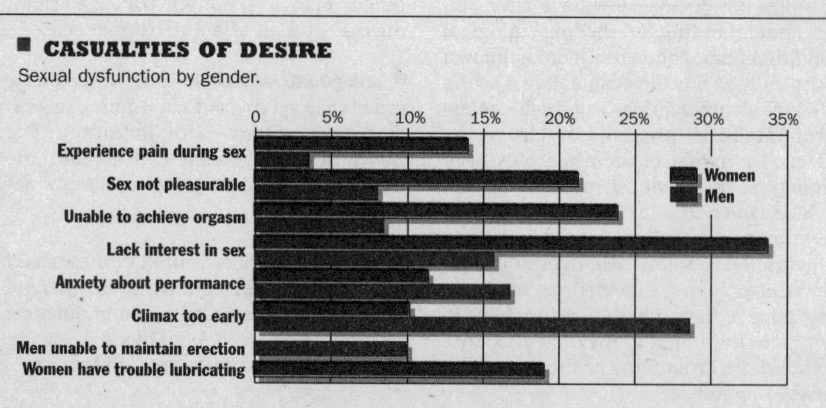

SOURCE: *The Social Organization of Sexuality: Sexual Practices in the United States,* University of Chicago Press, 1994.

in the medical community as being effective: Yohimbine, which is used to raise blood pressure; Trazodone, an antidepressant; and pentoxifylline, which makes the red blood cells more slippery to improve circulation in clogged arteries. Some experimenting is also being done with sub-lingual drugs that are dissolved under the tongue.

■ **TOPICAL MEDICATIONS:** Because it is difficult to predict the appropriate amount of drug to apply to the erective tissue, the topical approach is less effective than oral medication. But drugs like minoxidil (used for hair growth) and nitroglycerin can relax the blood vessels in the penis to induce an erection. Intra-urethral (applied via the urethra) drugs are being developed as well.

■ **VACUUM CONSTRICTIVE DEVICES:** A vacuum tube can be used to reduce the pressure around the penis and thus draw blood into it. Once an erection is attained, a rubber band is snapped around the base of the penis to retain the blood. It's a very effective method, but it does prevent ejaculation and can also be quite uncomfortable.

■ **PENILE PROSTHESES:** About 25,000 penile prostheses are inserted every year. There are two approaches. The first is a malleable rigid device that is inserted in the penis. The downside is that once the device is inserted, the penis remains eternally erect. A more complex inflatable device also can be inserted that includes an internal manual pumping device, which will allow more flexibility.

■ **VASCULAR SURGERY:** This is a bypass operation for people who are suffering from impotence brought on by blunt trauma to the artery leading to the penis. It is not effective in cases of impotence brought on by hardening of the arteries.

■ **INJECTIONS:** FDA approval is expected soon for drugs like prostaglandin-E that can be injected directly into the penis. They work like the nitric oxide that is released naturally during foreplay to dilate the blood vessels in the penis.

EXPERT Q&A

WHEN TO TAKE AN HIV TEST

If you are in a high-risk group, get tested now

Jim Graham, executive director of the Whitman Walker Clinic, which provides help to two out of three people living with AIDS in the Washington, D.C., metropolitan area, explains the test that identifies the HIV antibody that can lead to AIDS.

■ **Who should consider getting tested for HIV?**

Anyone who has been or is sexually active; anyone who is sexually active and not in a monogamous relationship; IV drug users; and anyone who has received a blood transfusion before the year 1985. Additionally, any person who does not know their HIV antibody status and who feels that they have been at risk for infection with HIV should consider testing.

■ **How is the test given?**

The Centers for Disease Control and Prevention have set guidelines, but not all doctors and hospitals follow them. Those guidelines recommend some type of prevention counseling before the test is given. Less than a tube of blood is then drawn. The labwork is done. The patient comes back for results and post-test counseling. At Whitman Walker, if the test is negative, that's the end of it. But if the results are positive, the test is repeated three times to make sure it's accurate before telling the patient. Once again, not all doctors and hospitals follow those guidelines; some just draw the blood and send it to the lab.

■ **What is the cost?**

There is no charge at Whitman Walker, but the test costs $30 to $70 at most places.

Once someone is exposed to HIV, how long does it take to show up on a test? Should he or she be tested again periodically?

It can take up to six months after the HIV virus enters the body before antibodies are produced. By six months, 99 percent of those infected with the virus will develop antibodies. But 95 percent of those who are infected with the virus will develop antibodies within three months after infection. Because of this window period for antibody development, people who have had unsafe sex or have shared needles three to six months before the test should consider re-testing.

Can people run into problems with their health or life insurance companies if they are tested and the results are positive?

Many life insurance companies require an HIV test as a coverage prerequisite. These companies often will not provide life insurance coverage to a person who has tested positive for HIV. Health insurance providers may drop a person from coverage or put a cap on benefits paid.

How confidential are the test results?

Many clinics that provide testing, including Whitman Walker, provide anonymous testing. This method provides no way of tracing who has tested positive. Some clinics provide testing that is only confidential and not anonymous.

FACT FILE:

AIDS DEATH TOLL

The Centers for Disease Control and Prevention estimates in 1995 that one million people in the United States are now infected with HIV, about one in 250 Americans. In 1994, HIV infection/AIDS was the ninth leading cause of death among people of all ages in the United States.

What are the latest methods for self-administration of tests at home? Are these tests now available? If not, when will they be?

To date, no home testing method has been approved by the Food and Drug Administration. Many home collection methods have been developed but are not yet available. Home collection kits will allow people to draw blood at home and mail the sample to a central testing center where results can be retrieved with a self-determined code. The conception of home testing has been criticized for many important reasons. In addition to inaccurate and misinterpreted results, home testing methods make it impossible to provide face-to-face counseling. Such counseling is critically important both before and after the test is taken and results are received.

Should newborn babies be tested?

Newborns should be tested if there is concern about the mother's risk of infection. However, because newborns have a quickly changing immune system, a baby with an HIV-positive result may later test negative.

If someone tests positive, what kind of care should he or she seek after the results come back?

Individuals who test positive should seek medical attention for treatment as well as counseling as needed. Individuals should also protect themselves from further infection and protect others from the virus. Precautions include following safe sex guidelines; never sharing needles or other drug works; reducing or stopping alcohol, cigarette, and drug use; eating well and getting plenty of rest and exercising; avoiding infections, especially those passed by sex; and not donating blood, plasma, sperm, or organs.

Should more people be tested to help curtail the spread of the virus?

Testing is one of the best methods for early detection of HIV. People who are aware of their HIV status can significantly help reduce the spread of HIV/AIDS by not putting others at risk.

STD'S

LOVERS AND OTHER STRANGERS

Sexually transmitted diseases can't just be kissed off

According to a recent study, men with two to four sex partners over a lifetime have a 1 in 29 chance of contracting a bacterial sexually transmitted disease such as syphilis or gonorrhea. For women with an equivalent number of partners, the risk is about twice as high. The patterns are similar for viral STDs such as genital herpes and hepatitis B. But men tend to have more partners than women. When that is taken into account, the chance of getting an STD is ultimately about the same for both sexes. Following are descriptions of the most common STDs from the Centers for Disease Control and Prevention:

BACTERIAL VAGINOSIS

Also called Gardnerella or Hemophilus.

■ **HOW SPREAD:** Through sexual intercourse and possibly through towels and wet clothing. A common cause of vaginitis.

■ **SYMPTOMS:** Grayish vaginal discharge is common. Untreated, it can cause reproductive problems such as abnormal Pap smears and urinary tract infections.

■ **TREATMENT:** Metronidazole.

CHLAMYDIA

Caused by the bacterium Chlamydia trachomatis. *Most common STD in the United States.*

■ **HOW SPREAD:** Vaginal or anal intercourse, mother to child during birth, hand-to-eye contact if hands have infected discharge.

■ **SYMPTOMS:** Appear 7 to 14 days after exposure. In women, it can cause infertility or pregnancy complications, vaginal discharge, painful urination, vaginal bleeding, bleeding after sex, and lower abdominal pain. In men, chlamydia causes burning during urination, urethral discharge, and inflammation of the urethra. Four-fifths of women have no symptoms; sexually active women may want to be screened periodically.

■ **TREATMENT:** Tetracycline. The Centers for Disease Control and Prevention now recommend Doxycycline as the treatment of choice because it only has to be taken twice a day. Erythromycin for pregnant women. Chlortetracycline for eye infections.

CRABS/PEDICULOSIS PEDIS

Caused by crablike lice that live in eyebrows, pubic, armpit, and chest hair.

■ **HOW SPREAD:** Physical contact with someone who is infected, or using towels, clothes, or bedding of a person who has crabs.

■ **SYMPTOMS:** Intolerable itching in the genital or other areas. The crabs can be seen by the naked eye, so it's easy to diagnose.

■ **TREATMENT:** A lotion called Kwell can be prescribed. After treatment, clean clothes, towels, and bed linen. The crab will die in 24 hours. If skin is irritated from itching, use aloe vera cream to ease the irritation.

GENITAL WARTS/HUMAN PAPILLOMA VIRUS

Caused by a virus similar to the one that causes skin warts.

■ **HOW SPREAD:** Sexual intercourse.

■ **SYMPTOMS:** Appears three weeks to eight months after exposure. Small, painless warts can appear on the labia, vulva, cervix, or anus in women. In men, warts appear on the penis or scrotum. Using a condom can help prevent infection.

■ **TREATMENT:** Dry ice or laser beam can burn off warts, or Podophyllin can be applied.

GONORRHEA

Caused by gonococcus, a bacterium.

■ **HOW SPREAD:** Sexual intercourse, oral sex, from mother to child during birth, from hand-to-eye contact. For women, from being inseminated by infected semen.

■ **SYMPTOMS:** Appear two days to three weeks after infection. In women, thick discharge, burning or painful urination, pain in lower abdomen, vomiting, fever, irregular periods, a rash, chills, fever, pain in the wrists and fingers, hands, feet, and toes. Some 80 percent of women have no symptoms. In men, thick milky discharge, pain during urination. Almost all men show symptoms.

■ **TREATMENT:** The CDC recommends ceftriaxone as treatment. Since people are often infected with gonorrhea and chlamydia at the same time, the CDC also recommends seven days of taking Doxycycline to treat chlamydia. Pregnant women should take Erythromycin; it's less effective, but safer.

HERPES

Two types of herpes are caused by the herpes simplex virus. Type I is characterized by cold sores and fever blisters on the mouth. Type II is characterized by sores and blisters on the genitals.

■ **HOW SPREAD:** Sexual intercourse or oral sex with someone who has an active infection. The disease is most contagious when sores exist, but infection can occur even when there are no symptoms.

■ **SYMPTOMS:** Appear 2 to 20 days after infection, but most people don't have symptoms until much later. Tingling, itching in the genital area, burning sensations, pain or feeling of pressure in the legs, buttocks or genitals, sores starting with one or more bumps that turn to blisters. Women can have sores on cervix with no noticeable symptoms. Blisters rupture in a few days and heal without treatment. Active sores may make urination painful. Also may be a dull ache or sharp pain in the genitals.

■ **TREATMENT:** No cure at present. CDC recommends keeping sores dry and clean. If very painful, xylocaine cream or ethyl chloride may be helpful. The antiviral drug acyclovir may reduce outbreak recurrence.

HIV INFECTION/AIDS

Caused by the HIV virus.

■ **HOW SPREAD:** Sexual intercourse, anal sex, blood transfusions, sharing of needles with an infected person. The virus is found in blood, semen, and vaginal secretions, so any contact with these bodily fluids with someone who is infected such as unprotected sexual intercourse could lead to infection.

■ **SYMPTOMS:** In both men and women, fatigue, weight loss, swollen glands, and skin problems such as seborrheic dermatitis. Bronchial infections, sores in the mouth, fevers, night sweats, loss of appetite, headaches, trouble swallowing. In women, recurrent yeast infections, chronic pelvic inflammatory disease, and severe genital herpes.

■ **TREATMENT:** There is currently no treatment for AIDS, which is fatal. But there are ways to stave off a full-blown AIDS outbreak. AZT and DDI are some drugs that are in use. The progress of the disease should be monitored by using a CD4 cell monitoring lab test.

NONGONOCOCCAL URETHRITIS (NGU)

Caused by Ureaplasma Urealyticum *bacterium.*

■ **HOW SPREAD:** Contracted through sexual intercourse. It can be found in apparently healthy people with no signs of infection.

■ **SYMPTOMS:** In men, symptoms include discharge from the penis and inflammation of the urethra. Some researchers think NGU causes pregnancy problems in women, but more research needs to be done.

■ **TREATMENT:** Tetracycline is the standard treatment. Doxycycline or Erythromycin may also be prescribed.

SCABIES

Caused by tiny parasitic mites.

■ **HOW SPREAD:** Sexual contact, towels, clothes and even furniture.

■ **SYMPTOMS:** Intense itching, red bumps on breasts, waist, genitals, buttocks, or hands.

■ **TREATMENT:** Kwell, which is also used to cure crabs. For pregnant women, Eurax.

SYPHILIS

Caused by a bacterium called spirochete.

■ **HOW SPREAD:** Sexual or skin contact with infected person, or from mother to unborn child. Spreads from open sores or rashes and can penetrate mucous membranes and broken skin anywhere on the body.

■ **SYMPTOMS:** Appear from 9 to 90 days after infection with a painless sore that looks like a pimple. In men, pimple could appear on penis or scrotum. Left untreated, could lead to rash over entire body, sore throat, swollen painful joints, aching bones, hair loss, or raised area around the genitals. After 10 to 20 years, bacteria can invade the heart and brain, causing heart disease, blindness, mental incapacity, crippling.

■ **TREATMENT:** Penicillin by injection, Doxycline, or tetracycline pills.

MENOPAUSE

THE CASE FOR ESTROGEN

The benefits and risks of hormone replacement therapy for women

For women facing menopause, hormone replacement therapy is becoming as common as children attending college or dieting. Nearly 4 in 10 menopausal women say they are taking estrogen, or estrogen and progestin, a substance that mimics a hormone similar to estrogen, to help relieve the discomforts of menopause. These symptoms include the sudden feeling of being overheated known as a "hot flash," as well as vaginal dryness, mood swings, thinning facial skin, headaches, and depression.

An important factor in helping keep the heart, bones, and skin healthy, estrogen production decreases sharply during menopause, which occurs at the average age of 51. Research has shown that women receiving a regular supplementation of estrogen during and after menopause have a significantly lower risk of heart disease, stroke, and osteoporosis, the debilitating condition that causes bones to become fragile and to break. Hormone replacement therapy (HRT) also helps spare many women the physical discomfort that can result from changes in the vagina during menopause. These changes, which include the loss of vaginal elasticity and lubrication, can ruin a woman's libido.

HRT is not without potential side effects, however. One large recent study has suggested that women who use HRT for five or more years after menopause run 30 to 40 percent more risk of developing breast cancer than those who don't. Taking progestin along with estrogen has been found to help protect the uterus against cancer in some studies, but it does not appear to protect against breast cancer.

In addition, the American College of Obstetricians and Gynecologists has reported that about 10 percent of women receiving HRT experience side effects that include breast tenderness, fluid retention, swelling, mood changes, and pelvic cramping.

Different dosages, hormone combinations, and ways of administering the hormones can be tailored to individual needs. Women in a high-risk group for heart disease or osteoporosis may be prime candidates for estrogen supplements. If a woman has a high risk of contracting breast cancer, her doctor may recommend a low-fat diet and regular exercise instead of estrogen therapy. For those who face a high risk of breast cancer, a doctor may also recommend tamoxifen, an estrogen-like drug that has favorable effects on cholesterol levels and prevents bone loss and breast cancer. But tamoxifen does seem to increase the risk of uterine cancer, and women taking it are advised to undergo periodic examinations to check for uterine changes.

Still more studies are now under way on the benefits and drawbacks of HRT, but most of them won't be completed until 2003. By then, another 20 million women will have entered menopause and will have had to decide whether the benefits of HRT outweigh its uncertainties. The answer is likely to depend on individual risk factors.

FACT FILE:

ESTROGEN AND HEART DISEASE

■ *A recent study of nearly 900 women over the age of 45 found that taking estrogen supplements after menopause significantly increased the level of "good" HDL cholesterol, which prevents heart disease. The level of "bad" cholesterol, LDL, dropped.*

EXPERT Q&A

HERE'S LOOKING AT YOU, DEAR

Sex will change, but it need not cease with aging

Growing older doesn't mean giving up a sex life. To the contrary, some of the most satisfying sexual experiences may come in later life. Dr. Robert N. Butler, professor of geriatrics at Mount Sinai Medical Center in New York and co-author of *Love and Sex after 60* (with Myrna I. Lewis, Ballantine, revised 1993) answers some questions about sexuality and aging.

■ What physical changes can people expect during sexual activity as they grow older?

Reaction time to auditory and visual stimuli increases as we age. It also takes longer for sexual arousal to occur, and it takes longer to complete intercourse. The time needed between sexual encounters is usually longer, too. But assuming good health and the presence of a partner who interests you and with whom you have a good relationship, desire remains strong and does not decline as a consequence of aging per se.

■ But isn't illness likely to interfere with sexual desire?

People of any age have to make adjustments during illness, and there are more likely to be illnesses the older we get. Illness saps energy and causes worry, which in turn makes people less preoccupied with sexuality. Some specific diseases have particularly adverse effects on sexuality. Diabetes is often associated with problems, for example, as is atherosclerosis, where fatty plaques in arteries and vessels reduce the supply of blood to the genital area in both men and women. This is detrimental because sexual excitation is dependent upon blood engorgement in the genitalia. In addition, important therapeutic medications like antihypertension prescriptions may take away sexual capability to some degree. These problem areas can be improved, however, with appropriate medical care. An older patient who is interested in sexuality should read up on the subject and bring up issues with a doctor. If the doctor doesn't seem comfortable, the patient may need to talk with a different doctor.

■ Are there benefits to maintaining an active sex life?

Social pressure tends to be negative toward sexuality and aging, and our society tries to deny that older people have any interest in sexuality. That attitude is built into the culture and with it comes kidding and jokes, anxious humor, and nervous laughter. But the desire for closeness and intimacy is very profound and goes on right through the end of life.

Older people often comment that no one ever touches them and they never have the chance to touch anyone else. That's especially true of older women because they tend to marry men three years older and they outlive men by about seven years. When somebody else thinks well of you, is attracted to you, and wants to be with you physically, it affirms your personhood.

There are physical benefits, too, but they're trickier to pinpoint because money hasn't exactly been poured into research. It seems as though the pain of arthritis, for example, may be relieved at least temporarily with sexual activity. And just as runners have highs that probably are related to endorphins in the brain, sexual activity, too, may produce a kind of high related to the central nervous system neurotransmitters.

■ How can older couples maintain their interest in sexual activity?

The way to keep the music playing, as the song goes, is for people to be concerned about each other and to remain interesting to their partners by continuing to learn and grow. Never downplay romance. People living together tend to take each other for granted and not date and not have fun, when they could go dancing, have an intimate dinner, or take trips together.

CHAPTER FOUR

EDUCATION

EXPERT QUOTES

"Teachers have discovered that if children are encouraged to use invented spelling, they can start writing in kindergarten."

—Sandra Wilde, author of *You Kan Red This!*

Page 338

"Very often in tracked schools, if you ask too many questions, you risk getting knocked down to the next level."

—Anne Wheelock, educational analyst and author of *Crossing the Tracks*

Page 352

"Few families understand how the college financial aid process works. Most people are just gambling."

—Kalman Chany, author of the *Princeton Review Student Access Guide to Paying for College*

Page 372

THE YEAR AHEAD: EXPECT many parents to "redshirt" their children by delaying their entry into kindergarten... **PAY ATTENTION** to the new content standards being developed by educators for your children... **ANTICIPATE** more interest in home schooling... **AVOID** the hype about computers in the classroom... **BEWARE** the rise in SAT scores as a result of changing the grading systems... **LOOK FOR** a backlash against grade inflation on college campuses...

K THROUGH 12

SCHOOL AGE, SCHOOL DAZE

When to start kindergarten is an increasingly complicated question

For many parents, there is no clear-cut answer to the question of when to start a child in school. Instead, the issue of whether a child is "ready" or not becomes tangled with questions about the merits of preschools, kindergarten transition programs, and the meaning of the battery of tests that children are typically expected to take today.

Many parents are "redshirting" their children by delaying their entry into kindergarten or first grade on the theory that their offspring are not yet ready for the classroom. In 1991, for instance, more than 20 percent of six-, seven-, and eight-year-old children were estimated to be behind other children their age in school, according to a study by Edith McArthur of the National Center for Education Statistics and Suzanne Bianchi of the Bureau of the Census.

Such trends, mostly the result of readiness decisions by parents and educational institutions, have led many states to raise the age by which they require a child to begin school, so that on the whole children start their kindergarten and first grade experiences at later ages today. In the vast majority of states, children must be five years old before they enter kindergarten; when Dwight D. Eisenhower was president, that age was four years, nine months—a significant difference at that stage in life.

The cut-off dates for determining enrollment eligibility have also been pushed back to the beginning of the school year, forcing younger children who would turn that age during the school year to delay enrolling for another year.

Thirty years ago, kindergarten children who would turn the appropriate age by February of that school year were allowed to enroll for the full school year; even as recently as 1979 only nine states required the age for kindergarten and first grade to be met before the beginning of October. Today most states have moved the cut-off date back to September.

"While 15 years ago it was considered appropriate to send a child to school at as early an age as possible, now the philosophy recommends waiting until a child is mature enough for academic work," according to researchers McArthur and Bianchi. But such a decision can often be quixotic, for many kindergarten and preschool programs have responded to the trend toward making first grade more academic by becoming more academic themselves.

PARENT'S GUIDE

THE KINDERGARTEN COUNTDOWN

When your child starts school may differ greatly, depending on the state in which you live. But just because a state allows a child to start kindergarten at age five, this need not mean your child must start then. Most states don't make school compulsory until a child turns six or even seven, and it is increasingly common for children to delay kindergarten until age six.

State[1]	Earliest permissible entrance age	Compulsory age for school to begin
ALABAMA	5 BY SEPT. 1	7
ALASKA	6 BY NOV. 2	7
ARIZONA	5 BY SEPT. 1	6
ARKANSAS	5 BY OCT. 1	5
CALIFORNIA	4 YRS., 9 MOS. BY SEPT. 1	6
COLORADO	5	7
CONNECTICUT	5 BY JAN. 1	7
DELAWARE	5 BY JAN. 1	5
DISTRICT OF COLUMBIA	5 BY DEC. 31	7
FLORIDA	5 BY SEPT. 1	6
GEORGIA	5 BY SEPT. 1	7
HAWAI'I	4 1/2, OR 5 1/2 IF 5 BY SEPT. 1	6
IDAHO	5 BY DEC. 31	6
ILLINOIS	5 BY SEPT. 1	7
INDIANA	5	7
IOWA	5 BY SEPT. 15	6
KANSAS	5 BY SEPT. 1	7
KENTUCKY	5 BY OCT. 1	6
LOUISIANA	5 BY SEPT. 30 (EXCEPT IN NEW ORLEANS)	6
MAINE	5 BY OCT. 15	7
MARYLAND	5 BY DEC. 31	5
MASSACHUSETTS	DISTRICT OPTION	6
MICHIGAN	5 BY DEC. 1	6
MINNESOTA	5 BY SEPT. 1	6
MISSISSIPPI	5 BY SEPT. 1	6
MISSOURI	5 BY JULY 1	7

State[1]	Earliest permissible entrance age	Compulsory age for school to begin
NEBRASKA	5 BY OCT. 15	7
MONTANA	5 BY SEPT. 10	7
NEVADA	5 BY SEPT. 30	7
NEW HAMPSHIRE	5 (CUT-OFF DATE DISTRICT OPTION)	6
NEW JERSEY	4 TO 6 (DISTRICT OPTION)	6
NEW MEXICO	5 BY SEPT. 1	5
NEW YORK	5 BY DEC. 1	6
NORTH CAROLINA	5 BY OCT. 16	7
NORTH DAKOTA	5 BY AUG. 31	7
OHIO	5 BY SEPT. 30	5
OREGON	5 BY SEPT. 1	7
PENNSYLVANIA	5 (CUT-OFF DATE DISTRICT OPTION)	8
RHODE ISLAND	5 BY SEPT. 31	6
SOUTH CAROLINA	5 BY SEPT. 1	5
SOUTH DAKOTA	5 BY SEPT. 1	6
TENNESSEE	5 BY SEPT. 30	7
TEXAS	5 BY SEPT. 1	6
UTAH	5 BY SEPT. 30	6
VERMONT	5 (CUT-OFF DATE DISTRICT OPTION)	7
VIRGINIA	5 BY SEPT. 30	5
WASHINGTON	5 BY AUG. 31	8
WISCONSIN	5 BY SEPT. 1	6
WYOMING	5 BY SEPT. 15	7

1. Red highlighting indicates states in which kindergarten attendance is mandatory.

SOURCE: The Education Commission of the States, Denver, Colo.

JUDGING TEACHING BY ITS RESULTS

What children should learn, defined in the new world of school reform

Even before the blistering report *A Nation at Risk* detailed the decline of America's public schools in 1983, educators, politicians, and parents had found many to blame for wrecking the nation's schools. A whole generation of school children have come and gone since then with little evidence that the finger pointing had much effect. Now, educators and policy makers seem committed to honing an approach called outcomes-based education, based on the idea that education should be judged by results, or outcomes, rather than inputs such as money or "seat-time," which is how teachers sometimes refer to the time their students spend in the classroom.

Federally sponsored efforts to identify what every student should know by grades 4, 8, and 12 have been a cornerstone of the Clinton administration's educational program, Goals 2000, which was approved by Congress in 1994. In the legislation, Congress set up a National Educational Standards and Improvement Council to "certify" the standards being developed by leading professional associations in each field with funding from the Department of Education. But the Clinton administration's effort has come under attack by those who fear too much federal meddling in the classroom. And the details, particularly of the history standards, have been enmeshed in politicking.

Most action today is in the states: Over 40 are in the process of adopting curricular content standards, drawing on a wide variety of sources, including the federally developed benchmarks. As states and school districts consider what standards to adopt, several related trends that could affect your child have emerged. They include:

- **NEW FORMS OF ASSESSMENT:** Essay writing replaces multiple-choice exams. Teachers keep examples of the students' written work in individual portfolios to document students' progress throughout the year. The new techniques are designed to better measure a student's critical skills and performance.

- **PRIVATIZATION:** In an effort to break bureaucracy, private firms are now running schools in California, Connecticut, Maryland, and Missouri. These companies are claiming success in cutting waste in maintenance services and administration, but their impact on academic achievement has received mixed reviews. In a variation on this theme, several well-known educators have formulated school improvement plans that have been adopted across school districts. The work is under the auspices of the New American Schools Development Corp., a nonprofit corporation founded in 1993.

- **TEACHERS AS COACHES:** Teachers lead students to solve problems on their own rather than serving as dispensers of information. Teachers' colleges are revamping courses and adopting alternative certification to attract talented individuals who don't necessarily have an education degree.

- **WRITING ACROSS THE CURRICULUM:** A growing group of teachers, working through the National Writing Project, are promoting writing as the key to understanding all subjects. School administrators also stress writing skills since such skills figure prominently in the kinds of open-ended assessment that are being used in lieu of traditional testing.

Will any of these new approaches really make a difference? For some perspective on the question, consider this call to arms: "The obvious fact is that our social life has undergone a thorough and radical change. If our education is to have any meaning for life, it must pass through an equally complete transformation." The speaker was educational philosopher John Dewey. The year: 1899.

LEARNING TO THINK LIKE LEONARDO

For a preview of where education reform is headed, check this out

Where did the dinosaurs go? How do plants get food? If your child starts asking these questions in kindergarten, he or she has begun the scientific inquiry that will pave the way for the study of science throughout high school. Similarly engaging questions are the hallmark of the standards-setting guidelines being developed by educators involved in everything from math to history to the arts.

■ **SCIENCE:** In the content recommendations recently drafted by leading scientists and educators in the report *National Science Education Standards,* scientific inquiry is the key to teaching science in kindergarten through 12th grade. The natural world becomes the textbook, as children observe changes. They can identify sequences of change and patterns—the change from day to night, for example. Teachers supply the connecting facts through demonstrations and discussions. The classroom, as a "community of learners," relies on students to help each other, collaborating whenever possible to set goals and plan activities and take responsibility for their own learning. At all levels students ought to be able to conceptualize, plan, and perform investigations. For a week-long lesson on sound, for instance, third-grade students design and build a musical instrument. The lesson culminates with a concert.

At the end of an investigation, teachers help students critique their results: How certain are they of their findings? Is there a better way to do the investigation? Should they do the experiment over? What are their sources of experimental error? Under the proposed standards, by the end of high school all students should understand and be able to explain the study of biological evolution, the molecular basis of heredity, interactions of energy and matter, population growth, the role of science and technology in local, national, and global challenges, and a host of other difficult consequences.

This new content, far from the old spoon-fed fact teaching, is difficult to assess. Tests are discouraged. Teachers are supposed to assess students' depth and breadth of knowledge through their explanations. To carry through with such ambitious change, many teachers may need considerable retraining themselves.

■ **HISTORY:** No effort to devise content standards has been more fraught with controversy than the recent report on teaching history. In the 271-page *National Standards for United States History,* Daniel Webster, the famous white male orator isn't mentioned, and Harriet Tubman, the eloquent former slave is. Most history teachers argue that students need to develop a view of history that includes blacks, women, and Native Americans, even if it portrays a not-so-glorious side of this nation's story. History, in this recasting, is the story of events, ideas, and places, not a saga populated by great men and just a few good women, as history textbooks have portrayed it in the past.

INSIGHT FOR EVERY AGE

New standards for the real world

In one typical science question being developed by the National Academy of Science's standards-setting panel, students are asked to predict how long a plant will live when planted in moist soil in a clear glass jar that is tightly covered and placed in a sunny window where the temperature is maintained between 60 degrees and 80 degrees Fahrenheit. The directions call for students "to use relevant ideas from the life, physical and Earth sciences."

And the intended answer?

There isn't a single correct one, actually. But the science educators hope that students in grades 5 through 8 will employ scientific concepts such as light, heat, and photosynthesis to analyze the problem, and that 12th graders will see the plant as a physical model of the Earth's ecosystem and view photosynthesis and respiration as complementary processes.

In another real-life example, intended to hone math skills of middle-schoolers, students are given the player statistics for four basketball stars in a National Basketball Association championship game. From the statistics, which include each player's points scored, assists, rebounds, field goals per scoring attempts, and minutes played, students are asked to find such things as the best percentage shooter in the game, and who snagged the most rebounds per minute.

As the panel of math experts stated: "A problem like this is ideally suited to the curious nature of middle school students and opens up a world of questions and investigations to them."

Unfortunately, much of what the standards-setters say every student should know is likely to be far over the heads of their intended age groups.

How many high school students, for instance, will be able to draw upon the ideas of religious groups such as the Virginia Baptists, mid-Atlantic Presbyterians, and millennialists, to assess how religion became a factor in the American Revolution? Which college students, for that matter, would be able to compare the power and significance of the Supreme Court in 1800 and 1820, although the question is rated a 7th-grade achievement in the history panel's report? Even a *Washington Post* reporter might find it taxing to explain to the panel's satisfaction the constitutional issues raised by the Watergate affair and to evaluate the effects of Watergate on public opinion.

But these are voluntary goals that teachers are meant to use as guidelines. Parents can use the standards, too, to spark some healthy debates at home. They are not being proposed as test questions to judge whether a student should graduate. The real test lies with textbook publishers, who must decide whether to rewrite their books to reflect the viewpoints and philosophy of the new standards.

As in the standards for other subjects, rote memorization is out and a focus on critical thinking skills is in. Students analyze a variety of sources, which might include their own family histories, draft records, or historical novels. Original documents ranging from the Declaration of Independence to the Immigration Reform and Control Act of 1986 allow students to develop their own opinions. Key activities to replace memorization include constructing chronologies, creating a narrative, and reconstructing historical arguments.

■ **MATH:** The math standards, developed in 1989 before standards became political hot potatoes, are regarded by many as the best and brightest model for others. They are clear, concise, and full of vignettes to illustrate their points. Their vital goals call for all students to learn to value mathematics; to learn to reason and communicate mathematically; to become confident

EXPERT SOURCES

WHERE TO GET THE PROPOSED STANDARDS

Booklets containing the standards being developed for the nation's schools come in seven core subjects. They attempt to describe all a student should know by a certain year and to illustrate the principles involved using vignettes. Prices for the booklets range from $9 to $25.

ART
MUSIC EDUCATORS NATIONAL COUNCIL
1806 Robert Fulton Drive
Reston, VA 22091
■ Ask for *National Standards for Art Education.*
☎ **800-828-0229**

CIVICS
CENTER FOR CIVIC EDUCATION
5146 Douglas Fir Rd.
Calabasas, CA 91302
■ Titled simply, *National Standards.*
☎ **800-350-4223**

ENGLISH
NATIONAL COUNCIL OF TEACHERS OF ENGLISH
1111 W. Kenyon Road
Urbana, IL 61801
■ Due in final form in the fall of 1995.
☎ **800-369-6283**

GEOGRAPHY
THE NATIONAL GEOGRAPHIC SOCIETY
P.O. Box 1640
Washington, DC 20013
■ Ask for *Geography for Life.*
☎ **202-775-7832**

HISTORY
UCLA NATIONAL CENTER FOR HISTORY IN THE SCHOOLS
10880 Wilshire Blvd
Suite 761
Los Angeles, CA 90021
■ Ask for *National Standards for United States History* for kindergarten through 4th grade or 5th through 9th grade. Standards for world history are also available.
☎ **310-825-4702**

MATH
NATIONAL COUNCIL OF MATHEMATICS
1906 Association Drive
Reston, VA 22091
■ Ask for *Curriculum and Evaluation Standards for School Mathematics.*
☎ **703-620-9840**

SCIENCE
NATIONAL ACADEMY OF SCIENCE
2101 Constitution Ave., N.W.
Washington, DC 20418
■ With the National Research Council, due in final form in fall, 1995.
☎ **202-334-1399**

of mathematical abilities; and to become mathematical problem-solvers.

In the 54 standards proposed for kindergarten through 12th grade, math educators are advocating revolutionary shifts away from rote memorization to focus on understanding real-life applications of mathematics. Take the study of statistics. In kindergarten through 4th grade, students are asked to explore basic statistical concepts. They may gather data on lunch preferences, for instance, and then chart the trends and analyze them.

By 5th through 8th grade, students should be able to use statistics in real-world situations to collect, organize, and describe data systematically; to construct, read, and interpret tables, charts, and graphs; to make inferences and convincing arguments that are based on data analysis; and to understand and appreciate the power that statistical methods can have in decision making.

By 12th grade, students should be able to interpret charts, tables, and graphs; use curve fitting to predict from data; understand and apply measures of central tendency, variability, and correlation; understand sampling; and design a statistical experiment to study a problem, conduct the experiment, and communicate the outcomes.

EXPERT Q&A

WHAT MAKES AN ALL-STAR SPELLER

Lots of reading and writing is the key to learning to spell better

For some people, good spelling comes naturally. But that may not be a talent that your child has inherited. Here, Sandra Wilde, an associate professor of education at Oregon's Portland State University and author of *You Kan Red This!* (Heinemann Press, 1992), advises parents on how their children can overcome spelling difficulties.

■ What makes some children good spellers, and others awful?

Two factors: One is that you have done a lot of reading; there is increasing evidence that seeing words over and over again in print increases the chance that you will know how to spell them. The other is natural spelling ability, which some people have more than others. Those who have the ability are more likely to be able to write a word and see that it's spelled correctly.

■ How can spelling be taught to both types?

Those who are naturally good spellers are going to teach themselves through reading. The ones who are not naturally good spellers must learn to proofread their writing, because when they get out into the world—applying for jobs and writing on the job—society expects 100 percent spelling accuracy.

■ How important is it that children spell correctly from the start?

Actually, the thinking now is that it's better at first not to focus on correct spelling. The term "invented spelling" refers to the spellings that children come up with on their own based on their knowledge of written language. A young kid writing the word "read" might write it "red." Teachers and researchers have discovered that if children are encouraged to use their own invented spelling, they can start writing in kindergarten or first grade. Through writing, they are teaching themselves about spelling, because they are thinking about "What sounds are in this word?" and "What letters would I use to spell this sound?"

Typically, if kids see words in print enough, they start spelling them correctly. In some ways, it's similar to learning how to talk. Really young children talk in baby talk and don't pronounce words correctly. We focus on the meaning instead, and eventually their speech gets better.

■ How valuable is learning spelling by rote—memorizing lists and taking spelling tests?

One of the problems with the traditional spelling test and spelling books, where kids have to learn 20 words a week, is that on average kids know how to spell two-thirds of the words before studying them, so they aren't really learning very much. Instead of doing a list of 20 words for each kid, tests should focus on words kids want to learn, which are often words they use in their own writing. I think 3 to 5 words per week is about right. Have kids get involved in choosing words, and get them asking, "What words would I like to learn?" I think this is especially valuable starting around 3rd grade when they know a lot of common words.

■ Do you like computer spell-checkers?

I think they're a really valuable tool, but not a panacea. They don't do much for really young kids, because their spellings are not precise enough for the computer to know what they were trying to spell. One problem is that they don't detect if you've used the wrong word. A lot of my college students will spell-check but not proofread, so I'll find instances where they use the word "their" which is spelled correctly, but the situation calls for the word "there." Spell-checkers are something I recommend for high school students and adults who are not naturally good spellers and need to fine-tune their spelling.

EXPERT LIST

CHILDREN'S CLASSICS NOT TO MISS

To encourage the reading of memorable books, the National Endowment for the Humanities asked some of the best public and private schools in the country several years ago for their lists of recommended books for students. Noting how frequently these lists included books that have been treasured for a generation or longer, the NEH decided to publish a compilation of the books that appeared most frequently on the lists they collected. The selections all date back to 1960 or before and have been organized into age-appropriate groupings by a panel of children's book specialists.

KINDERGARTEN THROUGH GRADE 3

Can be read to or by them.

Aesop
Fables
Atwater, Richard and Florence
Mr. Popper's Penguins
Bemelmans, Ludwig
Madeline series
Brown, Margaret Wise
Goodnight, Moon
Brunhoff, Jean de
The Story of Babar
Burton, Virginia Lee
Mike Mulligan and His Steam Shovel
Dalgliesh, Alice
The Bears on Hemlock Mountain
The Courage of Sarah Noble
Godden, Rumer
The Mousewife
Grahame, Kenneth
The Reluctant Dragon
Haywood, Carolyn
Betsy series
Kipling, Rudyard
Just So Stories for Little Children
Leaf, Munro
The Story of Ferdinand
Lear, Edward
Book of Nonsense
MacDonald, Betty
Mrs. Piggle-Wiggle
McClosky, Robert
Blueberries for Sal
Make Way for Ducklings
Milne, A. A.
The House at Pooh Corner
Now We Are Six
When We Were Very Young
Winnie-the-Pooh
Perrault, Charles
Cinderella
Potter, Beatrix
The Tale of Peter Rabbit
Rey, H. A.
Curious George series
Selden, George
The Cricket in Times Square
Seuss, Dr.
The Cat in the Hat
Stevenson, Robert Louis
A Child's Garden of Verses
Williams, Margery
The Velveteen Rabbit
Zion, Gene
Harry the Dirty Dog

GRADES 3 THROUGH 6

Adamson, Joy
Born Free
Alcott, Louisa May
Little Women
Anderson, Hans Christian
Fairy Tales
Bailey, Carolyn Sherwin
Miss Hickory
Barrie, J. M.
Peter Pan
Baum, L. Frank
The Wonderful World of Oz
Bond, Michael
A Bear Called Paddington
Boston, L. M.
The Children of Green Knowe
Brink, Carol Ryrie
Caddie Woodlawn
Burnett, Francis Hodgson
The Secret Garden
Butterworth, Oliver
The Enormous Egg
Clark, Ann Nolan
Secret of the Andes
Cleary, Beverly
Henry Huggins series
Coatsworth, Elizabeth
The Cat Who Went to Heaven
De Angeli, Marguerite
The Door in the Wall
De Jong, Meindert
The House of Sixty Fathers
The Wheel on the School
Dodge, Mary Mapes
Hans Brinker, or the Silver Skates
Du Bois, William Pene
The Twenty-One Ballons
Edmonds, Walter D.
The Matchlock Gun
Estes, Eleanor
Ginger Pye
Moffats series
Farley, Walter
The Black Stallion

■ **EXPERT LIST**

Field, Rachel
Hitty, Her First Hundred Years
Fritz, Jean
The Cabin Faced West
Gilbreth, Frank B. and Ernestine G. Carey
Cheaper by the Dozen
Gipson, Fred
Old Yeller
Grahame, Kenneth
The Wind in the Willows
Gray, Elizabeth Janet
Adam of the Road
Grimm, Jacob and Wilhelm
Grimm's Fairy Tales
Hawes, Charles
The Dark Frigate
Henry, Marguerite
King of the Wind
Misty of Chincoteague
Keith, Harold
Rifles for Watie
Kelly, Eric
The Trumpeter of Krakow
Kipling, Rudyard
Captains Courageous
The Jungle Book
Kjelgaard, Jim
Big Red
Knight, Eric
Lassie Come Home
Krumgold, Joseph
...And Now Miguel
Onion John
La Farge, Oliver
Laughing Boy
Lamb, Charles and Mary
Tales from Shakespeare
Latham, Jean Lee
Carry on, Mr. Bowditch
Lawson, Robert
Ben & Me
Rabbit Hill
Lenski, Lois
Strawberry Girl
Lewis, C. S.
Chronicles of Narnia series
Lindgren, Astrid
Pippi Longstockings series
Lofting, Hugh
Doctor Doolittle series
London, Jack
The Call of the Wild
White Fang
MacGregor, Ellen
Miss Pickerell series
McClosky, Robert
Homer Price
McSwigan, Marie
Snow Treasure
Meigs, Cornelia
Invincible Louisa
Minarik, Else Holmelund
Little Bear
Montgomery, L. M.
Anne of Green Gables
Mukerji, Dhan Ghopal
Gay-Neck, the Story of a Pigeon
Norton, Mary
The Borrowers series
O'Hara, Mary
My Friend Flicka
Pearce, Phillipa
Tom's Midnight Garden
Pyle, Howard
The Merry Adventures of Robin Hood
Richter, Conrad
The Light in the Forest
Sewell, Anna
Black Beauty
Sorenson, Virginia
Miracles on Maple Hill
Speare, Elizabeth George
The Witch of Blackbird Pond
Sperry, Armstrong
Call It Courage
Spyri, Johanna
Heidi
Steinbeck, John
The Red Pony
Stevenson, Robert Louis
Kidnapped
Treasure Island
Travers, Pamela L.
Mary Poppins series
Van Loon, Hendrik
The Story of Mankind
White, E. B.
Charlotte's Web
Stuart Little
Wilder, Laura Ingalls
Little House series
Wyss, Johann
The Swiss Family Robinson

■ **NEWBERY MEDAL WINNERS**

Each year, the Association for Library Service to Children, a division of the American Library Association, gives the Newbery Medal to the author of a single work in recognition of his or her outstanding contribution to children's literature. The most recent winners:

1990 NUMBER THE STARS
Lois Lowry, Dell, $3.99, grades 4–7

1991 MANIAC MAGEE
Jerry Spinelli, Thorndike Press, $3.95, grades 3–7

1992 SHILOH
Phyllis Reynolds Naylor, Dell, $3.99, grades 3–7

1993 MISSING MAY
Cynthia Ryland, Dell, $3.99, grades 5 and up

1994 THE GIVER
Lois Lowry, Houghton-Mifflin, $13, grades 7–9

1995 WALK TWO MOONS
Sharon Creech, Harper-Collins, $16, grades 3–7

■ EXPERT LIST

GRADES 7 AND 8

Alcott, Louisa May
Little Men
Bagnold, Enid
National Velvet
Blackmore, Richard D.
Lorna Doone
Boulle, Pierre
Bridge over the River Kwai
Bradbury, Ray
Dandelion Wine
Fahrenheit 451
The Illustrated Man
Martian Chronicles
Buchan, John
The Thirty-nine Steps
Bunyan, John
The Pilgrim's Progress
Carroll, Lewis
Alice's Adventures in Wonderland
Through the Looking Glass
Clark, Walter
The Ox-Bow Incident
Cooper, James Fenimore
The Deerslayer
The Last of the Mohicans
Curie, Eve
Madame Curie: A Biography
Dana, Richard Henry
Two Years before the Mast
Day, Clarence
Life with Father
Defoe, Daniel
Robinson Crusoe
Dickens, Charles
A Christmas Carol
Douglas, Lloyd C.
The Robe
Doyle, Arthur Conan
The Adventures of Sherlock Holmes
Dumas, Alexander
The Count of Monte Cristo
The Three Musketeers
Du Maurier, Daphne
Rebecca
Edmonds, Walter D.
Drums along the Mohawk
Ferber, Edna
Cimarron
Forbes, Esther
Johnny Tremain
Forester, C. S.
The African Queen
Hornblower series
Frank, Anne
Diary of a Young Girl
Frost, Robert
Poems
Gallico, Paul
The Snow Goose
Gunther, John
Death Be Not Proud
Guthrie, A. B.
The Big Sky
Haggard, H. Rider
King Solomon's Mines
Hansberry, Lorraine
A Raisin in the Sun
Hemingway, Ernest
The Old Man and the Sea
Hersey, John
A Bell for Adano
Hiroshima
The Wall
Heyerdahl, Thor
Kon-Tiki
Hilton, James
Goodbye, Mr. Chips
Lost Horizon
Hudson, W. H.
Green Mansions
Hughes, Richard
A High Wind in Jamaica
Hugo, Victor
The Hunchback of Notre Dame
Irving, Washington
The Legend of Sleepy Hollow
Keller, Helen
Story of My Life
Kennedy, John F.
Profiles in Courage
Kipling, Rudyard
Kim
Knowles, John
A Separate Peace
Lee, Harper
To Kill a Mockingbird
London, Jack
The Sea Wolf
Lord, Walter
A Night to Remember
Malory, Sir Thomas
Le Morte D'Arthur
Maxwell, Gavin
Ring of Bright Water
McCullers, Carson
Member of the Wedding
Michener, James
Bridges at Toko-Ri
Mitchell, Margaret
Gone with the Wind
Nordhoff, Charles and J. N. Hall
Mutiny on the Bounty
O'Dell, Scott
Island of the Blue Dolphins
Orczy, Baroness Emma
The Scarlet Pimpernel
Paton, Alan
Cry, the Beloved Country
Pyle, Howard
Men of Iron
Rawlings, Marjorie Kinnan
The Yearling
Renault, Mary
The King Must Die
Roberts, Kenneth
Northwest Passage
Saint-Exupery, Antoine de
The Little Prince
Wind, Sand and Stars
Saki
Stories
Schaefer, Jack
Shane
Scott, Sir Walter
Ivanhoe
Shelley, Mary
Frankenstein
Smith, Betty
A Tree Grows in Brooklyn
Steinbeck, John
The Pearl
Tortilla Flat
Stevenson, Robert Louis
The Black Arrow

■ EXPERT LIST

The Strange Case of Dr. Jekyll and Mr. Hyde
Stoker, Bram
Dracula
Thurber, James
The Thurber Carnival
Tolkien, J. R. R.
The Hobbit
The Lord of the Rings
Twain, Mark
Adventures of Huckleberry Finn
The Adventures of Tom Sawyer
A Connecticut Yankee in King Arthur's Court
Innocents Abroad
Life on the Mississippi
The Prince and the Pauper
Vern, Jules
Around the World in Eighty Days
Journey to the Center of the Earth
Mysterious Island
20,000 Leagues under the Sea
Wallace, Lewis
Ben-Hur
Washington, Booker T.
Up from Slavery
Wells, H. G.
The Time Machine
War of the Worlds
Wharton, Edith
Ethan Frome
Wilder, Thornton
The Bridge of San Luis Rey
Wister, Owen
The Virginian
Yates, Elizabeth
Amos Fortune, Free Man

GRADES 9 THROUGH 12

Agee, James
A Death in the Family
Anderson, Sherwood
Winesburg, Ohio
Austen, Jane
Emma
Northanger Abbey
Pride and Prejudice
Sense and Sensibility
Baldwin, James
Go Tell It on the Mountain
Balzac, Honore de
Le Pere Goriot
Beckett, Samuel
Waiting for Godot
The Bible
Old Testament
New Testament
Bolt, Robert
A Man for All Seasons
Brontë, Charlotte
Jane Eyre
Brontë, Emily
Wuthering Heights
Browning, Robert
Poems
Buck, Pearl
The Good Earth
Butler, Samuel
The Way of All Flesh
Camus, Albert
The Plague
The Stranger
Cather, Willa
Death Comes for the Archbishop
My Antonia
Cervantes, Miguel
Don Quixote
Chaucer, Geoffrey
The Canterbury Tales
Chekhov, Anton
The Cherry Orchard
Chopin, Kate
The Awakening
Collins, Wilkie
The Moonstone
Conrad, Joseph
Heart of Darkness
Lord Jim
The Secret Sharer
Victory
Crane, Stephen
The Red Badge of Courage
Dante
The Divine Comedy
Defoe, Daniel
Moll Flanders
Dickens, Charles
Bleak House
David Copperfield
Great Expectations
Hard Times
Oliver Twist
A Tale of Two Cities
Dickinson, Emily
Poems
Dinesen, Isak
Out of Africa
Dostoevski, Fyodor
The Brothers Karamazov
Crime and Punishment
Dreiser, Theodore
An American Tragedy
Sister Carrie
Eliot, George
Adam Bede
Middlemarch
Mill on the Floss
Silas Marner
Eliot, T. S.
Murder in the Cathedral
Ellison, Ralph
Invisible Man
Emerson, Ralph Waldo
Essays
Faulkner, William
Absalom, Absalom
As I Lay Dying
Intruder in the Dust
Light in August
The Sound and the Fury
Fielding, Henry
Joseph Andrews
Tom Jones
Fitzgerald, F. Scott
The Great Gatsby
Tender is the Night
Flaubert, Gustave
Madame Bovary
Forster, E. M.
A Passage to India
A Room with a View
Franklin, Benjamin
The Autobiography of

EXPERT LIST

Benjamin Franklin
Galsworthy, John
The Forsyte Saga
Golding, William
Lord of the Flies
Goldsmith, Oliver
She Stoops to Conquer
Graves, Robert
I, Claudius
Greene, Graham
The Heart of the Matter
The Power and the Glory
Hamilton, Edith
Mythology
Hardy, Thomas
Far from the Madding Crowd
Jude the Obscure
The Mayor of Casterbridge
The Return of the Native
Tess of the D'Urbervilles
Hawthorne, Nathaniel
The House of the Seven Gables
The Scarlett Letter
Hemingway, Ernest
A Farewell to Arms
For Whom the Bell Tolls
The Sun Also Rises
Henry, O.
Stories
Hersey, John
A Single Pebble
Hesse, Hermann
Demian
Siddhartha
Steppenwolf
Homer
Iliad
Odyssey
Hughes, Langston
Poems
Hugo, Victor
Les Miserables
Huxley, Aldous
Brave New World
Ibsen, Henrik
A Doll's House
An Enemy of the People
Ghosts
Hedda Gabler
The Master Builder
The Wild Duck
James, Henry
The American
Daisy Miller
Portrait of a Lady
The Turn of the Screw
Joyce, James
Portrait of the Artist as a Young Man
Dubliners
Kafka, Franz
The Castle
Metamorphosis
The Trial
Keats, John
Poems
Kerouac, Jack
On the Road
Koestler, Arthur
Darkness at Noon
Lawrence, D. H.
Sons and Lovers
Lawrence, Jerome and Robert E. Lee
Inherit the Wind
Lewis, Sinclair
Arrowsmith
Babbitt
Main Street
Llewellyn, Richard
How Green Was My Valley
Machiavelli
The Prince
MacLeish, Archibald
J.B.
Mann, Thomas
Buddenbrooks
The Magic Mountain
Marlowe, Christopher
Dr. Faustus
Maugham, Somerset
Of Human Bondage
McCullers, Carson
The Heart is a Lonely Hunter
Melville, Herman
Billy Budd
Moby Dick
Typee
Miller, Arthur
The Crucible
Death of a Salesman
Monsarrat, Nicholas
The Cruel Sea
O'Neill, Eugene
The Emperor Jones
A Long Day's Journey into Night
Mourning Becomes Electra
Orwell, George
Animal Farm
1984
Pasternak, Boris
Doctor Zhivago
Poe, Edgar Allan
Short Stories
Remarque, Erich
All Quiet on the Western Front
Rolvaag, O. E.
Giants in the Earth
Rostand, Edmond
Cyrano de Bergerac
Salinger, J. D.
The Catcher in the Rye
Sandburg, Carl
Abraham Lincoln: The Prairie Years
Abraham Lincoln: The War Years
Saroyan, William
The Human Comedy
Sayers, Dorothy
The Nine Tailors
Shakespeare, William
Plays and Sonnets
Shaw, George Bernard
Arms and the Man
Major Barbara
Pygmalion
Saint Joan
Sheridan, Richard B.
The School for Scandal
Shute, Nevil
On the Beach
Sinclair, Upton
The Jungle
Sophocles
Antigone
Oedipus Rex

■ EXPERT LIST

Steinbeck, John
East of Eden
The Grapes of Wrath
Of Mice and Men
Stowe, Harriet Beecher
Uncle Tom's Cabin
Swift, Jonathan
Gulliver's Travels
Thoreau, Henry David
Walden
Tolstoy, Leo
Anna Karenina
War and Peace
Trollope, Anthony
Barchester Towers
Turgenev, Ivan
Fathers and Sons
Twain, Mark
Pudd'nhead Wilson
Updike, John
Rabbit Run
Virgil
Aeneid
Voltaire
Candide
Warren, Robert Penn
All the King's Men
Waugh, Evelyn
Brideshead Revisited
A Handful of Dust
Wharton, Edith
The Age of Innocence
White, T. H.
The Once and Future King
The Sword in the Stone
Wilde, Oscar
The Importance of Being Earnest
The Picture of Dorian Gray
Wilder, Thornton
Our Town
Williams, Tennessee
The Glass Menagerie
A Streetcar Named Desire
Wolfe, Thomas
Look Homeward, Angel
Woolf, Virginia
Mrs. Dalloway
To the Lighthouse
Wouk, Herman
The Caine Mutiny
Wright, Richard
Black Boy
Native Son

EXPERT PICKS

PROUD VOICES FROM ACROSS THE AGES

Recommended classics from the African American experience

Few works can rival the power with which the following classics capture the African American experience. The selections and comments come from Henry Louis Gates, Jr., who is W.E.B. Du Bois Professor of the Humanities and Chairman of the Afro-American Studies Department at Harvard University.

THE AUTOBIOGRAPHY OF MALCOLM X
Malcolm X, with Alex Haley, 1965
■ A classic articulation of a life of protest.

LETTER FROM BIRMINGHAM JAIL
Martin Luther King, Jr., 1963
■ Articulates the case for justice and freedom, and the action required to achieve them in a racist society.

NARRATIVE OF THE LIFE OF FREDERICK DOUGLASS
Frederick Douglass, 1845
■ The prototype of the autobiography of the escaped slave.

THE SOUL OF BLACK FOLKS
W.E.B. Du Bois, 1903
■ Combines astute historical analysis with a lyric celebration of the black folk tradition to express perhaps more than any other single work the essence of African Americanism.

■ In addition to the works above, Gates suggests reading the fiction of such renowned African American authors as Charles Chestnutt, Jean Toomer, Nella Larsen, Richard Wright, Ralph Ellison, and Toni Morrison; and the poetry of masters such as Phyllis Wheatley and Langston Hughes.

EXPERT Q&A

FROM THE MOUTHS OF BABES

Language specialists believe second language training should begin early

The time when a little restaurant menu French was all the foreign language skill that most Americans assumed they needed has gone the way of the gold standard and a strong dollar. Today, foreign language ability is increasingly important in the global economy, and in many American cities you can go for hours without hearing English spoken. But U.S. schools lag far behind international counterparts in requiring foreign language training. Starting when a child is young is critical, argues Nancy Rhodes, who is associate director for English Language and Multi-Cultural Education at the Center for Applied Linguistics in Washington, D.C., and executive secretary of the National Network for Early Language Learning.

■ At what age is a child best suited to learn a second language?

There is a cut-off age around puberty. After 12 or 13, it is very difficult to learn a language and be able to speak it like a native speaker and develop a high level of fluency. Some studies comparing 2nd-grade learners with 8th-grade learners have found that eighth graders learn more quickly and can do more grammar than the 2nd graders can. The older students are more thorough learners.

That would be the case with any subject area. But young kids like playing with language, they like making new sounds. They're not inhibited or embarrassed by making strange sounds, so it's ideal for them to learn a foreign language. If you wait until kids are in adolescence, they are very inhibited and very worried about how they appear to their peers.

■ What sort of second language programs are available for young children?

Ideally, if one of the parents is bilingual, or if you live in a neighborhood where more than one language is spoken or you have a baby sitter that speaks another language, then the child can be exposed to another language at an early age. But for the majority of kids in the United States, that's not the case.

Typically, schools don't start foreign language teaching until about middle school or high school, but about a fifth of the elementary schools. teach some type of foreign language, either before or after school, or during the school day. It could be just an introduction or it could be an immersion experience. The successful programs are integrated into the school day so that everybody sees foreign language as part of the curriculum, not as some add-on that you only do if you have some extra time.

■ What is an immersion program?

Immersion is when the children receive all of their instruction or part of their instruction in the second language. The language is the medium of instruction, so they're not just learning a language, but they're learning all their content areas through the foreign language.

■ Does an immersion program require a special school?

No, but it requires a special program. About 150 public schools in the United States have implemented immersion programs: both partial immersion, where 50 percent of the day is in the foreign language, and total immersion, which starts out with 100 percent of the day in kindergarten and the first grade.

■ Do kids lag behind in their English when they spend all their time learning another language?

That is the most commonly asked question by parents—"What happens to their English?"—and it is a very reasonable question. Children in immersion programs are taught the regular school curriculum and they have to take all the standardized tests that the other kids take in English. By the time they get to 5th or 6th grade, they score as well or better in English than their peers who have been studying only in English. Studying another language helps you learn more about your native language. All of the research results show that it actually enhances your native language abilities. Immersion students score especially high in English vocabulary and reading comprehension, even though they have gotten very little direct English instruction.

■ Are there any other approaches to teaching a child a second language?

Besides the immersion model, there is the traditional foreign language in elementary schools approach (FLES). Those programs have differing goals, but most often their aim is to enable the child to speak about specific things relating to their school, their family, their friends, the weather—really basic things.

More and more though, these types of programs are learning from the immersion methodology and are starting to teach content from the regular curriculum. A third model is called foreign language experience, or FLEX, and that is where the children receive a smattering of four or five different languages. They're just introduced to the language and maybe a few basic phrases and some tidbits about the culture. It's supposed to expose the children to language in general and a few specific languages in particular so that when they go on to junior high or high school, they will know what they want to study in depth.

■ What if the school has no program? Are language tapes at all effective?

Listening to songs in different languages is fun for kids, but they're not going to learn to speak the language. What I would do myself if I had a child would be to find somebody in the neighborhood who spoke a different language, a child my child's age, and I would get them to play together. Kids learn so much from each other.

■ If a parent speaks the language that the child is learning, should the parent use it at home with the child?

There are some experts who say that when your child comes home from school, don't say "speak to me in Spanish." Especially at the beginning stage of language learning when the child is just going through a period where he's just supposed to be working on listening comprehension.

■ Are there any problems with language confusion?

Not at all. In general, children can learn five or six different languages. In fact, children in many other countries *do* learn five or six languages at once.

The important thing is to separate the languages for the kids. If the mother speaks English, for example, and the father speaks Spanish, they should try as much as possible to keep those roles the same so that the child will see that there are two separate languages.

FACT FILE:

THE TOP 10 TONGUES

The languages spoken most frequently at homes around the world, based on a 1992 world population of 5.5 billion.

	Native speakers	World pop. %
1. Mandarin Chinese	865 mil.	16%
2. English	334 mil.	6%
3. Spanish	283 mil.	5%
4. Arabic	197 mil.	4%
5. Bengali	181 mil.	3%
6. Hindi and Urdu*	172 mil.	3%
7. Portuguese	161 mil.	3%
8. Russian	156 mil.	3%
9. Japanese	125 mil.	2%
10. German	104 mil.	2%

*Same language, different alphabet.

SOURCE: Dr. William W. Gage, using information supplied in *Ethnologue: Languages of the World*, Summer Institute of Linguistics, 1988.

REFORM

WHAT "SCHOOL CHOICE" MEANS

There are more options than ever for public school kids

The traditional assumption that most children will attend school in their neighborhoods is far less true today than a generation ago. The move away from purely neighborhood schools began in the 1970s with court decisions mandating busing as a desegregation tool. The rise of magnet school programs, which early on were developed in some school districts to persuade families to accept busing, has fueled the trend. In the last few years, as public dissatisfaction with the quality of schools has mushroomed, the idea that families should be able to choose where to enroll their children based on program quality and not just location, has been embraced in many states and cities.

It's hard to understand your options unless you know the new vocabulary. The following terms represent variations on the school-choice theme now being debated wherever educators and politicians meet. The definitions are drawn from the Washington, D.C., think tank, the Heritage Foundation.

CHARTER SCHOOL—A "public" school created and operated by a group of teachers, or other qualified individual or groups of individuals, that is largely free from state and district oversight. A charter school differs from a magnet school in its method of creation and its autonomy.

CONTROLLED CHOICE—Choice that is limited by court-ordered desegregation guidelines. Example: The City of Boston must observe strict racial guidelines in city schools. Thus the choice program there limits parents to choices that do not upset the racial balance of a particular school.

FULL CHOICE—Includes private as well as public schools, but not necessarily religious schools.

INTERDISTRICT CHOICE—Students are permitted to cross district lines to attend schools. Some states, such as Colorado, allow interdistrict choice only among a limited number of districts.

INTRADISTRICT CHOICE—Open enrollment among the schools in one particular district. Also called transfers.

MAGNET SCHOOLS—Public schools offering specialized programs to attract students. This may be done as a voluntary method of achieving racial balances when districts are under court order to desegregate. Magnet schools offer students an option or substitute for their location-based school assignment.

OPEN ENROLLMENT—Parents in a state have the right to decide which public school their children will attend anywhere in the state, rather than having children assigned to a school based on location. With voluntary open enrollment, the district is not required to offer choice among its schools, but it can allow parents to choose a school. With mandatory open enrollment, the district must allow parents this option.

POST-SECONDARY ENROLLMENT OPTIONS—High school students (usually juniors or seniors) are permitted to enroll in courses at state universities or community colleges at government expense and to receive high school graduation credits and college credits for those courses. The money allocated for the child's education is used to pay for the courses selected, thus forcing high schools to compete with colleges to retain their students.

PRIVATE VOUCHER PROGRAMS—Programs supported by private individuals, businesses, and other groups that give vouchers to low-income children to attend the private school of their choice. The programs differ in the type of support they give to families and in the type of schools that are eligible.

HOME SCHOOLS

WHEN HOME IS THE SCHOOLHOUSE

Families dissatisfied with public schooling are doing it themselves

Until recently, home schooling was almost exclusively the refuge of born-again Christian families dissatisfied with the moral education that their children were receiving in the public schools. Of the estimated half-million students whose families are engaged in home schooling today, Christian fundamentalists still account for a large majority. But many of the newest converts to home schooling are motivated less by religious concerns than by the belief that they can do better than the public schools at developing their children's academic skills.

Fueling the move toward home schooling, whose ranks are growing at a rate of approximately 15 percent a year, has been the pronounced change in legal attitude on the part of the states. A decade ago very few states permitted home schooling even when a parent was certified as a teacher. Today every state allows home schooling in some form, although the amount of education required of a parent shouldering the teacher's role, the type of instructional materials that a family is expected to use, and the question of whether students have to take standardized tests differs from state to state.

Several important objections to home schooling have also been muted in recent months by the boom in personal computers and online information retrieval services. Families that may have felt hindered once because they lacked access to a library, specialized teachers, or the stimulation of other students, can now partake of all these things via the Internet or one of the commercial online services such as CompuServe and Prodigy.

Academy One, for instance, an educational service on the Internet, allows students to engage in electronic discussions of what they're studying with others nationwide. Home schoolers in Texas can tap into the Texas Education Network, an online service that makes available research materials and facilitates consultations with up to 27,000 Texas educators. One service known as Homer allows students to take courses and have their reports graded online. And many excellent software programs and CD-ROMs also have appeared to help teach reading, math, foreign languages, and typing.

Some families have even found a way to ensure that their home schoolers aren't shut out of the extracurricular activities that they would otherwise participate in at school. In many communities around the country, home school support groups are banding together to sponsor field trips and organize after-school sports leagues for their children. Some school districts have even begun to open up their extracurricular programs to home schoolers.

Advocates of home schooling point to several studies suggesting that home school students outperform their public school counterparts in standardized achievement tests. The fact that many colleges now allow home schoolers applying for admissions to submit "portfolios" of their work in lieu of academic transcripts has also helped the movement. Unless public schools can regain the confidence of the communities they serve, that trend is sure to increase.

EXPERT SOURCE

The Home School Legal Defense Association offers an up-to-date summary of home school laws in all 50 states for $20. Contact:

Home School Legal Defense Association, PO Box 159
Paeonian Springs, VA 22129
☎ 703-338-5600

EXPERT Q&A

NEW CITY, NEW SCHOOL

How to pick the best school for your child when moving to a new town

Each year, hundreds of thousands of families with school-age children move because of job opportunities or company relocations. Parents have to find new homes and safe neighborhoods, and just as important, they have to find new schools for their kids. Dr. William Bainbridge, president of SchoolMatch in Westerville, Ohio, helps about 28,000 families make this difficult decision every year. Here, he challenges the assumptions many people make when choosing new schools.

What are the best indicators for an outsider to use when picking a new school?

One thing is the education level of the parents in the community, because there is a high correlation between the education level of parents and the success of their children in school. This is quite different when you look at income levels and property values. For example, some college towns around the country have extremely high test scores and moderate income levels, because you have a bunch of college professors' children in school.

Give me a school with very high parent education level and I'll turn out good students at a very low cost. The youngsters in such a community are born with the expectation that their parents graduated from college and they should too. Plus the parents are more equipped to help them in homework, and the parents have a higher expectation level for the children.

What should parents look for in a school?

In addition to the high parent education level, they should look at the scholastic examinations themselves. Also look at the awards a school has won. And look at a school's accreditation. It's almost frightening to think that some people are being steered to non-accredited schools, which creates a major problem for children when they apply to college.

What awards reflect school quality?

We think that a state's department of education is very careful for the most part in the awards that they give each year for what they call blue ribbon schools and outstanding schools. The states select award-winning schools that we think are very good. Many private foundations give awards. But they usually specialize, awarding drug-free schools or schools with great computer programs.

What test scores should parents use to compare schools?

I think the college entrance exams are extremely important. It is not necessarily important that the school be in the top ten percent of the country, but I certainly think that if you want your youngster to go to college, it stands to reason that if the school is in the top third, that would be important. For elementary school children, there are about 11 different standardized tests around the country, and they are not intended to be used for comparison from school to school. I would rather look at the scholastic exams from high schools that the elementary schools feed into. Even the developers of the tests will tell you that achievement tests are not a very good way to compare schools, because they are normed differently.

How can you tell if a school is coasting on its reputation?

Look at the accrediting association's summary reports. If the school is in the Midwest, you might look at the North Central Association, for instance. The summary report generally makes recommendations as to what's going on and what the needs are for a school. You can find some glaring things. We did a study some years ago for *Money* magazine, where we took demographically identical schools, but one school had good test scores while the other did not. All a person had to do to find this out was to look at the final report of the accrediting association, which flat out said that in the school with worse test scores there was too much emphasis on athletics and that they had not replaced the director of instruction. A summary report is usually made public by a board of education at the end of an accrediting association's visit. These visits average about once every four years.

■ Is it better for a child if relocation takes place at the start of a new term?

We believe in mid-year relocations for small children, because it gives them a chance to meet other youngsters, so they don't have an isolated summer. Some people have the idea that it's better to relocate in June as soon as school is out. Frequently that child will spend the entire summer not knowing very many other youngsters. We think it is a better idea to go ahead and do the relocation mid-year in January and give them a chance to get acclimated to the school and to prepare for the unusually long summer vacation that we have in the United States. It also gives them a chance to meet some of their neighbors.

For high school kids, I don't see it makes much difference. However, it is important to finish a term or semester. The child could end up losing three or four credits if his or her courses are not available at the new school.

■ What are the biggest mistakes families make in picking a new school?

They listen to friends—what might be right for one family might not be right for another. Elementary and secondary schools are as different as colleges. Take the issue of school size. I think that's the biggest single issue that people ignore. Everyone understands its importance when choosing a college, but school size can be just as important in terms of a child's opportunity to participate on the elementary and secondary school level. Small schools tend to be less competitive, so if you want to make the volleyball team or the debate team, you've got a better shot. However, some of the specialized academic programs are not available at the small schools. I think it is most important to choose like-size schools. If you have a youngster in a school with 2,800 students, he or she is likely to be very unhappy in a school with 500. Conversely, the student in the school with 500 students is going to be very unhappy in the large school.

■ What advice do you have for a child being uprooted from a community and then dropped down in a new and unfamiliar situation?

I think it is very important for children to be involved in some activity, whether it is a musical, theatrical, or an athletic activity. The quicker the parents can get their child involved in an activity, the faster the child is going to make friends and be acclimated. Check out leadership programs such as student council and ask about competitive and non-competitive athletic programs.

■ Should the child be involved in the process of selecting a new school?

Absolutely. If the child can go to the school visits, I think that is great. Many schools, if asked, will assign a buddy. The teachers or principal arranges for your son or daughter to be taken around by another student who will spend time with your child for the first few days.

It is also important to look in metro areas at schools where they already have a high incidence of relocation, because they are probably better equipped to deal with it. You go into a lot of other places and the whole system seems to be stagnant and the same people have been there forever. The teachers and the students aren't used to having new kids on the block.

■ Is it important for parents to talk to teachers and ask questions about the curriculum?

Yes. I think it is more important though to talk to the administration. Check out computer hardware, text books, library resources, and teacher backgrounds. Ask if the curriculum emphasizes basic skills and if there is a diversity of program offerings. Ask if parent involvement is encouraged. If parents can't get an interview with a school principal when they are prospective parents, what's the situation going to be like when they are really there?

INDEPENDENT SCHOOLS

THE PREP SCHOOL MELTING POT

You don't have to be a New England WASP to go to Andover

In a state so racially and ethnically diverse that it has been called the Third World Capital of the World, it's not terribly surprising that some 48 percent of undergraduates at the University of California at Berkeley are students of color. But would you expect nearly two out of every five students at Phillips Exeter Academy to be from a minority background?

Although the famous New England prep school is among the most diverse private schools today, it reflects a growing trend. Enrollment by students of color at independent schools nationwide has risen from 9.8 percent a decade ago to 15.7 percent in the 1993–94 school year. At boarding schools, which have led the way in diversifying, the enrollment of students of color was 25.1 percent in 1993–94. The median tuitions at full boarding schools range from just under $11,000 to $20,600 at top boarding schools like Andover, but financial aid is rising, too: 16.6 percent of all independent school students received financial aid in 1993–94, with the average grant being $5,572 for the year. At Andover, 40 percent of the student body now receives some financial aid, and 9 percent receive full scholarships.

Along with the diversification of the student bodies at independent schools have come efforts to broaden faculty hiring and make the curriculum more diverse. Such trends don't make the private school experience as inclusive as riding the public transit system during rush hour, but they do make private school education a viable option for far more families than may appreciate it.

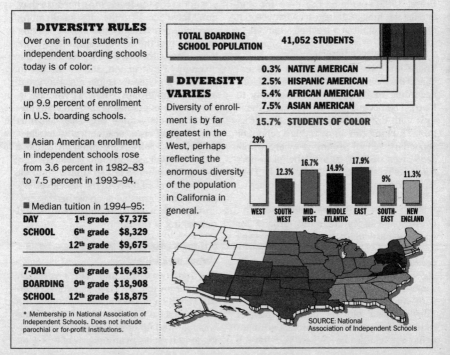

■ DIVERSITY RULES

Over one in four students in independent boarding schools today is of color:

■ International students make up 9.9 percent of enrollment in U.S. boarding schools.

■ Asian American enrollment in independent schools rose from 3.6 percent in 1982–83 to 7.5 percent in 1993–94.

■ Median tuition in 1994–95:

DAY SCHOOL	**1st grade**	**$7,375**
	6th grade	**$8,329**
	12th grade	**$9,675**
7-DAY BOARDING SCHOOL	**6th grade**	**$16,433**
	9th grade	**$18,908**
	12th grade	**$18,875**

* Membership in National Association of Independent Schools. Does not include parochial or for-profit institutions.

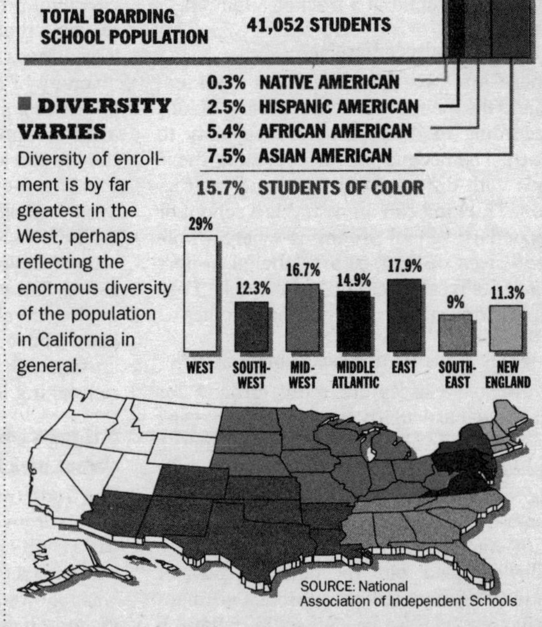

■ DIVERSITY VARIES

Diversity of enrollment is by far greatest in the West, perhaps reflecting the enormous diversity of the population in California in general.

SOURCE: National Association of Independent Schools

EXPERT Q&A

SHOULD STUDENTS BE TRACKED?

Academic pigeon-holing remains widespread despite controversies

Whether you knew it at the time or not, you probably have been academically tracked at some point in your educational career. According to a study by the National Association of Secondary School Principals, some form of academic tracking was found in 82 percent of the surveyed schools. Yet the practice remains highly controversial. Tracking expert Anne Wheelock, a policy analyst at the Edna McConnell Clark Foundation and the author of *Crossing the Tracks* (The New Press, 1992), explains the case for and against tracking and suggests what you can do to help a child in a tracked situation.

What is academic tracking?

There are two components to tracking. One is the identification and labeling of kids according to their perceived capacity to learn. The second part is providing those kids with different curricula and instruction. Tracking can apply to high school or secondary school programs where whole sequences of courses are labeled honors track, general track, or basic track. They have different names in different places.

Why is academic tracking so often used?

Untracked classes are more difficult for teachers, particularly teachers who haven't had the opportunities for professional development. Teachers who are used to teaching to the middle range of abilities in a classroom find that this doesn't work anymore with students of widely varying abilities. They're faced with the daunting task of rethinking their entire approach to managing the classroom. When you have a class with wide-ranging abilities, lecturing doesn't work. You have to engage all of the students' different abilities and talents.

Another argument is that schools should reflect the real world where people are sorted into different jobs all the time. The argument hinges on the belief that schools accurately gauge students' abilities with tracking. However, the most recent research shows that schools often make mistakes trying to place kids in the right tracks. You find some kids in the low groups who are scoring in the 99th percentile on achievement tests while some kids who are in the 20th percentile are in the high groups.

People support tracking because they believe that curricula get watered down in untracked classrooms. They argue that the kids from the higher tracks will miss more challenging material, because they have to wait for the kids from the lower tracks to catch up. This can be avoided, however, with the professional development of teachers.

How well does tracking work?

I think all students lose. The students who are not at the top levels lose, because they don't have access to the most challenging curriculum or usually the most engaging teaching that the school has to offer. In the lower tracks, the press for achievement, the diversity of instruction, and the access to interesting materials is just never as great as in the top groups. Students who are in the top tracks are losing, but they are losing in a more subtle way. They learn to avoid taking risks academically, intellectually, or socially. Very often in tracked schools, if you ask too many questions and reveal that you are not so smart, you risk getting knocked down to the next level. We learn from our mistakes, so we need to create climates in which asking questions and risk-taking is the norm.

Is there concrete evidence that untracked classes work better?

The most powerful and recent research comes from the U.S. Department of Education, which in 1988 began looking at the performance of eighth graders. Their status was followed up every two years, concluding in 12th grade. In an analysis of that data,

Robert Slavin of Johns Hopkins University and Jomills Braddock of the University of Miami looked at the test scores and academic records of students in the first interval from 8th to 10th grade and asked, "Does it make a difference if the students were in a tracked or untracked eighth grade?"

They found that it does make a difference, at least in terms of 10th-grade performance. The average- and low-scoring eighth graders in untracked classes were more likely in their 10th-grade year to get better grades and test scores than their comparable scoring peers who had been in tracked 8th-grade classes. They were also more likely to be in college-bound tracks than they would have been in if they had been tracked in eighth grade.

■ Is there anything parents with children in tracked schools should do about it?

They should fight like hell to get their kids in the top groups. And they should work with teachers to provide *all* the kids the opportunities available to those in the top groups. They should make sure that their child gets to go on field trips, learn research skills, solve interesting math problems, apply math in a variety of contexts and do lab experiments. They must also make sure that their child has access to computers and the library, and ask what kind of access it is. Often in tracked schools these opportunities to learn get distributed so that the top kids get more and the bottom kids get less.

■ What would you tell parents who worry about untracked classes?

Parents should ask, "What is my child going to learn, and how will I know if he or she has learned it?" They should ask, "How is the school going to use what it knows about gifted and talented programs in untracked classes?" By asking those questions, parents can guard against untracked classes being synonymous with watered-down classes.

A SCHOOL WHERE EVERYBODY KNOWS YOUR NAME

The case for the mega high school is being called into question

When it comes to schools, bigger is not better. Educators have long argued for smaller classes, and several researchers now are finding that the intimate environment that can make a class click also benefits a school as a whole.

The original arguments for large high schools go back to 1959 and a book by James Conant, the then-president of Harvard, arguing that very small high schools short-changed students because they were too small to afford such things as a science lab, advanced mathematics, and a full menu of electives.

Most high schools today have several thousand students and extensive curricular offerings. But recent research suggests little educational justification for large, comprehensive high schools.

"As schools get bigger, they tend to create demands for much higher levels of bureaucratic overhead," explains Anthony S. Bryk, an education professor at the University of Chicago. "Safety and disorder go up in large schools, and you have to hire police and extra assistant principals. All of the economic efficiencies that might attach to bigger buildings evaporate."

The optimum size for a high school may be in the range of 500 to 600 students, many experts believe. Studies indicate that there is less student absenteeism and classroom disorder, and lower drop-out rates in such schools. Teacher morale also tends to be higher, and at least in the period of transition from 8th to 10th grade, new research suggests that student achievement is higher in smaller schools.

"Smaller-sized schools tend to work because they create more engaging environments for students," Bryk says. "Large high schools are very anonymous places where students typically feel lost and often fall through the cracks."

EXPERT Q&A

THE CYBER SCHOOL

Computers are a waste if a school hasn't analyzed its mission

A school full of computers doesn't always signal that its students have an advantage over kids in otherwise woefully underwired surroundings. Pressured to buy the latest technologies, many schools are neglecting to outline just how the new equipment will be used in the classroom. Here, Martha Stone Wiske, co-director of Harvard University's Educational Technology Center, outlines what parents, teachers, and school administrators should consider before rushing to make their schools high-tech showcases.

What's the biggest mistake schools make when bringing technology into the classroom?

The biggest mistake schools make concerning educational technologies is focusing more on the technologies than on clarifying educational goals.

Computers and other new technologies are means not ends in themselves. Equipment purchased without a clear educational plan is likely to remain unused or to draw resources away from the real priorities. It is important that teachers and others who are expected to use new technologies play a central role in making decisions about how the new equipment will be used.

A second common mistake is spending money on computer hardware without setting aside sufficient funds for associated expenses such as software, furniture, supplies, wiring, and other renovations, and professional development. Of these, the last is most overlooked. That's the time to help teachers figure out how to incorporate technological innovations into their curriculum and practice.

How should computers be used in the classroom?

There are about as many ways to use computers to improve teaching and learning as there are good ways of teaching. Like books, computers can play a part in nearly any educational approach. Computers connected with databases (either online databases accessible through a telephone line or large databases on CD-ROMs) can be an excellent source of information. Word processing software packages are excellent general purpose tools that can help both teachers and students concentrate on expressing themselves clearly, rather than spending enormous amounts of time on the mechanics of writing. Graphing calculators and graphing software can help students see and manipulate quantitative relationships in multiple forms, as mathematicians do.

Such tools can help students understand mathematics as a means of representing and investigating ideas, rather than a set body of right answers. Special-purpose software, such as simulations and models, can enable students to investigate real world problems that are difficult or impossible to study directly. Drill and practice software may be helpful for the few things that need to be learned by rote memory, such as spelling, touch-typing, and number facts. Relatively little of the work to be done in schools is of this type, however.

How should teachers prepare for the introduction of new equipment?

Before teachers can use technology effectively, many factors need to be coordinated. They must know about hardware and software innovations that address their goals. Teachers must have time to become familiar with software, a process that may take hours of relaxed exploration. Teachers must also have access to the necessary equipment at times that are convenient. They must have time to design classroom materials, such as assignment and assessment worksheets that engage students with the technology in effective ways, and they must plan activities and orchestrate ways for students to make use of the technology. Students also may need to become familiar with software facilities and learn to play new roles in the classroom.

■ Can technology get in the way of what teachers can accomplish on their own?

Sometimes new technologies provide an interesting enrichment whose benefits are not really worth the expense and time they require. Calculating the cost of new technology should take account of the "opportunity costs." What else might teachers and students have done with their time and energy? What other opportunities were set aside in order to make use of new technology?

■ How can parents tell if computers are being used to educate their children or merely to entertain them?

Parents who want to know about their children's educational experiences at school should try to arrange to visit the school. Sometimes the best way is to offer to volunteer when the teacher asks for assistants. In some schools, parents are welcome to visit classes as long as they make arrangements in advance.

Because teaching is so complex and demanding, parents should be hesitant to leap to conclusions about the meaning and value of activities they observe. If they have serious doubts about what they see, they should try to raise questions with teachers. "I'm interested in knowing what my child's class is doing with computers. How does that fit in with the overall curriculum goals for this class? Do you think the computer-based work is valuable? Why, or why not? What do you think it would take to make the computer work more educationally worthwhile?"

If parents seek to understand a teacher's goals, concerns, plans, and problems, and they approach the situation with an open mind, they may learn ways in which to help teachers and schools carry out their very important and very difficult jobs.

■ There's a lot of talk about connecting schools to the Internet. How should schools view these new services?

Telecommunication certainly opens up many educational possibilities. These innovations can break through classroom walls, linking students with experts, fellow students and vast, readily updated databases around the world.

The potential is unlimited—and that is one of the biggest problems. When so much is possible, selecting or developing a truly educational use of telecommunications can be daunting. Most American schools now have at least one computer and a telephone line. With an inexpensive modem, these technologies make telecommunication possible. I would encourage teachers and parents to see that at least one beneficial use is made of these technologies before they press for extensive telecommunications access.

■ Should students be taught to program computers or to use computers as tools to help them with their traditional course work?

There are good arguments on both sides of this question. Many people believe that students should learn how to program computers so that they understand the nature of these machines and the instructions that humans must write to make them function. Some believe that learning how to break a problem into parts and to write a program to solve it fosters systematic thinking. Others say that we drive cars and use telephones without understanding much at all about how these technologies work. They may think that schools should concentrate more on teaching students to understand what they read, to write clearly, to gather and evaluate evidence, and to formulate and defend reasoned opinions.

Answers to the question about teaching computer programming ought to be developed through dialogue among teachers, administrators, parents, and students about what they want schools to do. The final answer is less important than the process of thoughtful debate within communities about how new technologies can support education.

GAP YEAR

TIME TO TAKE TIME OUT

Many students are taking a year off between high school and college

The fighting was over, the enemy had surrendered, and hundreds of thousands of American soldiers returned home after World War II to enroll in college as part of the GI Bill. There was a lot of worry at the time that student GIs, being older and more world-weary than the typical college freshman, would not fit in on campuses and wouldn't do well academically. But the maturity of the returning GIs and their eagerness to hit the books and get on with their lives made them classroom standouts.

There's no war now, there's not even a military draft, but the fact that taking time off between high school and college can sharpen a young person's focus and build the self-confidence necessary to excel in college is being discovered anew by many students and their families. At Harvard, for instance, as many as 50 to 60 students in the incoming freshman class of approximately 1,600 students will defer their admissions for a year.

"We would actually like to see more students do it," says William Fitzsimmons, who is an admissions officer for Harvard and Radcliffe. "Because virtually everyone who has ever done it has reported that it was one of the best experiences they have ever had."

For students considering a "gap year," the opportunities to broaden their perspectives are legion. Environmentalists can work in the Student Conservation Association, which places students in outdoor-oriented volunteer programs across the United States. Students interested in health care can try the Frontier Nursing Service, which provides a chance to work with and help people in rural Kentucky.

Those looking for overseas experiences can explore the International Internship Network. Whether you are interested in art, finance, or wine making, you can be placed in Spain, Israel, Germany, France, or Italy. Students seeking a more traditional academic year in a foreign culture can choose from among many boarding schools throughout England, India, and Australia.

Most students who take a year off complete the college admissions process as high school students and simply defer their matriculation for a year. But in some cases, students use their gap year to redo the application process, using their experience and new-found maturity to improve their chances of being accepted at the college of their choice.

A great starting point for planning a gap year is to consult *Time Out* (Simon & Schuster, 1992), a book by Robert Gilpin and Caroline Fitzgibbons that features hundreds of gap-year options from which you can choose. It includes detailed descriptions of the programs and a parcel of practical information about how to apply for the programs and what costs may be involved.

EXPERT SOURCE

One of the best ways to arrange a gap year for yourself or your child is to consult with Cornelius Bull of the Center for Interim Services in Cambridge, Mass. Bull charges a hefty one-time fee of $1,200, but he is very experienced at helping a student plan a gap-year sabbatical that involves several unusual educational adventures: ☎ 617-547-0980.

COLLEGE & GRAD SCHOOL

WHAT THE NEW SATs MEAN TO YOU

The tests have changed, and so has the scoring system

Three letters—S, A, and T—strung together form an acronym that manages to strike terror in the hearts of students and parents alike. The SAT, recently revised and renamed the Scholastic Assessment Test (the "A" used to stand for Aptitude), is the most widely used college entrance exam in the United States, with over one million high school students taking it in the last year alone.

The point of the SAT, its defenders maintain, is to predict a student's future college performance by testing reasoning skills in both verbal and mathematical areas. Unlike many other standardized tests, the SAT purportedly measures a student's potential for academic work rather than solely assessing knowledge already learned.

Critics claim, however, that the SAT does not measure skills so much as knowledge, and that knowledge is not a fair indication of future academic performance. Others contend that the SAT's method of assessing skills is inherently biased and unfair. What is indisputable is that the SAT is one of the key factors used by colleges and universities in making admissions decisions, and that a low SAT average can mean the difference between getting into the school you want and an also-ran.

To quiet critics, the exam's sponsor, the College Entrance Examination Board, working with the test's creator, the Educational Testing Service, undertook a major overhaul of the exam in 1995. The test was changed in name, format, content, and scoring for the first time in 20 years.

The revisions came after three years of "extensive research and field testing," according to the College Board. "The revised SAT recognizes the increased diversity of students in our educational system, as well as changes in how and what these students are being taught in secondary school," the board said.

The new reading comprehension section contains longer passages with more emphasis on analysis, and the revised math questions demand that students write their answers on a grid rather than pick a multiple choice answer. Beginning in April 1995, the scoring system was recalibrated as well. The purpose of the "re-centering" of test scores was to bring the average score for each section back to 500, which was the average when the scoring method was devised in 1941. Over the past four decades, average scores have dropped to the low to mid-400s.

The recalibrating means that by answering the same number of questions correctly, the average student will get approximately 80 extra points on the verbal section and 20 extra points on the math section. (As in the past, 1600 remains the perfect score for the math and verbal components combined.)

The grade inflation caused by the resetting of the scale is, of course, no secret to college admissions offices. Rather than increasing an individual's chance of being accepted by a school known for expecting high test scores, the revised scoring is supposed to give those who take the exam a better indication of how they did compared to others. If, for example, a student gets a 510 on the verbal exam, she will know that she scored a little above average.

How accurate is the test in predicting academic success? It depends. Some schools, such as Brown University, report that they have observed no marked correlation between scores and academic performance. At Harvard University, where the average combined SAT score is 1400, officials indicate that SAT scores are typically well correlated to academic performance, particularly during the freshman year.

But it is a mistake to make too much of SAT scores, warns Marlyn McGrath Lewis, Harvard's director of admissions. For a clearer picture of future academic success, Lewis says, it's essential to look at a bigger picture, which includes a student's high school grades, class rank, and extracurricular activities.

TEACHING TO THE TEST

Educators and test-makers dislike exam prep courses, but they work

Sure they're expensive. And maybe it's true that the same time spent in other academic or extracurricular pursuits could be just as valuable, if not more so, in helping one get into college. But SAT review courses by companies such as Princeton Review, Kaplan Educational Centers, Inc., and Sylvan Learning Centers do seem to raise test scores for many students. Independent audits conducted by two accounting firms, Price Waterhouse and Deloitte & Touche, concluded that students who took a preparation course raised their scores by approximately 125 points on average. Even the test maker, Educational Testing Service, concedes that a course may raise scores 30 to 50 points.

The premise of the test prep classes is that if students are familiar with the test and learn certain "tricks," they can improve their score substantially. The big commercial testing companies like Princeton Review, Kaplan, and Sylvan all offer group classes as well as individual tutoring for the SAT, the PSAT (the "P" in this case is for preliminary), and certain graduate school entrance exams. For the SAT, the cost of a course (generally 36 to 39 classroom hours) is about $700. Private tutoring runs about $75 per hour. All of the above are offered nationwide. You should consult a phone directory to find out if one or all operate in your area.

Before reaching into your wallet, however, you may want to investigate other possibilities that might fit your budget more easily. High schools, libraries, and community colleges increasingly offer their own versions of test prep courses for substantially less money. If you are trying to decide whether a $700 course is worth the money, ask the company you're considering whether there is an information session you can attend or a class you can visit. This normally costs nothing and might enlighten you as to what you are getting into.

HOWDJA DO?

Because of changes in the way the SATs will be scored after April 1995, average scores are likely to be about 80 points higher on the verbal part of the exam and 20 points higher on the math portion than in the past. As in the past, 1600 remains the perfect score for the math and verbal components combined.

AVERAGE SAT SCORES 1987–94

	VERBAL			MATHEMATICAL		
YEAR	**Men**	**Women**	**Total**	**Men**	**Women**	**Total**
1987	435	425	430	500	453	476
1988	435	422	428	498	455	476
1989	434	421	427	500	454	476
1990	429	419	424	499	455	476
1991	426	418	422	497	453	474
1992	428	419	423	499	456	476
1993	428	420	424	502	457	478
1994	425	421	423	501	460	479

SOURCE: Copyright 1994. College Entrance Examination Board.

ACING THE ACHIEVEMENT TESTS

Unlike the SATs, which are supposed to measure potential for academic performance, the College Board achievement tests are supposed to test student knowledge of a specific subject area. Following is the distribution of college board test results by percentage.

Score	English Comp.	Literature	American History	World History	Math I	Math II	Math IIC	Biology	Chemistry	Physics
700–800	4%	6%	4%	7%	6%	38%	42%	8%	16%	20%
600–699	21%	26%	23%	23%	28%	41%	39%	29%	30%	32%
500–599	33%	32%	35%	36%	36%	17%	15%	35%	32%	32%
400–499	29%	25%	28%	28%	24%	3%	3%	21%	19%	14%
300–399	11%	10%	10%	7%	6%	1%	1%	6%	3%	1%
200–299	1%	1%	0%	0%	0%	0%	1%	1%	0%	1%
MEAN SCORE	**520**	**532**	**526**	**539**	**500**	**662**	**674**	**555**	**582**	**604**

Score	French	French L/R*	German	German L/R*	Hebrew	Italian	Japanese L/R*	Latin	Spanish	Spanish L/R*
700–800	13%	6%	20%	5%	40%	23%	33%	14%	19%	9%
600–699	22%	17%	20%	20%	28%	22%	12%	23%	21%	22%
500–599	29%	29%	29%	31%	17%	25%	17%	29%	27%	34%
400–499	28%	36%	24%	32%	9%	22%	24%	30%	26%	28%
300–399	8%	11%	7%	12%	4%	7%	13%	30%	7%	8%
200–299	0%	0%	0%	0%	3%	0%	1%	5%	0%	0%
MEAN SCORE	**549**	**516**	**566**	**519**	**632**	**577**	**581**	**556**	**562**	**539**

*"Listing reading" tests, offered only at high schools, not at national test centers.
SOURCE: Copyright 1994, College Entrance Examination Board and Educational Testing Service.

ADMISSIONS

THE COMMON APPLICATION

More and more colleges are using a standardized application form

Everyone who has applied to college knows that the admissions process can be an arduous, time-consuming task. In an effort to simplify this process, 138 private colleges and universities across the country now accept the Common Application. In the past, the typical high school senior who applied to multiple schools often had to fill out redundant forms and compose a number of challenging essays. Now the student can fill out one form and answer a single essay question and then send copies to schools such as Harvard, Johns Hopkins, Swarthmore, Pomona, and New York University. (Public universities are not eligible.) When Harvard began accepting the Common Application in 1995, it experienced a 16 percent rise in applications, although that increase was not entirely due to the Common Application. But Harvard admissions officials credit the Common Application with improving the geographical diversity of its admissions pool and increasing the number of applicants with top grades and test scores.

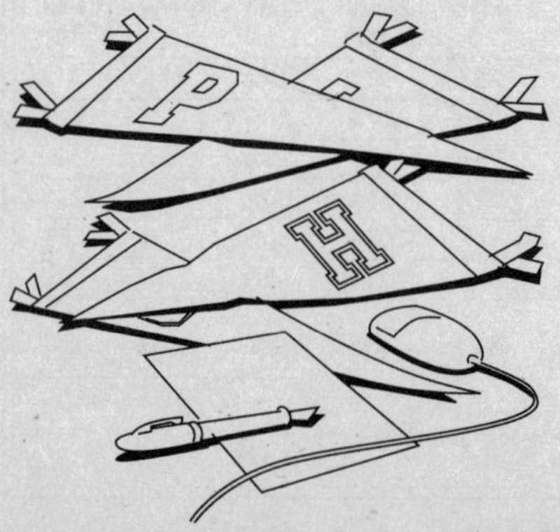

The Common Application is proving popular with many overburdened high school teachers and administrators, who need not submit as many versions of teacher evaluations and secondary school reports as a result. Some high school guidance counsellors worry, however, that students will be too cavalier about the number and types of schools they apply to as a result of the easier application process.

Just because a college accepts the Common Application doesn't mean that it is limited to asking questions that appear on the standard form. Many also require a supplemental form. Harvard, for example, requires candidates to identify more completely special academic, extracurricular, and vocational interests, to list non-academic honors, and to provide advanced placement test scores. The university also allows the candidate to send music tapes, slides of artwork, or samples of academic work, and gives applicants a chance to answer a second essay question should the topic required by the Common Application seem limited.

While the Common Application eliminates unnecessary paperwork, applications that are completely paperless will soon be common. The National Association of Secondary School Principals, which distributes the Common Application, has also begun making the forms available on computer disks. But not all colleges and universities are equipped to accept disks. In those cases, a printout of the application is acceptable.

In September of 1994, the College Board launched a program that allows students to apply via modem. Candidates can call up application forms and information from various colleges on computers available in their high school guidance offices. A version of the Common Application can also be accessed in this manner, and a second electronic application system is expected to be introduced by American College Testing in 1995. Says Margit Dahl, Yale University's director of admissions: "This is the wave of the future."

To obtain a copy of the Common Application and a list of colleges and universities that accept it, write: National Association of Secondary School Principals, 1904 Association Drive, Reston, VA 22091.

U.S. NEWS SURVEY

RATING AMERICA'S COLLEGES

The annual rankings can help you pick the right school for your needs

The publication of surveys rating the quality of American colleges and universities has become something of a cottage industry in recent years, but no guide is more eagerly awaited by students and parents each year than *U.S. News & World Report*'s rankings of America's best colleges.

To compile its ratings, *U.S. News* groups some 1,400 accredited colleges and universities into 14 categories of size, geographic whereabouts, and educational orientation, using guidelines adapted from the Carnegie Foundation for the Advancement of Teaching. It then surveys thousands of college presidents, deans, and admissions directors around the country for their assessment of the quality of peer institutions and combines that reputational data with objective information on an institution's selectivity in admissions, faculty resources, financial resources, graduation rates, and alumni satisfaction to arrive at rankings for schools in the different categories.

No ranking system can ever produce a wholly accurate measure of an institution's quality, of course, and a college that is appropriate for one student may be a poor match for another. The *U.S. News* survey is but one tool in helping students and their families pick the right college for their circumstances. Highlights of the *U.S. News* survey for 1994 appear on the following eight pages.

■ A FURTHER WORD ON METHODOLOGY

The *U.S. News* methodology for ranking colleges and universities has two components: a reputational survey taken among college administrators, together with a collection of more objective statistical measures of an institution's educational quality.

Reputation: According to *U.S. News,* college presidents, deans, and admissions directors from 1,400 schools participated in the 1994 survey of academic reputations. Participants were only asked to score institutions in the category to which their own schools belonged. The respondents were expected to assign each school to one of four quartiles based upon their assessment of a school's academic quality, and an average score was computed for each school.

Student selectivity: In measuring selectivity, the survey took into account the acceptance rate and actual enrollment of students offered places in the admissions process, the enrollees' high-school class ranks, and the average or midpoint combined scores on the SATs or ACTs.

Faculty resources: Faculty resources were judged by the ratio of full-time students to full-time faculty, excluding certain professional schools, as well as the percentage of full-time faculty with Ph.D's or other top terminal degrees, the percentage of part-time faculty, the average salary and benefits for tenured full professors, and the size of the undergraduate classes.

Financial strength: This was calculated by dividing the institution's total expenditures for its education program, including such things as instruction, student services, libraries and computers, and administration, by its total full-time enrollment.

Alumni satisfaction: This was a measure only weighed in the national universities and national liberal arts categories. It was derived from the average percentage of alumni giving during the two previous years. The data on alumni satisfaction do not appear in the tables that follow for space reasons, but were a factor in compiling the overall rankings.

EXPERT LIST

THE BEST COLLEGES IN AMERICA

Every year U.S. News & World Report *publishes a widely followed special report that ranks America's best colleges and universities by several objective measures such as test scores and student/faculty ratios, as well as by academic reputation. Highlights from the 1994–95 survey appear below.*

■ BEST NATIONAL UNIVERSITIES

The 229 national universities from which these top-ranked institutions were selected have comprehensive program offerings, place great emphasis on faculty research, and award many Ph.D's. For the fourth year in a row, Harvard finished first in this category in 1994.

Rank/School	Overall score	Academic reputation	Avg./mdpt. SAT/ACT score	Freshmen in top 10% of HS class	Acceptance rate	Student/ faculty rate	Education program per student
1. **Harvard University,** Mass.	100.0	1	1400	90%	16%	11/1	$37,219
2. **Princeton University,** N.J.	98.9	4	1322	90%	15%	8/1	$28,320
3. **Yale University,** Conn.	98.7	4	1355	95%	23%	10/1	$40,386
4. **Massachusetts Institute of Technology**	98.1	1	1380	96%	33%	10/1	$33,541
5. **Stanford University,** Calif.	97.5	1	1335	88%	22%	14/1	$33,629
6. **Duke University,** N.C.	97.1	9	1310	90%	28%	12/1	$27,206
7. **California Institute of Technology**	96.8	9	1415	98%	26%	7/1	$62,469
8. **Dartmouth College,** N.H.	95.4	16	1330	87%	26%	9/1	$26,619
9. **Columbia College,** N.Y.	95.3	9	1310	78%	29%	11/1	$30,639
10. **University of Chicago**	94.7	4	1300	68%	47%	7/1	$36,854
11. **Brown University,** R.I.	94.2	14	1310	87%	26%	13/1	$20,440
12. **Rice University,** Texas	94.0	21	1364	87%	19%	9/1	$22,836
13. **University of Pennsylvania**	94.0	16	1285	85%	42%	11/1	$25,765
14. **Northwestern University,** Ill.	93.7	14	1255	85%	42%	11/1	$26,385
15. **Cornell University,** N.Y.	93.2	9	1280	81%	37%	11/1	$22,480
16. **Emory University,** Ga.	90.4	31	1220	76%	49%	12/1	$28,457
17. **University of Virginia**	89.4	16	1225	74%	34%	13/1	$13,597
18. **Vanderbilt University,** Tenn.	89.9	26	1200	71%	60%	12/1	$23,850
19. **University of Notre Dame,** Ind.	88.5	37	1260	79%	48%	13/1	$13,936
20. **Washington University,** Mo.	88.3	26	1220	62%	69%	10/1	$45,702
21. **University of Michigan at Ann Arbor**	87.6	9	1185	66%	68%	22/1	$14,847
22. **Johns Hopkins University,** Md.	86.9	4	1310	75%	41%	9/1	$56,233
23. **University of California at Berkeley**	86.8	4	1230	95%	42%	16/1	$13,919
24. **Carnegie Mellon University,** Pa.	86.5	21	1245	60%	60%	9/1	$24,386
25. **Georgetown University,** D.C.	85.3	31	1240	71%	26%	13/1	$19,635
TIER ONE/SCHOOLS RANKED 26TH TO 57TH							
26. **Boston College,** Mass.		65	1210	66%	47%	17/1	$10,989
27. **Boston University,** Mass.		58	1150	45%	64%	16/1	$16,836
28. **Brandeis University,** Mass.		42	1215	48%	66%	10/1	$17,150
29. **Case Western University,** Ohio		42	1235	71%	81%	10/1	$19,733
30. **College of William and Mary,** Va.		37	1240	68%	44%	12/1	$9,534

■ **EXPERT LIST**

NATIONAL UNIVERSITIES Rank/School	Overall score	Academic reputation	Avg./mdpt. SAT/ACT score	Freshmen in top 10% of HS class	Acceptance rate	Student/ faculty rate	Education program per student
31. Colorado School of Mines		76	1200	65%	81%	14/1	$11,838
32. Georgia Institute of Technology		31	1240	89%	58%	19/1	$11,271
33. Lehigh University, Pa.		76	1140	40%	67%	13/1	$14,665
34. New York University		51	1145	70%	53%	11/1	$21,227
35. Penn State Univiversity at Main Campus		31	1096	48%	54%	18/1	$8,992
36. Pepperdine University, Calif.		107	1070	86%	53%	11/1	$16,185
37. Renesselaer Polytechnic Institute, N.Y.		51	1190	53%	83%	15/1	$15,605
38. Rutgers at New Brunswick, N.J.		42	1110	36%	55%	20/1	$10,474
39. SUNY at Binghampton, N.Y.		83	1150	60%	43%	18/1	$8,055
40. Tufts University, Mass.		51	1240	60%	47%	14/1	$18,981
41. Tulane University, La.		51	1168	47%	73%	13/1	$16,920
42. University of California at Davis		42	1075	95%	70%	22/1	$15,873
43. University of California at Irvine		58	1025	85%	69%	20/1	$15,934
44. University of California at Los Angeles		21	1154	93%	47%	19/1	$20,260
45. University of California at San Diego		42	1135	95%	59%	22/1	$17,674
46. University of California at Santa Barbara		65	1010	90%	85%	19/1	$9,475
47. University of Florida		42	1135	54%	71%	19/1	$14,737
48. University of Illinois at Urbana-Champaign		21	1150	52%	78%	18/1	$8,559
49. University of Iowa		37	25	23%	87%	22/1	$12,194
50. University of Minnesota at Twin Cities		26	1060	26%	58%	17/1	$16,122
51. University of North Carolina at Chapel Hill		16	1045	75%	41%	14/1	$15,893
52. University of Rochester, N.Y.		51	1140	56%	63%	13/1	$26,037
53. University of Southern California		42	1090	45%	69%	14/1	$17,007
54. University of Texas at Austin		21	1135	48%	65%	20/1	$7,837
55. University of Washington		26	1055	40%	55%	13/1	$16,527
56. University of Wisconsin at Madison		16	1085	36%	73%	15/1	$11,006
57. Wake Forest University, N.C.		76	1250	75%	42%	13/1	$41,766

■ BEST NATIONAL LIBERAL ARTS COLLEGES

The 164 liberal arts colleges from which these outstanding schools were picked are highly selective in their admissions and award more than 40 percent of their degrees in the liberal arts each year. Amherst, Williams, and Swarthmore have vied for the top ranking every year since 1987, with Amherst finishing first in 1994.

Rank/School	Overall score	Academic reputation	Avg./midpt. SAT/ACT score	Freshmen in top 10% of HS class	Acceptance rate	Student/ faculty Rate	Education program per student
1. Amherst College, Mass.	100.0	1	1335	83%	23%	8/1	$21,424
2. Williams College, Mass.	99.4	1	1350	81%	30%	9/1	$22,014
3. Swarthmore College, Pa.	98.1	3	1310	81%	39%	9/1	$23,975
4. Wellesley College, Mass.	97.1	3	1240	80%	43%	11/1	$21,409
5. Pomona College, Calif.	94.7	6	1330	80%	37%	9/1	$20,682
6. Bowdoin College, Maine	94.5	6	1200	76%	30%	11/1	$20,447
7. Haverford College, Pa.	94.5	10	1290	76%	44%	11/1	$17,021
8. Davidson College, N.C.	91.6	14	1230	77%	40%	12/1	$17,581
9. Wesleyan University, Conn.	91.5	6	1280	60%	41%	12/1	$16,262

■ EXPERT LIST

NATIONAL LIBERAL ARTS COLLEGES Rank/School	Overall score	Academic reputation	Avg./midpt. SAT/ACT score	Freshmen in top 10% of HS class	Acceptance rate	Student/ faculty rate	Education program per student
10. Carleton College, Minn.	91.3	3	1275	75%	59%	10/1	$17,960
11. Middlebury College, Vt.	91.2	14	1260	64%	34%	11/1	$21,426
12. Claremont McKenna College, Calif.	91.1	20	1270	71%	41%	10/1	$18,443
13. Smith College, Mass.	90.4	6	1175	51%	55%	10/1	$21,199
14. Bryn Mawr College, Pa.	89.3	10	1250	71%	55%	12/1	$17,449
15. Washington and Lee University, Va.	88.5	24	1251	68%	33%	9/1	$15,736
16. Vassar College, N.Y.	87.7	14	1235	53%	53%	10/1	$17,089
17. Grinnell College, Iowa	87.5	10	1265	56%	68%	10/1	$18,979
18. Colgate University, N.Y.	86.3	17	1200	46%	51%	11/1	$15,494
19. Oberlin College, Ohio	84.3	10	1225	50%	58%	10/1	$16.593
20. Colorado College, Colo.	84.0	24	1180	56%	49%	11/1	$14,664
21. Bates College, Maine	83.4	20	1225	53%	45%	10/1	$16,444
22. Trinity College, Conn.	83.0	27	1180	46%	59%	10/1	$18,034
23. Colby College, Maine	82.0	24	1175	58%	46%	10/1	$15,954
24. College of the Holy Cross, Mass.	81.2	40	1225	70%	56%	11/1	$12,138
25. Bucknell University, Pa.	80.4	27	1180	49%	58%	14/1	$13,675
TIER ONE/SCHOOLS RANKED 26TH TO 40TH							
26. Bard College, N.Y.		53	1230	50%	44%	10/1	$13,894
27. Barnard College, N.Y.		17	1205	53%	56%	10/1	$12,580
28. Connecticut College		32	1174	42%	51%	11/1	$14,773
29. Franklin and Marshall College, Pa.		32	1170	46%	65%	11/1	$15,797
30. Hamilton College, N.Y.		27	1138	40%	57%	10/1	$17,761
31. Kenyon College, Ohio		27	1170	44%	70%	11/1	$14,067
32. Lafayette College, Pa.		40	1130	36%	60%	11/1	$15,365
33. Lawrence University, Wis.		44	1155	50%	76%	10/1	$13,965
34. Macalester College, Minn.		20	1235	56%	51%	12/1	$14,213
35. Mount Holyoke College, Mass.		17	1128	47%	73%	9/1	$18,359
36. Rhodes College, Tenn.		36	1195	58%	80%	11/1	$13,388
37. Sarah Lawrence College, N.Y.		44	1215	57%	56%	6/1	$14,779
38. Scripps College, Calif.		36	1145	60%	74%	8/1	$18,372
39. Union College, N.Y.		44	29	49%	49%	12/1	$15,411
40. University of the South, Tenn.		36	1160	46%	67%	10/1	$18,784

■ BEST REGIONAL UNIVERSITIES:

The 500 institutions from which these standouts have been identified award a full gamut of bachelor's degrees, the majority in occupational and professional fields. Many also award graduate degrees. Schools in this category have been subdivided into four regions: North, South, Midwest, and West.

School	Overall score	Academic reputation	Student selection	Faculty resources	Finance resources	Grad. Rate rank	Alumni satisfaction
NORTH							
1. Villanova University, Pa.	100.0	1	7	8	21	4	36
2. Fairfield University, Conn.	99.3	3	10	14	11	6	18
3. Alfred University, N.Y.	93.7	9	6	27	4	34	17
4. University of Scranton, Pa.	93.2	9	12	32	33	7	2

■ EXPERT LIST

REGIONAL UNIVERSITIES School	Overall score	Academic reputation	Student selection	Faculty resources	Finance resources	Grad. Rate rank	Alumni satisfaction
5. **Trenton State College,** N.J.	90.7	9	1	17	50	16	114
6. **Manhattan College,** N.Y.	90.6	16	21	16	19	21	33
7. **St. Michael's College,** Vt.	88.8	16	23	36	20	12	9
8. **La Salle University,** Pa.	88.6	9	16	23	38	11	102
9. **Loyola College,** Md.	87.5	3	27	42	28	18	27
10. **Hood College,** Md.	87.3	3	30	39	9	37	10
11. **Ithaca College,** N.Y.	86.5	3	34	37	13	29	31
12. **Rutgers State U., at Camden,** N.J.	86.4	19	3	1	8	85	95
13. **St. Joseph's University,** Pa.	84.0	9	11	51	52	13	90
14. **Rochester Institute of Technology,** N.Y.	83.1	1	20	48	3	48	111
15. **Millersville University,** Pa.	81.3	33	9	15	77	41	53
SOUTH							
1. **University of Richmond,** Va.	100.1	1	1	1	3	1	9
2. **Stetson University,** Fla.	94.5	3	13	2	6	13	19
3. **Rollins College,** Fla.	94.4	3	15	7	4	4	23
4. **Mercer University,** Ga.	92.7	7	9	13	9	3	41
5. **Centenary College of Louisiana**	89.7	11	18	6	7	23	18
6. **Stamford University,** Ala.	88.7	3	6	19	14	36	36
7. **Loyola University,** La.	88.5	7	7	4	8	50	44
8. **James Madison University,** Va.	87.7	2	4	20	93	2	13
9. **Appalachian State Univiversity,** N.C.	85.0	11	14	5	70	17	42
10. **The Citadel,** S.C.	84.0	3	45	8	34	9	34
11. **Harding University,** Ark.	83.2	26	3	32	51	14	3
12. **Mary Washington College,** Va.	83.1	10	2	39	86	7	12
13. **University of N.C. at Charlotte**	78.5	7	30	10	63	32	81
14. **University of N.C. at Wilmington**	78.3	14	19	15	64	46	40
15. **Bellarmine College,** Ky.	77.3	26	22	47	46	8	10
MIDWEST							
1. **Valparaiso University,** Ind.	100.0	4	1	6	8	3	31
2. **Creighton University,** Neb.	97.3	1	20	7	1	7	8
3. **Drake University,** Iowa	97.3	2	10	1	6	20	28
4. **University of Dayton,** Ohio	94.7	5	22	10	3	4	27
5. **Calvin College,** Mich.	93.7	11	8	12	28	14	1
6. **Butler University,** Ind.	92.3	5	18	26	4	10	16
7. **John Carrol University,** Ohio	92.3	2	29	9	23	6	18
8. **University of Evansville,** Ind.	92.2	13	5	17	17	20	23
9. **Bradley University,** Ill.	90.1	5	17	24	25	9	37
10. **Drury College,** Mo.	89.6	22	7	11	5	43	3
11. **Baldwin-Wallace College,** Ohio	88.0	11	13	35	21	7	42
12. **North Central College,** Ill.	86.2	34	6	23	16	25	5
13. **University of Northern Iowa**	85.4	13	23	15	50	20	22
14. **Xavier University,** Ohio	82.2	5	45	44	12	10	10
15. **University of Saint Thomas,** Minn.	81.6	5	33	55	9	5	62
WEST							
1. **Trinity University,** Texas	100.0	1	1	1	1	3	16

■ EXPERT LIST

REGIONAL UNIVERSITIES School	Overall score	Academic reputation	Student selection	Faculty resources	Finance resources	Grad. Rate rank	Alumni satisfaction
2. **Santa Clara University,** Calif.	96.2	3	7	8	7	1	19
3. **Loyola Marymount University,** Calif.	93.1	5	13	5	6	6	40
4. **Linfield College,** Ore.	92.7	7	9	11	19	8	2
5. **Gonzaga University,** Wash.	91.7	3	15	9	14	16	6
6. **California Poly. at San Luis Obispo**	88.4	2	6	10	41	27	32
7. **St. Mary's College of California**	87.2	18	4	22	23	10	24
8. **Whitworth College,** Wash.	85.3	6	12	43	17	9	14
9. **University of Redlands,** Calif.	85.1	10	21	33	4	12	9
10. **Seattle Pacific University,** Wash.	84.4	14	11	35	10	18	15
11. **University of Portland,** Ore.	83.4	7	28	25	18	14	22
12. **Pacific Lutheran University,** Wash.	83.3	10	23	39	12	7	11
13. **Western Washington University**	81.5	14	10	18	58	22	39
14. **St, Mary's U. of San Antonio,** Texas	79.5	10	27	27	33	13	56
15. **Montana College of Min. Sci. & Tech.**	74.8	18	17	51	64	11	7

■ BEST REGIONAL LIBERAL ARTS COLLEGES

The 433 schools from which these colleges have been identified are generally less selective than the national liberal arts colleges. Some 60 percent of the bachelor's degrees they award are in occupational, technical, and professional fields.

School	Overall score	Academic reputation	Student selection	Faculty resources	Finance resources	Grad. Rate rank	Alumni satisfaction
NORTH							
1. **Susquehanna University,** Pa.	100.0	2	9	6	5	7	5
2. **Le Moyne College,** N.Y.	96.8	4	3	2	40	6	22
3. **Elizabethtown College,** Pa.	93.3	4	5	14	15	18	31
4. **Stonehill College,** Mass.	91.9	2	2	27	41	4	15
5. **Lebanon Valley College,** Pa.	88.9	16	10	10	28	14	13
6. **St. Anselm College,** N.H.	88.3	1	24	11	45	4	20
7. **Messiah College,** Pa.	86.5	16	4	26	36	8	17
8. **King's College,** Pa.	84.0	4	21	24	47	11	7
9. **Lycoming College,** Pa.	81.1	4	37	7	26	34	11
10. **Grove City College,** Pa.	80.9	10	1	32	83	2	47
SOUTH							
1. **Lyon College,** Ark.	100.0	3	1	1	1	54	22
2. **Roanoke College,** Va.	100.0	3	20	2	9	17	18
3. **Emory & Henry College,** Va.	99.4	1	25	4	25	8	3
4. **Columbia College,** S.C.	96.9	9	23	10	17	11	9
5. **Mary Baldwin College,** Va.	95.5	1	33	27	3	6	4
6. **John Brown University,** Ark.	94.5	18	6	20	30	13	28
7. **Maryville College,** Tenn.	92.0	9	15	8	15	64	5
8. **Louisiana College**	89.3	18	7	18	34	40	52
9. **Milligan College,** Tenn.	88.1	18	17	26	33	28	34
10. **Carson-Newman College,** Tenn.	88.0	7	8	44	57	22	35
11. **Florida Southern College**	88.0	7	29	9	64	21	58

EXPERT LIST

REGIONAL LIBERAL ARTS COLLEGES School	Overall score	Academic reputation	Student selection	Faculty resources	Finance resources	Grad. Rate rank	Alumni satisfaction
MIDWEST							
1. **St. Mary's College,** Ind.	100.0	4	5	1	4	2	27
2. **Hillsdale College,** Mich.	98.0	1	4	9	2	17	24
3. **Marietta College,** Ohio	96.9	17	2	2	11	4	30
4. **Ohio Northern University**	96.3	9	7	7	10	11	23
5. **St. Norbert College,** Wis.	95.8	1	18	5	26	6	10
6. **Millikin University,** Ill.	93.7	1	8	13	19	22	47
7. **Taylor University,** Ind.	93.6	9	1	24	38	3	20
8. **Otterbein College,** Ohio	92.8	4	12	19	30	8	32
9. **Mount Union College,** Ohio	92.2	17	13	4	35	12	13
10. **Augustana College,** S.D.	89.2	4	16	11	47	32	28
WEST							
1. **Evergreen State College,** Wash.	100.0	1	4	3	13	6	13
2. **Pacific Union College,** Calif.	93.9	8	7	9	5	5	18
3. **Oklahoma Baptist University**	86.5	2	2	17	37	19	9
4. **Concordia University,** Calif.	86.0	8	3	25	11	14	14
4. **LeTourneau University,** Texas	86.0	8	6	18	23	13	6
6. **Texas Lutheran College**	84.8	2	14	16	20	19	4
7. **Northwest Nazarene College,** Idaho	83.8	11	5	19	29	11	8
8. **College of Santa Fe,** N.M.	82.2	6	18	24	8	4	26
9. **George Fox College,** Ore.	80.6	2	16	26	17	17	7
10. **Schreiner College,** Texas	76.5	19	9	30	7	16	5

BEST SPECIALITY SCHOOLS

The 90 institutions from which these schools are drawn grant more than half their degrees in business, engineering, or the arts. Of the schools involved, 43 are in the arts, music, and design fields; 33 in business; and 14 in engineering. The group also includes the five service academies, but they are not ranked because they are so few in number.

School	Overall score	Academic reputation	Student selection	Faculty resources	Finance resources	Grad. Rate rank	Alumni satisfaction
THE ARTS							
1. **Juilliard School,** N.Y.	100.0	1	1	2	1	1	15
2. **Rhode Island School of Design**	82.9	2	10	12	18	2	3
3. **Art Center College of Design,** Calif.	82.2	3	13	9	7	7	7
BUSINESS							
1. **Babson College,** Mass.	100.0	1	1	1	1	2	4
2. **Bentley College,** Mass.	91.8	2	2	4	3	5	3
3. **Bryant College,** R.I.	83.1	3	4	3	6	7	16
ENGINEERING							
1. **Harvey Mudd College,** Calif.	100.0	1	2	1	1	1	1
2. **Cooper Union,** N.Y.	88.6	2	1	4	2	3	3
3. **Rose-Hulman Institute of Technology,** Ind.	87.6	2	3	2	4	2	2

SOURCE: *U.S. News & World Report, America's Best Colleges 1995 College Guide,* copyright U.S. News & World Report.

THE BEST VALUES ON CAMPUS

The best faculty and educational program in the world won't matter to you if you can't afford them. To enable families to relate the cost of attending to the quality of the education involved, U.S. News & World Report *developed a "best value" rating system that identifies colleges and universities that score high on overall quality as well as reasonableness of cost. The "best values" are based on an institution's "sticker price," the published price for tuition, room, board, and fees. For many students the actual price of attending that college will be less because of merit awards and need-based grants.*

NATIONAL UNIVERSITIES

Rank		Total Cost
	BEST VALUES	
1.	**University of Texas at Austin**	$9,507
2.	**Texas A&M University at College Station**	$9,293
3.	**Georgia Institute of Technology**	$11,371
4.	**University of Florida**	$11,270
5.	**University of Georgia**	$9,750
6.	**University of North Carolina at Chapel Hill**	$13,206
7.	**University of Tennessee at Knoxville**	$9,248
8.	**SUNY at Binghampton,** N.Y.	$11,508
9.	**University of Washington**	$12,417
10.	**University of Iowa**	$11,736
11.	**University of Wisconsin at Madison**	$13,386
12.	**Rice University,** Texas	$16,040
13.	**Rutgers State University,** N.J.	$13,161
14.	**University of Illinois at Urbana-Champaign**	$13,054
15.	**University of Nebraska at Lincoln**	$9,100
16.	**SUNY at Buffalo,** N.Y.	$11,705
17.	**University of Kansas**	$10,766
18.	**Iowa State University**	$10,936
19.	**Florida State University**	$10,740
20.	**University of Virginia**	$16,760
21.	**University of Minnesota at Twin Cities**	$13,107
22.	**SUNY at Stony Brook,** N.Y.	$11,557
23.	**SUNY at Albany,** N.Y.	$11,200
24.	**University of California at Berkeley**	$17,894
25.	**University of California at Los Angeles**	$17,163
	RUNNERS-UP	
	Baylor University, Texas	$10,940
	California Institute of Technology	$21,956
	Clemson University, S.C.	$11,726
	College of William and Mary, Va.	$17,766
	Colorado School of Mines	$17,004
	Indiana University at Bloomington	$14,145
	Miami University, Ohio	$13,614
	Michigan Technological University	$12,231
	Northwestern University, Ill.	$21,924
	Ohio State University at Main Campus	$13,799
	Ohio University	$12,081
	Penn State University at Main Campus	$14,775
	Purdue University at West Lafayette, Ind.	$13,546
	Rutgers State University at Newark, N.J.	$13,136
	University of Arizona	$11,716
	University of California at Davis	$17,358
	University of California at Irvine	$17,326
	University of California at San Diego	$18,434
	University of Michigan at Ann Arbor	$20,566
	University of Missouri at Columbia	$12,956
	University of Missouri at Rolla	$13,208
	University of Notre Dame, Ind.	$21,397
	Virginia Tech	$13,436
	Wake Forest University, N.C.	$18,210

NATIONAL LIBERAL ARTS COLLEGES

	BEST VALUES	
1.	**Washington and Lee University,** Va.	$18,724
2.	**Grinnel College,** Iowa	$20,680
3.	**Hendrix College,** Ariz.	$12,320
4.	**Centre College,** Ky.	$16,470
5.	**Davidson College,** N.C.	$22,534
6.	**University of the South,** Tenn.	$19,605
7.	**Amherst College,** Mass.	$25,332
8.	**Claremont McKenna College,** Calif.	$23,150
9.	**Wellesley College,** Mass.	$24,700
10.	**Colorado College**	$21,452
11.	**Carleton College,** Minn.	$23,375
12.	**Williams College,** Mass.	$25,560
13.	**Swarthmore College,** Pa.	$25,900
14.	**Pomona College,** Calif.	$25,120
15.	**Bowdoin College,** Maine	$25,240
16.	**Haverford College,** Pa.	$25,250
17.	**Wheaton College,** Ill.	$15,680
18.	**Wabash College,** Ind.	$17,370
19.	**Wesleyan University,** Conn.	$25,390
20.	**Macalester College,** Minn.	$20,782

RUNNERS-UP

School	Cost
Bates College, Maine	$25,180
Bryn Mawr College, Pa.	$25,290
Bucknell University, Pa.	$23,410
Colby College, Maine	$25,420
Colgate University, N.Y.	$25,220
College of the Holy Cross, Maine	$24,655
DePauw University, Ind.	$19,520
Earlham College, Ind.	$19,365
Furman University, S.C.	$17,622
Illinois Wesleyan University	$18,575
Kenyon College, Ohio	$23,540
Lawrence University, Wis.	$21,344
Middlebury College, Vt.	$25,920
Oberlin College, Ohio	$25,616
Rhodes College, Tenn.	$20,126
St. Olaf College, Minn	$18,100
Smith College, Mass.	$25,373
Trinity College, Conn.	$25, 280
Union College, N.Y.	$25,126
Vassar College, N.Y.	$25,335

REGIONAL UNIVERSITIES

BEST VALUES / SOUTH

Rank	School	Cost
1.	**The Citadel,** S.C.	$9,773
2.	**Appalachian State University,** N.C.	$10,064
3.	**Harding University,** Ariz.	$10,048
4.	**Marshall University,** W.V.	$9,434
5.	**Winthrop University,** S.C.	$9,792
6.	**Stamford University,** Ala.	$11,936
7.	**University of West Florida**	$10,166
8.	**University of North Carolina at Charlotte**	$11,050
9.	**Centenary College of Louisiana**	$12,746
10.	**James Madison University,** Va.	$12,538

NORTH

Rank	School	Cost
1.	**Trenton State College,** N.J.	$11,698
2.	**SUNY College at Geneseo,** N.Y.	$11,153
3.	**Rutgers State University,** N.J.	$13,008
4.	**Bloomsberg University of Pennsylvania**	$11,400
5.	**Millersville University of Pennsylvania**	$12,508
6.	**SUNY College at Oswego,** N.Y.	$11,671
7.	**SUNY College at Fredonia,** N.Y.	$11,329
8.	**Shippensburg University of Pennsylvania**	$12,118
9.	**St. Bonaventure University,** N.Y.	$15,778
10.	**University of Scranton,** Pa.	$18,545

WEST

Rank	School	Cost
1.	**Montana College of Mineral Sci. and Tech.**	$9,473
2.	**California Poly. at San Luis Obispo**	$12,277
3.	**Western Washington University**	$12,268
4.	**Abilene Christian University,** Texas	$10,740
5.	**St. Mary's University of San Antonio,** Texas	$12,866
6.	**California State Poly. at Pomona**	$12,486
7.	**Trinity University,** Texas	$17,530
8.	**California State University at Fresno**	$12,074
9.	**Gonzaga University,** Wa.	$17,550
10.	**University of Portland,** Ore.	$16,220

MIDWEST

Rank	School	Cost
1.	**Northeast Missouri State University**	$8,390
2.	**University of Northern Iowa**	$9,291
3.	**University of Michigan at Dearborn**	$10,116
4.	**Drury College,** Mo.	$12,525
5.	**Calvin College,** Mich.	$13,940
6.	**Valparaiso University,** Ind.	$15,510
7.	**Creighton University,** Neb	$15,336
8.	**University of Dayton,** Ohio	$16,050
9.	**Bradley University,** Ill.	$15,390
10.	**University of Minnesota at Duluth**	$12,612

LIBERAL ARTS COLLEGE

BEST VALUES / SOUTH

Rank	School	Cost
1.	**Mississippi University for Women**	$6,603
2.	**Louisiana College**	$8,606
3.	**Flagler College,** Fla.	$8,320
4.	**John Brown University,** Ariz.	$10,218
5.	**Dillard University,** La.	$10,350

NORTH

Rank	School	Cost
1.	**Grove City College,** Pa.	$8,992
2.	**York College of Pennsylvania**	$8,775
3.	**SUNY College of Purchase,** N.Y.	$11,677
4.	**Le Moyne College,** N.Y.	$16,200
5.	**Messiah College,** Pa.	$15,464

WEST

Rank	School	Cost
1.	**Oklahoma Baptist University**	$9,060
2.	**Evergreen State College,** Wash.	$10,957
3.	**Oklahoma Christian University**	$9,830
4.	**Texas Lutheran College**	$11,310
5.	**LeTourneau University**	$13,200

MIDWEST

Rank	School	Cost
1.	**College of the Ozarks,** Mo.	Free
2.	**Dordt College,** Iowa	$12,510
3.	**Augustine College,** S.D.	$14,359
4.	**Taylor University,** Ind.	$15,175
5.	**Bethel College,** Kan.	$12,320

METHODOLOGY NOTE: These ratings were based solely on the quality rankings for *U.S. News & World Report*'s 1994 edition of *America's Best Colleges,* divided by the total of tuition, fees, and room and board for the 1994–95 academic year. The higher the ratio of quality (a school's overall score) to price, the better the value. Because the best values are by definition at the better schools, only a proportion of all schools were considered.

EXPERT Q&A

LOOKING TUITION BILLS IN THE EYE

Know your options for meeting the staggering cost of college today

The average cost for a year at a private four-year college was $18,784 in the 1994–95 school year. Without some financial assistance from the government, educational institutions, or other private sources, more than half of college students would come up short at tuition time. Jack Joyce, Associate Director for Information and Training Services at the College Board, sponsors of the SATs and an organization dedicated to broadening access to higher education, has this advice for students and families on applying for financial aid.

■ Who is eligible for financial aid?

Well over half the students that are in college, and in some institutions, probably three-quarters of the students enrolled. But there is no one income number or other characteristic that determines a student's eligibility for aid.

■ How is financial aid eligibility determined?

At least two application forms and two formulas are used to determine a student's eligibility for financial aid. The most commonly used process starts with an application form that's called the Free Application for Federal Student Aid, or FAFSA. It collects a fairly limited amount of information on a family's income and assets. That information is used in the "federal methodology," which is a formula approved by Congress to determine a student's eligibility for federal financial aid programs.

Many colleges that have their own nonfederal financial aid collect some additional information on what is called the Financial Aid Form, or FAF. That form requests more details about a family's assets situation, including such things as home equity, and a little more information on other expenses the family has, such as medical and dental expenses. It is used to support a more traditional and sensitive need-analysis. This formula, known informally as the Institutional Methodology, was developed with the intent of providing a reasonable guideline as to a family's ability to contribute toward college costs.

■ Does it matter if the student is applying to a private or a state school?

In general, students applying to a state institution or public university where federal financial aid is all that is available would probably have to complete only the FAFA. If they are applying to private colleges or universities, they would also be asked to complete the FAF. Students should understand that forms and procedures *do* change from year to year. The FAFSA and FAF are being revised for 1995–96 financial aid determinations; 1996–97 requirements will be different. It's important for a student to ascertain what application forms are required for financial aid and what kind of deadlines the colleges, universities, and scholarship programs have.

■ Do both the federal and institutional methodologies look at stocks and other investments to see if a student qualifies?

There is no consideration of assets in the federal formula for a family whose taxable income is less than $50,000 and who files one of the simplified versions of the federal tax return, the 1040A or 1040EZ. For others, both methodologies collect and consider information on assets, including the value of stocks and bonds and anything else that would generate interest or dividend income.

■ How does family size affect a family's eligibility for financial aid?

The number of siblings and the size of the household is an important characteristic. The other important factor is the number of family members enrolled in college at the same time. A family might not be eligible for much financial aid this year, but next year, when the family's twins are enrolled, the family would suddenly be eligible for considerably more aid.

What are the major loan options and what are their differences?

The Stafford loan is the most widely available option. Right now it comes in two flavors. The first is available to families as part of the Federal Family Education Loan Programs (FFELP). The eligibility is determined by the school, which helps the family apply for the loan through a private lender, but the government pays the interest on the loan while the student is enrolled in school. For the past couple of years there's been a parallel program called the Federal Direct Student Loan Program. That program eliminates the private lender as the middle man and has the school not only determine eligibility for the loan but actually deliver the loan proceeds to the student. But from the student's perspective the differences are transparent. In both cases the terms are the same, the repayment obligation is the same, and the amount they can borrow is the same.

There is also the Perkins Loan Program, which is available to the neediest of students. The amount of money a college has for this program varies from school to school and depends on how many students an institution has applying for financial aid. Because it is intended for students with the highest need, it is a little more competitive than the Stafford program.

Are there any other loans?

Thanks to a major change in the FFELP and Direct Loan programs, a student who is not eligible for a loan based on need would still be eligible for an unsubsidized Stafford loan, in which the student would be responsible for the interest that accrues while she or he was in school. The student can either arrange to pay the interest while enrolled or have the interest capitalized while he or she attends school and then repay both principal and interest later. Compared to a commercial loan, it would still be an attractive option.

In addition, there is the Federal PLUS loan, which is available to parents as opposed to the students themselves. Right now a parent would be able to borrow as much as the full cost of education for a son or daughter, minus any financial aid, including subsidized or unsubsidized Stafford loans, regardless of income level. Repayment would generally begin within 60 days of the receipt of the loan. The interest rate is similar to the Stafford loan, but it's determined a little differently each year. Some families advocate home equity loans or home equity lines of credit as a more attractive option. There are others that have investments they may draw upon. But PLUS is a source for a number of parents.

THE HIGH COST OF COLLEGE

Tuition and fees account for about 62 percent of average total expenses at private four-year resident colleges; at public four-year resident institutions it is about 30 percent.

SECTOR		TUITION AND FEES	BOOKS AND SUPPLIES	ROOM AND BOARD	TRANS-PORTATION	OTHER EXPENSES	ESTIMATED TOTAL EXP.
TWO-YEAR	Resident	$1,298	$566	NA*	NA*	NA*	NA*
PUBLIC	Commuter			$1,746	$934	$1,095	$5,659
TWO-YEAR	Resident	$6,511	$552	$4,050	$569	$975	$12,647
PRIVATE	Commuter			$1,850	$908	$1,192	$11,013
FOUR-YEAR	Resident	$2,686	$578	$3,826	$592	$1,308	$8,990
PUBLIC	Commuter			$1,684	$892	$1,314	$7,154
FOUR-YEAR	Resident	$11,709	$585	$4,976	$523	$991	$18,784
PRIVATE	Commuter			$1,809	$844	$1,123	$16,070

*Sample too small to provide meaningful information.

SOURCE: College Entrance Examination Board, 1994.

FINANCIAL AID

MASTERING THE COLLEGE AID GAME

An insider's guide to maxing out financial aid

Most people who apply for financial aid for school have only a hazy idea of how colleges make their decisions. But there are some important facts everyone should know before they even sit down to fill out the forms. Kalman Chany, president of Campus Consultants Inc., a firm that guides parents through the financial aid process, and author of *The Princeton Review Student Access Guide to Paying for College 1995 Edition*, has these tips on how to qualify for the most financial aid possible.

■ **Understand the angles.** The theory is, the money goes where it's most needed. But people who better understand the system and how it works are going to get the most money. Few families understand how the aid process works. Most people are just gambling. Anyone can benefit, you just have to understand it.

■ **Don't rule out any school as being too expensive.** Private schools are more flexible, and may be able to offer more financial aid since they are not as regulated as state schools. If a family can afford $10,000 and it's looking at a $30,000 school, it might be eligible for $20,000 in financial aid.

■ **Think local.** If you really need the money, the worst thing you can do is go to a state school outside of the state in which you live. It's not popular and it's not good politically to give lots of aid to a student who is from out of state. The student isn't able to qualify for state aid. Instead, look at the state school in your state, or a private college in your state or out of state.

■ **Know the timeline.** The family income that the institutions will look at starts in January of the child's junior year in high school and ends in December of the child's senior year in high school. During that time, parents should be wary of selling stock, withdrawing from pensions prematurely, or withdrawing from IRAs prematurely.

■ **Put assets in the parent's name.** In aid formulas, the student's solvency is weighed more heavily than the parents.' If you want to hope for financial aid, put the money in the parent's name, not in the child's name.

■ **In divorce situations, assume the custodial parent has the onus.** The parent who had custody of the child for the previous 12 months before is the parent whose income will be scrutinized. In other words, the parent that the child lived with when the child was a senior in high school is the custodial parent. The custodial should fill out the financial aid forms. A handful of schools will look at both parents, but the majority don't.

■ **Postpone the wedding bells.** If a parent is planning on remarrying, he or she should wait until the child is out of college before heading to the altar. If a parent remarries, the step-parent's income will be analyzed as if it is that of a natural parent. This could cause financial aid to be lost.

■ **Don't rely on the school's financial aid administrator.** Financial aid administrators work for the school. They are going to put the school ahead of the family. Ask them what to do, how to save money, and they won't answer. They'll tell you the rules, but they put the needs of the school first.

■ **Save regularly.** Above all, parents should set aside as much money as they can on a regular basis. They should get into the habit of saving regularly. Parents shouldn't be intimidated by statistics quoting the astronomical cost of tuition. They should just save as much as they can, as regularly as they can.

EXPERT Q&A

DOING WELL BY DOING GOOD

The new national service program lets students earn tuition credits

AmeriCorps is a national service organization established by an act of Congress in September 1994. Its members participate in a variety of programs from tutoring at-risk youth to counseling crime victims, to building affordable housing. In exchange for service, members receive an array of benefits, including tuition assistance. Richard Allen, a White House spokesman for the program, explains what a student needs to know to participate:

■ What is AmeriCorps?

It is a national initiative that allows members to serve full- or part-time in more than 350 public service programs nationwide. In exchange for a year or two of service, members receive a modest living allowance, health coverage, and free education awards. Any American citizen or permanent resident of the United States who is 17 years or older is eligible, regardless of income.

■ How does it help pay tuition bills?

Participants receive living allowances roughly equal to minimum wage, while earning an educational award of $4,725 a year for up to two years for completing 1,700 hours of service. The award is $2,362 for part-time service. Students can use this credit within five years of completion of service to help pay for college, graduate school, or vocational training, or to repay a loan if they've already been to school.

■ Does the program have any other benefits?

In addition to the post-service award, participants will be gaining skills that will be useful in later life. They are developing the ability to make change in their communities and nurturing a lifetime commitment to service. The program is not that different from the Peace Corps, which many say is the most important experience in their lives.

■ What kinds of programs can participants be involved in?

There are 350 programs nationwide. They include Habitat for Humanity, the I Have A Dream Foundation, the American Red Cross, the Community on AIDS Partnership, and the New York Police Department. In the summer of 1993, a team of 88 members put together an outreach campaign that helped immunize 104,000 infants in Texas. In the summer of 1994, a group in Kansas City, Mo., working with the local police department, helped to close down 12 crack houses.

Depending on the program, you could serve for nine months or up to three years; full- or part-time; and before, during, or after college or job training. We try to give individuals the maximum amount of choice.

■ Are some programs more popular and more difficult to get into than others?

So far, there has been a strong demand for all the programs. We have had 200,000 inquiries for the first 20,000 spots! But each individual program has its own screening process. Some programs have a limited number of slots which they want to fill with some local people, and some people from outside the area. In addition, some applications require essays. There will be 20,000 people selected for AmeriCorps in '95, 33,000 in '96, and 47,000 in '97.

■ What is the application procedure?

Each program has a different answer. But if you are interested, you should call our number, ☎ 800-942-2677. When you receive a referral form, it will ask whether you want to receive literature on programs only in your local area, or from all over the United States. The form will also ask about your interests so we can tell what kinds of programs you might like. Programs that start in early fall begin recruiting in spring. Programs that start in January recruit in early fall or winter.

ENROLLMENT

YOUR BRILLIANT COLLEGE CAREER

It's not just a four-year hitch now, thanks to many pressures

In the lecture halls and common rooms of America's oldest and most prestigious universities, graduating with a bachelor's degree in four years has long been the tradition. But intellectual snobs might be surprised to find out that the four-year college degree is more an accident of American history than it is academic gospel.

When Harvard opened in 1636, it adopted the four-year system from Cambridge University in England. Little did Harvard know that Cambridge and Oxford Universities would be switching to three-year programs just a few years later. If the higher education system of the United States had been created just a few years later, today's academic Brahmins would be just as sure it takes three, not four years to produce an educated person.

In fact, increasingly, students are taking more than four years to obtain their college diplomas. A 1991 study done by the National Institute of Colleges and Universities shows that 43 percent of students graduating from private colleges and 64 percent of students graduating from public colleges took more than four years to obtain their degrees.

"We tend to see a lot more students stopping to do other things during their college careers," says Dr. Tim Sanford, assistant provost and director for institutional research at the University of North Carolina at Chapel Hill. "They take five or six years to graduate in that sense, but few are actually enrolled for longer than eight semesters."

The reasons for this trend are both academic and economic. A student may change his field of study, take more time, and end up in a more appropriate career. In others, students are taking lighter course loads per semester, in hopes of improving their chances to get into graduate school. Still others are obtaining dual degrees by taking extra time.

Taking more time to get a degree and earning money on the side is an economic necessity for some. According to a recent study by the Bureau of Labor Statistics, 51 percent of full-time college students held part-time jobs in 1993, compared with just 35 percent in 1972. What's more, many professional programs now have internship or practical experience requirements. Although taking the extra time to fulfill these can delay date of graduation, such requirements can provide valuable training that will benefit students in the future.

The high cost of tuition has other students rushing to finish their undergraduate degrees in less than four years as well. "We are seeing students graduating earlier rather than later," says Geoff Cox, vice provost for institutional planning at Stanford, where annual tuition, room, and board now tops $25,000. "Students have a lot of AP credits and they are learning there is nothing magic about four years. Some parents offer to pay for three years at Stanford, or four at a state university. People come to college for different reasons and students shouldn't be forced to stay for four years," Cox says.

Seventy-two schools now offer formal three-year programs leading to bachelor's degrees. Indiana's Valparaiso University, Vermont's Middlebury College, and Upper Iowa University are among them. "We are not doing it for internal financial reasons. It's an accelerated three-year international major," says Ronald Nief, a spokesman at Middlebury.

At Valparaiso, financial considerations are readily acknowledged. "These programs were first marketed as a way to save a year's tuition," says Katharine Anommaria, dean of the College of Arts and Sciences at Valparaiso. "But we market it as a way for the student to gain a year's earnings. It's mostly for highly motivated students, not something for everyone. But it should be an option. We need as many options as possible. Some students come in the door knowing it will take them eight years to graduate."

A VIEW FROM THE FRESHMAN QUAD

Politics is out, but smoking is up, and so is stress among today's students

Newt Gingrich, the former college instructor with a genius for political phrasemaking, will need more than a Contract with America to engage today's college students. The American Council on Education's annual poll of college freshmen found that in 1994 only 32 percent of the incoming class considered "keeping up with political affairs" an important goal in life, which was the lowest expression of interest in politics in the 25 years that the survey has been conducted. That was in contrast to 1990 when 42 percent gave politics a high priority, and 1966 when almost 58 percent did.

In the 1994 poll, conducted annually for the Council by the Higher Education Research Institute at the University of California, Los Angeles, only 16 percent said that they frequently "discuss politics." That was more than a third lower than in 1992 and almost a half lower than in 1968.

If political apathy has been the recent order of the day on campuses, that may be because of all the other things that have students worried. Tuitions, room and board, and fees increased an average of 6 percent in 1994, and borrowing heavily to foot the bills has become commonplace. The share of students who expressed doubt about their ability to pay for college hit an all-time high of almost 19 percent in 1994. That was 1.5 percent higher than in 1992, and more than double what it was in 1968.

Stress among students was pronounced. The ACE poll found that 24 percent of all incoming freshmen in 1994 reported feeling frequently "overwhelmed by all I have to do." That was a 50 percent increase over what it was for freshmen in 1985. The share of freshmen reporting that they frequently "felt depressed" also increased for the fourth consecutive year, and student assessments of their own emotional as well as physical health hit all-time lows.

On the other hand, beer-drinking among college freshmen dropped to only 53 percent in 1994; in 1981 more than 75 percent of incoming freshmen reported drinking beer at least occasionally. Public health experts attribute at least some of the recent decline to organizations such as Mothers against Drunk Driving, which have raised student awareness of the dangers of drinking while driving. Perhaps taking up the slack, anti-smoking efforts have been less successful on campuses. The percentage of freshmen classifying themselves as frequent smokers rose for the sixth time in seven years.

FACT FILE:

FRESHMAN ANGST

■ *In a recent survey of college freshmen, these objectives were considered to be essential or very important:*

Objective	%
1. Be very well off financially	73.7
2. Raise a family	70.6
3. Become authority in my field	65.2
4. Help others in difficulty	61.7
5. Get recognition from colleagues	53.2
6. Develop philosophy of life	42.7
7. Be successful in own business	40.9
8. Influence social values	40.2
9. Promote racial understanding	35.8
10. Keep up to date with politics	31.9

SOURCE: *The American Freshman: National Norms for Fall 1994*, Cooperative Institutional Research Program, American Council on Education, University of California, Los Angeles, 1994.

WHEN EVERY COURSE IS A GUT

Grade inflation has made academia like Lake Woebegone

In Garrison Keillor's fictional world of Lake Woebegone, all children are said to be above average. Grade inflation has made the groves of American academia a real-life equivalent. Despite the fact that college entrance examination scores have been slumping for many years, a study by Columbia Teachers College president Arthur Levine in the *Chronicle of Higher Education* has found that undergrad grade point averages have been increasing steadily. From 1969 to 1993, the proportion of students with gpa's of "A-" or higher almost quadrupled from 7 percent to 26 percent. Meanwhile, the number of students with gpa's of "C" or lower dropped from 25 percent to 9 percent in 1993. Today at elite institutions like Princeton and Stanford, grades below a "B" are rarely given.

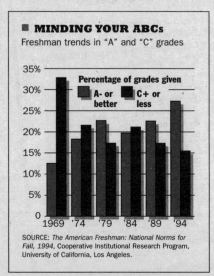

MINDING YOUR ABCs

Freshman trends in "A" and "C" grades

Percentage of grades given

A- or better / C+ or less

35% 30% 25% 20% 15% 10% 5% 0

1969 '74 '79 '84 '89 '94

SOURCE: *The American Freshman: National Norms for Fall, 1994,* Cooperative Institutional Research Program, University of California, Los Angeles.

Experts see several reasons for the upward trend in grades. Defenders suggest that colleges have ceased to issue failing grades in the hopes of encouraging grade-conscious students to experiment with a broader range of course offerings than they might otherwise dare. But some schools, feeling rising financial pressures, may be shying away from issuing flunking marks as a safeguard against losing tuitions, critics charge. Until recently, even a school as rich as Stanford University allowed students to withdraw from a course all the way up until the eve of the final exam, and permitted students to repeat a course an unlimited number of times before requiring a permanent recording of the final grade on a transcript. Both of these options enabled students to create picture-perfect transcripts and boost their graduate school acceptance records accordingly.

Grading study author Arthur Levine attributes the inflationary bias to a confusion of undergraduate and graduate grading systems. Graduate students, by definition, are assumed to be good students, Levine says, and that assumption has always been reflected in the high grades they are awarded. On campuses with extensive graduate programs, professors who teach both graduate and undergraduate courses carry over their more lenient graduate grading criteria to undergraduates, Levine believes.

There are signs that the inflationary psychology may finally have peaked, however. In a move hailed by editorial writers from coast to coast, Stanford recently announced that it was officially bringing back a flunking grade, though it chose to call it an "NP" (for No Pass) rather than an "F." Stanford had banished "F's" from its grading system in 1970. To further encourage truth-in-transcripts, the university also decided that a student having difficulty in a course could no longer drop out just before the final exam without having it recorded on his transcript. What's more, it will now only be possible to repeat a course once, and the fact that the course is being retaken must be entered on the student's transcript as an "RP" (for Repeat).

ROOMMATES YOU CAN LIVE WITH

Best friends don't always make good dorm mates says a new study

It is often said that only half of a college education takes places in the classroom. The other half is neither taught by professors, nor tested until after graduation. Part of that preparation for "the real world" is learning to live with roommates.

A recent study by Charles Hulick, a professor of educational psychology at Kentucky's Murray State University, suggests that many of the assumptions that college administrators have used to match up roommates may be faulty. Hulick found, for instance, that sharing similar personalities and values, two factors which housing officers (and marriage counselors) have traditionally considered important for happy communal living, in fact mean very little. The strongest predictor of dormitory contentment is agreement on the subject of visitors, Hulick discovered. Those who share similar views on having friends in the room are the most likely to be compatible roommates. Other obvious but often overlooked clues as to whether a match will work include (in order of importance) the students' views on the use of alcohol, bed-time preferences, the sharing of belongings, and the amount of time spent studying in the room.

Pairing a "morning person" with a "night owl" is asking for trouble, Hulick believes. The difference in their body clocks is likely to make communication between them difficult, he argues. Smoking habits and attitudes toward neatness can also be important sources of friction.

Several colleges are taking Hulick's research to heart. For instance, the University of California at Los Angeles is using a computer program to group students by "behavioral similarities." The program ensures that all members of a rooming cluster share similar views on smoking and drinking habits and sleep and study patterns. Once these basic determinations have been made, the university attempts to bring together students with common interests. Students may elect "theme houses" and "theme floors" that are especially oriented to "quiet," "fitness and well-living," or the "great outdoors," to name just a few.

Not all colleges are as sophisticated as UCLA about roommate placement, however. Some still pair students alphabetically, for instance. Whatever the policy, Hulick has this advice for new roommates:

- **Talk to your roommate.** You need not agree on everything to get along. Compromise is the key. Try to discuss issues before deciding to live together. If selection is beyond your control, set some ground rules before problems arise.

- **Go ahead and argue if you can't discuss an issue rationally.** Roommates who attempt to ignore gripes and stifle grievances usually end up fuming and finally boiling over. They also report the highest move-out rate.

- **Remember that your roommate need not be your best friend.** You can have a good relationship without being soulmates. Women tend to expect that their college roommate will be an intimate friend, while men are less disappointed when a close personal relationship fails to flourish. Mutual affection is less critical than mutual behaviors and preferences. In fact, a history of friendship may prevent the kind of honest communication that is necessary for roommates to coexist.

- **Use tact in voicing gripes.** In Hulick's study, male roommates were found to be more comfortable than women discussing complaints, but they have a tendency to divorce tact from candor. Sincere discussion benefits everyone; bruised feelings get roommates nowhere.

EXPERT TIPS

JUDGING CAMPUS SAFETY

The crime statistics required by the Feds don't tell the whole story

With the growing awareness of crime on campus, safety is joining curriculum quality and social life as one of today's hot student concerns. Here, Carl Stokes, director of law enforcement and safety at the University of South Carolina and president of the International Association of Law Enforcement Administrators, and Alan J. Lizotte, executive director of the Consortium for Higher Education Crime Research at the State University of New York at Albany, offer these tips for picking a safe campus.

■ **Don't assume campus crime statistics give a complete picture of a college's safety record.** Since 1992, federal legislation has required schools to report on the numbers of murders, forcible sex offenses, non forcible sex offenses, rapes, robberies, aggravated assaults, burglaries, motor-vehicle thefts, and liquor-law, drug, and weapons violations. However, schools are not required to report larceny, which Lizotte contends accounts for about 80 to 90 percent of campus crime. Moreover, college staff who are responsible for counseling students do not have to report crimes that they become aware through the course of their work. For instance, when a student who is sexually assaulted goes to a rape counseling center instead of the campus police, this offense may end up not being tallied by the college.

Schools also are not obligated to report crimes involving students which occur off campus. As a result, a school where a large number of students live in the community may have low crime statistics and appear safe, whereas a school where the majority of students live in college dorms may have relatively high crime statistics and appear unsafe, warns Lizotte. Keeping all of this in mind, what Lizotte looks for in the numbers is the incidence of drug, alcohol, and firearms violations. "If those three things are high," he says, "then everything else is likely to be high."

■ **Check out community crime rates.** They may be a more important consideration because colleges generally have on average one-tenth of the crime found in the surrounding community, Lizotte advises. To check a town's crime rates, look it up in the FBI's Uniform Crime Report at the library. But be aware that in a big city these statistics may make a school appear unsafe even though it is in safe part of town. For students who plan to live off campus, Carl Stokes says that campus security usually can tell students which areas of town cause the local police the most trouble.

■ **Check on a campus's physical safety features.** Good outdoor lighting systems have become standard on most college campuses. Many schools also have emergency call boxes placed around the campus, and some have begun to give their students beepers which can send a distress signal to campus police. Others have installed electronic door locks that require students to enter a special code or use their student ID to gain access to dormitories. A number of these systems alert campus security if doors are propped open for a certain length of time.

■ **Ask if the college has a crime awareness program.** It's an indication that a school is serious about preventing crime. A school has to try actively to counteract adolescent naiveté, Lizotte says. "College students are perfect targets, because they are unbelievably bad at protecting their property. They leave their doors unlocked at night and leave $3,000 notebook computers on the desk in the library while they go and get a drink of water."

GRAD STUDENT'S GUIDE

CLIMBING THE EDUCATIONAL LADDER

Nearly two million people are enrolled in graduate school today and many more are thinking about it. In the past quarter-century, the number of Americans who have earned master's degrees has increased 60 percent, to 350,000 each year. And no wonder. Several recent studies show that advanced degrees result in significantly higher incomes for their holders over a lifetime than for those with only a bachelor's degree. For those contemplating an advanced degree, here is a quick look at admissions prospects and test requirements in 40 major disciplines. The material is drawn from the 1995 edition of America's Best Graduate Schools *by* U.S. News & World Report.

AGRICULTURE AND NATURAL RESOURCES

89 graduate programs. Popular subdisciplines: agribusiness, food sciences, environmental studies.

■ **ADMISSIONS:** '93–'94 enrollment: 13,526 in master's programs; 10,588 in Ph.D. programs; about a third of Ph.D. enrollees are women. Master's in '93: 4,325; Ph.D.'s: 1,907. Sampling of acceptance rates: 34 percent at Purdue; 36 percent at Ohio State; 38 percent at Texas A&M.

■ **PREREQUISITES:** B.S. in sciences or related field. Chemistry and physics courses are recommended. Most programs require the GRE and a minimum grade point average of 3.0.

■ **TIPS ON GETTING IN:** Research experience is important. For plant genetics or agricultural economics, international experience such as the Peace Corps also is advantageous. Faculty letters of recommendation carry substantial weight.

ANTHROPOLOGY

166 graduate programs. Popular subdisciplines: applied anthropology, archaeology, human evolution.

■ **ADMISSIONS:** Estimated '93–'94 enrollment: 8,700; 50 percent of enrollees are women. Master's in '93:1,052; Ph.D.'s: 445. Sampling of acceptance rates: 15 percent at U. of Hawai'i; 24 percent at U. of Washington; 60 percent at SUNY at Binghamton.

■ **PREREQUISITES:** Most programs require the Graduate Record Examination. Anthropology courses are not always required; courses in history, biology, and research methods often will suffice instead.

■ **TIPS ON GETTING IN:** International experience and/or fieldwork is desirable and, in tandem with a foreign language, may help offset mediocre GPA or test scores. Personal statement is important and should focus on why you want to attend a particular school.

ARCHITECTURE

54 accredited programs. Popular areas of study: design, management, landscape architecture.

■ **ADMISSIONS:** '93–'94 enrollment: 5,349; 35 percent of enrollees are women. M.Arch's awarded in '94: 1,654. Sampling of acceptance rates: 13 percent at Princeton; 20 percent at Rice; 33 percent at U. of Illinois.

■ **PREREQUISITES:** Drawing or design courses are very desirable. Most schools require the Graduate Record Examination. At Princeton, successful applicants average 650 to 660 on each section of the GRE.

■ **TIPS ON GETTING IN:** Admission generally is based more on a candidate's design skill than on test scores or GPA. The student's portfolio is the most important element of the application package and should reflect experience in drawing, painting, and photography.

ART

86 accredited M.F.A. programs. Some 100 other non-accredited programs. Popular subdisciplines: drawing, painting, graphic design.

■ **ADMISSIONS:** '93–'94 enrollment in accredited programs: 4,548; 58 percent are women. Sampling of acceptance rates: 9 percent at U. of New Mexico; 21 percent at Art Institute of Chicago; 36 percent at U. of Iowa.

■ **PREREQUISITES:** A portfolio and a number of undergraduate studio hours as well as course work in art history are a must. GRE is usually not required, and there is no minimum GPA.

■ **TIPS ON GETTING IN:** The portfolio is the most important part of the application. Schools are looking for applicant's distinctive style. Letters of recommendation should come from faculty or other artists who can discuss an applicant's artistic talent.

BIOLOGICAL SCIENCES

235 Ph.D.-granting institutions. Popular subdisciplines: cell and molecular biology, genetics, immunology, ecology.

■ **ADMISSIONS:** '92–'93 enrollment: 54,437; 47 percent of enrollees are women. Ph.D.'s awarded in '93: 5,090. Sampling of acceptance rates: 23 percent at U. of Pennsylvania; 35 percent at U. of Texas at Austin; 51 percent at Case Western Reserve.

■ **PREREQUISITES:** B.S., including sufficient course work in chemistry, physics, and calculus. Most schools require GRE; some also want subject tests in biology or chemistry.

■ **TIPS ON GETTING IN:** Test scores above the 75th percentile are necessary for top schools. Independent research as part of a senior project or a summer research program is essential. Faculty letters of recommendation are extremely important.

BUSINESS

281 accredited schools. Popular subdisciplines: accounting, entrepreneurship, international management.

■ **ADMISSIONS:** '93–'94 enrollment: 122,203; 35 percent of enrollees are women. M.B.A.'s awarded in '93: 40,582. Sampling of acceptance rates: 23 percent at U. of Pennsylvania; 35 percent at U. of Texas at Austin; 51 percent at Case Western Reserve.

■ **PREREQUISITES:** Most business schools prefer two to four years of work experience. Graduate Management Admission Test generally required. Scores of at least 650 needed at top schools.

■ **TIPS ON GETTING IN:** Current trend is to consider an applicant's achievements as a whole and not concentrate on test scores and GRE. Demonstrated leadership skills are important; community volunteer work can serve as an example.

CHEMISTRY

313 graduate programs. Popular subdisciplines: physical, organic, inorganic, and biophysical chemistry.

■ **ADMISSIONS:** '92–'93 enrollment: 19,416; 34 percent of enrollees are women. Master's degrees awarded in '93: 1,683; Ph.D.'s: 2,139. Sampling of acceptance rates: 25 percent at Brown; 30 percent at Stanford; 35 percent at U. of Colorado.

■ **PREREQUISITES:** Successful applicants almost always are college chemistry majors; a major in a hard science is required. Most

■ GRAD STUDENT'S GUIDE

schools require GRE and subject test in chemistry.

■ **TIPS ON GETTING IN:** Students must take advanced courses in physical chemistry and biochemistry as well as math and have strong skills in computer science. Completion of research projects at the undergraduate level is extremely important.

COMPUTER SCIENCE

442 graduate programs. Popular subdisciplines: software engineering, artificial intelligence, robotics.

■ **ADMISSIONS:** '93–'94 enrollment: 32,000; 23 percent of enrollees in Ph.D. programs are women. Average number of master's awarded annually: some 9,000; Ph.D.'s: some 1,000. Sampling of acceptance rates: 5 percent at Carnegie Mellon; 10 percent at Brown; 15 percent at U. of Utah.

■ **PREREQUISITES:** A B.S. in computer science or related field with a GPA of 3.7 in the sciences is needed at most schools. GRE and computer science subject test are usually required.

■ **TIPS ON GETTING IN:** GRE score above 1300 is important, with the verbal score carrying considerable weight. Published research papers and research-oriented work experience can help make up for below-average test scores and grades.

CRIMINAL JUSTICE

More than 100 graduate programs. Popular subdisciplines: criminology, policing, corrections, private security.

■ **ADMISSIONS:** '93–'94 enrollment; 5,188; about one third of master's enrollees are women. Master's awarded in '91-'92: 1,240. Sampling of acceptance rates: 47 percent at Northeastern; 51 percent at SUNY at Albany; 65 percent at U. of Maryland; 70 percent at U. of Cincinnati.

■ **PREREQUISITES:** Most schools require familiarity with criminal justice or a related subject like sociology. Most schools require the GRE, but some will accept the Law School Admission Test.

■ **TIPS ON GETTING IN:** The most important criterion is GPA—3.3 is needed at some schools—and a minimum GRE score of 900. Interview is recommended for those with GPAs below 3.0. Courses in research methods, statistics, and law are helpful.

DENTISTRY

54 accredited dental schools. Popular subdisciplines: orthodontics, prosthodontics, periodontics.

■ **ADMISSIONS:** '93–'94 enrollment: 16,250; 37 percent of enrollees are women. D.D.S./D.M.D.'s awarded: 3,778. Sampling of acceptance rates: 6 percent at U. of Washington; 9 percent at Baylor College of Dentistry; 32 percent at Medical College of Georgia.

■ **PREREQUISITES:** Most schools require one year each of biology, organic chemistry, and physics. Dental Admission Test required. Score of at least 18 needed at top schools.

■ **TIPS ON GETTING IN:** Students with added science course work, particularly in biology, have an edge. A 3.3 to 3.5 GPA in science courses is needed. Schools look for good reading comprehension scores on the DAT. Work in a dentist's office helps.

DRAMA

69 accredited graduate programs. Popular subdisciplines: acting, directing, scene design.

■ **ADMISSIONS:** '93–'94 enrollment: 1,858; about half of enrollees are women. M.F.A. degrees awarded in '93: 417. Sampling of acceptance rates: less than 1 percent in acting at Florida State; 2 percent at U. of Missouri; 2 percent at Yale.

■ **PREREQUISITES:** Most schools require at least 1000 on the GRE and a 3.0 GPA, but many make exceptions for outstanding auditions and/or portfolios. Significant course work in area of study.

■ **TIPS ON GETTING IN:** The essential admission criterion for acting is the audition, while the portfolio is key for directing and scene design. For their audition, acting applicants should choose two contrasting pieces that demonstrate their performing range.

ECONOMICS

132 Ph.D. programs. Popular subdisciplines: industrial organization, finance, international trade.

■ **ADMISSIONS:** '93–'94 enrollment: 11,457; 28 percent of enrollees are women. Ph.D.'s awarded in '93: 930. Sampling of acceptance rates: 12 percent at Cornell; 33 percent at Boston U.; 35 percent at U. of Southern California.
■ **PREREQUISITES:** The GRE, two semesters of calculus, and at least one course in statistics are required. Most schools also require courses in econometrics and intermediate micro and macro theory.
■ **TIPS ON GETTING IN:** Top grades are needed in math and economics. Quantitative score on the GRE is significant; scores in the 700s needed for top programs. Strong recommendations highlighting applicant's research and problem-solving skills are important.

EDUCATION

220 Ph.D.-granting institutions. Popular subdisciplines: administration, primary education, counseling.

■ **ADMISSIONS:** '91–'92 enrollment: 197,000; 76 percent of master's enrollees and 60 percent of Ph.D.'s are women. Master's in '92: 92,668; Ph.D.'s: 6,864. Sampling of acceptance rates: 48 percent at U. of Illinois at Urbana-Champaign; 62 percent for master's at Harvard.
■ **PREREQUISITES:** Either GRE or Miller Analogies Test is required. GRE scores should average between 500 and 600 on each section; MAT scores should be in the mid-50s or higher.
■ **TIPS ON GETTING IN:** Test scores and GPA criteria vary widely; low scores won't necessarily eliminate an applicant. B.A. in education or substantial course work in the field applicant plans to teach is required. Evidence of working with children is also important.

ENGINEERING

219 graduate programs. Popular subdisciplines: electrical, mechanical, civil, and computer engineering.

■ **ADMISSIONS:** '93–'94 enrollment: 128,081; 15 percent of enrollees are women. Master's degrees awarded in '94: 31,943; Ph.D.'s: 6,458. Sampling of acceptance rates: 29 percent at Purdue; 41 percent at Texas A&M; 47 percent at U. of Michigan at Ann Arbor.
■ **PREREQUISITES:** Vast majority have bachelor's in engineering. GRE is generally required, but the engineering part is often not required. Top schools prefer quantitative scores in 650-750 range.
■ **TIPS ON GETTING IN:** Students can have a B.S. in a specific engineering field and still apply to a graduate program in another field. GPAs are generally in the 3.5 range at top schools. Summer engineering internships can boost applicant's chances.

ENGLISH

446 graduate programs. Popular subdisciplines: nationalism and post-colonialism, gender issues, 19th- and 20th-century American literature.

■ **ADMISSIONS:** '92–'93 enrollment: 128,081; 15 percent of enrollees are women. Master's in '92: 7,450; Ph.D.'s: 1,273. Sampling of acceptance rates: 4 percent at Stanford; 11 percent at U. of Washington; 22 percent at U. of Virginia.
■ **PREREQUISITES:** Writing samples and B.A. in English or related field. GRE and subject test in literature are required at most schools. Verbal scores in the 650s or higher are needed at top schools.
■ **TIPS ON GETTING IN:** Writing sample is a crucial part of the application. It should be related to desired area of study and show critical thinking and familiarity with recent

scholarship. Reading knowledge of at least one foreign language is strongly recommended.

FILM

34 schools offer the M.F.A. Popular subdisciplines: television production, film production, documentary filmmaking, screenwriting, animation.

■ **ADMISSIONS:** Estimated '93 enrollment: 1,500. Sampling of acceptance rates: 8 percent at Temple U.; 10 percent at U. of Southern California; 25 percent at Northwestern.

■ **PREREQUISITES:** Providing examples of artistic work is a must. GRE is required by most schools but is secondary to artistic work. Experience in a production company can be helpful.

■ **TIPS ON GETTING IN:** The most important part of an application is the artistic work. Most applicants send a 10-minute video, but other examples, such as scripts, are acceptable. Schools are looking for imagination and/or interesting point of view.

FOREIGN LANGUAGES

658 programs in 260 schools. Popular subdisciplines: literature, history, gender studies.

■ **ADMISSIONS:** '92–'93 enrollment: 13,230; 64 percent of enrollees are women. Master's in '92: 2,926; Ph.D.'s: 850. Sampling of acceptance rates: 28 percent at Columbia for East Asian languages; 60 percent at U. of Florida for German; 79 percent at U. of Wisconsin for French.

■ **PREREQUISITES:** A B.A. in the language applicant plans to study along with the GRE is usually required. GPA should be 3.5 or better and GRE verbal score 600 or better.

■ **TIPS ON GETTING IN:** Study or work abroad is considered vital. Typically, applicants have spent junior year abroad or lived in the country of interest. Statement of purpose is important; some schools require it in both English and the language to be studied.

GEOGRAPHY

135 graduate programs. Most popular subdisciplines: geographic information systems, using computers to map populations, geographic formations.

■ **ADMISSIONS:** '93–'94 enrollment: 3,701; about 35 percent of enrollees are women. Master's in '94: 577; Ph.D.'s: 123. Sampling of acceptance rates: 13 percent at Penn State; 20 percent at U. of Calif. at Santa Barbara; 27 percent at U. of Arizona.

■ **PREREQUISITES:** Most programs require scores above 1100 on the GRE and GPAs of 3.5. Research experience, in either the workplace or college, is considered important.

■ **TIPS ON GETTING IN:** Geography is defined as a science, so any course work in the sciences that familiarizes students with the research process is a plus. Computer science skills are very valuable as geography becomes increasingly computer driven.

GEOLOGY

336 graduate programs. Popular subdisciplines: hyrdrogeology, environmental geology.

■ **ADMISSIONS:** '92–'93 enrollment: 8,283; 28 percent of enrollees are women. Master's in '93: 1,272; Ph.D.'s: 496. Sampling of acceptance rates: 23 percent at Penn State; 40 percent at U. of Wisconsin at Madison; 60 percent at U. of Alabama.

■ **PREREQUISITES:** B.A. in geology or related science field; some schools require at least a 3.5 GPA in major. GRE is required at most schools, with combined verbal and quantitative scores above 1200.

■ **TIPS ON GETTING IN**: Faculty letters of recommendation carry strong weight; working as an undergraduate field assistant and other research experience can also boost chances. Students should have a broad background in the sciences.

■ GRAD STUDENT'S GUIDE

HEALTH SERVICES ADMINISTRATION

65 accredited programs. Popular electives: managed care, long-term care, home care, health care marketing.

■ **ADMISSIONS:** '92–'93 enrollment: 5,167; 58 percent of enrollees are women. Master's in '93: 1,616; Ph.D.'s: 45. Sampling of acceptance rates: 30 percent at Johns Hopkins U.; 33 percent at Trinity U. in Texas.
■ **PREREQUISITES:** Most schools require either the GMAT or GRE. An average of 600 on each portion of the GRE is preferred. The quantitative part is considered especially important.
■ **TIPS ON GETTING IN:** Accounting, statistics, finance, and economics courses are strongly recommended. Administrators must be able to discern patterns of disease and develop plans for preventive care, so computer and management skills also can help applicants.

HISTORY

134 graduate programs. Popular subdisciplines: 19th- and 20th-century American, gender, and social history.

■ **ADMISSIONS:** '93–'94 enrollment: 17,854; 39 percent of enrollees are women. Master's in '92: 2,754; Ph.D.'s: 644. Sampling of acceptance rates: 11 percent at U. of North Carolina at Chapel Hill; 20 percent at Brown; 33 percent at U. of Chicago.
■ **PREREQUISITES:** B.A. in history or substantial course work in the field. GRE is generally required, with average scores of 650 on each section.
■ **TIPS ON GETTING IN:** Statement of purpose and letters of recommendation are the most important elements of the application. The statement should indicate who you want to work with and why you want to attend that particular school.

INTERNATIONAL STUDIES

15 professional schools, but most universities offer degree programs. Popular subdisciplines: joint programs in business, law, or journalism.

■ **ADMISSIONS:** '93–'94 enrollment: 4,545 at professional schools; 48 percent of enrollees are women. Master's degrees awarded at professional schools in '93: 1,694. Sampling of acceptance rates: 20 percent at Tufts U.; 25 percent at Harvard.
■ **PREREQUISITES:** Students typically have a liberal arts background with an average GPA of 3.4. A GRE in the 1200 range and a foreign language are required at most schools.
■ **TIPS ON GETTING IN**: Many students take time off before entering the program. Applicants should try to get experience in region of interest. Strong language skills are a big plus; economics background can boost chances at some schools.

JOURNALISM

201 graduate programs. Popular subdisciplines: photo-, print, and broadcast journalism.

■ **ADMISSIONS:** '93–'94 enrollment: 11,153; 63 percent of master's degree enrollees are women. Master's degrees awarded in '92–'93: 2,838; Ph.D.'s: 150. Sampling of acceptance rates: 24 percent at Columbia; 51 percent at Indiana U.
■ **PREREQUISITES:** The GRE is usually required, though not at Columbia; for most programs, scores should be at least 500 on each section. Computer proficiency is increasingly important.
■ **TIPS ON GETTING IN:** Most students major in disciplines such as English, political science, or history. Statement of purpose is especially important. If the application requires a writing examination, knowledge of current events is essential.

LAW

177 accredited schools. Popular specialties: international, intellectual property, and environmental law.

■ **ADMISSIONS:** '93–'94 enrollment: 127,802; 43 percent of enrollees are

■ GRAD STUDENT'S GUIDE

women. J.D. degrees awarded in '93: 40,213. Sampling of acceptance rates: 17 percent for non-Texas residents at American U.; 34 percent at Brigham Young.

■ **PREREQUISITES:** The most common undergraduate majors are political science, history, and English. LSAT is required, with scores in the 160s needed for top schools.

■ **TIPS ON GETTING IN:** LSAT scores and undergraduate GPAs are very important. Those with GPAs below 3.0 need to do well on the LSAT. College writing courses are useful because of the amount of writing required of most lawyers.

LIBRARY SCIENCE

50 accredited programs. Popular subdisciplines: school and public librarian, information systems.

■ **ADMISSIONS:** '93–'94 enrollment: 14,304; 73 percent of enrollees are women. Master's and post-master's degrees awarded in '93: 5,005. Sampling of acceptance rates: 63 percent at U. of North Carolina at Chapel Hill.

■ **PREREQUISITES:** No specific major required; students usually have liberal arts background. GRE is generally required, with a score of at least 1000 needed; top schools may require a score of 1200.

■ **TIPS ON GETTING IN:** A background in computer science can strengthen an application. Most applicants have been in the workforce for several years. GPAs are not as important as relevant work experience.

MATHEMATICS

421 graduate programs. Popular subdisciplines: algebra, geometry, analysis.

■ **ADMISSIONS:** '92–'93 enrollment: 13,780; about one-fourth of enrollees are women. Ph.D.'s awarded in '93: 1,214. Sampling of acceptance rates: 15 percent at Rutger's; 33 percent at U. of Kansas; 72 percent at U. of Iowa.

■ **PREREQUISITES:** Few schools require B.S. in math, but most look for extensive course work in the discipline. GRE is required. Many schools also require the subject test in math.

■ **TIPS ON GETTING IN**: Faculty letters of recommendation dealing with applicant's ability to perform independent research carry significant weight. Computer science courses and experience are also extremely important.

MEDICINE

125 medical schools. Popular residency specialties: internal medicine, pediatrics, family medicine.

■ **ADMISSIONS:** '94–'95 enrollment: 67,072; 42 percent of enrollees are women. M.D.'s awarded in '94: 15,555. Sampling of acceptance rates: 3 percent at George Washington U.; 4 percent at Tulane U.; 8 percent at Oregon Health Sciences U.

■ **PREREQUISITES:** Medical College Admission Test is required. Double-digit scores are necessary for top schools, with GPAs of 3.5 or better in the sciences. Chemistry, physics, and biology courses needed.

■ **TIPS ON GETTING IN:** Because of the large number of applicants, schools pay close attention to test scores and GPA. Volunteer work or community service is extremely important to admissions boards looking for applicants with a passion for helping people.

MUSIC

More than 290 graduate programs. Popular subdisciplines: music education, voice, piano, strings, composition.

■ **ADMISSIONS:** '93–'94 enrollment: 14,285; nearly half of enrollees are women. Master's degrees awarded in '92–'93: 3,350; Ph.D.'s: 525. Sampling of acceptance rates: 20 percent at Julliard; 52 percent at San Francisco Music Conservatory; 70 percent at Indiana U.

■ **PREREQUISITES:** Most schools prefer a bachelor of music degree. Many, but

■ GRAD STUDENT'S GUIDE

not all, require GRE. Combined verbal and quantitative scores often are around 1100.

■ **TIPS ON GETTING IN:** Key element is the audition. Schools provide guidelines regarding selection of pieces. Students should follow them closely and not perform pieces that are too flashy for their technique or too advanced for their skills.

NURSING

214 accredited programs. Popular subdisciplines: nurse practitioner, critical-care nursing.

■ **ADMISSIONS:** '93–'94 enrollment: 33,637; almost 95 percent of enrollees are women. Master's in '93–'94: 7,653; Ph.D.'s: 365. Sampling of acceptance rates: 57 percent at U. of Colorado; 62 percent at Wayne State U.; 95 percent at U. of Nebraska Medical Center.

■ **PREREQUISITES:** While most schools require a bachelor's in nursing, those with programs geared to students' changing careers do not. GRE or MAT is required by most schools.

■ **TIPS ON GETTING IN:** GRE and GPA are the most important parts of an application. GRE scores on the verbal and quantitative sections should be 500 or better. Most applicants have nursing experience so statements of purpose are looked at closely.

PHARMACY

62 accredited Pharm.D. programs.

■ **ADMISSIONS:** 92–'93 enrollment: 6,820; 66 percent of enrollees are women. Pharm. D. degrees awarded in '93: 1,745. Sampling of acceptance rates: 25 percent at U. of Arizona; 42 percent at U. of Illinois at Chicago; 46 percent at Philadelphia College of Pharmacy and Science.

■ **PREREQUISITES:** Two years of course work in science or a B.S. in pharmacy. Some schools require the Pharmacy College Admission Test. Average composite score: 201.

■ **TIPS ON GETTING IN:** Schools pay close attention to the undergraduate transcript, particularly courses in hard sciences. For top programs, GPAs for the junior and senior years should be in the 3.3 to 3.5 range. Health-related experience is a big plus.

PHILOSOPHY

74 master's and 116 Ph.D. programs. Popular subdisciplines: medical ethics, logic, ancient Greek philosophy.

■ **ADMISSIONS:** '93–'94 enrollment: 4,999; about 30 percent of enrollees are women. Master's in '92: 555; Ph.D.'s: 282. Sampling of acceptance rates: 5 percent at U. of California, Berkeley; 9 percent at U. of Pittsburgh; 10 percent at Bowling Green State U.

■ **PREREQUISITES:** Bachelor's degree in philosophy not required but is the most common. Foreign language skills are important, particularly French, German, and ancient Greek. GRE is required.

■ **TIPS ON GETTING IN**: Substantial course work in philosophy, including history of philosophy, metaphysics, and ethics, is often needed. Students must have verbal and analytical skills, which they should exhibit in a statement of purpose.

PHYSICAL THERAPY

73 accredited programs. Popular subdisciplines: geriatrics, pediatrics, neurology.

■ **ADMISSIONS:** '93–'94 enrollment: 6,663; 72 percent of enrollees are women. Master's awarded in '94: 2,702. Sampling of acceptance rates: 14 percent at Temple U.; 17 percent at U. of Kansas Medical Center; 20 percent at U. of Southern California.

■ **PREREQUISITES:** GRE is required, with combined verbal and quantitative scores of 100. Course work in physics, chemistry, and biology also is needed.

■ **TIPS ON GETTING IN:** Voluntary experience in a health care setting is a must; it is preferable that applicants have a variety of experiences in acute care, rehabilitation, and outpatient settings. The

■ GRAD STUDENT'S GUIDE

statement of purpose is often used in making final admissions decision.

PHYSICS

262 graduate programs. Popular subdisciplines: condensed matter, high energy, and atomic physics.

■ **ADMISSIONS:** '93–'94 enrollment: 14,201; 15 percent of enrollees are women. Master's in '93: 1,797; Ph.D.'s: 1,369. Sample of acceptance rates: 14 percent at Johns Hopkins U.; 25 percent at U. of Maryland at College Park; 36 percent at U. of California at Santa Barbara.
■ **PREREQUISITES:** A B.S. in physics is recommended. GRE and subject test are usually required. A score above the 80th percentile on the subject test is needed to be competitive.
■ **TIPS ON GETTING IN:** Strong test scores, 3.5 GPA in physics and math, and letters of recommendation are most important. Letters should come from researchers—either faculty or scientists in the private sector with whom the applicant has worked.

POLITICAL SCIENCE

More than 200 master's and 130 Ph.D. programs. Popular subdiscipline: public policy.

■ **ADMISSIONS:** '93–'94 enrollment: 21,500; 32 percent of Ph.D. enrollees are women. Average number of master's awarded annually: 3,000; Ph.D.'s: 650. Sampling of acceptance rates: 8 percent at Yale U.; 11 percent at U. of California at San Diego.
■ **PREREQUISITES:** An undergraduate major in political science is quite common, but is not essential. GRE is required, and scores are usually above 600 on each section.
■ **TIPS ON GETTING IN:** Most schools pay close attention to grades, particularly in major fields, with GPAs of 3.3 to 3.5 common. Research work, particularly in public-opinion surveys or a senior thesis, looks very good on an application.

PSYCHOLOGY

450 accredited Ph.D. programs. Popular subdisciplines: clinical, counseling, and school psychology.

■ **ADMISSIONS:** '91–'92 enrollment: 37,440; 63 percent of Ph.D. enrollees are women. Ph.D.'s awarded in '93: 3,419. Sampling of acceptance rates: 4 percent at U. of Maryland; 6 percent at U. of Florida; 11 percent at U. of Texas at Austin.
■ **PREREQUISITES:** Although it is not required, the vast majority of applicants have an undergraduate degree in psychology. The GRE is generally required, along with the subject test.
■ **TIPS ON GETTING IN:** Psychology programs are very competitive, and undergraduate GPAs are often quite high—between 3.6 and 4.0. Average scores on each section of the GRE should be at least 650. Most students have prior research experience.

PUBLIC ADMINISTRATION

218 master's and 55 Ph.D. programs. Popular subdisciplines: urban planning, international administration, criminal justice administration.

■ **ADMISSIONS:** '92–'93 enrollment: 28,702; nearly half of enrollees are women. Master's in '93: 7,867; Ph.D.'s: 241. Sampling of acceptance rates: 27 percent at Howard U.; 31 percent at Michigan State U.; 55 percent at Syracuse U.
■ **PREREQUISITES:** Undergraduate majors are usually social and behavioral sciences. GRE is usually required; verbal and quantitative scores should each be in the 550 to 600 range.
■ **TIPS ON GETTING IN:** GPAs should be in the 3.5 range for top programs. Many successful applicants have several years of professional experience in public service. Volunteer experience or internships are particularly important when applicant is coming directly from college.

■ GRAD STUDENT'S GUIDE

PUBLIC HEALTH

27 accredited graduate schools. Popular subdisciplines: biostatistics, environmental health, epidemiology.

■ **ADMISSIONS:** '92–'93 enrollment: 13,329; 62 percent of enrollees are women. Master's awarded in '93: about 12,500. Sampling of acceptance rates: 45 percent at U. of Minnesota at Twin Cities; 53 percent at Harvard; 80 percent at Boston U.
■ **PREREQUISITES:** Although the GRE is preferred, some schools will accept standardized tests for other fields such as the GMAT or MACT. Some schools also require prior work in health care.
■ **TIPS ON GETTING IN:** Many applicants already have clinical degrees in medicine, nursing, or social work. Public health is a huge field, so applicants should know their specific area of interest. Since most applicants are older, work experience is important.

SOCIAL WORK

111 accredited master's programs. Popular subdisciplines: mental health, child welfare, corrections.

■ **ADMISSIONS:** '93–'94 enrollment: 32,195; 82 percent of enrollees are women. Master's awarded in '93: about 12,500. Sampling of acceptance rates: 13 percent at Hunter College (City University of New York); 16 percent at Ohio State U.; 79 percent at Washington U. in St. Louis.
■ **PREREQUISITES:** A liberal arts background with social science course work is considered very desirable. Some schools require GRE or Miller Analogies Test, but test scores are not considered crucial.
■ **TIPS ON GETTING IN:** Few people are admitted without paid or volunteer service in social service setting. The statement of purpose is important because it demonstrates motivation, direction, and how well the student communicates.

SOCIOLOGY

365 graduate programs. Popular subdisciplines: demography, stratification, criminology.

■ **ADMISSIONS:** '90–'91 enrollment: 5,137; 59 percent of enrollees are women. Master's degrees awarded in '91: 1,299; Ph.D.'s in 1993: 513. Sampling of acceptance rates: 10 percent at Indiana U.; 13 percent at Penn State; 20 percent at U. of Wisconsin at Madison.
■ **PREREQUISITES:** The GRE is required. Scores above 1100 and undergraduate courses in sociology are needed for most programs. Test scores are not as important as the overall application, though.
■ **TIPS ON GETTING IN:** Applicants should have at least one course each in research methods and statistics. Evidence of some kind of solid research experience, preferably in the social sciences, also is considered quite important.

VETERINARY MEDICINE

27 accredited programs. Popular subdisciplines: small animals, surgery, wildlife.

■ **ADMISSIONS:** '93–'94 enrollment: 8,810; 64 percent of enrollees are women. Doctorates of veterinary medicine awarded in '93: 2,074. Sampling of acceptance rates: 17 percent at Kansas State U.; 27 percent at Texas A&M; 31 percent at U. of Pennsylvania.
■ **PREREQUISITES:** The GRE generally is required and, often, the biology subject test as well. Top programs usually require GREs of at least 1100. Some schools require or accept the Veterinary College Admission Test or MCAT.
■ **TIPS ON GETTING IN:** The course requirements include physics, biology, organic chemistry, biochemistry, genetics, and calculus. GPA in sciences should be above 3.2. Applicants are expected to have some kind of experience working with animals.

CHAPTER FIVE

CAREERS

EXPERT QUOTES

"Those in the '74 Harvard business class that chose a career in a small business or struck out on their own were more successful."

—John Kotter, author of *The New Rules:How to Succeed in Today's Post Corporate World*

Page 415

"Financial rewards are overstated...There is much more power in non-monetary rewards."

—Robert Nelson, author of *1,001 Ways to Reward Employees*

Page 419

"In this period of downsizing, or to put it more nicely rightsizing, one always has to be prepared for the ax."

—Jim O'Connell, psychologist at a New York outplacement firm

Page 424

THE YEAR AHEAD: BE PREPARED for more job turmoil, less job security... **AVOID** manufacturing jobs, which will continue to slump... **SEEK** out jobs in the fast-growing service sector... **APPLY** for an internship to land a job... **DON'T EXPECT** more than a 4 percent raise... **PROTEST** because women still earn less than men... **ANTICIPATE** fewer perks... **SURF** the Internet for new job listings... **DON'T ANSWER** every question at a job interview... **RELAX** if you get fired...

GETTING STARTED

OUTLOOK

WHERE THE BEST JOBS WILL BE

The more education, the better your prospects—but it's a jungle out there

More job turmoil. Less job security. A need for better-prepared workers. That's the vision most career experts have for the next decade. The American economy will continue to be a powerful job-creating machine; the U.S. Department of Labor predicts that some 26.4 million jobs will be added to the economy by 2005, a 22 percent rise in total employment, to 147.5 million. But the new jobs won't be evenly scattered across the landscape, meaning there's more job restructuring on the horizon. In short, for better and for worse, the immediate future will look a lot like the recent past.

With automation and the movement of factory work overseas, jobs will stagnate or fall off in many areas that require little education. That means, for example, more tough times for apparel workers and machine feeders. Those without at least a high school diploma will find very few doors open. The fastest-growing areas require higher levels of skills and education. Three out of four of the fastest-growing job groups are executive, administrative and managerial, professional specialties, and technicians, according to the Labor Department.

Technical workers—those who diagnose diseases, who design and operate computer machinery used to make cars and planes, and those who develop and operate the sophisticated computer and telecommunications networks that are transforming business—are in the catbird seat. Technician jobs are expected to grow by 1.4 million between 1992 and 2005. There will be 500,000 new jobs for systems analysts alone. Nuclear medicine and EEG technologists' jobs are expected to rise by more than half. But the fabulous growth rates in the latter two specialized fields can be somewhat deceiving—because these fields are small, the growth translates into only several thousand new jobs a year, on average.

As always, changing demographics will help create future jobs: by 2005, the number of people aged 85 and older will grow about four times as fast as the total population, increasing the demand for health services. The graying of America, combined with medical improvements that will extend life spans, will keep the health service industry sizzling. Jobs will soar from 9.6 million to 13.8 million. Jobs in home health care, nursing homes, and offices and clinics of physicians and other health practitioners are expected to rise. Residential care institutions providing round-the-clock help

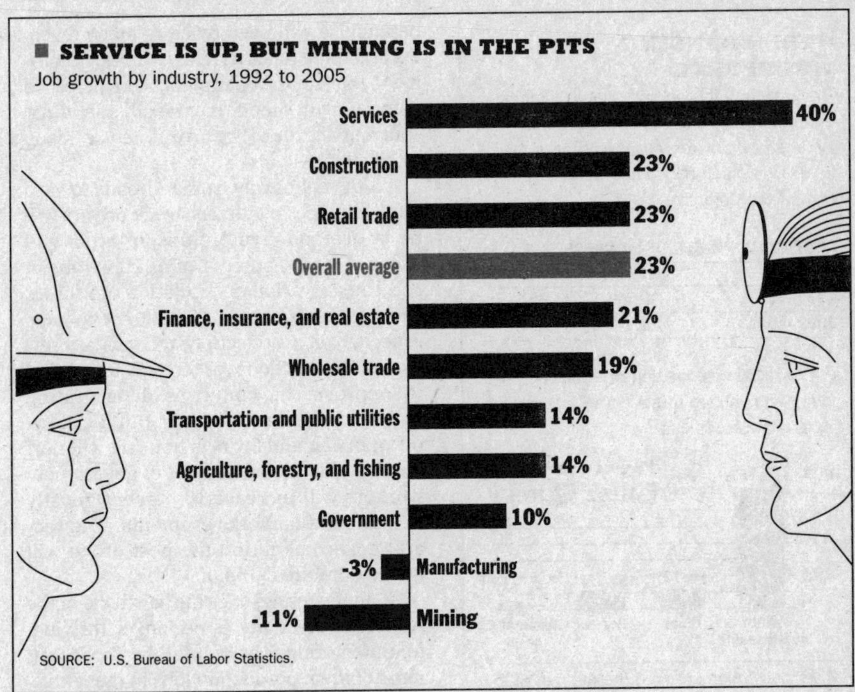

for the elderly are expected to be the fastest-growing industry in the whole economy. Other future hot spots: child day care and other social services, including elderly day care and family social services. One exception is hospitals, which will grow more slowly, due to cost-cutting competition in the industry.

Other service businesses will also continue to churn out jobs. Transportation, communications, utilities, retailing, government, finance, insurance, and real estate companies will account for almost two-thirds of all new jobs by 2005. Employment is expected to rise 40 percent in the services sector, to 54.2 million jobs. Aside from nursing care, other hot service jobs will be in data processing, management consulting, and social, legal, and engineering and management services. The strong demand for financial services will continue, giving a boost to finance, insurance, and real estate jobs. The fastest-growing areas will be in investment and mortgage banking and insurance. The future is less rosy for jobs in commercial banks and savings and loans.

A big chunk of the jobs created in the business services sector will come from temporary help agencies. Some 1.6 million workers already hold temp jobs, and their ranks are expected to grow 57 percent, to nearly 3 million. Of the temp workers, some 25 percent are highly skilled professionals. Wages generally are negotiable but average 15 to 20 percent less than salaries for similar permanent positions. Computer analysts, for example, earn about $23 an hour; clerical workers make about $10 an hour.

Temping may appeal to workers who want to mold jobs to their lifestyle but it also comes with headaches, such as finding affordable health insurance. Some temps can get coverage through a group plan offered by the National Association of Temporary Services, ☎ 703-549-6287. A bit of good news: about 30 percent of temporary jobs lead to full-time positions.

Despite the spotlight on high-tech careers, many of tomorrow's jobs will look much like today's. America will still need more gardeners, for example, than computer programmers in the years to come. The

■ THE CHANGING WORKFORCE

The growth in the women's labor force is expected to slow down, but it will still increase at a faster rate than that of men. In 1993, women accounted for 45.8 percent of the workforce.

GROWTH IN NUMBER OF WORKERS:

	WOMEN	MEN
1979–92	+30.7%	+13.9%
1992–2005	+24.2%	+13.8%

■ The racial composition of the labor force will continue to shift. The fast-growing group: Hispanics.

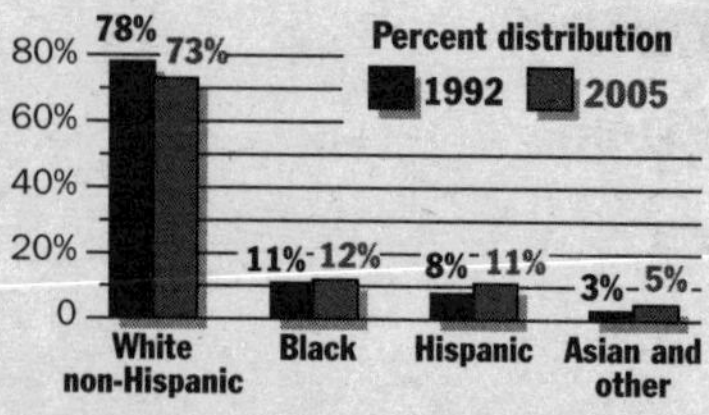

■ As baby boomers age, the number of people in the labor force between ages 45 and 64 will increase most rapidly.

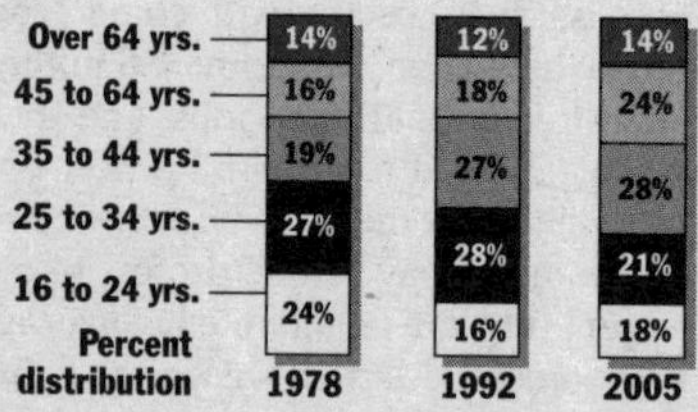

■ Most jobs through the year 2005 will become available as a result of replacement needs. Thus, even occupations with little or no employment growth still may offer many job openings.

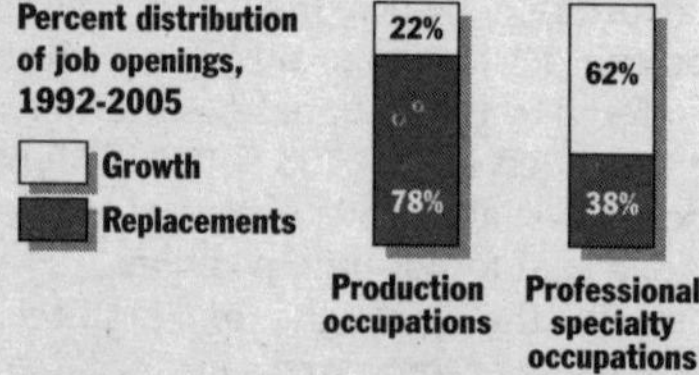

SOURCES: U.S. Bureau of Labor Statistics; Kim Cameron, University of Michigan.

nation also will need twice as many teachers and three times as many nurses, according to the Labor Department. And increased income will mean increased spending, spurring the need for five times as many retail clerks.

As the shift away from railroads toward road deliveries continues, truck drivers will be in demand. Truck transportation will account for 50 percent of all new jobs in this category. And deregulation of utilities should create some 117,000 new jobs, especially in water supply and sanitary services. Construction workers will be needed to improve the country's deteriorating roads, bridges, and tunnels. But the slowdown in demand for new housing will hurt home builders. The number of government workers will increase 10 percent, mostly in state and local governments. The federal government and the post office will lose a combined 154,000 jobs.

Manufacturing, once the backbone of the American economy, is no longer thriving. Manufacturing jobs will fall by 3 percent, most of them production jobs in the textile, metals, and automobile industries. Those in search of manufacturing jobs stand a better chance in the South. First Union Bank in Charlotte, N.C., found that the Northeast and West Coast lost more than 450,000 manufacturing jobs from 1992 to 1993 while the Southeast gained 23,000. Companies are lured to the South by lower costs, non-union labor, economic incentives, and a relaxed lifestyle. The area, particularly the Interstate 85 corridor from the Carolinas to Georgia, has been especially successful in attracting foreign manufacturers.

Not all states are created equal when it comes to serving as attractive places to start your own business. The Corporation for Enterprise Development, a nonprofit research organization in Washington, D.C., has ranked the 50 states based on 12 criteria, including taxes, state economy, and entrepreneurial environment. The most appealing state for starting a business was Colorado, followed Utah, Minnesota Delaware, and Pennsylvania. At the bottom: Arkansas, Oklahoma, Kentucky, Louisiana, and West Virginia, which was dragged down by low business vitality.

CAREER PLANNER'S GUIDE

THE 50 FASTEST-GROWING PROFESSIONS

The best job opportunities often are not where the most jobs are, but instead where the most growth is. Explosive growth in a relatively small pool indicates an industry in need of a rapid infusion of labor, and that means opportunities galore. The following statistics from the U.S. Bureau of Labor Statistics show the 50 professions expected to experience the fastest growth between 1992 and 2005.

JOB	JOBS IN 1992	NEW JOBS BY 2005	PERCENT GROWTH
1. HOME HEALTH AIDES The aging boomer population will seek more home care. The chronically ill will be treated at home, spurring the development of in-home medical technologies.	475,000	645,000	136%
2. HUMAN SERVICES WORKERS Facilities and programs for the elderly, the disabled, and families in crisis will expand rapidly.	189,000	256,000	136%
3. COMPUTER SCIENTISTS AND SYSTEMS ANALYSTS Employers will seek those with degrees in computer science to manage computer networks and information systems.	666,000	737,000	111%
4. PHYSICAL THERAPISTS New technologies will save more trauma victims and permit treatment of the disabled. An aging population more likely to have heart attacks, strokes, etc. will require help.	90,000	79,000	88%
5. PARALEGALS Demand will zoom as law firms and other employers of legal workers restructure. Expect keen competition as the number of paralegals exiting school exceeds job growth.	95,000	81,000	86%
6. MEDICAL ASSISTANTS An expanding health services industry will drive growth. High turnover and doctors' preference for trained personnel will increase demand for those with formal training.	181,000	128,000	71%
7. CORRECTION OFFICERS A growing number of inmates will require more guards and counselors.	282,000	197,000	70%
8. TRAVEL AGENTS With more leisure time, people will travel more. Business travel will increase as firms decentralize. Retiring boomers will create work for agencies specializing in cruise bookings.	115,000	76,000	66%
9. PRESCHOOL WORKERS High turnover, low pay, and difficult work will create job openings. Demand will grow as young women increasingly enter the labor force and parents seek quality child care.	941,000	611,000	65%
10. RADIOLOGIC TECHNOLOGISTS A new generation of diagnostic imaging equipment capable of detecting malignant tumors will increase treatments.	162,000	102,000	63%
11. MEDICAL RECORD TECHNICIANS The number of medical tests, treatments, and procedures will grow and third-party payers, courts, and consumers will increasingly scrutinize medical records.	76,000	47,000	61%
12. OPERATIONS RESEARCH ANALYSTS Emphasis on quantitative analysis in transportation, manufacturing, finance, and service industries will drive demand.	45,000	27,000	61%
13. OCCUPATIONAL THERAPISTS Medical advances will allow those with once critical problems to survive. Elderly boomers and disabled children entering special education programs will also spur growth.	40,000	24,000	60%
14. EEG TECHNOLOGISTS New tests and procedures will be developed as the aging population requires more sophisticated medical care.	6,300	3,400	54%
15. ACTORS, DIRECTORS, AND PRODUCERS New media outlets will need new material, but competition will remain intense because many are attracted to these careers and little formal training is necessary. Relatively few people will find regular employment.	129,000	69,000	54%
16. SECURITY GUARDS Concerns about crime, vandalism, and terrorism will increase demand. In-house jobs offer higher salaries and job security but contract security agencies will offer more opportunities.	803,000	408,000	51%

■ **CAREER PLANNER'S GUIDE**

JOB	JOBS IN 1992	NEW JOBS BY 2005	PERCENT GROWTH
17. SPEECH-LANGUAGE PATHOLOGISTS AND AUDIOLOGISTS The aging boomer population will drive demand, particularly as stroke-induced hearing loss and speech loss increases. Emphasis on early detection and prevention will also spur growth.	73,000	37,000	51%
18. FLIGHT ATTENDANTS More airline passengers mean more flight attendants. Competition will remain keen—those with at least two years of college and experience dealing with the public will have the best chances.	93,000	47,000	51%
19. NUCLEAR MEDICINE TECHNOLOGISTS Technological innovations and an aging population should increase demand.	12,000	6,000	50%
20. RESPIRATORY THERAPISTS AIDS epidemic and aging population will spur demand. Outlook is particularly good for those with neonatal care skills.	74,000	36,000	48%
21. PSYCHOLOGISTS Expect new programs for the elderly, the treatment of substance abuse, and criminal rehabilitation.	143,000	69,000	48%
22. GENERAL CONTRACTORS AND CONSTRUCTION MANAGERS Bigger and more complex construction projects and more spending on infrastructure—highways, bridges, dams, mass transit—will create work, especially for those with advanced degrees in construction science or management.	180,000	85,000	47%
23. RESTAURANT AND FOOD SERVICE MANAGERS The number of eating and drinking establishments will grow as population and leisure time increase and incomes rise.	496,000	227,000	46%
24. HEALTH SERVICE MANAGERS Most new jobs will be in hospitals, physicians' offices and clinics, nursing facilities, and home health care. Those with marketing skills will be especially attractive.	302,000	135,000	45%
25. NURSING AIDES AND PSYCHIATRIC AIDES Older people and those suffering from acute psychiatric or drug abuse problems will need help. Turnover will be high.	1,389,000	616,00	44%
26. TEACHER AIDES With the rising number of special education classes, the restructuring of schools and the increasing number of students who speak English as a second language, teachers are stretched to the limit.	885,000	381,000	43%
27. MANAGEMENT ANALYSTS AND CONSULTANTS Outsourcing will drive demand as firms look to expand markets, incorporate new technologies, and adapt to a changing labor force. Despite growth, job seekers will face keen competition.	208,000	89,000	43%
28. DENTAL HYGIENISTS Population growth, greater retention of natural teeth by middle-aged and elderly people, and rising incomes will spur demand. With increased workloads, dentists will need more help.	108,000	46,000	43%
29. SURGICAL TECHNOLOGISTS More people and more technology mean more operations. Growth will be fastest in clinics and doctor's offices, but the majority of jobs will continue to be in hospitals.	44,000	19,000	42%
30. REGISTERED NURSES More emphasis on primary care will create jobs—and high turnover as experienced nurses quit.	1,835,000	765,000	42%
31. HOTEL AND MOTEL DESK CLERKS More travelers will be checking in and out. High turnover, lots of part-time jobs.	122,000	50,000	40%
32. RECREATIONAL THERAPISTS More nursing homes, retirement communities, and adult day care services mean more opportunities.	30,000	12,000	40%
33. ANIMAL CARETAKERS (EXCEPT FARM) Prospects should be particularly good for graduates of training programs in veterinary technology.	103,000	41,000	40%
34. LICENSED PRACTICAL NURSES Prospects are excellent unless the number of those completing LPN training increases substantially.	659,000	261,000	40%
35. LOAN OFFICERS AND COUNSELORS A growing economy will increase the number of applications for commercial, consumer and mortgage loans.	172,000	68,000	40%
36. SOCIAL WORKERS The elderly, mentally ill, the disabled, and individuals and families in crisis will need help.	484,000	191,000	40%
37. DENTAL ASSISTANTS Dentists are expected to hire more assistants to perform routine tasks.	183,000	72,000	39%
38. INSULATION WORKERS Getting rid of asbestos in existing structures is still a big job. Turnover in this field is the highest of all construction occupations, possibly because of health concerns.	57,000	22,000	39%

■ CAREER PLANNER'S GUIDE

JOB	JOBS IN 1992	NEW JOBS BY 2005	PERCENT GROWTH
39. **CHEFS, COOKS, AND KITCHEN WORKERS** Increasingly, people like to eat out. Lots of turnover, however.	3,092,000	1,190,000	38%
40. **RECREATION WORKERS** More folks will want to stay fit and have fun. Few full-time jobs, but the outlook is good for seasonal and part-time.	204,000	78,000	38%
41. **SERVICE SALES REPRESENTATIVES** Growth will not keep pace with other service sectors because of the use of new technologies. Those with a college sales background or a proven sales record will do best.	488,000	185,000	38%
42. **SOCIAL SCIENTISTS AND URBAN PLANNERS** Increasing concerns over social issues will open horizons, even in non-academic settings.	258,000	95,000	37%
43. **PODIATRISTS** Physiological problems in aging boomers should drive demand.	15,000	5,500	37%
44. **MARKETING, ADVERTISING, AND PUBLIC RELATIONS MANAGERS** Increased global competition will drive demand for these highly coveted positions.	432,000	156,000	36%
45. **EMERGENCY MEDICAL TECHNICIANS** Old folks will need more service. High stress leads to high turnover.	114,000	41,000	36%
46. **COUNTER AND RENTAL CLERKS** Increased demand for dry cleaning, auto rental, and recreation will create jobs, particularly for part-timers.	242,000	88,000	36%
47. **PROPERTY AND REAL ESTATE MANAGERS** Opportunities will be best for those with degrees in business administration.	243,000	85,000	35%
48. **DISPENSING OPTICIANS** An aging population will need more corrective lenses. Most employees are young and move on after a year or two.	63,000	22,000	35%
49. **CHIROPRACTORS** Aging boomers will ache more.	46,000	16,000	35%
50. **AIRCRAFT PILOTS** Rapid growth, but heavy competition. Those most familiar with sophisticated equipment will do the best.	85,000	30,000	35%

■ WHERE THE JOBS WON'T BE

As any carriage maker will tell you, new technology is not necessarily good for business. Automation has displaced everyone from autoworkers to telephone operators, and others have found themselves as redundant as the Maytag repairman in an era where replacement is cheaper than repair.

JOB	JOBS IN 1992	NEW JOBS BY 2005	PERCENT GROWTH
1. **TELEPHONE REPAIRERS** Pre-wired jacks, modular telephones, and equipment that is cheaper to replace than to repair put repairers on hold.	40,000	20,000	50%
2. **COMPUTER AND PERIPHERAL EQUIPMENT OPERATORS** Automated data centers and omnipresent PCs spell bad news for operators of large mainframe systems.	296,000	122,000	41%
3. **COMMUNICATIONS EQUIPMENT REPAIRERS** Software is proving easier to repair than hardware.	108,000	41,000	38%
4. **PRIVATE HOUSEHOLD WORKERS** A run on nannies and maids has given rise to professional child care and household cleaning firms.	869,000	286,000	33%
5. **ROUSTABOUTS** Jobs for oil rig workers will be tapped out by automation, foreign oil supplies, and alternative energy sources.	33,000	11,000	33%
6. **TELEPHONE OPERATORS** Who needs an operator in the age of voice mail, automated switching stations, and voice-recognition technology?	314,000	89,000	28%
7. **SHOE AND LEATHER WORKERS** Cheap imported shoes will make replacement cheaper than repair, hobbling cobblers' efforts.	22,000	4,300	20%
8. **APPAREL WORKERS** Clothing firms find that offshore workers and automation suit them better.	986,000	183,000	19%
9. **TEXTILE MACHINERY OPERATORS** Like apparel workers, they're out of fashion.	1,218,000	204,000	17%
10. **FARMERS** Large, centralized operations threaten an employment drought, but rapid turnover may lead to a new crop of jobs.	1,218,000	204,000	17%

SOURCE: *1992–2005 Job Outlook*, Bureau of Labor Statistics, 1994.

FIRST JOBS

THE DIMINISHING VALUE OF DEGREES

Even four years at college doesn't guarantee you a running start

The stories are told on every college campus. An Ivy League graduate is folding T-shirts at the Gap, someone who wrote a senior thesis in economics is now delivering Domino's pizza, and a Phi Beta Kappa history major is still living with her parents, praying for even one response to the dozens of résumés already sent out.

A college diploma no longer guarantees job placement and success. Recent college grads currently outnumber the available jobs that require a degree. Employers aware of this surplus are demanding more than just a sheepskin from their prospective employees, and more recent grads are being left behind. The Bureau of Labor Statistics predicts that the trend will become more pronounced in coming years, with a dramatic increase in unemployment or "underutilization" after graduation, forcing grads into fields that require no college diploma.

EXPERT QUOTE

"Without the degree—without the learning and problem-solving skills that it certifies, without the web of connections that comes with it—a young person today...begins work with a handicap so large as to be almost, but not entirely, insurmountable."

—Robert Reich, U.S. Secretary of Labor

Which recent grads will have the edge? Experts advise that smart students will start thinking about their careers long before they actually march in cap and gown. That means coursework tailored to a specific career, meaningful on-campus activities, and summer internships with hands-on experience. Majors in engineering and the sciences are in the highest demand and will be rewarded with the highest wages.

A chemical engineering major is not a viable option for everyone, but there are ways that every college student can improve his or her career outlook. Basic computer proficiency is a must, and computer programming skills are an added attraction to employers. Those with fluency in a second or third language will also have an advantage, given the new international focus of many corporations, and knowledge of non-Romance languages like Japanese or Czech is especially desirable.

Willingness to relocate is an important factor, according to college recruiters, and job applicants should seriously consider smaller cities in the South and West that will offer the most job growth in the upcoming decade. Candidates should also consider small to medium-size companies, which will be hiring the most workers. Fewer of the big-name corporate recruiters are visiting campuses nationwide, according to the College Placement Council in Bethlehem, Pa.

Recent college graduates face a tough market, but the situation for those without degrees is even bleaker. Because of radical changes in the structure of the U.S. economy in the '80s, career outlooks are dismal for workers without a college education. Moreover, many of the jobs that don't require a degree will nonetheless be taken by "underutilized" college grads, leaving even fewer jobs for the high school grads.

College grads also receive the majority of high-paying jobs overall. In 1992, median earnings for college grads were $37,000 a year, compared with $21,000 for high school grads, and the average unemployment rate for college grads was 3 percent that year, compared with 8 percent for high school grads. That college sheepskin may not be worth as much as it once was, but you're still a lot better off with it than without.

BOOM TIMES FOR SPECIALISTS

The projected growth in college-level jobs between 1992 and 2005

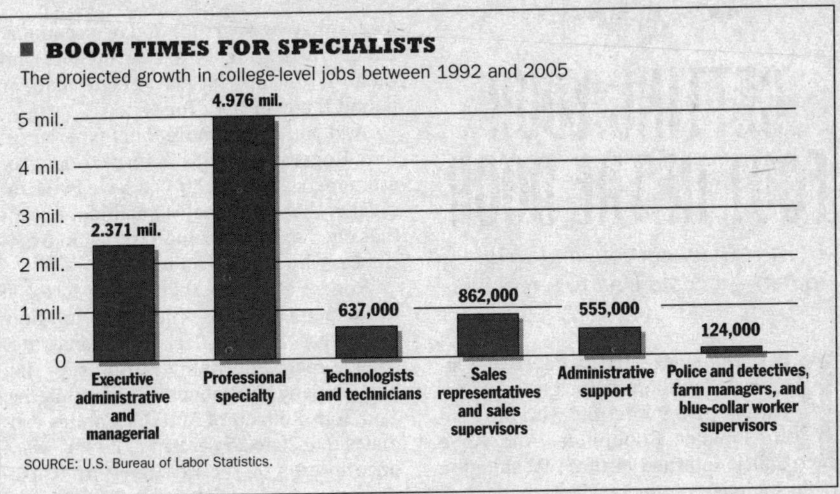

SOURCE: U.S. Bureau of Labor Statistics.

STARTING SALARIES FOR NEW GRADS

As your mother may have told you, a liberal arts major just won't pay the bills. Estimated starting salaries reveal the value of majoring in the sciences and modern technology.

Academic major	Estimated starting salary, 1993-1994
Chemical engineering	$40,689
Mechanical engineering	$35,713
Industrial engineering	$33,593
Computer science	$32,762
Nursing	$30,078
Geology	$28,689
Accounting	$28,022
Mathematics	$26,630
Marketing/sales	$24,782
Agriculture	$24,134
Business admin.	$23,950
Hotel, restaurant mgmt.	$23,855
Education	$22,898
Retailing	$22,195
Communications	$21.860
Advertising	$21,870
Human ecology/home economics	$21,353
Liberal arts	$21,124
Journalism	$20,837
Telecommunications	$20,821

SOURCE: Collegiate Employment Research Institute, Michigan State University.

AMERICA'S BIGGEST NEW JOB MARKETS

Start spreading the news: the biggest new-job markets are not in the Big Apple. Cities in the West and South will be offering more opportunities than the more traditional grad-magnets of the Northeast.

Metro area	Estimated annual increase in jobs, 1993–2015
Los Angeles-Long Beach, Calif.	1,273,000
Washington, D.C.	1,232,000
Atlanta, Ga.	1,194,000
Anaheim-Santa Ana, Calif.	1,189,000
Houston, Texas	1,062,000
Dallas, Texas	963,000
Phoenix, Ariz.	855,000
San Diego, Calif.	803,000
Seattle, Wash.	751,000
Tampa-St.Petersburg-Clearwater, Fla.	721,000
Minneapolis-St.Paul, Minn.	670,000
Boston-Lawrence-Salem-Lowell-Brockton, Mass.	626,000
Chicago, Ill.	617,000
Denver, Colo.	614,000
Philadelphia, Pa.	587,000
Orlando, Fla.	583,000
Riverside-San Bernardino, Calif.	558,000
Sacramento, Calif.	548,000
San Francisco, Calif.	522,000
Fort Lauderdale-Hollywood-Pompano Beach, Fla.	483,000

SOURCE: *Kiplinger's Personal Finance Magazine*, April 1994.

INTERNSHIPS

GETTING YOUR FOOT IN THE DOOR

The FBI wants you, and so do others—it could lead to a real job

Bill Clinton was once an intern in Senator J. William Fulbright's office. Patrick Ewing interned with the Senate Finance Committee. And Katie Couric interned at three Washington radio stations. Future presidents, basketball stars, and television personalities have an even wider variety of internships to choose from. Good jobs with good wages may be sparse in today's economy but internships aren't. You can do time with the FBI, run copy for David Letterman, or pound the gym floor for Nike.

And you'll gain more than experience. Ken Rogers, Boeing's intern/co-op program manager asks, "If you have two candidates that are equally qualified, except that one has a six-month internship experience, who would you hire?"

Rogers estimates that Boeing hires 50 to 70 percent of its interns as full-time employees. Hewlett-Packard's manager of college recruiting Kathy Burton says that her company hires about half of its interns. And Tom Rolston of Marvell Comics estimates that 20 to 25 percent of its staff were once interns. A recent survey by Northwestern University found that 26 percent of those hired by a variety of corporations had been interns—up from 17 percent in 1993. Says one former intern at CNN Sports: "You can't get hired at CNN Sports without having been an intern here."

Internships can also have down sides. About half of them pay little if anything, though some offer academic credit. And interns often are exploited by employers who benefit from their cheap labor, willingness to endure rotten working conditions, and tolerance for boring assignments. Of course, any job has its share of mundane tasks, but prospective interns should take care when selecting an internship to get a commitment that the majority of their time won't be spent in such a manner.

Mark Oldam, co-author with Samer Hamadeh of *America's Top 100 Internships* (Villard, 1994), suggests that interns cheerfully accept busywork in the beginning since many employers use it as a means of assessment. Once you've proved you're competent and diligent, you should then diplomatically request more substantive, challenging work. If the internship doesn't offer more rigorous work, says Sally Migliore, associate executive director of the National Society for Experiential Education, the intern should bring the problem to the attention of his or her supervisor. If that fails, try speaking to the internship coordinator.

FACT FILE:

DAVE BARRY DID THAT?

■ *Some former interns and where they interned:*

DAVE BARRY, syndicated columnist
Congressional Quarterly

HILLARY RODHAM CLINTON, first lady
Washington Research Project

SANDY GRUSHOW, president, Fox Ent.
Fox Entertainment

TOM HANKS, actor
Great Lakes Shakespeare Festival

JOHN F. KENNEDY, JR., lawyer
The Center for Democratic Policy, a Washington, D.C. think-tank

HENRY MULLER, editorial director of Time, Inc. and former managing editor of *Time* magazine
Life magazine

GEORGE STEPHANOPOULOS, senior adviser to President Clinton
Former Ohio Rep. Mary R. Oakar

EXPERT PICKS

TEN OF THE BEST INTERNSHIPS

Mark Oldman and Samer Hamadeh selected the following from their book, The Princeton Review Student Access Guide to America's Top 100 Internships *(Villard Books, $16). All are distinguished by offering little busywork. You can find the book and other, more local resources at many colleges around the country, which often allow non-students to use their placement offices as a resource.*

ABBOTT LABORATORIES
Manager of College Relations
Dept. 39K, Building AP6D
One Abbott Park Road
Abbott Park, IL 60064
☎ 708-937-7000

■ **THE JOB:** A health care products company, Abbott has a 12-week summer internship for college and graduate students at its headquarters near Chicago. Highly selective, Abbott accepts 150 to 200 interns to work in areas from manufacturing to product development, medical and pharmaceutical research, accounting, marketing, and other fields.
■ **THE REWARDS:** Free housing, travel, seminars. Salaries range from $340 to $1,000 per week.

ACADEMY OF TELEVISION ARTS & SCIENCES
Student Internship Program
5220 Lankershim Blvd
North Hollywood, CA 91601
☎ 818-754-2830

■ **THE JOB:** Best known for awarding the Emmy Awards, this highly selective eight-week program accepts 28 undergrads and recent college grads. Interns work in production, scriptwriting, film editing, public relations, animation, casting, and other areas.
■ **THE REWARDS:** Academy interns receive a $1,600 stipend and are honored at a party with the Academy governors. About 75 percent land good jobs in the television industry.

APPLE COMPUTER, INC.
Internship Program
College Relations
20525 Mariani Ave., MS 75-2J
Cupertino, CA 95014
☎ 408-996-1010

■ **THE JOB:** This highly selective program accepts 200 undergrads and grads for its 12-week summer program in Cupertino, near San Francisco.
■ **THE REWARDS:** Interns set their own hours, get one-day working vacations, participate in seminars, and receive discounts on Apple products. Salaries range from $600 to $1,100 per week.

BOEING
College Relations
PO Box 3707, MS 31-13
Seattle, WA 98124
☎ 206-3939-8472

■ **THE JOB:** Located in Seattle, this internationally known aircraft manufacturer accepts 100 to 250 college juniors and seniors for a summer or a six-month program. It was named the nation's top program in 1992 by the National Society of Black Engineers.
■ **THE REWARDS:** Interns receive $440 per week, $1,000 for housing, and weekly classes in which they learn airplane design.

INTEL CORP.
Staffing Department, FM4-145
PO Box 1141
Folsom, CA 95763
☎ 916-356-8080

■ **THE JOB:** About 1,000 interns work at Intel, which produces computer chips. College grads and undergrads spend eight weeks to eight months working in design, engineering, human resources, finance, and other areas in California, Arizona, New Mexico, and Oregon.
■ **THE REWARDS:** Interns earn $450 to $1,000 per week. They also get free round-trip travel, a rental car, and a $500 moving allowance. By 1996, 70 percent of all college graduates Intel hires will be former Intel interns.

EXPERT PICKS

LUCASFILM, LTD.
Human Resources
Intern Dept.
PO Box 2009
San Rafael, CA 94912
☎ 415-662-1999

THE JOB: Founded by "Star Wars" mastermind George Lucas, this highly selective program offers 9- to 12-week summer, spring, and fall internships to 15 to 20 juniors, seniors, and grads at its Skywalker Ranch or at its production facility in San Rafael, both near San Francisco.

THE REWARDS: Interns earn $4.25 per hour, or nothing at all in fall and spring, but do get to work in TV and film production, visual effects, commercials, model-making, games, finance, merchandising, and more. Interns attend advance screenings of Lucasfilm pictures, seminars, and company parties.

NATIONAL TROPICAL BOTANICAL GARDEN
Internship Program
PO Box 340
Lawai, Kauai, HI 96765
☎ 805-332-7361

THE JOB: In Kauai, Hawai'i, six college grad students spend 10 to 18 weeks in the summer, fall, or spring working in this garden's collections, research, administration, visitor's center and conservation programs. In addition to weeding and planting, interns conduct tours, have seminars with experts in botany and horticulture, and fly to Maui or other sites in Hawai'i for work and recreational activities.

THE REWARDS: Pay is $240 per week, and the NTBG provides free housing, seminars with horticultural experts, and even tree-climbing lessons.

TBWA
Internship Program
TBWA House
292 Madison Ave.
New York, NY 10017
☎ 212-725-1150

THE JOB: Located in New York, TBWA is one of the world's top 20 advertising agencies. Clients have included Absolut Vodka, Eagle Snacks, and Nissan. This moderately selective program accepts 8 to 12 interns for its 10-week summer internships in market research, account management, or media.

THE REWARDS: Interns get $225 per week and the chance to mingle with copywriters, client reps, and TBWA's president at weekly luncheon seminars and the company picnic.

U.S. DEPARTMENT OF STATE
Office of Recruitment
Student Programs
PO Box 9317
Arlington, VA 22219
☎ 703-875-7490

THE JOB: Year-round, the State Department places over 900 high school students, undergrads, recent grads, and grad students in internship positions in Washington, D.C., New York City, and over 250 embassies and consulates worldwide. Interns work in such areas as consular affairs, diplomatic security, economic affairs, human rights, and scientific affairs.

THE REWARDS: The State Department provides interns with tours of embassies, access to formal events and free overseas housing. Ten percent of interns are paid—from $325 to $440 per week.

THE *WASHINGTON POST*
Internship Program
1150 15th Street NW
Washington, DC 20071
☎ 202-334-6000

THE JOB: The *Post* runs a highly selective internship program wherein 15 to 20 college juniors, seniors, and grads report and write stories for the national, metro, business, sports, or style sections of the paper. Most successful applicants have had previous experience at other publications. Interns write at least one story a week, and many do front page stories four or five times over the summer.

THE REWARDS: Compensation is $730 a week and interns lunch with the likes of Bob Woodward, one of the two *Post* reporters who broke the Watergate scandal, and David Broder, a political columnist.

GETTING HIRED

JOB HUNTING IN CYBERSPACE

A thorough search these days should include some time online

Computers are encroaching on one of the last holdouts of personal contact, the job hunt. Many job seekers are trashing paper résumés and turning to videotapes, E-mail, and diskettes to pitch themselves to prospective employers, according to EnterChange Inc., an Atlanta-based outplacement firm. Companies are also increasingly flirting with listing job openings on computer networks and accepting résumés via computer linkup.

And, once resumes are in hand, many companies are using computers to do their hiring. Resource managers plug in key words to screen résumés for certain skills, degrees, and experience. The software programs then scroll through the résumés, placing those with the most key words at the top of the electronic pile. The Association of Human Resource Systems Professionals, a trade group in Dallas, says 10 percent of companies with more than 1,000 employees, including Disney and Xerox, now use résumé-scanning software.

How can you tap into the electronic job search? Big online services, including Prodigy, America Online, and CompuServe, offer areas for posting résumés and exchanging messages with other job hunters. Beyond that, there are three big online job banks. Help Wanted-USA, a two-year old database on America Online and the Internet, keeps a bank of 4,000 white-collar, mostly management jobs. Online Career Center, a fairly new player, provides access to Help Wanted-USA and about 4,000 additional openings posted by another 100 or so companies in search of mostly high-tech types. CompuServe's job database, called E-Span, posts some 2,000 openings sent in by employers seeking mostly professional and managerial workers.

Not surprisingly, techies are in big demand: About half of Online Career Center's listings are in technology fields. About one-third of Help Wanted-USA and E-Span's are also computer related, although the horizons are broadening. Prodigy has a smaller service, Online Classifieds, that posts a hundred or so.

Computer job hunts are still fairly new, so figures on their success rates are hard to come by. Still, say experts, a thorough job hunt should include a trip to cyberspace. Some employers believe anyone using bulletin boards must be a cut above the rest. Be sure your online résumé is short and snappy, advise experts. A brisk résumé is easy to skim and cheaper to download.

If you are a computer holdout, you can mail your résumé to one of the many database services that will try to match up your skills with company want ads. For a fee, the services will keep your résumé active for up to one year. One service, Career Database Inc., ☎ 508-487-2238, will hold your résumé and a four-page career profile active for one year for $50.

FACT FILE:

RÉSUMÉ ROULETTE

■ *Number of résumés received by AT&T each year: 1 million. Number of résumés received by Apple Computer each week: 3,000. Number of résumés received each week by large companies: 1,000.*

■ *Amount of time human resource managers say they spend reading most résumés: 30 seconds to 4 minutes.*

SOURCE: *Washington Post.*

JOB INTERVIEWS

WHAT YOU CAN'T BE ASKED

Sure, you want the job but you don't have to answer every question

Are you frequently sick? Have you ever been arrested? Do you have any addictions? Does stress sometimes affect your ability to be productive? If a job interviewer asks you any of these questions, he or she may have broken the law.

Increasingly, the job interview is becoming a legal minefield. In 1994 the Equal Employment Opportunity Commission issued 49 pages of new guidelines on how to conduct job interviews without running afoul of federal disability discrimination laws. The guidelines stemmed from the passage of the 1990 Americans with Disabilities Act (ADA), a landmark civil rights law for the country's disabled population. Employers are critical of the new guidelines, which they believe further muddy an already murky situation. The guidelines do contain some subtle distinctions. "Do you drink alcohol?" for example, is permissible. "How much alcohol do you drink per week?" is not.

An interviewer who is just trying to put an applicant at ease by asking a few personal questions can quickly cross into forbidden territory. How a question is asked can determine whether it is permissable or not. But, in general, any interview question may be considered illegal if it is used to discriminate or to judge a candidate in a manner that is not job-related. Following is a layman's guide to some of the things that you can and can't be asked. If you feel you've been discriminated against, you can call the Equal Employment Opportunity Commission, ☎ 800-669-4000.

CAN: Employers can ask you questions that relate specifically to your ability to perform the job with or without "reasonable accommodations." For example, if a job involves lifting weights, you may be asked whether or not you can lift those weights.

CAN'T: You can't be asked to take any medical or psychological test before being offered a job.

CAN: It is permissible to ask how many days you took off work the previous year, since the answer will not necessarily lead you to reveal any hidden disabilities.

CAN'T: You can't be asked any follow-up questions about a particular disability, even if you volunteer that you took time off from a previous job because of that disability.

CAN: You can be asked general questions about minor impairments, such as, "Do you have 20/20 vision?" If you admit your eyesight is not perfect, however, you do not have to say how bad your eyesight actually is.

CAN'T: You can't be asked about any addictions you may have.

CAN: You can be asked about illegal drug use and required to submit to drug tests. But you can only be asked about legal drug use (alcohol intake, supervised medications, etc.) if the prospective employer believes a positive drug test may have been the result of your taking prescribed medicines.

CAN'T: The results of tests you've taken to explore your honesty, taste, and habits can't be submitted to psychological analysis.

CAN: You can be asked to take a fitness test.

CAN'T: Your blood pressure or other medical tests can't be taken after a fitness test.

CAN: If a conditional offer of a job has been made, you may be required to undergo medical and psychological tests. But the offer can only be withdrawn if as a result of the tests it can be proven that any disability you may have would make you incapable of carrying out the job even after "reasonable accommodations" were made.

PAY & PERKS

HEY BOSS, CAN YOU SPARE A RAISE?

Don't count on getting much, even if you're doing a great job

The heady days of chunky annual pay raises went out with the greedy '80s. The typical raise for a job well done these days is about 4 percent, not much more than a cost-of-living increase. In 1994, the spread between the average raise and the consumer price index was a slim 1.7 percent, and it's projected to get slimmer still, to 0.8 percent for 1995. And, workers shouldn't expect a pay raise just for doing satisfactory work. You're going to have to prove you've done a spectacular job.

So who's making out like bandits? The guys in the corner office, that's who. The income gap between chief executive officers and average workers keeps getting wider. In 1980, according to *Business Week*, the average CEO earned 42 times what the average worker made ($624,996 vs. $15,008). A dozen years later, the chiefs were earning a staggering 150 times more than the troops in the trenches ($3.8 million vs. $24,411).

The bigger the company, the bigger the bucks for the guy at the top. The income gap between chief executives at big corporations and those at smaller companies grew in 1993, according to a study by William M. Mercer Inc., a human resources consulting firm. Total salary plus bonus for heads of small companies rose just 3.6 percent to a median $312,000 in 1993. By contrast, a Mercer survey of 350 Fortune 500 companies showed that they increased cash compensation for their CEOs in 1993 by 8.1 percent to a median $1,174,000.

Widening pay gaps are, in part, causing companies to look anew at how they reward employees. Traditional "tier" pay structures are fading fast. On the rise are more flexible "broadbanding" pay systems that cluster job categories into a handful of layers and consequently produce flatter and less

FALLING PAY RAISES

Ten-year trend: pay raises vs. consumer price index (CPI).

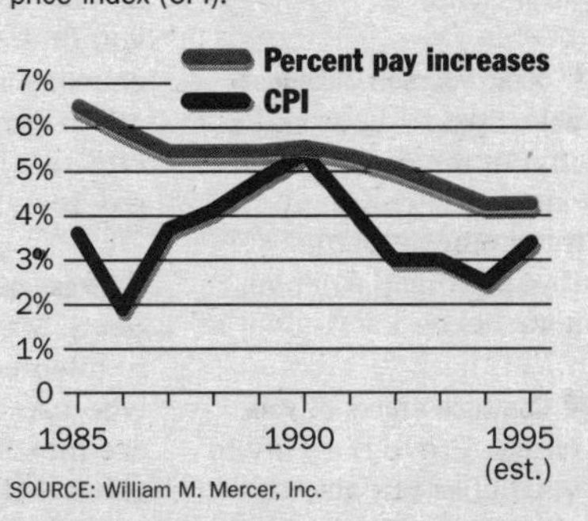

SOURCE: William M. Mercer, Inc.

hierarchical organizations. So far, only 8 percent of employers surveyed recently by Mercer use broadbanding of salary ranges, but 31 percent are considering a switch.

Companies also are experimenting with "skills-based pay," evaluation systems that determine raises by skills, not job title. Part of the reasoning is that this way workers will take more responsibility for their own career development. Many companies that are adopting skill-based or competency-based pay also are helping retrain employees.

"In this new world where skills and knowledge are what really counts, it doesn't make sense to treat people as jobholders. It makes sense to treat them as people with specific skills and to pay them for those skills," says Edward E. Lawler, a professor at the University of Southern California in Los Angeles, and an early proponent of skill-based pay.

So far, the approach has worked best with factory workers, but it also is spreading to white-collar jobs. Part of the problem: skills or competencies are not easy to measure at the managerial level. Still, many companies are giving it a shot; over half the Fortune 1000 companies now use skill-based pay in some form, according to a 1990 study.

Another innovation: the boss no longer is the sole judge of performance in many offices. Companies are calling on co-workers, customers—even subordinates—for so-called 360-degree feedback. By one estimate, a quarter of all companies now tap peers to review an employee. Some companies, like Honeywell, base raises on such reviews. Others, such as Sprint, use them to spawn ideas about how to improve skills.

Not everyone is pleased with 360-degree feedback. Critics say that sometimes being reviewed by so many people sends unclear or conflicting messages about an individual. One piece of advice from the experts: Demand anonymity if you are reviewing your own boss.

EXPERT TIPS

SEVEN GUARANTEED WAYS TO GET A RAISE

Just kidding. But, hey, why not give them a shot? Here's the best of the advice that's out there. Your particular strategy will depend on your spot on the totem pole.

- **Don't be shy, claim credit.** The farther down the rung you are, the more you need to do to make sure your boss knows about you.

- **Make yourself indispensable.** Spread your skills in a number of areas within the company. Your market value is tied to your particular set of skills.

- **Convince others of your talents.** Prove not only to your boss but also to customers, peers, and subordinates that you have special skills.

- **Don't make threats.** Your bluff may be called if you threaten to quit. But courting real offers from other firms can be an effective ploy in winning pay increases.

- **Stress quality and efficiency.** Managers hold on to talented staff; those who use assets wisely are most apt to be rewarded.

- **Don't compare yourself to a better-paid co-worker.** You're setting yourself up to be put down and have your co-worker's praises sung.

- **Choose the right industry.** A company that's downsizing isn't likely to hand out generous pay hikes. More often than not, pay raises are linked to industry-wide performance variables. Working extra hard in a floundering industry won't help.

WORKING STIFF'S GUIDE

WHAT 100 OCCUPATIONS PAY

Updated every two years by the Bureau of Labor Statistics, the Occupational Outlook Handbook *is a treasure trove of useful information. The book covers the training and education needed, earnings, working conditions, and employment prospects for jobs from accountant to zoologist. Below are the salaries of 100 occupations from that book. In real life, of course, salaries can vary considerably by region, level of experience, and other factors, but the list does give a good comparison of average incomes.*

TITLE	NO. OF JOBS	STARTING	MEDIAN	TOP
EXECUTIVE, ADMINISTRATIVE, AND MANAGERIAL OCCUPATIONS				
ACCOUNTANT	939,000	$28,000 yr.	$24,700 yr.	$84,000 yr.
FUNERAL DIRECTORS	27,000	NA	$41,393–$59,574 yr.	NA
HOTEL MANAGERS	99,000	NA	$59,100 yr.	NA
INSPECTORS	155,000	NA	$24,800–$59,300 yr.	NA
ADVERTISING MANAGERS	432,000	$21,000 yr.	$41,000 yr.	$79,000+ yr.
PERSONNEL MANAGERS	193,000	$22,900–$30,500 yr.	$37,000+ yr.	NA
RESTAURANT MANAGERS [1]	496,000	NA	$27,900 yr.	$45,000+ yr.
EXECUTIVE CHEFS [1]	496,000	NA	$33,600 yr.	$49,000 yr.
PROFESSIONAL SPECIALTY OCCUPATIONS				
ENGINEERS	1,354,000	$34,000–$54,000 yr.	$31,000–$57,300 yr.	$87,000+ yr.
ARCHITECTS	96,000	$24,000 yr.	$36,000–$50,000 yr.	$100,000+ yr.
ACTUARY	15,000	$31,800 yr.	$46,000–$65,000 yr.	NA
SYSTEMS ANALYSTS [2]	666,000	$18,300–$22,700 yr.	$42,100 yr.	$65,500+ yr.
MATHEMATICIANS	16,000	$28,400–$41,000 yr.	$43,070–$53,232 yr.	NA
STATISTICIANS	16,000	$40,000–$54,500 yr.	$51,893–$54,109 yr.	NA
BIOLOGICAL SCIENTISTS	117,000	$21,800 yr.	$34,500 yr.	$56,900+ yr.
CHEMISTS	92,000	$24,000–$48,000 yr.	$42,000–$60,000 yr.	NA
METEOROLOGISTS	6,100	$18,340–$40,229 yr.	$48,266 yr.	NA
ASTRONOMERS [3]	21,000	$30,000–$41,000 yr.	$65,000 yr.	$78,000 yr.
LAWYERS	626,000	$36,600–$80,000+ yr.	$134,000 yr.	$1mill.+ yr.
ECONOMISTS	51,000	$25,200 yr.	$65,000 yr.	$78,000+ yr.
PSYCHOLOGISTS	144,000	NA	$48,000–$76,000 yr.	NA
URBAN PLANNERS	28,000	$27,800 yr.	$42,000 yr.	$65,000+ yr.
SOCIAL WORKERS	484,000	NA	$30,000 yr.	NA
PROTESTANT MINISTERS	290,000	NA	$27,000 yr.[4]	NA
RABBIS	3,910	NA	$38,000–$60,000 yr.	NA
ROMAN CATHOLIC PRIESTS [5]	53,000	NA	$9,000 yr.[6]	NA
ARCHIVISTS	19,000	$18,300–$40,400 yr.	$46,000 yr.	NA
LIBRARIANS	141,000	$25,900 yr.	$37,900–$45,200 yr.	NA
ELEMENTARY SCHOOL TEACHERS	3,255,000	NA	$34,800 yr.[7]	NA
DENTISTS	183,000	NA	$85,000 yr.	$130,000 yr.
PHYSICIANS	556,000	$28,618–$36,258 yr.[8]	$139,000 yr.	$230,000+ yr.

■ WORKING STIFF'S GUIDE

TITLE	NO. OF JOBS	STARTING	MEDIAN	TOP
VETERINARIANS	44,000	$27,858 yr.	$63,069 yr.	NA
DIETITIANS	50,000	NA	$28,500–$40,000 yr.	NA
REGISTERED NURSES	1,835,000	NA	$34,424 yr.	$50,960+ yr.
NEWS ANCHORS	56,000	NA	$41,000 yr.	$163,000 yr.
REPORTERS	58,000	NA	$406–$654 wk.	$856+ wk.
TECHNICAL WRITERS [9]	283,000	$26,700 yr.	$35,000–$40,000 yr.	$45,400 yr.
PHOTOGRAPHERS	118,000	NA	$21,200 yr.	$49,200+ yr.
DANCERS (per performance)	18,000	$242	$587	NA

TECHNICIAN AND RELATED SUPPORT OCCUPATIONS

TITLE	NO. OF JOBS	STARTING	MEDIAN	TOP
EKG TECHNICIANS	31,000	NA	$17,222 yr.	$21,868 yr.
EMERGENCY MEDICAL TECHS.	114,000	$19,530–$24,390 yr.	$22,682–$28,079 yr.	$34,994 yr.
NUCLEAR MEDICAL TECHS.	12,000	NA	$32,843 yr.	$38,840 yr.
AIRCRAFT PILOTS	85,000	NA	$80,000 yr.	$165,000 yr.
AIR TRAFFIC CONTROLLERS	23,0008	$22,700 yr.	$53,800 yr.	NA
COMPUTER PROGRAMMERS	555,000	$18,300–$22,700 yr.	$35,600 yr.	$58,000 yr.
ENGINEERING TECHNICIANS	695,000	$14,600–$18,300 yr.	$20,900–$41,400 yr.	$42,436 yr.
PARALEGALS	95,000	$23,400 yr.	$28,200–$29,800 yr.	$37,600 yr.

MARKETING AND SALES OCCUPATIONS

TITLE	NO. OF JOBS	STARTING	MEDIAN	TOP
CASHIERS	2,747,000	$4.25 hr.	$219 wk.	$414+ wk.
COUNTER CLERKS	242,000	$4.25 hr.	$252 wk.	$514+ wk.
INSURANCE SALES AGENTS	415,000	NA	$30,100 yr.	$64,600+ yr.
REAL ESTATE AGENTS	397,000	NA	$507 wk.	$1,247+ wk.
TRAVEL AGENTS	115,000	$12,428 yr.	$15,610–$20,775 yr.	$25,007 yr.

ADMINISTRATIVE SUPPORT OCCUPATIONS

TITLE	NO. OF JOBS	STARTING	MEDIAN	TOP
BILL COLLECTORS	237,000	NA	$390 wk.	$640+ wk.
BANK TELLERS	525,000	NA	$14,800 yr.	$24,300 yr.
COMPUTER OPERATORS	266,000	$14,600–$16,400 yr.	$21,100 yr.	$38,700+ yr.
GENERAL OFFICE CLERKS	2,688,000	$12,700 yr.	$18,500 yr.	$23,800+ yr.
MAIL CLERKS	131,000	NA	$300 wk.	NA
MAIL CARRIERS	297,000	$23,737 yr.	$32,832 yr.	$33,952 yr.
SECRETARIES	3,324,000	$16,400 yr.	$26,700 yr.	$36,000 yr.
STENOGRAPHERS	115,000	NA	$410 wk.	$960+ wk.
TEACHER AIDES	885,000	NA	$8.31 hr.	NA
TELEPHONE OPERATORS	314,000	NA	$385 wk.	$561+ wk.
DATA ENTRY KEYERS [10]	1,238,000	$13,400 yr.	$20,000 yr.	NA

SERVICE OCCUPATIONS

TITLE	NO. OF JOBS	STARTING	MEDIAN	TOP
CORRECTIONS OFFICERS	282,000	$18,600 yr.	$23,200 yr.	NA
FIREFIGHTERS	305,000	NA	$636 wk.	$987+ wk.
GUARDS	803,000	$14,600–$16,400 yr.	$6–$11.15 hr.	$13.34+ hr.
POLICE OFFICERS	700,000	NA	$32,000 yr.	$51,200+ yr.
SHORT ORDER COOKS	714,000	NA	$5.99 hr.	NA
WAITERS	1.8 million	NA	$220 wk.	$380+ wk.

■ WORKING STIFF'S GUIDE

TITLE	NO. OF JOBS	STARTING	MEDIAN	TOP
BARTENDERS	382,000	NA	$250 wk.	$440+ wk.
DENTAL ASSISTANTS	183,000	NA	$332 wk.	$420+ wk.
COSMETOLOGISTS [11]	746,0001	NA	$20,000–$30,000 yr.	NA
PRESCHOOL WORKERS	941,000	NA	$260 wk.	$460+ wk.
FLIGHT ATTENDANTS	93,000	NA	$13,000–$20,000 yr.	$40,000 yr.
GROUNDSKEEPERS	884,000	NA	$275 wk.	$475 wk.
JANITORS	3,018,000	NA	$277 wk.	$477+ wk.
NANNIES [12]	896,000	$300–$375 wk.	NA	$900 wk.
MECHANICS, INSTALLERS, AND REPAIRERS				
ELEVATOR INSTALLERS	22,000	$370–$518 wk.	$740 wk.	$830 wk.
AUTOMOTIVE BODY REPAIRERS	202,000	NA	$401 wk.	$757+ wk.
AIRCRAFT MECHANICS	131,000	$18,300 yr.[13]	$32,500 yr.	$47,500+ yr.
MUSICAL INSTRUMENT TUNERS	12,000	NA	$20,000 yr.	$40,000 yr.
VENDING MACHINE REPAIRERS	20,000	NA	$5–$18 hr.	NA
CARPENTERS	990,000	NA	$425 wk.	$770+ wk.
CARPET INSTALLERS	62,000	NA	$375 wk.	$700+ wk.
ELECTRICIANS	518,000	NA	$550 wk.	$887+ wk.
PAINTERS	440,000	NA	$376 wk.	$703+ wk.
PLUMBERS	351,000	$9 hr.	$18.05 hr.	NA
PRODUCTION OCCUPATIONS				
BUTCHERS	349,000	NA	$310 wk.	$630+ wk.
JEWELERS	30,000	NA	$28,000 yr.	NA
MACHINISTS	359,000	NA	$492 wk.	$750+ wk.
TOOL AND DIE MAKERS	138,000	NA	$642 wk.	$911+ wk.
POWER PLANT OPERATORS	43,000	NA	$750 wk.	$960+ wk.
TREATMENT PLANT OPERATORS	86,000	NA	$26,200 yr.	$39,200 yr.
PRINTING PRESS OPERATORS	241,000	NA	$420 wk.	$710+ wk.
SEWING MACHINE OPERATORS	680,340	NA	$217 wk.	NA
UPHOLSTERERS	60,000	NA	$350 wk.	$670+ wk.
DENTAL LABORATORY TECHNICIANS	48,000	Just over min. wage [14]	$13.30 wk.	NA
PHOTO PROCESS OPERATORS	63,000	NA	$330 wk.	$520+ wk.
BUS DRIVERS	562,000	NA	$400 wk.	$721+ wk.
TAXI DRIVERS	120,000	NA	$313 wk.	$604+ wk.
TRUCK DRIVERS	2,720,000	NA	$12.92 hr.	NA

NOTES

1. Represents all restaurant and food service managers.
2. Includes computer scientists.
3. Includes physicists.
4. With benefits, this jumps to $44,000.
5 Approximately two-thirds of these are diocesan priests.
6. For diocesan priests with benefits, this number jumps to $29,000. However, religious priests take a vow of poverty and donate personal earnings to their order, which, in turn, supports them.
7. Those employed by public schools.
8. Salaries of medical residents, with $28,618 being the average for those in their first year of residency and $36,258 being the average for those in their sixth year of residency.
9. Includes all writers and editors. Includes camera operators.
10. Includes typists, word processors.
11. Includes barbers.
12. Includes all household workers.
13. With a license and employed by the federal government.
14. Trainees in dental laboratories.

SOURCE: *Occupational Outlook Quarterly*, Bureau of Labor Statistics, Spring 1994.

EQUAL OPPORTUNITY

WHY WOMEN STILL EARN LESS

The gap is narrowing, but men still make considerably more money

Penny by penny—a dime in the past decade—women's full-time wages have been approaching men's, but the gap amounts to more than pocket change in most fields. In 1993, women made up more than 40 percent of the workforce and earned an average of 76.8 cents to each dollar earned by men, up from 66.7 cents in 1983 based on weekly wages.

"The historic gap between women's and men's incomes has started to diminish," notes the U.S. government's Population Reference Bureau. "But many women do not share in these improvements."

Indeed, the wage gap between men and women exists for low-paid and high-paid jobs. Female dispatchers for rental cars, buses, security services, aircraft, etc., make up half of those in that job category but earn only 80 percent of what men do who perform the same jobs. Almost a third of all lawyers now are women. But they earn, on average, just under 84 percent of male lawyers' wages. "When we talk of comparing women's earnings with men's earnings, we find that no matter how we measure them, women's earnings are below those received by men," said the Department of Labor's Women's Bureau in 1993.

Education and work experience may explain some of the gap. Although the number of women attending law school has shot up dramatically in the past few decades, only after they've been practicing law for a while will the salary gap start to narrow further. Another statistic may be more revealing. Despite the increasing numbers of working women, men stay in the labor force for an average of 39 years, while women average 29 years. That, too, is changing. Women are taking less time out when having children: In 1991, 51.9 percent of women were working by the time their children were a year old, while only 17 percent were between 1961 and 1965.

Women are still virtually shut out of some sectors of the business world. According to Catalyst, a non-profit research and advisory group dealing with women in business and professions, only 6.2 percent of board seats on the Fortune 500 and Service 500 companies were held by women in 1993. In addition, according to a 1990 survey, women make up less than 5 percent of senior managers (vice presidents and those higher up) at those companies. Asked why, chief executives most frequently cited management's aversion to "taking risks" and a "lack of careful career planning and planned job assignments for women."

Paradoxically, the wage gap is narrowest in the few fields where a large percentage of the workers are women as well as in the occupations that have attracted few women workers. Female secretaries, stenographers, and typists earned 96.5 percent of the weekly wages of their male counterparts, who make up only 2 percent of that work force. Only 4 percent of mechanics and mechanical repairers are women. But they earn more than their male counterparts—$526 a week vs. $503.

BATTLE OF THE SEXES

The average weekly salaries of men and women in different fields:

Occupation	Male	Female
College and university teachers	$894	$689
Computer scientists	$879	$724
Elementary school teachers	$666	$586
Farm workers	$248	$232
General office supervisors	$730	$504
Insurance adjusters	$672	$414
Physicians	$1,186	$885
Police and detectives	$645	$576
Secretaries and typists	$399	$385
Truck drivers	$449	$331

SOURCE: *The American Workforce: 1992–2005,* Bureau of Labor Statistics, 1994.

MEDICINE

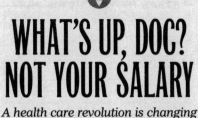

WHAT'S UP, DOC? NOT YOUR SALARY

A health care revolution is changing the lives—and income—of MDs

A quiet revolution is transforming the practice of medicine. States are moving toward providing access to health care for all at lower costs. Big hospitals are swallowing smaller local ones to form self-contained combines that are more efficient. And insurers are competing to trim costs and raise profits. What does all this price-squeezing mean for future doctors? As Princeton University professor Uwe E. Reinhardt puts it, "To become a physician now means you won't make as much money. Unless you have a real passion for medicine or an intellectual curiosity, I wouldn't recommend it."

Becoming a doctor is expensive. Medical school graduates commonly pile on between $50,000 and $100,000 in debt. And the initial monetary rewards aren't great, either. Residents, med school graduates who are in training, start out with an average $32,000 after putting in 80 to 100 hours a week. But that hasn't deterred people from flocking to medicine. From 1982 to 1992, the supply of doctors grew 32 percent, while the general population increased only 10 percent.

Two-thirds of new doctors each year are specialists. Being a specialists may be more professionally rewarding, and it is also where the money is. For doctors of all stripes, the average income came to $177,400 in 1992, up from $164,300 in 1990. But a huge chasm appears when you compare incomes for general practitioners with specialists. An average family doctor earned about $119,186 in 1992, compared to $309,556 for a radiologist. Between 1982 and 1992, income rose only 9 percent for general practitioners but jumped 29 percent for specialists.

The golden age of medicine may be over. Some 75 percent of doctors now participate in some type of managed-care group, focusing primarily on preventive care. When patients are kept healthy, expensive specialists are not needed, prices are kept in check, and the HMO (health maintenance organization) or PPO (preferred provider organization) profits. Primary care doctors who participate in HMOs often get incentives that are linked to making as few referrals to specialists as possible.

There are benefits associated with HMO alliances, including fewer administrative headaches, possibly shorter hours, and a steady flow of patients. But HMOs can be tight-fisted with salaries, too. A 1993 survey by Warren Surveys of Rockford, Ill., shows that a pediatrician on contract with an HMO made $98,000, compared to an average $123,870 in private practice.

What's the prognosis for the future? The picture is mixed. As the country moves increasingly toward a managed care system, generalists will be in demand. By 2000, there could be a shortage of 35,000 generalists. On the other hand, the supply of specialists will be about 30 percent more than needed, leading to a surplus of about 165,000 specialists, according to Dr. Jonathan P. Weiner of Johns Hopkins School of Public Health.

THE MEDICAL GAP

A selected breakdown of mean physician net income after expenses before taxes:

	1982	1992
All doctors	$97,700	$177,400
General practice	$71,400	$111,800
Internal medicine	$86,900	$159,300
Surgery	$128,600	$244,600
Pediatrics	$70,500	$121,100
Obstetrics/gynecology	$112,300	$215,100
Radiology	$133,300	$253,300
Psychiatry	$75,800	$130,700
Anesthesiology	$131,900	$228,500
Pathology	$106,500	$189,800

SOURCE: *Socioeconomic Characteristics of Medical Practice*, American Medical Association, 1994.

WHY GEOGRAPHY REALLY MATTERS

Where you work has a significant impact on how much you earn

No one chooses to be a teacher because of the money. But where you teach can have a significant impact on what you're paid, as well as the resources that are likely to be at your disposal. "We're the only nation [in the industrialized world] which has a highly decentralized system," notes Willis Hawley, dean of the College of Education at the University of Maryland at College Park. "Our system assigns different learning opportunities according to where children live."

Teachers in Connecticut, for example, earn twice as much as teachers in Mississippi. They reach the top of the pay scale in six to seven years, while teachers in some Southern states need 30 to 50 years to get to the top. Connecticut classrooms are also more likely to be better stocked, since school boards have more funds to disperse.

The contrasts are even starker when the United States is compared with Europe. Senior primary school teachers in Zurich, Switzerland, earn on average $18,000 more than U.S. teachers. At the high school level, Swiss teachers earn almost double what their American counterparts do.

Part of the explanation for the salary gap is that European teachers tend to be better trained. In most European countries, teachers are required to have two to three years of postgraduate study before qualifying to teach 11th and 12th grades. In the United States, a college degree is sufficient. Even so, the American Federation of Teachers reports that about 45 percent of American elementary teachers and 65 percent of high school teachers earn a master's degree by mid-career.

■ STATE OF TEACHER'S PAY

The average U.S. teacher earns $35,813

RANK/STATE	AVG. SALARY 1993–1994	PERCENT U.S. AVG.
1. CONNECTICUT	$50,389	140.7%
2. ALASKA	$47,902	133.8%
3. NEW YORK	$45,772	127.8%
4. NEW JERSEY	$45,582	127.3%
5. MICHIGAN	$45,218	126.3%
6. DISTRICT OF COLUMBIA	$43,014	120.1%
7. PENNSYLVANIA	$42,411	118.4%
8. CALIFORNIA	$40,636	113.5%
9. MARYLAND	$39,475	110.2%
10. ILLINOIS	$39,416	110.1%
11. RHODE ISLAND	$39,261	109.6%
12. MASSACHUSETTS	$38,960	108.8%
13. OREGON	$37,589	105.0%
14. DELAWARE	$37,469	104.6%
15. NEVADA	$37,181	103.8%
16. WISCONSIN	$36,644	102.3%
17. HAWAI'I	$36,564	102.1%
18. MINNESOTA	$36,146	100.9%
19. OHIO	$35,912	100.3%
20. WASHINGTON	$35,860	100.1%
21. INDIANA	$35,741	99.8%
22. VERMONT	$34,517	96.4%
23. NEW HAMPSHIRE	$34,121	95.3%
24. COLORADO	$33,826	94.5%
25. VIRGINIA	$33,472	93.5%
26. FLORIDA	$31,944	89.2%
27. ARIZONA	$31,825	88.9%
28. KANSAS	$31,700	88.5%
29. KENTUCKY	$31,639	88.3%
30. MAINE	$30,996	86.5%
31. WYOMING	$30,954	86.4%
32. IOWA	$30,760	85.9%
33. WEST VIRGINIA	$30,549	85.3%
34. TEXAS	$30,519	85.2%
35. TENNESSEE	$30,514	85.2%
36. MISSOURI	$30,324	84.7%
37. NORTH CAROLINA	$29,727	83.0%
38. NEBRASKA	$29,564	82.6%
39. SOUTH CAROLINA	$29,414	82.1%
40. GEORGIA	$29,214	81.6%
41. ALABAMA	$28,659	80.0%
42. ARKANSAS	$28,312	79.1%
43. MONTANA	$28,200	78.7%
44. UTAH	$28,056	78.3%
45. NEW MEXICO	$27,922	78.0%
46. IDAHO	$27,756	77.5%
47. OKLAHOMA	$27,612	77.1%
48. LOUISIANA	$26,243	73.3%
49. NORTH DAKOTA	$25,506	71.2%
50. SOUTH DAKOTA	$25,259	70.5%
51. MISSISSIPPI	$25,153	70.2%

SOURCE: American Federation of Teachers.

EMPLOYEE PERKS

SIDLING UP TO THE BENEFITS BAR

What'll it be—extra company-paid life insurance or a better health plan?

Welcome to the benefits smorgasbord. Chances are that your company benefits plan now offers you as many different choices as there are items at the salad bar in the company cafeteria. The number and range of options, of course, varies widely from company to company. Here are some of the things that are being served up.

■ **PENSION AND INVESTMENT PLANS:** The trend is toward "defined contribution plans," in which employee contributions are matched by the employer, and away from traditional "defined benefit" plans, which put a greater emphasis on the employer's guarantee of a retirement income. Defined contribution plans are "portable," meaning that you can take the money in it with you if you change jobs or go into business for yourself. Employees only benefit from old-fashioned pension plans as long as they stayed with the company a requisite number of years.

Defined contribution plans come in as many different varieties as Heinz condiments. Most popular of all are 401(k) plans (see "Pay Attention to Your 401(k)," page 146), which allow employees to contribute pre-tax income. Many companies also will match employee contributions. Under certain circumstances, you can tap into your 401(k) savings for unforeseen expenses. Profit-sharing plans enable employees to share in a company's success. Likewise, Employee Stock Ownership Plans (ESOPs) allow employees to purchase company stock at a discount or receive part of their salary in the form of company stock.

■ **HEALTH CARE:** To clip costs, companies are promoting "managed care" plans and trying to wean employees away from traditional so-called fee-for-service plans in which they were free to choose their own doctors. Employees increasingly are being asked to pay a larger percentage of the cost of their health plan, presenting a Hobson's choice: higher deductibles or higher premiums.

■ **LIFE INSURANCE:** Most companies offer some form of life insurance. The main differences are between plans that are fully employer paid and those that depend on employee contributions. Some companies offer a combination of both. Most core plans provide a cash payout equal to one times the employee's most recent annual salary, sometimes with a cash maximum. Often employees have the option of purchasing additional coverage.

■ **DISABILITY INSURANCE:** This benefit is more important than life insurance, since it is more likely you'll need to make use of it (see "The Nightmare Scenario," page 108). Employers differ in their formula for calculating short-term disability payments. Some use the "salary continuation method" in which employees receive their entire salary (or a percentage of their salary, depending on years worked) for a defined period of time before long-term disability benefits kick in. Other employers use the "accrual" method. Your benefits are based on the amount of time you've worked for the company. Long-term disability payments are generally a fixed percentage of your salary. Many employers allow you to purchase supplemental coverage.

■ **FLEXIBLE BENEFITS:** Increasingly, you can order your benefits a la carte. Each employee receives a certain number of credits and can use them as he or she sees fit. For instance, you may be able to "buy" extra vacation days with part of your salary, "sell" the credits for cash, or use them to

BIG BLUE'S BLUE RIBBON STANDARD

IBM has scotched its white-shirt and blue-suit dress code, but its employees still enjoy some pretty cushy perks. In Money *magazine's ranking of the companies with the best benefits, IBM came out on top, placing first in 1993 and second in 1994. Here's what IBMers get so you can compare how your benefits measure up to the Big Blue standard.*

RETIREMENT AND SAVINGS PLANS

■ IBM employees can choose between a traditional pension plan or a 401(k), which includes matched employer contributions. IBM will match 50 percent of employee contributions up to 6 percent of salary.

■ IBM also offers an Employee Stock Ownership Plan, or ESOP. The company pays out up to 10 percent of an employee's salary, depending on yearly revenues. In addition, employees participating in the ESOP can buy company stock for 85 percent of market share price.

HEALTH PLANS

■ IBM employees can choose between a range of health care and dental plans. Employees pay a flat fee of $0 to $25 a month for individuals and $12 to $60 a month for families, depending on the plan selected. The highest deductible amount is $750 for a family. Reimbursements cover 80 percent of costs for major medical; 100 percent for surgical and hospital costs.

■ Dental insurance costs $15 a month. The lifetime maximum coverage for dental work is $8,500.

LIFE AND DISABILITY INSURANCE

■ IBM's employer-paid life insurance pays out up to $50,000, based on length of service. Employees can make contributions toward additional life insurance of up to five times their salaries.

■ Short-term disability insurance provides full pay for up to one year.

■ Long-term disability options range from 50 to 66.66 percent of pay.

TIME OFF

■ IBMers get five weeks of vacaton after 20 years. Twelve holidays during the year. You can take parental personal leave for up to three years with benefits.

EXTRAS

■ Annual reimbursement of up to $250 for health and fitness programs or personal financial planning fees.

purchase extra life insurance or health insurance. Employees who are covered under their spouse's health plan might want to cash in their own health benefits and invest the money in a company stock purchase plan or some other savings options. A number of companies also allow employees to put a certain percentage of their pre-tax salary in "spending accounts" for health or "dependent" care. Some employers match these contributions.

■ **"FEEL GOOD" PERKS:** Ready-to-eat take-home meals. Dry cleaning on the premises. Company bank branches offering discount rate mortgages. These are just a few of the so-called time and convenience benefits some more enlightened companies are starting to offer overworked employees.

"With more companies cutting back on basic benefits like health care, such programs offer a relatively inexpensive way to help employees feel good about their employers," says Jack Bruner, a principal with Hewitt Associates, the giant benefits research firm. What's next? PepsiCo and Andersen Consulting offer "concierge" services that will take care of various errands for employees, from buying gifts to obtaining hard-to-get tickets to sports events.

EXPERT Q&A

WILL I GET MY JOB BACK?

What to do if you need to take time off to care for a loved one

All politicians say they are pro-family and now they have a law to prove it. The 1993 Family and Medical Leave Act (FMLA) stipulates that all government agencies and all private employers with more than 50 employees must provide up to 12 weeks of unpaid, job-protected leave for an employee for any of the following reasons: the birth or adoption of a child; the care of an immediate relative with a serious health condition; or medical leave for the employee if he or she is unable to work because of a serious health condition. Here, from the Labor Department's *Compliance Guide to the Family and Medical Leave Act*, are answers to some of the most commonly asked questions about the new law.

■ Does the law guarantee paid time off?

FMLA leave is generally unpaid. However, in certain circumstances the use of accrued paid leave—such as vacation or sick leave—may be substituted for the unpaid leave required by the law. FMLA is intended to encourage generous family and medical leave policies. For this reason, the law does not diminish more generous existing leave policies or laws.

■ Does FMLA leave have to be taken in whole days or weeks, or in one continuous block?

The FMLA permits leave for birth or placement for adoption or foster care to be taken intermittently, in blocks of time or by reducing the normal weekly or daily work schedule—subject to employer approval. Leave for a serious health condition may be taken intermittently when "medically necessary."

■ Are there employees not covered by the law?

Yes. An estimated 60 percent of U.S. workers (and about 95 percent of U.S. employers) are not covered by the law. To be eligible for FMLA benefits, an employee must: (1) work for a covered employer; (2) have worked for the employer for at least a year; (3) have worked at least 1,250 hours over the prior 12 months; and (4) work at a location where at least 50 employees are employed by the employer within 75 miles.

■ What do I have to do to request FMLA leave from my employer?

You may be required to provide your employer with 30 days' advance notice when the need for leave is "foreseeable." When the need for the leave cannot be foreseen, you must give your employer notice as soon as "practicable." You may be required to submit documentation—called a medical certification—from the health care provider treating you or your immediate family member.

■ Will I be allowed to return to my same job?

Ordinarily you will be restored to the same position you held prior to the leave, with the same pay and benefits, if the position remains available. You may be restored to an "equivalent" position rather than to the position you held before taking the leave, if the previous position is not available. An equivalent position must have equivalent pay, benefits, and terms and conditions of employment as the original job.

■ Do I lose all benefits when I take unpaid FMLA leave?

Your employer is required to maintain health insurance coverage on the same terms it was provided before the leave began. In addition, the use of FMLA leave cannot result in the loss of any employment benefit that accrued prior to the start of your leave.

■ What if I believe my employer is violating the law?

You have the choice of filing, or having another person file on your behalf, a complaint with the Employment Standards Administration, Wage and Hour Division, or you can elect to file a private lawsuit.

WORKING PARENT'S GUIDE

IS YOUR COMPANY FAMILY-FRIENDLY?

These days, parental leave is practically an entitlement at the most progressive companies. The following companies, taken from Working Mother *magazine's survey of the 100 best companies for working mothers, represent a cross-section of the most progressive family-friendly employers.*

Benefits	AT&T	Johnson & Johnson	Fel-Pro	Ben & Jerry's Homemade, Inc.	G. T. Water Products, Inc.
Employees	226,604	30,451	1,774	492	24
FAMILY LEAVE POLICIES					
Childbirth leave beyond FMLA	46 wks.	40 wks.	14 wks.	40 wks. with def. return date	14 wks. with disability pay
Includes some salary?	YES	YES	YES	YES	YES
Phase-back for new mothers? 1	YES	YES	YES	YES	YES
Paternal leave?	NO	NO	NO	2 wks. paid	NO
FLEXIBLE SCHEDULING POLICIES					
Flextime?	YES	YES	YES	YES	YES
Job sharing?	YES	YES	YES	NO	YES
Work at home?	YES	YES	YES	NO	YES
Compressed workweeks? 2	YES	YES	YES	YES	YES
Are part-time benefits full or pro-rated? 3	Full (25 hrs./wk.) pro-rated (17 hrs./wk.)	Some (19 hrs./wk.)	Pro-rated (24 hrs./wk)	Some (20 hrs./wk.)	Some (20 hrs./wk.)
CHILD AND ELDER CARE PROGRAMS					
On-site centers?	NO	Four centers, 520 children, $135–$164/wk.	40 children, $85/wk.	22 children, 10 to 14% of income	13 children, no charge
After school?	YES	NO	YES	NO	YES
Backup care?	YES	NO	YES	NO	YES
Direct child care subsidies?	NO	YES	NO	NO	NO
Funded community centers?	YES	YES	YES	NO	NO
Holiday care?	YES	YES	NO	NO	YES
On-site sick child care?	YES	NO	NO	NO	NO
Summer programs?	YES	YES	NO	NO	NO
OTHER BENEFITS					
Pre-tax set-asides? 4	YES	YES	YES	YES	NO
Tuition reimbursement?	NO	NO	UP TO $6,500	NO	NO
Scholarships for children?	YES	YES	NO	NO	NO
Adoption aid?	UP TO $2,500	UP TO $3,000	UP TO $5,000	NONE	UP TO $1,500
Research and referral service?	YES	YES	YES	NO	NO
Sick child days?	4	AS NEEDED	5	6	NONE
Elder care?	YES	YES	YES	NO	NO

1. Allows women to return to the workplace gradually after the birth of a child, working part-time or putting in hours at home.
2. Allows workers to put in 40 hours in less than five days, perhaps in four 10-hour days.
3. Employees can work certain hours per week below 40 (noted in parentheses) and still maintain some benefits.
4. Employees can use pre-tax salary dollars to pay for child care.

SOURCE: *The 100 Best Companies for Working Women,* Milton Moskowitz and Carol Townsend, *Working Mother,* October 1994.

SMART MOVES

THE NEW RULES OF SUCCESS

Forget big biz: Small companies are where the action is in the '90s

Has your career stalled or been phased out? You are not alone. Over the last twenty years, one-third of the 1974 graduating class of the Harvard Business School has been laid off or fired at least once. Nonetheless, the class today has a median income of $260,000 and nearly half are presidents, chairmen, or CEOs.

Harvard Business School professor John Kotter has tracked the Harvard grads over the years and documented how they beat the bad times in his new book, *The New Rules: How to Succeed in Today's Post Corporate World* (Free Press, 1995). Kotter found that, even for Harvard B-School grads, the traditional corporate career no longer ensures the stability or opportunity for growth that it once did. Many of the Class of '74 success stories played by new rules, many of which they did not learn in Harvard Business School. We asked Kotter to give us the lowdown.

■ What is the primary lesson of the business class of '74?

The single biggest route to success for most of the century was a narrow aisle up through a big company. The '74 class lies on the cusp of a major shift in capitalism. Today, small companies are better able to adapt to a more dynamic and rapidly changing world. That is why 62 percent of this class have selected careers with small companies.

■ What made the '74 class so successful?

Interestingly, it is not the Harvard degree or the intellectual capacity per se that characterized successful members of the '74 business class. Instead, what stood out was a drive to increase performance standards and a drive to continually learn.

■ What changes in the economy have necessitated the new rules for success?

The biggest change is the globalization of markets and the ensuing competition, which creates a more hazardous and volatile business environment. However, with the accelerating pace of change, there are also more opportunities for individuals to achieve success.

■ Does a career in big business mean a less fulfilling less well-paid job than a small business or entrepreneurial job?

Yes. Those in the '74 Harvard business class that chose a career in a small business or struck out on their own were more successful. In fact, most successful big companies are starting to resemble small companies in structure and style—the hierarchies are becoming less rigid, and different departments are more autonomous and more flexible than in the past. This means that people in big companies will have to assume more of the decision making and responsibility that their counterparts in small companies have, even though they generally will receive less compensation.

■ If most of Harvard's best and brightest left big business, who stayed?

Certainly there are a lot of very bright people left in big business. But big businesses are starting to fall apart. Nike, for instance, isn't that big of a company—they outsource much of their work.

■ Besides money, what is the major source of satisfaction for a career in a small company?

The major source of satisfaction the move toward entrepreneurship and small companies provides is being in charge, being able to shape your own destiny.

■ What about people who are reluctant to change jobs?

Because of changes in technology and the economy, most people will not have the opportunity to stick with one job, as their parents did. The modern-day worker has to assume more responsibility. The problem is that most of the population has been conditioned to prefer routines. Today many people are scared of change and when they see it they hide behind their desks and their roles.

■ Who stands most to gain by the new rules?

Whenever you have a stable environment the "in crowd" is favored. With unstable environments or times of great change such as we are experiencing now, the "out crowd" (anyone who has not been part of the status quo) has much greater opportunities than before.

■ What types of careers offer the most dynamic growth opportunities?

Some industries do offer more opportunities, but it is difficult to draw generalizations. A lot of older industries such as the apparel industry have huge opportunities. Four billion people on earth need apparel and the emerging middle class in India is going to need a lot of clothes from the garment industry.

■ Are there "must-have" skills in today's workplace?

As we go forward, it is going to be important to learn more about information technologies. But beyond skill, people have to learn to take initiative as well as be able to adapt to change.

■ What is the most important rule for success in today's post-corporate world?

In any job the question people have to ask is "Am I learning something?" It used to be that people thought in terms of companies, then they thought in terms of careers, but now they have to think in terms of life-long learning.

FACT FILE:

BEAUTY COUNTS

A recent study evaluated people on the basis of physical appearance. The results:

- *Those deemed unattractive earn, on average, 13 percent less than those deemed beautiful.*
- *Obese women tend to earn less, even after they lose weight. However, obesity is not a factor in men's earnings.*
- *But the overall effect of perceived attractiveness on earnings is the same for both men and women.*

SOURCE: The *Wall Street Journal*.

WORKING CONDITIONS

LOOKING FOR THE PERFECT JOB

America wants less work, more play, more family time, and better benefits

Feeling overwhelmed by the job-family-house juggling act? Are you willing to give up a higher salary for more time with family and flexible working conditions? If so, you're not alone. Across America, workers are opting for jobs that give them more control over their work schedules, more autonomy at the office and better dependent care benefits. The bottom line: Americans want more balance in their lives, more time to smell the roses.

It's no wonder, given that 42 percent of American workers went through downsizing and 28 percent saw cutbacks in their companies' management ranks in 1992 alone. Workers know that they can no longer depend on a job for life and a guaranteed pension. Without that security, they're no longer willing to commit themselves entirely to their jobs.

Does this mean that American workers are increasingly disloyal to their bosses? Hardly, but according to a Families and Work Institute (FWI) study on the changing American work force, American workers are more dedicated to their own jobs and their own well-being than to their supervisors or companies.

"Americans are looking for something different," notes FWI co-president Ellen Galinsky. "They want quality—in their own work, in their work environment, and in their relationships at home and work. And when they get it, they are more committed, productive employees."

The workplace may be more diverse than ever, but many workers still feel victimized by discrimination and believe unfair barriers are holding them back. While 15 percent of U.S. workers say they have experienced discrimination in their current jobs, more than one-fifth of minorities feel they have. Minority men and women, as well as white women, feel white men have the best chance at success. Overall, men are more confident in their opportunities than women. And workers seem ambivalent, at best, about diversity in the workplace. Galinsky's study suggests that most people prefer working with others of the same sex, race, and education. On the other hand, those already working in ethnically diverse environments prefer them.

Some habits are particularly resistant to change. Women still bear the brunt of household chores. They do most of the cooking, cleaning, shopping, paying bills, and child care. But when people living in dual-income homes were asked if the housework was evenly split, 43 percent of the men said yes, while only 19 percent of the women did. The division of labor inside the home is unlikely to change any time sooner—younger men are no more likely to do an equal share of the housework than older ones.

FACT FILE:

DAYDREAM NATION

The results of an Exec magazine survey of 3,000 readers about office daydreams:

- *Can you daydream while simultaneously talking with someone, including your boss?*

  YES 59% NO 41%

- *Do you ever daydream about being CEO of your company?*

  YES 73% NO 27%

- *Do you ever dream about having sex with a co-worker?*

  YES 77% NO 23%

WHAT WORKERS WANT

The following statistics are a snapshot of the hopes and aspirations of American workers as gleaned from a 1993 study by the Families and Work Institute. Here's what workers said when they were asked what they consider "very important" in finding the right job.

Open communications	65%
Effect on personal/family life	60%
Nature of work	59%
Management quality	59%
Supervisor	58%
Gain new skills	55%
Control over work content	55%
Job security	54%
Co-worker quality	53%
Stimulating work	50%
Job location	50%
Family-supportive policies	46%
Fringe benefits	43%
Control of work schedule	38%
Advancement opportunity	37%
Salary/wage	35%
Access to decision makers	33%
No other offers	32%
Management opportunity	26%
Size of employer	18%

HOW DO YOU SPELL SUCCESS?

Respondents were asked what being successful in their work life means:

Personal satisfaction from doing a good job	52%
Earning the respect or recognition of supervisors and/or peers	30%
Getting ahead or advancing in job or career	22%
Making a good income	21%
Feeling my work is important	12%
Having control over work content and schedule	6%

EQUAL PARTNERS?

How fair is your household's division of labor? A breakdown of who does the work in dual-income households:

	MEN	WOMEN
Cooking	15%	81%
Cleaning	7%	78%
Shopping	18%	87%
Paying bills	35%	63%
Repairs	91%	14%

EQUAL RESPONSIBILITY?

Inequality in child rearing continues despite the increase of working women:

Working women who say they take major responsibility for their children:	71%
Men who do:	5%

EQUAL OPPORTUNITY?

Managers were asked how they perceive their opportunities for professional advancement:

	MEN	WOMEN
Poor	7%	19%
Fair	9%	20%
Good	51%	34%
Excellent	33%	26%

WORKING HARD FOR THE MONEY: A ROUNDUP

- The average worker spends more than 45 hours a week on the job, including overtime and commuting.
- Eighty percent of workers say their jobs require them to work very hard, and 65 percent say they require working very fast.
- Forty-two percent of workers say they feel "used up" by the end of a workday.

SOURCE: *The Changing Workforce*, Families and Work Institute, 1993.

EXPERT Q&A

HOW TO KEEP WORKERS HAPPY

Money's nice but public approval from the boss counts for plenty

How workers feel about their work can make the difference between a successful firm and one that cannot keep up with the competition. Workers who do not feel they are valued are often reluctant to innovate, to work harder, to seek to become more efficient. Robert Nelson, a consultant at Blanchard Training and Development in San Diego, Calif., is a student of workplace psychology and the author of *1,001 Ways to Reward Employees* (Workman Publishing, 1994). We asked him for his advice.

How effective are financial rewards?

Financial rewards are overstated in both practice and in the perceptions of managers in thinking they are the most motivating to employees. There is a lot of evidence that says there are motivational aspects to money, but there is much more power in non-monetary rewards.

Then what are the most effective rewards?

The most motivating rewards tend to be initiated by one's manager and people one works most closely with. The best ones are personal, such as being specifically told in a timely way you did a good job by your manager. Fifty-eight percent of those surveyed said their manager seldom did this.

Second was being told this in writing by your manager. Then something else in writing, such as a note in the personnel file, something put in the company newsletter about you, a thank-you note to the family because your work has taken you away for some time. Public praise also tops the list.

What kind of public praise?

It could be as simple as bringing in a tub of ice cream. Ben and Jerry's give away ice cream to employees—two pints a week. To motivate employees you don't need money as much as you need managers to take the time to be thoughtful and creative. The general rule of thumb is you want to praise publicly and reprimand privately.

What are the benefits of behaving like this to your employees?

They're looking for ways to pay it back, through extra work, ways they can help customers, any number of ways. The reward system is not altruistic at all. You're doing it to get people to perform better. I'm not talking about manipulating people, I'm talking about finding out what motivates them. The more I do that, the more they want to work with me and do a good job for me.

Should rewards be limited to performance, or are all staff rewarded?

The ones that are best are performance-based. I always talk about starting there, but once the philosophy becomes part of your culture, not everything you do has to be performance-based. You can have general morale meetings. There are things you can do to help develop the whole culture. You can set up proposals that encourage people to catch each other doing things right, anyone can give formal praises to anyone else, they get it in writing, they get a plaque, at the end of the year they get dinner with the rest of the plaque winners in the company.

Would you reward management differently?

Motivation is a very personal thing. It changes with where you are in your life, in your career. People earning $200,000 per year, they want a chance to influence where the company's going. I find, in working with managers, as you work with people who are higher paid and perhaps better skilled, different things tend to motivate them—things like increasing responsibility, increased visibility, ownership, independence and autonomy. You've got to get to everybody. Everybody needs to feel special.

SELF-EMPLOYMENT

THE BEST OFFICE ON THE BLOCK

The joys and perils of working where you live

The phrase "cottage industry" is taking on new meaning. The ranks of the self-employed are swelling and they are choosing to work out of home offices. An astonishing 38 percent of all households, or 37 million, include a member performing income-generating work at home, according to Link Resources, a New York market-research firm. Many are refugees from corporate offices, either jettisoned during cutbacks or budding entrepreneurs dropping out to create their own jobs. They include consultants, freelancers, independent producers, contractors, and small-business operators of all kinds. All are attracted by the flexible hours, lower stress, and chance to be their own boss.

A successful home business can gross up to $100,000 in the first year. *Money* magazine recently surveyed a group of experts, including Paul and Sarah Edwards, authors of *The Best Home Businesses for the '90s* (G. P. Putnam's Sons, 1994), to find the home-based businesses most likely to succeed. The winners: editorial and publishing, temporary-employment agencies, repair services, and video production.

Starting up a home business need not be expensive. Depending on the business you can expect to shell out from $500 to $30,000. Often, part of the trick is to create the illusion that you're part of a much larger operation. Experts usually advise, for example, that you pony up for professionally designed and printed business cards, logos, and letterheads. Plain stationery and computer-generated letterhead and business cards look second-rate. Never use your home phone line for business calls. Get a separate business line. Live answering services or voice mail is preferable to answering machines, which are preferable to an unattended phone. In most parts of the country, home office workers can get office-like phone services for an extra $10 or so a month from the local phone company.

You probably already own a fairly good personal computer if you're going into business for yourself, but will you also need a copier, a fax machine, a printer, or a scanner? One new option is a multipurpose machine, which will print, fax, copy, and sometimes scan. Sales of these versatile machines are taking off: 140,000 were sold in 1994 and the number is expected to triple in the next 12 months. Hewlett-Packard's Officejet, $799, which combines a plain paper fax with 65 speed-dial numbers and a 20-page automatic document feeder, a monochrome inkjet printer, and a simple copier gets good reviews.

FACT FILE:

DO YOU FIT THE MOLD?

■ *Joe Mancuso, director of New York's Center for Entrepreneurial Management, a nonprofit consulting firm, researches people who go into business for themselves. He has found that they are most likely to be:*

- **Offspring of self-employed parents.**
- **Previously fired from more than one job.**
- **Immigrants or children of immigrants.**
- **Previously employed in businesses of fewer than 100 employees.**
- **The oldest child in the family.**
- **College graduates.**
- **Realistic, but not high risk-takers.**
- **Well organized.**

EXPERT SOURCES

WHERE TO TURN WHEN YOU'RE YOUR OWN BOSS

Joseph Anthony, author of Kiplinger's Working for Yourself: Full Time, Part Time, Anytime *(Kiplinger Books, 1993), recommends the following:*

BOOKS

KIPLINGER'S MAKE YOUR MONEY GROW
Theodore J. Miller, Kiplinger Books, 1993, $14.95
■ Advice on the financial planning needed by the self-employed.

MAKING THE MOST OF YOUR MONEY
Jane Bryant Quinn, Simon & Schuster, 1991, $27.50
■ Subtitled *The Complete Guide to Financial Planning*, another good source of advice for the self-employed.

WHAT COLOR IS YOUR PARACHUTE?
Richard Bolles, Tenspeed Press, annual, $14.95
■ This classic career guide offers insightful questions and worksheets that can help you determine whether going into business for yourself is the right choice.

ORGANIZATIONS

HEALTH INSURANCE ASSOCIATION OF AMERICA
■ Provides information on companies that sell major medical policies to individuals.
☎ **202-223-7780**

NATIONAL FEDERATION OF INDEPENDENT BUSINESS
■ The largest small business advocacy group in the country. Lobbies at the state and federal level on legislative positions determined by frequent membership polls. Dues are $100 and up per year, depending on desired level of contribution.
☎ **800-634-2669**

THE ROBERT WOOD JOHNSON FOUNDATION
■ The foundation's Health Care for the Uninsured Program helps pool small businesses seeking health coverage to bargain with hospitals and health maintenance organizations to provide benefits at a lower price.
☎ **609-452-8701**

U.S. SMALL BUSINESS ADMINISTRATION
■ The toll-free answer desk is a good place to turn for questions about financial management, business planning, and marketing. Offers programs and publications and can also provide specific advice for women and minorities in small business.
☎ **800-827-5722**

Canon's $800 Multipass 1000 comes complete with plain paper fax, PC fax, monochrome Bubble Jet printer, scanner, copier and telephone. Xerox, Brother, Okidata, and Panasonic also produce similar machines.

The biggest complaint among home office workers is a sense of isolation. For the self-employed, one remedy is to join a networking group or to communicate online with other home workers—on CompuServe's Working from Home, for example. For telecommuters who feel out of touch with headquarters, experts suggest visiting your company as often as possible, calling frequently, or sending E-mail messages.

Another problem home workers confront is separating their work from their personal life. Paul and Sarah Edwards, the home office gurus, suggest using a separate room or partition to separate your office from your living space. Set specific work hours, even though they need not be 9 to 5. Finally, just because you work at home doesn't mean you can also take care of the kids. Make child care arrangements.

FRANCHISES

THE BIG MAC ATTACK

A new study finds conventional start-up businesses often fare better

Every 17 minutes, a new franchise outlet opens somewhere in the United States. They range from auto and truck dealerships to soft drink bottlers to gyms and hardware stores, and their numbers have zoomed from 521,125 in 1990 to over 600,000 in mid-1995, according to the International Franchise Association. *Entrepreneur* magazine traditionally devotes its entire January issue to the 500 top franchises in the United States, but the 1995 issue lists nearly 900.

Why the mad rush? Conventional wisdom holds that franchising is a low-risk way to start a business. For a hefty investment, up to $600,000 or more for a McDonald's, for example, you get all the training and marketing support you need. Then, you manage your business and collect the revenues.

But that's not exactly the way it unfolds, according to a new study by Timothy Bates, an economics professor at Wayne State University. Bates tracked the performance of some 21,000 fledgling franchises for four years in the late '80s. His findings are startling: 35 percent of the franchises failed by 1991, compared with 28 percent of conventional start-ups. Franchisees whose companies survived earned just $14,900 a year, compared with $26,600 for other start-ups.

How can that be? Franchises have annual sales of $514,000, compared to $102,400 for non-franchises, and they are also better capitalized ($86,500 compared to $29,800). Bates draws several conclusions. For one thing, franchisees may be picking already saturated markets, or at least areas with tough competition. For another, perhaps franchisees aren't getting the much-touted management advice and support they need. Finally, says Bates, maybe it's all in the nature of the franchisee versus the self-starter: franchisees are inherently less likely to take risks.

The study is not cause to dismiss franchising altogether. After all, Bates found that nearly two-thirds of franchises do survive. But do look before you leap into a franchise. For starters, contact the Federal Trade Commission, ☎ 202-326-2161, which offers a free packet of information that includes the pros and cons of franchising and explanations of information that franchisors are required to disclose by law. Another good source for future franchisees: the International Franchise Association, ☎ 202-628-8000, in Washington, D.C.

■ THE FIVE HOTTEST FRANCHISES

Success magazine rates the top 100 franchises based on data including financial growth, corporate stability, and the continuing expansion of the franchisee network. Here are the top five.

Franchise name	Category	Total locations	Franchisee-owned loc.	Initial fee	Total investment
1. **GNC FRANCHISING INC.** ☎ 201-567-8500	Retail	1,553	371	$29,900	$75,001–$150,000
2. **AARON'S RENTAL PURCHASE** ☎ 216-380-4408	Retail	83	164	$29,000–$105,000	$150,001–$250,000
3. **CHOICE HOTELS INTERNATIONAL** ☎ 800-458-5912	Lodging	3,075	16	$32,500	Over $250,000
4. **BLIMPIE INTERNATIONAL INC.** ☎ 310-652-6393	Fast Food	679	1,323	$9,900–$23,900	Under $75,000
5. **SCHLOTZSKY'S INC.** ☎ 216-896-1122	Restaurants	321	526	$40,000	$75,001–$150,000

SOURCE: *Success* Magazine, November 1994.

EXPERT Q&A

ARE YOU A WORKAHOLIC?

As many as one in five Americans may suffer from work addiction

Everybody knows that spending too many hours on the job can lead to stress, bad nerves, ticks—even strokes and heart attacks. What is not so well known is that work, like alcohol, can actually be an addiction. Experts say up to 20 percent of the working population may be addicted to work. Here Barbara McConnell, a New York psychologist who has spent the last 13 years helping people conquer their work addiction, discusses what can be done about workaholism.

■ How is workaholism manifested?

In workaholism the person is usually functioning pretty well, but what happens is he reaches a point where he breaks down. The body is like any other machine—if you push it at 120 instead of 100, eventually you're going to have a problem.

■ What jobs and income levels are most effected by this?

At middle management and above you tend to see more workaholism. But in a compulsive society you can find "isms" anywhere. I feel there is a predisposition to it in a family, and children may be open to it in different ways. For example, in some families alcoholism skips a generation. Whatever you say about alcoholism is true of the other "isms." The effects of a workaholic parent are definitely in the children.

■ Are most workaholics men?

It's traditionally been more men. Men have been conditioned not to cry, to be deprived of a certain rich emotionality that comes with being human.

■ Is there any direct link between the number of hours worked and workaholism?

No. It's how you use your work that matters. You could have people who work 9 to 5, but then at home all they talk about is work. They have nothing else in their lives.

■ So is workaholism treatable?

Yes. Like alcoholism, workaholism is a self-diagnosed disease. With alcoholism, you must get people to say that it's not how much they drink, but how they use drink. Likewise, it's how you use work that matters. It should have a natural structure, a beginning, middle, and end. When people come in here [for treatment], they have no structure. I give them structure. You start by reducing the number of hours, controlling at least the mechanism of the disease. You have to help people curtail the number of hours and deal with the attendant emotions. A straightforward work problem takes about 12 weeks to resolve. Half the people I counsel do not leave; the other half I move, mainly because they're in a dysfunctional environment.

■ Could people go cold turkey?

No. I operate on the "little steps" theory. You slowly move them away from the negative behavior while you're detoxing their emotions.

FACT FILE:

FOUR TELLTALE SIGNS

■ *Four questions that you can ask yourself if you think you may be a workaholic:*

■ Do you use work life to avoid social commitments?

■ Does work life interfere with your family life?

■ Do you spend more than 50 hours a week at work?

■ Has working kept you from having interests and hobbies?

GETTING FIRED

WHAT TO DO IF YOU'RE CANNED

Relax, our expert says, this could be the biggest opportunity of your life

It's going to happen, you cannot avoid it—at some point in your career you will likely be fired or laid off. With many studies showing that most average American stays in a job for only five years, job loss has become a fact of life. Luckily, there is a lot you can do. We consulted Jim O'Connell, a psychologist at Drake Beam and Morrin, an outplacement firm in New York City, and found some reassuring advice.

What can one do to avoid getting canned?

In this period of downsizing or to put it nicely, rightsizing, one always has to be prepared for the ax. However, there are two important things one can do: (1) Keep up with all the developments in your field by reading journals and taking continuing education courses; (2) The best technique for avoiding "jobsolescence" is to initiate change instead of waiting for it.

What should you do if you hear that a firing or downsizing is imminent?

If you feel that your job is on the line, you should work out a severance plan—people fair better if they negotiate a severance package rather than wait for one to be presented to them. Also, always make sure that a lawyer reviews any papers and that you fully understand what you're agreeing to before you sign. In addition, while most people don't, you should keep a record of your evaluations and reports in case you think that you are being unfairly discharged. Keeping records will also be helpful in preparing your résumé.

Many managerial positions and some professions are becoming overly crowded or obsolete. What should you do if you're faced with one of these possibilities?

There are two types of job skills—work content skills, such as teaching history, and work transferable skills, such as teaching English. Most people have work transferable skills but they have to become aware of them and cultivate them to roll with the punches of today's changing workplace. Getting fired also provides a perfect opportunity to brush up on important computer and technical skills that will be important for all jobs in the future.

How does one cope with getting fired?

Don't take it personally. Most of the time it was something that was bound to happen. Getting fired can be an important time of renewal—a time to get your act together. This means that one should not call everybody one knows helter-skelter asking for a job.

In my work I've run across so many people who have never sat down and figured what they wanted to do when they grew up. People who take the time to evaluate and plan their lives are better able to mesh the jobs they choose with their dreams of what they want to do.

EXPERT SOURCE

Down and out and looking for a new job? You're red meat for headhunters. To find them, check out the *Directory of Executive Recruiters* (Kennedy Publications, $39.95), which provides information on search firms. *Executive Recruiter News* publishes a directory of 120 search firms that place executives temporarily ($19.95). For a copy, call ☎ 800-531-0007.

CHAPTER SIX

HOUSE & GARDEN

EXPERT QUOTES

"A bed should lie diagonal to the door. If not, occupants may be nervous and jumpy, traits that would affect their personal relationships."

—Sarah Rossbach, author of *Interior Design with Feng Shui*

Page 448

"It's better to cool grass down during the heat of the day [by watering]. It takes stress off the grass."

—Dale Haney, horticulturist for the White House

Page 470

"The key to training a dog to perform a stunt is the treat, the reward. That becomes the motivation."

—Steve Berens, Hollywood trainer to the canine stars

Page 478

THE YEAR AHEAD: ANTICIPATE a new burst of home renovation thanks to falling interest rates... **PROTECT** your front door, which is how most burglars break and enter homes... **SAMPLE** the outstanding 1991 Beaujolais or California Zinfandel vintages... **EXPECT** more use of home water filters to deal with tap water complaints... **SAVOR** the breeding of fruits and vegetables with old-fashioned flavors...

AROUND THE HOUSE

MAKING YOUR HOUSE A HOME

What the most popular alterations cost from coast to coast

You bought the place, but it needs work. Where should you start? Every house is different, of course, but some remodeling projects offer a better payback than others. Each year *Remodeling Magazine* puts some of the most popular home improvement projects to the test, asking real estate agents in 60 cities how much the project would add in the first year to a mid-priced house in an established neighborhood. The results are instructive: Buyers will pay for state-of-the-art kitchens, luxurious master bed and bath suites, family rooms, and extra bedrooms.

Here's a region-by-region breakdown of the projects. The estimates for construction costs come from two well-known publishers of estimating manuals, Home-Tech of Bethesda, Md., and R. S. Means Company, Inc., of Kingston, Mass. Keep in mind that the prices are averages; actual prices can vary widely depending on material, labor costs, and design.

MINOR KITCHEN REMODEL

■ **Project description:** Refinish cabinets; install new energy-efficient oven and cook top, new laminate counter tops and cabinet hardware, new wall coverings, and resilient flooring; and repaint the entire room.

REGION	JOB COST	RESALE VALUE	RECOUPED
East	$6,213	$6,143	99%
South	$5,134	$5,475	107%
Midwest	$5,804	$5,889	101%
West	$6,189	$6,661	108%
National	$5,835	$8,042	104%

MAJOR KITCHEN REMODEL

■ **Project description:** Update an outmoded 200-square-foot kitchen with design and installation of a functional layout of new mid-priced cabinets, laminate countertops, energy-efficient oven, cook top and ventilation system, microwave, dishwasher, garbage disposal, and custom lighting. Add new resilient flooring, wall coverings, and ceiling treatments. Kitchen features 30 lineal feet of cabinets and counter-top space, including a 3-by-5-foot island.

REGION	JOB COST	RESALE VALUE	RECOUPED
East	$18,277	$16,973	93%
South	$15,140	$15,147	100%
Midwest	$17,084	$15,265	89%
West	$18,178	$17,695	97%
National	$17,170	$16,270	95%

BATHROOM ADDITION

■ **Project description:** Add a second full bath to a house with one or one-and-a-half baths. The 6-by-8-foot bath is within the existing floor plan and in an inconspicuous spot that is convenient to the bedrooms. Include cultured marble vanity top, molded sink, standard bathtub with shower, low-profile toilet, lighting, mirrored medicine cabinet, linen storage, and ceramic floor tile. Walls in the tub/shower area get ceramic tile, with vinyl wallpaper elsewhere.

REGION	JOB COST	RESALE VALUE	RECOUPED
East	$9,554	$8,967	94%
South	$8,046	$8,852	110%
Midwest	$9,734	$8,679	89%
West	$9,486	$9,688	102%
National	$9,205	$9,046	98%

BATHROOM REMODEL

■ **Project description:** Update an existing 5-by-9-foot bathroom that is at least 25 years old with a new standard-size tub, a new commode, and a new solid-surface vanity counter with molded sinks. Also install new lighting, mirrored medicine cabinets, and ceramic floor tiles. The walls in the tub/shower area get ceramic tile, with vinyl wallpaper covering all other walls.

REGION	JOB COST	RESALE VALUE	RECOUPED
East	$6,841	$5,303	78%
South	$5,671	$5,050	89%
Midwest	$6,414	$5,069	79%
West	$6,848	$5,746	84%
National	$6,443	$5,252	82%

FAMILY ROOM ADDITION

■ **Project description:** In a style and location that is appropriate to the existing house, add a 16-by-25-foot, light-filled room on a new crawl space foundation with wood-joist floor framing. On exterior, match wood siding and fiberglass roof shingles on original house. Include drywall interior and batt insulation, 120 square feet of glass doors and windows, and hardwood tongue-and-groove flooring. Tie the entire

EXPERT TIPS

IF I HAD A HAMMER. . .

When not to do it yourself:

A thrifty homeowner decides to save money by refinishing his living room floors himself. He rents a sanding machine. He starts the job. He blows a fuse. As he troops back upstairs after flipping the switch, the newly activated sander grinds a hole through his floor.

The story will serve as fair warning for do-it-yourselfers who want to do it all. There are times when you just have to call a professional. Katie Hamilton should know. She and her husband, Gene, have fixed up 14 houses in the last 25 years. Here are the Hamiltons' lists of jobs they would do themselves and jobs for which they would seek professional help:

DO-IT-YOURSELF JOBS

■ Jobs with inexpensive tools and materials, such as indoor painting.

■ "Grunt" work jobs, which involve more sweat than materials, like removing paint, wallpaper, or tiles.

■ Jobs that require few skills, such as patching wall holes, caulking windows, and yard work.

JOBS TO HIRE OUT

■ Electrical, plumbing, and foundation work that must pass building codes—a licensed professional will know local requirements.

■ Projects with expensive building materials, such as hand-painted tile or high-end carpeting.

■ Dangerous jobs, such as installing a new roof.

addition into the existing heating and cooling system.

REGION	JOB COST	RESALE VALUE	RECOUPED
East	$28,848	$24,960	87%
South	$23,133	$20,560	89%
Midwest	$27,658	$23,580	85%
West	$29,247	$26,975	92%
National	$27,221	$24,019	88%

SUN SPACE ADDITION

■**Project description:** Add a 12-by-16-foot living space off the kitchen, dining room, or living room. Custom build on site including foundation. Walls and ceilings are mostly insulated glass, tinted or shaded if necessary for climate. Half the windows are for ventilation. Includes ceiling fan and tile floor. Ties into existing heating and cooling.

REGION	JOB COST	RESALE VALUE	RECOUPED
East	$25,229	$16,545	66%
South	$20,494	$14,305	70%
Midwest	$23,768	$15,882	67%
West	$25,236	$17,067	68%
National	$23,682	$15,950	67%

FACT FILE:

BUYING A HOUSE IS JUST THE FIRST STEP

■ *During their first year in a new house, homeowners spend an average of $1,000 on furniture and accessories. A look at some big-ticket items and when homeowners purchased them:*

	WHO OWNED HOME... Less than five years	More than five years
■**BOUGHT IN PAST YEAR**		
Bedroom furniture	18.6%	12.9%
Living room furniture	21.4%	16.8%
Washer	8.0%	5.3%
Dryer	6.3%	3.7%
Television	23.3%	19.9%
Lawn mower	8.0%	5.3%
■**DID IN PAST YEAR**		
Remodeled	23%	15.5%
Added a room	3.9%	3.2%
Painted exterior	19.6%	16.7%
Painted interior	36.2%	29.9%

NOTE: Excludes condos, co-ops, and mobile homes.
SOURCE: Simmons Market Research Bureau, Spring 1989; *American Demographics* magazine.

MASTER SUITE

■**Project description:** In a house with two or three bedrooms, add over a crawl space a 24-by-16-foot master bedroom with a walk-in closet, dressing area, master bath, whirlpool tub, separate ceramic tile shower, and a double-bowl vanity. Bedroom floor is carpeted; floor in bath is ceramic tile.

REGION	JOB COST	RESALE VALUE	RECOUPED
East	$29,005	$26,422	91%
South	$23,269	$22,008	95%
Midwest	$27,122	$23,556	87%
West	$28,826	$26,991	94%
National	$27,055	$24,744	91%

EXTERIOR REMODEL

■**Project description:** Replace 16 existing single-pane 3-by-5-foot windows with energy-efficient vinyl or vinyl-clad aluminum double-paned windows; cover 1,250 square feet of existing siding with new vinyl siding, including 200 lineal feet of trim. Apply 15 squares of new roofing over single layer of old roofing.

REGION	JOB COST	RESALE VALUE	RECOUPED
East	$16,815	$12,997	77%
South	$12,882	$9,876	77%
Midwest	$15,395	$11,629	76%
West	$16,709	$11,642	70%
National	$15,450	$11,536	75%

DECK ADDITION

■**Project description:** Add a 16-by-20-foot deck of pressure-treated pine supported by 4-by-4 posts set into concrete footings. Include a built-in bench, railings, and planter, also of pressure-treated pine.

REGION	JOB COST	RESALE VALUE	RECOUPED
East	$6,916	$5,008	72%
South	$5,965	$4,016	67%
Midwest	$6,665	$4,716	71%
West	$6,936	$5,390	78%
National	$6,620	$4,782	72%

ATTIC BEDROOM

■ **Project description:** In a house with two or three bedrooms, convert unfinished space in attic into a 15-by-15-foot bedroom and a 5-by-7-foot bathroom with a shower. Add four new windows, oriented to capture views and a 15-foot shed dormer. Insulate and finish ceilings and walls. Carpet unfinished floor. Add separate forced-air heating and air conditioning. Retain existing stairs.

REGION	JOB COST	RESALE VALUE	RECOUPED
East	$23,057	$18,549	80%
South	$18,273	$15,211	83%
Midwest	$21,907	$17,865	82%
West	$23,021	$21,170	92%
National	$21,565	$18,199	84%

HOME OFFICE ADDITION

■ **Project description:** Convert existing 12-by-12-foot room into home office, install custom cabinets configured for desk, computer work station, overhead storage, and 20 feet of plastic laminate desk. Rewire room electronic equipment, telephone lines. Include drywall interior and level-loop carpeting.

REGION	JOB COST	RESALE VALUE	RECOUPED
East	$8,662	$5,030	58%
South	$7,083	$3,398	48%
Midwest	$8,121	$4,945	61%
West	$8,589	$5,832	68%
National	$8,114	$4,801	59%

TWO-STORY ADDITION

■ **Project description:** Over a crawl space add a 24-by-16-foot, two-story wing with a first-floor family room and a second-floor bedroom and full bath. Features prefab fireplace in the family room, carpeted floors, 11 windows, drywall, and atrium-style exterior door. The 5-by-8-foot bathroom has a fiberglass bath/shower, standard-grade commode, ceramic tile flooring, and mirrored medicine cabinet; walls are papered.

REGION	JOB COST	RESALE VALUE	RECOUPED
East	$53,699	$44,545	83%
South	$44,430	$38,053	86%
Midwest	$50,410	$40,923	81%
West	$53,845	$46,233	86%
National	$50,596	$42,438	84%

NOTE: For a complete copy of the *1994–95 Cost vs. Value Report*, send check for $45.50 to Hanley-Wood, Inc., One Thomas Circle, NW, #600, Washington, D.C. 20005, Attn. Remodeling Reprints.

SOURCE: *Remodeling* magazine, October 1994.

■ HOW REMODELING PROJECTS DEPRECIATE

A new garage is your best bet for increasing the long-term value of your house.

PROJECT	PERCENTAGE OF ORIGINAL RENOVATION COSTS ADDED TO THE VALUE OF HOUSE AFTER		
	1 YEAR	3 YEARS	5 YEARS
Kitchen renovation	77%	62%	47%
Bathroom renovation	77%	62%	44%
Roof replacement	69%	52%	39%
Fireplace addition	76%	68%	61%
Swimming pool addition	53%	42%	31%
One-car garage	84%	78%	71%
Wood deck addition	79%	66%	55%
Solar room addition	72%	61%	53%
Living/dining/family room update	79%	59%	37%

SOURCE: Marshall & Swift National Cost-Reporting Service.

FURNITURE

FROM KLUTZ TO CARPENTER

Do-it-yourself kits are economical, easy, and the quality can surprise

In olden times, master cabinetmakers would spend months crafting chairs, desks, bureaus, and sideboards to grace the homes of their well-heeled clients. But today's resourceful furniture makers are pushing furniture that you can assemble by yourself, sometimes in just a few minutes.

Furniture-by-the-kit has come a long way. Sure, some ready-to-assemble (RTA, for short) kits still can drive you crazy as you sort screws, nuts, and grommets in various teacups. But with the best kits, the assembly agony is mercifully brief, and the chair doesn't wobble when you're done. Thanks to modern machinery, the pieces can be as well constructed as any in your home. Even a klutz will be able to assemble most items, though sometimes it will take some doing and some help. Lucie Young, a design writer who recently tested furniture kits for the *New York Times*, found that most of the half-dozen items she tested were "ingenious in their use of sophisticated technology and bold in their insistence on top-quality materials."

Although she hailed the designs as "nearly idiot-proof," the instructions were not always as clear as they could have been. Assembly time took from 2 to 35 minutes.

Kits generally include any special tools that you may need, glue, sandpaper, and stain. Prices are reasonable: about one-third the cost of a comparable finished product. An English hunt table from the Bartley Collection, for example, costs $675, compared with $1,700 finished. Many companies will sell you their finished pieces for about double the price. But think of the satisfaction you'll get if you put the item together with your own hands.

EXPERT SOURCES

ONE GRANDFATHER CLOCK TO GO, PLEASE

Here are some sources for furniture kits, and the company's specialties:

ADAMS WOOD PRODUCTS
Morristown, Tenn.
■ Tables, chairs, hutches, individual parts.
☎ **615-587-2942**

BARTLEY COLLECTION
Denton, Md.
■ Traditional 18th-century style furniture.
☎ **410-479-4480**

GRAND RIVER WORKSHOP
Des Moines, Iowa
■ Oak furniture. Bedroom furniture, bookcases, rolltop desks.
☎ **800-373-1101**

GREEN DESIGN
Portland, Maine
■ Light, airy designs. Bookcases, armchairs, tables, wood love seat.
☎ **207-775-4234**

SHAKER WORKSHOPS
Concord, Mass.
■ Shaker-style furniture and accessories, and a grandfather clock kit.
☎ **800-840-9121**

WOOD CLASSICS
Gardiner, N.Y.
■ Mahogany and teak outdoor furniture. Chairs, tables, swings.
☎ **800-385-0030**

YIELD HOUSE
North Conway, N.H.
■ Shaker-style tables, cabinets, sewing centers.
☎ **800-258-0376**

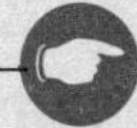

SHOPPER'S GUIDE

A PILGRIMAGE TO AMERICA'S FURNITURE MECCA

More than half of all America's furniture is made in a 200-square-mile region of North Carolina. Every spring, Bloomfield Hills, Mich., interior designer Kate Gladchun leads a group of shoppers from the Detroit suburbs on a trek to the nation's furniture mecca. The author of The Fine Furniture and Furnishings Discount Shopping Guide *(Resources, Inc., 1994), which includes some 300 outlets, Gladchun lists some of her favorites below:*

ATRIUM FURNITURE SHOWROOMS

High Point, N.C.

■ One of the largest home furnishings malls in the South. Atrium features four floors with more than 500 furniture and accessory lines represented.

☎ **910-882-5599**

HICKORY FURNITURE MART

Hickory, N.C.

■ Sixty galleries and factory outlets carry 500 lines of furniture, bedding, accessories, antiques, and collectibles, all at deep discounts. If you have only a short stay in North Carolina, this is the one store not to miss.

☎ **800-462-6278**

PRIBA FURNITURE

Greensboro, N.C.

■ More than 300 lines of furniture, discounted accessories, lamps, wall coverings, fabrics, carpets. Fliers are sent to customers on their mailing list announcing sales and specials.

☎ **800-334-2498**

SHAW FURNITURE GALLERIES

Randleman, N.C.

■ In business since 1940. Pays for your lodging if you purchase over a certain amount.

☎ **910-498-2628**

TURNER TOLSON

New Bern, N.C.

■ In business since 1887. Home and business furniture. Turner Tolson will pay for your lodging if you purchase over a certain amount.

☎ **919-638-2121**

WINDSOR FURNITURE GALLERIES

High Point, N.C.

■ Expert service and courteous design help.

☎ **910-812-8000**

YOUNG'S FURNITURE AND RUG COMPANY

High Point, N.C.

■ Specializes in upper-end furnishings. The staff includes nine interior designers, who are helpful and courteous.

☎ **910-883-4111**

ZAKI ORIENTAL RUGS

High Point, N.C.

■ Large showroom packed with more than 5,000 quality rugs, up to 16 by 26 feet, from Pakistan, India, China, Afghanistan, Portugal, and other countries.

☎ **910-884-4407**

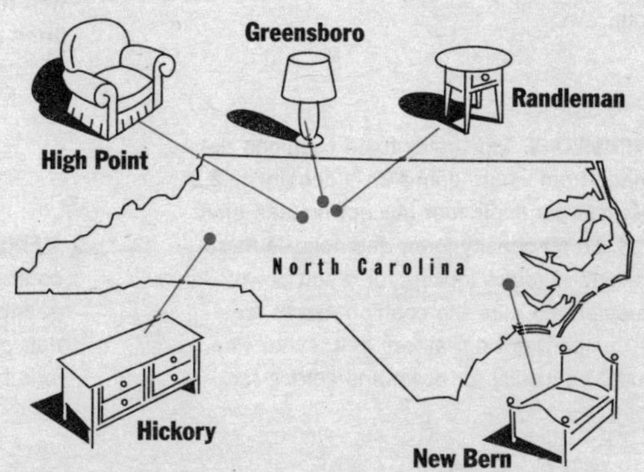

PUT A LITTLE SPRING IN YOUR SOFA

If you're in the market for a new sofa, you're probably wondering what makes a $2,000 sofa any different from one that costs a mere $600. The difference lies in the frame, padding, cushions, springs, fabric, and finish:

■ **PADDING:** Sofas often wear at the arms because the maker has scrimped on padding. The better sofas have a layer of cotton or polyfiber over a layer of foam. Cheaper sofas have fabric right on top of the foam.

■ **FABRIC:** The grade of a fabric determines the price, but is not a measure of the fabric's durability. Grades are based largely on fiber content and on how much waste results from matching the pattern. For durability, consider spending the extra $50 or so for treating the sofa with fabric protection.

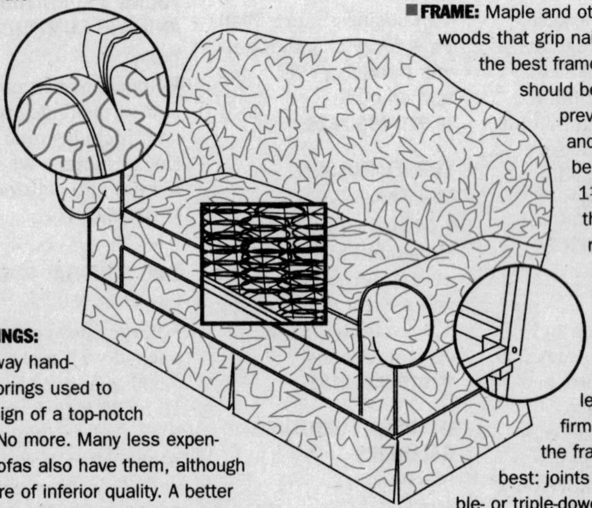

■ **FRAME:** Maple and other hardwoods that grip nails well make the best frames. The wood should be kiln-dried to prevent shrinkage and warping. The best frames are 1½ inches thick. (Experts refer to it as a 6/4 frame.) To keep a sofa from sagging, joints and legs must be firmly attached to the frame. The best: joints that are double- or triple-doweled at the top corners, and firmly attached with reinforcing blocks where the arms meet the seat.

■ **SPRINGS:** Eight-way hand-tied springs used to be a sign of a top-notch sofa. No more. Many less expensive sofas also have them, although they are of inferior quality. A better question: How many rows of springs are used in the seat? The best use four rows.

■ **CUSHIONS:** Top-quality foam cushions are made from virgin foam with a density of 2.2 pounds per cubic foot. Accept no less than 1.8. Lower-density foam deteriorates more quickly. If you're looking for a soft down cushion, be sure the cushion has at least 30 percent down feathers in it. Otherwise, you'll be paying for down and getting far less.

■ **FINISH:** Attention to detail counts. In high-quality sofas, seams are straight, pleats lie flat, corners fill out, and cushions have metal zippers.

CARPETING

WHAT'S HIDDEN UNDER THE RUG?

Some dealers lie like, well, a rug, so count the knots—and your change

Whether you are looking for basic wall-to-wall carpeting or a fancy oriental masterpiece, picking a good carpet can be a tough job. But you don't need the wisdom of Confucius or the patience of Job—just a little knowledge of what to look for:

■ **WALL-TO-WALL CARPETS:** The first decision is whether to choose wool or a synthetic. Wool is durable and takes color well, but it costs a lot more. Polyester carpeting used to flatten out with time, but the fibers have been improved and it now holds up pretty well.

The amount of yarn used to make the carpeting is another indication of quality—the more yarn that is used, the more durable the carpet will be. High traffic areas require a carpet with at least 50 ounces of yarn per square yard. Fibers that have been woven in will last longer than punched-in fibers. Finally, stain protection that has been built in to the carpet is preferable to protection that is sprayed on later.

■ **ORIENTAL CARPETS:** They are handmade, usually from wool or silk, in Iran, Pakistan, China, India, and Turkey, among other countries. Prices have dropped about 20 percent over the past two years, so unless you're buying ancient or rare oriental rugs, which can cost $50,000 or more, you can expect to pay a few hundred dollars for a small area rug and several thousand for a room-size rug. Iranian rugs are typically the priciest, partly because of their scarcity since the 1987 embargo on Iranian goods.

Handmade oriental carpets are almost always better investments than machine-made area rugs. They outlast machine-made carpets by many years yet don't cost considerably more. The number of knots per square inch is the usual measure of quality: 100 knots per square inch for a good rug, 300 knots for a better rug, and 600 or more for an exceptional rug. But counting knots can be deceiving. Some rugs, such as lesser grade Pakistani Bokharas, appear to have twice as many knots because the pile yarn is wrapped around the foundation twice.

Wool quality also is important. To test it, scratch the pile. If the rug sheds excessively, don't buy it. Imagine what foot traffic and vacuum cleaning will do to it.

■ **OUT, OUT DAMN SPOT**

Consumer Reports says these homemade brews will remove stains. For all, first blot spill, then place dry paper towels on the spot. Stand on them a minute, then apply the appropriate series of potions, blotting after each application. End with a cold water rinse and final blotting.

PASTA SAUCE OR SALAD DRESSING

1. 1 tsp. of dishwashing liquid to 1 cup of water.
2. 1 tbs. of ammonia to 1/2 cup of water.

RED WINE

1. 1 tsp. of dishwashing liquid to 1 cup of water.
2. 1 part vinegar to 2 parts water.
3. 1 tbs. of ammonia to 1/2 cup of water.

KOOL-AID

1. 1 tsp. of dishwashing liquid to 1 cup of water.
2. 1 tbs. of ammonia to 1/2 cup of water.
3. 1 part vinegar to 2 parts water.

UNIDENTIFIED SPILL

1. Soak with a dry- cleaning solvent.
2. 1 tsp. of dishwashing liquid to 1 cup of water.

SOURCE: *Consumer Reports* magazine, January 1991.

ELECTRONICS

WHEN TO FIX IT, WHEN TO TOSS IT

A handyman's advice on everything from answering machines to VCRs

Deciding whether to fix a faulty answering machine or trash a broken compact disk player can be a bewildering experience. Often what ails electronic equipment is minor: a stretched belt or not enough lubricant, for example. But if the warranty has run out on your machine, labor costs to repair it can be hefty. Manufacturers often quote labor charges of $100 or more to fix out-of-warranty equipment. And even getting an estimate on the job can cost as much as $80, though most repair shops will deduct that cost from the bill if you have them do the work.

Because electronic equipment repairs can be costly, you may be better off simply tossing out that broken TV or video cassette recorder. James L. Teeters, president of Atlantic Viewtronics Service Co., in Virginia Beach, Va., knows well when to junk an appliance and when to go ahead and have it repaired. Teeters, who's been in the electronics repair business for nearly 40 years, says that one rule of thumb applies to all electronic machinery: "If it's had a voltage surge, replace it. Fixing it is too costly."

ANSWERING MACHINE $40–$200

Average life: About five years.
What breaks: Aside from the batteries wearing down, the most common problem is a stretched manual drive belt.
Repair cost: $20 to $70; some batteries cost up to $20 to replace.

■ **TOSS IT:** Except for the newest solid state models with computer-chip memories, repairs can cost more than buying a new one. Replace obsolete machines, no matter what is broken. Toss it, too, if the warranty has expired.

CAMCORDER $500–$1,500

Average life: Indefinite. Requires cleaning and readjusting of motor and heads once a year.
What breaks: Wear and tear can cause gears to jam and tape heads to clog.
Repair cost: $150 to $250.

■ **TOSS IT:** When you want to replace it with a new model that has all the bells and whistles.

COMPACT DISK PLAYER $100–$1,000

Average life: About a year for a machine that cost up to $250; five to seven years for more expensive models.
What breaks: The optical block, which supplies the machine the power to read the disk; and the sled motor, which drives the unit in and out.
Repair cost: $100 to $175.

■ **TOSS IT:** When it's off the warranty and the optical block is broken.

TELEVISION $170–$4,500

Average life: Twelve years.
What breaks: Parts such as high-voltage transistors, transformers, and resistors. These components produce power and heat and get the most use.
Repair cost: $100 to 450.

■ **TOSS IT:** When the TV is more than 10 years old and has a fuzzy picture. Or if you paid less than $200 for it.

VIDEO CASSETTE RECORDER $150–$700

Average life: About 2 years for a less expensive VCR, but 15 years or more for more expensive models. Frequently using a nonabrasive head cleaner will help prolong the machine's life.
What breaks: The belt, gears, and power supplies.
Repair cost: $35 to $125.

■ **TOSS IT:** If the VCR is more than five years old or the repair bill is more than $125.

REPAIRS

WHEN THE FRIDGE IS ON THE FRITZ

Where to go and who to call when an appliance breaks down

If your furnace is cold, your fridge is hot, and your washing machine won't spin, all is not lost. You may even be able to fix them yourself—with a little help from the manufacturer. Many makers of household appliances have hotlines with technicians on hand to talk you through the repair (see "A Helping Hand," below). It could save you the $100 or so that a service call costs. For safety reasons, hot lines won't help on gas ranges and microwaves.

Before calling, be sure to jot down the appliance's model number, serial number and when you purchased it. You may also need to have an ohmmeter on hand, a little device that measures electrical resistance.

Of course, you may not be able to fix more complex problems, or you may simply find the innards of household appliances grotesque. If so, you're not alone. Consumers spent nearly $4 billion in 1993 for repairs to audio components and other electronic equipment, according to the Department of Commerce.

Aside from small local repair shops, big retailers like Sears, Roebuck & Co., which operates the nation's largest repair service, and Montgomery Ward & Co. have expanded their repair operations in recent years. The stores will fix national name-brand electronic equipment, whether under warranty or not, even for products not bought at their stores.

Radio Shack, a chain owned by the Tandy Corp., repairs 40 brands of electronic equipment, from Apple to Zenith, at any of its 6,500 stores across the country. Radio Shack will fix out-of-warranty consumer electronic equipment, including videocassette recorders, audio equipment, and computers. The rate: an $85 flat labor charge for any equipment, no matter what the problem. Parts are extra, but generally run about 50 percent of the labor charge.

■ A HELPING HAND

Some appliance company hotlines that can help you get your motor running:

■ FRIGIDAIRE CUSTOMER PRODUCT ADVICE LINE
Charge: Free
Hours: Monday through Saturday from 8 a.m. to 8 p.m. EST.
Appliances: All Frigidaire appliance models.
☎ **800-777-8349**

■ GENERAL ELECTRIC ANSWER CENTER
Charge: Free.
Hours: 24 hours, every day.
Appliances: GE, Hotpoint, and RCA refrigerators, washers, dryers, and ranges.
☎ **800-626-2000**

■ MAYTAG CUSTOMER ASSISTANCE
Charge: No charge, but you'll need to have a service manual close at hand when you call. The service manuals cost around $10.
Hours: Monday through Friday from 8 a.m. to 5 p.m. EST.
Appliances: All Maytag appliance models.
☎ **800-688-9900**

■ SEARS TECHNICAL ASSISTANCE
Charge: $9.95 allows you 30 days of unlimited calls.
Hours: 24 hours, every day.
Appliances: All Kenmore and major brand dishwashers, furnaces, washing machines, dryers, water heaters, refrigerators, and vacuum cleaners.
☎ **800-927-7957**

■ WHIRLPOOL CUSTOMER ASSISTANCE CENTER
Charge: Free
Hours: Every day from 7 a.m. to 11 p.m. EST.
Appliances: All Whirlpool appliance models.
☎ **800-253-1301**

SOME ALARMING FACTS ABOUT BURGLARS

There were almost 3 million burglaries in the United States in 1992, according to the FBI, but you needn't be a statistic. Burglars are about three times more likely to strike houses without security systems as those with them. Police most frequently recommend inexpensive systems that use magnets, installed in doors and windows, to survey entryways into the house. A bonus: Many insurance companies offer up to 30 percent off home insurance premiums if you install a system that will call your security company if there's a break-in.

■ **BURGLAR PROFILE: Roughly 91 percent are male and nearly two thirds are under 25 years old.**

■ Over half of all burglars come through the front door. Doors that are framed with glass panes are an easy target for burglars, who break the panes and reach through to open the door from the inside.

■ Some 43 percent of burglars come through first-floor windows or the back door.

■ Only 2 to 3 percent of break-ins are through second-floor windows or doors.

■ Household burglaries involve violence in only about 1 in every 25 break-ins.

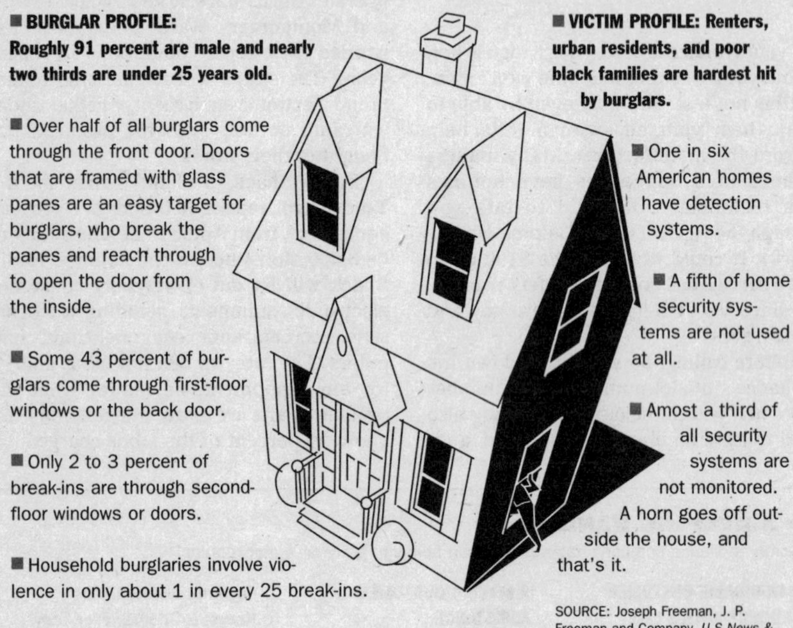

■ **VICTIM PROFILE: Renters, urban residents, and poor black families are hardest hit by burglars.**

■ One in six American homes have detection systems.

■ A fifth of home security systems are not used at all.

■ Amost a third of all security systems are not monitored. A horn goes off outside the house, and that's it.

SOURCE: Joseph Freeman, J. P. Freeman and Company, *U.S News & World Report.*

■ TO CATCH A THIEF

Home security specialists are working in the spirit of the genius who brought us X-ray specs and the joy buzzer. Melanie Franklin, founder of the gadget-laden *Safety Zone* catalog, ☎ 800-999-3030, says the following items are brisk sellers:

$19.95: A package of phony alarm-company decals; four for windows and two signs to post outdoors. Thieves presumably believe they are the real thing.

$119: Solar-powered outdoor security lights that turn on when they sense movement. The halogen security light goes for $69.95.

$129: An alarm that barks like a dog when it detects movement. The dog alarm can sense movement within 16 feet—even through a solid wall.

$329: Closed-circuit TV. Place the camera outside your house, hook up a wireless remote receiver to your TV, and watch the action. For $349, you can get the same system for the nursery with the camera disguised as a teddy bear.

EXPERT TIPS

DRINK NO WINE BEFORE ITS TIME

Budding oenophiles can start a modest cellar for $1,000. Here's how

Wine collecting is not an inexpensive hobby, but it doesn't require a huge upfront investment either. A beginner can start a wine collection simply by placing a case of wine on its side in a cool place. As your tastes become more refined, you can build a wine cellar and stock it with a wider selection.

Temperature is perhaps the most important element in maintaining wine at home. Experts advise keeping the wine in the coolest, driest part of your house. If that happens to be in your basement, stay clear of furnaces and damp areas along outer walls. High humidity will cause corks to mold and damage the wine. If a basement is not an option, try a cool closet or a dry corner of the garage. The ideal temperature range is between 50 and 60 degrees Fahrenheit. Every effort should be made to keep the temperature constant, although storing wine at 70 degrees or so for not more than a few weeks shouldn't harm it. The wine will simply mature faster.

To store your wine collection, place wine bottles on their sides in racks or bins. Simple metal or wood wine racks can be found for less than $50. Two sources of wine accessories are International Wine Accessories, ☎ 800-527-4072, and the Wine Enthusiast Catalog, ☎ 800-231-0100. Most wines, even the very best, reach their peak within 15 years.

When it comes to stocking your wine cellar, start with one bottle each of a variety of brands to find your favorites. A good red wine will have a balance of fruit, alcohol, acid, and tannin, which is produced by grape skins during fermentation. Some white wines have a crisp flavor with a touch of acidity. Others are highly aromatic. For descriptions of individual wines, try *The 1995 Ultimate Guide to Buying Wine* (M. Shanken Communications).

■ HOW DO YOU STOCK A WINE CELLAR FOR AROUND $1,000?

Stephen Tanzer, editor and publisher of *International Wine Cellar*, a bimonthly newsletter, drew up the following list. Tanzer advises buying three bottles of each and drinking the whites and the first group of reds within a year or two.

WHITE WINES

- *1993* **Domaine Delétang Montlouis Sec Les Batisses**, *Loire Valley*, **$14**
- *1993* **Columbia Winery Woodburne Cuvée Chardonnay,** *Washington, $11*
- *1993* **Lucien Crochet Chêne Marchand Sancerre,** *Loire Valley, $18*
- 1993 **Chalk Hill Sauvignon Blanc**, *Sonoma Co., $14*
- *1992* **Trimbach Riesling Réserve**, *Alsace, $12*
- *Non-vint.* **Cattier 1er Cru Brut Champagne**, *$25*

REDS

- *1993* **Etude Carneros Pinot Noir,** *Napa, $25*
- *1990* **Remelluri Rioja Reserva,** *Spain, $15*
- *1990* **Felsina Chianti Classico Riserva**, *Italy, $20*
- *1993* **Château d'Oupia Cuvée des Barons Minervois,** *Languedoc, $11*
- *1992* **Rothbury Estate Shiraz,** *Southeastern Australia, $10*
- *1993* **Ravenswood Old Vines Zinfandel,** *Sonoma County, $14*

AGEWORTHY REDS

- *1990* **Château Léoville-Barton,** *Bordeaux, $30*
- *1993* **Les Cailloux Châteauneuf du Pape,** *Rhone Valley, $20*
- *1991* **Pesquera Reserva Ribera del Duero**, *Spain, $25*
- *1990* **Altesino Brunello di Montalcino**, *Tuscany, $40*
- *1991* **Beringer Vineyard Cabernet Sauvignon Private Reserve,** *Napa Valley, $35*

THE WINE ADVOCATE'S VINTAGE GUIDE 1970-93

The following chart was put together by Robert M. Parker, Jr., for Wine Advocate. Parker warns that any vintage chart should be regarded as a very general, overall rating of a particular viticultural region. Such charts are filled with exceptions to the rule—astonishingly good wines from skillful or lucky vintners in years rated mediocre, and thin, diluted, characterless wines from incompetent or greedy producers in great years.

Regions	1970	1971	1972	1973	1974	1975	1976	1977	1978	1979	1980	1981
BURGUNDY												
St.Julien/Pauillac St. Est.	87 ●	82 ●	67 ●	65 ●	68 ●	89 ○	84 ●	73 ●	87 ●	85 ●	78 ●	85 ●
Margaux	85 ●	83 ●	71 ●	85 ●	74 ●	78 ○	77 ●	71 ●	87 ●	87 ●	79 ●	82 ●
Graves	87 ●	86 ●	75 ●	76 ●	76 ●	89 ○	71 ●	75 ●	90 ●	88 ●	78 ●	84 ●
Pomeroi	90 ●	87 ●	65 ●	70 ●	75 ●	94 ●	82 ●	72 ●	84 ●	86 ●	79 ●	86 ●
St. Emilion	85 ●	83 ●	65 ●	67 ●	62 ●	85 ●	82 ●	60 ●	84 ●	84 ●	72 ●	82 ●
Barsac/Saulemes	84 ●	86 ●	55 ●	65 ●	50 ●	90 ○	87 ●	50 ●	75 ●	75 ●	85 ●	85 ●
BURGUNDY												
Côte de Nuits (red)	82 ●	87 ●	86 ●	58 ●	64 ●	50 ●	86 ●	60 ●	88 ●	77 ●	84 ●	72 ●
Côte de Beaune (red)	82 ●	87 ●	83 ●	60 ●	62 ●	50 ●	86 ●	55 ●	86 ●	77 ●	78 ●	74 ●
White	83 ●	88 ●	84 ●	87 ●	75 ●	65 ●	86 ●	80 ●	88 ●	88 ●	75 ●	86 ●
RHONE												
N. Côte Rotie Hermitage	90 ●	84 ●	86 ●	72 ●	70 ●	73 ●	82 ●	72 ●	98 ○	87 ●	83 ●	75 ●
S. Châteauneuf du Pape	88 ●	82 ●	86 ●	74 ●	70 ●	60 ●	75 ●	70 ●	97 ●	88 ●	77 ●	88 ●
BEAUJOLAIS	—	—	—	—	—	—	86 ●	50 ●	84 ●	80 ●	60 ●	83 ●
ALSACE	80 ●	90 ●	55 ●	75 ●	74 ●	82 ●	90 ●	70 ●	80 ●	84 ●	80 ●	86 ●
LOIRE	—	—	—	—	—	—	86 ●	70 ●	85 ●	83 ●	72 ●	82 ●
CHAMPAGNE	85 ●	90 ●	NV	82 ●	NV	90 ●	90 ●	NV	NV	88 ●	NV	84 ●
ITALY												
Piedmont	84 ●	90 ●	50 ●	70 ●	85 ○	65 ●	67 ●	67 ●	95 ○	86 ●	70 ●	80 ●
Chianti	84 ●	88 ●	50 ●	68 ●	80 ●	84 ●	60 ●	72 ●	85 ●	75 ●	70 ●	82 ●
GERMANY	80 ●	90 ●	50 ●	67 ●	60 ●	85 ●	90 ●	70 ●	72 ●	84 ●	65 ●	82 ●
VINTAGE PORT	90 ●	NV	78 ●	NV	NV	82 ●	NV	95 ○	83 ○	NV	84 ○	NV
SPAIN												
Rioja	90 ●	74 ●	67 ●	86 ●	65 ●	84 ●	86 ●	70 ●	84 ●	79 ●	75 ●	87 ●
Penedes	—	—	—	—	—	—	—	—	—	—	85 ●	84 ●
AUSTRALIA New South Wales and Victoria			—	—	—	—	—	—	—	—	88 ●	85 ●
CALIFORNIA – NORTH COAST												
Cabernet Sauvignon	92 ●	70 ●	65 ●	88 ●	90 ●	85 ●	90 ○	84 ●	92 ●	80 ●	87 ●	85 ●
Chardonnay	83 ●	82 ●	84 ●	85 ●	75 ●	86 ●	80 ●	83 ●	86 ●	83 ●	88 ●	86 ●
Zinfandel	96 ●	60 ●	50 ●	86 ●	68 ●	80 ●	87 ●	85 ●	86 ●	83 ●	82 ●	82 ●
Pinot Noir	—	—	—	—	—	—	—	—	84 ●	80 ●	85 ●	83 ●
OREGON Pinot Noir	—	—	—	—	—	—	—	—	—	—	86 ●	86 ●
WASHINGTON Cabernet Sauvignon		—	—	—	—	—	—	—	—	—	—	—

RATING SYSTEM

90–100 = The finest
80–89 = Above average to excellent
70–79 = Average
60–69 = Below average
Below 60 = Poor

Red numbers = Top vintages

EXPLANATIONS OF SYMBOLS

● = Caution, may now be too old or irregular
○ = Early maturing
○= Still tannic and youthful
● = Ready to drink
NV = Non-vintage

SOURCE: Robert M. Parker, Jr., for the *Wine Advocate*, © 1995.

Regions	1982	1983	1984	1985	1986	1987	1988	1989	1990	1991	1992	1993
BURGUNDY												
St.Julien/Pauillac St. Est.	98 ●	86 ●	72 ○	92 ●	94 ○	82 ●	87 ○	97 ○	98 ○	75 ●	79 ○	86 ○
Margaux	86 ●	95 ●	68 ●	86 ●	90 ○	76 ●	85 ○	85 ○	90 ○	74 ●	75 ○	86 ○
Graves	88 ●	89 ●	79 ●	90 ●	89 ○	84 ●	89 ○	89 ○	90 ●	74 ●	75 ○	87 ○
Pomeroi	96 ●	90 ●	65 ●	88 ●	87 ○	85 ●	89 ○	95 ○	95 ○	60 ●	82 ●	88 ○
St. Emilion	94 ●	89 ●	69 ●	87 ●	88 ○	74 ●	88 ○	88 ○	98 ○	65 ●	75 ●	84 ●
Barsac/Saulemes	75 ●	88 ○	70 ●	85 ●	94 ○	70 ●	98 ○	90 ○	96 ○	70 ●	70 ●	70 ●
BURGUNDY												
Côte de Nuits (red)	82 ●	85 ●	78 ●	87 ●	74 ●	85 ●	86 ○	89 ●	92 ●	86 ○	78 ●	87 ○
Côte de Beaune (red)	80 ●	78 ●	70 ●	87 ●	72 ●	79 ●	86 ●	88 ●	90 ●	72 ○	82 ●	86 ○
White	88 ●	85 ●	80 ●	89 ●	90 ●	79 ●	82 ●	92 ●	87 ●	70 ●	92 ●	72 ●
RHONE												
N. Côte Rotie Hermitage	85 ●	89 ○	75 ○	90 ○	84 ○	86 ○	92 ○	96 ○	92 ○	92 ○	78 ○	65 ●
S. Châteauneuf du Pape	70 ●	87 ●	72 ●	88 ●	78 ●	60 ●	88 ●	96 ○	95 ○	70 ●	78 ●	89 ○
BEAUJOLAIS	75 ●	86 ●	75 ●	87 ●	84 ●	85 ●	86 ●	92 ●	86 ●	90 ●	77 ●	86 ●
ALSACE	82 ●	93 ●	75 ●	88 ●	82 ●	83 ●	86 ●	93 ●	93 ●	75 ○	85 ○	87 ●
LOIRE	84 ●	84 ●	68 ●	88 ●	87 ●	82 ●	88 ●	92 ●	90 ●	75 ●	80 ●	86 ●
CHAMPAGNE	90 ●	84 ●	NV	95 ●	89 ●	NV	88 ○	90 ●	87 ○	NV	NV	NV
ITALY												
Piedmont	92 ○	75 ●	65 ●	92 ○	78 ●	85 ○	90 ○	96 ○	96 ○	76 ○	74 ●	86 ○
Chianti	86 ●	80 ●	60 ●	93 ●	84 ●	73 ●	89 ○	72 ●	90 ○	73 ○	72 ●	74 ●
GERMANY	80 ●	90 ●	70 ●	85 ●	80 ●	82 ●	89 ●	90 ○	92 ○	85 ○	90 ●	87 ●
VINTAGE PORT	86 ○	92 ○	NV	95 ○	NV	NV	NV	NV	NV	90 ○	95 ○	NV
SPAIN												
Rioja	92 ●	74 ●	78 ●	82 ●	82 ○	82 ○	87 ○	90 ○	87 ○	76 ○	85 ○	87 ○
Penedes	87 ●	85 ●	86 ●	85 ●	77 ●	88 ○	87 ○	88 ○	87 ○	74 ○	82 ○	87 ○
AUSTRALIA	83 ●	76 ●	84 ●	86 ●	90 ○	87 ○	85 ○	88 ○	88 ○	89 ○	87 ●	87 ●
CALIFORNIA – NORTH COAST												
Cabernet Sauvignon	86 ●	76 ●	92 ●	92 ○	90 ○	90 ○	75 ○	84 ○	94 ○	94 ○	93 ○	91 ○
Chardonnay	85 ●	85 ●	88 ●	84 ●	90 ●	75 ●	89 ●	76 ●	90 ●	85 ●	92 ●	90 ●
Zinfandel	80 ●	78 ●	88 ●	88 ○	87 ○	90 ●	82 ●	83 ●	91 ●	91 ●	90 ●	90 ○
Pinot Noir	84 ●	85 ●	85 ●	86 ○	84 ●	86 ○	87 ●	85 ●	86 ○	86 ●	88 ●	88 ○
OREGON Pinot Noir	84 ●	90 ●	65 ●	87 ●	85 ●	72 ●	88 ●	86 ●	90 ●	87 ●	88 ●	89 ●
WASH. Cabernet Sauvignon	78 ●	92 ○	72 ●	85 ○	78 ●	85 ○	88 ○	92 ○	87 ○	65 ●	89 ○	87 ○

HOME HAZARDS

ENVIRONMENTAL HOMEFRONT

The keys to keeping your home free from radon, lead, or asbestos

Environmental pollution can make a mockery of the sanctuary of one's home. To advise potential homeowners of the environmental hazards that may be present in your home's walls, plumbing, and foundations, a group of government agencies and private organizations, including the Environmental Protection Agency, the Department of Housing and Urban Development, and the National Association of Realtors have joined forces to develop a primer for consumers. An adaptation follows:

RADON

Radon is a colorless, odorless, tasteless gas that occurs as a byproduct of the natural decay of uranium present in the Earth. It is present in varying quantities in the atmosphere and in soils around the world.

■ **Why is radon harmful?**

Radon gas breaks down into radioactive particles that remain in the air. Out of doors, radon is not a problem for human beings because the surrounding air allows the gas to diffuse in the atmosphere. But when radon gas and its decay products enter your home, they remain in circulation in the enclosed air. As you breathe these particles, they can become trapped in your lungs. As these particles continue to break down, they release bursts of energy (radiation) that can damage lung tissue. This damage can cause lung cancer.

■ **How does radon enter a home?**

Through small spaces and openings, such as cracks in concrete, floor drains, sump pump openings, wall/floor joints in basements, and the pores in hollow block walls. It also can seep into groundwater and remain entrapped there. There is greater potential for a radon problem if a home is supplied with water from a groundwater source (such as a well). The likelihood of radon in the water supply is greatly reduced for homes supplied with water from a municipal water supply.

■ **How does one test for radon?**

Preliminary screening test kits can be bought over the counter in many hardware, grocery, and convenience stores. Tests that measure the amount of radon in water normally require you to send a sample of tap water to a laboratory for analysis. State agencies should be consulted if the home water supply is a suspected source of radon.

When purchasing a radon detection kit, you should examine the package for indications that the kit has been approved by federal or state health, environmental protection, or consumer protection agencies. Short-term testing (ranging from a few days to several months) is one way to determine if a potential problem exists. Long-term testing (lasting for up to one year) is a more accurate way to determine if radon is present. Both short- and long-term testing devices are easy to use and relatively inexpensive.

What's an acceptable level of indoor radon?

The concentration of radon in air is measured in units of picocuries per liter of air (pCi/L). Estimates suggest that most homes contain from one to two picocuries of radon per liter of air. If preliminary tests indicate radon levels greater than 4 picocuries per liter of air in livable areas of the home, the Environmental Protection Agency recommends that a follow-up test be conducted. No level of radon is considered safe; there are risks even at very low levels. To put this into perspective, the EPA estimates that the risk of an annual radon level of 4 picocuries is equivalent to the risk from smoking 10 cigarettes a day or having 200 chest X-rays a year. A picocurie level of 40 is equivalent to smoking two packs a day, while a level of 100 is equal to 2,000 chest X-rays a year.

What does it cost to reduce the level of radon in a home?

The costs will depend on the number of radon sources, the amount of radon in the surrounding land or in the water supply, and the kind of construction used in the home. Normally, installing radon reduction equipment costs from several hundred dollars to several thousand dollars. If the treatment involves fans, pumps, or other appliances, operating costs for these devices also may increase monthly utility bills.

Is radon removal a "do-it-yourself project"?

Not usually. In some cases, homeowners should be able to treat the problem themselves; however, it is not always possible for homeowners to diagnose the source of

STATE RADON CONTACTS

Who to call if you suspect a problem:

	☎
ALABAMA	800-582-1866
ALASKA	800-478-4845
ARIZONA	602-255-4845
ARKANSAS	501-661-2301
CALIFORNIA	800-745-7236
COLORADO	800-846-3986
CONNECTICUT	203-566-3122
DELAWARE	800-554-4636
DISTRICT OF COLUMBIA	202-727-5728
FLORIDA	800-543-8279
GEORGIA	800-745-0037
HAWAI'I	808-586-4700
IDAHO	800-445-8647
ILLINOIS	800-325-1245
INDIANA	800-272-9723
IOWA	800-383-5992
KANSAS	913-296-1560
KENTUCKY	502-564-3700
LOUISIANA	800-256-2494
MAINE	800-232-0842
MARYLAND	800-872-3666
MASSACHUSETTS	413-586-7525
MICHIGAN	517-335-8190
MINNESOTA	800-798-9050
MISSISSIPPI	800-626-7739
MISSOURI	800-669-7236
MONTANA	406-444-3671
NEBRASKA	800-334-9491
NEVADA	702-687-5394
NEW HAMPSHIRE	800-852-3345 X4674
NEW JERSEY	800-648-0394
NEW MEXICO	505-827-4300
NEW YORK	800-458-1158
NORTH CAROLINA	919-571-4141
NORTH DAKOTA	701-221-5188
OHIO	800-523-4439
OKLAHOMA	405-271-5221
OREGON	503-731-4014
PENNSYLVANIA	800-237-2366
PUERTO RICO	809-767-3563
RHODE ISLAND	401-277-2438
SOUTH CAROLINA	800-768-0362
SOUTH DAKOTA	605-773-3351
TENNESSEE	800-232-1139
TEXAS	512-834-6688
UTAH	801-538-6734
VERMONT	800-640-0601
VIRGINIA	800-468-0138
WASHINGTON	800-323-9727
WEST VIRGINIA	800-922-1255
WISCONSIN	608-267-4795
WYOMING	800-458-5847

radon or to install systems that will reduce the level. Radon source diagnosis and mitigation normally require skills and tools not available to the average homeowner. When seeking a contractor to assist with a radon problem, consult local, county, or state government agencies for a recommendation of qualified radon reduction contractors.

LEAD

Lead is a metallic element found worldwide in rocks and soils. Its toxic effects have been known since ancient times. Recent research has shown that lead represents a greater hazard at lower levels of concentration than had been thought. Airborne lead enters the body when an individual breathes lead particles or swallows lead dust. Until recently, the most important source of airborne dust was automobile exhaust.

■ Why is lead harmful?

When ingested, lead accumulates in the blood, bones, and soft tissue of the body. High concentrations of lead in the body can cause death or permanent damage to the central nervous system, the brain, the kidneys, and red blood cells. Even low levels of lead may increase high blood pressure in adults. Infants, children, pregnant women, and fetuses are more vulnerable to lead exposure than others because the lead is more easily absorbed into growing bodies and their tissues are more sensitive to the damaging effects of the lead. Because of a child's smaller body weight, an equal concentration of lead is more damaging to a child than it would be to an adult.

■ Where is lead found in the home?

Lead can be present in drinking water, in paint used to decorate the interior or exterior of a home, in the dust within a home, and in soil around the home.

■ Are there acceptable levels for lead in drinking water?

Existing regulations set the maximum contamination level and goal at 50 micrograms per liter, but the EPA has proposed revising those standards to reflect new knowledge about the harmful effects of lead.

■ Can one tell by looking at the plumbing if water in a home will contain too much lead?

No. Visual inspection of pipe joints and solder lines is not an accurate means of determining whether or not decaying solder is a source of lead. The only way to determine lead levels in water is to test a sample of the water. Should homeowners suspect that lead is present in drinking water, or if they wish to have water tested, they should contact local, county, or state health or environmental departments for information about qualified testing laboratories.

■ How prevalent is lead-based paint?

According to the EPA, lead-based paint was applied to approximately two-thirds of the houses built in the United States before 1940; one-third of the houses built from 1940 to 1960; and to an indeterminate (but smaller) portion of houses that have been built since 1960.

■ How is lead-based paint harmful?

The health hazards to children from eating lead-based paint chips have been known for some time, but other sources of exposure to lead in household air and dust have been documented only recently. Lead can enter the air within a home when surfaces covered with lead-based paint are scraped, sanded, or heated with an open flame in paint-stripping procedures. Lead particles freed in fine dust or vapors settle into carpet fibers and fabric and can be recirculated by normal household cleaning and through the normal hand-to-mouth behavior of children, which results in the ingestion of potentially harmful amounts of any lead present in household dust. Lead also can enter household air from outdoor sources such as contaminated soil and from activities that require the use of solder.

■ How does one eliminate lead-based paint?

It is best to leave lead-based paint undisturbed if it is in good condition and there is little possibility that it will be eaten by children. Other procedures include covering the paint with wallpaper or some other building material, or completely replacing the painted surface. Pregnant women and women who plan to become pregnant

THE FILTERS THAT REFRESH

Home water filters don't all attack the same problems, so it's important to have your water tested before you choose a filter. Your options include:

■ **PHYSICAL FILTERS:** Designed to sift out particles such as dirt, sediment, and rust, these filters are usually made of fabric, fiber, ceramic, or other screening. They may be effective enough to remove particles as small as asbestos fibers, but they can't screen out all suspect organisms and so shouldn't be relied upon to filter microbiologically contaminated waters.

■ **ACTIVATED CARBON FILTERS:** These may improve your water's smell, taste, and appearance by removing some organic chemical contaminants. But they don't eliminate salts, metals, and most inorganic chemicals and should not be relied upon to treat water containing problem organisms. To avoid becoming sodden with chemical and bacterial impurities, they need to be changed at regular intervals.

■ **REVERSE OSMOSIS UNITS:** These systems have water pass through a membrane and collect in a storage tank. They are largely effective in removing most inorganic chemicals, including salts, lead, and other metals, asbestos, minerals, nitrates, and some organic chemicals. But they waste about 75 percent of the tap water run through them and slow the flow of water. The membranes also are susceptible to decay and failure and need periodic replacement.

■ **DISTILLATION UNITS:** By vaporizing water and then condensing it, these units eliminate most dissolved solids, including salts, metals, minerals, asbestos fibers, particles, and some organic chemicals. But they're not effective against all chemical impurities and bacteria, and the heating will raise energy bills.

■ **ULTRAVIOLET DISINFECTION:** Destroys bacteria and viruses. But it can't eliminate most chemical pollutants and, unless disinfection is regularly maintained, dissolved and suspended solids may keep the water from receiving enough exposure to ultraviolet light to be healthy.

SOURCE: Federal Trade Commission.

should not do this work. Professional paint removal is costly and requires everyone not involved in the procedure to leave the premises during removal and cleanup.

ASBESTOS

Asbestos is a fibrous mineral found in rocks and soil throughout the world. It has been used in construction because it is strong, durable, fire retardant, and an efficient insulator. Alone or in combination with other materials, asbestos can be fashioned into a variety of products that have numerous applications within the building industry, for example, for flooring, ceiling tiles, shingles, insulation, or as a fire retardant for heating and electrical systems.

■ **Why is asbestos dangerous?**

Once ingested, asbestos fibers lodge in the lungs. Asbestos persists in tissue and concentrates as repeated exposures occur. It can cause cancer of the lung and stomach after prolonged work-related exposure to it. The health effects of lower exposures in the home are less certain; however, experts are unable to provide assurance that any level of exposure to asbestos fibers is completely safe.

■ **When do asbestos-containing products in the home become a health risk?**

Home health risks arise when age, accidental damage, or normal cleaning, construction, or remodeling activities cause the asbestos-containing materials to crumble, flake, or deteriorate. When this happens, minute asbestos fibers are released into the air and can be inhaled. The fibers can cling to clothing, tools, and exposed flesh; cleanup operations can then dislodge the fibers and free them to circulate in the air.

■ Where in the home is asbestos found?

According to the EPA, many homes constructed in the United States during the past 20 years probably do not contain asbestos products. But asbestos is sometimes found around pipes and furnaces in older homes; in some vinyl flooring materials; in ceiling tiles; in exterior roofing shingles and siding; in some wallboards; mixed with other materials around pipes, ducts, and beams; in patching compounds or textured paints; and in door gaskets on furnaces, and ovens.

■ How can one tell if a home contains asbestos?

A professional trained in working with asbestos knows how to take samples properly and what corrective actions will be the most effective.

FACT FILE:

ART FOR SAFETY'S SAKE

Not all art supplies are safe to use, especially by children:

■ **Powdered clay is both toxic and an irritant.** *Talc-free, pre-mixed clay is a good alternative.*

■ **Permanent felt-tip markers may be toxic.** *Use water-based markers.*

■ **Epoxy glue is flammable and an irritant.** *Substitute white or yellow glue, school paste, or certain glue sticks.*

■ **Instant papier mâché is toxic and irritates.** *Newspaper and a simple flour paste will do just fine.*

SOURCE: Environmental Hazards Management Institute, Durham, N.H.

EPA regional asbestos coordinators can provide information on qualified contractors and laboratories. The federal government recently has required the labeling of new products containing asbestos and a phased-in ban of most asbestos products by 1996.

■ What should one do if asbestos is found?

Generally, if the material is in good condition and is in an area where it is not likely to be disturbed, you can leave the asbestos-containing material in place. Extreme care should be exercised in handling, cleaning, or working with material suspected of containing asbestos. If the material is likely to be banged, handled, or taken apart (especially during remodeling), homeowners should hire a trained contractor and reduce their exposure as much as possible.

■ Can you aggravate an asbestos problem by the things you do?

Common construction and remodeling operations can release varying amounts of asbestos fibers if the material being worked on contains asbestos. These operations include hammering, drilling, sawing, sanding, cutting, and otherwise shaping or molding the material. Routine cleaning operations (such as brushing, dusting, vacuum cleaning, scraping, and scrubbing) can also release hazardous fibers from asbestos-containing materials. Vinyl flooring products that contain asbestos can be cleaned in a conventional manner, but these products can release some asbestos fibers if they are vigorously sanded, ground, drilled, filed, or scraped. When properly installed on the exterior of a home, asbestos-containing products present little risk to human health. However, if siding is worn or damaged, spray painting it will help seal in the fibers.

■ How difficult is asbestos removal?

It depends on the amount of the product present, the percentage of asbestos it contains, and the manner in which asbestos is incorporated into the product. Total removal of even small amounts of asbestos-containing material is usually the last alternative. Homeowners should contact local,

ACCIDENTS DO HAPPEN

The National Safety Council reports that about 22,500 Americans died from accidents in the home in 1993. Falls caused nearly one-third of those deaths; fires and burns about a fifth, and all other types, about half. More than a third of those killed were 75 or older. Persons 25 to 44 made up about a fifth; children under 5 about one-tenth. Below are the leading causes of accidental death in the home in 1993, rounded to the nearest hundred.

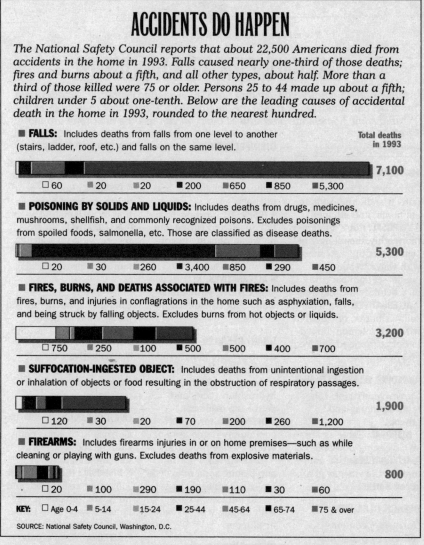

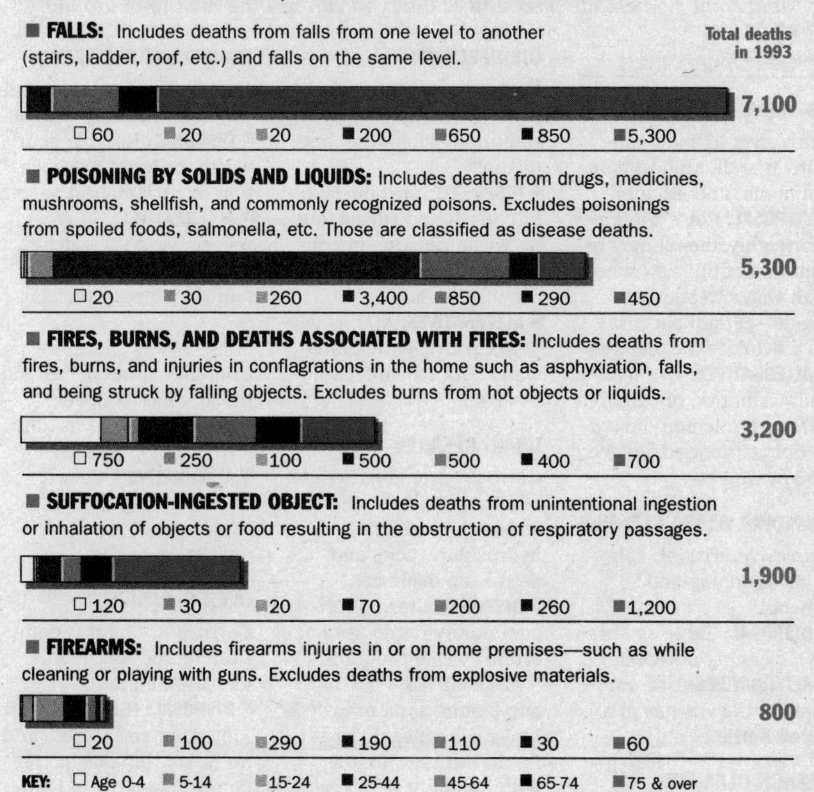
FALLS: Includes deaths from falls from one level to another (stairs, ladder, roof, etc.) and falls on the same level.
Total deaths in 1993
7,100
60 20 20 200 650 850 5,300
POISONING BY SOLIDS AND LIQUIDS: Includes deaths from drugs, medicines, mushrooms, shellfish, and commonly recognized poisons. Excludes poisonings from spoiled foods, salmonella, etc. Those are classified as disease deaths.
5,300
20 30 260 3,400 850 290 450
FIRES, BURNS, AND DEATHS ASSOCIATED WITH FIRES: Includes deaths from fires, burns, and injuries in conflagrations in the home such as asphyxiation, falls, and being struck by falling objects. Excludes burns from hot objects or liquids.
3,200
750 250 100 500 500 400 700
SUFFOCATION-INGESTED OBJECT: Includes deaths from unintentional ingestion or inhalation of objects or food resulting in the obstruction of respiratory passages.
1,900
120 30 20 70 200 260 1,200
FIREARMS: Includes firearms injuries in or on home premises—such as while cleaning or playing with guns. Excludes deaths from explosive materials.
800
20 100 290 190 110 30 60
KEY: Age 0-4 5-14 15-24 25-44 45-64 65-74 75 & over

SOURCE: National Safety Council, Washington, D.C.

state, or federal health or consumer product agencies before deciding on a course of action. To ensure safety and elimination of health hazards, asbestos repair or removal should be performed only by properly trained contractors.

Many home repair or remodeling contractors do not yet have the requisite training, experience, or equipment to work safely with asbestos. Furthermore, asbestos removal workers are protected under federal regulations that specify special training, protective clothing, and special respirators for these workers.

Source: Adapted from *A Home Buyer's Guide to Environmental Hazards*, a joint project of American Bankers Association, American Institute of Real Estate Appraisers, Department of Veterans Affairs, Department of Housing and Urban Development, Federal National Mortgage Association, Federal Deposit Insurance Corporation, Freddie Mac, Mortgage Bankers Association of America, Mortgage Insurance Companies of America, National Association of Realtors, National Council of Savings Institutions, Office of Thrift Supervision, Society of Real Estate Appraisers, The Appraisal Foundation, U.S. Environmental Protection Agency, and U.S. League of Savings Institutions.

ENVIRONMENTALIST'S GUIDE

FIRST YOU USE 'EM, THEN YOU LOSE 'EM

Many household products contain hazardous chemicals that, if not discarded properly, can do lasting harm to the environment. Here's how to dispose of them and some homemade alternatives that you can use the next time around.

HOUSEHOLD CHEMICALS

ABRASIVE CLEANER

Corrosive, irritant, contains trisodiumphosphate, ammonia, and ethanol.

■ **DISPOSAL:** Rinse container thoroughly, then it may be sent to landfill; also check with water treatment plants—certain bacteria may detoxify the material.

■ **ALTERNATIVES:** Use baking soda or borax, or rub area with half a lemon dipped in borax (toxic to children and pets).

AMMONIA-BASED CLEANER

Corrosive, irritant, contains ammonia and ethanol.

■ **DISPOSAL:** Same as abrasive cleaning powder.

■ **ALTERNATIVES:** Use undiluted white vinegar in a spray bottle.

BLEACH CLEANER

Corrosive, contains sodium or potassium hydroxide, hydrogen peroxide, sodium or calcium hypochlorite.

■ **DISPOSAL:** Fully use products, then dispose of waste thoroughly, can be at landfill.

■ **ALTERNATIVES:** For laundry, use 1/2 cup white vinegar, baking soda, or borax per load.

DISINFECTANT

Corrosive, contains diethylene or methylene glycol, sodium hypochlorite, and phenols.

■ **DISPOSAL:** If products are fully used and rinsed, and no waste remains in container, it may go to landfill, if necessary.

■ **ALTERNATIVES:** Mix 1/2 cup borax with 1 gal. boiling water. Not a disinfectant, however.

DRAIN CLEANER

Corrosive, contains sodium or potassium hydroxide, sodium hypochlorite, hydrochloric acid, and petroleum distillates.

■ **DISPOSAL:** Store until community organizes hazardous waste program.

■ **ALTERNATIVES:** Pour in 1/2 cup baking soda followed by 1/2 cup vinegar; let set for 15 minutes, follow with boiling water; snake or plunger.

FURNITURE POLISH

Flammable, contains diethylene, glycol, petroleum distillates, and nitrobenzene.

■ **DISPOSAL:** Same as drain cleaners.

■ **ALTERNATIVES:** Mix 3 parts olive oil to 1 part vinegar. For water stains, use toothpaste on damp cloth.

HOUSEHOLD BATTERY

Contains mercury, zinc, silver, lithium, and cadmium.

■ **DISPOSAL:** Recycle your waste, bring to a gas station or reclamation center.

■ **ALTERNATIVES:** Solar power, wind-up watches, rechargeables (may contain toxic heavy metals).

MOTHBALLS

Contain naphthalenes and paradichlorobenzene.

■ **DISPOSAL:** Same as abrasive cleaning powder.

■ **ALTERNATIVES:** Cedar chips or blocks; clean clothes well, put in airtight storage bag.

OVEN CLEANER

Corrosive, contains potassium or sodium hydroxide, and ammonia.

■ **DISPOSAL:** If products are fully used and rinsed, and no waste remains in container, it may go to landfill, if necessary.

■ **ALTERNATIVES:** Let mixture of 2 tbs. castile soap, 2 tsp. borax, and 2 cups water set in oven for 20 minutes; scrub with baking soda and salt.

PHOTOGRAPHIC CHEMICALS

Corrosive, irritant, contain silver, acetic acid, hydroquinone, sodium sulfite.

■ ENVIRONMENTALIST'S GUIDE

■ **DISPOSAL:** Should be safely stored until community organizes a hazardous waste program.
■ **ALTERNATIVES:** Unknown.

POOL CHEMICALS

Corrosive, contain muriatic acid, sodium hypochlorite, and algicide.
■ **DISPOSAL:** Rinse container thoroughly and it may be sent to landfill; check with water treatment plants, as certain bacteria may detoxify the material.
■ **ALTERNATIVES:** Disinfectants: ozone or UV-light system. pH: consult baking soda box for amount to add for proper pH.

RUG AND UPHOLSTERY CLEANER

Corrosive, contains naphthalene, perchloroethylene, oxalic acid, diethylene, and glycol.
■ **DISPOSAL:** Store until community organizes a hazardous waste program.
■ **ALTERNATIVES:** Clean immediately with soda water or baking soda paste, then vacuum (see "Out, Out Damn Spot," page 433).

TOILET BOWL CLEANER

Corrosive, irritant, contains muriatic (hydrochloric) or oxalic acid, paradichlorobenzene, and calcium hypochlorite.
■ **DISPOSAL:** Same as oven cleaner.
■ **ALTERNATIVES:** Coat bowl with paste of lemon juice and borax (toxic to children), let set, then scrub.

PAINTS

ENAMEL OR OIL-BASED PAINT

Flammable, toxic. Contains aliphatic and aromatic hydrocarbons, some pigments.
■ **ALTERNATIVES:** Latex or water-based paint.
■ **DISPOSAL:** Recycle wastes by bringing to service station or reclamation center.

LATEX OR WATER-BASED PAINT

May be toxic. Contains ethylene, glycol, glycol ethers, phenyl mercuric acetate, some pigments, resins.
■ **DISPOSAL:** Waste can be disposed of at some wastewater treatment plants where bacteria can detoxify the chemical; also may be recycled.
■ **ALTERNATIVES:** Latex without the above ingredients or limestone-based (whitewash) paint.

RUST-PROOFING COATING

Flammable, toxic. Contains methylene chloride, petroleum distillates, toluene, xylene, some pigments.
■ **DISPOSAL:** Should be safely stored until community organizes a hazardous waste program.
■ **ALTERNATIVES:** Unknown.

THINNERS, TURPENTINE

Toxic, flammable. Contain alcohol, acetone, esters, ketones, turpentine, petroleum distillates.
■ **DISPOSAL:** Check for disposal at local water treatment plants.
■ **ALTERNATIVES:** Use water in water-based paints.

PAINT AND VARNISH REMOVER

Flammable, toxic. Contains acetone, ketones, alcohol, xylene, toluene, methylene, chloride.
■ **DISPOSAL:** Wastes should be safely stored until community organizes hazardous waste program.
■ **ALTERNATIVES:** For lead-free paint, use sandpaper or scraper and heat gun.

WOOD PRESERVATIVE

Flammable, toxic. Contains copper or zinc naphthenate, creosote, magnesium cluorosilicate, petroleum distillates, chlorinated phenols (PCP).
■ **DISPOSAL:** Wastes should be safely stored until community organizes hazardous waste program.
■ **ALTERNATIVES:** Use water-based wood preservative. (May still contain some of the above ingredients.)

STAIN AND VARNISH

Flammable, toxic. Contains mineral spirits, gylcol ethers, ketones, toluene, xylene.
■ **DISPOSAL:** Wastes should be safely stored until community organizes a hazardous waste program.
■ **ALTERNATIVES:** Use latex or water-based finishes.

SOURCE: Environmental Hazards Management Institute, Durham, N.H.

FENG SHUI

THE ART OF WIND AND WATER

Ancient ideas of harmony with one's environment are winning converts

Ancient civilizations paid no attention to lead poisoning, much less radon or asbestos contamination, but they had many ideas about keeping in harmony with their physical environment. While some cultures use amulets to protect an individual and connect that individual with the spirit of life around them, others maintain that harmony with one's environment comes from careful planning of the space one occupies. No culture took this concern further than the Chinese, who for thousands of years have practiced the art of feng shui, which translated literally means "wind and water." The goal of feng shui is to create balanced and auspicious relationships between individuals and their environment, both natural and man-made. Correct placement of home, office, and the various features of each (furniture, walls, rooms, windows), as well as gravesites is thought to portend well for an individual's prosperity, physical and emotional health, and harmony with others. The belief is that the external arrangements of one's environment affect the ch'i (translated as breath), or life energy that is the spirit and vital force of people, animals, and nature alike.

風水

While in certain parts of Asia feng shui has been practiced for millennia, its introduction to the West is quite recent. As more Chinese investors come to American cities, architects, real estate agents, and business people have learned just how important feng shui can be to prospective buyers. Buildings with bad feng shui simply do not attract the same throngs of customers as those with good feng shui.

Each feng shui master has a different way of looking at the feng shui of a given space. Some use a feng shui compass (called a luopan), some use a mystical tool called a ba-gua, and some rely on intuition to assess the feng shui of a building or room.

For Westerners seeking better feng shui for their living spaces, here are some tips from feng shui expert Sarah Rossbach. Her books include *Living Color: Master Lin Yun's Guide to Harmony Through Color* (Kodansha, 1994), *Feng Shui: The Chinese Art of Placement* (Viking, 1991), and *Interior Design with Feng Shui* (Penguin, 1987).

■ **Use mirrors, crystal balls, and lights.** Mirrors can be used to cure a wide variety of feng shui ills. Outside a building they are hung to reflect bad feng shui, whether it be from a road aimed at the building, a tall neighboring building, or a funeral parlor. Inside, the bigger the mirror, the better. Mirrors are hung to reflect good views of water or gardens, to draw in light from the outside, and to increase the illusion of expanse and light.

Small-faceted crystal balls are also widely used in feng shui. They are said to bring to the resident the gift of farsightedness and good perspective. Lights are also powerful feng shui solutions. If, for example, one lives in an L-shaped house one would be well-advised to install a floodlight outside to square off the missing corner.

■ **Employ sound.** Wind chimes are the typical sound device used in feng shui. Traditionally, they disperse bad interior and exterior feng shui and redirect ch'i in a beneficial way.

■ **Embrace living objects.** Plants and flowers, whether they are real, silk, or plastic, send nourishing ch'i throughout the room. They are said to bring clients and money to

EXPERT TIPS

THE FENG SHUI OF FURNITURE

If the foot of your bed faces the door, it's your funeral.

Feng shui expert Sarah Rossbach offers these tips on arranging your furniture for good feng shui:

■ **BEDROOM:** Optimally, a bed should lie diagonal to the door so that the occupant has the widest possible view, and so that ch'i flows smoothly. If not, occupants may be nervous and jumpy, traits that would affect their personal relationships and their performance at work. If for some reason a bed cannot lie diagonally across from the door, a mirror can be hung to reflect the entrance. The bed should not be placed so that the foot of the bed faces the door (this position is reminiscent of a funeral position, thus bringing bad feng shui into the room).

■ **KITCHEN:** The most important consideration is the placement of the stove. The stove should be located so that the chef can easily see anyone entering. If a cook is startled by something or someone, a nervous chain reaction is sparked which could include familial discord.

■ **LIVING ROOM:** In general, both the hosts and the guests should face the door. Furniture placement is important in evoking the appropriate feel of the room—e.g., formal or cozy.

■ **BATHROOM:** The bathroom, a place where water—symbolic of money—enters and leaves, represents occupants' internal plumbing and finances. Avoid placing the toilet opposite the door or residents may suffer financial misfortune, health disorders, or miscarriages. A bathroom should be bright and open, as opposed to cramped and small.

businesses and restaurants, and in the home they can resolve design imbalances such as acute room angles that might be affecting the life of the inhabitants.

Fish bowls and aquariums are used to encourage nourishing and money-making ch'i (water symbolizes money). In offices fish are used to absorb bad luck, those with aerators being the most effective.

■ **Don't fear moving and heavy objects.** Electrically powered and wind-powered objects such as mobiles, windmills, and weathervanes often stimulate ch'i circulation and deflect the threatening ch'i of such things as roads and long hallways. Sometimes an object such as a stone or statue can help stabilize an unsettling situation (holding down a job or holding on to a relationship).

■ **Hang the flutes up.** Bamboo flutes historically were used to report peace and good news and have come to represent peace, safety, and stability. They must be hung with their mouthpieces facing down. They also symbolize protection and are thus hung in homes and stores to drive away thieves.

■ **Choose colors carefully.** Colors can be applied to various areas of a room or building to affect a specific aspect of one's life. Black is the color of the water element and thus connotes money and wealth; red is an auspicious color used in Chinese celebrations and weddings; white is the color of mourning and is thus avoided; yellow represents longevity; green is growth and tranquility. In the home pastel colors should be used: blue, pink, or green.

GARDENING

THE QUICK-THUMB GARDENER

New time-saving techniques are transforming the green thumb's art

The average American adult has a third less time for leisure than 20 years ago, according to a recently published book, *The Overworked American*, by Juliet Schor. But what free time there is, is increasingly being devoted to gardening. According to a recent survey, three out of every four American households participate in some type of regular gardening, making it the leading leisure-time activity in the United States.

As with everything else, however, time pressures are transforming the way many backyard gardeners are pursuing their avocation. Short-cuts are in much demand today, giving rise to what one gardening writer recently called "quick-thumb gardening." The object of these new techniques is to keep maintenance low, yet still get beautiful results.

The first principle of quick-thumb gardening is to start out small. Work up to larger gardens and beds once smaller ones are self-sustaining.

Careful plant selection also is crucial. Go with plants that are drought tolerant, disease resistant, and suited to your climate. More and more gardeners are turning to native plants because they are likely to thrive in their climate and region without chemical fertilizers and sprays. Your local public garden, agricultural extension agent, or state native plant society can tell you which plants are indigenous to your area.

Hurried gardeners should avoid "high-maintenance" plants such as hybrid roses or fruit trees that require lots of fertilizer, water, and spraying to keep them healthy. Plants that need staking and continual deadheading like dahlias, hollyhock, and delphinium also are impractical. Select shrubs and trees that don't have fruits or nuts to rake up. If you must grow high-maintenance plants, group them together so that they can be cared for in a single place.

If you don't want to spend time planting and pulling out annuals every spring and fall, hardy perennial flowers are a natural alternative. Although they will need to be divided every three years or so, they still save time and money in the long run.

Probably the most tedious of all gardening jobs is weeding, so all garden beds and pathways should be mulched once or twice a year to keep down weeds and keep soil moist, which also saves time on water-

■ WHERE THE GROWING ZONES FALL

Most plant catalogs specify the regions in which perennial plants thrive. The standard zones are defined by the minimum temperatures each region reaches in an average year; the 11 zones are shown.

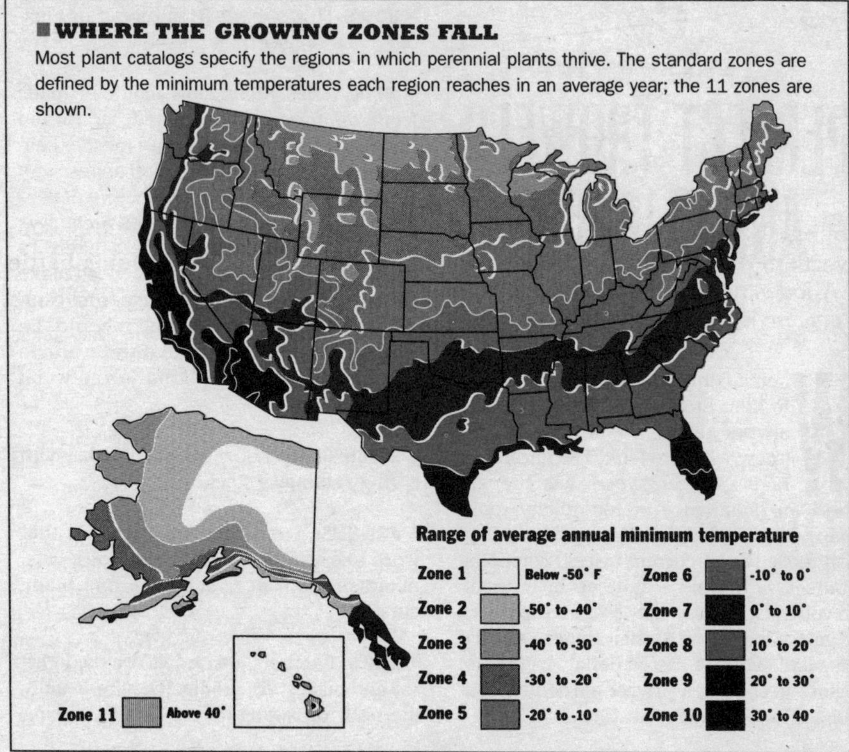

ing. In addition to organic mulches like compost, pine bark, and pine needles, there are new products that can virtually eliminate weeding without harmful chemicals. These synthetic landscape fabrics are spread out in garden beds and completely block weed growth. Unlike regular plastic mulches, they have microscopic holes that permit air and moisture exchange, keeping plants and soil healthy.

To cut down on lawn-maintenance time, many people are decreasing or even eliminating traditional grass lawns and instead installing low-maintenance plantings such as native trees, shrub borders, hardy ground cover, and native perennials and brick, stone, or concrete patios.

Watering chores can be reduced by using drip irrigation or soaker hoses instead of watering by hand or relying on overhead sprinklers. Soaker hoses are set down at soil level near plant roots. They save on water because water is emitted directly where it is needed and not lost to evaporation. You can cut down on regular fertilizer feedings of plants by using slow-release pellets that last throughout the growing season.

For people with limited space and time, raised bed gardens and container plantings are popular. They are easily planted and watered, and stay virtually weed-free. If you have a sunny back-door area, plants in containers right outside the door can be easy to water or harvest.

Look for tools and equipment that can save time, too. For example, a mulching lawn mower will save raking grass clippings, and some new mowers allow you to lime and fertilize as you mow.

For the truly hurried person, there's even a gardening trend called "ungardening," which promotes the idea that weeds, faded flower heads, and unpruned shrubs *enhance* a garden's charm. Nature isn't perfect, so why should your garden be?

EXPERT TIPS

PERFECT TROWELS AND CLIPPERS

Wooden handles cause fewer blisters, anvil pruners cut most sharply

When it comes to gardening tools, the Rolling Stones are wrong: you *can* always get what you want—if you know where to look. The gardening rage in recent years has brought forth an abundance of top-quality tools, many of them fashioned after classic English tools. But at current prices, equipping yourself fully can be quite an investment, so you must invest wisely. Here is the advice of gardening expert Alastair Bolton, who did his spadework at the National Arboretum before becoming a private gardening consultant in Washington, D.C.:

■ **HOSES:** Hoses made from rubber or Flexogen last longer than plastic ones.

■ **METAL TOOLS:** Metal tools should be made from tempered, heat-treated, or forged metal. Stainless steel tools are most expensive, but they are also the strongest and should last you a lifetime. Choose wooden-handled tools over metal ones whenever possible because they are less likely to cause blisters. Hickory and ash wood make the best handles. Handles made from Douglas fir will be weak and should be avoided. And make sure that there are no cracks or flaws of any kind in the wood before buying.

■ **PITCHFORKS:** Look for pitchforks with springy stainless steel tines.

■ **PRUNERS:** Anvil-type hand pruners that work like scissors make the sharpest cuts. Avoid pruners in which only one blade cuts.

■ **RAKES:** Bamboo lawn rakes are the lightest and easiest to handle. They're usually the best for raking leaves. But for raking

BUYER'S GUIDE

TOOLS AND EQUIPMENT TO DO THE JOB

Where to get a great rake or the best English spade

AMES LAWN AND GARDEN TOOLS
P.O. Box 1774
Parkersburg, WV 26102
■ Good selection of child-sized tools.
☎ **800-624-2654**

E. C. GEIGER
P.O. Box 285
Harlyesville, PA 19438
■ Tools, equipment, soil testers, fertilizers, etc.
☎ **215-256-6511**

LANGENBACK FINE TOOL CO.
P.O. Box 453
Blairstown, NJ 07825
■ Top-of-the line English and other imported tools.
☎ **201-362-5886**

A. M. LEONARD
P.O. Box 816
Piqua, OH 45356
■ Vast inventory for home and commercial gardening.
☎ **513-773-2694**

THE NATURAL GARDENING COMPANY
217 San Anselmo Ave.
San Anselmo, CA 94960
■ Tools, equipment, and organic gardening supplies.
☎ **415-456-5060**

SMITH & HAWKEN
25 Corte Madera
Mill Valley, CA 94941
■ Special line of gifts, clothes, and footwear.
☎ **415-383-2000**

leaves within flower beds, use a rake that is rubber-tipped. It won't damage the plants.

■ **ROTOTILLERS:** Unless you have a large garden, you should probably just rent a rototiller and chipper shredder once a year. Most rental centers now carry a variety of models. If you do decide to buy your own rototiller, look for models that you can easily handle and don't allow you to step on the area that was just tilled as you move it along the bed. Rear-tined (where wheels are in back) are best for difficult compacted or rocky soils.

■ **SHEARS:** Select hedge shears that have a self-sharpening blade. Those with short handles are lighter and easier to use.

■ **SHOVELS:** The best shovels and spades have a Y-brace handle to add strength by increasing leverage.

■ **TROWELS:** A narrow-bladed trowel, sometimes known as a rock-garden or transplanting trowel, will also work well for planting bulbs.

SUPERPLANTS FOR YOUR GARDEN

Today's fruits, vegetables, and flowers are being bred for perfection

Car designs are always being improved, so are tennis racquets and home computers. So why shouldn't the technology of a tomato plant or an impatiens be perfected? Each year horticulturists at botanical gardens, seed companies, and universities stake a claim to gardeners' gratitude by successfully breeding superior new varieties of flowers, vegetables, and fruits.

Take the plant officially known as the Tomato f1 Big Beef. Introduced in 1994, the Big Beef is a tomato plant that produces fruit earlier than other beefsteak types and maintains impressive yields throughout the growing season. Even late-season tomatoes

EXPERT SOURCES

WHERE TO GET THE YEAR'S BEST SEEDS

The first four companies offer by mail all three of the best new seeds selected annually by All-America Selections. The remainder offer at least one.

GEO. W. PARK SEED CO.
P.O. Box 31
Greenwood, SC 29647
☎ **803-941-4235**

J. W. JUNG SEED CO.
335 S. High St.
Randolph, WI 53957
☎ **414-326-3121**

OTIS TWILLEY SEED CO.
P.O. Box 65
Trevose, PA 19053
☎ **215-639-8800**

W. ATLEE BURPEE
300 Park Ave.
Warminster, PA 18974
☎ **800-888-1447**

CHAS. H. LILY CO.
P.O. Box 83179
Portland, OR 97283
☎ **503-289-5937**

EARL MAY SEED
208 N. Elm St.
Shenandoah, IA 51603
☎ **712-246-1020**

HARRIS SEEDS
P.O. Box 22960
Rochester, NY 14692
☎ **716-442-0410**

LAKE VALLEY SEED
5717 Arapahoe Ave.
Boulder, CO 80303
☎ **303-449-4882**

PLANTATION PRODUCTS
135 Belmont St.
South Easton, MA 02375
☎ **508-238-6213**

developed high on the plant are large, flavorful, and meaty. Or say your passion is for flowering perennials. You'll enjoy the "Lavender Lady," which is a new English lavender that blooms early and profusely.

Seed catalog aficionados know that each new season's editions carry wondrous claims for their new superplants. But if you're uncomfortable accepting the word of a catalog copywriter, you should be on the lookout for seeds that bear a commendation from All-America Selections (AAS), a nonprofit organization that annually cites what it regards as the best new gardening species. University horticulturists, seed companies, and backyard gardeners submit newly developed seeds to AAS, which then tests the entries at 55 locations across North America. The test sites include private and public gardens from Pennsylvania State University to Disney World.

"Anyone can enter their seeds as long as they are brand new and have never been sold anywhere in the world," says Nona Koivula, executive director of both All-America Selections and the National Garden Bureau in Downers Grove, Ill., which promotes the home garden seed industry. New varieties are matched against the closest comparisons currently on the market, and three winners are selected each year from the realm of vegetables, flowers, and bedding plants. The 1995 winners were all flowers: the petunia f1 Celebrity Chiffon-morn, the petunia f1 Purple Wave, and the *Rudbeckia hirta* Indian Summer.

So what will be the superplants of tomorrow? At W. Atlee Burpee Seed Company, the hunt is on for plants with more uniform growth patterns. Burpee also is encouraging the development of produce with old-fashioned flavors. One such fruit, the "Showing" watermelon, boasts an 11 percent sugar content and tastes "almost like a sugar lump," says Burpee representative Sharon Kaszan. In the past, breeders concentrated on developing hearty commercial varieties, paying relatively little attention to flavor, although that is what backyard gardeners value the most. But now, Kaszan says, "We are trying to get the breeders to understand that you need to breed for the home gardener, too."

EXPERT Q&A

A STARTER'S GUIDE TO SOWING SEEDS

Germination goes better when the soil is more than backyard dirt

Soil pH is just one of several factors that can determine whether a seed develops into a thriving plant or fails to grow at all. Maureen Heffernan, director of programs for the Cleveland Botanical Garden, explains here how the savvy gardener can give seeds a helpful head start in life:

■ When should I start seed?

Most seed packages come with full instructions on when to start the seed. As a rule of thumb, most annual vegetable and flower seed should be started about six to eight weeks before the average last frost date in your area.

■ What is the best soil medium?

Always use a germination mixture that has been specially formulated to spur growth. Homemade soil mixtures are easy to make and they are cheaper than buying premade ones, especially if you start large quantities of seed.

One of the best recipes is Cornell Peat-Lite, developed by horticulturists and agronomists at Cornell University. Its ingredients include: 1 bushel of shredded sphagnum peat meat; 1 bushel of horticultural vermiculite (no. 4–fine); 4 level tablespoonfuls of ammonium nitrate (a nitrogen source); 2 level tablespoonfuls of powdered superphosphate (20 percent); and 10 level tablespoonfuls of finely ground dolomitic limestone.

Never use soil from the yard or garden as your germination medium unless it is sterilized and combined with materials such as vermiculite, perlite, and horticultural sand. The mixture should be light and almost fluffy even after it is watered.

What is the right temperature for planting?

Most seedlings do best with "warm feet and cool heads." Make sure soil temperatures are at least 70° to 80°. Air temperature can be about 10 degrees cooler at night. Heat cables or heat mats are placed under germination containers to ensure soil temperatures that are evenly warm throughout. They are inexpensive and can be found in many garden-supply catalogs and most garden centers.

How much watering is necessary?

Water immediately after sowing seeds. Use a spritzer bottle to evenly moisten the surface. The most common mistake is applying too much or too little water. Just keep seeds and seedlings evenly moist and never allow seeds to dry out, even temporarily.

How much light do seeds need?

Some seeds need light to germinate, some need darkness. Once germinated, however, all seeds need bright light to develop. Light can come from a sunny window—south is best—or fluorescent lighting. Most seedlings need at least 12 to 16 hours of light each day.

EXPERT TIP

To sterilize a seed medium in an oven or microwave, you can use a medium-sized potato as your "sterility gauge." Place the soil medium in the oven at the same depth as you would need to fill a seed flat. When the potato is cooked enough to be eaten, the soil should be clean enough for your seeds.

—American Horticultural Society

If you are using fluorescent light, seedlings need about 15 to 20 watts per square foot of growing area. A double row of fluorescent tubes is enough for flats that are up to 16 inches wide. Place the light tube about 4 inches above the plants. Don't forget to raise the light tubes as the plants grow.

When should seedlings be thinned out or transplanted?

After the seedlings have germinated and developed at least two leaves, thin them out with scissors at soil level so remaining seedlings are an inch apart. If seedlings aren't thinned out, they will get crowded and become thin, weak, and disease-prone. Transplant seedlings to wider and deeper containers after they have developed at least two to four leaves. Transplanting allows seedlings to develop a stronger root system before being planted outdoors.

What kind of soil do seedlings need when they are moved outside?

Good growing soils are fertile, well drained, and well aerated. When you pick up a handful of earth, it should have a crumbly texture and be filled with worms and other enriching organisms. To prepare outside plots for planting, add at least 3 to 4 inches of organic matter to your garden beds every spring or fall. Work in the organic matter to a depth of at least 12 inches. If you are working with soil that has a lot of heavy clay or sand, add more organic matter and work it in several inches deeper, both in the spring and in the fall. If your soil is poorly drained, you may need to add sand or even put in drainage pipes.

What is the importance of soil pH?

A soil's pH number indicates its level of acidity (sourness) and alkalinity (sweetness). The pH scale ranges from 1 to 14 with 7 being neutral. Numbers below 7 indicate more acidic levels and numbers over 7 indicate alkaline conditions. Most garden plants, flowers, and vegetables prefer a slightly acidic soil pH of 6.2 to 6.8—about the same acidity as pure water. The pH scale is logarithmic, which means

TIPPING THE pH SCALES

Soil pH measures the relative acidity of the earth. Too much or too little, and your garden may suffer. Here's how to tip the scales in your favor.

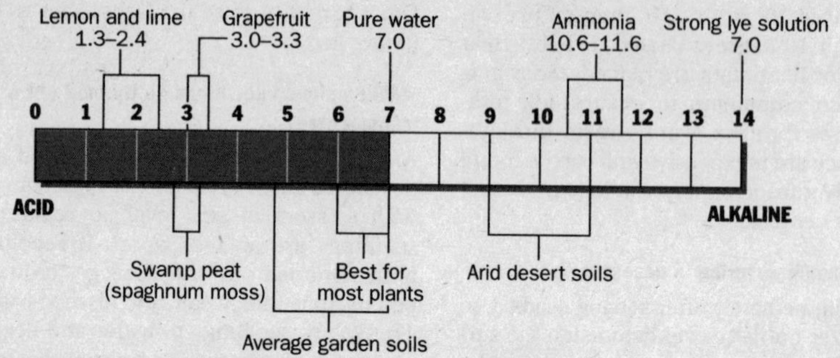

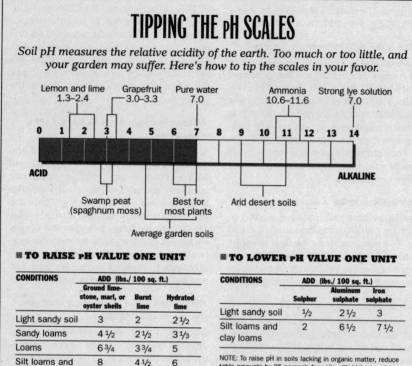

TO RAISE pH VALUE ONE UNIT

CONDITIONS	ADD (lbs./ 100 sq. ft.)		
	Ground limestone, marl, or oyster shells	Burnt lime	Hydrated lime
Light sandy soil	3	2	2 1/2
Sandy loams	4 1/2	2 1/2	3 1/3
Loams	6 3/4	3 3/4	5
Silt loams and clay loams	8	4 1/2	6

TO LOWER pH VALUE ONE UNIT

CONDITIONS	ADD (lbs./ 100 sq. ft.)		
	Sulphur	Aluminum sulphate	Iron sulphate
Light sandy soil	1/2	2 1/2	3
Silt loams and clay loams	2	6 1/2	7 1/2

NOTE: To raise pH in soils lacking in organic matter, reduce table amounts by 25 percent; for soils with high organic content, double the measurement.
SOURCE: American Horticultural Society.

that a soil pH of 5 is 10 times more acidic than a pH of 4.

How do I know what my soil pH is?

As a general rule, if you live in an area with little rainfall and high temperatures, like New Mexico or Arizona, you probably have alkaline soils. If you live in a region with a lot of rain and a temperate climate, as in the northeastern states, the soil is probably acidic. To get an exact soil pH reading, you will need to get your soil tested. Most county extension agencies will do such an analysis free of charge if you bring a sample to them. They are listed in the blue government services pages of the telephone book. Extension agencies can also analyze your soil's nutrient levels and let you know if you need to add any nutrients.

How reliable are pH home test kits?

Although they are not as accurate as soil-testing labs, home test kits will give you a fairly general pH measurement. You can buy such do-it-yourself soil testing kits from garden catalogs or from a well-stocked gardening center. Just be sure to follow all directions carefully to get the best results.

What should I do if the pH level is off?

Soil pH can be lowered—that is, made more acidic—by adding a combination of ground sulfur, aluminum sulfate, iron sulfate, and garden gypsum. In addition, pine needles, pine bark, and peat moss will slowly bring about slight drops in pH levels naturally. To raise pH, you can add agricultural or dolomitic limestone to your soil (see "Tipping the pH Scales," above).

TRENDS

MOTHER NATURE KNOWS BEST

Natural gardening is winning converts to the cause of ecology

Before there was Scott's Turf Builder, bioengineered tomatoes, and sprinklers that operate on timers, Mother Nature was already a pretty impressive ecologist when it came to designing self-sufficient habitats. Many gardeners are now honoring that wisdom by trying to imitate closely what nature does when left to its own devices. The movement, known as natural gardening, champions the use of biologically diverse indigenous plants, the restoration of wildlife habitats, and the reduction or elimination of chemical pesticides and herbicides. It also promotes designing landscapes to conserve water and developing naturally healthy and fertile soils by using compost and other organic soil supplements.

The native plant trend owes much to the severe droughts experienced in California and other parts of the country over the past decade. In the face of such dryness, gardeners saw their cultivated garden plants wither under the heat, yet at the same time noticed many wild plants growing beautifully in undeveloped areas. Their conclusion: native plants are often best suited for stressful environmental conditions. Hardy native plants, they also learned, rarely need any chemical fertilizers or sprays to stay healthy.

Another tenet of natural gardening is xeriscaping, which literally means dryscaping. The term refers to landscaping techniques aimed at conserving water in parched regions. Although originally developed in the West, xeriscaping methods are now used in all parts of the country to conserve water. Techniques include grouping plants according to water needs, using native plants, limiting lawn areas, and using mulches. When watering, xeriscapers recommend using drip irrigation or soaker hoses. The most committed even collect rainwater, and in very drought-stricken areas "gray water" collected from household laundries, showers, and sinks. (Don't bother with gray water unless you use biodegradable soaps.)

Many specialty nurseries now sell native plants for specific natural habitats such as Midwest prairies, Southwest deserts, and wetlands. Conservation groups like the National Wildlife Federation are also active in explaining the importance of planting vegetation that will attract and sustain butterflies, bats, birds, and other animals pushed out by housing and business development.

To get away from chemical pesticides, gardeners are also practicing integrated pest management. By using natural botanical pesticides, sticky traps, and other IPM techniques, the amount of chemicals necessary for a pest-free environment can be cut dramatically. Composting can serve much the same role in helping gardeners reduce the use of chemical fertilizers.

To be sure, Americans still spend close to $6 billion every year to keep their lawns looking emerald green and weed-free, and more chemicals are dumped on gardens and lawns each year than on all the farms of America. But with just small compost piles and meager water rations, wonderful plants may easily grow—if you are naturally inclined.

EXPERT QUOTE

We cannot in fairness rail against those who destroy the rain forest or spotted owl when we have made our own yards uninhabitable.

—*Sara Stein, author of* Noah's Garden: Restoring the Ecology of Our Own Backyards.

THE ORGANIC ALTERNATIVES

Organic fertilizers are substances derived from plants, animals, or minerals. They contain essential elements for plant growth. In contrast to synthetic fertilizers, they occur naturally, which means they may be physically processed but are never chemically altered or mixed with synthetic materials. To ensure effective use, consult these application guidelines from the American Horticultural Society, adjusting them when necessary to take into account soil conditions and the type of plants being raised.

FERTILIZER	APPLICATION RATE per 1,000 sq. ft.	USES
ALFALFA MEAL	40–50 lbs. (4 appl./yr.)	A "green manure." Breaks down easily to provide nitrogen.
BLOOD MEAL	10–30 lbs. (1 appl./yr.)	Readily available nitrogen; speeds decomposition of compost.
BONE MEAL	10–20 lbs. (1 appl./yr.)	Excellent source of phosphorus; raises pH. Good for fruits, bulbs, flowers.
CATTLE MANURE	30 lbs.	Valuable soil additive. If fresh, will burn.
COMPOST	2-inch depth (1 appl./yr.)	Valuable source of trace elements such as calcium, iron, magnesium, manganese, sulfur, and zinc.
COTTONSEED MEAL	20–30 lbs. (1 appl./yr.)	Acidifies soil; lasts 4-6 months.
FISH EMULSION	2 oz. per gal. water (2–3 spray appl./yr.)	A good "foliar spray," or liquid fertilizer, for early spring.
FISH MEAL	20 lbs. (1–2 appl./yr.)	Readily available nitrogen; speeds decomposition of compost.
SEAWEED	1 oz. per gal. water	Contains natural growth hormones.
SUL-PO-MAG	20 lbs. (1 appl./yr.)	High in potash. Recommended for plants suffering iron chlorosis.

SOURCE: American Horticultural Society.

■ CONVERTING FERTILIZER RATES

Fertilizers often are labeled with big-time planters in mind, but if you are planting only a small corner of your backyard, it's easy to convert the application rates. Gardening expert Dick Raymond says it's better to measure by volume than by weight when you are dealing with small quantities of fertilizer. The table at right shows how to convert rates assuming that two cups of fertilizer weigh about a pound—the standard weight of most commercially available fertilizers.

Area in square feet	Pounds of fertilizer to apply, where amount to be applied per acre is:		
	100 lbs.	400 lbs.	800 lbs.
100	0.25	1	2
500	1.25	5	10
1,000	2.50	10	20
1,500	3.75	15	30
2,000	5.00	20	40

SOURCE: *Down-to-Earth Gardening Know-How for the 90's*, Dick Raymond, Garden Way, 1991.

EXPERT TIPS

A MULCH FOR EVERY WEED

Black plastic and newspapers can keep your garden happy

Think of mulch as a protective blanket for your garden bed. It helps keep it cool in the summer and warm in the winter. A healthy layering of wood chips or pine needles can keep your garden appearing well maintained and attractive. But the principal reason to use mulch is to decrease weeds by smothering them. As a bonus, it can help to prevent soil-moisture loss.

Mulching also can provide an environmentally friendly outlet for all those grass clippings and raked leaves that many municipalities require to be recycled nowadays.

Here, Maureen Heffernan of the Cleveland Botanical Garden describes some of the different varieties of mulch, the depth at which they should be spread, and what they are best used for.

■ **BLACK PLASTIC** **one sheet**
Not very attractive, but highly effective. Black plastic totally smothers existing and emerging weeds and is great for warming soil in the spring. Make sure that enough water is penetrating the plastic to prevent the plants from drying out, though. Black plastic is most effective if it is used with drip irrigation.

■ **COMPOST** **1–8 in.**
Compost can be a combination of many of the other mulches found in this list. It has great color, costs nothing, and naturally enriches soil structure and fertility. Make sure not to put any diseased plants in the compost heap, though. The disease can spread easily to other, healthy plants.

■ **EVERGREEN BOUGHS** **8–24 in.**
They are a good winter covering for perennial beds. But be sure to remove them in the spring.

■ **GRASS CLIPPINGS** **3–6 in.**
A particularly good mulch for vegetable gardens. Do not use if the clippings were recently sprayed with herbicide, though.

■ **HAY** **6–12 in.**
Especially good for vegetable garden pathways. Salt hay has fewer weed seeds than regular hay.

■ **LANDSCAPE FABRICS** **one sheet**
These clear films are more porous than black plastic, and some are biodegradable. They are particularly good for foundation plantings.

■ **LEAVES** **3–5 in.**
Leaves make a great all around mulch and they're easy to come by. If they're shredded, pile them 6 to 8 inches higher so they don't blow away.

■ **PINE BARK** **2–5 in.**
When shredded, pine bark is good for acid-loving plants; 3- to 6-inch chips also are natural and attractive.

■ **PINE NEEDLES** **2–6 in.**
They have a lovely natural appearance and are excellent for increasing acidity in acid-loving plants like azaleas and rhododendrons.

■ **NEWSPAPERS** **½–2½ in.**
Best for informal areas like a vegetable garden. Don't use colored inks, and cover the newspaper with an organic mulch to weigh it down and to make it more attractive.

■ **STRAW** **3–9 in.**
Most often used in vegetable gardens and, of course, in between rows of strawberry plantings.

■ **WOOD CHIPS** **2–8 in.**
Nice appearance, but be sure to add extra nitrogen to the soil—wood consumes nitrogen when decomposing.

PESTS AND DISEASES

DOING BATTLE WITH BLIGHT

Stressed-out plants are the most vulnerable to external enemies

Diseases and pests know easy marks when they see them. When fallen fruit and leaves are left too long on garden beds, when plants are placed too close together and diseased vegetation isn't destroyed quickly, it's like hanging out a sign that says, "Unwelcome Visitors, Inquire Within." But pest and disease problems can be greatly minimized if you watch for danger signs and follow good cultivation practices.

The first principle of preventive maintenance, says plant pathologist Neil Pelletier, is to keep plants adequately watered, weeded, pruned, and fertilized. Plants that are well maintained and healthy will resist most attacks.

Diversifying what you plant, as well as where and when you plant, is also very helpful. By planting a variety of flowers and vegetables, you help ensure that even if one plant species is destroyed by disease or pests, there will still be an abundance of other plants. By rotating vegetable crops to different locations within the garden bed each year, a gardener reduces the risk that insect populations and diseases will infest an area where their favorite plants are most likely to be sited. If you're worried about a particular pest, find out from your local county extension office when that pest will be at its most destructive stage and plant before or after that time.

You can also use nature to repel nature by practicing what gardening writer Louise Riotte calls "companion planting." In this case, you fight fire with fire, or more precisely, odor. For example, many insect pests are repelled by strong-smelling plants such as marigolds, mint, basil, garlic, onions, chives, nasturtiums, and savory. Plant these

INSECTS THAT WILL SET YOU FREE

If you want to use natural predators to fight destructive bugs, here's a rundown of friendly enforcers and the garden pests that they can help control.

- **ASSASSIN BUG:** *Aphids, caterpillars, Colorado potato beetles, Japanese beetles, leafhoppers, Mexican bean beetles.*
- **ENCARSIA FORMOSA:** *Whiteflies.*
- **FIREFLIES:** *Mites, snails, slugs.*
- **GREEN LACEWINGS:** *Aphids, corn earworms, leafhoppers, mealybugs, mites, nymphs, scales, thrips, whiteflies.*
- **LADYBUGS:** *Aphids, chinch bugs, rootworms, scales, spider mites, weevils, whiteflies.*
- **MINUTE PIRATE BUGS:** *Aphids, spider mites, thrips, whiteflies.*
- **PRAYING MANTIS:** *Aphids, beetles, caterpillars, flies, leafhoppers.*
- **ROBBER, SYRPHID, AND TACHINID FLIES:** *Aphids, beetles, flies, grasshoppers, Japanese beetles, leafhoppers, mealybugs, scales, many varieties of caterpillar.*
- **SPIDERS:** *Almost all kinds of insects. (Be careful of poisonous species!)*
- **WASPS:** (Braconid, Chalcid, Ichneumon, and Trichogramma) *Armyworms, cabbage loopers, corn borers, cutworms, hornworms, fruitworms, harmful butterflies, and moths.*

in and around your vegetables and ornamental plants and they'll keep uninvited guests away.

If all this fails to stop incursions, construct barriers around plants to prevent pests from laying eggs nearby or crawling up plant stems. The barriers may include plant collars made of plastic, metal, or sticky tape. Why should you provide summer lodging for bad house guests?

THE BEST ORGANIC DISEASE FIGHTERS

Is your garden being overrun by hostile pests and diseases? Here's a natural arsenal to defend your turf:

■ **BACILLUS THURINGIENSIS (BT):** This natural biological control is sprayed on plants and soil to control caterpillar pests and is available at most garden centers. Follow package directions.

■ **BIODEGRADABLE SOAPS:** Composed of nonphosphate liquid soaps, they are mixed with water and sprayed on plants. Sometimes called insecticidal soap, biodegradable soaps like Safer and Reuter can control a wide range of pests such as aphids and mealybugs.

■ **BORDEAUX MIXTURE:** A classic organic spray that derives its name from decades of use in France's wine-growing region. It is effective for preventing most foliage fungal problems on fruits, vegetables, flowers, trees, and shrubs (see "Homemade Cures for Pests and Diseases," page 462).

■ **DIACIDE:** A mixture of diatomaceous earth and Pyrethrum (derived from the pyrethrum daisy). It will destroy aphids, beetles, leafhoppers, worms, caterpillars, and ants.

■ **DIATOMACEOUS EARTH:** A naturally occurring material with sharp, jagged edges. It is sprinkled around the base of plants to act as a barrier against soft- skinned pests like slugs.

■ **DORMANT OIL:** A petroleum-based substance that is applied in the fall to smother overwintering insects. It is particularly

BUYER'S GUIDE

THE BEST BUGS FOR THE BUCK

Where to get insects and other organic gardening supplies.

BOZEMAN BIO-TECH
P.O. Box 3146
Bozeman, MT 59772
■ Good selection of beneficial insects. Catalog contains detailed information.
☎ **406-587-5891**

EARLEE, INC.
2002 Highway 62
Jeffersonville, IN 47130
■ Wide selection of organic disease and pest formulations.
☎ **800-334-9184**

ECOLOGY ACTION
5798 Ridgewood Road
Willits, CA 95490
■ Organic insectides, soaps, fertilizers, good selection of organic gardening books. Write for a catalog.

NATURAL PEST CONTROL
8864 Little Creek
Orangevale, CA 95662
■ Comprehensive inventory of live, extremely vicious attack bugs. Write for a catalog.

PEACEFUL VALLEY FARM SUPPLY
11173 Peaceful Valley Rd.
Nevada City, CA 95959
■ Bugs, organic pesticides, fungicides, fertilizers. Write for a catalog.

PEST MANAGEMENT SUPPLY, INC.
P.O. Box 938
Amherst, MA 01004
■ Good selection, pest monitoring equipment.
☎ **800-272-7672**

EXPERT TIPS

HOMEMADE CURES FOR PESTS AND DISEASES

Organic gardening specialists recommend these do-it-yourself recipes for ridding your garden of unwanted visitors.

COOKING OIL SOLUTION

Effective against eggs and immature insects.

1 cup cooking oil
1 tbs. liquid dish soap

■ *Mix oil and soap. Use 2½ tsps. per 1 cup of water. Pour into a spray bottle and spray surface and undersides of leaves to smother insects. Apply once every 2 to 3 weeks until pest is gone.*

BAKING SODA SOLUTION

Usually effective in preventing foliage fungal problems, especially on roses.

1 tbs. baking soda
1 gal. water
½ tsp. insecticidal soap

■ *Dissolve baking soda in the water. Mix in the soap and pour into a spray bottle. Spray to cover the top and underside of foliage about twice a week from spring through early fall. It's a good idea to test this solution on just a few leaves before spraying an entire plant. Some plants may be sensitive and the solution strength may need to be diluted so the foliage does not discolor.*

GARLIC-PEPPER SOLUTION

Effective against a wide range of chewing insects and animals.

2 cloves garlic
1 tsp. liquid detergent
2 tsps. cooking oil
1 tbs. of cayenne pepper
2 cups water

■ *Combine ingredients in a blender and mix until the cloves are thoroughly pureed. Spray solution on affected plants. Reapply as needed.*

BORDEAUX MIXTURE

Effective against common fungal disease. Often used on small fruits.

2 heaping tbs. fresh hydrated spray lime
2 level tsps. copper sulfate crystals
3 gals. water

■ *Dissolve hydrated lime in 2 gallons of water. In a separate container, dissolve the copper sulfate in 1 gallon of water. Add the copper sulfate solution to the lime solution. This will give you a 3-gallon, slurrylike solution that can be strained through a cheesecloth directly into a sprayer. Spray to cover foliage. When dry, it forms an insoluble copper precipitate that prevents fungal spores from entering and infecting plants. Begin applications in spring, repeat once every 7 to 14 days through early fall. This mixture can cause injury to plants if used during cool and wet weather.*

effective against spider mites, scale, and aphids. Dormant oil is often used on fruit trees.

■ **LIME SULPHUR:** Useful in preventing fungal outbreaks on fruits, nuts, berries, and ornamental plants.

■ **LIQUID COPPER:** It controls powdery mildew, bacterial blights, and anthracnose on vegetables, fruits, and ornamental plants.

■ **PYRETHRUM:** A dust or spray made from a chrysanthemum species. Kills a variety of insects from aphids to caterpillars.

■ **ROTENONE AND SABADILLA:** Two botanical insecticides used to kill aphids, worms, borers, and other hard-to-kill pests.

■ **WETTABLE DUSTING SULPHUR:** A finely ground sulphur that is effective against many foliage diseases.

PLANTER'S GUIDE

CHOOSING VEGETABLES FOR EVERY TABLE

Planting should begin well before the last frost of the season. The following table provides a timetable for when vegetable seeds should be started.

Vegetable	Optimum temp. (°F)	Germination time (days)	Weeks relative to last frost to			Space between		Planting per person
			Sow inside	Transplant outside	Sow outside	Rows	Plants	
ASPARAGUS	60-85	21	7-8 BEF.	5-6 AFT.	†	3 FT.	15 in.	9-15 ROOTS
BEANS, BUSH	75-80	7	*	—	1 AFT.	24 in.	4 in.	10-15 FT.
BEANS, LIMA	85	7-10	*	—	2 AFT.	18 in.	6-8 in.	10-15 FT.
BEANS, POLE	75-80	7	*	—	1 AFT.	4 FT.	36 in.	3-5 HILLS
BEETS	75	7-14	8 BEF.	4 BEF.	1-2 BEF.	15 in.	3 in.	5-10 FT.
BROCCOLI	60-75	5-10	5-7 BEF.	3-4 BEF. to 3 AFT.	3-4 BEF.	30 in.	24 in.	5-10 PLANTS
BRUSSELS SPROUTS	68-75	5-10	10-12 BEF.	5-6 BEF.	5-6 BEF.	24 in.	18 in.	5-10 PLANTS
CABBAGE, CHINESE	50-75	10	10 BEF.	—	AFT.	18 in.	12 in.	5-10 PLANTS
CABBAGE, HEAD	68-75	5-10	7-9 BEF.	2-3 BEF.	1-4 AFT.	24 in.	18 in.	3-5 PLANTS
CARROTS	75	12-14	*	—	4-6 BEF.	14 in.	3 in.	5-10 ft.
CAULIFLOWER	68-86	5-10	6-8 BEF.	2-4 BEF.	†	24 in.	18 in.	3-5 PLANTS
CELERY	68-76	21-28	3-5 BEF.	3 AFT.	†	24 in.	6 in.	2-3 PLANTS
CORN, SWEET	70-86	7-10	*	—	1 AFT.	3 ft.	10 in.	15-25 ft.
CUCUMBERS	70-86	7-10	*	—	2 AFT.	6 ft.	48 in.	2-3 HILLS
EGGPLANT	70-86	10	4-6 BEF.	4-6 AFT.	†	3 ft.	24 in.	2-3 PLANTS
KALE	68-75	5-10	5-7 BEF.	0-2 BEF.	2-4 BEF.	18-24 in.	12-15 in.	5-10 ft.
LETTUCE, HEAD	68-70	7-1	1-6 BEF.	2 BEF. to 3 AFT.	4 BEF. to 4 AFT.	14 in.	10 in.	5-10 ft.
LETTUCE, OTHER	68-70	7-10	1-6 BEF.	2 BEF. to 3 AFT.	4 BEF. to 4 AFT.	14 in.	6 in.	5-10 ft.
MUSKMELONS	80-86	4-10	2-4 BEF.	0-3 AFT.	1 AFT.	6 ft.	36 in.	3-5 HILLS
OKRA	80-86	7-14	3-4 BEF.	3-4 AFT.	1-2 AFT.	2-4 ft.	10 in.	2 PLANTS
ONIONS	68-70	10-14	2-10 BEF.	5 BEF.to 3 AFT.	3-5 BEF.	15 in.	2 in.	10-15 ft.

HOW DEEP IS YOUR CABBAGE?

As a general rule, you should plant at a depth four times the seed's diameter.

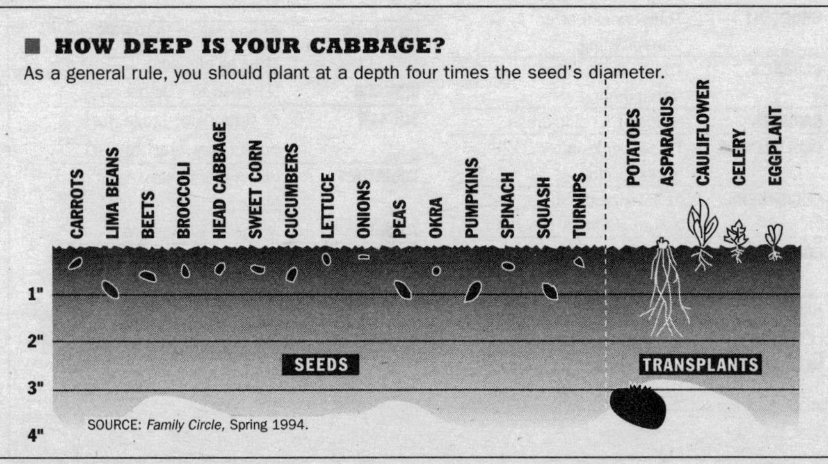

SOURCE: *Family Circle*, Spring 1994.

PLANTER'S GUIDE

VEGETABLE	OPTIMUM TEMP. (°F)	GERMINATION TIME (DAYS)	WEEKS RELATIVE TO LAST FROST TO			SPACE BETWEEN		PLANTING PER PERSON
			SOW INSIDE	TRANSPLANT OUTSIDE	SOW OUTSIDE	ROWS	PLANTS	
PARSNIPS	68-70	14-21	2-9 BEF.	4 BEF. to 3-4 AFT.	6-8 BEF.	18 in.	3 in.	10-15 ft.
PEANUTS	75-80	7-14	4-6 BEF.	AFT.	†	30 in.	12 in.	9-25 PLANTS
PEAS	65-70	7-14	*	—	2-4 BEF.	24 in.	8 in.	10-15 ft.
PEPPERS	75-85	10	2-4 BEF.	4-6 AFT.	†	24 in.	24 in.	2-3 PLANTS
POTATOES	65-70	10-14	*	—	1-3 BEF.	3 ft.	12 in.	50-100 ft.
PUMPKIN	68-75	7-10	1-2 BEF.	3-4 AFT.	2 AFT.	12 ft.	60 in.	3-5 HILLS
RADISH	65-70	5-7	*	—	2-4 BEF.	14 in.	2 in.	5-10 ft.
SALSIFY	65-70	7-20	4-12 BEF.	6 BEF. to 2 AFT.	†	14 in.	3 in.	10-15 ft.
SPINACH	68-70	7-14	*	—	3-5 BEF.	14 in.	3 in.	5-10 ft.
SQUASH, SUMMER	70-85	7-14	0-1 BEF.	4-5 AFT.	2 AFT.	3 ft.	48 in.	2-3 HILLS
SQUASH, WINTER	70-85	7-14	1-2 BEF.	3-4 AFT.	2 AFT.	6 ft.	60 in.	3-5 HILLS
SWEET POTATOES	75-85	18	6-8 BEF.	2-3 AFT.	†	3 ft.	12 in.	9-20 PLANTS
SWISS CHARD	68-75	7-14	*	—	1-2 BEF.	18 in.	9 in.	5-10 ft.
TOMATOES	75-80	7-14	5-7 BEF.	0-4 AFT.	†	3 ft.	36 in.	3-5 PLANTS
TURNIPS	65-70	7-14	*	—	2-4 BEF.	15 in.	3 in.	10-15 ft.
WATERMELONS	75-85	7-14	1-2 BEF.	1-4 AFT.	†	8 ft.	96 in.	3-5 HILLS

* Direct sowing in garden preferred †Transplant preferred

SOURCE: *Foolproof Planting*, 1990, Rodale Press editors and Anne Halpin; American Horticultural Society.

WHEN TO FERTILIZE YOUR VEGETABLE PLANTS

"Side-dressing" is simply a mid-season fertilizer boost. Here are the vegetables that require it.

ASPARAGUS	Before growth starts in spring, and after harvesting to promote fern growth.
BEANS*	No need to side-dress.
BEETS*	No need to side-dress.
BROCCOLI	Three weeks after transplanting.
CABBAGE	Three weeks after transplanting.
CARROTS*	No need to side-dress.
CAULIFLOWER	Three weeks after transplanting.
CUCUMBERS	At "stand-up" stage, just before they start to run.
EGGPLANT	When plants start to blossom.
KALE	Four weeks after planting.
LETTUCE*	No need to side-dress.
MUSKMELON	At "stand-up" stage, just before they start to run.
ONIONS	Four weeks and six weeks after planting.
PEAS*	No need to side-dress.
PEPPERS	When plants start to blossom.
POTATOES	At last hilling, before plants start to blossom.
SPINACH*	No need to side-dress.
SQUASH	At "stand-up" stage, just before they start to run.
TOMATOES	When plants start to blossom.
TURNIPS*	No need to side-dress.
WATERMELON	At "stand-up" stage, just before they start to run.

* Assumes that the fertilizer has been added to the rows before planting.

SOURCE: *Down-to-Earth Gardening Know-How for the 90's*, Dick Raymond, Garden Way, 1991.

PLANTER'S GUIDE

A BULB LOVER'S FAVORITE CHOICES

They can come back to brighten the same spot for decades, or you can dig them up and move them to a new home.

	Height (in.)	Planting depth (in.)	Planting time	Blooming time
SPRING-FLOWERING BULBS				
CROCUS *Crocus* species	3–5	3–4	EARLY FALL	EARLY SPRING
CROWN IMPERIAL *Fritillaria imperialis*	30–48	5	EARLY FALL	MIDSPRING
DAFFODIL *Narcissus* species	12	6	EARLY FALL	MIDSPRING
DUTCH IRIS *Iris xiphium*	24	4	EARLY FALL	LATE SPRING
FLOWERING ONION *Allium giganteum*	48	10	EARLY FALL	LATE SPRING
GRAPE HYACINTH *Muscari botryoides*	6–10	3	EARLY FALL	EARLY SPRING
HYACINTH *Hyacinthus orientalis*	12	6	EARLY FALL	EARLY SPRING
SNOWDROP *Galanthus nivalis*	4-6	4	EARLY FALL	EARLY SPRING
TULIP (early) *Tulipa* species	10–13	6	EARLY FALL	EARLY SPRING
TULIP (Darwin hybrid) *Tulipa* species	28	6	EARLY FALL	MIDSPRING
TULIP (late) *Tulipa* species	36	6	EARLY FALL	LATE SPRING
WILDFLOWER *Anemone blanda*	5	2	EARLY FALL	EARLY SPRING
SUMMER-FLOWERING BULBS				
ANEMONES *Anemone* species	18	2	**NORTH:** EARLY SPRING **SOUTH:** LATE FALL	LATE SUMMER
BUTTERCUP *Ranunculus*	12	2	SOUTH: LATE FALL	MIDSUMMER
CROCOSMIA *Crocosmia* species	24	4	APRIL-MAY	MID- TO LATE SUMMER
DAHLIA (dwarf varieties) *Dahlia* species	12	4	AFTER LATE FROST	LATE SUMMER
DAHLIA (large varieties) *Dahlia* species	48	4	AFTER LATE FROST	LATE SUMMER
GALTONIA *Galtonia candicans*	40	5	APRIL-MAY	MID- TO LATE SUMMER
GLADIOLUS (large flower) *Gladiolus* species	60	3–4	APRIL-JUNE	MIDSUMMER
GLADIOLUS (small flower) *Gladiolus* species	30	3–4	APRIL-JUNE	MIDSUMMER
LILY *Lilium* species	36–84	8	FALL OR EARLY SPRING	ALL SUMMER
TIGER FLOWER *Tigridia paronia*	16	3	EARLY SPRING	MID- TO LATE SUMMER

SOURCE: *Landscaping with Bulbs*, Ann Reilly, Storey Com Inc., 1988.

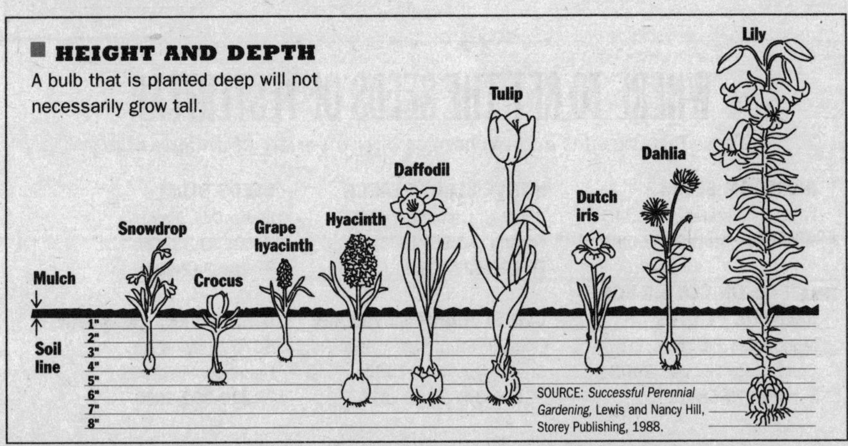

SPECIALTY SEEDS

THE JOY OF HEIRLOOMS

Antique seeds offer gardeners a lush, colorful alternative

Unable to grow the kind of zucchini or zinnias that abounded in your grandfather's garden? Perhaps you yearn for the juicy tomatoes you recall as a child. If so, then join the growing number of gardeners who have discovered the joy of cultivating antique crops.

Every year, backyard gardeners, historic-site groundskeepers, and a few mail-order companies make available their stock of antique or heirloom seeds. Many of them have been kept by the same family for as many as 150 years.

Modern gardening emphasizes compact plants with dense foliage and multipetaled flowers, explains Christie White, who supervises the horticulture program at Sturbridge Village, an 1830s small town recreated in Sturbridge, Mass. That means that owners of historic homes can't rely on modern hybrids for their gardens if they are sticklers for historical accuracy. Old Sturbridge Village offers Lady's Slipper seeds, for example, that are kissing cousins of today's New Guinea impatiens. But the Lady's Slipper grows to nearly 3 feet and produces beautiful salmon and white flowers.

Kent Whealy, who founded the Seed Savers Exchange in Decorah, Iowa, to promote the preservation of rare vegetable varieties, says antique plants provide a wealth of variation in colors, flavors, petal habit, and plant height. As for hardiness, Whealy says, "Anytime something is kept for 150 years in the same location, it usually develops a natural resistance to pests and disease."

Both Whealy and White recommend that gardeners start by growing beans and tomatoes, which are among the heartiest antique varieties. One favorite, the Brandywine Tomato, has unusual potato-leaved vines and produces medium-size fruit with thick, meaty walls and fine flavor. Another standout, the vigorous Scarlet Runner Bean, is a hit with antique gardeners because it attracts hummingbirds with its ornamental red flowers.

Keep in mind, however, that not all antique seeds are prize-winners—at least when it comes to disease and pest resistance. For example, novice gardeners should avoid some antique cucumber varieties because they are susceptible to bacterial wilts.

EXPERT SOURCES

WHERE TO GET THE SEEDS OF YESTERYEAR

These historic sites and exchanges offer a variety of antique seeds

HEIRLOOM SEEDS
Write for catalog: Box 245
West Elizabeth, PA 15088

JEFFERSON CENTER FOR HISTORIC PLANTS
Monticello, P.O. Box 316
Charlottesville, VA 22902
☎ **804-979-5847**

NATIVE SEEDS/SEARCH
2509 N. Campbell, #325
Tucson, AZ 85719
☎ **602-327-9123**

OLD STURBRIDGE VILLAGE
One Old Sturbridge Village Rd.
Sturbridge, MA 01566
☎ **508-347-3362 x270**

SEEDS BLUM
Idaho City Stage
Boise, ID 83706
☎ **208-342-0858**

SEED SAVERS EXCHANGE
3076 N. Winn Rd.
Decorah, IA 52101
☎ **319-382-5990**

EXPERT LIST

ROSES ROYAL ENOUGH FOR ROYALS

They are the Queens of the garden—here's how to select and care for them.

Over the 2,000-year history of rose cultivation, gardeners have developed countless variations of the 250 naturally occurring rose species. Roses come in almost every shape and size and can survive in most parts of the world. And, with the exception of the fabled blue rose, they can be found in every color of the rainbow.

Such history and variety have given roses an air of aristocracy, and like aristocrats, roses demand the best of living conditions wherever they happen to be. They need full sun, extremely well-drained, slightly acidic soil, and 1 or 2 inches of water per week to thrive. A balanced fertilizer mix like 10-10-10 should be applied monthly from spring through early fall, and a spray that combines a fungicide and insecticide should also be used every 7 to 10 days during the growing season. You should prune roses back about one-third to one-half in winter or early spring and remove any dead or broken canes.

As for selecting a specific variety of rose, if scent is your raison d'être, try the Arizona (a grandiflora), the Chrysler Imperial (a hybrid tea), or the Fragrant Cloud (also a hybrid tea). If your thumb is not fully greened, try hardy roses that require little maintenance, such as the Carefree Wonder (a shrub or climber), the Aquarius (a grandiflora), or the Double Delight (a hybrid tea).

For the rose gardener looking for the very best, here are the roses judged by the American Rose Society as the most prized in the land based on their color, shape, bloom size, fragrance, and ease of growth.

HYBRID TEAS

Largest of all the roses.

1. **First Prize**	PINK BLEND
2. **Peace**	YELLOW BLEND
3. **Granada**	RED BLEND
4. **Tiffany**	PINK
5. **Tropicana**	ORANGE-RED
6. **Mister Lincoln**	DARK RED
7. **Garden Party**	WHITE
8. **Double Delight**	RED BLEND
9. **Paradise**	MAUVE
10. **Lady X**	MAUVE

GRANDIFLORAS

Medium to large blossoms, but taller than hybrid tea.

1. **Queen Elizabeth**	PINK
2. **Pink Parfait**	PINK BLEND
3. **Sonia**	PINK BLEND

FLORIBUNDAS

Smaller than a grandiflora, but with more buds, the smallest floribundas grow in large sprays.

1. **Europeana**	DARK RED
2. **Little Darling**	YELLOW BLEND
3. **Iceberg**	WHITE
4. **Walko**	DARK RED

MINIATURES

The same as the floribunda, only with much smaller blossoms.

1. **Starina**	ORANGE-RED
2. **Beauty Secret**	RED
3. **Cinderella**	WHITE
4. **Toy Clown**	RED BLEND
5. **Magic Carousel**	RED BLEND

CLIMBERS

Large flowers that shoot right up the trellis. Can sometimes be shrubs.

1. **Galway Bay**	ORANGE-PINK
2. **Don Juan**	DARK RED
3. **Handel**	RED BLEND
4. **Dortmund**	MEDIUM RED
5. **May Queen**	LIGHT PINK

OLD GARDEN ROSES

From roses that were developed before the turn of the century. Many varieties.

1. **Rosa rubrifolia**	PINK
2. **Rosa hugonis**	YELLOW
3. **Koenigin**	PINK
4. **Sombreuil**	WHITE
5. **Tuscany**	MAUVE

HOUSE PLANTS

THE HEALING POWER OF PLANTS

They may help keep you healthy or speed recovery if you're already sick

Everyone knows that a pleasant environment can improve your mood, but recent research published by the People-Plant Council, an organization that studies the effects of plants on humans, goes a step further, suggesting that there are significant physical, mental, and even economic benefits to having plants in one's home or workplace. Several studies contend that plants can reduce stress, give people a sense of well-being, and even help make office workers more productive.

For instance, an investigation by V. I. Lohr, a horticulturist at Washington State University, found that indoor plants raise room humidity. This is good because medical studies have established that human colds occur more frequently at lower humidity levels. For both comfort and health reasons, humidity levels should be between 30 percent and 60 percent. At higher levels, molds, mildews, and moisture condensation are likely to occur.

Another atmospheric benefit was discovered in a recent study done in conjunction with the National Aeronautics and Space Administration. The research suggests that plants can "scrub" the air of certain toxins, thereby decreasing indoor air pollution.

One research project even showed that hospital patients who had flowers and plants in their rooms and windows that opened on parks or gardens often had faster recovery rates and better spirits than patients whose windows overlooked a parking lot or alley and who did not have plants.

PLANTER'S GUIDE

HOUSEPLANTS FOR EVERY WINDOW

How to match up a plant's light, temperature, and humidity needs to the location in your home or office that will best provide them.

NORTH WINDOWS: Receive no direct sun—but, if unobstructed, they do receive good light. Plants grown in a shaded north window during the winter months would appreciate extra light. When choosing plants for a dark window, remember that plants with variegated leaves require more light than ones with strictly green leaves. Consult the key on the next page.

Plant	Water	Temperature	Humidity	Fertilizer
CAST-IRON PLANT *Aspidistra elatior*	WD	I	MEDIUM	INTERMEDIATE
FERN, BIRD'S NEST *Asplenium nidus*	EM	I	HIGH	LOW
FIG *Ficus pumila*	EM	I	HIGH	LOW
PHILODENDRON, VELVET LEAF *Philodendron scandens var. micans*	W	I	HIGH	LOW
PRAYER PLANT *Maranta leuconeura*	EM	W	MEDIUM	INTERMEDIATE
SAGO PALM *Cycas revoluta*	W	I	MEDIUM	LOW
SPATHE FLOWER *Spathiphyllum*	EM	W	MEDIUM	INTERMEDIATE
WANDERING JEW *Zebrina pendula*	EM	I-W	MEDIUM	INTERMEDIATE

■ PLANTER'S GUIDE

■ EAST AND WEST WINDOWS: Both are excellent for growing houseplants. East windows tend to be cooler than west. If you can't grow the following plants in east or west windows, they should do fine in a south window—but add some shading during the day in the summer, especially for ferns.

Plant	Water	Temperature	Humidity	Fertilizer
BROMELIAD	W	I	MEDIUM	LOW
CAPE PRIMROSE *Streptocarpus*	W	I	HIGH	HIGH
FERN, BOSTON *Nephrolepsis exaltata*	W	I	HIGH	LOW
IVY, GRAPE *Cissus rhombifolia*	EM	I	MEDIUM	INTERMEDIATE
LILY, AMAZON *Eucharis grandiflora*	EM	I-W	MEDIUM	HIGH
LILY, KARRIR *Clivia minnata*	W	I	MEDIUM	INTERMEDIATE
LADY PALM *Rhapsis excelsa`*	W-EM	I	HIGH	INTERMEDIATE
NORFOLK ISLAND PINE *Araucaria heterophylla*	EM	C	MEDIUM	LOW
BEGONIA REX *Rex begonia*	EM	I	HIGH	HIGH
ROSARY VINE *Ceropegia woodii*	WD	I	LOW	INTERMEDIATE
RUBBER PLANT *Ficus elastica*	W	W	MEDIUM	LOW
SHAMROCK PLANT *Oxalis*	EM	I	MEDIUM	LOW
FIG, WEEPING *Ficus benjamina*	W	W	MEDIUM	LOW
VIOLET, AFRICAN *Saintpaulia*	W	I-W	MEDIUM	HIGH

■ SOUTH WINDOWS: South windows receive the most light. During the summer months they even can be too bright for many kinds of houseplants—you may need to shade them a bit. All of these plants, while preferring south windows, can also be grown in east or west exposures.

Plant	Water	Temperature	Humidity	Fertilizer
ALOE	WD	I	LOW	LOW
BEGONIA, TRAILING *Cissus discolor*	EM	I	MEDIUM	INTERMEDIATE
CACTUS	WD	I-W	LOW	LOW
GERANIUM *Pelargonium*	W	I	MEDIUM	LOW
GERANIUM, STRAWBERRY *Saxifraga stolonifera*	W	I	MEDIUM	LOW
IVY *Hedera helix*	EM	I	MEDIUM	INTERMEDIATE
IVY, GERMAN OR PARLOR *Senecio mikanioides*	WD	I	LOW	INTERMEDIATE
JADE PLANT *Crassula argentea*	W	I	LOW	LOW
PASSION FLOWER *Passiflora*	EM	I	MEDIUM	INTERMEDIATE
POMEGRANATE, DWARF *Punica granatum 'Nana'*	EM	I	MEDIUM	INTERMEDIATE
SHEFFLERA, HAWAI'IAN *Erassaia arboricola*	W	I	LOW	INTERMEDIATE

Key:

WATER:
- **WD:** Water thoroughly, let dry fully before rewatering.
- **W:** Water thoroughly but don't let it totally dry out before rewatering.
- **EM:** Keep soil evenly moist, but don't let it stand in water. Top inch of soil should always feel moist.

TEMPERATURE:
- **C:** Cool: 45° nights, 55° to 60° days.
- **I:** Intermediate: 50° to 55° nights, 65° to 70° days.
- **W:** Warm: 60° nights, 75° to 80° days.

HUMIDITY:
- **LOW:** 20 to 40 percent.
- **MEDIUM:** 40 to 50 percent.
- **HIGH:** 50 to 80 percent.

FERTILIZER:
- **HEAVY:** Use balanced fertilizer recommended for frequent feeding, feed each watering.
- **INTERMEDIATE:** Feed every other week with a balanced fertilizer.
- **LOW:** Feed about once per month with a balanced fertilizer.

SOURCE: *Landscaping That Saves Energy Dollars*, Ruth Foster, Globe Pequot, 1994.

LAWNS FIT FOR A PRESIDENT

A backyard briefing from the White House groundskeeper

You may not have to worry about helicopters leaving holes in your lawn or hundreds of reporters trampling through your rose garden, but White House horticulturist Dale Haney has some tips for starting and maintaining a lawn that will work anywhere. Haney has been keeping the grounds of the White House fit for presidents since 1974.

What steps should be followed in starting a healthy lawn?

The first thing is preparing the soil. Depending on your soil, you may have to add some nitrogen-rich fertilizer, but not too rich—say 8 to 12 percent—otherwise you'll promote top growth at the expense of root growth. Then you rototill it out and grade it following the contours of the yard. The next step is to seed and fertilize, generally about 1 pound of fertilizer and 6 pounds of grass seed per 1,000 square feet. After that, the most important thing is to keep the seed wet until germination, which takes two weeks in most cases.

When grass appears, what should be done?

Once it gets to be about 3 inches tall, cut it to 2 inches and after that start mowing it to about 3 inches. Don't spray for weeds until you've mowed it three or four times, otherwise you might damage the grass before it's established itself.

Once your lawn is established, what is the best maintenance schedule?

Mow once or twice a week after that. Also water once or twice a week.

What about fertilizer?

Fertilizer is important. Even in the heat of the summer, keep putting it down at a half-rate so you establish more root growth than top growth—especially if you're watering, because constant watering leaches nutrients from the soil.

You've got to be careful when you're watering in the summer, particularly at night. That's when you run into your fungus problems caused by standing water and high humidity. Conditions are just right for a fungus to drop in.

Is it harmful to water your grass during extreme heat?

I've heard that, too. But it's better to cool it down during the heat of the day. It takes stress off the grass and keeps the roots from coming up to the top instead of driving down.

Come fall, how should a lawn be prepared for winter?

In late August or early September of the lawn's first year, and every four or five years after that, you might want to rent a thatching machine to remove the lower layer of thatch [dead grass] and put down some more fertilizer and seed. That should get you ready for winter and a healthy lawn for next spring. Once your program is going, things should fall in place.

FACT FILE:

DROUGHT RESISTORS

According to the Lawn Institute, the following grasses do well in dry climates:

EXCELLENT	GOOD
Buffalograss	Fairway wheatgrass
Blue gama	Smooth brome
Bermudagrass	Western wheatgrass
	Fine fescue

PLANTER'S GUIDE

THE GRASS IS ALWAYS GREENER

To pick the best grass seed for your lawn, take into account the growing region (defined by humidity level and mean temperature), micro-climate (how much sun the lawn gets throughout the day), maintenance time, and expected foot traffic.

BAHIAGRASS — GULF COAST

Paspalum

■ *This wide, coarse-bladed grass is not particularly attractive, but its raggedness and deep root system make it good for erosion control.*

MICRO-CLIMATE	FOOT TRAFFIC	MAINTENANCE
Sunny to partly shady	High	Low

BENTGRASS — NORTHERN

Agrostis

■ *Often used on putting greens, this high-maintenance grass should be used only on low-traffic areas or where soft-soled shoes are worn.*

MICRO-CLIMATE	FOOT TRAFFIC	MAINTENANCE
Sunny to partly shady	Low	High

BERMUDAGRASS — SOUTHERN

Cynodon

■ *Fast-growing, this wide-bladed grass requires frequent edge-trimming, but will tolerate high traffic. Popular in the South for its vigor and density.*

MICRO-CLIMATE	FOOT TRAFFIC	MAINTENANCE
Sunny	High	Medium to high

BUFFALOGRASS — WEST CENTRAL

Buchloe

■ *Like wheatgrass, a native turf that is thick and rugged, requires low maintenance and will not grow over 4 or 5 inches if left unmowed.*

MICRO-CLIMATE	FOOT TRAFFIC	MAINTENANCE
Sunny	Medium	Low

CARPETGRASS — SOUTHERN

Axonopus

■ *Coarse but sensitive to wear, used primarily on hard-to-mow places because of its low maintenance and slow growth rate.*

MICRO-CLIMATE	FOOT TRAFFIC	MAINTENANCE
Sunny	Low	Low

CENTIPEDEGRASS — SOUTHERN

Eremochloa

■ *A good "middle-of-the-road" grass—easy to care for, will tolerate some shade, and is vigorous and attractive. It requires two seasons to grow.*

MICRO-CLIMATE	FOOT TRAFFIC	MAINTENANCE
Sunny to partly shady	Low	Low

KENTUCKY BLUEGRASS — NORTHERN

Poa

■ *The most popular of cool-season grasses for its beauty and ruggedness and flexibility. It will excel with minimum maintenance almost anywhere.*

MICRO-CLIMATE	FOOT TRAFFIC	MAINTENANCE
Sunny to partly shady	Medium to heavy	Low to high

PERENNIAL RYEGRASS — NORTHERN

Festuca

■ *This quick-growing and reasonably hardy grass is used in seed mixes to provide cover and erosion control while the other seeds take root.*

MICRO-CLIMATE	FOOT TRAFFIC	MAINTENANCE
Sunny to partly shady	Medium	Medium to high

■ PLANTER'S GUIDE

ST. AUGUSTINE GRASS — SOUTH ATLANTIC

Stenotaphrum

■ *Dense and spongy, it is prized for its high shade tolerance. Not available in seed form, but usually sold as fairly inexpensive sod.*

MICRO-CLIMATE	FOOT TRAFFIC	MAINTENANCE
Sunny to shady	Medium	Medium to high

TALL FESCUES — NORTHERN

Festuca

■ *Though it is a cool-season grass, this tough wide-bladed turf has good heat tolerance and grows well in areas with a steep range of weather. It is often used on playgrounds because of its extreme ruggedness.*

MICRO-CLIMATE	FOOT TRAFFIC	MAINTENANCE
Sunny to partly shady	Heavy	Medium

WHEATGRASS — HIGH PLAIN

Agropyron

■ *Thick and tough, this native grass grows on the high plains of the Northwest. It will withstand weather extremes and heavy traffic and requires mowing about once a month..*

MICRO-CLIMATE	FOOT TRAFFIC	MAINTENANCE
Sunny	High	Low

ZOYSIA — SOUTHERN

Zoysia

■ *Takes root very quickly and crowds out other grasses and weeds. It turns a not entirely unattractive straw yellow in cold weather and requires little maintenance in general.*

MICRO-CLIMATE	FOOT TRAFFIC	MAINTENANCE
Sunny to partly shady	High	Low to medium

SOURCE: Dr. H. A. Turgeon, Pennsylvania State University.

THE COMEBACK OF THE HAND MOWER

The old push mowers have been transformed by new technology

Lawnmowers have come a long way since the time when you needed real muscle power to push a gasoline-powered backyard model around your back-forty. Today, few of the 5 million power mowers sold annually require anything more than a gentle guiding hand to get them around a lawn, and at $250 and up, the pricier models can even "mulch" their own cuttings so you can leave shorn blades on the ground and skip the raking. But who has an acre of Kentucky bluegrass to worry about anymore? And aren't you getting a little tired of finding your mower out of gas or in need of a tuneup?

A hand-powered push mower may be just what you need. Today's version of the old wood and cast-iron models that were around back when the Model T was in vogue cost as little as $100, and they weigh less than half what their predecessors did. What's more, the new heat-treated alloy steel edge that's used to make the blades gives these mowers a scissor-like edge that seldom requires sharpening. So fine is the new push mowers' cut, in fact, that the clippings can be left to decompose on the lawn, cutting back on the need for chemical fertilizers. And since the new mowers don't pollute the air, they will be exempt from federal clean-air rules for gas mowers that may soon be introduced.

Top manufacturers of these high-tech push mowers include American Lawn Mower/Great States Corporation and Agrifab Inc., which specializes in the top-of-the-line models that are especially favored by groundskeepers and other lawn-maintenance perfectionists.

EXPERT SOURCES

A GARDENER'S BOOKSHELF

Even the greenest of green thumbs appreciate the advice of great garden reference books. Here, Maureen Heffernan (MH), program director of the Cleveland Botanical Garden, and Chip Tynan (CT), horticultural specialist at the Missouri Botanical Garden, nominate their favorites.

GENERAL REFERENCE

AMERICAN HORTICULTURAL SOCIETY ENCYCLOPEDIA OF GARDEN PLANTS
Christopher Brickell, ed., Macmillan, 1989, $49.95
■ A comprehensive volume of information on most of the trees, shrubs, flowers, and foliage plants grown in American gardens. MH

READER'S DIGEST ILLUSTRATED GUIDE TO GARDENING
Carroll C. Calkins, ed., Reader's Digest Association, 1989, $7.98
■ If you had access to no other source, you could develop some terrific skills with this book alone. It explains techniques in easily understood terms and provides excellent illustrations. CT

TREES AND SHRUBS

MANUAL OF WOODY LANDSCAPE PLANTS
Michael Dirr, Stipes Publishing, 1990, $31.95
■ An unsurpassed resource for concise information on the characteristics, culture, and habits of most of the trees, shrubs, and vines grown in the United States. CT

ANNUALS AND PERENNIALS

BURPEE AMERICAN GARDEN SERIES
Suzanne Bales and Burpee staff, Prentice Hall, 1993, $9 per volume
■ The annuals and perennials editions are excellent for beginning gardeners. Basic, reliable information on how to start seeds, plant, transplant, and maintain annuals and perennials with tips on creative garden and container designs. MH

MANUAL OF HERBACEOUS ORNAMENTAL PLANTS
Steven M. Still, Stipes Publishing, 1988, $48.80
■ This does for perennials what Michael Dirr's book does for woody plants. Concise and complete. CT

HOUSEPLANTS AND WILDFLOWERS

THE NEW HOUSE PLANT EXPERT
D.G. Hessayon, Sterling Publishing, 1992, $14.95
■ Most gardening books of British origin have limited value to American gardeners. This is the exception. Houseplants are houseplants the world over. CT

ORGANIC GARDENING

THE CHEMICAL-FREE LAWN
Warren Schultz, Rodale Press, 1989, $14.95
■ The best book on growing healthy lawns without major chemical dumping. Recommends regionally specific types of grass and grass cultivars. MH

THE ORGANIC GARDENER'S HOME REFERENCE
Tanya Denkla, Storey Com Inc., 1994, $19.95
■ All about growing fruits, vegetables, nuts, and herbs to peak quality, using organic techniques. CT

MISCELLANEOUS

THE COMPLETE SHADE GARDENER
George Schenk, Houghton Mifflin, 1984, $17.45
■ Creative garden design tips for shady sites and lists of plants that will grow in light to full shade. Also, complete information on how to grow each recommended plant. MH

GARDENING BY MAIL
Barbara Barton, Houghton Mifflin, 1994, $18.95
■ The ultimate source book for seeds, plants, equipment, and books. MH

PETS

GENETICS

THE PRICE OF BEING PUREBRED

Too much inbreeding has left many dogs walking basket cases

Bad genes plague every species, but most harmful traits are naturally selected out instead of being passed on from generation to generation. This has not been true for mankind's best friend, however. Over the past century, popular dogs have been defined by what looks good, as loosely defined by breed-specific dog clubs and the American Kennel Club. By breeding for external traits or idiosyncrasies, such as long or blunt faces, large or short sloping hips, or an odd eye color, consumers have unwittingly caused a proliferation of genetic disorders and undermined the genetic integrity of the dog species.

The origin of the domesticated dog is the subject of much debate. We do know that early humans kept the pups of wild animals, jackals, coyotes, and wolves as pets. But as these canines were domesticated, it was discovered that some were better than others at guarding, hauling, and herding. Humans began breeding selectively for these desirable traits. Only then were "breeds" created. But as dogs of similar genetic composition were bred over and over again, the gene pool became depleted, leaving behind hundreds of inheritable diseases and disorders: a deadly legacy that could be affecting your favorite canine.

Today, Americans own more than 20 million purebred dogs. As many as one in four of these purebreds are afflicted with genetic disorders that not only cause discomfort for dogs and distress for owners, but at worst can lead to disease and death. Great Danes suffer from heart defects, collies are prone to deafness, toy poodles often experience epilepsy, and Labrador retrievers have a high risk of dwarfism. In all, more than 300 genetic abnormalities have been found in dogs.

The problem is that the characteristics judges and clubs have deemed prize-winning are often detrimental to the animals' health. To demand huge heads on bulldogs can require that they be born unnaturally, through cesarean section. The wrinkled skin on shar-peis can make them prone to rashes.

To make matters worse, the best way to produce puppies with a specific external quality is to mate two dogs with that quality. Since the closest resemblances are found in families, dogs are often inbred, the mating of fathers and daughters or brothers and sisters being common practice.

YOUR DOG MAY SIT, BUT CAN IT STAND?

Bad posture may not land a dog in the doghouse in your view. But in some cases, your dog's posture may indicate real problems. A dog that's "down in front," for instance, may have a neuromuscular disorder and need to see a vet.

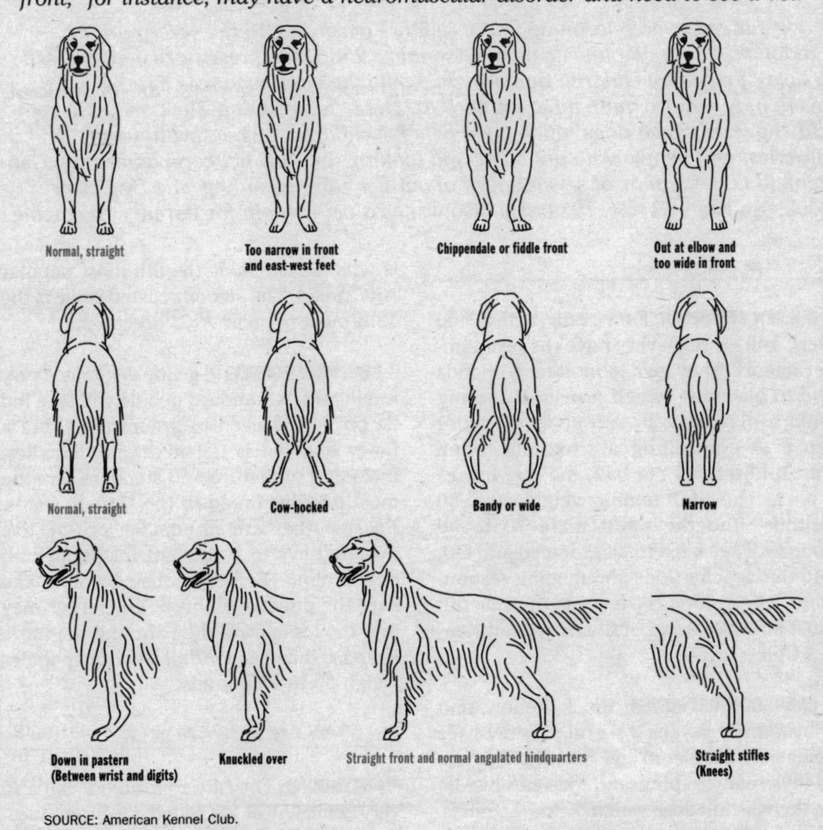

SOURCE: American Kennel Club.

Breeders also practice "line breeding," in which grandparents mate with their grandchildren, or cousins with each other. Both inbreeding and line breeding increase the likelihood of reproducing a desirable external trait. They also increase the likelihood of reproducing genetic disease.

The problem intensifies with overbreeding. Often a single desirable male, or even a set of desirable parents, will produce many litters. If it is later determined that the male, or the parents, have a genetic disease, it will have already been widely dispersed in the offspring. While early humans based the value of a dog on its ability to perform traditional tasks efficiently, today's dogs are evaluated on appearance alone. Because of inbreeding, line breeding, and overbreeding, many dogs can no longer even perform traditional tasks.

Who is to blame? Michael Fox, a veterinarian and animal behaviorist with the Humane Society, says, "It is the culture. A culture that regards dogs as commodities and recognizes purebreds as superior to mixed breeds."

DOG LOVER'S GUIDE

DOGS WITH AN ATTITUDE YOU'LL DIG

A dog's breed is no guarantee that it will act according to the veterinarian's handbook. Every dog has its own personality. But some breeds are better suited to being jostled by children than others, while the circumstances of other pet lovers may require quite different choices. Here, veterinarian Sheldon L. Gerstenfeld suggests which dogs make good pets for children, owners with active lifestyles, and people who are older and looking for easy pet companionship. Gerstenfeld is the author of seven books about pet care, including The Dog Care Book *(Addison-Wesley, 1989). He also writes a pet column for* Parents' *magazine.*

DOGS FOR CHILDREN

■ **GOLDEN RETRIEVER:** Easy-going, active, and alert, golden retrievers have the best temperaments. They love to interact with kids and to play ball, which provides a young child a playmate. It also gives a child a sense of controlling a situation—when the child throws the ball, the dog brings it back. The adult female weighs 50 to 60 pounds, and the adult male 70 to 90 pounds. They need to be groomed and fed, and that teaches kids about being responsible. The golden retriever is the seventh most popular breed of the American Kennel Club (AKC).

■ **LABRADOR RETRIEVER:** Black, yellow, and chocolate Labs are generally known for being even-tempered and friendly. They are always ready to play, and kids can just lie on them. Adult dogs weigh 60 to 70 pounds. They need grooming, so they also teach kids to be responsible.

Avoid the Chesapeake Bay retriever, which has a curlier coat. It isn't good with kids because it can be a little nasty and unpredictable and will bite more readily than the others. Labrador retrievers are the fifth most popular AKC breed.

■ **COLLIE:** These are sweet dogs. They're gentle and predictable and won't bite around your kids. They're easy to train and really want to please. Adult collies weigh about 50 pounds and their long hair requires grooming. The rough-coated collie, which is what Lassie is, is the 9th most popular AKC breed. The smooth-coated collie is the 13th most popular AKC breed.

■ **STANDARD POODLE:** A gentle dog that is very intelligent. A standard poodle will let a kid lie on it. You need to groom them, but a fancy hair cut is not necessary. Poodles, including miniature and standard, are the most popular breed in the United States. Because they are so popular, prospective owners have to watch out for puppy-mill degradation. Before choosing one, make sure the dog is well-bred. The larger they are, the less active they are and the more exercise they need. Adult standard poodles weigh 50 to 55 pounds.

DOGS FOR THE ACTIVE PERSON

■ **GREYHOUND:** They are a little aloof, but also very gentle. Most are adopted from the racetrack. Greyhounds have a regal personality and don't slobber with affection like a retriever. They're also very athletic, so they're good for active people. Adult greyhounds weigh 70 to 80 pounds. High-strung and easily upset by sudden movements at times, greyhounds are the 105th most popular AKC breed.

■ **BOXER:** Animated, with outgoing personalities, boxers respond readily to playfulness. They are the 24th most popular AKC breed. Prospective owners looking for a dignified dog, however, should be wary of the boxer: They tend to drool and snore.

■ DOG LOVER'S GUIDE

■ **TERRIER:** Terriers start out their morning as if they had eight cups of coffee, so they are good for an active person. I'd recommend the bull terrier, which was bred for pit fighting. They are always ready to frolic and so need firm training, but they are also known for their sweet personalities. The adult bull terrier weighs in at about 50 pounds. It is the 65th most popular AKC breed.

■ **ENGLISH COCKER SPANIEL:** These are sweet dogs, and they haven't been inbred. They're playful and alert at all times and great for children and active people. The English cocker spaniel is a medium-size dog with long hair. An adult usually weighs 23 to 25 pounds, 3 to 11 pounds more than its cousin, the American cocker spaniel. The English cocker is the 64th most popular AKC breed.

DOGS FOR OLDER PEOPLE

■ **CHIHUAHUA:** If they are from a good breeder, they will have a good personality. Chihuahuas have short hair, so they don't need a lot of grooming and so are a good choice for an older person living alone. The Chihuahua is the smallest of all the breeds. The barkless variety was once used by the Aztecs as a sacrificial animal to eradicate the sins of the dead. Chihuahuas can be yappy and clannish at times. An adult Chihuahua weighs about 3 pounds and is the 21st most popular AKC breed.

■ **MINIATURE POODLE:** These poodles are intelligent. And they're good for older people because they're small and don't shed a lot. They love attention. Again, the poodle is the most popular AKC breed, so owners have to make sure the dog is not inbred. All poodles are considered fast learners compared with other breeds, but generally the smaller they are the faster they learn. The adult miniature poodle weighs in at about 15 pounds.

■ **TOY POODLE:** These are good dogs for older people. Toy poodles love to be cuddled and are intelligent. They do have to be groomed, but they don't shed, so there's not much hair to clean up. The adult toy poodle weighs less than 10 pounds. It is the brightest of all the toys and will demand its owner's continuous attention. Because of the toy poodle's popularity, inbreeding can be a problem.

■ **YORKSHIRE TERRIER:** These dogs are small, easy to care for, and can be picked up. They weigh about 7 pounds and are about 7 inches tall, with long silky hair that drapes like a sheet over the body. Their coats require grooming, however, which may not be good for an elderly person who doesn't have the energy, or who has arthritis. The Yorkshire terrier is the 14th most popular AKC breed.

FACT FILE:

A DOG DEBT TO SOCIETY

■ *Dogs make wonderful companions, but they don't come free, as these cost estimates from the Humane Society of the United States indicate.*

Adopting a dog from a shelter	**$55**
First-year vaccinations	**$200**
Each year thereafter	**$65**
Initial training	**$50–$100**
Each year thereafter	**$50–$200**
Other annual veterinary care [1]	**$135**
Annual feeding	**$115–$400**
Annual toys, grooming supplies	**$160**
Grooming, per visit [2]	**$50**
Annual flea and tick care	**$80**
Daily boarding	**$21–$30**

1. 1991 figures. 2. Varies with size and breed.

EXPERT Q&A

WHEN THE MOVIE STAR IS A DOG

One of Hollywood's top canine trainers reveals his secrets

Do you have trouble getting your dog to perform even the most simple tricks? Does your pet have moxie that you don't know how to unleash? Consult Steve Berens, the trainer of some of Hollywood's biggest canine stars. Berens has 15 years' experience training leading dogs for movies such as *The Mask*, *Texasville*, and *Kuffs*. He learned the craft from his uncle, Ray Berwick, who trained the stars of the classic Alfred Hitchcock movie *The Birds*.

■ Is it better to have a professional train your pet or to do it yourself?

It doesn't help to send pets off somewhere unless you are part of the training. Dogs that are sent away come back and fall into the same old habits and routines again. It's best to do it yourself.

■ How would you start teaching obedience to a dog?

By doing leash work. You begin to control a dog naturally that way. Then you have to establish motivation by rewarding your dog with a pat on the head, playtime with a ball, or a treat. You have to be fair and consistent, just as you are with a child.

■ What is the best way to develop a bond with your pet?

The most important thing is to spend quality time—time during the day or at night, taking a walk or playing with a ball. It's important to establish communication with your animal. Five to 10 minutes a day is okay, but spend more if you can.

■ Is any special training required when there's a child in the house?

If you have a child in the house, you might want to approach a professional. If you have an aggressive dog, there are times when you might need to be careful around children. A lot of people want Labradors because they think the kids can jump up and down on the dog and it won't care. And of course there are times when kids will pull an ear. But it's very important for parents to teach their children to respect animals, too. Instead of getting someone hurt, it's always better to consult someone.

■ How have you been able to successfully break animals of their bad habits?

Sometimes it takes a long time. I am working with a Great Dane right now that I got from the pound. He was a bad growler and he pushed people around doing so. I had to break him of that habit because it is not good to have a growling dog on a movie set. I showed him a lot of love and did not meet his aggression with more aggression. Now he is totally normal. So punishment is not always the answer.

■ How can you get a dog to perform a stunt?

You have to break down the task. Every dog learns in different ways and at different speeds. But you have to continue to move the dog along. For example, in the jail scene from the movie *The Mask*, when the dog snatches the keys away from a sleeping guard and gives them to Jim Carrey, that routine was made up of 8 to 10 different moves. The dog had to walk over, stop, look around, jump up, and so on. You usually end up having the dog perform the whole thing from the beginning. But sometimes you have two trainers talking the dog through the routine. The key is the treat, the reward. That becomes the motivation for performing the routine.

■ What is the most difficult thing you have trained an animal to do?

I'm working on a movie now called *The Truth about Cats and Dogs*, in which I have to teach a dog to roller-skate. That has been very challenging.

PET TALK

CATS CHIRP WHEN STALKING BIRDS

Reading meaning into your cat's moves and meows

Your cat rolls over, and meows. He drools when you pet him. He avoids eye contact with your best friend. What is he trying to tell you? "Cats use a basic repertoire of sounds and body language to express emotions, intentions, needs, and wants," says Dr. Michael W. Fox, vice president of the Humane Society of the United States and author of *Understanding Your Cat* (St. Martin's Press, 1974). "A meow has a different meaning in a different context. A cat is aware of context."

For example, when a cat meows and then runs to the kitchen, you can be sure he wants to be fed. If a cat meows, makes eye contact, and raises its tail vertically, it probably wants to be picked up. When it brushes against you, meows, and then walks away with its tail in the air, it means "follow me." Think of a tour guide who holds an umbrella in the air. When a cat meows at the door and looks at the door knob, let him out. "Cats know you use the door knob to open the door," Fox says.

When a cat's tail is in an inverted "U" or it looks at you and flops over on one side, it wants to play. When its tail is arched toward its body during play, it is saying it's excited. Should it lash its tail, it means intense arousal. It may do this when it sees a bird or when it's being petted. It may also drool when it's being petted. If it lowers its head, gives a direct stare, and walks slowly forward, it's angry. When it crouches close to the ground, avoids eye contact, rises up on its four legs, arches its back and makes its hair stand on end, it's scared. "The classic Halloween cat is signaling fear," Fox says.

Sometimes a cat will wash itself after you've yelled at it. Is it trying to wash away its hurt? In fact, it's embarrassed. It may wash itself before a thunderstorm too, because it's anxious. "This is called 'displacement grooming.' Just as an adult will fidget with his pockets when he's anxious. It's a self-comforting behavior, like a child sucking his thumb," Fox explains.

When a cat makes chirping sounds, it probably has its eyes on a bird. A cat will usually make chirping sounds when it spots prey. When it avoids eye contact, it probably wants you to keep your distance.

Cats make 16 different vocal sounds. Fox describes them as murmur patterns, vowel patterns, and strained intensity sounds. A cat will make a murmuring sound, sometimes accompanied by purring when it's relaxed, when it has a goal in mind, such as being let outside, or when it's frustrated. A cat makes strained intensity sounds, such as hissing or growling, when fighting or mating.

A cat's eyes and ears are also good ways of finding out what kind of mood it's in. When its ears go back and its pupils enlarge, it is getting defensive. The more enlarged the pupils and the flatter its ears are on its head, the more defensive it is feeling. It may even bare its teeth if you keep it up.

Suppose your cat starts racing through the house with what Fox calls "the evening crazies." When all you see is the cat running around in circles, the cat is imagining it's out hunting in the jungle. It may pounce on imaginary prey or run around as if it's chasing a gazelle. "Cats have a great imagination," Fox says. What should Mr. or Mrs. Owner do when little Fluffy tears through the house? By all means, they should join in.

CAT LOVER'S GUIDE

FROM PHARAOH'S FAVORITES TO LOVING TABBIES

Cats have been everything from lap companion to religious idol through the ages. Here's the book on the best, brightest, most elegant, and most cuddly cats from which to choose when picking a pet.

■ **ABYSSINIAN:** One of the oldest known breeds, their slender, elegant, muscular bodies were often featured in paintings and sculptures in ancient Egyptian. Abyssinians have arched necks, large ears, almond-shaped eyes, and long, tapered tails. The Abyssinian's soft and silky medium-length coat is one of its most unique features. Each hair has two or three distinct bands of black or dark brown, giving the breed a subtle overall coat color and lustrous sheen. Abyssinians also can have a rich copper red coat. They are particularly loyal and make good companions.

■ **AMERICAN CURL:** The name comes from the breed's unique curled ears, which curl away from the head to make it look as if this cat is always alert. The American curl is moderately large, with walnut-shaped eyes. Its ears are straight at birth, and curl within 2 to 10 days. A relatively rare breed, the American curl usually weighs 5 to 10 pounds. Curls are short-haired, and their coats come in all colors possible. Even-tempered and intelligent with a playful disposition, American curls adore their owners and display affection in a quiet way. They adapt to almost any home, live well with other animals, and are very healthy.

FACT FILE:

TALLYING A TABBY'S TAB

■ *From the Humane Society of the United States, estimates of what it costs to be a cat owner on average:*

Adopting a cat from a shelter	**$25**
First-year vaccinations	**$200**
Each year thereafter	**$27**
Other annual veterinary care[1]	**$80**
Annual feeding[1]	**$145**
Annual kitty litter	**$78**
Annual toys, grooming supplies	**$160**
Daily boarding	**$10**

1. 1991 figures.

■ **AMERICAN SHORTHAIR:** The descendents of house cats and farm cats, American shorthairs are easy to care for and resistant to disease. They have big bones and are docile and even-tempered. The breed is strongly built, with an agile, medium to large body and big bones. They have a short, thick coat that ranges in colors from black to white to red to tabby.

■ **AMERICAN WIREHAIR:** Uniquely American, the breed began as a spontaneous mutation in a litter on a farm in New York in 1966. Its dense coarse coat is hard to touch and sets these cats apart from any other breed. Some also have curly whiskers. The breed is active and agile and has a keen interest in its surroundings. Although it is quiet and reserved, owners find the breed easy to care for.

■ **BALINESE:** Related to the Siamese, it has a long silky coat, but unlike most long-haired cats, its coat doesn't mat. Endowed with a long, muscular body, the Balinese can come in several colors, including seal point, blue point, and chocolate point. The Balinese is intelligent, curious, and alert. It is as affectionate and demonstrative as the Siamese, but it isn't as talkative and has a softer voice when it does speak up.

■ **BRITISH SHORTHAIR:** Perhaps the oldest natural English breed, the British shorthair is enjoying new popularity. These cats tend to be reserved, devoted, and good companions. Because of their dense coats, they also are easy to groom.

■ **BURMESE:** Known as the clown of the cat kingdom, the Burmese thrives on attention and is very gregarious. It has a compact body and a glossy coat that comes in several colors, including sable and champagne. Burmese live well with kids and dogs. They are smart, loyal, and devoted. Despite their hefty appetites, they seldom are fat. They *are* very expensive, though, costing as much as $1,500.

■ **CORNISH REX:** Considered "ultra-refined," the Cornish Rex has the body of a greyhound, huge ears set high on its head, and large eyes. It is surprisingly heavy and warm to the touch, with a very soft coat and muscular body. Not only do these cats fastidiously groom themselves, but they want to groom their human companions as well. If that's not to your liking, you may want another cat, because the problem may be impossible to eliminate. The Cornish Rex are highly intelligent and will adapt to almost any environment. They are skillful hunters, love children and dogs, and make superb pets. They generally like to be handled and are excellent choices for people who love cats but dislike cat hair, because they have an undercoat but no outer coat.

■ **DEVON REX:** Devons are considered a mutant breed. The mature female averages 6 pounds; the male averages 7.5 pounds. Devons have a full, wavy coat, large eyes, a short muzzle, prominent cheekbones, and huge low-set ears, which make them look a bit elfin. They are concerned for their owner's safety and are very curious. They refuse to be left out of anything, always knowing where they are going and what they will do there. People with allergies to cat hair can happily live with a Devon Rex because they do not shed.

■ **EXOTIC SHORTHAIR:** Sometimes called the "Teddy Bear" cat, exotic shorthairs require little maintenance because their medium-to-long coat does not mat. They are Persian-like in temperament and type but have an easy-to-care-for plush coat. They will jump in your lap to take a nap, but generally prefer cooler places to sleep. They are very quiet, but they will retrieve a toy until you get tired of throwing it.

■ **JAPANESE BOBTAIL:** The Japanese consider bobtails a symbol of good luck. They are medium-sized and muscular with a short tail which resembles a pom-pom or a rabbit's tail. They have high cheekbones, a long nose, and large ears. Born much larger than other cats, the sturdy breed learns to walk earlier than others and starts getting into mischief earlier as well. Active, intelligent, and talkative, their soft voices have a whole scale of tones; some people say they sing. They almost always speak when spoken to and enjoy a good game of fetch and riding around on their human companion's shoulders. Japanese bobtails are good travelers and good with dogs and children.

■ **KORAT:** They are quite rare, even in Thailand, where the breed originated. The Korat's oversized, luminous eyes have been called "dewdrops on a lotus leaf." The Korat is medium-sized with a hard body and a silverish blue coat. They have extraordinary powers of hearing, sight, and scent, are cautious, and dislike loud, sudden noises. They form an exceptionally strong bond to their human companions and enjoy being cuddled. They get along well with other cats, but might compete for the owner's affection if there is another cat.

■ **MAINE COON CAT:** The Maine coon cat was chosen as best cat at the first cat show ever held in America. It is a native American long-hair. Originally a working cat, it is a very good mouser. The Maine coon cat is solid and rugged and can endure a harsh climate, like Maine's. It has a smooth, shaggy coat and is known for its loving nature and great intelligence. The breed is especially good with children and dogs and has always been a popular and sought-after companion.

ORIENTAL SHORTHAIR: The extremely long Oriental shorthair is described by the Cat Fanciers' Association as "demonstrative and silly, as well as sinuous and sensuous. Its emerald eyes can gleam with wit, flash and arrogance." These cats are medium-sized and are choosy eaters at times. They are easy to care for and make a practical pet. The Cat Fanciers' Association says, "Their innate sensibility verges on psychic. Once communication is established, you'll never need an alarm clock, or wonder where the cat is when you arrive home from work."

PERSIAN: The most popular cat breed, Persians are known for their long, flowing coats, which require an indoor, protected environment. They need to be combed every day with a metal comb. They also need an occasional bath to prevent matting. Persians have a round massive head and a very round face. Their necks are short and thick and they have short, heavy legs and broad, short bodies. Persians don't like to jump and climb, but they are very responsive to affection. They have gentle personalities that fare better in secure, serene households than very busy ones. But given a little time, even they can adjust to a boisterous household with lots of children.

RUSSIAN BLUE: Fine-boned, with short hair and a regal appearance, Russian blues are clean, quiet cats that don't shed a lot. They are very intelligent and are well-attuned to the moods of their owners. They will tolerate being left alone all day while their human companions are at work, and generally do well in a house full of kids and dogs.

SIAMESE: Siamese cats are like dogs. They will fetch and do other tricks, talk a lot, and follow their owners around the house. They will also sit on your lap. They have blue eyes, and a dark, raccoonlike "mask" around them. They have pointed features—long svelte bodies and long tapered lines with coats that are short, finely textured, and close to the body. Siamese cats have persistent, distinctive voices and are intelligent, dependent, and affectionate. But be advised: because they have been highly inbred, Siamese cats can be extremely timid, unpredictable, or aggressive.

FACT FILE:

THEY'RE THE CAT'S MEOW

Cats don't have to be purebred to earn affection. Take these two household favorites:

CALICO: *Japanese sailors used to like to have a calico cat on their ships because they thought the cats warded off evil spirits. Calicos have characteristic three-colored patches—white, black, and red—on their coats. But the cat's personality is a little snitty.*

RED TABBY: *Two of the most popular red tabbies are Morris and the cartoon cat Garfield. The red tabby is a ginger or marmalade color with markings in even darker red. These cats are gentle and loving with people, but they're not good with other cats.*

PREVENTIVE CARE

SHOTS YOUR PET WILL APPRECIATE

Vaccinations will keep your dog or cat free of many common diseases

Since the discovery in the eighteenth century that it was possible to build up immunities against certain diseases in both people and animals by injecting them with tiny amounts of living virus, hundreds of vaccines have been created. By immunizing pets in their early months and bolstering the protection with annual "booster" vaccinations, pet owners can shield their animals from diseases that often are highly contagious to other animals and, in cases such as rabies, pose a serious threat to humans as well. Here, from the American Veterinary Medical Association, is a rundown of the diseases against which your dog or cat should be immunized.

BOTH CATS AND DOGS

■ **RABIES:** A viral disease that can attack the central nervous system of all warm-blooded animals, including humans. It is fatal if not treated. Most states require dog and cat owners to vaccinate their pets against rabies. The disease is transmitted by saliva, which is usually transferred by a bite from an infected animal and is frequently found in wild animals, such as skunks, raccoons, and bats.

There are two types of rabies—"dumb" and "furious." Both cause a departure from normal behavior. Animals with furious rabies will have a period immediately prior to death in which they appear to be "mad," frothing at the mouth and biting anything that gets in their way. Dumb rabies differs in that there is no "mad" period. Instead, paralysis, usually of the lower jaw, is the first sign. The paralysis spreads to limbs and vital organs and death quickly follows. Wild animals that are unusually friendly and appear to have no fear of man or domestic animals should be avoided and reported immediately to the police or animal control authorities.

Rabies is almost totally preventable by vaccination. Dogs and cats should receive an initial rabies vaccination by the age of three to four months. Protection lasts from one to three years. Regular booster vaccinations are required.

DOGS ONLY

■ **CANINE BORDETELLOSIS:** Caused by bacteria in the respiratory tracts of many animals, it is the primary cause of kennel cough. Besides the cough, some dogs suffer from a purulent nasal discharge. Transmission usually occurs through contact with other dogs' nasal secretions. Vaccination is generally administered by nasal spray.

■ **CANINE DISTEMPER:** A highly contagious viral disease, canine distemper is transmitted by direct or indirect contact with the discharges from an infected dog's eyes and nose. Direct contact is unnecessary because the virus can be carried by air currents and inanimate objects. Early signs are similar to those of a severe cold and often go unrecognized by the pet owner. The respiratory problems may be accompanied by vomiting and diarrhea. A nervous system disorder may also develop.

The death rate from canine distemper is greater than 50 percent in adult dogs and even higher in puppies. Even if the dog survives, distemper can cause permanent damage to a dog's nervous system, sense of smell, hearing, and sight. Partial or total paralysis is not uncommon.

■ **CANINE LEPTOSPIROSIS:** A bacterial disease that harms the kidneys and can result in kidney failure. Vomiting, impaired vision, and convulsions are all tipoffs. Transmission results from contact with the urine of infected animals, or contact with something tainted by the urine of an infected animal.

■ **CANINE PARAINFLUENZA:** A viral infection of the respiratory tract, it is frequently accompanied by other respiratory viruses and is usually spread through contact with the nasal secretions of other dogs.

■ **CANINE PARVOVIRUS (CPV):** A serious problem because the virus withstands extreme temperature changes and even exposure to most disinfectants. The source of infection is usually dog feces, which can contaminate cages and shoes and can be carried on the feet and hair of infected animals.

CPV attacks the intestinal tract, white blood cells, and heart muscle. Symptoms include vomiting, severe diarrhea, a loss of appetite, depression, and high fever. Most deaths occur within 48 to 72 hours after the onset of clinical signs. Infected pups may act depressed or collapse, gasping for breath. Death may follow immediately. Pups that survive are likely to have permanently damaged hearts.

■ **INFECTIOUS CANINE HEPATITIS:** Caused by a virus that can infect many tissues, the disease usually attacks the liver, causing hepatitis. In some instances a whiteness or cloudiness of the eye may accompany the disease. Another strain of the same virus can cause respiratory tract infections. These viruses are transmitted by contact with objects that have been contaminated with the urine from infected dogs. Infectious canine hepatitis is different from human hepatitis.

CATS ONLY

■ **FELINE PANLEUKOPENIA:** Also known as feline distemper, the disease comes from a virus so resistant that it may remain infectious for over a year at room temperature on inanimate objects. Spread through blood, urine, feces, nasal secretions, and fleas from infected cats, the virus causes high fever, dehydration, vomiting, and lethargy and destroys a cat's white blood cells. It is 50 to 70 percent fatal, but immunity can be developed through vaccination of kittens and annual boosters.

■ **FELINE LEUKEMIA VIRUS:** A disease of the immune system that is usually fatal, its symptoms include weight loss, lethargy, recurring or chronic sickness, diarrhea, unusual breathing, and yellow coloration around the mouth and the whites of the eyes. Confirmation of the virus requires a blood test. Fortunately, there is a new vaccine that provides protection.

■ **FELINE VIRAL RHINOTRACHEITIS, FELINE CALICIVIRUS, AND FELINE PNEUMONITIS:** All three are highly infectious viruses of the respiratory tract, for which vaccinations are available.

■ CALLING THE SHOTS ON YOUR PET'S HEALTH

The American Veterinary Medical Association recommends the following vaccination schedule:

DISEASE	AGE AT VACCINATION First (weeks)	Second (weeks)	Third (weeks)	Revaccination intervals (months)
■ **DOGS**				
DISTEMPER	6-10	10-12	14-16	12
INFECTIOUS CANINE HEPATITIS (CAV-1 or CAV-2)	6-8	10-12	14-16	12
PARVOVIRUS INFECTION	6-8	10-12	14-16	12
BORDETELLOSIS	6-8	10-12	14-16	12
PARAINFLUENZA	6-8	10-12	14-16	12
LEPTOSPIROSIS	10-12	14-16		12
RABIES	12	64		12 or 36*
CORONAVIRUS	6-8	10-12	12-24	12
■ **CATS**				
PANLEUKOPENIA	8-10	12-16		12
VIRAL RHINOTRACHEITIS	8-10	12-16		12
CALICIVIRAL DISEASE	8-10	12-16		12
RABIES	12	64		12 or 36
FELINE LEUKEMIA	10	12 & 24 or 13-14*		12

* Check with your veterinarian for type of vaccine.

SOURCE: American Veterinary Medical Association.

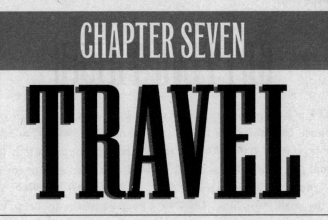

CHAPTER SEVEN

TRAVEL

"Hāna is the loveliest, most Hawaiian town in the islands."

—Susanna Moore, author of the *Hawaiian Trilogy*

Page 515

"When I dine, I filter out everything about the restaurant that's not food."

—Patricia Wells, restaurant critic of the *International Herald Tribune*

Page 531

"The best beaches aren't necessarily the most popular."

—Stephen Leatherman, director of the Laboratory for Coastal Research

Page 555

THE YEAR AHEAD: **FLY** American and Southwest, the two top-rated airlines... **EXPECT** air fares to rise moderately... **POP** a pill to get rid of jet lag... **ESCAPE** to Anguilla, new jewel of the Caribbean... **WHISK** through the Chunnel beneath the English Channel... **VISIT** Death Valley and Joshua Tree, America's newest national parks... **CANOE** along a rediscovered Indian trail... **CRUISE** on a new family-friendly ship...

GETTING THERE

AIR TRAVEL

THE BEST BIG AIRLINES TO FLY

Discovering which is tops isn't easy: Here are the facts to help you pick

Their ads brag that there's something special in the air, and in 1995 the National Institute for Aviation Research (NIAR) agreed. American Airlines won top carrier honors—as it has for four of the last five years. Southwest, which got top marks in the 1994 survey, slipped into second place (see "Comparing America's Big Airlines," opposite page).

The statisticians at NIAR, based at Wichita State University, have been rating airline performances since 1991. The scores are based on 19 weighted factors including such things as mishandled baggage, average cost per seat-mile, and on-time performance. The numbers are crunched according to a complicated formula and—voila—an "airline quality rating" is produced. Maybe the search for the best airline in the sky should end there.

Or maybe not. There are other players in the airline rating business, which like the skies, seems to be getting ever more crowded. *Condé Nast Traveler* conducts an annual survey of its readers' travel preferences. J. D. Power and Associates, a market research firm that annually canvasses business travelers, gave top marks to Delta and TWA in a 1993 survey. And in 1995, the Zagat survey, whose 30-point scale is gospel to discerning diners, weighed in as well.

Of the consumer preference surveys, the Zagat survey is the most comprehensive. Over 9,000 respondents were asked to evaluate airlines on the basis of comfort, service, timeliness, and food. Only one American carrier (Midwest Express) made it into the survey's top 10 of international and domestic airlines. The top three: Singapore Airlines, Swissair, and Cathay Pacific. Among domestic carriers, the Zagat survey rated Midwest tops, followed by Alaska Airlines, Kiwi International, and American.

So how should you choose your carrier? It depends on where you're going and what matters most to you. If, say, you've got to be in Seattle in the morning for a meeting, it's good to know that American—followed by United and Delta—bumps the fewest unwilling passengers. Southwest, Northwest, and American have the best on-time rates. If you're off to the beach and you only plan to wear your bikini, you might not care that the carriers with the best baggage-handling scores are Southwest, America West, and American.

EXPERT LIST

COMPARING AMERICA'S BIG AIRLINES

Each year, the National Institute for Aviation Research at Wichita State University analyzes 19 objective criteria and assigns each of America's big nine carriers an "airline quality rating." Below are the results of the 1995 NIAR report and some of the factors that went into those ratings.

Airline	☎	Mean airline quality rating	Average on time (percentage)	Bags mishandled per 10,000 passengers	Denied boardings per 10,000 passengers*	Average age of fleet (years)
1. AMERICAN	800-433-7300	0.225	.810%	48.2	0.4	8.77
2. SOUTHWEST	800-435-9792	0.211	.867%	42.1	3.8	8.02
3. UNITED	800-241-6522	0.123	.815%	56.7	0.5	11.18
4. DELTA	800-221-1212	–0.031	.804%	49.8	0.7	10.41
5. USAIR	800-428-4322	–0.148	.790%	61.5	2.1	11.58
6. NORTHWEST	800-225-2525	–0.210	.856%	60.9	0.6	17.56
7. AMERICA WEST	800-235-9292	–0.282	.804%	45.3	2.1	9.46
8. TWA	800-221-2000	–0.307	.800%	58.7	1.3	19.38
9. CONTINENTAL	800-525-0280	–0.574	.777%	66.7	1.8	14.47

* Not factored into airline quality rating.
SOURCE: National Institute for Aviation Research, Wichita, Kan.; U.S. Department of Transportation.

Southwest, American, and America West have the newest fleets. The average age of a Southwest plane is 8.62 years. TWA, Northwest, and Continental have the oldest. The average age of a TWA jet is 19.38 years.

For finicky flyers, amenities matter. Delta is non-smoking, even on international flights. It's hard to imagine choosing a carrier based on the airline's food. Zagat's respondents, however, found Kiwi's food "surprisingly good," and some travelers rejoiced that Alaska serves meals one "actually wants to eat." If you're fasting or dieting, try Southwest. It offers literally peanuts.

Many passengers, of course, opt for the cheapest fare, the one element not considered in the NIAR ranking because the market is constantly changing. But the Zagat survey concludes that Midwest Express, Alaska Airlines, and Kiwi International offer the best value.

Every flyer's paramount concern, of course, is safety. In that respect, 1994, the last year for which data were available as this book went to press, was not the best of years: 30 commercial airplanes crashed and 264 lives were lost. (In 1993, there were 32 commercial crashes, but only 25 deaths.)

So, which airlines are the safest? Generally, according to experts quoted in *Newsweek*, the odds of death are greater on commuter airlines. After calculating the odds of dying on one of the major carriers based on deaths in the past decade, *Newsweek's* experts concluded that American, Southwest, and TWA were the safest on domestic flights. But the statistics can be easily misconstrued. As the NIAR study notes, in 1994 only one in about 1.7 million passengers died in a commercial airline accident—and that was a bad year. (Over the past decade, the chance of being killed while flying was approximately one in 3 million.) Look at it another way: in 1994, it was 2.5 times more likely that you would be struck by lightning than die in an airplane crash.

DANGER ZONES

THE NOT-SO FRIENDLY SKIES

Lost bags may be the least of your worries in flying into some countries

When you are 30,000 feet in the air or bustling down a runway at 150 miles per hour, attention to detail becomes extremely important. A few seconds can mean the difference between a safe flight and a fatal collision. In the United States, you can rest assured that your flight has met strict safety standards set by an extremely vigilant Federal Aviation Administration, but when you travel abroad, you are sometimes at the mercy of more lax oversight bodies. Some may have failed to maintain air traffic control systems, and others may simply have abandoned regulation altogether.

That's why the FAA for the first time in 1994 released a list of nations whose governments failed to exercise sufficient safety oversight. FAA rules give carriers two alternatives: either they must make arrangements with an airline that is under the supervision of a country with approved air safety standards to fly passengers to the United States for them, or they must cease flights into the United States altogether.

Of the nine nations on the FAA list, three are in Africa—Gambia, Ghana, and Zaire. A recent study shows that the likelihood of dying in a plane crash there is 20 times higher than in the United States. The remaining six countries are in South or Central America. They are Belize, the Dominican Republic, Honduras, Nicaragua, Paraguay, and Uruguay.

Four additional countries—Bolivia, El Salvador, Guatemala, and the Netherlands Antilles—were also found not to be in compliance with international safety oversight standards, but the FAA has approved continued operations in the United States subject to heightened FAA inspections.

Not on the FAA list, but also cited as danger zones by travel experts are India, China, and Russia. Though their regulatory bodies meet FAA standards, all three nations suffer problems that an oversight agency can do little to remedy: political turmoil, deteriorating infrastructure, and a shortage of qualified pilots. In 1993 alone, for instance, 10 flights were hijacked in China. Let the flyer beware.

EXPERT PICKS

THE WORLD'S SAFEST AIRLINES

Some airlines are pretty safe, even in regions that would otherwise be considered unsafe. Below are the world's safest in 1994, as selected by the Dallas-based International Airline Passengers Association.

SAFEST LARGE AIRLINES

- **American**
- **British**
- **Delta**
- **Lufthansa**
- **Scandinavian System (SAS)**

SAFEST MID-SIZED AIRLINES

- **All Nippon**
- **America West**
- **Ansett Australia**
- **Canadian International**
- **Saudi Arabian**

SAFEST MEDIUM TO SMALL AIRLINES

- **Alaska Airlines**
- **Finnair**
- **Royal Dutch (KLM)**
- **Malaysian**
- **Swissair**

SAFEST SMALL AIRLINES

- **Cathay Pacific Airways**
- **Qantas Airways**
- **Sabena Belgian World Airlines**
- **Singapore**

JET SETTER'S GUIDE

IN AND OUT OF THE WORLD'S AIRPORTS

A 1993 poll of 6,548 transatlantic business travelers by the International Air Transport Association ranked international airports based on everything from lounge comfort to customs routines. Below are the results and some information to help you get out of the airport quickly.

Airport	Passengers in 1993 (x1,000)	Travel time to downtown	Lowest transit fare[1]	Cab fare[1]
1. AMSTERDAM ☎ 31-20-601-9111	21,275	20-25 mins.	Train: Dfl4.50 US$3	Dfl52 US$30
2. HOUSTON ☎ 713-230-3100	20,410	30-50 mins.	Metro-sked bus: US$1.25	US$29
3. SAN FRANCISCO ☎ 415-876-7809	32,737	20-25 mins.	Sam Trans Bus: 85¢	US$30
4. ATLANTA Hartsfield ☎ 404-530-6830	47,088	35-40 mins.	Airport Shuttle: US$8	US$15
5. TORONTO ☎ 613-990-5410	20,484	20-30 mins.	Airport Express: Can$10 US$7	Can$30 US$21
6. MONTREAL Mirabel ☎ 514-476-3010	2,412	45-60 mins.	Connaisseur: Can$14 US$10	Can$50 US$35
7. PARIS De Gaulle ☎ 33-14-862-1940	26,115	45-60 mins.	Metro: F5 US$1	F170 US$32
8. LONDON Gatwick ☎ 44-29-328-822	20,159	70-90 mins.	Flightline Bus: £6.50 US$9	£50 US$78
9. DALLAS/FT. WORTH ☎ 214-574-8888	49,970	30-40 mins.	Super Shuttle: US$13.50	US$28
10. LOS ANGELES ☎ 310-646-5252	47,845	30-35 mins.	RTD Bus: US$1.50	US$26
11. NEWARK ☎ 201-961-6000	25,613	30-45 mins.[2]	Olympia Trails Bus: US$7	US$30[3]
12. LONDON Heathrow ☎ 44-81-759-4321	47,899	30-50 mins.	Tube: £2.50 US$4	£28 US$44
13. FRANKFURT ☎ 49-69-6901	32,536	20-25 mins.	Airport Train: DM3.60 US$2	DM35 US$22
14. CHICAGO O'Hare ☎ 312-686-2200	65,078	25-60 mins.	Subway: US$1.50	US$25
15. DETROIT ☎ 313-942-3550	24,171	30-45 mins.	Commuter Co: US$12	US$28
16. BOSTON Logan ☎ 617-561-1800	24,215	15-25 mins.	City Bus: US85¢	US$15
17. WASHINGTON Dulles ☎ 703-661-2700	10,839	45-60 mins.	Washington Flyer: US$16	US$40
18. MIAMI ☎ 305-876-7000	28,660	20-25 mins.	TRI-RAIL: US$2	US$14
19. PARIS Orly ☎ 33-14-975-7933	25,368	40-45 mins.	Orlybus: F23 US$13	F130 US$78
20. NEW YORK JFK ☎ 718-244-4444	26,790	35-60 mins.	Airport Express: US$12.50	US$30[3]

1. Prices are based on U.S. exchange rate as of January 1, 1995. 2. To Manhattan. 3. Doesn't include tolls.
SOURCE: Ranked by the International Air Transport Association. Taxi, transit, and travel time information from *1994 Salk International's Airport Transit Guide* and individual airports; 1993 passenger flow information from Airports Council International.

EXPERT Q&A

WHEN BUMPED FROM A FLIGHT

How to turn bad news to good news when your plane is overbooked

The departure lounge is overflowing. The gate attendant announces the flight is overbooked. Should you accept the airline's offer for another flight? David S. Stempler, executive director of the International Air Passengers Association, offers some counsel.

What is overbooking?

For any given flight, a certain percentage of people will not show up for whatever reason. Airline companies track the average no-show rate for specific routes and overbook accordingly. If the no-show rate is usually about 10 percent, the airline then books the flight at 110 percent capacity.

How do I avoid being bumped from an overbooked flight?

You should get to the airport early, check in early, and get to the gate early. But watch out: sometimes just checking in at the gate doesn't necessarily count—your options change from airline to airline. Your best bet is to actually be on the plane as soon as possible. Possession is nine-tenths of the law.

If I volunteer to be bumped, what should I expect in the way of compensation?

Usually, the airlines start with the minimum that they can get away with, which is about $200. You're at the mercy of the lowest offer from other bidders though, so if the airline offers a free ticket, you should grab it. Be warned: the savvy traveler will ask when the next guaranteed trip to his destination is available or risk being stranded on stand-by. Also, ask yourself

A SNAPSHOT OF AMERICA'S CHRONICALLY LATE FLIGHTS

The worst offenders can change all the time, depending on the weather and the popularity of a given location over the year. The numbers below are for December 1994.

Airline	Flight No.	Origin	Destination	Arrivals over 15 mins. late*	Average lateness
SOUTHWEST	969	Las Vegas	Los Angeles	100.00%	39 mins.
SOUTHWEST	923	Oklahoma City	Phoenix	100.00%	58 mins.
SOUTHWEST	923	Phoenix	Los Angeles	96.43%	52 mins.
SOUTHWEST	1736	Spokane	San Francisco	93.55%	35 mins.
SOUTHWEST	1736	San Francisco	Burbank	90.32%	38 mins.
SOUTHWEST	923	St. Louis	Oklahoma City	89.68%	38 mins.
CONTINENTAL	1597	Greensboro/High Point	Atlanta	88.69%	25 mins.
CONTINENTAL	261	San Juan	Newark	86.24%	57 mins.
SOUTHWEST	1095	Los Angeles	Las Vegas	87.50%	45 mins.
US AIR	352	Miami	New York/LaGuardia	87.10%	28 mins.
AMERICAN	856	Dallas/Ft. Worth	Norfolk/Va. Beach	86.67%	40 mins.
CONTINENTAL	1416	Atlanta	Newark	85.19%	37 mins.
SOUTHWEST	1736	Burbank	Las Vegas	83.87%	38 mins.
US AIR	277	Philadelphia	Charlotte	83.87%	29 mins.
SOUTHWEST	1747	Tucson	Los Angeles	83.33%	32 mins.

* Delays caused by mechanical problems not included.

SOURCE: U.S. Department of Transportation.

what out-of-pocket expenses you will incur in waiting for the next plane, and if the airline will cover them.

■ What are my rights if I end up being bumped against my will?

When you buy a ticket, you've made a contract with the airline. Before you do anything, you have to make sure you've held up your end. Did you check in on time, for instance? Also, if the airline can get you to your destination within an hour of your originally scheduled time, it is free of any liability. Between one and two hours, though, it has to pay the amount of a one-way ticket to your destination (maximum $200). After that, the compensation doubles.

In all cases you get to keep the original ticket to use on another flight or can turn it in for a refund. Also, the Supreme Court has said that you can sue for compensatory damages to recoup whatever loss the delay might have cost you. If, for instance, being bumped forced you to miss a cruise that was paid for in advance, you can sue for the amount of that cruise, though the airline will probably try to get you to the cruise late rather than have to pay for the whole thing.

EXPERT SOURCES

GETTING IN TOUCH WITH AIRLINE WATCHDOGS

To find out more about different airlines, lodge a complaint, or educate yourself about passenger rights, consider these organizations:

U.S. DEPARTMENT OF TRANSPORTATION

■ Consumer and Community Affairs Office: Specializes in problems with baggage handling, overbooking, and delayed flights. Also releases monthly statistics based on consumer complaints and airline reports.
☎ **202-366-2220**

FEDERAL AVIATION ADMINISTRATION

■ Consumer Hotline: An FAA watchdog, the hotline is for complaints about problems with airport security, carry-on baggage, or the FAA itself.
☎ **800-322-7873**

■ Safety Hotline: To report violations of federal airport and airplane regulation or unsafe situations. Often the first stop for insider whistle-blowers.
☎ **800-255-1111**

AVIATION CONSUMER ACTION PROJECT

■ Founded in 1971 by Ralph Nader, ACAP researches consumer issues and publishes the brochure *Facts and Advice for Airline Passengers.* Will advise you about passenger rights and safety issues over the phone.
☎ **202-638-4000**

INTERNATIONAL AIRLINE PASSENGERS ASSOCIATION

■ Like members of the American Automobile Association, IAPA's 150,000 members can buy travel accident insurance or participate in the lost luggage retrieval assistance program. Their bi-monthly travel-safety alert is a good resource for international travelers worried about airline safety and other travel problems.
☎ **214-404-9980**

AMERICAN SOCIETY OF TRAVEL AGENTS

■ A travel trade organization, ASTA represents some 23,000 airlines, hotels, travel agents, rental car agencies, and other travel businesses around the world. Their consumer office can provide info about packing or preparing to travel abroad and also can informally mediate consumer disputes with ASTA members.
☎ **703 739-2782**

THE LAW OF SUPPLY . . .

Sure, average air fares have risen steadily since 1990, but they go up and down at the same times year after year, and that makes predicting prices a cinch. Jeanie Thompson-Smith, president of the Oregon-based travel consulting and auditing firm Topaz Enterprises, put together the numbers below that show what you always suspected: Fares are lowest during the spring and summer when the airlines have the most difficulty filling their planes.

AVERAGE DOMESTIC TICKET PRICES 1991–94

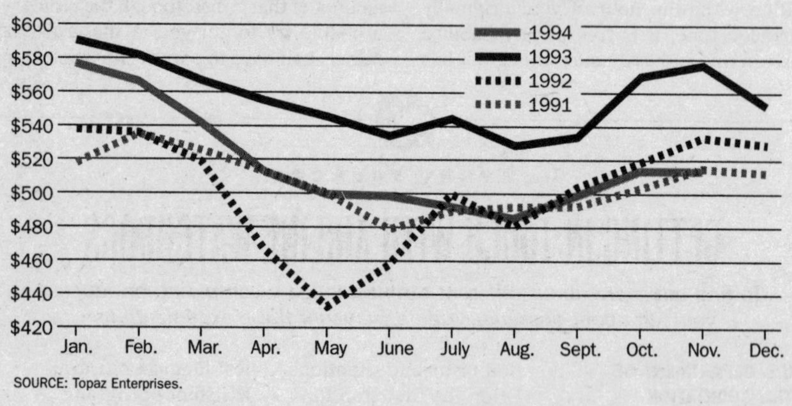

SOURCE: Topaz Enterprises.

. . . AND THE LAW OF DEMAND

Is this week's fare half of what you paid last week? Here's what to do:

You've already bought your ticket when you see the ad in the newspaper: a lower fare on the same route. Getting your ticket rewritten for the lower fare—and pocketing the savings—is not always possible. First you must meet all the qualifications listed in the ad in the small print: there must be the right numbers of days in advance of your trip; you must have been booked to travel when the fare applies; and there must still be seats available in the cheaper fare category. Even then, you might be charged $35 or so to have your ticket rewritten.

Don't give up if the first airline person who answers tells you your ticket is non-refundable and non-changeable, though. Insist on speaking with a supervisor. Also, move fast. The number of seats available at the lower fare is probably limited. Even if you meet all the restrictions, you will not be able to claim one of the cheap seats unless they are still unsold when you call.

A travel agent can give you further assistance. Some agents now guarantee you the lowest fare through use of a computer that monitors reservations systems overnight. Your agent may call you when a lower fare pops up. (You certainly won't hear about it from the airline.) If the agent is still holding your tickets, he or she could rewrite your ticket at the new price even before you open your morning paper.

EXPERT TIPS

DO'S AND DON'TS OF CHEAP FLYING

Coupons, regional airlines, and "split fares" can save you money

As the editor and publisher of *Best Fares* magazine, Tom Parsons has been studying the ins and outs of airline pricing and helping travelers fly cheaply since 1983. Here Parsons gives some money-saving tips.

DO

■ **Search for and use discount coupons.** Parsons says that airlines offer 350 to 400 unadvertised and unpublished travel deals every year. Most can be had by redeeming discount coupons that are distributed by retail outlets and with specific products. An example: people who bought three rolls of Kodak film at a Walgreens Drugstore recently could request a mail-in certificate redeemable for four $60-off coupons on American Airlines. This sort of coupon can usually be used during fare wars to further reduce already low prices.

■ **Look into niche and regional airlines.** Several small upstart airlines like Tower, ValuJet, and Kiwi now offer services between select areas at very low prices. They concentrate on specific pockets, usually only a handful of cities, and discount prices to to make up for their lack of name recognition and to encourage passengers to fly the short haul rather than drive.

■ **Take advantage of "split fares."** Surprisingly, splitting fares may enable a traveler to combine two cheap tickets for much less than the cost of the original single ticket, espe-

■ **IN SEARCH OF PEANUT FARES**

Upstart airlines are making a name for themselves by offering cheap fares on selected routes.

AIRLINE	HUB	MAJOR U.S. CITIES SERVED
AIR SOUTH ☎ 800-247-7688	Columbia, S.C.	Atlanta, Jacksonville, Miami, Myrtle Beach, Raleigh-Durham, St. Petersburg, Tallahassee
AMERICAN TRANS AIR ☎ 800-225-9919	Indianapolis	Boston, Chicago, Milwaukee, St. Louis
CARNIVAL AIR ☎ 800-824-7386	Doesn't operate on a hub system	Ft. Lauderdale, Los Angeles, Miami, Newark, New York, Tampa, West Palm Beach
FRONTIER ☎ 800-432-1359	Denver	Albuquerque, El Paso, Fargo, Missoula, Omaha, Las Vegas
KIWI INTERNATIONAL ☎ 800-538-5494	Newark	Atlanta, Chicago, New York, Orlando, Tampa
MIDWAY ☎ 800-446-6247	All flights go through Raleigh-Durham	Boston, Chicago, Ft. Lauderdale, Hartford, Philadelphia, New York, Newark, Orlando, Tampa, Washington, D.C.
RENO AIR ☎ 800-736-6247	Reno, San Jose	Anchorage, Chicago, Las Vegas, Los Angeles, Phoenix, Portland, San Diego, Seattle, Tucson, Vancouver
SPIRIT ☎ 800-736-6247	Detroit, Atlantic City	Atlantic City, Boston, Ft. Lauderdale, Orlando, Philadelphia, Tampa
SUN JET INTERNATIONAL ☎ 800-478-6538	Smyrna	Dallas, Ft. Lauderdale, Long Beach, Newark, Orlando, St. Petersburg
TOWER AIR ☎ 800-221-2500	New York (JFK)	Los Angeles, Miami, New York, San Francisco
VALUJET ☎ 800-825-8538	Atlanta	Chicago, Columbus, Dallas–Ft. Worth, Detroit, Ft. Lauderdale, Ft. Myers, Hartford, Indianapolis, Jacksonville, Louisville, Memphis, Miami, Nashville, New Orleans, Orlando, Philadelphia, Raleigh-Durham, Savannah, Tampa, Washington, D.C.

SOURCE: Individual carriers.

THE GUY SITTING NEXT TO YOU PAID LESS

The price of an airline seat isn't locked till the plane leaves the ground. Below is a snapshot of what people paid on a recent American Airlines flight from Miami to New York on take-off—the average fare: $196.89.

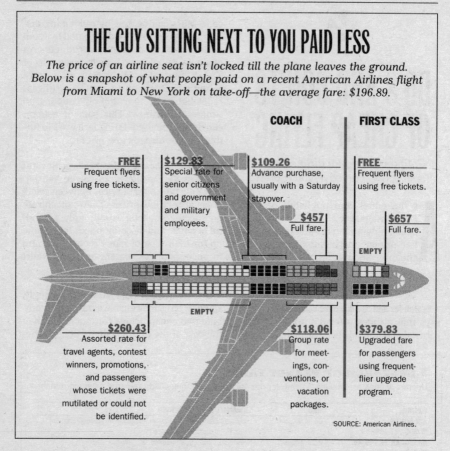

COACH

FIRST CLASS

FREE Frequent flyers using free tickets.

$129.83 Special rate for senior citizens and government and military employees.

$109.26 Advance purchase, usually with a Saturday stayover.

FREE Frequent flyers using free tickets.

$457 Full fare.

$657 Full fare.

EMPTY

EMPTY

$260.43 Assorted rate for travel agents, contest winners, promotions, and passengers whose tickets were mutilated or could not be identified.

$118.06 Group rate for meetings, conventions, or vacation packages.

$379.83 Upgraded fare for passengers using frequent-flier upgrade program.

SOURCE: American Airlines.

cially with the aforementioned rise of niche markets. Rather than buying a single ticket from Dallas to Kansas City, for example, Parsons suggests that a consumer look into flying from Dallas to Tulsa, Oklahoma, and then from Tulsa to Kansas City.

■ **Consider flying to and from alternative cities.** Some air routes are significantly cheaper than others. If you are willing to make the journey to and from an out-of-the-way airport before and after a long trip, you may be able to save big. A one- or two-hour drive, according to Parsons, can take as much as 70 percent off of a single ticket price. Washington, D.C. flyers should consider making the trek to nearby Baltimore, and Chicago flyers should look into flying by way of Milwaukee.

DON'T

■ **Buy tickets immediately.** Most discount fares need only be purchased 14 days in advance. Buying sooner may simply mean a loss of future savings. People who buy early can't get any money back when prices drop. Buy tickets immediately only if you wish to travel during busy holidays like Christmas or New Year's Day.

■ **Always pick a flight time.** Tell travel and reservation agents that cheap is more important than, say, arriving at nine in the morning. The relationship between time and cost is not always obvious, so you should inquire about the least expensive times to fly a chosen route—some times cost more than others, and some special fares only apply at specific times.

FREQUENT FLYERS

THOSE FREE MILES ARE FLYING AWAY

Airlines are making it harder and harder to get freebies

Remember the days when 20,000 frequent flyer miles bought you a free flight anywhere in the United States? No longer. In the last five years, veteran frequent flyer mile gatherers have watched their stashes slowly but surely devalue. Travelers who have been saving their miles for a rainy day are in danger of being washed out.

More than 200 billion of the trillion miles awarded since the inception of frequent flyer programs remain unredeemed, and airlines are making it harder for travelers to do so by raising the number of miles needed to claim a free trip, lowering the number of miles awarded on popular routes, imposing expiration dates on miles awarded, and limiting the seats available for coupon award tickets.

The savvy flyer can still beat the miles crunch, though. If you need an extra five thousand or ten thousand miles to get a coupon, you can get them without flying by using a credit card or long-distance telephone carrier aligned with a frequent flyer program. Travelers who need fewer miles can take advantage of the many hotels, car rental agencies, and airline frequent flyer clubs that have ongoing frequent flyer promotions. Hotels and car rental companies listed in airline frequent flyer newsletters often offer double mileage promotions, while airline clubs such as TWA Ambassador's Club award 5,000 miles for a one-year membership.

Beyond these backdoor methods, travelers would do well to compare their frequent flyer programs with other major programs. Where there is a choice, it pays to sign up and fly with those programs that are the most lucrative.

EXPERT LIST

HOW FREQUENT FLYER PROGRAMS STACK UP

Here's how Randy Peterson, editor of Inside Flyer *magazine, rates the airlines' frequent flyer programs. Peterson has analyzed frequent flyer programs since their inception in the 1980s.*

PROGRAM	Grade	EASE OF EARNING		BLACKOUT		SEAT AVAILABILITY		Customer service	Hotel partners	Tie-ins
		Dom.	Int.	Dom.	Int.	Dom.	Int.			
Northwest WorldPerks	B+	B+	A	B	A	A	C	A–	B	B
American AAdvantage	B+	B+	C	A	C	A	C	C	A	A
USAIR Frequent Traveler	B	B	B	A	C	A	C	B	A	B
United Mileage Plus	B	B+	C	B	C	A	C	A	A	A–
America West Flight Fund	B	B	A	B	B	A	C	A–	B-	B–
Alaska Mileage Plan	B	B	B	B+	C	A–	C	B–	B	A–
Continental OnePass	B	B+	B	C	D+	B	C	A–	B	B+
Delta Frequent Flyer	B–	B	C–	C	D	A	C	A–	A	B–
TWA Freq. Flight Bonus	C+	B–	C	C	D	B	C	B	C	B
Southwest Company Club	C	C	NA	A	NA	A	NA	A–	F	F

AIR FARES

FOUR WAYS TO FLY FOR LESS

Couriers, rebaters, consolidators, and charters are cheap—but tricky

In 1959, when *How to Travel without Being Rich* was a hot seller, a 10-day trip from New York to Paris including air fare, lodging, and sightseeing cost $553. Today, that price would elude even the most serious of cost-cutters. But bargains still abound for creative travelers willing to do a modicum of research.

AIR COURIERS

The absolute cheapest way to fly is as a courier. Although most large courier companies such as Federal Express and UPS use their own couriers, smaller companies use "freelance couriers". A typical courier fare can be as low as one-fourth of the regular airline economy class fare. Last-minute tickets are especially cheap—one courier company recently listed a fare from Los Angeles to Tokyo of $100. A full-fare ticket would cost around $1,800.

In exchange for a drastically reduced fare, couriers have minimal duties. It works like this: After booking a flight with a company, the courier meets a representative of the company at the airport two to four hours before departure. The agent hands baggage checks for the cargo and other paperwork over to the courier. The courier then boards the plane and, on arrival at his international destination, accompanies the cargo through customs. Once through customs, the courier hands over the paperwork to the company agent. After that he is free to go.

■ **DRAWBACKS:** Because air courier companies use a courier's allotted baggage space for cargo, couriers generally are limited to carry-on baggage only. More important, courier travel can be unreliable. On rare occasions, for instance, courier companies will cancel or postpone their shipments because of last-minute cargo changes. In this instance, if a courier does not have flexible travel plans and cannot wait for the next courier flight, he or she may have to buy a full-fare economy ticket from a regular airline.

■ **WHERE TO GO:** Most courier flights leave from New York, Los Angeles, San Francisco, or Miami. The best way to find them is to join the International Association of Air Travel Couriers, ☎ 407-582-8320. A one-year membership is $45. With membership, you get a bi-monthly bulletin and access to twice-daily updates of available courier flights online or via fax.

FACT FILE:

AROUND THE WORLD, CHEAPLY

■ *Want to go around the world? Buy a "round-the-world" ticket from a consolidator or any airline that offers them. They require that you keep traveling in the same direction and that you stay with two or three designated carriers. Otherwise, you have the same flexibility in your itinerary as you would if you had bought individual tickets—and paid a lot more. Prices can reach $6,000, but many consolidators sell them for as low as $1,600.*

CONSOLIDATORS

Consolidators are the Price Club of airline travel—large brokerage houses which buy blocks of tickets from airlines at wholesale prices and then pass the savings on to individual flyers. Airlines sell to consolidators at reduced prices because they fear that the tick-

THE PROS AND CONS OF CHEAP FLYING

What's more important to you? On-board comfort? Ease of payment? Here are the trade-offs for different discount flights.

	AIRLINE (sale price)	REBATER	CONSOLIDATOR	CHARTER	COURIER
AFFORDABILITY	$ $ $ 1/2	$ $ $	$ $	$ $	$
CANCELED FLIGHT OPTION	Next available flight on any airline	Next available flight on any airline	May be required to fly only on issuing airline	Company must supply plane or flight, long wait possible	You are on your own
AMENITIES	Seat assignments and special meals	Seat assignments and special meals	No seat assignments or special meals	Crowded seating and no special meals	No seat assignments or special meals
FREQUENT FLYER MILES	Yes	Yes	Yes	No	Generally no
CREDIT CARD PAYMENT ALLOWED	Yes	Yes	Depends on consolidator, may be 3% surcharge	Generally yes	No
TICKET RESTRICTIONS	Saturday stayover and 7- to 21-day advance purchase	Saturday stayover and 7- to 21-day advance purchase	None	None	Length of stay may be restricted

ets would otherwise go unsold. Consolidators buy seats mostly on established carriers for flights that are headed to overseas destinations. Travelers booking flights with consolidators can save anywhere from 20 to 50 percent off the price of a regular ticket.

DRAWBACKS: Most consolidators are reliable, but to protect against illegitimate businesses, travelers should use a credit card whenever possible. Consolidator tickets are non-refundable, so a traveler who cannot use his or her ticket will most likely end up eating the fare. Consolidator tickets typically are not honored by other airlines, so ticket holders who miss their flights or whose flights are canceled will have to wait for another flight on the issuing airline. Also, flights generally are not direct and sometimes have as many as three stops.

WHERE TO GO: Travel agents rarely volunteer information about consolidator tickets. Should a travel agent plead ignorance, it may help to suggest that he look up the fare in *Jax Fax*, ☎ 800-952-9329, a monthly newsletter that lists consolidator fares and is widely distributed to travel agents. Consolidator fares are also listed in small print ads in the travel sections of major newspapers like the *New York Times* and *USA Today*. For flights originating in Europe, the Air Travel Advisory Bureau in London, ☎ 44-1-636-5000, has a complete listing of consolidators (or, as they are called in Britain, "bucket shops").

CHARTER FLIGHTS

Charter flights offer savings that are competitive with consolidator tickets, but generally they are only for non-stop routes. Charter companies are able to profit by running less often than regularly scheduled airline flights and by booking to complete capacity. On transatlantic flights especially, travelers can expect to save between $200 and $400.

Charters also are a good alternative for those who like to fly first class but don't want to pay for it. *Consumer Reports Travel Letter* editor Ed Perkins says, "One of the best values around is the premium class service on some of the transatlantic charters. First class on charter planes is a third of the price of regular airlines with many of the same amenities."

AN AIR COURIER SAMPLER

Three of the larger courier brokers and some of their most popular routes

	NOW VOYAGER ☎ 212-431-1616	JUPITER ☎ 310-670-5123	HALBART ☎ 305-593-0260
DEPARTURE POINT	New York	Los Angeles	Miami
POPULAR ROUTES	Rome, London, Milan, Rio de Janeiro	Seoul, Hong Kong, Singapore, Melbourne	Rio de Janeiro, Lima, Madrid, Mexico City, Santiago
AIRLINES COMMONLY USED ON THOSE ROUTES	Al Italia, Continental, TWA, Varig	United States, Japan	American, Ladeco, Varig
AVERAGE LENGTH OF STAY	One week	Two weeks	One week
BAGGAGE ALLOTMENT	One carry-on	One carry-on	Two carry-on
REQUIREMENTS	Must be 18, $50 registration fee	Must be 18, no criminal record, $35 registration fee	Must be 18
COMMENT	Cheapest fares are between New Year's Day and March 15	Call two months in advance for a specific travel date	Cheap fares for flights on extremely short notice

SOURCE: Individual brokers.

■ **DRAWBACKS:** Infrequency of flights and overcrowding of planes are common complaints. If a charter flight is canceled close to departure, there usually are no other planes available, nor will a charter ticket be honored on another airline. Travelers can often have a lengthy wait for another flight, or worse, will have to pay full fare on a regular airline. Also, despite the aforementioned first-class options, charter flights are not known for luxury service. The meals often come in a brown bag, and you're packed in like the proverbial sardine.

■ **WHERE TO GO:** Travel agencies are an excellent source for charter listings. Charter companies also advertise heavily in the travel sections of major newspapers. Martinair Holland, ☎ 800-366-4655, Tower, ☎ 800-221-2500, and Balair Ltd., ☎ 800-322-5247, get high marks from Perkins for first-class service.

REBATERS

Rebaters are "no-frills" travel agents who pay the ticket buyer all or part of the commission they are paid by airlines for selling the ticket. Rebaters profit by charging a flat fee for making a reservation and issuing a ticket to the buyer. A traveler headed from New York to Stockholm might be quoted a round-trip fare of $800. By using a rebater, the fare would drop to $750. The reason: Rebaters refund their commission, in this case, $80 or 10 percent of the fare. They then tack on a $20 fee to issue the ticket and sometimes an extra $10 to make the reservation. Still, the total price of the ticket is $50 less than it would have been with a regular travel agent.

■ **DRAWBACKS:** For the money saved by using a rebater, a traveler gives up a lot in service. The only function a rebater will perform is making a reservation and issuing a ticket. All other travel details, such as seat assignments, hotel reservations, and ground transportation, will need to be made by the traveler. "The amenities a consumer loses using a rebater instead of a full-service travel agent are not worth the savings unless you are buying expensive tickets," Perkins says.

■ **WHERE TO GO:** One of the most prominent rebaters is Travel Avenue in Chicago, ☎ 800-333-3335. In addition, *Consumer Reports Travel Letter,* ☎ 800-234-1970, lists major rebaters throughout the country once a year.

EXPERT Q&A

A CURE FOR JET LAG AT LAST?

A non-prescription pill can help you readjust to a different time zone

Recent reports have suggested that travelers can avoid jet lag altogether by taking melatonin, a non-prescription medication. We consulted with Dr. Richard Dawood, author of *Traveler's Health: How to Stay Healthy All Over the World* (Random House, 1994), and a contributing editor to *Condé Nast Traveler* magazine.

■ What is melatonin and how does it work?

The substance melatonin is actually a natural hormone that all humans carry. In recent years scientists have come to a clearer understanding of how this substance is a crucial regulator of the human body clock. The hormone is released into the bloodstream according to a daily cycle that is determined by your body clock as it is influenced by darkness. During the day, melatonin secretion is suppressed by light; at nightfall, the pineal gland begins to secrete melatonin into the bloodstream.

Jet travel through different time zones interferes with this natural process because the body is left releasing melatonin on its old schedule. The body clock takes anywhere from 1 to 12 days to adjust, depending on the number of time zones a person has traveled. (One time zone generally produces one day of jet lag.)

■ When should one take melatonin?

Studies have shown and scientists now believe that a supplemental dose of melatonin helps to bring body functions into sync with the day/night rhythm of the new time zone. Timing of the dosage is critical to its success, however. In trials, the best results occurred when subjects took the pill 30 to 90 minutes before bedtime on the day of the arrival and each day of travel thereafter as needed. In other words, travelers who are taking an overnight flight should not take the pill until the evening of the day they arrive.

■ Where does one buy melatonin?

Melatonin is widely available in a synthetic form that can be purchased as a nutritional supplement at health food stores, but there is no mention of jet lag relief on the bottle. The reason: Food supplements are not subjected to FDA approval as long as there are no claims regarding health effects advertised on the bottle. Melatonin can be ordered from Ecological Formulas, Concord, Calif., for $12.95 plus $1.50 for shipping for 60 capsules, ☎ 800-888-4585.

■ Are there any side effects?

Synthetic melatonin has very few known side effects, apart from the fact that it has a mild contraceptive effect on some women. Travelers who have allergies to other drugs or are taking other medications should consult their physicians before trying the pill, as should anyone who has any kind of special concern about it.

EXPERT TIPS

If you don't care to try the melatonin, here are some other jet lag remedies:

- **Begin observing mealtimes of your destination as soon as possible on your day of travel.**
- **Avoid alcohol while traveling.**
- **Avoid caffeine while traveling.**
- **Drink a pint of liquids during flight.**
- **Sleep according to the schedule of your destination.**

ALL ABOARD THE ORIENT EXPRESS

Eight incredible rail journeys that take you to Hell and the Outback

For nearly thirty years, George Drury has been traveling the great rail lines of the world, both as a writer and head librarian for *Trains Magazine,* and as a life-long lover of a rapidly disappearing way of looking at the world. Here is a highly subjective listing of some of his favorites, based on the scenery outside, the service inside, and the ever-intangible "romance factor."

THE CALIFORNIA ZEPHYR
Chicago to Oakland

■ The original California Zephyr of 1949 was conceived as a "cruise train"—the journey was just as important as the destination and took 8 to 10 hours longer than the competition. Its successor continues that tradition by scheduling the three-day trip to time the best scenery with daylight hours, leaving Chicago in the afternoon and arriving in Denver the following morning so you wake up to see the breathtaking beauty of the Rockies. Along the way is the passage through the Sierra Nevadas and a fine view of San Francisco Bay. "It offers Amtrak's largest helping of scenery," says Drury.

Amtrak ☎ **800-872-7245**

THE CARIBOO DAYLINER
British Columbia, Canada

■ The fourteen-hour trip from North Vancouver to Prince George includes some spectacular and seldom-seen scenery through the Coast Mountains and up the Fraser River Valley. For a day trip, travelers can get off in Lillooet to return to North Vancouver by sunset. BC Rail runs the trains daily in the summer and three times a week in the winter. The cars are not particularly luxurious, but their enormous windows allow the scenery to work its magic. Reserved seats include a meal.

BC Rail ☎ **604-631-3500**

COPPER CANYON
Mexico

■ This line along the edge of Mexico's spectacular Copper Canyon (four times the size of the Grand Canyon) and through the Sierra Madres was proposed at the turn of the century as a short route from Kansas City to the Pacific and completed 60 years and one revolution later. The 14-hour trip includes a 15-minute stop to view the rugged canyon bottom. Stay overnight in Los Mochis for the return trip, or—if you're ambitious—make the somewhat unpredictable trip overland and by ferry to Baja California.

Book via Columbus Travel ☎ **800-843-1060**

INDIAN PACIFIC
Sydney to Perth

■ This three-day trip covers 2,720 miles, from the Pacific through the Blue Mountains west of Sidney and across the outback to Perth and the Indian Ocean. Most of the journey is spent in the austere beauty of the Nullarbor Plains, where one stretch of track goes 297 miles without a curve. Passengers can kick back in luxuriously refurbished lounge cars as they watch wild kangaroos leap across the outback. "One of the attractions," says Drury, "is going completely across something."

Book via ATS Tours ☎ **800-423-2880**

THE OSLO-TRONDHEIM-BODO-NARVIK
Norway

■ Surprisingly enough, Hell is located near the Arctic Circle. It is a small town nestled in the Dovre Mountains of Norway, just a few miles from Trondheim and not nearly as unpleasant as its namesake. Norwegian State Railways operates several day trains and a night train through the mountains. The scenery is austere, but the trains are comfortable and well-equipped. Sharp-eyed travelers may sight the occasional musk ox.

Book via DER Tours ☎ **800-782-2424**

RHAETIAN RAILWAY BERNINA LINE
The Swiss Alps

■ This train descends some 4,000 feet as it makes its way from Chur, Switzerland, across the Bernina Pass and into Tirano, Italy—all without the reassuring traction that cog railways offer. It is the highest crossing of the Alps by any rail line. The train itself is not particularly exciting, but the scenery is unsurpassed. There is no dining car, but travelers have about an hour in Italy to buy ice cream before the return trip. Eurail passes are valid, or travelers can make reservations at any Swiss train station. The express line travels each way once a day. Book through a travel agent or call the rail line in Switzerland for details.

Rhaetian Railway ☎ 011-41-81-221124

THE TRANS-SIBERIAN RAILWAY
Moscow to Vladivostock

■ A seven-day journey into the Far East on the world's longest continuous rail line. Of the regular trains on this route, the Rossiya is the best. It's not luxurious, but it does offer sleeping berths and a dining car. The entire trip can be exhausting, so you may want to take it in bits and pieces. A consortium of Eastern and Western businessmen have put together a charter train, called the Rhythm, that runs the same route on occasion and offers world-class dining and the height of luxury. "The best part of the trip," says Drury, "is finding out that a country that was once absolutely forbidden is absolutely beautiful."

Book via Blue Heart Travel ☎ 800-882-0025

VENICE SIMPLON-ORIENT-EXPRESS
Paris to Budapest or Venice

■ "Perhaps the ultimate experience in pampered land travel," Drury says of this most famous of train lines. Murder is rare, but fine dining and classic details like posh, overstuffed upholstery are not. The cars have been restored so authentically that most of them do not have air conditioning. (You may want to avoid travel during the hottest months.) The dining car service is that of a four-star restaurant. Uniformed, gold-braided stewards will go out of their way to make your trip a comfortable one. Drury recommends the southbound line for scenery, but adds you should take the trip for "what's inside the windows."

Orient Express ☎ 800-524-2420

CHUNNEL IF BY LAND, FERRY IF BY SEA

London and France are joined by land for the first time since the Ice Age.

After years of work drilling the 31-mile tunnel out of the chalk bedrock beneath the English Channel, the $16 billion Chunnel—shorthand for Channel tunnel—opened in 1994 with non-stop service between London and Paris.

The 300-mile trip takes about three hours on the new 186-mph Eurostar bullet trains. That's substantially faster than a direct flight when you include taxi time from the airport to downtown.

You can't drive through the chunnel, but you will be able to transport your car on a train at prices that are competitive with those of regular ferries. Le Shuttle—the Franco-Anglo name for the car-train—will cost about $300 for one car to go one way. Service is scheduled to start in late 1995, with a crossing-time just a few minutes under that of a standard hovercraft ferry.

Passenger fares are less competitive. A direct flight from London to Paris can be had for as little as $130, while the lowest-priced Eurostar ticket is about $150. But for those looking for convenience and service, Eurostar may be just the ticket.

American travelers can buy Eurostar tickets through a travel agent or through ticket broker Britrail Travel International, ☎ 800-677-8585, or in New York City, ☎ 212-575-2667.

TRAVELER'S GUIDE

TAKE THE A-TRAIN . . . OR TAKE THE B-TRAIN IF YOU LIKE

Countries all over the world offer passes that guarantee unlimited, flexible travel at a set price for a specified period, and it often only takes one or two trips for you to come out ahead by buying one. Below are some of the options.

AUSTRALIA

Travel between most tourist sites in this vast nation requires an overnight trip, making air travel a practical option in many cases, but the view of the outback is better from ground level.

■ **PRICE RANGE:** The AustrailPass, with unlimited travel on all ROA railways, ranges from $326 for 14 days in economy class to $825 for 30 days in first class. Austrail flexi-passes run from 8 days of travel in 60 days (economy) for $255 to 15 days of travel in 60 days (first class) for $593. Some routes are restricted. The Kangaroo Road 'n' Rail Pass includes limited travel on Greyhound Pioneer buses and ranges from $491 to $1,148. All passes must be bought outside Australia.

■ **TRAIN TIP:** Wildflower fans must see the spectacular blooms along the Indian-Pacific line from Sydney to Perth in September and October.

ATS Tours ☎ 800-423-2880

CANADA

Train travel in this sprawling nation isn't a particularly efficient means of transport, but the Canadian line through the Rockies is popular among rail buffs for its spectacular views. The Canrail Pass allows unlimited coast-to-coast economy-class travel on VIARail lines for 12 days within a 30-day period.

■ **PRICE RANGE:** During the low season (Jan. 6–May 31 and Oct. 1–Dec. 14) passes are $270 for adults and $247 for those under 25 or over 60. During the high season, they are $395 and $356. Canrail passes are not honored Dec. 15 to Jan. 5. Purchase passes from VIARail, Amtrak, or a travel agent.

■ **TRAIN TIP:** In 1992, Canada's national passenger railway launched a restored, stainless steel fleet of passenger cars built in the '50s. The cars retain their art deco sleekness, but are updated with showers and advanced suspension systems.

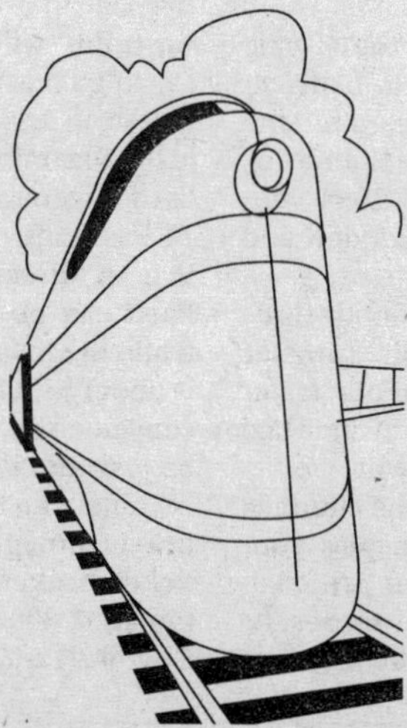

VIARail ☎ 800-561-3949

EUROPE

A way of life for the teeming masses of backpack-toting college grads that storm Europe every summer, the Eurail pass is valid in 17 countries in Continental Europe (a notable exception is Britain). The cheaper Europass covers three to five of the following nations: France, Germany, Spain, Italy, and Switzerland. All passes must be purchased in the United States and are good for 6 months from the time of purchase. Any travel agent can order passes.

■ **PRICE RANGE:** Eurailpass runs from $348 for 5 days of travel in 60 days to $1,398 for 90 days of unlimited travel. Youth passes are available for those under 26 and range from $255 to $768. Europass prices range from $280 for 5 days of travel in 60 days in three countries to $650 for 15

■ TRAVELER'S GUIDE

days of travel in 60 days in five countries.

■ **TRAIN TIP:** If you're in a hurry, try the French TGV. It set the world record for passenger rail speed at 320 mph in 1990 and averages 130 mph on regular passenger routes.

Rail Europe ☎ 800-438-7245

INDIA

Rail travel is a popular but slow alternative to India's sometimes harrowing airline system. Indrail passes are available in three classes: air-conditioned first class (sometimes includes a sleeper), regular first class or air-conditioned chair car (different cars, same pass), and second class (which tends to be very crowded). The definition of "first class" varies from line to line. Tickets must be purchased outside of India.

■ **PRICE RANGE:** From $30 for a 1-day pass (second class) to $975 for a 90-day unlimited travel pass (air-conditioned first class).

■ **TRAIN TIP:** Many lines here rely on ancient telexes to confirm reservations; travelers often are stranded when the telex fails.

Hari World Travel
☎ 212-957-3000

JAPAN

If you intend to do even minimal travel in Japan, a train pass is a great investment. An ordinary 7-day pass costs less than a round-trip ticket from Tokyo to Osaka, and the extensive Japan Railway (JR) system rivals that of Continental Europe for speed and convenience. JR passes come in two flavors: green (first class) and ordinary (economy). Both include travel on most Shinkansen (bullet trains), some buses, and the ferry between Honshu and Miyajima.

■ **PRICE RANGE:** From $270 for a 7-day ordinary pass to $780 for a 21-day green pass. Children 6 to 11 are half-price. Passes must be purchased outside Japan.

■ **TRAIN TIP:** A 7-day train pass costs about as much as a cab from Narita airport to downtown Tokyo. Don't take a cab.

TBI Tours ☎ 800-223-0266

UNITED KINGDOM

Britain is not included in Eurail packages, but it does offer several rail passes of its own. Among them are the Britpass, the BritGermany Pass, the BritIreland Pass, and the BritFrance Pass. All include travel in Wales and Scotland, and some include ferry travel. All passes must be purchased in the United States and are good for six months from the time of purchase. A travel agent can provide details and order passes.

■ **PRICE RANGE:** Britpasses range from $189 for 10 days of travel in 30 days (economy) to $715 for 30 days of unlimited travel (first class).

■ **TRAIN TIP:** The "Chunnel" beneath the English Channel opened in 1994, allowing direct travel from London to Brussels, Paris, and Amsterdam.

Brit Rail ☎ 212-575-2667
Rail Pass Express
☎ 800-551-1977

U.S.A.

Despite government subsidies, Amtrak has had trouble competing with airlines in most areas except along the Eastern Seaboard and parts of the West Coast, so it has abandoned many less popular lines. Train travel enthusiasts might consider Amtrak's All Aboard America fares, though. They are good for 45 days, but you must choose your itinerary in advance and are allowed only three stopovers.

■ **PRICE RANGE:** Amtrak divides the nation into three regions: east, west and central. Tickets range from $179 (off-peak) for travel in one region to $329 (peak) for travel in all three regions. Peak season is from June 17 to August 21. There is a 50 percent discount for children 2 to 15 and a 15 peercent discount for seniors over 62.

■ **TRAIN TIP:** Amtrak began the first regularly scheduled transcontinental train service in U.S. history in 1993. The Sunset Limited makes the 3,000-mile journey from Miami to Los Angeles in just 69 hours.

Amtrak ☎ 800-872-7245

GETTING THERE ON THE CHEAP

There are bargains galore for seniors, students, and small children

Face it, working world, airlines might drop their rates or offer special packages from time to time, but they won't bend over backwards to court you. The story is different, however, for senior citizens, students, and small children. Travel industry executives know that many working men and women have to fly on business, but younger and older travelers still need to be wooed. Accordingly, there are several excellent discounts available for young and not-so-young travelers. Outlined below are some the best.

AIRLINE DEALS AND DISCOUNTS

■ **SENIORS:** Most North American airlines offer coupon books good for travel within the United States and Canada. The books come in sets of four and eight, with each coupon redeemable for a single, one-way flight. They cost about $600 for four, and about $1,000 for eight. Those who fly only short distances might not want to buy these coupons, but they do offer considerable savings on expensive and coast-to-coast routes. Since the prices and services are similar on each airline, choose the one that serves cities you expect to visit most.

■ **STUDENTS:** Several airlines have their own discount "clubs" for students. American Airlines offers students deals through the National Collegiate Travel Club. For $50 a year, students receive three certificates valid for travel within the continental United States. One certificate can only be used by the student to either depart from or arrive at an airport near the student's college. The other two certificates can be used by the student or his or her parents, but only for flights between school and home. Of course, there are several restrictions with this plan.

USAir offers rates as low as $29 to students traveling distances under 750 miles to entice them to fly rather than drive.

Full-time students who carry American Express cards can enroll free in the company's "Student Privileges" program. It offers discount certificates on Continental Airlines, some of which can be used on international flights or by companions.

■ **CHILDREN:** Infants under the age of 2 travel free on almost all domestic airlines. They are expected to travel on a parent's or guardian's lap, and can only be placed in a seat if one is available. With USAir, children between 2 and 11 can use senior coupons when they are accompanied by seniors also using coupons.

TRAIN DEALS AND DISCOUNTS

■ **SENIORS:** Amtrak passengers 62 and older can get coach tickets 15 percent off, but only between Monday and Thursday. The discount does not apply to Auto-train, Metroliner, sleeper car, Club service, or Custom Class passengers.

■ **STUDENTS:** Students 12 to 25 can get big discounts on rail and ferry tickets in Europe and beyond by showing an International Student ID Card. The cards are available for under $20 from the International Education Exchange. They offer no savings in the United States, though.

■ **CHILDREN:** Amtrak passengers 2 and under can ride on a parent's lap for free, while children 2 to 15 can ride at half-price with an adult or other child who is paying regular, adult ticket prices.

OVERNIGHTING DEALS AND DISCOUNTS

■ **SENIORS:** Many hotels already offer senior discounts to guests either 60 or 65 and older, but some increase their discounts for members of the American Association of Retired Persons. The AARP admits anyone over 50, so membership means senior rates for some not-so-senior travelers. AARP membership also brings discounts on rental cars, sightseeing tours, and cruises. The annual membership fee is $8.

Other seniors' clubs, such as the National Alliance of Senior Citizens and the Silver Keys, offer discounts as well.

Several hotel chains have created their own seniors' clubs. They sometimes offer big savings, but deals vary greatly, according to a recent study by the *Consumer Reports Travel Letter.* Hilton's Senior Honors offers up to 50 percent off nightly rates, but charges $50 for one year and $35 each year thereafter. Red Roof's RediCard +60 program entitles guests to a 10 percent discount over its regular senior discount for a $10 lifetime-membership fee. Several other clubs, including Best Inns' Senior First Club and Hampton Inn's Lifestyle 50 Club, offer free membership but with reduced savings.

Seniors who want to combine travel with classroom learning can vacation for very little through the Elderhostel program. Participants, who must be at least 60, spend one to four weeks on a college campus, studying a variety of subjects, eating in dining halls, and sleeping in student housing. Room and board is just over $300 a week in the United States and Canada.

National Park enthusiasts 62 or older can pay $10 for a lifetime Golden Age Pass, good at all U.S. national parks for 50 percent off all recreation fees—a good deal for seniors who enjoy camping but not the standard $8 to $10 daily rates.

■ **STUDENTS:** Many hotels are increasing the maximum ages for free stays with accompanying parents from 12 to 18. Holiday Inn Express even lets 19-year-olds in free.

For students seeking shelter sans parents, American Youth Hostels (AYH) provide an inexpensive bed and the opportunity to meet other travelers. A $25 AYH membership is not required, but it does reduce the $5 to $12 cost for a bed for the night by a few dollars. The majority of hostel guests are between 18 and 30, but there is no age requirement. Children under 12 receive reduced rates at many youth hostels, but they must be accompanied by a parent of the same sex.

■ **CHILDREN:** Many hotels permit children to stay free when their parents or guardians pay regular rates. Children under 16 are admitted free to all U.S. national parks.

EXPERT TIPS

HOW TO GET LOW HOTEL RATES

You don't have to pay top dollar to get top-notch service

■ **Request all the basic discounts.** Discounts are often avaiable to senior citizens, members of automobile associations, and military personnel. But those who are eligible have to ask for them.

■ **Ask for a still lower rate.** Hotels are often willing to reduce rates if doing so will fill empty rooms. *Money* magazine reports that budget motels have an average occupancy rate of 62 percent. That's a lot of rooms in need of filling; don't be afraid to ask the check-in manager for a still lower rate.

■ **Call a reservation service.** By purchasing rooms in bulk at reduced prices, these services pass savings on to you—usually 25 percent to 50 percent off the regular rates on mid-priced and luxury rooms. Some of the larger services:

Hotel Reservations Network
☎ 800-964-6835

Quikbook
☎ 800-789-9887

Room Exchange
☎ 800-846-7000

RECREATIONAL VEHICLES

THE NEW KINGS OF THE ROAD

Why not take a home with you on your next vacation?

To all those hip folks who wouldn't be caught dead in an RV: think again. Kids love 'em. A 1993 poll by the University of Michigan found that 36 percent of 18- to 34-year-olds plan to purchase a recreational vehicle in the near future, a higher proportion than any other age group. Of course, older folks still love 'em too—people 55 and older represent more than half of all RV owners. Still, sales of the kind of folding camping trailers that are popular with entry-level buyers increased by 46 percent in 1993—record growth in an industry that generates $10 billion in annual retail sales.

Why? Those who had already purchased RVs cited comfort (easy-swivel captain's seats!), convenience (no lost luggage!), and a "good value" (home cooking every night!) as their primary motivations. And of course, there is the simple thrill of trekking across the nation as our pioneer ancestors did: with a kitchen in the back seat and a bed in the trunk.

Driving an RV may be convenient—if you're up to the task of parallel parking—but buying one can be a daunting task. RVs cost anywhere from $30,000 for a basic trailer to upward of half a million dollars for those deluxe custom buses favored by rodeo stars and country western singers.

Options vary widely, from handy dashboard cup holders to deluxe built-in home entertainment centers. The only thing that doesn't vary much, in fact, is the mileage, which is universally bad—about 8 to 10 miles per gallon at best.

With so many choices available, you may want to rent an RV first to see what kind of amenities you will require on the road and, more important, to see if gypsy life is really all that you and your traveling companions had dreamed.

EXPERT SOURCES

WHERE TO GO TO GET GOING

Resources for joining a new American subculture

MONK
Four issues, $10, "Lifetime after lifetime" subscription, $100 (includes first reincarnation)
■ Billed as "The World's Only Mobile Magazine," *Monk* is the witty, occasional publication of two RV nomads, James Crotty and Michael Lane. Each issue (there are about four per year) tells of their latest adventures on the road with their cat, the Dolly Lama (not to be confused with the Tibetan Dalai).
☎ **212-465-3231**

GOOD SAM CLUB
■ Sort of an American Automobile Association for RV owners. Good SAM offers campground discounts, mail forwarding service, insurance, roadside assistance, and tour packages to nearly 940,000 members.
☎ **800-234-3450**

RECREATIONAL VEHICLE INDUSTRY ASSOCIATION
■ The RVIA can put you in contact with a local RV dealer and will also send you a free 16-page guide for first-time campers.
☎ **800-477-8669**

EXPERT TIPS

TRAILER PARK A' GO-GO

Buying a new home? Make sure you kick the tires first. Michael Lane, who with James Crotty has edited the nomadic RV journal Monk *for nearly a decade, here shares some tips for first-time renters or buyers.*

BATHROOM You will want space to move around without bumping your head, so save by skipping the bathtub—a shower is all you need. RV toilets have two pedals, one to fill the bowl, and one to flush it into a storage tank.

BEDROOM A lot of RVs come set up with a vanity sink in the bedroom. It is a waste of space. And forget about those sliding closet doors. They buckle and become useless as the frame settles.

KITCHEN: Cabinets should open upward or have solid latches to prevent them from popping open in transit. Also, make sure the fridge switches from battery to propane power. And get a big one, you'll want the space.

DRIVER'S SEAT: You'll spend a lot of time here. Make sure you have comfortable arm rests and good back support.

TANKS: Get big water tanks, at least 100 gallons. You can go through 100 gallons in less than two days. Likewise, make sure that your "gray water" tank (for water that's already been used) has at least a 50-gallon capacity.

SPARE TIRE: The spare should be easily accessible. Some are mounted in such a way that it takes three people to get at them. You won't always be able to get roadside assistance.

SEWAGE Make sure that the sewage hose is at least 10 feet long or that the dealer includes an extension so that it will reach out-of-the-way dump sites.

ENGINE: Size counts. A 454 engine is big and it's worth it. If you get a small engine, you will really suffer going up hills. As for the other kind of power, the standard 12-volt deep-cycle battery should be powerful enough to keep your electrical system running for about a day without being recharged.

LODGING

THE CHEAPEST PLACES TO SLEEP

Here's what you'll find inside America's budget motels

They all look the same when you're cruising the Interstate at 65, but there is a world of difference between budget motel chains. True, travelers don't go to them for the amenities, but some budget chains are a lot more budget-oriented than others, and some go out of their way to buck the budget stereotypes. La Quinta Inn chains, for example, offer free coffee and Danish to guests—no great leap for mankind, but a little nicety almost unheard of at budget motels just a few short years ago.

The table below tells what each of the 12 biggest budget motel chains has to offer. Senior citizens, for example, might want to note which chains don't offer senior discounts, while CNN fanatics can learn where to turn in for their daily fix.

For those travelers who want specific recommendations, both *Consumer Reports Travel Letter (CRTL)* and *Money* magazine sent their reporters nationwide in search of the best budget motels. They judged motel chains according to comfort, convenience, cleanliness, price, and safety. Of the 12 chains listed below, both publications gave high marks to Comfort Inn, Hampton Inn, La Quinta Inns, and Super 8. *CRTL* also selected Red Roof Inns, and *Money* liked Travelodge-Thriftlodge.

THE 12 BIGGEST MOTEL CHAINS

CHAIN (Locations*)	DISCOUNTS	EXTRAS	COMMENTS
Comfort Inn (1,300) ☎ 800-424-6423	SENIOR, AAA	POOL, FREE BREAKFAST	*Money* says 90 percent have saunas, 75 percent restaurants.
Courtyard-Marriott (215) ☎ 800-321-2211	SENIOR	CTV, POOL	*CRTL* notes spacious 300-square-foot rooms.
Days Inns (1,400) ☎ 800-325-2525	SENIOR, AAA	POOL	Quality varies. Some offer big savings for seniors.
Econo Lodge (800) ☎ 800-424-6423	SENIOR AAA		So "Econo" it takes a deposit to place non-credit card calls.
Hampton Inn (350) ☎ 800-426-7866		CTV, FREE BREAKFAST	*Frequent Flyer* magazine gives it high marks for quality and looks.
Howard Johnson (560) ☎ 800-446-4656	SENIOR	POOL	*CRTL* notes tiny guest rooms that average 110 square feet.
La Quinta Inns (220) ☎ 800-531-5900	SENIOR, AAA	CTV, POOL, FREE BREAKFAST	Attractive. All are run by live-in husband-wife teams.
Motel 6 (760) ☎ 800-440-6000		CTV, POOL	*New York Times* notes barren rooms.
Red Roof Inns (210) ☎ 800-843-7663	SENIOR		*New York Times* called it "brightly lit but cheerless."
Scottish Inns (400) ☎ 800-251-1962			Stands out for its high level of dissatisfaction in *CRTL* poll.
Super 8 (1,000) ☎ 800-848-8888	TRUCKER	CTV, POOL	One guest describes rooms as decent, yet "Spartan."
Travelodge-Thriftlodge (800) ☎ 800-255-3050		CTV	*Money* cites spacious rooms.

* Approximate figures.

EXPERT PICKS

THE BEST ROAD ATLASES

To keep you from losing your bearings before hitting the road, we called on veteran cartographer Dewey Hicks, formerly of the National Geographic Society and the Defense Mapping Agency, for his advice on the best atlases. Hicks suggests that you steer clear of older versions of whichever atlas you choose—an up-to-date map is the only defense against ever-changing road names and detours. Hicks's evaluations:

■AAA ROAD ATLAS 1995
American Automobile Association, $7.95
AAA is geared for specifics with more cities than other atlases and efficient local maps. The price is smaller type and more clutter. Highway exit information is better than Rand McNally's, but huge indices on each page cut down on map space. (AAA will provide members with a detailed, custom-made "Triptic" for your next road trip that includes current detours, lodging information, and roadside attractions.)
Overall rating: 6

■AMERICAN MAP CORPORATION 1995 ROAD ATLAS
American Map Corp., $6.95
Although AMC's atlas has strong sections on vacation spots and parks, the symbols, roads, and lettering are all too large; the result is a hard-to-read atlas. At 8 by 11 inches, though, it is smaller and more convenient than others. It contains fewer local maps—50 as compared with 300 in most others—and even the ones it includes are of marginal use.
Overall rating: 4

■GOUSHA NEW DELUXE 1995 ROAD ATLAS
H. M. Gousha, $7.95
Hicks loves this atlas's legend and found its state maps easy to read. The master and individual indices are a handy feature. The individual map index doesn't encroach on map space as it does in the AAA Atlas. Local maps are decent, as are those of larger metropolitan areas. Glossy pages make it more durable. A smaller version with much of the same info is also available for a dollar less.
Overall rating: 7

■MOBIL 1994 ROAD ATLAS TRIP PLANNING GUIDE
H. M. Gousha, $7.95
This is basically the Gousha atlas, barring the inclusion of a superior legend and the mysterious exclusion of a master index. For the same price, however, Mobil includes great sections on tourist attractions, local radio, weather, and state histories, which Hicks found very useful compared with the usual fluff most competitors include. If you're traveling with inquisitive kids, this atlas will help.
Overall rating: 8

■RAND MCNALLY 1995 ROAD ATLAS
Rand McNally, $8.95
This is Hicks's top choice. It provides excellent maps and is reputedly kept most up-to-date. Intelligent use of color helps orient you quickly, and symbols are aptly used. City insets are merely functional. There are also comprehensive sections on tourist information, national and regional parks, and area lodging. A more compact, spiral bound edition is also available for $7.95.
Overall rating: 8

HOT SPOTS

THE PERFECT CARIBBEAN ISLAND

We've scoured the azure sea and discovered nine gems for the '90s

Although there are 26 territories, countries, or commonwealths in the Caribbean, there are hundreds of individual islands, some of them spectacular. The bad news for sun worshippers and pleasure seekers is there are very few islands left that are "undiscovered." The good news is times change—governments are overthrown, new resorts are built, airlines add new routes. Beaches once occupied by fully armed U.S. Marines are now filled with sunbathers carrying weapons no more lethal than sunblock. And the new beauty spots aren't hard to find. A veritable army of travel writers is constantly on the lookout for the poshest, cheapest, most environmentally correct, most decadent—or whatever else—spot.

With this in mind, we set out to find the "hot" islands of the Caribbean by meticulously tracking everything that has been written about this vacationer's paradise. What emerges is a startling consensus about where the sybarite of the '90s will find the most sun and fun. We've shied away from bigger, more commercial islands such as Jamaica, Barbados, St. Martin, and Aruba, looking instead for places off the beaten track. Here's what we discovered:

ANGUILLA

Anguilla is considered by many to be the new St. Barts, the super-expensive Francophone hangout that's been the glitterati's island of choice. Like St. Barts, Anguilla is small, just 16 miles long and 3.4 miles wide, and has probably the best beaches in the Caribbean. The island is long and completely flat, resembling a finger. Its tone is somewhat less intimidating than St. Barts. There still are reasonably priced places to stay and eat, and there is a significantly large local population, which means you are just as likely to share your table with a Rastafarian as with a movie star.

BEST BEACHES: There are over 30 white sandy stretches. Highlights among them: **Shoal, Rendezvous Bay, Maunday's,** and **Meads.** The best coral reef for snorkeling is at **Sandy Isle,** just offshore from Sandy Ground.

PRICE GUIDE

Per person per day, double occupancy:

$ = $70 to $150 per night
$$ = $150 to $250
$$$ = $250 to $350
$$$$ = $350 to $450
$$$$$ = $450 and up

A FLYER'S PRIMER TO THE CARIBBEAN

Our nine favorite islands are out of the way, so changing planes at least once is *de rigeur.* American Airlines, with a hub in San Juan, Puerto Rico, is the primary Caribbean carrier.

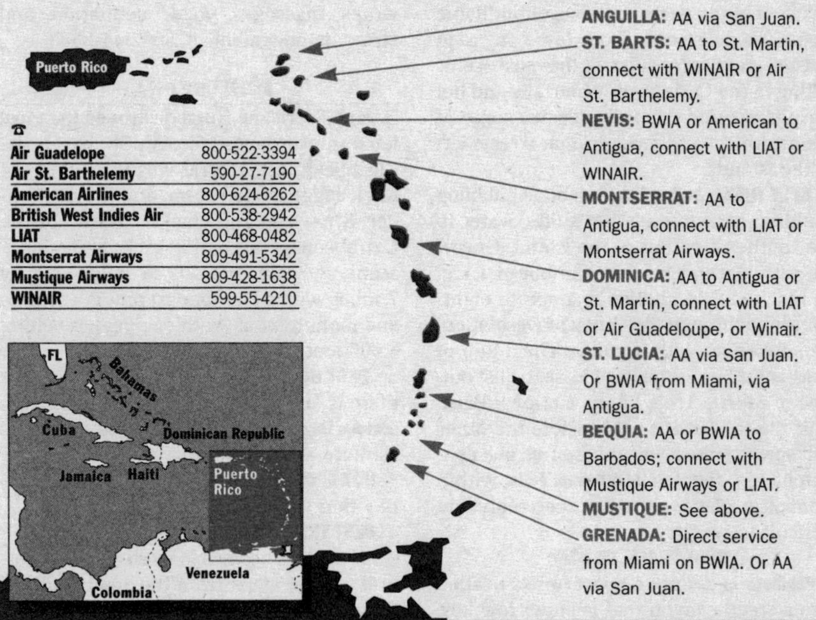
Puerto Rico
FL
Bahamas
Cuba
Dominican Republic
Jamaica
Haiti
Puerto Rico
Venezuela
Colombia
ANGUILLA: AA via San Juan.
ST. BARTS: AA to St. Martin, connect with WINAIR or Air St. Barthelemy.
NEVIS: BWIA or American to Antigua, connect with LIAT or WINAIR.
MONTSERRAT: AA to Antigua, connect with LIAT or Montserrat Airways.
DOMINICA: AA to Antigua or St. Martin, connect with LIAT or Air Guadeloupe, or Winair.
ST. LUCIA: AA via San Juan. Or BWIA from Miami, via Antigua.
BEQUIA: AA or BWIA to Barbados; connect with Mustique Airways or LIAT.
MUSTIQUE: See above.
GRENADA: Direct service from Miami on BWIA. Or AA via San Juan.

☎	
Air Guadelope	800-522-3394
Air St. Barthelemy	590-27-7190
American Airlines	800-624-6262
British West Indies Air	800-538-2942
LIAT	800-468-0482
Montserrat Airways	809-491-5342
Mustique Airways	809-428-1638
WINAIR	599-55-4210

Sandy Island Enterprises, a boat service, can get you there, ☎ 809-497-5643.

HOT SPOT: Johnnos is a beachfront restaurant with a great view of the sailboat races, picnic tables, grilled lobster, and beer.

BEST TREK: Journey to **Windward Point,** at the eastern tip of the island; walk through the former Katouche Plantation at Crocus Bay and around the 100-acre salt pond at Sandy Ground.

BEST PLACES TO STAY:

$$$$ Mailiouhana, the island's most highly touted resort, is situated on a cliff overlooking Meads Bay. Formal and chic, it has two staffers for every guest. ☎ 800-835-0796

$ Rendezvous Bay, with 47 beach cottages sprawled over 60 wild acres, is the island's first seaside resort. There is no room service, however. ☎ 800-274-4893

BEQUIA

This tiny 7-square-mile island has been popular with yachters because of its laid-back ambience and picturesque, hill-sheltered harbor. The island's casual pace was threatened by the recent construction of an airport, but the place hasn't changed much; it's just easier to get to. The island is refreshingly unglitzy and a great bargain.

BEST BEACHES: Lower Bay, a classic Caribbean beach with white sand, palm trees, and a five-minute swim to the island's most accessible snorkeling reef.

HOT SPOT: De Reef, the Lower Bay beach bar, is popular with locals who go for the island's home brew, Hairoun beer.

BEST PLACE TO STAY:

$ Frangipani is a century-old West-Indies-style family inn nestled into a hill overlooking the harbor. The best rooms have private baths and face the garden. ☎ 809-458-3255

DOMINICA

The largest of the windward islands, Dominica shoots up from the sea in a series of formerly volcanic peaks and slopes. It has no white beaches, no serious resorts, and no night life. Though it has long been a haven for divers and hikers, eco-travelers have tried to keep quiet about the wonders of a vacation on Dominica. Three-quarters of the island consists of untillable slopes rising steeply from low-lying rain forests, making for some of the most scenic hiking in the Caribbean. Waterfalls and hot springs abound. Underwater are some of the healthiest and most dramatic reefs left in the islands.

BEST TREKS: Boiling Lake is a huge bubbling cauldron of extremely hot sulfur water in the southeast corner of the island. One of the natural wonders of the Caribbean, it can be reached by a challenging six- to eight-hour hike through the Valley of Desolation. Be sure to go with a guide. The 140-foot **Trafalgar Falls** is northeast of Roseau, just outside of Morne Trois Pitons National Park. Half the falls are icy cold while the other half spring from a volcanic source at a consistent 104 degrees. **Middleham Falls,** within Dominican National Park, is spectacular but difficult to reach.

BEST PLACE TO STAY:

$ **Papillote** is a unique guest house nestled into a steep canyon that is super low key, informal, and eco-sensitive. The hot water is fed from a real hot spring. Rooms are spare but comfortable; the food is traditional Caribbean. ☎ 809-448-2287

GRENADA

For many Americans, this island still conjures images of U.S. troops landing on its beaches. That's kept its prices somewhat lower than on many other islands, but all the important amenities are there.

BEST BEACH: Grand Anse.

HOT SPOT: The **open-air market**, on Saturdays in Grenada's capital, St. George's, is a colorful mélange of tropical fruits and island crafts.

BEST TREKS: Grand Etang, a 3,800-acre park about 20 minutes from St. George's, has at its center **Grand Etang Lake.** The lake is the crater of an extinct volcano and is surrounded by mountains that are prime bird-watching territory. **Seven Sisters Waterfalls** has seven cascades, each with deep, cool pools, but should be toured with a guide.

BEST PLACE TO STAY:

$$$ **La Source** is one of the few real spas in the Caribbean. It offers individually designed menus and a range of spa treatments including mud baths, seaweed wraps, massages, yoga, meditation, and stress management. ☎ 800-544-2883

MONTSERRAT

Before Hurricane Hugo destroyed the most famous recording studio (Air Studios) in the Caribbean, Montserrat was the habitat of Mick Jagger, Elton John, and Stevie Wonder. Known as the emerald island of the Caribbean because of its rich, green landscape, the tiny island is 11 miles long by 7 miles wide. The topography is volcanic and mountainous, with one peak reaching 3,000 feet. Striking views abound.

BEST BEACH: There are few beaches, but there is one nice white sand crescent: **Rendezvous Bay,** an excellent place to rent a villa, as there are few hotels.

HOT SPOT: Rootsman, a beach bar on Carr's Bay that serves the local "Bush" rum.

BEST TREKS: Mount Chance, a 3,002-foot volcanic peak, is accessible by a strenuous natural trail of steps from the road south of Plymouth. The hike takes about an hour and a half and offers stunning views. **Galway's Soufrière** no longer spouts lava, but the still-active volcano bubbles springs and sulfur. A hike to the Soufrière from the village of St. Patrick's takes about two hours by road and trail. A guide is required. **The Great Alps Falls** drops into a 70-foot gorge. A 45-minute hike starts in St. Patrick's, and winds uphill about a mile. There is a small, swimmable pool at the bottom. Guides are recommended for all trips. Tours can be arranged by the Montserrat Tour Guides Association, ☎ 809-491-3160.

BEST PLACE TO STAY:

$$ The **Vue Point Hotel** has 28 individual cottages sloping down the hill above Old Road Bay. ☎ 800-235-0709

MUSTIQUE

The popularity of this island, whose name means "mosquito," stems from the fabulously wealthy and famous people who own houses on it, among them: Mick Jagger, David Bowie, and Princess Margaret.

EXPERT PICKS

BAREFOOT ON A BAREBOAT

If you're going to the Caribbean to to take in the ocean, why not skip the land altogether? Charters generally last a week to 10 days. Weekly rates run from $1,900 to $6,000 during the high season and as little as half that in the off-season. The only requirement is that you have at least one proficient sailor in your group (though it's probably better to have more). If your skills aren't up to snuff, you can hire a skipper at $80 to $120 a day. Here, Yachting *magazine executive editor Kenny Wooten picks the top outfitters.*

CARIBBEAN YACHT

■ One of the older and better-established charter companies, CYC is based in St. Thomas in the U.S. Virgin Islands.
☎ **800-225-2520**

CATAMARAN CHARTERS

■ Catamarans are fast, stable, and roomier than most monohull boats. With cabins in the four corners of the two hulls, they can sleep more people with greater privacy. Catamaran Charters has the largest catamaran fleet in the Caribbean, with bases in the British Virgin Islands, Martinique, Guadeloupe, and St. Martin.
☎ **305-462-6506**

THE MOORINGS

■ The world's largest charter company, with six Caribbean bases. The company's in-house travel agency can make all of your travel arangements.
☎ **800-535-7289**

NAUTOR'S SWAN

■ Based in St. Martin, its fleet is made up entirely of Swans, which are considered the luxury sedan of yachts. The outfitter also offers "Learn to Sail" and "Learn to Cruise" programs.
☎ **800-356-7926**

STARDUST MARINE

■ A French company, Stardust's large and relatively new fleet includes a sizable number of catamarans. Stardust offers a complimentary first night on the boat or in a hotel.
☎ **800-634-8822**

SUNSAIL

■ This company has eight bases throughout the Caribbean, but not every type of boat is available at every location.
☎ **800-327-2276**

SUN YACHT CHARTERS

■ Sun is the only major bareboat company that offers a full-service base in Antigua. Other locations include the British Virgin Islands and St. Martin.
☎ **800-772-3500**

BEST BEACH: Macaroni Beach.

HOT SPOT: Basil's Bar, an upscale but casual bar. Check out the Wednesday night "jump-up" (buffet) with reggae band and jam. For celebrity watching, try the tiny Anglican church on Easter and Christmas.

BEST PLACE TO STAY:

$$$$ The Cotton House, a former 18th-century plantation house, is the island's only hotel. ☎ 809-456-4777

NEVIS

Just two miles away from St. Kitts and a 50-minute charter flight from St. Barts, Nevis is more laid back than either. The Four Seasons opened a fantastically expensive resort here in 1991 with a Robert Trent Jones golf course, but the rest of the island is still relatively poor, sleepy, and charming. For people looking for a more old-fashioned Caribbean experience sans condos, night life, and duty-free shops, Nevis is a good choice. The former plantation houses are the best places to stay.

BEST BEACHES: Pinney's, a 6-mile stretch of sand, and **Newcastle Bay beach** are great for snorkeling. All the beaches on the island are white sand.

HOT SPOT: The 25-mile main road that circumnavigates the island. The circuit takes two hours to complete.

BEST TREK: Nevis Peak, a 3,232-foot-high mountain, sits in the island's center. **Hamilton Trail,** a popular two-and-a-half hour hike to its peak, traverses part of a rain forest and leads to spectacular views of surrounding islands. Guides can be found through the Nevis Historical and Conservation Society. ☎ 809-469-5786

BEST PLACES TO STAY:

$$$ **Montpelier Plantation Inn** is a large stone house with eight ocean-view bungalows, a lap pool, and a shuttle to Pinney's Beach. Princess Di recently pitched up for some rest and relaxation. ☎ 809-469-3462

$$$ **The Hermitage,** built in 1780, is the oldest building on Nevis. Among its amenities: a stable of eight thoroughbred horses ready for guests to ride. ☎ 809-469-3477

ST. BARTS

The choicest of the Caribbean islands, because of its French flavor, beautiful beaches, swanky gourmet restaurants, and extremely high ratio of celebrities. The island also has the most hair-raising airplane landing and the highest prices in the Caribbean.

BEST BEACHES: Gouverneur Beach, Colombière Beach, Grand Saline Beach, and **Flamands Beach** (in that order). Colombière Beach on the northwest coast can only be reached by boat or trail. The trail starts at Flamands Beach, at the west end, and is about a 20-minute hike. Bring food and drink as the beach is totally uninhabited. A word to the prudish: bathing suits (top and bottom) are optional on the island.

HOT SPOT: Chez Maya, a très chic beachside restaurant in Gustavia with Vietnamese and Caribbean cuisine. A celebrity hangout.

BEST PLACES TO STAY:

$$$$ **Guanahani** is far from the airport and Gustavia, the main town, but it boasts a gorgeous beach, 16 pools, and is good for families. ☎ 011-590-27-6660

$ **Hostellerie des Trois Forces** is a small inn nestled in the eastern slope of Morne du Vitet. ☎ 011-590-27-6125

ST. LUCIA

This sleepy island looks more like Hawai'i than it does most of the Caribbean. Two cone-shaped mountains, Gros Piton and Petit Piton, are perched right next to each other on the southwestern coast, dominating the landscape.

BEST BEACHES: Divers should check out **Anse Chastanet's Beach.** For sunbathing, try instead **Reduit Beach** on the northern end of the island.

HOT SPOT: Grosislet, a neighborhood on the northern end of the island, holds a street fair and jump-up (dance) on Friday nights. Local vendors and restaurateurs sell their best dishes while tourists and locals mingle, eat, and dance. When you're there, be sure to try the very tasty St. Lucian lager, Piton beer.

BEST TREKS: Gros Piton has a 2,619-foot climb to the summit, which should be taken with a guide. The St. Lucia National Trust, ☎ 809-452-5005, can arrange for tours. **Frigate Islands Nature Preserve,** off St. Lucia's eastern coast, is home to the frigate—the magnificent bird that can be seen nesting and roosting from May to July. It is also the home to the boa constrictor, among other exotic creatures. There's another small preserve on the Maria Islands: **Sulfur Springs,** located in Soufrière at the southwestern part of the island, is a 7-acre site of volcanic craters filled with bubbling, sulfurous steam.

BEST PLACES TO STAY

$$$$ **Jalousie Plantation** is a relatively new and controversial resort located between the Pitons. Environmentalists did not want the area between the two mountains developed. The luxurious individual cottages have their own plunge pool and all the modern amenities. ☎ 800-392-2007

$$-$$$ **Anse Chastenet,** facing the Pitons, has a more casual atmosphere. Rooms don't have modern amenities such as TVs, telephones, or air-conditioning—but they *do* have incredible views. ☎ 800 223-1108

EXPERT PICKS

MY PRIVATE HAWAI'I

Susanna Moore, who grew up in Honolulu, writes lyrical novels about the Hawai'i of her childhood, filled with island mythology, colors, and scents. Her Hawai'ian Trilogy includes: My Old Sweetheart, The Whiteness of Bones, *and* Sleeping Beauties *(published by Knopf). Some of her favorite off-the-beaten-track places:*

THE ACADEMY OF ART
900 S. Beretania St., Honolulu
☎ 808-532-8700

■ A small, light-filled museum built around several courtyards, with an especially ravishing collection of Japanese art. My father, who is a doctor, used to leave me there in the hot, hot afternoons while he made his rounds.

THE BERNICE PAUAHI BISHOP MUSEUM
1525 Bernice St., Honolulu
☎ 808-847-3511

■ One of the childhood places most loved, most visited, perhaps because it was there that I first literally discovered who I was and, thanks to the walls of ethnographic and geographic maps and charts, where I was.

BROKE THE MOUTH CAFE
1148 Bishop St., Honolulu
☎ 808-524-0355

■ The best local food in the islands (there is another in Hilo, Hawai'i). The name is Pidgin English for food so good that the mouth breaks with joy, and overuse. Like Pidgin itself, the food is a combination of cultures—Chinese, Hawai'ian, Portuguese, Japanese.

HĀLAWA VALLEY

■ The easternmost point of Moloka'i, island of sorcery. There are two waterfalls at the back of the valley with sacred bathing pools of ice-cold water.

HĀNA

■ The loveliest, most Hawai'ian town in the islands. It is a verdant, tropical, and the place of many old legends.

HANAKĀPĪ'AI TRAIL

■ It begins at Hā'ena on the island of Kaua'i. It is a narrow, difficult trail along the treacherous Nāpali Coast, mountains on one side, ocean on the other. During the rainy season (early spring), it is dangerous. It once took me four hours to crawl on my hands and knees in the rain the last half-mile.

HANAPĒPĒ

■ This sleepy farm town on Kaua'i sits at the mouth of a muddy river that flows through a narrow valley of taro patches and vegetable farms. There is a great bar and a general store selling rubber fishing shoes and preserved mango seed.

HILO

■ A small town on the slopes of Mauna Kea on the Big Island known for its beautiful bay and orchids. It is the place where those interested in preserving the best of Hawai'i seem to settle.

THE KAWAIKŌ'I STREAM

■ In the mountains of Kōke'e on Kaua'i, the trail winds along the bank of a stream, through stands of bamboo, cedar, wild ginger, orchids, and ferns. It is the most romantic, most perfect walk in Hawai'i.

POLIHALE
A mile-long state beach at the westernmost end of Kaua'i

■ To reach it, you drive through dry ranchland and dense cane fields. The water can be very dangerous. The sand is so hot that you must wear shoes to walk from the keawe groves to the water's edge. At the north end, where I like to swim, are big sea turtles and sometimes sharks, perhaps because it is the ancient site of an *heiau* for the dead, where bodies once were thrown from the rocks into the sea below.

SMOOCHER'S GUIDE

THE PERFECT PLACES TO PUCKER

A kiss is just a kiss? We suspected otherwise, and Paula Begoun and Stephanie Bell—authors of The Best Places to Kiss *guides (Beginning Press), which cover Northern California, New England, New York City, Southern California, the Northwest, and Hawai'i—confirmed our suspicions. Begoun and Bell based their ratings on the location's ambience, privacy, comfort, and surrounding splendor. Following are those places that received the highly coveted "four lips" rating.*

NEW ENGLAND

CATHEDRAL OF THE PINES

Rindge, N.H.

♥ An extraordinary outdoor cathedral built on a hilltop with views of Mount Monadnock; the walls are the forest and the sky is the ceiling. Multifaith services are held at an outdoor altar. **Free**

☎ **603-899-3300**

CHILLINGSWORTH RESTAURANT

Brewster, Mass.

♥ A romantic restaurant with outstanding five-course gourmet dinners. It has the feel of a private manor, brims with art and antiques, and is lit by candles and fireplaces. **$$$$$**

☎ **508-896-3640**

NORUMBEGA

Camden, Maine

♥ This inn is an elegant stone castle by the sea. King-size beds, antique furniture, and a fabulous ocean view make for regal romance. **$$$$$-$$$$$$**

☎ **207-236-4646**

NEW YORK CITY

THE ST. REGIS HOTEL

♥ Reminiscent of a private mansion, albeit large at 350 rooms, this hotel oozes opulence. Each room has its own sitting area, a tremendous marble bathtub big enough for two, and Egyptian cotton sheets and down pillows on the bed. **$$$$$$**

☎ **212-753-4500**

SIGN OF THE DOVE

♥ You'll feel as at home in black tie as you would in everyday garb at this elegant but eclectic restaurant. Fabulous food and four different rooms with different moods. The most romantic: the Music Room. **$$$$-$$$$$**

☎ **212-861-8080**

THE PACIFIC NORTHWEST

THE HERB FARM

Fall City, Wash.

♥ Part restaurant, part herb garden, part gift and plant shop, the Herb Farm, 35 miles southwest of Seattle, is a gourmet's paradise in all its fragrant splendor. Reservations must be made six months in advance. **$$$$$$**

☎ **206-784-2222**

WESTWINDS B & B

San Juan Island, Wash.

♥ The ultimate place to kiss in the Northwest, this wood-and-glass home sits at the top of a tree-laden hill, on the west side of San Juan Island. There are breathtaking views of the Olympic Mountains and the Strait of Juan de Fuca. The house is rented to only one couple at a time. **$$$**

☎ **360-378-5823**

STRATHCONA PROVINCIAL PARK

Vancouver Island, B.C.

♥ Sheltered in the heart of Vancouver Island, Strathcona's legendary wilderness covers over 220

KEY:	RESTAURANTS*	LODGINGS
$		$75 and under
$$	$25 and under	$75 to $90
$$$	$25 to $50	$90 to $125
$$$$	$50 to $80	$125 to $175
$$$$$	$80 to $110	$175 to $250
$$$$$$	$110 and up	$250 and up

*Prices are for dinner for two, excluding liquor.

■ SMOOCHER'S GUIDE

hectares. The park is blissfully isolated. **Free**
☎ **604-337-5121**

NORTHERN CALIFORNIA

THE HUNTINGTON HOTEL
San Francisco

♥ Originally built as a luxury apartment building, the hotel has 140 luxuriously appointed rooms and a superbly gracious staff. **$$$$$-$$$$$$**
☎ **800-227-4683**

CHATEAU DU SUREAU
Oakhurst

♥ An authentic French provincial country estate located 20 miles south of Yosemite. The wooded grounds have meandering stone walkways, fountains, and a swimming pool. The rooms feature beautiful linens and stone fireplaces. **$$$$$$**
☎ **209-683-6860**

SOUTHERN CALIFORNIA

SIMPSON HOUSE INN
Santa Barbara

♥ A beautifully renovated Victorian mansion amidst sprawling oaks, flowering gardens, and manicured lawns. Each of its 13 guest rooms and 4 garden cottages is beautifully appointed. Included in the cost are breakfast and evening wine. **$$$-$$$$$**
☎ **800-676-1280**

TWO BUNCH PALMS
Desert Hot Springs

♥ This is the pinnacle of tranquillity and self-indulgence. Guests check into this plush, 44-villa spa for a few days of luxurious pampering. The grounds offer a swimming pool, tennis courts, and secluded rock grotto pools that are fed by mineral hot springs. **$$$$$$**
☎ **619-329-8791**

HAWAI'I

HAWAI'I VOLCANOES NATIONAL PARK
Hawai'i

♥ There is nothing like hot, bubbling lava, gurgling in its crater, erupting down the mountain and spilling into the cool sea, to inspire passion. Also, don't be surprised if the earth moves—rumbling earth is a normal part of life here. **Free**

HOLULOA INN IN HOLULOA
Holuloa, Hawai'i

♥ This three-story cedar inn stretches gracefully across the upper portion of a working cattle ranch and coffee farm. Enfolded by fig, papaya, and plumeria trees, the inn has breathtaking views of Kailua Bay and the Pacific. The best spot for kissing is the rooftop gazebo. **$$-$$$**
☎ **808-324-1121**

KAILUA PLANTATION HOUSE
Kailua, Kona

♥ A bed-and-breakfast with the luxury of a superior hotel, this two-story mansion is perched atop a black lava beach, offering exquisite views of the Pacific surf. All five guest rooms have spectacular views; some have their own Jacuzzis. **$$$-$$$$**
☎ **808-329-3727**

PAVILLIONS AT SEACLIFF
Kilauea, Kaui

♥ A private home for rent, this is a complete retreat, usually for three couples. The 7 manicured acres boast unobtructed vistas of rolling surf, three ocean-view master suites, a blue-tiled pool, a tennis court, an exercise room, and a putting green. **$$$**
☎ **808-826-7244**

POHALI PARK BEACH
Mana, Kaua'i

♥ A 15-minute ride down a dirt road will bring you to this velvety sand beach under the sheer cliffs of the Napali coastline. At dusk you might even have it to yourselves. **Free**

HOTEL HANA-MAU
Hana, Maui

♥ Once owned by millionairess Carolyn Hunt, each of the hotel's 96 bungalows scattered over the Hana hillside feature plush furniture, large soaking tubs, and a private patio. **$$$$$$**
☎ **800-321-4262**

BANYAN TREE RESTAURANT
Kapalua, Maui

♥ A casual restaurant with excellent Italian food. They serve lunch only, but the ocean views and tasty pasta can inspire delicious kissing for dessert. **$$$**
☎ **808-669-6200**

VACATION VILLAS

THIS PALACE COULD BE YOURS

It's easier than you think to rent a place abroad—and getting easier

Ann Waigand and her husband and their two children did a modest amount of sightseeing during a recent stay in France's Loire Valley. But not the usual kind. For example, one evening Waigand, who publishes the newsletter *Educated Traveler,* and her family took a leisurely 15-minute drive from their house to watch the sunset over Chambertin, a 15th-century chateau, the roof of which Leonardo da Vinci designed to look like the skyline of a city. Generally, though, the Waigands stayed closer to home—in this case, a restored 19th-century pigeon house on the grounds of an estate. By the end of the week, everyone in the village knew everyone in the family. "If you are sick and tired of sightseeing," Waigand explains, "[renting] is the perfect antidote; you just *live.*"

Renting a villa has long been part of a typical vacation for Europeans, especially the British. And with the growth of worldwide vacation home rental agencies in the United States, Americans too are finding it easy to get in on the act. No longer does one need to know foreign languages or have years of expatriate experience. Many agencies can make all the arrangements here—even down to car rentals.

What's the allure? Instead of trying to take in a whole country in a couple of weeks of frenzied traveling, or staying in look-alike resort hotels with other travelers, renting abroad immerses travelers in the day-to-day life of the natives. Renters may not enjoy the services of a hotel, but they will enjoy the privacy of their own place and amenities such as private garden or pool that go with an established residence.

There's also an economic incentive to renting abroad, according to Gail Richards of the travel newsletter the *Hideaway Guide:* "The myth is that renting vacation homes abroad is only for the rich and famous, [but] many British and European vacation homes are affordable for the middle-income bracket."

Indeed, in comparison with most resort hotels, where a single room can run $100 a day or more, vacation home rental offers substantial savings. The typical rental for four to six people is $700 to $1,200 per week in season—about $30 per person per day—and even less in the off-season. You also can save money on budget-busting restaurants by shopping at farmers' markets and eating at home (at least most of the time).

For the best deals, travelers should rent in an area that is not "in season." Condos in the Costa del Sol in Spain that cost $600 a week in August, for example, cost a mere $200 a week in January. In ski areas such as the Swiss Alps, prices usually dip in the summer and are especially cheap in the spring and fall. In Europe, the farther south and the farther inland one goes, the cheaper the prices will be—except in July and August, when roving hordes of northern Europeans in search of sun and beaches drive up rental prices by 30 to 40 percent.

Europe isn't the only place one can rent a vacation home. In fact, it may not even be the best place. Mexico and the Caribbean offer vacation homes equipped with American appliances and American standards of cleanliness. In Europe, many homes, especially in rural areas, may not have the amenities that Americans are used to. Most rural French farmhouses and even chateaus don't have air-conditioning, washing machines, or even screen windows. The service in Europe also tends to be much less attentive; in the Caribbean and Mexico, property agents usually are at your beck and call.

RENTER'S GUIDE

WHERE THE VILLAS ARE

The best way to save money on a vacation rental home is to bypass the middleman. You can save 20 to 30 percent by renting directly through the owner. Options include writing the local tourist board or looking through the classified sections of college alumni magazines. Rental agencies, on the other hand, offer the convenience of an experienced pro minding the details. Some resources:

RENTAL AGENCIES

If you use a rental agency, it's a good idea to choose one with a local agent based near the town in which you intend to rent. That way, you'll have someone to contact in case anything goes wrong.

AT HOME ABROAD
New York, N.Y.

■ Caters to an upscale market. Rates range from $3,500 to $50,000 per month, although many of their Caribbean and Mexican villas also are available by the week. Requires a $50 registration fee. At Home Abroad is the agent for Mick Jagger's retreat, Stargrove, on the West Indies island of Mustique. Rent is $9,000 a week during peak winter months.
☎ **212-421-9165**

BARCLAY INTERNATIONAL
New York, N.Y.

■ Specializes in apartment rentals in most of the major cities around the world. Properties include suites at some luxury hotels. A free catalogue is available.
☎ **800-845-6636**

BRITISH TRAVEL INTERNATIONAL
Elkton, Va.

■ Offers properties in France, England, and Italy. A color catalog is available for a small fee.
☎ **800-327-6097**

CREATIVE LEISURE INTERNATIONAL
Petaluma, Calif.

■ Properties primarily in Hawai'i, the Caribbean, and Mexico. Will arrange everything from airfare to babysitting.
☎ **800-426-6367**

EUROPA LET
Ashland, Ore.

■ Listings in Europe, Mexico, Hawai'i, the Caribbean, and the Pacific islands. A good choice for sailors seeking seaside homes. There is a $25 booking fee.
☎ **800-462-4486**

HOMES AWAY
Toronto, Canada

■ A relatively new branch of Butterfield and Robinson, which is well known for organizing hiking and biking trips, offers houses not usually for rent—an old silk farm, for example.
☎ **800-678-1147**

INTERHOME
Fairfield, N.J.

■ In its 30th year and with over 20,000 listings, Interhome is one of the oldest and largest home rental agencies in the world. Hot spots include the northern Croatian coast (safely away from the war zone), Poland, and the Czech Republic.
☎ **201-882-6864**

RENT A HOME INTERNATIONAL
Seattle, Wash.

■ Offers an estimated 25,000 listings around the world in Europe, Australia, and Asia. Prices range from $600 to $25,000 per week. Does not have as detailed information on its properties as many other agencies. Several catalogs are available for small fees.
☎ **206-789-9377**

VILLAS INTERNATIONAL
San Francisco, Calif.

■ Listings include a villa on Phuket island in Thailand that costs from $1,200 to $1,600 per week, but they specialize in properties in Europe and the Caribbean.
☎ **800-221-2260**

■ RENTER'S LIST

HOME EXCHANGE

An economical way to take a vacation. Usually there is a listing fee, but other arrangements are left to the homeowners.

INTERVAC
San Francisco, Calif.

■ International and domestic listings.
☎ **800-756-4663**

HIDEAWAYS INTERNATIONAL
Littleton, Mass.

■ Listings include owners of resort and vacation properties in Europe, the United States, and the Caribbean. Members also get special discounts.
☎ **617-486-8955**

VACATION EXCHANGE CLUB
Key West, Fla.

■ The club offers a free information package.
☎ **800-638-3841**

RENTING BY COUNTRY

Renting through an institution abroad can be challenging. But it also can lead to savings by cutting out the middleman.

DENMARK

■ **Scandinavia DanCenter:** Offers Danish rentals only. Material is written in German and Danish. Write: Sotorbet 5, DK 1371, Copenhagen, Denmark, or call ☎ 45-3333-0102.

■ **ScanAm World Tours:** Rents throughout Scandinavia. Write: 933 Highway 23, Pompton Plains, NJ 07444, or call ☎ 800-545-2204.

ENGLAND

■ **Heritage of England Country Homes:** The organization specializes in country houses and will arrange airfare and car rental. Write: 153 W. 13th St., New York, NY 10011 or call ☎ 212-242-2145.

■ **The Landmark Trust:** A charitable trust that preserves buildings by carefully restoring them and renting them to vacationers. Rentals include everything from medieval halls to concrete bunkers. A catalog of properties is available for $35. Write: Shottesbrooke, Maidenhead, Berkshire SLX 3SW, England, or call ☎ 44-162-88-25925.

■ **National Trust Enterprises:** Determined travelers can find real bargains at this branch of the National Trust, which is aimed more toward British nationals. Prices range from $183 per week in the off-season to $1,725 in the summer, mostly for old farm workers' cottages on beautiful estates. Write: The Travel Trade Department, PO Box 536, Melksham Wiltshire, England SN128SX. Or call the Royal Oak Foundation, a sister organization in New York City, ☎ 212-966-6565.

FRANCE

■ **Federation Nationale des Gites de France:** A nonprofit institution founded in 1955 to preserve old country houses and bolster rural economies through tourism. The network consists of over 50,000 houses and apartments—or *gites*. *Gites* are not available in cities. They are more modest dwellings and not always available in prime vacation areas. Write: 35 Rue Godot de Mauroy, 75009, Paris, France, or call ☎ 14-742-25-43.

■ **The French Experience:** It rents more upscale French *gites*. In the high season, July and August, the company's prices range from $400 to $750 per week. For information, write: 370 Lexington Ave., New York, NY 10017, or call ☎ 212-986-1115.

ITALY

■ **Cuendet U.S.A.:** Full-service rental agency with more than 1,500 listings from farmhouses to castles and villas. A catalog costs $18. Write: 165 Chestnut St., Allendale, NJ 07401, or call ☎ 201-327-2333.

SCOTLAND

■ **National Trust for Scotland:** For information, write: 5 Charlotte Square, Edinburgh, Scotland EH2 4DU, or call ☎ 44-1-226-5922

SWEDEN

■ **Varmland Tourist Board:** The board specializes in rentals in Sweden's Lake District. For information, write: V. Torgatan 26, 65300, Karlstad, Sweden, or call ☎ 46-54-195901.

THERE'S A SMALL HOTEL . . .

Looking for charm in New York, London, and Paris? Look no further!

Many guides offer reliable listings of large, luxury hotels with established reputations. But for those who put a premium on charm and prefer lodging on a more personal scale, we've culled some of the smaller hotels that are catching travel writers' eyes. Prices are in U.S. dollars as of early 1995 and don't include taxes or fees.

NEW YORK

Convention-goers may head for the Hilton and heads of state to the Waldorf Astoria, but there's a mini-boomlet in smaller, neighborhood hotels in the Big Apple.

THE LOWELL

28 E. 63rd St. ☎ 800-221-4444 FAX 212-319-4230

■ Sets high standard for solicitous service and elegant comfort. Mostly suites, many with fireplaces, all with kitchenettes. Near Madison Avenue shops and galleries. Doubles from $355. Suites from $455 to $1,500.

HOTEL WALES

1295 Madison Ave. ☎ 800-428-5252
FAX 212-860-6000

■ Civilized, unpretentious atmosphere. Close to the Met, Guggenheim, Cooper-Hewitt museums, and upper East Side shopping. Doubles from $145 with continental breakfast. Suites from $170 to $250.

THE ROYALTON

44 W. 44th St. ☎ 800-635-9013
FAX 212-869-8965

■ Chic, custom decor. Convenient to theater district, shops. Doubles from $255. Suites from $380.

THE SURREY

20 E. 76th St. ☎ 212-288-3700 FAX 212-628-1549

■ Large, pleasant rooms, all with kitchenettes. Ideal for families and for longer stays. Near Frick, Whitney museums, Central Park. Two-person studios from $205. Four-person suites from $395.

THE ELYSEE

60 E. 54th St. ☎ 800-535-9733 FAX 212-753-1066

■ Attentive service, carefully appointed rooms. Midtown location near business, shopping, top restaurants. Doubles from $195 with continental breakfast.

THE FRANKLIN

164 E. 87th St. ☎ 212-369-1000 FAX 212-369-8000

■ Imaginative, up-to-the-minute styling of smallish rooms at reasonable prices. Vibrant neighborhood with abundant boutiques, antiques. Doubles from $135 with continental breakfast.

LONDON

These days there's a virtual explosion of small and elegant townhouse hotels all over town. A selection of some of the choicest in different settings and price ranges:

47 PARK STREET

47 Park St. W1 ☎ 44-171-491-7282 FAX 44-171-491-7281

■ Edwardian townhouse in chic Mayfair with spacious rooms and 24-hour room service from the celebrated Le Gavroche restaurant, both owned by the Roux family. Doubles from $369. Suites from $596.

HAZLITT'S

6 Frith St. W1 ☎ 44-171-434-1771 NO FAX

■ Three antique-filled, 18th-century terraced houses off lively and fashionable Soho Square. Near Oxford Street and the Royal Opera House. Singles from $160. Doubles from $205.

THE MILESTONE

1-2 Kensington Court W8 ☎ 44-171-917-1000
FAX 44-171-917-1010

■ A handsome 19th-century house, carefully restored with 58 luxury suites and a health spa. Overlooks

Kensington Gardens and Kensington Palace. Suites from $330.

CANNIZARO HOUSE
W. Side, Wimbledon Common SW 19 ☎ 44-181-879-1464
FAX 44-181-879-7338

■ Elegantly furnished Georgian house with ornamental lake and gardens. Well-situated for the Wimbledon tournament in June. Doubles from $188 to $275.

NUMBER 16
16 Sumner Place SW7 ☎ 44-171-589-5232
FAX 44-171-584-8615

■ Adjoining Victorian townhouses with a conservatory and a large rear garden. Near Sloane Square, Knightsbridge. Bed and breakfast from $94 to $133.

HALKIN HOTEL
5 Halkin Place SW1 ☎ 44-171-333-1000
FAX 44-171-333-1100

■ Sleek and sophisticated Italian design in a modern townhouse-style hotel. No public rooms except restaurant. Doubles from $298 to $376.

DORSET SQUARE
39 Dorset Square, NW1 ☎ 44-171-723-7874
FAX 44-171-724-3328

■ An elegant country house atmosphere with modern conveniences. On a handsome garden square near Regent's Park, Oxford St. Bed and breakfast from $98 to $228.

L'HOTEL
28 Basil St., SW3 ☎ 44-171-589-6286
FAX 44-171-225-0011

■ Informal with small, attractive rooms. Children welcome. Close to Harrod's, Hyde Park, Buckingham Palace. Bed and breakfast from $98 to $228.

THE FIELDING HOTEL
4 Broad Court, Bow St. ☎ 44-171-836-8305
FAX 44-171-497-0664

■ An 18th-century building houses this charming, cozy hotel. Reasonable prices. On a quiet street in the heart of Covent Garden. Near the Royal Opera House and West End. Bed and breakfast from $60 to $115.

PARIS

The Parisian hotel scene is perpetually transforming itself as sophisticated new entries and updated old favorites help fill the insatiable demand for intimate places with charm and desirable addresses.

MONTALEMBERT
3 Rue de Montalembert, 7th Arr. ☎ 331-45-48-68-11
FAX 331-42-22-58-19

■ Luxuriously redesigned rooms may be either Empire or modern in style. Convenient to the Musée d'Orsay and St.-Germain-des-Pres. Doubles from $345.

PAVILLON BASTILLE
65 Rue de Lyon, 12th Arr. ☎ 331-43-43-65-65
FAX 331-43-43-96-52

■ Petite and ultramodern. Offers compact rooms with many features at bargain prices. In courtyard opposite Bastille Opera House. Doubles or singles from $160.

HOTEL RELAIS MEDICIS
23 Rue Racine, 6th Arr. ☎ 331-43-26-00-60
FAX 331-40-46-83-39

■ An urban country inn with Provençal charm on the Place de l'Odéon, near the Luxembourg Gardens. Doubles from $246.

HOTEL LE TOURVILLE
16 Ave. de Tourville, 7th Arr. ☎ 331-47-05-62-62
FAX 331-47-05-43-90

■ Good-sized rooms combine antiques and modern comforts. A few have private terraces. Between the Champs de Mars and the Invalides. Doubles from about $150.

HOTEL GRANDE TURENNE
6 Rue de Turenne, 4th Arr.
☎ 331-42-78-43-25 FAX 331-42-74-10-72

■ Refurbished small hotel near lovely Place des Vosges with smallish rooms, new bathrooms, breakfast buffet. Doubles from $140.

HOTEL MONTAIGNE
6 Ave. Montaigne, 8th Arr.
☎ 331-47-20-30-50 FAX 331-47-20-94-12

■ Sleek elegance with views across the Seine to the Eiffel Tower. Convenient to haute couture houses. Doubles from $330 to $350.

EXPERTS' PICKS

THE BEST PLACES TO BED DOWN IN AMERICA

Here are the top-ranked hotels from four of the most respected travel authorities. The American Automobile Association (AAA) and the Mobil Travel Guide *both release a yearly list of the nation's best hotels. Also in the hotel rating game are two well-known travel publications: the* Hideaway Report*, a newsletter, and* Condé Nast Traveler *magazine. AAA and Mobil utilize roving teams of inspectors, whereas* Hideaway *and* Condé Nast *rely on reader polls. To appear on our list, a hotel had to receive top marks from at least two of the four authorities we consulted. Only eight hotels—checked in red—made it on to all four lists.*

HOTEL	HIDEAWAY	CONDÉ NAST	AAA	MOBIL
AUBERGE DU SOLEIL, Rutherford, Calif. ☎ 800-348-5406	✓	✓		
THE BOULDERS, Carefree, Ariz. ☎ 203-868-0541	✓	✓	✓	
THE BROADMOOR, Colorado Springs, Colo. ☎ 800-634-7711		✓	✓	✓
THE CARLYLE, New York, N.Y. ☎ 800-227-5737	✓	✓		✓
THE CLOISTER, Sea Island, Ga. ☎ 800-732-4752	✓	✓	✓	
C LAZY U RANCH, Granby, Colo. ☎ 303-887-3344			✓	✓
FOUR SEASONS, Boston, Mass. ☎ 800-332-3442	✓	✓	✓	
FOUR SEASONS, Chicago, Ill. ☎ 800-332-3442	✓	✓	✓	✓
FOUR SEASONS, CLIFT, San Francisco, Calif. ☎ 800-332-3442	✓	✓	✓	✓
FOUR SEASONS, Washington, D.C. ☎ 800-332-3442	✓	✓	✓	
FOUR SEASONS, RESORT, Maui, Hawai'i ☎ 800-332-3442	✓	✓	✓	
FOUR SEASONS, HOTEL, Newport Beach, Calif. ☎ 800-332-3442		✓	✓	
FOUR SEASONS, New York, N.Y. ☎ 800-332-3442	✓	✓	✓	
FOUR SEASONS, Philidelphia, Pa. ☎ 800-332-3442		✓	✓	
FOUR SEASONS, Seattle, Wash. ☎ 800-332-3442	✓	✓	✓	
GRAND WAILEA BEACH RESORT, Wailea, Hawai'i ☎ 800-233-1234		✓	✓	
THE GREENBRIER, White Sulphur Springs, W.V. ☎ .800-624-6070	✓	✓	✓	✓
HALEKULANI, Honolulu, Hawai'i ☎ 800-367-2343	✓	✓	✓	
HOTEL BEL AIR, Los Angeles, Calif. ☎ 800-648-4097	✓	✓		✓
HYATT REGENCY, Maui, Hawai'i ☎ 800-233-1234		✓	✓	
INN AT LITTLE WASHINGTON, Washington, Va. ☎ 703-675-3800	✓	✓	✓	✓
THE LITTLE NELL, Aspen, Colo. ☎ 800-525-6200	✓		✓	
LODGE AT KOELE, Lanai, Hawai'i ☎ 800-321-4666	✓	✓		
LODGE AT PEBBLE BEACH, Pebble Beach, Calif. ☎ 800-654-9300	✓	✓		
MANSION AT TURTLE CREEK, Dallas, Texas ☎ 800-527-5432	✓	✓	✓	✓
MARRIOTT'S CAMELBACK INN, Phoenix, Ariz. ☎ 800-242-2635			✓	✓
MAUNA LANI BAY, Kohala Coast, Hawai'i ☎ 800-367-2323	✓	✓	✓	
MEADOWOOD, St. Helena, Calif. ☎ 800-458-8080	✓	✓		
THE PENINSULA, Beverly Hills, Calif. ☎ 800-262-9467		✓	✓	✓
THE PHOENCIAN, Scottsdale, Ariz. ☎ 800-888-8234	✓	✓		✓
RITZ CARLTON BUCKHEAD, Atlanta, Ga. ☎ 800-241-3333	✓	✓	✓	
RITZ CARLTON, Boston, Mass. ☎ 800-241-3333	✓	✓		
RITZ CARLTON, Chicago, Ill. ☎ 800-241-3333	✓	✓	✓	
RITZ CARLTON, Laguna Niguel, Calif. ☎ 800-241-3333	✓	✓	✓	✓
RITZ CARLTON, Naples, Fla. ☎ 800-241-3333	✓	✓	✓	✓
RITZ CARLTON, San Francisco, Calif. ☎ 800-241-3333	✓	✓	✓	✓
STOUFFER WAILEA BEACH RESORT, Maui, Hawai'i ☎ 800-992-4532		✓	✓	
ST. REGIS, New York, N.Y. ☎ 800-759-7550	✓		✓	
SCOTTSDALE PRINCESS, Scottsdale, Ariz. ☎ 800-223-1818		✓	✓	
VENTANA, Big Sur, Calif. ☎ 800-628-6500	✓	✓		
WILLIAMSBURG INN, Williamsburg, Va. ☎ 800-447-8679		✓		✓
WINDSOR COURT, New Orleans, La. ☎ 800-262-2662	✓	✓	✓	

WASHINGTON

WHERE TO HAIL THE CHIEF

Forget the monuments. Here are President Clinton's hangouts

Most visitors to the nation's capital, of course, don't get to say a personal hail to the chief. But your odds improve considerably if you know where the president hangs out. Fortunately, Bill Clinton is more peripatetic than most recent occupants of the Executive Mansion. Here are some spots where you might catch a glimpse of him:

■ **THE MORNING CONSTITUTIONAL:** To be like Bill, you'll have to hit the pavement between 6 a.m. and 7 a.m. and hoof it at an eight-minute mile. For security reasons, the first runner has to vary his route, but his favorite places to pass are **The Mall,** the **Capitol Building,** and **Haines Point** in Potomac Park.

■ **THE CAPITOL:** Except for the State of the Union address every January, the president doesn't regularly come to call on the legislative branch—especially now that the Republicans have taken over. But he does limo up from time to time. The Capitol Building is open and free to tour seven days a week. If you prefer, you can wander about on your own from 9 a.m. to 4:30 p.m. Call your senator or congressman for tickets to view open sessions of Congress. For tour information, call ☎ 202-225-6827.

■ **THE PENTAGON:** In most cases, the generals come to the Oval Office, but when the commander in chief does visit—usually on weekends—he scoots over the **Memorial Bridge.** Even if the president isn't coming to call, there's no better place to see your tax dollars at work. Hour-long tours are available weekdays. For tour information, call ☎ 703-695-1776. A nine-iron shot up the freeway is the **Army-Navy Country Club,** where the president often goes for a round of golf. Unfortunately, it's members only.

■ **PRESIDENTIAL PRAYERS:** The first family often attends 11 a.m. services on Sunday at the **Foundry United Methodist Church** at 1500 16th Street NW. If, however, they are trying to avoid anti-abortion protesters, they may hit **St. John's Episcopal Church** at 1525 H St. NW for an earlier service. For their first Christmas in town, the Clintons went to the **Washington National Cathedral.** Although not a publicly funded building as the name might suggest, this 50-year-old ongoing project is an architectural masterpiece. Gargoyles gracing the walls include the Yuppie and the Crooked Politician. For general information, call ☎ 202-364-6616.

■ **WINING AND DINING:** One of the President's favorites is **The Bombay Club** at 815 Connecticut Ave. NW, ☎ 202-659-3727, near the White House. Clinton brought German Chancellor Helmut Kohl to **Filomena** at 1063 Wisconsin Ave. NW, ☎ 202-337-2782 to satisfy their mutual scongili fixation. **Galileo's** at 1110 21st St. NW, ☎ 202-293-7191, found space one evening for the Clintons and actors Paul Newman, Joanne Woodward, and Tim Robbins. Reserve early. For Valentine's Day, the president took the first lady to the ever-popular **Red Sage** at 604 14th St. NW, ☎ 202-638-4444. When Vice President Al Gore and his wife Tipper double-dated with the First Couple, they first hit **RT's** at 3804 Mount Vernon Ave. in nearby Alexandria, Va., ☎ 703-684-6010. Then they danced the night away at **The Birchmere,** a great place for live music also in Alexandria, 3901 Mt. Vernon Ave., ☎ 703-549-5919.

■ **THE WHITE HOUSE:** Bill Clinton sleeps here—most nights, anyway. The private residence is off limits, but several areas, including the Blue and East rooms, have been completely redone by an Arkansan decorator and are open to the public. Notify your congressman or senator six to eight weeks before you want to visit and you can get reserved tickets for a longer tour, often including a visit to the redecorated Oval Office. For general information, call ☎ 202-456-7041.

KID PICKS

A PINT-SIZED VIEW OF DISNEY WORLD

Our nine-year-old expert tells you the attractions not to miss

What's an American childhood without the ritual pilgrimage to Disney World, the magic mecca in Orlando. Sure, you can consult the many guides to Disney World that line the shelves of any bookstore. But all these tomes were written by adults for adults. Would you trust anyone over 13 to tell you about Space Mountain? To remedy these deficiencies, we sent Nicholas Bernstein, age 9, to check out the scene along with two of his cousins—Allison, also age 9, and Laura, age 8, for a kid's-eye view. Nicky's report:

First of all: Leave your parents at home. I'm not suggesting that you hop on a plane all by yourself, but if you can, go with your grandparents. The trouble with parents is that they are always telling you not to do this, not to do that, to stop fighting with your brother or sister, or to improve your manners. Grandparents, on the other hand, just let you have fun and they don't care so much what you eat. One day, for example, all we had for lunch were cookies-and-cream milk shakes.

My second piece of advice: three days is not enough. We left Wednesday and came back Sunday, so we had about three-and-a-half days to see stuff. We saw lots of things and went on lots of rides but not nearly enough. I'd suggest that you convince whoever is taking you to stay for five or so days. That way you get to try lots of things, go on your favorite rides more than once, and still have enough time for swimming and just goofing around.

Here's the best way to plan your day: Leave your hotel early in the morning. You want to walk through the gates just as the park is opening. That way you'll get to the best rides before long lines form. Plan on having lunch either at the park or back at your hotel. (The turkey dogs weren't very good.) Take a rest, read, or go swimming, then head back to the Magic Kingdom, EPCOT, or wherever, late in the afternoon.

Now, here's what you must see. I've rated each attraction; ★★★★★ is tops.

THE MAGIC KINGDOM

★★★★ **SPACE MOUNTAIN:** This is a very scary, exciting, fast, and dark ride. The reason it's scary is that it's so dark inside that you can't see the track the car is on. You don't know where you're going—just like when I'm driving with my mom, but even scarier. I'd say kids eight and up would really like this, but younger kids might be too afraid. The line doesn't look long from outside, but it is. It moves pretty fast. Plan on waiting 25 to 45 minutes no matter when you arrive.

★★★ **THE HAUNTED MANSION:** This ride is more fun than scary—although they do try to scare you. Hands pop out of graves, ghosts peek around corners, and there are lots of illusions. Kids 4 to 10 will like this. It's a long wait, usually about 25 minutes.

★★★★ **SPLASH MOUNTAIN:** Be prepared for a 45-minute wait; this is one of the most popular rides in the Magic Kingdom. With scenes of Brer Rabbit, Brer Bear, and Brer Fox along the side, you race through swamps, caves, and bayous. The climax is a five-story drop into the briar patch. You get wet, but not that wet. Kids four and under might get too scared by the ending, though they'll enjoy everything else. It's a good ride, but not worth waiting over 40 minutes.

EPCOT CENTER

★★★★★ **HONEY, I SHRUNK THE AUDIENCE:** A short scientist wins an award for a shrinking invention. During a demonstration of his experiment, however, everything goes wrong. Instead of shrinking a family's luggage, he ends up shrinking the audience. Among other things, a scary cat almost eats you, and a snake slithers by. There are lots of special effects that make you think it's real. Good for all ages, including parents, though three-year-olds might get scared.

Don't worry about long lines—over 500 people can fit in every 20 minutes or so.

★★★★ **THE LIVING SEAS:** One of the most educational attractions in the park, but it's also a lot of fun. You learn about fish and manatees—a huge, endangered species that looks like a cross between an elephant and a whale. You see divers feeding all sorts of fish, including sharks and dolphins. Usually not much of a wait.

MGM STUDIOS

★★★★★ **INDIANA JONES EPIC STUNT SPECTACULAR:** You should get here either before 11 a.m. or after 5 p.m., because even though the Stunt Theater can hold 2,000 people, it is almost always filled. The show is funny and exciting. The stunts are as spectacular as they are in the movies. Great for all ages, but boys will probably like this more than girls.

★★★★ **DISNEY-MGM ANIMATION STUDIO:** Walter Cronkite (I've never heard of this guy, but my grandfather says you can believe everything he says) and Robin Williams (he was terrific in *Mrs. Doubtfire,* which you can rent at Blockbuster Video) take you around the studios showing you exactly how cartoons are made. At one point, Robin Williams goes to Never-Never Land with Peter Pan. You see the animators drawing and lots of other neat things. It's interesting for older people (like my grandparents) but also not too complicated for younger people (like me). And there usually isn't much of a line.

★★★ **THE MAKING OF THE LION KING:** You see who draws all the characters, see the people who become the characters' voices, and get a good idea about how the movie was put together. It's a lot like the Animation Studio, but seeing both gives you a much better idea of how it all works. Arrive 10 minutes before the show starts to be sure to get in. Good for all ages.

★★★★ **STAR TOURS:** A robot takes you on his first flight but things get totally out of control. Your ship shakes, rattles, and rolls as you hurl through space at warp speed. You're attacked by meteors but you get back to your base safely. A super ride. Plan to wait about 20 minutes.

★★★ **TWILIGHT ZONE TOWER OF TERROR:** Don't go if you get scared, but if you're up to it, it's great. You take an elevator up to the fifth floor of the Hollywood Towers Hotel and then things start getting weird. Before it's over, you're not sure which way is up.

LAS VEGAS ISN'T JUST FOR GAMBLING

America's Sin City reinvents itself as a family resort.

The slot machines spew quarters reassuringly, but across the lobby, a 20-foot barge is making its way through artificial mists into what appears to be an Egyptian tomb. The Luxor, a large glass pyramid with a miniature river running through it, is one of four new mega-resorts that cater to families. Meanwhile, the initial Vegas family resort and parent to the Luxor, Circus Circus, recently built a $90 million theme park. The '90s are here; it's makeover time in Sin City.

In just the past 10 years, the budget-boosting magic of legalized gambling has swept across the country, revitalizing ailing post-industrial cities and bringing untold wealth to once obscure Indian reservations. To compete, Las Vegas is turning itself into a kind of Disney World Mark II. From the Camelot-themed Excalibur to MGM's 33-acre amusement park, to Treasure Island's reenactments of naval duels with full-sized replicas of pirate ships, the new hotels offer Disneyesque fun while still providing the adult games that Las Vegas is known for.

Las Vegas's biggest payoff for families is the price. That's because the hotels still make most of their money through gambling. Some shows are expensive, but lodging and food are cheap—all the better to lure parents to the gambling table.

HAUNTED HOUSES

WHERE THE GHOULS ARE

A guide to the skeletons in America's closet

Dennis William Hauck, an international authority on paranormal phenomena, deems these haunted places as being among the most noteworthy in the United States. More can be found in his book, *The National Directory of Haunted Places* (Athanor Press, 1995).

CHATHAM MANOR Fredericksburg, Va.

■ A love affair was brought to an end here by George Washington. An aristocratic English friend of the owner thought that a trip across the ocean would end his daughter's romance with a commoner. But her suitor followed and the lovers plotted an elopement. Washington, who happened to be staying at Chatham, learned of the romance and had the man arrested. The girl returned to England and was married; her ghost came back and today haunts the grounds.

CHEESMAN PARK Denver, Colo.

■ Formerly Mount Prospect Graveyard, a cemetery for criminals and epidemic victims. In 1893, the city hired an inept undertaker to remove the 6,000 to 10,000 bodies buried there. Chaos ensued. Corpses were broken into pieces to fit smaller caskets, body parts were mixed up, and many of the graves were looted. The remaining bodies were simply plowed over. The spirits are still upset over that one.

PIKE PLACE MARKET Seattle, Wash.

■ The underground ramps of this shopping plaza are haunted by the ghost of an American Indian, Kickisomolo, daughter of Chief Seattle. In 1854, the chief prophesied that once his tribe was gone, its spirits would continue to haunt their former homeland.

USF CONSTELLATION Baltimore, Md.

■ The frigate, built in 1797, was the first commissioned ship in the U.S. Navy. It got off to a bad start. In 1799, a sailor was tied to a gun and blown to bits for falling asleep on his watch. His ghost and that of the captain who ordered the execution haunt the ship today.

WHALEY HOUSE San Diego, Calif.

■ Recognized as an official haunted house by the state of California, the two-story brick house was built by Thomas Whaley in 1857. Whaley rented part of his house to the town of San Diego to be used as a county courtroom and department of records. It soon became the center of a power dispute that ended in its being ransacked and the Whaley family terrorized by disgruntled townspeople. Later, Whaley tried in vain to collect damages. Today, Whaley family ghosts account for strange noises and mysterious lights.

THE WHITE HOUSE Washington, D.C.

■ Of its many haunted rooms, the most interesting is the Lincoln bedroom. Lincoln was likely the most mystical of our presidents. He regularly sought advice from deceased world leaders through a medium.

WINCHESTER HOUSE San Jose, Calif.

■ This 160-room house has 950 doors and was actually built for ghosts by Sarah Winchester. In 1884, her husband and only child died. When Sarah went to a medium to try to contact their spirits, he suggested that she build a house for all the spirits of the people killed by the rifle that bore her husband's name. Much of the building is based on the number 13, and there are many blind passageways to deter evil spirits. Winchester left instructions in her will that ghosts continue to be welcomed.

DINER'S GUIDE

TEN TOP TONGUES' TASTES OF CHOICE

It's a big country with food that's getting better all the time, so coming up with the best restaurants in America could be a daunting task. We tackled it by asking the food critics in 10 cities their favorites. Prices listed are for dinner.

RESTAURANT ▸ Address ☎ **Phone** **$** Prices ‖ **Cuisine** ▸ *Critic's comment*

■ **ATLANTA:** Hordes will flock to Atlanta for the 1996 Summer Olympics. Christiane Lauterbach, the dining critic for *Atlanta Magazine*, suggests some of the finer places to dine.

BRASSERIE LE COZE ▸ 3393 Peachtree Rd., Lenox Square Mall ☎ **404-266-1440** ‖ French Bistro **$** Entrees **$10 to $20**
▸ *Best French restaurant in town; authentic, unpretentious food.*

BUCKHEAD DINER ▸ 3073 Piedmont Rd. ☎ **404-266-1440** ‖ American **$** Entrees **$7.50 to $17.50**
▸ *The glamour spot of the Big Peach, creative American cuisine coupled with visiting celebrities such as Elton John.*

THE DINING ROOM ▸ 3434 Peachtree Rd. NE, ☎ **404-237-2700** ‖ Creative continental **$** Prix fixe, **$56, $80 w/ wine.**
▸ *The best restaurant in Atlanta; renowned chef Gunter Seeger creates daring and fresh seasonal cuisine.*

FLYING BISCUIT CAFE ▸ 1655 McClendon Ave. at Clifton Rd. ☎ **404-687-8888** ‖ Southern-reg. **$** Entrees **$5.95 to $12.95**
▸ *The best breakfast, available all day, great biscuits, vegetarian specialties, and full-scale dishes as well.*

THE HORSERADISH GRILL ▸ 4320 Powers Ferry Rd. ☎ **404-255-7277** ‖ Southern-reg. **$** Entrees **$8.95 to $18.95**
▸ *Traditional southern cooking translated for the modern world.*

■ **BOSTON:** Mat Schaffer, the restaurant critic for *Boston Magazine*, makes his picks.

GRILL 23 & BAR ▸ 161 Berkeley St. ☎ **617-542-2255** ‖ American **$** Entrees **$18 to $28**
▸ *Try the prime sirloin; it's aged 21 days and grilled to taste.*

CARL'S PAGODA ▸ 23 Tyler St. ☎ **617-357-9837** ‖ Chinese **$** Entrees **$4.75 to $17.95**
▸ *Asking for the menu at this hole-in-the-wall Cantonese restaurant brands you a neophyte so remember: tomato soup, clams in black bean sauce, fried oysters, whole steamed fish, ginger lobster, chicken and broccoli, Carl's special steak, scrambled eggs and shrimp, Chinese sausage and broccoli, and pork lo mein with Carl's rice.*

EAST COAST GRILL ▸ 1271 Cambridge St., Cambridge ☎ **617-491-6568** ‖ American **$** Entrees **$11.75 to $18.25**
▸ *Aggressively seasoned meats, poultry, seafood cooked over wood. Served in a crowded, noisy, fun atmosphere.*

HAMERSLEY'S BISTRO ▸ 553 Tremont St. ☎ **617-423-2700** ‖ French Provencale **$** Entrees **$19 to $28**
▸ *Simple, sophisticated, honest, delicious food; the cassoulet and seafood will transport you to Provence.*

ROWES WHARF RESTAURANT ▸ 70 Rowes Wharf ☎ **617-439-3995** ‖ New England **$** Entrees **$18 to $35**
▸ *Exceptional cuisine well worth the price; try the house-cured maple-smoked Atlanta salmon.*

■ **CHICAGO:** Phil Vitell, the restaurant critic for the *Chicago Tribune*, names his top picks.

ARUNS ▸ 4156 N. Kedzie Ave. ☎ **312-539-1909** ‖ Thai **$** Entrees **$13.95 to $23.95**
▸ *A beautiful dining room with museum-quality art is combined with culinary excellence.*

EVEREST ▸ 440 South La Salle St. ☎ **312-663-8920** ‖ French **$** Entrees **$28 to $32**
▸ *Located on the 40th floor of a building. Try the pork cheeks with lentils.*

TOPOLOBAMPO FRONTERA GRILL ▸ 445 N. Clark St. ☎ **312-661-1434** ‖ Mexican **$** Entrees **$14 to $21,** Grill, **$8 to $17**
▸ *Two restaurants in one space, Topolobampo is a smaller, more upscale dining room, while Frontera is more crowded and casual. Both offer unsurpassed regional Mexican food.*

TRIO ▸ 1625 Hinman Ave., Evanston ☎ **708-733-8746** ‖ Fusion-American **$** Entrees **$23 to $38**
▸ *Brilliant cross-cultural cuisine served in dazzlingly artistic presentations often including slabs of granite or marble.*

VIVERE ▸ 71 W. Munroe ☎ **312-332-4040** ‖ Italian **$** Entrees **$16 to $22**
▸ *Light, stylishly presented, contemporary Italian food.*

■ **DINER'S GUIDE**

■ **DALLAS:** *Dallas Morning News* lifestyles editor Dotty Griffith's favorites are less upscale than the renowned Mansion at Turtle Creek, and a little more off the beaten path.

CITY CAFE ▸ 5757 W. Lovers Lane ☎ **214-351-2233** | Regional American **$** Entrees **$13 to $19.**
Seasonally based, creative food with a menu that changes every two weeks.

MATT'S RANCHO MARTINEZ ▸ Lakewood Plaza 6312 La Vista Dr. ☎ **214-823-5517** | Tex-Mex **$** Entrees **$7.25 to $15.75**
Stupendous chiles rellenos.

THE PALM RESTAURANT ▸ 701 Ross Ave. at Market ☎ **214-698-0470** | American **$** Entrees **$14 to $25**
Steaks, lobsters, and the beautiful people crowd.

STAR CANYON ▸ 3102 Oaklawn Ave, Suite 144 ☎ **214-520-7827** | New Texas **$** Entrees **$14 to $23**
Sophisticated food with Texas roots. Favorite dish: chilled shrimp and jicama soup with fresh buttermilk and basil.

SONNY BRYAN'S ▸ 2202 Inwood Rd. ☎ **214-357-7120** | Traditional Bar-B-Q **$ $5 to $12**
Ribs and brisket so good that people often stop in on their way to the airport.

■ **LOS ANGELES:** Irene Virbila, the restaurant editor for the *Los Angeles Times*, made picks that varied as much in style as they did in price—from under $10 all the way up to $300.

THE BAR BISTRO AT CITRUS ▸ 6703 Melrose Ave. ☎ **213-857-0034** | French **$** Entrees **$9.50 to $17.50**
French comfort food from the same kitchen as Michel Richard's French-California flagship, Citrus.

CAMPANILE ▸ 624 S. La Brea Blvd. ☎ **213-938-1447** | California-Mediterranean **$** Entrees **$15 to $26**
Great breakfasts and lunches. At dinner try the flattened grilled chicken with parsley salad or the bistecca fiorentina.

CHINOIS ON MAIN ▸ 2709 Main St., Santa Monica ☎ **310-329-9025** | East-West fusion **$** Entrees **$19 to $29**
Wolfgang Puck's—the creator of L.A. restaurant/institution, Spago—best restaurant yet.

GINZA SUSHI-KO ▸ 218 N. Rodeo Dr., Beverly Hills 90210 ☎ **310-247-8939** | Japanese **$** Entrees **$200 to $300**
The most expensive restaurant in Los Angeles, this exquisite little sushi bar has the fish flown in daily from Japan.

VALENTINO ▸ 3115 Pico Boulevard, Santa Monica ☎ **310-829-4313** | Italian **$** Entrees **$18 to $25**
Possibly the best Northern Italian restaurant in North America. Instead of ordering from the menu, ask chef Piero Selvaggio to prepare a series of small courses.

■ **MIAMI:** Not just for grandparents anymore, Miami these days is hot, filled with celebrities, models, and great restaurants. Geoffrey Tomb, a restaurant critic at the *Miami Herald*, surveys the scene.

CHEF ALLEN'S RESTAURANT ▸ 19088 N.E. 29th Ave., ☎ **305-935-2900** | Fusion-American **$** Entrees **$22.95 to $29.95**
Don't miss the 16-ounce veal chop with double mustard sauce, wild-mushroom risotto, and ginger-flavored calabaza.

DIDIERS ▸ 2530 Ponce de Leon Blvd., Coral Gables ☎ **305-567-2444** | Neo-French **$** Entrees **$14.75 to $23.95**
Lush, earthy combinations such as essence of farm cream in lentils with poached salmon.

LE SANDWICHERIE ▸ 229 14th St. ☎ **305-532-8934** | Casual fare **$** Entrees **$5 to $10**
Open till 5 a.m. on weekends, this sidewalk joint is as likely to serve people in tuxedoes as cab drivers.

OSTERIA DEL TEATRO ▸ 1443 Washington Ave. ☎ **305-538-7850** | Italian **$ $14 to $24**
Excellent Italian food and maybe the best restaurant in town. Emphasis is on seafood.

THE RALEIGH RESTAURANT ▸ 1775 Collins Ave. ☎ **305-534-1775** | Creative American **$** Entrees **$9 to $19**
A 1940s gem; the ghost of Esther Williams lives here. Sit outside and order the warm goat cheese–potato cakes.

■ **NEW YORK:** Five restaurants, impossible! That was Florence Fabricant, a food and restaurant columnist for the *New York Times*, who couldn't get her list down to five. We let her cheat a little.

CITÉ ▸ 120 W. 51st St. ☎ **212-956-7100** | Fusion French **$** Entrees **$19.50 to $26.50**
The food here reflects chef Claude Proistros's great French heritage intertwined with the vibrancy of his 10 years in Brazil—all in a fun, relaxed atmosphere.

GOTHAM BAR AND GRILL ▸ 12 E. 12th St. ☎ **212-620-4020** | American **$** Entrees **$10 to $32**
The finesse of Alfred Portale's food arranged in breathtaking pinnacles matches the celebratory, high-ceilinged space in which it is so deftly served.

■ **DINER'S GUIDE**

LE BERNADIN ▸ 155 W. 51st St. ☎ **212-489-1515** ‖ French **$** Entrees **$68**

Sublime seafood. Two greats: Winey sea bass with mashed potatoes or silken roast cod.

LE CIRQUE ▸ 58 E. 65th St. ☎ **212-794-9292** ‖ French **$** Entrees **$22 to $32**

A wondrous restaurant, tiny copper casseroles with exotic mushrooms, a simple bouquet of vegetables bathed in olive oil, and heady lobster risotto.

NOBU ▸ 105 Hudson St. ☎ **212-219-0500** ‖ Fusion **$** Dinner **$45 to $50**

The most inventively delicious food in town: Deep-fried kelp adorns roasted lobster nuggets or caviar on seared tuna.

REMI ▸ 145 W. 53rd St. ☎ **212-581-4242** ‖ Italian **$** Entrees **$15 to $28**

Francesco Antonnuci unerringly commands pasta, risotto, foie gras, anchovies, duck, salmon, and zabaglione.

■ **SAN FRANCISCO:** The challenge of good eating in San Francisco is the transient nature of restaurants there, says Michael Bauer, the restaurant critic at the *San Francisco Chronicle.* His picks:

THE FRENCH LAUNDRY ▸ 6040 Washington St., Yountville ☎ **707-944-2380** ‖ French **$** Prix Fixe **$49**

The $49 menu includes five courses all reminiscient of a three-star country restaurant in France.

FRINGALE ▸ 570 Fourth St. at Bryant ☎ **415-543-0573** ‖ French **$** Entrees **$10 to $15**

The best casual French restaurant in San Francisco; don't miss the mussels flecked with parsley and fried garlic.

MASAS ▸ 648 Bush St. ☎ **415-989-7154** ‖ French **$** Prix Fixe **$68 to $75**

A great special-occasion restaurant with a four- to six-course classic French menu.

YANK SING ▸ 427 Battery St. ☎ **415-781-1111** ‖ Chinese **$** Entrees **$10 to $15**

Unparalleled dim sum, minced squab in crunchy lettuce cups, and Peking duck with sweet, doughy buns.

ZUNI CAFE ▸ 1658 Market ☎ **415-552-2522** ‖ American **$** Entrees **$10 to $28**

Great people-watching and casual food. Signature dishes: chicken with bread salad and hamburger on foccacia.

■ **SEATTLE.** Tom Sietsema, the food and restaurant critic for the *Seattle Post-Intelligencer,* defines his favorite restaurants by the ones he returns to over and over again. Five of his regulars:

CAFE CAMPAGNE ▸ 1600 Post Alley ☎ **206-728-2233** ‖ French **$** Entrees **$6.95 to $14.95**

A fantastic, gourmet meal-to-go place with a tiny bar serving samplings of upscale wine and appetizers.

LAMPREIA ▸ 2400 First Ave. ☎ **206-443-3301** ‖ American **$** Entrees **$19 to $22**

A luxurious and seasonal menu; opt for the cheese course after dinner, which includes handcrafted local samples.

MACRINA BAKERY ▸ 2408 First Ave. ☎ **206-448-4032** ‖ American **$** Entrees **$8 to $20**

The bakery is well known for its rustic loaves and European coffee cakes, but the witty little cafe adjoining the bakery also turns out excellent lunches and dinners.

PIROSMANI ▸ 2220 Queen Ann Ave. ☎ **206-285-3360** ‖ Georgian **$** Entrees **$16-$22**

Inspired food from the Republic of Georgia, which also embraces the sunny flavors of the Mediterranean.

THE HERB FARM ▸ 32804 Southeast Issaquah–Fall City Rd., Fall City ☎ **206-784-2222** ‖ Regional **$** Prix Fixe **$115**

An extraordinary restaurant 30 minutes east of Seattle. The prix fixe price includes nine herb-infused courses.

■ **WASHINGTON:** Phyllis Richmond, the food critic for the *Washington Post,* recommends:

GALILEO ▸ 1110 21st St., NW ☎ **202-293-7191** ‖ Italian **$** Entrees **$18 to $28**

Chef Roberto Donna's pappardelle and risotto with first-of-the-season alba truffles are famous.

INN AT LITTLE WASHINGTON ▸ Middle & Main St., Washington, Va. ☎ **703-675-3800** ‖ New American **$** Full course **$78 to $98**

Self-taught American chef Patrick O'Connell coaxes wonders out of local ingredients such as Virginia ham, Chesapeake Bay crabs, berries, and herbs. A bit of a drive from the District.

JEAN-LOUIS AT THE WATERGATE ▸ 2650 Virginia Ave., NW ☎ **202-298-4488** ‖ French **$** Full course **$45 to $95**

Fans know to make sure that Jean-Louis will be in town when they make a reservation

KINKEAD'S ▸ 2000 Pennsylvania Ave., NW

EXPERT LIST

TWENTY FANTASTIC MEALS WORTH THE JOURNEY

Choosing the very best among the multitude of great chefs and cuisines is not for the faint-hearted. Undaunted, International Herald Tribune *food critic Patricia Wells spent a year traveling the globe to do just that. Her method: "When I dine, I filter out everything about the restaurant that's not food: its reputation, my preconceived notions or previous experiences, other people's opinions, even the service and the room in which I dine. I focus only on the look, the aroma, the taste, the texture of the food. The restaurant wins or loses on the basis of my physical and emotional response." Concerned at the outset whether she'd know when she'd found the finest example of a country's cuisine, Wells wrote in presenting her choices, "I needn't have worried. When the big one comes along, the earth moves." Picking 10 favorites from the thousands of more casual restaurants with superb food was a far tougher assignment, she says. Her choices:*

FINE DINING

1. JOEL ROBUCHON
59 Avenue Raymond-Poincare
Paris 16, France
☎ 47-27-12-27

2. RESTAURANT FREDY GIRARDET
1 Route d'Yverdon
Crissier, Switzerland
☎ 21-634-0505

3. LAI CHING HEEN
The Regent, Salisbury Road,
Hong Kong
☎ 721-1211

4. LE LOUIS XV-ALAIN DUCASSE
Hotel de Paris, Place du Casino, Monte Carlo
☎ 92-16-30-01

5. OSTERIA DA FIORE
San Polo-calle del Scaleter
Venice, Italy
☎ 41-721-308

6. JIRO
Chuo-ku, Ginza 4-2-15,
Tsukamoto Sozan Building,
B1, Tokyo, Japan
☎ 3535-3600

7. GUY SAVOY
18 Rue Troyon
Paris 17, France
☎ 43-80-40-61

8. TAILLEVENT
15 Rue Lamennais
Paris 8, France
☎ 45-63-96-01

9. RESTAURANT DANIEL
20 East 76th St..
New York, NY
☎ 212-288-0033

10. DA CESARE
12 Via Umberto
Albaretto della Torre, Italy
☎ 173-520-141

CASUAL DINING

1. AL FORNO
577 South Main St.
Providence, R.I.
☎ 401-273-9767

2. LA TUPINA
6 Porte de la Monnaie
Bordeaux, France
☎ 56-91-56-37

3. FRONTERA GRILL
445 N. Clark St.
Chicago, IL
☎ 312-661-1434

4. CITY CHIU CHOW
E. Ocean Ct., 98 Granville Rd., Tsim Sha Tsui East
Kowloon, Hong Kong
☎ 723-6226

5. CA L'ISIDRE
Les Flors 12
Barcelona, Spain
☎ 441-1139

6. THE SEAFOOD RESTAURANT
Riverside, Padstow, Cornwall
PL28 8BY, England
☎ 841-532-485

7. CHECCHINO DAL 1887
30 Via Monte Testaccio
Rome, Italy
☎ 6-574-6318

8. CIBREO
8R Via del Verrocchio
Florence, Italy
☎ 55-234-1100

9. VIRIDIANA
Juan de Mena 14
Madrid, Spain
☎ 523-4478

10. LE CAMELEON
6 Rue de Chevreuse
Paris 6, France
☎ 43-20-63-43

SOURCE: *International Herald Tribune.*

NATURAL TREASURES

THE 10 MOST POPULAR PARKS

Getting away from it all in America's backyard

If the national parks were in it for the money, business would be booming. Last year, 273 million people visited them, and in the next decade that figure is expected to double. Today, however, roads are closing, gift shops are being razed, and new construction is at a standstill throughout the park system. That's because the National Park Service's previous strategy of luring visitors with resort hotels and new roads worked too well, resulting in the traffic jams, pollution, and honky-tonk resort accommodations that now plague many of the national parks.

To stave off the major ecological threat that tourism has become, the Park Service is putting the brakes on all environmentally degrading tourism and instead focusing on preservation. The urban ills that the Park Service is attempting to eliminate are especially prevalent in the 10 most popular of America's 52 national parks, which account for more than half the system's visitors.

That means that finding a spot to pitch a tent or hook up a trailer is not always going to be easy, especially during the summer. Some campsites are on a first-come, first-served basis. For others, you may need to contact the park directly through the National Park Service's Mistix system, ☎ 800-365-2267. Following are the 10 most popular national parks ranked by popularity (as of 1994) and a description of the more interesting tracks they have to offer—beaten or otherwise.

1. GREAT SMOKY MOUNTAINS NATIONAL PARK

107 Park Headquarters Rd., Gatlinburg, TN 37738, ☎ 615-436-1200

9.3 million visitors per year ☛ *800 square miles* ☛ *Largest national park east of the Rockies*

A world unto itself, Great Smoky Mountains National Park has over 1,500 species of flowering plants, 10 percent of which are considered rare, and over 125 species of trees—more than in all of Europe. In addition, there are 200 species of birds, about 50 species of fish, and 60 species of mammals, including wild hogs and black bears.

A hike or drive from mountain base to peak is equivalent to the entire length of the Appalachian Trail from Georgia to Maine in terms of the number of species of trees and plants—every 250 feet of elevation is roughly equivalent to 1,000 miles of distance on the trail. A quarter of the

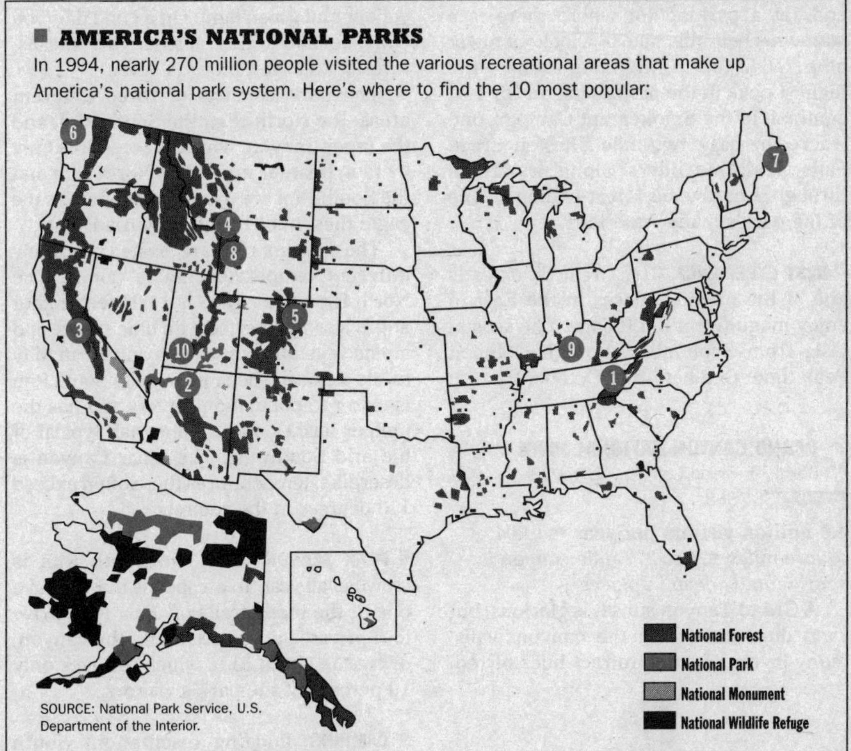

■ AMERICA'S NATIONAL PARKS

In 1994, nearly 270 million people visited the various recreational areas that make up America's national park system. Here's where to find the 10 most popular:

SOURCE: National Park Service, U.S. Department of the Interior.

park is virgin forest, the largest concentration east of the Mississippi. Some of the trees are up to 8 feet in diameter.

In addition to its natural attributes, Great Smoky Mountains is one of the most interesting national parks historically, with farms, churches, cabins, and working grist mills left by the mountain people who moved away when the park was established in 1934. The park has been designated a United Nations International Biosphere Reserve as well as a World Historical Site.

■ PEAK SEASON TIPS: During the summer, in the lower elevations, expect haze, humidity, and afternoon temperatures in the 90s—and terrible traffic jams. Cades Cove, the less spectacular but more historically interesting section of the park, is generally less crowded in the summer.

■ CAMPING: Reservations are required May 15 through October 31 for Elkmont, Smokemont, and Cades Cove campgrounds. Contact Mistix. Sites at other campgrounds are on a first-come, first-served basis. Stays of up to 7 days are allowed from mid-May through October, and up to 14 days the rest of year. Rarely filled are the Look Rock and Cosby campgrounds, which are in more remote parts of the park. Also of note is the LeConte Lodge, located on the park's third-highest peak (elevation, 6,593 feet), a six-hour hike from the main road. Accommodations are in cabins with no electricity or running water, but do include beds and hot meals. The lodge is open from late March through mid-November, ☎ 615-429-5704.

■ BEST ONE-DAY TRIP: Entering the park from Gatlinburg, continue on US 441, and stop at the Newfoundland Gap, where there are spectacular views of the mountains. From there, turn onto Clingmans Dome Road (closed in the winter), which ends at a parking lot where there is a strenuous half-mile hike to a lookout tower atop 6,643-foot Clingmans Dome—the highest peak in the park. Back on US 441, continue to the Smokemont Campground where the easy, two-mile Chasten Creek Falls Trail meanders along a stream through a hardwood forest ending at one of the park's many waterfalls.

■ **BEST EXPERIENCE:** The Great Smokies is one of the premier places in the East to enjoy magnificent fall foliage. The season lasts from September through October. Peak time: October 15 to October 31.

2. GRAND CANYON NATIONAL PARK

PO Box 129, Grand Canyon, AZ 86023
☎ 602-638-7888

4.6 million visitors per year ☛ *1,904 square miles* ☛ *The 277-mile canyon is nearly a mile deep in places*

A Grand Canyon sunset is glorious, but even during the day, the canyon walls' many layers of stone refract hues of red, yellow, and green light. On a good day, you can see 200 miles across vast mesas, forests, and the Colorado River.

The park consists of three different areas: the North Rim, the South Rim, and the Inner Canyon, which is accessible only by foot, boat, or mule. The North Rim and the South Rim are only 9 miles apart as the eagle flies, but 214 miles by road.

The different rims are located in entirely different temperate climate zones. The North Rim on average is 1,000 feet higher and is heavily forested with blue spruce and alpine vegetation. It is open only from May to late October. The more popular South Rim is closer to population centers and has the juniper bushes and Gambel oak typical of the arid Southwest. The Inner Canyon is desertlike; temperatures there often exceed 110 degrees in the summer.

EXPERT TIP

One- and two-day mule rides are a (somewhat bumpy) alternative to hiking the Grand Canyon. Avoid rides in the summer, when temperatures can reach 118 degrees. Two-day trips start at the South Rim, for information about rides there, write:

Grand Canyon Trail Rides
Box 1638
Grand Canyon, AZ 86023

For North Rim rides:

National Park Reservations
PO Box 699
Grand Canyon, AZ 86023
☎ 602-638-2401 summer
☎ 801-679-8665 winter

■ **PEAK SEASON TIPS:** The South Rim is crowded all year. To escape the masses, take one of the many trails off East Rim Drive to a private spot overlooking the canyon, or try the North Rim, which receives only 10 percent of the park's visitors.

■ **CAMPING:** Lodging reservations South Rim, including Phantom Ranch, ☎ 602-638-2401. North Rim Lodging reservations: ☎ 801-568-7686. Recorded general park info is available at ☎ 602-638-7888.

■ **BEST ONE-DAY TRIP:** The West Rim Drive offers wonderful views of the main canyon. In the summer, it is open only to buses, which can be taken from the visitor center. A paved trail runs along the South Rim offering an easy hike. All hikes into the canyon are strenuous. Of them, only the Bright Angel and the South Kaibab trails are regularly maintained.

■ **BEST EXPERIENCE:** A raft ride down the Colorado River is a great way to enjoy the splendor of the canyon. Motorboat trips take 7 to 10 days, raft trips take 10 to 12 days, and trips on wooden dories usually last 18 days, though 3- to 8-day partial trips can be arranged. Write the park superintendent for a complete list of outfitters licensed by the National Park Service.

SURE WAYS TO BEAT THE CROWDS

Travel in the off-season has its own rewards—and its own perils

Traffic on the main roads slows to a crawl, people are everywhere. Morning drive time in New York City? No, it's the summer rush to the nation's most popular national parks. Traffic has gotten so bad at some parks that tourists can spot wildlife simply by looking where other cars have pulled over to the side of the road to gawk.

The surest way to beat the crowds is to visit in the off-season. From June through October, Great Smoky National Park typically gets over a million visitors a month, but roughly half that number visit in the months between November and April, when temperatures in the lower elevations average about 50 degrees and occasionally reach into the 70s—perfect hiking weather, in other words.

There are other off-season rewards, too. At Rocky Mountain National Park, the bighorn sheep come down from higher elevations in May to feed on the mud deposits, and wildflowers there are spectacular in the spring. Yosemite National Park's waterfalls rush from the melting winter snows. In the fall, the foliage in many parks is absolutely superb. September is the sunniest month at Rocky Mountain National Park. And Grand Teton National Park is open all winter, allowing access to excellent cross-country skiing.

Of course, seasonal difficulties abound. There are, for instance, sudden snowstorms at Yellowstone National Park as early as September. And spring weather at Zion National Park is unpredictable; flash floods are not uncommon. Mammoth Cave can be especially dank in the dead of winter.

If such perils are too daunting for you, it is possible to avoid the masses in the summer simply by venturing into the backcountry. Most visitors don't wander very far from their cars.

3. YOSEMITE NATIONAL PARK

PO Box 577, Yosemite National Park, CA 95389, ☎ 209-372-0200

3.8 million visitors per year ☛ *1,170 square miles* ☛ *Home of the giant sequoia*

Yosemite's majestic granite peaks, groves of ancient giant sequoia trees, and waterfalls (including Yosemite Falls, which at a height of 2,425 feet is the nation's highest) inspired some of the earliest attempts at conservation in the United States. In 1864, Congress enacted laws protecting the valley. Journalist Horace Greeley, who visited that year, noted that he knew of "no single wonder of Nature on earth which can claim a superiority over the Yosemite." And naturalist John Muir, whose efforts led to the park's formation, said of the valley, "No temple made with hands can compare with Yosemite."

The enormous park occupies an area comparable to Rhode Island, with elevations of up to 13,114 feet.

■ **PEAK SEASON TIPS:** During the busy summer months, forgo the sights and splendors of the seven-mile Yosemite Valley, which attracts the hordes.

■ **CAMPING:** Of the 18 campgrounds in Yosemite, the 5 main ones in the valley offer "refugee-style camping"—over 800 campsites crammed into a singularly unspectacular half-mile. For more space and better views, head for the hills and try one of the eight Tioga Road campgrounds. There also are five tent camps about a day's hike from one another on the High Sierra Loop Trail. Campers can obtain meals, showers, and cots there. Reservations via Yosemite Reservations, ☎ 209-454-2002, are advised.

Reservations also are required year-round in Yosemite Valley's auto campground and for Hodgdon Meadow, Crane Flat, and Tuolumne Meadows campgrounds. All other campgrounds are operated on a first-come, first-served basis. Camping reservations may be made up to, but no earlier than, eight weeks in advance through Mistix. Reservable campsites fill up quickly from mid-May to mid-September. Your best bet for snagging a spot is to start calling the Mistix reservation number at 7 a.m. Pacific Standard Time eight weeks in advance of the date you want to camp.

■ **BEST ONE-DAY TRIP:** Avoid the congested route to Yosemite Valley. Instead, grab a tour bus and get off either at shuttle stop 7, for an easy half-mile, 20-minute hike to Lower Yosemite Falls, or shuttle bus stop 8, for a strenuous one- to three-hour round-trip hike to Upper Yosemite Falls. Other sites include the Native American Yosemite Village and El Capitan, a 3,000-foot face crawling with little black specks which, on closer inspection, turn out to be rock climbers.

4. YELLOWSTONE NATIONAL PARK

PO Box 168, Yellowstone National Park, WY 82190, ☎ 307-344-7381

2.8 million visitors per year ☛ *3,472 square miles* ☛ *The largest concentration of geysers and hot springs in the world*

The center of what is now Yellowstone Park erupted 600,000 years ago, obliterating all life and scattering ash for thousands of miles around. The explosion left behind a 28-by-47-mile crater that contained the world's greatest concentration of geothermal phenomena, including hot springs, fumaroles, steam vents, mud pots, and over 300 geysers. Among the geysers is Steam Boat, which shoots columns of water a record 350 feet high.

Yellowstone is the second largest park in the lower 48 states, encompassing an area larger than the states of Delaware and Rhode Island combined. It is also the oldest park in the country, established in 1872. It has the largest mountain lake (Yellowstone Lake, with 110 miles of shoreline); the biggest elk population in America (90,000 strong); and is the last place in the country where there is a free-ranging herd of bison (3,500 of the woolly beasts).

■ **PEAK SEASON TIPS:** This is one of the coldest parks in the continental United States. Be prepared for winter weather at any time of the year. The park receives half its visitors in July and August, overcrowding the roads and limited visitor facilities. The solution: head for the backcountry. Most visitors never venture far from their cars.

■ **CAMPING:** The 13 campgrounds are available on a first-come, first-served basis except for Bridge Bay, where reservations can be made through Mistix. They often fill early in late summer. Winter camping is available only at Mammoth Campground.

■ **BEST ONE-DAY TRIP:** From the west entrance, drive along Grand Loop Road to the mile-long Upper Geyser Basin, where boardwalks and trails run among the most outstanding geothermal phenomena in the world. Continue on to Yellowstone Lake.

EXPERT TIP

The dramatic domes and soaring pinnacles in Yosemite make it one of the best places in the world for rock climbing. The Yosemite Mountaineering School and Guide Service offers beginning through advanced classes in the summer, ☎ 209-372-1244.

5. ROCKY MOUNTAIN NATIONAL PARK

Superintendent, Estes Park, CO 80517
☎ 303-586-1206

2.9 million visitors per year ☛ *414 square miles* ☛ *One of the highest regions in the country: 114 mountains above 10,000 feet*

On both sides of Rocky Mountain National Park's 44-mile Trail Ridge Road, the highest paved road in America, are craggy snow-capped mountain peaks shrouded in clouds, alpine fields ablaze with wildflowers, and crystal-clear mountain lakes. Elk, deer, moose, coyotes, marmots,

EXPERT TIP

Yellowstone is one of the few national parks where snowmobiles are permitted. In addition, snow coaches—winter buses on skis—provide a unique way to travel. Call TW Recreational Services Inc. for information on snow coaches and snowmobile rentals, ☎ 307-344-7311.

ptarmigan, and the bighorn sheep—the symbol of the park—can often be seen.

■ **PEAK SEASON TIPS:** The road to Bear Lake is one long traffic jam in the summer. Consider spending most of your time on the west side of the park; it's less spectacular but also less crowded, and there are better opportunities to see wildlife.

■ **CAMPING:** There are five campgrounds in the park, each with a seven-day camping limit. For reservations to Moraine Park and Glacier Basin campgrounds, call Mistix. The other three are available on a first-come, first-served basis. In the summer, Timber Creek, on the west side of the park, is recommended—it doesn't fill up until about 1:30 p.m. Aspenglen and Longs Peak, where one begins the ascent to the summit, are often full by 8 a.m. Privately owned campgrounds also are available.

■ **BEST ONE-DAY TRIP:** For a sampling of the varied topography, take Fall River Road to the Alpine Visitors Center at Fall River pass, 11,796 feet above sea level. Drive back along Trail Ridge Road. If time permits, turn off Trail Ridge road onto Bear Lake Road, which winds past lakes and streams to Bear Lake, where there is an easy 2/3-mile nature walk around the lake and a 1.1-mile hike to Dream Lake. A less-crowded trail nearby is the Glacier Gorge Junction Trail to Alberta Falls. Those who are in peak physical condition may want to attempt Long's Peak Trail, a strenuous, 8-mile hike. A third of the 15,000 people who attempt it every year don't make it—at 14,000 feet, there is 40 percent less oxygen in the air.

■ **BEST EXPERIENCE:** Eighty percent of the park's trails can be ridden on horseback, and there are two historic ranches at the center of the park. Horses can be rented from livery concessions in Glacier Basin and Moraine Park. For a list of nearby ranches, many of which offer accommodations, write: Colorado Dude and Guest Ranch Association, PO Box 6440, Cherry Creek Station Rd., Denver, CO 80206.

6. OLYMPIC NATIONAL PARK

600 East Park Ave., Port Angeles, WA 98362
☎ 360-452-4501

2.68 million visitors per year ☛ *1,441 square miles* ☛ *The best example of virgin temperate rain forest in the country*

On a relatively isolated peninsula with no roads traversing it, Olympic is one of the most pristine of the nation's parks. It has been referred to as the "last frontier." It divides into three distinct environments: rugged coastline, virgin temperate rain forest, and rugged mountains, at the foot of which is the largest intact strand of coniferous forest in the lower 48 states. The park also plays host to 60 active glaciers.

■ **PEAK SEASON TIPS:** Though three-quarters of the precipitation falls from October 1 to March 31, Olympic still receives more rain than any other area in the United States. Always bring rain gear.

■ **CAMPING:** Nestled in thickets of spruce, the main coastal campgrounds of Kalaloch and Mora provide privacy and a sense of wilderness. For an even greater sense of solitude, try one of the two smaller campgrounds, Ozette Lake or Ericson's Bay. (The latter is accessible only by canoe.) All of the coastal campgrounds are available on a first-come, first-served basis.

The Hoh campground is the largest in the rain forest. The four smaller campgrounds, especially the 29-site July Creek campground on Quinault Lake, have more privacy and better wildlife-watching.

On the mountain, the Deer Park campground, at an elevation of 5,400 feet, feels remote but it is accessible by car and provides an excellent base from which to explore the mountains.

Most of the 17 developed mountain campgrounds are available on a first-come, first-served basis, but group reservations at Kalaloch and Mora campgrounds can be made through either the Kalaloch park ranger, ☎ 360-962-2283, or the Mora park ranger, ☎ 360-374-5460.

■ BEST ONE-DAY TRIP: On a drive up Route 101, you can take in the park's harbor seals, gigantic driftwood, and tide pools teeming with activity along the coast. On the right, you'll pass a sign for the world's largest cedar tree. Switch off onto the spur road to the Hoh Rain Forest Visitor Center. There is a 3/4-mile round-trip hike that winds through the dense rain forest at the end of the road. Back in your car, turn onto the road to the Mora Campground, where there are several short scenic trails along the beach.

■ THE BIGGEST PARKS

The largest parks cover more ground than some of our smallest states

NATIONAL PARK OR STATE	ACRES
1. Wrangell–St. Elias, Alaska	8,331,604
2. Gates of the Arctic, Alaska	7,523,888
3. Denali, Alaska	5,000,000
4. Katmai, Alaska	3,716,000
5. Death Valley, Calif.	3,367,628
6. Glacier Bay, Alaska	3,225,284
CONNECTICUT	**3,118,080**
7. Lake Clark, Alaska	2,636,839
8. Yellowstone, Wyo.	2,219,790
9. Kobuk Valley, Alaska	1,750,421
10. Everglades, Fla.	1,506,499
11. Grand Canyon, Ariz.	1,217,158
12. Glacier, Mont.	1,013,572
13. Olympic, Wash.	922,163
14. Big Bend, Tex.	801,163
15. Joshua Tree, Calif.	793,954
RHODE ISLAND	**675,200**

SOURCE: *Backpacker Magazine*, December 1994.

7. ACADIA NATIONAL PARK

PO Box 177, Bar Harbor, ME 04609
☎ 207-288-3338

2.66 million visitors per year ☛ *54 square miles* ☛ *The highest coastal mountains on the east coast*

The park is made of two islands and a peninsula: Mount Desert Island (which is accessible by a land bridge), Isle au Haut, and Schoodic Peninsula.

Artists and writers flocked to Mount Desert Island in the 1850s, attracted by its dramatic natural beauty and the rustic life it offered. Later, in the Gay '90s, wealthy vacationers, inspired by the paintings, came and built "cottages" of a level of opulence that the country had not seen before. Many of the cottages were burned to the ground in the great fire of 1947, but the magnificent landscape that the painters celebrated remains—jagged, granite cliffs with forests of birch and pine that grow right up to the coastline.

The park's proximity to the ocean gives it a milder climate than that of the mainland, which helps it to sustain more than 500 varieties of wildflowers and makes it one of the best places on the Eastern Seaboard to take in fall foliage. The park also is known as "The Warbler Capital of the United States." Over 275 species of birds, including 26 varieties of warblers as well as the endangered peregrine falcon, inhabit the park.

■ PEAK SEASON TIPS: Expect nothing but bumper-to-bumper traffic on the Park Loop Road on the east side of Mount Desert Island in the summer. To avoid crowds, try the island's much less crowded but only slightly less spectacular western side. Also consider taking a ferry trip either to Baker Island or to Isle au Haut. June is the best month to see birds in the spruce, fir, and hardwood forests. August is the best month for sea birds.

OUR NEWEST NATIONAL PARKS

These desert lands are an oasis for those thirsting after beauty

Two new national parks and a new national preserve belie popular myths about American desert lands. Created by the 1994 California Desert Protection Act, Death Valley National Park, Joshua Tree National Park, and Mojave National Preserve, all in California's Mojave Desert, are not simply cactus-strewn sandboxes. In fact, they are practically teeming with some 700 species of plants and 760 species of wildlife, some of which are extremely rare. And cultural artifacts also appear on the arid landscape, from mysterious ancient pictographs to the "Boeing burial ground," where the aircraft manufacturer has laid several 747s to rest.

Gas, water, food, and telephones are few and far between, though, and summer daytime temperatures average more than 100 degrees. Make sure you consult a map carefully before you travel. The best months for visiting are October through May.

DEATH VALLEY NATIONAL PARK
Death Valley, CA 92328, ☎ 619-786-2331

■ At 5,000 square miles, it is now the largest national park in the lower 48 states. Badwater, the lowest and hottest place in the United States, is located here, but many of the mountains in the park can be chilly, even in the summer. Notable sites include Eureka Valley's 700-foot sand dunes and Scotty's Castle, the opulent home of an early prospector. Death Valley is probably the most visitor-friendly of the new national parks, with hotels, campgrounds, and even a golf course within its boundaries.

JOSHUA TREE NATIONAL PARK
74485 National Monument Dr.
Twentynine Palms, CA 92277
☎ 619-367-7511

■ Ansel Adams shot some of his most famous landscape photographs here. Home of the gnarly, 20- to 40-foot Joshua tree, it is also a world-famous spot for rock-climbing. Although there are adequate camping facilities in the park, one might want to stay instead in Twentynine Palms or Palm Springs for the comforts of civilization.

MOJAVE NATIONAL PRESERVE
Lake Mead National Recreation Area
601 Nevada Highway, Boulder City, NV 89005
☎ 702-293-8918

■ Initially proposed as a national park, but downgraded to a national preserve to allow hunting. With 19 mountain ranges, groves of white fir and Joshua trees, limestone caves, and extensive, ancient petroglyphs, there is plenty to keep one occupied. Of the new parks, however, the Mojave is probably the least equipped for visitors, with only two campgrounds and no towns nearby.

■ **CAMPING:** The Blackwoods campground on the east side of Mount Desert Island is exceptionally well-landscaped with 310 campsites interspersed among groves of trees. It is open all year. Reservations via Mistix are advised.

On the less-crowded west side is the 200-site Seawell campground, which is open only during the summer. You have to hike in from a parking lot to reach it, but the serenity of nearby roads that are less traveled makes it well worth the extra effort. Sites there are available on a first-come, first-served basis only.

Particularly remote are Isle au Haut's five small lean-to shelters, which are perfect for escaping the cars and crowds without sacrificing convenience. The ferry there lands at a nearby hamlet where one can obtain provisions.

■ BEST ONE-DAY TRIP: From the visitor center, take Park Loop Road to the 3.5-mile road that leads to Cadillac Mountain, where a short, paved trail winds around the 1,530-foot mountain, the highest coastal mountain in the nation. Back on Park Loop Road, turn around and continue down the East Coast. Stop at Sand Beach—it's a good place for a dip, and the 1.4-mile Great Head Trail there offers a moderate hike around a rocky, forested peninsula. Continue on Park Loop Road to Route 3 and turn onto Route 198. Keep an eye open for Hadlock Pond Carriage Road Trail where there is a 4-mile loop across three granite bridges. This trail goes past the highest waterfall in the park and is one of the best places to enjoy the spring blooms.

■ BEST EXPERIENCE: Take the charming carriage ride through the park that is offered by the Wild Wood Stables near Jordan Pond, ☎ 207-276-3622.

If carriages are too old-fashioned for you, this also is one of the few national parks where snowmobiles are allowed. The network of carriage roads provides excellent terrain.

EXPERT TIP

Maine's windjammers breeze past parts of the rugged coastline that are best left unhiked. The hand-crafted schooners can carry anywhere from 12 to 25 passengers. On summer trips, they leave Monday morning and return Saturday, visiting places such as the scenic Isle au Haut. For more information, write:

Maine Windjammer Assoc.
PO Box 317B
Rockport, ME 04856.

8. GRAND TETON NATIONAL PARK

PO Drawer 170, Moose, Wyoming 83012
☎ 307-739-3300

2.57 million visitors per year ☛ *485 square miles* ☛ *Best part of the beautiful Teton range*

There are not many places in the world where you can literally stand next to a mountain. Foothills usually intervene. Imagine then Grand Teton, where the mountains rise sharply out of the relatively flat Jackson Hole Valley like stark, granite skyscrapers.

Another geological oddity formed during the ice age, Jackson Hole Valley looks as if some gargantuan infant sculpted it out of Play-Doh. When the valley formed, little driblets from the glaciers formed rocky deposits, called moraines, around the six sparkling mountain lakes that were incongruously punctured into the landscape.

Winding gently through this strange valley is the Snake River, along the banks of which grow willows, cottonwoods, and the blue spruces in which bald eagles prefer to nest. Beavers have built dams up and down the river, forming wetlands that have an incredibly dense concentration of wildlife, including bears, elk, moose, trumpeter swans, sandhill cranes, and Canada geese.

■ PEAK SEASON TIPS: From June through August, most of the crowds can be found near Jenny Lake, which has sand beaches and sometimes is warm enough for a quick swim.

■ CAMPING: Campgrounds are generally open from late May to October. In summer, Jenny Lake campground fills the fastest and has a seven-day camping limit—the other five parks have two-week limits. Camping at all six campgrounds is available on a first-come, first-served basis except at Colter Bay Trailer Village, where reservations are required, ☎ 307-543-2855.

■ BEST ONE-DAY TRIP: Beginning at the south entrance on Route 191, stop at Mentor's Ferry and the Chapel of the Transfiguration for a look at the dwellings of some of the area's first pioneers. Then drive north along Teton Park Road to

EXPERT SOURCES

THE BEST NATIONAL PARK GUIDES

The National Park Service publishes a handsome series of park guides with color photographs, maps, and illustrations from $2.50 to $7.50. For more information, call ☎ 304-535-6018. Some other excellent sources:

THE COMPLETE GUIDE TO AMERICA'S NATIONAL PARKS
Jane Bangley McQueen, ed., National Park Foundation, biannual, $14.95
■ Short on description, but contains practical information on permits, fees, and monthly weather conditions.

NATIONAL GEOGRAPHIC GUIDE TO THE NATIONAL PARKS OF THE UNITED STATES
Elizabeth L. Newhouse, ed., National Geographic Society, 1992, $24
■ Small enough to fit in your parka pocket and packed with information, itineraries, and maps of all the national parks. Informative and interesting, it is available by mail order only, ☎ 800-638-4077.

THE NATIONAL PARK SYSTEM MAP AND GUIDE
U.S. Government Printing Office, 1995, $1.25
■ A map with listings of every unit in the system and information on facilities and accommodations. Available from the Consumer Information Center, PO Box 100, Pueblo, CO 81002.

THE NATIONAL PARKS INDEX
U.S. Government Printing Office, 1993, $5
■ Statistics and summaries of the historic and natural features of each park. Write: U.S. Superintendent of Documents, U.S. Government Printing Office, Washington, DC 20402, and request GPO publication no. 024-005-01123-4.

NATIONAL PARKS: LESSER-KNOWN AREAS
U.S. Government Printing Office, 1995, $1.75
■ Brief descriptions of less well-known but in many cases no less spectacular parks. Available through the Consumer Information Center.

NATIONAL PARKS VISITOR FACILITIES AND SERVICES
National Parks Hospitality Association, annual, $4.05 (Kentucky, $4.26)
■ Addresses and phone numbers for most concessionaires in national parks and info about lodging, mountaineering schools, horseback riding, and whale watching. Send check to: Conference of National Park Concessionaires, Mammoth Cave, KY 42259.

Lupine Meadow and take the spur road to the trail head, where there is a difficult hike to Amphitheater Lake near the timberline. Attempt this only if you are in good shape. Head back up Teton Road for a stop at South Jenny Lake, which is located at the bottom of the tallest Teton peak. An easy six-mile hike there circles the lake and affords spectacular views of the mountain. Finally, stop at Colter Bay for a one-mile hike that loops around the wetlands and provides good opportunities for viewing the wildlife up close.

■ **BEST EXPERIENCE:** In winter, horse-drawn sleighs take visitors to see the herd of 11,000 elk that live in the valley.

9. MAMMOTH CAVE NATIONAL PARK

Superintendent, Mammoth Cave, KY 42259
☎ 502-758-2328

2.4 million visitors per year ☛ *82 square miles* ☛ *The largest cave on earth*

Inside the world's largest cave's 335 miles of charted passageways are 70-foot chambers, Indian artifacts, an underground river, and some plant and animal species that have been isolated from the outside world for more than a million years. In fact, there are five species of animals unique to the cave.

Mammoth Cave has intrigued man for thousands of years. Native Americans first came 4,000 years ago and continued to use it for about 2,000 years. Tourists started visiting after the War of 1812, and by the mid-1800s it was one of the most popular tourist sites in the country.

Two-thirds of the park is composed of distinctive karst topography—the type of land surface that forms above a cave that features sinkholes, cave entrances, and "disappearing" streams. There are nearly 100 sinking streams called "pnors" that disappear abruptly into holes in the ground.

■ **PEAK SEASON TIPS:** The cave, of course, is the main attraction. It is always best to reserve cave trips in advance.

■ **CAMPING:** Houchins Ferry (no trailer hook-ups) and Denison Ferry (tent sites only, no water) sites are available on a first-come, first-served basis. Reservations are needed for Maple Spring Group Campground sites, ☎ 502-758-2328.

■ **BEST ONE-DAY TRIP:** A great variety of cave trips in terms of length and difficulty are available, some lasting an hour, others most of the day. After or before your cave trip, take a short hike on the 3/4-mile Cedar Sink Trail to see good examples of karst topography. You may also want to take the one-hour boat trip down the Green River or a walk along the Cave island nature walk, part of which also goes along the river.

■ **BEST EXPERIENCE:** Various cave trips are operated throughout by the National Park Service and are offered every day in the summer and on some weekends in the spring and fall. Be warned: Caving involves stooping, bending, and crawling. Helmets and lights are provided, but visitors should bring their own knee pads. Long pants and boots are required, and gloves are recommended. Make reservations no earlier than 56 days before and no later than one hour before you wish to tour the cave. For reservations in the United States or Canada, call ☎ 800-967-2283.

10. ZION NATIONAL PARK

Springdale, UT 84767, ☎ 801-772-3256

2.4 million visitors per year • *229 square miles* • *The 319-foot Kolub Arch is the world's largest sandstone formation*

Nineteenth-century Mormons named the main canyon in this park Zion after the Heavenly City and gave religious names to many of the rock formations. With its brilliantly shaded sandstone cliffs, wide variety of flowers, and strange geological formations, the park does indeed look otherworldly. Some of the park's outstanding features include massive stone arches, hanging flower gardens, forested canyons, and isolated mesas.

The varied topography and plant life of the canyon have been caused by differences in the amount of water that reaches the various parts of the park. The little micro-environments shelter a wide variety of animals, from black bears to lizards.

■ **PEAK SEASON TIPS:** Expect exceedingly unpleasant traffic jams on summer weekends when temperatures climb to over 100 degrees and over 5,000 cars visit the park. The west side generally is less crowded.

■ **CAMPING:** Watchman Campground is open all year, but reservations are necessary, ☎ 801-772-3256. The South Campground is open only in the summer. It is operated on a first-come, first-served basis and has restrooms and a disposal station. Lava Point Primitive Campground is usually open May to October and offers camping by reservation for groups of nine people.

■ **BEST ONE-DAY TRIP:** A spectacular stretch of Utah Route 9 descends 2,000 feet in 11 miles into the park. As you enter the half-mile wide canyon, the road turns into Zion Canyon Scenic Drive and runs north to the Temple of Sinawava. Riverside Walk, an easy 2-mile round trip and the most popular trail in the park, begins here.

ALL OF AMERICA'S CROWN JEWELS

The parks, how to get in touch with them, and their claims to fame

NATIONAL PARK ☎ Telephone number for information **Claim to fame** *Special activities*

ALASKA

DENALI ☎ 907-822-5234 **Mt. McKinley, N. America's highest mountain** *Dog sledding, cross-country skiing, hiking*

GATES OF THE ARCTIC ☎ 907-456-0281 **Greatest wilderness in N. America** *River running, fishing, mountaineering*

GLACIER BAY ☎ 907-697-2232 **Tidewater glaciers, wild terrain from ice to rain forest** *Sea kayaking, fishing*

KATMAI ☎ 907-246-3305 **Alaskan brown bears, the world's largest carnivores** *Sport fishing, kayaking*

KENAI FJORDS ☎ 907-224-3175 **300 sq.-mile Harding Ice Field, varied rain forest** *Sea kayaking, charter boats*

KOBUK VALLEY ☎ 907-442-3890 **Entirely north of the Arctic Circle** *Canoeing, exploring archeological sites*

LAKE CLARK ☎ 907-781-2218 **Headquarters for red salmon spawning** *Charter river trips, fishing*

WRANGELL-ST. ELIAS ☎ 907-822-5234 **Chugach, Wrangell & St. Elias Mtns. meet here** *Rafting, x-country skiing*

AMERICAN SAMOA

PARK OF AMERICAN SAMOA ☎ 808-541-2693 **Paleotropical rain forests, coral reefs** *Bird watching, sunbathing*

ARIZONA

GRAND CANYON ☎ 602-638-7888 **The mile-deep canyon itself** *River rafting, hiking, mule rides*

PETRIFIED FOREST ☎ 602-524-6228 **Petrified trees, Indian ruins** *Self-guiding auto tours, photography*

ARKANSAS

HOT SPRINGS ☎ 501-623-1433 **Some 950,000 gals. of water a day flow through 47 thermal springs** *Hot baths*

CALIFORNIA

CHANNEL ISLANDS ☎ 805-658-5700 **Seabirds, sea lions, and unique plants** *Scuba diving, bird watching*

DEATH VALLEY ☎ 619-786-2331 **Lowest point in Western Hemisphere** *Photography, jeep riding, horseback riding*

JOSHUA TREE ☎ 619-367-7511 **20- to 40-foot Joshua trees, stunning dunes** *Wildlife watching, nature walks*

KINGS CANYON ☎ 209-565-3341 **The enormous canyons of the Kings River** *Hiking, photography*

LASSEN VOLCANIC ☎ 916-595-4444 **Huge lava-flow mountains, steaming sulfur vents** *X-country, downhill skiing*

REDWOOD ☎ 707-464-6101 **Redwood forests and 40 miles of scenic coastline** *Whale watching, guided kayaking*

SEQUOIA ☎ 209-565-3341 **Giant Sequoias include General Sherman, the largest living tree** *Hiking, fishing*

YOSEMITE ☎ 209-372-0200 **Granite peaks and domes, and the nation's highest waterfall** *Skiing, rock climbing*

COLORADO

MESA VERDE ☎ 303-529-4461 **Pre-Columbian cliff dwellings and other artifacts** *Guided lectures, exhibits*

ROCKY MOUNTAIN ☎ 303-529-4461 **Trail Ridge Rd., highest in the lower 48** *Mountain climbing, horseback riding*

FLORIDA

BISCAYNE ☎ 305-247-7275 **Pristine wilderness, living coral reefs** *Glass-bottom boat tours, snorkeling, scuba*

DRY TORTUGAS ☎ 305-242-7700 **Largest all-masonry fort in the west** *Fishing, snorkeling, scuba diving*

EVERGLADES ☎ 305-242-7700 **Largest remaining subtropical wilderness in U.S.** *Backcountry canoeing, fishing*

HAWAI'I

HALEAKALA ☎ 808-572-9306 **Inactive volcano, chain of pools linked by a waterfall** *Sunrise and sunset watching*

HAWAI'I VOLCANOES ☎ 808-967-7311 **Devastation from recent eruptions** *Backpacking, bird watching*

KENTUCKY

MAMMOTH CAVE ☎ 502-758-2328 **Longest recorded cave system in the world** *Cave tours, cave boating*

ALL OF AMERICA'S NATIONAL PARKS

Park	☎	Highlight	Activities
MAINE			
ACADIA	207-288-3338	**Cadillac Mountain, highest on East Coast north of Brazil**	*Boat tours, skiing*
MICHIGAN			
ISLE ROYALE	906-482-0984	**The largest island in Lake Superior**	*Lake kayaking, hiking*
MINNESOTA			
VOYAGEURS	218-283-9821	**Thirty lakes and over 900 islands**	*Canoeing, x-country skiing, ice-skating*
MONTANA			
GLACIER	406-888-5441	**Nearly 50 glaciers, glacier-fed streams, lakes**	*Excursion-boat cruises, snowshoeing*
NEVADA			
GREAT BASIN	702-234-7331	**Ice field on 13,063-ft. Wheeler Peak, Lehman Caves**	*Fishing, climbing, spelunking*
NEW MEXICO			
CARLSBAD CAVERNS	505-785-2232	**U.S.'s deepest cave (1,593 ft.), and largest chambers**	*Guided cave tours*
NORTH DAKOTA			
THEODORE ROOSEVELT	701-623-4466	**The arid Badlands, Roosevelt's Elkhorn Ranch**	*Fishing, photography*
OREGON			
CRATER LAKE	503-594-2211	**Deepest lake in the U.S. (1,932 feet)**	*Boat tours, snowmobiling, x-country skiing*
SOUTH DAKOTA			
BADLANDS	605-433-5361	**The scenic western badlands**	*Hiking, wildlife watching*
WIND CAVE	605-745-4600	**Beautiful limestone cave and the scenic Black Hills**	*Spelunking, cave tours, hiking*
TENNESSEE			
GREAT SMOKY MOUNTAINS	615-436-1200	**Loftiest range in the East, diverse plant life**	*Hiking, photography*
TEXAS			
BIG BEND	915-477-2251	**Rio Grande passes through canyon walls for 118 miles**	*Horseback riding, fishing*
GUADALUPE MOUNTAINS	915-828-3251	**Portions of world's most extensive fossil reef**	*Hiking, historic sites*
UTAH			
ARCHES	801-259-8161	**Giant arches, pinnacles change color as the sun shifts**	*Interpretive walks, auto tours*
BRYCE CANYON	801-834-5322	**Colorful, unusually shaped geologic forms**	*X-country skiing, snowshoeing*
CANYONLANDS	801-259-7164	**Canyons of Green, Colorado rivers**	*Mountain biking, backcountry drives, rafting*
CAPITOL REEF	801-425-3791	**Waterpocket Fold, a 100-mile-long wrinkle in earth's crust**	*Hiking, photography*
ZION	801-772-3256	**Unusual geologic formations–Kolub Arch, world's largest at 310 feet**	*Hiking, photography*
VIRGINIA			
SHENANDOAH	703-999-2243	**The scenic Blue Ridge Mountains**	*Skyline Drive, horseback riding, nature walks*
VIRGIN ISLANDS			
VIRGIN ISLANDS	809-775-6238	**Secluded coves, white beaches fringed by lush hills**	*Snorkeling, swimming*
WASHINGTON			
MOUNT RAINIER	206-569-2211	**Greatest single-peak glacial system in U.S.**	*Skiing, snowshoeing, climbing*
NORTH CASCADES	206-856-5700	**Half the glaciers in the U.S., 318 are active**	*Backpacking, hiking*
OLYMPIC	206-452-0330	**One of the biggest temperate rain forests in the world**	*Mountain climbing, fishing*
WYOMING			
GRAND TETON	307-733-2880	**The flat Jackson Hole Valley and the Teton mountains**	*Hiking, climbing, skiing*
YELLOWSTONE	307-344-7381	**World's largest concentration of geothermal phenomena**	*Skiing, snowmobiling*

SOURCE: National Park Service; individual parks.

EXPERT PICKS

MOTHER NATURE'S DELUXE ABODES

National park lodges show off the best of rustic architecture

In addition to the largest canyons, the biggest geysers, and the most pristine wildernesses, America's national parks contain some of the best-preserved rustic hotels in the United States. These capacious lodges were built with stones and trees hewn directly from the stunning landscapes they occupy in an attempt to recreate the great outdoors indoors. Park architects drew on the ideas of noted landscape architects such as Frederick Law Olmsted, eschewing straight lines and sophisticated accoutrements and instead building soaring lobbies, gnarled log balconies, four-story, stone fireplaces and log furniture that harkened back to pioneer days.

Rustic architecture reached its apotheosis during the 1930s with numerous WPA projects designed to put men to work and promote national parks. Many of the buildings are now either national landmarks or on the National Register as some of the most beautiful places to stay in the country. The rooms are as comfortable as those of any fine urban abode, but the hotels remain what their creators intended: one of man's most ambitious attempts to build on a grand scale in harmony with nature.

Here, Harvey Kaiser, vice president of Syracuse University and author of *Landmarks in the Landscape,* a history of park architecture, recommends the most beautiful lodges in the country. All are either national landmarks or on the National Register; many have undergone major renovations. Because of their popularity, some lodges may be difficult to reach by telephone, so we've included fax numbers and addresses to write for more information.

AHWAHNEE HOTEL (1925)
Yosemite National Park
☎ 209-252-4848 FAX 209-456-0542

■ Its asymmetrical rock columns and varied levels convey the impression of a mountain range. The concrete exterior is dyed red to match the redwood forest. The floor-to-ceiling stained glass windows offer splendid views of the soaring walls of Yosemite Valley. Open year-round, rooms from $208. Write: Yosemite Reservations, 5410 E. Home Ave., Fresno, CA 93727.

BRYCE CANYON LODGE (1925)
Bryce Canyon National Park
☎ 801-586-7686 FAX 801-586-3157

■ Atop a mesa overlooking the colorfully hued stone walls of Bryce Canyon, the lodge and adjacent cabins are classic examples of rustic architecture. A wave-patterned, cedar-shingle roof, stone masonry, wrought-iron chandeliers, and liberal use of solid log beams (one measures 52 feet) give an Old West feel. Open April 15 to November 1, rooms from $70 to $104. Write: TW Recreational Services, 451 North Main St., PO Box 400, Cedar City, UT 84720.

EL TOVAR LODGE (1905)
Grand Canyon National Park
☎ 602-638-2401 FAX 602-638-9247

■ Only 50 feet from the South Rim of the Grand Canyon, El Tovar was one of the first railroad destination resorts. Original promotional literature described it as a combination of "Swiss Chalet and Norway villa." With Indian murals and crafts throughout, it is among the most eclectic hotels in the national parks. Today, it is also one of the most luxurious, with first-rate service and gourmet meals. Open year-round, rooms from $115 to $275. Write: Grand Canyon National Park Lodges, PO Box 699, Grand Canyon, AZ 86023.

LAKE MCDONALD LODGE (1913)
Glacier National Park
☎ 406-226-5551 FAX 406-226-4404

■ This mountainous lake region, so similar to the Swiss Alps, inspired architects to build one of the premier examples of Swiss chalet hotel architecture in the United States. Lying atop a small rise, the western façade of the hotel faces out across Lake McDonald, the largest lake in the park, with views of the magnificent snow-capped mountain beyond. Open May to October, rooms from $51 to $91. Write: Glacier Park, Inc., Reservations, Dial Corporate Center, Phoenix, AZ 85077.

NORTH RIM LODGE (1927)

Grand Canyon National Park
801-586-7686 FAX 801-586-3157

■ Lying on the edge of the North Rim, the lodge with adjacent cabins offers an inexpensive alternative to El Tovar. It is built into the side of the rim; its several levels actually step down from the canyon rim. The many terraces and observation decks offer breathtaking views of the canyon. Also notable is the oversize fireplace on the eastern terrace—big enough for an adult to walk into. Open mid-May through mid-October, rooms from $55 to $83. Write: Reservations, TW Recreational Services, Inc., 451 North Main St., PO Box 400, Cedar City, UT 84720.

OLD FAITHFUL INN (1904)

Yellowstone National Park
☎ 307-344-7311, FAX 307-344-7456

■ The first national park building constructed in an architectural style harmonious with the grandeur of the surrounding landscape, this hotel boasts a seven-story-high log lobby. Many rooms have views of the world-famous Old Faithful geyser nearby. Open May 5 to October 22, rooms from $67 to $291. Write: TW Recreational Services Inc., PO Box 165, Yellowstone National Park, WY 82190.

OREGON CAVES CHATEAU (1934)

Oregon Caves National Monument
☎ 503-592-3400 FAX 503-592-6654

■ Located in the Siskiyou Mountains next to the entrance to the only limestone cave formation in Oregon, this hotel actually spans a small gorge; the fourth floor is at road level. The fireplace, according to a recent study, is one of the largest in the state if not on the entire West Coast. Also of note is a stream that runs through the first-floor dining room and disappears outside into a lush green forest. Open March 11 to May 22 and September 7 to December 31 at "bed- and-breakfast" rate of $59; open May 23 to September 6 as a full-service hotel, rooms from $79. Write: Oregon Caves Company, PO Box 128, Cave Junction, OR 97523.

PARADISE INN (1916)

Mount Rainier National Park
☎ 360-569-2275 fax 360-569-2770

■ One of the earliest ski resorts in the country, Paradise Inn lies at an elevation of 5,400 feet. The exterior has a lovely, shimmering silver quality due to the use of timbers that were aged 30 years before construction. Significant are the hand-crafted artistry and gothic feeling reminiscent of northern European woodwork. Open May 17 to October 1, rooms from $88 with bath, $62 without. Write: Mount Rainier Guest Services Inc., 55106 Kernahan Rd. East, PO Box 108, Ashford, WA 98304.

STANLEY HOTEL (1909)

Rocky Mountain National Park
☎ 303-586-3371 FAX 303-586-3673

■ A regular stop for world leaders such as the emperor of Japan—but still affordable—this Neo-Georgian hotel provides Old World elegance in the heart of the Rockies. Canopy beds and antique furniture are found throughout the unique rooms. Although unlike the rustic landmark hotels on the list, Kaiser felt that it was too magnificent to leave out. Open year-round, rooms from $69 to $124. Write: Stanley Hotel, PO Box 1767, Estes Park, CO 80517.

WAWONA HOTEL (1876)

Yosemite National Park
☎ 209-252-4848 FAX 209-456-0542

■ This hotel predates the rustic movement, but it is the largest existing Victorian hotel complex within a national park, and one of the best preserved in the United States. The hotel complex also contains the studio of Thomas Hill, one of the last great painters of the Hudson River School. Open April 1 to November 25 continuously and intermittently the rest of the year, rooms from $86.25 with bath, $63.75 without. Write: Yosemite Reservations, 5410 E. Home Ave., Fresno, CA 93727.

EXPERT LIST

THE BEST PLACES ON THE PLANET

The United Nations has declared these sites to be vital to humanity

Without doubt, the most difficult landmark designation to obtain is that of a World Heritage site. Established by the United Nations Education, Scientific, and Cultural Organization's general conference in 1972, the World Heritage Convention chooses sites that members feel have such outstanding value that "safeguarding them concerns humanity as a whole." Today there are 358 designated World Heritage sites in 81 countries. Signatories to the convention not only agree to forever preserve sites located within their own territory, but also to respect designated sites in other countries. Following is a list of the 18 sites included on the list in the United States.

CULTURAL SITES

■Cahokia Mounds State Historic Site, Illinois

The low bluffs and alluvial terraces of this region were inhabited by large numbers of pre-Columbian people. Here they built a major agricultural and trading base that extended 1.2 million square miles, to include Monk's Mound, probably the largest prehistoric earthen site in the New World. The mound is larger at the base than the greatest of the Egyptian pyramids, although, at 108 feet, it is not as tall.

■Chaco Culture National Historical Park, New Mexico

The pinnacle of pre-Columbian civilization in the United States, this site is also the largest, with over 2,800 archeological sites and the ruins of 13 major pueblo villages.

■Independence Hall, Pennsylvania

This two-story, red brick structure was the seat of the U.S. government through the 1780s until 1790, when Washington, D.C., was designated the capital.

■La Fortaleza and San Juan Historic Sites, Puerto Rico

Both sites are part of the fortifications that surround San Juan and together make up the largest historic fortifications in the Americas. La Fortaleza dates from the mid-16th century, evolved into a 19th-century palace, and today is the residence of Puerto Rico's governor.

■Mesa Verde, Colorado

This site has the most complete record of the Anasazi culture in existence, including ceremonial shrines and residences that range from one-room houses to enormous cave villages.

■Monticello and the University of Virginia, Virginia

Jefferson drew his ideals of universal freedom, self-determination, and self-fulfillment from Greek and Roman precepts. Here he built stunning neoclassical structures that embody those ideals. Monticello, his home, was built between 1784 and 1809, and the university was built between 1805 and 1824.

■Statue of Liberty, New York

This symbol of freedom was presented to the United States by the government of France on the occasion of the first centennial in 1876. The 151-foot figure is dressed in a Roman toga with a torch in her right hand. In her left is a tablet marked July 4, 1776. She is stepping forward from shackles of slavery—a broken chain lies below her feet.

■Pueblo de Taos, New Mexico

Taos is a pre-Hispanic town that has successfully retained many of its early traditions. It was founded by the Anasazi Indians of

■ EXPERT LIST

the prehistoric period, and remarkably today most of the multitiered adobe buildings have retained their original forms, changed only by the addition of a few new external doors and windows, and modern fireplaces.

NATURAL SITES

■ Everglades National Park, Florida
The largest subtropical wilderness in the United States, the Everglades are a haven for over 800 vertebrates. In addition, the park has one of the greatest natural history and environmental education centers on earth.

■ Grand Canyon National Park, Arizona
The Grand Canyon's walls, a mile deep at some points, are a geological record that reaches back some 2 billion years. Also in the area are ruins from the ancient peoples who lived in this rugged environment.

■ Great Smoky Mountains National Park, North Carolina and Tennessee
In addition to one of the last great virgin forests in North America, this park contains one of the largest collections of fungi, mosses, and lichen in the world.

■ Hawai'i Volcanoes National Park, Hawaii
Here, active volcanoes rise directly from the Pacific Ocean floor. They have provided the best records and understanding of volcanic activity on earth. Also throughout the park are numerous archeological sites that indicate the understandable reverence early Hawai'ian peoples had for the volcanoes.

■ Mammoth Cave National Park, Kentucky
The largest cave system on earth, with hundreds of miles of charted chambers. In fact, the known chambers are 10 times as extensive as the next-largest cave system.

■ Olympic National Park, Washington
The park contains one of the largest temperate rain forests remaining on the planet. Its relative isolation on a peninsula accounts for the park's many rare plant and animal species.

■ Redwood National Park, California
The park contains the three largest trees on earth—the largest is 468 feet. Redwood also has archeological sites stretching back to 300 B.C., including well-preserved semi-subterranean plank houses, sweathouses, and crematoriums.

■ Wrangell–St. Elias National Park, Alaska
Contains the largest number of glaciers and greatest collection of peaks over 16,000 feet on the continent. One of the most unspoiled national parks in the United States.

■ Yellowstone National Park, Idaho, Montana, and Wyoming
The central third of the oldest national park in the United States is the largest volcanic crater on earth. In addition there are 27 fossilized forests, and over 10,000 geysers.

■ Yosemite National Park, California
The multitude of glacial features found here is virtually unmatched in the world.

EXPERT SOURCE

Stunning photographs and essays by world-renowned figures about all 358 World Heritage Sites can be found in *Masterworks of Man & Nature: Preserving Our World Heritage*, published by Harper-MacRae with UNESCO and IUCN. The hardcover book costs $35.

NATIONAL TRAILS

PATHS ACROSS THE NATION

Some are no wider than a fat guy, but all are of scenic or historic value

While they may not have hiked it top to bottom, most Americans have heard of the Appalachian Trail. Many are unaware, though, that the Appalachian belongs to a much larger system of trails. In 1968, Congress passed the National Trails Assistance Act to establish a national trail system. The trails fall into two categories: national scenic trails, which are protected scenic corridors for outdoor recreation, and national historic trails, which recognize prominent past routes of exploration, migration, and military action and may consist of no more than a series of roadside markers. The entire system includes 17 trails and covers most of the country.

NATIONAL SCENIC TRAILS

Benton Mackay, the man who created the Appalachian Trail, thought it should be no wider than the space required by the average fat man. The majority of the trails are open to hikers only, although some allow mountain bikes and horses. Many are works in progress and have significant sections closed to the public. Call ahead to inquire about available sections, allowable modes of transportation, and camping permits.

APPALACHIAN NATIONAL SCENIC TRAIL

Appalachian Trail Conference
PO Box 807, Harpers Ferry, WV 25425
☎ 304-535-6331

Length: *2,144 miles* ☛ The first interstate recreational trail, the Appalachian was conceived in 1921 by Benton McKay as a national preserve parallel to the East Coast. Beginning in Georgia and ending in Maine, the trail hugs the crest of the Appalachian Mountains and is open only to hikers. There are shelters every 6 to 12 miles, making it possible to hike the entire span without leaving the trail. Approximately 175 people hike the entire length of the trail every year, while millions of other hikers find inspiration and adventure on shorter segments.

CONTINENTAL DIVIDE NATIONAL SCENIC TRAIL

U.S. Forest Service, PO Box 7669
Missoula, MT 59807, ☎ 406-329-3511

Length: *3,100 miles* ☛ The Continental Divide Trail provides spectacular backcountry travel through the Rocky Mountains from Mexico to Canada. It is the most rugged of the long-distance trails. About 75 percent of the entire 3,100 miles is finished in some form, and the Forest Service hopes to complete the rest by the year 2000. (It is possible for the more adventurous to hike from border to border now, though). The longest continuous finished stretch reaches 795 miles from Canada through Montana and Idaho to Yellowstone National Park, and there is another solid 400-mile stretch through Colorado. The trail is open to hikers, pack and saddle animals, and, in some places, off-road motorized vehicles.

FLORIDA NATIONAL SCENIC TRAIL

U.S. Forest Service, 325 John Knox Rd.
Suite F100, Tallahassee, FL 32303
☎ 904-942-9300

Length: *1,300 miles* ☛ The Florida Trail extends from Big Cypress National Preserve in South Florida to just west of Pensacola in the northern part of the Florida Panhandle. Formed in 1964, the trail will eventually extend through Florida's three national forests to Gulf Islands National Seashore in the western panhandle. The trail passes through America's only subtropical landscape, making it especially popular with winter hikers and campers. Side-loop trails connect to nearby historic sites and other points of interest. At present, Forest Service officials estimate that about 600 miles of the trails are in place and open to public use.

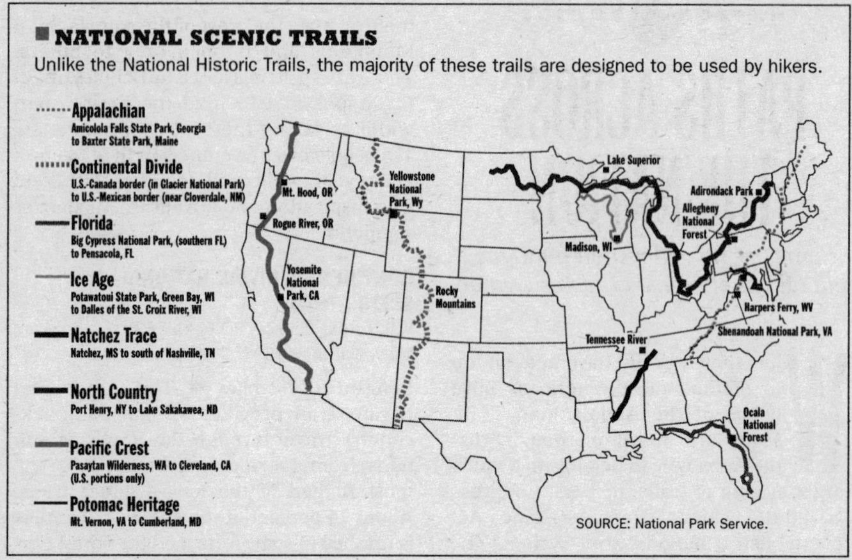

NATIONAL SCENIC TRAILS

Unlike the National Historic Trails, the majority of these trails are designed to be used by hikers.

SOURCE: National Park Service.

ICE AGE NATIONAL SCENIC TRAIL

National Park Service, 700 Rayovac Dr., Suite 100, Madison, WI 53711

☎ 608-264-5610

Length: *1,000 miles* ☛ At the end of the Ice Age, some 10,000 years ago, glaciers retreated from North America and left at their southern edge a chain of moraine hills made of rocks and gravel that the glaciers had accumulated along their journey. In Wisconsin, this band of hills zigzags across the state for 1,000 miles from Lake Michigan to the St. Croix River. Almost half the trail is open to the public, and certain sections are sometimes even used for marathons, ski races, and super long-distance running across the trail's rough terrain.

NATCHEZ TRACE NATIONAL SCENIC TRAIL

Natchez Trace Parkway,
RR 1, NT 143, Tupelo, MS 38801

☎ 800-305-7417

Length: *110 miles* ☛ The trail lies within the boundaries of the as yet uncompleted Natchez Trace Parkway, which extends 450 miles from Natchez, Miss., to Nashville, Tenn. The parkway will commemorate the historic Natchez Trace, an ancient path that began as a series of animal tracks and Native American trails. It was later used by early explorers, "Kaintuck" boatmen, post riders, and military men, including Andrew Jackson after his victory at the Battle of New Orleans. Segments near Nashville (26 miles), Jackson (20 miles), and Rocky Springs, which is near Natchez (15 miles), are close to completion. There also are about 20 shorter "leg-stretcher" trails throughout. The Park Service hopes to connect the entire 450 miles within the next 10 to 20 years.

NORTH COUNTRY NATIONAL SCENIC TRAIL

National Park Service, 700 Rayovac Dr., Suite 100, Madison, WI 53711

☎ 608-264-5610

Length: *3,200 miles* ☛ Conceived in the mid-1960s, the North Country Trail links the Adirondack Mountains with the Missouri River in North Dakota. The trail journeys through the grandeur of the Adirondacks, Pennsylvania's hardwood forests, the canals and rolling farmland of Ohio, the Great Lakes shorelines of Michigan, the glacier-carved lakes and streams of northern Wisconsin and Minnesota, and the vast plains of North Dakota—not to mention nine national forests and two national parks. Park officials say that about half of the trail is now completed for hiking.

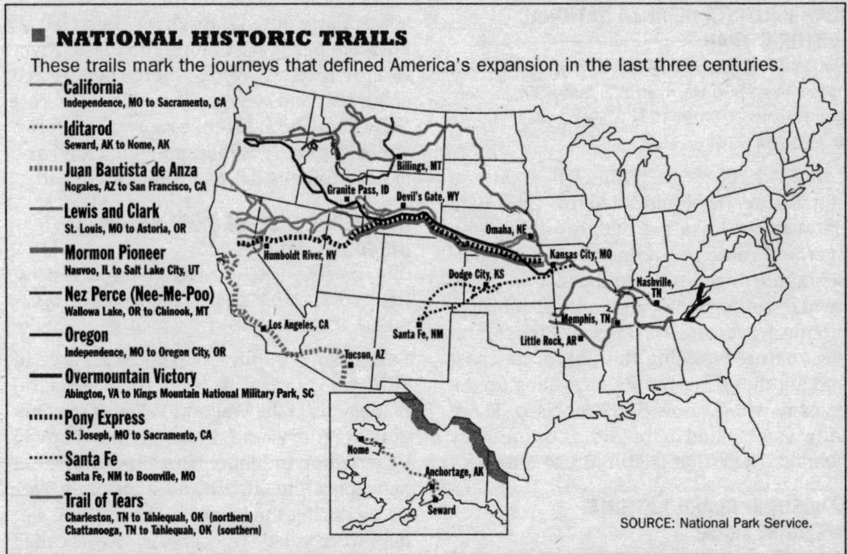

■ **NATIONAL HISTORIC TRAILS**

These trails mark the journeys that defined America's expansion in the last three centuries.

SOURCE: National Park Service.

PACIFIC CREST NATIONAL SCENIC TRAIL

U.S. Forest Service Outdoor Recreation Center, Jackson Federal Building, 915 Second Ave., Suite 442, Seattle, WA 98174
☎ 206-220-7450

Length: *2,638 miles* ☛ Running along the spectacular shoulders of the Cascade and Sierra Nevada mountain ranges from Canada to Mexico, the Pacific Crest Trail is the West Coast counterpart to the Appalachian National Trail. It passes through 25 national forests and seven national parks.

POTOMAC HERITAGE NATIONAL SCENIC TRAIL

C&O Canal National Historic Park, PO Box 4, Sharpsburg, MD 21782
☎ 301-739-4200

Length: *700 miles* ☛ The trail commemorates the unique mix of history and recreation along the Potomac River. Although it was established only in 1983, park officials say that much of it is already in place: the 18-mile Mount Vernon Trail in Virginia, the 70-mile Laurel Highlands Trail in Pennsylvania, and the 184-mile towpath of the Chesapeake and Ohio Canal. The last 20 or so miles of the trail along the Chesapeake and Ohio provide a wonderful bicycle ride that ends in the heart of Washington, D.C.

NATIONAL HISTORIC TRAILS

National historic trails are somewhat more conceptual than national scenic trails. Their objective is to preserve any historic remnants of the trail rather than provide a continuous footpath across its entire length. The "trails" often are no more than a series of roadside signs that direct travelers to historic sites or markers, though foot trails do appear from time to time at the roadside stops. The main exception to this description is the Iditarod in Alaska.

IDITAROD NATIONAL HISTORIC TRAIL

Iditarod Trail Committee, PO Box 870800, Wasilla, AK 99687 ☎ 907-376-5155

Length: *2,450 miles* ☛ The trail was made famous by prospectors and their dog teams during the Alaska gold rush at the turn of the century. Most of the trail is usable only during Alaska's six-month winter, when rivers and tundra are frozen. Each year, the 1,150-mile Iditarod sled dog race is run along the trail from Anchorage to Nome. Other events include the 210-mile Ididasport race for skiers, mountain bikers, and snowshoers, and the Alaska Gold Rush Classic Snowmachine Race. A network of shelters is being installed by the Bureau of Land Management and the Iditarod Trail Committee.

JUAN BAUTISTA DE ANZA NATIONAL HISTORIC TRAIL

National Park Service, Western Region Division of Planning, 600 Harrison St., Suite 600, San Francisco, CA 94107
☎ 415-744-3968

Length: *1,200 miles* ☛ In 1775, a party of 200 Spanish colonists led by Col. Juan Bautista de Anza set out to establish an overland route to California. The band of 30 families, a dozen soldiers, and 1,000 head of cattle, horse, and mule spent three months traversing the deserts of the Southwest before reaching the California coast and another three months traveling up the coast to what is now San Francisco. There they established a presidio, or military headquarters, that is still in use today.

LEWIS AND CLARK NATIONAL HISTORIC TRAIL

National Park Service, 700 Rayovac Dr., Suite 100, Madison, WI 53711
☎ 608-264-5610

Length: *3,700 miles* ☛ President Thomas Jefferson in 1803 doubled the area of the United States by purchasing from France 885,000 square miles of land west of the Mississippi. The following year he commissioned Meriwether Lewis and William Clark to explore and map his $125 million "Louisiana Purchase." They took the Missouri River upstream from what is today Wood River, Ill., crossed over several other rivers, and reached the Pacific Ocean at the mouth of the Columbia River in 1805. State, local, and private interests have established motor routes, roadside markers, and museum exhibits telling the Lewis and Clark story along the route.

MORMON PIONEER NATIONAL HISTORIC TRAIL

National Park Service, PO Box 45155, Salt Lake City, UT 84145 ☎ 801-539-4093

Length: *1,300 miles* ☛ Mormon emigration was one of the principal forces of settlement of the West. Seeking refuge from religious persecution, thousands of Mormons in 1846 left their settlement in Nauvoo, Ill., where church-founder Joseph Smith had lived. They spent the next winter in the Council Bluffs, Iowa, and Omaha, Neb., areas. Early in 1847, Brigham Young led an advance party west along the Platte River to Fort Bridger, Wyo., where they turned southwest and eventually came to the Great Salt Lake. The 1,624-mile route through five states generally is marked with a logo and closely follows the trail's historic route.

NEZ PERCE (NEE-ME-POO) NATIONAL HISTORIC TRAIL

U.S. Forest Service, Nez Perce National Historic Trail Coordinator, PO Box 7669, Missoula, MT 59807 ☎ 406-329-3511

Length: *1,170 miles* ☛ The Nez Perce in 1877 were forced to leave their ancestral homelands in the Wallowa Valley of the Oregon Territory and move to the Lapwai Reservation in Idaho. Hostilities broke out between white settlers and some of the Nez Perce during the journey. Three of the settlers were killed. The U.S. Army was called in, and five bands of the Nez Perce, one of them led by Chief Joseph, headed north across the Rocky Mountains hoping to find refuge in Canada. They eluded capture for months, but just short of reaching the Canadian border in Montana, they were captured by the army and forced to settle in Oklahoma. Within two years, they were returned to Idaho and Washington. Joseph became an eloquent spokesman for peace until his death in 1904.

OREGON NATIONAL HISTORIC TRAIL

U.S. Forest Service Outdoor Recreation Center, Jackson Federal Building, 915 Second Ave., Suite 442, Seattle, WA 98174
☎ 206-220-7450

Length: *2,170 miles* ☛ As the harbinger of America's westward expansion, the Oregon Trail was the pathway to the Pacific for fur traders, gold seekers, missionaries, and emigrants of every stripe. Beginning in 1841 and over a span of two decades, an estimated 300,000 emigrants undertook the five-month journey from Kansas to Oregon. The trail corridor still contains some 300 miles of discernible wagon ruts and 125 historic sites. The approximate route can be followed by automobile, and opportunities are available to travel by foot, horse, or mountain bike in many places.

EXPERT LIST

AN UP-CLOSE LOOK AT AMERICAN HISTORY

Historian James M. McPherson, whose Civil War history Battle Cry of Freedom *won the 1989 Pulitzer Prize, considers these the nation's most interesting sites:*

ANTIETAM NATIONAL BATTLEFIELD
Sharpsburg, Md.
■ The first invasion of the North was stopped here in 1862. At the battle's end, more men had been killed or wounded than on any other day of the Civil War.

APPOMATTOX COURT HOUSE NATIONAL HISTORICAL PARK
Appomattox, Va.
■ On April 9, 1865, General Robert E. Lee surrendered to General Ulysses S. Grant here. Although it would be several weeks before the Confederacy fell, the surrender in effect ended the war.

BOSTON NATIONAL HISTORICAL PARK
Boston, Mass.
■ The birth of the American Revolution is commemorated here. The 2.5-mile Freedom Trail connects 16 National Historic Park sites, including the Old North Church and the Paul Revere House.

COLONIAL WILLIAMSBURG
Williamsburg, Va.
■ From 1699 to 1776, Williamsburg was the capital of England's oldest, largest, richest, and most populous colony. Today the Colonial Williamsburg Foundation preserves 173 acres of the original 220-acre town just as it was on the eve of the Revolution.

FREDERICKSBURG AND SPOTSYLVANIA COUNTY BATTLEFIELDS MEMORIAL NATIONAL MILITARY PARK
Fredericksburg, Va.
■ The site of four major battles of the Civil War. Notable sites include the Jackson Shrine, the house where Stonewall Jackson died.

GETTYSBURG NATIONAL MILITARY PARK
Gettysburg, Penn.
■ The greatest battle of the Civil War was fought here from July 1 to July 3, 1863—a repulse of the second attempted Confederate invasion of the North and the turning point in the war.

HAGLEY MUSEUM AND LIBRARY
Wilmington, Del.
■ Part of the original du Pont Mills Estate and Gardens, built on 240 acres along the Brandywine River. Sights include a restored workers' community and the Potterworks, where some of the first power tools were used.

LOWELL NATIONAL HISTORIC PARK
Lowell, Mass.
■ America's first large-scale planned industrial community was founded here in 1826, introducing high-volume manufacturing to the United States. McPherson notes the town belongs to the time before industrialization turned ugly.

SHILOH NATIONAL MILITARY PARK
Shiloh, Tenn.
■ The site of the daring surprise attack by the Confederates and the massive counteroffensive by the Union Army. The park and National Cemetery overlook the Tennessee River.

VICKSBURG NATIONAL MILITARY PARK
Vicksburg, Miss.
■ A 47-day siege here ended July 4, 1863, with the surrender of Vicksburg, giving the North control of the Mississippi River. Sites include the USS *Cairo*, an ironclad Civil War gunboat.

OVERMOUNTAIN VICTORY NATIONAL HISTORIC TRAIL

Contact: Sycamore Shoals Historical Park, 1651 W. Elk Ave., Elizabethton, TN 37643
☎ 615-543-5808

Length: 300 miles ☛In the fall of 1780, citizens of Virginia, Tennessee, and North Carolina formed a militia to drive the British from the southern colonies. This trail marks their 14-day trek across the Appalachians to the Piedmont region of the Carolinas. There they defeated British troops at the Battle of Kings Mountain, setting in motion events that led to the British surrender at Yorktown and the end of the Revolutionary War. Much of the trail has become road and highway; only a 20-mile portion remains as a foot trail across the mountains. In most places roadside signs indicate proximity to the trail. A guide to the seven walking sections of the trail is available.

SANTA FE NATIONAL HISTORIC TRAIL

Contact: National Park Service, Long Distance Trails Group Office–Santa Fe, PO Box 728, Santa Fe, NM 87504, ☎ 505-988-6888

Length: 1,203 miles ☛After Mexican independence in 1821, U.S. and Mexican traders developed the Santa Fe Trail using American Indian travel and trade routes. It quickly became a commercial and cultural link between the two countries. It also became a road of conquest during the Mexican and Civil wars. With the building of the railroad to Santa Fe in 1880, the trail was largely abandoned. Of the 1,203 miles of the trail route between Old Franklin, Mo., and Santa Fe, N.M., more than 200 miles of wagon ruts remain visible; 30 miles of them are protected on federal lands.

TRAIL OF TEARS HISTORIC TRAIL

Contact: National Park Service, Long Distance Trails Group Office–Santa Fe, PO Box 728, Santa Fe, NM 87504 ☎ 505-988-6888

Length: 2,200 miles ☛ After many years of pressure from white settlers, 16,000 Cherokees from the southeastern states were moved by the U.S. Army in the late 1830s to lands west of the Mississippi River. Various detachments followed different routes west to the Oklahoma Territory. Thousands died along the way. Today the designated trail follows two of the principal routes: a water trail (1,226 miles) along the Tennessee, Ohio, Mississippi, and Arkansas rivers; and an overland route (826 miles) from Chattanooga, Tenn., to Tahlequah, Okla.

CALIFORNIA NATIONAL HISTORIC TRAIL

Contact: Oregon-California Trails Association, 524 S. Osage St., Independence, MO 64050
☎ 816-252-2276

Length: 5,665 miles ☛The California Trail has been aptly described as a great rope stretching from the Missouri River to the California gold fields. One would have to describe the rope as quite frayed, though, both at the ends and in the middle. The trail is commonly thought of as a single and direct line across the western United States that was trampled by fortune seekers during the gold rush of 1849. In fact, it was a collection of competing routes developed in the decade prior to the gold rush by land-seeking emigrants. Officially opened in 1992 and awesome in length, the entire system includes an estimated 320 historical sites, including forts, trading posts, and the natural landmarks that guided emigrants.

THE PONY EXPRESS TRAIL

Contact: National Park Service, Western Region Division of Planning, 600 Harrison St., Suite 600, San Francisco, CA 94107
☎ 415-744-3968

Length:1,666 miles ☛During its 18 months of operation, riders for the privately owned Pony Express carried mail between St. Joseph, Mo., and San Francisco in an unprecedented 10 days. The horse-and-rider relay system became the nation's most direct and practical means of east-west communications before the telegraph. The trail proved the feasibility of a central overland transportation route that could be used year-round, paving the way for the construction of a cross-country railroad. Approximately one-third of the 150 relay stations, where the Pony Express riders were allowed exactly two minutes to exchange mail with the station master, show identifiable remains and are historical sites along the trail.

EXPERT LIST

THE SURF IS THUMBS UP

"Dr. Beach" picks his favorite coastlines for swimming, snorkeling, and sunsets:

A few too many beach towels encroaching on your territory, menacing schools of jellyfish, or glass shards glistening in the sand can make your trip to the shore a far cry from a day at the beach. Dr. Stephen Leatherman, who is the director for the Laboratory for Coastal Research at the University of Maryland, ranks the nation's beaches every year. Known as Dr. Beach, Leatherman uses 50 criteria—from sand softness and frequency of mosquitoes to wind speed and number of sunny days—to determine America's top 20.

Pollution is most likely to bring demerits to coastal retreats. "No one's going into water that has floating garbage," notes Leatherman. He also has found that swimmers like warm surf (70 to 75 degrees) and clear water. "Even though clouded water might merely be the result of a river or marsh nearby, we have to downgrade for sediment."

Surprisingly, California beaches don't make the grade. Leatherman cites big waves that run the risk of crushing small children, water that rarely registers over 65 degrees, and beaches that are too crowded.

In fact, crowds are a key factor wherever you go. Leatherman says, "The best beaches aren't necessarily the most popular. For example, the most popular beach in the country is Jones Beach, Long Island. Over 10 million people visit each year. I've flown over in a helicopter and the beach looks like a giant patchwork quilt."

Here are Dr. Beach's most recent picks. He takes first-place beaches out of the running every year because "top beaches will always be top beaches."

BEST BEACHES 1995

1. St. Andrews, Fla.
2. Caladesi Island St. Park, Fla.
3. Kailua, Hawai'i
4. St. George Isl. St. Park, Fla.
5. St. Joseph Peninsula State Park, Fla.
6. Kaunaoa, Hawai'i
7. Wailea, Hawai'i
8. Hulopoe, Hawai'i
9. Cape Florida, Fla.
10. Ft. Desoto Park, Fla.
11. Delnor-Wiggins Pass, Fla.
12. Perdido Key, Fla.
13. Ocracoke Island, N.C.
14. Sand Key Park, Fla.
15. Westhampton Beach, N.Y.
16. East Hampton Beach, N.Y.
17. Hanalei, Kaua'i, Hawai'i
18. Kaanapali, Maui, Hawai'i

BEST SUNSETS

1. Sanibel Island, Fla.
2. Sunset Bay Beach, Ore.
3. Santa Barbara, Calif.

BEST SWIMMING

1. St. George Island St. Park, Fla.
2. Grayton Beach, Fla.
3. Assateague State Park, Md.

BEST SNORKELING

1. Hanauma Bay, Oahu, Hawai'i
2. Molokini Island, Maui, Hawai'i
3. John Pennekamp St. Park, Fla.

BEST CAMPING

1. (Tie) Ft. Stevens St. Park and Jessie M. Honeyman St. Park, Ore.
2. Barking Sands Beach, Kaua'i, Hawai'i
3. St. Joseph Peninsula State Park, Fla.

BEST FISHING

1. St. George Island St. Park, Fla.
2. Cape Hatteras, N.C.
3. Kona Coast, Big Island, Hawai'i

ALL TIME CHAMPS

1992. Bahia Honda, Fla.
1993. Hapuna, Hawai'i
1994. Grayton Beach, Fla.

ADVENTURE

TRAILS OF NATIVE AMERICANS

Where the traffic is low on America's original superhighways

"The weekend traffic is approaching bumper to bumper," says David Jenkins, director of conservation and public policy for the American Canoe Association. And no wonder. *Canoe Magazine* estimated in 1992 that some 14 million Americans participate in some form of paddling sport every year, be it canoeing, whitewater kayaking, sea kayaking, or rafting. To make matters worse, more and more rivers are polluted or unsuited for paddling. For every mile of American river that's preserved, say experts, 85 miles are plugged with concrete.

Traffic jams on America's waterways are nothing new, however. America's history is full of the canoe exploits of adventurers such as René-Robert La Salle, who discovered and named Louisiana, and Jacques Marquette, the French explorer and Jesuit priest who first reported accurate data on the course of the Mississippi. And the Europeans, of course, were only taking their cue from early Native Americans, who perfected canoe travel and used rivers much more than overland routes.

The good news: Many of the routes originally mapped by Native Americans remain in, or have been restored to, pristine condition. Native Trails (PO Box 240, Waldoboro, ME 04572, ☎ 207-832-5255) works to preserve pre-mechanized travel routes. Below are its top eight picks for canoe routes you can still travel today that look much as they did centuries ago.

BOUNDARY WATERS

Grand Portage, Minn., to International Falls, Minn. Length: 160 miles

10 days ☛ The key highway for Native Americans and Canadian Voyageurs in the rich fur trade west of the Great Lakes. The route is still a wild chain of granite-reefed lakes and backwater rivers, little changed from the days of the bitter rivalry between the Northwest and Hudson Bay companies. Though little whitewater skill is needed, good judgment on wind-whipped lakes and stamina for portages are necessities.

COOSA TRAIL

Carters, Ga., to Coosa, Ga. Length: 150 miles

Seven to 10 days ☛ Next to Carters, Ga., is the archeological site of Little Egypt, where 16th-century Spanish explorer Hernando de Soto raided the temples that crowned the city of Coosa's earthen pyramids. The raid yielded no gold, so de Soto marched on, leaving behind only the plague of smallpox, inadvertently destroying the Coosa people. The pristine route allows for keen appreciation of this former center of the Native American kingdom.

EASTERN OHIO TRAIL

Cleveland, Ohio, to Marietta, Ohio
Length: 270 miles

15 days ☛ The Cuyahoga River was so polluted in 1967 that it caught fire. Today, it is a model of recovery. Its valley leads south to waterfalls and an old portage route to the Tuscarawas and Muskingum River system. French explorers, settlers, and the Ohio Canal all followed the water trail to the Ohio River. Though no longer wild, the scenery is still beautiful as the rivers wind through the western edge of the Appalachians.

MISSOURI BREAKS

Fort Benton, Mont., to James Kipp Recreation Area, Mont. Length: 160 miles

Seven days ☛ Much of the upper Missouri has become a series of shallow, windswept lakes, hostile to canoes. This federally protected section escaped that fate. The painted cliffs of the Badlands hem the river from Virgelle to the end. Good current and few rapids make this an easy, scenic trip.

NORTHERN FOREST CANOE TRAIL

Old Forge, N.Y., to Ft. Kent, Maine
Length: 680 miles

1 to 2 months ☛ Like the Appalachian Trail, it traverses the wildest regions remaining in the Northeast. Some sections are not marked, but the trail is usable throughout—beginning where the St. John and Fish rivers meet at Fort Kent and following more than 15 rivers across the Adirondacks, Vermont, New Hampshire, and ending in Maine. Some sections are easy, others are broken by difficult rapids. Intermediate (class III) whitewater skills are needed to do the entire route. There are at least 30 mandatory portages on the trail.

POTOMAC HERITAGE TRAIL

Old Town, Md., to Piscataway National Park, Md.
Length: 200 miles

Eight to 10 days ☛ The Potomac was the Native American's major highway through the Appalachians. Most miles are easy, but

■ A QUICK GUIDE TO WHITEWATER RAPIDS

River conditions can vary widely and unpredictably. The following ratings were developed to give those unfamiliar with a river a feel for what they are getting into—before they get into it.

■ **CLASS I: Flat water, some current.**

■ **CLASS II: Small waves.**

■ **CLASS III: Big waves, requires maneuvering through "hydraulic holes" in which the water breaks back on itself over a rock.**

■ **CLASS IV: Big waves, many rocks, and very fast, powerful water. Requires precise maneuverability. Not fun to swim in if you make a mistake.**

■ **CLASS V: Pushing the limits of navigability, should be done only by experts. Extremely steep gradient of river: 30- to 40-foot drops. Mistakes or capsizing will result in injury or possibly death.**

■ **CLASS VI: Pushing the absurd. Paddlers on the West Coast define it as not runnable. Those on the East recommend it only for experts, lunatics, or both. Injury or death is a distinct possibility.**

EXPERT SOURCES

LEARNING HOW TO PADDLE

Dennis Stuhaug, editor of Canoe & Kayak *magazine, tells you where to find out more about canoeing or kayaking before getting on the water.*

PADDLING CLUBS

Paddling clubs are a good way to get your feet wet. Those looking for a club close to home should call:

THE AMERICAN CANOE ASSOCIATION

■ The largest paddling association in the country, it sets instructor certification tests and general water safety standards.

☎ **703-451-0141**

NORTH AMERICAN PADDLE SPORTS ASSOCIATION

■ Also covers kayaking. Can put you in touch with a club near you.

☎ **414-242-5228**

OUTFITTERS

Be sure the outfitter has a trained staff, a clean safety record, and is affiliated with a national paddling organization such as those above. To locate one near you, call:

AMERICA OUTDOORS

■ Lists recreational opportunities with premier backcountry outfitters on public lands and waterways.

☎ **615-472-2205**

NATIONAL ASSOC. OF CANOE AND LIVERY OUTFITTERS

■ A professional organization that will put you in contact with members.

☎ **606-472-2205**

PADDLING SCHOOLS

For those who prefer to have some easy experience on the water before embarking on a more challenging trip with an outfitter. Canoe and kayak retailers sometimes offer classes and can also be good sources of other information, including local water conditions. For schools near you refer to:

CANOE & KAYAK MAGAZINE

$3.99 per issue, $17.97 per year (6 issues)

■ All the news you need, and useful listings and ads from a variety of outfitters and schools.

☎ **800-692-2663**

rapids and falls break the river at Harpers Ferry and between Seneca and Georgetown. Many of the falls require portages for other than expert canoers. The last portion of the trip, just before Georgetown, is in tidewater, so paddlers need to plan their trip according to tidal charts.

ROGERS RETREAT

Newport, Vt., to Williams River Landing near Bellows Falls, Vt. Length: 260 miles

Ten days ☛ Charts one of the boldest initiatives of the French and Indian War: the attack on St. Francis, Quebec, by Robert Rogers and his rangers. Experience the agony of victory by climbing slowly up the Clyde River, racing and portaging down the Nulhegan and Connecticut rivers, then up the Johns River to portage the Ammo for a long downriver run to where the Rangers finally reached a safe retreat. The route is difficult but rewarding.

WISCONSIN TRAIL

Menasha, Wis., to Prairie du Chien, Wis. Length: 240 miles

14 days ☛ Indian guides introduced this route to Europeans in the middle of the 16th century. The route has pretty, if not particularly wild, scenery starting with Lake Winnebago, ascending the slow-moving Fox River, and finally following the Wisconsin River past the Baraboo Range and into the hills of western Wisconsin. Some short portages at a few dams are required along the way.

KAYAKING

A CHAMPION'S FAVORITE RIVERS

Where to go for the best whitewater kayaking in the country

Whitewater kayaking is not a sport for the timid. One of the first things any good kayaker learns, in fact, is "the roll," in which one spins the kayak upside down, placing oneself briefly but entirely under water. As a member of the U.S. Whitewater Team and the 1987 winner of the World Whitewater Championships in France, Bruce Lessels has had plenty of experience rolling his kayak. Here, Lessels, who also is the author of the *Whitewater Handbook* (AMC Books, 1994) and the president of the Zoar Outdoor Kayaking School in Charlemont, Mass., lists seven of his favorite places to kayak in the United States.

TUOLUMNE RIVER

Stanislaus National Forest, California

Located near Yosemite National Park in a pristine land reserve, the Tuolumne has 6 miles of expert-only class IV and class V rapids at top. Below are 18 miles of slightly less demanding class IV rapids.

■ **Permits:** Granted to only 80 people per day to prevent overcrowding. For permit and river condition information, call the Groveland Ranger District in Stanislaus National Forest, ☎ 209-962-7825.

ROGUE RIVER

Southwestern Oregon

Expert kayakers love this river for its class IV and class V rapids. But warm water and a 40-mile run of class II to class V rapids also make it fun for novices.

■ **Schools:** Sundance Expeditions Kayak School and Rafting Company, based in Merlin, Ore., offers a nine-day introductory course. ☎ 503-479-8508.

■ **Permits:** A limited number are given out through a lottery system with a January 31 deadline for the Memorial Day through Labor Day season, ☎ 503-479-3735.

MIDDLE FORK OF THE SALMON RIVER

Central Idaho

A paddler's favorite, the Middle Fork is 98 miles of remote, wild river appropriate for beginning, intermediate, and advanced kayakers. The water is warm, many of the beaches are sandy, and along the way are excellent hiking, great trout fishing, and beautiful hot springs.

■ **Permits:** For private permit information or a list of area outfitters, call the U.S. Forest Service, Middle Fork Ranger District, ☎ 208-879-5204.

THE CLARK'S FORK OF THE YELLOWSTONE RIVER

Southwestern Montana

The whitewater and scenery are awesome, but non-expert paddlers should steer clear; the river's 37 miles of class IV and V rapids have proven deadly for even the most advanced kayakers. Wildlife is plentiful.

■ **Permits:** Because there is not a problem of overuse, no permits are required. For more information, call the Jackson Hole Kayak School, ☎ 800-733-2471.

RIO GRANDE

Big Bend National Park, Texas

Unlike most other American rivers, the Rio Grande is runnable all year. Hot springs warm the water to a perennially comfortable 70 degrees, making the river inviting to even the wimpiest of beginners. Rapids range from class II to class III, but the temperature and scenery make the river popular even with advanced kayakers.

■ **Permits:** Required for all paddlers and can be obtained on-site at Big Bend National Park. For more information, call the Park Service at Big Bend, ☎ 915-477-2393.

CHATTOOGA RIVER

South Carolina and Georgia

Deliverance was filmed here. The Chattooga's rapids are some of the most challenging on the East Coast, and the scenery some of the most beautiful. Few have suc-

EXPERT PICKS

WHITEWATER AROUND THE WORLD

"The most scared I have ever been on the water was while making A River Wild *in Montana," says Arlene Burns, a member of the U.S. Women's Whitewater Team and one of the world's foremost experts on whitewater rafting, who was Meryl Streep's double in the 1994 film. Whitewater rafting isn't for the faint of heart, but it doesn't usually call for stunt doubles, either. Here are some of Burns's picks of the world's most unforgettable rafting spots.*

BIO BIO RIVER
Chile

■ Jungle scenery, the Mapuchi Indians, and warm water are the draws for this classic rafting river.

CHATKAL RIVER
Uzbekistan

■ This big-water (class IV and class V rapids) river flows through the snow-capped Tienshan mountain range down south to Kisilkum, where the land is lush, and finally dwindles into desert. The mountain and valley communities that lined the Chatkal were victims of Stalin's forced relocation policies, and the abandoned orchards and farms along the river give it a haunting quality. After the put-out, a trip to nearby Samarkand, one of the world's oldest cities, is a must.

KARNALI RIVER
Nepal

■ The Karnali originates in the Kialash area of Tibet, which Hindus and Buddhists believe to be the navel of the earth. From an altitude of 15,000 feet, the river descends some 350 miles through glaciers high in the Himalayas to the flatlands of Nepal.

TATSHENSHINI RIVER
Alaska

■ The icy waters of the Tatshenshini frighten off a lot of rafters, but the rapids usually are mild, making the possibility of an unexpected swim unlikely. Located in the St. Alais coastal range, the river offers a mild float marked by passing glaciers, grizzly bears, black bears, bald eagles, and osprey.

ZAMBESI RIVER
Zimbabwe

■ The Zambesi is renowned as the biggest commercially run whitewater in the world. Rafters put in directly beneath the spectacular Victoria Falls and travel on through the narrow basaltic (volcanic formation) gorges that separate Zimbabwe from Zambia. Warm weather and beautiful, sandy beaches invite frequent swimming, but be careful—hippos and crocodiles are a real threat.

cessfully navigated the treacherous class IV section, and many have sustained critical injuries in the attempt.

■ **Schools:** Beginners come here for the Nantahala Outdoor School in Bryson City, N.C. For details, call ☎ 704-488-2175.

■ **Permits:** Kayakers running the river on their own can obtain the required permits at the put-in at the U.S. Route 76 Bridge near Clayton, Ga.

SHEENJEK RIVER
Arctic National Wildlife Refuge, Alaska

Although the rapids on this river usually do not exceed class II, the temperature and volume of the water combined with the remoteness of the site make this almost a class III challenge. The area is accessible only by seaplane.

■ **Permits:** For information, call the Arctic National Wildlife Refuge, ☎ 907-456-0250.

SCUBA DIVING

BEST PLACES TO TAKE A PLUNGE

Whether you're a novice or expert, here are some spots not to miss

Diving has gone mainstream. These days, wet suits are so fashionable that women's swimsuit designers often take their cues from the fluorescent colors and slick shapes of diving wear. That means more outfitters, schools, and resorts than ever before. We asked Steve Blount, executive editor of *Scuba Diving* magazine, for his recommendations of the half-dozen best spots for divers of varying abilities to take the plunge.

NOVICE DIVERS

JOHN PENNEKAMP CORAL REEF STATE PARK, FLORIDA KEYS

Best time to go: May through September.

Clear, calm, and warm water; rich, varied animal life; and plentiful reefs that are mostly protected by state parks and marine sanctuaries make the Florida Keys the most popular dive destination in the world. Park officials estimate that 1.5 million tourists visit John Pennekamp State Park; most of them are divers.

■ **DIVE OPERATORS AND LODGING:** The park's "in-house" dive operator is the Coral Reef Park Rental Company, ☎ 305-451-6322.

WASHINGTON-SLAGBAII NATIONAL PARK, BONAIRE

Best time to go: October through April.

A part of the Netherlands Antilles just off the North Coast of South America, Bonaire has one of the first and most successful marine parks in the Caribbean. There are dozens of dive sites that slope gently from down 60 feet or more and are covered with a psychedelic array of mounding corals and purple and yellow, human-sized tube sponges.

■ **DIVE OPERATORS AND LODGING:** Most hotels operate their own diving operation or have an agreement with one. The dive center at the Sand Dollar Condominium and Beach Club, ☎ 800-288-4773, was given five stars by the Professional Association of Dive Instructors (PADI).

INTERMEDIATE DIVERS

THE CAYMAN ISLANDS

Best time to go: October through April.

The three islands of this British dependency make up the tip of a submarine ridge that plunges more than a mile into the Caribbean. The best dives are at depths of 60 to 90 feet. Sights include huge basket sponges, sheet coral, and plenty of big fish.

■ **DIVE OPERATORS AND LODGING:** One-week dive packages at the Grand Bay Club Condominiums on Grand Cayman can be reserved through Sea Safaris Travel, Inc., ☎ 800-821-6670. Divers also can consult the PADI Travel Network, ☎ 800-729-7234, for other dive operators and lodging on the Caymans.

COZUMEL, MEXICO

Best time to go: December through August.

Cozumel is particularly popular with Americans. Intermediate or experienced divers are drawn to a deep wall that starts at about 60 feet below sea level and is a sheer drop as far as the eye can see—and lateral visibility in this clear water ranges 150 feet or more. Big fish abound and evolving coral can be seen in huge spirals and pinnacles. Divers should be careful of the powerful current along the wall, though.

■ **DIVE OPERATORS AND LODGING:** Dive Paradise in Cozumel offers half-day dives, ☎ 800-308-5125. The Galapagos Inn is popular with divers and offers one-week diving packages, ☎ 800-847-5708.

ADVANCED DIVERS

CHU'UK LAGOON, MICRONESIA

Best time to go: Good all year.

Most people know this Pacific lagoon as

WHERE TO LEARN TO BLOW BUBBLES

Four ways to get yourself certified

Most countries require that you be certified before you strap on your tanks and dive in, and for good reason—mishandled equipment or an error in judgment in the lower depths can lead to a life-threatening case of the bends. Here are three ways to get certified, and a fourth way to dip your toe into diving without making a three-week commitment.

■ **CERTIFICATION CLASSES:** They are usually offered at the local dive shop or YMCA. The three- to six-week programs combine classroom instruction, pool-time, and open-water dives in an ocean or other body of water with currents and waves. Look for programs certified by one of the two largest American diving associations, the National Association of Underwater Instructors (NAUI), or the Professional Association of Diving Instructors (PADI). Both set clear standards for everything from equipment to instructor credentials. Also, try to meet your instructor before committing to the class. Diving is a high-risk activity; a novice needs to feel comfortable with the instructor. Tuition, equipment, and textbook should run about $250.

■ **RESORTS:** Most resorts that offer diving also offer on-premise certification classes. They usually last three to four days and cost $350 to $450. You should make sure that the program is certified by NAUI or PADI before signing on.

■ **AT-HOME INSTRUCTION WITH ON-SITE DIVE:** A combination program for those who live in cold-weather climates. You do all your instruction at home in an indoor pool, and then do your open-water test at a resort with a referral program. Costs vary widely.

■ **PASSPORT PROGRAM:** For people who want to try diving but don't want to commit the time or money to getting certified, these half- or one-day programs review the basics and conclude with an open-water or shore-dive accompanied by the instructor. The cost is usually about $50.

Truk. In 1993, though, the state legislature changed the name to its native roots, Chu'uk. In 1944, the U.S. Navy caught a huge fleet of Japanese merchant ships at anchor in the lagoon and sank them. Divers who are comfortable with depths of a hundred feet and more can see airplanes, trucks, tanks, and other war remnants.

■ **DIVE OPERATORS AND LODGING:** The Truk Continental Hotel and the Micronesia Aquatics Dive Shop offer seven-day lodging and dive packages. For reservations call Sea Safaris Travel, Inc., ☎ 800-821-6670.

THE GALAPAGOS ISLANDS

Best time to go: October through May.

The Galapagos Islands are part of Ecuador, located off the west coast of South America. The warm Humboldt current, named for the German explorer who discovered it in 1800, collides with colder Pacific waters all around the Galapagos, making for a mélange of wildlife. Divers can see tropical parrotfish, penguins, and one-of-a-kind sea-diving iguanas. The islands are a national park, so there are no hotels. Divers must visit on specially designed live-aboard boats.

■ **DIVE OPERATORS AND ACCOMMODATIONS:** See and Sea Travel in San Francisco specializes in live-aboard diving trips. It offers a 10-day trip to the Galapagos Islands. Divers looking for other live-aboard outfitters should consult the PADI Travel Network, ☎ 800-729-7234.

RANCH VACATIONS

HOMES ON THE RANGE

Dude ranches offer everything from luxury living to cattle herding

In the movie *City Slickers*, Billy Crystal plays a thoroughly urbanized man who transcends a midlife crisis by spending a week at a working cattle ranch. The movie was a fantasy, but the idea is catching on; aging baby boomers have been rushing west with an abandon not seen since the Gold Rush of '49.

Dudes (those not ranchers or descended from ranchers) searching for traditional ranch activities like horseback riding and cattle driving have plenty of ranches to choose from. Frontier outposts they're not—many offer hot tubs, gourmet cooking, and professional massages after a long (or short) day in the saddle.

Following are some of the outstanding ranches highlighted in Gene Kilgore's *Ranch Vacations* (John Muir Publications, 1994), the most comprehensive guide to America's ranches currently available. For copies of the book, which lists over 200 ranches, call ☎ 800-472-6247.

DUDE RANCHES

BAKERS BAR M — $–$$

Adams, Ore.

Teddy Roosevelt fished here. Later 20th-century guests can still enjoy the river and a hot springs pool on this 2,500-acre ranch on the Umatilla River in the Blue Mountains of northeastern Oregon. ☎ **503-566-3381**

CROSSED SABRES RANCH — $$

Wapiti, Wyo.

Established in 1898 as a stagecoach stop, Crossed Sabres exudes Old West ambiance. The ranch requires a minimum stay of one week. ☎ **305-587-3750**

KLICKS' K BAR RANCH — $–$$

Augusta, Mont.

One of the best and oldest ranches in the West. Getting to this high country hideaway requires a half-hour float plane ride across Gibson Lake or a ride by saddle horse on a mountain trail. ☎ **406-467-2771** (summer) and ☎ **406-562-3589** (winter)

NORTH LAND RANCH RESORT — $–$$$

Kodiak, Ala.

Located in the emerald green Kalsin Valley with the Pacific Ocean on one side and mountains on the other, North Land is a 31,000-acre cattle and horse ranch with spectacular Alaskan scenery. The mood is low key and the wildlife is first rate. Excellent fishing and riding. ☎ **907-486-5578**

SKYLINE GUEST RANCH — $$–$$$

Telluride, Colo.

The owners have deeded this ranch nestled in the high meadows and aspen-rich peaks of the San Juan Mountains to the Nature Conservancy. ☎ **303-728-3757**

PACK TRIPS

RIMROCK RANCH — $–$$

Cody, Wyo.

Five- to 10-day pack trips into nearby Yellowstone National Park and Shoshone National Forest. Also great fishing in the North Fork of the Shoshone River and on Buffalo Bill Lake. Guides cook the trout you catch on an open fire. ☎ **307-587-3970**

OLD GLENDEVY RANCH — $$

Glendevy, Colo.

Glendevy combines pack trips with a stay at the ranch. There's excellent fishing as well on 3 miles of private shoreline at McIntire Creek. ☎ **303-435-5701**

APPROXIMATE 1996 RATES PER PERSON PER DAY:

$ = $100 and below
$$ = $100–$150
$$$ = $150–$250
$$$$ = $250–$300
$$$$$ = $300 and up

EXPERT LIST

THE TOP 10 RODEOS IN NORTH AMERICA

The rodeo has been called "the circus of the west," but its roots are in the hard work of everyday ranching; those rodeo clowns don't just entertain the kids, they also keep the rodeo pit safe by distracting unruly broncos when the stars hit the ground. Rodeo organizers try to make the danger worth it by competing to offer the biggest purses and draw the biggest stars. Below are the 10 biggest in North America as of 1994.

RODEO	TOTAL PURSE	LOCATION	WHEN
1. NATIONAL FINALS RODEO	$2,573,675	Las Vegas, Nev.	December
2. HOUSTON LIVESTOCK SHOW	$330,649	Houston, Texas	February/March
3. DODGE NATIONAL CIRCUIT FINALS	$231,428	Pocatello, Idaho	March
4. RENO RODEO	$124,500	Reno, Nev.	June
5. ORIGINAL COORS RODEO SHOWDOWN	$120,000	Phoenix, Ariz.	October
6. CALGARY STAMPEDE	$118,750	Calgary, Alberta	July
7. CHEYENNE FRONTIER DAYS	$117,000	Cheyenne, Wyo.	July
8. SOUTHWESTERN EXPOSITION AND LIVESTOCK SHOW AND RODEO	$112,000	Ft. Worth, Texas	January/February
9. NATIONAL WESTERN RODEO	$109,000	Denver, Colo.	January
10. SAN ANTONIO STOCK SHOW AND RODEO	$100,020	San Antonio, Texas	February

SOURCE: Professional Rodeo Cowboys Association, Colorado Springs, Colo.

SEVEN LAZY P **$$–$$$**
Choteau, Mont.

A low-key, family-owned ranch specializing in pack trips and located on the North Fork of the Teton River. ☎ **406-466-2044**

WORKING CATTLE RANCHES

BAR H BAR **$$**
Soda Springs, Idaho

Bar H Bar has 2,000 head of beef cattle on 9,000 acres in the Bear River Range of the Wasatch Mountains, bordering the Caribou Cache National Forest. Guests participate in calving, branding, fence mending, cattle drives, and salting and doctoring beef for market. ☎ **208-547-3082**

CHEYENNE RIVER **$**
Douglas, Wyoming

A working cattle and sheep ranch with over 8,000 acres in the wide-open prairie of eastern Wyoming. Usually only one family or couple at a time stay at the ranch and participate in cattle drives, changing pastures, calving and sheep shearing (in April), and branding and lambing (in May). ☎ **307-358-2380**

PONDEROSA CATTLE COMPANY AND GUEST RANCH **$**
Seneca, Ore.

A historic 120,000-acre cattle ranch located in a magnificent valley in eastern Oregon. Dudes can herd, change pastures, check fences, and practice roping. ☎ **800-331-1012**

SPANISH SPRINGS **$$**
Ravendale, Calif.

A working cattle ranch, Spanish Springs boasts 5,000 cows and 20 horses on 70,000 acres in Northern California's rugged high-desert country near Nevada. Wild horses also are seen on occasion. ☎ **800-272-8282**

FLY-FISHING RANCHES

BIG HOLE RIVER OUTFITTER $$$$–$$$$$
Wise River, Mont.

One of the best fly-fishing outfits in North America. A maximum of 10 guests receive personal attention and instruction suited to their ability, with one guide to no more than two guests. ☎ **406-832-3252**

CRESCENT H RANCH $$$–$$$$
Wilson, Wyo.

An upscale ranch with an international fly-fishing reputation. Guides take guests to the ranch's private spring creeks, the nearby South Fork in Idaho, or the Firehole and Yellowstone rivers in Yellowstone National Park. ☎ **307-733-3674**

CRYSTAL CREEK LODGE $$$$$
Dillingham, Alaska

For people who like to fish, like to fly, and who don't like to rough it, this is the place. A premier lodge with upscale amenities, and daily fly-in/fly-out fishing in five planes and two helicopters at remote sites. ☎ **800-525-3153**

ELK CREEK LODGE $$$$$
Meeker, Colo.

Offers extensive private land and fishing water in northwestern Colorado—over 100 log-dammed pools in Elk Creek, on six private miles of the White River, and on Trapper Lake, the second largest natural lake in Colorado. ☎ **303-878-5454**

CROSS COUNTRY/SNOWMOBILE

FRYING PAN RIVER RANCH $$$–$$$$
Meredith, Colo.

Thousands of acres of untracked snow in the Rockies. Excellent but challenging backcountry skiing as well as a winter fly-fishing program. There's an outdoor hot tub, too. ☎ **303-927-3750**

LONE MOUNTAIN RANCH $$$
Big Sky, Mont.

Seventy-five kilometers of meticulously groomed trails for every ability level. Highlights include guided all-day ski trips into Yellowstone Park. ☎ **406-995-4644**

OWN YOUR OWN TEPEE

Or stay in one overnight at these beautiful campgrounds

Need a tepee? Don and Marcy Ellis will be glad to custom-design one for you, or just as happy to instead use designs originated by the Cheyenne, Sioux, Crow, and Blackfoot nations. The tepees range from 9 to 24 feet in height and are available from White Buffalo Lodges, ☎ 406-222-7390. If you don't have room in your backyard or the $270 to $2,000 asking price, check out these sites where the Ellises' handiwork is available for inexpensive overnight stays.

BOZEMAN HOT SPRINGS KOA CAMPGROUND
Bozeman, Mont.

▲ Four teepees are set up every summer near a group of mineral pools on the edge of the Gallatin River. Base price is $20 per night. ☎ **406-586-6492**

LOLO HOT SPRINGS
Lolo, Mont.

▲ This campground near Missoula gets a bit chilly in the winter, but its eight tepees circle a toasty open fire. Inside are Coleman lanterns, wood chip–covered floors, and optional cots. Base price is $25 per night. ☎ **406-273-2290**

SAGE AND CACTUS VILLAGE
Lusk, Wyo.

▲ A rugged bed and breakfast on the McGee Ranch in Niobrara County. The eight-tepee camp sits on a bluff overlooking the Cheyenne River and offers campfires at night and a western breakfast in the morning. Base price is $40 per night. ☎ **307-663-7653**

VISTA VERDE GUEST AND SKI TOURING RANCH **$$$–$$$$**
Steamboat Springs, Colo.

A romantic winter getaway with indoor-outdoor hot tubs, sauna, and exercise equipment. ☎ **800-526-7433**

LUXURY

ALISAL GUEST RANCH **$$$–$$$$**
Solvang, Calif.

A secluded 10,000 acres, 40 miles northwest of Santa Barbara. Thirty miles of riding trails, a par 72 championship golf course, and seven tennis courts. ☎ **800-425-4725**

RANCHO DE LOS CABALLEROS **$$–$$$**
Wickenburg, Ariz.

One of the premier ranch resorts with an 18-hole championship golf course. First-rate service. ☎ **602-684-5484**

TRIPLE CREEK **$$$$–$$$$$**
Darby, Mont.

A luxurious, adults-only mountaintop guest ranch with a romantic atmosphere and gourmet cuisine. ☎ **406-821-4664**

FAMILY AND KIDS

CHEROKEE PARK RANCH **$$–$$$**
Livermore, Colo.

Offers a tremendous diversity of activities for all ages and three full-time counselors for ages 3 through 12. ☎ **800-628-0949**

PARADISE GUEST RANCH **$$–$$$**
Buffalo, Wyo.

A traditional dude ranch full of children's programs. Kids under 6 will be completely supervised if parents desire. ☎ **307-684-7876**

PEACEFUL VALLEY LODGE AND RANCH RESORT **$$–$$$**
Lyons, Colo.

A two-to-one staff to guest ratio and an extensive program for kids three and up, with a nursery and supervised children's program in the summer. ☎ **800-955-6343**

WHITE STALLION RANCH **$–$$**
Tucson, Ariz.

Some 3,000 acres surrounded by rugged desert mountains. Kids will enjoy the ranch's petting zoo. ☎ **800-782-5546**

EXPERT SOURCES

ACROSS THE PLAINS WITHOUT SHOCK ABSORBERS

A journey across the high plains by covered wagon can take travelers back to the time when pioneers headed west seeking new land and new lives. The pace is slow and chuckwagon food is the norm, but some groups offer modern conveniences such as showers and rest rooms. Below are a few of the outfitters recommended by Gene Kilgore in his book Ranch Vacations.

FLINT HILLS OVERLAND WAGON TRAIN TRIPS
PO Box 1076
El Dorado, KS 67042
☎ 316-321-6300

HONEYMOON TRAIL CO.
458 S. Main
Moccasin, AZ 86022
☎ 602-643-7292

FORT SEWARD WAGON TRAINS, INC.
PO Box 244
Jamestown, ND 58402
☎ 701-252-6844

MESSENGER BROTHERS
5915 U.S. Route 30
Cheyenne, WY 82001
☎ 307-638-6888

OREGON TRAIL WAGON TRAIN
Route 2, Box 502
Bayard, NE 69334
☎ 308-586-1850

REDINGTON LAND & CATTLE
Cascabel Ranch
HC 1, Box 730
Benson, AZ 85602
☎ 602-212-5555

SAFARIS

WHERE THE WILD THINGS ARE

A noted zoologist's guide to Africa's best game-watching

Most of us know Africa from the movies. In the '70s, *Born Free*, the film about Joy Adamson, her husband, and their lion Elsa, spawned a whole generation of lion lovers. In the '80s, there was *Out of Africa* and *Gorillas in the Mist*, romantic and beautiful depictions of African bush and gorillas, respectively. No doubt, Hollywood is at least partly responsible for the heightened craze for safaris. The enormous growth in the tourist industry in Africa, however, has not been without consequence. Many large game parks and reserves are so crowded that where there are animals, there are lines. Others have fared worse. Crowds, for example, have driven elephants out of the Masai Mara reserve in Kenya. But wild Africa survives; it's still possible to witness the activity of herds of wildebeest, elephant, and zebra there, and prides of lions still roam, searching for their nightly kill.

Dr. Richard Estes is one of the world's foremost experts on the social ecology of African animals. He is an associate at the Peabody Museum of Archeology and Ethnography at Harvard University and the chairman of the World Conservation Union's Antelope Specialist's Group, as well as the author of *The Safari Companion, A Guide to Watching African Mammals* (Chelsea Green Publishing, 1993). Here's his animal-by-animal guide to the best game-watching in Africa.

CHEETAH

■ **Where they live:** Usually found in low density in sub-Saharan savannas and arid zones where suitable prey occurs.

■ **Best places to see them:** Masai Mara NR and Amboseli NP, Kenya; Etosha NP and private game ranches in Namibia; Serengeti NP, Tanzania.

■ **Active time:** The most diurnal cat, usually rests during the heat of the day.

CHIMPANZEE

■ **Where they live:** In rain forests, savanna woodlands, and montane forests (a kind of mountain forest) from Guinea, north of the Congo River through central Africa to Tanzania. Pygmy chimpanzees live in the rain forest south of the Congo River.

■ **Best places to see them:** Gombe NP, Mahale Mountains NP, Tanzania; Kibale Forest, Uganda.

■ **Active time:** Generally spend about half the day feeding, with a midday siesta.

ELEPHANT

■ **Where they live:** Used to live everywhere south of the Sahara that had enough water and trees, but over three-quarters of the population were destroyed in the last two decades by ivory poachers. The survivors live mostly in protected parks.

■ **Best places to see them:** Chobe NP and Moremi GR, Botswana; Etosha NP, Namibia; Kruger NP, South Africa; Hwange NP, Zimbabwe. (The Masai Mara GR in Kenya is popular, but few elephants remain.)

■ **Active time:** Feeds 16 hours a day and sleeps 4 to 5 hours. Bathes daily, but can abstain several days if no water is available.

GAZELLE

■ **Varieties:** The Grant's gazelle is large with pale-to-dark tan coloring and white underparts. The Thomson's gazelle is smaller, with cinnamon coloring, a rump patch smaller than a Grant's, and bold, black side stripes and facial markings.

■ **Where they live:** The Somali-Masai Arid Zone, from southern Sudan and Ethiopia to northern Tanzania, and from the Kenya coast to Lake Victoria (Grant's). Somali-

GUIDE TO ABBREVIATIONS:

NP = National park
NR = Nature reserve
GR = Game reserve

Masai arid zone and adjacent northern savanna, from northern Tanzania to northern Kenya, with an isolated population in Sudan (Thomson's).

■ **Best places to see them:** Amboseli NP, Masai Mara NR, Meru NP, Nairobi NP, Samburu-Isiolo NR, Shaba NR, Sibiloi NP and Tsavo NP, Kenya; Ngorongoro Conservation Area, Serengeti NP and Tarangire NP, Tanzania (Grant's). Amboseli NP, Masai Mara NP, Nairobi NP and Nakura NP, Kenya; Ngorongoro Crater, Serengeti NP and Tarangire NP, Tanzania (Thomson's).

■ **Active time:** Day and night, peak activity generally early in the day, though.

GIRAFFE

■ **Where they live:** Used to be found wherever trees occurred throughout the arid and dry-savanna zones south of the Sahara. Eliminated from most of the West African (Senegal) and southern Kalahari range (South Africa and southern Botswana) but are still fairly common, even outside wildlife preserves.

■ **Best places to see them:** Too numerous to mention; most approachable along roads in popular national parks.

■ **Active time:** Females spend just over half the day grazing, males slightly less. Night is spent resting, especially during the darkest hours.

GORILLA

■ **Varieties:** The mountain gorilla has a long and silky coat, while the western or eastern gorilla has a shorter, sparser coat.

■ **INTO AFRICA**

Ready to live the wild life? *Outside* magazine recommends the following outfitters to take you on a safari Into Africa:

Abercrombie & Kent	☎ **800-323-7308**
Africa Adventure Co.	☎ **800-882-9453**
African Portfolio	☎ **212-737-0144**
African Travel	☎ **800-421-8907**
Baobab Safari Co.	☎ **800-835-3692**
REI Adventures	☎ **800-662-2236**
Wilderness Travel	☎ **800-368-2794**

■ **Where they live:** Cameroon, the Central African Republic, the lowland rain forest of Congo, Equatorial Guinea, and Gabon (western lowland); eastern Zaire; and in the adjacent highland areas near Rwanda's border and isolated pockets of rain forest (eastern lowland). Also Rwanda, Uganda, and Zaire (mountain).

■ **Best places to see them:** Eastern Zaire, especially Kahuzi-Biega NP and Virunga NP.

■ **Active time:** The average group of gorillas spends a little under a third of the day feeding, a little under a third traveling, and a little over a third resting, mainly at midday.

HIPPOPOTAMUS

■ **Where they live:** Used to be found everywhere south of the Sahara where adequate water and grazing conditions occurred. Now largely confined to protected areas, but still survive in many major rivers and swamps.

■ **Best places to see them:** Almost any park or reserve with sizable lakes or rivers bordered by grassland.

■ **Active time:** Hippos walk from 2 to 6 miles during their nightly forage. After five hours of intensive grazing, they return to water beds before dawn to spend the day digesting and socializing.

LION

■ **Where they live:** Throughout Sub-Saharan Africa, except in deserts and rain forest.

■ **Best places to see them:** Most major NPs and GRs have them, but the best places are the Ngorongoro Conservation Area and the Serengeti NP, both in Tanzania.

■ **Active time:** Lions spend nearly 20 hours a day "reserving energy," and hunt most actively early and late at night, carrying over a couple of hours into daybreak. Lions become active any time day or night, hungry or gorged, if easy prey presents itself.

RHINOCEROS

■ **Varieties:** Black and white.

■ **Where they live:** Formerly widespread in the northern and southern savanna, Sahel, Somali-Masai, and southwest arid zones. Human population growth and poaching

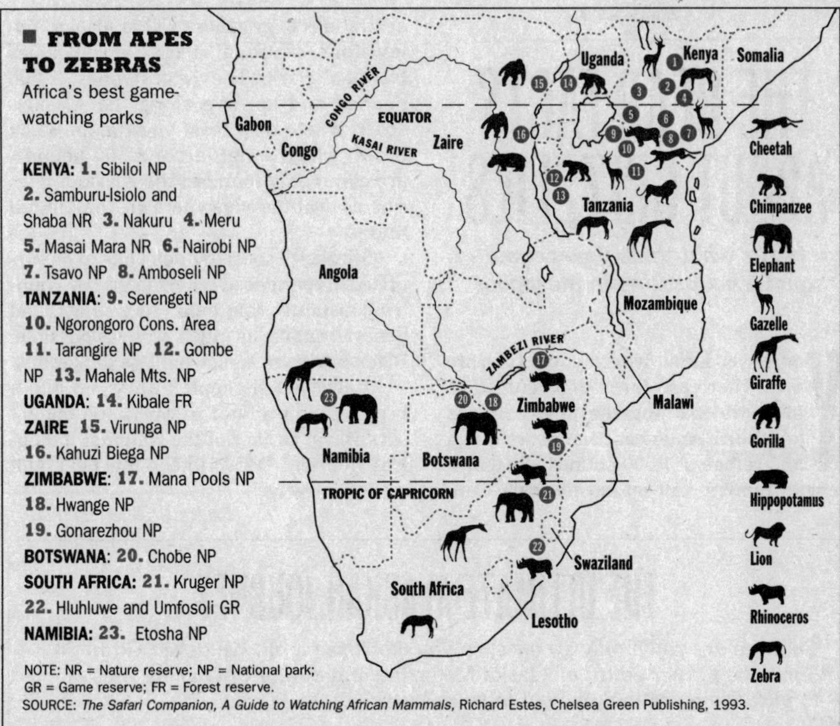

(rhino horns are valued as an aphrodisiac in Asian and Arab countries) have led to a steady decline. Now endangered everywhere, including Namibia, South Africa, and Zimbabwe.

■ **Best places to see them:** Nairobi NP, Solio Ranch GR, Kenya; Ngorongoro Crater, Tanzania. (Other good possibilities include Kruger NP and Hluhluwe GR, South Africa; Gonarezhou NP and Mana Pools NP, Zimbabwe.)

■ **Active time:** The rhino is most active early and late in the day, but it also moves and feeds at night. Least active during the hottest hours.

ZEBRA

■ **Varieties:** The Grevy's zebra has a distinct pattern of narrow stripes with a bullseye on the rump and wider stripes on the neck and chest. The mountain zebra is distinguished by large ears and a distinctive gridiron pattern on the rump. The plain's zebra is smaller than the Grevy's.

■ **Where they live:** Restricted to the Somali arid zone of Ethiopia, Somalia, and Kenya. The only substantial population (several thousand) lives in Kenya's northern frontier district (Grevy's). Cape mountain zebras inhabit the southwestern and southern Cape Province in South Africa. Hartmann's race, another subspecies of the mountain zebra, are found in southern Angola and Namibia (mountain). Southeastern Sudan to South Africa and west to Angola, in Somali-Masai arid zone (plains).

■ **Best places to see them:** Meru Sibiloi NP and Samburu-Isiolo NR, Kenya (Grevy's). Mountain Zebra NP, South Africa (mountain). Too numerous to list but Etosha NP, Namibia, and Ngorongoro Crater, Tanzania, are some places where one can get very close (plains).

■ **Active time:** Active both day and night. Zebras graze an hour or so at a time at night. In early morning, they begin treks of up to 10 miles before settling again for the night.

WILDLIFE

THE BEAR FACTS ABOUT GRIZZLIES

Here's what to do if you come upon a bear sitting in the woods

You never know where you'll run into one. There are three different kinds of bears roaming the polar regions and North America. Polar bears weigh an average of 1,500 pounds, are excellent swimmers, and eat mostly seals. Concentrations of grizzlies exist in Alaska, Yellowstone National Park, and Glacier National Park. The largest ones, 1,600 pounds and up, live along the Alaskan coast, where they feast on salmon. Black bears, which weigh around 300 pounds, are commonly found in the Alaskan interior as well as elsewhere in the United States.

Grizzlies, especially, don't like to be surprised. Experienced hikers in grizzly country constantly ring bells, sing songs, and generally make as much noise as possible. Black bears are somewhat less dangerous.

"I always tell people if they run into a bear on the trail not to worry too much," says David Graber of the National Biological Service. "Most likely the bear will meander away."

THE ULTIMATE ALASKAN JOURNEY

Chances are you'll only go once, so you won't see it all. We asked Grant Sims, the former editor of Alaska Magazine *and author of* Leaving Alaska, *to pick some destinations not to be missed.*

■ **BROOKS RANGE:** Fly to Bettles, above the Arctic Circle. Much of Alaska is too soggy to hike during the peak travel months of May through September, so the best overland trips combine hiking with rafting or canoeing. The sunny, southern Brooks Range offers gentle terrain and rivers that are tamer than many in other parts of the state. Sourdough Outfitters can get you started, ☎ 907-692-5252.

■ **KACHEMAK BAY:** Hike in the Kenai Mountains, fish in the bay's abundant waters, and birdwatch. The Cook Inlet has the second highest tide in the world. Stay at the beautiful Kachemak Bay Wilderness Lodge, which features the usual stunning views and not-so-usual, delicious gourmet food, ☎ 907-235-8910.

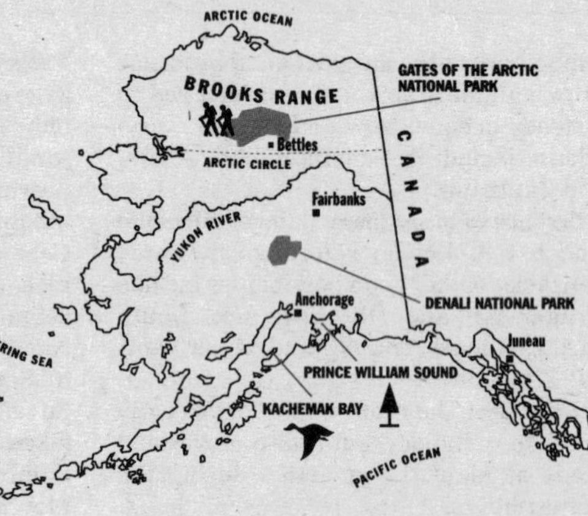

■ **PRINCE WILLIAM SOUND:** The area has almost entirely recovered from the 1989 *Exxon Valdez* disaster. Spend your days touring the sound in a sailboat, whale watching, hiking through old-growth coast rain forests and sea kayaking in glacial bays and fjords. Alaska Wilderness Sailing Safari Outfitters, ☎ 907-835-5679, can make all the arrangements.

For information on other outfitters, hotels, and inns, or an Official State Guide and Vacation Planner, contact the Alaska State Division of Tourism, ☎ 800-862-5275.

Here's some more specific advice from a Denali National Park publication:

■ **Never run:** Bears can run more than 30 mph—faster than an Olympic sprinter. Running can elicit a chase response from otherwise non-aggressive bears.

■ **An unaware bear:** If the bear is unaware of you, move quickly and quietly away from it. Give the bear plenty of room, allowing it to continue its own activities undisturbed.

■ **An aware bear:** If the bear is aware of you, but has not acted aggressively, back away slowly, talking in a calm, firm voice while slowly waving your arms. Bears that stand up on their hind legs are usually trying to identify you and are not threatening.

■ **An approaching bear:** Do not run; do not drop your pack. A pack can help protect your body in case of an attack. To drop your pack may encourage the bear to approach people for food. Bears occasionally make "bluff charges," sometimes coming to within 10 feet of a person before stopping or veering off. Stand still until the bear stops and has moved away, then slowly back off. Climbing trees will not protect you.

■ **If a bear touches you:** If a brown bear does actually make contact with you, curl up in a ball, protecting your stomach and neck, and play dead. If the attack is prolonged, however, change tactics and fight back vigorously. If it is a black bear, do not play dead at all; fight back.

EXPLORING THE LAST FRONTIERS

Walk on glaciers, see the penguins—and don't forget a heavy sweater.

The earth's polar caps are seemingly forbidding expanses of uncharted, pristine land. But there is a way to drink in their icy beauty without suffering the indignities of dog-sledding or snowshoeing: Take a cruise.

Operators now run tours to both poles, usually hiring a naturalist to come along to help tourists identify the myriad wildlife the poles have to offer. Days are spent zooming between glaciers on motorized rubber "Zodiac" rafts observing hundreds of species of birds, penguins (south), polar bears (north), whales, dolphins, and seals. Evenings tend to be devoted to lectures.

The weather isn't as bad as you might think, especially at the South Pole. Ron Naveen, editor of a newsletter about Antarctica and a frequent visitor, says he wears just a heavy sweater most of the summer. Some adventurous travelers have even taken an invigorating, if brief, plunge into the icy waters. But Naveen notes, "The weather is extremely unpredictable and tends to be stormy."

Only specially designed ships make the journey. "Antarctic travel requires extremely heavy boats with ice-breaking capacities," explains Naveen. "These boats require many tons of motor fuel. This is both expensive and, unfortunately, bad for the environment."

The emphasis in polar cruises is more on ruggedness than luxury. The cost, nonetheless, remains high—$5,000 and up for a one-week journey. Naveen says that the growing number of visitors to Antarctica is both a good and a bad thing. "Antarctica is an extremely fragile ecosystem. It is very difficult to visit the area with little or no impact," says Naveen. On the other hand, he adds, "The more people that see the place, the more people that will want to help protect it."

■ **OUTFITTERS TO THE POLES**

Mountain Travel/Sobek	☎ 800-227-2384
Clipper Adventure Cruises	☎ 800-325-0010
Special Expeditions	☎ 800-762-0003
Overseas Adventure Travel	☎ 800-221-0814

ECOTOURISM

HOW GREEN IS YOUR TRIP?

Lots of tours say they're environmentally correct. Not all of them are

The term "ecotour" is about as widely abused as the term "fat-free." Yet the ecotourism industry is exploding as citizens of the world become more environmentally conscious. Indeed, a 1994 *Condé Nast Traveler* survey found that more than 35 million Americans said they were likely to take an ecotour within the next three years. So how do responsible travelers ensure that their tour is environmentally friendly? The following tips are an amalgamation of the advice of environmental travel journalists who have sought to answer just that question.

FACT FILE:

LOVE, ECOSTYLE

■ Ecotraveler Magazine's *favorite spots to protect the earth and get a good start on your marriage—not necessarily in that order:*

- **Harmony Resort, St. John**
- **Seven Spirit Bay, Australia**
- **Inn of the Anasazi, New Mexico**
- **Post Ranch Inn, Big Sur**
- **Lapa Rios, Costa Rica**
- **Point Pleasant Resort, St. Thomas**
- **Sundance, Utah**
- **Moorea Beachcomber Parkroyal, French Polynesia**

WHAT YOU CAN DO

■ Seek a tour that educates: Guides should be knowledgeable about the destination's wildlife and history, and lectures, slide shows, and videos should be an inherent part of the trip.

■ Don't disturb the wildlife: "Take only pictures, and leave only footprints." Remain on marked pathways and be particularly cautious around fragile systems such as coral reefs, mosses, and lichens.

■ Practice low-impact travel: Avoid littering of any kind, and make sure your tour operator has made provisions to carry back garbage generated by the trip.

WHAT TOUR OPERATORS CAN DO

■ Support indigenous peoples: Especially in disadvantaged areas, they should utilize local businesses, employ indigenous peoples, and make financial contributions to local conservation activities.

■ Build in harmony with the land: Hotels and lodges should use local materials to blend with the land around them.

HOME AND AWAY, BOYCOTT THESE

■ **CORAL AND SEA TURTLE PRODUCTS:** Including jewelry, eggs, and skin cream.

■ **MOST REPTILE SKINS:** Particularly those from Latin America, the Caribbean, China, and Egypt.

■ **PRODUCTS MADE OF PANGOLIN:** Pangolin is another word for anteater.

■ **IVORY:** Especially worked ivory from elephants and from marine mammals, such as whales, walruses, and narwhals.

■ **BIRDS:** All live birds, as well as any wild bird feathers and skins used in or as artwork (including mounted birds).

■ **FUR:** Particularly that of spotted cats such as the snow leopard or jaguar.

SOURCE: Endangered products are from *The Audubon Society Travel Ethic For Environmentally Responsible Travel*, National Audubon Society, New York.

CRUISES

FLOATING RESORTS

THE BIGGEST SHIPS ON THE SEA

It doesn't matter where you go when you take your resort with you

The 76,000-ton *Sun Princess* is the newest, biggest cruise ship in the world—10 city blocks long and 11 stories high. It has everything you would find at a good Club Med: six spas, a high-tech fitness center, three swimming pools, five dining areas, a teen center and disco—even a computerized virtual-reality golf center. With these amenities, who cares about the destination?

Apparently nobody. Most of the megaships spend their time island-hopping instead of doing something useful like crossing the Atlantic or discovering new continents. But this hasn't prevented the biggest growth in the cruise business since the golden age of ocean liners more than half a century ago. By 2000, as baby boomers retire and seek out new ways to spend their leisure time, 8 million passengers annually are projected. And the cruise industry is scrambling to build them accommodations.

The *Sun Princess* is expecting a sister soon, and it will be dwarfed in 1997 by a 100,000-ton giant. The Walt Disney Company also is getting into the fray with its own cruise line and two 2,400-passenger vessels. All told, at least 28 ships are scheduled to be launched through 1998—6 or 7 of which will take their place among the world's largest. The boom will add more than 44,000 passenger berths, a 40 percent gain over current capacity.

And the ships won't just be bigger, they'll be better, too. They will answer complaints about cramped '70s-style megaships with larger cabins and fewer passengers—the *Sun Princess* is 7,000 tons larger than the *Norway*, currently the world's second largest ship, but it carries almost 100 fewer passengers. Food and service may vary, but most of the new crop will be equipped with state-of-the-art technology like environmentally friendly waste systems and big brother video surveillance systems to keep an eye on the kids. Entertainment will include Broadway musicals, dancing, lectures—sometimes even art exhibits by first-rate (and often unaffordable) artists like David Hockney and Robert Motherwell.

More affordable will be fares on the older ships, which are expected to remain steady at about $175 to $225 per person per day, including return air fare. The new ships will be big in every way, commanding prices of 25 percent to 30 percent above average.

SAILOR'S GUIDE

HOW THE BIG 10 CRUISE SHIPS STACK UP

Size counts when you're dealing with an ocean. Here are the the biggest of the big, ranked by size, with comments from a variety of guides, travel agents, and the lines themselves:

SUN PRINCESS

Princess Cruise Line

■ **WHO:** 1,950 passengers, mostly singles and young or middle-aged couples. 900 crew.

■ **WHERE:** Winter port in Ft. Lauderdale. Summer port in Vancouver. Seven-day cruises to Caribbean and Alaska.

■ **ON BOARD:** High-tech innovations include a computerized virtual reality golf center, but even basic facilities are impressive.

NORWAY

Norwegian

■ **WHO:** 2,370 passengers, families, older couples, a few singles. 870 crew.

■ **WHERE:** Base port in Miami. Seven-day cruises to the Eastern Caribbean.

■ **ON BOARD:** Once the flagship of France, but recently added cabins are overcrowding public spaces and the food and service are not what they used to be. Still a classic though: Irregular cabins distinguish it from today's look-alikes. Also excellent children's facilities and exciting nightlife.

MAJESTY OF THE SEAS

Royal Caribbean

■ **WHO:** 2,744 passengers, mostly singles and young or middle-aged couples. 822 crew.

■ **WHERE:** Base port in Miami. Seven-day cruises to the Western Caribbean.

■ **ON BOARD:** One of the classier mega-ships with glitzy decor and a swingin' crowd. The "Shipshape" fitness program can help you work off the gourmet meals. Not a good ship for those prone to cabin fever: quarters are small.

MONARCH OF THE SEAS

Royal Caribbean

■ **WHO:** 2,744 passengers, mostly singles and young couples. 822 crew.

■ **WHERE:** Base port in San Juan. Seven-day trips to the Southern Caribbean.

■ BY THE NUMBERS:

A look at how the 10 biggest cruise ships stack up

SHIP	TONNAGE	CABINS	PASSENGERS*	CREW
1. Sun Princess	77,000	1,011	1,950	900
2. Norway	76,049	1,016	2,370	870
3. Majesty of the Seas	73,941	1,177	2,744	822
4. Monarch of the Seas	73,941	1,177	2,744	822
5. Sovereign of the Seas	73,192	1,177	2,744	808
6. Ecstasy	70,367	1,020	2,594	920
7. Fantasy	70,367	1,022	2,364	920
8. Fascination	70,367	1,020	2,040	920
9. Sensation	70,367	792	1,596	678
10. Legend of the Seas	70,000	NA	2,068	732

* Passenger capacity is based on double occupancy.

SOURCE: Individual cruise lines.

■ SAILOR'S GUIDE

■ **ON BOARD:** The ship offers exceptionally smooth sailing. Similar in construction to sister ships *Majesty* and *Sovereign*, but with a better layout of public rooms and an excellent library.

SOVEREIGN OF THE SEAS

Royal Caribbean

■ **WHO:** 2,524 passengers, mostly singles and young or middle-aged couples. 808 crew.

■ **WHERE:** Base port in Miami. Seven-day cruises to the Eastern Caribbean.

■ **ON BOARD:** The older sister ship to *Monarch* and *Majesty*: offers the same festive atmosphere, but with awkward layout that gives an overcrowded feel. Mostly small cabins, except for the 12 penthouse suites on the bridge deck.

ECSTASY

Carnival

■ **WHO:** 2,594 passengers, younger singles with some families. 920 crew.

■ **WHERE:** Base port in Miami, three-day cruises to the Bahamas and four-day cruises from Key West to Cozumel.

■ **ON BOARD:** As with most of the Carnival ships, the food and service on board are average, but the festive atmosphere makes up for it with splashy neon and chrome decorations and big, Broadway-style theatrical productions. The *Ecstasy* also has excellent children's care facilities.

FANTASY

Carnival

■ **WHO:** 2,594 passengers, mostly younger singles. Special attention to newlyweds. 920 crew.

■ **WHERE:** Base port in Port Canaveral, three- to four-day cruises to the Bahamas.

■ **ON BOARD:** Similar to sister-ship *Ecstasy*. Spectacular public areas include the "Cats Lounge" where tables are enclosed in huge cat food containers and "Cleopatra's Bar," with Egyptian mummies.

FASCINATION

Carnival

■ **WHO:** 2,594 passengers, mostly younger singles and younger families. 920 crew.

■ **WHERE:** Base port in San Juan. Seven-day cruises to the lower Caribbean.

■ **ON BOARD:** A Carnival fleet standout. Casino is huge, as are cabins. The theme: Hollywood. Mannequins of movie stars are displayed around the ship.

SENSATION

Carnival

■ **WHO:** 2,594 passengers, mostly younger singles. Special attention to newlyweds. 920 crew.

■ **WHERE:** Base port Miami. Seven-day cruises alternating between Eastern and Western Caribbean.

■ **ON BOARD:** Vegas theme. More elaborate entertainment than most Carnival ships. Also: the Fantasia lounge—black and gold decor featuring stylized lips and eyes in the furnishings.

LEGEND OF THE SEAS

Royal Caribbean

■ **WHO:** 2,068 passengers. 732 crew.

■ **WHERE:** Base port NA, 7- to 10-day cruises to Hawai'i, Alaska, San Juan.

■ **ON BOARD:** The latest addition to the pack. Offers massive, open deck-space including an 18-hole golf course and the solarium—an indoor/outdoor public area that features a swimming pool and whirlpool, elaborate landscaping, and fine dining.

■ **TO BOOK:**

Carnival Cruise Line
Carnival Place
3655 N.W. 87th Ave.
Miami, FL 33178
☎ 800-327-9501

Norwegian Cruise Line
95 Merrick Way
Coral Gables, FL 33134
☎ 800-327-7030

Princess Cruises
10100 Santa Monica Blvd.
Los Angeles, CA 90067
☎ 800-568-3262

Royal Caribbean Cruise Line
1050 Caribbean Way
Miami, FL 33132
☎ 800-327-6700

SIGNING UP

BOOKING PASSAGE MADE EASY

Who to talk to and what to say for big savings on fares

Booking passage on a cruise ship can sometimes be so confusing that if you didn't need a vacation when you started, you will definitely need one by the time you set sail. Some cruise lines don't even book directly, and those that do often neglect to point out ways you can save. Where is a cruiser to turn?

A travel agent can do the job—and can book flights, cars, and hotels as well—but members of the National Association of Cruise Agents or agents affiliated with Cruise Lines International Association have even greater expertise about ships, and often offer discounts that regular travel agents can't.

Some alternatives without the bells and whistles offer even better deals. Cruise discounters aren't the type to sit down with you and help you plan your cruise, but they do offer a wide variety of discounts on a limited number of ships. They are best for repeat cruise customers who know what they want.

Then there are cruise clubs, which are limited to dues-paying members and specialize in large, last-minute discounts. Dues usually range from $20 to $50 annually. Before you join, though, make sure the club really offers the discounts it claims.

No matter who you use to book your cruise, you will be able to get a better deal if you come across as a seasoned sailor who knows the ropes. Here are eight strategies to consider:

■ **BOOK EARLY.** You get a bargain rate—sometimes as much as 50 percent off—and you are first in line to be upgraded to a better cabin.

■ **BOOK OFF-SEASON.** You can get as much as half off if you sail when the crowds don't. Cruises from September until December 14 offer bargain prices as do those sailing during the first three weeks of January. Some deals are available in mid-season from April until July.

■ **JOIN A PAST PASSENGER CLUB.** If you've cruised on the same line before, you could be in line for cruise discounts, free shore expeditions, cabin upgrades, and dinner at the captain's table. Even if your cruise line doesn't have a past passenger club, make sure you inform them you've sailed before. You may get special treatment.

■ **SAIL STANDBY.** If you sail standby, a category A cabin on American Hawaii Cruises is yours for almost half off the brochure price, and they will guarantee your reservation 21 days before departure. Norwegian Cruise Lines' Sea Saver program offers discounts about a month before sailing if space is still available.

■ **LOOK AT TRAVEL MAGAZINES.** They carry ads for cruise discounters in the back. *Cruise* magazine is available at ☎ 800-888-6088.

■ **LOOK FOR SENIOR CITIZEN DISCOUNTS.** The older set often qualify for discounts, especially off-season. For more information, call the American Association for Retired People Travel Service, ☎ 800-421-2255.

■ **BOOK AS A GROUP.** Most ships offer discounts to groups of 10 to 15. And they sometimes throw in a free cabin for the group leader.

■ **BOOK AT THE LAST MINUTE.** If you can't book early, your best bet for getting a bargain is booking late. Choices may be limited, but check with cruise discounters.

■ **KNOW YOUR AGENT.** If you're interested in a particular cruise line, call it and ask for the names of agencies in your area. Agencies that fill ships often get price breaks. East Coast agencies may have better rates on Caribbean cruises; West Coast agencies on Alaska and Pacific cruises.

ON BOARD

CHOOSING THE RIGHT CABIN

You could end up paying a lot for a view of the lifeboats

Nothing can ruin the perfect cruise like lousy quarters. A berth next to the engines, underneath the jogging track, or within earshot of the disco, for instance, can ruin your night if you're a light sleeper. On the other hand, you need not reserve the most deluxe stateroom to rest in comfort. Indeed, cruise brochures can sometimes be misleading. The description of one ship's most expensive cabin promises "three picture windows," but neglects to point out that nearly half of the view is blocked—or that passengers walking by can stare inside. To avoid similar disasters, consider the following when selecting a cabin:

■ **SIZE:** Cabins costing the same can differ in size, particularly on older ships. Cabins midship on older vessels are usually the largest, but ask your travel agent to supply you with the dimensions of several cabins within the class you want. Don't be fooled by the magnified photos in brochures; compare them with the deck plans to get an idea of the actual size.

■ **LOCATION:** On some of the largest ships, the cabins can be quite a distance from the

EXPERT PICKS

MY FAVORITE CABINS, SHIP BY SHIP

The author of Water Trips *and other travel books, Ted Scull has logged over 870 nights on ships. Here are some of his favorites:*

THE CANBERRA
P&O Cruises
■ Features the rare single cabin. Cheaper than a double, you avoid the surcharge of a single passenger in a double cabin. These splendid cabins have handsome, solid wood furniture and beautiful trim. They cost $200 to $300 per person per day. Book via Golden Bear Travel.
☎ **800-451-8572**

THE DELTA QUEEN
Delta Queen Steamboat Co.
■ The outside deluxe cabins on the sun deck of this Mississippi steamboat built in 1926 have brass beds, sofas, shuttered windows, and stained glass on the tops of the windows. Your private deck chair sits outside your door—"It's like having a cabin at the beach," says Scull. Cabins cost $350 to $500 per person per day.
☎ **800-543-1949**

QUEEN ELIZABETH II
Cunard Lines
■ Cabins B1 and B2 are the best kind of traditional cabin—spacious wood-paneled rooms with hallways, separate trunk rooms, and elliptical portholes. A perk: access to Queen's Grill restaurant, the highest-rated restaurant on the ship. Cabins cost $550 to $800 per person per day.
☎ **800-221-4770**

THE ROTTERDAM
Holland America
■ The deluxe outside cabins have original wood trim, batik bedspreads and matching curtains. A good value: cabins cost $350 to $500 per person per day.
☎ **800-426-0327**

DECK BY DECK

Your cabin's location can have a profound effect on your enjoyment of a cruise. The higher you go, for example, the more likely you are to suffer the ill effects of the ship's pitching and rolling. On the other hand, if you are too close to the night life, you might not get much sleep. No two ships are alike, but here is what you generally can expect on various decks.

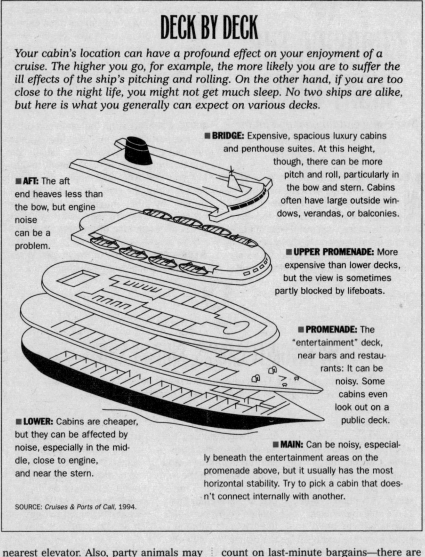

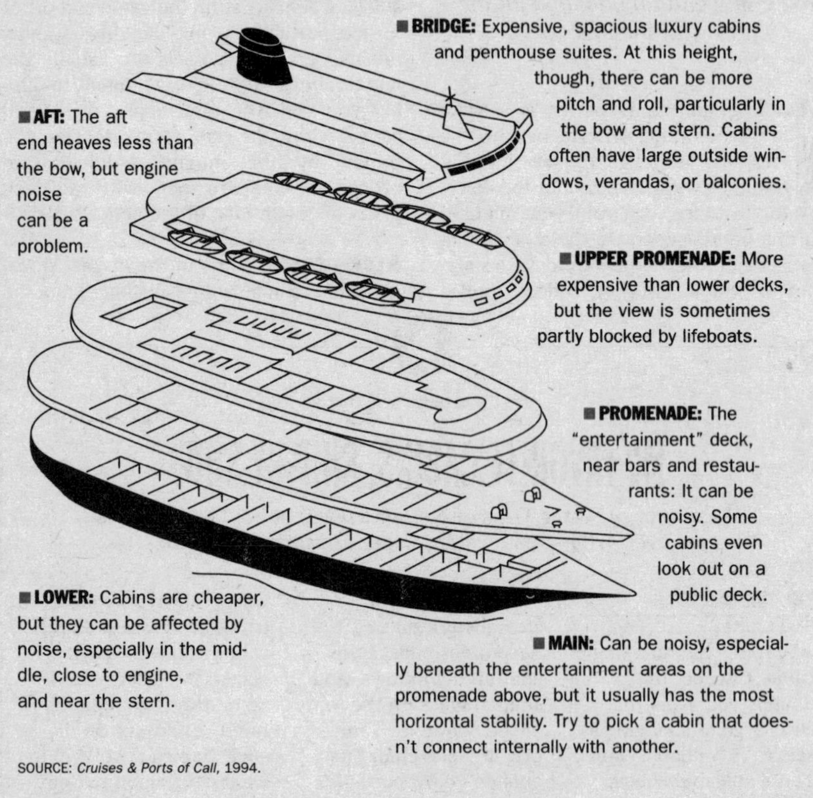

■ **BRIDGE:** Expensive, spacious luxury cabins and penthouse suites. At this height, though, there can be more pitch and roll, particularly in the bow and stern. Cabins often have large outside windows, verandas, or balconies.

■ **AFT:** The aft end heaves less than the bow, but engine noise can be a problem.

■ **UPPER PROMENADE:** More expensive than lower decks, but the view is sometimes partly blocked by lifeboats.

■ **PROMENADE:** The "entertainment" deck, near bars and restaurants: It can be noisy. Some cabins even look out on a public deck.

■ **LOWER:** Cabins are cheaper, but they can be affected by noise, especially in the middle, close to engine, and near the stern.

■ **MAIN:** Can be noisy, especially beneath the entertainment areas on the promenade above, but it usually has the most horizontal stability. Try to pick a cabin that doesn't connect internally with another.

SOURCE: *Cruises & Ports of Call,* 1994.

nearest elevator. Also, party animals may want to be close to the disco, but party poopers will want to avoid it and other clearly noisy night spots. Study the deck plan carefully before choosing.

■ **PRICE:** Booking far in advance also puts you in line for an upgrade if an unsold higher-priced cabin becomes available at the price you paid. (Make sure your travel agent has you on the upgrade list.) Don't count on last-minute bargains—there are fewer of them than there used to be.

■ **BARGAIN CABINS:** Outside cabins with views that are blocked by lifeboats or other obstructions often are discounted. Cabins that accommodate four people are, of course, cheaper per person than the standard room. Also, if you don't intend to spend much time in your cabin, consider one with no view at all.

FAMILY TRAVEL

CRUISING WITH THE KIDS

Some ships are theme parks that cater to children of all ages

There have always been reasons to take kids on a cruise, of course. Exotic new ports daily will intrigue children with even the shortest of attention spans, and such exposure can be an educational introduction to new cultures. But cruise lines seeking boomer business have been upping the family ante in the last few years with a whole new slew of services that roll summer camp, theme park, and sophisticated island resort into one package—and then sweetening the pot with third- and fourth-person discount rates for families on a budget.

A typical approach is that of Premier's "Big Red Boat," otherwise known as the *Starship Atlantic*. There's batting practice on the sports deck, games and crafts at the children's center, a ping-pong tournament, karaoke singing, and even rehearsals for children's theater productions at the Premier theater. And, in keeping with the theme-park theme, crew members dress as Loony Tunes characters.

Spending your vacation with Bugs Bunny or Tweety Bird probably isn't your idea of a good time, so the ship also offers dawn-to-dusk baby-sitting service and the usual cruise activities for adults. Everyone has a good time, and parents can rest assured that it is exceedingly difficult to lose a child on a cruise ship.

Of course, some ships would rather the kids did get lost, or at least were kept quiet. Even some ships that do welcome children are not as well prepared to deal with their needs as others—the playroom may be no more than a corner in a public area with a few toys and children's programs may be offered only in the summer, if at all. When you book a cruise, always ask what their child policy is.

Among the mega-cruisers that welcome children, Norwegian's *Norway*, Carnival's *Fantasy*, and Royal Caribbean's *Legend of the Seas* stand out for their facilities for kids. If a classic cruise is more your style, try the *Queen Elizabeth II*. It offers the best of both worlds: first-class dining and entertainment for mom and dad, and top-notch care by English nannies (of course) for the kids. Other first-rate family ships are listed in "Where the Kids Are All Right," below.

FAMILY CRUISER'S GUIDE

WHERE THE KIDS ARE ALL RIGHT

Here we list some favorite cruise ships for families. All offer year-round activities and most have baby-sitting available on a regular basis.

STARSHIP ATLANTIC

Premier

■ **WHO:** 1,600 passengers, mostly families. 550 crew.
■ **WHERE:** Base port in Port Canaveral. Mostly three- to four-day cruises to the Bahamas.
■ **ON BOARD:** Spacious public areas and roomy cabins (some accommodate up to four people). Largest recreation center in the industry: "Pluto's Playhouse." Activities from 9 a.m. to 9:30 p.m. with group baby-sitting from 9:30 p.m. to 1 a.m. Separate price scale for single parents.

MV ROYAL MAJESTY

Majesty

■ **WHO:** 1,501 passengers, mixed. 525 crew.
■ **WHERE:** Base port in

■ FAMILY CRUISER'S GUIDE

Miami. Three- to four-day cruises to the Bahamas and Boston–St. George's, Bermuda.

■ **ON BOARD:** No glitz here. Teak and brass accents, tasteful furnishings. Superb children's program covers ages 2 to 12 and includes autograph hunts, movies, slumber parties, and dance lessons. No teen program. One drawback: small cabins.

SEA BREEZE

Dolphin

■ **WHO:** 1,250 passengers, good mix of singles, couples, and families. 410 crew.

■ **WHERE:** Base port in Miami. One-week cruises to Eastern and Western Caribbean.

■ **ON BOARD:** A more intimate ship. Public space can be crowded, but the cabins are comfortable and spacious. Children's programs (geared to ages 2 to 12, no teen programs) focus on learning, with lessons in ship navigation, marine life, and the various ports of call.

UNIVERSE

World Explorer

■ **WHO:** 550 passengers, many retired professionals and families. 200 crew.

■ **WHERE:** Base port in Vancouver. Two-week cruises around Alaska.

■ **ON BOARD:** Cultured, tasteful entertainment and wide variety of educational lectures. The *Universe* also boasts the largest library afloat, over 12,000 volumes. Ship's personnel make it clear they do not take primary responsibility for children. There is a drop-off children's center, but no baby-sitting or off-ship supervision.

FAIRSTAR

P&O Holidays

■ **WHO:** 1,598 passengers, mostly Australian and British passengers, many families. 460 crew.

■ **WHERE:** Base port in Sydney, Australia. Cruises of different lengths around the South Pacific.

■ **ON BOARD:** A little crowded at full capacity. The decor is pleasant, if unremarkable, but that doesn't detract from festive atmosphere. The big draw is exotic ports: Bali, the Whitsunday Islands in Queensland, and the Samari Islands in Papua, New Guinea. Kids will love the newness of it all, and the children's program is excellent.

INDEPENDENCE

American Hawaii

■ **WHO:** 798 passengers, varied, with many families. 350 crew.

■ **WHERE:** Base port in Honolulu. One-week trips through Hawai'ian Islands.

■ **ON BOARD:** The atmosphere is casual: not a lot of boisterous partying here. The cabins are showing signs of age but are comfortable and spacious. Activities exclusively for kids include hula dancing lessons, lei making, and lessons in playing the ukulele. There is also a special Hawai'ian teacher called a Kumu to teach Hawai'ian history and music.

■ TO BOOK:

Premier Cruise Line
PO Box 573
Cape Canaveral, FL 32920
☎ 800-327-7113

Majesty Cruise Line
901 South America Way
Miami, FL 33132
☎ 800-532-7788

World Explorer Cruises
555 Montgomery,
Suite 1400
San Francisco, CA 94111
☎ 800-854-3835

P & O Holidays
Book via International
Cruise Connection
☎ 800-433-8747

American Hawaii Cruises
Two North Riverside Plaza,
Suite 200
Chicago, IL 60606
☎ 800-765-7000

Dolphin Cruise Line
901 South America Way
Miami, FL 33132
☎ 800-222-1003

EDUCATIONAL TRAVEL

MIND-EXPANDING VOYAGES

Journey to the ends of the earth and to the center of the mind

"Broad, wholesome, charitable views of men and things cannot be acquired by vegetating in one little corner of the earth all one's lifetime."

—Mark Twain, *The Innocents Abroad*

Twain's words are the credo of a rapidly expanding niche of the cruise business that caters to those seeking adventure, education, and comfort in equal measures. Instead of long, boozy nights at the gambling tables of the *Love Boat*, these travelers traipse through the ancient ruins of Pompeii or encounter primitive Indonesian tribes.

Educational cruise ships are usually smaller than the mega-ships used for ordinary cruises. Some carry 50 passengers or fewer. They generally have shallower drafts that enable them to anchor in ports that cannot accommodate bigger vessels. And on many trips, smaller specialized landing boats are taken along to carry travelers to more remote locations. On a New York Botanical Gardens–sponsored trip down the Amazon River in Brazil, for example, voyagers spend four to six hours a day exploring the shorelines in motorized canoes. Accommodations may not be luxurious, but most ships are perfectly comfortable.

Only the most adventurous travelers would venture unaccompanied to many of these destinations. Take heart: University professors and other experts lecture nightly onboard most cruises.

"What makes an educational cruise really interesting and exciting is gaining access to culture and places that would otherwise be quite inaccessible," explains Terry Shaller, the director of Harvard Alumni Travel.

With the guidance of an expert, educational cruises allow passengers to retrace the Mediterranean voyage of Odysseus, follow the Nile, explore Antarctica, and visit some of the primitive island cultures of the South Pacific. Many colleges and universities now sponsor trips for alumni and various museums, organizations, and environmental groups have teamed up with cruise lines and travel agencies to offer trips to exotic locations.

There are so many choices, in fact, that you will need to do your homework to match the right destination to the right cruise line. One factor to consider: the lecturer who's coming along with you. Like college tuition, passage isn't cheap. Costs range from $250 to $500 per person per day. You can save by skipping alumni- or museum-sponsored trips and booking directly through an educational cruise company. Alumni associations often provide world-renowned members of their university's own faculty for the cruises, but the cruise companies through which the museum or alumni association trip has been chartered often have their own knowledgeable experts for much less.

Following are some of the more popular trips offered today by leading outfitters. To get you into the spirit of the journey, we've also included a list of recommended reading.

THE VOYAGE OF ODYSSEUS

Recreate the ancient sailor's struggle against the plans of Zeus with a voyage (sans sea monsters) around the Mediterranean. Begin at an excavation site in Turkey believed to be where the ancient city of Troy was located, then travel on to Malta, Pompeii, and Tunisia. Though you most likely won't be seduced by the goddess Calypso, you will be transfixed by the beauty of this ancient sea.

- **WHEN:** April to December.
- **WHO:** Classical Cruises, Swan Hellenic.
- **RECOMMENDED READING:** *The Odyssey*, Homer; *Gods, Graves and Scholars*, C. W. Ceram, Vintage, 1986, $10; *The Spirit of Mediterranean Places*, Michel Butor, Marlboro Press, 1987, $9.

THE NILE: CRADLE OF CIVILIZATION

Cruise the 600 miles from Cairo to Aswan and see the famous step pyramid of Djoser at Sakkara, the temple at Luxor, the botanical gardens on Kitchener Island, and the Temple of Horus—the best-preserved temple in Egypt.

■ **WHEN:** Avoid the scorching summer season and March and April sandstorms.
■ **WHO:** Swan Hellenic.
■ **RECOMMENDED READING:** *The Rediscovery of Ancient Egypt*, Peter A. Clayton, Thames & Hudson, 1983, $15.99; *Egypt in Late Antiquity*, Roger S. Bagnall, Princeton, 1983, $29.95.

A CRUSADE THROUGH THE DARK AGES

Cruise up the Rhine, Main, and Danube Canal to visit the perfectly preserved medieval town of Rothenburg-ob-der-Tauber. Stop at Duernstein to see a Benedictine abbey, then on to Vienna, Bratislava, and Budapest. Don't miss the thousand-year-old cathedral city of Bamberg on the Regnitz River.

■ **WHEN:** Avoid the crowded summer and winter tourist seasons.
■ **WHO:** Classical Cruises, Swan Hellenic.
■ **RECOMMENDED READING:** *The Danube*, Claudio Magris, Farrar & Straus, 1989, $11.95; *The Viennese: Splendor, Twilight, and Exile*, Paul Hofmann, Doubleday, 1988, $12.95.

THE UNSPOILED WILD OF THE NORTHWEST

Follow the Strait of Georgia from Vancouver up the coast of British Columbia to historic Wrangell and on to Juneau (accessible only by sea or air). Don't miss Haines, which has the world's largest concentration of bald eagles, or Glacier Bay, with its breathtaking fjords. Last stop: Victoria, the "City of Gardens."

■ **WHEN:** June to September.
■ **WHO:** Special Expeditions, World Explorer, Clipper Cruises.
■ **RECOMMENDED READING:** *Alaska*, James A. Michener, Random House, 1988, $6.99; *A Naturalist's Guide to the Arctic*, E. C. Pielou, U. of Chicago, 1994, $19.95.

WHALE-WATCHING OFF THE BAJA STRIP

Sailing along the Baja peninsula off California and Mexico offers an opportunity to see dolphins, sea lions, and finback and blue whales. You can sometimes get close enough to whales to touch them. Strap on a mask and snorkel for an up-close look at the wildlife and beautiful coral reefs.

■ **WHEN:** January through April.
■ **WHO:** Special Expeditions.
■ **RECOMMENDED READING:** *Log from the Sea of Cortez*, John Steinbeck, Penguin Books, 1977, $7; *The Forgotten Peninsula*, Joseph Wood Krutch, U. of Arizona Press, 1986, $12.95.

THE EVER-EVOLVING GALAPAGOS ISLANDS

Just off the coast of Ecuador are the islands where Charles Darwin did his ground-breaking studies in the nature of evolution. Here's a great chance to observe the fauna that inspired him; many of the island's animals will let you walk right up to them.

■ **WHEN:** Any time.
■ **WHO:** Adventure Associates.
■ **RECOMMENDED READING:** *Voyage of the Beagle*, Charles Darwin, Penguin, $9.95; *The Beak of the Finch*, Jonathan Weiner, Random House, 1994, $25.

THE DRAGONS OF INDONESIA

Cruise to the Indonesian isles of Bali, Komodo, and the lesser Sundas. Stops include visits to the palace of the Sultan in Rabu Dompu. During an afternoon on the Komodo islands, you will probably encounter a 10-foot long Komodo dragon, the last of the prehistoric giant monitor lizards. And on the island of Sumbwa, the Duo Donnggo people continue to live as their ancestors did more than a thousand years ago.

■ **WHEN:** March through October.
■ **WHO:** Abercrombie & Kent.
■ **RECOMMENDED READING:** *South Pacific Handbook*, David Stanley, Moon, 1993, $19.95; *Indonesia: Paradise on the Equator*, Kal Muller and Paul Zach, St. Martin's Press, 1988, $35.

EXPERT SOURCES

WHO WILL GUIDE YOU ACROSS THE SEA?

These well-regarded cruise companies get high marks from travelers and sponsor some of the educational cruises described on these pages

ABERCROMBIE & KENT INTERNATIONAL
1520 Kensington Rd.
Oak Brook, IL 60521
■ One of the posher outfits. Year-round cruises to the Indonesian Spice Islands, the Nile, and Antarctica. They cruise elsewhere, but without the educational bent.
☎ **800-323-7308**

ADVENTURE ASSOCIATES
13150 Colt Rd., Suite 110
Dallas, TX 75240
■ Year-round cruises to the Galapagos and the rivers of Ecuador on vessels, from small yachts to larger 110-person ships. Aboard are scientists and botanists who specialize in unique ecosystems.
☎ **800-527-2500**

CLASSICAL CRUISES
132 East 70th St.
New York, NY 10021
■ Features big name professors like Harvard's Emily Vermeule. Some ships are too big to provide access to remote locations and intimate conversation. Otherwise first-rate, especially for Mediterranean programs.
☎ **800-252-7745**

SPECIAL EXPEDITIONS
720 Fifth Avenue
New York, NY 10019
■ Specializes in natural history trips. Two flat-hulled boats (capacity: 110 each) ply the Alaskan coast in the summer and Baja California in the winter.
☎ **800-762-0003**

SWAN HELLENIC CRUISES
c/o Esplanade Tours
581 Boylston St.
Boston, MA 02116
■ One of the pioneers of educational cruising, this British company offers educational cruises along the Danube, Mosel, and Rhine. Also famous for their Mediterranean and Nile cruises.
☎ **800-426-5492**

WORLD EXPLORER CRUISES
555 Montgomery St.
Suite 1400
San Francisco, CA 94111
■ Their 550-passenger *Universe* is bigger than most educational cruise ships, and at a good price to boot. Summer cruises to Alaska.
☎ **800-854-3835**

THE SACRED CITIES OF SOUTHEAST ASIA

Journey down the Mekong River past the ruins of Angkor, the temples of Borobudu, and on to the island of Bali. An unusual experience for Western travelers, but it doesn't have to be an apocalypse or journey into the heart of darkness if it is planned properly.

■ **WHEN:** January and February.
■ **WHO:** Classical Cruises.
■ **RECOMMENDED READING:** *Southeast Asia: Past and Present,* D. R. Sardesai, Westview, 1994, $24.95.

OFF TO ANTARCTICA

Cruise from the Argentine coast down to the final frontier at the bottom of the world: Antarctica. Try to score a cruise with Sir Ranulph Fiennes, one of the world's great explorers and an authority on the area. Look for whales, sea elephants, penguins, and fur seals along the way.

■ **WHEN:** November to February.
■ **WHO:** Abercrombie & Kent.
■ **RECOMMENDED READING:** *The Epic Crossing of the Antarctic Continent,* Ranulph Fiennes, Delacorte Press, 1994, $21.95.

EXPERT SOURCES

GETTING TO KNOW WHERE THE CRUISE SHIPS GO

A few of our favorite guides to seafaring trips:

GENERAL CRUISING

BERLITZ COMPLETE GUIDE TO CRUISING AND CRUISE SHIPS
Douglas Ward, Macmillan & Sons, 1994, $17.95
■ One of the best, with overview of cruising history and a comprehensive evaluation of most ships plying the world's seas and rivers based on 400 individual factors. Stuffed with every cruising statistic that one could ever want.

THE TOTAL TRAVELER BY SHIP
Ethel Blum, Graphic Arts Center, 1993, $16.95
■ Lots of personal observations by Blum. Not nearly as detailed as Berlitz, but gives a sense of life aboard most of the major ships with a personal touch that many of the other guides lack.

CONSUMER REPORTS TRAVEL BUYING GUIDE
Ed Perkins, ed., Consumers Union, 1994, $8.95
■ A great source that includes a useful overview of how to get good deals on cruises and an extensive list of cruise discounters and cruise clubs.

FODOR'S CRUISES AND PORTS OF CALL
Daniel and Sally Grotta, Fodor's Travel Publications, Inc., 1993, $18
■ A lively guide to many of the major cruise ships. Easy to use, informative about the different destinations, and a good source for descriptions of the different ship's facilities.

FIELDING'S CRUISES
Antoinette Deland and Anne Campbell, Fielding Worldwide, Inc., 1994, $16.95
■ The next best guide after Berlitz. A highly readable book with personal observations by some real cruise pros who tell it like they see it. Includes extensive descriptions of the various cruise ship destinations available.

FAMILY TRAVEL

SUPER FAMILY VACATIONS
Martha Shirk and Nancy Kleeper, Harper Perennial, 1992, $14
■ Cruising is just one of the family vacations covered in this well-written and highly informative book by an award-winning reporter for the St. Louis *Post-Dispatch*.

FAMILY TRAVEL TIMES
$12 per issue, $40 per year (4 issues)
■ Information about family travel that includes much about cruises. The publisher, Travel with Your Children, also publishes *Cruising with Children* ($22, or $14 with subscription), which provides answers to just about any question you could dream of regarding children and cruising.
☎ **212-206-0688**

EDUCATIONAL TRAVEL

THE EDUCATED TRAVELER
$39 per year (6 issues)
■ This 10-page newsletter offers advice for the adventurous traveler. In a recent issue: submarine cruises. Includes a directory of museum-sponsored trips.
☎ **800-648-5168**

THE GUIDE TO ACADEMIC TRAVEL
Shaw Guides, 1992, $16.95
■ Extensive listings of educational tours and adult learning and language vacations that are sponsored by various universities and cultural organizations.
☎ **800-247-6553**

CHAPTER EIGHT

SPORTS

"[*Cobb*] is the most arresting book-length portrait of a baseball person I've ever read."

—Roger Kahn, author and baseball aficionado.

Page 593

"This game is so much in the mind. What you believe will work for you will work."

—Frank Thomas, technical director of the United States Golf Association

Page 617

"One of the most common errors is buying a bike that is too large."

—Geoff Drake, editor of *Bicycling Magazine*

Page 630

THE YEAR AHEAD: BET that baseball fans will still be stewing about the strike... **WELCOME** the football Rams to St. Louis and the Raiders back to Oakland... **CHEER** for two new basketball franchises in Toronto and Vancouver... **ANTICIPATE** that American women athletes will shine at the Olympics... **EXPECT** the U.S. to win more medals than any other country for the first time since 1968... **LOOK** for new golf clubs to rival Big Bertha... **PEDAL** a mountain bike down a ski slope... **TRY** kite buggying—if you dare...

A FAN'S GUIDE

TAKE ME OUT TO THE BALL GAME

Where to sit, where to park, and what to eat at major league parks

A hot summer Sunday afternoon, the sun blazing overhead, and you're at the game watching your favorite team. Of course, you can still get peanuts and popcorn, and there's beer. But why not try the barbecued ribs, the kielbasa, or the sushi. Here's an insider's guide to all of America's major league ball parks—with tips about where to sit, where to park, and what to eat. And, oh yes, some stats about your favorite team.

AMERICAN LEAGUE EAST

BALTIMORE ORIOLES

Last World Series title: 1983. Last League title: 1983. Last Division title: 1983.

■ **ORIOLE PARK AT CAMDEN YARDS:** 48,079 capacity, grass surface, built in 1992. Modern amenities with old-time charm.

■ **FAN NOTES:** Arrive at least 45 minutes early to get one of the stadium's 5,000 parking spots. Although many players have tried to reach the B&O Warehouse over the right field fence, only Ken Griffey, Jr. has during a home run hitting contest. Former O's first baseman Boog Powell operates a wildly successful barbecue stand inside the stadium, near the Eutaw Street entrance. ☎ **410-685-9500**

BOSTON RED SOX

Last World Series title: 1918. Last League title: 1986. Last Division title: 1990.

■ **FENWAY PARK:** 33,871 capacity, grass surface, built in 1912. A baseball classic.

■ **FAN NOTES:** Avoid pole seats. Otherwise, virtually all seats in the grandstand are good. Best bleacher seat: the red one in row 33, where Ted Williams's 502-foot homer landed in 1946. Fenway franks are a legend, but more for tradition than taste. Don't wear a Yankees shirt. Sections 32 and 33 are no-drinking and no-smoking. The screen behind home plate to protect fans was the first of its kind. ☎ **617-267-8661**

DETROIT TIGERS

Last World Series title: 1984. Last League title: 1984. Last Division title: 1987.

■ **TIGER STADIUM:** 52,416 capacity, grass surface, built in 1912. Surely on its last legs.

■ **FAN NOTES:** No on-site parking. However, there are several cheap parking lots nearby. Seating is closer to the playing field than in any other park. Only stadium in the majors with double-decker bleachers. 125-foot-high flagpole in deep center field is the highest outfield obstacle in play in major

YOU MAKE THE CALL

Doug Harvey, an umpire for 47 years, 20 of them in the majors, has seen it all. Here, Harvey explains some commonly misunderstood rules.

■ **BALK:** The most recent rule requires the pitcher to come to a complete stop with his hands in front of him before throwing the pitch. Once the pitcher has his hands together in front of him he has to either throw or step off the rubber—he can't wind up again.

■ **INFIELD FLY:** The rule prevents the infielder from making a cheap double play. Applied when there are men on first and second or first, second, and third and there are fewer than two outs. The batter hits a fly ball that an infielder can catch with "normal effort." The umpire can call the batter out even before the ball is caught or hits the ground.

■ **INTERFERENCE:** When the offense interferes with a defensive play. For example, a runner interferes with the fielder catching a ball. The penalty is an automatic out.

■ **OBSTRUCTION:** When the defense impedes the progress of the offense around the bases—the second baseman can stand in front of a runner and not even touch him and it's still interference. This rule is only enforced if the runner fails to attain his base because of the obstruction. The penalty is the award of a base by the umpire.

■ **FAIR/FOUL BALL:** A ground ball must pass inside the foul line when it passes the bases. It can then pass into foul territory and still be fair. With fly balls, if the ball is caught while in fair territory but the fielder reaches into foul territory to catch it, it is foul. If the fielder is in foul territory and reaches into fair territory to catch the ball, then the ball is fair.

league history. Sign above visitors' clubhouse reads "Visitors' Clubhouse—No Visitors Allowed." Second-to-last stadium to have lights. ☎ **313-962-4000**

NEW YORK YANKEES

Last World Series title: 1978. Last League title: 1981. Last Division title: 1981.

■ **YANKEE STADIUM:** 57,545 capacity, grass surface, built in 1923. It may be the "House that Ruth Built," but George Steinbrenner, the team's current owner—to say nothing of George Castanza of the TV hit *Seinfeld*—wants one *he* built.

■ **FAN NOTES:** Parking around the stadium is difficult. Second and third decks were added to left-center in the winter of 1927. The food court on the lower level is the best. Stadium monuments and plaques commemorate, among others, Joe DiMaggio, Lou Gehrig, Babe Ruth, Pope Paul VI (for his 1965 visit), and Pope John Paul II (who visited in 1979). ☎ **718-293-6000**

TORONTO BLUE JAYS

Last World Series title: 1993. Last League title: 1993. Last Division title: 1993.

■ **SKYDOME:** 50,516 capacity, artificial surface, built 1989. The best of the domes.

■ **FAN NOTES:** The parking is expensive and the tickets are difficult to get. To avoid a long wait on the phone, write for tickets several weeks in advance. Or try the ticket window at Gate 9 on game days. The 200-level seats are probably the best. Avoid those in the 500 level, which can be dizzying. Home of North America's largest McDonald's. ☎ **416-341-1111**

AMERICAN LEAGUE CENTRAL

CHICAGO WHITE SOX

Last World Series title: 1917. Last League title: 1959. Last Division title: 1993.

■ **COMISKEY PARK:** 44,321 capacity, grass surface, built in 1991. A nice, new place, but not as charming as the old place.

■ **FAN NOTES:** Located in a residential neighborhood, so parking is difficult. Wind shifts wreak havoc with the ball, benefiting hitters. All seats are half-price for Monday games. The same architects also designed new stadiums in Baltimore, Cleveland, and Denver. Dirt from the original Comiskey field was recycled here. ☎ **312-924-1000**

CLEVELAND INDIANS

Last World Series title: 1948. Last League title: 1954. Never won a Division title.

■ **JACOBS FIELD:** 42,400 capacity, grass surface, built in 1994. Modern and cozy. Shows off Cleveland's skyline.

■ **FAN NOTES:** Located in one of the poorer areas of the city, the new park has contributed to the revitalization of downtown. Difficult stadium in which to hit doubles. Offers 75 different foods (hence the wider than normal seats), including deli, baked goods, and a new southwestern menu. Kidsland, an area for youngsters, is in the lower deck in right field.
☎ **216-241-5555**

FACT FILE:

STADIUM FARE: BUY ME SOME SUSHI AND EVIAN

■ *Red hots and cold beer still reign supreme at baseball games, but some fans have moved on:*

■ **BALTIMORE:** *Crab cakes and baseball's only Kosher stand.*
■ **COLORADO:** *"Organic" franks.*
■ **FLORIDA:** *Empanadas and Cuban sandwiches.*
■ **LOS ANGELES:** *Sushi.*
■ **MONTREAL:** *Kojax Souvlaki.*
■ **MILWAUKEE:** *Bratwurst.*
■ **OAKLAND:** *Caesar salad with garlic breadsticks.*
■ **ST. LOUIS:** *Toasted ravioli.*
■ **SAN DIEGO:** *Fish tacos.*
■ **SAN FRANCISCO:** *Chinese chicken salad and black bean chili.*

KANSAS CITY ROYALS

Last World Series title: 1985. Last League title: 1985. Last Division title: 1985.

■ **KAUFFMAN STADIUM:** 40,625 capacity, grass surface, built in 1973. Always a good stadium, now even better with grass.

■ **FAN NOTES:** More than enough parking. No bad seats in the house. Half-price reserved seats on Mondays and Thursdays. Waterfalls and fountains run for 322 feet on the embankment overlooking right-center. The Boja, the 125-tree forest, lies beyond the left-center fence. Best visibility for hitters in the majors. ☎ **816-921-8000**

MILWAUKEE BREWERS

Never won a World Series. Last League title: 1982. Last Division title: 1982.

■ **COUNTY STADIUM:** 53,192 capacity, grass surface, built in 1953. It's showing its age.

■ **FAN NOTES:** Plenty of cheap parking. World-class tailgating parties. Bratwurst's secret sauce is so popular, it's sold in local grocery stores. The worst seats are the four or five rows at the back of the first deck. Jose Canseco is the only player to have hit a home run over the left field roof. Mascot Bernie Brewer slides into a huge beer stein for every home team homer. ☎ **414-933-1818**

MINNESOTA TWINS

Last World Series title: 1991. Last League title: 1991. Last Division title: 1991.

■ **HUBERT H. HUMPHREY METRODOME:** 56,783 capacity, artificial surface, built in 1982. Very loud, but keeps out the cold weather.

■ **FAN NOTES:** Arrive early and park on the street using eight-hour meters. Power hitter's park. Violent rainstorms on April 27, 1986 caused the scoreboard and roof to sway. On May 4, 1984 Dave Kingman hit a ball through the roof. More home runs tend to be hit when the air-conditioning is turned off. ☎ **612-375-7444**

AMERICAN LEAGUE WEST

CALIFORNIA ANGELS

Never won a World Series or League title. Last Division title: 1986.

ANAHEIM STADIUM: 64,593 capacity, grass surface, built in 1966. It's not the prettiest thing in Southern California.

■ **FAN NOTES:** Even at sellouts parking lots are rarely full. Scalping laws are strictly enforced. Replaced an orange and eucalyptus tree farm. Considered a power hitter's park. ☎ **714-634-2000**

OAKLAND ATHLETICS

Last World Series title: 1989. Last League title: 1990. Last Division title: 1992.

■ **OAKLAND–ALAMEDA COUNTY STADIUM:** 47,313 capacity, grass surface, built in 1966. Neither offensive nor delightful.

■ **FAN NOTES:** Try to arrive at least half an hour before the game to get a parking spot. Good sightlines from just about every seat. Tickets are available on a walk-up basis for most games. Arguably the best grass in baseball. Possible to watch game for free from concourse behind the field seats by looking between wooden slats on cyclone fence. Large foul territory makes this the best pitcher's park. ☎ **510-638-0500**

SEATTLE MARINERS

Never won a World Series, League, or Division title.

■ **KINGDOME:** 59,702 capacity, artificial surface, built in 1976. Not even the weather outside could be this dreary. Dark and cavelike.

■ **FAN NOTES:** Although there are few parking spots, there are also few fans. Every Sunday home game is seniors' day—fans over 62 can buy two tickets for the price of one. In the summer of 1994, parts of the roofing tiles fell on the playing surface, closing the stadium for the season. Only stadium to have Funny Nose–Eye Glasses night. Seven fair balls have bounced off speakers and remained in play. Four batted balls hit off speakers and were caught for outs. ☎ **206-628-3555**

TEXAS RANGERS

Never won a World Series, League, or Division title.

■ **THE BALLPARK IN ARLINGTON:** 48,100 capacity, grass surface, built in 1994. May be the best of the new parks.

■ **FAN NOTES:** Parking is easy. The benches from the old Arlington Stadium were removed and placed in the bleachers. Check out the Walk of Fame on your way into the stadium. You can eat and watch the game from TGI Friday's, located behind the upper home run porch in right field. With the right-field foul pole only 325 feet from home plate and the fence only 8 feet high, it pays to be a lefty. ☎ **817-273-5222**

NATIONAL LEAGUE EAST

ATLANTA BRAVES

Last World Series title: 1957 (as Milwaukee Braves). Last League title: 1992. Last Division title: 1993.

■ **ATLANTA–FULTON COUNTY STADIUM:** 52,709 capacity, grass surface, built in 1965. Braves will move to Atlanta Centennial Olympic Stadium after the '96 Summer Games.

■ **FAN NOTES:** The stadium is on its last legs. Field level offers the best chance to catch fouls. The new stadium will seat 45,000 to 47,000, with seating concentrated on the infield. ☎ **404-683-6100**

FLORIDA MARLINS

Never won a World Series, League, or Division title.

■ **JOE ROBBIE STADIUM:** 47,662 capacity, grass surface, built in 1987. With the Miami heat, the Marlins should be playing in a dome.

■ **FAN NOTES:** Parking is no problem; the lot was built to handle 70,000 football fans. Spectators can purchase tickets for future games through ticket vendors roaming the stadium. Sightlines from the lower-level seats between the infield edge and the foul poles present a problem. Many Latin-oriented dishes. Sections 134 and 403 are designated no-alcohol, no-smoking, family sections. ☎ **305-626-7400**

MONTREAL EXPOS

Never won a World Series or League title. Last Division title: 1981.

■ **OLYMPIC STADIUM:** 46,500 capacity, artificial surface, built in 1976. The place is literally falling apart. Originally built for track and field.

■ **FAN NOTES:** Has Canada's largest indoor parking garage under the stadium. Scalping, although illegal, is quite visible. This stadium, built for the 1976 Olympics, had a retractable dome roof added in 1989 which improves offense by keeping out cold weather. Plaque inside and Jackie Robinson statue at main entrance commemorate the city where Robinson starred as a Montreal Royal. ☎ **800-463-9767**

NEW YORK METS

Last World Series title: 1986. Last League title: 1986. Last Division title: 1988.

■ **SHEA STADIUM:** 55,601 capacity, grass surface, built in 1964. Somewhat of an eyesore; you can watch the planes land at LaGuardia Airport.

■ **FAN NOTES:** Parking is not difficult. Avoid the last two or three rows of the loge and mezzanine levels. Upper-deck sections 10 to 16, between home and third base, are designated no-alcohol. Designed to expand eventually to 90,000 seats. One of the first dual-sport stadiums. Worst visibility for hitters in the major leagues. ☎ **718-507-8499**

PHILADELPHIA PHILLIES

Last World Series title: 1980. Last League title: 1993. Last Division title: 1993

■ **VETERANS STADIUM:** 62,382 capacity, artificial surface, built in 1971. An ugly and impersonal stadium.

■ **FAN NOTES:** Park in the Spectrum lot next door or take the subway from downtown. Try to avoid the 700-level seats down the foul lines. Highest seats are much too far from the action. Stadium is known to have the loudest boos and smallest hot dogs in baseball. Worst playing surface in the majors. Park's shape is called an "octorad" by the architects. The first ball here was dropped from a helicopter on April 10, 1971. ☎ **215-463-1000**

NATIONAL LEAGUE CENTRAL

CHICAGO CUBS

Last World Series title: 1908. Last League title: 1945: Last Division title: 1989.

■ **WRIGLEY FIELD:** 38,765 capacity, grass surface, built in 1914. A Chicago landmark. Fans love it.

■ **FAN NOTES:** Parking is almost nonexistent. Bleacher seats are the most popular. A rivalry exists between those in right field and those in left field, but both sides agree to throw back opposing teams' home run balls. After the game a blue flag with a white W or a white flag with a blue L is flown to signify a win or loss by the Cubs. A strong breeze off the lake favors pitchers. The ball park had no lights until 1988. ☎ **312-404-2827**

CINCINNATI REDS

Last World Series title: 1990. Last League title: 1990. Last Division title: 1990.

■ **RIVERFRONT STADIUM:** 52,952 capacity, artificial surface, built in 1970. Just another cookie-cutter stadium.

■ **FAN NOTES:** You can park in the lot underneath the stadium or across the river in Covington, Ky. Hot dogs are still only a dollar. First stadium to paint metric distances on the outfield walls. Emblem in left center signifies where Pete Rose's major league record 4,192nd base hit landed. Heavy winds off the Ohio River help right-handed hitters. ☎ **513-421-7337**

HOUSTON ASTROS

Never won a World Series or League title. Last Division title: 1986.

■ **ASTRODOME:** 53,821 capacity, artificial surface, built in 1965. No charm.

■ **FAN NOTES:** Plenty of parking. The second major league covered stadium—the first was the field under the Queensboro 59th Street Bridge in New York

FACT FILE:

A LITTLE ORGAN MUSIC

■ *Those old Wurlitzer organs still grind out "Take Me Out to the Ball Game" at most parks. But some fans like singing to a different beat.*

■ **MILWAUKEE:** *"Roll Out the Barrel."*
■ **ST. LOUIS:** *The Anheuser-Busch Theme Song.*
■ **SEATTLE:** *"Louie, Louie."*
■ **TEXAS:** *"Cotton-Eyed Joe."*

WHERE THE BOYS OF SPRING HANG OUT

Here are the places to catch a game before the regular season starts:

League	Stadium	Capacity	Ticket information
AMERICAN LEAGUE EAST			
BALTIMORE ORIOLES	Al Lang Stadium, St. Petersburg, Fla.	7,004	☎ 813-894-4773
BOSTON RED SOX	City of Palms Park, Fort Myers, Fla.	6,850	☎ 813-334-4700
DETROIT TIGERS	Marchant Stadium, Lakeland, Fla.	7,027	☎ 813-499-8229
NEW YORK YANKEES	Fort Lauderdale Stadium, Fla.	8,340	☎ 305-776-1921
TORONTO BLUE JAYS	Grant Field, Dunedin, Fla.	6,218	☎ 813-733-0429
AMERICAN LEAGUE CENTRAL			
CHICAGO WHITE SOX	Ed Smith Stadium, Sarasota, Fla.	7,500	☎ 813-287-8844
CLEVELAND INDIANS	Chain O'Lakes, Winter Haven, Fla.	7,042	☎ 813-291-5803
KANSAS CITY ROYALS	Baseball City Stadium, Davenport, Fla.	7,000	☎ 813-424-2500
MILWAUKEE BREWERS	Compadre Stadium, Chandler, Ariz.	10,000	☎ 602-895-1200
MINNESOTA TWINS	Lee Co. Sports Complex, Fort Myers, Fla.	7,500	☎ 800-338-9567
AMERICAN LEAGUE WEST			
CALIFORNIA ANGELS	Diablo Stadium, Tempe, Ariz.	9,785	☎ 602-678-2222
OAKLAND ATHLETICS	Phoenix Stadium, Phoenix, Ariz.	8,500	☎ 602-392-0074
SEATTLE MARINERS	Peoria Stadium, Peoria, Ariz.	10,000	☎ 602-784-4444
TEXAS RANGERS	Charlotte Co. Stadium, Port Charlotte, Fla.	6,026	☎ 813-625-9500
NATIONAL LEAGUE EAST			
ATLANTA BRAVES	Municipal Stadium, West Palm Beach, Fla.	7,200	☎ 407-683-6100
FLORIDA MARLINS	Spacecoast Stadium, Melbourne, Fla.	7,200	☎ 407-633-9200
MONTREAL EXPOS	Municipal Stadium, West Palm Beach, Fla.	7,500	☎ 407-684-6801
NEW YORK METS	St. Lucie Co. Stadium, Port St. Lucie, Fla.	7,400	☎ 407-871-2115
PHILADELPHIA PHILLIES	Jack Russell Stadium, Clearwater, Fla.	7,195	☎ 215-463-1000
NATIONAL LEAGUE CENTRAL			
CHICAGO CUBS	HoHoKam Park, Mesa, Ariz.	8,963	☎ 800-638-4253
CINCINNATI REDS	Plant City Stadium, Plant City, Fla.	6,700	☎ 813-752-7337
HOUSTON ASTROS	Osceola County Stadium, Kissimmee, Fla.	5,100	☎ 407-933-2520
PITTSBURGH PIRATES	McKechnie Field, Bradenton, Fla.	6,562	☎ 813-748-4610
ST. LOUIS CARDINALS	Al Lang Stadium, St. Petersburg, Fla.	7,600	☎ 813-896-4641
NATIONAL LEAGUE WEST			
COLORADO ROCKIES	Hi Corbett Field, Tucson, Ariz.	7,726	☎ 602-327-9467
LOS ANGELES DODGERS	Holman Stadium, Vero Beach, Fla.	6,500	☎ 407-569-4900
SAN DIEGO PADRES	Peoria Stadium, Peoria, Ariz.	10,000	☎ 602-878-4337
SAN FRANCISCO GIANTS	Scottsdale Stadium, Scottsdale, Ariz.	10,000	☎ 602-990-7972

City used by the New York Cubans. The roof originally had clear panes of glass but the glare prevented fielders from seeing the ball so the ceiling was painted. The grass then died and AstroTurf was introduced. The first AstroTurf game was played here against the Dodgers on April 8, 1966. ☎ **713-799-9555**

PITTSBURGH PIRATES

Last World Series title: 1979. Last League title: 1979. Last Division title: 1992.

■ **THREE RIVERS STADIUM:** 47,972 capacity, artificial surface, built in 1970. Just a plain vanilla ball park. Pittsburgh deserves much better.

■ **FAN NOTES:** Parking problems when there's

a larger-than-average crowd. Tailgate parties are a Pittsburgh tradition. Stands are close to the action. Sections 177 to 183 in the lower-deck left field are no-smoking and one section is also no-alcohol. Numbers painted on seats in right field upper deck indicate where Willie Stargell's home runs landed. Named Three Rivers because it is located on a site that was an island during the French and Indian Wars at the confluence of the Allegheny, Monongahela, and Ohio rivers. ☎ **412-321-2827**

ST. LOUIS CARDINALS

Last World Series title: 1982. Last League title: 1987. Last Division title: 1987.

■ **BUSCH STADIUM:** 57,000 capacity, artificial surface, built in 1966. A cookie-cutter stadium that doubles as an oven in summer.

■ **FAN NOTES:** There's plenty of parking, but it's difficult to leave. Summertime games can be brutal. Fans from Missouri and four neighboring states make for brisk advance sales, especially for Cubs games. Because of overhanging seats, those in the back of the loge reserve are a little dreary. Can see the Gateway Arch from the top deck in right field. Line drive park due to quick turf and deep center field. Also home of the National Bowling Museum. Used to house the football team, but a new stadium across town will serve that purpose now. As a result, the AstroTurf is slated for removal in the next couple of years in favor of natural grass. ☎ **314-421-4060**

NATIONAL LEAGUE WEST

COLORADO ROCKIES

Never won a World Series, League, or Division title.

■ **COORS FIELD:** 45,200 capacity, grass surface, built in 1995. Yet another great new stadium.

■ **FAN NOTES:** Limited parking. Possibly the most spectacular view in baseball; the Rocky Mountains are visible beyond the left-field fence. Home team has the distinct advantage of being accustomed to Denver's mile-high atmosphere. Tickets will be harder to get now that the Rockies no longer play in the much larger Mile High Stadium. ☎ **303-762-5437**

LOS ANGELES DODGERS

Last World Series title: 1988. Last League title: 1988. Last Division title: 1988.

■ **DODGER STADIUM:** 56,000 capacity, grass surface, built in 1962. Doesn't show its age, meticulously maintained.

■ **FAN NOTES:** Parking lots funnel efficiently into nearby freeways. Top-deck seats are much too far from the action. Dodger Dogs are required eating. A classic pitcher's park. Originally built to be expanded to 85,000 seats. ☎ **213-224-1400**

SAN DIEGO PADRES

Never won a World Series title. Last League title: 1984. Last Division title: 1984.

■ **SAN DIEGO JACK MURPHY STADIUM:** 46,510 capacity, grass surface, built in 1967. The best of the multi-purpose stadiums.

■ **FAN NOTES:** The team isn't great, but the ballpark is. Stadium parking lots have the second most spaces in the league. Although all seats are unobstructed, fans in pavilion seats can't see the main scoreboard. Rubio's fish tacos are a big hit. Different branches of the armed forces often take over whole sections and try to outchant each other. Stadium is named after the sports editor who campaigned to bring major league baseball to town. ☎ **619-283-4494**

SAN FRANCISCO GIANTS

Last World Series title: 1954 (as the New York Giants). Last League title: 1989. Last Division title: 1989.

■ **CANDLESTICK PARK:** 60,000 capacity, grass surface, built in 1960. Not even earthquakes can rid the world of the Stick.

■ **FAN NOTES:** Parking is expensive. Arrive early to avoid bottlenecks. The left-field bleacher seats are not terrific. Try the Polish sausage. Field is occasionally covered in fog. It's usually easy to get tickets the day of the game. Named for jagged rocks and trees that rise from the tidelands like giant candlesticks. In the 1960s many fans arrived by boat. Known for its tremendous winds. Few home runs because of cold temperatures. ☎ **415-467-8000**

SOURCES: *The Complete Four Sport Stadium Guide*, the sports staff of *USA Today*, Tom Dyja, ed., Fodor's Travel Publications, 1994; *Total Baseball*, John Thorn and Pete Palmer, eds., Time Warner, 1991; *Baseball 1994 Yearbook*, Mike Nahrstedt, ed., Sporting News Publishing Co., 1994; individual sports clubs.

EXPERT SOURCES

THE BEST BASEBALL BOOKS

We asked several well-known commentators on the national pastime to recommend a handful of books about the sport from among the dozens published recently. Our panel: Bob Costas, the NBC sportscaster and journalist; Daniel Okrent, author of 9 Innings: The Anatomy of a Baseball Game *(Houghton Mifflin, 1994) and managing editor of* Life *magazine; and Roger Kahn, author of* The Boys of Summer *(HarperCollins, 1971), one of the most celebrated baseball books of all time. Here are their choices:*

COBB
Al Stump, Workman Publishing, 1994, $24.95
■ This biography of perhaps the most talented and meanest man ever to don a pair of spikes was the only book to appear on all our experts' lists. Cobb received loads of attention as the source for the 1995 movie of the same name. But this account, based on the author's extraordinary firsthand access to Cobb, is no mere accompaniment. Roger Kahn calls it "the most arresting book-length portrait of a baseball person I've ever read."

THE CATCHER WAS A SPY: THE MYSTERIOUS LIFE OF MOE BERG
Nicholas Dawidoff, Pantheon, 1994, $24
■ It has been said that Berg could speak a dozen languages but couldn't hit in any of them. Dawidoff, a first-time author who has written for *Sports Illustrated* and the *New Yorker,* meticulously traces Berg's life in and out of baseball, including his World War II service as an OSS agent charged with assessing Hitler's nuclear bomb capability. Daniel Okrent says, "It's a real achievement of scholarship as well as a fascinating book."

CRACKING THE SHOW
Thomas Boswell, Doubleday, 1994, $23
■ The newest collection of essays and articles by the *Washington Post*'s baseball columnist, considered by many knowledgeable fans to be among the best in the business today.

LORDS OF THE REALM: THE "REAL" HISTORY OF BASEBALL
John Helyar, Villard, 1994, $6.99
■ This look at the business of baseball offers compelling portraits of the men and women who have owned baseball teams and ruled the sport from the commissioner's chair. Helyar (co-author of the best-selling *Barbarians at the Gate*) is an accomplished reporter with a fine eye for detail. The lords and ladies of baseball provide a treasure trove of material.

OCTOBER 1964
David Halberstam, Villard, 1994, $24
■ Another of Halberstam's loving looks at a pivotal baseball season. This time he chronicles the year that marked the end of the Yankee dynasty.

SHADOWS OF SUMMER: CLASSIC BASEBALL PHOTOGRAPHS 1869–1947
Text by Donald Honig, Viking Studio Books, 1994, $60
■ If you're looking for a recent coffee table book for your favorite baseball fan, this is it. Not the most publicized recent picture book on the sport (that would be *Baseball,* the companion to Ken Burns's mammoth PBS documentary), but the one our experts recommend.

FOOTBALL

EVERY SUNDAY CAN BE SUPER

What every fan needs to know at the stadium or in front of the tube

At another time and place—say, 19th-century France—Sunday afternoons were reserved for a stroll in the park "en famille." In late 20th-century America during fall and early winter, the pastime is football. Men and boys—and increasingly women and girls—are huddled before the TV sets or, if they are lucky enough, at the stadium itself watching hulking grown men throw themselves at each other. Not since the Romans put a gladiator in a ring with a lion has a sport been so brutal and so popular. Here's where to park, where to sit, and what kind of bread to get next time you go to the circus.

AMERICAN FOOTBALL CONFERENCE East

BUFFALO BILLS

Never won a Super Bowl title (despite four appearances in the championship game). Last Conference title: 1994.

■ **RICH STADIUM:** 80,091 capacity, artificial surface, built in 1973.

■ **FAN NOTES:** For on-site parking—and tailgate parties—arrive at least two hours before game time. Food is standard—but, surprisingly, no buffalo wings. Because of snow and freezing temperatures, most home games are played near the beginning of the season. Seats provide possibly the best sightlines in the league. ☎ **716-649-0015**

INDIANAPOLIS COLTS

Last Super Bowl title: 1971. Last Conference title: 1971.

■ **RCA DOME:** 60,127 capacity, artificial surface, built in 1984.

■ **FAN NOTES:** There are 44,300 parking spots within a square mile of this downtown dome. Local fans get a lot more excited about high school basketball than than they do about football. Tickets are readily available on most game days. Avoid the nosebleed seats in the top row—the view is terrible. Ma & Pa's Barbecue is the food favorite. ☎ **317-297-7000**

MIAMI DOLPHINS

Last Super Bowl title: 1974. Last Conference title: 1985.

■ **JOE ROBBIE STADIUM:** 73,000 capacity, grass surface, built in 1987.

■ **FAN NOTES:** The stadium offers shuttle service from its distant parking lots. Oftentimes there are 20,000 tickets available on game day. Avoid the upper deck on the visiting team's side unless you really want a sunburn. The 5,000 seats in the family section are a good deal. There's fast food galore, but also several traditional Cuban choices. ☎ **305-620-5000**

NEW ENGLAND PATRIOTS

Never won a Super Bowl. Last Conference title: 1986.

■ **FOXBORO STADIUM:** 60,794 capacity, grass surface, built in 1971.

■ **FAN NOTES:** The stadium has 18,500 licensed parking spots and almost as many potholes in the lots. Getting out can be miserable. The food's improving, but you might do better at one of the local restaurants. Attendance has been impressive considering how the team has fared. Surprisingly, the most expensive seats are obstructed by the players. ☎ **508-543-1776**

NEW YORK JETS

Last Super Bowl title: 1969. Last Conference title: 1969.

■ **GIANTS STADIUM:** 76,891 capacity, artificial surface, built in 1976.

■ **FAN NOTES:** Parking is no problem but getting back into Manhattan after the game can take over an hour. Fans are knowledgeable, loud, and occasionally downright obnoxious. Most seats are taken by season ticketholders and otherwise hard to get. ☎ **516-538-7200**

AMERICAN FOOTBALL CONFERENCE Central

CINCINNATI BENGALS

Never won a Super Bowl title. Last Conference title: 1989.

■ **RIVERFRONT STADIUM:** 60,389 capacity, artificial surface, built in 1970.

■ **FAN NOTES:** On-site parking is sold out on a seasonal basis. Instead, arrive early to get into one of the surrounding parking areas. Because the stadium is small, tickets can be hard to get. Your best bet may be the 700 lower end-zone seats that go on sale at the conclusion of the Reds' baseball season. The majority of the tickets not sold on a seasonal basis are in the upper deck. Watch out: Some of the more expensive seats, although well situated for baseball fans, are not as good for football fans. ☎ **513-621-3550**

CLEVELAND BROWNS

Never won a Super Bowl or Conference title.

■ **CLEVELAND MUNICIPAL STADIUM:** 78,512 capacity, grass surface, built in 1931.

■ **FAN NOTES:** Try to arrive at least an hour before the game for hassle-free parking. Tailgating is extremely popular here. Hot dogs with local Bertram's mustard are also popular. The "Dawg Pound," 6,000 end-zone seats where fans are knowledgeable, vocal, and often wear rubber dog-masks, is what gives this stadium its flavor. Because this place is so big, it's often possible to get tickets for non-division games. ☎ **216-891-5000**

HOUSTON OILERS

Never won a Super Bowl or Conference title.

■ **ASTRODOME:** 62,439 capacity, artificial surface, built in 1965.

■ **FAN NOTES:** Fans have nicknamed the dome "The House of Pain"—for the Oilers' style of football, not for the dome's amenities. Parking is easy and inexpensive. More than 2,500 sight-obstructed seats were removed in 1993, but try to avoid the back rows in the upper deck. Scalping is legal in Texas, but not on stadium grounds. Instead, try the Yellow Pages under "Tickets." ☎ **713-797-1000**

JACKSONVILLE JAGUARS

Never won a Super Bowl or a Conference title. The team was formed in 1995.

■ **JACKSONVILLE STADIUM:** 73,000 capacity, grass surface, built in 1995.

■ **FAN NOTES:** Bears little resemblance to the Gator Bowl it once was. Now luxurious and plush, many of the seats are situated between the 30-yard lines. There is little on-site parking, but plenty on nearby streets. Limited single-game tickets may be available. Scalping is illegal but not unheard of. ☎ **904-633-6000**

PITTSBURGH STEELERS

Last Super Bowl title: 1980. Last Conference title: 1980.

■ **THREE RIVERS STADIUM:** 59,600 capacity, artificial surface, built in 1970.

■ **FAN NOTES:** Only 4,000 on-site parking spots, but there are many lots in the nearby North Side. Iron City Beer and Primanti Brothers hoagies are local favorites. Season tickets haven't been available since 1972. Single-game tickets usually are gone also. Try to stay between the 30-yard lines. Scalpers tend to be found on the North Side. ☎ **412-323-1200**

FACT FILE:

SUPER BOWL WINNERS AND LOSERS

■ *Several teams have lost big on Super Bowl Sunday, but at least they got there. The San Francisco '49ers have struck gold the most. The Dallas Cowboys have won four and lost four.*

MOST WINS	
San Francisco	5
Dallas	4
Pittsburgh	4
Oakland/ LA	3
Washington	3

MOST LOSSES	
Buffalo	4
Dallas	4
Denver	4
Minnesota	4
Miami	3

AMERICAN FOOTBALL CONFERENCE West

DENVER BRONCOS

Never won a Super Bowl. Last Conference title: 1990.

■ **MILE HIGH STADIUM:** 76,273 capacity, grass surface, built in 1948.

■ **FAN NOTES:** Denver is football mad. Virtually all games are sold out. Arrive at least two hours early to beat the crowds. Sightlines are good from all seats. If you're able to get a ticket, try for sections 301 through 346 in the third level. As far as scalping goes, it's a seller's market. ☎ **303-433-7466**

KANSAS CITY CHIEFS

Last Super Bowl title: 1970. Last Conference title: 1970.

■ **ARROWHEAD STADIUM:** 77,872 capacity, artificial surface, built in 1972.

■ **FAN NOTES:** The crowd is one of the league's loudest; many fans paint their faces and sport the team's colors. Parking is plentiful but you should still get here early. Those seeking sun like to sit in the north stands. Scalpers often cause traffic jams. ☎ **816-924-9400**

LOS ANGELES RAIDERS

Last Super Bowl Title: 1984. Last Conference title: 1984.

■ **STADIUM: UNCERTAIN.**

■ **FAN NOTES:** As this book went to press, the team was contemplating a move back to Oakland, which it left in 1982, for the 1995–96 season. The team would play at the Oakland–Alameda County coliseum, which would be expanded to 65,000 seats.

SAN DIEGO CHARGERS

Never won a Super Bowl. Last Conference title: 1995.

■ **SAN DIEGO JACK MURPHY STADIUM:** 60,836 capacity, grass surface, built in 1967.

■ **FAN NOTES:** There's ample parking. You can eat well— sushi, Rubio's fish tacos, and Häagen-Dazs ice cream. Very few tickets are available on game day, depending on how the Chargers fare. The lowest seats in the lower level are too low. Bleacher seats are added to the end zones following the end of the baseball season. ☎ **619-280-2121 or 619-563-8281**

SEATTLE SEAHAWKS

Never won a Super Bowl or Conference title.

■ **KINGDOME:** 66,400 capacity, artificial surface, built in 1976.

■ **FAN NOTES:** Plenty of close-in parking. Besides the usual stadium fare, there's Ezell's fried chicken and Seattle's own Starbucks coffee. Season tickets were once impossible to get, but now have become available. Seattle's a football town; fans are knowledgeable and loud. The 200-level seats are a good deal. However, the 100-level seats closest to the field are slightly obstructed. ☎ **206-827-9766**

NATIONAL FOOTBALL CONFERENCE East

ARIZONA CARDINALS

Never won a Super Bowl or Conference title.

■ **SUN DEVIL STADIUM:** 73,521 capacity, grass surface, built in 1958.

■ **FAN NOTES:** Cardinals games are a great place to get a tan and the parking is easy. Sometimes the upper-deck seats get a refreshing cool breeze. Only 27,000 seats have backs; however, seat backs can be rented. No alcohol is sold after halftime. ☎ **602-379-0102**

DALLAS COWBOYS

Last Super Bowl title: 1994. Last Conference title: 1994.

■ **TEXAS STADIUM:** 65,024 capacity, artificial surface, built in 1971.

■ **FAN NOTES:** Cowboys tickets are more valuable than Texas oil and tough to come by. Home of the famous Dallas Cowboys cheerleaders. Texas Stadium has 52 full concession stands. Recently, police have clamped down on scalpers, so if you do run into one, be prepared to pay a pretty penny. ☎ **214-579-5000**

NEW YORK GIANTS

Last Super Bowl title: 1991. Last Conference title: 1991.

■ **GIANTS STADIUM:** 77,311 capacity, artificial surface, built in 1976.

■ **FAN NOTES:** This may be the league's best football facility. The parking lot may be the largest in the league. But leaving the stadium is a complete headache. Games are always sold out. There are no bad seats.

■ THE OLDEST GRUDGE MATCHES

Some match-ups mean more than others. Here's a look at the longest-running rivalries in the NFL, where they stand, and when you can catch the action.

THE RIVALRY	WON/LOST RECORD	FIRST MET	MATCHES IN '95
1. **Chicago Bears vs. Green Bay Packers**	Bears **81–70–6**	1921	Sept. 11, Nov. 2
2. **Chicago Bears vs. Detroit Lions**	Bears **75–50–5**	1930	Nov. 19, Dec. 4
3. **Green Bay Packers vs. Detroit Lions**	Packers **64–57–7**	1930	Oct. 15, Oct. 29
4. **New York Giants vs. Washington Redskins**	Giants **71–50–3**	1932	Oct. 29, Dec. 10
5. **New York Giants vs. Philadelphia Eagles**	Giants **64–54–2**	1933	Oct. 15, Nov. 19
6. **Washington Redskins vs. Philadelphia Eagles**	Redskins **66–47–5**	1934	Oct. 8, Nov. 25

Dress warmly; winds off the Hudson River—Hudson Hawks as they are called—can be bone chilling. Local legend has it that Teamsters boss Jimmy Hoffa is buried in one of the end zones. His body has never been found. ☎ **201-935-8222**

PHILADELPHIA EAGLES

Never won a Super Bowl. Last Conference title: 1981.

■ **VETERANS STADIUM:** 65,187 capacity, artificial surface, built in 1971.

■ **FAN NOTES:** Philly fans are opinionated, loud, and loyal. Games always sell out. Cheese steaks and soft pretzels are popular. While stadium lots accommodate up to 10,000 cars, there is plenty of parking close by. The worst seats are in sections 100 through 112, 125, and 152 through 166; 700-level seats are too far away. If you want to get in, plan on paying scalpers big bucks. ☎ **215-463-5500**

WASHINGTON REDSKINS

Last Super Bowl title: 1992. Last Conference title: 1992.

■ **ROBERT F. KENNEDY MEMORIAL STADIUM:** 56,454 capacity, grass surface, built in 1961.

■ **FAN NOTES:** The team has gone downhill recently, but Washington fans still love them, even though owner Jack Kent Cooke plans to move the team to the suburbs. Parking is adequate. Tailgating is popular because the food inside the gate is lousy. The first 10 rows at field level offer a good view of those players not in the game. ☎ **202-546-2222**

NATIONAL FOOTBALL CONFERENCE **Central**

CHICAGO BEARS

Last Super Bowl title: 1986. Last Conference title: 1986.

■ **SOLDIER FIELD:** 66,950 capacity, grass surface, built in 1928.

■ **FAN NOTES:** Arrive at least two hours early to get a parking spot. Most seats are taken by season ticketholders. If you can get into a game, try to get a seat in the middle of the east side of the stadium. The view is good and you can somewhat avoid the winds, which can be unbearable late in the season. Avoid seats in the far corners. ☎ **312-663-5100**

DETROIT LIONS

Never won a Super Bowl or Conference title.

■ **PONTIAC SILVERDOME:** 80,500 capacity, artificial surface, built in 1975.

■ **FAN NOTES:** The size of the Silverdome makes it easy to get tickets—and tough to sell out games. That means that often the only way to see a game is to go. In addition to 10,000 on-site parking spots, there are several lots within half a mile of the stadium. ☎ **313-335-4151**

GREEN BAY PACKERS

Last Super Bowl title: 1968. Last Conference title: 1968.

■ **LAMBEAU FIELD:** 59,543 capacity, grass surface, built in 1957.

■ **FAN NOTES:** Tickets are tough to get. All seats have good sightlines. Fans arrive up to three hours before games. Stadium lots often fill quickly but nearby neighborhood lots are available. Seats are very close to the field. Once October comes, wear your warmest clothes. **Green Bay:** ☎ **414-496-5719** **Milwaukee:** ☎ **414-342-2717**

MINNESOTA VIKINGS

Never won a Super Bowl. Last Conference title: 1977.

■ **METRODOME:** 63,000 capacity, artificial surface, built in 1982.

■ **FAN NOTES:** Fans are sometimes too quiet. Games usually sell out. However, tickets are usually available the week before. There is no stadium parking, but plenty in nearby lots. None of the seats have obstructed views. The seats around the top of the stadium are as good a bargain as you can get. ☎ **612-333-8828**

TAMPA BAY BUCCANEERS

Never won a Super Bowl or Conference title.

■ **TAMPA STADIUM:** 74,296 capacity, grass surface, built in 1976.

■ **FAN NOTES:** In most cases you can just walk up to the ticket window and get a seat. The best bet for parking is in the free lot across the street at the Tampa Bay Center. None of the seats have obstructed views, and neither do they have protection from the rain and sun. The stadium's west side is usually in the shade in the second half. ☎ **813-870-2700**

NATIONAL FOOTBALL CONFERENCE West

ATLANTA FALCONS

Never won a Super Bowl or Conference title.

■ **GEORGIA DOME:** 70,500 capacity, artificial surface, built in 1992.

■ **FAN NOTES:** All seats are the same price. There are 17,000 parking spots in the nearby vicinity. However, team officials discourage driving to games because of the horrendous traffic. Avoid upper-deck seats outside the 20-yard lines, especially behind the end zone. ☎ **404-223-8000**

CAROLINA PANTHERS

Team was formed in 1995 and has never won a Super Bowl or Conference title.

■ **CLEMSON STADIUM:** 81,473 capacity, grass surface, built in 1942.

■ **FAN NOTES:** Home of the Clemson Tigers. The Panthers will move into their own stadium in 1996. ☎ **704-358-7000**

NEW ORLEANS SAINTS

Never won a Super Bowl or Conference title.

■ **LOUISIANA SUPERDOME:** 69,065 capacity, artificial surface, built in 1975.

■ **FAN NOTES:** This place is so large that the Astrodome could fit inside of it. The parking garage only holds 5,000 cars, but there are 10,000 spots within walking distance. Since it's the only game in town, Saints tickets are in demand. Fans are loud, abundant, and party-loving. Even the highest seats are pretty good. ☎ **504-522-2600**

SAN FRANCISCO 49ERS

Last Super Bowl title: 1995. Last Conference title: 1995.

■ **CANDLESTICK PARK:** 66,513 capacity, grass surface, built in 1960.

■ **FAN NOTES:** Now that the team is hot, tickets are almost impossible to get. Vegetarians and seafood lovers can pig out. Without prepaid parking, plan to park in one of the 10,000 spots close by. The best seats are on the east side, between the 40-yard lines, around 20 rows up. Try to avoid the seats in the back rows of odd-numbered sections 1 through 21 or even-numbered sections 2 through 8. Those who know say the best place to get tickets is at local sports bars. ☎ **415-468-2249**

ST. LOUIS RAMS

Never won a Super Bowl. Last Conference title: 1980

■ **STADIUM:** 65,000 capacity, artificial surface, built in 1995.

■ **FAN NOTES:** The Rams have left Los Angeles. They will play their first game in St. Louis on October 22, 1995. The city has been without a team since the mid-'80s, when the Cardinals moved to Phoenix. Designers are already considering adding more seats to the brand new stadium. As of press-time for this book, the stadium remains unnamed. ☎ **314-982-4267**

SOURCES: *The Complete Four Sport Stadium Guide*, the sports staff of *USA Today*, Tom Dyja, ed., Fodor's Travel Publications, 1994; *Total Baseball*, John Thorn and Pete Palmer, eds., Time Warner, 1991; *Baseball 1994 Yearbook*, Mike Nahrstedt, ed., Sporting News Publishing Co., 1994; individual sports clubs.

BASKETBALL

A WHO'S WHO OF HOOPSTERS

Michael Jordan's back—here's where you'll catch the action

When the Basketball Association of America and National Basketball League merged just after the 1948–49 season, the National Basketball Association (NBA) was born. But it wasn't until the early '80s, with players like Larry Bird, Magic Johnson, and Michael Jordan, that the NBA exploded in popularity. Now Michael Jordan has come and gone and come back again. In 1995 the NBA will add expansion teams in Vancouver and Toronto. Here's the lineup for the 1995–96 season.

EASTERN CONFERENCE — Atlantic Division

BOSTON CELTICS

Last League title: 1987. Last Conference title: 1986.

■ **FLEET CENTER:** 18,400 capacity. This spanking new arena will have its debut in 1995. It replaces the much-loved but dangerously dilapidated Boston Garden. ☎ **617-523-3030**

MIAMI HEAT

Never won a League or Conference title.

■ **MIAMI ARENA:** 15,200 capacity. Enthusiastic fans coupled with a small arena raise both the intensity and the noise level. Good seats are hard to come by. Avoid the seats farthest from the floor. ☎ **305-577-4328**

NEW JERSEY NETS

Never won a League or Conference title.

■ **BYRNE MEADOWLANDS ARENA:** 20,029 capacity. Overall, there are really no bad seats. Often quiet. Don't miss the potato knishes. ☎ **201-935-8888**

NEW YORK KNICKERBOCKERS

Last League title: 1973. Last Conference title: 1994.

■ **MADISON SQUARE GARDEN:** 19,763 capacity. The essence of New York—big and loud. Without season tickets, scalpers are the primary, but expensive, way of getting tickets. Check along Seventh and Eighth avenues, between 31st and 34th streets. Seats lack legroom. ☎ **212-465-6000**

ORLANDO MAGIC

Never won a League title. Last Conference title: 1995.

■ **ORLANDO ARENA:** 16,010 capacity. Tickets have been difficult to get since the first game in the 1989–90 season. But since superstar Shaquille O'Neal joined the team, it's been nearly impossible. Sightlines are good, seats are comfortable, and decibel level is high. Sections 226 and 227 offer a good view for a low price. ☎ **407-649-2255**

PHILADELPHIA 76ERS

Last League title: 1983. Last Conference title: 1983.

■ **THE SPECTRUM:** 18,618 capacity. One of the oldest NBA arenas. If you're looking for a good deal, check out sections B, L, O, and Y in the corners. Avoid the upper-deck sections. Try the soft pretzels with mustard and, of course, the cheese steaks. ☎ **215-339-7676**

WASHINGTON BULLETS

Last League title: 1978. Last Conference title: 1979.

■ **USAIR ARENA:** 18,756 capacity. Tickets have become much harder to get since the team signed Juwan Howard and traded for Chris Webber, former members of Michigan's Fab Five. Sections 203 through 209, 217, and 219 through 223 are good bargains if you can't get center court seats closer to the floor. ☎ **301-622-3865**

EASTERN CONFERENCE — Central Division

ATLANTA HAWKS

Last League title: 1958. Last Conference title: 1961.

■ **THE OMNI:** 16,368 capacity. Tickets usually are available with no problem on game nights. For a reasonable price, sections 206 through 212 and 224 through 230 offer great views. Avoid sections 201, 235, 236, and 217 through 219. Fans go for the chicken wings, smoked sausage, and specialty coffee. ☎ **404-827-3865**

CHARLOTTE HORNETS
Never won a League or Conference title.

■ **CHARLOTTE COLISEUM:** 23,698 capacity. Unbelievably loud hometown fans. Usually the only seats available are those closest to the roof. The Coliseum gets kudos for having the most diverse array of concessions and the lowest prices. ☎ **704-357-0489**

CHICAGO BULLS
Last League title: 1993. Last Conference title: 1993.

■ **UNITED CENTER:** 21,500 capacity. Tickets were hard to come by for the new arena before Michael Jordan set foot in the building. Now, you can pretty much forget about it. Good food—if you get in. ☎ **312-455-4000**

FACT FILE:

WINNERS AND LOSERS

■ *Most NBA titles*

Boston Celtics	16
Minneapolis/Los Angeles Lakers	11
Philadelphia/ San Francisco/ Golden State Warriors	4
Chicago Bulls	3
Philadelphia 76ers	3

■ *Most losses in NBA finals*

Minneapolis/Los Angeles Lakers	13
New York Knicks	5
Boston Celtics	3
St. Louis Hawks	3
Philadelphia 76ers	3
Philadelphia/ San Francisco/ Golden State Warriors	3
Washington Bullets	3

CLEVELAND CAVALIERS
Never won a League or Conference title.

■ **GUND ARENA:** 21,500 capacity. Most games sell out. Sixty percent of the seats are in the lower concourse, close to the action. Sammy's at the Arena is one of the best restaurants downtown. ☎ **216-420-2000**

DETROIT PISTONS
Last League title: 1990. Last Conference title: 1990.

■ **THE PALACE OF AUBURN HILLS:** 21,454 capacity. As the Pistons add young talent, it's getting harder to get a seat. Check out sections 201 and 202, 214 through 215, and 229 through 230. ☎ **313-337-0100**

INDIANA PACERS
Never won a League or Conference title.

■ **MARKET SQUARE ARENA:** 16,530 capacity. Tickets are rare—the Pacers are popular and the arena is small. Try upper-deck aisles 5 through 8 and 17 through 20. ☎ **317-263-2100**

MILWAUKEE BUCKS
Last League title: 1971. Last Conference title: 1974.

■ **BRADLEY CENTER:** 18,633 capacity. Tickets available most game nights. Stay away from sections 431 through 435 and 409 through 413. ☎ **414-227-0500**

TORONTO RAPTORS
1995–96 expansion team

■ **SKY DOME:** 22,500 capacity. Raptors are scheduled to play here for three years until a new stadium is built. ☎ **416-366-3865**

WESTERN CONFERENCE Midwest Division

DALLAS MAVERICKS
Never won a League or Conference title.

■ **REUNION ARENA:** 17,502 capacity. Occasionally the crowd comes to life. The seats in sections 106, 110, 120, and 124 offer some of the best views in the place. ☎ **214-939-2800**

DENVER NUGGETS
Never won a League or Conference title.

■ **McNICHOLS SPORTS ARENA:** 17,171 capacity. Nuggets games have increas-

MARCH MADNESS: THE FINAL FOUR

From 64 to 4: the National Collegiate Athletic Association (NCAA) men's and women's Final Four games offer some of the most exciting basketball action of the season. The 1996 men's Final Four is scheduled at the Meadowlands (N.J.) Arena March 30 through April 1; the women's will be held at the Charlotte (N.C.) Coliseum March 30 and 31. Some recent champs and the runners-up:

	MEN		WOMEN	
				67 CONNECTICUT
OKLAHOMA ST. 61	**UCLA 89**	1995	**67 CONNECTICUT**	56 ALABAMA
ARKANSAS 75	ARKANSAS 78		63 VIRGINIA	63 VIRGINIA
N. CAROLINA 68				62 LOUISIANA TECH
ARKANSAS 91				89N. CAROLINA
ARIZONA 82	**ARKANSAS 76**	1994	**60 N. CAROLINA**	74 PURDUE
DUKE 70	DUKE 72		59 LOUISIANA TECH	69 LOUISIANA TECH
FLORIDA 65				66 ALABAMA
N. CAROLINA 78				60 TEXAS TECH
KANSAS 68	**N. CAROLINA 77**	1993	**84 TEXAS TECH**	46 VANDERBILT
MICHIGAN 81	MICHIGAN 71		82 OHIO ST.	73 OHIO ST.
KENTUCKY 78				72 IOWA
DUKE 81				78 STANFORD
INDIANA 78	**DUKE 71**	1992	**78 STANFORD**	62 VIRGINIA
MICHIGAN 76	MICHIGAN 51		62 W. KENTUCKY	84 W. KENTUCKY
CINCINNATI 72				72 SW MISSOURI ST.
DUKE 79				68 TENNESSEE
UNLV 77	**DUKE 72**	1991	**70 TENNESSEE**	60 STANFORD
KANSAS 79	KANSAS 65		67 VIRGINIA	61 VIRGINIA
N. CAROLINA 73				55 CONNECTICUT

ingly become the place to be. The upper-deck seats in sections 1, 3, 5, 29, 31, 33, 35, 59, 61, and 63 provide a good view at a low price. ☎ **303-893-3865**

HOUSTON ROCKETS

Last League title: 1995. Last Conference title: 1995.

■ **THE SUMMIT:** 16,611 capacity. A tough ticket to get since the Rockets won the 1994 championship. Good sightlines; no seat is more than 128 feet from the court. A million-dollar upgrade vastly improved the arena's concessions: besides the popular margarita bar, sought-after treats include barbecued brisket and fajitas. ☎ **713-627-0600**

MINNESOTA TIMBERWOLVES

Never won a League or Conference title.

■ **TARGET CENTER:** 19,006 capacity. Good seats are usually available on game day. Try Minnesota's own fried walleye fish sandwich. ☎ **612-673-1313.**

SAN ANTONIO SPURS

Never won a League or Conference title.

■ **ALAMODOME:** 20,640 capacity. Large crowds, but some tickets are usually available on game nights. The upper level is opened for big games, increasing capacity to 35,000. Bargain seats in the upper deck are possibly the best buy in the NBA. ☎ **210-554-7787**

UTAH JAZZ

Never won a League or Conference title.

■ **DELTA CENTER:** 19,911 capacity. The tickets are tough to get. The fans are quiet but loyal. Although illegal in Salt Lake City, scalping is allowed on the grounds of the Delta Center. ☎ **801-355-3865**

WESTERN CONFERENCE **Pacific Division**

GOLDEN STATE WARRIORS

Last League title: 1975. Last Conference Title: 1975.

■ **OAKLAND COLISEUM ARENA:** 15,025 capacity. Games have sold out since 1989. Try the grilled sausages or one of the several varieties of local micro-brewery beers on tap. ☎ **510-638-6300**

LOS ANGELES CLIPPERS

Never won a League or Conference title.

■ **LOS ANGELES MEMORIAL SPORTS ARENA:** 16,005 capacity. Tickets usually are available, and cheaper than for the more glamorous crosstown rival, the Lakers. Check out the middle-concourse seats in sections 1 through 4, 14 through 18, and 28A through 30. ☎ **213-748-0500**

FACT FILE:

WHERE STARS ARE BORN

■ *Each year, the NBA fulfills a small group of college players' dreams by drafting them to play in the big time. These collegiate athletic conferences provide the league with the most players.*

1. Atlantic Coast Conference	13.4%
2. Big East Conference	11.8%
3. Big 10 Conference	10.5%
4. Southeastern Conference	9.2%
5. Pacific 10 Conference	7.4%
6. Big 8 Conference	6.1%
All the rest	41.6%

LOS ANGELES LAKERS

Last League title: 1988. Last Conference title: 1991.

■ **THE GREAT WESTERN FORUM:** 17,505 capacity. The most expensive tickets in the league are readily snapped up by Hollywood's finest. Check out the $500 floor seats for the rich and famous. Park nearby; you don't want to walk around here at night. ☎ **213-480-3232**

PHOENIX SUNS

Never won a League title. Last Conference title: 1993.

■ **AMERICA WEST ARENA:** 19,023 capacity. You'll feel close to the action from just about anywhere, but avoid sitting behind the baskets at any level. ☎ **602-379-7867**

PORTLAND TRAIL BLAZERS

Last League title: 1977. Last Conference title: 1992.

■ **THE ROSE GARDEN:** 21,300 capacity. This new arena opens for the 1995–96 season. It is expected to be modern and impressive. ☎ **503-231-8000**

SACRAMENTO KINGS

Last League title: 1951. Last Conference title: 1951.

■ **ARCO ARENA:** 17,317 capacity. Built for basketball; great sightlines from all seats. One of the toughest tickets in the League. Because of the arena's isolated location, scalping hardly exists. ☎ **916-928-6900**

SEATTLE SUPERSONICS

Last League title: 1979. Last Conference title: 1979.

■ **SEATTLE CENTER COLISEUM:** 17,700 capacity. Closed in 1995 for renovations, but it will reopen in time for the 1995–96 season. ☎ **206-283-3865**

VANCOUVER GRIZZLIES

1995–96 expansion team.

■ **GM PLACE:** 20,000 capacity. A new arena for a new team. ☎ **604-688-5867**

SOURCES: *The Complete Four Sport Stadium Guide*, the sports staff of *USA Today*, Tom Dyja, ed., Fodor's Travel Publications, 1994; *Total Baseball*, John Thorn and Pete Palmer, eds., Time Warner, 1991; *Baseball 1994 Yearbook*, Mike Nahrstedt, ed., Sporting News Publishing Co., 1994; individual sports clubs.

HOCKEY FAN'S GUIDE

THE FASTEST GAME ON ICE

The top eight teams in each conference qualify for the Stanley Cup playoffs, the outcome of which determines the League's champion. At least one team from each division makes the playoffs. These division leaders are seeded first and second. One plays eight, two plays seven, and so on. The divisions:

TEAM • First season in NHL • *Stanley Cups (most recent win)* [1] • **Stadium** • Capacity ☎ **Ticket information**

EASTERN CONFERENCE Atlantic Division

FLORIDA PANTHERS • 1993–94 • *0* • **Miami Arena** • 14,500 ☎ **305-358-5885**

NEW JERSEY DEVILS • 1974–75 • *1 (1995)* • **Meadowlands Arena** • 19,040 ☎ **201-935-3900**

NEW YORK ISLANDERS • 1972–73 • *4 (1983)* • **Nassau Coliseum** • 16,927 ☎ **516-888-9000**

NEW YORK RANGERS • 1926–27 • *4 (1994)* • **Madison Square Garden** • 18,200 ☎ **212-465-6741**

PHILADELPHIA FLYERS • 1967–68 • *2 (1975)* • **The CoreStates Spectrum** • 17,380 ☎ **215-336-2000**

TAMPA BAY LIGHTNING • 1992–93 • *0* • **ThunderDome** • 26,000 ☎ **813-229-8800**

WASHINGTON CAPITALS • 1974–75 • *0* • **USAir Arena** • 18,130 ☎ **301-386-7000**

EASTERN CONFERENCE Northeast Division

BOSTON BRUINS • 1924–25 • *5 (1990)* • **The Fleet Center** • 17,200 ☎ **617-227-3200**

BUFFALO SABRES • 1970–71 • *0* • **Crossroads Arena** • 29,000 ☎ **716-856-8100**

DENVER [2] • 1979–80 • *0* • **McNichols Arena** • 17,171 ☎ **303-893-6700**

HARTFORD WHALERS • 1978–79 • *0* • **Hartford Civic Center** • 15,635 ☎ **800-469-4253**

MONTREAL CANADIENS • 1917–18 • *23 (1993)* • **Montreal Forum** • 21,400 ☎ **514-932-2582**

OTTAWA SENATORS • 1993–94 • *0* • **Ottawa Civic Centre** • 10,585 ☎ **613-721-4300**

PITTSBURGH PENGUINS • 1967–68 • *2 (1992)* • **Civic Arena** • 17,537 ☎ **412-323-1919**

WESTERN CONFERENCE Central Division

CHICAGO BLACKHAWKS • 1926–27 • *3 (1961)* • **United Center** • 17,742 ☎ **312-559-1212**

DALLAS STARS • 1967–68 • *0* • **Reunion Arena** • 16,914 ☎ **214-467-8277**

DETROIT RED WINGS • 1926–27 • *7 (1955)* • **Joe Louis Arena** • 19,275 ☎ **313-396-7544**

ST. LOUIS BLUES • 1967–68 • *0* • **Kiel Center** • 18,500 ☎ **314-291-7600**

TORONTO MAPLE LEAFS • 1917–18 • *13 (1967)* • **Maple Leaf Gardens** • 15,642 ☎ **416-977-1641**

WINNIPEG JETS • 1979–80 • *0* • **Winnipeg Arena** • 15,405 ☎ **204-982-5304**

WESTERN CONFERENCE Pacific Division

MIGHTY DUCKS OF ANAHEIM • 1993–94 • *0* • **Arrowhead Pond of Anaheim** • 17,250 ☎ **714-704-2500**

CALGARY FLAMES • 1972–73 • *1 (1989)* • **Olympic Saddledome** • 20,230 ☎ **403-777-4646**

EDMONTON OILERS • 1979–80 • *5 (1988)* • **Northlands Coliseum** • 17,503 ☎ **403-471-2191**

LOS ANGELES KINGS • 1967–68 • *0* • **Great Western Forum** • 16,005 ☎ **310-419-3870**

SAN JOSE SHARKS 1991–92 • *0* • **San Jose Arena** • 17,190 ☎ **408-287-9200**

VANCOUVER CANUCKS • 1970–71 • *0* • **GM Place** • 20,000 ☎ **604-280-4400**

NOTES: 1. As of the end of the 1994–95 season. 2. Formerly the Quebec Nordiques; not yet renamed. The conference and division for the new Denver team have not, as of early summer of 1995, been established.

OLYMPICS '96

LOOKING AHEAD

LET THE GAMES BEGIN

The big story will be the dominance of American women athletes

The Olympics turn 100 years old in 1996, and the city of Atlanta will celebrate by staging the biggest Summer Games ever. More athletes (nearly 11,000) and teams from more countries (196) are expected to compete in the 1996 Olympiad than in any before. Upward of 11 million tickets will be sold for Olympic events, more than at the 1992 Summer Games and the 1994 Winter Games combined.

If the Atlanta Games are distinguished by any single feature, it may be for their emphasis on women's sports. Nearly 3,800 female athletes are expected to compete at the 1996 Summer Games, 25 percent more than the number of women who participated at the '92 Games in Barcelona. Women's softball and soccer will appear as Olympic medal sports for the first time in Atlanta; women also will compete in the other sports debuting in Olympic competition in 1996: mountain biking and beach volleyball. The number of teams participating in both the women's basketball and women's volleyball competitions will grow from 8 to 12 as well, putting the women's games on a par with the men's events.

If women's sports get more attention at the 1996 Summer Games, Americans are likely to bask in the spotlight. U.S. teams have dominated recent international competition in the new women's sports of softball and soccer, and America's female gymnasts are at the peak of their sport right now. And for the first time, thanks to the creation of a new national women's basketball team, the U.S. Olympic squad will have played as a unit for months prior to the Games, rather than weeks, as in the past.

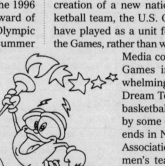

IZZY, the mascot of the 1996 Olympic Summer Games

Media coverage of the 1992 Games in Barcelona overwhelmingly focused on the Dream Team, the American basketball team that was led by some of the greatest legends in National Basketball Association history. The U.S. men's team in Atlanta will again feature pro basketball's best, and it will almost certainly crush its competition once again. Magic Johnson and Michael Jordan are

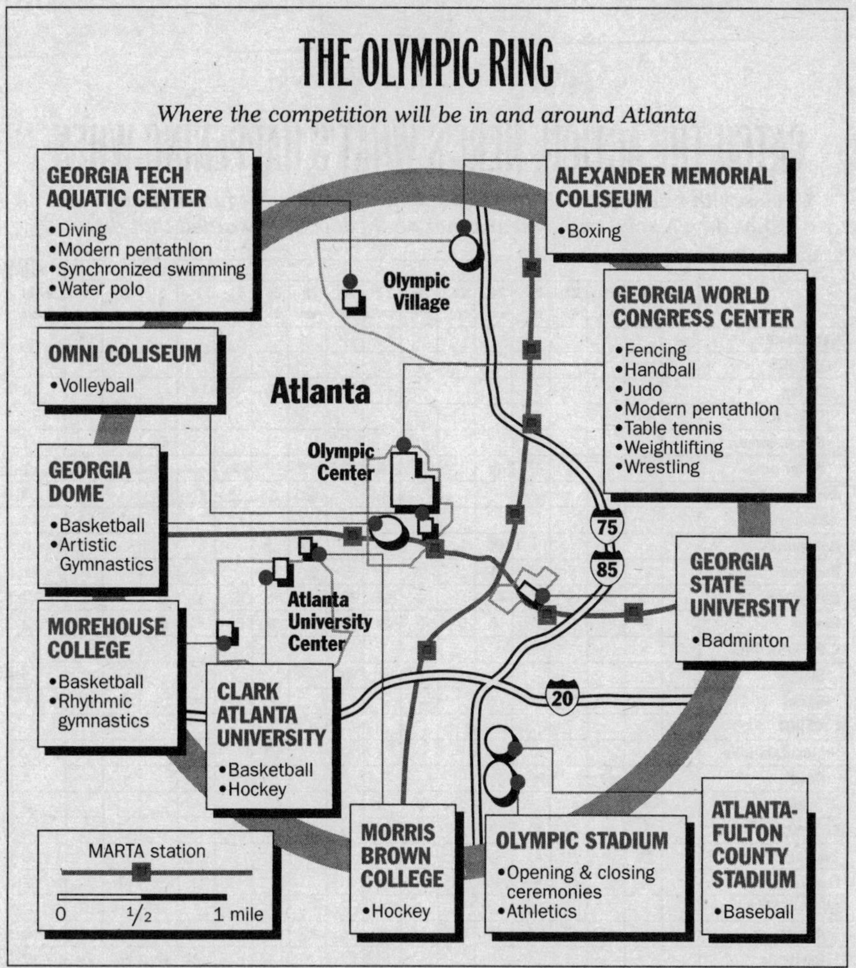

eligible; whether or not they will play is another question. Even so, the team will probably be a much more modest story this time around, letting other sports and athletes share more evenly in the spotlight.

If you're seeking drama, look to the swimming pool, where American women will challenge the recent dominance of the Chinese women, several of whom have come under scrutiny for using performance-enhancing drugs. And look to the gymnastics arena, where the American women will seek to end the historic supremacy of their Russian counterparts in the team competition. And as always, look to the track oval, where what has often been called the world's biggest track meet unfolds with its quadrennial display of speed and might.

Because the former Soviet republics will all be competing separately in Atlanta, the United States has a solid chance to win more medals than any other country, which it has not done since 1968 in an Olympics in which teams from the former Eastern bloc competed. But it is far from a sure bet; the Olympic Games seem to get more and more democratic every year. More countries won medals at the last two Summer Olympics than at all of the previous Summer Games combined.

SPECTATOR'S GUIDE

CATCH THE ACTION: HERE'S WHAT'S HAPPENING WHEN

Circles with numbers in them show the number of event finals taking place that day. A solid circle means that no medals are awarded that day.

	JULY													AUGUST				Total
	19 FRI	20 SAT	21 SUN	22 MON	23 TUE	24 WED	25 THU	26 FRI	27 SAT	28 SUN	29 MON	30 TUE	31 WED	1 THU	2 FRI	3 SAT	4 SUN	event finals
Ceremonies	●																●	
AQUATICS																		
Diving								●	❶	●	❶	●	❶	●	❶			4
Swimming		❹	❹	❺	❺	❺	❺	❹										32
Synch. swim.												●			❶			1
Water polo		●	●	●	●	●		●	●	❶								1
Archery											●	●	❶	❶	❷			4
Athletics								❸	❸	❻	❻		❹	❻	❻	❾	❶	44
Badminton						●	●	●	●	●	●	●	❷	❸				5
Baseball		●	●	●	●	●	●		●	●	●	●		●	❶			1
Basketball		●	●	●	●	●	●	●	●	●	●	●	●	●	●	❶	❶	2
Boxing		●	●	●	●	●	●	●	●	●		●	●	●	●	❻	❻	12
CANOE/KAYAK																		
Slalom									❷	❷								4
Sprint												●	●	●	●	❻	❻	12
CYCLING																		
Mountain Bike												❷						2
Road			❶										❶			❷		4
Track						❶	❶	●	❸	❸								8
Equestrian			●	●	●	❶		❶	●	❶	●		●	❶		❶	❶	6
Fencing		❶	❷	❷	❶	❷	❷											10
Football		●	●	●	●	●	●		●	●			●	❶	●	❶		2
GYMNASTICS																		
Artistic		●	●	❶	❶	❶	❶			❺	❺	●						14
Rhythmic														●	❶	●	❶	2
Handball						●	●	●	●	●	●	●	●	●	●	❶	❶	2
Hockey		●	●	●	●	●	●	●	●	●	●	●	●	❶	❶			2
Judo		❷	❷	❷	❷	❷	❷	❷										14
Modern pentathlon												❶						1
Rowing			●	●	●	●	●	●	❼	❼								14
Shooting		❷	❷	❶	❷	❷	❷	❷	❷									15
Softball			●	●	●	●	●	●	●		●	❶						1
Table tennis					●	●	●	●	●	●	❶	❶	❶	❶				4
Tennis					●	●	●	●	●	●	●	●	●	●	❷	❷		4
VOLLEYBALL																		
Beach					●	●	●	●	❶	❶								2
Indoor		●	●	●	●	●	●	●	●	●	●	●	●	●	●	❶	❶	2
Weightlifting		❶	❶	❶	❶	❶		❶	❶	❶	❶	❶						10
Wrestling		●	❺	●	❺							●	❺	●	❺			20
Yachting				●	●	●	●	●	●	❷	❷	❸	❷	❶				10
EVENT FINALS	**0**	**10**	**17**	**12**	**17**	**15**	**13**	**13**	**20**	**29**	**16**	**9**	**17**	**15**	**20**	**30**	**18**	**271**

OLYMPIC EVENTS

GOING FOR THE GOLD

Our sport-by-sport rundown of what to watch for in the big events

The summer Olympics is the world's biggest sporting event. For 16 days in 1996, nearly 11,000 atheletes will vie for 1,933 medals in 37 sports. The Olympic motto is *Citius, Altius, Fortius,* which means faster, higher, stronger. Here's where to find those qualities in 15 of the Olympic's most-watched sports.

BASEBALL

The American pastime was an exhibition sport until the 1992 Summer Games in Barcelona, and will be played in Atlanta for just the second time as a full-fledged Olympic sport. Olympic baseball, a round-robin competition, is played in essentially the same manner as the American League game (with a designated hitter batting in place of the pitcher). One difference: The players are allowed to use aluminum bats.

■ **THE COMPETITORS:** Eight men's teams with 20 players each. Baseball is one of the last holdouts against open professionalism in the Olympics. Major league players are barred from Olympic competition, as are players from openly professional leagues in countries like Japan (although Cuban and other players who compete in quasi-professional industrial leagues are permitted to play, a source of irritation to baseball officials in the United States and around the world). As in the past, the American team will be made up of top college athletes.

■ **WINNERS IN 1992:** Cuba, Taiwan, and Japan won the gold, silver, and bronze medals, respectively.

■ **VIEWING HINTS:** There is mercy for overmatched teams in Olympic baseball. Games are ended after the seventh inning if a team trails by 10 or more runs.

■ **WHO TO WATCH IN ATLANTA:** Cuba, Japan, and the United States.

BASKETBALL

Olympic basketball closely resembles NCAA basketball: The five-member teams play two 20-minute halves, zone defense is allowed, and each player is permitted five fouls before being disqualified. The distance of a three-point field goal is 20 feet, 6.1 inches, compared to 19 feet, 9 inches in college and 22 feet in the NBA.

■ **THE COMPETITORS:** Twelve teams for men and 12 teams for women, made up of 12 players each. The U.S. men's team in Atlanta will be made up entirely of NBA stars; for the first time, the U.S. women will be drawn mainly from a national women's team, which will play together from September 1995 until the Atlanta Games.

■ **WINNERS IN 1992:** The Dream Team, led in scoring by Charles Barkley and Michael Jordan and in spirit by Magic Johnson, won its games by an average of more than 43 points and captured the gold. Croatia and

FACT FILE:

BIGGER AND BETTER

■ *Some 11.2 million tickets will be sold for events at the 1996 Summer Games, more than at the 1994 Winter Games and 1992 Summer Games combined.*

■ *From a logistical standpoint, putting on the Olympic Games in Atlanta will be the equivalent of staging eight Super Bowls a day for 17 days.*

Lithuania won the silver and bronze. The U.S. women's team settled for the bronze in the 1992 games, falling in the semifinals to the eventual gold-medal champion, the Unified Team from the former Soviet Union. China won the silver.

■ **VIEWING HINTS:** Watch for opponents to try to slow down the speedy American men and women by holding the ball and playing zone defenses.

■ **WHO TO WATCH IN ATLANTA:** The U.S. men's team should easily sweep to gold again, with only token opposition coming from Eastern European teams like Croatia and Lithuania. The U.S. women's team will battle China and Russia for the top medals.

BOXING

Each nation is allowed to enter a boxer in each of 12 weight classes. The winner of the final bout in each weight class wins the gold, the loser gets the silver, and the losers of the two semifinal bouts each get bronzes. Knockouts are rare in Olympic bouts, which consist of three, three-minute rounds; instead, boxers try to rack up points by throwing a lot of punches. The force of the blow does not matter. Because knockouts occur so infrequently, the relatively subjective opinions of the panel of judges are crucial, so almost every Olympics includes its share of contested decisions. But an electronic scoring system used for the first time in Barcelona cut down on the number of controversial judgments. A "split decision" occurs when the three judges disagree on the winner, with two voting for one boxer and the third favoring the other.

■ **THE COMPETITORS:** There will be 364 boxers from dozens of countries.

■ **WINNERS IN 1992:** Cuban boxers won 7 of the 12 boxing golds, Germans captured 2, and American, Irish, and North Korean boxers took the rest.

■ **VIEWING HINTS:** Fight fans familiar only with the heavyweight brand of professional boxing are often surprised by the extent to which strategy, footwork, and speed, rather than brute force, hold sway in Olympic boxing. Injuries are rare because boxers are required to wear headgear.

■ **WHO TO WATCH IN ATLANTA:** If Cuba does not boycott, which it did the last time the Olympics were held in America, its boxers will be heavily favored in many weight classes.

CYCLING

Olympic cycling can be breathtaking to watch, particularly in the track events where riders dart around a banked oval at sizzling speeds—with no brakes. Olympic cyclists also compete on the open highway in road events. There are a total of 12 events: 5 track events for men and 3 for women, and 2 road events each for men and women. For the first time, the 1996 Games will include a mountain bike competition (replacing the 100-kilometer team time trial) in which 50 men and 30 women will race about 70 kilometers (more than 40 miles) over a rugged course. Another Olympic first in Atlanta: professional cyclists will be allowed to compete.

■ **THE COMPETITORS:** In road events, 240 male athletes and 85 female athletes will compete. In track events, 152 men and 54 women. And in mountain biking, 50 men and 30 women.

■ **WINNERS IN 1992:** Germany won three of the seven golds in men's events; Italy captured two of them, and Spain and Great Britain the others. Women from Australia, Germany, and Estonia won the three women's events.

■ **VIEWING HINTS:** Strategy matters as much as speed in Olympic cycling. You'll frequently see a cyclist riding close behind another competitor. He's not hiding, he's "drafting"—letting the competitor take on as much of the wind resistance as possible. Also, watch for riders to suddenly burst out of a pack in an attempt to pull away from the rest in a maneuver called a "breakaway."

SPECTATOR TICKETS WORTH THEIR WEIGHT IN GOLD

Want to see the '96 games in person? It's not too late—if you're not too picky

By now early birds have snatched up most of the best tickets and the choicest accommodations. But if you've just decided to venture to Atlanta for the 1996 Summer Games, it's probably not too late.

Although the Atlanta Committee for the Olympic Games (ACOG) has set aside 4 million tickets for Olympic sponsors and patrons, another 7 million are for public consumption—more than the total available for the 1984 Games in Los Angeles. Tickets first went on sale through the mail in May 1995. Since requests have been filled on a first-come, first-served basis, the best seats for many prime events are long gone. But the sponsors of the Games expect to sell fewer than two-thirds of all available tickets, so plenty should remain—just don't get your heart set on seeing hot-ticket events like the gymnastics or men's basketball finals, or the opening ceremonies. Mail-order sales continue until December 1, 1995; phone sales begin in February 1996, and box-office sales start in June 1996. For more information, call ☎ 404-744-1996.

Getting tickets may be a breeze compared with the other major challenge: finding a place to stay. If at all possible, stay with friends or family in or near Atlanta; if you can't, your options include:

■ **HOTEL ROOMS:** These will be difficult to come by at this late date; many of metropolitan Atlanta's 55,000 hotel rooms are set aside for those who got their tickets early. If you really want a hotel room, try other Georgia cities like Gainesville (53 miles away) or Macon (84 miles) or surrounding major cities like Birmingham, Ala. (120 miles). Private agencies such as Event Management Travel, ☎ 800-695-366, may be able to provide access to hotel rooms and other Atlanta-area accommodations.

■ **PRIVATE HOMES:** ACOG has set up a useful network called Private Housing 1996, ☎ 404-455-0081, through which Atlanta residents can rent their homes to Olympic visitors. More than 8,000 houses and 3,000 apartments are participating, at prices ranging from $150 to $425 per bedroom per night. Accommodations in private homes may also be available through private agencies such as International Bed and Breakfast Reservation Service, ☎ 800-473-9449 and RSVP Grits, ☎ 800-823-7787.

■ **COLLEGE DORMS:** Some local colleges and universities also are opening their dormitories to out-of-towners. For more information, call ☎ 404-744-1996.

■ **WHO TO WATCH IN ATLANTA:** Among the women, Germany, Australia, France, and the United States; among the men, Italy, Germany, Australia, and the Netherlands.

DIVING

The Olympics feature two diving competitions each for men and women: the 3-meter springboard and the platform, which is equivalent to leaping from three stories up. Competitors perform dives in six categories: forward, backward, reverse, inward, twisting, and, in platform only, armstand. The divers in each event compete in a preliminary round, and the top dozen finishers compete in the finals.

■ **THE COMPETITORS:** Seventy men and 70 women from two dozen countries.

■ **WINNERS IN 1992:** Chinese divers won three of the four golds. An American, Mark Lenzi, won the fourth in the men's springboard competition.

■ **VIEWING HINTS:** Seven judges rate each dive on a scale of 0 to 10. The high and low scores are discarded, and the rest are multiplied by 0.6 and by the degree of difficulty for each dive, which can range from 1.2 to 3.5. Divers lose points for bending their limbs and for even the slighest splash when they hit the water.

■ **WHO TO WATCH IN ATLANTA:** China, the United States, Russia, and Germany. But Canada, Mexico, Australia, and several former Soviet republics could challenge.

GYMNASTICS

Artistic gymnastics, as the sport of Olga Korbut and Mary Lou Retton is called, is something of a misnomer. It is artistic, but it is also enormously athletic and powerful. The men participate in team and individual competition in six events: floor exercise, parallel bars, horizontal bar, pommel horse, still rings, and vault. The women compete in four: floor exercise, balance beam, uneven parallel bars, and vault. Five judges rate their performances, with 10.0 a perfect score. One gold medal is awarded in the men's and women's team competition; one gold is awarded to an individual male and female in the all-around competitions; and gold medals are awarded for each of the six individual events for men and the four events for women. In rhythmic gymnastics, female gymnasts perform choreographed routines with equipment such as pieces of rope, hoops, balls, clubs, and ribbons. For the first time in Atlanta, the event will include a group competition, in which five athletes from a country work together as a cohesive unit.

■ **THE COMPETITORS:** Twelve men's teams and 12 women's teams of 7 gymnasts each, plus 24 other competitors who qualify individually. There also are 12 women's teams in rhythmic gymnastics.

■ **WINNERS IN 1992:** The Unified Team won both the men's and women's team combined exercises. China and Japan took the men's silver and bronze, and Romania and the United States medaled in the women's competition. In individual competition, Trent Dimas won a gold in the men's horizontal bar and Shannon Miller won two silvers and two bronzes for the United States.

■ **VIEWING HINTS:** "Compulsories" are the predesigned routines that contain specific movements required of all gymnasts; to "stick" a dismount is to land it solidly, without taking a step or wavering.

■ **WHO TO WATCH IN ATLANTA:** For the men, Russia, China, and Japan; for the women, Russia, Romania, and the United States.

FACT FILE:

THE TOP TEAMS FROM THE 1992 GAMES

■ *The Unified Team, made up of most of the former republics of the Soviet Union, captured more medals than any other country at the '92 Games.*

	Gold	Silver	Bronze	Total
1. Unified Team	45	38	29	112
2. United States	37	34	37	108
3. Germany	33	21	28	82
4. China	16	22	16	54
5. Cuba	14	6	11	31
6. Hungary	11	12	7	30
7. South Korea	12	5	12	29
8. France	8	5	16	29
9. Australia	7	9	11	27
10. Spain	13	7	2	22

SOCCER (FOOTBALL)

At the 1992 Olympics, for the first time ever, male soccer players had to be under 23 years of age. The age limit was designed by the Federation Internationale de Football Association, which governs the sport worldwide, to preserve the prestige and uniqueness of the World Cup as the international soccer showplace. At the 1996 Olympics, each team will be permitted three wild-card players of any age, a change designed to add a little splash to the Olympic soccer

■ SUMMER OLYMPICS TV SCORECARD

NBC paid a record $456 million for rights to broadcast the 1996 Summer Games in Atlanta, even though the network lost upward of $100 million on the 1992 Games. The network got hammered in 1992 partly because few events were aired live in prime-time owing to the time difference in Barcelona, and partly because of its disastrous pay-per-view Triplecast, which few Americans purchased. This time around, the network is banking on the fact that it can air almost all the marquee events during prime hours and that Olympic ratings soared in 1984, the last time the games were held in the United States.

Year	Network	Site	Rights Fee	Hours	Ratings
1996	NBC	Atlanta	$456 mill.	168.5 (est.)	NA
1992	NBC	Barcelona	$401 mill	161	17.5
1988	NBC	Seoul	$300 mill.	179.5	16.9
1984	ABC	Los Angeles	$225 mill.	180	23.2

competition by allowing some of the world's most recognizable players to compete. Women's soccer debuts as an Olympic sport in Atlanta.

■ **THE COMPETITORS:** Sixteen men's teams of 18 players each; 8 women's teams of 16 players each—11 play per side at any one time.

■ **WINNERS IN 1992:** Spain, Poland, and Ghana captured the gold, silver, and bronze in the men's soccer.

■ **VIEWING HINTS:** Olympic soccer is virtually identical to the World Cup game that millions of Americans watched when the event was played in the United States for the first time in 1994. Some Americans think the game moves too slowly and is too low scoring; soccer enthusiasts say it is just difficult to televise.

■ **WHO TO WATCH IN ATLANTA:** Likely challengers for the men's gold include Brazil, Spain, Italy, Mexico, and possibly the United States. The American women have dominated international competition, but face challenges from Norway and Germany.

SOFTBALL

The first-ever medal competition in this fast-growing sport. If your primary exposure to softball has been the league your office team plays in, Olympic women's softball will shock you. Some of it will look familiar: pitches are tossed underhand, and the basic rules are the same. But pitchers hurl the ball at more than 60 miles an hour and can throw many of the same curves and change-ups that baseball pitchers do. And the pitchers stand just 40 feet from the plate on a significantly smaller diamond, so the game is very fast.

■ **THE COMPETITORS:** Eight women's teams of 15 players each; 10 play on the field at one time.

■ **WINNERS IN 1992:** U.S. women have dominated international competition, winning the last three world championships including the 1994 event in St. John's, Newfoundland.

■ **VIEWING HINTS:** As in baseball, the focus in fast-pitch softball is on the confrontation between the pitcher and the batter. In the slow-pitch game, the final scores resemble football and dozens of home runs are commonplace, but here the pitcher has the edge, and shutouts are frequent. Watch the pitch curve in and out, up and down—and watch for batters to get completely fooled by the change-up pitch.

■ **WHO TO WATCH IN ATLANTA:** The U.S. women are the heavy favorites, but top competition is expected from China, Australia, and Canada.

SWIMMING:

Gold medals will be awarded in 13 individual events each for men and women, plus three relays for men and two for women. The individual events range from 50-meter sprints to nearly mile-long races for the men. The swimmers get better virtually every year: Winners at Barcelona set Olympic or world records in 10 of the 16 men's events and eight of the 15 women's events. The Chinese women—accused of attaining their recent world dominance with the help of performance-enhancing drugs—will be under heavy scrutiny.

■ **THE COMPETITORS:** A veritable army—450 men and 450 women—will represent their countries in the swimming events, more than in any sport besides track and field.

■ **WINNERS IN 1992:** Of the 16 men's events, the United States won six golds, the Unified Team five, Hungary two, and Canada, Australia, and Spain one each. In the women's events, the United States won five golds, China four, Hungary three, and Japan, the Unified Team, and Germany one each.

■ **WHO TO WATCH IN ATLANTA:** Russia, Hungary, and the U.S. should lead the men's competition, while China and the United States should vie most strongly for the women's golds, with Hungary challenging, too.

TENNIS

Tennis players are among the most recognizable Olympic athletes. In many sports, fans don't learn much about their Olympians until the Games themselves, but they will know many of the tennis players from watching Wimbledon and the U.S. Open. Olympic tennis consists of four draws—men's singles and doubles and women's singles and doubles. The winner of each championship match gets the gold, the loser of that match gets the silver, and the losers of the two semifinal matches each get bronzes. The men's matches are three-out-of-five sets, the women's best two-of-three sets, with no tiebreaker in the last set for men or women.

■ **THE COMPETITORS:** Coming to the net will be 96 men and 96 women.

■ **WINNERS IN 1992:** American women swept the golds in Barcelona, with Jennifer Capriati besting Steffi Graf in women's singles and Gigi and Mary Jo Fernandez defeating Conchita Martinez and Aranxta Sanchez-Vicario of Spain in doubles. Mark Rosset of Switzerland was the surprise winner in the upset-crazy men's singles tournament, topping home-country favorite Jordi Aresse of Spain, and Boris Becker and Michael Stich won the doubles gold for Germany, topping the South African duo of Wayne Ferreira and Piet Norval. Goran Ivanisevic won the first medals ever for the nascent country of Croatia, taking bronzes in men's singles and in doubles (with countryman Goran Prpic).

■ **WHO TO WATCH IN ATLANTA:** American men have topped the tennis rankings in recent years. They are most likely to be challenged by the Germans and French. A youthful U.S. women's squad should face stiff competition from players from Spain and Germany.

TRACK AND FIELD

By far the Olympics' biggest and most diverse competition, with 24 events for men and 19 for women. New events at the '96 Games include the triple jump for women and a 5,000-meter women's race replacing the 3,000-meter run. From the electrifying speed of the sprints and sprint relays to the grueling endurance of the marathon and the remarkable diversity of the athletes in the 10-sport decathlon, track and field has something for everyone, which explains why it is the Olympics' most watched event.

■ **THE COMPETITORS:** Some 1,300 male and 776 female athletes from scores of countries.

■ **WINNERS IN 1992:** Thirteen countries won gold medals in the 24 events of the men's competition, led by the United States with eight. Athletes from 10 countries won golds in women's events, including four

WHERE ARE THEY NOW?

Every Olympics produces its breakthrough stars, who burst into the nation's consciousness with a stellar performance or remarkable story. Who will be Atlanta's Nadia Comaneci? Its Greg Louganis? Who knows? But we can tell you what has become of some heroes of Olympics past.

RAFER JOHNSON

1960: Olympic record in decathlon.
NOW: Corporate spokesman and president of the California Special Olympics.

OLGA KORBUT

1972: Two golds in gymnastics.
NOW: Teaches gymnastics to 7- to-9-year-olds in Atlanta.

MARK SPITZ

1972: Seven swimming golds, more than any Olympic athlete.
NOW: Broadcaster and actor. His 1992 comeback effort failed, but he swam faster at age 41 than at 17.

FRANK SHORTER

1972: Marathon gold.
NOW: Makes and distributes running clothes. Will provide NBC commentary for marathon in Atlanta.

NADIA COMANECI

1976 and **1980:** Five golds, three silvers, and a bronze in gymnastics.
NOW: Engaged to Bart Conner, former U.S. gymnast. They plan to open a gymnastics school in Oklahoma.

BRUCE JENNER

1976: Set decathlon world record.
NOW: Actor, race-car driver, motivational speaker, father of eight.

MARY LOU RETTON

1984: Won first gold ever for an American female gymnast.
NOW: Corporate spokeswoman and aspiring actress (*Naked Gun 33 1/3*).

FLORENCE GRIFFITH-JOYNER

1988: 100-meter and 200-meter golds in track.
NOW: Co-chair of the President's Council on Physical Fitness.

GREG LOUGANIS

1984 and **1988:** Swept men's diving events.
NOW: First high-profile, openly gay athlete to acknowledge that he has AIDS.

each to the United States and the Unified Team.

■ **VIEWING HINTS:** Track meets are sometimes confusing to watch in person because several events often occur at the same time. But television has always made Olympic track a treat by focusing on one event at a time.

■ **WHO TO WATCH IN ATLANTA:** The American men and women should once again challenge for many golds, with chief competition coming from the Russians and athletes from such African countries as Kenya and Namibia. But so many more countries are competing and excelling in track that the track competition is among the more wide-open in the Olympics.

VOLLEYBALL

Like softball, this is another sport that will stun you with its quickness and athleticism if you're accustomed to seeing it played at company picnics. A team may only score points when it is serving, games are played to 15 points, and a team must win three games to take the match. The rules will be changed slightly in this Olympics, though. Teams must still win games by two points, but there's now a 17-point—a team wins a game if it gets ahead 17–16. In the fifth game of a match, a point is awarded on every serve, not just when the serving team wins the point, and the 17-point ceiling is not in effect.

■ **THE COMPETITORS:** Twelve teams of 12 players each for men and women; teams play 6 to a side at a time. Beach volleyball—which features only 2 players to a side—will debut as an Olympic sport in Atlanta, with 24 men's teams and 16 women's teams.

■ **WINNERS IN 1992:** Brazil, the Netherlands, and the United States took the gold, silver, and bronze in men's volleyball; Cuba, the Unified Team, and the United States captured first, second, and third, respectively, in the women's competition.

■ **VIEWING HINTS:** Watching volleyball, one's eyes are naturally drawn to the spiker, whose dramatic, powerful smashes are the home runs of volleyball. But to best understand and appreciate the game, watch the seemingly less exciting setter, who is in fact the most important player on the court. This is the player who makes the passes that set up the spikers' shots.

■ **WHO TO WATCH IN ATLANTA:** A wide-open competition among the men, featuring Brazil, Russia, Japan, Cuba, and the United States. Among the women, Brazil, Russia, Cuba, China, and the United States will challenge for the gold.

WATER POLO

Not unlike hockey, the game is played in a pool instead of on ice. Players must tread water at all times and cannot touch the sides or bottom. Except for the goaltender, players may handle the ball with only one hand at a time. The teams play four 7-minute quarters, and the offensive team must shoot the ball within 35 seconds of gaining possession. Water polo is surprisingly physical with lots of maneuvering for position in front of the goal. Most fouls result in a free throw from the point of the offense; but players can be excluded for 20 seconds for more serious breaches, like kicking or holding an opponent who doesn't have the ball. Teams average between 6 and 10 goals per game.

■ **THE COMPETITORS:** Twelve teams of 13 players each; seven (including a goaltender) play at a time.

■ **WINNERS IN 1992:** Italy, Spain, and the Unified Team.

■ **VIEWING HINTS:** The "hole set" (also called a two-meter man) is like the center in basketball; he stations himself in front of the opponent's goal, dishing passes back out to perimeter players and releasing quick shots from close range. The "hole guard" defends the hole set. A "swim-off" starts each quarter: the players line up at their respective goal lines; the referee releases the ball into the middle of the pool, and the players rush to get it.

■ **WHO TO WATCH IN ATLANTA:** The United States, which finished fourth in Barcelona, and Germany, Australia, Cuba, and Hungary are likely to challenge the 1992 medalists (most members of the 1992 Unified Team will play for Russia) for the gold in 1996.

WEIGHTLIFTING

No fancy Nautilus machines for these muscle-bound guys. They compete in two events with appropriately violent names: the clean-and-jerk and the snatch. The clean-and-jerk contains two motions: one that takes the enormous weight to the lifter's shoulders, and another that thrusts it over his head. The snatch is more difficult because there is no middle point: the lifter raises the barbell from the ground to over his head in one abrupt motion. At the games in Atlanta, every gold-medal lift will set an Olympic record: The International Weightlifting Federation established a new set of weight classes in 1993, so all marks set at the 1992 Games and before are obsolete.

■ **THE COMPETITORS:** Some 240 athletes from dozens of countries, lifting in 10 weight classes.

■ **WINNERS IN 1992:** The Unified Team won five golds, while Bulgaria, South Korea, Turkey, Greece, and Germany each captured one.

■ **WHO TO WATCH IN ATLANTA:** Russia, Germany, Poland, and, in the lighter weight classes, China.

WRESTLING

The two kinds of Olympic wrestling, Greco-Roman and freestyle, bear almost no resemblance to the farcical "sport" that features Hulk Hogan and the like. The aim is the same: pin your opponent by holding his shoulders to the mat for a half-second. In Olympic wrestling, pins are dramatic but relatively rare. Instead, wrestlers accumulate points for a series of techniques and maneuvers, including takedowns (bringing an opponent to the mat) and reversals (moving from underneath an opponent to controlling him from above). If a match is tied after five minutes or if no wrestler has accumulated three points or more during that time, a three-minute overtime will ensue. The primary difference between the two styles of wrestling: in Greco-Roman, competitors may not grasp their opponents below the waist or use their legs in any wrestling move.

■ **THE COMPETITORS:** Some 360 athletes, divided among 10 weight classes each in Greco-Roman and freestyle.

■ **WINNERS IN 1992:** In Greco-Roman, the Unified Team won three golds, Hungary two, and Turkey, South Korea, Norway, Germany, and Cuba one each; in freestyle, wrestlers from the United States and the Unified Team each took three golds, North Koreans won two, and Cuban and South Korean grapplers each captured one.

■ **WHO TO WATCH IN ATLANTA:** Turkey, Russia, Cuba, Iran, South Korea, and Germany in freestyle; Russia, Ukraine, Poland, Bulgaria, and former Soviet republics like Moldova and Azerbaijan in Greco-Roman.

EXPERT SOURCES

FOLLOWING THE OLYMPIC ACTION

Your best bet for following the games is the daily paper. But if you want a little history, or you prefer information straight from the source, try these:

PUBLICATIONS

THE COMPLETE BOOK OF THE OLYMPICS
David Wallechinsky, Little, Brown & Company, 1992, $14.95
■ Filled with knowing commentary and a flood of statistics and records.

OFFICIAL SPORTS GUIDE TO THE 1996 OLYMPIC GAMES
The editors of Pindar Press, 1996, price NA
■ Rules and history, published in cooperation with the Atlanta Committee for the Olympic Games and International Olympic Committee.

OFFICIAL TV VIEWERS' GUIDE TO THE 1996 OLYMPIC GAMES IN ATLANTA
The editors of Pindar Press, 1996, $15.95
■ A 112-page preview of events and athletes.

THE OLYMPICS: A HISTORY OF THE MODERN GAMES
Allen Guttmann, U. of Illinois Press, 1992, $24.95
■ Thoughtful analysis of the games from a top sports historian.

THE OLYMPIC FACTBOOK
The editors of Visible Ink Press, 1996, $15.95
■ The only guide to the games that is formally sanctioned by the U.S. Olympic Committee.

ONLINE

OLYMPICS ON THE NET
WORLD WIDE WEB: *http://www.atlanta.olympic.org*
■ For the first time, sports fans can follow the Olympic Games in cyberspace. The home page of the Atlanta Committee for the Olympic Games, sponsor of the Atlanta Games, can be reached on the World Wide Web at the Internet address listed above.

FROM OLYMPIA TO ATLANTA

The games began nearly three millennia ago in ancient Greece, but the modern Olympics will be just 100 years old in 1996

776 B.C. The ancient Olympics are held in Olympia, Greece, for the first time. They are staged every four years for nearly 10 centuries, until A.D. 394, when Emperor Theodosius the Great abolishes what he considers to be a pagan rite.

1892: Baron Pierre de Coubertin, a French industrialist, proposes an athletics competition based on the uncorrupted ancient Olympics.

1896: With the financial backing of a wealthy Greek architect named Georgios Averoff, the first modern Olympic Games are held in Athens. Hundreds of athletes from 13 countries compete; winners receive a gold medal and an olive branch from the King of Greece, and the most celebrated event, the marathon, is won by a Greek peasant.

1906: After poorly organized Olympiads in 1900 and 1904 flop, Greece stages the Intercalated (Interim) Games. The event's success keeps the Olympic movement alive.

1916: The Olympics are canceled because of World War I.

1928: Women compete in track-and-field events for the first time.

1936: Although Jews in various countries urge a boycott—narrowly defeated in the United States—the Summer Games in Berlin go on. Hitler's attempts to use the Olympiad to prove Aryan superiority are foiled as the U.S. track team, led by six black athletes including Jesse Owens, wins 12 gold medals to 4 for the Germans. This Olympiad also marks the first time that the Olympic torch is carried from Olympia to the site of the Games.

1940: The Summer and Winter Games, both initially awarded to Japan, are moved when Japan invades China, then canceled because of World War II. No Games are staged in 1944 either.

1952: The Soviet Union participates in the Olympics for the first time.

1968: Although boycotts and protests had disrupted the Games before, the Mexico City Olympics are considered to mark the beginning of the Olympics' most openly political era. Two American sprinters, Tommie Smith and John Carlos, thrust their black-gloved fists in the air on the victory stand to call for more power for black Americans. The IOC suspends them and orders them to leave the country. Meanwhile, Mexican police kill hundreds of protesting students who are part of a national strike.

1972: Stunning performances in Germany by Olga Korbut, a Soviet gymnast, and Mark Spitz, an American swimmer, are overshadowed by the murder of two Israeli athletes and the kidnapping of nine others by Arab terrorists. Television captures the drama as the remaining athletes and several of their captors are killed in a shoot-out at the Munich airport.

1980: Sixty-four nations, including the United States, boycott the Moscow games to protest the Soviet invasion of Afghanistan.

1984: Most Soviet-bloc countries boycott the Summer Games in Los Angeles. The United States easily dominates the competition, and the Games turn a profit for the first time.

GAMES

THE QUEST FOR A BETTER CLUB

Will Big Bertha and ping irons make you a scratch player?

Alchemists in the Middle Ages believed that a substance known as the philosophers' stone would transform base metals into gold or silver. Add the substance to lead or some other cheap metal, they believed, and through a magical process laden with philosophical and religious implications, a much more valuable metal would emerge. The elusive search for such a substance—and for the accompanying riches—occupied them for centuries. Many golfers are on a modern-day quest for the philosophers' stone, spending thousands of dollars on the latest equipment in a desperate attempt to improve their game.

That money might better be spent on a lesson or two from a golf pro—equipment isn't nearly as important as technique in golf. Nonetheless, manufacturers of golf equipment seize on the search for ever more sophisticated equipment, churning out advance after advance, claiming to add distance or control to a duffer's game. "Most of the new products on the market are purely style rather than substance," says Frank Thomas, technical director for the U.S. Golf Association. "This game is so much in the mind. In general, what you believe will work for you will work, because it will increase your confidence."

While some of the alleged technological advances of the last decade border on the ridiculous, some actually *have* made a difference. Mirroring the move to bigger racquets in tennis, for example, the trend to bigger clubs has won out on the links. The vast majority of golf clubs produced today have oversized heads, offering a larger effective hitting area—commonly known as a "sweet spot"—making bad hits more likely to fly straight.

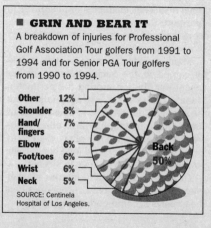

■ GRIN AND BEAR IT

A breakdown of injuries for Professional Golf Association Tour golfers from 1991 to 1994 and for Senior PGA Tour golfers from 1990 to 1994.

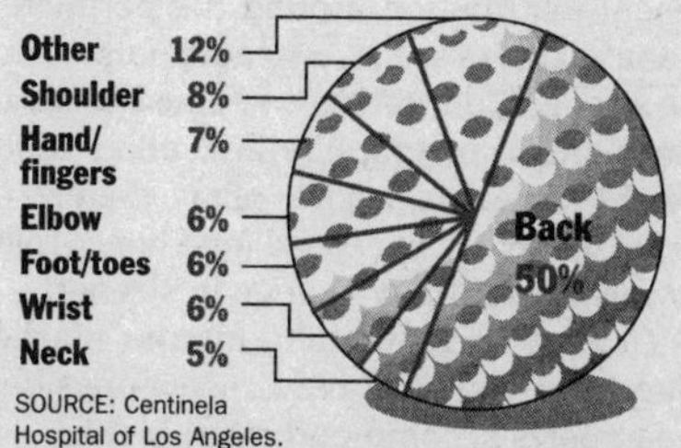

SOURCE: Centinela Hospital of Los Angeles.

HOW MANY DIMPLES ARE ON YOUR BALL?

What's the difference between cheap golf balls and pricy ones? Not much

If choosing among the dizzying number of woods, irons, and putters doesn't make your head spin, picking out a golf ball to hit with them will. Manufacturers all claim their balls will add length, increase or decrease spin, lift the height of drives or—you get the idea.

Golf balls vary in size, compression, dimple configuration, and core and cover material. But the most significant difference is between two-piece and three-piece balls. Three-piece (or wound) balls were the originals; they feature a rubber or liquid center wrapped in thin rubber thread, and are typically covered in rubber or another soft material. They are softer and spin more, giving skillful golfers more control of the ball, but they tend not to be durable. Two-piece balls, introduced in the late 1960s, have a solid core and no thread. Because they are harder, they travel further, but some of them feel as if you're playing with rocks.

If you want extra distance, two-piece balls may be for you; if you play a finesse game, you may prefer a wound ball. Or you might check out recent innovations: some new three-piece balls have more durable covers and some new two-piece balls have higher spin rates.

Manufacturers are constantly seeking an edge in the marketplace. Wilson's new Ultra 500 ball has 500 dimples, compared to the standard 380, which it insists provides greater accuracy and distance. HPG's Laser TDX has dimples with a bump in the middle, which it promises will "let the good player work the ball." But Frank Thomas, technical director for the U.S. Golf Association, which sets golf ball standards, says you shouldn't necessarily believe the hype about these or any other balls. The 400 top balls, he says, all test within 10 yards of the maximum distance permitted by the USGA.

In the same vein, it is uncommon to find a wood today that is actually made of wood; metal woods, crafted from steel, graphite, titanium, or other compounds, now dominate the market. The switch to metal heads has enabled manufacturers to distribute the weight around the perimeter of the head, also providing an expanded sweet spot.

Many of today's irons also have a cavity carved in the back, allowing further weight distribution around the perimeter. Manufacturers are also steadily improving the strength, durability, and consistency of shafts made of graphite and other lightweight materials, which allow golfers to increase their swing speed (and hence their power) without any change in strength.

Dozens of new clubs hit the market every year. Here are a few recent ones that the experts recommend most highly:

■ **WOODS:** Since 1991, Callaway Golf's Big Bertha driver has dominated the fairways, and its big heads and boron-graphite shaft have been imitated dozens of times over. Several experts say they have spotted Big Bertha's toughest competitor yet: Taylor Made's Bubble Burner, which has taken weight from the grip and distributed it along the shaft. With more weight near the end of the club, says Kim Casey, a buyer in the golf shop at Congressional Country Club in Potomac, Md., the Bubble Burner gives the golfer about 10 percent quicker swing speed. She and others believe the Burner could knock Big Bertha from the peak of drivers within a few years.

■ **IRONS:** Big heads and back cavities came to irons several years ago, so the recent innovations in these clubs have primarily been a matter of fine tuning. Manufacturers are experimenting by expanding the size and shape of the back cavity and placing different patterns on the club face, for example. Ping irons, which started the back-cavity trend, are still leading the market, but among the newer irons recommended by our experts are Cobra's King Cobra Sr. for older players, Lynx's Black Cat, and Nicklaus's The Bear, which is reportedly flying out of stores.

■ **PUTTERS:** "Feel" is the byword in putters now as always and manufacturers are promoting clubs that give golfers a greater sense of control over their painstaking work on the greens. They're experimenting with materials designed to offer a softer feel (Gary Player's PP12 putter is made of aluminum bronze) and with clubs that give a player aural feedback (Karsten's Ping-n-Ping makes a "ping" noise when it is hit solidly, and Cliker Golf's ASP Echo mallet has a rear "echo chamber"). Perhaps the most popular new putter is the Odyssey Dual Force Rossie, which has a soft black insert made of a thermoplastic substance that is supposed to cushion the ball's impact and reduce its skid off the putter.

For all the technological advances in equipment, real and exaggerated, the advice of most golf experts remains the same: Check out what the better players are using. Ask your local pro to check out your swing, and use clubs that match up well with your stroke and skills. And most of all, use the clubs you have confidence in, and stick with them. "You get people who try out every new gimmick that comes out, but chances are they're going to go back to their old favorites or the simplest designs," says Congressional's Casey.

Golfers' never-ending search for the perfect club is very profitable. In 1988 Callaway Golf had $5 million in sales. Sales climbed to $54 million in 1991, when the company introduced the Big Bertha line of woods, and to $125 million in 1992. So the search for the philosophers' stone has been very good for the golf industry. But has it been good for the golfer? Just remember this: Alchemists all but abandoned their search for the stone in the 18th century.

DIFFERENT STROKES FOR DIFFERENT FOLKS

Golf may be the only sport in which people of differing ability can compete fairly. That's because handicapping allows golfers to shave strokes off their scores depending on the quality of their games and the difficulty of the courses on which they're playing.

In simple terms, your handicap is the number of strokes by which you typically exceed par over 18 holes. But the system now used by the U.S. Golf Association for figuring a handicap is far from simple. Each golfer has a USGA handicap index that ranges from +3.4 for outstanding golfers who regularly score under par to 40.4 for players whose scores soar well over 100.

Under USGA regulations, only a golf club can calculate your handicap index. Each course has its own handicap table, based on the course's difficulty. By checking where your index falls on the course's handicap table, you can determine how many strokes to subtract from your score in that day's round. The tougher the course, the greater the deduction.

■ **SELECTED HANDICAPS**

Maury Povich, *talk-show host,* **4**
Michael Jordan, *basketball star,* **6**
Orel Hershiser, *baseball pitcher,* **6**
Dan Quayle, *former vice president,* **8**
Jimmy Connors, *tennis star,* **11**
Robert Allen, *CEO of AT&T,* **12**
Bill Clinton, *president,* **13**
John Denver, *musician,* **15**
Danny Sullivan, *race-car driver,* **15**
Louis Gerstner Jr., *CEO of IBM,* **18**
Bill Murray, *comedian,* **18**
Clint Eastwood, *actor,* **19**
George Bush, *former president,* **20**

SOURCE: Celebrity Golf Association.

DUFFER'S GUIDE

THE TOUGHEST COURSES IN AMERICA

The magazine Men's Journal *recently set out to find the 10 toughest public and resort courses in America. They ranked the courses on the basis of USGA-recognized slope ratings; courses with identical slopes were ranked by yardage. All slopes and distances are from the most difficult men's tees. Their findings:*

1. KOOLAU GOLF COURSE

Kaneohe, Hawaii

■ Distance and demoralizing hazards make this course, designed in 1992 by Dick Nugent, the nation's toughest. The 474-yard, par 4, 18th hole carries over a ravine to a narrow landing guarded by a 330-yard waste bunker. Head pro Parris Ernst says, "Whatever your handicap is, that's how many balls you'll need." ☎ **808-236-1463**

2. RIDGE & CANYON

La Paloma Country Club, Tucson, Ariz.

■ La Paloma, designed by Jack Nicklaus in 1986, comprises three 9-hole desert courses: Ridge, Canyon, and Hill. The toughest 18-hole combo is Ridge and Canyon. The tee on Ridge 4, a 199-yard par 3, is 50 feet above the peninsula green, perched on the edge of a cliff with desert all around. It's like trying to hit a table top from a five-story building. ☎ **602-229-1500**

3. THE LAGOON LEGEND

Marriott's Bay Point Resort, Panama City Beach, Fla.

■ The aesthetics of the hazards, mounds, and water make this a great place to relax—if you're not worried about your score. If scoring, your despair will only be magnified by number 18, a 382-yard run on St. Andrew Bay that island-hops from tee station to fairway to green. Designed in 1986 by Bruce Devlin and Robert vonHagge. ☎ **904-235-6909**

4. PGA WEST: TPC STADIUM COURSE

La Quinta, Calif.

■ Beware of the 19-foot-deep bunker protecting the 16th green: Because of its chasmlike trap, the 571-yard par 5 is known as San Andreas Fault. Designed by Pete Dye in 1986. ☎ **619-564-7170**

5. THUNDER HILL GOLF COURSE

South Madison, Ohio

■ More difficulty per dollar than any other in the top 10. Designed in 1976 by Fred Slagle, the course features 75 lakes. Number 9 is a whopping 246-yard par 3 that crosses a lake; bring an extra ball to the tee. ☎ **216-298-3474**

6. BLACKWOLD RUN: RIVER COURSE

Kohler, Wis.

■ Named the best course in Wisconsin by *Golf*

■ PAR FOR THE COURSES

How America's toughest courses stack up

Course	Slope	Yardage	Par	Greens fee
1. Koolau	155	7,310	72	$85–$100
2. Ridge & Canyon	152	7,088	72	$95[1]
3. The Lagoon Legend	152	6,942	72	$40–$70
4. PGA West	151	7,261	72	$75–$190
5. Thunder Hill	151	7,223	72	$25–$30
6. Blackwold Run	151	6,991	72	$91,cart $14
7. Ocean Course	149	7,371	72	$75–$130[2]
8. The Bear Acme	149	7,065	72	$40–$100
9. Shattuck	148	6,701	71	$35; cart $10
10. Thoroughbred	147	6,900	72	$55

1. Must be a guest at Westin La Paloma. 2. Less for guests at the resort; add $19 for carts.

■ DUFFER'S GUIDE

Digest, Pete Dye's 1988 design calls for target golf: Pot bunkers and severe mounds wait patiently for you to miss a fairway or green. Number 9 is a 337-yard par 4 that has three landing areas off the tee that get progressively riskier and provide three options for playing the hole. ☎ **414-457-4446**

7. THE OCEAN COURSE

Kiawah Island Resort, Kiawah Island, S.C.

■ Pete Dye's 1988 design for this wide-open beach course has an aesthetic upside (ocean views from every hole) and a practical downside (no break from the ocean winds). Head pro Greg French says, "All you'll hear is the wind, some birds, the ocean, and profanity." Number 17 is a 197-yard par 3 that carries over a lake; 30,000 balls were retrieved from it last year. ☎ **803-768-2121**

8. THE BEAR. ACME

Grand Taverns Resort, Mich.

■ No two holes are similar and not one is easy. Number 4's back tees are rarely used, even in tournaments. Architect Jack Nicklaus (1985) drew lots of criticism for the Bear's difficulty, so when a Michigan pro named Brent Veenstra shot a course-record of 62 in 1992, Nicklaus said "Thank God. Maybe now those SOBs will get off my back." ☎ **616-938-1620**

9. SHATTUCK GOLF COURSE

Jaffrey, N.H.

■ Rated the best in New Hampshire by *Golf Digest.* It takes 33 bridges to navigate the water. They come into play on 16 holes. Number 5 is a 612-yard par 5. Designed by Brian Silva, 1991.
☎ **603-532-4300**

10. THOROUGHBRED GOLF CLUB

Rothbuy, Mich.

■ Part of a dude ranch, holes here are heavily wooded to protect horses from stray balls. Designed by Arthur Hills in 1993.
☎ **616-893-4653**

SOURCE: David Willey, *Men's Journal,* May 1994.

THE BEST 18 HOLES IN ONE GOLF COURSE

Take 3 from Augusta, 1 from Pebble Beach, and 14 others and voilà:

Do you dream of driving the fairways and putting the unforgiving greens of Augusta National Golf Club, the vaunted home of The Masters? Unless you're one of the selective club's 300 members or a lucky friend, you're probably out of luck. But a course near Houston can offer you a taste of Augusta and some of the country's other top links. Tour 18 in Humble, Texas, replicates to near-perfection holes from 16 well-known courses, including Pebble Beach, Doral, Pinehurst, Merion, and the three-hole "Amen Corner" from Augusta National.

The course's designers have copied the layout and vegetation of each hole in exacting detail say golfers who've played Tour 18 and the originals. Doing so was no simple task: Building the course to match the terrain of the original holes required about a half-million cubic yards of bulldozed earth, twice the amount needed for a typical golf course.

Tour 18 is opening a second course in Flower Mound, Texas, 15 miles north of the Dallas-Fort Worth Airport. The hillier locale will enable the course to display 11 new holes from such courses as Muirfield Village, Medina, and Pine Valley, including some that were impossible to construct on the flatter Houston site.

The greens have proved lucrative for Tour 18: Duffers played 65,000 rounds in 1993, the course's first full year in business. A round costs $58.99 on weekdays, and $80.41 on weekends and holidays.

TENNIS

HOW TO PICK A RACQUET

Get a grip on the most important equipment in the game

"Buying a tennis racquet is the most complex thing imaginable," says Warren Bosworth, racquet consultant to stars like Ivan Lendl, Pete Sampras, and Martina Navratilova, and chairman of Bosworth International, a racquet-testing company. "All consumers have to do is walk into a sporting goods store and see a wall of racquets to be confused." We asked Bosworth for a private lesson in racquet picking. Here's what he told us:

You naturally look for an exact fit in shoes, clothes, and everything else you buy. Do the same with racquets, which are individualized instruments that must be chosen carefully. Don't worry about all the marketing, the technology, or even the industry guides suggesting a particular type of racquet for a particular type of player. Instead, start with some racquets suggested by your local pro or some friends and take a three-step approach:

First, simplify your understanding of the racquet. Realize that the racquet is simply a setup of three independent systems—the frame, the strings, and the handle.

Second, plan to customize. Any racquet can be made more or less powerful by adjusting the three systems—handle size and shape, overall weight and balance, and string type and tension. So plan to adjust the systems of any racquet you buy depending on what you want the racquet to do.

And third, try the racquet out. For some reason, demo-ing racquets is not a common practice among tennis consumers. Don't just buy something off the shelf. Pro shops and stores usually have demos available for testing, and friends will often let you use their favorite racquet. The greater variety you test, the more intelligent the decision will be as to which one is more effective. Also, don't limit your play-testing to racquets. Test different strings and tensions as well. Here are some factors to consider as you go about your tests.

■ **RACQUET FACTORS:** Be guided by your preference and the racquet's playability. Today's wide body is to the old conventional racquets what a bazooka is to a popgun, but the power has come at the sacrifice of arm and control problems. For those seeking a balance between power and control, conventional wisdom suggests that the wider the body, the more inherent power; the more conventional the racquet, the more control. But don't oversimplify: this formula can be drastically affected by materials, how the weight is distributed, and other, more complex engineering factors.

Weight also is a critical factor. Too heavy a racquet will strain your wrist, arm, elbow, or shoulder, but the new ultralights have also been a principal cause of injury because they are just too light to overcome the impact of the ball. Balance, whether the racquet is head-heavy or handle-heavy, will similarly affect playability and your arm.

FACT FILE:

TENNIS ELBOW, ANYONE

■ *Fewer than 5 percent of those who get tennis elbow play tennis, according to Tennis Magazine. Golfers, violinists, and surgeons also suffer from it. If you get tennis elbow (an inflammation or tiny tear of the muscle in the forearm), wait 20 minutes to let your body heat return to normal, then use ice to reduce the pain. Severe pain may need a prescription of cortisone.*

CUSTOMIZING YOUR RACQUET

Tips on getting the best from your racquet from racquet expert Warren Bosworth

FRAME: Adjust the weight and balance with lead tape in strategic places. Avoid putting it on top if the racquet is already too head-heavy. It is fairly easy to add weight, far less so to eliminate it, so while taking care to avoid buying too light a racquet, make absolutely certain you don't buy one that is too heavy.

STRINGS: Don't settle for whatever strings are in the racquet. Choose your own, on the advice of the pro, and then take advantage of stringing offers or other opportunities. Play-test new strings whenever you can.

HANDLE: If the handle is turning in the hand after contact, it might be that it is too small or that its shape isn't suited to you. Perhaps the butt cap is too large or too small for the hand to feel comfortable. Alter the handle by unwrapping the grip, changing the shape or size of the underhandle with suitable tape, and then rewrapping. Or similarly change the butt cap by building it up with tape or shaving it down. If you experience excessive wear on the thumb, the racquet is moving around a lot in the hand.

Finally, there are many types of grip materials. Experiment with the one that is the most comfortable and effective.

STRING FACTORS: Strings are the most important part of the racquet in regard to storing energy and influencing the spin of the ball. But one need only look at the variety available to see that they also represent an even greater dilemma to the consumer than perhaps racquets do.

Essentially, you have two choices— gut and synthetics. If you purchase gut, expect to pay anywhere from $40 to $60. When you venture into synthetics, the costs drop to $10 to $40, but the variations soar.

Generally synthetics are thought to last longer, but you really have to take into account climate and humidity (dry weather is better for strings), surface (clay is harder on strings), the type of racquet (some have grommets, or stringholes, that are harder on strings than others) and the type of player you are (spin players are harder on their strings).

Gauge, or string thickness, is as critical as string type. Thicker gauges—that is, fatter strings—last longer. The thinner ones provide more feel. As a rule, recreational players should expect to get several months out of a set of strings before they break or lose flexibility, while more competitive players may have to string more often.

Ask the pro's advice on tension.. He or she will help you find the optimum tension range for your racquet, your game, and your comfort. The looser the strings, the more power. Tighter may give more spin control, but also may add shock. Until you know what you like, seek the guidance of a racquet stringer certified by the U.S. Racquet Stringers Association.

COST FACTORS: Expect to spend $150 to $250 for a standard retail purchase. Racquets often are discounted, though, so shop around. Look for last year's model, which is often just as good. Whatever you buy, buy two if you can. That way, you won't be out of action when a string breaks.

TENNIS PLAYER'S GUIDE

WHERE THE BALL MACHINES NEVER STOP

When their volleys need sharpening or their second serve droops a bit, the top players in the world go back to school, often high-tech tennis compounds overseen by doting roving professors of the net. Whether you're a novice or a club player, you also can enroll in camps, clinics, and academies that will lift your level of play, if not bombard you with a million balls. Since the tennis camp boom in the early 1970s, only a select number of schools have emerged as leaders in the United States and Canada. Some are run like boot camps, while others resemble—or are part of—country clubs, north-wood retreats, or beachside resorts. David Butwin has played and trained at many of the best tennis facilities around the world. Here's his guided tour of the camps. Most offer multiday packages, with prices starting at about $100 a day, including tennis and lodging. The two John Gardiner camps are by far the priciest of the lot.

AMELIA ISLAND PLANTATION TENNIS ACADEMY

Amelia Island, Fla.

■ There is no multiday school, but you can piece together daily two-hour clinics—and then hop over to the beach. The academy aims to eliminate errors and keep the points alive. ☎ **904-261-6161**

AMHERST TENNIS CAMP

Amherst, Mass.

■ Long-running boot camp thriving since early 1970s on Amherst College's ivied campus. Rousing drills on 36 courts refine existing strokes. Three half-hour private lessons included. With junior camps (ages 10 to 17) operating nearby, perfect for families. Option to live, eat off-campus. ☎ **800-526-6388**

COLONY BEACH & TENNIS RESORT

Longboat Key, Fla.

■ Clubby tennis hangout (touring pros come and go) stages clinics on long weekends twice a month except busy March and April. Morning drills, supervised match play afternoons, and lots of time for the fine white beach. Condo bungalows are comfortable, if tightly bunched. ☎ **800-237-9443**

HARRY HOPMAN/ SADDLEBROOK INTERNATIONAL TENNIS

Wesley Chapel, Fla.

■ Noted for its junior program, Hopman also trains adults on a regimen developed for kids: fast-moving drills stressing preparation and conditioning. With tiring pace and resort toys at hand (two pools, two golf courses, full fitness center), half-day sessions are enough. ☎ **800-729-8383**

INN AT MANITOU

McKellar, Ontario

■ Solid instruction at a lovely lakefront setting 150 miles north of Toronto. Attractive 33-room inn, serving fine food, open May to October. Manitou-Wabing sports and arts camp nearby. ☎ **705-389-2171**

JOHN GARDINER'S TENNIS RANCH IN CARMEL VALLEY

Carmel Valley, Calif.

■ The John Gardiner flagship operation in California (12 years older than Scottsdale) may provide the most elegant tennis vacation in the country. Favored by 50-plus country clubbers happy with jacket-and-tie edict at dinner. Teaching is highly personalized, and food is tops. The catch: $1,600 to $1,700 for one week. Open April 1 to December 1. ☎ **408-659-2207**

JOHN GARDINER'S TENNIS RANCH ON CAMELBACK

Scottsdale, Ariz.

■ Chic, expensive, formal, and beginning to show its age, the ranch is drawing a somewhat younger clientele, singles among

■ EXPERT LIST

them, and is updating the food. The instruction remains spirited and thorough. Sunday through Sunday weeks from $1,620. ☎ **800-245-2051**

JOHN NEWCOMBE'S TENNIS RANCH

New Braunfels, Texas

■ The ex-star isn't always around, but his tactics are in evidence. Stroke improvement, not conditioning, is stressed at this 28-court complex, 30 minutes from San Antonio. Popular weekend package (two nights, three clinics, all meals), in cottage or condo. ☎ **800-444-6204**

KILLINGTON SCHOOL FOR TENNIS

Killington, Vt.

■ Director Barry Stout does things differently; he videotapes every stroke (with immediate classroom analysis) and starts with the volley, something downplayed at most camps. Pick from two-, three-, and five-day packages; Green Mountains are a cooling backdrop. Open May through September. ☎ **800-343-0762**

LA QUINTA HOTEL GOLF & TENNIS RESORT

La Quinta, Calif.

■ Michael Bolton or Danny DeVito may be on the next court at this hideaway near Palm Springs. Old Hacienda serves as clubhouse for 21 hard, 6 grass, 3 Har-Tru courts. ☎ **800-854-1271**

LODGE OF THE FOUR SEASONS

Lake of the Ozarks, Mo.

■ Intensive tennis instruction in beautiful Missouri lake country. Led by guru Dennis Van der Meer with a special focus on doubles play. The rambling resort offers four indoor courts, as well as boating, riding, and golf. ☎ **800-843-5253**

NICK BOLLETTIERI TENNIS ACADEMY

Bradenton, Fla.

■ Best known for its junior program, academy offers adults novel drills and classroom sessions to simplify and improve strokes. On full package you stay in condominium clusters by the courts and eat hearty, if ordinary, meals. ☎ **800-872-6425**

STAN SMITH TENNIS ACADEMY

Hilton Head, S.C.

■ Ace player of a generation ago, Smith appears only at Thanksgiving week clinic, but his classic game serves as model for all instruction at handsomely landscaped Sea Pines Racquet Club. Classes are held only three hours a day, leaving time for beach, golf, and biking. ☎ **800-845-6131**

STRATTON TENNIS SCHOOL

Stratton Mountain, Vt.

■ Director Kelly Gunterman's program incorporates techniques gleaned from many top clinics. Learn movement and footwork by seeing a lot of balls. Two-day clinics from mid-May to Columbus Day (with Saturday-Sunday the most popular). Golf, riding, and sailboard schools offer a diversion. ☎ **800-843-6867**

TOPNOTCH AT STOWE

Stowe, Vt.

■ Sweat it out in style at this posh northern Vermont inn. Tom Salmon's efficient clinics are particularly beneficial for beginners. Use off-court time for riding, biking, exercising in deluxe fitness center, or antiquing. Clinics open all winter on four indoor courts. ☎ **800-451-8686**

VAN DER MEER TENNIS CENTER

Hilton Head, S.C.

■ For everyone from tot to pro. Let the staff tailor a day, weekend, or week package (at either on-premises spartan Tennis Center or nearby Shipyard Plantation resort). Try to reserve a periodic clinic taught by master Dennis Van der Meer, who will spot your flaws in minutes. ☎ **800-845-6138**

VIC BRADEN TENNIS COLLEGE

Coto de Caza, Calif.

■ Braden relies on high-tech props (lots of video) and a dogmatic teaching style that stresses topspin. ☎ **800-422-6878**

SOURCE: Adapted from *Travel & Leisure* magazine. Reprinted with permission of the author.

BACKYARD GAMES

SPORTS FOR A SUMMER DAY

You'd play a lot more if you could remember the rules: Here they are

Baffled about how to keep score in badminton? Not sure how to set up the croquet wickets? Unclear on the difference between a leaner and a ringer in horseshoes? Don't know whether or not you have to win the serve before getting a point in volleyball? Here are the basic rules and regulations for four popular pastimes. So go ahead and dig out the equipment you've stashed in a musty basement corner and hit the backyard or beach.

BADMINTON

Badminton was popular in England in the 1870s, after being imported from India (where it was called *poona*) by British army officers. The eighth duke of Beaufort introduced the game to English society at his estate, called Badminton, in Gloucester. Hence the name. Now, it is the national sport of Indonesia, Malaysia, and Singapore and a backyard favorite in the United States and Canada.

Badminton is similar to tennis. The object is to volley, with light racquets, a shuttlecock or bird (a small, hemispheric cork with a tail of 14 to 16 feathers) until it is missed by your opponent or hit out of bounds. The game can be played indoors or outdoors, by two or four people.

■ THE RULES: The initial serve goes from the right half of the court to the half diagonally opposite. The serving team continues to serve until losing a rally or committing a fault. A fault occurs if you serve overhand,

■ BADMINTON

The basic equipment and layout for a regulation game.

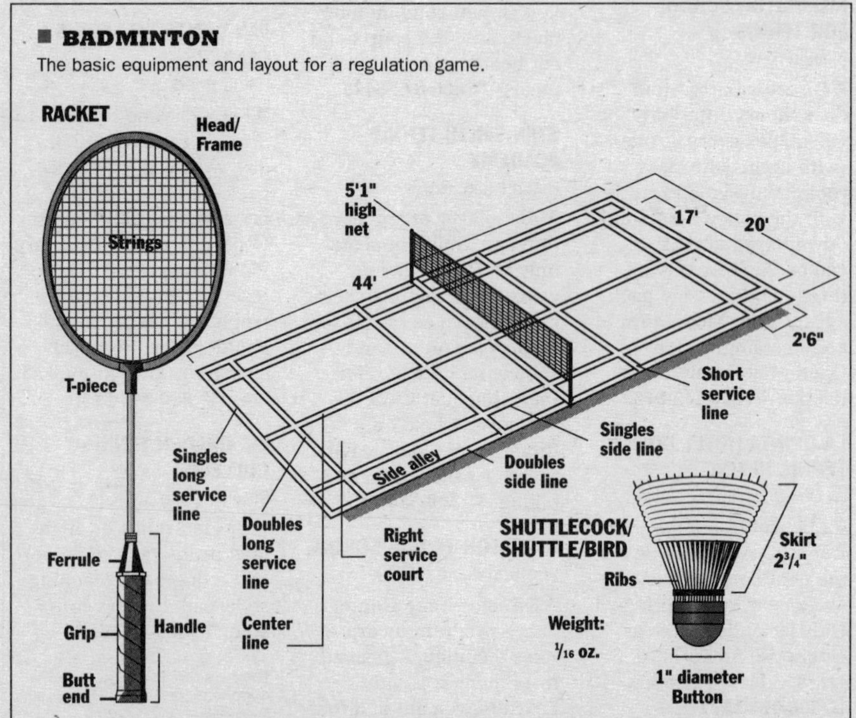

touch the net, or do not serve diagonally across the court. Points may only be scored by the serving team. In doubles, a player serves until his team commits a fault, at which time the teammate gains the serve. Following each game, the players switch sides. The winning side serves first.

■ **SCORING:** All doubles and men's singles games are played to 15 or 21 points, while women play to 11. The first player or team to win two games wins the match. If a match goes to three games, the players switch sides when the score reaches 8 in a 15-point game and 6 in an 11-point game. In a 15-point game, the team to reach 13 first has the option of extending the game to 18 points if the score becomes tied at 13. In 11-point games, the score may be extended to 12 if the game becomes tied at either 9 or 10. In a one-game match to 21 points, the score may be extended to 24 if there is a tie at 19 or extended to 23 if the game is tied at 20.

CROQUET

The game probably originated in France in the 17th century. It became popular in England and Ireland during the 19th century and made its way to the United States in about 1870. It was one of the first games in which women and men competed on an even basis. There are three leading modern versions of the game: American lawn croquet, English croquet, and roque. Most croquet balls are made of wood, but better balls are made of hard rubber or plastic. The mallet head may be of wood or other material.

■ **THE RULES:** There are two courses: nine wickets and two stakes or six wickets and one stake. In the American nine-wicket game, the court is fitted to the area available. The English court has definite boundaries and locations for the six wickets and peg (see diagrams, below). A toss determines who gets which color. These colors are usually painted on the stake, or peg,

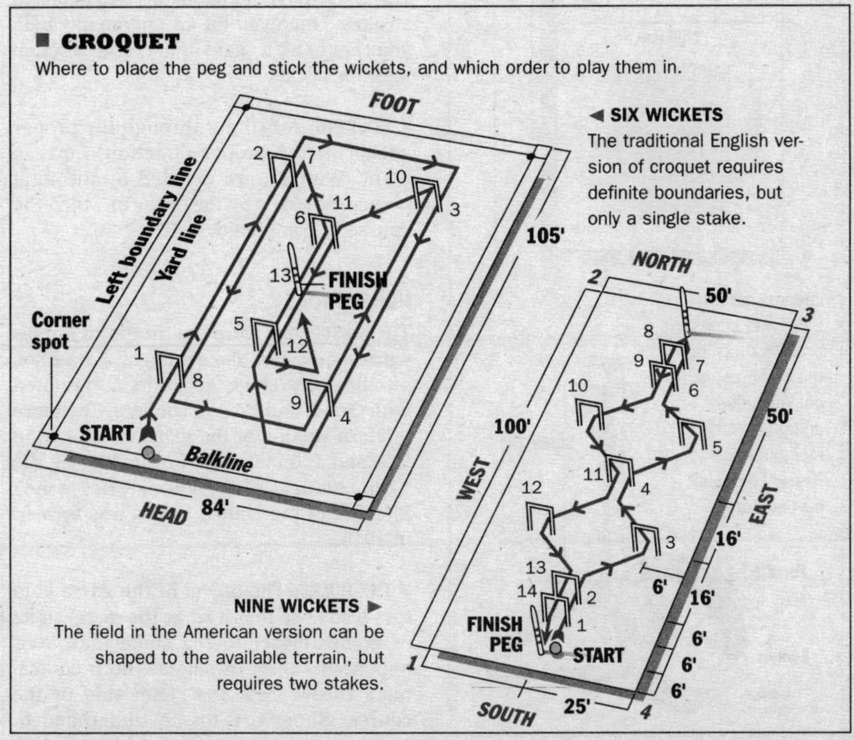

■ **HORSESHOES**

A regulation course and a look at leaners.

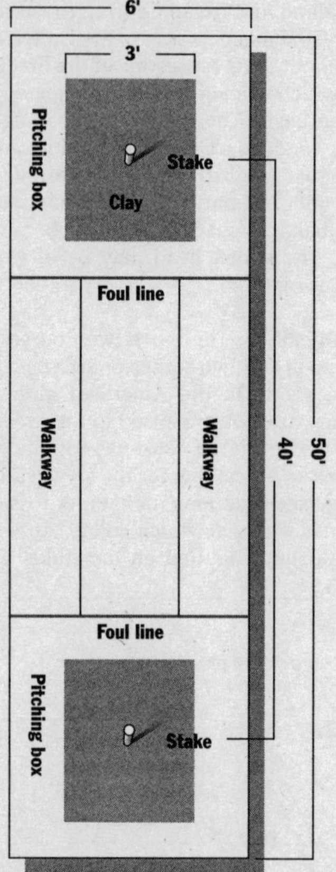

Leaners, or hobbers, and shoes actually touching the stake count only as close shoes. In informal games, a leaner can count for two points.

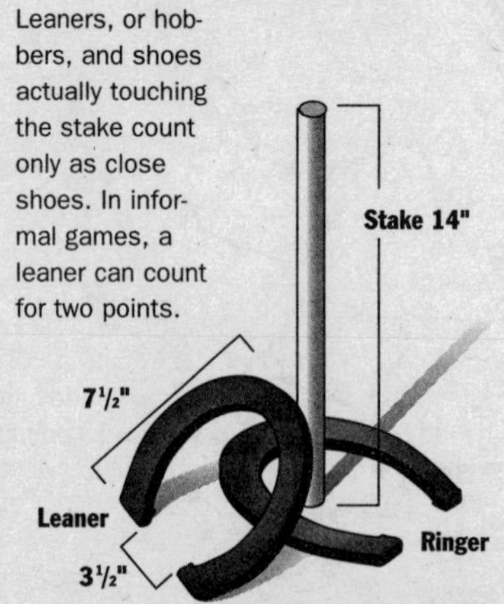

and control the order of play. Players—two to eight people can play at one time—use balls of the color allocated to them. The first striker hits the ball with his mallet at the balkline or home stake, depending on what course one is playing on. Subsequent players do likewise. The course leads through the wickets, or hoops. The strikers alternate turns.

Your turn continues as long as you drive the ball through the proper wicket. If you fail to go through a wicket or hit another player's ball, you lose your turn. You also lose your turn if your mallet hits the wicket or the ground, but not the ball, or if your mallet accidentally hits another player's ball.

A striker makes a roquet by knocking his ball into an opponent's. If you do so, you have three options: (1) You may place your ball against your opponent's and, putting your foot on your ball, drive your opponent's ball away; (2) You can drive both balls; or (3) you can simply place your ball ahead of your opponent's and take two strokes. Once you hit an opponent's ball, you cannot hit it again until you go through another wicket.

■ **SCORING:** A ball put through the proper wicket in the proper direction scores a point. Winners are decided by the total points scored or by the order in which the course is completed.

HORSESHOES

The early Celts were the first to fit horses with shoes. But the game of horseshoe pitching, by some accounts, originated with Greek and Roman soldiers. The more modern version of the game developed in England and mainland Europe during the 17th century. The National Horseshoe Pitchers of the United States was formed in 1915.

■ **THE RULES:** The object of the game is to toss a shoe so that it rings the metal stake or comes closer to the stake than your opponent's toss. In singles, both contestants throw from the same side of the course. Shoes are tossed underhanded.

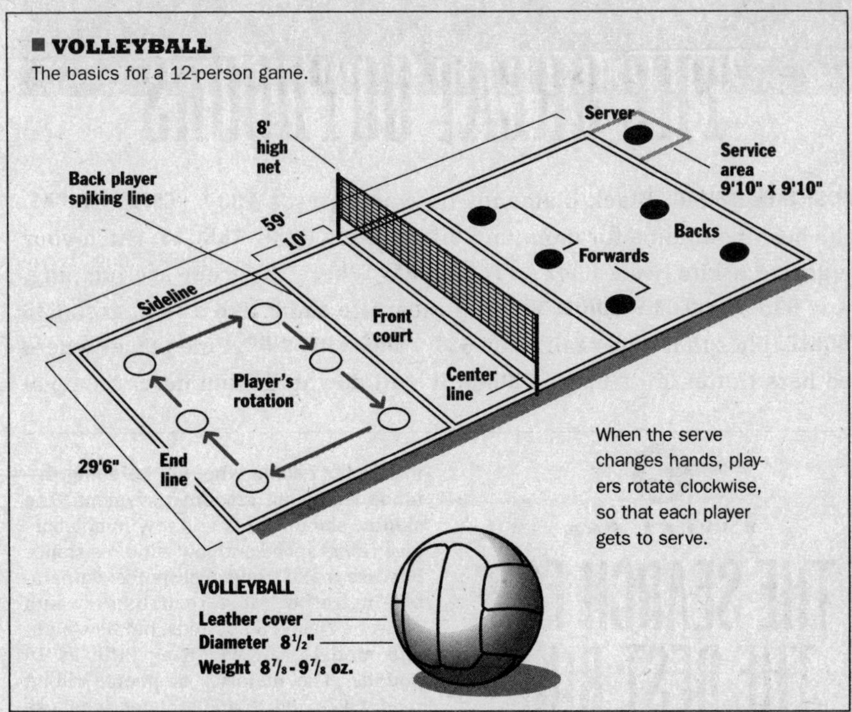

Each pitcher is allotted two tosses in an inning. The pitcher who scores in an inning leads off the next.

■ **THE RULES:** Each ringer is worth three points. Each shoe closer than an opponent's is worth one point, but shoes only score when landing within 6 inches of the stake. If an opponent's shoe knocks a ringer off, it loses value. Two points are awarded if you land two shoes closer than any of your opponents. Leaners, or hobbers, and shoes actually touching the stake count only as close shoes. (In informal games, a leaner can count for two points.) Singles matches are usually played to 50 points, doubles matches to 21.

VOLLEYBALL

Volleyball originated in Holyoke, Massachusetts, in 1895. William G. Morgan, physical director of the Young Men's Christian Association in Holyoke. is credited with the invention of the game. It's been modified since and now is played indoors and outdoors and is included in the Olympics.

■ **THE RULES:** There are six people on each team—usually three forward and three back. The height of the net varies: 8 feet high for men, 7½ feet high for women, and sometimes lower for kids. The players can hit the ball to each other before hitting it back over the net. However, the ball can only be hit a maximum of three times on one side of the net. A player may not hit the ball twice in a row.

■ **SCORING:** Points are scored by hitting the ball into the opposing court in a way so the competition cannot return it. The team serving gains one point for doing this and continues serving. If the receiving team does it, it wins the right to serve. A game is 15 points, but it must be won by two points, thus a 14-to-14 tie continues until either team gains a two-point advantage. When the serve changes hands, players rotate clockwise, so that each player gets to serve.

THE GREAT OUTDOORS

EXPERT Q&A

THE SEARCH FOR THE BEST BIKE

What to look for if you're riding up a mountain or over to the corner store

A stroll into today's bike shop is not for the faint of heart. The days of banana seats and coaster brakes are long gone, replaced by the likes of titanium steel frames and shock-absorbing suspension forks. But don't be intimidated—or fooled. Inside that shop, there is a bike that is exactly what you need—and lots more that you don't need. Here to guide you through the maze of bike styles and sizes and help you pick one that best suits your needs (and pocketbook) is the editor of *Bicycling* magazine Geoff Drake.

■ **How do I know what type of bike I need?**

There are three types of bikes: road, mountain, and hybrid. Each is built for a certain type of riding. A breakdown:

ROAD BIKES: The lightest and fastest of the three bicycle types, these bikes are primarily for people who will be doing distance riding on smooth pavement. The skinny, smooth tires and low handlebars give riders speed and low wind resistance but also make some cyclists feel vulnerable in traffic. Most road bikes weigh between 20 and 30 pounds, but new high-end models can weigh as little as 18 pounds. The majority of people riding road bikes today are athletes who use them for training purposes.

MOUNTAIN BIKES: Mountain bikes, created by outdoors enthusiasts in Northern California, are now the most popular bike in the United States. The upright seating, fat, knobby tires, and easy gearing make these bikes ideal for off-road riding. But even if you live in the heart of the city and only occasionally hit a trail, mountain bikes offer comfort and stability. If you use your bike only for riding with the kids or short trips around town, a mountain bike is probably better suited to your needs than a road bike.

HYBRID BIKES: Hybrids, relative newcomers to the bike market, are rapidly gaining in popularity. Hybrids combine the upright seating and shifting of mountain bikes, but offer the thin, smooth tires of road bikes for speed. Many people like the versatility a hybrid offers; you can ride on some less-challenging trails, and also make better time than you would on a mountain bike. But don't buy a hybrid if you are a serious

■ THE NUTS AND BOLTS OF MOUNTAIN BIKES

Bike shops are dangerous places for those with an itchy wallet finger. There are hundreds of bike accessories you could purchase, but a much smaller number that you actually need. Here are a few of the basics, and some exotic innovations:

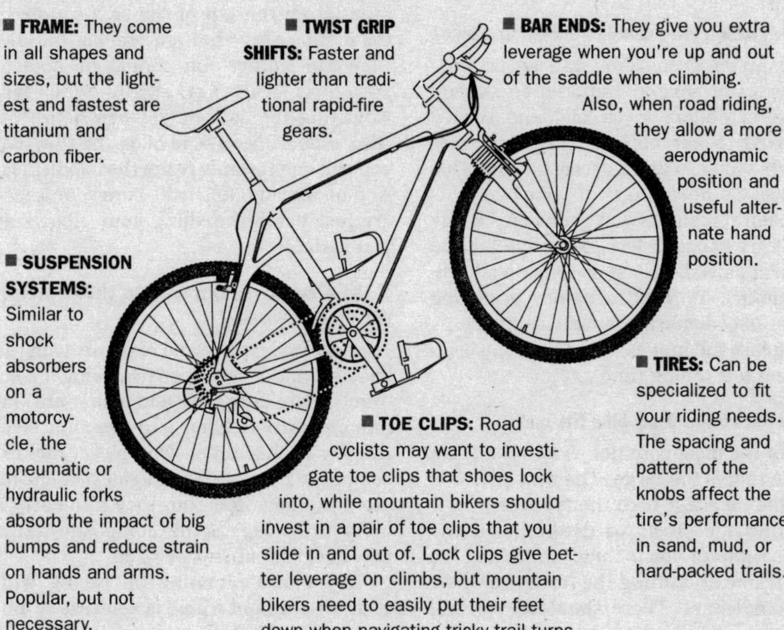

■ **FRAME:** They come in all shapes and sizes, but the lightest and fastest are titanium and carbon fiber.

■ **TWIST GRIP SHIFTS:** Faster and lighter than traditional rapid-fire gears.

■ **BAR ENDS:** They give you extra leverage when you're up and out of the saddle when climbing. Also, when road riding, they allow a more aerodynamic position and a useful alternate hand position.

■ **SUSPENSION SYSTEMS:** Similar to shock absorbers on a motorcycle, the pneumatic or hydraulic forks absorb the impact of big bumps and reduce strain on hands and arms. Popular, but not necessary.

■ **TOE CLIPS:** Road cyclists may want to investigate toe clips that shoes lock into, while mountain bikers should invest in a pair of toe clips that you slide in and out of. Lock clips give better leverage on climbs, but mountain bikers need to easily put their feet down when navigating tricky trail turns.

■ **TIRES:** Can be specialized to fit your riding needs. The spacing and pattern of the knobs affect the tire's performance in sand, mud, or hard-packed trails.

■ BUYING A HELMET

Wearing a bike helmet is no longer nerdy. In fact, in many cities it's the law.

■ The majority of bike-related deaths are caused by head injuries—injuries that could easily be avoided if cyclists wore helmets. But a helmet won't do you any good if it doesn't fit properly.

■ The experts suggest buying a helmet that feels snug, but not uncomfortable.

■ The strap under your chin should feel snug, but loose enough to open your mouth wide enough to take a drink of water.

■ The helmet should touch the head at the crown, sides, front, and back and should not roll backward or forward on the head when you push up.

■ Remember that you can make a tight helmet looser by inserting smaller sizing pads or sanding down existing pads.

cyclist: the limitations on both roads and trails will frustrate you. If you want to ride on challenging trails, the hybrid's frame and thin tires can't handle the challenge. And if you want to take it on the open road, you'll be battling wind resistance the whole ride.

■ How much money should I spend on a bike?

Bikes aren't cheap. You can spend anywhere from several hundred to several thousand dollars for a high-end model. It's hard to purchase a bad bike today, though—you can find a decent bike for $300 to $400. So don't worry if your budget is tight, but remember you get what you pay for. Don't expect a less-expensive bike to perform as well or last as long as a high-end model. Your extra money is buying lighter, sturdier frames, and components (like gears and brakes) that can take a beating and last a long time.

■ How do I know if my bike fits me?

One of the most common errors is buying a bike that is too large. The best advice is buy the smallest bike that you can comfortably ride. Tests to determine if the size is right for you include: straddling the bike frame and lifting the front tire up by the handlebars. There should be several inches of clearance between your crotch and the bike frame, 1 to 2 inches for a road bike, and at least 3 to 4 inches for a mountain bike. For more precise sizing, measure your inseam and then multiply by .883. The result should equal the distance from the top of the seat saddle to the middle of the bottom bracket spindle.

When riding, you should be able to straighten—but not strain—your leg. Adjusting the seat height can help this. Also, especially on road bikes, be sure that you can comfortably reach the handlebars. And on a road bike, make sure your knees are just barely brushing your elbows as you pedal.

■ There are so many frames to choose from. What's best for me?

Frames vary in price and expense, with the heaviest and least expensive being a steel frame. More expensive and lighter are aluminum, carbon fiber, and titanium steel frames, in that order. One-piece, molded composite frames are the lightest of all and are a hot new item, but they also carry a hefty price tag. Some composite-frame bikes cost as much as $3,250.

If you are planning on racing with your bike, a light frame is a necessity. But for weekend riders, it is merely a luxury that will make your ride somewhat more enjoyable.

■ Which bikes do you recommend?

Bike models come and go, and what's hot this year may be outdated by next year. The surest way to purchase a quality bike is to avoid the hot gimmicks and new names, and stick with companies that produce high-quality bikes year-in and year-out.

For mountain and hybrid bikes, try Trek and Cannondale, which are two of the biggest American companies. Also try GT, Specialized, and Schwinn.

For road bikes: Specialized and Trek are always reliable. For sure-fire winners that will put a dent in your wallet, look overseas to the Italian-made bikes. Some bike shops carry Pinarello and De Rosa, which are top-of-the line—and the most expensive. They often cost as much as $5,000.

FACT FILE:

BIKING COAST TO COAST

■ *Depending on your route, it takes 60 to 90 days. The Adventure Cycling Association in Missoula, Mont., ☎ 406-721-8754, recommends three routes:*

The TransAmerica Tour: *Williamsburg, Va., to Portland, Ore.* 4,450 miles

The Northern Tier: *Seattle, Wash., to Bar Harbor, Maine.* 4,500 miles

The Southern Tier: *San Diego, Calif., to St. Augustine, Fla.* 3,135 miles

BIKING

BLACK DIAMONDS ON WHEELS

When the snow melts, mountain bikers head for the ski resorts

Ski resorts aren't just for ski bums anymore. In fact, many of the nation's ski resorts are keeping their doors (and lifts) open all summer long so that mountain bike enthusiasts can enjoy the same thrills, jumps, and speeds that skiers do during the winter months.

Capitalizing on the popularity of mountain biking, 130 of the nation's ski resorts currently offer summer biking programs. Mountain bike aficionado Stan Zukowski of *Bicycling* magazine has put together a best of the best list (below), but for a complete list of the ski resorts offering mountain biking, refer to the May 1995 issue of *Bicycling* (available at ☎ 800-666-2806).

All of the resorts on Zukowki's list offer breathtaking scenery and challenging rides, not to mention a lift up the mountain (you may be adventuresome, but you're no fool). Shuttle service, gondolas, or chairlifts generally bring bikers to the top of the mountain, where they are free to roam the miles of ski trails, logging roads, and national parkland that adjoins many ski resorts. The riding ranges from intermediate to expert. If you've never been on a mountain bike before, 11,000 feet above sea level on a narrow downhill trail is not a good place to learn.

No matter what your skill level, you may experience a flat tire or an accident while on a trail, and many of the resorts offer emergency repair and rescue. Besides the exhilarating rides, one of the biggest attractions of ski resort biking is the off-season prices. Lodging that would cost you several hundred dollars during prime ski season can run as little as $40 a night off-season.

EXPERT PICKS

TAKING MOGULS ON A BIKE

Stan Zukowski of Bicycling *magazine picks his favorite resorts for mountain biking. Prices quoted are as of 1995.*

MOUNT SNOW, VERMONT
■ Sixteen miles of trails on the mountain, but bikers also enjoy access to many miles of adjoining land. The vertical drop is 1,700 feet. $17 for one trip up, $25 for an all-day ticket.
☎ **800-245-7669**

VAIL, COLORADO
■ Four miles of downhill riding, many more miles of trails traversing the mountain and on access roads. Vertical drop: almost 3,000 feet. All-day gondola ticket $18.
☎ **303-476-5601**

CRESTED BUTTE, COLORADO
■ Adjacent to Gunnison National Forest, which offers bikers 600,000 acres of riding territory. Ranges from $6 to $15 by the hour or by the day for trail access only.
☎ **303-349-2333**

BRIAN HEAD RESORT, UTAH
■ Sixty miles of single-track trails from 11,300-foot summit. $10 for an all-day lift pass. $39.95 gets a room and lift pass.
☎ **801-677-2035**

MAMMOTH MOUNTAIN SKI AREA, CALIFORNIA
■ Vertical drop of 3,100 feet. Over 55 miles of trails. $15 for a half-day ticket, $25 for all-day.
☎ **619-934-2571**

THRILLS

HITCH YOUR BUGGY TO A KITE

Is there life after bungee jumping? The latest thrill blowing in the wind

If you're ready to tackle a new high-speed sport, consider the newest activity for thrill-seekers: kite buggying. In this sport, a large kite is used to propel a low-to-the-ground tricycle. The buggy's "pilot" flies a rip-stop nylon kite with his hands while steering the buggy with his feet. The result: the wind's force pulls the pilot and his gear across an open area (usually a beach) at speeds of up to 50 mph.

Humans have used wind-powered transportation for centuries, but the most recent kite-propulsion craze was born with the lightweight, durable kites of the 1970s. Creative kite flyers experimented with a variety of kite-propelled vehicles—from inline skates to ice carts. Then Peter Lynn, a designer from New Zealand, built the steel tricycle that today is the vehicle of choice.

The sport claims some 500 enthusiasts nationally, according to Fran Gramkowski, co-chairman of the American Kite-flyers Association's power flying committee. The first North American kite buggy racing championships are scheduled for September 1995, and Gramkowski expects the sport to explode in popularity as more novice kite flyers discover it. In an effort to educate those flyers, the AKA publishes the *Powerflying Manual*, a 16-page booklet of safety and instructional information. The booklet costs $2 for members and $5 for nonmembers and can be ordered by calling the AKA at ☎ 800-252-2550.

Keep in mind that kite buggying can be dangerous and is not recommended for those with no kite-flying experience, says Tim Waters, a spokesman for AKA. Experts at the AKA say inexperienced kite-flyers should learn how to fly a two- or four-line soft kite before they try kite buggying. Even after mastering the kite, it's still best to learn buggying from an experienced teacher. A local kite specialty store can help you find one.

GUARANTEED TO GET THE BLOOD FLOWING

A sampler of popular and only seemingly death-defying diversions:

BALLOONING
$100 to $175 per person
■ An hour flight, depending on the wind, can take you from under a mile to over 10, reaching an average height of 500 feet. No training is necessary—the pilot takes care of everything.

SKYDIVING
$150 to $300 per person
■ Many options. Tandem ride: jumper is attached to instructor's harness—requires minimal ground training. Static line: chute is deployed automatically. Accelerated free fall: instructors hold you until chute opens.

WATERSKIING
$50 to $100 per person
■ Ski school can teach you everything from slaloming, kneeboarding, and jumping to barefoot waterskiing. Cost depends on how many events you want to learn.

HANG GLIDING
$50 to $100 per person
■ Lookout Mountain in Rising Farm, Ga., a top-rated flight school, costs $99 for a day's class that includes five flights off a gently sloped hill.

BUNGEE JUMPING
$10 to $25 per person
■ Jumper usually must weigh at least 80 pounds. States may have age regulations. Rebounds make one jump feel like three.

WHERE THE TROUT ARE JUMPING

A guide to some of the nation's best fishing holes

A friendly fly fisherman may give you directions to his favorite fishing hole, but a smart one will guard his spot like gold. Fly fishermen tend to be tightlipped about where the fish are biting, so finding a good fishing spot can seem overwhelming to those just starting out. But we've done some of your work for you and compiled a list of some of the country's best fly fishing rivers. While there are thousands of good fishing holes around the country, fly fishing experts at the Federation of Fly Fishers and *Fly Fisherman* magazine recommended these rivers as surefire winners. If none of them are within an easy drive, the experts recommend asking a local fly shop for advice. But ask where the best river access is, they say, not where a particular hole is. Easy access will allow you to roam up and down the river with the fish, as opposed to being confined to a single fishing spot.

ALAGNAK RIVER, Alaska

■ The Alagnak, with its giant trout and amazing scenery, is just one of Alaska's many fishing pleasures. If you tire of the river, the region also offers excellent lakes and ponds.

AU SABLE RIVER, Michigan

■ One of the few midwestern rivers to make the list, the Au Sable is a good bet for all kinds of trout. But midwesterners shouldn't bemoan a lack of fishing holes. The tributaries to the Great Lakes offer great pike and small mouth bass fishing.

BEAVERKILL RIVER, New York

■ Bass prefer the warmer waters of lakes and ponds, and are more common in the East. This is one of the best bass rivers in the country. Use a dry fly. You may also catch some small rainbow trout.

BIGHORN AND MADISON RIVERS, Montana

■ Montana is the Mecca of fly fishing, and these two Montana rivers are considered the best of the best. Trout thrive in the cool, mountain waters. Fish these waters with dry or wet flies for brown and rainbow trout. The average catch is about 10 to 12 inches.

GREEN RIVER, Vermont

■ Good for rainbow and brown trout, with a few bass.

JACKSON RIVER, Virginia

■ The Jackson River is an easy day trip from Washington, D.C., or Richmond, Va. It is considered one of the best trout streams in the area.

LOWER DESCHUTES RIVER, Oregon

■ This cold water stream is teeming with trout and bass. Catches average 1 to 4 pounds for the trout and 6 to 10 pounds for the bass.

SAN JUAN RIVER, New Mexico

■ The San Juan is respected as one of the premier big-trout rivers in the country. Rainbow trout are plentiful. But so are annoying crowds of fishermen. The best time to fish the San Juan is in the off-season (late fall or early spring).

SUSQUEHANNA RIVER, Pennsylvania

■ Some portions of the Susquehanna are polluted, but the river (which winds through Pennsylvania, New York, and Maryland) offers excellent small mouth bass fishing.

■ **EDITOR'S NOTE:** For stories and guides to the best canoeing, kayaking, and white-water rafting rivers in the United States, see pages 556 through 561 in the Travel chapter.

ANGLER'S GUIDE

WHERE TO LEARN TO THINK LIKE A FISH

To catch a fish, you have to think like a fish—so make like a fish and join a school. The quickest way to learn the art of fly fishing is to sign up for a class. One day of fly fishing school can prevent 30 years of mistakes and prepare you to hook the big one in a matter of days. There are lots of choices. John Randolph, editor of Fly Fisherman *magazine, compiled this list of his favorite schools around the country. Prices quoted are as of 1995.*

ALLENBERRY RESORT INN
Boiling Springs, Pa.

■ Fly fisher-wannabes in Philadelphia and Washington, D.C., have to travel only about two hours. Students split their time between taking classes and fishing on a heavily stocked stream. Because of the school's proximity to major urban areas, the students tend to be young professionals. Three days for $395, lodging included.
☎ **717-258-3211**

CREATIVE SPORTS ENTERPRISES
Pleasant Hill, Calif.

■ Creative Sports students spend a week fishing on the Snake River in Idaho, which is one of the best spots in the world. The fish there are wild (not bred), so it's more difficult, but not impossible, for beginners to catch them. Most students are affluent professionals. One week for $1,850, includes everything.
☎ **510-938-2255**

THE FLY BOX
Bend, Ore.

■ This is a good option for locals who don't have a lot of time and are checking out fly fishing for the first time. If you're planning on a half-day lesson, do some preparatory reading before you get there. Half day for $90; one-day, private lesson for $145.
☎ **503-388-3330**

JOAN AND LEE WULFF FISHING SCHOOL
Lew Beach, N.Y.

■ This is one of the only schools conducted by a woman, Joan Wulff. But men and women alike are guaranteed excellent instruction here, and the location, on the Beaverkill River, is convenient for commuting New Yorkers. Three days for $400, lodging not included.
☎ **914-439-4060**

KAUFMANN'S FLY FISHING EXPEDITIONS
Portland, Ore.

■ Located on the Deschutes River, which is only two and a half hours from Portland. Three days on the Deschutes River for $395, accommodations included. Three days—two in the shop, one on the river—for $75.
☎ **503-639-6400**

L.L. BEAN FLY FISHING SCHOOLS
Freeport, Maine

■ L.L. Bean may be the best introduction to fly fishing in New England. You'll split your days between fishing on the Grand Lake Stream and attending seminars on everything from tackle to entomology. The emphasis may be on bass fishing because of the ponds and streams you'll be fishing on, but the techniques are universal. There are classes for all levels of experience, and the student-instructor ratio is very low. Three days for $395, lodging not included, or five days for $1,195, everything included.
☎ **207-865-4761**

THE ORVIS COMPANY
Manchester, Vt.

■ Orvis is the oldest fly fishing company in the United States, which means that you get history and tradition along with excellent instruction on the Battenkill River. Several other Orvis shops across the country also offer first-rate classes.

FLIES THAT NEVER FAIL

They have funny names, but fish find them most alluring

Rule number one for aspiring fly fishermen: never say the word "worm" to another fisherman. Instead, try peppering your conversation with words like hopper, nymph, or woolly bugger (a few commonly used flies). You'll fit right in.

Fly fishermen fish with imitation insects (flies) instead of worms or minnows, and pride themselves on the intricacy and variety of their flies. To ease your transition into the large and sometimes intimidating world of flies, here is a quick guide to some of the most popular and successful flies, according to fly guru John Bailey. From his fly shop in Livingston, Mont., Bailey has been supplying fly fishermen with his hand-tied flies for decades. He's also a fly-tier to the stars: he served as a consultant and fly fishing instructor for Robert Redford's movie *A River Runs through It.*

WOOLLY BUGGER

❋ One of the most universal flies, the woolly bugger works for both trout and bass on eastern and western waters. The woolly bugger is a streamer fly, which means it replicates minnows that swim below the surface.

MUDDLER MINNOW

❋ Like the woolly bugger, the muddler is a streamer that works on both trout and bass, but it is more effective on streams than it is on lakes.

ADAMS

❋ Good for trout fishing, the Adams is a dry fly, which means it floats on top of the surface like an insect.

ROYAL WULFF

❋ Another dry fly for trout. The white wings on this one allow you to keep an eye on it even in rough or choppy waters.

HARE'S EAR NYMPH, PRINCE NYMPH, BITCH CREEK NYMPH, AND DAMSEL

❋ Nymph flies imitate aquatic insects in a particular developmental stage. Although nymphs are primarily for trout, the bitch creek nymph is good for both trout and bass, but is rarely used in eastern waters. The damsel is best for catching lake trout.

ELK HAIR CADDIS

❋ Another good dry fly for trout. This one is made out of real elk hair. Because elk hair is hollow, the fly floats well.

DAVE'S HOPPER

❋ This fly, named for fly fishing expert Dave Whitlock, replicates a grass hopper, floats on the surface, and can be used in most places.

Responding to the growing number of women interested in fishing, Orvis has started a school exclusively for women. The crowd here tends to be slightly younger, even with some children included in the classes. Three days for $395, lodging included.
☎ **800-235-9763**

SAGE/WINSLOW
Bainbridge Island, Wash.

■ Like Orvis, Sage has other locations in the West, making it convenient for those not in the Seattle area. Sage is one of the top rod makers in the country, so you receive excellent instruction in the fundamentals of tackle and equipment. Half-day clinic for $40, or one day for $85.
☎ **206-842-6608**

If none of these schools fits your budget or schedule, chances are your local fly shop offers classes of its own—or try joining a local fly fishing club, which may offer free or cheap instruction.

BIRD WATCHING 

WHERE BIRDS FLOCK TOGETHER

All the right places from coast to coast for spotting species

Virtually every setting—coastline, open prairie, big city park—makes for rewarding bird-watching. One of the joys of the sport is how little equipment it requires. Binoculars and a comprehensive field guide are all you need, though a telescope is best for observing waterfowl and other stationary birds. Roger F. Pasquier, an author of several books on birds, works at the Environmental Defense Fund. He chose the following locales as among America's best for bird watching. For information, call or write the sources below.

ARANSAS NATIONAL WILDLIFE REFUGE

Box 100, Austwell, TX 77950 ☎ 512-286-3559

The 54,000-acre refuge is most famous for its rarest bird, the whooping crane. More than 100 of this highly endangered species (there are only 150 left in the world) are usually here between mid-October and early April, visiting from breeding sites in Alberta. Visitors can view them only at a distance by boat. Five companies run cruises in season. For information, call Rockport Chamber of Commerce, ☎ 512-729-6445.

CAPE MAY POINT

Cape May Bird Observatory, Box 3, Cape May Point, NJ 08212 ☎ 609-884-2626

■ The southern tip of New Jersey acts as a funnel for migratory birds between the Atlantic Ocean and Delaware Bay. Mid-August into November, flocks follow the coastline south. North of Cape May, at Stone Harbor Point, look for herons and egrets in spring and summer. The nearby Edwin Forsythe National Wildlife Refuge at Oceanville is a haven for waterfowl and shorebirds from fall through spring.

CAVE CREEK CANYON

U.S. Forest Service, Portal Ranger Station, Box 126, Portal, AZ 85632 ☎ 602-558-2221

■ One of many outstanding birding locations in southern Arizona. Cave Creek contains a wide variety of species in a small area. Of special interest are the many essentially Mexican birds that do not venture farther north of the border, including hummingbirds and the painted redstart.

CENTRAL PARK, NEW YORK CITY

Urban Park Rangers, 1234 Fifth Ave., New York, NY 10028 ☎ 212-427-4040

■ Like its counterparts in other dense cities, Central Park serves as a green oasis, especially important to migratory birds in spring and fall. Late April through May is peak season; on a good day, 70 or more species can be seen, including thrushes, vireos, warblers, orioles, tanagers, and other migrants from the tropics. The Ramble, a wooded area on the north side of the park's main lake, lures most species. The reservoir is a winter favorite of ducks and gulls.

BLACKWATER NATIONAL WILDLIFE REFUGE

2145 Key Wallace Dr., Cambridge, MD 21613 ☎ 410-228-2677

■ One of several outstanding sites on the Eastern Shore of the Chesapeake Bay. Thousands of migrating ducks and geese congregate in the refuge mid-October through November and mid-February through March (as long as the ponds aren't frozen). Bald eagles are permanent residents.

CHEYENNE BOTTOMS WILDLIFE MANAGEMENT AREA

Dept. of Wildlife and Parks, Cheyenne Bottoms, Rte. 3, Box 301, Great Bend, KS 67530 ☎ 316-793-7730

■ This western Kansas wetland is an important locale for waterfowl and other birds dependent on marshes. Thousands of ducks and geese use the bottoms, and as many as 15,000 American white pelicans land here during migration.

DAUPHIN ISLAND

Audubon Bird Sanctuary, Box 848, Dauphin Island, AL 36528
☎ 205-861-2120

■ This 14-mile barrier island near Mobile is one of many landfalls along the Gulf Coast known for the vast numbers of northbound migrants every spring that need to rest and feed after their long flight across the Gulf of Mexico. The 164-acre Audubon Bird Sanctuary is one of the best birding spots on the island. Shorebirds, terns, and marsh birds can be seen much of the year in the mudflats, lagoons, and other wetlands.

EVERGLADES NATIONAL PARK

40001 State Rd., 9336, Homestead, FL 33034
☎ 305-242-7700

■ Some 2,200 square miles of wetland encompassing most of the undeveloped parts of southern Florida. A system of paved roads, trails, and boardwalks allows access to marshes and patches of woods. Many species of herons, egrets, and other wading birds are abundant. In spring and summer the spectacular swallow-tailed kite glides overhead. Many Everglade birds are tame enough to be photographed easily.

GRAND TETON NATIONAL PARK

Drawer 170, Moose, WY 83012
☎ 307-739-3399

■ The park combines spectacular scenery and diverse habitats typical of the Rockies. The endangered trumpeter swan breeds here. Note the regular replacement of one species by a close relative as the elevation changes—a progression you can see among the jays (including the black-billed magpie and Clark's nutcracker), nuthatches, chickadees, thrushes, and sparrows.

HAWK MOUNTAIN SANCTUARY

Hawk Mountain Sanctuary Association, Rte. 2, Box 191, Kempton, PA 19529 ☎ 610-756-6961

■ This site along the Kittatinny Ridge (the eastern chain of the Appalachians), located 35 miles from Reading, is on a flight path for migrating birds of prey. Late August through November, all eastern North American species of hawks, eagles, and falcons take this aerial highway in numbers.

MONTEREY PENINSULA

Pacific Grove Museum of Natural History, 165 Forest Ave., Pacific Grove, CA 93950 ☎ 408-648-3116

■ The municipal wharf and the Coast Guard pier and breakwater allow for good views of saltwater ducks, gulls, and alcids (murres, guillemots, and other puffinlike birds). From Point Pinos, you can see shearwaters and alcids over the sea. Along the rocky shore look for Pacific coast species, including the black oystercatcher, the surfbird, and the wandering tattler.

MOUNT DESERT ISLAND

Acadia National Park, PO Box 177, Bar Harbor, ME 04609 ☎ 207-288-3338

■ Habitats include oceanside cliffs, sphagnum bogs, spruce and fir forests, and bare mountain peaks, all accessible by roads and trails. Excellent birding throughout the year: common eiders, black guillemots, bald eagles, northern ravens, and gray jays. May through August, 20 wood warbler species and many other migrants from the tropics nest here. In winter, sea ducks are easily visible in the harbors.

TULE LAKE

Klamath Basin National Wildlife Refuges, Rte. 1, Box 74, Tulelake, CA 96134 ☎ 916-667-2231

■ Three national wildlife refuges—Lower Klamath, Clear Lake (not open to the public), and Tule Lake—are oases for waterbirds in the semidesert near the Oregon border. The refuges support significant breeding populations of grebes, ducks, gulls, terns, and cormorants. Rarely seen sage grouse live in the dry uplands.

YOSEMITE NATIONAL PARK

Box 577, Merced, CA 95389 ☎ 209-372-0200

■ Elevations in the Sierra Nevada range from 2,000 to 13,000 feet, providing a cross section of habitats. Many birds typical of more northerly forests are easy to see, including the great gray owl and pine grosbeak. Rare in the East, they coexist with typical Rockies denizens like the calliope hummingbird and others. Spring and summer are the best seasons.

SOURCE: Adapted from *Travel & Leisure* magazine, August 1994. Reprinted with permission of the author.

IT'S DOWNHILL FROM HERE

The best resorts have greens, blues, and blacks all over

Looking for lots of expert terrain? Head to Jackson Hole, Mad River Glen, or Mammoth Mountain. Deep powder? Your best bets are Alta, Grand Targhee, or Snowbird. Kids love skiing at Smuggler's Notch, Beaver Creek, and Snowmass, while teen activities are excellent at Sugarloaf, Breckenridge, or Killington. The ski schools are highly rated at Taos, Beaver Creek, and Deer Valley, while scenery alone is enough reason to go to Lake Louise or Telluride. Crowds are seldom found in Solitude or Big Sky, and the weather is consistently fine at Purgatory, Alpine Meadows, and Squaw Valley. Wonderful European ski villages are at Vail and Whistler/Blackcomb, while art aficionados might prefer Aspen or Taos. It's funky and western in Steamboat, and an old mining town waits in Red River. Gamble at Heavenly or "party-on" at Whiteface/Lake Placid. You'll eat well on the mountain in Sun Valley or dine happily in the town of Stowe.

Of course, all these areas have multiple attributes and flaws, as well. The process of weighing them all to get a ranking is, of course, purely subjective. In fact, the table at left shows how three major ski magazines obtained dramatically different results. Here are some of the pros and cons of the ski areas that made *Ski* magazine's top 10 list. We've noted readers' top preferences at the different resorts.

1. VAIL, Colorado

The perennial favorite for *Ski* readers, Vail is a complete resort. Twenty-five lifts service 4,000-plus acres, including the seven bowls on the back side that often hold powder for days after a storm. The town is huge, too, with 41,305 beds and plenty of options for shopping, dining, or partying. Vail appeals to a wide range of people, from Europeans and Hollywood celebrities to dishwashing ski bums and snowboarding home-boys—ensuring big crowds throughout the season and lots of votes in readers' polls. Prices are sky-high, too.

■ **TOP RATINGS:** Snow conditions and grooming, terrain, challenge, fair weather, food, lodging, après-ski, and family programs.

2. TELLURIDE, Colorado

Although tough to get to, there is great scenery and a funky small-town atmosphere in Telluride. The front side looms over the town with a 3,165-foot vertical rise and plenty of bump skiing, while the back side slopes away to the mountain village. Overall, this is an excellent ski mountain with plenty of terrain variety, and relatively few people crowding it.

■ **TOP RATINGS:** Terrain, lifts and lines, challenge, and fair weather.

■ **THE BEST PLACES TO SKI**

How the nation's top resorts stack up, according to the readers of *Ski, Skiing,* and *Snow Country* magazines.

Area	Ski magazine	Snow Country	Skiing magazine
Vail, Colo.	1	2	1
Telluride, Colo.	2	NA	10
Aspen (Highlands), Colo.	3	6	6
Alta, Utah	4	NA	5
Whistler/Blackcomb, B.C.	5	1	3
Snowbird, Utah	6	NA	17
Snowmass, Colo.	7	NA	6
Taos Ski Valley, N.M.	8	NA	8
Mammoth Mtn., Calif.	9	4	18
Steamboat, Colo.	10	3	2
Park City, Utah	19	5	NA
Beaver Creek/Vail, Colo.	14	7	1
Keystone, Colo.	18	8	NA
Squaw Valley, Calif.	30	9	13
Breckenridge, Colo.	31	10	NA
Sun Valley, Idaho	22	NA	4
Banff/Lake Louise, AB	36	NA	7
Killington, Vt.	27	NA	9

3. ASPEN HIGHLANDS, Colorado

Aspen Highlands has the highest vertical lift in Colorado (3,800 feet) and two new high-speed quad lifts to service it. There is good variety of terrain, and experts love the two steep ridges that provide innumerable challenges. At the foot of the lifts is one of America's great ski towns, with plenty of restaurants, bars, and jet setters.

■ **TOP RATINGS:** Snow conditions and grooming, terrain, value, challenge, and fair weather.

4. ALTA, Utah

Alta gets 500-plus inches a year, draped over challenging terrain. The lift prices are low, too, but that's largely because the resort owner has resisted the urge to modernize. Old and slow lifts result in lineups on the weekends. The local amenities are limited, but Salt Lake City is just 45 minutes away.

■ **TOP RATINGS:** Snow conditions and grooming, terrain, value, challenge, fair weather, and accessibility.

5. WHISTLER/BLACKCOMB, British Columbia

These two close-by Canadian resorts boast long runs, wide open terrain, lots of variety, and breathtaking vistas. The service and on-slope lodging are first class, and there are excellent children's programs. The village is car-free with easy strolling between shops and nightspots. But proximity to the Pacific often means wet snow.

■ **TOP RATINGS:** Terrain, lifts and lines, challenge, food, lodging, après-ski.

6. SNOWBIRD, Utah

Like Alta a mile up the road, Snowbird gets 500-odd inches of bone-dry powder each year. The terrain is steep (3,100 feet vertical), and features excellent chutes and gullies. There is also an enlarged intermediate section and a separate area for families and beginners. Local après-skiing options are limited, but not as limited as Alta's.

■ **TOP RATINGS:** Snow conditions and grooming, terrain, challenge, fair weather, and accessibility.

■ VITAL STATS FOR SKI BUMS

Here are the key stats on America's top-rated ski resorts. The list includes all the resorts mentioned in the rankings by the three top ski magazines at left. For lift ticket prices and other travel and lodging information, call the individual resorts.

Area	☎ Information & reservations	Vertical rise (ft.)	Skiable acres	% slopes that are: Exp.	Int.	Beg.	Number of lifts	Snowfall (in. /yr.)
Vail, Colo.	800-525-2257	3,250	4,014	32%	36%	32%	25	335
Telluride, Colo.	800-525-3455	3,522	1,050	21%	47%	32%	10	300
Aspen (Highlands), Colo.	800-262-7736	3,635	530	23%	48%	29%	9	300
Alta, Utah	801-742-3333	2,050	2,500	25%	40%	35%	8	500
Whistler/Blackcomb, B.C.	604-932-3434	7,000	5,522	25%	55%	20%	26	360
Snowbird, Utah	800-453-3000	3,100	1,570	20%	30%	50%	7	500
Snowmass, Colo.	800-598-2005	4,087	2,500	8%	52%	40%	16	300
Taos Ski Valley, N.M.	800-776-1111	2,612	1,094	24%	25%	51%	11	320
Mammoth Mtn., Calif.	800-367-6572	3,100	3,500	30%	40%	30%	31	335
Steamboat, Colo.	800-922-2722	3,685	2,500	15%	54%	31%	20	325
Park City, Utah	801-649-8111	3,100	2,200	17%	49%	34%	14	350
Beaver Creek, Colo.	800-525-2257	3,340	1,125	18%	39%	43%	10	330
Keystone, Colo.	800-222-0188	2,340	1,737	9%	59%	32%	19	230
Squaw Valley, Calif.	800-545-4350	2,850	4,200	25%	45%	30%	33	450
Breckenridge, Colo.	800-221-1091	3,340	1,125	20%	31%	49%	10	330
Sun Valley, Idaho	800-635-8261	1,322	2,054	38%	45%	31%	17	150
Banff/Lake Louise, AB	403-256-8473	3,250	4,000	25%	45%	30%	9	144
Killington, Vt.	800-621-6867	3,150	860	45%	20%	35%	20	252

SOURCE: Individual resorts.

7. SNOWMASS, Colorado

Just down the road from the town of Aspen, Snowmass is a "family area," with vast intermediate terrain (lots of cruising runs) and an excellent ski school.

■ **TOP RATINGS:** Snow conditions and grooming, terrain, challenge, fair weather, food, lodging, après-ski, and family programs.

8. TAOS SKI VALLEY, New Mexico

Taos is a hybrid resort, combining European flair with southwestern charm. Steep is the operative word, with long mogul runs and out-of-bounds skiing on Kachina Peak, but there is plenty of intermediate terrain, too. The ski school is consistently ranked as one of the country's best. There are on-slope hotels and restaurants, but a far greater selection exists in the nearby town of Taos.

■ **TOP RATINGS:** Snow conditions and grooming, terrain, lifts and lines, challenge, fair weather, and family programs.

9. MAMMOTH MOUNTAIN, California

This huge resort is aptly named. At last count there were 31 lifts and 150 runs, many of them above the tree line. There is extensive snowmaking in addition to an average annual snowfall of 340 inches. And it's only a five-hour drive from Los Angeles.

■ **TOP RATINGS:** Snow conditions and grooming, terrain, challenge, and fair weather.

10. STEAMBOAT, Colorado

The area is known for its tree-skiing, dense aspen glades that hold powder beautifully. There also is a great ski school, especially for kids, and above-average possibilities for dining and nightlife. But the most prominent feature about Steamboat is the working ranch-town atmosphere.

■ **TOP RATINGS:** Snow conditions and grooming, terrain, lifts and lines, challenge, lodging, and family programs.

FOLLOW THE POWDER HOUNDS

For the ultimate thrill, try helicoptering into the backcountry

Tired of icy, crowded slopes that end at the concessions all too soon? Consider powder skiing. Skiing the virgin snow of the backcountry isn't easy, but for many of those who have made the effort, it's been the thrill of a lifetime.

There are a few ways to do it. You can climb into the backcountry yourself with skins on your skis and get one, maybe two, runs in a day, or you can hitch a ride. Helicopters are faster and incredibly scenic, but they are also expensive ($250 to $400 per day) and vulnerable to weather problems. Snow cats are cheaper ($150 to $200 per day) and more dependable, but they haven't the speed or range of helicopters. Helicopter and snow cat reservations are required sometimes far in advance. Skiers should be at least strong intermediates. Safety is a legitimate concern, but the precautions are usually thorough. The machines are frequently and rigorously tested to meet high performance standards, and powder hounds seldom ski alone. Before you begin skiing, you'll each be given a radio receiver and instructions on how to find one another using it, in case of an avalanche or other mishap. Once on the mountain, the guide is careful to examine the snow before you ski, sometimes digging deep holes to study the critical layering of the snow. The result of this is a commendable industry safety record that belies the occasional, much-publicized incident.

The development of new wider skis called "fat boys" is making backcountry skiing easier. Their width provides superior flotation and handling in most conditions, and users don't tire nearly as fast.

If you go, dress for the occasion. It's best to wear a one-piece ski suit with elastic wrist and ankle closures. Bring at least two pairs of gloves and an extra hat. And prepare yourself physically—start training at least a month in advance.

CHAPTER NINE

ENTERTAINMENT

EXPERT QUOTES

"Comedy Central is getting better all the time. The humor is more topical now that the channel has 60 percent original programming."

—Greg Murphy, cable TV editor, *TV Guide*

Page 650

"Sharing a movie with your children shows them that you're not just seating them in front of the TV to give yourself a break."

—Nell Minow, "The Movie Mom"

Page 666

"If you're going to start with one opera, make it *Carmen*."

—Ted Libbey, commentator on the National Public Radio show, *Performance Today*

Page 672

THE YEAR AHEAD: EXPECT progress on reducing television violence... **ENJOY** the scramble to establish interactive TV and get new cable programming channels on your system... **LISTEN** to Mario Cuomo in his new career as a radio talk show host... **WATCH** Tom Hanks try to threepeat as Best Actor at the Oscars... **VISIT** the new Rock and Roll Hall of Fame and Museum... **WIN** at blackjack. Here's how...

ON THE AIR

PROGRAMMING

SAYING NO TO TV MAYHEM

Televised violence is making us more fearful, if not more violent

In the 1976 movie *Network*, an aging television newscaster done in by poor ratings rants during his farewell broadcast, "I'm mad as hell and I'm not going to take it anymore." That defiant scene may have its '90s counterpart in the television viewing public's current dismay over the amount of violence on television. According to a recent poll by *Time* magazine, over half the American public is "very concerned" about the amount of violence depicted in TV shows, movies, and popular music. Nearly three-quarters of those polled said they believe the depiction of violence numbs people to its effects and that it tells people that violence is fun and acceptable.

That violence has become a nearly ubiquitous feature on our TV screens is beyond dispute. One recent study (see box, opposite page) by the Center for Media and Public Affairs, a Washington, D.C.–based research group that monitored a day of programming on major broadcast and cable channels in its local market, found 2,605 acts of violence in a single 18-hour period. Other studies have estimated that by the time the average child finishes grade school, he or she will likely have witnessed 100,000 acts of TV violence.

Psychologists and criminologists can't be certain that watching TV violence encourages violent behavior, but hundreds of studies show an association between television violence and aggressive behavior in the young. One often-cited study by University of Michigan psychologist Leonard D. Eron found that the amount of TV violence watched by a group of young boys was a better predictor of how aggressive they would be when they grew up than how their parents had otherwise raised them. The more TV violence the subjects had watched, the more aggressive and more likely to commit a crime they were a decade later.

Other studies have suggested that children who are exposed to violent media show a greater willingness to hurt others afterward, particularly if they were considered highly aggressive to begin with. Some psychologists and law-enforcement officials insist, however, that it is difficult to establish a cause-and-effect relationship between TV watching and violent behavior. There are too many other societal factors, such as family breakdown and a lack of positive role models, to pin much blame on fictional TV violence, they argue.

The bigger impact may come from local TV news, not entertainment programming,

and may be more on those who are frightened by what they see than on those who are moved to emulate it. Dr. George Gerbner, a leading expert on TV violence at the Annenberg School for Communication at the University of Pennsylvania, has found that heavy TV watchers are more likely to worry about the safety of their own neighborhood and to own guns for protection.

"The contribution of television to the committing of violence is relatively minor," Gerbner said in a recent *New York Times* interview. "Whereas the contribution of television to the perception of violence is much higher. People are almost paralyzed by fear."

The revulsion against media violence is sparking a variety of protests against the companies that produce or air it. The attacks span the political spectrum from the Clinton White House to Republican politicians such as Robert Dole and former Education Secretary William Bennett. And groups as disparate as the Christian Film and Television Commission, the New York Urban League, and the National Political Congress of Black Women are getting into the act.

There are indications that the backlash is beginning to have some effect. Both the TV networks and cable industries have asked independent organizations to help them monitor on-air violence better, and their reports, due near the end of 1995, are expected to show some decline in the amount of TV violence. Significantly, some advertisers are reported to be balking at sponsoring shows known for violence or other controversial material. Citizens' groups are likely to step up the pressure.

Consumers who are "mad as hell" should consider the advice of New Jersey Senator Bill Bradley, who said in a recent *Time* magazine interview: "If you see something that offends you, find out who the sponsor is, find out who's on its board of directors....Send a letter to the members of the board at their homes and ask whether they realize they are making huge profits from the brutal degradation of other human beings. Then send a copy of that letter to all of their neighbors and friends....You have to try to introduce into the functioning of the market a moral sensibility that is usually absent."

ESCALATING VIOLENCE

Number of scenes of violence shown on 10 channels in a single 18-hour period.

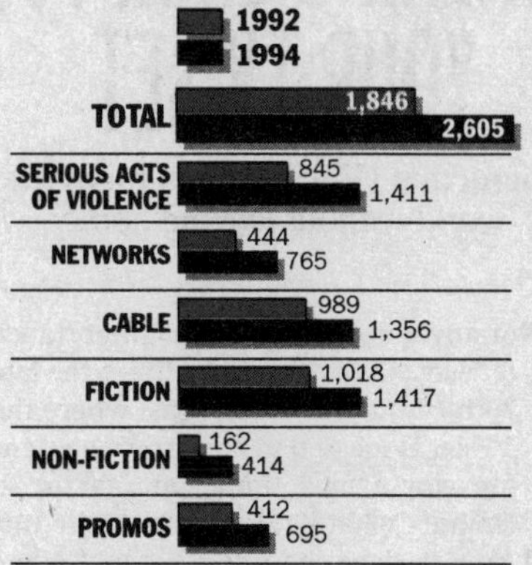

BROADCAST BREAKDOWN

The hourly rate of scenes of violence.

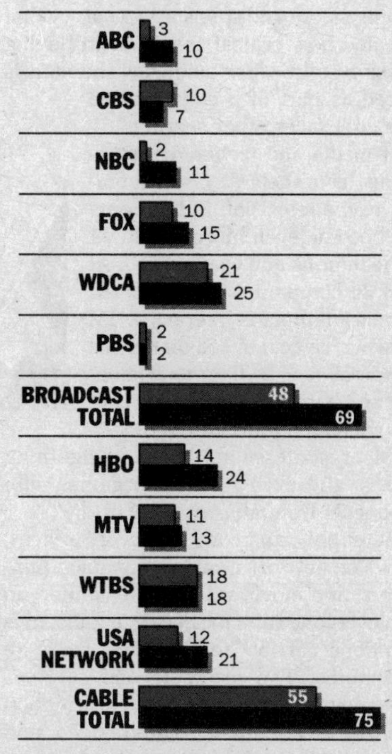

SOURCE: Center for Media and Public Affairs.

TALKING BACK TO YOUR TV SET

Interactive TV will let you roam the world without leaving home

For anyone who doubts the importance of television to American life in the late 20th century, consider this: where the TV set is located in a person's home is the single most important factor in determining what kind of furniture to buy and how to decorate one's home. "When we design our living rooms, we do so under the assumption that the sofa will face the TV," says Pamela Diaconis, a spokesperson for IKEA, the world's largest home furnishings store and sponsor of a survey that revealed how critical the TV is in buying decisions. "In other countries the sofa is placed as part of a conversation area so it faces other seating."

If media and technology companies have their way, this attention to the television in the home will become even more dominant in the months and years ahead. At least 30 companies have initiated serious attempts at interactive TV, allowing viewers to call up movies of their choice, do their food shopping and banking at home, seek out and exchange information of personal or professional value at lightning speeds, and even play video games with opponents from all over the world.

To supply this cornucopia of services, television networks, cable companies, publishers, and movie studios are teaming up with everyone from local and long-distance telephone carriers to computer software companies. The products and services being developed for this new "information highway" will combine audio, video, and text in multimedia formats that allow a viewer not only to see and hear what's being piped into their homes, but to ask questions, talk back, and tailor the information content and viewing experience to fit their own personal tastes and needs.

In the interactive age, consumers will find themselves freed from the strictures of scheduled television and cable programming because many of the new information services will be available on demand, 24 hours a day, by merely pushing a button or entering a code electronically on your home video terminal.

Whether that terminal will be a TV set with computer intelligence or a computer that can also behave like a television set is not yet clear. The fact that all programming in the new era will be delivered to the home in digital form is likely to render obsolete our old definitions of what a television set and a computer are.

One harbinger of the interactive world is Time Warner's "Full Service Network" (FSN), which has been operating in a few Orlando, Fla., homes since late 1994. FSN operates like a cable system running off a standard remote control, but when you turn on the TV set, you are greeted with a rotating three-dimensional carousel that displays a menu of interactive viewing choices from cable programming and movies to shopping and games. The carousel and its menus work in full-motion video, lending great immediacy to what might otherwise be just a static screen.

The movie menu is stocked with thousands of titles. Point the remote at the one you want to watch, and it comes up within seconds. The pause, rewind, and slow-motion functions are all on the remote, making a VCR unnecessary. If you want to watch the news, there's FSN's News Exchange, where viewers can find in the index any previously aired broadcast of CNN or NBC Nightly News and decide which stories they wish to view. For those who want to create their own nightly news, a list of icons on the screen allows you to collect your favorite sports teams' results, stock prices, weather in a particular area of the country, movie reviews, or nearly any other information you desire.

CLIMBING INTO YOUR TV SET

Get yourself onto Letterman, Donahue, or Oprah on your next trip to the Big Apple, Chi Town, or La-La Land. Here's what you need to do to get tickets:

IN NEW YORK

THE LATE SHOW WITH DAVID LETTERMAN

Ed Sullivan Theater
1697 Broadway
New York, NY 10019
☎ 212-975-4321

■ In June 1995, tickets were sold out through December 1995. Despite the show's name and airtime, taping starts at 5:30 p.m., Monday through Friday. Stand-by tickets are given out each weekday at the Ed Sullivan Theater box office, starting at noon, and are limited to one per person. You must be 16 or older to make the cut.

DONAHUE

30 Rockefeller Plaza
New York, NY 10012
☎ 212-664-6500

■ Shows are taped on Tuesday, Wednesday, and Thursday. You must be at least 16 years old. To get free tickets, send a postcard with your name, address, and telephone number at least a month in advance.

RICKI LAKE SHOW

401 Fifth Ave.
New York, NY 10016
☎ 212-889-7091

■ Ricki's studio audience is the youngest and most energized on the talk show circuit. To participate, mail a postcard with the number of tickets you'd like.

SATURDAY NIGHT LIVE

30 Rockefeller Plaza
Room 1719
New York, NY 10012
☎ 212-664-4444

■ Hard to get, so plan ahead. Taping is at 11:30 p.m., with an open dress rehearsal earlier in the day. Reserved tickets for both are distributed by lottery; get standby tickets at 9:15 a.m. Saturday in front of the GE Theater. You must be at least 12 to attend.

IN CHICAGO

OPRAH WINFREY SHOW

☎ 312-591-9595

■ All you have to do is call one month in advance to reserve a free seat. You will be asked to give your name and phone number, and someone will call you to confirm if they have a seat on the day you'd like.

IN LOS ANGELES

THE TONIGHT SHOW WITH JAY LENO

300 Alameda Avenue
Burbank, CA 91523
☎ 818-840-2222

■ Write at least three weeks in advance.You will receive your tickets 10 days before you are scheduled to be on the air, provided you are at least 16 years old. The tickets say you should be at the taping by 4 p.m., but those who know say it's best to be there by 3 p.m.

The shopping functions are even more extensive. Select the shopping menu from the carousel, and you'll be asked to choose a store. Select your neighborhood grocery and you'll see a wide video view of the layout. You can scan the rows, homing in and retreating from items as you wish. Want to check the price on a box of cereal? Rotate the product, examine the price, ingredients, or anything else on the label. If you already know what you want, call up a product index, point your remote, and the item appears before your eyes. For $10, a company called Shopper Vision will take your order and deliver the goods to your home, no matter how large or small the delivery.

Is all this convenience worth it? That depends on the price, of course, and neither Time Warner nor its competitors know yet how much interactivity will cost to offer on a mass scale, much less what consumers will be willing to pay for it on a monthly basis. Ultimately, the future of interactive TV rests not with the companies developing it, but with the consumers who must decide if it's worth their time and money.

EXPERT LIST

YOU'RE ENTITLED TO YOUR OPINION, CALLER

It's hard to dispute that television is the dominant media in today's world. But there is one forum where radio still rules: the call-in show. There are over 2,000 radio talk shows on the local level, and a growing number of nationally syndicated shows. Here, according to Talkers Magazine *editor Michael Harrison, are America's 25 most important radio talk show hosts. See the map for where they're located.*

GLORIA ALLRED (1)
KABC, Los Angeles, Calif.
High profile, ultra-liberal, feminist attorney. Stands up for women, gays, and minorities.

JIM BOHANNON (2)
Washington, D.C. Syndicated
Served many years in shadow of Larry King as backup, a gentleman now heard late nights on hundreds of stations.

NEAL BOORTZ (3)
WSB, Atlanta, Ga.
An attorney with an independent anti-big-government stance, represents the libertarian attitude that is so popular among talk radio hosts and listeners.

CHARLIE BRENNAN (4)
KMOX, St. Louis, Mo.
Moderate whose use of the power of talk radio as a peacemaker has earned him significant credibility.

DR. JOY BROWNE (5)
New York, N.Y. Syndicated
Long-running talk radio psychologist. Serious, clinical, and professional, a ratings-getter with a strong and loyal following.

DAVID BRUDNOY (6)
WBZ, Boston, Mass.
Longtime favorite in Boston, but heard across the Northeast. An intellectual, recently revealed to be gay and HIV positive.

ALAN COLMES (7)
New York, N.Y. Syndicated
A left-of-center humorist who proves that talk radio is not dominated by conservatives.

BLANQUITA CULLUM (8)
Washington, D.C. Syndicated
A single, female, Hispanic, business owner, and political conservative with some of the best Washington connections.

BOB GRANT (9)
New York, N.Y. Syndicated
Highly rated, acid-tongued, conservative veteran of the Big Apple radio wars.

KEN HAMBLIN (10)
Denver, Colo. Syndicated
This powerful black conservative voice incites controversy among members of his own race and

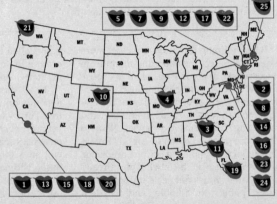

THE VOICE OF AMERICA

Everbody's talking, but they're talking more in New York City and Washington, D.C., than anywhere else in the nation.

■ EXPERT LIST

strikes hard at many of the issues white hosts cannot touch.

CHUCK HARDER (11)
White Spring, Fla. Syndicated
☻ The king of the conspiracy theorists. Independent and iconoclastic. He is heard on several hundred small- to medium-market stations.

DON IMUS (12)
New York, N.Y. Syndicated
☻ Long-running "bad boy" of radio, has evolved from early pioneer of risqué comedy to modern-day sociopolitical irreverence. Enjoys unique, ongoing, on-air relationship with President Clinton.

MICHAEL JACKSON (13)
KABC, Los Angeles, Calif.
☻ More than 25 years' service to talk radio broadcasting—still a strong liberal voice in an ocean of conservatives.

VICTORIA JONES (14)
WWRC, Washington, D.C.
☻ One of few still-rare female hosts of a morning drive show in a top-10 market. Being located in the nation's capital makes this British-born generalist even more important.

TOM LEYKIS (15)
Los Angeles, Calif. Syndicated
☻ This one-of-a-kind "outsider" covers both political and social issues in an irreverent manner that is quickly making him a national sensation among young adult listeners.

G. GORDON LIDDY (16)
Fairfax, Va. Syndicated
☻ The controversial Watergate figure brings colorful history to the airwaves and surprises many with his eloquence and gentlemanly manner in representing conservative political views.

RUSH LIMBAUGH (17)
New York, N.Y. Syndicated
☻ The king of talk radio, clearly its biggest star who has grown far beyond the medium and become a contemporary cultural icon.

MICHAEL REAGAN (18)
Los Angeles, Calif. Syndicated
☻ The son of Ronald Reagan and Jane Wyman would be a major talk radio powerhouse even if he didn't come from such luminous roots. Armed with facts and opinions that always make for a provocative and lively political show.

NEIL ROGERS (19)
WIOD, Miami, Fla.
☻ Openly gay, stream-of-consciousness, oftentimes vindictive gabber. Talks about life, sex, gambling, drinking, and many of his personal hangups and opinions.

DR. LAURA SCHLESSINGER (20)
Los Angeles. Nationally synd.
☻ She is on the cutting edge of a new wave of relationships—a psychologist with an attitude. Many stations are programming her to counter Rush Limbaugh.

MIKE SIEGEL (21)
KKVI, Seattle, Wash.
☻ Quintessential talk radio muckraker and political activist, keeps local politicians and press honest.

HOWARD STERN (22)
New York, N.Y. Syndicated
☻ A contemporary cultural phenomenon who makes political incorrectness and social inappropriateness an art form. The prototype of what has come to be known as the "shock jock."

ARMSTRONG WILLIAMS (23)
Washington, D.C. Syndicated
☻ Black, inspirational, strong religious overtones, politically conservative. The top radio voice in the black self-determination movement.

BRUCE WILLIAMS (24)
Arlington, Va. Syndicated
☻ Self-described as "vanilla," Williams is the ultimate self-help and jack-of-all-trades advice giver.

JERRY WILLIAMS (25)
WRKO, Boston, Mass.
☻ One of the original talk-radio populists. Williams has had enormous political influence in New England.

SOURCE: *Talkers Magazine*, February 1995.

CABLE WATCHER'S GUIDE

ON THE VIEWING MENU FOR TODAY

Cable television may never be as ubiquitous in American homes as the telephone, but 61 million U.S. households now subscribe to cable TV service, and the average monthly cable bill is $18. A plethora of new basic cable channels have been proposed in recent months, covering everything from arts and antiques to autos, cowboys, and parenting, but getting carried on local cable systems and attracting large enough audiences to be economically viable is a struggle. Some of television's most original programming is being offered on pay-cable channels today. But some of Hollywood's most mediocre fare finds time slots on these services, too. Here, Greg Murphy, cable TV manager for TV Guide, *describes what the major cable channels offer by way of entertainment.*

BASIC CABLE

AMERICAN MOVIE CLASSICS

42 million subscribers

■ Vintage movies from the '30s to the '70s. Movies are uninterrupted, uncut, and uncolorized. Also some original programming. Kudos to AMC's series, *Movies That Changed My Life*, with celebs like Jesse Jackson and Carly Simon talking about films that influenced them.

AMERICA'S DISABILITY CHANNEL

15 million subscribers

■ Three hours of entertainment and information programming every day, all open-captioned, and all in sign language.

ARTS & ENTERTAINMENT NETWORK

54 million subscribers

■ Biographies, documentaries, and mysteries dominate the A&E schedule. The programming is consistently quality fare.

BLACK ENTERTAINMENT TELEVISION

34 million subscribers

■ Music videos make up a large part of the schedule, but there's programming of interest to African Americans that can't be found elsewhere, like vintage black films and informational programs.

BRAVO

10 million subscribers

■ A mix of independent, foreign, and classic films, as well as dance, jazz, and documentaries. A favorite: *TV Too Good for TV*, which showcases canceled network programming such as *Twin Peaks* and *Brooklyn Bridge*.

CNBC

47 million subscribers

■ Business news all day, talk all night.

CABLE NEWS NETWORK

60 million subscribers

■ Best known for coverage of late-breaking and international news, CNN's other strengths are underestimated. Special reports and news features are among the best in the news business.

CNN HEADLINE NEWS

49 million subscribers

■ Terrific for busy news addicts: all the news in 30 minutes. Headline News has exchange agreements with hundreds of international broadcasters, making the channel a powerbroker in the industry. Continuous stock market ticker across the bottom of the screen is replaced by a sports wire at night.

C-SPAN

57 million subscribers

■ C-SPAN covers both houses of Congress and all major government activity without interruption or analysis. The best political event coverage anywhere.

COMEDY CENTRAL

25 million subscribers

■ Getting better all the time. The humor is more topical now that the chan-

■ CABLE WATCHER'S GUIDE

nel has 60 percent original programming. *Mystery Science Theater 3000* and Britain's *Absolutely Fabulous* have become cult hits.

COUNTRY MUSIC TELEVISION
16 million subscribers

■ Riding the crest of the rising popularity of country music. Videos and variety specials make up most of the programming.

THE DISCOVERY CHANNEL
58 million subscribers

■ Eighteen hours per day of nonfiction: science, nature, culture, history. [Eds. note: Much of the programming looks like PBS, but there have been some compelling original documentaries recently.]

E! ENTERTAINMENT TELEVISION
20 million subscribers

■ The televised equivalent of *People Magazine*. Dangerously addictive. A must for the entertainment industry and the people who care about it.

ESPN
60 million subscribers

■ All sports programming. ESPN is 15 years old this year and, at the moment, America's largest cable network. It just spawned ESPN2, with more coverage of exotic sports and a new look.

THE FAMILY CHANNEL
55 million subscribers

■ There used to be a lot of shoot-'em-ups on this holier-than-thou channel. That's all changed. It's now a dependable mix of family programming.

HOME SHOPPING NETWORK
21 million subscribers

■ Offers 24-hour shop-at-home services. Lots of celebrities push lots of products.

THE LEARNING CHANNEL
17 million subscribers

■ Not to be confused with children's programming. It's cooking, gardening, home improvement, and documentaries.

LIFETIME
58 million subscribers

■ Entertainment and informational programming of interest to women.

MTV
56 million

■ Music-video driven and slightly irreverent, but socially responsible. The Rock the Vote campaign that aired before the 1992 presidential election was a significant force in motivating young voters.

NICKELODEON
55 million subscribers

■ There are two networks here: Nickelodeon and Nick at Nite. Nickelodeon credits its success to a "decidedly kids' point-of-view." Nick at Nite airs classic television shows like *I Love Lucy* and *The Dick Van Dyke Show*. Like the other MTV-owned networks, Nickelodeon has shown a strong commitment to social responsibility in its programs.

QVC NETWORK
42 million subscribers

■ Shop by phone, at a discount. QVC's look is more upscale than its myriad of smaller competitors. Q2 is coming soon.

THE SCI-FI CHANNEL
10 million subscribers

■ Sci-fi the way you remember it: a terrific mix of funky (often outdated) series, movies, and animation. They recently started producing original movies.

TBS SUPERSTATION
59 million

■ The original "superstation." Not surprisingly, this broadcast independent-gone-national looks like a broadcast independent. Thank God for the action film genre and Atlanta Braves baseball.

TNN
51 million subscribers

■ Country music and country livin'. This is not a video channel; there's entertainment news, cooking, crafts, comedy specials, and interviews. Weekends feature sports programming.

TURNER NETWORK TELEVISION
56 million subscribers

■ TNT borrows heavily from the Turner/MGM

■ CABLE WATCHER'S GUIDE

library. There are also original films, cartoons, and NBA and NFL sports. It's a nice mix.

THE TRAVEL CHANNEL
18 million subscribers

■ At present the only network devoted exclusively to travel, though a number of competitors are trying to enter the field. Parent company Landmark Communications has been upgrading the programming since it took over in 1992.

USA NETWORK
60 million subscribers

■ The highest rated among the cable networks. What makes it different? More original movies than any other network, fresh episodes of old series, original game shows, U.S. Open tennis, and WWF wrestling.

VH-1
45 million subscribers

■ Major changes in VH-1. The past included lots of comedy, fashion news, and interview specials. The future sees a return to good ol' music videos.

WGN
38 million subscribers

■ Chicago's equivalent of TBS, only with Cubs baseball.

WWOR
13.5 million subscribers

■ The New York equivalent of TBS, featuring Mets baseball.

THE WEATHER CHANNEL
52 million subscribers

■ Extremely useful. You get a local weather report within 5 minutes of turning on your TV. Also great during natural disasters.

PAY CABLE CHANNELS

CINEMAX
6 million subscribers

■ Second to older sibling HBO in ratings, Cinemax's programming schedule is perfect for avid VCR users, with features like Not on Home Video Week. There's a different movie genre showcased each day of the week, and 1,000 titles air between Memorial and Labor Day.

THE DISNEY CHANNEL
6 million subscribers

■ The great children's programming is no surprise, but Disney offers some exceptional concert programming, classic movies, and compelling specials after 9 p.m.

ENCORE
3.5 million subscribers

■ This is the brash newcomer to pay cable. Movies are not exactly first run, but they are uncut and commercial-free for a fraction of the cost of other pay cable networks.

HOME BOX OFFICE
17.6 million subscribers

■ Quality and diversity are the cornerstones of the largest and oldest pay-TV service. HBO is distinguished by award-winning original movies (*The Josephine Baker Story, Barbarians at the Gate,* and *Stalin* won Emmies), music specials (Michael Jackson, Madonna, and Streisand have all played exclusively for HBO), documentaries, series, and sports. Their ad slogan of a few years ago, "Simply the Best," wasn't far off.

THE MOVIE CHANNEL
11.9 million subscribers

■ Exclusively movies from this sister to Showtime. A favorite feature: no more than 5 minutes between each film. The next favorite feature: festivals like the No-Repeat Movie Marathon and programming blocks like Joe-Bob's Drive-In Theater (with humorist Joe Bob Briggs) and VCR Overnight.

SHOWTIME
11.9 million subscribers

■ Blockbuster movies are at the core of Showtime's programming schedule, but the real value of Showtime lies in original programming. Anthologies such as *Shelly Duvall's Bedtime Stories, The Red Shoe Diaries,* and *The Showtime 30-Minute Movie* are exceptional. Showtime is also seriously committed to family viewing, dominating the ACE awards for children's programming.

THE MOVIES

GREAT FILMS

MUST-SEE FLICKS FOR ALL TIME

The Librarian of Congress wants to protect our film heritage

If you were Noah, and you could only save a limited number of movies from being washed away by time, which would you find a place for aboard your ark? The question is not as fanciful as it sounds. Many classics are at risk of being lost forever—not from flooding, but from the deterioration of the fragile celluloid on which they were printed. Fewer than 20 percent of the features from the 1920s, for example, survive in complete form today. In light of such loss, film preservation has become a major issue for film historians and movie buffs alike.

In 1988, Congress stepped into the fray with the National Film Preservation Act, which established a National Film Registry as a cinematic ark of sorts—a safe haven for the best the movies have to offer. The law authorizes the Librarian of Congress and a National Film Preservation Board to select up to 25 films a year for participation in an extensive preservation program.

Members of the 18-person board tend to be movers and shakers in the film industry (directors Martin Scorsese and John Singleton have been representatives), but their recommendations are just that: recommendations. Anyone is allowed and encouraged to nominate films for the Registry. But the ultimate decision rests with the Librarian of Congress, James H. Billington.

"This selection process should not be seen as the 'People's Choice Awards,'" Billington recently explained. Instead, he says, he chooses the films that "continue to have historic, cultural, or aesthetic significance, and, just as important, represent other films deserving of recognition."

For a survey of what American filmgoers have found great, good, and just plain entertaining over the years, see the lists of films in the National Film Registry on the following pages.

EXPERT TIP

To submit a nomination to the National Film Registry, write:

National Film Registry
Library of Congress
Motion Picture, Broadcasting, and Recorded Sound Division
Washington, D.C. 20540

EXPERT LIST

MOVIES THAT MAKE IT TO THE HALL OF FAME

On your next trip to the video store, bring back something that's really great. Listed below are the feature films in the National Film Registry, organized by category, along with a brief description of the entries and any Oscars they may have won. Most of these films are available on video cassette, as indicated by the icon. Films marked with an asterisk were made before the 1927 inception of the Academy Awards.

COMEDY

ADAM'S RIB

George Cukor, b&w, 1949, 101m

■ Spencer Tracy and Katharine Hepburn are at their best as a husband-and-wife legal team on opposite sides of a case.

ANNIE HALL

, Woody Allen, color, 1977, 94m

■ One of the best romantic comedies ever made. Woody Allen stars and directs himself, Diane Keaton, and Tony Roberts through the minefield of relationships in New York and Los Angeles.

■ **OSCAR:** Best Actress, Director, Screenplay, Picture.

THE APARTMENT

, Billy Wilder, b&w, 1960, 125m

■ Jack Lemmon stars in this fantastic satire as an insurance clerk who loans his apartment to his superiors for their extramarital affairs. All's well until he falls for one of the women. Shirley MacLaine and Fred MacMurray co-star.

■ **OSCAR:** Best Art Direction/Set Decoration, Director, Editing, Screenplay.

THE BANK DICK

Eddie Cline, b&w, 1940, 73m

■ W. C. Fields's classic comedy about a reluctant drunk-turned-hero.

BIG BUSINESS

James Horne, b&w, 1929, 30m

■ A Laurel and Hardy short in which they try to sell Christmas trees in July.

BRINGING UP BABY

, Howard Hawks, b&w, 1938, 102m

■ Katharine Hepburn and Cary Grant star in the kind of great slapstick comedy that just doesn't get made anymore.

DAVID HOLZMAN'S DIARY

, Jim McBride, b&w, 1967, 71m

■ Clever satire on the pretensions of cinema verité. A filmmaker explores the truth in his life by making a film about himself.

DR. STRANGELOVE (OR, HOW I LEARNED TO STOP WORRYING AND LOVE THE BOMB)

, Stanley Kubrick, b&w, 1964, 93m

■ Peter Sellers plays three roles in this brilliant black comedy about nuclear bombs. George C. Scott, Slim Pickens, and James Earl Jones contribute great comic performances, too. Nominated for Best Picture.

DUCK SOUP

, Leo McCarey, b&w, 1933, 70m

■ The best of the Marx Brothers films. Strangely, it was a box-office disaster when first released.

THE FRESHMAN*

, Sam Taylor and Fred Newmeyer, b&w, 1925, 70m

■ Harold Lloyd stars as a college nerd who'll do anything to be popular. Little does he know that people aren't laughing with him, but at him.

THE GENERAL

, Buster Keaton, b&w, 1927, 74m

■ Keaton stars as an engineer trying to retake his stolen locomotive during the Civil War. His silent magnetism dominates the whole film.

THE GOLD RUSH*

, Charlie Chaplin, b&w, 1925, 100m

■ Chaplin stars as well as directs this historical comedy. Includes the brilliantly inventive "dance of the dinner rolls."

■ EXPERT LIST

HIS GIRL FRIDAY
Howard Hawks, b&w, 1940, 92m
■ A newspaper comedy based on the oft-filmed Ben Hecht and Charles MacArthur book, *The Front Page*. Cary Grant and Rosalind Russell have combustible chemistry as a battling reporter and her editor.

IT HAPPENED ONE NIGHT
Frank Capra, b&w, 1934, 105m
■ Clark Gable and Claudette Colbert fall in love one night. Frank Capra directs in the patent "feel-good" style he invented.
■ **OSCAR:** Best Screenplay, Actor, Actress, Director, Picture.

MODERN TIMES
Charlie Chaplin, b&w, 1936, 87m
■ Chaplin's classic industrial satire features the Little Tramp stuck in an automated nightmare. It probably means more to today's technology-flooded viewers than it did to the moviegoers of 1936.

A NIGHT AT THE OPERA
Sam Wood, b&w, 1935, 92m
■ A Marx Brothers musical comedy with a love story tacked on for good measure. Fortunately, the romance doesn't spoil the Brothers' weird brand of antic fun.

NINOTCHKA
Ernst Lubitsch, b&w, 1939, 110m
■ A comedy starring Greta Garbo? The lady with the scowl plays a Soviet commissar checking up on some comrades in Paris. It's still good lightweight entertainment.

SAFETY LAST*
Fred Newmeyer and Sam Taylor, b&w, 1923, 78m
■ A Harold Lloyd picture about an up-and-comer in the big city. His famous building-climbing scene (Lloyd did his own stunts) stunned early audiences and still keeps viewers on the edge of their seats.

SOME LIKE IT HOT
Billy Wilder, b&w, 1959, 120m
■ A comedy classic. Jack Lemmon and Tony Curtis witness a mob hit and flee to the safe haven of an all-girl band—as girls. Marilyn Monroe is the lead singer of the band in her best performance.
■ **OSCAR:** Best Costume Design.

SULLIVAN'S TRAVELS
Preston Sturges, b&w, 1941, 90m
■ Sturges sends a jaded Hollywood director out into the real world with nothing but a dime in his pocket. Clever satire featuring Veronica Lake.

TROUBLE IN PARADISE
Ernst Lubitsch, b&w, 1932, 83m
■ The story of two jewel thieves who fall in and out of love.

DRAMA

THE AFRICAN QUEEN
John Huston, color, 1951, 105m
■ Bogart and Hepburn travel downriver through Africa. Scripted by James Agee, this is a near-perfect film.
■ **OSCAR:** Best Actor.

ALL ABOUT EVE
Joseph L. Mankiewicz, b&w, 1950, 138m
■ This look at the New York theater scene features a great leading performance from Bette Davis. Also stars Marilyn Monroe and George Sanders.
■ **OSCAR:** Best Director, Picture, Sound, Supporting Actor.

FACT FILE:

OSCAR'S ALL-TIME FAVORITES

■ *The distinction of being the all-time biggest Oscar winners is shared by:* **Ben Hur 1959** *and* **West Side Story 1961** *Each was honored in 11 categories, including Best Picture and Director. So striking was the dancing in West Side Story that a special Oscar was awarded for choreography.*

■ EXPERT LIST

THE BIRTH OF A NATION*
D. W. Griffith, b&w, 1915, 175m
■ Director John Singleton nominated it for preservation in hopes that the disturbing glorification of the KKK would serve as a lesson for younger Americans and a reminder for older ones.

THE BLACK PIRATE*
Albert Parker, b&w, 1926, 122m
■ Silent buccaneer film written by and starring Douglas Fairbanks, Sr. It's silly, mindless fun.

THE BLOOD OF JESUS
Spencer Williams, Jr., color, 1941, 50m
■ Williams wrote, directed, and starred in this well-told story of a husband who accidentally shoots his wife.

BONNIE AND CLYDE
Arthur Penn, color, 1967, 111m
■ Warren Beatty and Faye Dunaway reinvented the gangster picture as the infamous crime duo. The final shoot-out in slow motion is one of the most memorable scenes in American film. Also stars Gene Hackman and Estelle Parsons.
■ **OSCAR:** Best Cinematography, Supporting Actress.

CASABLANCA
Michael Curtiz, b&w, 1942, 102m
■ The standard by which every movie romance will forever be judged. Bogart and Bergman are magic at every turn.
■ **OSCAR:** Best Director, Picture, Screenplay.

THE CHEAT*
Cecil B. DeMille, b&w, 1915, 60m
■ A silent melodrama about a high-society woman who loses her shirt and her honor to a Japanese lender.

CITIZEN KANE
Orson Welles, b&w, 1941, 119m
■ The single most influential American film. The story of newspaper tycoon Charles Foster Kane still tops many lists of the greatest films of all time, and it established Orson Welles as the premier talent of his generation.
■ **OSCAR:** Best Original Screenplay.

FACT FILE:

HEAVEN WILL WAIT

■ *Only two films have ever won Oscar's quintuple crown by being fêted in all five top categories: best picture, director, screenplay, actor, and actress. They were:*

1934 It Happened One Night

1975 One Flew over the Cuckoo's Nest

CITY LIGHTS
Charlie Chaplin, b&w, 1931, 81m
■ Considered Chaplin's masterpiece, the actor's little tramp befriends a blind woman and does all he can to help her. The finale will bring tears to your eyes.

THE COOL WORLD
Shirley Clarke, b&w, 1963, 125m
■ A disturbing, early look at ghetto life. Clarke follows a gang leader on his symbolic pursuit of a gun through the mean streets of Harlem. Every urban film since owes something to this one.

A CORNER IN WHEAT*
D. W. Griffith, b&w, 1909, 1 reel
■ Griffith contrasts the lives of the rich and poor by examining a wheat farmer and a Wall Street broker. The startling ending culminates in the death of the farmer. Based on the writings of Frank Norris.

THE CROWD
King Vidor, b&w, 1928, 90m
■ An examination of a working-class family in a wealthy world. Vidor's best work.

DODSWORTH
William Wyler, b&w, 1936, 101m
■ From the Sinclair Lewis novel of the same name. The finely crafted story follows Walter Huston as Dodsworth, a

■ EXPERT LIST

self-made millionaire and automobile mogul.
■ **OSCAR:** Best Interior Decoration.

THE GODFATHER
Francis Ford Coppola, color, 1972, 175m
■ The unforgettable first chapter in the Corleone family saga. Marlon Brando stars as the title character, with Al Pacino, James Caan, Talia Shire, Diane Keaton, and Robert Duvall. A great film.
■ **OSCAR:** Best Actor, Adapted Screenplay, Picture.

THE GODFATHER, PART II
Francis Ford Coppola, color, 1974, 200m
■ Robert De Niro joins the star-studded cast as the young Don Corleone, but it's Al Pacino as Michael who eclipses everyone with a skillful, complicated performance. In a break from tradition, the sequel is just as good as the original.
■ **OSCAR:** Best Adapted Screenplay, Art Direction/Set Decoration, Director, Picture, Supporting Actor, Screenplay.

GONE WITH THE WIND
Victor Fleming, color, 1939, 222m
■ Clark Gable and Vivien Leigh star in the epic telling of the last days of the Civil War. Politically incorrect? Sure. But it remains a beautiful, compelling, and thoroughly entertaining film.
■ **OSCAR:** Color Cinematography, Interior Decoration, Screenplay, Editing, Supporting Actress, Actress, Director, Picture.

THE GRAPES OF WRATH
John Ford, b&w, 1940, 129m
■ Henry Fonda is brilliant and Ford is at his best. Adapted from the Steinbeck classic about Okies fleeing the Dust Bowl.
■ **OSCAR:** Best Supporting Actress, Director.

GREED*
Erich Von Stroheim, b&w, 1924, 133m
■ Von Stroheim's tale of corruption must have been a wonder in its original nine-hour length. Even in the VCR-friendly two-hour version, it's a magnificent remnant from the silent era.

HOW GREEN WAS MY VALLEY
John Ford, color, 1941, 118m
■ The story of a Welsh mining family told by 13-year-old Roddy McDowall.
■ **OSCAR:** Best Interior Decoration, Black and White Cinematography, Supporting Actor, Director, Picture.

I AM A FUGITIVE FROM A CHAIN GANG
Mervyn Leroy, b&w, 1932, 90m
■ The story of an honest man convicted of a crime he didn't commit. This was one of the first films to explore this subject, and Paul Muni's performance pulls it all together.

INTOLERANCE*
D. W. Griffith, b&w, 1916, 175m
■ An ironic title, considering the controversy surrounding Griffith's work. This story is an amalgam of four tales of intolerance: two historical, two modern.

IT'S A WONDERFUL LIFE
Frank Capra, b&w, 1946, 129m
■ Jimmy Stewart finds out what the world would be like if he had never been born. A Christmas classic with an ending as sweet as Santa himself.

THE ITALIAN*
Reginald Barker, b&w, 1915, 78m
■ The tragic turn-of-the-century tale of an immigrant Italian family in New York.

KILLER OF SHEEP
Charles Burnett, b&w, 1977, 83m
■ Set in South Central L.A., Burnett follows Stan, an aging man struggling to keep his values while the world falls around him. It's a complex tale, beautifully told.

THE LADY EVE
Preston Sturges, b&w, 1941, 94m
■ Barbara Stanwyck stars as a con making the moves on the wealthy but nerdy Henry Fonda. Subtle humor pervades the script and the lead performances are first-rate.

LASSIE COME HOME
Fred Wilcox, color, 1943, 90m
■ Elizabeth Taylor and

■ EXPERT LIST

Roddy McDowall star, but Lassie steals the show. Perfect family viewing, even 50 years later.

LAWRENCE OF ARABIA
David Lean, color, 1962, 221m
■ Peter O'Toole gives one of the greatest debut performances in film history as T. E. Lawrence, and David Lean tells the lengthy story with remarkable ease. See it on a large screen if possible.
■ **OSCAR:** Best Art Direction/Set Decoration, Color Cinematography, Sound, Score, Editing, Director, Picture.

THE LEARNING TREE
Gordon Parks, color, 1969, 107m
■ Gordon Parks became the first black director of a major studio film with this autobiographical project. The former *Life* photographer directed, produced, wrote the script, and scored the film himself.

LETTER FROM AN UNKNOWN WOMAN
Max Ophüls, b&w, 1948, 90m
■ Romance starring Joan Fontaine and Louis Jourdan. Director Ophüls gives the film a European feel and stylized look.

THE MAGNIFICENT AMBERSONS
Orson Welles, b&w, 1942, 88m
■ Orson Welles's dark portrait of a midwestern family in decline, from the Booth Tarkington novel. Was nominated for Best Picture, but is still overshadowed by the classic *Citizen Kane;* don't miss it.

MARTY
Delbert Mann, b&w, 1955, 91m
■ The tiny but touching story of a Bronx butcher (Ernest Borgnine) who finds love unexpectedly. Paddy Chayefsky's script keeps this from being an ordinary love tale, and Borgnine gives (by far) his best performance.
■ **OSCAR:** Best Screenplay, Actor, Director, Picture.

FACT FILE:

BIG WINNERS

■ *Only six have won Best Actor twice:*

Marlon Brando
On the Waterfront
The Godfather
Gary Cooper
High Noon
Sergeant York
Tom Hanks
Philadelphia
Forrest Gump
Dustin Hoffman
Kramer vs. Kramer
Rain Man
Fredric March
Best Years of Our Lives
Dr. Jekyll and Mr. Hyde
Spencer Tracy
Captains Courageous
Boys Town

MIDNIGHT COWBOY
John Schlesinger, color, 1969, 113m
■ The only X-rated film to win Best Picture, *Cowboy* is hardly as shocking today as it was then. Dustin Hoffman and Jon Voight star as small-time hustlers who become friends. New York never looked seamier than through director Schlesinger's lens.
■ **OSCAR:** Best Adapted Screenplay, Director, Picture.

MOROCCO
Josef von Sternberg, b&w, 1930, 92m
■ Marlene Dietrich's first Hollywood film casts her as a cabaret singer stuck in Morocco. Gary Cooper goes along for the ride.

MR. SMITH GOES TO WASHINGTON
Frank Capra, b&w, 1939, 129m
■ Capra and Jimmy Stewart (as Jefferson Smith) team up to tell the story of a scoutmaster turned senator who brings old-fashioned values back to Capitol Hill. It's every politician's dream role.
■ **OSCAR:** Best Screenplay.

NASHVILLE
Robert Altman, color, 1975, 159m
■ Altman at his best. With a large ensemble cast at his disposal, the director

■ EXPERT LIST

examines American life and the way it was lived in the '70s with acute wit and style.
■ **OSCAR:** Best Song.

NOTHING BUT A MAN
Michael Roemer, b&w, 1964, 95m
■ A quiet look at racial prejudice in the South. Melodrama is kept to a minimum, as director Roemer examines the complexities of black life.

ON THE WATERFRONT
Elia Kazan, b&w, 1954, 108m
■ Marlon Brando stars as Terry Malloy, a boxer-turned-longshoreman. Disgusted by the mob corruption that his older brother (Rod Steiger) has introduced him to, Brando sums himself up with one of the most desperate lines in the movies: "I coulda' been a contender."
■ **OSCAR:** Best Art Direction/Set Decoration, Black and White Cinematography, Editing, Screenplay, Supporting Actress, Actor, Director, Picture.

ONE FLEW OVER THE CUCKOO'S NEST
Milos Forman, color, 1975, 129m
■ *Cuckoo's Nest* and *It Happened One Night* are the only two films to have swept the five major Oscar categories. Jack Nicholson is an inmate at a mental institution who brings the other patients back to life. Based on Ken Kesey's novel. Look for a great early-career performance from Danny DeVito.
■ **OSCAR:** Best Screenplay, Actor, Actress, Director, Picture.

PATHS OF GLORY
Stanley Kubrick, b&w, 1957, 86m
■ Kubrick's specialty, an anti-war movie. Kirk Douglas stars as a World War I sergeant forced to defend three of his troops against charges of cowardice.

A PLACE IN THE SUN
George Stevens, b&w, 1951, 120m
■ Elizabeth Taylor, Montgomery Clift, and Shelly Winters star as the three points of a love triangle.
■ **OSCAR:** Best Black and White Cinematography, Costume Design, Score, Editing, Screenplay, Director.

FACT FILE:

BIGGER WINNERS

■ *Katharine Hepburn has been named Best Actress four times:*
Morning Golory
Guess Who's Coming to Dinner
The Lion in Winter
On Golden Pond

■ *John Ford, won four Oscars for directing:*
The Informer
Grapes of Wrath
How Green Was My Valley
The Quiet Man

THE POOR LITTLE RICH GIRL*
Maurice Torneur, b&w, 1917, 64m
■ Mary Pickford gives an extraordinary performance as a girl with everything but her family's love.

THE PRISONER OF ZENDA
John Cromwell, b&w, 1937, 101m
■ From the Anthony Hope novel about a power struggle in a small European kingdom. Ronald Colman stars, and Mary Astor, Douglas Fairbanks, Jr., and David Niven also put in appearances.

RAGING BULL
Martin Scorsese, b&w, 1980, 128m
■ Many critics hailed this drama about boxer Jake LaMotta as the best film of the '80s. Robert De Niro gives a fantastic performance as LaMotta, portraying the character from his 20s as a fighting machine to his dissolute later years.
■ **OSCAR:** Best Editing, Actor.

REBEL WITHOUT A CAUSE
Nicholas Ray, color, 1955, 111m
■ The classic tale of teen angst and alienation. James Dean stars in the role that made him an American legend.

■ EXPERT LIST

SALT OF THE EARTH
Herbert Biberman, b&w, 1954, 94m

■ Deals with a miners' strike in New Mexico from a staunchly pro-union perspective. During the McCarthy era, it was attacked as Communist propaganda.

SCARFACE
Howard Hawks, b&w, 1932, 93m

■ Like the remake, it was censored at first because of its violent content. Hawks's film was the best gangster film until *The Godfather.* Paul Muni plays a Capone-like mob man with deep affection for his sister.

SHADOWS
John Cassavetes, b&w, 1959, 87m

■ Cassavetes's first directorial effort. The picture follows a light-skinned black girl through life in New York City. Lelia Goldoni turns in a strong lead performance.

SHERLOCK, JR.*
Buster Keaton, b&w, 1924, 45m

■ Keaton plays a projectionist with Walter Mitty–like dreams of being a great detective. He walks from the booth onto the screen and enters a fantasy drama. Besides being Keaton's greatest display of skill as a director, the "fourth-wall" fusion of reality and fantasy has been copied by everyone from Woody Allen to Schwarzenegger.

SUNSET BOULEVARD
Billy Wilder, b&w, 1950, 100m

■ A cavalcade of Hollywood's greats appear in this black comedy about Norma Desmond, played by Gloria Swanson in her defining role, a silent film star who's got nothing left. As a Broadway musical starring Glenn Close, it was a hit in 1994.
■ **OSCAR:** Best Art Direction/Set Decoration, Screenplay, Score.

SWEET SMELL OF SUCCESS
Alexander Mackendrick, b&w, 1957, 96m

■ Burt Lancaster and Tony Curtis star in a story about a newspaper gossip columnist (Lancaster) and the press agent who'll do anything for him (Curtis). An excellent musical score by Elmer Bernstein of *Magnificent Seven* fame.

TABU
F. W. Murnau and Robert Flaherty, b&w, 1931, 81m

■ Equal parts ethnography and drama. The story follows a young diver and his unrequited love for a woman declared "taboo" by the gods.
■ **OSCAR:** Best Cinematography.

TAXI DRIVER
Martin Scorsese, color, 1976, 112m

■ Robert De Niro plays Travis Bickle, a disturbed taxi driver who can't stand New York and goes berserk. Scorsese's portrait of vigilantism proved strangely prophetic when John Hinckley cited the film as one reason for his assassination attempt on Ronald Reagan. Co-stars Jodie Foster, Cybill Shepherd, and Harvey Keitel.

TEVYE
Maurice Schwartz, b&w, 1939, 96m

■ Later known as *Fiddler on the Roof,* this is the original story of a Jewish dairyman whose lifestyle is changed by his daughter's wishes to marry outside the faith. From the Sholom Aleichem story.

WHERE ARE MY CHILDREN?*
Lois Webber and Phillips Stanley, b&w, 1916, 72m

■ A silent "social" film from woman director Lois Webber, starring Tyrone Power, Sr. Daring, in that it takes a pro-birth control, anti-abortion stand in the early 20th century.

THE WIND
Bud Greenspan, b&w, 1928, 74m

■ Lillian Gish stars as a girl who marries a farmer to escape her family. One of the last great silent films.

WITHIN OUR GATES*
Oscar Micheaux, b&w, 1920, 79m

■ The earliest surviving film by an African American director. A mixed cast explores racial issues that didn't bubble to the cultural surface for decades.

■ EXPERT LIST

A WOMAN UNDER THE INFLUENCE
John Cassavetes, color, 1974, 147m
■ Gena Rowlands and Peter Falk star in the story of a woman who is cracking up.

HORROR

CAT PEOPLE
Jacques Torneur, b&w, 1942, 73m
■ Simone Simon is a dressmaker who believes she's infected with a panther curse in this creepy, well-directed thriller.

FRANKENSTEIN
James Whale, b&w, 1931, 71m,
■ Boris Karloff's performance as Mary Shelley's monster is still the best, Robert De Niro's friendly monster in the Kenneth Branagh version included.

FREAKS
Tod Browning, b&w, 1932, 64m
■ Director Browning explores relationships between sideshow freaks in this strange horror film. The real story is the humanity of the freak characters, many of whom are real-life sideshow performers.

KING KONG
Merlan Cooper and Ernest Shoedsack, b&w, 1933, 105m
■ Big ape rampages through New York until he reaches the Empire State Building. A camp classic.

PSYCHO
Alfred Hitchcock, b&w, 1960, 109m
■ Anthony Perkins stars as Norman Bates, motel proprietor and neighborhood psychotic. Thirty years and several hundred slasher imitators later, Psycho still provides some terrifyingly good screams.

MUSICALS

AN AMERICAN IN PARIS
Vincente Minnelli, color, 1951, 113m
■ Gene Kelly stars in this entertaining musical as a GI-turned-painter. Features a stunning, 17-minute ballet sequence with classic Kelly dancing.

■ **OSCAR:** Best Art Direction/Set Decoration, Color Cinematography, Score, Screenplay, Picture.

CARMEN JONES
Otto Preminger, color, 1954, 105m
■ Oscar Hammerstein II adapted the film from Bizet's opera. Harry Belafonte and Dorothy Dandridge turn in good performances.

FOOTLIGHT PARADE
Lloyd Bacon, b&w, 1933, 100m
■ James Cagney plays a struggling stage director trying to out-do himself (and sound movies) with every musical number.

GIGI
Vincente Minnelli, color, 1958, 116m
■ Leslie Caron is Gigi, a harlot-in-training with Louis Jourdan on her mind. One of the last great movie musicals.
■ **OSCAR:** Best Art Direction, Color Cinematography, Costume Design, Score, Song, Screenplay, Director, Picture.

LOVE ME TONIGHT
Rouben Mamoulian, b&w, 1932, 104m
■ The Rodgers & Hart musical that introduced "Isn't It Romantic" (sung by Maurice Chevalier) to the film world.

MEET ME IN ST. LOUIS
Vincente Minnelli, color, 1944, 133m
■ Set at the 1903 World's

FACT FILE:

WOMEN ON THE EDGE

■ *Four women directors have had films nominated for Best Picture. They are:*

Randa Haines
1987 **Children of a Lesser God**
Penny Marshall
1990 **Awakenings**
Barbra Streisand
1991 **Prince of Tides**
Jane Campion
1993 **The Piano**

None, alas, were winners.

■ EXPERT LIST

Fair in St. Louis. Director Minnelli's musical tracks a family through their expectant, turn-of-the-century lives. Judy Garland carries the picture, although child-star Margaret O'Brian was given a special Oscar for her performance.

SINGIN' IN THE RAIN
Gene Kelly and Stanley Donen, color, 1952, 103m
■ The greatest movie musical ever. Kelly's performance of the title song is deservedly one of the most famous scenes in film. Donald O'Connor, Debbie Reynolds, Cyd Charisse, and Rita Moreno give great performances, too.

TOP HAT
Mark Sandrich, b&w, 1935, 97m
■ Ginger Rogers and Fred Astair in their best form. "Cheek to Cheek" and "Top Hat, White Tie, and Tails" are just two of the great songs performed. Look for Lucille Ball in a small early role.

THE WIZARD OF OZ
Victor Fleming, color/ b&w, 1939, 101m
■ An American classic based on L. Frank Baum's novel of the same name. Judy Garland stars as Dorothy in the role of a lifetime. The music is instantly hummable, the performances unforgettable. A perfect film.
■ **OSCAR:** Best Song, Score.

YANKEE DOODLE DANDY
Michael Curtiz, b&w, 1942, 126m
■ James Cagney stars in the story of composer George M. Cohan. Cagney proved he could play something other than a gangster in this sweet musical.
■ **OSCAR:** Best Score, Sound, Actor.

MYSTERY & SUSPENSE

BADLANDS
Terrence Malick, color, 1974, 94m
■ Before Oliver Stone's *Natural Born Killers,* there was *Badlands.* Director Malick's creepy thriller stars Martin Sheen and Sissy Spacek as a murderer and his companion. Loosely inspired by a Nebraska killing spree in 1958.

CHINATOWN
Roman Polanski, color, 1974, 131m
■ Jack Nicholson and Faye Dunaway in one of Hollywood's greatest executions of film-noir. John Huston, Dianne Ladd, and Burt Young co-star.
■ **OSCAR:** Best Original Screenplay.

DETOUR
Edgar Ulmer, b&w, 1946, 69m
■ Ulmer was one of the first low-budget, independent filmmakers. His craft is at its sharpest in this film noir about a drifter, who is played superbly by Tom Neal.

DOUBLE INDEMNITY
Billy Wilder, b&w, 1944, 106m
■ Fred MacMurray stars as an insurance salesman who joins Barbara Stanwyck in a plot to kill her husband for his insurance. Suspense films don't get any better than this.

FORCE OF EVIL
Abraham Polonsky, b&w, 1948, 100m
■ Noir classic starring John Garfield as a mob lawyer caught between crime and brotherly love. A tremendous performance by Garfield, a too-often underrated actor.

THE MALTESE FALCON
John Huston, b&w, 1941, 101m
■ Bogart is Sam Spade, a P.I. investigating the web of deceit and murder spun around a priceless statue. With a supporting cast featuring Peter Lorre, Mary Astor, and Sydney Greenstreet, this is the best of P.I. flicks.

THE MANCHURIAN CANDIDATE
John Frankenheimer, b&w, 1962, 126m
■ Frank Sinatra gives his best performance as an Army man who knows more than he thinks he does in Frankenheimer's thrilling adaptation of the Richard Condon novel. The plot revolves around conspiracy and brainwashing at the highest levels of American government.

EXPERT LIST

THE NIGHT OF THE HUNTER
Charles Laughton, b&w, 1955, 93m

■ Robert Mitchum plays a terrifying preacher trying to kill his step-kids. This is one scary flick, and Mitchum turns in a creepy, career-defining performance.

OUT OF THE PAST
Jacques Torneur, b&w, 1947, 97m

■ A small film noir starring Robert Mitchum and Kirk Douglas. Mitchum plays a P.I. who gets involved with a gangster's girl. Douglas plays the formidable gangster.

SHADOW OF A DOUBT
Alfred Hitchcock, b&w, 1943, 108m

■ Joseph Cotten stars as Uncle Charlie, a loving relative who may have a murderous secret to hide. Hitchcock's personal favorite.

SUNRISE
F. W. Murnau, b&w, 1927, 110m

■ The story of a farmer who plots to murder his wife. The silent film featured innovative camerawork for the times.
■ **OSCAR:** Best Actress.

TOUCH OF EVIL
Orson Welles, b&w, 1958, 108m

■ Director Welles also stars as the corrupt sheriff of a seedy Mexican border town. Charlton Heston, Janet Leigh, and a host of other stars also appear.

THE TREASURE OF THE SIERRA MADRE
John Huston, b&w 1948, 126m

Humphrey Bogart, Walter Huston, and Tim Holt go prospecting for gold and discover the worst in human nature.
■ **OSCAR:** Best Screenplay, Supporting Actor, Director.

FACT FILE:

WHEN IN DOUBT, NOMINATE

■ *The most nominated films in Oscar history are:*

All About Eve	**14**
From Here to Eternity	**13**
Judgment at Nuremberg	**13**
Mary Poppins	**13**

The big winner among them was:
From Here to Eternity **8 awards**
The most disappointed was:
Judgment at Nuremberg **2 awards**
But even that looked sensational compared with:
The Turning Point *and* **The Color Purple,** *which were each nominated 11 times and took home nothing.*

VERTIGO
Alfred Hitchcock, color, 1958, 126m

■ Jimmy Stewart is an ex-cop hired to shadow Kim Novak. He has vertigo. To reveal anything more would be criminal.

SCIENCE FICTION

BLADE RUNNER
Ridley Scott, color, 1982, 122m

■ An art-house favorite starring Harrison Ford as an everyday cop in a nightmarish future that resembles L.A. Cast features Darryl Hannah, Sean Young, Edward James Olmos, and Rutger Hauer. The production design is superb.

E.T. THE EXTRA TERRESTRIAL
Steven Spielberg, color, 1982, 115m

■ This touching adventure of a boy and his alien could only come from the imagination of Steven Spielberg. Henry Thomas as Eliot gives the best child-performance ever in a film, and the superior cast (including Debra Winger as the voice of E.T.) makes this *the* classic of '80s pop-cinema.
■ **OSCAR:** Best Sound, Visual Effects, Score.

INVASION OF THE BODY SNATCHERS
Don Siegel, b&w, 1956, 80m

■ One of the most influential sci-fi horror movies. Aliens replace

■ EXPERT LIST

people with duplicates hatched from pods. Don't watch it alone.

STAR WARS

George Lucas, color, 1977, 121m

■ "A long time ago, in a galaxy far, far away," sci-fi fantasies were drive-in jokes. Then director George Lucas came along and made outer space into a world populated by heroes and monsters drawn from Greek mythology. The special effects set a new standard for film technology.

■ **OSCAR:** Best Art/Direction/Set Decoration, Costume Design, Editing, Sound, Visual Effects, Score.

2001: A SPACE ODYSSEY

Stanley Kubrick, color, 1968, 139m

■ The groundbreaking film that took viewers into a future where machine and man are equals. Besides being a visual feast, the philosophical and theological issues raised within make it one of the touchstone films of a generation.

■ **OSCAR:** Best Visual Effects.

WESTERNS

HELL'S HINGES*

William S. Hart and Charles Swickard, b&w, 1916, 65m

■ Director Hart was the first master of the western, and this fine film had more to do with shaping the formula of the genre than any other.

HIGH NOON

Fred Zinneman, b&w, 1952, 85m

■ The clock ticks down on sheriff Gary Cooper as an old nemesis turns his wedding day into a nightmare. Great suspense and good acting; Cooper won his second Oscar for the role.

■ **OSCAR:** Best Editing, Song, Score, Actor.

MY DARLING CLEMENTINE

John Ford, b&w, 1946, 97m

■ Henry Fonda plays Wyatt Earp in the best version of the oft-filmed shoot-out at the O.K. Corral.

RED RIVER

Howard Hawks, b&w, 1948, 133m

■ One of the most frequently underrated westerns. John Wayne plays a leathery rancher with surprising skill. Montgomery Clift co-stars in his first film role.

RIDE THE HIGH COUNTRY

Sam Peckinpah, color, 1962, 93m

■ Two gunmen are hired to guard a stash of gold. One has honorable intentions, one doesn't. Starring Randolph Scott and Joel McCrea in their final screen roles.

THE SEARCHERS

John Ford, color, 1956, 119m

■ John Wayne plays a racist old Confederate in search of his niece (Natalie Wood) who was abducted by Indians. Both Wayne and director Ford are in peak form.

SHANE

George Stevens, color, 1953, 117m

■ A great drama from the Jack Schaeffer novel of the same name. Alan Ladd as the lonesome gunfighter is fantastic.

■ **OSCAR:** Best Color Cinematography.

FACT FILE:

COWBOYS IN PARADISE

■ *The first western to win an Oscar for Best Picture was Cimarron, in 1930. But despite all the gun-slinging, cattle thieving, posse riding, and damsel saving that took place on the silver screen, it took over 60 years to show that cowboys could ride home again with Oscars for Best Picture for a western:*

Kevin Costner, starring and directing,
1990 Dances with Wolves

and Clint Eastwood, starring and directing,
1992 Unforgiven

CRITICS

MEET THE BLURB WRITERS

Sometimes reviews say more about reviewers than about the movies

Trying to spend your movie-ticket dollar wisely? The blurbs in movie ads can be as deceptive as cineplex "butter." If the names attached to "Wonderful," "Heart Warming," and "Best of the Year" mean nothing to you, here's the skinny on the critics who do the dissin'.

■ **MIKE CLARKE,** *USA Today*: Clarke's not easily impressed by art-house pretensions. On the other hand, he shows a weakness for movies with big budgets and big stars.

■ **MICHAEL MEDVED,** *New York Post:* The author of a conservative indictment of movie sex and violence, Medved's tastes favor family-styled entertainment. Trust him when you're taking the kids.

■ **TERRENCE RAFFERTY,** *New Yorker:* Rafferty has inherited the mantle of his predecessor, Pauline Kael, as Hollywood's most demanding critic. If he likes a major studio film, it's probably good. He's much less discriminating with art flicks.

■ **CARRIE RICKEY,** *Knight-Ridder:* Tough to please. She gets more excited by risk-takers (good or bad) than recycled formulas.

■ **JOEL SIEGEL,** *Good Morning America:* Call him an optimist, but he loves almost everything. If you're going to the theater based only on his blurb, you're asking for it.

■ **GENE SHALIT,** *Today Show:* He's not "blurbed" as much as he used to be, which means he's become more critical of big films. Beware, however; occasionally he still gets carried away with his raves.

■ **KENNETH TURAN,** *Los Angeles Times:* Turan is pretty cynical, as befits a critic in Hollywood's backyard. But when he praises a movie, he means it.

EXPERT SOURCES

A GUIDE TO THOSE WHO WRITE THE GUIDES

LEONARD MALTIN'S MOVIE AND VIDEO GUIDE
Leonard Maltin, Signet Books, 1994, $17.95
■ The well-regarded critic lists more than 19,000 films with brief reviews and information about the filmmakers.

ROGER EBERT'S VIDEO COMPANION
Roger Ebert, Andrews & McMeel, 1994, $14.95
■ For people who love to read and argue about movies. Included are 1,250 reviews as they originally appeared in the *Chicago Sun-Times* (Ebert's home paper).

VIDEO HOUND'S GOLDEN RETRIEVER
Martin Connors and Julia Furtaw, Visible Ink, 1994, $17.95
■ *Golden Retriever* includes major award information underneath its capsule reviews of 22,000 films. Thirteen indices help your search.

VIDEO MOVIE GUIDE 1995
Mick Martin and Marsha Porter, Ballantine Books, 1994, $7.99
■ Organized by movie theme (drama, comedy, etc.) rather than alphabetically. Cross-listed indices help you find the films of your favorite director or star.

KID FLICKS

MAKING MOVIES MEANINGFUL

How parents can turn their children on to what films have to teach

Sick of children's movies that are chewing gum for the mind? You don't have to succumb to the latest Hollywood formula flicks. Classic movies that once were available only on scratchy prints in art houses or riddled with commercials on the "Late Late Show" now appear in video stores, as rich as Rembrandts. Films that enchant, thrill, even teach, are there for parents who know where to look. Writer Nell Minow, aka "The Movie Mom," has been organizing film festivals for her children for many years. She offers these tips on changing your children's movie watching habits for the better:

■ **ENTICE THEM.** Parents need to get children interested before the movie begins. Tell them what the challenge or conflict in the movie is, but don't tell them how it turns out. Children love to watch the movies that were their parents' (and grandparents') favorites when they were the children's ages.

■ **CHALLENGE THEM.** Make sure that every movie they see is one that you feel is worth the two hours it takes away from other things. Then challenge them to challenge the film. Ask them why the character is behaving in the way shown and what they would do in that situation. Discuss with them how the movie springs its surprises and makes them feel suspense. This not only teaches them about narrative and point of view, it helps to teach them critical thinking.

■ **PREPARE THEM.** No matter how bright and well-educated a child is, he or she is unlikely to be able to follow the plot of a feature film without some kind of introduction. Give them a general overview of the situation, issues, and the characters. If they ask questions, give them more details without spoiling the ending. Sometimes, with younger children, it helps to read a book together on the same subject. With musicals, it's a good idea to listen to the record a few times before going to see the movie.

■ **CONNECT WITH THEM.** Pick a movie that relates to the child's interests or experience in some way. If you have visited (or plan to visit) New York, try *On the Town,* where three sailors have one day to see the city. If the child loves baseball, try *Pride of the Yankees.* Many classic children's books have been made into movies. Children who have read *The Secret Garden, Little Women,* or *The Phantom Tollbooth* will especially enjoy the movies.

■ **WARN THEM.** Older movies do have the advantage of telling their stories without the kind of language, violence, or nudity that led to the development of the rating system in the late 1960s. But they sometimes reflect attitudes that clash with today's values, particularly about women and minorities. Even an objectionable movie has some value if it prompts a discussion. It may give you a chance to point out aspects of your own past or to talk about values without sounding as though you are preaching. This provides a perfect chance to discuss the issues and to explore the history that surrounded the movie's presentation of these attitudes.

■ **JOIN THEM.** Sharing a movie with your children shows them that you are not just seating them in front of the TV to give yourself a break. Watching a wonderful movie together becomes part of the common experience that you will always treasure having with your children.

VIDEO LOVER'S GUIDE

THE MOVIE MOM'S FAVORITE FLICKS

No one should grow up without seeing the cinematic treasures of childhoods' past. Movie-mom Nell Minow, creator of the Mom Filmfest for her family in McLean, Va., explains why these classics will be hits with children.

CHILDREN UNDER SEVEN

RABBIT EAR SERIES

1980–

■ Narrated by some of the finest contemporary actors, this collection of classic children's stories includes *The Elephant's Child*, read by Jack Nicholson, *The Velveteen Rabbit*, read by Meryl Streep, and *Anansi the Spider*, read by Denzel Washington.

SHARI LEWIS VIDEOS

1984 to 1991

■ The best thing about these delightful videos by longtime children's entertainer Shari Lewis is that they involve the children, with interesting activities that get little couch potatoes off the couch.

tom thumb

1957

■ The tale of a boy no bigger than a thumb is brought to life with former gymnast Russ Tamblyn in the title role. He is as irresistibly charming as his "very own song," as one of the musical numbers suggests. Villains Terry Thomas and Peter Sellers try to get the diminutive hero to steal for them, but a good fairy thwarts them.

DISNEY ANIMATION CLASSICS

1937 to 1961

■ Older movies like *Snow White* (1937), *Pinocchio* (1940), *Cinderella* (1950), *Alice in Wonderland* (1951), *Peter Pan* (1953), *Sleeping Beauty* (1959), and *101 Dalmatians* (1961) hold up exceptionally well, with gorgeous pre-computer animation and excellent music. Some children may be frightened by the villains, but familiarity with the story can help.

FOR OLDER CHILDREN

CAPTAINS COURAGEOUS

1937

■ A wealthy and spoiled young boy traveling on a luxurious ocean liner is washed overboard and rescued by a sailor on a fishing boat. Forced to stay on the boat until it returns to shore, he learns the importance of earning respect from others, and from himself. There is a sad death, but the story ends with the boy becoming close to his father for the first time. Spencer Tracy stars in an Oscar-winning performance, with Lionel Barrymore, Mickey Rooney, and Freddie Bartholomew.

CHARIOTS OF FIRE

1981

■ This is the true story of two athletes who raced in the 1924 Olympics, one a privileged Jewish student at Cambridge, the other a missionary from Scotland. Wonderfully evocative of the time and place, with superb performances, the movie shows us the source of the runners' determination—for one, a need to prove himself, for the other, a connection to God. The movie won the Oscar for Best Picture.

THE DAY THE EARTH STOOD STILL

1951

■ A mysterious spaceship arrives in Washington in this Cold War classic. A man and a robot are inside, bringing a message that humans must stop making nuclear weapons. They are befriended by a young boy whose father was killed in WW II, and by a scientist. But not everyone wants peace, and it is up to the heroes to save the world from itself.

FANTASTIC VOYAGE

1966

■ A team of scientists is shrunk to microscopic size in order to perform emergency surgery in this exciting adventure. They must battle everything from white blood cells (attacking them as though they were an infection) to an onboard traitor, to time itself, as they race to complete the operation and leave the body before the effects of the shrinking ray wear off and they return to normal size. Exciting and fun, this movie also teaches about the inner workings of the body.

LILIES OF THE FIELD

1966

■ A black itinerant handyman (Sidney Poitier) driving through the Arizona desert stops at a small farm to ask for some water. The farm is the home of a small group of nuns, recent refugees from Eastern Europe. When this movie was made in the midst of the early 1960s civil rights battles for integration and tolerance, a black man in the leading role made it seem that the movie was about race. Some 30 years later, we see that race is just one of many differences the characters must understand in order to work together.

THE MAGNIFICENT SEVEN

1963

■ Seven gunfighters join forces to protect a small Mexican farm community from bandits in this classic western (based on the Japanese movie *The Seven Samurai*). Yul Brynner and Steve McQueen lead the group. This is a thrilling American epic, with an unforgettable score.

THE MIRACLE WORKER

1962

■ The true story of Annie Sullivan, who found a way to reach her pupil, Helen Keller, a deaf and blind girl. Until Sullivan (Anne Bancroft) arrives, Helen (Patty Duke) is allowed to run completely wild. Sullivan's fierce determination to find a way to communicate with Helen is looked upon by the family with reactions ranging from tolerant to scornful. Duke and Bancroft deservedly won Oscars for their roles. The moment when Helen realizes that language means something is one of the most indelible in movie history.

THE MUSIC MAN

1962

■ A traveling salesman (Robert Preston, repeating his Broadway role) comes to a small town in Iowa, planning to sell them a dream of a boys' band and skip town with the money. The skeptical town librarian (Shirley Jones) is the only one who isn't dazzled. As they fall in love, to some of the most joyously gorgeous music ever written, she learns about the importance of dreams from him, and he learns about the importance of responsibility from her.

A NIGHT AT THE OPERA

1935

■ Harpo, Chico, and Groucho Marx bring their sublime anarchy to perhaps its most appropriate venue—the opera. Groucho is a fast-talking fortune-hunter, and as usual chasing dim dowager Margaret Dumont. When she agrees to bring two opera stars to America (sweet Kitty Carlisle and cruel Walter Woolf King), Harpo, Chico, and romantic lead Allan Jones stow away. This movie contains many classic routines. The slapstick is zany and the wordplay riotous.

SOUNDER

1972

■ A rare movie about a loving and intact black family, this beautiful film about the coming of age of a young man in the South of the 1930s is a quiet classic.

TO KILL A MOCKINGBIRD

1961

■ A story of prejudice and injustice as seen through the eyes of a little girl, the daughter of a lawyer (Gregory Peck) who defends a black man against a trumped-up charge of assault in 1930s Georgia. The sense of time and place—not just the time in history, but the time in the lives of the little girl and her brother—is extraordinary. One of the best movies about childhood ever made.

EXPERT SOURCES

VIDEOS THAT ARE HARD TO FIND

The variety of unusual videos that can be ordered through the mail is staggering. While Blockbuster Video might have 140 copies of True Lies, *very often the major video rental chains don't carry a single copy of harder-to-find films. For those videophiles looking for the obscure, whether for rental or purchase, mail-order houses are often the best bet. Some outlets rent and sell only through membership deals, while others are happy to deal with one-time customers.*

ALTERNATIVE VIDEOS
P.O. Box 270797
Dallas, TX 75227
☎ 214-823-6030

■ Specializes in films for those of African descent. The catalog is free, but there's a $25 basic membership charge before you can rent or purchase.

THE BRAUER BETA CATALOG
26 Emery Lane
Woodcliff Lake, NJ 07675
☎ 800-962-7722

■ For those who still insist on clinging to the ol' Beta machine. There's a free catalog, and they sell packs of blank tapes.

COLUMBIA HOUSE
1400 N. Fruitridge Avenue
Terre Haute, IN 47811
☎ 800-262-2001

■ Good deals at first, but read the agreement and respond to your mail—monthly selections are sent unless you say in advance that you don't want them. Free catalog.

CRITICS' CHOICE VIDEO
P.O. Box 749
Itasca IL 60143
☎ 800-367-7765

■ The free catalog of 2,500 titles is the tip of the iceberg; some 42,000 unlisted titles are available via another special 900 number. Call for information.

DAVE'S VIDEO, THE LASER PLACE
12114 Ventura Blvd.
Studio City, CA 91604
☎ 800-736-1659

■ Ten percent discount on all discs. Dave's insists it can and will find any title currently available on the laser disc format. Catalog available on request.

FESTIVAL FILMS
2841 Irving Ave. S.
Minneapolis, MN 55408
☎ 612-870-4744

■ Specializes in foreign titles at lower-than-average prices. The price of the $2 catalog is applied to your first purchase.

FILMIC ARCHIVES
The Cinema Center
Botsford, CT 06404
☎ 800-366-1920

■ One of the few mail-order houses that only sells to teachers. Three free catalogs: one each for teachers of English, history, and kindergarten through 8th grade.

KEN CRANE'S LASER DISC SUPERSTORE
1521 Beach Blvd.
Westminster, CA 92683
☎ 800-624-3078

■ The superstore claims to have over 100,000 titles available—with an updated list every week. Every purchase is automatically discounted by 10 percent.

MONDO MOVIES
255 W. 26th St.
New York, NY 10001
☎ 212-929-2560

■ The avant-garde specialists, from raunchy B-movies to hard-to-find, experimental art-shorts. Free catalog.

SCIENCE FICTION CONTINUUM
P.O. Box 154
Colonia, NJ 07067
☎ 800-232-6002

■ The name says it all. The catalog costs $1.

WHOLE TOON CATALOG
P.O. Box 369, Department LM
Issaquah, WA 98027
☎ 206-391-8747

■ Sheer heaven for animation lovers, the $2 catalog specializes in hard-to-find imports.

MUSIC & MUSEUMS

LIVING WITH THE MUSIC MASTERS

Building blocks for a classical CD collection, from Bach to Gershwin

"Music is about emotions," says Ted Libbey, commentator on the weekly National Public Radio show "Performance Today," "it helps us grow." And, Libbey says, classical music "has a particular richness because it goes back centuries." Libbey is the author of the recently published book *The NPR Guide to Building a Classical CD Collection* (Workman Publishing Co., 1994). Following are the composers that Libbey would make the building blocks of any classical music collection and why he thinks so.

JOHANN SEBASTIAN BACH (1685–1750)

Bach has had a huge influence on music history, much greater than any of his contemporaries would have guessed. He was known mainly as an astounding keyboard virtuoso and a very prolific composer. What has emerged in the two and a half centuries since his death, however, is the absolutely amazing spiritual power of his compositions. There is a beauty of construction and a kind of clarity of conception and detail that goes far beyond what any other composer of the baroque period achieved.

WOLFGANG AMADEUS MOZART (1756–1791)

Mozart is his favorite, Libbey says, because of the sense of humanity that comes out in the music. People say he was a divine genius, and it's true. But he was also very human. With all the formality of the 18th century, he could evoke tragedy in music and make it burn with emotion. He was a virtuoso keyboardist, the greatest of his age. At the same time he played the violin well enough that he could have had a career as Europe's leading violinist. In his operas he conveys to the listener an understanding of an emotional or dramatic state probably more acutely than any other composer of all time.

JOSEPH HAYDN (1732–1809)

Haydn was the most powerful innovator of the later 18th century. In the field of symphonies, he was the leader. He grew the form from a lightweight suite to a very thoroughly worked-out and highly contrasted musical expression for a large orchestra. For Haydn, music was something of a game, and so there are wonderful jokes in his music. He didn't probe the tragic dimension as much as Mozart did, but he was a pioneer in creating the classical style.

LUDWIG VAN BEETHOVEN (1770–1827)

Beethoven was a classical composer who can also be called the first Romantic. He made things more subjective. His music not only conveyed emotions or imagery, but very precise emotions from his own soul as well. Working on the basis of what Mozart and Haydn had done, Beethoven reinvented the string quartet and symphony and expanded their meaning dramatically. His instrumentals set the standards for the entire 19th and 20th centuries. Like an undertow in the ocean, they pull you in.

FRANZ SCHUBERT (1797–1828)

Schubert was the great song writer in music history; his melodies pin down a state of emotion so effectively. His music is more concerned with contemplation than drama. It puts a very high value on the beauty of sound. Indeed, what you hear in Schubert's music is the beginning of a Romantic concept of sound as color. His music inhabits regions. It's not in a hurry to go from one place to another in a straight line. It's like seeing a strange landscape.

FREDERIC CHOPIN (1810–1849)

There has never been a closer connection between a composer and an instrument than with Chopin and the piano. There is an Italian quality to some of his works: he treated the piano as a human voice. There is an undertone of darkness in much of what he wrote, but also a surreal beauty and lightness to it all—an imaginative release from life.

PIOTR ILYICH TCHAIKOVSKY (1840–1893)

Tchaikovsky has been diminished by the musicologists as a little bit too hysterical and trite in his music. But when you listen to his music, it's not surprising that it's among the most popular. It's music of immediate emotional impact. His ballets—*Sleeping Beauty*, *Swan Lake*, *The Nutcracker*—are among the greatest ever written. His symphonic music has a richness and translucency to it. Many of his musical ideas are almost commonplace, like a simple scale, but he clothed them so gloriously that they come out as very powerful expressions.

CLAUDE DEBUSSY (1862–1918)

Debussy was one of the most profound thinkers in the history of music. He did so much to create modernity. He had an ear for sonority that was completely original. He was influenced by the orchestra of cymbals and gongs from Indonesia that he heard at the World's Fair in Paris. It revolutionized his thinking about sound and resulted in some of the most extraordinary writing for the piano ever. The essential Debussy is in the quiet floating pieces like "Prelude to the Afternoon of the Faun." People tend to compare Debussy to the impressionist painters, but it's more accurate to compare him to the symbolist poets. Most of his work takes a literary point of departure.

GEORGE GERSHWIN (1898–1937)

Gershwin was a lot like Schubert. He was a wonderful melodist. His tunes are all over our musical consciousness. He wrote "Rhapsody in Blue" when he was 25. As he got older, he got more of a sense of organization and structure without losing that freshness he always possessed. His opera, *Porgy and Bess*, is probably the great American opera. It's a tragedy his life ended so early. He still conveys something of the American spirit, especially of the roaring '20s, that no one else has captured in quite the same way.

EXPERT PICKS

10 CLASSICAL CDs NO ONE SHOULD MISS

If you're ready to start a disk library, Ted Libbey, of National Public Radio's classical music broadcast, "Performance Today," suggests these CD recordings for the beginning collector:

BACH: B-Minor Mass
Monteverdi Choir, English Baroque Soloists/ John Eliot Gardiner. Deutsche Grammophon Archiv

■ This is the best of Bach, the best of the baroque era, and one of the greatest works in all of music. Gardiner's magnificent period-instrument account is colorful and light on its feet, yet it conveys the lofty grandeur of Bach's musical conception.

MOZART: Piano Concertos Nos. 23 and 24
Clifford Curzon, piano; London Symphony Orchestra/ István Kertész. London Weekend Classics

■ Swiss conductor Charles Dutoit once said of Mozart's operas and concertos that they are the summit of creation. Here, two musicians with remarkable insight into Mozart team up to scale the heights.

HAYDN: Symphonies Nos. 92 (Surprise) and 104 (London)
Royal Concertgebouw Orchestra/ Sir Colin Davis. Philips Insignia

■ Two of Haydn's most brilliant symphonies—full of wit and wisdom, and yes, surprises—from the set of 12 he wrote as a capstone to his career as an orchestral innovator. They receive sparkling performances from Davis and the Dutch orchestra.

BEETHOVEN: Symphony No. 6 (Pastorale)
Columbia Symphony Orchestra/ Bruno Walter. Sony Classical

■ A recollection of Beethoven's happy thoughts on visiting the country, this is one of the most profound and appealing works in the symphonic literature. Walter's wonderful, youthfully fresh, and exuberant performance has the glow of deep spiritual maturity.

SCHUBERT: Trout Quintet; MOZART: Clarinet Quintet
Rudolf Serkin, piano; Harold Wright, clarinet; with string players from the Marlboro Festival. Sony Classical

■ Mozart's radiant quintet is full of gentleness and pathos. Schubert wrote his "Trout" on a summer vacation, and its sunny informality makes it the perfect counterpart. In these loving performances, the recording offers a wonderful introduction to the realm of chamber music.

CHOPIN: Ballades and Scherzos
Arthur Rubinstein. RCA Red Seal

■ These are the most substantial single-movement pieces Chopin wrote. They are notable for their wealth of content and formal command. If there's one sure bet in this repertory, it's Rubinstein, whose fiery readings combine drama and poetry with mesmeric effect.

BIZET: Carmen
Baltsa, Carréras, Van Dam, Ricciarelli; Chorus of the Paris Opera, Berlin Philharmonic/Herbert von Karajan. Deutsche Grammophon

■ If you're going to start with one opera, make it *Carmen*, which is one of opera's greatest achievements. Completed by Bizet when he was only 36, it's full of memorable melodies, fascinating situations, and gripping drama. Karajan and his colleagues give a polished account that revels in the beauty and color of the score.

■ **EXPERT PICKS**

TCHAIKOVSKY: Piano Concerto No. 1; RACHMANINOFF: Piano Concerto No. 2
Van Cliburn, piano; RCA Symphony Orchestra/Kirill Kondrashin; Chicago Symphony Orchestra/Fritz Reiner. RCA Red Seal
■ Thrills abound in these evergreen performances of two spectacular Romantic piano concertos. Riding these warhorses for all they are worth, the young Van Cliburn shows why he is one of the greatest virtuosos this country has ever produced. Since they were first issued 35 years ago, these accounts have never been out of print.

DEBUSSY: La Mer; SAINT-SAENS: Organ Symphony
Boston Symphony Orchestra/Charles Munch. RCA Victor "Living Stereo"
■ Debussy's majestic portrait of the sea, the greatest work of musical Impressionism, is paired with Saint-Saëns' blockbuster symphony. This is French music at its best, passionately performed by Munch and the greatest "French" orchestra ever assembled.

GERSHWIN: Rhapsody in Blue, An American in Paris; BERNSTEIN: Candide Overture, Symphonic Dances from West Side Story
Leonard Bernstein, pianist and conductor; Columbia Symphony Orchestra and New York Philharmonic. Sony Classical
■ The classics of 20th-century American music. Bernstein leads a sultry, ideally jazzy performance of Gershwin's "Rhapsody," and gives a bracing account of *An American in Paris*. No one compares with him as an interpreter of his own music.

WHAT JAZZES WYNTON MARSALIS

Jazz, with its mix of bracing intellectuality and moving lyricism, has long been known as America's classical music. Few have done more to foster that reputation than trumpeter Wynton Marsalis, who is renowned both for his classical and his jazz playing. As the artistic director of Jazz at the Lincoln Center, Marsalis has been at the forefront of creating a jazz "canon," music that is undeniably classic, if not indeed classical. Here, the master trumpeter picks his 10 favorite jazz albums by the greats who inspired him.

LOUIS ARMSTRONG	*The Hot Fives (any recording)*	*Columbia*
LOUIS ARMSTRONG	*The Hot Sevens (any recording)*	*Columbia*
COUNT BASIE	*The Original American Decca Recordings*	*MCA/Decca*
ORNETTE COLEMAN	*The Shape of Jazz to Come*	*Rhino/Atlantic*
JOHN COLTRANE	*Crescent*	*Impulse*
MILES DAVIS	*Kind of Blue*	*Columbia*
DUKE ELLINGTON	*The Far East Suite*	*RCA*
THELONIOUS MONK	*It's Monk's Time*	*Columbia*
JELLY ROLL MORTON	*The Pearls*	*RCA*
CHARLIE PARKER	*The Complete Dial Recordings*	*Style/Stash*

EXPERT LIST

MUSIC FESTIVALS THAT WILL MAKE YOU SING

As the former European cultural critic for the New York Times *and now the director of the Lincoln Center Festival in New York, John Rockwell has been one of the most respected voices in the music world for many years. Below is his selection of the best music festivals in the world, based both on the high quality of the music and the special atmosphere of the locations. They are arranged according to when they fall on the annual calendar.*

UNITED STATES

NEW ORLEANS JAZZ AND HERITAGE FAIR
P.O. Box 53407
New Orleans, LA 70153

■ **End of April through first week in May:** A wonderful, vital, and diverse jambalaya of folk and commercial popular music.

OJAI MUSIC FESTIVAL
PO Box 185
Ojai, CA 93024

■ **Memorial Day Weekend:** Spiffy performances of challenging contemporary music in a gorgeous southern California setting. Special festivities in 1996 to mark its 50th anniversary.

SPOLETO FESTIVAL
PO Box 157
Charleston, SC 29402

■ **End of May to early June:** A charming, historic city playing host to a lively and diverse variety of performing arts.

LINCOLN CENTER FESTIVAL
70 Lincoln Center Plaza
New York, NY 10023

■ **Summer '96 (dates to be determined):** Starting in 1996, Lincoln Center will offer a wide variety of innovative and traditional performances led by both Lincoln Center constituents and visiting artists from around the world.

SANTA FE OPERA
PO Box 2408
Santa Fe, NM 87504

■ **Summer '96 (dates to be determined):** The most diverse, attractive summer opera festival in the United States, partly for the opera and partly for the location, which is out-of-doors and offers spectacular scenery for a backdrop.

TANGLEWOOD MUSIC FESTIVAL
Before June 9:
c/o Symphony Hall
301 Massachusetts Ave.
Boston, MA 02115
After June 9: West St.
Lenox, MA 01240

■ **Early July to mid-August:** Summer home of the Boston Symphony and the granddaddy of all orchestral U.S. music festivals.

NEXT-WAVE FESTIVAL
70 Lafayette Street
Brooklyn, NY 11217

■ **Mid-October to mid-December:** A fall festival concentrating on post-modern performance events of all kinds. Held at the Brooklyn Academy of Music.

EUROPE

VIENNA FESTIVAL
Box office: Wiener Festwochen,
11 Lehargasse, A-1060
Vienna, Austria

■ **Early May to early June:** The festival concentrates on avant-garde innovations, but runs concurrently with the gala performances at the Vienna State Opera.

GLYNDEBOURNE FESTIVAL OPERA
Lewes, East Sussex
BN8 5UU, England

■ **Late May to late August:** Now in a handsome new theater. Interesting in its repertory and productions. Expect to see England's finest in formal wear, but don't worry about stuffiness—the atmosphere is lightened by picnics amidst contented cows.

DROTTNINGHOLM COURT THEATER
Forestallningar, Box 27050
102 S1 Stockholm, Sweden

■ **Late May to early September:** This pocket-sized the-

■ EXPERT LIST

ater, the only fully functioning, unimproved baroque theater in the world, offers charming performances of 18th-century opera on period instruments. During the intermissions one can walk on the rolling lawns of Sweden's royal palace.

ALDEBURGH FESTIVAL
Aldeburgh Foundation
High St., Aldeburgh, Suffolk
1P15 5AX, England

■ **Early to late June:** Founded by Benjamin Britten and now led by the composer Oliver Knussen, Aldeburgh offers an attractive repertory in a lovely, although somewhat marshy, site.

AIX-EN-PROVENCE FESTIVAL
Palais de l'Ancien Archeveche
13100 Aix en Provence, France

■ **Early to late July:** Although it has been struggling financially, this is still a lovely festival in a lovely town in the heart of Provence.

SAVONLINNA OPERA FESTIVAL
Olavinkatu 27, SF-57130
Savonlinna, Finland

■ **Early to late July:** The festival takes place in a brooding medieval castle in the midst of the Finnish lake district. The operas are always quite good and often very innovative. Especially striking is the sunlight which, due to the far-northern latitude, lasts almost until midnight.

SALZBURG FESTIVAL
A-5010 Salzburg
Postfach 140, Austria

■ **Late July to late August:** Spiritually, if not chronologically, the mother of all festivals. Recently it has become revitalized under the imaginative leadership of Gerad Mortier.

RICHARD WAGNER FESTIVAL, BAYREUTH
Postfach 100262
D-95402 Bayreuth, Germany

■ **Late July to late August:** This festival is not the finest artistic fettle under the direction of Wolfgang Wagner, and not of much use to anyone who dislikes his grandfather's music, but it is still an extraordinary experience for those who do.

ROSSINI OPERA FESTIVAL
Via Rossini 37, 1-61100
Pesaro, Italy

■ **Mid- to late August.** A relatively recent addition to the list of major festivals. Pesaro offers a familiar and exotic Rossini, with top-flight singers in the midst of Italy's Adriatic vacation land.

EDINBURGH FESTIVAL
Edinburgh International Festival
21 Market St., Edinburgh
EH11BW, Scotland

■ **Mid-August to early September.** A sprawling, city-wide festival with a "manic" fringe. Edinburgh always has interesting offerings, and the offerings are becoming increasingly so under the recent direction of Brian McMaster.

■ **WHERE IT'S AT WHEN IT'S HOT**

When the city's stifling and the tempo slow, a jazz festival may be the perfect escape from the doldrums. There are over 200 jazz festivals staged nationwide between May and September. Here are 7 of the largest, most popular events and when they will take place in 1996.

FESTIVAL	WHERE	WHEN	☎ TICKETS
Playboy Jazz Festival	Los Angeles, Calif.	June 17-18	310-449-4070
J.V.C. Jazz Festival	New York, N.Y.	June 23 to July 1	212-787-2020
J.V.C. Jazz Festival	Newport, R.I.	Aug. 11-13	212-787-2020
Long Beach Jazz Festival	Long Beach, Calif.	Aug. 11-13	310-436-7794
Chicago Jazz Festival	Chicago, Ill.	Aug. 30 to Sept. 3	312-427-1676
Montreux Detroit Jazz Festival	Detroit, Mich.	Sept. 1-4	313-963-7622
Monterey Jazz Festival	Monterey, Calif.	Sept. 15-17	800-307-3378

EXPERT LIST

BILLBOARD'S GREATEST HITS

How many times did you crank up the jukebox with the top singles of all time? Are any of the 100 most popular albums of all time in your collection? Billboard *magazine has been ranking America's favorite pop records since the late '50s.*

SINGLES

The most popular singles since Billboard *began keeping charts on August 4, 1958.*

1. **I Will Always Love You,** *Whitney Houston, 1993*
2. **End of the Road,** *Boyz II Men, 1992*
3. **The Sign,** *Ace of Base, 1993*
4. **You Light Up My Life,** *Debby Boone, 1977*
5. **Physical,** *Olivia Newton-John, 1981*
6. **The Twist,** *Chubby Checker, 1960*
7. **Mack the Knife,** *Bobby Darin, 1959*
8. **Endless Love,** *Diana Ross & Lionel Richie, 1981*
9. **Hey Jude,** *The Beatles, 1968*
10. **Bette Davis Eyes,** *Kim Carnes, 1981*
11. **That's the Way Love Goes,** *Janet Jackson, 1993*
12. **The Theme from "A Summer Place,"** *Percy Faith, 1960*
13. **Jump,** *Kris Kross, 1992*
14. **Can't Help Falling in Love with You,** *UB40, 1993*
15. **Dreamlover,** *Mariah Carey, 1993*
16. **Every Breath You Take,** *The Police, 1983*
17. **Night Fever,** *Bee Gees, 1978*
18. **Eye of the Tiger,** *Survivor, 1982*
19. **Tossin' and Turnin',** *Bobby Lewis, 1961*
20. **I Want to Hold Your Hand,** *The Beatles, 1964*
21. **Tonight's the Night (Gonna Be Alright),** *Rod Stewart, 1976*
22. **Informer,** *Snow, 1994*
23. **Shadow Dancing,** *Andy Gibb, 1978*
24. **Say Say Say,** *Michael Jackson and Paul McCartney, 1983*
25. **Battle of New Orleans,** *Johnny Horton, 1959*
26. **I Love Rock 'N Roll,** *Joan Jett & the Blackhearts, 1982*
27. **Ebony & Ivory,** *Paul McCartney & Stevie Wonder, 1982*
28. **Flashdance...What a Feeling,** *Irene Cara, 1983*
29. **Le Freak,** *Chic, 1979*
30. **I'm a Believer,** *The Monkees, 1967*
31. **Baby Got Back,** *Sir Mix-a-Lot, 1992*
32. **Freak Me,** *Silk, 1992*
33. **Call Me,** *Blondie, 1980*
34. **Whoomp! (There It Is),** *Tag Team, 1993*
35. **Billie Jean,** *Michael Jackson, 1983*
36. **(Everything I Do) I Do It for You,** *Bryan Adams, 1991*
37. **I Heard It through the Grapevine,** *Marvin Gaye, 1967*
38. **Lady,** *Kenny Rogers, 1979*
39. **Aquarius/Let the Sunshine In,** *The 5th Dimension, 1969*
40. **Black or White,** *Michael Jackson, 1993*
41. **It's All in the Game,** *Tommy Edwards, 1951*
42. **Centerfold,** *J. Geils Band, 1982*
43. **My Sharona,** *The Knack, 1979*
44. **Are You Lonesome To-night,** *Elvis Presley, 1960*
45. **I'd Do Anything for Love (But I Won't Do That),** *Meatloaf, 1993*
46. **Alone Again (Naturally),** *Gilbert O'Sullivan, 1972*
47. **Stayin' Alive,** *Bee Gees, 1977*
48. **Save the Best for Last,** *Vanessa Williams, 1992*
49. **I Just Want to Be Your Everything,** *Andy Gibb, 1977*
50. **The Power of Love,** *Celine Dion, 1993*
51. **Hero,** *Mariah Carey, 1993*
52. **The First Time Ever I Saw Your Face,** *Roberta Flack, 1972*
53. **Nel Blu Dipinto Di Blu (Volare),** *Domenico Modugno, 1958*
54. **Another One Bites the Dust,** *Queen, 1980*
55. **Joy to the World,** *Three Dog Night, 1971*
56. **Hot Stuff,** *Donna Summer, 1979*

■ EXPERT LIST

57. **(Just Like) Starting Over,** *John Lennon, 1980*
58. **I'll Be There,** *The Jackson 5, 1970*
59. **I Can't Stop Loving You,** *Ray Charles, 1962*
60. **Bridge over Troubled Water,** *Simon & Garfunkel, 1970*
61. **When Doves Cry,** *Prince, 1984*
62. **Silly Love Songs,** *Wings, 1976*
63. **Upside Down,** *Diana Ross, 1980*
64. **Bump 'N Grind,** *R. Kelly, 1993*
65. **Maggie May/Reason to Believe,** *Rod Stewart, 1971*
66. **All Night Long (All Night),** *Lionel Richie, 1983*
67. **Sugar, Sugar,** *The Archies, 1969*
68. **Bad Girls,** *Donna Summer, 1979*
69. **Again,** *Janet Jackson, 1993*
70. **Sugar Shack,** *Jimmy Gilmer & the Fireballs, 1963*
71. **Like a Virgin,** *Madonna, 1984*
72. **Love Is Blue,** *Paul Mauriat, 1968*
73. **Venus,** *Frankie Avalon, 1959*
74. **Cathy's Clown,** *Everly Brothers, 1960*
75. **It's Now or Never,** *Elvis Presley, 1960*
76. **How Deep Is Your Love,** *Bee Gees, 1977*
77. **Weak,** *SWV, 1993*
78. **In the Year 2525,** *Zager & Evans, 1969*
79. **Big Bad John,** *Jimmy Dean, 1961*
80. **Big Girls Don't Cry,** *Four Seasons, 1962*
81. **Jump,** *Van Halen, 1984*
82. **I Will Survive,** *Gloria Gaynor, 1978*
83. **If I Ever Fall in Love,** *Shai, 1992*
84. **To Sir with Love,** *Lulu, 1967*
85. **Crazy Little Thing Called Love,** *Queen, 1980*
86. **All for Love,** *Bryan Adams/Rod Stewart/Sting, 1993*
87. **It's Too Late/I Feel the Earth Move,** *Carole King, 1971*
88. **Rush Rush,** *Paula Abdul, 1991*
89. **Raindrops Keep Fallin' on My Head,** *B. J. Thomas, 1970*
90. **People Got to Be Free,** *The Rascals, 1968*
91. **Total Eclipse of the Heart,** *Bonnie Tyler, 1983*
92. **Knock Three Times,** *Dawn, 1971*
93. **My Sweet Lord/Isn't It a Pity,** *George Harrison, 1971*
94. **Abracadabra,** *Steve Miller, 1982*
95. **American Pie,** *Don McLean, 1972*
96. **All That She Wants,** *Ace of Base, 1993*
97. **Another Brick in the Wall (Part II),** *Pink Floyd, 1980*
98. **Da Ya Think I'm Sexy?,** *Rod Stewart, 1979*
99. **Maneater,** *Daryl Hall & John Oates, 1982*
100. **I Swear,** *All-4-One, 1994*

ALBUMS

The rankings reflect sales between March 24, 1956, and June 25, 1994.

1. **Thriller,** *Michael Jackson, 1984*
2. **My Fair Lady,** *Original Cast, 1964*
3. **Calypso,** *Harry Belafonte, 1975*
4. **Rumours,** *Fleetwood Mac, 1977*
5. **West Side Story,** *Soundtrack, 1961*
6. **South Pacific,** *Soundtrack, 1958*
7. **Please Hammer Don't Hurt 'Em,** *M.C. Hammer, 1990*
8. **Purple Rain,** *Prince & the Revolution/Soundtrack, 1984*
9. **Dirty Dancing,** *Soundtrack, 1987*
10. **Saturday Night Fever,** *Bee Gees/Soundtrack, 1977*
11. **Born in the U.S.A.,** *Bruce Springsteen, 1985*
12. **The Bodyguard,** *Whitney Houston/Soundtrack, 1992*
13. **Blue Hawaii,** *Elvis Presley/Soundtrack, 1961*
14. **Ropin' the Wind,** *Garth Brooks, 1991*
15. **The Sound of Music,** *Soundtrack, 1965*
16. **Some Gave All,** *Billy Ray Cyrus, 1994*
17. **Synchronicity,** *The Police, 1981*
18. **The Sound of Music,** *Original Cast, 1959*
19. **Mary Poppins,** *Soundtrack, 1964*
20. **The Button-Down Mind of Bob Newhart,** *Bob Newhart, 1960*
21. **Faith,** *George Michael, 1987*
22. **The Music Man,** *Original Cast, 1957*
23. **Whitney Houston,** *Whitney Houston, 1985*
24. **Mariah Carey,** *Mariah Carey, 1990*
25. **Tapestry,** *Carole King, 1971*
26. **Sgt. Pepper's Lonely Heart's Club Band,** *The Beatles, 1967*
27. **Around the World in 80 Days,** *Soundtrack, 1958*

EXPERT LIST

28. **Forever Your Girl,** *Paula Abdul, 1988*
29. **More of the Monkees,** *The Monkees, 1967*
30. **Frampton Comes Alive!,** *Peter Frampton, 1977*
31. **Hi Infidelity,** *REO Speedwagon, 1980*
32. **To the Extreme,** *Vanilla Ice, 1990*
33. **Business as Usual,** *Men at Work, 1982*
34. **The Kingston Trio at Large,** *The Kingston Trio, 1959*
35. **Peter, Paul, & Mary,** *Peter, Paul, & Mary, 1964*
36. **Slippery When Wet,** *Bon Jovi, 1986*
37. **Songs in the Key of Life,** *Stevie Wonder, 1976*
38. **Whipped Cream & Other Delights,** *Herb Alpert's Tijuana Brass, 1966*
39. **Modern Sounds in Country and Western Music,** *Ray Charles, 1962*
40. **The Wall,** *Pink Floyd, 1980*
41. **Hysteria,** *Def Leppard, 1987*
42. **The Monkees,** *The Monkees, 1967*
43. **Days of Wine and Roses,** *Andy Williams, 1963*
44. **A Hard Day's Night,** *The Beatles, 1964*
45. **Hair,** *Original Cast, 1968*
46. **Camelot,** *Original Cast, 1960*
47. **Elvis Presley,** *Elvis Presley, 1956*
48. **4,** *Foreigner, 1983*
49. **Gigi,** *Soundtrack, 1958*
50. **The Music from Peter Gunn,** *Henry Mancini, 1959*
51. **Blood, Sweat & Tears,** *Blood, Sweat & Tears, 1969*
52. **Appetite for Destruction,** *Guns 'N Roses, 1987*
53. **Grease,** *Soundtrack, 1979*
54. **Dr. Zhivago,** *Soundtrack, 1967*
55. **Girl You Know It's True,** *Milli Vanilli, 1988*
56. **Abbey Road,** *The Beatles, 1970*
57. **Judy at Carnegie Hall,** *Judy Garland, 1962*
58. **Sing Along with Mitch,** *Mitch Miller & the Gang, 1959*
59. **Bad,** *Michael Jackson, 1987*
60. **Sold Out,** *The Kingston Trio, 1960*
61. **Whitney,** *Whitney Houston, 1987*
62. **Can't Slow Down,** *Lionel Richie, 1983*
63. **Don't Be Cruel,** *Bobby Brown, 1988*
64. **What Now My Love,** *Herb Alpert & the Tijuana Brass, 1966*
65. **Brother in Arms,** *Dire Straits, 1985*
66. **Music Box,** *Mariah Carey, 1993*
67. **Hotel California,** *Eagles, 1977*
68. **Going Places,** *Herb Alpert & the Tijuana Brass, 1966*
69. **The First Family,** *Vaughn Meader, 1962*
70. **Asia,** *Asia, 1982*
71. **The Graduate,** *Simon & Garfunkel/Soundtrack, 1967*
72. **The Joshua Tree,** *U2, 1987*
73. **Tchaikovsky: Piano Concerto No. 1,** *Van Cliburn, 1958*
74. **Meet the Beatles,** *The Beatles, 1964*
75. **No Jacket Required,** *Phil Collins, 1985*
76. **Miami Vice,** *TV Soundtrack, 1985*
77. **The King and I,** *Soundtrack, 1956*
78. **Belafonte,** *Harry Belafonte, 1956*
79. **Footloose,** *Soundtrack, 1984*
80. **Love Is the Thing,** *Nat King Cole, 1957*
81. **Johnny's Greatest Hits,** *Johnny Mathis, 1958*
82. **Calcutta,** *Lawrence Welk, 1961*
83. **Janet Jackson's Rhythm Nation 1814,** *Janet Jackson, 1989*
84. **The Long Run,** *The Eagles, 1979*
85. **G.I. Blues,** *Elvis Presley/Soundtrack, 1960*
86. **Here We Go Again!,** *The Kingston Trio, 1960*
87. **Led Zeppelin II,** *Led Zeppelin, 1970*
88. **The Singing Nun,** *The Singing Nun, 1963*
89. **Goodbye Yellow Brick Road,** *Elton John, 1973*
90. **Bridge over Troubled Water,** *Simon & Garfunkel, 1970*
91. **Tattoo You,** *The Rolling Stones, 1981*
92. **Abraxas,** *Santana, 1970*
93. **Cosmo's Factory,** *Creedence Clearwater Revival, 1971*
94. **American Fool,** *John Cougar, 1982*
95. **Unplugged,** *Eric Clapton, 1992*
96. **Breakfast in America,** *Supertramp, 1987*
97. **Jesus Christ Superstar,** *Various, 1971*
98. **Oklahoma!,** *Soundtrack, 1957*
99. **Glass Houses,** *Billy Joel, 1980*
100. **janet,** *Janet Jackson, 1993*

SOURCE: *Billboard* magazine.©1994 BPI Communications,Inc.

MUSIC LOVER'S GUIDE

WHEN STORE-BOUGHT ISN'T GOOD ENOUGH

For some of the greatest blues, jazz, rock, and country music, mail order is where it's happening. Most record companies sell their wares through record stores, but many smaller labels—as well as a few big ones—also put out catalogs. Ordering through a catalog removes the middleman, meaning lower prices for the consumer and less filtering of your music choices by retail record store buyers. Independent distributors are another great resource, especially if you are trying to track down a rare or out-of-print recording. Here are some of the best catalogs from labels and independent distributors in a variety of musical styles, selected by Josh Tyrangiel of Vibe *magazine.*

BOMP!! RARE RECORDS
P.O. Box 7112
Burbank, CA 91510

■ The Bomp!! catalog may not look like much from the outside (it's a few pieces of copy paper stapled together newsletter-style), but its contents are a pleasant surprise for the indie-rock lover. There's lots of hard-to-find music available at reasonable prices, as well as a selection of thematically related books, magazines, and videos. The Bomp!! catalog is not available by phone, so you either have to find a record or book store that carries it, or send a written request to their Burbank address.

CADENCE, THE REVIEW OF JAZZ & BLUES
Cadence Building
Redwood, NY 13679
☎ 315-287-2852

■ *Cadence* is both a catalog and a magazine. Every month, it dedicates about 100 pages to jazz. There are features, extensive artist interviews, and dozens of record reviews. But it's the 40 pages of rare albums for sale that really make *Cadence* special. Each title is listed in a no-nonsense, phone-book style; over 9,000 titles indexed and alphabetized by record label. *Cadence* can be found in a few select specialty record stores, or it can be ordered for $3 at the phone number above. A year's subscription (12 issues) is $30.

DOUBLE TIME JAZZ RECORDS
1211 Aebersold Drive
New Albany, IN 47150

■ Another well-organized jazz outlet, it offers nearly 5,000 titles. All eras of jazz are represented, but Double Time is especially good at locating out-of-print items. Write to receive a catalog.

MUSIC IN THE MAIL
P.O. Box 1
Brightwaters, NY 11718

■ Music in the Mail is for serious classical collectors only. Several hundred classical labels are represented in their catalog (including Telarc, Chandos, and Harmonia Mundi). They offer a wide variety of hard-to-find new and used CDs. They also feature an extensive selection of LPs. (Though the format has fallen out of favor in most markets, many audiophiles swear by the sonic superiority of vinyl.) Prices are reasonable, and requests are shipped once a month. The catalog costs $1.

RHINO CATALOG
10635 Santa Monica Blvd.
Los Angeles, CA 90025
☎ 800-357-4466

■ The label bills itself as the top archival record label in the country; the extensive catalog bears out that claim. It covers music from the '50s to the '90s, with a great selection of funk anthologies and rock compilation albums. A recent catalog featured thick sections of Cajun music, zydeco, New Orleans r&b, folk, world music, country and west-

■ MUSIC LOVER'S GUIDE

ern, blues, jazz, vocals, contemporary classical, soundtracks, spoken word, comedy, and holiday music. The catalog is free. Requests are handled at the 800 number.

ROUNDER RECORDS
One Camp St.
Cambridge, MA 02140
☎ 617-354-0700

■ A small label with a lot of character. Rounder releases a consumer catalog about once every eight weeks, filled with eclectic zydeco, blues, and world music titles.

TIME WARNER & SONY SOUND EXCHANGE
45 N. Industry Court
Deer Park, NY 11729
☎ 800-521-0042

■ Sound Exchange is a catalog released seasonally by entertainment mega-corps Sony and Time Warner. What it lacks in hipness it more than makes up for in utility. There's an artist index across from the order form that allows you to quickly scan for what you want, and there are several pages of $7.98 CDs. Diversity is also a plus; the catalog offers a moderate selection of titles in rock, pop, easy-listening, old-time radio and nostalgia, jazz, humor, world beat, classical, and country. Catalogs and orders are facilitated through the 800 number.

GENERATIONAL JUKEBOX

Your parents still love Frank Sinatra. Listening to the White Album or the Mothers of Invention still transports you back to the '60s. But don't assume because you're no longer in college that the only spot on the FM dial that you'll be happy is an Oldies station. A travel guide for music in the '90s:

If you like	You ought to hear
BEATLES	*Gin Blossoms, Green Day, Robyn Hitchcock, Matthew Sweet*
MILES DAVIS	*De La Soul, Tremendous Vegetables, A Tribe Called Quest*
BOB DYLAN	*Beck, Billy Bragg, Counting Crows*
ROBERTA FLACK	*Anita Baker, Toni Braxton, Celine Dion*
GRATEFUL DEAD	*Blues Traveler, God Street Wine, Dave Matthews Band, Phish*
JIMI HENDRIX	*Big Head Todd and the Monsters, Nirvana, Pearl Jam, Soundgarden*
GEORGE JONES	*David Ball, Alan Jackson, Sammy Kershaw, Lyle Lovett, John Michael Montgomery*
LED ZEPPELIN	*L7, Living Colour, Metallica, Smashing Pumpkins, Soundgarden*
JONI MITCHELL	*Shawn Colvin, Sheryl Crow, Nanci Griffith, k.d. lang, Sarah McLachlan, Jane Silberry*
PINK FLOYD	*Aphex Twin, The Orb*
ROLLING STONES	*The Mekons, Liz Phair, Paul Westerberg*
SLY & THE FAMILY STONE	*Arrested Development, The Beastie Boys, Dee-Lite, Lenny Kravitz, Red Hot Chili Peppers*
THE TEMPTATIONS	*Boyz II Men, Shai, Jodeci*
VELVET UNDERGROUND	*The Breeders, Luna, R.E.M., Stereolab, Jesus & Mary Chain, Mazzy Star, Sonic Youth*
LAWRENCE WELK	*Kenny G, John Tesh, Yanni*

SOURCE: Adapted from the *Washington Post's Fast Forward* magazine, November 1994 and additional reporting.

PILGRIMAGES

THE CHURCH OF ROCK 'N ROLL

If you loved, or missed, rock's early years, try the new Hall of Fame

So you've already criss-crossed the country. And you've hit all of the meccas of American culture. And you just don't have the energy to follow the Dead or make Lollapalooza your life. No problem. Unearth those tapes you used to listen to when you wore those hot pants! Pack the car with ones that make you feel like a voodoo child!! Take along your prized Fender Telecaster, and drive yourself through all the fields of gold until you reach Cleveland, Ohio, home of the Rock and Roll Hall of Fame....

The concept for a museum dedicated to the history of rock and roll was born over a decade ago, with the creation of the Rock and Roll Hall of Fame Foundation. Founded by a group of music industry moguls, the foundation honors men and women who have made unique contributions to rock and roll. In 1986, after a nationwide search for an appropriate location, Cleveland, Ohio, was chosen as the home of the Rock and Roll Hall of Fame and Museum. The doors open in September 1995.

If James Brown's stage costume, Pete Townshend's battered acoustic guitar, Big Joe Turner's passport, or Grace Slick's dress from Woodstock aren't enough of a draw, it's worth the trip to Cleveland to see the creation of one of the world's most famous architects. Designed by I. M. Pei, who also renovated the Louvre, the rock museum has not only exhibition areas and archival facilities, but also indoor and outdoor concert areas, and a working studio where visiting DJs can conduct live broadcasts.

Inside the dramatic cantilevered spaces, the exhibits are likely to delight not only the most diehard rock fans, but also the most technologically sophisticated of visitors with the way high-tech wizardry has been blended with good, old-fashioned story-telling to show how rock and roll helped shaped today's culture.

The collections spotlight Hall of Famers by including materials that cover the entire scope of each individual's life and work, as well as portraying rock and roll in the context of the society that gave birth to and felt the impact of such high-decibel stars as the Rolling Stones, the Beatles, Janis Joplin, Jimi Hendrix, and James Brown.

Museum officials embrace the good, the bad, and the ugly; the major music scenes, and the music's impact on the way we live are all covered in exhibitions.

This is no mere Hard Rock Cafe. The museum's special features include a multimedia presentation that leads visitors through a recording session; a series of ongoing film presentations and focused exhibits that provide in-depth information on artists, historical periods, and current events; an interactive database featuring "The 500 Songs That Shaped Rock and Roll"; a three-dimensional display that traces the history of fashion in rock and roll; and tons of memorabilia collected by fans or donated by the legends themselves.

LOCATION

The museum is located on the shore of Lake Erie in downtown Cleveland's North Coast Harbor at 1040 East 9th St., Cleveland, Ohio 44114.

As of May 1995, ticket price had not yet been determined. For the latest information, call ☎ 800-349-7625.

MUSEUMGOER'S GUIDE

THE NEWEST JEWELS IN THE CULTURAL CROWN

Museums are no longer the dusty fusty repositories of fine arts that you may remember visiting as a child. Now the walls are coming down as museums increasingly take note of developments in the outside world. "Multi-cultural," "high tech," and "pop" are today's watch words on the cultural beat, and new museums have clearly heard the call. From new high-tech kiosks where one can see how an artifact such as a ceremonial Indian flute was used in its original context to grain elevators that one can climb into, the new museums are offering fresh perspectives on the historical and the everyday. Here, Donald Garfield, senior editor of Museum News, *the official news magazine of the American Association of Museums, recommends the following recently built museums. Also included are outstanding additions to existing museums.*

AMERICAN AND MODERN ART

KEMPER MUSEUM OF CONTEMPORARY ART AND DESIGN

Kansas City, Mo.

■ The museum, a block from the beautiful campus of the Kansas City Art Institute, features work by such artists as David Hockney, Bruce Nauman, Nancy Graves, Georgia O'Keeffe, and Thomas Hart Benton. It is strong on interaction between artists and the community and offers many discussion groups with contemporary artists. ☎ **816-561-4852**

SAN FRANCISCO MUSEUM OF MODERN ART

San Francisco, Calif.

■ One of the two most significant post-modern museums of the last five years—the other is in Seattle. Designed by world-renowned architect Mario Botta, the modernist structure doubles the current exhibit space in the Veterans Building. ☎ **415-357-4000**

SEATTLE ART MUSEUM

Seattle, Wash.

■ Designed by the celebrated post-modern architect Robert Venturi, this is the other most significant museum built in the last five years. It does not have an encyclopedic collection of art like New York's Metropolitan, but its African American and Native American collections are among the most impressive in the country. ☎ **206-625-8900**

ANDY WARHOL MUSEUM

Pittsburgh, Pa.

■ A fabulous example of what can be done when a seven-story warehouse is turned into a museum. Architect Richard Gluckman also designed the avant-garde Dia Foundation in New York. The museum features the history and creative works of Andy Warhol, the father of pop art. ☎ **412-237-8300**

WEXNER CENTER FOR THE VISUAL ARTS

Columbus, Ohio

■ An important and controversial museum due to architect Peter Eisenmann's post-modern aesthetic. This architectural marvel mimics the street grids of Columbus, as well as the streets on the Ohio State campus. Following the grids, the structures inside the museum have no 90-degree angles—even the stairs are slanted. Although there are no permanent collections, many rotating shows visit here regularly. ☎ **614-292-3535**

FREDERICK R. WEISMAN ART MUSEUM

Minneapolis, Minn.

■ A visionary metallic museum on the campus of the University of Minnesota, the only one in the United States designed by celebrated architect Frank Gehry. It continues the tradition of the private collection, in this case, Frederick Weisman's. It is especially strong in American art between 1900 and 1950. ☎ **612-625-9494**

HISTORY

AMERICAN HERITAGE CENTER AND ART MUSEUM

Laramie, Wyo.

■ On the campus of the University of Wyoming, the center is housed in architect Antoine Predock's new conical-shaped centennial complex, which is reminiscent of an Indian teepee. The attached art museum is a Pueblo-inspired design. It contains a variety of fine arts exhibits and features Native American and cowboy art and artifacts. ☎ **307-766-3497**

BEIT HASHOAH MUSEUM OF TOLERANCE

Los Angeles, Calif.

■ This museum explores the horrors of the 20th century: genocide, the Holocaust, and racism, through audio and visual displays. ☎ **310-553-9036**

MICHAEL C. CARLOS MUSEUM

Atlanta, Ga.

■ Part of the Emory University Museum of Art and Archaeology. First-rate collections of art and artifacts from classical antiquity, including the Egyptian, Roman, Grecian, and Pre-Columbian periods. In the forefront of technology, this museum by architect Michael Graves is developing interactive kiosks in the galleries, where one can call up the history of an artifact and see in a video how it was used in its original context. ☎ **404-727-4282**

HOLOCAUST MUSEUM

Washington, D.C.

■ Based on an idea rather than a collection, this museum chronicles the Holocaust through many extraordinary audiovisual displays. ☎ **202-653-9220**

MINNESOTA HISTORY CENTER

St. Paul, Minn.

■ More than just a museum, this is also a library, an archive, and a research center. The museum explores all aspects of Minnesota history. Among the various interactive exhibits is a model grain elevator you can climb into, the better to understand how grain is processed. It also features an important collection of Native American art. ☎ **800-657-3773**

NATIONAL CIVIL RIGHTS MUSEUM

Memphis, Tenn.

■ The museum makes use of audiovisual displays to document the Civil Rights movement. It starts with the slave revolts and ends in the motel (now part of the museum) where Martin Luther King was assassinated. ☎ **901-521-9699**

VALENTINE RIVERSIDE MUSEUM

Richmond, Va.

■ Associated with the Valentine History Museum, the Riverside Museum is geared toward the family. It has a Colonial Williamsburg quality to it, along the lines of a theme park, but with a strong historical basis. ☎ **216-781-7625**

THE WARM SPRINGS TRIBAL MUSEUM

Warm Springs, Ore.

■ The magazine *American Anthropologist* described the museum as having just about the finest exhibitions in the United States. It tells the story of three tribes, the Paiute, the Wasco, and the Warm Springs. The narration along the way is by tribal elders. ☎ **503-553-3331**

MISCELLANEOUS

CHILDREN'S MUSEUM OF HOUSTON

Houston, Texas

■ Where does the food on the dinner plate come from? How do televisions work? What is gravity? The answer to these and other questions can be found at hundreds of interactive exhibits at this award-winning children's museum designed by architect Robert Venturi. ☎ **713-522-1138**

PARLOR GAMES

CUT THE DECK, PLEASE

A quick review of how to play poker, gin rummy, spades, and solitaire

If you want to learn how to play bridge, you need to either read a book or take lessons. But here are the rules—and some tricks of the trade—for popular card games that almost anyone can play. That's no guarantee, of course, that you'll draw good cards, but at least you'll be prepared to call the other guy's bet.

POKER (FIVE-CARD DRAW)

Poker pits one player against another. Casinos that provide poker tables make their money by taking a percentage of the winnings or charging by the hour for the use of their table and dealer. If you are not an expert, a casino is definitely not the place to test your skill. Better to wager chips or change in the comfort of your own home.

There are hundreds of card games based on slight modifications of standard poker or "five-card draw." Common variations include adding wild cards, changing the way in which players bet, and altering the size of each hand. The goal is always the same: get a better hand (selection of cards) than the other players.

To play five-card draw, shuffle a regular 52-card deck and deal 5 cards to each of three to seven players. Typically each player pays a small sum, called an "ante," for the privilege of seeing his or her hand. All bets (and antes) are placed in the pot, a pile of money in the center of the table.

Players bet on their cards in a clockwise fashion, starting at the dealer's left. The first player has several betting options:

- **FOLD:** Throwing in his or her cards and sitting out the rest of the hand. Any time a player folds at this stage, the ante remains in the pot and goes to the winner.
- **BET:** Placing a wager in the pot.
- **PASS:** Choosing not to make a wager and allowing the next player to go.

If the first player doesn't make a bet, then the next player has the same options. Once a player has made a bet, however, other players may no longer pass, and are required to do one of the following:

- **FOLD**: And lose one's bets and ante.
- **CALL**: Match the other player's bets by placing an equal wager into the pot.
- **RAISE**: Place a higher wager than others have bet into the pot. All other players will need to match this raised bet in order to stay in the game.

After a round of betting, all remaining players are then allowed to exchange up to three of their cards with those from the top of the remaining deck in the same order that the cards were dealt. At this time, the players have a second round of betting. After this round, all remaining players show their cards to each other. The player with the highest hand wins the entire pot.

Cards are ranked in the following order, from lowest to highest: 2, 3, 4, 5, 6, 7, 8, 9, 10, Jack, Queen, King, Ace. The box at right helps illustrate the ranking. Each level of the table beats ALL hands below it. For example, even the lowest straight (2, 3, 4, 5, 6) will beat the highest three of a kind (Ace, Ace, Ace, King, Queen).

If two players have the same type of hand, the one with higher cards wins the hand. For example, a player with a 9, 9, 9, Jack, 2 (three 9s) would beat a player with a 6, 6, 6, Ace, Queen (three 6s). Extra cards, such as the Ace, Queen, Jack, and 2 in this example, only matter when two players have identical winning combinations. For example, a player with a 9, 9, 5, 5, King (two pair, with a King) would beat a player with a 9, 9, 5, 5, Queen (two pair, with a Queen).

■ LOW-HAND POKER

The rules for this game are identical to poker, except for an exciting 180-degree switch. In low-hand poker, it is the player with the lowest (and not the highest) hand who wins. The lowest hand possible is a 2, 3, 4, 5, 7, which is known as a "seven-high" hand. There is no such thing as a six-high, because a 2, 3, 4, 5, 6 would make a straight. In this game, it is common to see players discarding Aces and pairs of cards to rid themselves of their beastly hand.

■ HIGH-LOW POKER

Two players split the pot—the one with the highest hand and the one with the lowest hand. If all but one player folds, then the entire pot goes to the winner.

■ FIVE-CARD STUD

Unlike draw, this game begins by dealing only two cards to each player. One of these cards is face down and one is face up, in plain view of all players at the table. Each

■ WHAT BEATS WHAT

Hand	Cards	Number possible	Odds of obtaining
ROYAL FLUSH The highest straight flush—10, J, Q, K, A all of the same suit	10 ♦ TEN, J JACK, Q QUEEN, K KING, A ♦ ACE	4	1:649,739
STRAIGHT FLUSH A straight, and all five cards are of the same suit	7 ♥ SEVEN, 8 ♥ EIGHT, 9 ♥ NINE, 10 ♥ TEN, J JACK	40	1:64,973
FOUR OF A KIND Four cards of the same value with one extra	K KING, 6 ♣ SIX, 6 ♦ SIX, 6 ♥ SIX, 6 ♠ SIX	624	1:4,164
FULL HOUSE Three cards of one value and two of another	4 ♠ FOUR, 4 ♥ FOUR, 4 ♦ FOUR, J JACK, J JACK	3,744	1:693
FLUSH Five cards of the same suit, such as five spades	10 ♠ TEN, 8 ♠ EIGHT, 5 ♠ FIVE, 3 ♠ THREE, K KING	5,108	1:508
STRAIGHT Five cards in a sequence of different suits, such as 5-6-7-8-9	5 ♥ FIVE, 6 ♣ SIX, 7 ♣ SEVEN, 8 ♦ EIGHT, 9 ♠ NINE	10,200	1:254
THREE OF A KIND Three cards of the same value with two extra	3 ♠ THREE, 8 ♣ EIGHT, A ♣ ACE, A ♠ ACE, A ♥ ACE	54,912	1:46
TWO PAIR Two pairs of cards with one extra	2 ♦ TWO, 7 ♠ SEVEN, 7 ♦ SEVEN, Q QUEEN, Q QUEEN	123,552	1:20
ONE PAIR (Two of a kind) Two cards of the same value with three extra	10 ♠ TEN, K KING, 5 ♦ FIVE, 9 ♦ NINE, 9 ♣ NINE	1,098,240	1:1.37
HIGH CARD In a hand with no winning combination of cards, the highest card	2 ♥ TWO, 3 ♦ THREE, 5 ♣ FIVE, 10 ♣ TEN, K KING	1,302,540	1:1

player is allowed to look at his or her face-down card, and then a round of betting ensues. Betting starts with the player showing the highest card. After this round, another card is placed face up for each player (so that each player has two cards showing and one hidden card) and there is another round of betting. Again, betting starts with the player showing the highest cards. This pattern continues until each player has five cards. At any time during the game, a player can fold and the person with the highest hand at the end wins.

SEVEN-CARD STUD

This is an extremely lively and often high-stakes game. It is played in a similar fashion to five-card stud, except that the game begins by dealing three cards to each player—two are face down and one is face up. Rounds of betting are then interspersed with receiving additional face-up cards until each player has two face-down cards and four face-up cards. At this time, a final card is dealt face down and the final round of betting occurs.

Players can use any of their seven cards to make their best five-card hand. The catch to this game is that the odds are thrown haywire. Having seven cards makes it much easier to achieve good hands. It is common to see full houses, straights, and flushes.

BASEBALL

Baseball is a popular variation on seven-card stud, which makes the chances of achieving a high hand ridiculously easy. The game has wild cards, ones that can represent any other card in the deck at the player's discretion. In the game, all 3s and 9s (the number of strikes and innings in baseball) are wild. But they come with a price; a player must either purchase 3s and 9s (at a pre-determined price) if they are dealt these cards face up or they must fold the hand. If a player is dealt a 4 face up (the number of balls in baseball), they are immediately dealt another card face down.

Because of the wild cards in baseball, and the possibility of having more than seven cards (if a 4 is dealt), it is common for players to obtain the absurd "five of a kind." For example, a hand of 5, 5, 5, 3, 9 would be five 5s. Five of a kind is the highest hand possible, and beats a royal flush.

BLACKJACK

The object of blackjack is to have a hand with a point value that is higher than the dealer's. You must do this without going over 21 points, which is why the game is also known as Twenty-one. A player or dealer with 22 points or more has busted and automatically loses the hand. All numbered cards are worth their face value; picture cards (Jacks, Queens, and Kings) are worth 10 points each; and Aces are worth either 1 or 11—which the player gets to determine. Suits and colors are disregarded in the game.

Before each deal, all players make their bets, if you're playing at a casino. Two cards are then dealt to everybody including the dealer, who is dealt one card face down. A player whose first two cards add up to 21 (e.g., an Ace and a Queen) has a Blackjack and is immediately paid 3–2, unless the dealer also has a Blackjack. Whenever a dealer and player tie, it is known as a push, and neither one wins the hand.

Once everyone has been dealt, players have several options to choose from. The best move depends both on what you have been dealt and on the one exposed card of the dealer's hand. A player can:

- **HIT:** Take an additional card.
- **STAND:** Take no additional cards.
- **DOUBLE DOWN:** Double the original bet and take only one additional card.
- **SPLIT:** When a player has been dealt two cards of identical value (e.g., two 9s), he can choose to double the original bet and play the two cards as two separate hands.
- **CLAIM INSURANCE:** When a dealer is showing an Ace, players are invited to claim insurance that the next dealer's card will be worth 10 (and thus Blackjack). Insurance involves risking half the amount of the original bet and pays off at two to one, if the dealer has a Blackjack.
- **SURRENDER:** Forfeit the hand and lose half of the original bet. (Not an option in many casinos.)

HOW TO WIN AT BLACKJACK

You got to know when to hold 'em, and know when to fold 'em.

■ **Always hit when you have been dealt 8 or less.** You have no chance of busting, and you need to get closer to 21.

■ **Always stand on hard hands of 17 or more, regardless of what the dealer is showing.** A hard hand is a hand that either has no Aces or has an Ace or Aces that must be worth only one point because to be worth more would mean a bust (e.g., a 6, a Jack, and an Ace). If you hit, odds are you will bust.

■ **Always hit if you have 16 or less and the dealer's card is a 7, 8, 9, 10, or Ace.** These are the best cards and it is likely that the dealer will beat you. Although you have a good chance of busting, it is worth the risk of getting closer to 21.

■ **Always stand on hard hands of 12 or more if the dealer's first card is a 2, 3, 4, 5, or 6.** These are the worst cards and it is likely that the dealer will bust. But, you don't win if you bust first!

■ **Always stand on soft 19s and 20s.** A soft hand is one that has an Ace that can still be valued at either 1 or 11. Don't risk losing the good hand.

Once all players are either satisfied with their hands or have busted, the dealer proceeds. Unlike the players, who get to make choices, the dealer must proceed according to set rules: drawing on any hand that is less than 17 and standing on anything 17 or higher.

■ GIN RUMMY

Gin Rummy (or simply "Gin") is one of the most popular two-handed card games. It not only can be played for money but is fun to play in its own right. All 52 cards are used. Suits, however, do not play a role in the game. Face cards are worth 10 points each; numbered cards are worth their face value; and Aces are worth one point each. One common variation, however, is to allow Aces to be either high or low. Usually when this is done, Aces are worth 15 points instead of one. The object is to get rid of the cards in your hand by creating sets of three or more cards that can be "melded." Timing is important, though—the sets are played differently depending on who melds his or her cards first. The sets can be formed in two ways:

■ **SERIES:** Three or more cards form a series in sequential order, such as a 4-5-6-7 or a 10-J-Q.

■ **MATCHING SETS:** This is when cards are put in groups of the same value, such as an 8-8-8 or an A-A-A-A.

To play the game, 10 cards are dealt to each of two players and the remainder of the deck is placed in a pile between them. The dealer turns over the top card from this pile and places it face up to begin a discard pile. The second player then has the option of taking this card and switching it with one of the cards in his hand or passing and giving the dealer the same option. If the dealer also passes, the second player takes the card that is on the top of the pile—so that momentarily there are 11 cards in his hand. One of the 11 cards is then placed face up on top of the discard pile.

The dealer must then either take the card that has been discarded or the next card from the deck. This continues until a player decides to end the round of play, by melding his or her cards to reveal the hand.

Here's where it gets complicated. The first player to meld or "knock" must have fewer than 10 points in hand that are *not part of sets.* For example, after several rounds of drawing cards, a player might knock with the following hand: 5-5-5 (a set), 8-9-10-J (another set), and A, 2, 2, K (not a set). This player can discard the King and then meld with the set of 5s, the 8 through Jack sequence, and five points (A+2+2).

The second player then must meld his or her cards, too. In doing so, the second player has the added advantage of being able to play cards off the first player's hand.

For example, the second player might have the following hand: 2-3-4, 9-9-9, 4, 5, 8, Q. The 2 through 4 sequence and the 9s would be played in their own right. However, the Q could also be played off the 8 through Jack sequence of the first player, as would the 5 with the three 5s. This would leave the second player with only 12 unused points (4+8). The player who knocked would earn the difference between the two hands, or seven points (12-5).

If a player knocks and then is beat (or underscored), then the second player gets an additional 25 points for the feat. If a player melds an entire hand, with no extra cards, then he is entitled to say "gin" and obtains an extra 25 points. The winner of each round deals the next hand.

The game continues until one player reaches 100 points (or any pre-determined score). To play for money, players typically bet a certain sum per point. For example, a final score of 105 to 80 would result in 25 points to the winner.

■ SPADES

Spades can be played by three people, but four is ideal. The goal is to score as many points as possible by collecting "tricks."

To begin, the entire 52-card deck is dealt evenly to each of the players. If there are four players, each will have 13 cards. The first round is begun by whoever has the 2 of clubs, which is laid in the center of the table. The player to his or her left then must lay down any card of the same suit. The next player does likewise, and the next, till each has laid a card. The highest card wins the trick. (Aces are played high in spades; 2 is the lowest.)

If a player doesn't have a card in the suit that is being played, he or she may trump the trick by playing a spade. However, if any of the following players in that round also has no cards in the original suit, he or she may "trump the trump" with a higher spade. (No one may open with a spade until spades have been "broken"—that is, played as a trump.) The winner of the book plays the next card, and the round continues till all 13 books have been played.

Scoring is what makes spades challenging. Each trick is worth 10 points. After a hand is dealt, players must make a bid on how many tricks they expect to get based on the strength of the cards they were dealt.

EXPERT SOURCES

TO HELP YOU BEAT THE ODDS

CAN YOU WIN?: THE REAL ODDS FOR CASINO GAMBLING, SPORTS BETTING, AND LOTTERIES
Mike Orkin, W. H. Freeman, 1991, $11.95
■ For mathematically minded gamblers. The odds in everything from football pools to slot machines. Also covers the "house edge" on casino games.

SCARNE'S NEW COMPLETE GUIDE TO GAMBLING
John Scarne, Simon & Schuster, 1986, $18
■ Besides offering an in-depth look at the rules of various games, it explains popular swindling methods, such as crooked dice, three-card monte, trimmed decks, and marked cards. A decade old, but still a pleasurable read and useful resource.

WINNING BLACKJACK FOR THE SERIOUS PLAYER
Edwin Silberstang, Cardoza, 1993, $9.95
■ For those who wish to know the "right move to make." Tells when to hit, stand, double down, or split, based on both your hand and the dealer's.

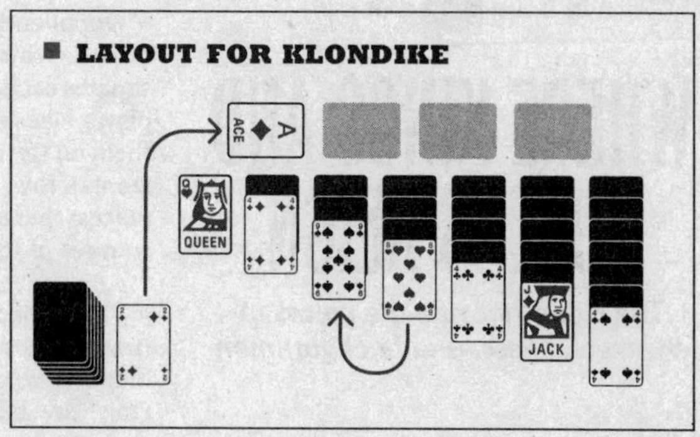

■ LAYOUT FOR KLONDIKE

Because each player in a four-person game has 13 cards, there are 13 possible tricks (130 points). A player who found among his or her 13 cards a couple of Kings, some Queens, and several spades of any value, would rightly feel justified in making a high bid because those cards are all likely to make a trick. The catch: If a player has a strong hand and so bids, say, 6 tricks, that player must make at least those 6. If not, he or she will instead lose 60 points (–10 points for each trick bid).

On the other hand, if the player makes over the amount bid, say 7 tricks instead of the 6 bid, he or she receives only a single point for each extra trick—in this case 61 points. Another catch: if a player receives more than 10 of those extra single points, he or she loses 100 points. This is called "sandbagging."

A player who is behind by more than 100 points may bid "blind six," a bid of six made before the cards are even dealt. If the six are made, the player receives 100 points; if not, the player loses 100 points.

Players can play as many hands as they like to a preset score. About 500 points is a good goal for a satisfying evening.

■ SOLITAIRE

Klondike is the most common form of solitaire in the United States—so common in fact, that it is often known simply as "solitaire." In reality, there are many varieties of solitaire which, as the name implies, refers to any card game played by one person.

To play Klondike, deal one card face up from a standard deck. Then deal six additional cards face down, to form a row to the right of the first card. Next a card is dealt face up on top of the second card in the row, and five more cards are dealt face down on top of the remaining piles to the right. This pattern continues until 28 cards have been used and there are seven piles or columns of cards, ranging from one card (in the left column) to seven cards (in the right column). The remainder of the deck is placed face down on the table.

Cards are then shifted from one column to another to form descending sets (from King to 2) that alternate by color (red-black or black-red). In the example above, the red 8 can be placed on top of a black 9. Then, the card beneath the 8 can be flipped over. If a red 10 were to appear, then the 9 and 8 could be placed on top of the 10, allowing the player to flip over more cards.

Aces are immediately removed from the layout when they appear, and are used as starting points to build ascending sets. These sets are based on suit, rather than the black-red pattern already described. In this example, the Ace of diamonds has been set aside for this purpose. If the two of diamonds appears, it will be placed on top of the Ace, and then the 3 of diamonds, and so on. The game is won if all four of these Ace piles are built into Ace-through-King sequences.

If one of the seven columns ever becomes empty because all of its cards have been shifted, a King (and anything stacked beneath it) can be moved to the column to fill the empty space. Once there are no cards that can be moved, cards are taken three at a time from the remainder of the deck, and played off on any of the columns if possible. If you can play the top card, you can play the next one as well. The cards that can't be played are set aside, face up. When the entire deck has been played through three times, the game is over.

A variation on the game, which many people use to make it easier, involves flipping the discard pile over and going through the cards a second time, or even a third time before calling it a loss.

BOARD GAMES

WHERE KINGS AND QUEENS REIGN

The rules that rule the pieces in checkers, chess, and backgammon

The most exciting board games require a unique mix of brains and imaginative brawn. In the best of matches, the rules metamorphose from simple mathematical variations into the physics of a new world in which pawns become warriors and you are the mastermind behind a war in which everything good and decent is at stake. Here are the rules that govern the battlefield.

HOPSCOTCHING THE CHECKER BOARD

Learning to play checkers is child's play, but devising strategies to beat a good player takes skill and lots of practice. The winner, of course, is the first one to capture all of an opponent's men or to block them so that they can't move. To test your mettle, follow these instructions:

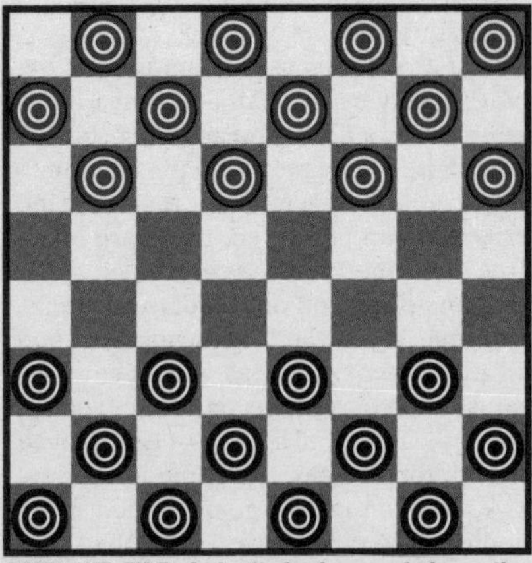

RANK AND FILE: In both checkers and chess, the rows across are known as ranks; the columns as files. In checkers, only the red squares are used.

■ Opponents face each other across the board, which has eight rows of eight squares each, alternately red and black. One player takes the red pieces, or men, and puts them on the black squares in the three horizontal rows nearest him. The opponent places the black checkers on the black squares in the three rows facing him.

■ The opponents take turns—black goes first, then red—moving a man forward diagonally toward the opponent's side. Only the black squares are used. With each turn, a player moves one man to an adjacent empty square. When one player's man comes up against an enemy checker and there is an empty space behind it, the player jumps over the enemy, landing on the unoccupied square. The captured checker is removed from the board.

■ One man can jump two or more enemy pieces consecutively, by moving diagonally left or right after the first jump, as long as there are empty spaces to land on between each jump. A checker that makes it to any square in the opponent's first row becomes a king. The checker gets crowned by a man of the same color that is not in play. The king can move, and jump, forward and backward.

THE MIND FIELDS OF CHESS

When it comes to drama, intrigue, and byzantine rules, few games can match chess, which is thought to date back to sixth-century India or China. Odds are you won't become the next Bobby Fischer, who at age 15 was the youngest international grand master in history, but here are the rules that will take you to the endgame: capturing the enemy's king.

■ Opponents face each other across the board, which has eight rows of eight squares each, alternately white and black. Each player gets 16 pieces of one color, black or white. From least to most important, the pieces are: 8 pawns, 2 knights, 2 bishops, 2 rooks (or castles), 1 queen, and 1 king.

■ Place the board so that each player has a light square at the nearest right-hand corner. In the row closest to you, place in order from left to right: rook, knight, bishop, queen, king, bishop, knight, and rook. Line up the pawns next to each other in the row directly in front these pieces.

■ A piece can move only into a square that's not occupied by another piece owned by the same player. If an enemy piece occupies the square, it is captured. You remove the captured piece from the board and put your piece in its place.

■ A pawn moves forward one square at a time, except for its first move when it can go one or two squares. A knight makes an L-shaped move, going two squares forward, backward, or sideways, then another square at a right angle. It's the only piece that can jump over another piece. A bishop goes diagonally forward or backward, but has to stay on the same color. A rook moves forward, backward, or sideways, for any distance. The queen is a potent force. She moves forward, backward, sideways, and diagonally for any number of squares in one direction. The king's moves are like the queen's except that he moves one square at a time, as long as it's unoccupied or not under attack by an enemy piece.

■ When a king is under attack by an enemy piece, the king is in check. The player whose king is in check has several options: to move the king to safety, to capture the attacker, or to move another piece to a square between the king and the attacker. If a player can't take any of these moves, the king is captured or "checkmated," and the game is over.

■ Pieces capture an opponent's man by moving as they normally do, except for the pawn. It can capture any of its opponent's pieces that are diagonally next to and ahead of it.

■ A pawn can also take an enemy pawn "en passant," or in passing. Say an opponent starts by moving his pawn two squares, instead of one, putting it next to one's pawn. You can take that piece by moving diagonally to the square directly behind it. But do it immediately: you can't wait for your next turn.

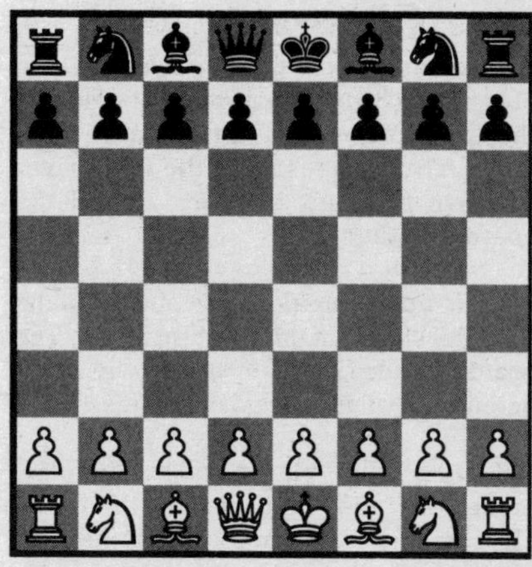

King moves Queen moves Bishop moves

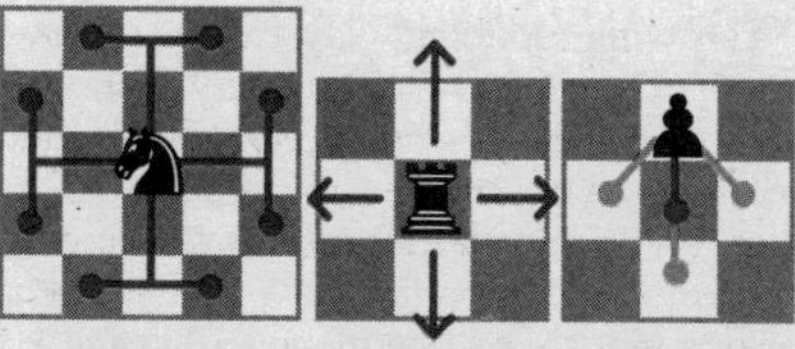

Knight moves Rook moves Pawn moves

MANUEVERS: The six chess pieces can move in a variety of ways. The knight, however, is the only one that can actually move through other pieces. That ability, combined with its unusual moving pattern, makes it an endgame linchpin.

■ Once in each game, in a move called castling, a king gets to move two spaces. Castling is done only if the king is not in check, there are no pieces between the king and a rook, and neither piece has yet made a move. The two-part move is done by moving the king two squares toward the rook and then putting the rook on the square passed over by the king. Castling counts as one move.

THE FINER POINTS OF BACKGAMMON

Backgammon is a game played by two players, each with 15 markers or stones—these days checkers can be used in a pinch. The object is to be the first player to move all one's markers around the board and then off it.

■ To set up, the markers are placed on the board as shown in the diagram below. The board is divided into four "tables" with numbered triangular spaces, or "points."

■ To play, each player rolls a die. The higher one goes first. Players then take turns rolling two dice to determine how many spaces to move the stones, with black moving around the board in one direction and white moving in the opposite direction. The numbers on each die can be combined so that one piece moves the total amount indicated. Alternatively, each die's value can be applied separately to a single marker.

■ Throwing "doubles" (say, two 4s), allows a player to move twice as many points as shown on the dice—in this case, either four markers can be moved four spaces each, one can be moved four spaces and one 12 spaces, two can be moved 8 spaces each, or one marker can be moved 16 spaces.

■ There is no limit to the number of markers of the same color that may stay on one point, but markers of opposite colors may not occupy the same point. If two or more markers are on a point, the point is closed—a marker of the opposite color can't land there. However, a point occupied by only one marker is open and is called a "blot." If an opponent lands on a blot, the other player must move his or her man to the bar between the two halves of the board and can play no other man till the one on the bar reenters. To do so, the player must make a roll of the dice that corresponds to a space on the other player's inner table that is open or blotted.

■ Once all of a player's 15 men have entered his or her "inner table" (the opposite side of the board from which the player began), the player may begin bearing off by rolling the dice and removing any men that occupy spaces indicated by the roll. If a player rolls 5 and 4, for example, he or she may remove one of the men that occupy point 5 and one of the men that occupy point 4. If the number is higher than any of the occupied points, the player may remove a man from the next highest point. Double 6s are an especially good roll at this point. Play continues till one of the players has removed all of his or her men.

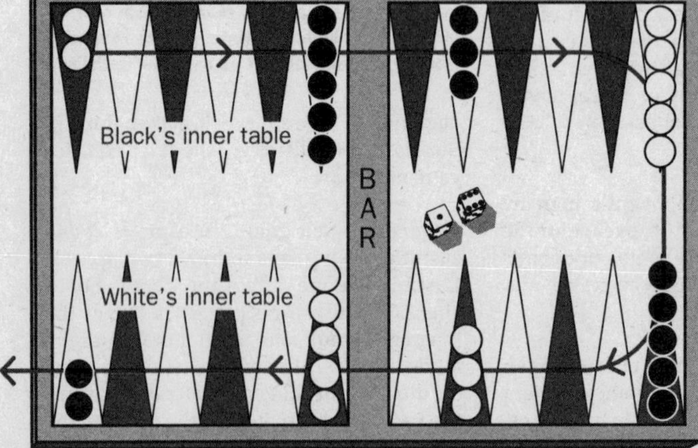

BACKGAMMON: Board is shown in the starting position. The goal is to move your men from your opponent's inner table to your own inner table on the opposite side of the board. White moves in the direction indicated by the arrows, black moves in the opposite direction. When all of your men reach your inner table, you may begin bearing them off by throwing dice that (hopefully) correspond to the number assigned each point.

CHAPTER TEN

AUTOS

EXPERT QUOTES

"Tell the salesperson you expect him to make a profit but you're not going to send him on his next trip to Hawai'i."

—W. James Bragg, author of *In the Driver's Seat: The New Car Buyer's Negotiating Bible*

Page 699

"A lot of play in the steering wheel indicates that the steering system will probably need to be replaced."

—Rick Rinaman, Indy 500 pit crew chief

Page 712

"The smooth driver is always better than the aggressive driver. I try to tell people, think of yourself as the ideal chauffeur."

—Jackie Stewart, three-time world racing champion

Page 714

THE YEAR AHEAD: LOOK FOR sport-utility vehicles that have the comforts of a living room... **DISCOVER** the advantages of leasing rather than buying your next new car... **EXPECT** more experimentation by auto dealers with no-dicker pricing policies... **WATCH FOR** more women car salespersons... **APPRECIATE** the continuing quality improvements in U.S.-made cars... **BE CAUTIOUS** about the discontinuation of the 55 mph speed limit in most states...

BUYING & LEASING

STEER YOUR WAY THROUGH THE '90S

Cars are safer and more reliable but prices have made leasing attractive

It may be a cliché to say that you can tell what frame of mind Americans are in by what kind of cars they're driving, but it's a cliché with good reason. It doesn't take a Ph.D. to notice that the big tail fins and automatic transmissions cars boasted in the '50s reflected a national mood that was pretty upbeat. Or that when Volkswagen beetles and psychedelic vans commandeered the highways in the '60s, they signaled that the winds were blowing in a different direction.

What now, then? The '80s, a decade in which the president insisted it was morning in America again, yet the rich folk all seemed to drive German-born BMWs and Mercedes-Benzes, and those who weren't made the Honda Accord America's number-one-selling car, are now an automotive memory. But their legacy lives on in minivans, antilock brakes, and customer satisfaction surveys that hold all car makers to Japanese standards of quality.

The face of the '90s has several significant new wrinkles, however. Leasing rather than buying has become increasingly commonplace, as the average purchase price of a new car pushed past $20,000 in 1994. Fancy sports-utility vehicles with four-wheel drive are crowding out luxury car sales as Baby Boomers gravitate to transportation that will allow them to ferry a car pool or cross a mountain without having to scrimp on leather upholstery or audiophile compact disk systems. Japanese and German car sales have also slowed significantly as the quality of American autos has become more competitive and sharp swings in foreign exchange rates have made products made in Japan and Germany more expensive for American consumers.

All these trends are likely to become even more pronounced before inevitably giving way to new consumer patterns. Take auto leasing, which has been the car industry's way of keeping monthly auto payments affordable (see "When Leasing Makes Sense," page 704) even though the average sales

THE QUALITY LEADERS

The research firm J. D. Power and Associates in 1994 asked more than 44,000 owners of new cars and light trucks to evaluate their autos 90 days after they had purchased them. The average number of new car problems per 100 vehicles was 110 in 1994, compared with 107 in 1993. For light trucks the average number of reported problems was 126, compared with 129 in 1993. Here are the 50 models that had the least problems:

1994 PROBLEMS PER 100	
Lexus LS 400	32
Lexus GS 300	48
Lexus SC 300/SC 400	52
Geo Prizm	56
Acura Legend	57
Infiniti J30	61
Mercury Grand Marquis	61
Toyota Camry	63
Toyota Tercel	67
Lexus ES 300	68
Lincoln Town Car	68
Toyota Paseo	69
Toyota Previa	71
Nissan Maxima	72
Buick Park Avenue	76
Saturn Sedan	76
Toyota Corolla	76
Ford Crown Victoria	78
Volvo 960	78
Oldsmobile 98	79
Saturn Coupe	79
Toyota T100	79
Buick LeSabre	80
BMW 5-Series	81
Ford Explorer	83
Eagle Summit	84
Ford Ranger	84
Infiniti Q45	84
Mercedes-Benz SL-Class	85
Mazda MX-5 Miata	86
Mercedes-Benz C-Class	86
Toyota 4-Runner	86
Honda Civic	89
Lincoln Mark VIII	89
Mazda Protege	89
Oldsmobile Cutlass Ciera	89
Cadillac DeVille/Concours	90
Volvo 940	90
BMW 7-Series	91
Buick Century	91
Mercedes-Benz S-Class	92
Toyota Celica	92
Honda Accord	93
Mercedes-Benz E-Class	94
Saturn Wagon	95
Lincoln Continental	96
Ford Taurus	97
Mercury Sable	97
Nissan Sentra	97
Pontiac Grand Am	97

THE BEST-MADE CARS FOR THE PRICE	
Under $12,000	Toyota Tercel
$12,001–$17,000	Geo Prizm
$17,001–$22,000	Mercury Grand Marquis
$22,001–$29,000	Buick Park Avenue
$29,000–higher	Lexus LS 400

SOURCE: J. D. Power and Associates, 1994.

price of a new car has risen from about $14,000 five years ago to just over $20,000 at the end of 1994. According to CNW Marketing/Research, a Bandow, Ore., firm that follows the auto business, one in four new car sales in 1994 were financed by leases, but by 1998, that will reach two of every five cars sold.

For those who would rather own than lease a car, leasing may still have created a benefit for them. That's because the industry's dependence on two- and three-year leases to move their wheels in recent times has created excellent opportunities for used car buying; there will be a huge pool of well-maintained late-model cars whose leases have expired coming onto the used car market in the next two years. With all that supply on hand, used car buyers should find the prices attractive.

Sport-utility vehicle shoppers, who sometimes have had to pay premiums of several thousand dollars to obtain an upscale four-wheel drive vehicle in the face of dealer shortages in the past, should find lots more choice and better prices in the future. Instead of standing by while American makers of sports-utility vehicles such as the Ford Explorer, Jeep Grand Cherokee, and Chevrolet Blazer take a deep bite out of their luxury car sales, everyone from Mercedes-Benz and BMW to Toyota and Honda are searching for ways to compete in the sports-utility field. Christopher Cedergren, a leading industry analyst at AutoPacific Group, predicts that sales of compact sport-utility vehicles will increase almost 40 percent by 1996, while luxury car sales will grow no more than a third of that.

EXPERT PICKS

THE BEST CARS OF 1995

When it comes to picking winners and awarding prizes, Americans take a back-seat to nobody. And when it comes to rating cars, the magazines Car and Driver *and* Automobile Magazine *are among the first places car lovers turn for the last word. Here are the cars their editors picked as the very best of model year 1995.*

$12,000 TO $18,000

GEO PRIZM LSI

Front-engine, front-wheel drive, 5-passenger. Base: $12,340

■**COMMENT:** The Prizm LSi is as good as many automobiles twice its price, and it's a revelation every time we drive one. It steers better, grips better, and goes better than its price leads us to believe. *AUTOMOBILE MAGAZINE*

CHRYSLER NEON SPORT

Front-engine, front-wheel drive, 2-door coupe. Base: $13,567

■**COMMENT:** Like the original Volkswagen GTI, which pretty much defined the genre—frugal, front-wheel drive economy cars pumped up with hot-blooded mechanicals—the Neon Sport coupe wins your heart with pyrotechnic performance while convincing your wallet with sound financial reasoning. *AUTOMOBILE MAGAZINE*

FORD CONTOUR SE / MERCURY MYSTIQUE

Front-engine, front-wheel drive, 5-passenger, 4-door sedan. Base: $15,695

■**COMMENT:** No other American car in this class has ever driven like the Contour V-6 we had. It was compact and tight, hammered together more like a Saab than a Tempo from the rent-a-car place. It was alert and agile, and it answered the controls like a European sport sedan. *AUTOMOBILE MAGAZINE*

MAZDA MX-5 MIATA

Front-engine, rear-wheel drive, 2-door, sports car. Base: $16,450

■**COMMENT:** If you don't have fun driving a Miata, you probably don't have a pulse. At 60 mph, the engine purrs happily in fifth gear. Grab the fist-sized shifter and switch to third, and the purr changes to a rasp. Plant your foot on the floor, and the rpm can easily climb to 7,000. With your hair flying in the wind and a panoramic view, it's hard to imagine a better car anywhere. *CAR AND DRIVER*

FORD PROBE 24V GT

Front-engine, front-wheel drive, 2-door, 4-passenger sports car. Base: $16,545

■**COMMENT:** A beautifully integrated package—practical, comfortable, and easy to drive quickly. Its price is within reach of most new car buyers. *AUTOMOBILE MAGAZINE*

HONDA ACCORD

Front-engine, front-wheel drive, 5-passenger, 2- or 4-door sedan. Base: $15,180–$23,000

■**COMMENT:** As always, the Accord offers a satisfying combination of practicality, comfort, and refinement that seems to push the right buttons with both ordinary commuters and demanding enthusiasts. *CAR AND DRIVER*

$18,000 TO $25,000

CHRYSLER CIRRUS LXI

Front-engine, front-wheel drive, 5-passenger, 4-door sedan. Base: $19,600

■**COMMENT:** The Cirrus has a sophisticated control-arm suspension to provide a winning combination of precise handling and a smooth ride. At a base price of $19,600 for a completely loaded Cirrus LXi, this car provides tremendous value. *CAR AND DRIVER*

ACURA INTEGRA GS-R

Front-engine, front-wheel drive, 2+2-passenger, 3-door coupe. Base: $21,070

■**COMMENT:** A first-time winner last year, the Acura Integra GS-R captivated us again with its combination of practicality and performance. *CAR AND DRIVER*

■ EXPERT PICKS

NISSAN MAXIMA SE

Front-engine, front-wheel drive, 5-passenger, 4-door sedan. Base: $21,989

■ **COMMENT:** It may not be lust at first sight with the Maxima SE, but after your first drive, you'll want one...for the engine, a free-revving 190-bhp, 3.0-liter V-6 that provides bulletlike speed. You'll want one for the slick shifter and clutch, the precision steering, the enthusiastic handling, and the overall refinement. But you have to think practically. So go ahead and buy it. The build quality is exemplary, the backseat generous, and the price reasonable. *AUTOMOBILE MAGAZINE*

$25,000 TO $35,000

HONDA PRELUDE VTEC

Front-engine, front-wheel drive, 2+2-passenger, 2-door coupe. Base: $25,350

■ **COMMENT:** This is the fourth consecutive win for the Prelude and the third for the VTEC model, which brings the same finely developed hardware to sports coupes that the Accord brings to family sedans.
CAR AND DRIVER

MAZDA MILLENIA S

Front-engine, front-wheel drive, 5-passenger sedan.
Base: $31,400

■ **COMMENT:** Mazda engineers are more imaginative and far braver than most, and they turn out great work. But the people we really need to thank are their product planners, who gave us out-of-the-mainstream cars like the RX-7, the Miata, and now the sleek, all-of-a-piece Millenia S....We think this package is a cut above family cars as superior as the Toyota Camry and the Honda Accord.
AUTOMOBILE MAGAZINE

BMW 325I AND M3

Front-engine, rear-wheel drive, 5-passenger, 2- or 4-door sedan. Base: $31,920–$36,642

■ **COMMENT:** Those who genuinely enjoy the act of driving and still demand a practical, compact sedan will have a tough time finding a better choice than one of these three-series Bimmers.
CAR AND DRIVER

$35,000 AND ABOVE

MERCEDES-BENZ C280

Front-engine, rear-wheel drive, 5-passenger luxury sedan. Base: $36,300

■ **COMMENT:** Blessed with a compliant, agile, confidence-inspiring suspension that employs double wishbones in front and five links in the rear, the C280 becomes more beautiful as its speed increases. An automobile that feels merely solid and capable on the interstate sprouts the wings of angels when the roads snake through the mounts....The steering is trustworthy and the brakes are strong.
AUTOMOBILE MAGAZINE

MAZDA RX-7

Front-engine, rear-wheel drive, 2-passenger, 3-door coupe. Base: $37,363

■ **COMMENT:** In miserable weather or for long trips, the RX-7 is not ideal. But for Sunday morning excitement in the mountains, this $37,363 sports car is one of our favorites.
CAR AND DRIVER

LEXUS SC300

Front-engine, rear-wheel drive, 2+2-passenger, 2-door coupe. Base: $41,000

■ **COMMENT:** A luxury coupe should provide the comfort of a luxury sedan, with a rear seat that is at least somewhat usable, and an extra helping of performance and style. The $41,000 Lexus serves up all of those qualities to perfection. *CAR AND DRIVER*

NISSAN 300ZX TURBO

Front-engine, rear-wheel drive, 2-passenger, 3-door coupe. Base: $41,283–$43,510

■ **COMMENT:** The bottom line is that the $42,000 300ZX is a 155-mph sports car that a hard-core enthusiast can drive effortlessly as a daily commuter, which is exactly why we fell in love with it when we put 30,000 miles on one during a long-term test. *CAR AND DRIVER*

JAGUAR XJ6

Front-engine, rear-wheel drive, 5-passenger luxury sedan. Base: $53,450

■ **COMMENT:** Surrounds you with leather and wood and

■ EXPERT PICKS

wool and with the ambience of an exclusive private club. Its road manners...are a ride engineer's ideal...what a Jaguar sedan should be.
AUTOMOBILE MAGAZINE

SPORT-UTILITY VEHICLES

LAND ROVER DISCOVERY

Front-engine, all-wheel drive, 7-passenger sport-utility vehicle. Base: $29,350

■ **COMMENT:** It has a strong 3.9-liter V-8 engine and a long list of standard equipment....In a world where everyone including Ford is trying to build a better Ford Explorer, the Discovery has the sort of oddball personality that grabs our attention and won't let go.
AUTOMOBILE MAGAZINE

MINIVANS

FORD WINDSTAR

Front-engine, front-wheel drive, 7-passenger minivan.
Base: $23,000

■ **COMMENT:** The Holy Grail for a minivan buyer. It is carlike to drive, so you don't feel so much like you are piloting a school bus. It has lots of room—seating seven easily....It is low enough to the ground that you can step in comfortably while carrying an infant or other bulky package. And it is plush, comfortable, even for a minivan, luxurious inside, so you don't feel surrounded by hard plastic.
AUTOMOBILE MAGAZINE

Sources: *Automobile Magazine,* February 1995; *Car and Driver,* January 1995.

■ YOUR CAR'S RESALE VALUE FIVE YEARS LATER

The percentage to the right of each vehicle represents how much of its original value the vehicle will retain at the end of five years. Resale value is based on the car's rate of depreciation. Vehicles with better resale values have slower rates of depreciation.

HIGHEST RESALE VALUE

■ SUBCOMPACT	
Saturn SC Coupes	69%
Acura Integra RS Coupe	64%
Toyota Celica ST Liftback	62%
■ COMPACT	
Saturn SL Sedans Series	65%
Honda Accord DX Sedan	64%
VW Jetta GL 10 Sedan	61%
■ MIDSIZE	
Nissan Maxima Series	61%–58%
Toyota Camry XLE Sedan	58%
Volkswagen Passat GLX	55%
Mazda 626 DX Sedan	55%
■ LARGE	
Buick LeSabre Custom	53%
Chrysler Concorde	51%
Dodge Intrepid Sedan	51%
■ LUXURY	
Lexus LS 400	67%
Lexus GS 300	67%
Mercedes Benz E420	66%
■ SPORT	
Porsche 911 Carrera Cabriolet	64%
Mitsubishi 3000GT	61%
Chevrolet Corvette	59%
Mercedes SL320 Roadster	59%
■ SMALL WAGON	
Honda Accord LX	65%
Saturn SW	65%
Toyota Corolla DX	62%
■ MIDSIZE–LARGE WAGON	
Toyota Camry LE	58%
Subaru Legacy L	57%
Volkswagen Passat GLX	55%

LOWEST RESALE VALUE

■ SUBCOMPACT	
Hyundai Scoupe	47%
Eagle Summit DX Coupe	48%
Chrysler LeBaron GTC Convert.	48%
■ COMPACT	
Oldsmobile Achieva S Series II Coupe	43%
Dodge Spirit Sedan	45%
Buick Skylark Custom Sedan	46%
■ MIDSIZE	
Ford Taurus SHO Sedan	43%
Oldsmobile Cutlass Ciera SL	45%
Mercury Sable LS Sedan	45%
■ LARGE	
Oldsmobile 88 LSS Sedan	46%
Buick Roadmaster Lmt. Sedan	48%
■ LUXURY	
Alfa Romeo 164	46%
Lincoln Continental	47%
Cadillac Deville	47%
■ SPORT	
Pontiac Firebird Formula Coupe	49%
Porsche 928 GTS	49%
Subaru SVX L	50%
Nissan 300ZX 2+2 Coupe	52%
■ SMALL WAGON	
Ford Escort LX	52%
Mercury Tracer	52%
Subaru Impreza AWD	52%
■ MIDSIZE–LARGE WAGON	
Ford Taurus LX	47%
Volvo 940	48%
Mercury Sable LS	49%

SOURCE: *The Complete Car Cost Guide,* IntelliChoice, 1995.

EXPERT TIPS

GET A BARGAIN ON YOUR DREAMBOAT

A car-buying pro reveals how to get the best deal in town

No-dicker auto dealerships are increasingly common today, thanks to the one-price-fits-all success of General Motor's Saturn division and a growing number of other dealerships. But if the deals at such showrooms are fair, they are seldom great, say experts. And 85 percent of all new car purchases are still negotiated. But there's no reason why your neighbors the Joneses should get a better deal than you. Here, W. James Bragg, author of *In the Driver's Seat: The New Car Buyer's Negotiating Bible* (Random House, 1993) and founder of the car buying information service, Fighting Chance, outlines what you need to know to push a dealer eager to negotiate to the limit.

■ **Know the real cost of the car you like before walking into the showroom.** Forget the sticker price. The dealer invoice represents what the dealer really paid the manufacturer for the car. In addition, you need to know if there are any factory-to-dealer incentives—money that the manufacturer passes along to dealers to get them to push a particular model. Dealers can hide incentives from the consumer and use them on promotions, or they can pass them along as discounts. The average range for factory-to-dealer cash on a vehicle is $500 to $1,000. Then there are "holdbacks." This is extra profit that most manufacturers keep from the dealer until the car is sold, ranging from 2 percent of the base invoice to 3 percent of the full sticker price. "Once you know those three things," says Bragg, "you are as close to nirvana as you're ever going to be."

■ **Show the salesmen you know what they know.** Bragg suggests making a worksheet with all your pricing information and taking it with you. "Tell the salesperson," Bragg says, "that you know what your dealer invoice is and you know about this incentive. You expect him to make a profit, but you're not going to send him on his next trip to Hawaii." To calculate the price you should be offering, subtract any manufacturer incentives from the dealer invoice then add back the manufacturer's price for any options or accessories. To allow for dealer profit, Bragg then adds to this price about $200 to $600 for cars retailing from $10,000 to about $27,000. For cars in the high twenties to $40,000, he adds $500 to $1,200. For a luxury car retailing for around $50,000, he adds $2,000 to $3,000.

■ **Offer your price, and then bite your tongue.** Let the salesman have the next word. "If you talk next," says Bragg, "it shows you're uncertain or insecure." And if the dealer doesn't like the price, give him your phone number and leave. Frequently, the salesman will stop you before you get in your car. Be prepared for him to ask, "How do you expect me to make any money?" Counter this tactic by reminding him that you know about the profit hidden in the holdback.

■ **Know the supply and demand for the car you want.** The industry trade magazine, *Automotive News,* found at most libraries, carries

FACT FILE:

SHOWROOM INEQUITIES

■ *According to a 1991 article in the Harvard Law Review, when white women go car shopping, they pay markups 40 percent higher than white men. The situation is even worse for African American men and women, who pay two to three times the markup that white men do.*

sales figures for different makes and models. Knowing that a dealer desperately needs you to buy his cars can be a real confidence builder. You should tell the salesman when you know a model is not moving from the lot, Bragg says; "His mouth will hit the chair, because he is not aware of this. He's just trying to figure out how he can hustle you." Sometimes this information is not helpful, however. The demand for a Chevy Suburban is so intense that you literally have to wait in line and pay what the dealer asks, he says.

■ **Work two or three dealers for the same car.** Let each know that they are competing for your business. Bragg knows of people who have priced cars by fax and phone. He claims 40 to 60 percent of the dealers will respond to an offer given in this manner. The bottom line, he says, is who wants to sell cars this month or who wants to play games.

■ **Negotiate the price before discussing financing and trade-ins.** If you bargain on the price of your trade-in too early, the dealer may give you a great deal on the used car. But, Bragg says, the salesperson is trained to get this money back on the price of the new car. Dealers end up giving you the wholesale price on your trade-in no matter what they tell you, he adds.

If you're planning on paying cash, avoid being up front about it. This tells the salesman that he won't be making money on financing. That means that the salesman, again, will try to squeeze you on the price of the car.

■ **Shop for cash and then the car.** On average, a dealer makes more money from financing a car than selling a car. Bragg encourages car buyers to check on financing terms with their banks or credit unions so they can be sure that the dealer has put together a good financing package.

■ **Research insurance prices.** Knowing how much you are going to pay in insurance premiums can really help you determine the true price of a car (see "The Other Car Payment Not to Forget," page 708).

EXPERT SOURCES

WHERE TO GET A FIX ON PRICES

Invoice prices can be found in two annuals, The Complete Car Cost Guide *(IntelliChoice, Inc.) or* Edmund's New Car Price Guide *(Edmund Publications). The services below will mail or fax you that and more for $11 to $23.*

CAR PRICE NETWORK
■ Everything from dealer invoices and factory rebates to market overviews and negotiating tips.
☎ **800-227-3295**

CAR/PUTER
■ Information about dealer invoices and factory rebates.
☎ **800-992-7404**

CENTER FOR THE STUDY OF SERVICES
■ Its biweekly newsletter, *Car Deals,* provides info on factory incentives for $4.50 a copy.
☎ **202-347-7283**

CONSUMER REPORTS NEW CAR PRICING
■ Dealer invoice, factory rebates, negotiating tips.
☎ **800-933-5555**

FIGHTING CHANCE
■ Like Car Price Network, it offers dealer invoices, factory rebates, market overviews, and negotiating tips.
☎ **800-288-1134**

INTELLICHOICE
■ Dealer invoice, factory rebates, resale values, and ownership costs.
☎ **800-227-2665**

■ **Leave your checkbook and credit cards at home.** This will help you avoid making an impulse buy. Also, be wary of giving dealers too much information. They may ask for your name, address, Social Security number, and driver's license number. If you take a test drive, the dealer has the right to see your license. But he doesn't have the right to photocopy it, says Bragg. The right information allows the dealer to run a credit report, which may divulge who else has requested one. "If they don't see any other car dealers on the report, they will think that you are not making this [the car buying] competitive."

■ **Don't let sales teams play good cop, bad cop.** Many times the salesperson will act as if he is on your side, competing with the sales manager to secure the best price. He leaves to discuss your offer with the manager and then comes back with sleeves rolled up, saying that he did his best but that the manger needs a few hundred bucks more. Don't let this back-and-forth routine continue. "The object is to wear you down and keep you from buying a car from somebody else," Bragg says.

Instead, ask to speak directly with someone who can negotiate the price, or tell the salesperson that you know his game and to stop wasting your time. If it continues, tell him you will shop elsewhere. Typically, you can avoid these games if you reveal that you are an educated customer. In fact, Bragg says, "They would rather sell you a car and get you the hell out of there, so you don't contaminate their other customers."

■ **Avoid being taken at the end of the deal.** Here's where the dealer tries to sell you extra undercoating, corrosion protection, and fabric protectant. "You need this stuff like a moose needs a hat rack," Bragg says.

The same is true of extended warranties (see box). Plan to drive your new car until its wheels fall off. If you do decide to buy an extended warranty, only buy one that is sponsored by the manufacturer, he says. You should offer no more than half the retail price and pay no more than two-thirds.

THE EXTENDED SERVICE CONTRACT SCAM

They're sometimes called service contracts and at other times extended service warranties. But by whatever name, long-term protection for a new car against future repair costs is almost always a bad decision. That's because most new cars today are reliable and many come with manufacturer's warranties that cover most major service problems you're likely to encounter in a car's early years.

But if you worry about buying a lemon, find the very prospect of maintaining a car daunting, or expect to be driving your new vehicle well into the next century, find out what that extended service contract covers before signing on. You need to know not only how much more the extended warranty covers over the manufacturer's basic warranty but also where you are allowed to get your repairs done and how the shop will be paid, says Robert Ellis of the Center for the Study of Services, a consumer group in Washington, D.C.

"Even if you want an extended service contract, you don't have to buy it where you buy your car. You should shop competitively," Ellis advises. A study in the Center's publication, *Consumer's Checkbook,* found the price on an identical service contract has been known to range from $400 at one dealer's to more than $1,200 at another dealer's down the street. Even so, the magazine says, the average payout on a contract is less than $200. A second study, by *Consumer Reports,* indicates that companies offering extended service contracts spend only 4 cents to 15 cents on service for every dollar they charge for coverage. When it comes to extended service contracts, you generally don't get what you paid for.

BUYING SERVICES

LET OTHERS DO THE DICKERING

If you hate negotiating with dealers, let those who love it help you

Fed up with high-pressure sales tactics and unsure they are getting the best prices, many new car shoppers are turning to buying services. A 1993 study by research firm J. D. Power and Associates found that more than 1 in 20 new car buyers purchased a car through such a service, and most said they would do so again.

Working with a pool of dealers, the services try to secure the best possible deals they can for their clients. Doris Ehlers, an account director with J. D. Power, says it's hard to track how much such sevices save consumers, but the best of them promise to return all fees if the customer finds a better price on the same model. Some services, however, receive financial benefits from dealers. They should, of course, be avoided.

CarBargains, on the other hand, is entirely nonprofit. Sponsored by the Center for the Study of Services in Washington, D.C., the group will seek bids from dealers in your area and send you their quote sheets, showing how much above or below the factory invoice each dealer has agreed to sell. To close the deal, however, the customer must visit the lot to work out with the sales manager such details as the value of the trade-in. The service costs $135.

James Boerger of Consumers Automotive will deliver the car right to your driveway. Dealers, he says, take advantage of showroom visits to sell needless extras such as extended warranties and underbody protection. And Ashley Knapp, founder of AutoAdvisor, not only believes in getting his customers the best prices but also in helping them choose the right car. While this advice comes with a price, it can save a lot of time, Knapp says—the average car buyer with a college degree spends at least 16 hours shopping.

EXPERT SOURCES

BIDDERS THAT WANT TO EARN YOUR BUSINESS

The best auto-buying services are those whose fees are paid by the customers, not the car dealers. Among the best known are:

AUTO ADVISOR
■ Cost of $359 includes one-hour consultation. Enhanced services are up to $679 for one-week delivery. You may price more than one car at a time. Prices guaranteed.
☎ **800-326-1976**

AUTOMOBILE CONSUMER SERVICES
■ Costs $75 per vehicle plus a percentage of savings between sticker price and purchase price. Total costs average about $295.
☎ **800-223-4882**

CAR BARGAINS
■ A nonprofit service. Will solicit bids from five dealers in your area for only $135. Includes dealer quote sheets, financing info, service contracts, and the value of your used car.
☎ **800-475-7283**

CONSUMERS AUTOMOTIVE
■ Fees are $195 for a car with a sticker price up to $15,000, $295 for a car $15,000 to $30,000, and $395 for more expensive cars. Prices guaranteed.
☎ **703-631-5161**

CONSUMER WATCH

LEMON OWNERS GET A REPRIEVE

If the car you buy is a dud, you may qualify for a refund or replacement

Your car is only a year old but it won't start on rainy days. It stalls if you drive it for over an hour and has windshield wipers that swing into action with no human intervention. What is a lemon-owner to do about such luck?

All states now have passed "lemon laws," and although each state's law varies, most agree on one point: If a car has to be taken to the shop for the same repair four times, it's a lemon.

Depending on where you live, that may entitle you to ask the manufacturer for a refund or replacement. In some cases you may have to pay a fee for using the car, but that fee should only apply to the mileage driven until the first repair attempts, according to the Center for Auto Safety, a consumer watchdog organization in Washington, D.C.

To make sure you can take advantage of the lemon law in your state, it is crucial that you keep good records of car repairs and can show that you have tried to fix the same problem at least four times unsuccessfully. You'll need records documenting when the car was taken in to the repair shop, the mechanical problems involved, and the repairs made, including which parts were replaced and how much labor was required. When writing a car maker, enclose copies of your shop repair orders, which should provide much of the necessary information.

If the manufacturer refuses to give you a refund or a replacement car even though you qualify under your state lemon law, you may have to consider legal action. You can get a lemon lawyer referral by writing: CAS Lemon Lawyers, at The Center for Auto Safety, 2001 S Street, N.W., Suite 410, Washington, D.C. 20009, ☎ 202-328-7700.

TO GET LEMON AID

	☎
ALABAMA	800-392-5658
ALASKA	907-562-0704
ARIZONA	602-542-5763
ARKANSAS	501-682-2341
CALIFORNIA	916-322-3360
COLORADO	303-866-5189
CONNECTICUT	203-566-7002
DELAWARE	302-577-3250
DISTRICT OF COLUMBIA	202-727-7080
FLORIDA	800-321-5366
GEORGIA	404-656-3790
HAWAII	808-587-3222
IDAHO	208-334-2424
ILLINOIS	217-782-9011
INDIANA	800-382-5516
IOWA	515-281-5926
KANSAS	913-296-3751
KENTUCKY	502-573-2200
LOUISIANA	504-342-9638
MAINE	207-626-8849
MARYLAND	410-528-8662
MASSACHUSETTS	617-727-8400
MICHIGAN	517-373-1140
MINNESOTA	612-296-3353
MISSISSIPPI	800-281-4418
MISSOURI	800-392-8222
MONTANA	406-444-3553
NEBRASKA	402-471-0087
NEVADA	702-688-1800
NEW HAMPSHIRE	603-271-3641
NEW JERSEY	201-504-6226
NEW MEXICO	505-827-6060
NEW YORK	518-474-5481
NORTH CAROLINA	919-733-7741
NORTH DAKOTA	800-472-2600
OHIO	800-282-0515
OKLAHOMA	405-521-4274
OREGON	503-378-4732
PENNSYLVANIA	215-560-2414
RHODE ISLAND	401-274-4400
SOUTH CAROLINA	803-734-9452
SOUTH DAKOTA	800-300-1986
TENNESSEE	615-741-4737
TEXAS	214-742-8944
UTAH	801-530-6601
VERMONT	802-656-3183
VIRGINIA	804-786-2042
WASHINGTON	206-587-4240
WEST VIRGINIA	800-368-8808
WISCONSIN	608-266-0765
WYOMING	307-777-7825

EXPERT Q&A

WHEN LEASING MAKES SENSE

Auto leasing is a cheap way to drive an expensive vehicle

Leasing a car can be a smooth ride if you map out your route in advance. Here, Randall McCathren, executive vice president of Bank Lease Consultants, Inc., a consulting company that deals with auto lease financing, and the author of *Automobile Lending and Leasing Manual* (Warren, Gorham & Lamont, 1989) steers you toward your destination.

■ What is the difference between buying and leasing a car?

When you lease a car, you have no obligation for the car when you reach the end of the lease term on the closed-end lease (if you have observed the mileage and wear-and-tear restrictions). You have a guaranteed trade-in value equal to the end-of-term lease balance, and if you want to keep the car, you can exercise your purchase option. When you buy a car, there is no guaranteed trade-in value any time you want to terminate the loan and trade in the car.

■ What are the advantages to leasing a car?

Leasing has become attractive to people who understand the benefits of cash conservation and guaranteed trade-in value. Leasing traditionally requires no down payment, though some special manufacturer-lease programs require 5 to 10 percent down to get the financial terms being offered. Leasing has much lower payments than financing because the consumer only pays for depreciation, or the portion of the vehicle expected to be used up, rather than for the total price of the vehicle. The higher the down payment on the lease, the lower the monthly payment. The guaranteed value means the customer can walk away from the vehicle when the lease is up without obligation even if the vehicle is worth less than projected.

Another benefit of leasing is deferring the purchase decision until after you've driven the vehicle for a while. Even consumers who think they want to keep the vehicle for 10 years are better off leasing if for three to five years first, then deciding whether or not they want to keep it for the full 10 years.

■ Why are people hesitant to lease a car?

Leasing can be very confusing. Unfamiliar words, lengthy technical contracts, and manipulative sales techniques can make shopping for a lease more difficult than shopping for a car. With no capitalized cost disclosure (which is analogous to the selling price in a purchase) and no annual percentage rate (APR) disclosure, it's difficult to be comfortable that you've gotten a good deal. Also, some consumers have misunderstood or ignored their responsibilities or the economic reality of the lease.

■ What are some of those responsibilities and economic realities?

For example, if consumers put down $1,000 less and pay $50 to $75 a month less on a five-year lease than a five-year loan, they can't expect to have the same lease balance after three years as they would have had on the loan.

Some lessees plan to terminate early when the structure of the lease is intended to avoid building equity. If lessees pay for 15,000 miles per year and drive 25,000, they can't expect to drop the car off with no obligation—if they had purchased the car, its trade-in value would certainly be lower because of the extra mileage. The same is true in cases of excess wear and tear.

Finally, as in any business there are some unscrupulous lessors who try to take advantage of customers. Excessive charges for early termination and wear and tear are the two biggest areas of abuse. One or two bad apples can create a lot of negative publicity.

READING THE FINE PRINT ON A LEASE

Monthly payments are just the beginning

Randall McCathren, executive vice president of Bank Lease Consultants, Inc., a consulting firm that tracks trends in auto lease financing, advises that, in addition to monthly payment, which is the main shopping comparison consumers use, potential lessees should consider these variables:

■ **CAPITALIZED COST:** Don't lease the car without getting it in writing. Leasing has $300 to $500 of costs not found in loans (such as contingent liability insurance and credit insurance) so expect to pay at least that much more than for a purchase. The other benefits of leasing may also be worth a higher purchase price, particularly a highly subsidized rate, but remember that capitalized cost can be negotiated just like the selling price of the vehicle.

■ **RESIDUAL VALUE:** This is the predicted value of the car at the end of the lease term, and it's guaranteed. Recognize that the higher it is, the more likely it is that the lessor will lose money at the end. If you don't know if the lessor is in the business long-term or is ethical, beware of high residual values.

■ **PERMITTED MILEAGE:** The standard is 15,000 miles per year. If you expect to drive less, you should be able to negotiate a lower monthly lease payment.

■ **EARLY TERMINATION RIGHT AND CHARGE:** Look for a lease that permits early termination and has a constant yield (where interest is earned at the same rate every month and is precalculated), at least after the first 12 months.

■ **PURCHASE OPTION:** Look for a residual value fixed-price purchase option or, if you can find it, the lesser of the wholesale value and the residual value.

■ **EXCESS MILEAGE CHARGE:** Make sure it is reasonable if you drive extra miles. For a car worth up to $15,000, you shouldn't pay more than 10 cents per extra mile. For a car worth $15,000 to $30,000, excess mileage shouldn't cost more than 15 cents a mile, and for cars above $30,000, no more than about 18 cents a mile.

■ **TERM:** Don't sign a lease for longer than you plan to drive the car. The guaranteed value only benefits you at the end of the term. Never plan to terminate early. If you can't afford payments on the shorter term, choose a less expensive car.

■ **LIABILITY AFTER CASUALTY LOSS:** Ask if the lease includes "gap insurance." If not, don't pay more than $200 for coverage and consider self-insuring the risk.

■ **How can I make sure that I'm getting a good deal?**

Negotiate the purchase price first. Get it in writing. Then negotiate the lease and get a statement of the capitalized cost in writing. If the dealer or independent leasing company says they don't know what the capitalized cost is or that there isn't one, take your business elsewhere. Shop around and talk to a number of lessors. Compare rates and terms before making a decision. When you're ready to lease, don't agree to a longer term than you reasonably expect to keep the vehicle. Don't choose a car so expensive that you won't be able to pay for the early termination if you need to.

And make sure you're comfortable with the vehicle. A great lease on a car you don't really want is not a good deal.

CRASH TEST DUMMY'S GUIDE

HOW YOUR CAR DOES IN A CRUNCH

Each year the National Highway Traffic Safety Administration conducts crash tests of new cars under conditions that are the equivalent of having a head-on collision with an identical vehicle at 35 mph. The tables below include results for cars tested for the first time in 1995 as well as results for previously tested vehicles that were essentially the same cars being sold in model year 1995. Vehicles should be compared only to other vehicles in the same weight class—if a light vehicle collides head-on with a heavier vehicle at 35 mph, for example, the occupants in the lighter vehicle would experience a greater chance of injury than indicated. Vehicles are classified by the estimated chance of injury for the driver or passenger, and receive a one- to five-star rating, with five stars indicating the best protection.

VEHICLE	AIRBAG	DRIVER PASSENGER
LIGHT-COMPACT PASSENGER CARS		
ACCURA INTEGRA 4-dr. sedan, 2,709 lbs.	YES YES	★★★★ ★★★
OLDSMOBILE ACHIEVA 2-dr. sedan, 2,806 lbs.	YES NO	★★★★ ★★★
SUBARU LEGACY 4-dr. sedan, 2,654 lbs.	YES YES	★★★★ ★★★★
TOYOTA COROLLA 4-dr. sedan, 2,553 lbs.	YES YES	★★★★ ★★★★
TOYOTA TERCEL 4-dr. sedan, 2,176 lbs.	YES YES	★★★ ★★★★
VOLKSWAGEN JETTA III 4-dr. sedan, 2,725 lbs.	YES YES	★★★ ★★★
MID-WEIGHT PASSENGER CARS		
AUDI A6 4-dr. sedan, 3,373 lbs.	YES YES	★★★★★ ★★★★★
BUICK CENTURY 4-dr. sedan, 3,049 lbs.	YES NO	★★★★ ★★★★
CHEVROLET CAMARO 2-dr. Hb., 3,408 lbs.	YES YES	★★★★★ ★★★★★
CHEVROLET MONTE CARLO 2-dr. sedan, 3,284 lbs.	YES YES	★★★★ ★★★★
DODGE INTREPID 4-dr. sedan, 3,254 lbs.	YES YES	★★★★ ★★★★
FORD CONTOUR 4-dr. sedan, 3,020 lbs.	YES YES	★★★★★ ★★★★
FORD MUSTANG 2-dr. sedan, 3,119 lbs.	YES YES	★★★★ ★★★★
FORD THUNDERBIRD 2-dr. sedan, 3,460 lbs.	YES YES	★★★★★ ★★★★★
MAZDA MILLENIA 4-dr. sedan, 3,150 lbs.	YES YES	★★★★ ★★★★★
MERCEDES-BENZ C220 4-dr. sedan, 3,190 lbs.	YES YES	★★★★ ★★★★
PONTIAC GRAND-PRIX 2-dr. sedan, 3,189 lbs.	YES YES	★★★★ ★★★
SAAB 900 4-dr. Hb., 3,210 lbs.	YES YES	★★★★ ★★★★
TOYOTA CAMRY 4-dr. sedan, 3,128 lbs.	YES YES	★★★★ ★★★
VOLKSWAGEN PASSAT 4-dr. sedan, 3,124 lbs.	YES YES	★★★★ ★★★★
VOLVO 850 4-dr. sedan, 3,241 lbs.	YES YES	★★★★★ ★★★★
HEAVY PASSENGER CARS		
ACURA LEGEND 4-dr. sedan, 3,550 lbs.	YES YES	★★★ ★★★★
CHEVROLET CAPRICE 4-dr. sedan, 4,177 lbs.	YES YES	★★★ ★★
CHRYSLER NEW YORKER 4-dr. sedan, 3,589 lbs.	YES YES	★★★★ ★★★★
FORD CROWN VICTORIA 4-dr. sedan, 3,866 lbs.	YES YES	★★★★ ★★★★★
INFINITI J-30 4-dr. sedan, 3,640 lbs.	YES YES	★★★★ ★★★★
LEXUS GS-300 4-dr. sedan, 3,765 lbs.	YES YES	★★★ ★★★
LINCOLN TOWN CAR 4-dr. sedan, 4,080 lbs.	YES YES	★★★★★ NA
OLDSMOBILE AURORA 4-dr. sedan, 3,993 lbs.	YES YES	★★★ ★★★
PONTIAC BONNEVILLE 4-dr. sedan, 3,558 lbs.	YES YES	★★★★★ ★★★
LIGHT TRUCKS		
CHEVROLET S-10 BLAZER 4-dr. 4x4, 4,156 lbs.	YES NO	★★★ ★
FORD BRONCO 2-dr. 4x4, 4,783 lbs.	YES NO	★★★★★ ★★★★★
ISUZU RODEO 4-dr. 4x4, 4,021 lbs.	NO NO	★★ ★★★
JEEP CHEROKEE 4-dr. 2,983 lbs.	YES NO	★★★★ ★★★★

■ **CRASH TEST DUMMY'S GUIDE**

VEHICLE	AIRBAG	DRIVER / PASSENGER
JEEP GRAND CHEROKEE 4-dr. 4x4, 3,748 lbs.	YES / NO	★★★★ / ★★★
JEEP WRANGLER 2-dr. 4x4, 2,896 lbs.	NO / NO	★★ / ★★★★
NISSAN PATHFINDER 4-dr. 4x4, 3,932 lbs.	NO / NO	★ / ★★★
TOYOTA 4-RUNNER 4-dr. 4x4, 4,114 lbs.	NO / NO	★ / ★★★★
LIGHT TRUCKS		
DODGE DAKOTA PU 2-dr., 3,924 lbs.	YES / NO	★★★★★ / ★★★★
DODGE RAM 1500 PU 2-dr., 4,489 lbs.	YES / NO	★★★★★ / NA
FORD F150 PU 2-dr., 4,444 lbs.	YES / NO	★★★★★ / ★★★★★
ISUZU PU 2-dr., 2,840 lbs.	NO / NO	★★★ / ★★★★
MITSUBISHI MIGHTY MAX PU 2-dr., 2,731 lbs.	NO / NO	★★★ / ★★★
NISSAN PU 2-dr., 2,793 lbs.	NO / NO	★★★ / ★★★★
TOYOTA PU 2-dr., 2,563 lbs.	NO / NO	★★ / ★★★★

VEHICLE	AIRBAG	DRIVER / PASSENGER
TOYOTA T100 PU 2-dr., 3,382 lbs.	YES / NO	★★★★ / ★★★★
VANS		
CHEVROLET BEAUVILLE SPORT VAN 5,031 lbs.	YES / NO	★★★ / ★★★
DODGE CARAVAN 3,457 lbs.	YES / YES	★★★★ / ★★★★
DODGE RAMVAN 2500 4,162 lbs.	YES / NO	★ / ★★★
FORD AEROSTAR VAN 3,670 lbs.	YES / NO	★★★★ / ★★★
FORD ECONOLINE VAN 5,166 lbs.	YES / NO	★★★★ / ★★★
FORD WINDSTAR VAN 3,801 lbs.	YES / YES	★★★★ / ★★★★★
NISSAN QUEST VAN 3,855 lbs.	YES / NO	★★★★ / ★★★
PONTIAC TRANSPORT VAN 3,708 lbs.	YES / NO	★★★★ / ★★★
TOYOTA PREVIA VAN 3,644 lbs.	YES / YES	★★★★ / ★★★

SOURCE: National Highway Traffic Safety Administration, 1995.

COLLISIONS IN THE REAL WORLD

Most accidents involve moving cars, not fixed barriers. The crash impact isn't the same.

A car need not be expensive to protect you in a crash. A recent study of the crashworthiness of cars under "real-world" conditions found that two moderately priced American sedans—the Chevrolet Lumina and the Ford Taurus—held up better in crash tests at 40 mph than more expensive European sedans such as the Volvo 850 and Saab 900.

Government crash tests currently smash cars into fixed barriers at 35 mph to assess how well air bags and seat belts protect a vehicle's occupants. But over half of all accidents involve cars colliding with each other at different angles, so the Insurance Institute for Highway Safety used a technique known as an "offset test" to simulate what would happen to the structural integrity of a car traveling 40 mph if it collided with another car at an angle such as near the driver's door or behind the headlights. At the right is how the 14 midsize cars ranked in the Insurance Institute's tests:

GOOD (in order of finish)

- Chevrolet Lumina
- Ford Taurus
- Volvo 850

ACCEPTABLE

- Toyota Camry
- Subaru Legacy
- Honda Accord
- Mazda Millenia

MARGINAL

- Saab 900

POOR

- Ford Contour
- VW Passat
- Chevrolet Cavalier
- Mitsubishi Galant
- Chrysler Cirrus
- Nissan Maxima

AUTO SHOPPER'S GUIDE

THE OTHER CAR PAYMENT NOT TO FORGET

Some are far better than others when it comes to savings

The cars listed to the right are grouped alphabetically by make. Next to each model is Allstate's rating of that car's insurance cost when compared with other models in the same price range. The five rating groups range in price from "much better than average" to "much worse than average." The guide compares similarly priced cars because consumers tend to shop for cars in a certain price range.

Generally, the more expensive a car is, the more it costs to insure. That's because higher-priced cars cost more to repair and are more likely to be targeted by thieves. Thus, a Toyota Celica rated "average" will cost more to insure than a Chevrolet Beretta rated "average." But there are exceptions. For example, a Honda Civic may cost about the same to insure as an Audi 90, even though the Civic's suggested retail price is about $11,000 less.

The examples below illustrate this relationship in three price ranges. For the sake of comparison, insurance costs were calculated using identical rating factors.

■ Sticker Price: $12,501 to $15,000

Better than average	Buick Skylark	$723
Average	Chevrolet Beretta	$775
Worse than average	Honda Civic	$837

■ Sticker Price: $15,001 to $20,000

Better than average	Plymouth Voyager	$843
Average	Toyota Celica	$911
Worse than average	Acura Integra	$927

■ Sticker Price: $20,000 to $30,000

Better than average	Audi 90	$837
Average	Infiniti G20	$927
Worse than average	Dodge Stealth	$1,165

NOTE: Based on a suburban Chicago married male driving a 1995 vehicle. Premiums are annual and vary by individual.

SOURCE: *Make & Model: Your New Car Guide to Insurance Values,* Allstate Insurance, 1995.

MAKE	INSURANCE COSTS
■ ACURA	
NSX•◊	AVERAGE
Integra•◊	WORSE THAN AVERAGE
Legend•◊	WORSE THAN AVERAGE
Vigor•◊	WORSE THAN AVERAGE
■ AUDI	
90 Series•◊	BETTER THAN AVERAGE
A6•◊	AVERAGE
Cabriolet•◊	AVERAGE
S6•◊	AVERAGE
■ BMW	
530 Series•◊	AVERAGE
540 Series•◊	AVERAGE
740 Series•◊	AVERAGE
750 Series•◊	AVERAGE
840 Series•◊	AVERAGE
850 Series•◊	AVERAGE
M3 Series•◊	AVERAGE
525 Series•◊	WORSE THAN AVERAGE
318 Series•◊	MUCH WORSE THAN AVERAGE
325 Series•◊	MUCH WORSE THAN AVERAGE
■ BUICK	
LeSabre•◊	BETTER THAN AVERAGE
Regal•◊	BETTER THAN AVERAGE
Riviera•◊	BETTER THAN AVERAGE
Roadmaster•◊	BETTER THAN AVERAGE
Skylark•◊	BETTER THAN AVERAGE
Century•◊	AVERAGE
Park Avenue•◊	AVERAGE
■ CADILLAC	
Concours•◊	BETTER THAN AVERAGE
DeVille•◊	BETTER THAN AVERAGE
Fleetwood	BETTER THAN AVERAGE
Seville•◊	BETTER THAN AVERAGE
Eldorado	AVERAGE
■ CHEVROLET	
Astro Vans•◊	BETTER THAN AVERAGE
Caprice•◊	BETTER THAN AVERAGE
Lumina APV•◊	BETTER THAN AVERAGE
Lumina Sedan•◊	BETTER THAN AVERAGE

■ AUTO SHOPPER'S GUIDE

MAKE	INSURANCE COSTS
Tahoe•◊	BETTER THAN AVERAGE
Beretta•◊	AVERAGE
C and K Series Pickups•◊	AVERAGE
Cavalier•◊	AVERAGE
Corsica•◊	AVERAGE
G Series Vans•◊	AVERAGE
Impala SS•◊	AVERAGE
Monte Carlo•◊	AVERAGE
S-10 4WD Pickups•◊	AVERAGE
Suburban•◊	AVERAGE
Blazer•◊	WORSE THAN AVERAGE
Corvette•◊	WORSE THAN AVERAGE
S-10 2WD Pickups•◊	WORSE THAN AVERAGE
Camaro•◊	MUCH WORSE THAN AVERAGE
■CHRYSLER	
Town & Country Vans•◊	MUCH BETTER THAN AVERAGE
New Yorker•◊	BETTER THAN AVERAGE
Cirrus•◊	AVERAGE
Concorde•◊	AVERAGE
LeBaron•◊	AVERAGE
LHS•◊	AVERAGE
Sebring•◊	AVERAGE
■DODGE	
Caravan•◊	MUCH BETTER THAN AVERAGE
Avenger•◊	AVERAGE
Dakota Pickups•◊	AVERAGE
■EAGLE	
Ram Vans & Wagons•◊	BETTER THAN AVERAGE
Vision•◊	BETTER THAN AVERAGE
Intrepid•◊	AVERAGE
Neon•◊	AVERAGE
Ram Pickups•◊	AVERAGE
Spirit•◊	AVERAGE
Stratus•◊	AVERAGE
Talon•◊	AVERAGE
Viper	AVERAGE
Stealth•◊	WORSE THAN AVERAGE
Summit•◊	WORSE THAN AVERAGE

MAKE	INSURANCE COSTS
■FORD	
Aerostar Vans & Wagons◊	BETTER THAN AVERAGE
Bronco•◊	BETTER THAN AVERAGE
Crown Victoria•◊	BETTER THAN AVERAGE
Econoline Vans & Club Wagons•◊	BETTER THAN AVERAGE
Explorer•◊	BETTER THAN AVERAGE
F Series 4WD Pickup◊	BETTER THAN AVERAGE
Taurus•◊	BETTER THAN AVERAGE
Aspire•◊	AVERAGE
Contour•◊	AVERAGE
Escort Excl. GT, Standard◊	AVERAGE
F Series 2WD Pickup◊	AVERAGE
Ranger Pickup•◊	AVERAGE
Thunderbird•◊	AVERAGE
Windstar•◊	AVERAGE
Escort GT•◊	WORSE THAN AVERAGE
Probe•◊	WORSE THAN AVERAGE
Escort Standard◊	MUCH WORSE THAN AVERAGE
Mustang•◊†	MUCH WORSE THAN AVERAGE
■GEO	
Prizm•◊	WORSE THAN AVERAGE
Metro•◊	MUCH WORSE THAN AVERAGE
Tracker	MUCH WORSE THAN AVERAGE
■GMC	
Safari Vans•◊	MUCH BETTER THAN AVERAGE
Yukon•◊	MUCH BETTER THAN AVERAGE
Suburban•◊	BETTER THAN AVERAGE
Sierra Pickups•◊	AVERAGE
Sonoma 4WD Pickups•◊	AVERAGE
Jimmy•◊	WORSE THAN AVERAGE
Rally and Vandura Vans•◊	WORSE THAN AVERAGE
Sonoma 2WD Pickups•◊	WORSE THAN AVERAGE
■HONDA	
Accord•◊	AVERAGE

LEGEND: • Antilock brakes ◊ Airbag

† Significantly worse than other models in "much worse" category

■ AUTO SHOPPER'S GUIDE

MAKE	INSURANCE COSTS
Del Sol•◊	AVERAGE
Odyssey•◊	AVERAGE
Passport	AVERAGE
Civic•◊	WORSE THAN AVERAGE
Prelude•◊	MUCH WORSE THAN AVERAGE
■ **HYUNDAI**	
Accent•◊	AVERAGE
Elantra•◊	AVERAGE
Sonata•	WORSE THAN AVERAGE
Scoupe	MUCH WORSE THAN AVERAGE
■ **INFINITI**	
All Models•◊	AVERAGE
■ **ISUZU**	
Rodeo◊	AVERAGE
Pickups	WORSE THAN AVERAGE
Trooper•◊	WORSE THAN AVERAGE
■ **JAGUAR**	
All Models•◊	AVERAGE
■ **JEEP**	
Cherokee•◊	AVERAGE
Grand Cherokee•◊	AVERAGE
Wrangler•	AVERAGE
■ **LEXUS**	
All Models•◊	WORSE THAN AVERAGE
■ **LINCOLN**	
Continental•◊	BETTER THAN AVERAGE
Mark VIII•◊	AVERAGE
Town Car•◊	AVERAGE
■ **MAZDA**	
626•◊	AVERAGE
Millenia•◊	AVERAGE
MPV◊	AVERAGE
MX-5 Miata•◊	AVERAGE
MX-6•◊	AVERAGE
929•◊	WORSE THAN AVERAGE
MX-3•◊	WORSE THAN AVERAGE
Pickups•◊	WORSE THAN AVERAGE
Protege•◊	WORSE THAN AVERAGE
RX-7•◊	WORSE THAN AVERAGE
■ **MERCEDES-BENZ**	
200 Series•◊	AVERAGE
300 Series•◊	AVERAGE
400 Series•◊	AVERAGE
600 Series•◊	AVERAGE
500 Series•◊	MUCH WORSE THAN AVERAGE

MAKE	INSURANCE COSTS
■ **MERCURY**	
Cougar•◊	BETTER THAN AVERAGE
Grand Marquise•◊	BETTER THAN AVERAGE
Sable•◊	BETTER THAN AVERAGE
Villager•◊	BETTER THAN AVERAGE
Mystique•◊	AVERAGE
Tracer•◊	AVERAGE
■ **MITSUBISHI**	
Diamante•◊	AVERAGE
Eclipse•◊	AVERAGE
Expo•◊	AVERAGE
Galant•◊	AVERAGE
Pickups	WORSE THAN AVERAGE
3000 GT•◊	MUCH WORSE THAN AVERAGE
Mirage◊	MUCH WORSE THAN AVERAGE
Montero•◊†	MUCH WORSE THAN AVERAGE
■ **NISSAN**	
Quest•◊	BETTER THAN AVERAGE
Altima•◊	AVERAGE
Maxima•◊	AVERAGE
200SX•◊	WORSE THAN AVERAGE
240SX•◊	WORSE THAN AVERAGE
Pickups	WORSE THAN AVERAGE
Sentra•◊	WORSE THAN AVERAGE
300ZX•◊†	MUCH WORSE THAN AVERAGE
Pathfinder	MUCH WORSE THAN AVERAGE
■ **OLDSMOBILE**	
88•◊	BETTER THAN AVERAGE
98•◊	BETTER THAN AVERAGE
Achieva•◊	AVERAGE
Aurora•◊	AVERAGE
Cutlass Ciera, Cutlass Cruiser•◊	AVERAGE
Cutlass Supreme•◊	BETTER THAN AVERAGE
Silhouette•◊	BETTER THAN AVERAGE
■ **PLYMOUTH**	
Voyager•◊	BETTER THAN AVERAGE
Acclaim•◊	AVERAGE
Neon•◊	AVERAGE
■ **PONTIAC**	
Trans Sport•◊	MUCH BETTER THAN AVERAGE
Bonneville•◊	BETTER THAN AVERAGE
Grand Am•◊	AVERAGE
Grand Prix•◊	AVERAGE
Sunfire•◊	AVERAGE
Firebird•◊	WORSE THAN AVERAGE

■ AUTO SHOPPER'S GUIDE

MAKE	INSURANCE COSTS
■ **PORSCHE**	
All Models•◊	AVERAGE
■ **SAAB**	
900 Series•◊	AVERAGE
9000 Series•◊	BETTER THAN AVERAGE
■ **SATURN**	
All Models•◊	AVERAGE
■ **SUBARU**	
Impreza•◊	AVERAGE
Legacy•◊	AVERAGE
SVX•◊	AVERAGE
■ **SUZUKI**	
Samuri	AVERAGE
Sidekick	AVERAGE
Swift•◊	WORSE THAN AVERAGE
■ **TOYOTA**	
4 Runner•	MUCH WORSE THAN AVERAGE
Avalon•◊	AVERAGE
Camry•◊	AVERAGE
Celica•◊	AVERAGE
Corolla•◊	WORSE THAN AVERAGE
Land Cruiser•◊†	MUCH WORSE THAN AVERAGE
MR2•◊	AVERAGE
Paseo•◊	AVERAGE
Pickups 2WD Excl. T100 Series	MUCH WORSE THAN AVERAGE
Pickups 4WD Excl. T100 Series	WORSE THAN AVERAGE
Previa•◊	BETTER THAN AVERAGE
Supra•◊	WORSE THAN AVERAGE
T100 Pickups•◊	MUCH WORSE THAN AVERAGE
Tercel•◊	MUCH WORSE THAN AVERAGE
■ **VOLKSWAGEN**	
Cabriolet•◊	AVERAGE
Euro Van•	AVERAGE
Golf III•◊	AVERAGE
GTI VR6•◊	AVERAGE
Jetta III•◊	AVERAGE
Passat•◊	MUCH WORSE THAN AVERAGE
■ **VOLVO**	
850 Series•◊	AVERAGE
940 Series •◊	AVERAGE
940 Series Turbo•◊	MUCH BETTER THAN AVERAGE
960 Series•◊	AVERAGE

SOURCE: *Make & Model: Your New Car Guide to Insurance Values*, Allstate Insurance, 1995.

CHOOSING AN INSURER

Compare rates from the biggest

If you live in a non-competitive insurance state like Massachusetts or Texas, rates are controlled by an insurance commission or rating bureau, and all insurers are required to charge the same premium. However, in all other states rates are competitive and can vary dramatically.

One thing you should factor into your evaluation of a prospective insurer is its reputation when it comes to the speedy processing of claims. To do so, check with the Better Business Bureau or local repair or body shops to find out which insurers have the best and worst reputation.

The largest auto insurers in the United States are listed below. To make sure you are getting the most competitive rates, call a few of them for quotes and compare them with the offerings of smaller companies and independent agents.

	☎
■ **Aetna**	**800-872-3862**
■ **Allstate**	**708-402-5000**
■ **Farmers**	**510-847-3100**
■ **Geico**	**800-841-3000**
■ **ITT Hartford**	**203-547-5000**
■ **Liberty Mutual**	**800-225-2390**
■ **Nationwide**	**800-882-2822**
■ **State Farm**	**800-942-0526**
■ **Travelers**	**203-277-0111**
■ **USAA**	**800-531-8100**

EXPERT TIPS

AN INDY GUIDE TO USED CAR BUYING

Be a pro when you kick the tires of an auto you're considering owning

Marlboro-Penske team member Rick Rinaman has been the pit crew chief for two-time Indianapolis 500 champion Emerson Fittipaldi since 1990. Here are Rinaman's tips on what to look for mechanically when shopping for a used car.

■**FLUIDS:** Check the front CV joints, the front wheels, and the wheel wells for grease. Bearing grease in the wheel wells may indicate bad seals that need replacing. If you get into replacing CVs, you start getting up in the dollars.

If there are any problems with seals, there will be oil spots on the ground. Be sure to look for leaks around the seals in the rear end.

If someone's selling the car, he's probably changed the oil in it. If he hasn't, you want to look at the filter and see if it's been on there for a million miles. It's very easy to change an oil filter and if you put a new filter on, it stays clean for a lot of miles. If it hasn't been changed recently, you'll be able to tell right away if the owner's been taking care of the engine.

■**EXHAUST:** A car that has a lot of miles on it is going to show a lot of rust and what-not in the exhaust system. You don't want to get an exhaust system that has areas that have been spot-welded. The muffler might not leak while you're test-driving it, but a couple miles down the road, it could just fall off.

The best way to check for a rusted-out muffler is to actually get down underneath the car and grab the muffler. When exhaust systems start to go, you can actually crush them with your hands.

■**BODY CONDITION:** First of all, open the door to get a better look at the body. Any part in there that looks like it's new or is covered with fresh paint is an indication that the car has been in an accident—which means you're looking at possible alignment problems.

If the rear panels have been repainted, they may also have been body-puttied to cover up damage or rust. You could get into trouble with that.

■**SUSPENSION:** Check for rust around all the suspension parts. A lot of old cars rust at the top mounting plates from the top of the shocks—especially in the front, where it's pretty visible once you lift the hood and look past the engine at the plates. The struts may actually push through the metal.

■**TIRES:** Unless the seller has put on a new set of tires, which is probably very unlikely, you can tell a lot from tire wear. If the wear is sort of wavy with high and low spots in the tires, for example, you have bad shocks and they need to be looked at. If you have wear on the sides, on the other hand, you have front alignment problems.

■**STEERING:** A lot of play in the steering wheel shows a lot of hard wear and indicates that the steering system will probably need to be replaced. If there are two inches of play and the tires aren't turning, watch out—the problems go beyond the steering system.

■**BRAKES:** Check the brake pads for wear. A hard-driven car is going to show on the brakes. Check the rotors for scars. A lot of times, people buy a used car and they have to have their rotors ground because they're pretty rough.

■**INTERIOR:** There are a lot of people who say they don't like smoking in their car, so keep that in mind.

If the vinyl or any part of the interior console is cracked, then you know it's been outside in the sun a lot.

A CHECKLIST FOR AVOIDING GRIEF

You don't have to get yourself covered with grease to tell quickly whether a car has been well maintained. The following tips for reading a car's history will save you lots of headaches later:

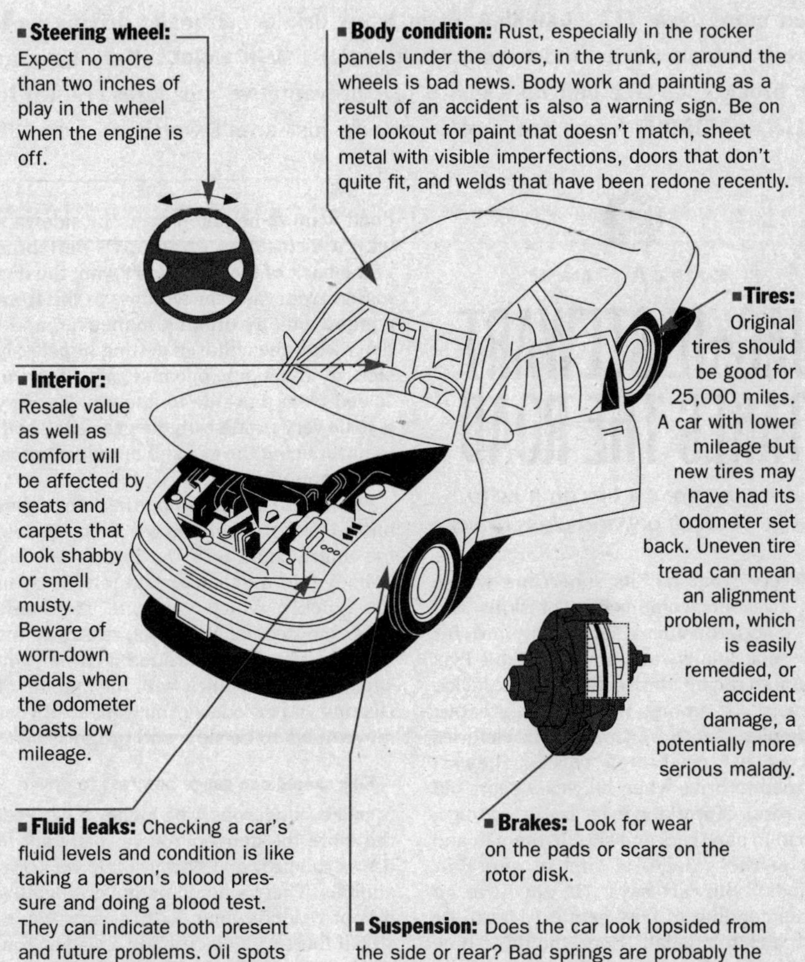

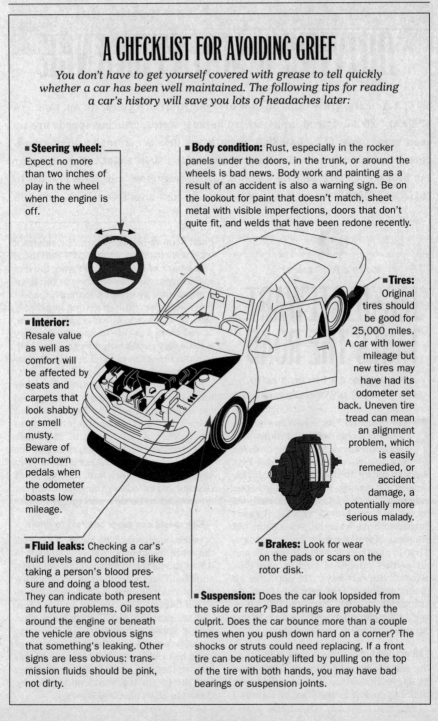

- **Steering wheel:** Expect no more than two inches of play in the wheel when the engine is off.

- **Body condition:** Rust, especially in the rocker panels under the doors, in the trunk, or around the wheels is bad news. Body work and painting as a result of an accident is also a warning sign. Be on the lookout for paint that doesn't match, sheet metal with visible imperfections, doors that don't quite fit, and welds that have been redone recently.

- **Tires:** Original tires should be good for 25,000 miles. A car with lower mileage but new tires may have had its odometer set back. Uneven tire tread can mean an alignment problem, which is easily remedied, or accident damage, a potentially more serious malady.

- **Interior:** Resale value as well as comfort will be affected by seats and carpets that look shabby or smell musty. Beware of worn-down pedals when the odometer boasts low mileage.

- **Fluid leaks:** Checking a car's fluid levels and condition is like taking a person's blood pressure and doing a blood test. They can indicate both present and future problems. Oil spots around the engine or beneath the vehicle are obvious signs that something's leaking. Other signs are less obvious: transmission fluids should be pink, not dirty.

- **Brakes:** Look for wear on the pads or scars on the rotor disk.

- **Suspension:** Does the car look lopsided from the side or rear? Bad springs are probably the culprit. Does the car bounce more than a couple times when you push down hard on a corner? The shocks or struts could need replacing. If a front tire can be noticeably lifted by pulling on the top of the tire with both hands, you may have bad bearings or suspension joints.

DRIVING & MAINTENANCE

EXPERT Q&A

JACKIE STEWART TAKES THE ROAD

A racing great's tips on how to make yourself a world-class driver

Every sport has its superstars whose awesome combination of skills and competitiveness set a standard for generations to come. In Grand Prix auto racing, the Scottish driver, Jackie Stewart, is among the sport's greatest champions, with 27 Grand Prix victories during his celebrated career. Stewart learned to drive when he was 9 years old as a result of working in his father's garage. "I had to park cars and shuttle them in and out of the garage, at first at very low speeds," Stewart says. "It gave me an understanding of how gentle I had to be with a clutch pedal." Here, the three-time world champion shares his tips on how you can make yourself a better driver.

■ What's the key to being a good driver?

The smooth driver is always better than the aggressive driver. I try to tell people, think of yourself as the ideal chauffeur. I don't want to be taken from the sidewalk with a dislocation of granny's vertebrae in the back of the car. I don't want the dog tossed from the rear window to the front window on any braking maneuver, and I don't want the children getting hopelessly sick in the back because my steering sawed from one side to another. The key is to be very gentle with the gas pedal, both in introducing the gas and in reducing forward motion.

The same applies to putting the brakes on and taking the brakes off. Everyone told me that I could jerk the brakes on, but nobody told me that I could release them too quickly, which you can. The same applies to steering. When you're turning the steering wheel to go around a corner, you shouldn't be too quick with the amount of steering you introduce. You want all of your movements to be slow and progressive.

■ How should one gauge how fast to drive?

Speed is dangerous. The higher the speed, the more the danger. You've really got to drive cautiously and slowly within your own abilities. There's no damn good tailgating if your reaction time doesn't allow you to stop if there's an obstruction ahead of you. You are probably totally misjudging your lack of ability to handle speed. If I say to a man he's a very poor driver or a very poor lover, he would never be convinced he was bad at either one, but in fact there are many bad drivers in the world and I assume there are also some bad lovers.

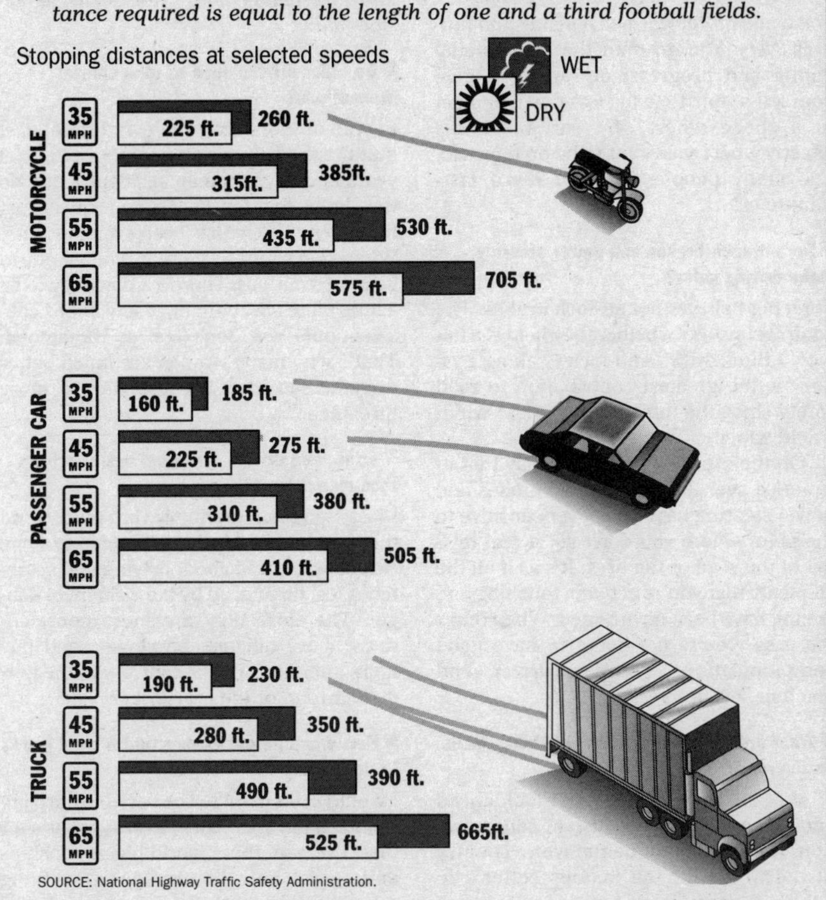

■ Are posted speed limits a good guide to how fast you can drive and still be safe?

The speed limits are a very good indicator, but sometimes because of lack of visibility, rain, or the winter, driving at the designated speed limit is too fast. The dynamics of an accident are far beyond what anybody can imagine. At 30 mph, for example, if you're not wearing seat belts, the impact of hitting a solid object is the same as falling out of a fourth-story window in the United States.

■ What is the best technique for changing lanes and passing?

You can only accelerate when you know that the lane you're meshing with is clear. If you're not addressing your rear-view mirrors correctly and using them positively and then being even more than careful, there's no good in pulling out at all. You don't go right up to the back of the vehicle in front and then make an aggressive move to the right or left in order to change lanes and pass. You've got to give plenty of warning and make a very smooth transition to join that other lane or undertake a passing maneuver.

■ What is the best approach to cornering?

You come off the gas pedal gently and progressively. You go onto the brake pedal gently and progressively and you give yourself ample time to slow down and get to a speed where you can recognize exactly where you want to be on the road. Too many people act as if it's a last-minute effort.

■ Do anti-lock brakes and power steering make driving safer?

I'm a big believer in anti-lock brakes. The controversy over whether they help is a fallacy. I think ABS (Anti-lock Braking System) is the greatest contribution to road safety since the introduction of the windshield wiper.

On the other hand, I would say that in America over the years power brakes and power steering have been over-sensitive to the point where you don't get a real feeling of the road or the tires. It's as if all the elements that you're actually touching and feeling have been novocained. When that's the case, you're not going to have good communications between driver and machine, or vice versa.

■ What are the most common mistakes made on the road?

First of all, most people don't look ahead enough, and that's because of concentration. America might be the worst country in the world for the famous coffee cup holder. It seems as if the driver of every car I look into has a coffee cup in his hands. It's absolutely ridiculous. If it spills the wrong way, it's going to burn the person, and he or she is going to overreact, which is probably going to cause an accident on its own. You can't possibly drive with one hand and avoid a child who jumps out in front of you or another vehicle that gets into your path. You've got to have both hands on the steering wheel—I need both hands on the wheel. Other common mistakes include turning across other traffic without giving the other cars enough space, or turning suddenly across somebody else's path when the folks behind you are in the process of overtaking. That's a common one. So is lane-changing without knowing that there's a car suddenly alongside you.

■ Do older drivers need to take special precautions?

People of more mature years often boast that they've been driving for more than 30 years and never had an accident. Little do they know that for the last majority of that time everyone else has been avoiding them. When you're more mature, you've got to be more cautious. There's a tendency to be a little more absent-minded and not as conscientious. You don't feel as threatened. That's why many women are much better drivers than men because they're more threatened.

■ So women drivers are often better drivers than men drivers?

Most men think driving is very macho and they can handle anything. Women to some extent are scared about driving and sometimes feel threatened by the element of danger. Therefore they are more conscientious, more diligent, go slower, and pay more attention. This is contrary to the normal cartoon of the lady driver.

■ How can a parent ensure that a child learns to drive well?

I would send them to the very best driving school in the area. There's no substitute for that. I've won three world championships and I sent both of my sons to driving schools. Don't teach them yourself. A parent, a boyfriend, a relation, is simply not the way to go.

■ Which professional race care driver did you most admire when you were racing?

Jim Clark, a fellow Scot (and two-time World Grand Prix champion). He was the best driver I ever raced against. He was the smoothest and he just did the best job in the most unspectacular fashion. It's making the driving effortless that's the key to great driving.

HIGHWAY DRIVING

HURRY UP AND GET THERE

Speed limits are up in most states—cruising speeds are up even more

"America is a country that doesn't know where it is going but is determined to set a speed record getting there," quipped Laurence J. Peter, author of *The Peter Principle,* in 1977. Peter was speaking metaphorically, but a new study of American driving habits underscores his point: The report by *Prevention* magazine shows that 55 percent of drivers on the nation's highways today exceed the posted speed limits, up from 44 percent in 1983. Moreover, the national speed limits on federally funded highways in urban and rural areas (55 mph and 65 mph, respectively) are likely to be repealed soon.

Better roads have played a role in this speeding up of American traffic, as has a return to larger, more powerful cars, according to Jerry Scannell, president of the National Safety Council. But the main reason, he suggests, is that police are too busy fighting other crime to enforce speed laws.

"Speeding initially increased in the western part of the country," says Scannell, "where the highways are long, flat, and straight." The raising of speed limits in many rural areas has not only encouraged speeding but led to increases in automobile-related fatalities in states with 65 mph speed limits, Scannell argues.

Despite these developments, motor vehicle-related death rates nationwide have actually been declining for some years now. In 1994, for example, there were 41,300 such deaths in the United States, according to the National Safety Council. Calculated as a death rate per 100 million vehicle miles, this was only about one-half of what it was in 1980 and one-third of what it was in 1960.

The recent decline in vehicle-related fatalities can't be credited to improvements in driver attentiveness. One-third of those in the *Prevention* survey said that they try to read maps and directions while driving, and nearly two-thirds said that they change cassette tapes or radio stations.

Part of the improvement in death rates can be attributed to higher seat belt use. In the *Prevention* survey, 73 percent said they always wear a seat belt when sitting in the front seat of a car; in 1983 only 19 percent reported doing so.

The other big factor, experts say, has been the raising of the legal drinking age to 21 in some states. "The number of people who drink and drive has steadily decreased," says Scannell, who gives much of the credit to Mothers against Drunk Driving, or MADD. While 56 percent of all automobile fatalities were alcohol-related in 1983, it was down to 44 percent in 1993. But studies have shown that drivers who imbibe enough to be presumed tipsy under the laws of most states are at least 48 times more likely to die in a traffic accident than those who avoid the beer or bottle.

FACT FILE:

FEELING DROWSY

One in four drivers has dozed off at the wheel at some point, according to a recent survey by the Institute for Traffic Safety Management and Research. The study found:

- **About 1 in 14 men are involved in reported accidents because of sleepiness, compared with fewer than 1 in 100 women.**
- **Snorers are more likely to nod off while driving, perhaps because they are generally less well rested, according to the study's authors.**

HOLDING YOUR LIQUOR

Percentage of alcohol in the blood one hour after drinking

Examples of alcoholic drinks	Amount of alcohol (oz.)	Body weight (lbs.) 100	120	140	160	180	200
Three Dubonnet cocktails	3.0	.252	.208	.176	.152	.134	.119
Four Bloody Marys, Daiquiris, or Whiskey Sours	2.8	.234	.193	.163	.141	.124	.110
Two glasses Fish House Punch	2.6	.217	.178	.151	.130	.114	.101
Three Martinis or Manhattans or glasses malt liquor	2.4	.199	.163	.138	.119	.104	.092
Two Maitais or Mint Juleps	2.2	.181	.149	.125	.108	.094	.083
Four champagne cocktails	2.0	.163	.134	.113	.097	.084	.075
Two Margaritas	1.8	.146	.119	.100	.086	.057	.066
Two Martinis or Manhattans	1.6	.128	.104	.087	.075	.065	.057
Two highballs, Bloody Marys	1.4	.110	.089	.075	.063	.055	.048
Two 3 oz. glasses fortified wine (port, vermouth, etc.)	1.2	.092	.075	.062	.052	.045	.039
Two glasses beer	1.0	.075	.060	.049	.041	.035	.030
One Black Russian	0.8	.057	.045	.037	.030	.025	.021
One Sloe Gin Fizz	0.6	.039	.030	.024	.019	.015	.012
One 1 oz. cordial or liqueur	0.4	.021	.015	.011	.008	.006	.004

THE MEANING OF TIPSY

The figures in red represent the blood alcohol content past which you shouldn't drive:

BLOOD ALCOHOL CONTENT	EFFECTS ON FEELING AND BEHAVIOR	EFFECTS ON DRIVING ABILITY
.40 .20 .19 .18	At this point, most people have passed out.	Hopefully, driver passed out before trying to get into vehicle.
.17 .16 .15 .14 .13	Major impairment of all physical and mental functions. Irresponsible behavior. Euphoria. Some difficulty standing, walking, and talking.	Distortion of all perception and judgment. Driving erratic. Driver in a daze.
.12 .11 .10	Difficulty performing gross motor skills. Uncoordinated behavior. Definite impairment of mental abilities, judgment, and memory.	Judgment seriously affected. Physical difficulty in driving a vehicle.
.09 .08 .07	Feeling of relaxation. Mild sedation. Exaggeration of emotions and behavior. Slight impairment of motor skills. Increase in reaction time.	Drivers take too long to decide and act. Motor skills (such as braking) are impaired. Reaction time is increased.
.06 .05 .02	Absence of observable effects. Mild alteration of feelings, slight intensification of existing moods.	Mild changes. Most drivers seem a bit moody. Bad driving habits slightly pronounced.

SOURCES: National Clearinghouse for Alcohol and Drug Information; National Safety Council.

EXPERT TIPS

KEEPING YOUR CAR BREAKDOWN-FREE

With the average cost of a new car over $20,000, maintenance is crucial

Cars just aren't made the way they used to be. Thanks to Total Quality Management, they're made better. But not even the most demanding of auto makers has figured out a way to keep a car running if it's not properly maintained. And with the average price of a new car now exceeding $20,000, the price of neglect can wreak havoc with your budget. To keep your garage bills down and your wheels running smoothly, Robert Livingstone, director of Automotive Services at the American Automobile Association, recommends the following maintenance schedule.

■ **Check the brakes for wear once a year.** The front brakes wear out more quickly than the back brakes, particularly in the city, where you have to start and stop in traffic. Many repair shops have free safety checks. Replacing worn brake pads should cost $80 to $90, including labor. If the pistons have to be rebuilt or replaced, that would cost anywhere from $150 to $600.

■ **Change the oil and oil filter every three months, or every 3,000 to 4,000 miles.** Oil lubricates and cools the engine. When it becomes dirty, it's doing its job. But if it gets too contaminated, it can cause more wear on the engine than there should be. An oil change will usually cost $20 to $40 at a garage. Manufacturers typically recommend standard oil, which is defined as meeting manufacturers' specifications. Synthetic oil is blended better and only needs changing once a year, but it's considerably more expensive. If the auto manufacturer stipulates that the oil be changed at certain intervals, and you don't do so, the manufacturer won't accept liability if the car breaks down.

■ **Replace the air and fuel filters when they are dirty, or once a year.** The fuel filter takes particles from the gas tank and filters it so it doesn't clog fuel injection equipment. It also stops water that may build up in the fuel injection system. Replacing the fuel filter should cost about $55: about $20 for the filter and about a half-hour to an hour of labor, depending on where it is located.

Air filters screen out dirt from the engine and keep the air in the engine clean. They need to be replaced once a year unless you live in extremely dusty conditions. Filters cost $10 to $15 and take only a couple minutes of labor to replace.

■ **Replace spark plugs every 30,00 miles.** Spark plugs ignite the mixture of fuel and air in the combustion cylinder. They are like the pilot light on a gas stove. If they're not replaced from time to time, the car may not start or may be sluggish or jerky. Depending on how many cylinders your car has, it takes about one and a-half hours of labor, at anywhere from $45 to $60 per hour.

■ **Check the battery regularly.** The average life of a battery is two to three years, possibly longer. A new one costs about $60. Corroded connections need cleaning or replacing. If you don't have the maintenance-free variety, be sure to check the water.

■ **Replace radiator and heater hoses every two years.** The radiator and heater hoses are made of rubber, so they can get brittle and crack, which is when they fail. It's usually the bottom radiator hose that goes; it's the hardest to see and is not regularly looked at. A replacement hose costs $10 to $20, plus about one and a half hours of labor at $40 to $60 an hour. But replacing hoses before they go can save as much as $1,000 in repairs on an overheated engine. Sometimes a garage will replace the hoses at the same time as it replaces antifreeze.

■ **Change the antifreeze mixture every two years.** The cooling system includes the radiator, heater core, hoses that attach the engine, and the antifreeze mixture. In a place where there are extreme conditions, the antifreeze mixture should be changed once a year. To flush and refill the antifreeze mixture takes about an hour. Some specials might cost $49.99. Otherwise, it can cost up to $80 to $90.

■ **Leave the air-conditioner alone unless it's not cooling.** There are three major parts of an air-conditioner that can go bad. A problem with the condenser or evaporator will cost $250 to $300; a problem with the compressor $350 to $400. If you need more freon, the likely bill will be about $60.

■ **Check the exhaust system regularly.** The rubber mounts that hold the exhaust system sometimes need to be replaced if they're worn. Wear is more likely if you take a lot of short trips, but in some cases, mounts will never need replacing. The exhaust system should also be checked for leaks at least once a year on late-model cars, and twice a year on older cars. In the height of summer or winter, the windows are closed; if there's a leak in the exhaust system, you could be breathing the fumes. A garage will normally check your system free of charge. A new exhaust system costs about $600.

■ **Check tires at least once a month for proper pressure and other problems.** Low tire pressure cuts gas mileage and affects the car's stability and safety. Tires also should be inspected for bulges or cuts on the side wall. Sometimes a tire is wearing unevenly, and there are rough edges. If you use a full-service gas station, they usually check the tire for free. You don't have to take the tires off.

■ **Rotate your tires every 10,000 miles or once a year.** It costs $20 to $30, but if you don't do it, your tires will wear out a lot faster.

■ **Replace wiper blades once a year.** Do it before rainy season. If you get new blades ($10 to $15) you can insert them into the arm yourself. You can replace the whole unit for $20 to $30. It's about 15 minutes of labor. A repair shop may install them for free.

■ **Check vehicle lights regularly, especially during winter.** To get the brake lights replaced, it costs about $3 for a bulb. It's about a half-hour's work. Changing the brake light in some cars can be done in 2 or 3 minutes. In the winter, it's especially important to make sure the headlights are working properly. Depending on the type of headlights, it will take 15 minutes to a half-hour to change them. Normally a new bulb will cost $10 to $15.

■ **Replace the clutch on a manual transmission every 60,000 to 100,000 miles.** If you ride the clutch excessively, replacement will be needed sooner. Expect to pay from $350 to $450 for a new clutch.

FACT FILE:

THE FIX-IT FACTOR

■ **ENGINE OVERHAUL:** *If the engine is worn out, making a lot of noise, blowing smoke, or has no power, it might need an overhaul. That's when an engine gets rebuilt to the manufacturer's specification. For a 4-cylinder engine, it might cost $2,000 to $3,000. For an 8-cylinder it can get up to $4,000. That's when you have to evaluate if it's worth putting that much money into the vehicle.*

■ **AUTOMATIC TRANSMISSION:** *The automatic transmission should be serviced every 25,000 miles. Symptoms of automatic transmission failure are that the vehicle feels as if it lacks power, is going nowhere, or is making grinding noises. The majority just won't drive. If you have a transmission failure, it could cost $1,200 to $3,000.*

CHAPTER ELEVEN

COMPUTERS

EXPERT QUOTES

"The typical notebook serves up only about one-third the computing performance of a comparably priced desktop computer."

—The editors of *PC Magazine*

Page 735

"Let kids test-drive products, listen to them when they tell you something is uncomfortable."

—Carol Ellison, education editor of *Home PC* magazine

Page 751

"The National Enquirer has nothing on this place."

—Seth Godin, author of *The Internet White Pages*

Page 776

THE YEAR AHEAD: **KNOW** that computer prices will continue to drop... **EXPECT** better, faster machines every six months or so... **HERALD** the new, cheaper Macintosh clones... **CONSIDER** adding memory to handle the latest software... **GET READY** for the debut of the Microsoft online network... **SAY GOODBYE** to black-and-white monitors... **TRY OUT** touch-sensitive pads on notebook computers... **SAMPLE** some of the glitzy new CD-ROMs... **SURF** the World Wide Web with an easy-to-use browser...

HARDWARE

THE BASICS

THE ANATOMY OF A COMPUTER

You too can talk like a nerd once you've mastered a few basic terms

You don't have to take a programming course or lock yourself up for days on end attempting to decode technical manuals to understand the basic principles on which computers operate. There are virtually no moving parts inside a computer, just electronic messages zipping along. Here's a quick course on how those messages get from place to place.

■ **CD-ROM DRIVE:** Most new computers come with CD-ROM drives, which make your machine multimedia-ready (for more information, see "The Sound and the Fury," page 732).

■ **CENTRAL PROCESSING UNIT (CPU):** The CPU does most of the computer's work; you have probably heard people calling the CPU by one of its more familiar names, the "processing chip" or "processor." In PCs, most CPUs are based on processors manufactured by Intel Corp.'s 80X86 series ("X" stands for a number from 2 to 4). But since folks in the computer industry like to shorten nomenclature, you'll often hear a PC referred to as a "286," "386," or "486." The higher the number, the more powerful the PC. To make things a bit more complicated, however, the fastest and newest Intel processor doesn't have a number at all; it's called the Pentium processor. People don't generally refer to Macs by the speed of the processor—they just identify Macs by model ("Macintosh SE," "Mac II," and so on).

■ **CHASSIS:** This is the metal or plastic case that covers everything inside your computer.

■ **CLOCK SPEED:** Near the CPU there is a little crystal called a clock. It whirs around, which speeds up the processing power of the computer. The speed at which the clock whirs is called—tada!—the clock speed, and it's measured in Megahertz (Mhz). When you see an advertisement for a PC, and it reads something like 486/25, the "25" part refers to the clock speed—the faster the clock speed, the faster the computer.

■ **EXPANSION SLOTS:** There may come a time when you want to add extra stuff, called peripherals, onto your computer—sound, a CD-ROM drive, a scanner, an internal modem. When this time comes, you will be glad that your computer has

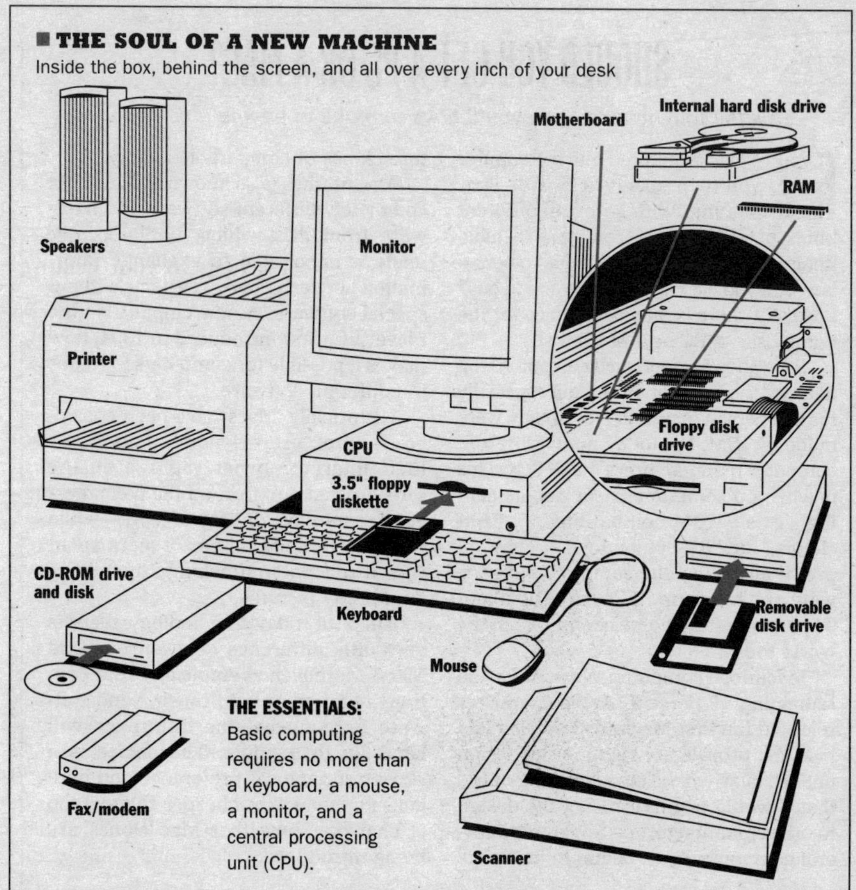

expansion slots, which are simply empty slots that are usually located at the back of your computer. The slots are designed to accommodate special expansion cards that either add functionality to your computer by themselves or allow peripherals like modems and CD-ROMs to "talk" to your computer. Some computers have as many as eight expansion slots, others have as few as three. When you buy a computer, make sure it comes with enough free expansion slots so that you'll have room to grow; a safe number of free slots is between three and five.

■ **FLOPPY DISK DRIVES:** Those one or two doors on the front of your desktop computer are floppy disk drives, and they are made for floppy disks—smaller versions (in physical size and storage space) of your hard disk. Floppy disks are handy because they let you carry your data around from computer to computer, unlike hard disks which stay inside the computer all the time. Floppy disks come in two sizes: $3\frac{1}{2}$-inch and $5\frac{1}{4}$-inch. Some computers have two disk drives for both sizes, but most computers now have just one $3\frac{1}{2}$-inch drive, because that's the most popular size. Floppy disks get their name from the flexible mylar disks that are inside their plastic casings.

■ **HARD DISK:** You'll probably never see your hard disk (it's nestled inside your computer), but you'll use it all the time. The

SHOULD YOU GET A PC OR A MAC?

It's the toughest decision you'll have to make in buying a computer

If you've ever wandered into a computer store, you've probably left with your head spinning. With so many different kinds of computers—Compaq, Toshiba, Zenith, IBM, Apple, and countless others—how will you ever know which one to buy? Basically, there is only one choice for the home user: a PC or a Macintosh.

PC stands for "personal computer," the name of the first computer built especially for one person to use. PCs originally were made by IBM, but today many different computer manufacturers make PCs. This is why you sometimes hear people calling PCs "IBM-compatibles," "IBM clones," or "PC-compatibles." They all pretty much use the same type of software and hardware. PCs make up about 90 percent of the home computers in the world today.

Macintosh computers account for the remaining 10 percent. Apple Computer released the first Macintosh in 1984 and held the proprietary rights to its design until 1995, when the company announced that it would begin licensing the design to other manufacturers. Since then, several companies have begun to manufacture clones of comparable quality.

Macintoshes (also known as Macs) use completely different software and hardware from PCs, which, until recently, made it impossible to exchange information between the two systems without special software. A new chip, called the Power PC, first introduced in 1994, now makes it possible for computers to "read" the different software.

Historically, Macs have been considered more "user-friendly" than PCs—their interface (what you see on the screen when you turn on the computer) is more intuitive or easy to learn—while PCs are for folks who care more about speed and data-crunching capabilities than pretty pictures.

But with today's technology, there is very little difference between PCs and Macs. Moreover, as Apple and IBM continue to hammer out licensing and software agreements, the difference will continue to dwindle. The choice is a matter of personal preference and budget—PCs tend to be cheaper. But that too is changing now that Mac clones are being introduced.

hard disk stores all the letters, reports, spreadsheets, and other documents that you work on, as well as all your applications (the software that makes it possible for you to create those documents). When you store something on your hard disk, it's like making an audio recording on a cassette tape—the information is scratched on the disk's magnetic surface ("writing") and when you want to look at that information, the disk plays it back to you ("reading") like a song on a tape. The amount of storage space a hard disk has is measured in Megabytes (MB) and most computers today aren't sold with less than a 250 MB hard drive. A word to the wise: Get a hard disk with as much memory as you can afford.

■ **KEYBOARD:** A computer keyboard is different from that of a typewriter. Many have "function" keys, labeled F1 through F12, that you can program to carry out various—you guessed it—functions. Most have "arrow" keys that let you move the cursor (that blinking bar or square) around the monitor's screen, a "delete" key, and other specialized keys that allow you to give the computer information that it can understand.

■ **MONITOR:** Monitors come in different sizes and resolutions; most come in color or monochrome (for more info, see page 730). A computer monitor may look like a single component, but it's actually two: the monitor itself and something called a

EXPERT TIPS

BUY NOW OR SAVE LATER?

Prices are always dropping. Here's how to figure when you should buy.

The planned obsolescence cycle in the computer industry is about every six months. That means every half year—when a newer, better, cheaper computer comes out on the market—you'll be slapping yourself on the forehead for not having waited longer to buy. Or should you have waited? Here's how to decide.

■ Did you need a computer yesterday, and can you afford it today? If you answered "yes" to both questions, then go for it. You may want to compare prices, but you're best off buying now so that you can get started working as soon as possible. If, however, you're just perusing your options, you can search at a more leisurely pace and wait for better deals. Remember, too, computers never really become obsolete; thousands of decade-old IBM PCs are in use today. A computer isn't likely to break down because it is old. Indeed, a computer is more likely to have problems in its first months of life than to die of old age.

■ Do you know what you want? If you're sure that you want a Compaq Pentium/75 MHz PC with at least 20 MB RAM, a 540 MB hard drive, and a double-speed CD-ROM drive, you're clearly well-informed, have assessed your requirements, and have found a machine to suit them. If, however, you're likely to go into a computer store and say to a sales rep, "I'm looking for a computer," stop! You may be sold a computer that will not best suit your needs. Wait, research, and do some careful self-analysis before you lay down your credit card.

■ Have you thought about major future developments? Take software, for example. You may think that you don't need a lot of RAM for the applications you're likely to run, but if you'll want to upgrade to multimedia (see "The Sound and the Fury," page 732) or Windows 95 (see "In the Belly of the Beast," page 741), you'll need 8 MB at least, preferably 16 MB.

display adapter. The display adapter is a card that fits into one of your computer's expansion slots; it produces the video for the monitor. When you buy a computer, it will come with both of these components—but if, someday, you want to buy a bigger, better monitor, you'll probably have to buy a new display adapter, too.

■ **MOTHERBOARD:** This circuit board is where the CPU, RAM, and the other "brains" of the computer live. It's called the motherboard because it has to do the most work.

■ **MOUSE:** Some older PCs didn't come with these, but today most do—and Macs have always come with them. A small, plastic gizmo with one or several buttons on top, the mouse attaches to your computer with a cord. Using a mouse is just an easier way of moving the cursor around the screen. Moving the mouse around with your hand, you'll see an arrow or some other symbol (sometimes something called an "I-bar") on your screen corresponding with your movements; when you click on the left-hand mouse button at a certain spot, the arrow or symbol will put the cursor there. Some computers come with a trackball instead of a mouse; it's a different design, but it does the same thing. Mice and trackballs can also carry out more complex commands.

■ **RANDOM ACCESS MEMORY (RAM):** A computer's RAM—often just called "memory"

SAVE EARLY, SAVE OFTEN

A computer crash can be devastating—unless you've stored stuff elsewhere

Computers are not invulnerable. They lose things just like the rest of us. The best way to prevent file loss is to copy any important data onto removable storage media—a fancy way of saying you're backing stuff up on something other than your hard disk. What should you use to make back-up copies? There's no lack of choices: floppy disks, optical disks, tape drives, CD-ROM drives, and others. Here are the pros and cons of the various alternatives:

■ **FLOPPY DISKS:** Floppy disks are the most common back-up medium, and if you're just backing up a single PC, they're generally the best. A floppy stores a lot less data than a hard disk (between 360 KB to 1.4 MB) and, at a dollar or less each. About 10 years ago, 5 1/4-inch floppies were the standard; today, however, 3 1/2-inch floppies are far more popular. If you're working with databases or massive graphics files, you'll need a bunch of floppies to back up everything.

■ **CARTRIDGES:** Usually called Bernoulli or Syquest drives after the two biggest manufacturers, these are basically hard disks enclosed in hard plastic cases. They fit into their own external drive (which does not come with most computers, so you'll have to buy one). They can hold up to 105 MB and cost between $75 and $100, but they're far too slow to use as your primary storage medium.

■ **CD-ROM:** They look just like the compact discs you play on your stereo, and they work like them, too. CD-ROM stands for Compact Disc, Read-Only Memory, which means that, although you can call up files on this medium, you can't copy anything onto it. CD-ROM discs store graphics libraries, multimedia programs, large databases, and other programs that take up a lot of space. They can store up to 680 MB of data—enough to hold the complete contents of an encyclopedia.

■ **TAPE CARTRIDGES:** These look like audio cassette tapes and work in basically the same way. It's not practical, however, to use tape cartridges as your primary storage medium because, just like audio cassettes, it takes too long to locate just the track you need. For backups and archives, though, they're great, and they're also cheap—about $20 for a 220 MB cartridge. Look for the QIC80 standard.

■ **OPTICAL DISKS:** Optical disks store more information than all of the above—up to a gigabyte (1,000 MB), depending on the model. But they're much slower than hard drives or floppies. That makes optical disks great for long-term storage but inappropriate as a primary storage device.

—is the brain power a computer needs to let you work on several programs at once. RAM is measured in Megabytes (MB), and the more memory you have, the more programs you'll be able to use—faster—at the same time. To be most efficient, don't get a computer with less than 8 MB of RAM (otherwise, your programs will run sluggishly). If you need more RAM (and you may, especially if you use a lot of graphics applications), you can always buy more. RAM comes in physical units called SIMMs (Single In-line Memory Modules), which look like little plastic rectangles with computer chips on them. One SIMM can hold 1 MB, 4 MB, or 16 MB of memory. Before you buy your computer, ask the salesperson how much RAM you can add to the system; the ideal number is 64.

HARD DRIVES

GETTING MORE ON YOUR MACHINE

Can't fit anything else on your computer? Add another drive

Think of it as computing's law of manifest destiny: No matter how much space you have on your hard disk, you'll find a way to use it up. When you're beginning to feel cramped, your first plan of action should be to compress the files on your disk—a utilities program will allow you to do this (see "Software that does the Dirty Work," page 743). But it may be time to add a bigger and faster hard drive. Most reliable hard drive manufacturers—among them Maxtor, Connor, and Seagate—sell their wares through mail-order houses and major retail outlets. Here's what to look for.

■ **Get the drive with the greatest storage capacity that you can afford.** You can expect to pay $500 or less for a 500 MB hard disk for a Mac or PC (in general, though, you'll find Mac hard drives are a trifle more expensive). Drives of 300 MB to 500 MB are standard. But if you plan to do a lot of desktop publishing, upgrade to multimedia, electronically save the faxes that you receive on your computer, or use any kind of graphics-heavy applications, consider opting for 850 MB or better.

■ **Go as fast you can.** Most drives have a 10-millisecond to 14-millisecond average access time. Access time is how long it takes the hard disk to find the information that you have requested. Anything more than 14 milliseconds is not worth considering.

A drive with something called a cache or a hard disk caching controller can make your drive's response time even speedier. The caching feature automatically recognizes which information you are accessing most and keeps that data front and center so that every time you want to call it up, your hard drive doesn't have to waste time searching its entire inventory to find it.

A good transfer rate—4 MB or faster—will also speed things up. The transfer rate is the amount of time it takes for the hard drive to send information through the drive's interface.

■ **Make sure the hard drive's interface is compatible with your computer.** A hard drive's interface determines how it will talk to the rest of your computer. If you're a Mac user, SCSI (Small Computer Systems Interface—pronounced "scuzzy") is your only choice. But if you use a PC, you can choose between SCSI and IDE (Integrated Drive Electronics) drives, with SCSI being the interface of choice if you want a drive of more than 500 MB. Most PCs are spacious, which means that you don't have to get rid of your old drive to make room for the new one: You will just have two drives available to you.

Macintoshes, however, are smaller creatures, so you'll either have to remove the old drive to install a new internal one, or you just add an external drive.

A note: There are two kinds of SCSI drives—SCSI-1 and SCSI-2. Both will work on any computer that accepts SCSI, but older machines are more likely to utilize SCSI-1. SCSI-2 is the new standard. It is more efficient and, with the proper upgrades, can be adapted to most computers.

■ **Make sure it fits.** Internal hard drives are installed in an empty drive bay in your computer's chassis that is similar, and often next to, the floppy bay. Most hard drives are 3 1/2 inches, the same size as the most popular floppy disk format. Adding an internal drive isn't hard, but if you've never done it before, you would do best to ask the advice of your friendly neighborhood computer guru. Adding an external drive is even easier—just plug it in.

SHOPPING

WHERE TO BUY YOUR COMPUTER

There is no end of choices. Here's how to get the best deal

Mom and Pop computer shops, massive computer warehouses, second-hand dealers, mail-order houses—you could fill a New York City phone book listing all the places that sell computers. So, where's the best place to buy the computer of your dreams? That depends largely on your preferences, disposition—and budget. Here's a quickie guide to the main computer stores, arranged by type, and their advantages and drawbacks.

■ **RETAIL SHOPS:** You probably live close to one of these living-room-sized store fronts. The chief advantage: You're likely to get attentive service. You will probably find that the sales staff is happy to load the requisite software into your new computer and check to make sure all the components are in working order before you bring it home. Local shops frequently have repair technicians on hand too, so if your computer misbehaves, you can drop it off to be fixed, rather than shipping it to the manufacturer. Of all venues, retail stores tend to be the most expensive and least comprehensive in terms of stock. The staff might be willing to order computers or components for you, but you'll have to pay for that service.

■ **DISCOUNT WAREHOUSES:** These are the supermarkets of computer sales. Computer discount stores carry most of what you see advertised in magazines and newspapers—and at bargain prices. If you have a good idea of what you want before you go in, you can get a great deal. The downside is that you aren't likely to get the kind of service that you receive at smaller stores. But since most computers come with all the software and manuals you need to get up and running, the lack of sales support is not a big problem.

■ **STEREO AND HOME ELECTRONICS SHOPS:** Many are beginning to sell computers and computer equipment. It's possible to find a bargain computer here, but make sure to buy a well-known brand name and a sufficient parts and labor warranty. The staff at these stores may be able to hook you up with an amplifier that'll make your Jimi Hendrix riffs scream, but you shouldn't assume that they'll be able to fix your hard drive.

■ **MAIL-ORDER OR DIRECT MARKET HOUSES:** Some of the best in the market—including Dell and Gateway—built their empires via mail-order houses. The easiest way to track down the names and numbers of mail-order houses is to scan the ad pages of computer magazines. Not only can you get computers at great prices, but you can also ask the mail-order people to custom-build you one according to your specifications—at no extra charge. Your machine will be sent to you via UPS, usually within a couple of weeks.

Of course, there are a few caveats. Because you can't just drop by a mail-order house to get your computer fixed if it ever breaks down, you need to be sure that you buy from a reputable company. Ask friends about their dealings with various houses. Also, prepare a list of questions and call up the company's technical support hotline before you talk to the sales staff. Take note of how long you have to wait before a live person helps you and how responsive the support staff is—good indicators of the service to come.

■ **USED COMPUTERS:** If you're on a budget, don't need the fanciest system on the market, and don't care about warranties or service with a smile, consider buying a used computer. Since computers have virtually no moving parts, they're not as risky to purchase used as, say, a car. You can find real bargains if you're willing to do some research. You might also try calling the American Computer Exchange, a service that matches computer buyers and sellers, ☎ 800-786-0717.

EXPERT LIST

THE BEST BRAND FOR YOUR MONEY

Who's the best computer manufacturer? It depends on your price range. We asked Tin Albano, staff editor at PC Magazine, to give us the inside skinny on who makes the best computers. Albano says that finding a good company isn't difficult; it's more a matter of deciding how much you can spend and where you want to shop—by mail order or at a store.

TOP OF THE LINE

If you can afford it, buy one of the top-of-the-line computers made by the companies listed below. They also offer less expensive models, but those lower-end machines don't always offer the most bang for your buck. These computers are available in almost all computer super stores. Almost no business is done directly.

APPLE COMPUTER INC.
One Infinite Loop
Cupertino, CA 95014
☎ 800-776-2333

COMPAQ COMPUTER CORP.
PO Box 692000, M120208
Houston, TX 78727
☎ 800-345-1518

HEWLETT-PACKARD
3000 Hanover St.
Palo Alto, CA 94304
☎ 800-752-0900

IBM PERSONAL COMPUTER CORP.
Route 100
Somers, NY 10589
☎ 800-772-2227

MICRON COMPUTER INC.
915 East Karchner Rd.
Nampa, ID 83687
☎ 800-388-6334

SECOND TIER

Purchased at retail store or ordered from a mail-order company, these machines aren't necessarily second rate—they're just a tad less glamorous and pricey. These are good choices if you're on a budget but want solid, state-of-the art equipment. As always, however, compare prices before buying.

RETAIL

DIGITAL EQUIPMENT CORP.
146 Main St.
Maynard, MA 01754
☎ 800-722-9332

NEC TECHNOLOGIES INC.
1414 Massachusetts Ave.
Boxborough, MA 01719
☎ 800-632-4636

PACKARD BELL ELECTRONICS, INC.
31717 La Tienda Dr.
Westlake Village, CA 91362
☎ 800-733-5858

MAIL ORDER

DELL COMPUTER CORP.
2214 West Braker Lane
Suite D
Austin, TX 78758
☎ 800-289-3355

GATEWAY 2000 INC.
610 Gateway Dr.
North Sioux City, SD 57049
☎ 800-846-2000

TANGENT COMPUTER INC.
197 Airport Blvd.
Burlingame, CA 94010
☎ 800-800-5550

ZEOS
1307 Industrial Blvd.
Minneapolis, MN 55413
☎ 800-423-5891

THIRD TIER

If you don't need cutting edge components, computers from the following companies are reliable and inexpensive options. All can be purchased from a store or from the company directly.

ACER AMERICA CORP.
2641 Orchard Pkwy.
San Jose, CA 95134
☎ 800-368-2237

AST RESEARCH INC.
16215 Alton Pkwy.
Irvine, CA 92718
☎ 800-876-4278

COMPUADD COMPUTER CORP.
12303 Technology Blvd.
Austin, TX 78727
☎ 800-627-1961

MONITORS

IN SEARCH OF A SHARP IMAGE

A buyer's guide to finding the best monitor

It generally strikes after you start buying lots of graphics-packed software for your new computer, and perhaps a sound card, and you begin to think, "This stuff would really look great if I had a big color monitor." You've been bitten by the bigger-better-color bug. Before you make an impulsive purchase, arm yourself with an understanding of the ways that moniters are differentiated.

■ **COLOR:** Get a color monitor. A monochrome monitor is certainly serviceable, but all your programs—even word processing—will look better in color. Moreover, many new software programs are unintelligible in black and white because their interface depends on color coding.

■ **RESOLUTION:** Display resolution refers to the number of dots of light (called pixels) that a monitor can display—the higher the resolution, the clearer the picture. The absolute minimum display resolution standard for monitors is 640 pixels across the screen and 480 pixels down. Instead of rattling off those numbers, people in the computer industry call that resolution "VGA" (Video Graphics Adapter).

VGA monitors are pretty outdated at this point, though. You'll be much happier with an "SVGA" or "Super VGA" monitor. SVGA monitors aren't much more expensive than VGA, and the extra investment is worth it.

■ **DOT PITCH:** The distance between each pixel on the monitor's screen is measured in millimeters. The smaller the dot pitch, the crisper the image. If you really want a clear image, go with a dot pitch of 0.28 millimeters or less. You might hear a salesperson refer to dot pitch as "stripe pitch." Don't worry, it's pretty much the same thing.

■ **SIZE:** Like television sets, monitors are measured in inches by the diagonal length of the cathode ray tube inside. The current standard is 14 inches, but as more people buy multimedia computers (which come equipped with CD-ROM drives, sound and video cards, and speakers), the standard is increasing to 17 inches.

Monitors do get bigger—up to 24 inches—but mega-monitors are really for people who work every day with desktop publishing packages or huge spreadsheets, which require a different driver, or software program, for each program you use.

If you're updating from a 14-inch monitor, and you're the average user (you do a lot of word processing, some spreadsheet work, and would like to update to a multimedia system), go with a 17-inch monitor.

■ **FLICKER:** Monitor flicker can cause eye stress and headaches, so it's worth your while to buy a monitor that uses technology to prevent it. The watchwords here are "vertical refresh rate" and "interlacing." Vertical refresh rate refers to the number of times that the screen is repainted from

EXPERT TIP

Monitor dirty? Here's what the editors of *PC Commuting* suggest: Clean it with Windex, ammonia, or even vinegar—but don't use alcohol. And spray your cleanser on a rag first, then clean the monitor. Otherwise you'll remove the coating on your screen.

ARE MONITORS REALLY A MENACE?

Worries that monitors emit dangerous levels of radiation have made front-page news. How can you protect yourself?

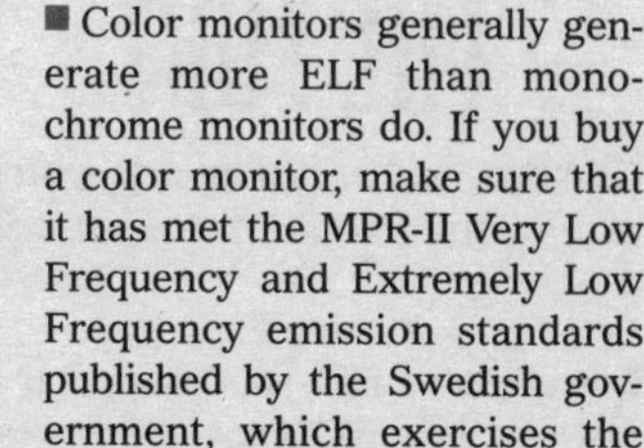

The type of radiation in question is called extremely low frequency (ELF), which is emitted in low doses from computer monitors. Although no studies have proven that health problems arise directly from using monitors frequently, ELF from other sources (such as electrical transmission and distribution lines) has been linked with increased incidents of childhood cancer.

Should you worry about being exposed to ELF if you use a monitor? Experts disagree. The best tactic in protecting yourself against potentially harmful ELF radiation is to exercise "prudent avoidance" and arm yourself with some facts:

■ Because ELF's electromagnetic field is elliptically shaped, the greatest concentration of radiation is emitted not from the front of the monitor, but from the back and sides. Make sure that you're at least several feet away from monitors on either side and in back of you.

■ Color monitors generally generate more ELF than monochrome monitors do. If you buy a color monitor, make sure that it has met the MPR-II Very Low Frequency and Extremely Low Frequency emission standards published by the Swedish government, which exercises the most stringent regulations on monitors of any country. Monitors that have been approved bear the MPR-II seal.

■ Screen shields—transparent screens that fit over your monitor—block the electrical component of ELF radiation, not true magnetic, about two feet. Even if you use a screen shield, you still need to sit away from your monitor and make sure that you're several feet away from other monitors around you.

■ Liquid crystal display (LCD) screens, which are used in most notebook and laptop computers, do not emit any ELF radiation.

top to bottom and is measured in Hertz (Hz). The higher number, the better. If you use a Macintosh, or use Windows with your PC, you want a monitor that has a vertical refresh rate of 72 Hz or higher; otherwise, you'll be plagued by constant flicker.

Interlacing refers to the monitor's refresh method. Interlaced monitors refresh every other line of the picture on your monitor's screen, then go back and repaint the lines in between. A noninterlaced monitor, however, paints the whole screen at once, which means less flicker. Our advice: Get a noninterlaced monitor with a vertical refresh rate of at least 72 Hz.

■ **IMAGE MANIPULATION:** The more ways you can finesse the picture on your screen, the better the image quality. Almost all monitors come with a basic set of controls: brightness, contrast, horizontal and vertical positioning, and image size. But if you're opting for a color monitor, you might want to look for controls that let you adjust the intensity of colors and reduce moiré patterns—those weird, wavy lines that wiggle around in areas of solid color. Look for "color connection" and "digital" controls.

Soon, you'll be able to buy super-fancy software-based controls that you operate from your computer. New isn't always better, though—particularly if you're on a budget. A good old-fashioned thumbwheel control that sharpens a beautiful image beats an average image with digital controls any day.

MULTIMEDIA

THE SOUND AND THE FURY

With some extra hardware, you can make your PC act like an arcade

Once you've had your computer for a while, the novelty of word processing, electronic tax programs, and spreadsheets begins to wear off. You'll start leafing through computer magazines, reading reviews of interactive CD-ROM packages, and soon you'll be spending Saturdays test-driving multimedia applications at the local computer store. Then, you'll know: it's time to get a multimedia machine.

Luckily, you don't need to buy a new computer to get it (though many computers sold today come standard with CD-ROMs and other multimedia essentials). You can buy a multimedia upgrade kit for $500 or less. Here, the editors of *Family PC* magazine explain how to pick one.

WHAT TO LOOK FOR

A multimedia upgrade kit contains a CD-ROM drive, sound card, speakers, and software that turns your computer into a multimedia marvel. CD-ROM disks are the natural media for multimedia software; they can handle the massive amounts of sound and image data that make up multimedia applications. If you don't have a speedy drive, the images on CD-ROMs will move sluggishly on your screen; make sure your kit includes at least a double-speed CD-ROM drive. As this book was going to press, "quad-speed" drives were emerging as the new industry standard. But few current CD-ROM programs exploit the faster drives' ability to deliver smoother video.

The sound card enables your computer to play back speech, music, and sound effects, and also provides the connector and circuitry for hooking up the CD-ROM drive to your computer; it fits into an expansion slot inside your CPU. Insist on a 16-bit, Sound Blaster–compatible card. As with stereos, the speakers that come with the upgrade kits range from the amazing to the abysmal.

Make sure that your kit meets with the "MPC 2" standard. This standard is set by an independent body of multimedia publishers called the Multimedia PC Marketing Council, who decide which products are and aren't acceptable. You may run across kits that advertise MPC 1 approval; this standard was set in 1991 and is now out of date.

DOING IT YOURSELF

Beware: All multimedia upgrade kits promise do-it-yourself, easy installation. But if you're not the type who enjoys tinkering under the hood of your car, installing an upgrade kit can be a nightmare. Our advice: Have the kit installed professionally.

Some dealers offer free installation when you buy a kit, but they'll charge extra for the kit itself. Other dealers charge an installation fee, usually between $20 and $50, if you buy the kit from their store—about $70 if you bought it elsewhere.

If you insist on doing it yourself, here are a few hints:

- Watch out for static electricity. As you shuffle across the carpet of your den, you can build up a static electrical charge in excess of 10,000 volts—more than enough to fry the brains of your computer. Before you touch any of the components of the upgrade kit, ground yourself by touching the metal chassis of your computer and its power supply; this will discharge any static electrical buildup. Also, handle all cards by their plastic edges to avoid touching any of the metal parts or exposed circuits.

- Read the instruction manual thoroughly before you get started.
- Find the technical support number of the manufacturer, and note when you can call. Don't attempt installation while support is unavailable, or you could run into serious snags and have nowhere to turn.

GETTING IT ALL DOWN ON PAPER

How to choose between dot matrix, ink jet, and laser machines

The electronic age may promise to package all communication into bits and bytes, but we're still a long way off from becoming a paperless society. Printers get more technologically sophisticated every year, and sales keep climbing. Fortunately for the beginner seeking a printer, there are really only four categories from which to choose: good, better, best, and color. Or, to use the computer industry's classification system: dot matrix, ink jet, laser, and color. The basics:

■ **DOT MATRIX:** Oldies but goodies, these printers did not produce very glamorous output when they first appeared on the market a decade or so ago. Their print resolution was so low that you could actually see all the dots that made up each character. Today, dot matrix technology has improved to the point that some high-end machines can print characters at what's called "near letter quality," which means that while it's not laser quality, it's still pretty good.

Besides print quality, there are three good reasons to buy a dot matrix printer: They're inexpensive (you can buy a new one for under $200), they can print multilayer forms and carbons (unlike lasers or ink jets, dot matrixes have printer heads that can hammer impressions through several sheets of paper), and they are very sturdy and reliable.

Unlike ink jet and laser printers (which use cut-sheet paper, the type you use in a photocopying machine), most dot matrix printers use what is called continuous form paper, which is joined by perforation at the top and bottom and has holes on either side of every page. The quality of dot matrix output depends largely on what type you buy: 9-pin, which prints 9 dots per character, or 24-pin, which prints out 24 dots per character. Nine-pins are less expensive than 24-pins, but the print quality usually is not as good.

Dot matrixes also are classified by speed, which is measured in characters per second (cps). The higher the cps, the faster the printer. This quote, however, is always based on the rate of printing in draft mode: the lowest-resolution font on dot matrix printers. The rate always drops for printing near-letter quality fonts. Look for a dot matrix that has a cps of 200 or better.

One drawback of dot matrix printers is that they're noisy. Although most dot matrixes have hoods to buffer the clamor or employ some kind of noise-reduction technology, they still make a racket compared to ink jet and laser printers. Also, if you plan to print out a lot of professional documents—any that will contain graphics or letter-quality fonts—you should probably spend a little more and go for an ink jet.

■ **INK JET PRINTERS:** Perfect for those who want laser-like quality but don't have the cash to buy one, ink jet printers can be found for less than $300. With improved technology, ink jet printers can produce output at the same resolution as respectable, mid-range laser printers. Their speed is measured by pages per minute (ppm). What's more, ink jets are light (in fact, many are portable) and practically noiseless.

Ink jets have print heads composed of tiny nozzles that spray jets of ink onto the page, creating letter-quality characters and good-looking graphics. But don't be fooled: There is a difference between ink jet and laser output. When the nozzles spray ink onto the page, they spatter slightly around the edges of each character. While you might need a magnifying glass to detect this, even the naked eye can tell that ink jets' output is a bit fuzzier than lasers'. Still, ink jets are fine for many professional jobs.

■ **LASER PRINTERS:** Laser technology is not simple, which makes choosing a laser printer a slightly more complicated proposition. The three things to look for when you go laser printer shopping are language, resolution, and speed.

Although some speak both, most laser printers speak one of two languages: PostScript or Printer Control Language (PCL). These are programming languages—software—which determine how your printer communicates with your computer. PostScript printers specialize in handling graphics and layout designs; these machines are, however, more expensive than PCL printers. PCL printers are appropriate for most people.

The output quality of laser printers is measured in dots per inch (dpi). In 1994, the standard was 300 dpi; as this book went to press in mid-1995, it was 600; in the next few years, it will be 1,200 dpi. The higher the dpi, the crisper and more typeset-perfect the output.

Speed is measured in pages per minute (ppm). Usually, the printer's name will tell you how fast it prints; for example, the HP LaserJet IIP (a popular low-end laser printer in Hewlett-Packard's LaserJet series) prints at two pages per minute. But keep in mind that if your document is graphics-heavy, printing can take up to twice as long as advertised.

A few years ago, you couldn't buy a laser printer for under $1,000; now, you can find new 300 dpi laser printers now for as little as $300 at discount computer warehouses. You will, however, pay more for a reliable, top-of-the-line printer made by Hewlett-Packard, the laser printer leader.

■ **COLOR PRINTERS:** You can have color in almost any printer. There are color dot matrixes, ink jets, lasers, and—if you need museum-quality color—thermal wax transfer. Since these printers are costly, they are really only appropriate for professional graphics artists.

Color dot matrixes use color ribbons, and thus produce a fairly limited range of colors. They are, however, cheap, starting at around $400. Color often is offered as an option on regular monotone dot matrixes as well. Ink jets offer more professional-looking color printing and don't cost much more than standard monotone ink jets; prices start at about $500. If you want a color laser printer, however, your cost is going to shoot up quickly. While you can find a new monochrome laser printer for about $300, color laser printers start at about $2,000.

PRINTERS YOU CAN PACK IN YOUR BRIEFCASE

If you're on the road a lot, tucking a printer into your briefcase for emergency reports and faxes can come in handy. But be careful: Crafty computer folk can make anything sound portable. To be truly portable, a printer should be 10 pounds or lighter, including its sheet feeder, and it should also include a battery option so that you can print anywhere.

Although portables are available in dot matrix, ink jet, or thermal fusion versions, your best bet probably is ink jet. (Laser printers aren't yet available in portable versions.) Not only is the print quality of ink jets superior, but printing is also quick, quiet, and inexpensive. Thermal fusion, which uses the same technology as high-end thermal transfer printers, requires specially made, high-priced paper but doesn't deliver any extras in print quality.

EXPERT Q&A

SIZING UP SMALL COMPUTERS

Portable computers are big in the market. Here's what you get

Seems like everybody's going mobile. According to *PC Magazine*, over a quarter of 1994's overall PC sales were notebooks, and you can expect that number to expand at Malthusian rates from now on. With more and more people working away from the office—at home, on the road, in planes and trains, and other far-flung locations—portable computers are compact, convenient, and are getting so powerful that many people are beginning to use them as their primary computers. But other than the size difference, what's to know about portable computers? We asked some of the editors of *PC Magazine* to give us the lowdown on the downsized machines.

■ What's the difference between portable and desktop computers?

Portables are smaller. It sounds like a ridiculously obvious point, but if you're talking components, that's about the only real difference between desktops and portables. You will, however, have to pay more for those components in miniature. While prices of portables are falling steadily, you'll still pay about a third more for a portable (specifically, a notebook) than you would for a desktop. Why? It's the price of design ingenuity. It takes some pretty fancy engineering to cram all those goodies into a compact package. The other difference is power. By and large, turbo-powered computing always hits the desktop market before it shrinks to portable sizes. In other words, don't expect the same kinds of bells and whistles that you see on desktops now (e.g., internal CD-ROM drives or 1GB hard drives) to be standard fare on a portable until at least next year.

■ What's the difference between a PowerBook, laptop, notebook, and subnotebook?

Actually, it's pretty straightforward. PowerBooks are made by MacIntosh; this is the company's registered trademark for its line of portable computers which, different from PCs, are not based on Intel chips. Everything else is a PC of varying shape and weight. Laptops are the heaviest (7 pounds or more) and, while they enjoyed a period of popularity in the late 1980s, they're outdated at this point; if you're in the market for a laptop, your best bet is to check the classified section for secondhand sales.

The PC version of the PowerBook is generically known as the notebook, and it's currently the most popular, practical class of portable. They're slim, weigh less than seven pounds, and many have processing capabilities on a par with powerful desktop PCs. Subnotebooks are smaller versions of notebooks, about half their weight—great for assiduous notetakers and e-mail communicators, but because subnotebooks have such cramped keyboards and tiny screens, they're not appropriate for people who write all the time. And subs are definitely not right for budget-buyers, who will find better bargains in laptop and notebook computers.

■ What should you look for in a notebook?

The typical configuration in an average PC-based notebook now includes the following: a 486 DX2/50 CPU, 340 MB hard disk, a $9\frac{1}{2}$-inch dual-scan passive color screen, a PCMCIA slot (credit-card-size drives for modems), a $3\frac{1}{2}$-inch floppy drive, built-in trackball—all weighing in at about $6\frac{1}{2}$ pounds. The average time for battery life on notebooks and PowerBooks is about three hours, but some machines can go up to seven. Remember, though, that heavy-duty batteries can saddle you down—they weigh up to half a pound. Make sure that the weight you're quoted for the portable

EXPERT TIPS

BATTERIES THAT KEEP ON GOING...AND GOING

Learning about how batteries work can save you trouble on the road, or wherever you're tethered to your computer. Here's what the experts advise:

■ **PUT IT TO SLEEP.** If you're not going to be working on a file for several minutes, don't turn off the laptop (the energy required to boot it up again drains battery juice). Most portable computers have energy-saving utilities that will lull the machine into "sleep mode" after several minutes of non-use, but if you don't have this feature, simply close the cover or use the Suspend/Resume switch.

■ **KEEP THE LIGHT LOW.** A bright monitor setting drains 20 to 65 percent of your computer's energy; keep your screen as dim as is comfortable.

■ **AVOID USING PERIPHERALS.** Switching between your CD-ROM drive, modem—even floppy drive—wastes a lot of energy. Try to work only from your hard disk, and save files as infrequently as possible; constant saving can eat up to 80 percent of a battery's power.

■ **TREAD LIGHTLY ON YOUR HARD DRIVE.** The type of software you use and the amount of RAM in your computer affect how often the disk drive is used and therefore the running time of the battery. If you increase the amount of RAM on your computer, say, from 4 MB to 8 MB, the battery will last longer. Also, some programs rely more heavily on the hard drive than others.

■ **PREVENTIVE CARE.** When you buy a new, uncharged battery, charge and discharge it two to four times before taking it on a trip. To discharge a battery, unplug your AC-adapter and leave your laptop on (idle) for a few hours. Discharge it fully before recharging. Also, don't let batteries go dormant too long; unplug your AC-adapter every so often while you're working on your laptop at home, and always disconnect it when you're not using the machine. Discharging and recharging your battery periodically will lengthen its life.

■ **WATCH FOR NEW DEVELOPMENTS.** New technologies are producing lighter batteries that run longer on a single charge. Within the past year, manufacturers introduced lithium ion batteries, which last longer, can be recharged more often, and retain more of their charge during storage than nickel-metal hydride batteries. They are, however, more expensive.

machine includes the weight of the battery and its adapter.

■ **What if I wait until next year to get a notebook?**

As always, waiting a year will get you more computing power for less money. A typical notebook configuration in the next year or so will probably include a 75-MHz Pentium CPU, an 800 MB hard disk, a 9 1/2 inch active-matrix color screen, PCMCIA fax/modem, a touch-sensitive pad (instead of a trackball or mouse, this is a pad that you just press with your finger to get the cursor moving on-screen), and a lithium battery with longer battery life. Is it worth the wait? As always, if you know what you want—and have the cash—go for it.

EXPERT Q&A

HOW MODEMS WORK

The speed is far more important than the brand

The consensus among hardcore computer users is that a computer without a modem is just a glorified typewriter. You don't have to master the technology of a modem, but a little knowledge about them will go a long way in making your PC more than a fancy paperweight. We asked Andrew Kantor, associate editor of *Internet World*, a magazine that covers everything associated with the Internet, for a quick primer and some expert advice.

What is a modem?

A modem is a device that allows your computer to send information to other computers through telephone lines. The word "modem" is a contraction of "modulator-demodulator," which describes the device's process of sending and receiving that information. Modems convert your computer's digital information into pulses of electricity, which are expressed in sequences of high and low tones. That's why, when your modem is connecting, you hear weird screeches coming from it: Those screeches are the high and low tones going really, really fast over the phone lines.

How is a modem's speed measured?

By bits per second (bps) or kilobits per second (Kbps). A bit is equivalent to one electrical pulse, and all modems use algorithms called compression schemes to crunch bits together, which makes transmission faster and more efficient. If the compression scheme is v.32, for example, the modem has a speed of 9600 bps; if it's v.32 bis, it supports 14.4 Kbps, and if it's v.34, the modem can support 28.8 Kbps.

What speed modem should the average user buy?

The fastest you can afford. Even if your online service supports only up to 9,600 bps, buy a 14.4 Kbps modem because you can bet that in the next few months the higher speed will be supported. The modems on the market now range from 9,600 bps to 28.8 Kbps. There are older modems that support speeds between 1,200 bps and 4,800 bps, but they're incredibly slow; you can buy a newer, faster modem for about $100, and prices on older modems are constantly dropping because the technology keeps getting faster.

But here's the hitch: You can only connect as fast as the slowest access speed. In other words, even if you have a 28.8 Kbps, or VFAST, modem, you'll only access information at 9,600 bps if that's the highest speed your online service supports. It works the other way, too. If you have a 2,400-bps modem, and your service supports 9,600 bps, you'll still only connect at 2,400 bps. Still, always buy the fastest modem you can afford because, in the long run, it will save you time and money. The faster you can receive and send information, the less time you will spend online per task.

What is the difference between the various brands?

Speed. Other than that, there is really no difference in terms of performance. Different brands might offer you different bells and whistles—the power switch is in the back on this one, it's up front on that one—but those features only have to do with preference, not with things that you actually need.

The only difference in terms of compatibility is Macintosh versus PC, and there, the choice is simple: If you have a Mac, buy a modem made for Macs, and if you have a PC, buy a PC modem. All but one brand of modems on the market are based on the same chipset, so they're basically all the same. Just look for one with the best warranty, and find a good dealer that will allow you to return the modem if you have a problem with it.

■ What is the difference between external and internal modems, and which should you buy?

Again, there is really no viable performance difference between internal and external modems—it's a matter of personal preference. If you have a computer that's about a year old, you might, for example, want to get an internal modem because it's convenient. An internal modem just looks like a circuit board with a lot of chips and stuff on it; all you have to do is open up your computer and stick the board in its slot. And, then, you never have to think about it: You don't have to carry it around, it won't take up space on your desk, and you can control the on-and-off switch and volume by software. If you have a laptop that's about a year old, it probably is equipped with something called a PCMCIA slot on the side of the machine. This slot is made to hold a modem about the size of a credit card, which is compact and easy to tote around.

External modems look like palm-sized rectangular boxes; they're encased in either plastic or metal. There are a few compelling reasons to buy an external modem, the first of which is that if you do have an older computer, you might not have a slot for an internal board, and thus you have no choice. But you might also want the flexibility of transporting it. For example, if you have a desktop computer at the office, but you bring a laptop with you on business, it makes sense to buy an external so that you can swap it from one computer to the other.

Also, if you're really a computer nerd, you might want to save the slot space inside your PC. The average PC has six to eight open slots, into which you can insert video cards, sound cards—all kinds of peripherals to beef up your PC. If you want to save the slots for things like that, buy an external modem.

■ WHAT YOUR MODEM IS TELLING YOU

A guide to those blinking lights, be they vertical or horizontal.

- **HS HIGH SPEED**—Your modem is set to communicate at its highest speed.
- **AA AUTO ANSWER**—Your modem is set to answer incoming calls.
- **CD CARRIER DETECT**—Your modem is connected to another modem.
- **OH OFF HOOK**—Your modem is in use, either answering an incoming call or placing an outgoing one.
- **RT** or **RX RECEIVE DATA**—Your modem is receiving data from another modem.
- **ST** or **SX SEND DATA**—Your modem is sending data to another modem.
- **MR MODEM READY**—Your modem is on.
- **TR TERMINAL READY**— A hardware connection exists between your computer and your modem.

■ Should you buy a modem that has data and fax capability?

Definitely. These days, in fact, you probably can't find a modem now that doesn't have both. And the advantage of having faxing capability is that you can send computer-generated faxes directly from your computer, and you can receive them—just print them out for hard copies. All you need is a good faxing software package. Most modems come with a basic fax software package, but you can buy a really good one for about $80.

■ How do you connect your modem to go online?

Just plug the power cord into the wall, and the phone line into a phone jack. Turn it on. Then call up an online service (see "The Big Five Online Services," page 763). That's it.

USER'S GUIDE

WARNING: COMPUTING CAN BE HAZARDOUS TO YOUR HEALTH

If you type 50 words a minute for an hour, you'll have pecked out some 18,000 keystrokes. Keep that up all day, five days a week, and you're giving your digits and wrists a hard-core workout. Typing's repetitive movements can lead to muscle strain, pain, and weakness in the hands, arms, and wrists—all of which are signs of carpal tunnel syndrome and other repetitive stress injuries (RSI). And that's not all. A bad chair or posture can cause back and neck strain, and staring at your monitor (especially if it's a flickery one) is a great way to give yourself a pounding headache, not to mention ruin your eyes.

PREVENTING REPETITIVE STRESS INJURIES

BEHAVIOR MODIFICATION

■ Make sure that your keyboard is lower than your elbows; your wrists should be slightly higher than your fingers.

■ Don't over-curl your fingers, drop, or twist your wrists—you'll put too much stress on your hands' muscles and tendons. When you're at the keyboard, keep your fingers just slightly curled and sit up straight.

■ Avoid tendonitis in the elbow (also known as tennis elbow) by making sure that your arms rest comfortably on the armrests of your chair and that your elbows do not jut out at an awkward angle. Ideally, your elbows should bend at 90 degrees. The best chairs let you adjust the armrests to fit your body size.

■ Do you peck at the keyboard, using only a few fingers to do all the work? This can cause muscle strain. Learn to touch-type and you'll reduce the pain and double your typing speed.

■ Take plenty of breaks (at least five minutes every hour).

PRODUCTS TO TRY

■ Investing in a wrist-rest—a device that elevates your hands so that your wrists remain straight while typing—is a great way to help prevent RSI. They range from the simple (a foam pad, about $10) to the sophisticated (plastic shackles, $25 and above). Wrist-rests are sold at many computer stores. Don't want to spend the dough? Try a rolled up towel instead.

■ Dozens of keyboards claim to be ergonomic, and some of them actually deliver on that promise. The most comfortable keyboards are Kinesis Ergonomic Keyboard (☎ 206-455-9220) and Microsoft's keyboard.

■ **KEYBOARDING**

Three common incorrect practices and their symptoms:

TWISTING: Long muscles forced to stretch around elbow, stressing muscles in hands and arms.
SYMPTOMS: Elbow inflammation, throbbing forearm, loss of dexterity in ring and little fingers.

OVER-CURLED FINGERS: Continosly flexed muscles that contract cause nerve compression in the wrist
SYMPTOMS: Pain in the wrist and forearm, tingling or numbness in the fingers.

DROPPED WRISTS: Tendons press agains the nerves in the wrist weakening the thumb, index and ring fingers.
SYMPTOMS: Numbness, tingling in the fingers at night, swelling of wrist and/or thumb.

■ COMPUTER USER'S GUIDE

PREVENTING EYE STRAIN

BEHAVIOR MODIFICATION

■ Keep at least 20 inches between your eyes and monitor, and adjust the monitor's angle so that you don't have to crane your neck to look at the screen. If you wear bifocals, adjust your monitor so that you're looking down.

■ The light that you work by should be diffuse and overhead. A light source coming from the side, or worse, from behind, will make you squint; over time, you'll develop headaches from eyestrain.

■ It sounds kinds of obvious, but have you adjusted the brightness and contrast on your screen? This often overlooked solution can save you from squinting at a screen that ís either too dim or too bright.

■ Contact lenses may cause eyestrain in people who stare at a computer screen for hours on end. Try using your glasses instead. Photo-sensitive lenses soften the glare from the screen.

PRODUCTS TO TRY

■ Nothing is harder to look at than a bright monitor; it can cause headaches as well as eye strain. Look for add-on screen filters to correct that problem, such as the ones that are available from Less Gauss.

■ Is your monitor's screen flickering? If so, it's causing strain on your eyes. A monitor that flickers usually has a low vertical refresh rate or a high dot pitch (see "In Search of a Sharp Image," page 730); it's probably time to get a new monitor.

PREVENTING BACK AND NECK STRAIN

BEHAVIOR MODIFICATION

■ Bad posture is the most common reason for neck and upper back pain. So learn to sit straight, don't slouch, and keep shoulders relaxed (but not dropped forward).

PRODUCTS TO TRY

■ If you're looking for a computer desk (anything that costs more than $100 is probably called a workstation), keep a few important points in mind: Get one that you can raise and lower from 27 to 29 inches. Make sure it has an adjustable and sliding keyboard holder—one that is a couple of inches below the table level. Finally, spend the extra bucks and get something solid—there's nothing more headache-inducing than a wobbly PC.

■ If you tend to slouch at your desk, try the $49.95 Nada Chair, a contraption that forces you to sit straight (call ☎ 800-722-2587 for more information).

■ Looking for a new chair? Make sure the backrest is adjustable and tilts backward. Also look for lumbar support, armrests, adjustable height, and easy-rolling wheels.

■ **POSTURE**

Computer workstations can be equipped to insure good posture and proper alignment.

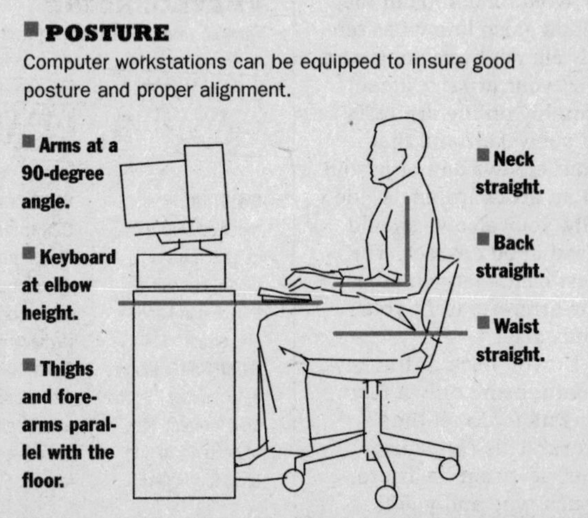
■ Arms at a 90-degree angle.
■ Keyboard at elbow height.
■ Thighs and fore-arms parallel with the floor.
■ Neck straight.
■ Back straight.
■ Waist straight.

SOFTWARE

OPERATING SYSTEMS

IN THE BELLY OF THE BEAST

Software that lets you tell your computer what to do

There are two kinds of software: application software and operating system software. Applications, which are individually purchased packages that serve a specific function such as word processing or game playing, get all the glory. But it's really the operating system (OS) that keeps everything together. Your OS sits quietly in the background, telling your computer how to handle programs and files. If you've used a computer at all, you've used an operating system of some kind.

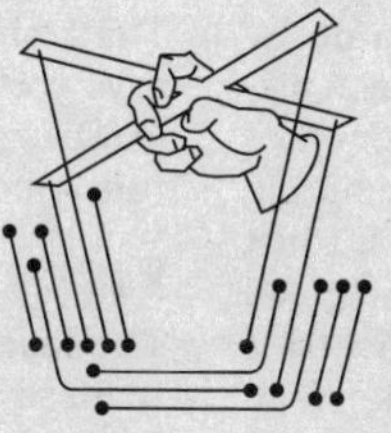

There are only a few operating systems available to the average user. For PCs, there are three: MS-DOS (which can work with a program called "Windows"), OS/2, and Microsoft Windows 95, scheduled for release in August 1995. For Macs, there is only one: Macintosh Operating System. The selection is limited because software companies have to design their applications specifically to work with a particular operating system. That's why you see applications listed as Windows-, DOS-. or Macintosh-compatible. If software companies had to write applications for a zillion different operating systems, they wouldn't have any time to design new and different applications.

So which operating system is the best one for you? The good news is that you don't have to make that decision if you don't want to: Operating systems usually come with computers when you buy them. If you bought a PC today, it would certainly come with DOS and, chances are, the manufacturer would throw Windows in, too. All Macs come with Mac OS. Nonetheless, choices are proliferating. Operating systems come in versions. Macintosh System 7.1 and most recently 7.5, for instance, will run all the same programs, but they offer slightly different features. Likewise, PC-users can choose between different versions of Microsoft's offerings or opt instead for OS/2. Each OS has its strengths and weaknesses; some have a lot of neat features but are hard to navigate, while others are just the opposite. An OS may promise to integrate everything from faxing to e-mailing to multimedia from one menu, but if there aren't many applications that work with it, it's of little use. Here's what the major systems have to offer:

MS-DOS

All IBM clones use the operating system MS-DOS, which stands for Microsoft Disk Operating System. The irony, of course, is that MS-DOS—usually just called DOS—is sold by Microsoft, not IBM. Microsoft founder and president Bill Gates designed it for IBM as an undergraduate student at Harvard, shortly before he dropped out. IBM let him keep the licensing rights, and the rest is history.

DOS's way of interacting with you—its "interface"—is a bit inscrutable. When you turn on a PC running DOS, you will see a black screen and something that looks like this: C:\> This weird-looking symbol, called a "C-prompt," is DOS's way of telling you that it is ready for you to tell it what to do: Run your word processing program, double your hard disk space, check for viruses—whatever. In DOS, you have to type DOS commands if you want the computer to do anything. If you type "help" at the C-prompt, DOS will give you a complete list of commands and explanation of each.

Few people want to go through the trouble of learning DOS commands to use their PCs. That's why, in the mid-1980s, Microsoft came out with Microsoft Windows. Windows is pretty and user-friendly. Instead of typing out commands at the C-prompt, you tell Windows what to do by clicking on an icon (a thumbnail-sized picture that represents an application or other function) with a mouse or other pointing device. But Windows is not an OS; it's just a prettier interface, a GUI (pronounced gooey), or Graphical User Interface (it's called that because it has graphics). Windows runs "on top" of DOS, masking its ugly duckling interface.

Today, most people who use PCs run Windows on top of MS-DOS. Windows is easier to use and nicer to look at than DOS. And, unlike DOS, Windows lets you run several applications at once, a feature called "multi-tasking." Finally, there are more neat applications designed for the Windows interface than for DOS's.

OS/2

Not long after the debut of Windows, IBM (with some help from Microsoft) decided to launch its own OS, one that would combine the workhorse power of DOS and the good looks of Windows. They called it OS/2 (for "Operating System 2"). Although OS/2 has, by most reports, lived up to its promise, it hasn't had much success in the consumer marketplace. The success of Windows has overshadowed it; there just aren't enough applications written for OS/2 to make it truly viable. But now, IBM has re-dressed OS/2, scaled it down in price and power, added an automatic online connection, and called it something else: Warp. Since it's still new, and there are relatively few applications written for it, the verdict is still out on Warp.

WINDOWS 95

This is where things start getting a bit complicated. The Windows that we were talking about before is a GUI than runs on top of DOS. Microsoft has, however, developed a kind of Windows that is a bona fide OS, called Windows 95. For PC users, Windows 95 is a coup. It has a more user-friendly interface. It runs and manages applications faster and more efficiently, and it automatically figures out which peripherals you have attached to your computer. But the best part is that it connects you online from the moment you install it. The problem is that even though Microsoft says you don't, you really need at least a 486-based machine with 8 MB of RAM to run Windows 95.

MACINTOSH OPERATING SYSTEM

The Macintosh Operating System revolutionized the face of computers: It was the first OS GUI. That's why, when the Mac debuted in the mid-80s, it practically caused riots. Finally, an operating system that was easy—even fun—to use. Based on icons instead of command lines, mice instead of keyboards, Mac OS made computing "user-friendly," a feature for which people were willing to pay quite a bit, even if it meant skimping on the processing power offered by PCs. Mac OS was so popular, in fact, that PCs tried to imitate it with Windows. For a while, the joke in the computer industry was that IBM really stood for "I wanna Be a Mac."

SOFTWARE THAT DOES THE DIRTY WORK

Doctor, housekeeper, management consultant: That is what a broad class of software called utilities are to your computer. Caught a computer virus? A utility can usually detect it and zap it. Lost a file? A utility can track it down. Need extra room for storage? A utility can double your hard disk size. Here are some utilities programs to consider.

■ **GENERAL HOUSEKEEPING:** Norton Utilities is far and away the best general utilities package around. It not only helps you manage your files, but its Disk Doctor feature can fix almost anything that's gone wrong with your hard disk. A second choice: PC Tools has the same types of programs that Norton Utilities has, as well as some others.

■ **VIRUS PROTECTION:** The least damaging computer viruses—self-propagating programs that spread through online services or infected floppy discs—cause annoying glitches. The most deadly viruses, however, can wipe out your entire hard disk.

Effective anti-virus programs include Norton Anti-Virus from Symantec, Untouchable from Fifth Generation Systems, and Central Point Anti-Virus. If you have a PC, check out the antivirus protector that you already have on DOS 6.0; it can handle most viruses just fine.

You can get equally excellent programs like Viruscan, Clean-Up, and VShield at bargain rates from McAfee Associates, who distributes them as shareware—software that can be downloaded free of charge or for a nominal fee.

■ **FILE COMPRESSION:** Compression software squeeze your files so that they take up less room on your hard disk. The most popular compression program is Stacker, by Stac Electronics. If you have a PC and DOS 6.0, you already have a compression utility: DoubleSpace. But Stacker is more sophisticated. PKZIP and PKUNZIP are popular shareware utilities for PC files.

■ **RAM UTILITIES:** Real RAM is expensive, but some utilities can fake an increase for substantially less. Connectix RAM Doubler, for instance, does exactly that, allowing you to keep more programs open at once.

■ **SCREEN SAVERS:** They don't really save your screen. Most computers come with a collection built-in, but you can buy programs featuring everything from flying toasters to cartoons from Gary Larson's "The Far Side."

Mac Operating System has been through several incarnations—the latest is called System 7—which, like Windows 95, has networking power, but it has always been designed to work with Macintosh computers and software only. The advantage of this design is what's called "plug and play": Since everything is controlled by one company, you never have to worry about whether or not different software or hardware will work with your Mac. It just does. But now that nearly everyone is computer-literate, Macs don't attract the way they used to. Sure, people still want their computers to be easy to use, but now that most computers are easy to use, people want more power and more applications.

So, the tables have turned: Macs now want to be IBMs. In partnership with IBM, Macintosh is not only beginning to license Mac OS to clone manufacturers, but it's also designing a totally new operating system (code-named "Copland"), which—not surprisingly—will be designed like OS2/Warp and Windows 95.

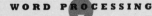

WORD PROCESSING

TYPING HAS NEVER BEEN SO EASY

Mail merge, grammar-check, and instant résumés are some options

At this point, every serious package has a spell-checker as standard fare, but other writing tools, like a thesaurus and a grammar checker, may still be considered separate options by some companies. Here's a list of features to look for in word processors.

■ **AUTOMATIC FOOTNOTES:** Numbers footnotes and places them at the bottom of the page, or wherever you prefer.

■ **AUTOMATIC INDEXER AND TABLE OF CONTENTS:** Creates an index for your manuscript. You can tag key words that you want to include in the index, and the indexer will place them there, with the appropriate page number. If page numbers change as you edit the document, the indexer updates the information. The contents function scans all the headings in your manuscript and lists them, with page numbers, in a table of contents.

■ **AUTOMATIC STYLE FORMATTING:** This feature offers a variety of document templates, which may include one for a fax cover sheet, résumé, business letter or memo, newsletter (with multiple columns) and, of course, a regular document. This is very handy when you need to make professional-looking documents in a hurry and you neither have the time nor the talent to design them yourself. But this feature also allows you to design your own templates, too.

■ **AUTOMATIC ENVELOPE AND LABEL MAKER:** Each word processor varies in sophistication where this feature is concerned. The most basic lets you input the name and address of the addressee, automatically creating an envelope or label with that information, plus your name and return address. More robust word processors incorporate mail merge functions (see below) and let you input multiple return addresses.

■ **FILE PREVIEW AND OUTLINING:** File preview lets you take a close-up or an at-a-distance view of what your document will look like when it's printed. The outlining feature lets you concentrate on just headings or the first lines of each paragraph.

■ **GRAPHICS EDITING AND SUPPORT:** This lets you import graphics (pictures, charts) into your document, automatically wrapping text around them. This is a must if you create presentations or newsletters.

■ **CUSTOMIZABLE MACROS:** A macro is a mini-program that you design for shortcuts. For example, if you type a certain phrase frequently ("To: B. Smith. From: S. Thomas"), you can create a macro to do it for you in one or two keystrokes (Ctrl-X, for instance).

■ **MAIL MERGE:** Handy for home-based businesses, this feature lets you zip through mass mailings by letting you merge a form letter with your database of names and addresses.

■ **GRAPHING AND DRAWING MODULES:** Some word processors have extra features (sometimes called "modules") that let you design graphs and drawings to enhance your documents, automatically wrapping text around the graphic.

■ **SAVING IN DIFFERENT FORMATS:** This feature translates a document created in another word processing program, and lets you save it in your own word processor's format.

■ **THESAURUS, GRAMMAR-CHECKER:** A thesaurus offers synonyms for words you select; a grammar-checker, well, checks your grammar.

EXPERT PICKS

DO YOU HAVE THE WRITE STUFF?

Which word processing program is best for you? Kay Yarborough Nelson, author of Slick Tricks for Word for Windows *and* Friendly Macintosh, *and Edward Mendelson, Columbia University English professor and contributing editor of* PC Magazine, *pick the cream of the crop. The best packages are expensive: expect to pay between $100 and $400. The good news is you can't really make a mistake: all the programs listed are good. Because word processing packages are updated so frequently, we haven't listed specific versions. The features referred to were available as this book went to press in mid-1995.*

FOR PCS WITH WINDOWS

AMIPRO

Lotus Development

■ This Windows-based application is an excellent graphics handler and a powerful desktop publishing application. You can create graphs and tables without having to dip into a separate module to do it. It's also very easy to use, a plus for the beginner.
☎ **800-343-5414**

MICROSOFT WORD FOR WINDOWS

Microsoft Corp.

■ Arguably the best text editor ever. You can cut and paste text in between several documents; its menus are helpful and robust; and it has several intelligent, automated editing features—like automatically correcting misspelled words as you type.
☎ **800-426-9400**

WORDPERFECT FOR WINDOWS

WordPerfect Corp.,

■ With easy-to-program macros—miniature programs that allow you to design short cuts—for just about every feature, this is a great package for people who love to customize their word processors. It also has great document handling features. Without leaving the program, you can create directories on

DIRT-CHEAP WORD PROCESSING

You don't need all the options? Here's a few DOS-based cheapies under $25

WEBSTER'S WORD PROCESSOR

Cosmi Corp.

■ The king of thrifty word processors, Webster's (no relation to the dictionary) is full-featured enough for all word processing tasks. It's got spell-checking, a thesaurus, and a feature that corrects widows and orphans.
☎ **310-833-2000**

SWIFT WORD PROCESSOR

Cosmi Corp.

■ This is a cinch to learn. Commands are selected either from pull-down menus or Alt-key combinations. You can't italicize, bold-face, or change the style of the text in any way, though, and the spell-checker will report mistakes, but it won't correct them.
☎ **310-833-2000**

EASY WORKING: THE WRITER

Spinnaker Corp.

■ Offers everything Swift does, but its features are more robust. Text is displayed on the screen exactly the way it will appear on the page, including margin settings and page breaks. The spell-checker is worse than Swift's, though.
☎ **800-323-8088**

HOW TO BE THE NEXT GUTENBERG

This software lets you design pages like a pro. But is that really necessary?

Desktop publishing (DTP) software allows you to create page layouts that only a few years ago could have been done only by professional typesetters and printers. Typical users of DTP software are production designers in the publishing industry (like the ones who produced this book), who use the programs to lay out and produce magazine covers and pages, complete with all the photos, text, and fancy formatting they require.

Do you need DTP? Probably not. DTP came into vogue when word processors were still fairly basic, but today's high-end word processors are very sophisticated; they're built to handle just about every design feature you'd be likely to use for newsletters and the like. If you find you're pushing your word processor to the max, though, you might want to look into a professional DTP package. Most cost around $500. One caveat: DTP software hogs hard disk space (not to mention RAM), so make sure your computer is powerful enough to handle it.

■ LEADING DESKTOP PUBLISHING PACKAGES

FRAMEMAKER Frame Technologies	☎ **800-843-7263**
MICROSOFT PUBLISHER Microsoft Corp.	☎ **800-426-9400**
PAGEMAKER Aldus	☎ **800-945-4480**
QUARKXPRESS Quark	☎ **800-788-7835**
VENTURA PUBLISHER Ventura	☎ **800-822-8221**

your hard disk, rename, copy, and create a list of documents that you work with frequently.
☎ **800-321-4566**

FOR PCS WITH DOS ONLY:

MICROSOFT WORD FOR DOS
Microsoft Corp.

■ It offers many of the same features as WordPerfect for DOS, but it's not as elegant in looks or file handling. It does, however, have a lot of short-cut keys, so if you're a crackerjack typist, you may prefer it over its competitors.
☎ **800-426-9400**

WORDPERFECT FOR DOS
WordPerfect Corp.

■ This package is so good-looking, you almost feel as though you're in Windows—you can even use a mouse, if you want to. It's also the best word processor for DOS.
☎ **800-321-4566**

FOR MACINTOSHES

MACWRITE PRO
Claris

■ Though not as feature-rich as other Macintosh word processors, MacWrite Pro is a bargain (you can find it for under $100). With a communications link, you can send e-mail directly from the word processor. Also has great search-and-replace features and graphics capabilities. Features like grammar-checker and outlining cost extra.
☎ **800-544-8554**

WORD FOR THE MACINTOSH
Microsoft Corp.

■ Probably the best of the Mac word processors, Word for the Macintosh boasts every feature that its Windows counterpart does. (This book was edited in Word.)
☎ **800-426-9400**

WORDPERFECT FOR THE MACINTOSH
WordPerfect Corp.

■ For point-and-click addicts, WordPerfect for the Macintosh has a toolbar for everything—mail merges, formatting, fonts, tables, and more. But it still isn't as good as its Windows counterpart.
☎ **800-321-4566**

EXPERT TIP

THE BOTTOM LINE ON SPREADSHEETS

These days there's hardly a number that the best programs can't crunch

It's hard to find a bad spreadsheet program, says *PC Magazine* contributing editor Craig Stinson, because all of the major players are capable of heavy lifting. Here's Stinson's list of things to check before you buy:

■ **ANALYSIS AND MODEL BUILDING:** A good spreadsheet application can analyze numbers and interpret them in a way that allows you to build models based on the data. Clues that tell you whether or not a spreadsheet can do this are number of data entry tools, function library, ability to annotate, special features that organize and consolidate data, as well as features that let you access databases.

■ **CHARTING:** This feature transforms your data into different types of charts, for presentation purposes. Look at the number and quality of chart formats that the spreadsheet offers, its ability to automate simple charting tasks, and options such as customizable titles, notes, multiple typefaces, objects, colors, and shading.

■ **WORKSHEET PRESENTATION:** Make sure that the application produces board-room quality documents, on screen and on paper. Generally, if the program offers a print previewer, a number of preconfigured document styles, as well as a broad range of fonts, shading, ruling, color options, it's up to snuff.

■ **LINKING:** Make sure that the spreadsheet application you buy lets you import data from other spreadsheet and nonspreadsheet applications. In other words, can you cut information from your word processing application and paste it into your spreadsheet?

■ **CUSTOM DESIGN:** Once you become a spreadsheet whiz, you may want to have the option of making macros—programming keys on your keyboard to carry out certain functions automatically. Each spreadsheet application has its own "macro language" that lets you do this. Before you buy the software, examine the macro language: Does it seem easy to learn? Does it let you program the keys to carry out a wide variety of commands, such as bring up different screens, menus, or icons?

DOWN WITH DATABASES

Unless you run the census, a spreadsheet is probably all you need

Most people use spreadsheets to keep track of numbers, so what do you need database software for? Chances are, you don't need it. Database software is mainly a power tool for power users. These programs accept huge amounts of data and sort it according to type. Relational databases, the most powerful of the lot, can link information from different files and come with built-in programming languages that let you custom-design features, formats, and other things that you probably wouldn't use unless you were in charge of inventory for Macy's national headquarters or organizing information for the U.S. Census.

Today's advanced spreadsheets are taking over many of the tasks that once belonged exclusively to databases, such as sorting and linking. So, unless you handle a huge amount of data, a spreadsheet may be all you need.

ALL-IN-ONE SOFTWARE

Now you can get different programs bundled together. Is it a good deal?

Supermarkets were a revolutionary innovation: Instead of going to the butcher, the milkman, and the green- grocer, you could pick up everything you needed in one massive emporium. The computer industry has begun to catch on to the concept: selling word processing, spreadsheet, and database software all bundled together in one tidy package.

There are low-end, one-stop shopping packages (for people who just want the basics) and high-end suites with all the bells and whistles for big spenders and power users. Sounds great, but which is right for you? And is it worth getting the whole package when you won't use all the programs?

THE SWEETEST SUITES

INTEGRATED SOFTWARE

CLARIS WORKS	Claris	☎ 800-325-2747
BETTER WORKING EIGHT IN ONE	Spinnaker Software	☎ 800-323-8088
LOTUS WORKS	Lotus Development	☎ 800-343-5414
MICROSOFT WORKS	Microsoft Corp.	☎ 800-426-9400
PFS: FIRST CHOICE	Spinnaker Software	☎ 800-323-8088
WORDPERFECT WORKS	WordPerfect	☎ 800-451-5151

SUITES

PERFECT OFFICE	Novell Inc.	☎ 800-331-0877
LOTUS SMART SUITE	Lotus Development Corp	☎ 800-343-5414
MICROSOFT OFFICE PROFESSIONAL	Microsoft Corp	☎ 800-426-9400

INTEGRATED SOFTWARE

Buying integrated software is kind of like buying an integrated stereo system—a boom box with tapes. You're paying for convenience, not top-notch components. Similarly, you won't find lots of state-of-the-art features in the modules of integrated software packages, but you'll probably be quite satisfied if you just want a product that's practical, convenient, and economical. Integrated packages usually cost less than individual programs. Most are well under $200; some are as low as $50.

One of the drawbacks of integrated software is that all of its programs are designed exclusively for that package. In other words, when you buy, say, WordPerfect Works, you aren't getting the latest version of WordPerfect for your word processor; you're getting a watered-down version designed specifically to fit into the integrated package. The good news, however, is that every module of an integrated package works similarly, so once you've learned how to use one, you've essentially learned how to use them all.

SUITES

If you use two or more of the programs included in these packages, suites are a sweet deal. All the major software companies—Microsoft, Lotus, and Novell (WordPerfect's parent company)—combine their latest word processing, spreadsheet, and database programs (some even throw in e-mail and presentation graphics software, too). No watered-down versions here; it's all top-notch, turbo-powered stuff. Suites range in price—from about $500 to $900 on the street. A single word processing program can cost about the same.

Currently, suites are really just bundles of stand-alone programs: The programs inside are great on their own, but they don't work together very well. (Ironically, integration is handled better by the low-end packages). Future generations of suites will offer more uniformity so you won't have to learn how to use three or five separate programs.

MONEY MANAGER'S GUIDE

PROGRAMS THAT DO EVERYTHING—EXCEPT MAKE MONEY

Stumped by a money matter? There are more than two dozen software programs to help you organize your financial affairs by computer. Some simply handle record keeping, banking, and check writing; others help you plan your budget, choose a portfolio of stocks, bonds, and mutual funds, and then buy and sell them for you. For tax season, there are tax programs with scores of income tax forms and money-saving tips. How do you choose? We've compared top-selling software in four categories: record keeping and banking; financial planning; investing; and tax preparation. The prices we indicate are suggested retail prices, but you can generally get the software for 20 to 30 percent less at discount stores.

RECORD KEEPING AND BANKING

For basic financial chores like paying bills, keeping records, and budgeting, these programs fit the bill. All can print checks and envelopes and track a stock or mutual fund portfolio. Quicken and Money-Counts can get price quotes electronically from online data services for about $15 a month. Beyond that, here's how they compare:

QUICKEN

Intuit, $29.95

DOS • WINDOWS • MAC

■ The top-selling personal finance software. Excels at budgeting and graphing what happens to your money. Makes it easy to pay bills, track expenses, graph the results, and budget your income.

☎ 800-624-9060

QUICKEN DELUXE

Intuit, $49.95

WINDOWS

■ The upgraded deluxe version has a home inventory feature and a tax-link assistant that categorizes taxable items.

☎ 800-624-9060

MICROSOFT MONEY

Microsoft, $24.95

WINDOWS

■ Good for beginners who want to create a budget by using their spending patterns as a guide. Its online banking ability also makes it appealing to more sophisticated investors.

☎ 800-426-9400

MONEYCOUNTS

Parsons Technology, $49

DOS • WINDOWS

■ One of the few packages that includes a general ledger and a trial balance. Allows you to keep large mailing lists and to address envelopes and labels; useful if you're a small business owner or fund-raiser for an organization.

☎ 800-223-6925

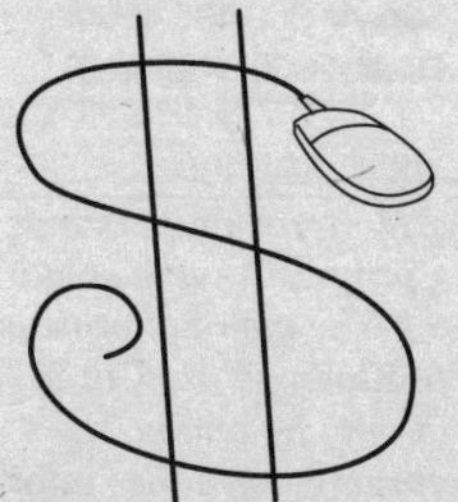

FINANCIAL PLANNING

These programs offer tools for choosing investments. They allow you to pick a goal, such as paying for college tuition, then figure out how much you need to save to meet it. You can put together a portfolio of stocks or funds and track its performance. You can also handle specific tasks, like analyzing life insurance.

WEALTHBUILDER

Reality Online, $49.95

WINDOWS • MAC

■ Everything you need to put together a thorough financial plan. Designed with *Money Magazine*, the program scopes out your financial philosophy—from very conservative to very aggressive—by asking questions about your holdings. It has financial data on thousands of stocks, bonds, and mutual funds.

☎ 800-346-2024

■ EXPERT LIST

MANAGING YOUR MONEY
Meca, $39.95
DOS • WINDOWS • MAC

■ Advice from financial planning guru Andrew Tobias. Strong on managing your portfolio and investments.
☎ 800-288-6322

KIPLINGER SIMPLY MONEY
Computer Associates, $34.95
WINDOWS

■ Helpful tips from the folks who publish *Kiplinger's Personal Finance* magazine on how to manage your money. Good graphics. Easy to learn with clear, lively commentary.
☎ 800-225-5224

PERSONAL INVESTING

These programs are for experienced investors; they offer little on-screen advice. They let you screen stocks, bonds, or mutual funds and then manage your portfolio. All except Pulse let you trade securities by modem through discount brokerage houses.

REUTERS MONEY NETWORK
Reality Online, $24.95 (Free with WealthBuilder)
Windows

■ Good choice for mutual fund watchers. Lets you sort through a database of more than 17,000 stocks, bonds, and certificates of deposit. The program suggests CDs, mutual funds, and money market funds that fit your investment goals.
☎ 800-346-2024

PULSE
Equis International, $195.00
DOS

■ Allows you to break down your holdings by any category you designate, such as asset type. Easy to navigate.
☎ 800-882-3040

CAPTOOL
Techserve, $149.00
DOS

■ For the serious investor who is primarily interested in individual stocks. Does sophisticated calculations, such as your stock (but not bond) portfolio's internal rate of return.
☎ 800-826-8082

EQUALIZER
Charles Schwab, $59
DOS

ON-LINE XPRESS
Fidelity Investment, $49.95
DOS • WINDOWS

■ For those who have accounts with Schwab or Fidelity, these programs let you place orders before the market opens, though they don't offer much advice on choosing stocks. Both offer 10 percent off the firms' standard discount brokerage commissions for customers who trade with the software.
☎ **Schwab:** 800-435-4000
☎ **Fidelity:** 800-544-8888

TAX PREPARATION

Nearly 3 million personal tax programs were sold in 1993. The average price is $30. Kiplinger TaxCut is sold only by phone. Returning consumer information cards is especially useful for buyers of tax software, which is updated yearly. Manufacturers can then send information about new editions. The price of all tax software, of course, is tax deductible.

TURBOTAX
Intuit, $42.00
DOS • MAC • WINDOWS

■ The top seller. Visual displays are easy on the eye. Good at finding deductions.
☎ 800-964-1040

ANDREW TOBIAS' TAXCUT
Meca, $29.95
DOS • MAC • WINDOWS

■ Simple to follow instructions from finance writer Andrew Tobias. Makes it easy to move from one tax form to another and back.
☎ 800-284-3694

KIPLINGER TAXCUT
Meca, $39.95
DOS • MAC • WINDOWS

■ More guidance than Tobias' TaxCut. Tips on just about everything, even tricky questions. Also included: Kiplinger Tax Estimator program for tax planning and a tax guide on Sure Ways to Cut Your Taxes.
☎ 800-365-1546

PERSONAL TAX EDGE
Parsons Technology, $19.00
DOS • MAC • WINDOWS

■ Good for filers with fairly simple returns. A bargain, but offers little advice.
☎ 800-223-6925

EXPERT Q&A

COMPUTERS AND YOUR KIDS

How to get them started, and how to get them to stop

The odds are better than even that your kids are more at home with a computer than you are. But in case they're not, Carol Ellison, education editor at *Home PC* magazine, offers some advice about how to make your home computer as comfy as a teddy bear.

■ Do children really need special equipment to make them comfortable?

Probably not, but it's not a bad idea to get it. Since kids are starting out on computers much earlier than their parents, you want to make the experience of learning how to use them a comfortable one. Give some attention to ergonomics: Kids are a lot smaller than you are and may be happier with products that are designed for them.

■ What should parents consider when purchasing hardware for kids?

First of all, how much is the child going to use the computer? If she or he will be using it a lot, you might want to think about buying a smaller mouse. And there is another question: How old is the child? A pre-schooler's fingers probably aren't big or strong enough to manipulate a mouse for an extended period of time, whereas older kids—between seven and eight years old—can probably safely use adult mice. When a child is sitting at a computer, his or her wrists and arms should be fairly flat: Check to see if your kid is "aligned" properly. If not, you may want to look into products, such as wrist rests or special hand rests that can snap onto mice.

Also, the issue might not be with what you buy, but with how you use it. What kind of chair is the child using? If the chair is too low, the child will have to strain to reach for the keyboard, which, over time, can cause back and neck problems. You may want to investigate buying a chair that is designed for kids.

■ How should parents go about buying items?

It's a great idea to take the kids shopping with you. Let kids test-drive products, listen to them when they tell you something is uncomfortable. At the same time, take their suggestions with a grain of salt. Often, kids just want to get what looks cool.

■ Are there any special rules about how long kids should stay on the computer?

Kids probably have to take breaks more often than adults: every 15 minutes is a good rule. You don't have to make them feel as though you're nagging them, either. If, for example, your child is working on a drawing program, ask him or her to print out the finished picture and be ready with crayons or pens to color it in. If kids are playing a game in teams, the 15-minute break is a good time to get up, move around, and trade spots. Remember: Computing can be an isolating, sedentary activity. Make sure kids are socializing and exercising enough.

FACT FILE:

CAMPING, CANOEING... AND COMPUTING?

■ *Summer computer camps are becoming hot spots for technologically inclined tots. According to Family PC, the top three are:*

Future Kids	☎ **800-765-5000**
The Technology Camp of Epiphany	☎ **206-329-0217**
Computer-Ed High Tech Camp	☎ **617-938-6970**

PARENT'S GUIDE

SOFTWARE FOR TRENDY TOTS

Buying good software for your kids is like finding suitable television shows for them: You've got to weed out the junk, then make a parent-child compromise. Carol Ellison, education editor at Home PC *magazine, picks her favorites, the best programs for kids 10 and under, which we've listed roughly by age group.*

THE PUTT-PUTT SERIES

Putt-Putt Joins the Parade, Putt-Putt Goes to the Moon, Putt-Putt's Fun Pack

Humongous Entertainment, $39.95 each, ages 3–8

■ Putt-Putt. a little purple car, is the all-time most popular computer character with preschoolers. Children move Putt-Putt around through various scenes, mazes, and activities.There is a lot of problem-solving, and most parents appreciate the message: you've got to be nice to others in order to get anywhere.

PLAYROOM

Broderbund Software, $49.95, ages 3–7

■ An adventure game for preschoolers in which kids maneuver Pepper Mouse through various doorways. Behind each is a new surprise and challenge: In one, kids can illustrate a monster, in another, design an ecosystem. Playroom also folds in fun counting and picture-recognition games.

LIVING BOOKS SERIES

Living Books Software, $49.95, ages 3–7

■ Living Books has been in the educational multimedia business from the start, and the company has perfected the art of creating kids' storybooks on CD-ROM. From "Grandma and Me" to "Aesop's Fables" to Dr. Seuss's tales, Living Books CDs are excellent: fun to play with, easy to use, and most important, wonderfully readable.

READER RABBIT SERIES

Reader Rabbit's Ready for Letters, Reader Rabbit 1, Reader Rabbit 2, Reader Rabbit 3, Reader Rabbit's Interactive Reading Journey, Reader Rabbit's Reading Development Library

The Learning Company, Ready for Letters $35, Reader Rabbit 1, 2, and 3, $35-$50, Reader Rabbit Journey, $99, Library, $45, ages 2–9

■ This is a series of four programs: In each, the child plays with Reader Rabbit, a reporter for *The Daily Skywriter,* its boss, editor Ed Word, and the rest of the staff of the newspaper. Most are reading programs, though Reader Rabbit 3 does start kids on writing. It is a nice program for two reasons. First, the protagonist is gender-neutral and kids don't seem compelled to assign one to it. Second, Reader Rabbit grows with the kids. In the first application, for example, kids learn the alphabet along with Reader Rabbit.

MILLIE'S MATHHOUSE

Edmark, $36.99, ages 2–6

■ These programs teach teeny-tinies about very basic math, reading, and science. Kids learn how to recognize numbers, shapes, sounds, and animal groups as cartoon characters guide the way. They've got animation, humor, music, and a lot of intelligence.

KID PIX

Broderbund Software, $49.95, ages 4–12

■ In this drawing program, you can choose from 20 brushes called "wacky brushes." One wacky brush, for example, leaves a trail of stars; another is a drippy brush, which leaves paint streaking down the screen. There is also a talking alphabet; kids punch a letter on the keyboard and the computer tells what letter it is.

KID WORKS

■ PARENT'S GUIDE

Davidson & Associates, $49.95, ages 4–10

■ Kid Works lets kids write, illustrate, print out, and listen to stories that they make up themselves; little kids can use icons, bigger kids can type. To draw, kids can choose from lots of different backgrounds (a farm, woods, underwater scene, a blank slate, and others).

THE TREASURE SERIES
Treasure MathStorm, Treasure Mountain, Treasure Cove, Treasure Galaxy
The Learning Company, $45 each, ages 5–9

■ In Treasure MathStorm a snowy storm has blown away all the treasures and put the crown in a deep freeze. To restore things to a state of normalcy, kids have to do math and logic problems. In Treasure Mountain, kids focus on reading, as well as math and thinking skills. Treasure Cove concentrates on reading, science, reasoning, and math. Treasure Galaxy is a cosmic math program that focuses on problem solving.

TREEHOUSE
Broderbund Software, $35, ages 6–10

■ A bunch of different games that kids like to do by themselves (parents are not allowed in the treehouse, remember?). Kids hone their reading skills, as well as learn about everything from money to

music—they can even stage their own play.

COUNTING ON FRANK
EA*Kids, $59.95, ages 7–12

■ This program was written to answer the question: "Why do we have to learn math?" Frank is a dog, whose adventures lead him to math problems. For example, Frank's friend Billy—a little boy—wonders what would happen if he were to grow twice as big as he is now. The program also shows kids how to use a calculator and how to make estimates.

OPERATION NEPTUNE
The Learning Company $35 DOS, $45 DOS CD, ages 8–12

■ This is an all-in-one action-adventure-math game. Kids have to use math and logic skills to protect the ocean from becoming polluted by the toxic chemicals that are emitted by a space capsule that has fallen into the sea.

CARMEN SANDIEGO SERIES
Where in the World is Carmen Sandiego? Where in the USA...? Where in Time...? Where in America's Past...? Where in Space...?
Broderbund Software World, $35-$50, ages 8 and up

■ Carmen Sandiego is a thief; kids play detective with the Acme Detective Agency, and their mission is to track down Carmen and her gang of henchmen, and then return the booty to its proper place. The games are packed with almanacs and travel guides, so kids have to do research to win the game, which they may sometimes resent. Kids are more likely to pick up historical factoids than learn about history, but they do learn how to use reference books. The games are a bit tough intellectually on eight-year-olds.

OREGON TRAIL, OREGON TRAIL II
MECC $49.95, ages 10 and up

■ The first Oregon Trail is the oldest game in the computing world. Basically, kids have to navigate the Oregon Trail, circa the 1800s, when the first pioneers journeyed on it. They start in St. Louis and head to the Pacific Northwest. It is a game of strategy and history. The players have to decide what they're going to purchase: how many guns, spare wagon wheels, what kind of food, medicine. They have the option of buying it now or later down the trail. Kids are confronted

HOW TO CHILDPROOF YOUR COMPUTER

Its easier than you think to keep kids away from your files

Sharing the home computer with your brood seems like a good idea, both financially and familially—until your seven-year-old deletes an important business report from your hard disk. There are, however, several inexpensive ways to prevent the "I didn't mean to do it" syndrome.

■ **HARDWARE SOLUTIONS:** A solid hardware solution to kid intervention is hard disk partitioning. If you're a computer whiz, you have probably done this already; otherwise, you're best off taking your computer to a good service store. Disk partitioning allows you to divide a single hard disk into several drives, assigning one to kids, the other to adults. When kids boot up the computer, they're automatically routed into the drive assigned to them; password protection prevents them from accessing the adult's space.

If you decide on this option, just make sure that you have a hard drive that is large enough to divide. A 400 to 500 MB drive can be divided in half, leaving adults enough hard disk space to run powerful applications, while still providing kids with enough power to run games; anything less may compromise functionality. For true division, you can buy two external hard drives: one for parents and one for kids.

■ **SOFTWARE SOLUTIONS:** Give your kids their own desktop software. Kid Desk, from Edmark, ☎ 800-426-8056, is a graphical interface—computerese for what appears on your computer screen after you turn it on—that looks like a child's desk. Like the Microsoft Windows or Macintosh desktop, Kid Desk displays icons for those applications that your children use, and identifies parents' territory with a single icon, which is password protected. If parents want to access their own applications from Kid Desk, they simply click on the adult icon, type in their secret code, and return to their own desktop interface.

Launch Pad, Berkeley Systems, ☎ 800-877-5535, works in the same way, but kids are given the option of selecting one of several desktop wallpaper designs: a spaceship, dinosaurs, a castle, a unicorn, or a creepy old haunted house. If you have a multimedia PC, Launch Pad runs neat features for kids, such as a talking clock and calculator, as well as a mini-recording studio that lets children record

with obstacles: breaking an axle, running out of food, running into bad weather. Often, they'll die from one or many causes (smallpox, starvation, an accident), which serves to instruct them on how to plan better for the next game. Oregon Trail II is similar, but kids can choose from 15 historical trails, including the Santa Fe.

STUDENT WRITING CENTER

The Learning Company, $60–$70 depending on system, ages 10 and up

■ This is a word processor designed for students. There is a journal-entry area that kids can password-protect from parents. It also has neat features that mimic adult programs. For instance, there is a feature that automatically formats a bibliography, but it instructs kids on what information needs to be in a bibliography. The spell-checker and grammar-checker are more rigorous than adult versions. The grammar-checker, for example, will ask kids to make decisions about which punctuation and syntax to use, explaining correct and incorrect responses. The new Student Writing and Research Center includes an abridged Compton's multimedia encyclopedia.

EXPERT LIST

ROAMING THROUGH THE CD-ROMS

Like miners to the gold rush, book publishers, game developers, Hollywood types, and even business application programmers are packing their wares into multimedia CDs. But just because the box says it's multimedia doesn't mean that it's good. Anyone with an idea, the right computer gear, and the $1.50 that it takes to cut a CD can market a multimedia product. The bottom line: For every hundred multimedia CDs, there might be one worth buying. To find the best ones, 38 PC Magazine staff members sorted through the proverbial haystack. Their picks are sorted into five groups: reference, home, rec room, coffee table, and office. (For the best software for kids, see "Software for Trendy Tots" on page 752.) The choices are listed alphabetically by title. Except when otherwise indicated, the list price is indicated. Mail-order houses and some retailers, of course, discount heavily.

REFERENCE

Here are dictionaries, encyclopedias, and other information-rich titles.

A.D.A.M. THE INSIDE STORY

A.D.A.M. Software Inc., estimated street price, $39

■ An easy-to-understand, fun-to-use multimedia tour of human anatomy, narrated by primogenitors Adam and Eve.

AMERICAN HERITAGE TALKING DICTIONARY

SoftKey International, $59.95

■ Based on *The American Heritage Dictionary of the English Language*, this volume can do what the print version can't: enunciate pronunciations. You can also search for definitions by typing in words, and add the CD to the menu of your Windows-based processor.

BEETHOVEN AND BEYOND

The Voyager Company, $24.95

■ A complete and beautifully organized multimedia

course on the composer's life, works, and place in history, as well as a survey of 19th-century Western music, which includes essays on other composers.

BERLITZ LIVE! SPANISH

Sierra On-Line, estimated street price, $110

■ Learn to speak survival-level Spanish by listening, repeating, and conversing in a series of well-organized lessons. Cultural insights, as well as a dictionary, are included.

BEYOND THE SAMBATYON: THE MYTH OF THE TEN LOST TRIBES

Creative Multimedia, estimated street price, $30

■ Created with the Museum of the Jewish Diaspora in Tel Aviv, this CD details the history of the famous fable and, documentary-style, tracks the origins of Jewish groups in every continent, using excellent photographs and a variety of primary sources.

THE COMPLETE MULTIMEDIA BIBLE

Compton's NewMedia, $49.95

■ Based on the King James version, this Bible packs a bit more pizzazz than the print version. The full text of the Old Testament and the New Testament is searchable by keyword and supplemented by videos, photos, and narration by James Earl Jones.

COMPTON'S INTERACTIVE ENCYCLOPEDIA, 1995 EDITION

Compton's NewMedia, estimated street price, $70 to $90

■ Combining 35,000 articles, over 7,000 photos, 80 videos, as well as maps, charts, and more than 14 hours of audio, this latest

■ EXPERT LIST

version of Compton's is the best yet.

FRANK LLOYD WRIGHT: PRESENTATION AND CONCEPTUAL DRAWINGS
Oxford University Press, $1,500

■ You'll need a powerful computer and a passion for the architect to appreciate this presentation, but if you do, you'll find in this CD the most complete compilation of Wright's works anywhere. It includes all of the drawings in the Frank Lloyd Wright archives and many from private collections.

HER HERITAGE, A BIOGRAPHICAL ENCYCLOPEDIA OF FAMOUS AMERICAN WOMEN
Cambrix Publishing, estimated street price, $29

■ With more than 1,000 biographies of American women of note, this CD offers enlightening entries—as well as short films—on its remarkable subjects.

LOST TREASURES OF THE WORLD WITH STAN GRIST,
Follgard CD Visions Inc., $49.95

■ Treasure-hunter Stan Grist gives tips on hunting and discusses some of his more exciting exploits in videos, text, and slideshows. Amateur archeologists can scour the 5,000 Treasures database, which lists the approximate sites of yet-to-be-discovered treasures.

MICROSOFT ENCARTA '95
Microsoft Corp., estimated street price, $100

■ Organized by category—physical science and technology, geography, history, and others—this version of Encarta is more comprehensive than its predecessor and easier to navigate. It has fabulous multimedia elements; includes a dictionary and a thesaurus.

MULTIMEDIA SPACE EXPLORER
Betacorp, $39.95

■ The complete history of NASA in a well-organized, visually stunning CD.

THE 1995 GROLIER MULTIMEDIA ENCYCLOPEDIA
Grolier Electronic Publishing, estimated street price, $89

■ It's not as easy to use as Encarta, but Grolier's CD is still remarkable and comprehensive. This latest version offers essay-like presentations on subjects such as The Artist in the Modern Era, Explorers, and Horizons of Discovery.

PC GLOBE MAPS 'N' FACTS
Broderbund Software Inc., estimated street price, $35

■ With new maps, charts, and statistical data, this latest version of the CD is a great homework-helper for kids ages 12 and older.

POWER JAPANESE 2.0
Bayware Inc., estimated street price, $165 to $199

■ In learning Japanese, hearing (and pronouncing) is everything. This CD provides excellent drilling and dialogue in well-designed audio lessons, as well as a word processor that lets students practice writing in Japanese characters.

THE RANDOM HOUSE UNABRIDGED ELECTRONIC DICTIONARY
Random House Reference and Electronic Publishing, $79

■ Powerful search tools, etymologies, illustrations, and word pronunciations make this latest version of the great dictionary even better than before.

THE ROSETTA STONE LEVEL 1A RUSSIAN; THE ROSETTA STONE POWERPAC
Fairfield Language Technologies. Level Ia Russian, $395; PowerPAC, $99

■ Level 1a Russian uses the submersion technique to teaching language—that is, you start learning Russian by listening, speaking, and associating words with pictures, instead of getting drilled-and-grilled. The most amazing part is that it really works. PowerPAC offers English, Spanish, German, Russian, and French, and teaches in much the same way.

3D ATLAS
ABC/EA Home Software, $79.95

■ From a spinning three-dimensional globe, you can zero in on any country to view maps, read population and trade sta-

■ EXPERT LIST

tistics, photographs, and other information.

THE 20TH CENTURY VIDEO ALMANAC
Mindscape Inc., $49.95

■ Spanning world history from 1890 to 1994, this CD captures many of the most important events of this century on video.

VIETNAM
Medio Multimedia, $59.95

■ A remarkably thorough and compelling study of the war and surrounding events and issues, this CD covers all points of view and includes the complete text of George Herring's *America's Longest War*.

FOR THE HOME

This section includes CDs covering home improvement, gardening, and leisure activities.

HOME PC LIBRARY; PC LIBRARY
Allegro New Media, $59.95 and $99.95, respectively

■ The multimedia compilation of answers to the most frequently asked questions, Home PC Library covers entertainment technology, hardware, home office issues, online services and more; PC Library covers the business market (spreadsheets, word processors, and more).

THE ART OF MAKING GREAT PASTRIES
Cambrix Publishing, estimated street price, $28

■ 101 recipes, along with videos on tips and techniques.

4 PAWS OF CRAB
Live Oak Multimedia Inc., $44.95

■ This Thai cookbook teaches you how to whip up everything from fresh Thai tofu soup with greens to stir-fried mushrooms in oyster sauce, with video demonstrations and cultural notes accompanying the recipes.

KITTENS TO CATS
Villa Crespo Software Inc., $49.95

■ A multimedia owner's manual for feline fanatics, Kittens to Cats covers training, behavior, health, grooming, nutrition, choosing a kitten, and more.

MARTIAL ARTS EXPLORER
FutureVision Multimedia Inc., $49.95

■ Part game, part research text, this title invites you to explore a fictional martial arts expert's collection and library on the nonfictional history, philosophy, and practice of these Eastern disciplines.

MICROSOFT AUTOMAP ROAD ATLAS 4.0
Microsoft Corp., estimated retail price, $39.95

■ Map out your trip from start to finish with this complete road atlas; the program automatically calculates your route (choose from scenic, fastest, shortest) and the time it will take you to travel. It also provides you with information on hotels/motels, rest areas, national parks, and historical sites that are along the way.

POPULAR MECHANIC'S NEW CAR BUYER'S GUIDE
Books That Work/Hearst New Media, $49.95

■ All the stats—including dealer costs, manufacturer's suggested retail price, options lists (with prices), engine and drivetrain specs, and more—on new cars and light trucks.

RAND MCNALLY TRIPMAKER
Rand McNally New Media, $79.95

■ A complete road-trip planner, this CD automatically maps out the best route according to your specifications; it also offers off-road attractions, including museums, shopping, historical sites, stuff for kids, and more.

3D HOME ARCHITECT CD-ROM
Broderbund Software Inc., estimated street price, $70

■ Re-do your kitchen, design your dream

■ EXPERT LIST

house—this CD is a powerful plotting and designing program that takes you through the entire process, including tips from *American HomeStyle Magazine* and 50 Home-Pro video clips.

TOTAL HEALTH—BODY AND MIND
SoftKey International, $79.95

■ It can't supply human encouragement, but this CD can assess your physical shape and dietary and nutritional deficits and get you started on a tailor-made weekly regimen.

UNDERSTANDING EXPOSURE: HOW TO SHOOT GREAT PHOTOGRAPHS
DÌAMAR Interactive Corp., $79.95 with companion book; CD-ROM only, $59.95

■ Expert Bryan Peterson teaches amateurs and pros alike about lens choice, film speed, aperture, shutter speed, and more.

FOR THE REC ROOM

Here are the hottest games and other forms of entertainment with little or no educational value.

BOB DYLAN: HIGHWAY 61 INTERACTIVE
Graphix Zone Inc., $59.95

■ A beautifully conceived tribute to the beatnik bard and his ballads.

CHUCK JONES' PETER AND THE WOLF
Time Warner Interactive, $29.95

■ Delightful animation, a classic score, and a time-honored tale make this CD a family favorite.

DARK FORCES
LucasArts Entertainment Co., estimated street price, $55

■ Everything you loved about Star Wars (compelling characters, complex plot, adventure, excellent music) is on this CD—and it's interactive.

DAZZELOIDS
The Voyager Co., $40

■ The "Dazzeloids" are the cartoon heroes of the two interactive storybooks on this title, and they're everything kids' characters should be: weird, wacky, funny, smart, musical, and ethical (not goody-goody).

DOOM II: HELL ON EARTH
GT Interactive Software/id Software, estimated street price, $39 to $49

■ The computer game to rule all computer games goes to the second level—and CD-ROM: It's more realistic, faster-paced, and filled with more gory details. (Cool!)

FLASH TRAFFIC CITY OF ANGELS
Time Warner Interactive, $29.95

■ You: wise-cracking FBI agent. Your mission: track down terrorists and disarm nuclear bomb. Our advice: for adults only.

JOHNNY MNEMONIC
Sony Imagesoft, estimated street price, $70

■ The cyberpunk hero stars in a game-cum-multimedia movie; super-cool effects and a full-throttle plot make this CD a good choice for anyone who thrives on overdrive.

MICROSOFT CINEMANIA '95
Microsoft Corp., estimated street price, $60

■ Quite simply, this is the best movie database on CD-ROM, with reviews by critics Leonard Maltin, Roger Ebert, and Pauline Kael, and video clips, sound bites, and cinema trivia.

MICROSOFT COMPLETE NBA BASKETBALL
Microsoft Corp., estimated street price, $50

■ This is not a game, sports fans—it is, however, a terrific collection of NBA stats, historic moments, and video clips of memorable games.

MONTY PYTHON'S COMPLETE WASTE OF TIME
7th Level Inc., estimated street price, $50

■ Marvelously pointless and hilarious, this CD belongs in the drives of Monty Python devotees.

MTV'S CLUB DEAD
Viacom New Media, estimated street price, $60

■ A role-playing game, this CD stars you as Sam Frost, virtual reality specialist, on an assignment to solve a high-tech crime. Bond-style gadgets and unexpected plot

■ EXPERT LIST

twists will keep you absorbed in alternate reality for hours.

NASCAR RACING
Papyrus Design Group Inc., estimated street price, $55 to $65

■ Rubber-burners, rev those engines: choose from nine tracks and race for one day or map out the whole season.

NHL HOCKEY '95
Electronic Arts, $59.95

■ Every hard-hitting detail has been perfected to make this game as realistic as you can get without full-body padding.

RELENTLESS: TWINSEN'S ADVENTURES
Electronic Arts, $59.95

■ Help little Twinsen save the world from the nefarious Dr. Funfrock. A cleverly designed control panel lets you change Twinsen's mental disposition as well as his movements.

THE RESIDENTS FREAK SHOW
The Voyager Company, $49.95

■ Characters from circus sideshows tell their stories through the songs, photo albums, and video clips of the underground rock group, The Residents.

SIMCITY 2000 CD COLLECTION
Maxis, estimated street price, $70

■ You are the mayor of a major metropolis and must manage everything from natural disasters to urban planning. You'll have your hands full: If you're not judicious and attentive, your voting public may riot and impeach you.

SPORTS ILLUSTRATED MULTIMEDIA ALMANAC, 1995 EDITION
StarPress Multimedia, estimated street price, $40

■ All the stats, highlights, low-points, and events from the last year and a half in sports.

STAR TREK: THE NEXT GENERATION INTERACTIVE TECHNICAL MANUAL
Simon and Schuster Interactive, $69.95

■ The ultimate trekkie tour of the Enterprise: Explore Captain's Quarters, Ten Forward, the Bridge, the Ready Room, and key hulls of the mothership.

TRANSPORT TYCOON
MicroProse Software, estimated street price, $58

■ As the president of a major transportation company, you've got to develop and maintain roads, rails, airports, bridges, and tunnels within budget and for serious profit.

UNDER A KILLING MOON
Access Software Inc., $99.95

■ You play down-and-out P.I. Tex Murphy in a script that runs like the best tongue-in-cheek, slap-stick film noir movies, and since each character in the game is played by a real-life actor (including Margot Kidder and James Earl Jones), you really feel as though you're in one.

U.S. NAVY FIGHTERS
Electronic Arts, $59.95

■ Complete with high-flying action, flight simulation, and copilots who swear like sailors. Puts you in the cockpit for the virtual ride of your life.

WARREN MILLER'S SKI WORLD
Multicom Publishing, $49.95

■ Ace skiing instructor Warren Miller shows instructional videos for all levels, clips of the pros on the slopes, and a guide to the world's top ski resorts.

WING COMMANDER III
Origin Systems, estimated street price, $55 to $70

■ Fight alien invaders to save the Earth and command dozens of death-defying flying missions; the cast includes you (played by Mark Hamill) and a host of other stars.

XPLORA 1 PETER GABRIEL'S SECRET WORLD
Interplay Productions, estimated street price, $60

■ One of the most ingenious implementations of

■ EXPERT LIST

multimedia yet, this CD is a coup for Gabriel fans: It includes full-length videos, discographies, interviews with the musician and his collaborators, and footage from his performances.

FOR THE COFFEE TABLE

This section includes multimedia titles that would also make wonderful, large-format, hard-cover picture books. (Indeed, some of them were books before they were CDs.)

AMERICAN VISIONS
Creative Labs Inc., $39.95

■ A tour of the Roy R. Neuberger collection of 20th-century art, with information and photos of the artists, the collector's commentary, and discussion of the historical context for the works.

ANTARCTICA
Cambrix Publishing, estimated street price, $29

■ The white continent, in all its icy beauty and ecological complexity.

A BRIEF HISTORY OF TIME
Creative Labs Inc., $59.95

■ The best-selling book on astronomy and physics is beautifully illustrated and explored; author Stephen W. Hawking narrates.

THE DEAD SEAS SCROLLS REVEALED
Logos Research Systems, $59.95

■ More a compelling documentary than a CD-ROM, this title investigates the history and meaning of the artifacts using over an hour of video clips and three-dimensional animation that lets you zoom in on the scrolls.

GREAT ARTISTS
Attica Cybernetics, $59

■ Featuring 40 artists whose works hang in the National Gallery in London, this title explores the work and method of great European painters; search for definitions of artistic terms by clicking on them.

MATERIAL WORLD: A GLOBAL FAMILY PORTRAIT
StarPress Multimedia, estimated street price, $40

■ The consummate multimedia coffee-table book, this title is the collaborative effort of 16 photojournalists who document the lives, rituals, and possessions of families in 13 countries.

PEOPLE WEEKLY: 20 AMAZING YEARS OF POP CULTURE
The Voyager Co., $29.95

■ The life and times of the stars and local heroes, as covered by the chronicler of pop culture since 1974.

SAFARI
Medio Multimedia Inc., $59.95

■ Narrated by wildlife photographer and writer Jonathan Scott, this CD covers Kenya's Masai Mara National Reserve in living color and glorious detail.

SMALL BLUE PLANET: THE CITIES BELOW; SMALL BLUE PLANET: THE REAL PICTURE ATLAS, VERSION 2.0.
Cambrix Publishing, estimated street price, $29 and $39, respectively

■ The first CD takes you above America's largest cities for a bird's-eye view; the second features satellite photographs of geographical hot spots.

THE ULTIMATE FRANK LLOYD WRIGHT
Byron Preiss Multimedia Company Inc./Microsoft Corp., $59.95

■ An introductory survey of the master architect, this CD combines biographical and historical information, photographs, videos, and sound.

THE WAY THINGS WORK
DK Multimedia, estimated street price, $50

■ David Macaulay's classic book comes to CD-ROM, with animations and illustrations so clear and engaging that it makes learning about physics, electricity, and other lofty scientific principles fun.

WORLD VISTA ATLAS
Applied Optical Media Corp., $49.95

■ Based on the latest Rand McNally maps, statistics, and photos, and music samples from the Smithsonian's Folkways Collection, this atlas provides a complete—and stunning—worldview.

■ EXPERT LIST

FOR THE OFFICE

You'll find all types of business-enhancing multimedia here.

CAMBIUM SOUND CHOICE, VOLUME 2
Cambium Development Inc., $69

■ This collection packs an assortment of musical sound bites for professional business presentations. Original recordings, the 29 samples range from hard rock to classical.

COREL GALLERY 2
Corel Corp., $99

■ A library of professional clip-art, this CD offers 500 photos, 500 fonts, and 50 percent more clip-art than the previous version.

COREL STOCK PHOTO LIBRARY
Corel Corp., $995

■ 20,000 royalty-free photos on over 200 subjects.

HP SUPPORT ASSISTANT
Hewlett-Packard Co., $395 per year

■ For the office that is heavily endowed with Hewlett-Packard equipment, this subscription-service CD includes detailed technical support for printers, PCs, servers, and network products.

MICROSOFT DEVELOPER'S NETWORK CD
Microsoft Corp.,$195 (Level I), $495 (Level II)

■ Must-buys for Microsoft developers, these two disks contain volumes of

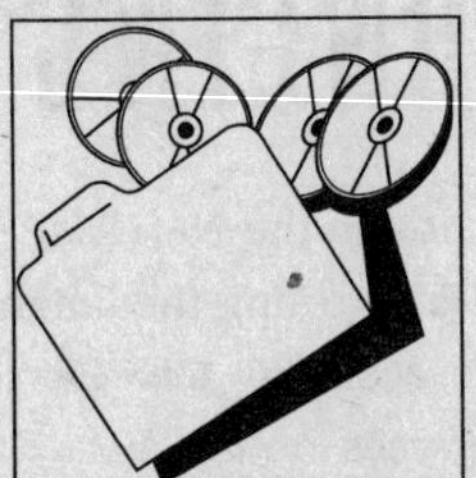

technical information collected from books, magazines, and online services.

MICROSOFT TECHNET
Microsoft Corp.,$299 (single-user license), $699 (unlimited user license); updated CD released monthly

■ A great subscription service for tech departments, two disks answer all technical questions about Microsoft products and include patches and updates for software.

MULTIMEDIA BUSINESS 500, RELEASE 2
Allegro New Media, $49.95

■ Based on the 1995 edition of *Hoover's Handbook of American Business*, this CD compiles corporate profiles and relevant financial information on 500 top U.S. companies; with a subscription to Prodigy, you can link to current stock quotes.

MULTIMEDIA MBA SMALL BUSINESS EDITION
SoftKey International, $149.95

■ A collection of information, videos, slide shows, and photographs, this CD offers advice of interest to small-business owners.

MULTIMEDIA TYPING INSTRUCTOR
Individual Software Inc., estimated street price, $29

■ This CD teaches typing in the kind of environment on-the-fly business folk are most familiar with: an airport lobby. Once you've described your typing skills in a passport, you're moved to a simulated airport seat to begin your lesson; the program tracks your progress, critiquing your speed and accuracy.

PHONEDISC POWERFINDER '95
Digital Directory Assistance Inc., $249

■ With 90 million listings and powerful searching capabilities, finding a number on this CD is easier than dialing information.

PHOTODISC SIGNATURE SERIES
PhotoDisc Inc., estimated street price, $299 per CD

■ Several hundred first-rate photographs are arranged by subjects such as "Colors" and "Children of the World"; you can search for an image by keyword.

SELECT PHONE
Pro CD Inc.,$299

■ Like PhoneDisc, this volume is an extensive electronic dialing directory; the company also offers other operator-like CDs, including Free Phone (800 directory), Canada Phone, and Home Phone.

ONLINE

CHOOSING AN ONLINE SERVICE

Each option has its own distinct flavor, population, and price

Joining the online community can be like moving into a city about six times the size of Manhattan: With an estimated 25 million people now working, talking, and traveling in cyberspace, how do you carve out a niche for yourself, meet the people you want to meet, and get the information that you need? Like any neighborhood, each online service has its own distinct flavor, population, services, and price range.

After deciding on the features you want—and what you can afford—you can start browsing. For business use, *PC Magazine* gives CompuServe Information Services its "Editors' Choice," praising the service for its "breadth and depth of forums, databases, files, and services." Compuserve now offers connections to Internet news groups, which can be useful. But if you are after a family-oriented online service, you might want to consider Prodigy Information Service, which the editors of *PC World* recommend for its "good financial conferences, as well as a host of domestic conferences on subjects such as cooking, child care, and shopping." Its other virtues include an interactive ESPN link and services for kids.

America Online generally gets rave reviews from the popular press, but trade publications don't rate it as highly. It is the online choice if fun is what you're after: chat forums with people from around the country and transcontinental computer games.

Delphi Internet Service, a comparatively small service, provides inexpensive Internet access and lets its members create their own forums on any subject they choose, though it's not as user-friendly as some of the other services. Delphi also offers "R-rated celebrity" images that you can download. GEnie is also relatively small, but *PC Week* reports that it "offers access to a solid package of business services" (with access to Dow Jones News/Retrieval Service), as well as an array of family and hobby forums. And new services are popping up all the time. Apple's new eWorld (the Macintosh connect to the online world) has a friendly interface based on the metaphor of a town—for example,

THE BIG FIVE ONLINE SERVICES

What you get online depends on what you want. Here's a comparison guide of the big five online services by pricing, hardware, and software requirements, and what each has to offer:

	America Online	CompuServe	Delphi	GEnie	Prodigy
☎	800-827-6364	800-848-8199	800-695-4005	800-638-9636	800-776-3449
PRICING					
Basic monthly fee	$9.95	$9.95	$10.00	$8.95	$9.95
HARDWARE/SOFTWARE					
Max. access speed (bits per second)	28.8	28.8	14.4	14.4	28.8
DOS support	YES	YES	NO	YES	YES
Microsoft Windows support	YES	YES	YES	YES	YES
Macintosh support	YES	YES	NO	YES	YES
BASIC FEATURES					
Searchable full-text magazine databases	1	8	0	1	0
Searchable full-text newspaper databases	4	5	2	6	9
Health information databases	3	7	8	5	1
Financial Services	I	I	I	I	I
Official Airline Guide (OAG)	I	I	I	I	0
Entertainment information databases	37	14	15	30	6
TOPICAL FORUMS*					
Approximate total	280	900	250	250	175
Health	5	8	8	4	2
Hobbies	20	50	18	6	5
Social and political	16	4	17	5	1
Professional	13	20	17	10	5
Education	16	7	9	4	3

* Numbers subject to frequent change.

SOURCE: Individual services.

click on the mail truck to get your e-mail, or click on the mall to go shopping. The new 800-pound gorilla is Microsoft's new online service, which is planned for launch in the summer of '95 at the same time that the new version of Windows—Windows 95—is introduced. And for the truly adventurous (and technologically inclined) there's always the Internet (see "A Beginner's Guide to the Net," page 764).

So, peruse the market: All the companies listed on this page will send you free information packets on request (see "The Big Five Online Services," above). Then, after looking over the material, set up an account with one of the online services, buy and install a modem (see "How Modems Work," page 737), and start exploring your new digs and meeting your neighbors.

EXPERT Q&A

A BEGINNER'S GUIDE TO THE NET

If Columbus were alive today, he would be exploring this new world

Think of it as a vast new kingdom. You get there through your computer and your modem. But once you've arrived, an enormous landscape is spread out before you. When you go, what roads you take, what winding paths you follow, and when you return is all up to you. We asked Rick Ayre, executive editor of *PC Magazine*, the leading trade journal, for a background briefing about how to get started on a great adventure in cyberspace.

■ What is the Internet?

The Internet is a mass of computer networks that are linked globally. It was originally started by university professors and the military about 20 years ago to share information and talk with each other over their computers, instead of by mail or phone. Today, more than 20 million people from all kinds of backgrounds are using it. There are still a huge number of academic forums, but there are also tons of nonacademic topics. There is a list for people who want to talk about the TV show "The Simpsons," for example. There are also more resources—the Library of Congress is on the Internet, as are most university libraries in the United States, and many abroad. You can exchange information with people from around the world, from Hollywood to Hong Kong.

■ Who runs the Internet?

No one. There is no "Internet Corp.," per se. Instead, it's a massive, community-maintained system created by the people who participate in it.

This is a double-edged sword. On the one hand, there's no place or no one you can go to and file a complaint if you're having a hard time, if you feel the information is disorganized, or if someone is acting up—there simply are no rules on the Internet. On the other hand, this means you can say anything you want, you have access to a tremendous amount of information and you can, if you choose, provide information of your own.

This is not to say that there isn't a mode of decorum or etiquette on the Net, as it's called; there is. But it's something that you learn by experimenting and having conversations with people in different "areas," just as you would in real life. Think of the Internet as a huge city encompassing many neighborhoods and cultures; while there is a way that one behaves in a big city in general, one also modifies one's manner and manners to suit individual neighborhoods.

■ How does one connect to the Internet?

There are a number of ways. First, obviously, you need a modem and a free phone line to plug into it. Then you need to connect to a network that is connected to the Internet (see box): These are called access, or service, providers. Most universities, and more and more companies, have direct connections to one of these access providers already. If you're a student or an employee at a fair-sized company, just call up the internal computer services department and get them to give you an Internet account.

If you are a single user, you can get an account with a dial-up provider—there are hundreds of these around the country. They usually charge you a flat rate of about $25 per month, with unlimited online time. They will give you an account, which lets your modem dial-up their computer, which is already connected to the Internet.

The third way—and probably the best way for beginners—is to access the Internet through a gateway on one of the big on-line services like America Online, CompuServe, GEnie, Prodigy, or Delphi. Basically, all you do is call up one of these companies' toll-free numbers and ask it to send its software. Most of them have a free trial period, which gives you time to explore what the service has to offer, as well as time to investigate the Internet.

■ What is the difference between the Internet and an online service?

Remember, the Internet is owned by no one; online services are major corporations. They might use the same kind of technology as the Internet to link people's computers together, but they are self-contained entities.

Think of online services as private clubs or associations: You've got to pay dues and fees, and in return, you get to use their facilities, socialize with members, and take advantage of their services. Those services might include special groups for children, access to the Dow Jones news wire, a forum hosted by Rush Limbaugh, or access to the Internet. Some services have more limited Net access than others. For example, there are a number of pornographic groups on the Net; some services may filter these out, so their members can't access them. Generally, the big online services try to give access to those Internet groups they think their members will be interested in.

■ How is the information on the Internet organized?

Well, it is and it isn't. The Internet is sort of an information anarchy. But there are some organizing principles. Electronic mail is the chief way of communicating on the Internet. Everyone has a different address, just like a house or an apartment, that describes who and where you are (see "Getting Caught in the Web," page 766). If you want to regularly receive and e-mail messages on a particular topic, you sign up for mailing lists, which are the addresses of people who have similar interests—anything from neurobiology to "Beavis and Butt-head." Then, there are the UseNet News groups, which are like bulletin board services, and there are about 4,500 of them. News and communications on everything from business in Japan to feminist social groups are UseNet News groups.

SIGNING UP FOR THE INFOBAHN

You can't just ring up the Internet and hop on. You need an account to gain access to the information superhighway. Here are your options.

■ PERMANENT CONNECTION: Your computer is connected directly to a network that is actually a part of the Internet, so you don't even have to have your modem call a number to get connected. Since these accounts are designed to accommodate a lot of users, and they are very expensive (upward of $10,000 a year), usually only big companies and universities have this type of account.

■ DIAL-IN CONNECTION: Also called a SLIP (Serial Line Internet Protocol) or PPP (Point-to-Point Protocol), dial-in connections are the next best thing to a permanent connection. Your modem dials up an Internet server directly.

■ DIAL-UP CONNECTION: Your modem dials up the computer of a service provider that has a permanent connection. It's kind of a twice-removed connection to the Internet—you're connected to a computer that's connected to a network that's connected to the Internet.

■ MAIL CONNECTIONS: This account is only for e-mail. If you are a member of CompuServe, America Online, or any of the computer bulletin boards that are connected to the Internet, you already have such an account.

THE INTERNET

GETTING CAUGHT IN THE WEB

Lost in cyberspace? Here's a tool that can help you find your way

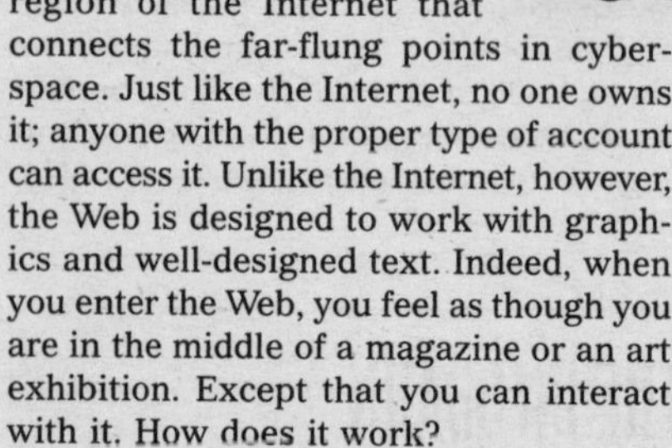

You've discovered the Internet (see previous story) but you feel lost in cyberspace. So many choices. What's a budding cybernaut to do? Try the World Wide Web—usually just called "the Web," a growing region of the Internet that connects the far-flung points in cyberspace. Just like the Internet, no one owns it; anyone with the proper type of account can access it. Unlike the Internet, however, the Web is designed to work with graphics and well-designed text. Indeed, when you enter the Web, you feel as though you are in the middle of a magazine or an art exhibition. Except that you can interact with it. How does it work?

Just as each person on the Internet has an address, so does each "site." When you type in a site address, your modem transports you to a "home page," the welcome mat of a Web site. The home page looks like a page in an illustrated book, and it usually offers a list of features. Key words and images on the home page are highlighted in color type (called hypertext). By clicking on a hypertext word or image, you're transported to a new page in the site (or to another site altogether), which provides more information about the topic that that word or image describes.

For example, let's say you enter the address for Pathfinder, the Web site of Time Warner. You will be transported to Pathfinder's home page, which offers a menu box containing symbols (or icons) for all the magazines the company has launched on the Web. Click on the *People Weekly* icon, and you go from the Pathfinder home page to that of *People*. Scrolling through the table of contents, you see the name "O.J. Simpson" highlighted; click on it and your screen displays the magazine's latest update on the athlete's murder trial. Within the article, other names may be highlighted. If you click on them, you will be transported to articles covering those personalities, or you may be transported to another site altogether, such as a computer bulletin board devoted to discussing the trial. Where you go on the Web depends entirely on what you click on. Here is a list of what you'll need for traveling in the Web.

■ **A COMPUTER THAT HANDLES GRAPHICS:** If you want to get the most out of your Web travels, it's best to have a computer that can handle graphics and hypertext. For that reason, your interface (also called an operating system) should be graphical. All Macintosh computers have graphical interfaces; graphical interfaces for PCs include Microsoft Windows or OS/2/ Warp. (To learn more about operating systems, see page 741.)

■ **A SPEEDY MODEM:** Since it can take a while for big graphics to make their way across phone lines, you're best off with a modem that can process quickly; get a modem that runs at 14.4 kbps or higher. (For more information about modems, see page 737.)

■ **A SLIP OR PPP ACCOUNT:** To access the Web, you need a special, turbo-powered type of Internet account; these cost more than regular accounts (usually about $10–$15 more per month). Tell your Internet provider that you'd like add SLIP (Serial Line Internet Protocol) or PPP (Point-to-Point Protocol) to your account.

■ **A BROWSER:** This is special software that lets you access, view, and search for sites on the Web. Browsers are available as shareware—meaning that they can be downloaded free or for a nominal charge from the Internet.

E-MAIL

THE ONLINE POSTAL SERVICE

Forget licking envelopes. Here's how to zap messages to your pals

Most people go online to talk, and since you can't hear anyone in cyberspace (not yet, anyway), the way most people "talk" is through e-mail. Short for electronic mail, e-mail is exactly what it sounds like: letters that you write, send, and read from your computer. E-mail has at least two things to recommend it: it's fast and cheap.

"Messages can be delivered within seconds, so you don't have to wait a week or two while your letter is being delivered to France or Japan or wherever," writes Peter Kent, author of *The Complete Idiot's Guide to the Internet* (Alpha Books, $19.95). "You don't have to worry about time zones, figuring out exactly when your friend or colleague is getting up, to make a call. Also, you can respond whenever you want to." The cost is often cheaper than sending a message by mail, and it's almost always cheaper than placing a phone call.

Like regular mail, e-mail has its own protocols. "The Internet is a massive global network," Kent writes, "so you have to be very specific—sometimes even more specific than you would be in addressing a letter—in telling the Net where you want your message sent."

Your address is made up of two parts: your log-in name (whatever name you type in to get online) and your domain's name (where your computer is located on the Internet). These two segments are separated by an @ sign. Consider the following example: *sgthomas@echonyc.com.* The first part, sgthomas, is the log-in name; echonyc.com is the domain name. If you're trying to give somebody this address over the phone, you'd say "S.G. Thomas at echo NYC dot com."

Commercial online services or e-mail services work slightly differently. Here's the rundown of some of the bigger ones:

- **COMPUSERVE:** Members are assigned numbers. Find addressee's number, then type: *number@compuserve.com*
- **PRODIGY:** *loginname@prodigy.com*
- **AMERICA ONLINE:** *loginname@aol.com*
- **GENIE:** *loginname@genie.geis.com*
- **MCIMAIL:** *number@mcimail.com*

EXPERT SOURCES

LOST IN CYBERSPACE?

An old-fashioned book may be your best bet. Two of our favorites:

THE INTERNET DIRECTORY
Eric Braun, Ballantine Books, 1994, $25

■ Braun takes a fairly technical approach to navigating the Net, with a close look at news services, library catalogs, gopher sites, and useful custom document retrieval systems.

THE INTERNET YELLOW PAGES
Harley Hahn and Rick Stout, McGraw Hill, 1995, $29.95

■ With entries that range from the bizarre ("The Jihad to Destroy Barney on the Web") to the dryly utilitarian ("Russian Swear Words and Algebra Assistance"), this is an accessible road map to even the most obscure exits.

TECH TALK

LEARNING THE LANGUAGE ONLINE

A glossary of online terms and symbols that'll get you fluent in no time

Talking in cyberspace is not impersonal; you just have to know how to speak the language. People express emotions online with "emoticons," symbols that denote happiness, sadness, anger, and other garden-variety, as well as complex, feelings. Abbreviations are short cuts for commonly used online idioms: slang, in other words. Online etiquette requires knowing the language; you would be well-advised to learn the following emoticons and abbreviations before you go online, just as you would study a bit of useful French before you travel to France.

FREQUENTLY USED ABBREVIATIONS

word Asterixes that flank a word in the same way that quotation marks are used for emphasis in lieu of underlining or boldfacing.

<bg> Big grin.

<g> or <G> Grin.

AFKB Away from keyboard.

BTW By the way.

f2f Face to face, used when you're referring to meeting an online friend in person, or when you'd like to.

FAQ Frequently Asked Questions (see below).

IMHO In my humble opinion.

IMNSHO In my not so humble opinion.

IOW In other words.

IRL In real life.

ITRW In the real world.

LOL Laughing out loud.

MorF? Male or female? Used when your online name is gender-neutral.

OTF On the floor (laughing).

RTFM Read the f***ing manual, usually in response to a question you could have figured out on your own.

WRT With regard to.

YMMV Your mileage may vary.

FREQUENTLY USED TERMS

Browser—Software, such as Mosaic or Netscape, for PC Windows- or Mac-users that allows one to point and click one's way around the World Wide Web instead of using UNIX commands. (See page 768.)

Bulletin board service (BBS)—Cheaper than major online services, BBSes are generally run by a small number of people as a hobby, bringing together people who share a common interest; most are regional. Generally, you join a BBS by paying an annual fee (between $30 to $50 a year), as well as an hourly online fee (35¢ to $2.50 an hour). To find lists of BBSes (there are thousands of them), consult your local computer users' group, a computer store, or magazines such as *Boardwatch Magazine*, ☎ 303-973-4222, or *Computer Shopper*, ☎ 212-503-3500.

Frequently Asked Questions (FAQ)—Electronic handbooks filed at most Usenet newsgroups that answer most questions you'll have about that site. Read them before you participate to avoid getting flamed.

Finger—An Internet tool that gives you information on the identity (name, online location, last log-in) of another Internet user.

Flame—An inflammatory statement that is often rude, and occasionally crude. Flames are common on online services and the Internet. Newcomers sometimes are flamed for ignoring "netiquette." When two or more people send flames back and forth over a period of days, it's considered a "flame war."

Gopher—A search tool that helps you find files, services, and sites on the Internet by listing them in menu form. People at the University of Minnesota developed the software, so they got to name it (after their mascot).

■ COMMONLY EXPRESSED EMOTICONS

Here are some codes for getting your point across in cyberspace conversations

:-)
Smile; happy; "I'm joking."

:-(
Frown; sadness; "Bummer."

:(or :)
Variations of :-) or :-(

:-D
Big, delighted grin.

;-)
Wink; denotes pun or sly joke.

:-P
Sticking out your tongue.

:-O
Yelling, or completely shocked.

%-)
Confused but happy; drunk or under influence of controlled substances.

:-|
Can't decide how to feel; no feelings either way.

:'-(
Crying.

:'-)
Crying happy tears.

:-] or :-}
Sarcastic smile.

:-\
Mixed feelings, but mostly happy.

:-/
Mixed, but mostly sad.

:-()
Can't (or won't) stop talking.

%-(
Confused and unhappy.

[] or {}
Hug.

* Kiss.

{{{***}}}
Hugs and kisses.

:-&
Tongue-tied.

:-X
Lips are sealed.

:-)~ Drooling.

|-O
Yawning or snoring.

B-)
User wears horn-rimmed glasses.

:-#
User wears braces.

-:-)
User has a mohawk.

+-:-)
User is the Pope or holds some Christian office.

C=:-)
User is a chef.

Home page—The reception area for World Wide Web sites (see below). A home page welcomes you, lists the site's features and areas, and gives you a menu of choices that you can access.

Hypertext—Highlighted text in a file that is linked electronically to another file. Point and click on a word, and a new file pops up. Hypertext is the primary means of navigating the World Wide Web (see below).

Internet Relay Chat (IRC)—Instead of exchanging messages via e-mail, this tool lets you talk in "real time" with people. It's a typed, instead of spoken, conversation.

Lurk—To read posts in a Usenet newsgroup (see below) for a time without posting—virtually listening in on conversations without participating in them. Lurking is encouraged when you first join a newsgroup to get a sense of the atmosphere and conversations, but if you lurk for too long, you may inspire suspicion and get flamed.

Telnet—This nifty tool lets you log onto various sites or services on the Internet and use their computers—and the games, databases, files, and programs—as if they were on your own computer. Telnet systems can be public or private.

Usenet newsgroups—The group of over 7,000 Internet discussion groups, whose topics range from Elvis to toxic waste to computer programming.

World Wide Web (WWW)—This tool is like Gopher, only it's more sophisticated. You can search globally for articles, services, databases—for the most part, whatever you like—by pointing and clicking through hypertext menus.

POTPOURRI

WHO'S GOT THE BEST INFO

Where to find the good stuff about investing, health, kids, and shopping

Everywhere you turn these days, you hear how much information is available online. There's a lot out there but is it any good? We took a hard look at the offerings of the three major online services—Compuserve, Prodigy, and America Online—and the Internet in several areas of keen interest—investing, health, shopping, and children. Here are our findings:

INVESTING

Don't fire your stockbroker just yet. Online investing services can't replace the expertise of a professional investor, but they can help teach you how to manage and invest your money effectively. You can bank, track stocks and mutual funds, research companies, keep up on insider industry gossip, and even trade online. America Online's offerings come standard with a paid subscription to the service; they are also the most basic. CompuServe provides the most comprehensive investment services, but some are "extended services" (there is an extra charge for using them). Prodigy, the close runner-up, also offers basic and pay-to-use services.

AMERICA ONLINE

■ **STOCK INFORMATION:** StockLink (click on "Quotes & Portfolios" in the Personal Finance menu) provides the current or closing price, the change during the day, the day's low and open, yesterday's close, volume, 52-week high and low, and the price-to-earnings ratio. Just enter the stock's symbol, and the entire quote pops up (if you don't know the symbol, you can click on a button that says "Lookup Symbol" to get it). By clicking on the Hoover's company profiles button, for example, you can get more information about the company. If you want to track a stock that you own, or one that you're just interested in following, StockLink lets you add it to your electronic portfolio. A certified financial planner and investment advisers oversee several financial advice forums for amateurs.

■ **MUTUAL FUNDS INFORMATION:** The Morningstar Mutual Fund Analysis lets you research over 4,000 funds. You also can pull up Morningstar's "Top 25 Overall Mutual Funds" to help you pick one that's right for you. (See "The 140 Top Mutual Funds," page 39.)

■ **ONLINE TRADING:** Click on the TradePlus Gateway icon, and you're zipped to the real-world trading arena. TradePlus Gateway connects you to E*Trade, one of the oldest computerized stock trading services in the country. Once on E*Trade, you have access to the New York Stock Exchange (NYSE), NASDAQ's national and over the counter (OTC) markets, and other regional exchanges.

■ **MARKET NEWS:** Located in the Market News & Indicators section, "Market Briefs" gives you an overview of the day's markets, including the NYSE Composite Index and the Dow Jones Industrial averages.

■ **BUSINESS NEWS:** AOL's Financial Newsstand offers business news from the *Chicago Tribune*, *New York Times*, *Worth* magazine, *Investor's Business Daily*, *Business Week*, and more.

COMPUSERVE

■ **STOCK INFORMATION:** As with AOL's StockLink, features like Issues/Symbol Lookup, Select Quotes, and Basic Quotes enable you to look up company symbols and get a complete listing of stocks, bonds, and securities. You also can set up a sample portfolio to track stocks.

■ **MUTUAL FUNDS INFORMATION:** The Fund Watch Online service tracks the performance of mutual funds and is managed by the editors of *Money Magazine*. You can follow over 1,900 mutual funds, searching for information by name or symbol. You also can specify your criteria, and the service will track down appropriate funds.

■ **INVESTMENT ANALYSIS:** CompuServe's Investment analysis feature provides you with information on more than 10,000 companies.

■ **MARKET QUOTES/HIGHLIGHTS:** This service offers Current Market Snapshot (a look at the day's Dow Jones Industrials, Standard & Poor's 500 Index, NASDAQ Composite, London Gold Fix, and the rate of the dollar against the yen, deutsche mark, and pound); Historical Stock/Fund Pricing (daily, weekly, or monthly prices on securities listed for the past 12 years); Highlights—Previous Day (from NYSE, AE, and OTC markets); and Commodity Markets (access to several databases that provide historical information on commodities performance).

■ **ONLINE INVESTING:** E*Trade Securities, Quick & Reilly, and Spear Rees & Company are discount brokerage firms available through CompuServe, whose fees are lower online than off-line. Some of them will allow you to do your own trading.

■ **BUSINESS NEWS:** Business Database Plus, available for about $15 per hour, plus $1.50 per article retrieved, is a database that includes the full-text articles from over 500 business and trade publications.

■ **INVESTMENT ADVICE:** CompuServe's Financial Forums are a good place to ask a question. These discussion groups have members both novice and expert in finance and investing.

■ **FINANCIAL SOFTWARE:** You can download free software from the Financial Software Library, whose holdings range from mortgage calculators to a variety of recordkeeping packages.

PRODIGY

■ **STOCK AND MUTUAL FUND INFORMATION:** Quote Track lets you create and track your own portfolio. You can create multiple tracks, each with up to 50 securities. The Company News feature, which is linked to Quote Track, gives you current business news, and Company Reports provide profile information. In addition to Quote Track, Prodigy also offers Trade Line, managed by *Investment Dealer's Digest*, which includes historical trading information over a five-year period.

■ **INVESTMENT ADVICE:** For high-level analysis (and $14.95 a month), check with Strategic Investor, a service managed by *Market Guide*. Wall Street Edge ($19.95 a month) offers the combined wisdom of several hundred insider newsletters, magazines, and research organizations.

HEALTH

There are reams of health information online—from medical reference books to discussion groups, whose members not only exchange health tips but also upload useful articles and information that they've researched.

AMERICA ONLINE

■ **THE BETTER HEALTH & MEDICAL FORUM** (*keyword: HEALTH*) offers the Home Medical Guide, containing information on diseases, disorders, and treatments. The forum also features discussion groups, such as: Lifestyles and Wellness; Mental Health and Addictions; Human Sexuality; Patients' Rights; Health Reform and Insurance; Seniors' Health and Caregiving; and Alternative Medicine. AOL also offers Health News, a database of health-related articles, as well as Health Focus, where journalists and lay folk alike share articles, insights, and information on medical issues.

COMPUSERVE

■ **HEALTHNET** (*Go HNT-289*) offers the HealthNet Reference Library, which is similar to AOL's Better Health and Medical Forum. In the Health/Fitness section, CompuServe offers the online version of the *The Consumer Reports Complete Drug Reference*, as well as several discussion groups whose topics range from Attention Deficit Disorder to 12-Step Programs. Another feature of the section, Health DataBase Plus is a professional medical periodicals library; you can search for articles by entering keywords, and download matches for $1.50 apiece.

PRODIGY

■ **HEALTH/FITNESS:** Prodigy offers several bulletin boards devoted to health issues

(Health & Lifestyles, Medical Support, Crohn's & Colitis, and Keeping Fit), as well as online medical resources such as *Consumer Reports Health and Fitness* (the online version of the reference book) and HealthNews (a database of health-related articles). Another database, Health Topics, offers easy-to-understand articles on the following topics: Wellness; Children; Brain and Behavior; Diseases; Exercise and Sports; and Hot Topics (a sampler of late-breaking health news reports).

THE INTERNET

The U.S. government, as well as some universities, support several health-related bulletin boards, some of which you must dial up directly (which means a toll-call if you don't live in the area) and some to which you can telnet, a communications mode that allows you to access various sites as if they were on your own computer. Here are some of the better health boards on the Net.

■ **FDA ELECTRONIC BULLETIN BOARD:** Monitored by the U.S. Food and Drug Administration, this board offers news about drug safety, information on approved products, new information about AIDS, and articles on medical consumer issues.
MODEM: 800-222-0185 or 301-594-6857
TELNET: *fdabbs.fda.gov*

■ **NIH INFORMATION CENTER:** The National Institutes of Health bbs offers a vast quantity of information on diseases (articles, studies, and fact-sheets) as well as updates on goings-on at the institutes.
MODEM: 800-644-2271 or 301-480-5144

■ **ABLE INFORM BBS:** Funded by the National Institute on Disability and Rehabilitation Research (NIDRR), this board offers five databases full of lengthy articles and other useful information about disabilities and treatments.
MODEM: 301-589-3563

■ **ARIZONA HEALTH SCIENCES LIBRARY:** From its home page on the World Wide Web, you can link to a number of different databases, ranging from those devoted to public health issues, nutrition, smoking cessation, pediatric care, as well as the library itself. To access:
WORLD WIDE WEB: *http://amber.medlib.arizona.edu*

KIDS AND TEENS

Children master computers at an early age—and online services know it. All of the major commercial companies offer games and educational forums for elementary schoolers on up to teenagers.

PRODIGY

■ **JUST KIDS:** Prodigy is by far the strongest service for kids. The Just Kids screen includes several categories: Games, Kids' Talk, Stories, Activities, Kids' News/Info, Humor, and Contests/Quizzes. In Activities, young children can explore interactive maps from National Geographic or take a tour of a NASA mission with NOVA. And Homework Helper provides online encyclopedias, background news, and other reference sources, as well as access to newspapers and PBS. The Reading Magic section, for example, offers illustrated stories that let children direct the narrative by choosing plot options along the way.

■ **BULLETIN BOARD FOR KIDS:** Angst-ridden teenagers everywhere can vent on Prodigy's Bulletin Board for Kids, discussing everything from dating to homework to parents (parents may lurk, but aren't invited to post messages to this sometimes excruciatingly frank forum).

AMERICA ONLINE

■ **KIDS ONLY ONLINE (KOOL):** Allows the 5- to 14-year-old set to meet and communicate with each other in forums and occasional real-time conferences. From KOOL, kids can access KidsNet, a clearinghouse for children's audio, video, radio, and television programming. *National Geographic,* the Smithsonian Institution, the Cartoon Network, Compton's Encyclopedia, and Disney's *Adventure Magazine* also have sections here, but unlike Prodigy's version, this one is geared to junior and high school kids and isn't as graphically appealing. Kids also have access to Teacher Pager to get help on homework.

UNCLE SAM WANTS YOU IN CYBERSPACE

Is government just as bureaucratic online as it is off? Find out for yourself:

President George Bush was awestruck by supermarket check-out technology. President Bill Clinton regularly checks his own e-mail messages.

The times, they have a-changed, and now, most of the federal government is online. Technological advancement aside, however, the federal government is still, well, the federal government: Accessing government bulletin boards is not always easy or inexpensive.

Here are some of the more user-friendly government services. For a more complete guide to what the government can do for you online, try *Washington Online: How to Access the Government's Electronic Bulletin Board Services* by Bruce Maxwell (Congressional Quarterly, Inc., $19.95).

■ **FEDWORLD:** Managed by the National Technical Information Service, FedWorld acts as a gateway to over 100 federal bulletin board services, including those devoted to business and economic data, the Census, health-related issues, and agriculture as well as being a source itself. It's relatively easy to use and is the place to start any search for government-related information.

MODEM: 703-321-8020.
FTP: *ftp.fedworld.gov.* **TELNET:** *fedworld.gov.*
WORLD WIDE WEB: *http://www.fedworld.gov.*

■ **CONSULAR AFFAIRS BULLETIN BOARD:** Managed by Overseas Citizens Services, this is a terrific resource for Americans who live or who are planning to travel abroad. The board has information on everything from updates on political and health-care considerations in foreign countries, to how to get a visa or a passport, to emergency services for Americans abroad. It can be accessed through FedWorld, or, to dial directly:
MODEM: 202-647-9225.

■ **CONSUMER INFORMATION CENTER BBS:** Managed by the U.S. General Services Administration, this bulletin board has dozens of publications online ranging from "AIDS and the Education of Our Children" to "Your Rights When Purchasing Products by Mail or Phone." The administration's comprehensive book on consumer protection, *Consumer's Resource Handbook*, is also online. Accessible through FedWorld, or to dial directly:
MODEM: 202-208-7679.

■ **CAREER CENTER:** Provides career and summer job information for high school students. Kids also have access to résumé templates and a cover letter library. There's also College Board information about individual colleges, financial aid, and entrance exams.

COMPUSERVE

■ **THE Y-DRIVE:** Short for Youth Drive, CompuServe's forum for the younger set is run by kids. In it there are topical discussions, as well as library forums sponsored by the Family Channel, games, and educational and multimedia software. The level of discussion is geared to the 11 to 16 age group.

■ **FORUMS:** Associated Press Online and CENDATA can help with homework or general interest research. The Dinosaur Forum and the Earth Forum offer discussion for all ages, often of real scientific issues (as opposed to the latest Barney song). And children's software publisher Broderbund has a forum for those interested in games.

SHOPPING

Behold the newest malls. All the commercial online services now offer 24-hour keyboard shopping. And the Internet is full of shopping opportunities, too—if you know where to look. Shop-

ping online is like ordering from a catalog—sort of. Some stores show their wares with photographs, or (more often) with cartoon-style graphics, but in general, products are described in text-only lists. Most companies are just testing the venue to see what kind of profits online shopping will yield. In other words, don't expect to see all your favorite garments from the Spiegel catalog when you enter its cyber-boutique. And, as yet, there is no way to ask real-time questions about availability, sizes, and colors. You can post e-mail questions to a sales representative, but don't expect an instant response. What's safe to buy online? Generally, anything you'd feel comfortable ordering from a catalog or gift service. That is, items like flowers, books, CDs, and gift foods are reliable, but you may want to think twice before you order a refrigerator. Once you find what you want, ordering is generally fairly easy. The good thing about electronic malls: They're always open.

PRODIGY

All the tried-and-true brand names—Sears, J.C. Penney, Lands End, Spiegel—as well as the Home Shopping Network are available, and it's probably the easiest online mall to navigate. Prodigy's online mall sends you e-mail receipts to confirm that your package has been ordered and shipped out—a nice touch and an efficient, paperless way to keep track of purchases.

Gift Reminder and Gift Sender services are handy for the forgetful gift-giver. Enter up to 50 events (such as birthdays and holidays) and their dates, and Gift Reminder will e-mail you in advance to prompt you to buy. Gift Sender is a sampler of 400 gift ideas, from choice-cut meats to teddy bears.

Some best buys recommended by *Computer Life*: Sheets, towels, and sundry household items at Sears and J.C. Penney.

COMPUSERVE

With J.C. Penney, Sears, and Lands End, as well as Gift Sender, the gift-finding/shipping service, CompuServe's electronic mall (called simply, "Electronic Mall") has 170 merchants and a broader variety of merchandise than Prodigy, but its interface is not as attractive. There are precious few pretty pictures, and shopping consists mainly of reading lists. Even so, CompuServe's selection is the broadest and most sophisticated of the online shopping bazaars. CompuServe also offers a convenience that Prodigy does not: It stores your credit card information for future purchases, so you don't have to type it out every time you order something.

Top items: Artsy gifts from the Metropolitan Museum of Art and tasty meats and condiments from Omaha Steaks.

AMERICA ONLINE

Talk about mark-up inflation: Where Prodigy and CompuServe stop charging you for connect time the minute you enter the mall, AOL keeps the meter running.

AOL's chief draw is Shopper's Advantage, a name-brands-for-cheap warehouse offering 250,000 products. Penny Wise is a convenient place to order office supplies, but you'll get an even better selection and savings by dialing up the company's own toll-free bulletin board service (BBS), ☎ 800-752-3012. AOL also recently opened the Global Plaza, which contains all the goods from the Home Shopping Network.

Top items: Office supplies at Penny Wise Office Products.

THE INTERNET

The shopping experience on the Net is like every other experience on the Net: Great stuff—if you can find it. There is an overwhelming number of shops, but they're scattered far and wide in cyberspace, and there is no mall map to guide you along. One plus: Since most Internet stores are setting up shop as commercial Web sites, many have taken advantage of the graphics and hypertext technology, producing professional-looking pages that rival glossy catalogs.

The bad news is that ordering products on the Net is rare. Generally, shoppers browse for items and then phone to order.

Top items: Anything from the Home Shopping Network.

SHAREWARE

SOFTWARE THAT'S UP FOR GRABS

You can download everything from spreadsheets to games online

If you've ever bought a shirt and then returned it because it didn't fit right, you understand the basic principle of shareware. Shareware refers to any software package that programmers post online for people to copy onto their own computers and try free (or for very little up front). If you like it, you're expected to pay for it; if you don't like it, you're on your honor to notify the author and delete the program from your computer.

In many cases, shareware programs are just as good as commercial offerings and are available in almost every category of software, from spreadsheets to word processors to Personal Information Managers (PIMs)—and a ton of games. You can get shareware from a computer user's group or directly from the author, but the most common source is an online bulletin board service.

Shareware programs cost anywhere from $5 to $200; on average, you'll pay about $50, much less than you'd pay for a comparable commercial package. Most authors will let you try out their package for a week or so, and often the program that you get to evaluate won't be the absolute final product (it might, for example, have certain limits that the full-feature program does not); this is the author's way of encouraging you to purchase the real thing.

If you haven't paid after a reasonable amount of time, look out. The honor system of shareware is basic "netiquette," and if you violate it, be prepared for a flood of reminders, which will become increasingly angry, and rightfully so—you're stealing the author's property.

Once you pay, the author of the program will send you a manual, most often in electronic form; sometimes you'll also get a printed version of it. You will then be put on a mailing list to get updates or new versions of the program; you might also be sent a set of new disks. Trying out shareware is a great way to save money on software and lets you look at cutting-edge programs before they're snapped up by big companies. "Doom," one of the world's most popular computer games, started out as shareware and is still available at dozens of sites on the Internet and online services.

Sometimes, programmers feel magnanimous and decide to give away their programs free. This kind of software is called freeware or public domain software, and it's posted as such on online bulletin services. Freeware and public domain software are generally simple programs, like macros—keyboard shortcuts for functions—in other software, or basic organizers. Unlike shareware, public domain and freeware really is free—no salesperson will call.

■ COMPANIES THAT SHARE

These companies can provide you with a list of shareware and public domain software; call the following numbers for more information.

	☎
CWI	**800-777-5636**
PC-SIG	**800-245-6717**
Public Brand Software	**800-426-3475**
Public Software Library	**800-242-4775**
Shareware Express	**800-346-2842**
ZiffNet (on CompuServe)	**800-848-8199**
America Online	**800-827-6364**

For overall information about shareware and public domain software, subscribe to the *Free Software Foundation Newsletter.*

E-MAIL the message *SUBSCRIBE* to *info-gnu-request@prep.ai.mit.edu*

Macintosh users:
FTP: *sumexaim.stanford.edu-info-mac.*

DOS and Windows users:
FTP: *ftp.cica.indiana.edu.*

EXPERT LIST

THE BEST PLACES TO HANG OUT ONLINE

Whatever your obsession, there's a place to indulge it online. The editors and writers of Computer Life *magazine considered the offerings on every service from America Online to CompuServe to GEnie, plus the Internet and independent Bulletin Board Services (BBSes) to come up with this list of their favorite places to visit online. Their picks are arranged by subject.*

FOR TV AND MOVIE FANS

Seth Godin, author of The Internet White Pages *and* E-Mail Addresses of the Rich and Famous, *picks the best places for fans of the boob tube and silver screen to hang out.*

■ **Best place to gossip about stars:** If you want down and dirty showbiz gossip, head for the Internet newsgroup *alt.showbiz.gossip. The National Enquirer* has nothing on this place.

■ **Best place to meet stars:** Prodigy's bulletin board Ask the Stars (*JUMP: GUEST*) hosts such tinsel town luminaries as Mel Gibson, all of those kids from 90210, Mick Jagger, and others.

■ **Best place to pick a video:** The Internet Movie Database is an online database for readers of the Internet newsgroup *rec.arts.movies.* It's filled with all the information you'd ever want to know about motion pictures.
WORLD WIDE WEB: *http://www.-msstate.edu/movies*

■ **Best place for armchair film critics:** CompuServe's ShowBiz Media forum (*GO SHOWBIZ*) gets crowded, but its discussions of movies, films, and the industry in general are fascinating and informed. Proof: even movie reviewer Roger Ebert hangs out here.

■ **Best place to meet a television producer:** The creator of Warner Brothers' sci-fi television series "Babylon 5," Michael Straczynski, frequents GEnie's Science Fiction Roundtable (type *SFRT2* at the system prompt). Ask him questions about the series, writing, whatever, and he'll usually respond. Sometimes, he'll even dangle hints about upcoming episodes.

■ **Best place for odd movie legends:** Rumors, myths, and real-life accounts are demystified, de-bunked, and confirmed on the Internet's Movie Legend's Database, from weird facts about "The Wizard of Oz" to startling revelations concerning "The Little Mermaid." To get there:
FTP: *cathouse.org /pub/cathouse/urgan.legends/movies*

■ **Best places to talk about late night talk shows:** Discussion of the world of late-night talk show hosts is all the rage on the Net, espe-

■ **GETTING THERE**

Online services use different terms to indicate how to search content. AOL's is KEYWORD. Prodigy's is JUMP. CompuServe's is GO. Other terms of address used throughout:

E-MAIL is how you send people messages online.
FTP means file transfer protocol. It is the Internet address of a site that has files you can download to your computer.
MODEM followed by a phone number indicates a bulletin board service (BBS) that you can have your modem dial directly.
TELNET allows you to log onto another computer and use the software there as if it were on your own computer.
WORLD WIDE WEB is the multimedia component of the Internet. The addressing system always begins with http://.

■ EXPERT LIST

cially in the newsgroups *alt.fan.letterman*, *alt.fan.jayleno*, *alt.fan.conan-obrien*, and the catchall *alt.tv.talkshows.late*. One of the best sources for information and opinion about late night is in the electronic newsletter *Late Show News*. This weekly guide lets you in on what's happening in late-night TV and in the industry at large. To subscribe, send the message: *SUBSCRIBE LATE-SHOW NEWS* to *listserv@mcs.net*.

FOR SPORTS FANS

Writer David Norack, a contributor to Computer Life, *spends a lot of time online trading stats, reliving great plays, and arguing about the Red Sox with fellow sports fans. Here are his favorite sports haunts online.*

■ **Best place for instant scores:** Prodigy and the cable sports channel ESPN have teamed up to provide ESPNet (*JUMP: ESPN*). It's the virtual sports hangout.

■ **Best place for Joe Montana fans:** Prodigy's National Football League Online Fan Club (*JUMP: NFL*) puts gridiron enthusiasts in touch with NFL players, breaking football stories, and exclusive information on the game.

■ **Best place for replays:** Delphi's Sports Connection Online SIG (at the system prompt type *SPORTS CONNECTION*) offers a database of sports audio clips that you can download and play on almost any PC or Mac.

■ **Best place for a pickup game:** CompuServe's Sports Forum (*GO SPORTS*) has Fantasy Sports simulations that let you play everything from baseball to hockey to football with other cyber-jocks.

■ **Best place to argue about the Dallas Cowboys:** America Online's Grandstand (*KEYWORD: GRANDSTAND*) is a place for sports fans to talk, write, and roar about happenings both on and off the field, court, or rink.

■ **Best place to wrestle:** The Online Sports BBS of Toronto has its own professional wrestling league, where members can role-play as Hulk Hogan (or his manager). The service also provides 24-hour sports news and stats. **MODEM:** 416-928-3339

FOR LITERATI AND GROUPIES

Dylan Tweney, author of The Traveler's Guide to the Information Highway, *identifies the best of the high-brow culture inner sanctum-sanctorums online. Jason Snell, the founding editor of the online magazine* InterText, *points out the hippest places for pop-culture addicts to hang out.*

■ **Best place for pop music groupies:** Find out if there is a Musical Mailing List (Internet e-mail) for your favorite band. These e-mail missives are circulated among an intimate group of fans who discuss concerts, new recordings, group gossip, and the like. You can get a list of the mailing lists in the Usenet newsgroup *rec.music.misc* by selecting Search for Topic and entering *MAILING LIST*. Or to find out when your beloved band is coming out with its new CD, subscribe to the Internet e-mail list NEWRELEASES, which gives you an updated listing of what's coming up when every week. To subscribe, send the message *SUBSCRIBE NEWRELEASES* to *new-releases-request@cs.uwp.edu*.

■ **Best place to read everything you should have read in college:** Project Gutenberg on the Internet is converting public-domain literature into electronic form and distributing it as far and as wide as possible, free. In addition to all of Shakespeare's works and the King James Bible, there are dozens of other classics of literature, philosophy, and history. **FTP:** *mrcnext.cso.uiuc.edu*, log in as "anonymous," and go to the directory */pub/etext*. Or **E-MAIL:** *SUB GUTENBERG YOUR NAME* **TO** *listserv@uiucvmd.bitnet*.

EXPERT LIST

Best place to view online cartoon art: Two comic strips are available online: "Doctor Fun" by David Farley (a "Far Side"-style one-panel strip) and "NetBoy" by Stafford Side (a "Life in Hell"-style multipanel strip). You get the best view from the Web, so for "Doctor Fun" go to:
WORLD WIDE WEB: *http://sunsite.unc.edu/Dave/drfun.html*
For "NetBoy" go to:
http://www.interaccess.com/netboy.html.
Also available in digital format is Scott Adams's syndicated cartoon "Dilbert" on America Online (*KEYWORD: DILBERT*). Adams, an AOLer, also writes an entertaining periodic e-mail newsletter about the comic strip. His e-mail address:
scottadams@aol.com

Best place for literati: CompuServe's Literary Forum (*Go LITFORUM*) is the hangout for aspiring and published writers, book lovers, and lit-addicts in general. Favorite sections are Poetry&Lyrics, Mystery&Suspense, and Romance/Historical. The forum also offers an online writing workshop.

Best place for alternative reading material: Zines meet cyberspace. These electronic newsletters range in subject from political satire to historical research, and many intriguing and odd-ball topics in between. You'll find them on CompuServe's Electronic Frontier Forum (*Go EFFSIG)*, in the Zines from the Net library; on AOL (*KEYWORD: PDA*), in the Software Libraries–Palmtop Paperbacks/Ezine libraries; and on the Internet at:
FTP: *//ftp.etext.org/pub/-Zines/*

Best place to find a good bookstore: The atmosphere is definitely highbrow in the Internet newsgroup *rec.arts.books*, but it's not inaccessible—everyone here just loves books.

RELIGIOUS RETREATS

Preacher's daughter and Computer Life *editor Chris Shipley guides us to her favorite online meditation rooms and soap-box pulpits.*

Best place for choir practice: AOL's The Front Porch Room (*KEYWORD: RELIGION*) is a virtual church social. Here, followers of every religion are invited to share their beliefs "in a heated but polite" manner. Even pagans gather on the porch (every Thursday at 10 p.m. EST). The choir practices the first Sunday of the month for two hours beginning at 8:30 p.m. EST.

Best place to argue about evolution: Section 8 of CompuServe's Religion Forum (*Go RELIGION*) is home to an interfaith dialogue where the intelligentsia and charismatic meet to debate everything from the divinity of Jesus and the context of Paul's writings to speaking in tongues and the right- or wrong-headedness of evolutionism.

Best place to pray: Think of Prodigy's Religion Concourse (*JUMP: RELIGION CONCOURSE)* as an online prayer circle. A small group gathers in the Prayer Line area to request others' prayers for themselves and their families and friends. Each request is met with support, concern, and hope for speedy answers to these community prayers.

Best place to spread the gospel of the Internet: Come worship the almighty processor in the Internet newsgroup *alt.religion.computers.* The group often splits between the fundamentalist Windows users and born-again Mac disciples. If using a PC is a religious experience for you, you belong here.

Best place to meet a goddess: If your religion is woman-earth-goddess-centric, share your inner light with the members of the Internet usegroup *alt.mythology.* This fascinating group discusses everything from the

EXTRA! EXTRA! READ ALL ABOUT IT

All the news that's fit to appear on your computer screen

Some 50 newspapers already are online, and untold online magazines, web sites, and bulletin boards serve up a smorgasboard of news. To get your cybernews, you've got to sign up for the online service that carries it—or, if the newspaper of your choice is on the Internet, you've got to get an Internet account and sign up for "delivery" online. Many of the newspapers on online services charge a few dollars per hour, while those on the Internet charge a flat rate. Rosalind Resnick, editor and publisher of "Interactive Publishing Alert," a monthly newsletter that tracks trends and developments in electronic newspaper and magazine publishing, picks the best of online newspaper offerings.

■ **ACCESS ATLANTA:** A joint venture of Prodigy and *The Atlanta Constitution-Journal*, Access Atlanta wants to be your hometown paper in cyberspace. You'll find news from lists of births, deaths, home sales, and day care centers to the length of the tour at the CNN Center. Click a yellow square on a subway map and find out what's happening at Peachtree Center; page through a transportation index to find the fastest route there.
Price: $6.95 a month, $4.95 for Prodigy members.

■ **@TIMES:** The *New York Times'* joint venture with America Online is an electronic version of the paper's popular "Arts and Leisure" section. Rather than reproduce the entire paper online, the *Times* has created a world-class entertainment guide to help both New Yorkers and out-of-town visitors plan their nights and weekends in the Big Apple. Thanks to its interactive format, @times gives *Times* fans much much more than they can get in the daily paper—and far more easily. @times' message boards let readers swap notes on everything from "The Flintstones" to books on the Times' "Best Seller" lists. There is also a searchable archive of current and past *Times* reviews.
Price: Free to America Online subscribers.

■ **NANDO.NET:** The *Raleigh News and Observer's* NandO.net is the most ambitious Internet newspaper published so far. Besides daily news, NandO.net readers get the full text of U.S. Supreme Court decisions, plus advance access to the paper's classified ads, a legislative bill-tracking system, and unlimited use of the Internet.
Price: $15 per month for users with Internet accounts, $30 for newspaper and Internet access.

Descent of Ishtar to the Netherworld to the influence of the goddess on modern religions.

FOR HOBBYISTS

Rosalind Resnick, editor and publisher of Interactive Publishing Alert, *an online monthly newsletter, has many hobbies, but the one to which she devotes most time is searching for new hobby groups online. The ones she visits most:*

■ **Best place to learn to tat:** Whether you've got a knack for knitting or craving to crochet, there's somebody on Crafts Forum (*Go CRAFTS*) who shares your interest. The forum features "live" quilting bees every Tuesday night at 10 p.m., EST.

■ **Best place for amateur historians, family chroniclers, and arm-chair archeologists:** In CompuServe's Living History Forum (*Go LIVING*), enthusiasts from all over the world talk about history, archeology, and the cultures and mores of times past. Try Prodigy's Genealogy Bulletin Board (*JUMP: GENEALOGY BB*) or CompuServe's Genealogy

■ EXPERT LIST

Forum (*Go ROOTS*) to discover new branches of your family tree.

■ **Best place to buy Kurt Cobain's autograph:** Want to buy (or sell) Richard Nixon's autograph or bid via e-mail on a "guaranteed authentic" photo of Harrison Ford? Go to the Internet's *alt.collecting.autographs*.

■ **Best place to find collectibles:** Prodigy's Collecting Bulletin Board (*Jump: COLLECTING BB*) hosts discussions of just about every conceivable collectible—from artwork, antiques, and books to glass, coins, comics, stamps, and toys.

■ **Best place for bonsai tips:** The Internet newsgroup *alt.arts.bonsai*.

■ **Best place for car buffs:** *Alt.hotrod* is the hottest place on the net to get the lowdown on low-riders, racing oils, pressure sensors, and other super boosters.

■ **Best place for sci-fi junkies:** GEnie's three sci-fi forums (type *SFRT* at the system prompt) give equal time to readers, writers, and viewers. Attend a "live" writer's workshop on Wednesday nights at 10 p.m., EST or mind-meld with Trekkies at Star Trek night on Tuesdays, also at 10 p.m., EST.

■ **Best place to talk trivia:** Log-on to America Online's Trivia Forum (*KEYWORD: TRIVIA*). In addition to engaging in trivial discussions, you can also compete in trivia games with fellow members.

■ **Best place to strain your brain:** Wise guy, eh? Hang out in CompuServe's Mensa Forum (*Go MENSA*)—you might change your mind.

TO FIND LOVE, INTRIGUE, OR JUST GOOD, CLEAN FUN

Computer Life *contributing editor by day, cruiser of online singles hangouts by night, Nancy Tamosaitis points out who's naughty and nice on the singles scene.*

■ **Best gay and lesbian hangout:** GLIB is a nonprofit, cooperative information and communications resource serving the gay, lesbian, and bisexual community. It's got information on health, law, social events, the arts, and local and national news items of interest to the gay community. For more information, call:
☎ 703-379-4568
MODEM: 703-578-4542

■ **Best places to meet older (over 65-years old) men:** America Online's SeniorNet (*KEYWORD: SENIOR*) is the place to find ROMEOs: Retired Older Men Eating Out. The forum is the place for seniors who like computers and online socializing; members can get technical support, organize social events, and just engage in lively discussions.

■ **Best place to get tied up:** If bondage is your beat, but you're turned off by the blatantly hostile atmosphere on the Internet's *alt. Sex.bondage*, try the independent BBS The English Palace. The group's membership is 40 percent female. The Palace is the largest fetish bulletin board on the East Coast.
MODEM: 908-739-1755

■ **Best place to hang out nude:** The Natural Connection for nudists promotes the clothing-optional lifestyle, which "is serious business to us" says Pat O'Brien, the board's system operator. Users post messages about their experiences and opinions on items of interest to nudists. Contact Pat O'Brien at:
☎ 414-426-2357
MODEM: 414-426-2110

■ **Best place to talk to single New Yorkers:** The men and women of ECHO (acronym for East Coast Hang Out) are a cerebral—frequently bitingly witty—community who connect on topics from politics, love, psychology, to virtual reality. Their favorite topic: New York City. Eighty percent of ECHOids live there—and love it.

EXPERT TIPS

WHEN BAD THINGS HAPPEN ONLINE

Anyone can receive unwanted sexual advances. Here's what to do:

Every city has a red light district, and with a population of some 20 million, the online metropolis has more than its share of seedy neighborhoods: from sexually explicit chat forums to pornographic photos to wayward lonely-hearts roaming the net in search of something slightly more lewd than love. Just as in the real world, women and children are more likely to be the targets of unwanted sexual advances from strangers. Sandra Donnelly, founder of Women Online—a popular women's forum of ZiffNet (on CompuServe)—offers some tips on avoiding the net's danger zones.

CALL THE CYBER-COPS. Major online commercial services employ SysOps (short for "System Operators") to make sure that everything runs smoothly. This includes responding to subscribers' complaints of sexual harassment or inappropriate advances. If an offender consistently singles you out, make sure that you save the harassing messages and note the sender's ID or account number; this way, when you e-mail the SysOp, you'll have proof and a positive identification. Generally, such creeps have targeted more than one person, so your complaint probably will be one of many, and the offender's service will be cut off.

Reporting sexual harassment on the more chaotic Internet is not as easy. Since there is no central management, there is no policing. One way to cool a hot pursuit is to screen your messages with a kill filter, which automatically deletes e-mail from specified sender IDs; icy silence is sometimes the best response. You can also change your own ID, or broadcast the offender's behavior and ID to people online. A group flame—in which a large group of people simultaneously and strongly reprimand someone for bad behavior—can be highly effective in putting a perpetrator in his (or her) place.

In general, however, it is probably not worth your time to report every isolated incident, unless you find a certain message so repugnant that you feel its sender deserves serious punishment. Come-ons are common in cyberspace, and however irritating, they are generally as harmless as drive-by whistles from a carload of teenage boys. Use your judgment.

HEED WARNING SIGNS. Don't participate in chat forums, conferences, boards, or lists with telltale titles. The Internet's UseNet news groups alt.bondage and alt.beastiality, for example, are to be avoided unless you're ready and willing to be exposed to some pretty racy material. The subject may sound funny to you, but to the people who subscribe to that group, it's quite serious—and if you post a message, or even lurk in that area, you are inviting advances.

WARN CHILDREN ABOUT TALKING TO STRANGERS. Kids should know not to respond to any questions that seem inappropriate. Online creeps can hide behind their anonymity, pretending that they are children themselves. It's one thing for a cyber-friend to ask what your child's school is like; it's another to ask for the specific location, when classes end, and what route he takes home. In general, it's best to make it a rule that kids are not allowed to go online unless an adult is at home. That way, if kids sense something funny going on, adults can check the offending messages, save the sender's ID, and take due action.

EXPERT SOURCES

TRAVEL BOOKS FOR CYBERSPACE

First-timers and certifiable scouts alike need a trusty guidebook to navigate the Net. Tin Albano, book review editor of PC Magazine, *recommends the following to suit all ranges of experience.*

FOR BEGINNERS

ZEN AND THE ART OF THE INTERNET
Brendan P. Kehoe, Prentice Hall, 1994, $23.95
■ The best introductory guide to the Internet. It wastes little time with cute graphics or long lists. It's strictly a how and where book.

THE INTERNET FOR DUMMIES
John R. Levine, IDG Books, 1994, $19.95
■ This book is one of the best ways to get started on the Net. It covers everything from getting hooked up to using the myriad search and navigation tools.

EXPLORING THE WORLD OF ONLINE SERVICES
Rosalind Resnick, Sybex Inc., 1993, $17.95
■ An excellent intro to Prodigy and CompuServe. Includes ways to keep costs down.

FOR ADVANCED USERS

THE INTERNET GUIDE FOR NEW USERS
Daniel P. Dern, McGraw-Hill, 1995, $40.00
■ The title is a misnomer; this is no beginner's book. Rather, it's a top-notch reference guide to the history, tools and features of the Internet. Besides the basics, the guide gives plenty of information on using UNIX (the operating system of choice on the Net), and guides to security, commercial services, and software.

NET GUIDE
Michael Wolff and Peter Rutten, Random House Reference and Electronic Publishing, 1994, $19
■ One of the more complete, well-organized guides to online topics, it contains listings of over 4,000 special-interest forums available on CompuServe, GEnie, and the Internet.

USING COMPUTER BULLETIN BOARDS
John Hedtke, MIS Press, 1994, $29.95
■ The first half of this clearly written book takes you through the BBS labyrinth and explains how to log on, navigate through the features and conferences. The second half, for more advanced users, introduces various BBS software, such as Fido, Wildcat!, and PC Board.

MAGAZINES

PC NOVICE
$2.95 per issue, $24 for one year (12 issues)
☎ 800-848-1478

HOMEPC
$8 per issue; $21.97 for one year (12 issues)
☎ 800-829-0119
■ Both of these cover the computer world in a newbie-friendly tone.

MACWORLD
$2.50 per issue; $30 for one year (12 issues)
☎ 800-234-1038

MACUSER
$3.95 per issue; $19.97 for one year (12 issues)
☎ 800-627-2247
■ Both offer in-depth reviews, along with expert forecasts of where various computer-related markets are headed. The equivalents for PC users are *PC Magazine* and *Windows Sources*.

WIRED
$4.95 per issue, $39.95 for one year (12 issues)
☎ 415-222-6200
■ Anyone interested in how computers are affecting the world should read this. Full of cultural insights, the skinny on the industry, and reviews of neat stuff.

CHAPTER TWELVE

THE U.S.A.

EXPERT QUOTES

"People aren't with Clinton on the issues and they aren't with him on character."

—Michael Barone, editor of the *Almanac of American Politics*

Page 784

"When [James Monroe] left the presidency, he spent almost all his time suing the federal government."

—Henry Graff, Columbia University history professor

Page 801

"I still have a dream. It is a dream deeply rooted in the American dream."

—Martin Luther King, Jr., Speech on the steps of the Lincoln Memorial

Page 857

THE YEAR AHEAD: **BET** that the Republicans will keep control of Congress... **EXPECT** Bill Clinton will face a very tough time getting another term... **COUNT ON** more Republican governors... **VOTE** because almost half of all eligible Americans don't... **ANTICIPATE** that New York and California will be the abortion capitals of the country... **DRIVE** carefully in California, Texas, and Florida, the states with the most traffic accident deaths... **WATCH** Americans continue to move West...

ELECTION '96

THE REPUBLICANS COME ON STRONG

The GOP made huge gains in '94—chances are they'll make more

Soothsayers beware. Few predicted the landslide that swept the country in the 1994 mid-term election, wresting control of both the Senate and the House from the hands of Democrats for the first time in four decades. Will the Republicans be able to make further gains in 1996 or will the Democrats regain lost ground? Consider the historical tea leaves.

■ THE PRESIDENCY

When Bill Clinton was elected by a narrow plurality of 43 percent of the popular vote in 1992, the Democrats took control of the White House for the first time in 12 years. Democrats have occupied the White House for 21 years of the postwar period and Republicans for 29, but prior to 1992, Democrats had controlled the White House for only four of the previous 24 years. Franklin D. Roosevelt was the last Democrat elected to a second term—off course, he was elected to third and fourth terms as well.

Michael Barone, editor of the *Almanac of American Politics*, argues that Clinton has a tough road ahead. "People aren't with him on the issues and they aren't with him on character," Barone says.

Besides, a new political calendar may also give challengers an edge (see "The 1996 Primary Trail," page 788). More states will hold their primaries early, so by late spring of 1996 it should be clear who the Republican and Democratic nominees will be. That means they will have more time to plot strategy and raise money for the general election.

■ THE CONGRESS

Prior to the 1994 elections, Republicans had not held both houses of Congress since 1953. The '94 Democratic rout was hailed by some analysts as evidence of a sea change in American politics. Indeed, since the election the Republicans have picked up two more Senate seats with the high-profile defections of Sens. Richard Shelby (formerly D-Ala.) and Ben Nighthorse Campbell (formerly D-Colo.). The current Republican edge: 54 to 46.

Of the 33 Senate seats up for grabs in '96, 18 are currently held by Republicans and 15 by Democrats. But political analysts reckon that 11 of those 18 Republican seats are likely to remain in GOP hands. Only two of the 15 seats currently held by Democrats are considered safe. For a state-by-state rundown of the '96 races, see "The Republican Revolution (Part One)," page 789.

WHAT'S UP FOR GRABS IN '96

All 335 House seats, 33 Senate seats, 11 gubernatorial spots, and one spot in the Oval Office are up for election on November 5, 1996. Red highlighting indicates states that gave Bill Clinton their electoral votes in 1992.

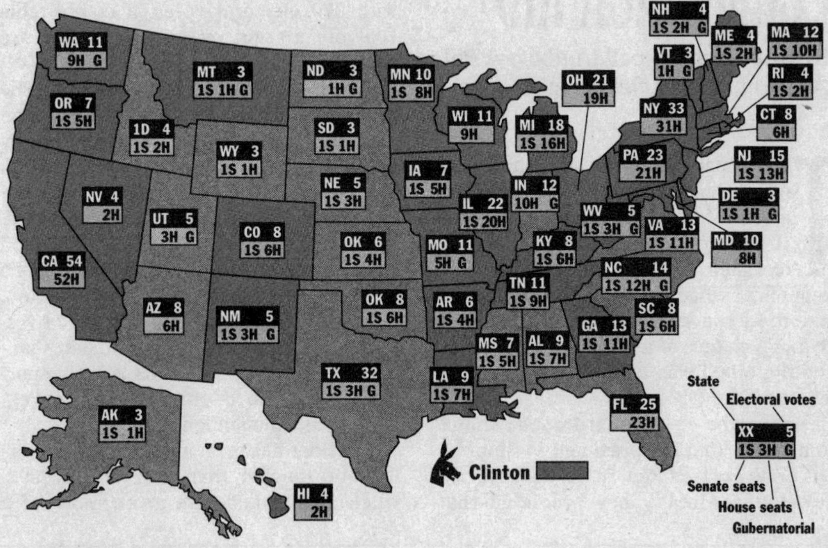

TRENDS TO WATCH

- The number of Americans identifying themselves as Democrats has been declining since 1962. Meanwhile, the number of Republican voters is on the rise.

- Republicans continue to make gains in large southern states such as Florida, North Carolina, and Texas.

- Clinton is in deep trouble in seven of the states he won in 1992, according to *The Cook Report*. The states—Georgia, Louisiana, Kentucky, Montana, Nevada, New Hampshire, and Tennessee—will have a total of 52 electoral votes in the upcoming election.

- No Republican has ever won the party's nomination without winning the New Hampshire primary.

Republicans seem likely to keep control of the House, as well. "People are tending to vote more of a straight ticket in the 1990s than they used to," Barone notes. Nevertheless, if there is any fallout from the "Republican Revolution," it is most likely to be felt in the House. All 435 seats are up for grabs in 1996. The current party lineup: 231 Republicans, 203 Democrats, and one Independent. For a region-by-region breakdown of the race, see "The Republican Revolution (Part Two)," page 791.

■ THE STATEHOUSE RACES

The Republicans occupy 31 governor's mansions. Maine is held by an independent. The governors of Kentucky, Louisiana, and Mississippi are up for reelection in 1995. The first two are currently held by Democrats; Kirk Fordice of Mississippi is a Republican. In 1996, 11 more states will choose governors. Seven are currently controlled by Democrats and four by Republicans. Once again, the odds favor the Republicans (see "A Who's Who of Governors," page 792).

THE PRESIDENCY

RETURN OF THE COMEBACK KID?

Early indicators spell trouble for Bill Clinton, but the field is wide open

The campaign is already well under way. As this book went to press in the summer of 1995, President Clinton had already indicated that he would seek reelection (no surprise there) and nine Republicans had declared their intent to take the job away from him. And there's always a chance of a third party challenge like the one Texas billionaire Ross Perot mounted in 1992.

So far, the electoral arithmetic shows some signs that the president is slipping. *The Cook Political Report*, a well-respected newsletter, already has predicted that Clinton is likely to lose seven states that he won in 1992—Georgia, Louisiana, Kentucky, Montana, Nevada, New Hampshire, and Tennessee.

Even if that turns out to be the case, victory could still be within Clinton's grasp. He easily defeated George Bush in 1992 with 370 electoral votes, a comfortable 100-vote margin over the 270 that are needed to win.

There are not many good omens for the president in the results of the 1994 mid-term elections, however. Democrats did poorly all across the country, but particularly in the West and Midwest, regions that were crucial to Clinton's '92 victory. All told, Democrats lost eight Senate seats and 55 House seats, the most for any party since 1980 and 1948, respectively. In addition, polls show that a growing number of voters are willing to consider a third party candidate, and voter registration groups report that large numbers of new voters are registering as independents.

Presidential primaries will come earlier and quicker than they did in 1992, when candidates were given more of a

WHO REALLY ELECTS THE PRESIDENT

Just in case you forgot how the Electoral College works

The authors of the Constitution devised the Electoral College to act as a kind of buffer between the masses and the ultimate process of selecting a president. The voters would choose electors for their state on a predetermined election day and then those individuals, along with electors from other states, would then take it upon themselves to choose the president.

Today, the Electoral College is a body of 538 people. Each state receives a number of electoral votes equal to the number of senators and representatives in its congressional delegation, and Washington, D.C., which has no congressional representation, gets three votes. A candidate needs 270 electoral votes, slightly more than a majority, to be elected president. The candidate who wins a majority of a state's popular vote wins all of its electoral votes. As a result, the electoral vote tends to exaggerate the popular support of the winner.

If no candidate receives a majority of the votes of the Electoral College, the election will be decided by the House of Representatives. This has only happened once, so far, when in 1824 Andrew Jackson won the popular vote in a four-way race but John Quincy Adams was elected president by the House. In 1876, Rutherford B. Hayes lost the popular vote but won the presidency by a single electoral vote. (For more information, see "They Had the Right Stuff," page 798.)

breather to raise the funds that would carry them through to the final stretch (see "The 1996 Primary Trail," page 788). More than 70 percent of the Republican delegates to the national convention will be chosen before March 1996. In the past, primary battles have continued until as late as June. The thinking now is that if the primaries end early, the likely nominee can concentrate on fund-raising and strategy for the general election.

No one expects the summer political conventions to be anything more than television-friendly coronations of already decided-upon candidates. Nonetheless, the amount of air time the TV networks give to the conventions has been steadily declining in recent years. In 1992, none of the three major networks bothered with gavel-to-gavel coverage of the conventions. The Republicans are scheduled to meet in August in San Diego; the Democrats in Chicago in August. Republicans will try to avoid a replay of the '92 convention in Houston, when the party's right-wing sounded themes that alienated much of the general electorate. For their part, Democrats will strive to wipe out memories of their last convention in Chicago in 1968, which was marred by violent, highly politicized clashes between police and Vietnam War protesters.

Want to get an early lead on who is going to come out ahead on Election Day, November 5, 1996? Presidential debates may be interesting but there is little evidence that they significantly shape an election's outcome. The second presidential debate of 1992, whose innovative format allowed for questions from the audience for the first time, attracted the largest U.S. television audience ever, beating out the final episode of M*A*S*H in 1983. But Clinton was ahead in the polls before and after the debate. Historically, Labor Day polls have been most accurate when one candidate had a strong lead, such as in the 1984 election. In 1980, Jimmy Carter led in the polls past Labor Day but was soundly defeated by Ronald Reagan in November. Various seers tout their prediction methods, but all of their records have been spotty. Guess you'll just have to wait and see.

THE PRESIDENTIAL SWEEPSTAKES

A look at how the popular vote has been reflected in the electoral vote in the last 50 years

		DEMOCRAT		REPUBLICAN		
Popular	Electoral		YEAR		Electoral	Popular
60.8%	**523**	**Roosevelt**	1936	Landon	8	36.5%
54.7%	**449**	**Roosevelt**	1940	Willkie	82	44.8%
53.4%	**432**	**Roosevelt**	1944	Dewey	99	45.9%
49.6%	**303**	**Truman**	1948	Dewey	189	45.1%
44.4%	89	Stevenson	1952	**Eisenhower**	**442**	**55.1%**
42.0%	73	Stevenson	1956	**Eisenhower**	**457**	**57.4%**
49.7%	**303**	**Kennedy**	1960	Nixon	219	49.5%
61.1%	**486**	**Johnson**	1964	Goldwater	52	38.5%
42.7%	191	Humphrey	1968	**Nixon**	**301**	**43.4%**
37.5%	17	McGovern	1972	**Nixon**	**520**	**60.7%**
50.1%	**297**	**Carter**	1976	Ford	240	48.0%
41.0%	49	Carter	1980	**Reagan**	**489**	**50.7%**
40.6%	13	Mondale	1984	**Reagan**	**525**	**58.8%**
45.6%	111	Dukakis	1988	**Bush**	**426**	**53.4%**
43.0%	**370**	**Clinton**	1992	Bush	168	37.4%

SOURCE: *Statistical Abstract of the United States: 1994*, U.S. Department of Commerce.

THE 1996 PRIMARY TRAIL

Party nominations for the presidency generally aren't settled in smoke-filled rooms. Instead, delegates, who usually (but not always) are pledged to a certain candidate, are selected in state-level primaries and caucuses and then go on to the national conventions to vote for a nominee. The Republican National Convention will be held August 10-16 in San Diego. The Democratic National Convention will be August 27-29 in Chicago.

Date[1]	Event	Delegates	
Feb. 6	Louisiana Caucus	27R	
Feb. 12	Iowa Caucus	25R	48D
Feb. 20	New Hampshire Primary	16R	20D
Feb. 24	Delaware Primary	12R	14D
Feb. 27	Arizona Primary	39R	
	North Dakota Primary	18R	
	South Dakota Primary	18R	15D
March 2	South Carolina Primary	37R	
March 5	American Samoa Caucus		3D
	Colorado Primary	27R	49D
	Connecticut Primary		53D
	Georgia Primary	42R	76D
	Idaho Caucus		18D
	Maine Primary		23D
	Maryland Primary	32R	68D
	Massachusetts Primary		93D
	Minnesota Caucus		76D
	Rhode Island Primary		22D
	Vermont Primary	12R	15D
	Washington Caucus		74D
March 7	New York Primary	102R	244D
	Missouri Caucus		76D
March 7-21	North Dakota Caucus		14D
March 9	Alabama Primary		54D
	Alaska Caucus		13D
	South Carolina Primary		49D
March 9-11	Democrats Abroad Caucus		7D
March 10	Nevada Caucus		18D
SUPER	Florida Primary	98R	152D
TUESDAY	Hawai'i Caucus		20D
March 12	Louisiana Primary		59D
	Massachusetts Primary	37R	
	Mississippi Primary	32R	38D
	Oklahoma Primary	38R	44D
	Rhode Island Primary	16R	
	Tennessee Primary	37R	68D
	Texas Primary/Caucus	123R	194D
March 17	Puerto Rico Primary	14R	
March 19	Illinois Primary	69R	164D
	Michigan Primary	57R	128D
	Ohio Primary	67R	147D
	Pennsylvania Primary		167D
	Wisconsin Primary		79D
March 23	Wyoming Caucus		13D
March 25	Utah Caucus		24D
March 26	California Primary	163R	363D
	Connecticut Primary	27R	
March 30	U.S. Virgin Islands Caucus		3D
April 2	Kansas Caucus	31R	36D
	Wisconsin Primary	36R	
	Minnesota Caucus	33R	
April 7	Puerto Rico Primary		51D
April 13	Virginia Caucus		79D
April 23	Pennsylvania Primary	73R	
April 26	Alaska Convention	19R	
May 2	Nevada Caucus/Convention	14R	
May 3	Maine Caucus	15R	
May 4	Wyoming Caucus	20R	
May 5	Guam Caucus		3D
May 7	D.C. Primary	14R	17D
	Indiana Primary	52R	74D
	North Carolina Primary	58R	84D
May 14	Nebraska Primary	24R	25D
	W. Virginia Primary	18R	30D
May 21	Arkansas Primary	20R	
	Oregon Primary	23R	47D
May 28	Arkansas Primary		36D
	Idaho Primary	23R	
	Kentucky Primary	26R	51D
	Washington Primary	36R	
June 4	Alabama Primary	39R	54D
	Montana Primary	14R	16D
	New Jersey Primary	48R	104D
	New Mexico Primary	18R	25D
June 11	North Dakota Primary	18R	
DATES NOT YET DETERMINED			
	American Samoa[2]	4R	
	Guam[2]	4R	
	Hawai'i Caucus	14R	
	Missouri Caucus	35R	
	Nevada Caucus	14R	
	U.S. Virgin Islands Caucus	4R	
	Utah Convention	28R	
	Virginia Caucus	53R	
TOTAL DELEGATE VOTES:		Republicans 2,013	
		Democrats 4,313[3]	

1. As of June 9, 1995. Dates and delegate allotments subject to change. 2. Method not yet determined. 3. Includes 776 unpledged officials, called "Super Delegates."
SOURCE: Republican and Democratic National Committees.

EXPERT LIST

THE REPUBLICAN REVOLUTION (PART ONE)

The Republicans currently hold 54 seats in the U.S. Senate; the Democrats, 46. In '96, 33 seats are up for grabs. Of those, 15 are currently held by Democrats. Four of the Democratic seats are considered toss-ups, with an additional nine seats in varying degrees of jeopardy. Of the 18 Republican seats up for grabs, on the other hand, 11 seem sure to remain in Republican hands. We asked Elizabeth Wilner, managing editor of The Cook Political Report, *a respected political newsletter, for a state-by-state assessment of the '96 races.*

ALABAMA
OPEN
■ Democrat Howell Heflin, who won 61 percent of the vote in 1990, is retiring. With the South becoming ever more conservative, Democrats will have a hard time holding on.

ALASKA
Ted Stevens (R)
■ Four-term incumbent Stevens won two-thirds of the vote in 1990 and is expected to win again in 1996.

ARKANSAS
OPEN
■ Democrat David Pryor, who ran unopposed in his last election, is stepping down. But the seat is likely to stay Democratic.

COLORADO
OPEN
■ The only open Republican seat in 1996 with the retirement of Hank Brown. The state's junior senator, Ben Nighthorse Campbell, recently jumped parties to the GOP. The Democrats' chance of picking up this seat depends on whether they can field a candidate with statewide name recognition.

DELAWARE
Joseph Biden (D)
■ Three-termer Biden won his last race by a comfortable 63 percent and is going into election season as one of only two Democratic senators considered a safe bet for reelection. (The other: Jay Rockefeller of West Virginia.)

GEORGIA
Sam Nunn (D)
■ Nunn was unopposed in 1990, but he is likely to face a wide field which could become still wider if he in fact retires, as some have speculated he will.

IDAHO
Larry Craig (R)
■ A solid Republican seat, incumbent Craig is expected to win easily.

ILLINOIS
OPEN
■ With the retirement of Democrat Paul Simon, this is one of the biggest battlefields of '96. Illinois has been following the more rightward tilt of the rest of the country. The state's junior senator, Carol Moseley Braun, is the only African American in the Senate.

IOWA
Tom Harkin (D)
■ Harkin is likely to keep his seat. Complacent Democrats might be wise to take note: Harkin, who won his last election with 54 percent of the vote, is the only Democrat left in the state's congressional delegation.

KANSAS
Nancy Kassebaum (R)
■ The daughter of 1936 Republican presidential nominee Alf Landon, Kassebaum is a shoo-in; she garnered 74 percent of the votes in her 1990 race.

KENTUCKY
Mitch McConnell (R)
■ McConnell won 52 percent of the vote in 1990 and should retain his seat.

LOUISIANA
OPEN
■ Democrat Bennett Johnston is retiring. The race to succeed him is a toss-up.

■ EXPERT LIST

Still, Louisiana, like the rest of the South, is becoming more Republican.

MASSACHUSETTS
John Kerry (D)
■ Kerry won 57 percent of the vote in 1990 and is likely to hold onto his seat.

MAINE
William S. Cohen (R)
■ Despite the presence of several challengers, Cohen's hold on this seat looks solid.

MICHIGAN
Carl Levin (D)
■ Levin faces an uphill battle. The seat leans Democratic, but Levin could be dragged down by Clinton's poor ratings in Michigan.

MINNESOTA
Paul Wellstone (D)
■ This is likely to be one of the more vicious races of 1996. First-termer Wellstone faces a Republican field dominated by former-Sen. Rudy Boschwitz, from whom Wellstone took his seat in 1990 by a minuscule margin.

MISSISSIPPI
Thad Cochran (R)
■ Incumbent Cochran is running unopposed.

MONTANA
Max Baucus (D)
■ This is one of the five Democratic seats rated a toss-up. Baucus won a fourth term in 1990 with 68 percent of the vote, but his vote for the 1994 crime bill has made him vulnerable to a conservative constituency opposed to the assault weapons ban. Historically, however, Montana leans Democratic.

NEBRASKA
OPEN
■ Democrat Jim Exon is retiring after three terms. Nebraska hasn't had a Republican senator in over a decade, but this time they have a good shot at electing one.

NEW HAMPSHIRE
Bob Smith (R)
■ In this conservative New England state, the GOP will likely prevail.

NEW JERSEY
Bill Bradley (D)
■ The former basketball great may hang up his political sneakers. He was elected by a bare majority in 1990; look for surprises.

NEW MEXICO
Pete Domenici (R)
■ As his approval rating reaches 75 percent, he should be easily reelected.

NORTH CAROLINA
Jesse Helms (R)
■ The ever-controversial Helms will probably keep his seat, but it's not a sure thing.

OKLAHOMA
Jim Inhofe (R)
■ Inhofe won his seat in a special election in 1994, following the resignation of Democrat David Boren. He should get reelected.

OREGON
Mark Hatfield (R)
■ Hatfield was the lone GOP holdout against the balanced budget amendment. He may retire, but if he runs, he'll win.

RHODE ISLAND
Claiborne Pell (D)
■ The 77-year-old Senate aristocrat may retire to the manor. But the seat should remain in Democratic hands.

SOUTH CAROLINA
Strom Thurmond (R)
■ The state is among the most Republican in the country. Whether or not Thurmond, who is 92, runs again, the Republicans are likely to hold on to this seat.

SOUTH DAKOTA
Larry Pressler (R)
■ Pressler is the only incumbent Republican whose reelection chances are rated a toss-up. One factor: South Dakota leans Republican in presidential years.

TENNESSEE
Fred Thompson (R)
■ Ex-actor and Watergate counsel Thompson was elected in 1994 to serve the final two years of Vice President Al Gore's Senate term. The chances are good that he'll be reelected.

THE REPUBLICAN REVOLUTION (PART TWO)

A region-by-region look at the battle for the House

The Republicans captured control of the House of Representatives for the first time in over 40 years in the 1994 elections and currently hold 231 of the total 435 seats. Leading the charge was Newt Gingrich, the Georgian who is now Speaker of the House, who pledged nothing less than a Republican revolution. We asked Norman J. Ornstein, a congressional scholar and fellow at the American Enterprise Institute, whether the Gingrich forces are likely to prevail again in '96. Here's how he sees things shaping up region by region:

■ **THE SOUTH:** The region has changed remarkably over the last 30 years from being an overwhelmingly Democratic base to one where Republicans are now more dominant. Because of redistricting and changing voting patterns among white voters, white Democrats are becoming a dying breed. If the Democrats are reduced to largely black districts, then the South will become a Republican base.

A historical comparison is instructive: In 1960, Democrats held 94 percent of the seats in the South—about a quarter of the House. Now the number of seats has increased, from 104 in 1960 to 125 seats today. Democrats currently make up 48.8 percent of the southern House delegation. Thus, the proportion of seats held by Democrats has been cut in half as the number of seats has increased. If you look back to the era of Democratic dominance in Congress, it was built on a southern base. If the Democrats don't have that base, they will have headaches.

■ **THE WEST:** This is the most competitive region in the country. The Rocky Mountain states (which include Colorado, Montana, and Wyoming) were a Democratic stronghold in the '50s. Now, Democrats have only 25 percent of them. The other area that matters in the West is the Pacific region (Oregon, Washington, and California). It was there and in the South that the Democrats took the biggest hit in '94. They went from holding almost two-thirds of the seats there to less than half.

■ **THE MIDWEST:** Republicans could do well here. The Democrats suffered significant losses in the Midwest in '94. The area currently is divided evenly between the two major parties.

■ **THE NORTHEAST:** We've seen almost a complete reversal from back in the '30s and '40s. In the early part of this century, New England was a major base for the Republican party, along with the Plains states. Now they are the strongest regions for the Democrats. The Northeast as a whole is likely to see the least political change in the near future.

TEXAS
Phil Gramm (R)
■ Although Gramm is also running for the Republican presidential nomination, Texas law permits him to keep his reelection bid open at the same time. In any case, the seat is considered safe for the GOP.

VIRGINIA
John Warner (R)
■ Warner won his 1990 election with 81 percent of the vote, but intra-party feuding could cause him trouble—he refused to back GOP Senate nominee Oliver North in 1994. Still, the seat will likely stay in Republican hands.

WEST VIRGINIA
Jay Rockefeller (D)
■ The only Democrat-held seat, besides that of Joe Biden of Delaware, that is considered safe.

WYOMING
Alan Simpson (R)
■ Simpson is a shoo-in for reelection.

VOTER'S GUIDE

A WHO'S WHO OF GOVERNORS

With the Republican Congress promising to turn many federal programs over to the states, the residents of governor's mansions could gain increased importance. Three gubernatorial seats are up for grabs in 1995 (Kentucky, Louisiana, and Mississippi) and 11 more will be fought for in 1996 (Delaware, Indiana, Missouri, Montana, New Hampshire, North Carolina, North Dakota, Utah, Vermont, Washington, and West Virginia). Following is a quick sketch of the current office holders and the outlook for upcoming elections.

STATE ★ Next election ★ **Governor** • **Party** • Terms (date first elected) • **% of vote won** ★ Salary • Previous occupation

ALABAMA ★ 1998 ★ **Fob James, Jr.** **R** 2 (1979) • **50.5%** ★ $81,151 • Business executive

ALASKA ★ 1998 ★ **Tony Knowles** **D** 1 (1994) • **41.2%** ★ $81,648 • Mayor of Anchorage

ARIZONA ★ 1998 ★ **Fife Symington** **R** 2 (1990) • **52.4%** ★ $60,000 • Business executive/CEO

ARKANSAS ★ 1998 ★ **Jim Guy Tucker** **D** 1 (1992) • **59.8%** ★ $60,000 • Lieutenant Governor

CALIFORNIA ★ 1998 ★ **Pete Wilson** **R** 2 (1990) • **55.4%** ★ $120,000 • U.S. Senator

COLORADO ★ 1998 ★ **Roy Romer** **D** 3 (1986) • **55.3%** ★ $70,000 • State Treasurer

CONNECTICUT ★ 1998 ★ **John G. Rowland** **R** 1 (1994) • **36.1%** ★ $78,000 • U.S. Representative

DELAWARE ★ 1996 ★ **Thomas R. Carper** **D** 1 (1992) • **65%** ★ $95,000 • U.S. Representative

ELECTION OUTLOOK: *Count on Carper being reelected.*

FLORIDA ★ 1998 ★ **Lawton Chiles** **D** • 2 (1990) • **50.9%** ★ $101,764 • U.S. Senator

GEORGIA ★ 1998 ★ **Zell Miller** **D** 2 (1990) • **51%** ★ $91,092 • Lieutenant Governor

HAWAI'I ★ 1998 ★ **Benjamin J. Cayetano** **D** 1 (1994) • **36.6%** ★ $94,780 • Lieutenant Governor

IDAHO ★ 1998 ★ **Phil Batt** **R** 1 (1994) • **2.2%** ★ $75,000 • State Chair, Idaho Republican Party

ILLINOIS ★ 1998 ★ **Jim Edgar** **R** 2 (1990) • **64.1%** ★ $103,097 • Illinois Secretary of State

INDIANA ★ 1996 ★ **Evan Bayh** **D** 2 (1988) • **62%** ★ $77,200 • Indiana Secretary of State

ELECTION OUTLOOK: *Bayh is required to retire under term limit rules. A generally Republican state, Indiana tends to lean that way even more so in a presidential election year. Still, with former Vice President Dan Quayle and his wife, Marilyn, having removed their names from the list of possible contenders, the race is considered a toss-up.*

IOWA ★ 1998 ★ **Terry Branstad** **R** 4 (1982) • **57.1%** ★ $76,700 • Lawyer/Lieutenant Governor

KANSAS ★ 1998 ★ **Bill Graves** **R** 1 (1994) • **64%** ★ $76,476 • Kansas Secretary of State

KENTUCKY ★ 1995 ★ **Brereton Jones** **D** 1 (1991) • **65%** ★ $86,352 • Developer/Horse breeder

ELECTION OUTLOOK: *Jones is retiring under current state law that limits governors to one four-year term, although his successor will be allowed to serve up to two terms. Only one Republican has held the statehouse since the Civil War, but the GOP has been making gains in the Blue Grass State.*

LOUISIANA ★ 1995 ★ **Edwin Edwards** **D** 4 (1971) • **61%** ★ $73,440 • U.S. Representative

ELECTION OUTLOOK: *Edwards is retiring, leaving this race wide open. While Louisiana's "jungle primary" system (one primary for all parties with a run-off election if necessary) has traditionally been more challenging for Republicans, the climate has been warmer for the GOP of late. The state recently legalized gambling and it could be a campaign issue.*

MAINE ★ 1998 ★ **Angus King** **I** 1 (1994) • **35.8%** ★ $70,000 • Businessman/Public television host

MARYLAND ★ 1998 ★ **Parris N. Glendening** **D** 1 (1994) • **50.2%** ★ $120,000 • County Executive

MASSACHUSETTS ★ 1998 ★ **William F. Weld** **R** 2 (1990) • **70.9%** ★ $75,000 • Asst. Atty. General

MICHIGAN ★ 1998 ★ **John Engler** **R** 2 (1990) • **61.5%** ★ $112,025 • State Senate Majority Leader

MINNESOTA ★ 1998 ★ **Arne Carlson** **R** 2 (1990) • **63.5%** ★ $109,053 • State Auditor

VOTER'S GUIDE

STATE ★ Next election ★ **Governor** • **Party** • Terms (date first elected) • **% of vote won** ★ Salary • Previous occupation

MISSISSIPPI ★ 1995 ★ **Kirk Fordice** **R** 1 (1991) • **51%** ★ $75,600 • Businessman/CEO

☛ **ELECTION OUTLOOK:** *Fordice has presided over criminal and educational reforms and is popular within the state. He's likely to be reelected.*

MISSOURI ★ 1996 ★ **Mel Carnahan** **D** 1 (1992) • **59%** ★ $90,312 • Lieutenant Governor

☛ **ELECTION OUTLOOK:** *Carnahan has the advantage of being the incumbent and has the edge. But Missouri is becoming increasingly conservative.*

MONTANA ★ 1996 ★ **Marc Racicot** **R** 1 (1992) • **51%** ★ $90,312 • State Attorney General

☛ **ELECTION OUTLOOK:** *Incumbent Racicot is considered a shoo-in.*

NEBRASKA ★ 1998 ★ Ben Nelson **D** 2 (1990) • **74.1%** ★ $65,000 • Lawyer

NEVADA ★ 1998 ★ Bob Miller **D** 2 (1990) • **53.9%** ★ $90,000 • Lieutenant Governor

NEW HAMPSHIRE ★ 1996 ★ **Steve Merrill** **R** 2 (1992) • **70%** ★ $86,235 • State Atty. General

☛ **ELECTION OUTLOOK:** *Merrill is expected to have no problems keeping his job in one of the most Republican states in the country.*

NEW JERSEY ★ 1997 ★ **Christine Todd Whitman** **R** 1 (1993) • **50%** ★ $85,000 • CEO

NEW MEXICO ★ 1998 ★ **Gary E. Johnson** **R** 1 (1994 • **49.5%** ★ $90,000 • Business owner

NEW YORK ★ 1998 ★ **George E. Pataki** **R** 1 (1994) • **48.9%** ★ $130,000 • State Senator

NORTH CAROLINA ★ 1996 ★ **James B. Hunt Jr.** **D** 3 (1976) • **53%** ★ $123,300 • Lawyer

☛ **ELECTION OUTLOOK:** *Hunt has a 70 percent job approval rating and is likely to keep his job.*

NORTH DAKOTA ★ 1996 ★ **Ed Schafer** **R** 1 (1992) • **58%** ★ $68,280 • Businessman

☛ **ELECTION OUTLOOK:** *Incumbent Schafer is expected to have few problems holding on to the statehouse.*

OHIO ★ 1998 ★ **George V. Voinovich** **R** 2 (1990) • **71.9%** ★ $115,752 • Mayor of Cleveland

OKLAHOMA ★ 1998 ★ **Frank Keating** **R** 1 (1994) • **46.9%** ★ $70,000 • General Counsel, HUD

OREGON ★ 1998 ★ **John Kitzhaber** **D** 1 (1994) • **52.7%** ★ $80,000 • President of State Senate

PENNSYLVANIA ★ 1998 ★ **Tom Ridge** **R** 1 (1994) • **45.1%** ★ $105,000 • U.S. Representative

RHODE ISLAND ★ 1998 ★ **Lincoln C. Almond** **R** 1 (1994) • **47.2%** ★ $69,900 • Foundation President

SOUTH CAROLINA ★ 1998 ★ **David Beasley** **R** 1 (1994) • **50.5%** ★ $101,959 • Speaker pro tempore, South Carolina House of Representatives

SOUTH DAKOTA ★ 1998 ★ **William J. Janklow** **R** 3 (1978) • **55.4%** ★ $74,649 • State Atty General

TENNESSEE ★ 1998 ★ **Don Sundquist** **R** 1 (1994) • **54.3%** ★ $85,000 • U.S. Representative

TEXAS ★ 1998 ★ **George W. Bush** **R** 1 (1994) • **53.5%** ★ $99,122 • Oil and gas executive

UTAH ★ 1996 ★ **Michael O. Leavitt** **R** 1 (1992) • **42%** ★ $70,000 • Insurance executive

☛ **ELECTION OUTLOOK:** *Leavitt squeaked by in 1992 with a bare plurality, but should have an easier time getting re-elected in Republican Utah. Leavitt, 43, is the youngest of the governors up for reelection.*

VERMONT ★ 1996 ★ **Howard Dean** **D** 2 (1992) • **70%** ★ $85,977 • Physician/Lieutenant Governor

☛ **ELECTION OUTLOOK:** *Incumbent Dean, who has been maintaining a high profile in the wake of Republican attacks on federal social programs, is likely to retain his seat.*

VIRGINIA ★ 1997 ★ **George F. Allen** **R** 1 (1993) • **58%** ★ $110,000 • U.S. Representative

WASHINGTON ★ 1996 ★ **Mike Lowry** **D** 1 (1992) • **52%** ★ $121,000 • U.S. Representative

☛ **ELECTION OUTLOOK:** *This could be one of the messiest races of the election season. Lowry is facing charges of sexual harassment from a former employee and could be challenged in a primary. Democrats will have a hard time holding on.*

WEST VIRGINIA ★ 1996 ★ **Gaston Caperton** **D** 2 (1988) • **56%** ★ $90,000 • Insurance executive

☛ **ELECTION OUTLOOK:** *Incumbent Caperton is term-limited, but the Democrats shouldn't have much trouble in this overwhelmingly Democratic state.*

WISCONSIN ★ 1998 ★ **Tommy G. Thompson** **R** 3 (1986) • **67.4%** ★ $92,283 • State Senator

WYOMING ★ 1998 ★ **Jim Geringer** **R** 1 (1994) • **58.7%** ★ $70,000 • State Senator

VOTER TURNOUT

WHY DOESN'T ANYBODY VOTE?

Turnout has been down since 1960, but it may be turning around

Women vote in greater numbers than men. White Americans vote more often than Blacks or Hispanics, and more senior citizens than those in their 20s go to the polls. Yet as a nation, Americans are far more likely to avoid the ballot box than citizens of most other industrial democracies.

FACT FILE:

VOTER TURNOUT IN PRESIDENTIAL YEARS

■ *Political analysts bemoan the low voter turnout in the United States, which peaked in 1960. But the '92 elections saw increased turnout for the first time since the Reagan landslide in 1984. Turnout in non-presidential years tends to be lower.*

YEAR	Total pop. that was of voting age	Proportion that voted
1948	95.6 million	51.1%
1952	99.9 million	61.6%
1956	104.5 million	59.3%
1960	109.7 million	62.8%
1964	114.1 million	61.9%
1968	120.3 million	60.9%
1972	140.8 million	55.2%
1976	152.3 million	53.5%
1980	164.6 million	52.6%
1984	174.5 million	53.1%
1988	182.8 million	50.1%
1992	189.0 million	55.2%

SOURCE: *Statistical Abstract of the United States: 1994*, U.S. Department of Commerce.

The greatest voter turnout in an American election was in 1960, when 63 percent of eligible voters went to the polls. Since then, voter turnout has slipped. The 1992 presidential election, however, was something of an aberration—55 percent of eligible voters turned out, the highest percentage since 1960. Optimists cite the '92 vote as evidence of the renewed interest of the American electorate. Others aren't convinced. Off-year election turnout figures are significantly lower.

In Western Europe, turnouts of 75 to 90 percent are the norm. In May 1995, more than 85 percent of French voters went to the polls to choose a new president. Voter participation declined significantly in Germany between 1976 and 1990 from 91 percent to 76 percent—still significantly higher than the U.S. numbers. According to the Congressional Research Service of the U.S. Congress, which measured voter turnout in industrial nations in the mid-1980s, the United States was surpassed by only Switzerland (48.9 percent turnout in 1985) in voter lethargy. America was dwarfed by such civic-minded nations as Belgium (93.6 percent turnout in 1985) and Australia (94.2 percent turnout in 1984). Voting is compulsory in both countries.

Curtis Gans, director of the Committee for the Study of the American Electorate attributes the difference in voter participation partly to the fact that the United States is a less class-oriented society than Europe. Fewer Americans see the significance in the triumph of one party over another. "We don't have class-based parties," Gans notes. "People think they can pick themselves up by their bootstraps," which lessens their stake in the outcome of elections.

It probably doesn't help that historically it's been harder to register to vote in the United States. However, voter turnout rates have stayed lower even as it has gotten easier to cast a ballot. Civil rights legislation, of course, wiped out discriminatory voting requirements such as literacy tests. The new "Motor Voter" law, enacted at the beginning of 1995, which guarantees registration by mail and at cer-

HOW TO GET INTO POLITICS

Well, you might try voting—or giving money to the candidates of your choice

The process of registering to vote just got easier—at least for the residents of the 46 states to which the recently passed "Motor Voter" bill applies. The new law, which took effect on January 1, 1995, mandates states to allow eligible voters to register by mail, at motor vehicle registries (hence the name), and at certain other state agencies including bureaus of public assistance. Minnesota, Wisconsin, and Wyoming were exempt from the law because they offer same-day registration on Election Day already, according to Matt Farrey, Project Manager of the League of Women Voters Education Project in Washington, D.C. North Dakota, which does not bother registering its small voting population, also was exempt.

Three states, Virginia, Vermont, and Arkansas, have been given an extra year to reconcile their state laws to be in compliance with the bill. Eight states—including California, Illinois, and Pennsylvania—have filed suits against the law, claiming they can't afford to comply with it without federal funds. However, the California suit has already been rejected by a federal court and the challenges are considered unlikely to prevail.

Eligible voters should contact their State Secretary's office, town hall or county election office, or local League of Women Voters branch for more information. For those who are housebound or will be out of their district on voting day, absentee ballots usually are available from the same sources.

SO YOU WANT TO GIVE MONEY

Money seems to amplify the voice of the electorate substantially, so you may want to consider supporting the candidate that supports your views. But before you write a check to your favorite candidate or political party, you better know the rules limiting campaign donations.

According to Federal election laws, individuals may give no more than as follows: $1,000 to each candidate or candidate committee in an election (primaries and general elections count separately), $20,000 to a national party committee per calendar year, and $5,000 to any other political committee per calendar year. Foreign nationals are prohibited from donating to campaigns in the United States. For more information, contact the Federal Election Commission, ☎ 800-424-9530.

tain mobile sites, should make registration easier still in most states (see box, above).

Besides, demographic trends seem to favor increased voter participation. Generally the higher the level of education, the greater the degree of residential stability, and the older the electorate, the higher the voter turnout will be. The U.S. population generally is better educated, staying put, and graying—but, except for the 1992 blip, still shying away from the ballot box. Gans is left with only one conclusion: "You've got to say that the decline of participation has to do with motivation." In a word, apathy.

All segments of the American electorate, however, aren't equally apathetic. In every presidential election since 1980, both the number and proportion of eligible women voters that vote has exceeded those of men, according to figures from the Center for the American Woman and Politics at Rutgers University. And U.S. Census figures show that college-educated Americans are twice as likely to vote as those without a high school diploma.

What will motivate the rest of America to vote? Gans suggests that an attempt at civil political dialogue and voter education could help decrease the level of cynicism. Politicians who are in touch with and responsive to the needs of ordinary Americans, Gans says, might be just the ticket.

EXPERT SOURCES

KEEPING TABS ON YOUR LEGISLATORS

How closely does that campaign rhetoric match the reality? You can't monitor every vote of your Representative personally, but there are organizations that do just that and more on a regular basis. We've listed some of the most influential interest groups in the country; whether you want to join their cause and lobby Congress or merely find out what your elected officials are up to, these organizations can help. An asterisk indicates groups that rate members of Congress.

BUSINESS AND LABOR

AFL-CIO COMMITTEE ON POLITICAL EDUCATION*
815 16th St. NW
Washington, D.C. 20006
☎ 202-637-5101
■ The nation's most powerful labor group, it's actually a federation of local, state, and national unions.

U.S. CHAMBER OF COMMERCE*
1615 H St. NW
Washington, D.C. 20062
☎ 202-659-6000
One of the big three pro-business lobbying groups. Had its heyday during the Reagan administration.

NATIONAL ASSOCIATION OF MANUFACTURERS
1331 Pennsylvania Ave. NW
Suite 1500
Washington, D.C. 20004
☎ 202-637-3000
The most politically middle-of-the-road of the big three. Its members are, not surprisingly, large manufacturing firms.

NATIONAL FEDERATION OF INDEPENDENT BUSINESS
600 Maryland Ave. SW, #700
Washington, D.C. 20024
☎ 202-554-9000
■ Champions the interests of small, independent businesses and is closest to the grass roots of the big three business groups.

CIVIL RIGHTS

NATIONAL RAINBOW COALITION, INC.
1700 K St. NW, #800
Washington, D.C. 20006
☎ 202-728-1180
■ Founded by the Rev. Jesse Jackson, this group is best known for its advocacy of racial and ethnic tolerance.

CONSUMER GROUPS

COMMON CAUSE
2030 M St. NW #300
Washington, D.C. 20036
☎ 202-833-1200
■ Among other things, Common Cause advocates public financing of congressional campaigns and ethics in government. It has been a player in the recent debate about campaign finance reform.

CONSUMER FEDERATION OF AMERICA*
1424 16th St. NW, #604
Washington, D.C. 20036
☎ 202-387-6121
■ This federation of 240 organizations claims to stand up for the rights of average consumers in Congress and before federal regulatory agencies.

THE ENVIRONMENT

NATIONAL WILDLIFE FEDERATION
1400 16th St. NW, #610
Washington, D.C. 20036
☎ 202-797-6800
■ One of the most powerful public advocates for the environment and endangered species.

FAMILY ISSUES

THE CHRISTIAN COALITION *
P.O. Box 1990
Chesapeake, VA 23327
☎ 804-424-2630
■ The coalition has mobilized thousands of Christian activists around the country in support of a host of conservative issues. Leader Ralph Reed has been scoring points as one of Washington's savviest operators. TV evangelist Pat Robertson is the power behind the scenes.

NATIONAL ABORTION REPRODUCTIVE RIGHTS ACTION LEAGUE*
1156 15th St. NW, Suite 700
Washington, D.C. 20005
☎ 202-973-3000
■ The most prominent

■ EXPERT SOURCES

organization supporting reproductive choice and safe, legal abortions.

NATIONAL RIGHT TO LIFE COMMITTEE*
419 7th St., NW, Suite 500
Washington, DC 20004
☎ 202-626-8800
■ The other side of the abortion battle. The committee opposes abortion, euthanasia, and infanticide, and supports abortion alternative programs.

GUNS

NATIONAL RIFLE ASSOCIATION*
11250 Waples Mill Rd.
Fairfax, VA 22030
☎ 703-267-1000
■ The self-appointed defender of the Second Amendment, the NRA knows how to flex its muscle in Washington. It is one of the most powerful PACs in the country.

JEWISH CAUSES

AMERICAN ISRAEL PUBLIC AFFAIRS COMMITTEE
440 First St. NW, #600
Washington, D.C. 20001
☎ 202-639-5200
■ A powerful voice in Congress on issues that affect the future of Israel

AMERICAN JEWISH CONGRESS
2027 Massachusetts Ave. NW
Washington, D.C. 20036
☎ 202-332-4001
■ Along with AIPAC, the most prominent lobbying force in Washington for Jewish affairs. Promotes civil rights and religious freedom.

SENIOR CITIZENS

AMERICAN ASSOCIATION FOR RETIRED PERSONS
601 E Street, NW
Washington, D.C. 20049
☎ 202-434-2277
■ Arguably the most vocal public interest group of them all, and certainly one of the most powerful, this senior citizens' organization is legendary for its legislative savvy. Its magazine, *Modern Maturity,* has the largest circulation of any in the country.

HOW TO E-MAIL YOUR CONGRESSPERSON

They may be inside the Beltway, but that doesn't mean they're out of touch

It's January 1997 and Washington is buzzing with new and returning Hill staffers, White House aides, and, oh, yes, newly elected officials. Here's how to find out what they are up to via the Internet. For further information about online government offerings, see "Uncle Sam Wants You in Cyberspace," page 773.

■ **CONGRESS:** At last count, 32 senators and 89 representatives have gone online. Their e-mail adressess, as well as the text of House bills, the Bill of Rights, and election results are available on the World Wide Web and at several gopher sites:
WWW: *http://www.house.gov/*
GOPHER: *gopher//ftp.senate.gov.70/*

■ **THE WHITE HOUSE:** If you wish to communicate with the President and his minions, the White House has its own World Wide Web site. Here you can see up-to-the-minute press releases and transcripts of presidential speeches, get information on White House tours and other events at the mansion, and send a message to the president. Among the more trivial web arcana is a sound bite of Socks the cat meowing.
WWW: *http://www.whitehouse.gov/*

■ **GENERAL:** The increasingly useful Yahoo directory on the World Wide Web offers several hypertext links on its government sites page. Among them are CapWeb, Thomas, and Project Vote Smart, which offers ratings of members of Congress by several different organizations and other useful general information.
WWW: *http://www.yahoo.com/Government/*

PRESIDENTS

THEY HAD THE RIGHT STUFF

A composite look at the 42 fellows who have led the nation thus far

Gerald Ford once commented on the early days of his troubled presidency, "I guess it just proves that in America, anyone can be president." Of course, it helps if you're white, male, and protestant. Following are some of the traits that America's top executives have had in common, and a few that they haven't.

■ **PLACES OF ORIGIN:** The most fertile producer of American presidents is Virginia, where 8 presidents were born, followed by Ohio (7), Massachusetts (4), and New York (4). All together, 19 states conspired to produce the 42 presidents thus far elected. Where did successful presidential candidates live at the time of their election? New York leads with 8 candidates, followed by Ohio (6), and Virginia (5). Six presidents were born in log cabins—Andrew Jackson, Zachary Taylor, Millard Fillmore, James Buchanan, James Garfield, and, of course, Abraham Lincoln.

■ **RELIGION:** Nearly all of the presidents were born Protestants. John Kennedy, the first Roman Catholic elected to the office, was the sole exception. The most common sect of presidents is Episcopalian (11), followed by Presbyterian (7) and Unitarian (4). The four Baptist presidents (Warren Harding, Harry Truman, Jimmy Carter, and Bill Clinton) have all served in the 20th century. Thomas Jefferson was a Deist. Andrew Johnson and Abraham Lincoln had no affiliation with an organized religion.

■ **EDUCATION:** The president with the least formal education was Andrew Jackson (his wife taught him how to read). Woodrow Wilson was the only president with a Ph.D.—a degree in history from Johns Hopkins. Twelve presidents made it to the highest office with no college degree at all, but only one (Truman) served in the 20th century. Harvard boasts the greatest number of presidential alumni (5), followed by Yale, Princeton, and William and Mary, each of which claims two graduates.

■ **PROFESSION:** Thirteen presidents were practicing lawyers, and over half of the 42 presidents had training in the law. Seven were former soldiers and 3 were professors. Andrew Johnson was a tailor, Herbert Hoover was an engineer, and Ronald Reagan was an actor. Two presidents served as university presidents—Woodrow Wilson at Princeton and Dwight Eisenhower at Columbia.

MARRIAGE AND FAMILY: Nearly all of America's presidents have been married; James Buchanan is the sole exception. Eight presidents, however, were widowed before or during their terms of office. Two presidents, Grover Cleveland and Woodrow Wilson, were married while in the White House. George Washington, James Madison, Andrew Jackson, James Polk, James Buchanan, and Warren Harding were the only presidents not to have children—although there is some evidence that Harding fathered an illegitimate child while in office and Jackson took in a Native American child orphaned following a raid on a Florida settlement when Jackson was a general. Grover Cleveland is the only president to admit to fathering an illegitimate child.

ELECTIONS: Two presidents won office despite losing the popular vote. In 1824, John Quincy Adams lost the electoral vote and the popular vote. He received 30 percent of the popular vote to Andrew Jackson's 40 percent in a four-person race. The outcome was decided in the House of Representatives. In 1876, Rutherford B. Hayes lost the popular vote to Samuel Tilden by over 250,000 popular votes but squeaked into office by just one electoral vote.

John Kennedy beat Richard Nixon by a mere 118,000 votes in the 1960 election. In 1968, Nixon beat Hubert Humphrey by only 510,000 votes. The three biggest landslides went to Franklin Roosevelt in 1936, Richard Nixon in 1972, and Ronald Reagan in 1984. Both Nixon and Reagan carried all but one state and the District of Columbia.

LIFE AFTER THE WHITE HOUSE: John Quincy Adams was elected to Congress, where he served for 17 years. Andrew Johnson was elected to the U.S. Senate. Jimmy Carter served as an international mediator.

DEATHS: Three presidents, John Adams, Thomas Jefferson, and James Monroe, died on July 4, the anniversary of the signing of the Declaration of Independence, in which all three had taken part.

Eight presidents have died while still in office. Four of them—Abe Lincoln, James Garfield, William McKinley, and John Kennedy—were assassinated. William Harrison, Zachary Taylor, Warren Harding, and Franklin Roosevelt all died of natural causes. Harrison died one month after taking office, from pneumonia that developed from a cold that he caught on Inauguration Day, after speaking for two hours in a freezing rainstorm.

PRESIDENTIAL PERCENTAGES

Some factors are more important than others

MALE OF THE SPECIES	42	100.0%
PROTESTANT	38	90.5%
MARRIED	41	97.6%
STUDIED LAW	28	66.6%
OWNED DOGS	22	52.4%
OVER SIX FEET	18	42.9%
FROM VIRGINIA	8	19.0%
NAMED JAMES	6	14.3%
HAD A BEARD	5	12.0%
WENT TO HARVARD	5	12.0%
OWNED PET RACCOONS	2	5.0%

ODDS AND ENDS: Nine presidents owned slaves. Two presidents, Millard Fillmore and Andrew Johnson, were indentured servants during their childhoods. Fillmore was indentured to two different textile craftspeople; he bought his freedom at the age of 19.

Jefferson was perhaps the most inventive president. Among his many inventions: a dumbwaiter for moving food into rooms from the kitchen; the lazy susan; swivel chairs; and a pedometer. John Adams swam in the Potomac. John Quincy Adams produced a small volume of poetry in 1832. Zachary Taylor's warhorse, Old Whitey, wandered around on the White House lawn.

A PARADE OF PRESIDENTS

So far, there have been 42 presidents and 45 vice presidents of the United States. Sixteen of the presidents served more than one term.

PRESIDENT	VICE PRESIDENT	TERM OF OFFICE		PARTY AFFILIATION	AGE AT INAUG.
1. George Washington	John Adams	April 30, 1789	March 3, 1797	Federalist	57
2. John Adams	Thomas Jefferson	March 4, 1797	March 3, 1801	Federalist	61
3. Thomas Jefferson	Aaron Burr George Clinton	March 4, 1801	March 3, 1809	Dem.-Rep.	57
4. James Madison	Elbridge Gerry	March 4, 1809	March 3, 1817	Dem.-Rep.	57
5. James Monroe	Daniel D. Tompkins	March 4, 1817	March 3, 1825	Dem.-Rep.	58
6. John Quincy Adams	John C. Calhoun	March 4, 1825	March 3, 1829	Dem.-Rep.	57
7. Andrew Jackson	Martin Van Buren	March 4, 1829	March 3, 1837	Democrat	61
8. Martin Van Buren	Richard M. Johnson	March 4, 1837	March 3, 1841	Democrat	54
9. William Henry Harrison	John Tyler	March 4, 1841	April 4, 1841	Whig	68
10. John Tyler [1]		April 6, 1841	March 3, 1845	Whig	51
11. James K. Polk	George M. Dallas	March 4, 1845	March.3, 1849	Democrat	49
12. Zachary Taylor	Millard Fillmore	March 5, 1849	July 9, 1850	Whig	64
13. Millard Fillmore [1]		July 10, 1850	March 3, 1853	Whig	50
14. Franklin Pierce	William R. King	March 4, 1853	March 3, 1857	Democrat	48
15. James Buchanan	John C. Breckinridge	March 4, 1857	March 3, 1861	Democrat	65
16. Abraham Lincoln	Hannibal Hamlin Andrew Johnson [2]	March 4, 1861	April 15, 1865	Republican	52
17. Andrew Johnson [1]		April 15, 1865	March 3, 1869	Democrat	56
18. Ulysses S. Grant	Schuyler Colfax Henry Wilson	March 4, 1869	Nov. 22, 1875	Republican	46
19. Rutherford B. Hayes	William A. Wheeler	March 4, 1877	March 3, 1881	Republican	54
20. James A. Garfield	Chester A. Arthur	March 4, 1881	Sept. 19, 1881	Republican	49
21. Chester A. Arthur [1]		Sept. 20, 1881	March 3, 1885	Republican	50
22. Grover Cleveland	Thomas A. Hendricks	March 4, 1885	March 3, 1889	Democratic	47
23. Benjamin Harrison	Levi P. Morton	March 4, 1889	March 3, 1893	Republican	55
24. Grover Cleveland	Adlai E. Stevenson	March 4, 1893	March 3, 1897	Democrat	55
25. William McKinley	Garret A. Hobart Theodore Roosevelt	March 4, 1897	March 3, 1901	Republican	54
26. Theodore Roosevelt [1]	Charles W. Fairbanks	March 4, 1901	March 3, 1909	Republican	42
27. William Howard Taft	James S. Sherman	March 4, 1909	March 3, 1913	Republican	51
28. Woodrow Wilson	Thomas R. Marshall	March 4, 1913	March 3, 1921	Democrat	56
29. Warren G. Harding	Calvin Coolidge	March 4, 1921	Aug. 2, 1923	Republican	55
30. Calvin Cooolidge [1]	Charles G. Dawes	Aug. 3, 1923	March 3, 1929	Republican	51
31. Herbert Hoover	Charles Curtis	March 4, 1929	March 3, 1933	Republican	54
32. Franklin D. Roosevelt	John N. Garner Henry A. Wallace, Harry S Truman	March 4, 1933	April 12, 1945	Democrat	51
33. Harry S Truman	Alben W. Barkley	April 12, 1945	Jan. 20, 1953	Democrat	60
34. Dwight D. Eisenhower	Richard M. Nixon	Jan. 20, 1953	Jan. 20, 1961	Republican	62
35. John F. Kennedy	Lyndon B. Johnson	Jan. 20, 1961	Nov. 22, 1963	Democrat	43
36. Lyndon B. Johnson [1]	Hubert H. Humphrey	Nov. 22, 1963	Jan. 20, 1969	Democrat	55
37. Richard M. Nixon	Spiro T. Agnew Gerald Ford	Jan. 20, 1969	Aug. 9, 1974	Republican	56
38. Gerald Ford [1]	Nelson Rockefeller	Aug. 9, 1974	Jan. 20, 1977	Republican	61
39. James Earl Carter	Walter F. Mondale	Jan. 20, 1977	Jan. 20, 1981	Democrat	52
40. Ronald Reagan	George Bush	Jan. 20, 1981	Jan. 20, 1989	Republican	69
41. George Bush	Dan Quayle	Jan. 20, 1989	Jan. 20, 1993	Republican	64
42. William J. Clinton	Al Gore	Jan. 20, 1993		Democrat	46

1. Term includes part of predecessor's term. 2. A Democrat elected as vice-president with the Republican Lincoln on the National Union ticket.

EXPERT Q&A

THE MAKING OF THE PRESIDENCY

Two leading scholars reflect on how the office has changed in 200 years

How has the institution of the presidency evolved since George Washington took office in 1789? We spoke with two leading historians to find out. Henry Graff, Professor Emeritus at Columbia University and one of five members of the JFK Assassination Record Review Board, has been teaching a course on the presidency since the '50s. Stephen Ambrose, a history professor at the University of New Orleans, is the author of biographies of Dwight Eisenhower and Richard Nixon.

■ How has the presidency changed over the years?

GRAFF: It was created by Washington, who was very conscious that he was the first president, and that everything he did would create a precedent. If there hadn't been a strong figure in the beginning, the office would not have evolved the way it did. The president was known then as the "Great White Father."

With the exception of Washington and Lincoln, most people didn't know what the president looked like during the 19th century. With the exception of Lincoln, the president was not the center of news until Teddy Roosevelt's time. The institution has been accentuated by television. There is hardly a television broadcast that isn't done from the driveway of the White House. Teddy Roosevelt was the first to put "The White House" on his stationery.

The creation of the presidency was discussed at the Constitutional Convention, but the details were an afterthought not formally voted upon. The term of the office wasn't even decided. At the beginning of the 20th century, the president became known as the head of party, head of government, and chief of state.

The president also has assumed an enormous legislative role. There was less legislation during the 19th century, largely because this was before the enlargement of the country. The "Montesquieu" model of the Founding Fathers was seen as compartmentalized, but it didn't work that way. We do not really have the vaunted separation of powers.

■ Have there been times when the president was less important?

AMBROSE: There was a lack of preeminence in presidents between Madison and Lincoln, and during the post–Civil War period, with the exception of times of real crises in the country. Now we're in a similar situation, but we're not at all geared to it. Today we have a press and electronic media that are completely geared to covering the presidency and maintaining expensive staffs at the White House, but it's almost irrelevant, because all the action is in Congress. Whoever won the election of 1992 was going to find great frustration. The job is really not all that important, not as it has been. It's not a question of personality.

■ What distinguishes the presidents of the 20th century?

GRAFF: In the 20th century, the president has been expected to have a program. The New Nationalism of Teddy Roosevelt, the New Freedom of Wilson. The New Frontier, The New Deal, The Fair Deal. Prior to the 20th century, the vision thing was not something presidents were expected to have.

■ What influences a president's ability to succeed?

AMBROSE: It does not have much to do with their characteristics. It has more to do with crises and whether the president can convince the country that there is a crisis. Clinton, for example, could not convince the country that there was a crisis in health care. Franklin Roosevelt, on the other hand, was more successful in persuading people of the need for social security. And

Teddy Roosevelt was able to convince the country that there was a crisis in conservation, so he accomplished a lot.

It also takes something else that's lacking today: money in the bank. Eisenhower was a successful president, a builder. But not since Eisenhower have we run the kind of surpluses we ran at that time.

What makes a good president?

GRAFF: A president has to be both extraordinary and ordinary in all dimensions: in his political performance, in his personal performance, in his family performance, in his television appearances. It is difficult to do. On television, he comes across as too ordinary; when he is reclusive, he is seen as too distant.

AMBROSE: Power of articulation, believability and credibility, and an ability to show concern are very important. Basic honesty. Does character matter? I think it does. Washington, Grant, and Jackson are examples of soldiers who have been successful. Indecisiveness certainly is a great weakness in the White House. That applies to both Carter and Clinton.

EXPERT PICKS

FIRST-RATE PRESIDENTS AND FASCINATING FIRST LADIES

Who were the most successful presidents? The most interesting? The most overrated? And what about the first ladies? We asked historians Henry Graff and Stephen Ambrose for the answers. Their picks are listed in chronological order.

MOST SUCCESSFUL

Stephen Ambrose chooses:

GEORGE WASHINGTON: He established precedence and assured the democratic future of the republic. He gave us stability after a long war, during the difficult period following the Articles of Confederation.

THOMAS JEFFERSON: He oversaw the Louisiana Purchase. (A vast territory west of the Mississippi that the United States purchased from the French emperor, Napoleon, for a mere $15 million.)

ANDREW JACKSON: Jackson brought the common man into the White House. His attack on the Bank of America, and on monopoly capitalism gave new meaning to the evolving political traditions of the Republic.

ABRAHAM LINCOLN: The reasons are obvious. The author of the Gettysburg Address, he presided over the country during the biggest threat to its future and saw it through.

THEODORE ROOSEVELT: A champion of conservation, he created the national park system and successfully negotiated the Panama Canal Treaty.

FRANKLIN D. ROOSEVELT: He rallied a country that badly needed it. He gave hope where there had been only fear, led us through the greatest war of our history, and his conduct during the war was right, for the most part.

DWIGHT D. EISENHOWER: He was a builder who constructed our national highway system. He put a final seal on the reforms of the New Deal, in the face of members of his own party who wanted to get rid of it. He kept the welfare program and vastly expanded social security, putting the program above politics.

LYNDON B. JOHNSON: He did more for black America than any president since Lincoln. There were some excesses, but he would have been a great president if it wasn't for the war in Vietnam.

■ EXPERT PICKS

MOST INTERESTING

Henry Graff chooses:

■ **JAMES MONROE:** He was known as "The last of the cocked hats," the last of the revolutionary figures. It was said that part of his popularity was that he looked like George Washington. He redid the White House with modern elegance after it was reconstituted following the War of 1812, when it was burned by the British. When he left the presidency, he spent almost all of his time suing the federal government for real and imagined reimbursements he claimed were due him. He was always in debt, from which he was finally bailed out when he sold his library to Congress. These were the first volumes of the Library of Congress.

■ **JAMES K. POLK:** Like Truman, he was an unknown who came out of nowhere. He was the only Speaker of the House to become President. He ran a war (the Mexican War), successfully imposing it on an unwilling Congress. He oversaw the largest land acquisition after the Louisiana Purchase (New Mexico, California, and Oregon). He said he would not run for a second term—and kept his word.

■ **GROVER CLEVELAND:** A major figure in the post–Civil War era. He wrestled with the development of the civil service, with the new role of American finance, and with U.S. relations with the rest of world finance. He was a symbol of America as a growing place in the world, a transitional figure. He was hounded for having gone fishing on Memorial Day, and for giving back the Confederate flag to Southern veterans.

■ **FRANKLIN D. ROOSEVELT:** The greatest and most interesting president. A man of great personal courage. He had been out of politics and had risen again when he came to office in 1932. For all the disingenuousness that he could display, for all the double-talk he employed, people trusted him. He was not transparent, and there are still things about him that we do not know.

OVERRATED PRESIDENTS

Stephen Ambrose chooses:

■ **JOHN F. KENNEDY:** He had no major accomplishments and took a lot of high risks that were in part excessive, particularly the Cuban Missile crisis.

■ **RONALD REAGAN:** For putting us in a terrible debt situation. If you had to put it down to one issue it would be the "Star Wars" program. Lowering taxes while increasing defense was a major error.

INFLUENTIAL FIRST LADIES

Henry Graff chooses:

■ **MARTHA WASHINGTON:** She was spunky, social, with a sense of decorum, and she had an impact on the presidency from the very beginning.

■ **SARAH CHILDRESS POLK:** A power at dinners, she was serious, had a strong working relationship with her husband, and a strong Protestant work ethic (and no use for dancing or theater). She was as forceful as Hillary Clinton, a voracious reader who was independent and educated, and cultivated friendships with strong men (including former and future Presidents Andrew Jackson and Franklin Pierce) and women in Washington.

■ **LOUISE TAFT:** She was very instrumental in her husband's nomination to the presidency.

■ **ELEANOR ROOSEVELT:** A strong partner to Franklin in the White House, she was well-traveled, compassionate, and tirelessly worked for a variety of women's and children's causes, as well as helping to mobilize the war effort.

■ **ROSALYNN CARTER:** The first to take solo diplomatic missions, she concurred with Betty Ford's belief that the first lady ought to be a paid position.

EXPERT SOURCES

A PRESIDENTIAL READING LIST

The following books are lauded by historians and pundits as the best sources of information about the institution and the individuals that make up the presidency

GENERAL BOOKS

PRESIDENTIAL POWER AND THE MODERN PRESIDENTS: THE POLITICS OF LEADERSHIP FROM ROOSEVELT TO REAGAN
Richard E. Neustadt, Free Press, 1990, $22.95
■ The classic. A prominent Harvard professor looks at the leadership abilities of presidents from WW II to the end of the Cold War.

THE PRESIDENTIAL CHARACTER: PREDICTING PERFORMANCE IN THE WHITE HOUSE
James David Barber, Prentice-Hall, 1972, $15.95
What characteristics affect the ability of presidents to lead and succeed? Barber looks at the inhabitants of the White House from Washington to Carter and singles out the patterns associated with successful presidential performance.

FIRST LADIES
Betty Boyd Caroli, Oxford University Press, 1987, $13.95
■ An in-depth look at presidential wives from Martha Washington to Nancy Reagan, including an examination of the origins of the term first lady, a look at the role's controversies, and a study of the role's evolution.

BIOGRAPHIES

WASHINGTON: THE INDISPENSABLE MAN
James Thomas Flexner, Little, Brown & Co., 1969, $14.95 (abridged)
■ Originally four volumes, but even the abridged version is exhaustive in its account of Washington's life from the French and Indian War to his death in 1799.

JEFFERSON AND HIS TIME
Dumas Malone, Little, Brown & Co., 1967–1981, $15.95 per volume
■ Six volumes. Winner of the Pulitzer Prize for History in 1975, this is one of the most detailed accounts of Jefferson's presidency, as well as his earlier and later careers.

THOMAS JEFFERSON: A LIFE
Willard Sterne Randall, Henry Holt & Co., 1993, $16
■ This recent work by an investigative reporter claims to uncover new material and challenge previously held assumptions about Jefferson's life, philosophy, and moral beliefs. It stirred quite a bit of controversy on its release.

JAMES MONROE: THE QUEST FOR NATIONAL IDENTITY
Harry Ammon, U. of Virginia Press, 1990, $18.95
■ A complete account of Monroe's life, from his birth in Virginia in 1758 and his early army career through the Confederation Congress and the presidency.

ANDREW JACKSON AND THE COURSE OF AMERICAN EMPIRE
Robert Remini, Penguin, 1988, $27.95
■ From his childhood to the presidency. An examination of both character and historical context.

THE AGE OF JACKSON
Arthur M. Schlesinger, Jr., Little, Brown, 1945, $15.95
■ Beautifully written, this is the definitive account of the impact of Jackson's two terms on the evolving democratic traditions of 19th-century America.

THE PRESIDENCY OF JAMES K. POLK
Paul Bergeron, University Press of Kansas, 1987, $25
■ One of the most important works about the Polk presidency. An examination of Polk's emergence as a political leader.

EXPERT SOURCES

HERNDON'S LIFE OF LINCOLN
Willard H. Herndon, Da Capo Press, 1983, $14.95
■ Lincoln from the perspective of his law partner.

MORNINGS ON HORSEBACK
David G. McCullough, Simon & Schuster, 1981, $14.95
■ The author of the best-selling biography of Harry Truman examines Teddy Roosevelt's early career.

THEODORE ROOSEVELT
Henry F. Pringle, Harcourt Brace & Co., 1931, $13.95
■ The definitive, Pulitzer Prize–winning biography.

THE WARRIOR & THE PRIEST: WOODROW WILSON & THEODORE ROOSEVELT
John M. Cooper, Jr., Belknap Press, 1990, $14.50
■ Delves into the character of the two most influential presidents of the early 20th century.

WOODROW WILSON: A BIOGRAPHY
August Heckscher, Collier Books, 1991, $18
■ A *New York Times Book Review* "Notable Book of the Year," and a revealing look at Wilson.

ROOSEVELT 1882–1940: THE LION AND THE FOX
James M. Burns, Harcourt Brace & Co., 1984, $16.95
■ The first of two volumes, it covers FDR's early life and through to the New Deal.

NO ORDINARY TIME: FRANKLIN AND ELEANOR ROOSEVELT: THE HOME FRONT IN WORLD WAR II
Doris Kearns Goodwin, Simon & Schuster 1994, $30
■ This Pulitzer Prize-winning new study explores the relationship of Franklin and Eleanor, and the impact of their partnership on a country at war.

TRUMAN
David G. McCullough, Simon & Schuster, 1992, $15
■ This recent best-selling Pulitzer Prize winner examines the life and times of Truman from World War I and Kansas City machine politics through the Korean War.

EISENHOWER: SOLDIER AND PRESIDENT
Stephen Ambrose, Simon & Schuster, 1990, $16
■ An abridged version of the exhaustive two-volume work originally published as *Eisenhower.*

A THOUSAND DAYS: JOHN F. KENNEDY IN THE WHITE HOUSE
Arthur M. Schlesinger, Jr., Houghton Mifflin, 1965, $7
■ One of the most detailed and informed accounts of the Kennedy administration as told by renowned historian Schlesinger, who was a White House insider during the Kennedy administration.

MEANS OF ASCENT: THE YEARS OF LYNDON JOHNSON
Robert A. Caro, Random House, 1991, $15
■ Second in a planned multi-volume series. Traces Johnson through his military sevice and focuses on the 1948 Texas Senate race.

NIXON: THE EDUCATION OF A POLITICIAN, 1913–1962
Stephen Ambrose, Simon & Schuster, 1987, $16
■ The first of a three-volume biography, the book traces the youthful development and career of this "complex, ambivalent, and contradictory" politician.

RICHARD MILHOUS NIXON: THE RISE OF AN AMERICAN POLITICIAN
Roger Morris, Henry Holt & Co., 1990, $15.95
■ A finalist for the National Book Critics Circle Award and the 1990 National Book Award.

AT THE HIGHEST LEVELS: THE INSIDE STORY OF THE END OF THE COLD WAR
Michael Beschloss and Strobe Talbott, Back Bay Books, 1993, $12.95
■ A comprehensive description of presidential foreign policy making; in this case, the delicate behind-the-scenes negotiations between presidents George Bush and Mikhail Gorbachev and their respective foreign secretaries, James Baker and Eduard Shevardnadze, at the end of the Cold War.

■ EXPERT SOURCES

FOR YOUNG READERS

FACTS ABOUT THE PRESIDENTS: A COMPILATION OF BIOGRAPHICAL AND HISTORICAL DATA
Joseph Nathan Hale, H.W. Wilson, 1974[1]
■ A great homework reference—a dictionary with two sections, the first includes a chapter on each president from Washington through Nixon, including statistics about each. The second section includes a tabulation of data about the presidents, plus an alphabetical listing of presidential and vice-presidential candidates.

PRESIDENTS OF THE UNITED STATES
Jane McConnell and Burt McConnell, Crowell, 1956[1]
■ The story of the life of each of the presidents from Washington to Truman is told against the historical backdrop of America's political and economic changes.

GEORGE WASHINGTON: THE MAN WHO WOULD NOT BE KING
Stephen Krensky, Scholastic, 1991, $2.95
■ Chockablock with pictures and illustrations from the National Archives, the book explains the beginning of the republic and traces the life of the founding father and his influence on future presidencies.

GEORGE WASHINGTON: FRONTIER COLONEL
Sterling North with illustrations by Lee Hines, Random House, 1957[1]
■ This is not a complete biography, but instead an entertaining portrayal of Washington's early life and his frontier experience as a colonel during the French and Indian War.

ANDREW JACKSON AND HIS AMERICA
Milton Meltzer and F. Watts, 1993, $16.40
■ *Kirkus Reviews* called this "a scathing portrayal of the man who presided over an era when slavery became more deeply entrenched, native Americans were driven from their eastern homelands, and U.S. citizens flooded Texas in anticipation of its annexation." For readers ages 11 and up.

ABRAHAM LINCOLN
Ingri D'Aulaire and Edgar Parin, Dell, 1939, $10
Winner of the Caldecott Medal, this classic illustrated book is targeted toward children in the primary grades.

LINCOLN: A PHOTOBIOGRAPHY
Russell Freedman, Houghton Mifflin, 1987, $7.95
■ An account of Lincoln's life from his boyhood to his assassination in 1865, the book contains dozens of carefully chosen photos and illustrations. It won the John Newbery Medal for Children's Literature.

ABE LINCOLN: LOG CABIN TO WHITE HOUSE
Sterling North, Random House, 1956, $4.99
■ A classic description of the poverty and other barriers that Lincoln surmounted to reach the White House.

BULLY FOR YOU, TEDDY ROOSEVELT
Jean Fritz, G.P. Putnam's Sons, 1991, $15.95
■ A look at Roosevelt's adventurous life, including accounts of his hobbies: hunting, exploring the wilds of South America, and fighting in Cuba, as well as his political life.

FRANKLIN D. ROOSEVELT: PORTRAIT OF A GREAT MAN
Gerald W. Johnson, Morrow, 1967[1]
■ Illustrated with 30 photographs. "Perhaps the most interesting aspect of the book," said the now-defunct *Saturday Review* magazine, "is the picture it gives of the political struggles of the beginner."

JOHN F. KENNEDY: COURAGE IN CRISIS
John W. Selfridge, Fawcett, 1989, $3.95
■ Part of the *Great Lives Series* for middle school students, the book examines the "courage and conviction" of Kennedy's life and presidency.

1. No longer in print—check your local library.

STATES & CITIES

PORTRAIT OF A NATION

America's population is growing, graying, and moving West

Americans love statistics about themselves. Hardly a day passes without a poll being released. Here, gleaned from the pages of the *Statistical Abstract of the United States*, the national data book published annually by the Department of Commerce, are some other facts and figures that describe how we live and how the country is changing.

■ **HEADCOUNT:** When the first estimate of the population was made in 1790, some 3.9 million people were living in the continental United States. According to the 1990 census, the U.S. population was almost 249 million, an increase of nearly 10 percent from the 1980 figure. The United States is the third most populous country in the world; only China and India have more people.

■ **THE MELTING POT:** During the 20th century, the greatest number of legal immigrants flooded our shores between 1901 and 1910—8.8 million people came to call America home. The second greatest wave—7.3 million—arrived during the '80s. Figures are available only through 1992, but the immigration rate doesn't seem to be dropping off in the '90s. The greatest number of new immigrants are coming from Mexico, Vietnam, and the Philippines.

■ **WHO WE ARE:** In 1992, women accounted for 51 percent of the population. The male-female ratio isn't projected to change much for the next 50 years. The median age of the entire population was 33.4 years. Just shy of 83 percent of Americans are white, 12.6 percent black, and 4.5 percent "other." People of Hispanic origin account for 9.5 percent of the population.

■ **WHERE WE LIVE:** Almost 80 percent of the population live in metropolitan areas. (New York, Los Angeles, and Chicago are the country's three largest cities.) The fastest-growing areas of the country are the Rocky Mountain states and the Southeast. New England, the Middle Atlantic states, and the Midwest either are losing population or growing at a much slower pace.

■ **WHAT WE EARN:** The median income for a white family in 1993 was $38,909; for a black family $21,161. Almost a third of black families are below the poverty level; only 9 percent of white families. Nationwide, 12 percent of American families are living below the poverty level.

CITIZEN'S GUIDE

THE STATES OF THE UNION

The United States continue in the great tradition of regionalism in which they were founded. A look at what sets them apart—and what binds them:

ALABAMA

The Heart of Dixie

★ **Montgomery**
BIRD: Yellowhammer
FLOWER: Camellia
ESTABLISHED: Dec. 4, 1819

AREA: 50,750 sq. miles 28th
POPULATION: 4,218,792 22nd

White	73.6%
Black	25.3%
Hispanic	0.6%
Asian or Pacific Islander	0.5%

■ BIGGEST CITIES

Birmingham: 265,968 pop. The "Football Capital of the South."
Mobile: 196,278 pop. The state's only seaport.
★**Montgomery:** 187,106 pop. The first capital of the Confederacy in 1861.

■ MONEY MATTERS

PER CAPITA INCOME: $17,106.
TAXES: Income, 2–5%; Sales, 4%; Gas,16 cents per gallon; Cigarettes, 16.5 cents per pack.

■ RED-LETTER DATES

1540: Spanish explorer Hernando de Soto explores the region.
1881: Tuskegee Institution is founded by Booker T. Washington. George Washington Carver later conducts groundbreaking agricultural research there.
1955: Rosa Parks refuses to give up her seat on a bus in Montgomery, leading to a bus boycott and a court ruling declaring segregation on buses to be unconstitutional.

■ SONS & DAUGHTERS

Hank Aaron, baseball player.
Helen Keller, author and educator.
Harper Lee, author.
☎ **TOURISM:** 800-252-2262

ALASKA

The Last Frontier

★ **Juneau**
BIRD: Willow Ptarmigan
FLOWER: Forget-me-not
ESTABLISHED: Jan. 3, 1959

AREA: 570,374 sq. miles 1st
POPULATION: 606,276 49th

White	75.5%
Black	4.1%
Hispanic	3.2%
Asian or Pacific Islander	3.9%

■ BIGGEST CITIES

Anchorage: 226,338 pop. Founded in 1915 as a railroad construction headquarters, the city is now home to 40 percent of Alaska's residents.
Fairbanks: 30,843 pop. It is the northernmost city in the United States.
★**Juneau:** 26,751 pop. Light planes tour the 1,500-square-mile Juneau Icefield, studded with nearly 40 glaciers.

■ MONEY MATTERS

PER CAPITA INCOME: $23,008.
TAXES: Income, none; Sales, 1–7%; Gas, 8 cents per gallon; Cigarettes, 29 cents per pack.

■ RED-LETTER DATES

1741: Discovered by Vitus Bering and Alexei Chirikuv.
1867: Sold to the United States by Russia for $7.2 million on March 30 after negotiations by Secretary of State William Seward. Purchase ridiculed as "Seward's Folly."
1989: The *Exxon Valdez* strikes Bligh Reef in Prince

■ AIDS

The states with the most people with AIDS, and the number of cases in each as of year-end 1994:

NEW YORK	83,197
CALIFORNIA	78,084
FLORIDA	43,978
TEXAS	30,712
NEW JERSEY	25,089

SOURCE: The Centers for Disease Control, Dec 31, 1994.

■ CITIZEN'S GUIDE

William Sound causing a 45-mile oil spill, the largest in U.S. history.

■ **SONS & DAUGHTERS**

Susan Butcher, sled-dog racer.
Vitus Bering, explorer.
☎ **TOURISM:** 907-465-2010

ARIZONA

Grand Canyon State

★ **Phoenix**
BIRD: Cactus Wren
FLOWER: Saguaro Cactus blossom

ESTABLISHED: February 14,1912
AREA: 113,642 sq. miles 6th
POPULATION: 407,5052 24th

White	80.8%
Black	3.0%
Hispanic	18.8%
Asian or Pacific Islander	1.5%

■ **BIGGEST CITIES**

★**Phoenix:** 983,403 pop. One of the country's fastest-growing cities.
Tucson: 405,390 pop. A veritable melting pot—residents of Native American, Spanish, Mexican, and Anglo backgrounds.
Mesa: 288,091 pop. Founded by Mormons in 1883.

■ **MONEY MATTERS**

PER CAPITA INCOME: $18,119.
TAXES: Income, 3.8–7%; Sales, 5%; Gas, 18 cents per gallon; Cigarettes, 18 cents per pack.

■ **RED-LETTER DATES**

1539: Spanish Franciscan friar Marcos de Niza enters area searching for the legendary Seven Cities of Gold.
1821: Spain cedes Arizona to Mexico. The United States takes state over in 1848 at the end of the Mexican war.
1973: New Cornelia Tailings, one of the world's largest dams, is finished.

■ **SONS & DAUGHTERS**

Alice Cooper, musician.
Barbara Eden, actress.
Geronimo, Apache chief.
Linda Ronstadt, singer.
☎ **TOURISM:** 800-842-8257

ARKANSAS

Land of Opportunity

★ **Little Rock**
BIRD: Mockingbird
FLOWER: Apple Blossom

ESTABLISHED: June 15, 1836
AREA: 52,075 sq. miles 27th
POPULATION: 2,452,671 33rd

White	82.7%
Black	3.0%
Hispanic	0.8%
Asian or Pacific Islander	0.5%

■ **BIGGEST CITIES**

★**Little Rock:** 175,795 pop. The state's historic, cultural, and economic center.
Fort Smith: 72,798 pop. The town's national historic site commemorates the founding, in 1817, of one of the American West's earliest forts.
North Little Rock: 61,741 pop. Its Old Mill is the only backdrop from the movie, *Gone With the Wind,* that still is in existence.

■ **MONEY MATTERS**

PER CAPITA INCOME: $15,994.
TAXES: Income, 1–7%; Sales, 4.5%; Gas, 18.5 cents per gallon; Cigarettes, 31.5 cents per pack.

■ **RED-LETTER DATES**

1686: First settlement, at Arkansas Post, by the French under Henri de Tonty.
1861: Arkansas secedes from Union—after the Civil War has begun.
1957: Governor Orval Faubus calls out the National Guard to prevent desegregation of Little Rock's Central High School. President Eisenhower sends in federal troops to enforce the court ruling.

■ **SONS & DAUGHTERS**

Bill Clinton, 42nd president of the United States.
Maya Angelou, poet, author.
Hattie Caraway, first woman senator.
☎ **TOURISM:** 800-628-8725

CALIFORNIA

Golden State

★ **Sacramento**
BIRD: California Valley Quail
FLOWER: Golden Poppy

ESTABLISHED: Sept. 9, 1850
AREA: 155,973 sq. miles 3rd

■ CITIZEN'S GUIDE

POPULATION: 31,430,697 1st

White	69.9%
Black	7.4%
Hispanic	25.8%
Asian or Pacific Islander	9.6%

■ **BIGGEST CITIES**
Los Angeles: 3,484,398 pop. City of Angels and celluloid dreams. Residents hail from more than 140 countries.
San Diego: 1,110,549 pop. 70 miles of beaches and three world-famous animal parks.
San Jose: 782,248 pop. The virtual capital of "Silicon Valley."

■ **MONEY MATTERS**
PER CAPITA INCOME: $21,884.
TAXES: Income, 1–11%; Sales, 6%; Gas, 18 cents per gallon; Cigarettes, 37 cents per pack.

■ **RED-LETTER DATES**
1848: California Gold Rush begins.
1906: Earthquake and fire April 18–19 kills 503 and leaves $350 million in damages in its wake.
1992: Rioters cause up to $1 billion in damage to south-central Los Angeles following the acquittal of four policemen in the videotaped beating of motorist Rodney King.
1994: O.J.Simpson goes on trial for the double murder of his former wife, Nicole, and her friend, Ronald Goldman.

■ **SONS & DAUGHTERS**
Shirley Temple Black, actress, ambassador.
Jack London, author.
Sally Ride, astronaut.
Tom Seaver, baseball player.
☎ **TOURISM:** 800-862-2543

COLORADO

Centennial State

★ **Denver**
BIRD: Lark Bunting
FLOWER: Columbine
ESTABLISHED: August 1, 1876
AREA: 103,729 sq. miles 8th
POPULATION: 3,655,647 26th

White	88.2%
Black	4.0%
Hispanic	12.9%
Asian or Pacific Islander	1.8%

■ **BIGGEST CITIES**
★**Denver:** 467,610 pop. The Mile-High City and the capital of the Rocky Mountain region.
Colorado Springs: 281,140 pop. At the foot of Pike's Peak—the highest of the Rocky Mountains.
Aurora: 222,103 pop. Settled in 1891, it now hosts a bustling fishing-tackle industry.

■ **MONEY MATTERS**
PER CAPITA INCOME: $21,475.
TAXES: Income, 5% of federal taxable income; Sales, 3%; Gas, 22 cents per gallon; Cigarettes, 20 cents per pack.

■ **RED-LETTER DATES**
1706: Territory is claimed by Juan de Ulibarri for Spain.
1806: Lt. Zebulon M. Pike explores the area, discovers his eponymous peak.

■ **SONS & DAUGHTERS**
Jack Dempsey, boxer.
Douglas Fairbanks, actor.
Anne Parrish, writer.
☎ **TOURISM:** 800-265-6723

CONNECTICUT

Constitution State, Nutmeg State

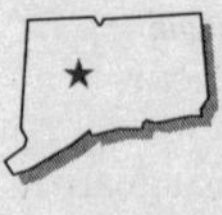

★ **Hartford**
BIRD: American Robin
FLOWER: Mountain Laurel
ESTABLISHED: Jan. 9,1788
AREA: 4,845 sq. miles 48th
POPULATION: 3,275,251 27th

White	87%
Black	8.3%
Hispanic	6.5%
Asian	1.5%

■ **BIGGEST CITIES**
Bridgeport: 141,686 pop. Home of the Barnum Museum, dedicated to showman P.T. Barnum.
★**Hartford:** 139,739 pop. The Old State House here is the nation's oldest.
New Haven: 130,474 pop. Home of Yale University.

■ **MONEY MATTERS**
PER CAPITA INCOME: $27,957.
TAXES: Income, 4.5%; Sales, 6%; Gas, 30 cents per gallon; Cigarettes, 47 cents per pack.

■ **RED-LETTER DATES**
1639: Now nicknamed the "Constitution State," Con-

■ CITIZEN'S GUIDE

necticut developed the Fundamental Orders, on which much of the Constitution was later based.
1703–1875: Connecticut had two capitals: Hartford and New Haven. Since 1875, the General Assembly has met solely in Hartford.
1878: First commercial telephone exchange in New Haven.

■ SONS & DAUGHTERS
Nathan Hale, officer of the American Revolution.
Harriet Beecher Stowe, author.
Katharine Hepburn, actress.
☎ **TOURISM:** 800-282-6862

DELAWARE

First State, Diamond State

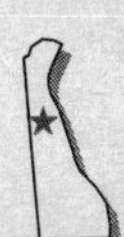

★ **Dover**
BIRD: Blue Hen Chicken
FLOWER: Peach Blossom
ESTABLISHED: Dec. 7, 1787
AREA: 1,955 sq. miles 49th
POPULATION: 706,351 46th

White	80.3%
Black	16.9%
Hispanic	2.4%
Asian or Pacific Islander	1.4%

■ BIGGEST CITIES
Wilmington: 71,529 pop. Becoming a national banking center.
★**Dover:** 27,630 pop. A local tavern here was the site of the Delaware convention ratifying the federal Constitution.
Newark: 26,464 pop. Home of the University of Delaware.

■ MONEY MATTERS
PER CAPITA INCOME: $21,735.
TAXES: Income, 3.2–7.7%; Sales, none; Gas, 22 cents per gallon; Cigarettes, 24 cents per pack.

■ RED-LETTER DATES
1609: Henry Hudson discovers Delaware.
1802: E. I. du Pont opens gunpowder mill, setting foundation for state's chemical industry.

■ SONS & DAUGHTERS
Thomas Garrett, abolitionist.
Annie Jump Cannon, astronomer.
Randy White, football player.
☎ **TOURISM:** 800-441-8846

FLORIDA

Sunshine State

★ **Tallahassee**
BIRD: Mockingbird
FLOWER: Orange Blossom
ESTABLISHED: March 3, 1845
AREA: 53,997 sq. miles 26th
POPULATION: 13,952,714 4th

White	83.1%
Black	13.6%
Hispanic	12.2%
Asian or Pacific Islander	1.2%

■ BIGGEST CITIES
Jacksonville: 672,971 pop. Features a 12-mile River-

■ GROWING PAIN
Folks are fleeing D.C., perhaps to take a gamble on Nevada

	NET CHANGE IN POPULATION 1980-1992
DISTRICT OF COLUMBIA	–8.3%
WEST VIRGINIA	–7.2%
IOWA	–3.8%
NORTH DAKOTA	–2.9%
WYOMING	–1.0%
PENNSYLVANIA	1.1%
ILLINOIS	1.6%
LOUISIANA	1.7%
MICHIGAN	1.9%
NEBRASKA	2.0%
OHIO	2.1%
KENTUCKY	2.6%
SOUTH DAKOTA	2.6%
INDIANA	3.1%
NEW YORK	3.1%
MISSISSIPPI	3.7%
MASSACHUSETTS	4.5%
MONTANA	4.5%
ARKANSAS	4.7%
CONNECTICUT	5.5%
MISSOURI	5.6%
RHODE ISLAND	5.7%
OKLAHOMA	5.9%
WISCONSIN	6.1%
NEW JERSEY	6.2%
ALABAMA	6.3%
KANSAS	6.4%
TENNESSEE	9.5%
MINNESOTA	9.6%
MAINE	9.9%
VERMONT	11.7%
IDAHO	12.9%
OREGON	12.9%
SOUTH CAROLINA	15.4%
DELAWARE	16.2%
NORTH CAROLINA	16.3%
MARYLAND	16.6%
VIRGINIA	19.6%
HAWAI'I	19.8%
COLORADO	19.9%
NEW HAMPSHIRE	21.1%
NEW MEXICO	21.4%
GEORGIA	24.0%
UTAH	24.0%
TEXAS	24.3%
WASHINGTON	24.5%
CALIFORNIA	30.5%
FLORIDA	38.3%
ARIZONA	41.1%
ALASKA	46.3%
NEVADA	66.9%

SOURCE: *County and City Data Book*, U.S. Department of Commerce, 1994.

walk, lined with restaurants and shops.
Miami: 358,548 pop. The art deco–spattered South Beach is the place to see and be seen.
Tampa: 280,015 pop. The MOSI Science Center's $35 million expansion will make it the largest science center in the Southeast.

■ **MONEY MATTERS**
PER CAPITA INCOME: $20,710.
TAXES: Income, none; Sales, 6%; Gas, 4 cents per gallon; Cigarettes, 33.9 cents per pack.

■ **RED-LETTER DATES**
1538: Ponce de Leon, looking for the "Fountain of Youth," finds Florida instead.
1958: *Explorer I,* the first U.S. earth satellite is launched Jan. 31 at Cape Canaveral.
1983: Sally Ride, the first American woman in space, blasts off in the space shuttle *Challenger* from Cape Canaveral.
1992: State attorney Janet Reno is appointed the first female U.S. attorney general.

■ **SONS & DAUGHTERS**
Charles and John Ringling, circus entrepeneurs.
Faye Dunaway, actress.
Jim Morrison, singer.
☎ **TOURISM:** 904-487-1462

■ **HEALTH CARE**
The five states with the highest percentage of residents that had health insurance in 1992.

HAWAII	94.0%
MINNESOTA	91.9%
CONNECTICUT	91.9%
NORTH DAKOTA	91.7%
PENNSYLVANIA	91.5%

SOURCE: U.S. Bureau of the Census.

GEORGIA

Empire State of the South, Peach State

★ **Atlanta**
BIRD: Brown Thrasher
FLOWER: Cherokee Rose
ESTABLISHED: Jan. 2, 1788
AREA: 57,919 sq. miles 21st
POPULATION: 7,055,336 11th

White	71.0%
Black	27.0%
Hispanic	1.7%
Asian or Pacific Islander	1.2%

■ **BIGGEST CITIES**
★**Atlanta:** 394,017 pop. Will host the 1996 Summer Olympics.
Columbus: 179,278 pop. The Lunchbox and Collectibles Museum serves up thousands of lunch boxes dating from 1900.
Savannah: 137,560 pop. The largest urban historic landmark district in the country.

■ **MONEY MATTERS**
PER CAPITA INCOME: $19,203
TAXES: Income, 1–6%; Sales, 4%; Gas, 7.5 cents per gallon; Cigarettes, 12 cents per pack.

■ **RED-LETTER DATES**
1835: Gold discovered on Indian territory. Indians forced to cede land.
1864: Union General William T. Sherman captures Savannah in the Civil War.
1945: President Roosevelt dies of a cerebral hemorrhage at age 63 in Warm Springs.

■ **SONS & DAUGHTERS**
Martin Luther King, Jr., civil rights leader.
Margaret Mitchell, author of *Gone with the Wind.*
Juliette Gordon Low, founder of the U.S. Girl Scouts.
☎ **TOURISM:** 800-847-4842

HAWAI'I

The Aloha State

★ **Honolulu**
BIRD: Hawai'ian Goose
FLOWER: Hibiscus
ESTABLISHED: August 21, 1959
AREA: 6,423 sq. miles 47th
POPULATION: 1,178,564 41st

White	33.4%
Black	2.5%
Hispanic	7.3%
Asian or Pacific Islander	61.8%

■ **BIGGEST CITIES**
★**Honolulu:** 377,059 pop. Its name means "protected harbor."
Hilo: 37,808 pop. Hawai'i's main port.

■ CITIZEN'S GUIDE

Kailua: 36,818 pop. Plays host to several world-class deep-sea fishing tournaments.

■ MONEY MATTERS

PER CAPITA INCOME: $23,378.
TAXES: Income, 2–10%; Sales, 4%; Gas, 16 cents per gallon; Cigarettes, 60 cents per pack.

■ RED-LETTER DATES

1820: King Kamehameha III and his chiefs create the area's first constitution and a legislature that sets up a public school system.
1835: Sugar production begins. It soon becomes the islands' dominant industry.
1893: Final monarch, Queen Liliuokalani, is deposed.

■ SONS & DAUGHTERS

Bernice Pauahi Bishop, Princess, heiress to close to 9 percent of the land in the Hawai'ian islands.
Salevaa Antinoe (Konishiki), sumo wrestler.
Hiram L. Fong, first Chinese-American senator.
☎ **TOURISM:** 800-464-2924

IDAHO

Gem State

★ **Boise**
BIRD: Mountain Bluebird
FLOWER: Syringa
ESTABLISHED: July 3, 1890

AREA: 82,751 sq. miles		11th
POPULATION: 1,133,034		42nd
White		94.4%
Black		0.3%
Hispanic		5.3%
Asian or Pacific Islander		0.9%

■ BIGGEST CITIES

★**Boise:** 135,506 pop. Touted as the "City of Trees."
Idaho Falls: 48,226 pop. Located where Snake River narrows and drops into a waterfall.
Pocatello: 47,914 pop. Was made famous in a Judy Garland song.

■ MONEY MATTERS

PER CAPITA INCOME: $17,540.
TAXES: Income, 2–8.2%; Sales, 5%; Gas, 21 cents per gallon; Cigarettes, 18 cents per pack.

■ RED-LETTER DATES

1896: Butch Cassidy robs a bank near Montpelier on August 13, getting away with $7,165.
1936: Sun Valley, the home of the world's first alpine skiing chairlift, is established as a ski resort.
1982: Legislature is first in the nation to outlaw the insanity plea for defendants.

■ SONS & DAUGHTERS

Ezra Pound, poet.
Sacajawea, guide on Lewis and Clark expedition.
Gretchen Frasier, 1948 Olympic gold medalist in skiing.
Gutzon Borglum, sculptor, carved Mt. Rushmore.
☎ **TOURISM:** 800-635-7820

ILLINOIS

The Prairie State

★ **Springfield**
BIRD: Cardinal
FLOWER: Native Violet
ESTABLISHED: Dec. 3, 1818

AREA: 55,593 sq. miles		24th
POPULATION: 11,751,774		6th
White		78.3%
Black		14.8%
Hispanic		7.9%
Asian or Pacific Islander		2.5%

■ BIGGEST CITIES

Chicago: 2,783,726 pop. The "Windy City." Early Native American inhabitants called it "Chicaugou."
Rockford: 139,426 pop. Nicknamed "The Forest City" for its tree-lined streets.
Peoria: 113,504 pop. Its Heart of Illinois Fair brings some 200,000 people to town every year.

■ MONEY MATTERS

PER CAPITA INCOME: $22,534.
TAXES: Income, 3%; Sales, 6.25%; Gas,19 cents per gallon; Cigarettes, 44 cents per pack.

■ RED-LETTER DATES

1846: Mormons, after fighting for right to practice polygamy, leave Nauvoo in western Illinois (now on Route 96) for Salt Lake City, Utah.
1886: A labor battle for an eight-hour work day in Chicago erupts into the Haymarket Riot.
1992: Carol Moseley

Braun becomes the first black woman to be elected to the U.S. Senate.

■ **SONS & DAUGHTERS**
Jane Addams, social worker.
Ernest Hemingway, author.
Betty Friedan, feminist.
Ronald Reagan, president.
☎ **TOURISM:** 800-223-0121

INDIANA

Hoosier State

★ **Indianapolis**
BIRD: Cardinal
FLOWER: Peony
ESTABLISHED: Dec. 11,1816

AREA: 35,870 sq. miles 38th
POPULATION: 5,752,073 14th

White	90.6%
Black	7.8%
Hispanic	1.8%
Asian or Pacific Islander	0.7%

■ **BIGGEST CITIES**
★**Indianapolis:** 731,327 pop. The Musical Arts Center conducts the longest continuous opera program in the Western Hemisphere.
Fort Wayne: 173,072 pop. Includes Indiana's largest shopping mall and Johnny Appleseed's gravesite.
Evansville: 126,272 pop. Houses Old Evansville Antique Mall, one of the two largest antique malls in southern Indiana.

■ **MONEY MATTERS**
PER CAPITA INCOME: $19,161.
TAXES: Income, 3.4%; Sales, 5%; Gas, 15 cents per gallon; Cigarettes, 15.5 cents per pack.

■ **RED-LETTER DATES**
1731–32: The French build a trading post at Vincennes.
1763: France cedes the area to Britain.
1811: General William H. Harrison defeats Tecumseh's Indian troops.

■ **SONS & DAUGHTERS**
Frank Borman, astronaut.
Cole Porter, songwriter.
Twyla Tharp, dancer and choreographer.
David Letterman, talk-show host.
Jane Pauley, TV personality.
☎ **TOURISM:** 800-289-6646

IOWA

Hawkeye State

★ **Des Moines**
BIRD: Eastern Goldfinch
FLOWER: Wild Rose
ESTABLISHED: Dec. 28, 1846

AREA: 55,875 sq. miles 23rd
POPULATION: 2,829,252 30th

White	96.6%
Black	1.7%
Hispanic	1.2%
Asian or Pacific Islander	0.9%

■ **BIGGEST CITIES**
★**Des Moines:** 194,540 pop. In the heartland of America, it's the three-time winner of the All-American City award.
Cedar Rapids: 111,659 pop. Features a Czech village with traditional bakeries, meat market, and shops.
Davenport 97,509 pop. Buffalo Bill Cody lived here, and his father's 1847 homestead and a memorial museum remain.

■ **MONEY MATTERS**
PER CAPITA INCOME: $18,324.
TAXES: Income, 0.4–9.98%; Sales, 5%; Gas, 20 cents per gallon; Cigarettes, 36 cents per pack.

■ **RED-LETTER DATES**
1673: Jacques Marquette and Louis Jolliet claim area for France.
1803: The United States gains control of this territory as part of Thomas Jefferson's Louisiana Purchase from the French.
1869: Terrace Hall mansion built by Iowa's first millionaire.

■ **SONS & DAUGHTERS**
Ann Landers and Abigail Van Buren, advice columnists.
Norman Borlaug, Nobel Peace Prize winner.
Henry A. Wallace, FDR's vice president.
☎ **TOURISM:** 800-345-4692

KANSAS

Sunflower State, Free State

★ **Topeka**
BIRD: Western Meadowlark
FLOWER: Native Sunflower
ESTABLISHED: Jan. 29,1861

AREA: 81,823 sq. miles 13th
POPULATION: 2,554,047 32nd

White	90.1%
Black	5.8%
Hispanic	3.8%
Asian or Pacific Islander	1.3%

■ CITIZEN'S GUIDE

■ BIGGEST CITIES

Wichita: 304,011 pop. A major aircraft industry center.

Kansas City: 149,767 pop. Not to be confused with much larger sister city in Missouri. The state constitution was drafted here.

★**Topeka:** 119,883 pop. Home of the Menninger Clinic, a leader in treatment of mental illness.

■ MONEY MATTERS

PER CAPITA INCOME: $19,874.

TAXES: Income, 4.4–7.75%; Sales, 4.9%; Gas, 18 cents per gallon; Cigarettes, 24 cents per pack.

■ RED-LETTER DATES

1874: Mennonites from Russia bring Turkey Red wheat to the state; Kansas is now a leading wheat-producing state.

1953: Kansas playwright William Inge's work, *Picnic,* wins Pulitzer Prize.

■ SONS & DAUGHTERS

Gwendolyn Brooks, poet.

Walter P. Chrysler, automobile manufacturer.

Amelia Earhart, aviator.

☎ **TOURISM:** :800-252-6727

KENTUCKY

Bluegrass State

BIRD: Cardinal

FLOWER: Goldenrod

ESTABLISHED: June 1, 1792

AREA: 39,732 sq. miles 36th

POPULATION: 3,826,794 23rd

White	92.0%
Black	7.1%
Hispanic	0.6%
Asian or Pacific Islander	0.5%

■ BIGGEST CITIES

Louisville: 269,063 pop. Home of the legendary Kentucky Derby horse races.

Lexington-Fayette: 225,366 pop. The town's first race course was established around 1788.

Owensboro: 53,549 pop. The last public hanging in the United States took place here on August 14, 1936.

■ MONEY MATTERS

PER CAPITA INCOME: $16,954.

TAXES: Income, 2–6%; Sales, 6%; Gas,15 cents per gallon; Cigarettes, 3 cents per pack.

■ RED-LETTER DATES

1774: First permanent American settlement west of the Allegheniés, in Harrodsburg.

1775: Explorer Daniel Boone clears the Wilderness Trail on his way west.

1875: The first Kentucky Derby is held on May 17 in Louisville.

■ SONS & DAUGHTERS

Muhammad Ali, boxer.

Louis D. Brandeis, Supreme Court Justice.

Abraham Lincoln, president.

Diane Sawyer, broadcast journalist.

☎ **TOURISM:** 800-225-8747

■ ABORTION

American women underwent 1,528,930 abortion procedures in 1992. A breakdown by state:

CALIFORNIA	304,230
NEW YORK	195,390
TEXAS	97,400
FLORIDA	84,680
ILLINOIS	68,420
MICHIGAN	55,580
NEW JERSEY	55,320
PENNSYLVANIA	49,740
OHIO	49,520
MASSACHUSETTS	40,660
GEORGIA	39,680
NORTH CAROLINA	36,180
VIRGINIA	35,020
WASHINGTON	33,190
MARYLAND	31,260
DISTRICT OF COLUMBIA	21,320
ARIZONA	20,600
COLORADO	19,880
CONNECTICUT	19,720
TENNESSEE	19,060
ALABAMA	17,450
MINNESOTA	16,180
OREGON	16,060
INDIANA	15,840
WISCONSIN	15,450
LOUISIANA	13,600
MISSOURI	13,510
NEVADA	13,300
KANSAS	12,570
HAWAI'I	12,190
SOUTH CAROLINA	12,190
KENTUCKY	10,000
OKLAHOMA	8,940
MISSISSIPPI	7,550
ARKANSAS	7,130
RHODE ISLAND	6,990
IOWA	6,970
NEW MEXICO	6,410
DELAWARE	5,730
NEBRASKA	5,580
MAINE	4,200
UTAH	3,940
NEW HAMPSHIRE	3,890
MONTANA	3,330
WEST VIRGINIA	3,140
VERMONT	2,900
ALASKA	2,370
IDAHO	1,710
NORTH DAKOTA	1,490
SOUTH DAKOTA	1,040
WYOMING	460

SOURCE: *County and City Data Book,* U.S. Dept. of Commerce, 1994.

■ CITIZEN'S GUIDE

LOUISIANA

Pelican State

★ **Baton Rouge**
BIRD: Eastern Brown Pelican
FLOWER: Magnolia
ESTABLISHED: April 30, 1812

AREA: 43,566 sq. miles	33rd
POPULATION: 4,315,085	21st
White	67.3%
Black	30.8%
Hispanic	2.2%
Asian or Pacific Islander	1.0%

■ BIGGEST CITIES

New Orleans: 496,938 pop. Site of the new world's first major trade center.
★**Baton Rouge:** 219,531 pop. The new state capitol building is the tallest in the nation—34 stories.
Shreveport: 198,525 pop. The state fair is held here every fall.

■ MONEY MATTERS

PER CAPITA INCOME: $16,588.
TAXES: Income, 2–6%; Sales, 4%; Gas, 20 cents per gallon; Cigarettes, 20 cents per pack.

■ RED-LETTER DATES

1803: Napoleon sells Louisiana to the United States for $11,250,000 in bonds plus $3,750,000 for American citizens with claims against the French government.
1815: British troops, unaware that a peace treaty had been signed in December of 1814, attack U.S. entrenchments near New Orleans on Jan. 8. The troops of General Andrew Jackson, also unaware of the treaty, defeat them in the Battle of New Orleans.

■ SONS & DAUGHTERS

Louis Armstrong, musician.
Lillian Hellman, playwright.
Paul Prudhomme, chef.
☎ **TOURISM:** 800-334-8626

MAINE

Pine Tree State

★ **Augusta**
BIRD: Chickadee
FLOWER: White Pine Cone and Tassel
ESTABLISHED: March 15, 1820

AREA: 30,865 sq. miles	39th
POPULATION: 1,240,209	38th
White	98.4%
Black	0.4%
Hispanic	0.6%
Asian or Pacific Islander	0.5%

■ BIGGEST CITIES

Portland: 64,358 pop. Home of Henry Wadsworth Longfellow, who called it "the beautiful town that is seated by the sea."
Lewiston: 39,757 pop. Home of Bates College.
Bangor: 33,181 pop. Home of best-selling horror author Stephen King and the country's oldest symphony orchestra.

■ MONEY MATTERS

PER CAPITA INCOME: $18,775.
TAXES: Income, 2–8.5%; Sales, 6%; Gas, 19 cents per gallon; Cigarettes, 39 cents per pack.

■ RED-LETTER DATES

1819: Maine votes to separate from Massachusetts, adopts state constitution.
1802: Bowdoin College opens.
1977: The Penobscott, Passamaquoddy, and Maleseet Indians sue for recovery of their native lands. They eventually settle for $81.5 million.

■ SONS & DAUGHTERS

F. Lee Bailey, defense attorney, television personality.
Dorothea Dix, social reformer.
☎ **TOURISM:** 800-533-9595

MARYLAND

Old Line State, Free State

★ **Annapolis**
BIRD: Baltimore Oriole
FLOWER: Black-eyed Susan
ESTABLISHED: April 28, 1788

AREA: 9,775 sq. miles	42nd
POPULATION: 5,006,265	19th
White	71.0%
Black	24.9%
Hispanic	2.6%
Asian or Pacific Islander	2.9%

■ BIGGEST CITIES

Baltimore: 736,014 pop. Oriole Park at Camden Yards, opened in 1992, is a hit.
Rockville: 44,835 pop. Burial place of F. Scott and Zelda Fitzgerald.
Frederick: 40,148 pop. Boasts some 33 blocks of historic homes and mansions.

■ CITIZEN'S GUIDE

■ **MONEY MATTERS**
PER CAPITA INCOME: $23,920.
TAXES: Income, 2–6%; Sales, 5%; Gas, 23.5 cents per gallon; Cigarettes, 36 cents per pack.

■ **RED-LETTER DATES**
1649: Religious freedom granted all Christians in Toleration Act. Overturned following a Puritan revolt.
1786: Delegation from five states meets in Annapolis to call a convention to draft a constitution.
1814: British bombard Fort McHenry in unsuccessful attempt to capture Baltimore. Francis Scott Key inspired to pen the "Star-Spangled Banner."

■ **SONS & DAUGHTERS**
Benjamin Banneker, abolitionist, inventor.
Billie Holiday, singer.
Rachel Carson, writer.
☎ **TOURISM:** 410-333-6611

MASSACHUSETTS

Bay State, Old Colony

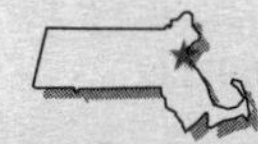

★ **Boston**
BIRD: Chickadee
FLOWER: Mayflower
ESTABLISHED: February 6, 1788
AREA: 7,838 sq. miles 45th
POPULATION: 6,041,123 13th

White	89.8%
Black	5.0%
Hispanic	4.8%
Asian or Pacific Islander	2.4%

■ **BIGGEST CITIES**
★**Boston:** 574,283 pop. Teeming with history, from Paul Revere's House to Faneuil Hall.
Worcester: 169,759 pop. Boasts 13 colleges and universities and one of the country's leading small art museums.
Springfield: 156,983 pop. The birthplace of basketball.

■ **MONEY MATTERS**
PER CAPITA INCOME: $24,475.
TAXES: Income, 5.95/12.0%; Sales, 5%; Gas, 21 cents per gallon; Cigarettes, 51 cents per pack.

■ **RED-LETTER DATES**
1620: Pilgrims, seeking religious freedom, found the colony of Plymouth.
1636: Harvard, the oldest university in the country, is founded on October 28.
1682: Twenty women accused of being witches are executed in Salem.

■ **SONS & DAUGHTERS**
John Adams, John Quincy Adams, John F. Kennedy, presidents.
Susan B. Anthony, suffragist.
Emily Dickinson, poet.
☎ **TOURISM:** 617-727-3201

MICHIGAN

Great Lakes State, Wolverine State

★ **Lansing**
BIRD: Robin
FLOWER: Apple Blossom
ESTABLISHED: Jan. 26, 1837
AREA: 56,809 sq. miles 22nd
POPULATION: 9,496,147 8th

White	83.4%
Black	13.9%
Hispanic	2.2%
Asian or Pacific Islander	1.1%

■ **BIGGEST CITIES**
Detroit: 1,027,974 pop. The only American city ever to surrender to a foreign power (Britain, in the War of 1812).
Grand Rapids: 189,126 pop. A leader in the logging industry.
Warren: 144,864 pop. First called Hickory, then Aba, now it's Warren, and a major automotive manufacturing center.

■ **MONEY MATTERS**
PER CAPITA INCOME: $20,542
TAXES: Income, 4.6%; Sales, 4%; Gas, 15 cents per gallon; Cigarettes, 25 cents per pack.

■ **RED-LETTER DATES**
1843: A frame capitol is constructed in Lansing; replaced with a brick one in 1854.
1897: Olds Motor Company founded by Ransom

■ **OLD FOLKS**
The five states with the greatest number of residents that are over 65.

CALIFORNIA	3.1 million
FLORIDA	2.4 million
NEW YORK	2,4 million
PENNSYLVANIA	1.8 million
TEXAS	1.7 million

SOURCE: American Association of Retired Persons.

■ CITIZEN'S GUIDE

E. Olds. Today, it's the Oldsmobile Division of General Motors.
1943: Race riot in Detroit on June 21 leaves 700 injured and 34 dead.

■ **SONS & DAUGHTERS**
Francis Ford Coppola, movie director.
Earvin "Magic" Johnson, basketball player.
Gilda Radner, comedian.
☎ **TOURISM:** 800-543-2937

MINNESOTA

North Star State, Gopher State

★ **St. Paul**
BIRD: Common Loon
FLOWER: Pink and White Lady-Slipper
ESTABLISHED: May 11, 1858
AREA: 79,617 sq. miles 14th
POPULATION: 4,567,267 20th

White	94.4%
Black	2.2%
Hispanic	1.2%
Asian or Pacific Islander	1.8%

■ **BIGGEST CITIES**
Minneapolis: 368,383 pop. Home of the Minnesota Twins and Vikings.
★**St. Paul:** 272,000 pop. Cafesjian's Carousel, displayed in the state fair from 1914 to 1990, is now used year-round in Town Square Park.
Bloomington: 86,453 pop. Forty-five miles of parks includes the Minnesota Valley National Wildlife Refuge.

■ **MONEY MATTERS**
PER CAPITA INCOME: $21,017
TAXES: Income, 6–8.5%; Sales, 6.5%; Gas, 20 cents per gallon; Cigarette, 48 cents a pack.

■ **RED-LETTER DATES**
1873: Grasshoppers invade. The infestation lasts five years.
1980: The Minnesota-based 3-M Company introduces Post-it™ Notes.
1987: Minnesota Twins win the World Series. They take the title again in 1991.

■ **SONS & DAUGHTERS**
Walter F. Mondale, vice president.
Bob Dylan, folk singer.
Jessica Lange, actress.
☎ **TOURISM:** 800-657-3700

MISSISSIPPI

Magnolia State

★ **Jackson**
BIRD: Mockingbird
FLOWER: Magnolia
ESTABLISHED: Dec. 10, 1817
AREA: 46,914 sq. miles 31st
POPULATION: 2,669,111 31st

White	63.5%
Black	35.6%
Hispanic	0.6%
Asian or Pacific Islander	0.5%

■ **BIGGEST CITIES**
★**Jackson:** 196,637 pop. Named for Andrew Jackson. Originally known as Le Fleur's Bluff.
Biloxi: 46,319 pop. Includes Beauvoir, the last home of Jefferson Davis, president of the Confederacy.
Greenville 45,226 pop. Gambling was legalized in 1990; the Cotton Club and Las Vegas Casinos—like all others in the state—operate 24 hours a day, 7 days a week.

■ **MONEY MATTERS**
PER CAPITA INCOME: $14,708.
TAXES: Income, 3–5%; Sales, 7%; Gas, 18 cents per gallon; Cigarettes, 18 cents per pack.

■ **RED-LETTER DATES**
1861: Mississippi secedes from Union.
1935: Singer Elvis Presley is born in a two-room house in Tupelo.
1962: As 3,000 troops put down riots, James Meredith becomes the first black student to enter the University of Mississippi.

■ **SONS & DAUGHTERS**
Charles and Medgar Evers, civil rights leaders.
Oprah Winfrey, talk show host, actress.
William Faulkner, Nobel Prize–winning novelist.
☎ **TOURISM:** 601-359-3297

MISSOURI

Show-Me State

★ **Jefferson City**
BIRD: Bluebird
FLOWER: White Hawthorn
ESTABLISHED: Aug. 10,1821
AREA: 68,898 sq. miles 18th

■ CITIZEN'S GUIDE

POPULATION: 5,227,640	15th
White	87.7%
Black	10.7%
Hispanic	1.2%
Asian or Pacific Islander	0.8%

■ BIGGEST CITIES

Kansas City: 435,146 pop. The Nelson Gallery, one of the nation's largest art museums, houses Oriental art and modern French paintings.
St. Louis: 396,685 pop. The 630-foot Gateway Arch stretches majestically above the city. Home of beer-manufacturing giant, Anheuser-Busch.
Springfield: 140,494 pop. At the edge of the Missouri Ozark Mountain expanse. Home of the Bass Pro Shop, the world's largest sporting goods center.

■ MONEY MATTERS

PER CAPITA INCOME: $19,559.
TAXES: Income, 1.5–6%; Sales, 4.225%; Gas, 13 cents per gallon; Cigarettes, 17 cents per pack.

■ RED-LETTER DATES

c. 1735: First settlement by French at St. Genevieve.
1804: Lewis and Clark set off from St. Louis.

■ SONS & DAUGHTERS

Josephine Baker, singer, dancer
Miles Davis, musician, composer.
Ginger Rogers, actress, dancer
Mark Twain, journalist, author.
☎ **TOURISM:** 314-751-4133

MONTANA

Treasure State

★ **Helena**
BIRD: Western Meadowlark
FLOWER: Bitterroot
ESTABLISHED: Nov. 8, 1889
AREA: 145,556 sq. miles 4th

POPULATION: 856,047	44th
White	92.7%
Black	0.3%
Hispanic	1.5%
Asian or Pacific Islander	0.5%

■ BIGGEST CITIES

Billings: 81,151 pop. Founded by the Northern Pacific Railroad, it's named for the company's president, Frederick Billings.
Great Falls: 55,097 pop. Western painter and sculptor Charles M. Russell's art studio is still here.
Missoula: 42,918 pop. University of Montana was founded here in 1893.

■ MONEY MATTERS

PER CAPITA INCOME: $17,413.
TAXES: Income, 2–11%; Sales, none; Gas, 24 cents per gallon; Cigarettes, 18 cents per pack.

■ RED-LETTER DATES

1876: In the Battle of Little Big Horn, Cheyenne and Sioux Indians kill General Custer and more than 200 of his troops. It was the last major victory for Native Americans in the war for American lands.
1880: Copper is discovered in Butte.

■ AUTO WRECKS

Some 40,300 Americans died in motor vehicles in 1992.

	MOTOR VEHICLE DEATHS IN 1992
CALIFORNIA	3,816
TEXAS	3,057
FLORIDA	2,480
NEW YORK	1,800
PENNSYLVANIA	1,545
OHIO	1,440
ILLINOIS	1,375
GEORGIA	1,323
MICHIGAN	1,295
NORTH CAROLINA	1,262
TENNESSEE	1,155
ALABAMA	1,001
MISSOURI	985
INDIANA	902
LOUISIANA	871
VIRGINIA	839
KENTUCKY	819
ARIZONA	810
SOUTH CAROLINA	807
NEW JERSEY	766
MARYLAND	664
WASHINGTON	651
WISCONSIN	644
OKLAHOMA	619
MISSISSIPPI	604
ARKANSAS	587
MINNESOTA	581
COLORADO	519
MASSACHUSETTS	485
OREGON	464
NEW MEXICO	461
IOWA	437
WEST VIRGINIA	420
KANSAS	387
CONNECTICUT	296
NEBRASKA	270
UTAH	269
NEVADA	251
IDAHO	243
MAINE	213
MONTANA	190
SOUTH DAKOTA	161
DELAWARE	140
HAWAI'I	128
NEW HAMPSHIRE	123
WYOMING	118
ALASKA	106
VERMONT	96
NORTH DAKOTA	88
RHODE ISLAND	79
DISTRICT OF COLUMBIA	NA

SOURCE: *County and City Data Book*, U.S. Dept. of Commerce, 1994.

■ CITIZEN'S GUIDE

1906: A sugar refinery is built in Billings, bringing in Japanese, Russo-German, and Mexican workers.

■ **SONS & DAUGHTERS**

Gary Cooper, actor.
Evel Knievel, daredevil motorcyclist.
Jeannette Rankin, first woman elected to Congress.
☎ **TOURISM:** 800-548-3390

NEBRASKA

Cornhusker State

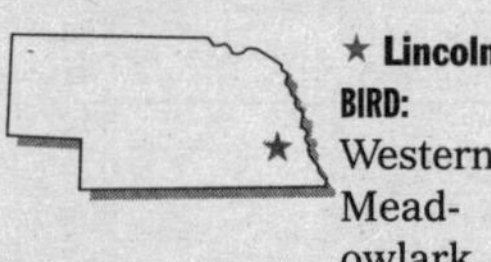

★ **Lincoln**
BIRD: Western Meadowlark
FLOWER: Goldenrod
ESTABLISHED: March 1, 1867
AREA: 76,878 sq. miles 15th
POPULATION: 1,622,858 36th

White	93.8%
Black	3.6%
Hispanic	2.3%
Asian or Pacific Islander	0.8%

■ **BIGGEST CITIES**

Omaha: 335,795 pop. President Gerald Ford's boyhood home.
★**Lincoln:** 191,972 pop. Fourteenth-floor capitol's observation deck provides a bird's-eye view of the city.
Grand Island: 39,386 pop. The Heritage Zoo on 7.5 acres is open April to October.

■ **MONEY MATTERS**

PER CAPITA INCOME: $19,757
TAXES: Income, 2.62–6.99%; Sales, 5%; Gas, 26 cents per gallon; Cigarettes, 34 cents per pack.

■ **RED-LETTER DATES**

1854: Treaty with Omaha Native Americans is reached, and a land rush ensues.
1865: Union-Pacific transcontinental railroad begun in Omaha.

■ **SONS & DAUGHTERS**

Fred Astaire, dancer, actor.
Marlon Brando, actor.
Gerald Ford, president.
☎ **TOURISM:** 800-228-4307

NEVADA

Sagebrush State, Battle Born State, Silver State

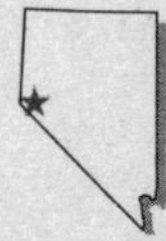

★ **Carson City**
BIRD: Mountain Bluebird
FLOWER: Sagebrush
ESTABLISHED: Oct. 31, 1864
AREA: 109,806 sq. miles 7th
POPULATION: 1,457,028 39th

White	84.3%
Black	6.6%
Hispanic	10.4%
Asian or Pacific Islander	3.2%

■ **BIGGEST CITIES**

Las Vegas: 258,295 pop. Home of the one-armed bandit. More than 86,000 couples were married in over 30 chapels in 1993.
Reno: 133,850 pop. Originally a trading post on the wagon trails, it is now teeming with casinos and restaurants.
Henderson: 64,942 pop. Take a self-guided tour through the Ethel Mo Chocolate Factory, or visit the Kidd Marshmallow Factory.

■ **MONEY MATTERS**

PER CAPITA INCOME: $22,747.
TAXES: Income, none; Sales, 6.5%; Gas, 22.25 cents per gallon; Cigarettes, 35 cents per pack.

■ **RED-LETTER DATES**

1859: Discovery of the Comstock Lode of gold and silver.
1931: State legalizes gambling. Today, Nevada has the nation's highest per capita gambling revenue.

■ **SONS & DAUGHTERS**

Andre Agassi, tennis player.
Patty Sheehan, golfer.
Robert Caples, painter.
☎ **TOURISM:** 800-638-2328

NEW HAMPSHIRE

Granite State

★ **Concord**
BIRD: Purple Finch
FLOWER: Purple Lilac
ESTABLISHED: June 21, 1788
AREA: 8,969 sq. miles 44th
POPULATION: 1,136,820 40th

White	98.0%
Black	0.6%
Hispanic	1.0%
Asian or Pacific Islander	0.8 %

■ **BIGGEST CITIES**

Manchester: 99,567 pop. It is the home of the New Hampshire Symphony Orchestra.

■ CITIZEN'S GUIDE

Nashua: 79,662 pop. Air traffic control for all of New England and upstate New York is provided from the Federal Aviation Agency Center here.
★**Concord:** 36,006 pop. Home of President Franklin Pierce.

■ MONEY MATTERS

PER CAPITA INCOME: $22,169.
TAXES: Income, 5%; Sales, none; Gas, 18 cents per gallon; Cigarettes, 25 cents per pack.

■ RED-LETTER DATES

1652: Massachusetts Bay Colonists declare 200 miles around today's Nashua as Massachusetts territory.
1805: One of the nation's first textile mills opens.
1808: Concord becomes the state capital.

■ SONS & DAUGHTERS

Daniel Chester French, sculptor of Lincoln Memorial.
John Irving, author.
Sharon Crista McAuliffe, teacher and astronaut who perished in space shuttle *Discovery* disaster.
☎ **TOURISM:** 800-386-4664

NEW JERSEY

Garden State

★ **Trenton**
BIRD: Eastern Goldfinch
FLOWER: Violet
ESTABLISHED: Dec. 8, 1787

AREA: 7,419 sq. miles		46th
POPULATION: 7,903,925		9th
White	79.3%	
Black	13.4%	
Hispanic	9.6%	
Asian or Pacific Islander	3.5%	

■ BIGGEST CITIES

Newark: 275,221 pop. The Newark Museum inclues American, Tibetan, and Oriental works.
Jersey City: 228,537 pop. The Hudson Waterfront Museum features a 1914 railroad barge.
Paterson: 140,891 pop. Produced first workable revolver, first steam locomotive, and engine of the *Spirit of St. Louis.*

■ MONEY MATTERS

PER CAPITA INCOME: $26,967.
TAXES: Income, 2–7%; Sales, 6%; Gas, 10.5 cents per gallon; Cigarettes, 40 cents per pack.

■ RED-LETTER DATES

1804: Vice president Aaron Burr kills rival Alexander Hamilton in a duel in Weehawken.
1825: John Stevens of Hoboken builds first steam locomotive.
1869: John Wesley Hyatt of Newark invents celluloid film.

■ SONS & DAUGHTERS

Bud Abbott and Lou Costello, comedians.
Sarah Vaughan, singer.
William Carlos Williams, physician and poet.
☎ **TOURISM:** 800-537-7397

■ BEER BELLIES

States that consume the most 12-ounce beers.

	Annual beers per capita
NEVADA	431
NEW HAMPSHIRE	355
WISCONSIN	322
ARIZONA	309
FLORIDA	301

SOURCE: *USA Today.*

NEW MEXICO

Land of Enchantment

★ **Sante Fe**
BIRD: Piñon Bird
FLOWER: Yucca (Our Lord's Candles)
ESTABLISHED: Jan. 6, 1912

AREA: 121,365 sq. miles		5th
POPULATION: 1,653,521		37th
White	75.6%	
Black	2.0%	
Hispanic	38.2%	
Asian or Pacific Islander	0.9%	

■ BIGGEST CITIES

Albuquerque: 384,736 pop. Native American dances are performed at the Indian Pueblo Cultural Center.
Las Cruces: 62,126 pop. Historic Mesquite and Alameda districts include the original 1849 townsite.
★**Sante Fe:** 55,859 pop. It features five state museums.

■ MONEY MATTERS

PER CAPITA INCOME: $16,333
TAXES: Income, 1.8–8.5%; Sales, 5%; Gas, 22 cents per gallon; Cigarettes, 21 cents per pack.

■ CITIZEN'S GUIDE

■ **RED-LETTER DATES**
1610: New capital of Santa Fe is founded by Governor Don Pedro de Peralta.
1898: Teddy Roosevelt recruits his New Mexico "Rough Riders."
1945: The first atomic bomb is exploded on July 16 in Alamogordo.

■ **SONS & DAUGHTERS**
William Hanna, animator.
Nancy Lopez, golfer.
Victorio, Apache chief.
☎ **TOURISM:** 800-545-2040

NEW YORK

Empire State

★ **Albany**
BIRD: Bluebird
FLOWER: Rose
ESTABLISHED: July 26, 1788

AREA: 47,224 sq. miles 30th
POPULATION: 18,169,051 2nd

White	74.4%
Black	15.9%
Hispanic	12.3%
Asian or Pacific Islander	3.9%

■ **BIGGEST CITIES**
New York City: 7,322,564 pop. The Big Apple—the Great White Way, the Statue of Liberty, and great museums. The subway has the most stations of any in the world—469.
Buffalo: 328,123 pop. Noted for its sophisticated architecture, with works by Frank Lloyd Wright and Louis Sullivan.
Rochester: 231,636 pop. Birthplace of the Kodak camera.

■ **MONEY MATTERS**
PER CAPITA INCOME: $24,771.
TAXES: Income, 4–7.875%; Sales, 4%; Gas, 8 cents per gallon; Cigarettes, 56 cents per pack.

■ **RED-LETTER DATES**
1626: Peter Minuit buys Manhattan for goods valued at $24 and names it New Amsterdam.
1848: Lucretia Mott and Elizabeth Cady Stanton lead the Women's Rights Convention in Seneca Falls.
1886: The Statue of Liberty, a gift from the French, is dedicated.
1993: A bomb explodes in an underground parking lot in the World Trade Center on February 26; six people are killed, more than 1,000 are injured.

■ **SONS & DAUGHTERS**
Jonas Salk, polio researcher.
Chico, Groucho, Harpo, Zeppo Marx, comedians.
Margaret Sanger, birth control leader.
☎ **TOURISM:** 800-225-5697

NORTH CAROLINA

Tar Heel State, Old North State

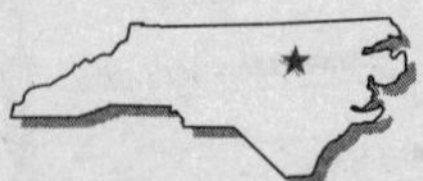

★ **Raleigh**
BIRD: Cardinal
FLOWER: Dogwood
ESTABLISHED: Nov. 21, 1789
AREA: 48,718 sq. miles 29th
POPULATION: 7,069,836 10th

White	75.6%
Black	22.0%
Hispanic	1.2%
Asian or Pacific Islander	0.8%

■ **BIGGEST CITIES**
Charlotte: 395,934 pop. The last full Confederate cabinet meeting was held here in 1865.
★**Raleigh:** 207,951 pop. Named for Sir Walter Raleigh, it's known for its many tree-lined streets.
Greensboro: 183,521 pop. Hosts approximately 500 factories, including Wrangler jeans and No Nonsense pantyhose.

■ **MONEY MATTERS**
PER CAPITA INCOME: $18,688.
TAXES: Income, 6–7.75%; Sales, 4%; Gas, 22 cents per gallon; Cigarettes, 5 cents per pack.

■ **RED-LETTER DATES**
1775: The Mecklenburg Declaration of Independence is signed; the colonies' joint effort follows a year later.
1960: Four black college students refuse to leave a Woolworth's counter in Greensboro after being denied service. Sit-ins begin; more than 70,000 students, black and white, participate.

■ **SONS & DAUGHTERS**
Jesse Jackson, clergyman, civil rights leader.
Dolley Madison, first lady.
Thelonious Monk, musician, composer.
☎ **TOURISM:** 800-847-4862

■ CITIZEN'S GUIDE

NORTH DAKOTA

Peace Garden State

★ **Bismarck**
BIRD: Western Meadowlark
FLOWER: Wild Prairie Rose
ESTABLISHED: Nov. 2, 1889
AREA: 68,994 sq. miles 17th
POPULATION: 637,988 47th

White	94.6%
Black	0.6%
Hispanic	0.7%
Asian or Pacfic Islander	0.5%

■ BIGGEST CITIES

Fargo: 74,111 pop. Features Yukers Farm, the state's only children's museum.
Grand Forks: 49,425 Home to the University of North Dakota and the North Dakota Museum of Art.
★**Bismarck:** 49,256 The North Dakota Heritage Center chronicles Dakota past and present.

■ MONEY MATTERS

PER CAPITA INCOME: $17,123.
TAXES: Income, 14% of federal income tax liability; Sales, 5%; Gas, 18 cents per gallon; Cigarettes, 44 cents per pack.

■ RED-LETTER DATES

1790's: White traders make contact with area's Hidatsa and Mandan Indian tribes.
1829–1867: Fort Union is the largest of a string of trading posts along the northern rivers.
1984: The Freedom Mine, the state's largest, producing 40 percent of its lignite, opens.

■ SONS & DAUGHTERS

Louis L'Amour, novelist.
Lawrence Welk, band leader.
Angie Dickinson, actress.
☎ **TOURISM:** 800-435-5663

OHIO

Buckeye State

★ **Columbus**
BIRD: Cardinal
FLOWER: Scarlet Carnation
ESTABLISHED: March 1, 1803
AREA: 40,953 sq. miles 35th
POPULATION: 11,102,198 7th

White	87.8%
Black	10.6%
Hispanic	1.3%
Asian or Pacific Islander	0.8%

■ BIGGEST CITIES

★**Columbus:** 632,910 pop. The nation's largest state fair is held every August.
Cleveland: 505,616 pop. Boasts approximately 80 libraries.
Cincinnati: 364,040 pop. Over 4,000 acres of parks.

■ MONEY MATTERS

PER CAPITA INCOME: $19,627.
TAXES: Income, 0.743–7.5%; Sales, 5%; Gas, 22 cents per gallon; Cigarettes, 24 cents per pack.

■ RED-LETTER DATES

1833: Oberlin College becomes the first institution of higher education in the United States to adopt a coeducation policy. In 1835, it refuses to bar students due to race.
1832–1850: Harriet

■ POOR FOLKS

Some 40 million Americans fell below the poverty line in 1993

	NUMBER OF POOR (x1,000)	Percent state pop.
DIST. COLUMBIA	158	26.4%
LOUISIANA	1,119	26.4%
MISSISSIPPI	639	24.7%
WEST VIRGINIA	400	22.2%
KENTUCKY	763	20.4%
ARKANSAS	484	20.0%
OKLAHOMA	662	19.9%
TENNESSEE	998	19.6%
SOUTH CAROLINA	678	18.7%
CALIFORNIA	5,803	18.2%
FLORIDA	2,507	17.8%
ALABAMA	725	17.4%
NEW MEXICO	282	17.4%
TEXAS	3,177	17.4%
NEW YORK	2,981	16.4%
MISSOURI	832	16.1%
ARIZONA	615	15.4%
MAINE	196	15.4%
MICHIGAN	1,475	15.4%
MONTANA	127	14.9%
NORTH CAROLINA	966	14.4%
SOUTH DAKOTA	102	14.2%
ILLINOIS	1,600	13.6%
GEORGIA	919	13.5%
WYOMING	64	13.3%
PENNSYLVANIA	1,598	13.2%
IDAHO	150	13.1%
KANSAS	327	13.1%
OHIO	1,461	13.0%
WISCONSIN	636	12.6%
INDIANA	704	12.2%
WASHINGTON	634	12.1%
OREGON	363	11.8%
MINNESOTA	506	11.6%
NORTH DAKOTA	70	11.2%
RHODE ISLAND	108	11.2%
NEW JERSEY	866	10.9%
MASSACHUSETTS	641	10.7%
UTAH	203	10.7%
IOWA	290	10.3%
NEBRASKA	169	10.3%
DELAWARE	73	10.2%
VERMONT	59	10.0%
COLORADO	354	9.9%
NEW HAMPSHIRE	112	9.9%
NEVADA	141	9.8%
MARYLAND	479	9.7%
VIRGINIA	627	9.7%
ALASKA	52	9.1%
CONNECTICUT	277	8.5%
HAWAI'I	91	8.0%

SOURCE: U.S. Bureau of the Census.

■ CITIZEN'S GUIDE

Beecher Stowe lives in Cincinnati and writes much of *Uncle Tom's Cabin* there.
1852: African Americans first vote in Cincinnati; the nation follows 18 years later.

■ **SONS & DAUGHTERS**
Neil Armstrong, first man to walk on the moon.
Erma Bombeck, columnist.
Annie Oakley, markswoman.
☎ **TOURISM:** 800-282-5393

OKLAHOMA

Sooner State

★ **Oklahoma City**
BIRD: Scissor-tailed Flycatcher
FLOWER: Mistletoe
ESTABLISHED: Nov. 16, 1907
AREA: 68,679 sq. miles 19th
POPULATION: 3,258,069 28th

White	82.1%
Black	7.4%
Hispanic	2.7%
Asian	1.1%

■ **BIGGEST CITIES**
★**Oklahoma City:** 444,719 pop. Its "Frontier City" tourist attraction stages simulated gunfights.
Tulsa: 367,302 pop. One of the nation's largest city-owned parks, Mohawk Park, sprawls over 2,800 acres.
Lawton: 80,561 pop. The grave of Geronimo, who died at Fort Sill, is located here, as are the fort and a military museum.

■ **MONEY MATTERS**
PER CAPITA INCOME: $17,035
TAXES: Income, 0.5–7%; Sales, 4.5%; Gas, 17 cents per gallon; Cigarettes, 23 cents per pack.

■ **RED-LETTER DATES**
1825: Creek Indian Archie Yahola convened first council meeting under an oak tree that still stands in Tulsa's Creek Nation Council Oak Park.
1889: The United States opens state to white settlement. Some 50,000 settlers converge the first day.
1928: The largest oil strike to date is hit in Oklahoma City.
1995: Over 160 people are killed in the largest terrorist incident in U.S. history when a bomb is set off at an Oklahoma City federal building.

■ **SONS & DAUGHTERS**
Ralph Ellison, writer.
Ron Howard, actor, director.
Jeane Kirkpatrick, diplomat.
☎ **TOURISM:** 800-652-6552

■ **BIGGEST DUMPS**
The states with the most hazardous waste sites

NEW JERSEY	108
PENNSYLVANIA	101
CALIFORNIA	96
NEW YORK	85
MICHIGAN	77

SOURCE: *National Priorities List*, Environmental Protection Agency, May 1994.

OREGON

Beaver State

★ **Salem**
BIRD: Western Meadowlark
FLOWER: Oregon Grape
ESTABLISHED: Feb. 14, 1859
AREA: 96,003 sq. miles 10th
POPULATION: 3,086,188 29th

White	92.8%
Black	1.6%
Hispanic	4.0%
Asian or Pacific Islander	2.4%

■ **BIGGEST CITIES**
Portland: 471,328 pop. Known as the "City of Roses" for local Washington Park's 500 varieties.
Eugene: 119,235 pop. Home to the University of Oregon and the Hult Performing Arts Center.
★**Salem:** 113,325 pop. The state's capitol is open for public tours.

■ **MONEY MATTERS**
PER CAPITA INCOME: $19,447
TAXES: Income, 5–9%; Sales, none; Gas, 24 cents per gallon; Cigarettes, 38 cents per pack.

■ **RED-LETTER DATES**
1841–1860: Emigrants cross the 2,000 miles from Missouri to western Oregon on the Oregon Trail.
1870s: Railroads come to Oregon.
1913: Governor George Oswald declares the state's beaches public property. Nearly 400 acres are open, year-round, to this day.

■ CITIZEN'S GUIDE

■ **SONS & DAUGHTERS**
Matt Groenig, cartoonist.
Linus Pauling, chemist.
Ken Kesey, writer.
☎ **TOURISM:** 800-547-7842

PENNSYLVANIA

Keystone State

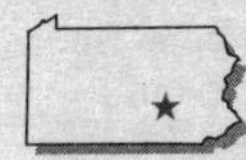

★ **Harrisburg**
BIRD: Ruffed Grouse
FLOWER: Mountain Laurel
ESTABLISHED: Dec. 12, 1787
AREA: 44,820 sq. miles 32nd
POPULATION: 12,052,367 5th

White	88.5%
Black	9.2%
Hispanic	2.0%
Asian or Pacific Islander	1.2%

■ **BIGGEST CITIES**
Philadelphia: 1,585,577 pop. Home of the Liberty Bell and Independence Hall, where the Declaration of Independence and Constitution were written,
Pittsburgh: 369,879 pop. Has more golf courses per capita than any other U.S. city.
Erie: 108,718 pop. The Port of Erie is Pennsylvania's only lake port.

■ **MONEY MATTERS**
PER CAPITA INCOME: $21,241 **TAXES:** Income, 2.95%; Sales, 6%; Gas, 12 cents per gallon; Cigarettes, 31 cents per pack.

■ **RED-LETTER DATES**
1794: Militia of 15,000 suppresses "Whisky Rebellion" of Pennsylvania farmers protesting liquor tax.
1892: Strike at Carnegie steel mills in Homestead results in 18 shooting deaths of guards, strikers, and spectators.
1979: Major accident at Three Mile Island's nuclear reactor near Middletown.

■ **SONS & DAUGHTERS**
Louisa May Alcott, novelist.
Daniel Boone, frontiersman.
Margaret Mead, anthropologist.
Betsy Ross, flagmaker.
☎ **TOURISM:** 800-847-4872

RHODE ISLAND

Little Rhody, Ocean State

★ **Providence**
BIRD: Rhode Island Red
FLOWER: Violet
ESTABLISHED: May 29,1790
AREA: 1,045 sq. miles 50th
POPULATION: 996,757 43rd

White	91.4%
Black	3.9%
Hispanic	4.6%
Asian or Pacific Islander	1.8%

■ **BIGGEST CITIES**
★**Providence:** 160,728 pop. Home to Brown University and the Rhode Island School of Design.
Warwick: 85,427 pop. Its Rocky Point is one of New England's oldest shore resorts.
Cranston: 70,060 pop. Settled in 1636, it's named for Samuel Cranston, governor of Rhode Island from 1698 to 1727.

■ **MONEY MATTERS**
PER CAPITA INCOME: $21,203.
TAXES: Income, 27.5% of federal income tax liability; Sales,7%; Gas, 28 cents per gallon; Cigarettes, 44 cents per pack.

■ **RED-LETTER DATES**
1774: Rhode Island abolishes slavery.
1763: Touro Synagogue, the oldest in the United States, is built.
1824: First strike by women, by the weavers of Pawtucket.

■ **SONS & DAUGHTERS**
Anne Hutchinson, religious leader.
Roger Williams, clergyman and founder of Rhode Island.
Spalding Gray, writer, conversationalist.
☎ **TOURISM:** 800-556-2484

SOUTH CAROLINA

Palmetto State

★ **Columbia**
BIRD: Carolina Wren
FLOWER: Yellow Jessamine
ESTABLISHED: May 27, 1788
AREA: 30,111 sq. miles 40th
POPULATION: 3,663,984 25th

White	69.0%
Black	29.8%
Hispanic	0.9%
Asian or Pacific Islander	0.6%

■ **BIGGEST CITIES**
★**Columbia:** 98,052 pop. One of the nation's first planned cities.

EDUCATION

Public elementary and secondary school expenditures in 1993 (x 1,000):

CALIFORNIA	$28,387
NEW YORK	$22,917
TEXAS	$18,555
PENNSYLVANIA	$13,148
FLORIDA	$11,645
OHIO	$11,289
MICHIGAN	$10,816
NEW JERSEY	$10,564
ILLINOIS	$10,043
VIRGINIA	$6,014
INDIANA	$5,821
WASHINGTON	$5,816
GEORGIA	$5,646
WISCONSIN	$5,609
NORTH CAROLINA	$5,594
MASSACHUSETTS	$5,470
MINNESOTA	$5,022
MARYLAND	$4,932
CONNECTICUT	$4,107
MISSOURI	$3,966
ARIZONA	$3,508
LOUISIANA	$3,442
OREGON	$3,382
COLORADO	$3,375
TENNESSEE	$3,333
KENTUCKY	$3,158
SOUTH CAROLINA	$3,055
ALABAMA	$2,805
OKLAHOMA	$2,726
IOWA	$2,642
KANSAS	$2,575
WEST VIRGINIA	$1,890
ARKANSAS	$1,825
MISSISSIPPI	$1,769
UTAH	$1,510
NEBRASKA	$1,449
NEW MEXICO	$1,453
MAINF	$1,357
NEVADA	$1,233
HAWAI'I	$1,077
ALASKA	$1,058
NEW HAMPSHIRE	$1,021
IDAHO	$957
RHODE ISLAND	$904
MONTANA	$868
VERMONT	$684
DELAWARE	$673
SOUTH DAKOTA	$627
DIST. OF COLUMBIA	$621
WYOMING	$621
NORTH DAKOTA	$547

SOURCE: *Statistical Abstract of the United States*, U.S. Department of Commerce, 1994.

CITIZEN'S GUIDE

Charleston: 80,414 pop. Its historic district boasts more than 2,000 preserved and restored buildings.
North Charleston: 70,218 pop. Industrial heart of the South Carolina low country.

MONEY MATTERS

PER CAPITA INCOME: $16,810
TAXES: Income, 2.5–7%; Sales, 5%; Gas, 16 cents per gallon; Cigarettes, 7 cents per pack.

RED-LETTER DATES

1729: South Carolina officially separates from North Carolina.
1828: Local government declares states' right to abolish federal law.
1865: The "March to the Sea" rampage of Union General William T. Sherman destroys Columbia.

SONS & DAUGHTERS

Mary McLeod Bethune, educator.
Dizzy Gillespie, jazz trumpeter.
Ronald McNair, astronaut.
☎ **TOURISM:** 803-734-0122

SOUTH DAKOTA

Coyote State, Mount Rushmore State

★ **Pierre**
BIRD: Ring-necked Pheasant
FLOWER: American Pasque
ESTABLISHED: Nov. 2, 1889
AREA: 75,896 sq. miles 16th

POPULATION: 721,164 45th

White	91.6%
Black	0.5%
Hispanic	0.8%
Asian or Pacific Islander	0.4%

BIGGEST CITIES

Sioux Falls: 100,814 pop. The Great Plains Zoo includes wild dogs of America and the Australian outback.
Rapid City: 54,523 pop. The city's well-thought-out design extended to its wide streets so horses and ox-drawn wagons could turn around more easily.
Aberdeen: 24,927 pop. *The Wizard of Oz* author L. Frank Baum moved his family here in 1888.

MONEY MATTERS

PER CAPITA INCOME: $17,977
TAXES: Income, none; Sales, 4%; Gas, 18 cents per gallon; Cigarettes, 23 cents per pack.

RED-LETTER DATES

1743: The French Verendrye brothers are the first white people to enter the state, claiming the region for their king.
1876: Wild Bill Hickok is gunned down while playing a poker game. He's buried beside Calamity Jane in a local cemetery.
1892: "The Star-Spangled Banner" makes its official debut at Fort Meade.

SONS & DAUGHTERS

Sitting Bull, a Sioux chief.
Gladys Pyle, first Republican woman elected to the U.S. Senate.
☎ **TOURISM:** 800-732-5682

■ CITIZEN'S GUIDE

TENNESSEE

Volunteer State

★ **Nashville**
BIRD: Mockingbird
FLOWER: Iris
ESTABLISHED: June 1, 1796
AREA: 41,220 sq. miles 34th
POPULATION: 5,175,240 17th

White	83.0%
Black	16.0%
Hispanic	0.7%
Asian or Pacific Islander	0.7%

■ BIGGEST CITIES

Memphis: 610,337 pop. The home of the King—Elvis Presley.
★**Nashville-Davidson:** 510,784 pop. Resident Andrew Jackson served in the House of Representatives and the Senate before going on to become the nation's seventh president.
Knoxville: 165,121 pop. Gateway to the Great Smoky Mountains.

■ MONEY MATTERS

PER CAPITA INCOME: $18,415.
TAXES: Income, 6%; Sales, 6%; Gas, 21 cents per gallon; Cigarettes, 13 cents per pack.

■ RED-LETTER DATES

1870s: A series of yellow fever epidemics sweeps Memphis, bankrupting the city.
1925: John T. Scopes is found guilty of teaching evolution to Dayton high school students. He is fined $100.
1968: Martin Luther King, Jr. is assassinated at a motel in Memphis on April 4.

■ SONS & DAUGHTERS

James Agee, writer.
Davy Crockett, frontiersman.
Aretha Franklin, singer.
Wilma Rudolph, sprinter.
☎ **TOURISM:** 800-836-6200

TEXAS

Lone Star State

★ **Austin**
BIRD: Mockingbird
FLOWER: Bluebonnet
ESTABLISHED: Dec. 28, 1845
AREA: 261,914 sq. miles 2nd
POPULATION: 18,378,185 3rd

White	75.2%
Black	11.9%
Hispanic	25.5%
Asian of Pacific Islander	1.9%

■ BIGGEST CITIES

Houston: 1,630,864 pop. Named for Sam Houston, the general who won Texas's independence from Mexico, it's now one of the nation's largest seaports.
Dallas: 1,007,617 pop. The first settler built a single cabin here in 1841. Twenty years later, the "town" had only doubled in size. Today it's the Southwest's largest banking center.
San Antonio: 935,933 pop. Its fiesta in April includes 10 days of parades, street dancing along the popular River Walk, and fireworks.

■ MONEY MATTERS

PER CAPITA INCOME: $19,134.
TAXES: Income, none; Sales, 6.25%; Gas, 20 cents per gallon; Cigarettes, 41 cents per pack.

■ RED-LETTER DATES

1836: The defenders of the Alamo are wiped out by Santa Anna, the Mexican dictator ruling the territory, in a 13-day siege. Later Sam Houston's Texans defeat Santa Anna at San Jacinto and declare independence.
1963: President John F. Kennedy is shot as he

■ HIGH SCHOOL GRADUATES

The states with the highest percentage of students graduating from public high schools...

MINNESOTA	89.2%
IOWA	87.6%
NORTH DAKOTA	87.5%
NEBRASKA	87.2%
MONTANA	85.5%

...and the lowest:

TEXAS	56.0%
SOUTH CAROLINA	58.1%
MISSISSIPPI	62.1%
DIST. OF COLUMBIA	62.8%
GEORGIA	63.7%

SOURCE: National Center for Education Statistics, U.S. Department of Education, 1992.

■ CITIZEN'S GUIDE

rides in a motorcade through Dealey Plaza in Dallas.
1993: An unsuccessful raid on the Branch Davidian compound in Waco kills four federal agents; the ensuing 51-day siege ends with Davidians setting fire to the compound. Seventy-two members, including 17 children, perish.

■ **SONS & DAUGHTERS**
Alvin Ailey, choreographer.
Carol Burnett, comedian.
Sandra Day O'Connor, first woman to be appointed to the Supreme Court.
Dan Rather, TV newscaster.
☎ **TOURISM:** 800-452-9292

UTAH

Beehive State

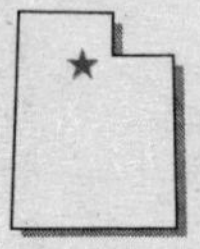

★ **Salt Lake City**
BIRD: California Seagull
FLOWER: Sego Lily
ESTABLISHED: Jan. 4, 1896

AREA: 82,618 sq. miles 12th
POPULATION: 1,907,936 35th

White	93.8%
Black	0.7%
Hispanic	4.9%
Asian or Pacific Islander	1.9%

■ **BIGGEST CITIES**
★**Salt Lake City:** 159,936 pop. Headquarters of the Church of the Latter-Day Saints (the Mormons).
West Valley City: 86,976 pop. A business center located in the Salt Lake Valley.
Provo: 86,835 pop. Founded in 1850 as Fort Utah, named for the Native American Ute tribe.

■ **MONEY MATTERS**
PER CAPITA INCOME: $16,138.
TAXES: Income, 2.55–7.2%; Sales, 5%; Gas,19 cents per gallon; Cigarettes, 26.5 cents per pack.

■ **RED-LETTER DATES**
1847: Brigham Young, leader of the Mormon church, looks out over Salt Lake Valley and proclaims it "the right place."
1977: Convicted murderer Gary Gilmore becomes the first American to be put to death since 1967.
1982: Barney Clark receives first permanent artificial heart.

■ **SONS & DAUGHTERS**
Roseanne Arnold, actress.
Butch Cassidy, outlaw.
Donny and Marie Osmond, entertainers.
☎ **TOURISM:** 801-538-1467

■ **INMATES**
States with largest prison populations in 1992.

STATE	INMATES
CALIFORNIA	109,496
NEW YORK	61,736
TEXAS	61,178
FLORIDA	48,302
MICHIGAN	39,019
OHIO	38,378
ILLINOIS	31,640
GEORGIA	25,290
PENNSYLVANIA	24,974
NEW JERSEY	22,653

SOURCE: *Statistical Abstract of the United States*, U.S. Department of Commerce, 1994.

VERMONT

Green Mountain State

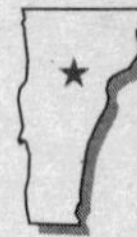

★ **Montpelier**
BIRD: Hermit Thrush
FLOWER: Red Clover
ESTABLISHED: March 4, 1791

AREA: 9,249 sq. miles 43rd
POPULATION: 580,209 48th

White	98.6%
Black	0.3%
Hispanic	0.7%
Asian or Pacific Islander	0.6%

■ **BIGGEST CITIES**
Burlington: 39,127 pop. Renaissance of the waterfront has become complete with boat trips and bike path.
Rutland: 18,230 pop. Features the Norman Rockwell Museum.
South Burlington: 12,809 pop. In 1995, the city celebrated its 130th birthday—it separated from the city of Burlington in 1865.

■ **MONEY MATTERS**
PER CAPITA INCOME: $19,442.
TAXES: Income, 25% of federal income tax liability; Sales, 5%; Gas,15 cents per gallon; Cigarettes, 20 cents per pack.

■ **RED-LETTER DATES**
1777: Vermont's first constitution abolishes slavery and gives all men the right to vote.
1791: Vermont becomes the first state after the original 13 to join the Union.

■ CITIZEN'S GUIDE

■ **SONS & DAUGHTERS**
Chester A. Arthur, Calvin Coolidge, presidents.
Rudy Vallee, singer.
Richard Morris Hunt, architect.
☎ **TOURISM:** 800-837-8668

VIRGINIA

Old Dominion

★ **Richmond**
BIRD: Cardinal
FLOWER: Dogwood
ESTABLISHED: June 25,1788
AREA: 39,598 sq. miles 37th
POPULATION: 6,551,522 12th

White	77.4%
Black	18.8%
Hispanic	2.6%
Asian or Pacific Islander	2.6%

■ **BIGGEST CITIES**
Virginia Beach: 393,069 pop. First Landing Cross marks where the Jamestown colonists first set foot in the New World in 1607.
Norfolk: 261,229 pop. The naval base, established in 1917, is now the largest naval installation in the world.
★**Richmond:** 203,056 pop. Thomas Jefferson designed part of the Virginia State Capitol.

■ **MONEY MATTERS**
PER CAPITA INCOME: $21,544.
TAXES: Income, 2–5.75%; Sales, 4.5%; Gas, 17.5 cents per gallon; Cigarettes, 2.5 cents per pack.

■ **RED-LETTER DATES**
1716: The first theater in the colonies opens in Williamsburg.
1775: In Continental Congress on June 7, Virginia's Richard Lee moves for a resolution to be passed that becomes the Declaration of Independence.
1831: Slave Nat Turner leads a local slave rebellion that kills 57 whites. Troops, in turn, hang Turner and kill 100 slaves.

■ **SONS & DAUGHTERS**
Arthur Ashe, tennis player.
Russell Baker, columnist.
Ella Fitzgerald, singer.
☎ **TOURISM:** 800-847-4882

WASHINGTON

Evergreen State

★ **Olympia**
BIRD: Willow Goldfinch
FLOWER: Coast Rhododendron
ESTABLISHED: Nov. 11, 1889
AREA: 66,581 sq. miles 20th
POPULATION: 5,343,090 18th

White	88.5%
Black	3.1%
Hispanic	4.4%;
Asian or Pacific Islander	.45%

■ **BIGGEST CITIES**
Seattle: 516,259 pop. Peer out over the 605-foot Space Needle's observation deck at the city below.
Spokane: 117,196 pop. Every year the Spokane

■ **CRIME VICTIMS**
Violent crime victims in 1992 as a percentage of state population.

DISTRICT OF COLUMBIA	2.83%
FLORIDA	1.21%
NEW YORK	1.12%
CALIFORNIA	1.12%
MARYLAND	1.00%
LOUISIANA	.99%
ILLINOIS	.98%
SOUTH CAROLINA	.94%
NEW MEXICO	.94%
ALABAMA	.87%
TEXAS	.81%
MASSACHUSETTS	.77%
MICHIGAN	.77%
TENNESSEE	.75%
MISSOURI	.74%
GEORGIA	.73%
NEVADA	.70%
NORTH CAROLINA	.68%
ARIZONA	.675
ALASKA	.66%
OKLAHOMA	.62%
DELAWARE	.62%
COLORADO	.58%
ARKANSAS	.58%
KENTUCKY	.54%
WASHINGTON	.53%
OHIO	.53%
KANSAS	.51%
OREGON	.51%
INDIANA	.51%
CONNECTICUT	.50%
PENNSYLVANIA	.43%
MISSISSIPPI	.41%
RHODE ISLAND	.40%
VIRGINIA	.38%
NEBRASKA	.35%
MINNESOTA	.34%
WYOMING	.32%
UTAH	.29%
IDAHO	.28%
IOWA	.28%
WISCONSIN	.27%
HAWAI'I	.26%
WEST VIRGINIA	.21%
SOUTH DAKOTA	.20%
MONTANA	.17%
MAINE	.13%
NEW HAMPSHIRE	.13%
VERMONT	.11%
NORTH DAKOTA	.08%

SOURCE: *Statistical Abstract of the United States,* U.S. Department of Commerce, 1994.

■ CITIZEN'S GUIDE

Music and Allied Arts Festival attracts artists and musicians from the entire Pacific Northwest.
Tacoma: 176,664 pop. Its Point Defiance Park of 700 acres is the second largest city park in the nation.

■ MONEY MATTERS

PER CAPITA INCOME: $21,773.
TAXES: Income, none; Sales, 6.5%; Gas, 23 cents per gallon; Cigarettes, 54 cents per pack.

■ RED-LETTER DATES

1889: A fire in Seattle destroys its entire business district.
1974: Spokane hosts the World's Fair.
1980: The volcano, Mt. St. Helens, erupts on May 18. Two more eruptions follow on May 25 and June 12, killing 60 and causing upward of $3 billion in damage.

■ SONS & DAUGHTERS

Carol Channing, actress.
Hank Ketcham, cartoonist.
Robert Motherwell, artist.
Judy Collins, singer.
☎ **TOURISM:** 800-544-1800

WEST VIRGINIA

Mountain State

★ **Charleston**
BIRD: Cardinal
FLOWER: Big Laurel
ESTABLISHED: June 20, 1863
AREA: 24,087 41st
POPULATION: 1,822,021 34th

White	96.2%
Black	3.1%
Hispanic	0.5%
Asian or Pacific Islander	0.4%

■ BIGGEST CITIES

★**Charleston:** 57,287 pop. Several area glass factories give tours. Home of the University of West Virginia.
Huntington: 54,844 pop. Founded in 1870 by railroad magnate Collis P. Huntington.
Parkersburg: 33,862 pop. Once an Indian hunting ground, it is now home to paper, plastics, and glassware industries.

■ MONEY MATTERS

PER CAPITA INCOME: $16,148.
TAXES: Income, 3–6.5%; Sales, 6%; Gas, 20.5 cents per gallon; Cigarettes, 17 cents per pack.

■ RED-LETTER DATES

1797: Salt furnace constructed in Malden; salt becomes a large export to the rest of the country.
1818: Charles Town officially established as Charleston.
1913: Charleston's first chemical company founded.

■ SONS & DAUGHTERS

Pearl S. Buck, author.
Martin R. Delany, first black army major.
Chuck Yeager, test pilot and Air Force general.
Mary Lou Retton, Olympic gold-medal gymnast.
☎ **TOURISM:** 800-225-5982

WISCONSIN

Badger State

★ **Madison**
BIRD: Robin
FLOWER: Wood Violet
ESTABLISHED: May 29, 1848
AREA: 54,314 sq. miles 25th
POPULATION: 5,081,658 16th

White	92.2%
Black	5.0%
Hispanic	1.9%
Asian or Pacific Islander	1.1%

■ BIGGEST CITIES

Milwaukee: 628,088 pop. Its name is derived from the Algonkian Indian word *Millioke,* meaning "beautiful land." Major beer manufacturing center.
★**Madison:** 191,262 pop. Home to the University of Wisconsin.
Green Bay: 96,466 pop. The smallest city in the nation to sponsor a professional football team.

■ MONEY MATTERS

PER CAPITA INCOME: $19,811.
TAXES: Income, 4.9 to 6.93%; Sales, 5%; Gas, 23.2 cents per gallon; Cigarettes, 38 cents per pack.

■ RED-LETTER DATES

1854: The Republican Party is formed in Ripon.
1954: Junior Republican Senator Joseph McCarthy 100 years later leads hearings that allege Communist activity in the U.S. Army. He was censured by the Senate later that year.

■ CITIZEN'S GUIDE

■ **SONS & DAUGHTERS**
Orson Welles, actor, director.
Charlotte Rae, actress.
Frank Lloyd Wright, architect.
Georgia O'Keeffe, painter.
☎ **TOURISM:** 800-432-8747

WYOMING

Equality State

★ **Cheyenne**
BIRD: Western Meadowlark
FLOWER: Indian Paintbrush
ESTABLISHED: July 10, 1890
AREA: 97,105 9th
POPULATION: 475,981 50th

White	94.2%
Black	0.8%
Hispanic	5.7%
Asian or Pacific Islander	0.6 %

■ **BIGGEST CITIES**
★**Cheyenne:** 50,008 pop. It annually hosts the world's largest outdoor rodeo.
Casper: 46,742 pop. Stages the Casper Classic Bicycle Race in July, one of the nation's toughest.
Laramie: 26,687 pop. Houses the University of Wyoming Art Museum.

■ **MONEY MATTERS**
PER CAPITA INCOME: $19,724.
TAXES: Income, none; Sales, 4%; Gas, 9 cents per gallon; Cigarettes, 12 cents per pack.

■ **RED-LETTER DATES**
1869: First women's suffrage law passed here December 10.
1870: 57-year-old housewife Esther Hobart Morris appointed justice of the peace, becoming the first woman to hold public office in the United States.
1872: Yellowstone National Park, the nation's first, is founded by Congress.

■ **SONS & DAUGHTERS**
Esther Morris, first female judge.
Jackson Pollock, painter.
Jedediah Smith, mountain man.
Nellie Tayloe Ross, first woman elected governor of a state.
☎ **TOURISM:** 800-225-5996

WASHINGTON, D.C.

Justitia Omnibus (Justice to All)

BIRD: Wood Thrush
FLOWER: American Beauty Rose
AREA: 61 sq. miles 51st
BECAME U.S. CAPITAL: Dec. 1, 1800
POPULATION: 570,175

White	30%
Black	65.8%
Hispanic	5.4%
Asian or Pacific Islander1	8%

■ **MONEY MATTERS**
PER CAPITA INCOME: $29,836.
TAXES: Income, 6 to 9.5%; Sales, 6%; Gas, 20 cents per gallon; Cigarettes, 65 cents per pack.

■ **RED-LETTER DATES**
1800: Federal government moves from Philadelphia to new home in the District of Columbia.
1814: The British storm the city and set fire to the Capitol and the White House. President James Madison and his wife Dolley flee to Virginia. It is the first and last time in U.S. history that a foreign power takes control of Washington.
1865: Abraham Lincoln is shot to death by John Wilkes Booth on April 14 at Ford's Theater.
1963: Dr. Martin Luther King, Jr. leads 200,000 in a march on Washington for equal rights for blacks and delivers his stirring "I Have a Dream" speech.

■ **SONS & DAUGHTERS**
Hank Aaron, baseball great.
Helen Keller, author and educator.
Coretta Scott King, civil rights leader.
☎ **TOURISM:** 202-727-4511

■ **GHOSTS**

The Ghost Research Society in 1993 attempted to determine which states had the most haunted houses, graveyards, or other spooky locations. The top 5 picks:

	HAUNTED LOCATIONS
VIRGINIA	69
CALIFORNIA	56
NEW YORK	29
OHIO	28
ILLINOIS	22

SOURCE: *National Register of Haunted Locations*, Ghost Research Society, 1994.

■ FROM HERE TO THERE ACROSS AMERICA

Mileages between major U.S. cities	ATLANTA	BOSTON	CHICAGO	CLEVELAND	DALLAS	DENVER	DETROIT	HOUSTON	KANSAS CITY	LOS ANGELES	MIAMI	MINN.-ST. PAUL
ATLANTA Ga.		1,084	715	727	826	1,519	741	875	882	2,252	662	1,136
BOSTON, Mass.	1,084		976	643	1,868	2,008	706	1,961	1,442	3,130	1,547	1,399
CHICAGO, Ill.	715	976		349	936	1,017	297	1,073	505	2,189	1,386	416
CLEVLAND, Ohio	727	643	349		1,225	1,373	173	1,356	799	2,487	1,365	769
DALLAS, Texas	826	1,868	936	1,225		797	1,194	241	505	1,431	1,394	940
DENVER, Colo.	1,519	2,008	1,017	1,373	797		1,302	1,038	604	1,189	2,126	871
DETROIT, Mich.	741	706	297	173	1,194	1,302		1,326	752	2,448	1,395	693
HOUSTON, Texas	875	1,961	1,073	1,356	241	1,038	1,326		746	1,564	1,306	1,181
KANSAS CITY, Mo.	882	1,442	505	799	505	604	752	746		1,631	1,485	435
LOS ANGELES, Calif.	2,252	3,130	2,189	2,487	1,431	1,189	2,448	1,564	1,631		2,885	2,033
MIAMI, Fla.	662	1,547	1,386	1,365	1,394	2,126	1,395	1,306	1,485	2,885		1,786
MINNEAPOLIS ST. PAUL, Minn.	1,136	1,399	416	769	940	871	693	1,181	435	2,033	1,786	
NEW ORLEANS, La.	518	1,625	938	1,132	495	1,292	1,143	349	809	1,947	881	1,228
NEW YORK, N.Y.	863	217	818	502	1,649	1,852	632	1,742	1,223	2,911	1,325	1,261
OMAHA, Neb.	1,027	1,451	477	816	681	540	745	931	185	1,668	1,686	371
PHILADELPHIA, Pa.	776	308	767	425	1,561	1,770	588	1,648	1,141	2,829	1,231	1,179
PORTLAND, Ore.	2,873	3,229	2,250	2,599	2,145	1,347	2,523	2,368	1,953	1,016	3,438	1,830
RENO, Nev.	2,611	2,953	1,980	2,310	1,849	1,038	2,239	1,975	1,654	475	3,217	1,782
ST. LOUIS. Mo.	582	1,188	293	545	643	858	514	780	254	1,942	1,231	553
SALT LAKE CITY, Utah	1,959	2,431	1,411	1,796	1,240	501	1,725	1,502	1,105	704	2,621	1,309
SAN DIEGO, Calif.	2,230	3,119	2,210	2,476	1,421	1,243	2,445	1,578	1,706	125	2,817	2,138
SAN FRANCISCO, Calif.	2,554	3,198	2,233	2,563	1,791	1,267	2,492	1,984	1,903	383	3,238	2,077
SEATTLE, Wash.	295	3,163	2,184	2,533	2,222	1,426	2,457	2,445	1,984	1,193	3,469	1,691
WASHINGTON, D.C.	641	443	696	358	1,414	1,707	525	1,501	1,066	2,754	1,096	1,116

NEW ORLEANS	NEW YORK	OMAHA	PHILADELPHIA	PORTLAND	RENO	ST. LOUIS	SALT LAKE CITY	SAN DIEGO	SAN FRANCISCO	SEATTLE	WASHINGTON, D.C.	
518	863	1,027	776	2873	2611	582	1,959	2,230	2,554	295	641	**ATLANTA,** Ga.
1,625	217	1,451	308	3229	2953	1,188	2,431	3,119	3,198	3,163	443	**BOSTON,** Mass.
938	818	477	767	2250	1980	293	1,411	2,210	2,233	2,184	696	**CHICAGO,** Ill.
1,132	502	816	425	2599	2310	545	1,796	2,476	2,563	2,533	358	**CLEVELAND,** Ohio
495	1,649	681	1,561	2145	1849	643	1,240	1,421	1,791	2,222	1,414	**DALLAS,** Texas
1,292	1,852	540	1,770	1347	1038	858	501	1,243	1,267	1,426	1,707	**DENVER,** Colo.
1,143	632	745	588	2523	2239	514	1,725	2,445	2,492	2,457	525	**DETROIT,** Mich.
349	1,742	931	1,648	2368	1975	780	1,502	1,578	1,984	2,445	1,501	**HOUSTON,** Texas
809	1,223	185	1,141	1,953	1,654	254	1,105	1,706	1,903	1,984	1,066	**KANSAS CITY,** Mo.
1,947	2,911	1,668	2,829	1,016	475	1,942	704	125	383	1,193	2754	**LOS ANGELES** Calif.
881	1,325	1,686	1,231	3,438	3,217	1,231	2,621	2,817	3,238	3,469	1,096	**MIAMI,** Fla.
1,228	1,261	371	1,179	1,830	1,782	553	1,309	2,138	2,077	1,691	1,116	**MINNEAPOLIS-ST. PAUL,** Minn.
	1,406	994	1,312	2,654	2,350	690	1,735	1,879	2,300	2,731	1,165	**NEW ORLEANS,** La.
1,406		1,295	89	3,088	2,789	969	2,275	2,900	3,082	3,025	232	**NEW YORK,** N.Y.
994	1,295		1,213	1,749	1,499	439	938	1,788	1,726	1,824	1,150	**OMAHA,** Neb.
1,312	89	1,213		3,006	2,707	887	2,193	2,818	2,960	2,943	141	**PHILADELPHIA,** Pa.
2,654	3,088	1,749	3,006		666	2,207	768	1,137	611	175	2,943	**PORTLAND,** Ore.
2,350	2,789	1,499	2,707	666		1,908	516	576	222	856	26,44	**RENO,** Nev.
690	969	439	887	2,207	1,908		1,359	1,931	2,157	2,238	812	**ST. LOUIS** Mo.
1,735	2,275	938	2,193	768	516	1,359		812	730	924	2,130	**SALT LAKE CITY,** Utah
1,879	2,900	1,788	2,818	1,137	576	1,931	812		525	1,314	2,743	**SAN DIEGO,** Calif.
2,300	3,082	1,726	2,960	611	222	2,157	2,157	525		786	2,897	**SAN FRANCISCO,** Calif.
2,731	3,025	1,824	2,943	175	856	2,238	2,238	1,314	786		2,880	**SEATTLE,** Wash.
1,165	232	1,150	141	2,943	2,644	812	812	2,743	2,897	2,880		**WASHINGTON,** D.C.

DOCUMENTS

THE MAYFLOWER COMPACT

The roots of the Constitution are found in a hastily written charter

CAPE COD, NOV. 11, 1620—The principle of government by written contract was established in the New World in part because of a mix-up in directions. A band of devout religious separatists, now known as the Pilgrims, decided in 1620 to leave England for what they hoped would be the more religiously tolerant shores of the Colonies. To help with expenses, they joined a larger group of non-separatists in an agreement with a joint stock company to settle in the colony of Virginia. After a seven-week journey aboard the Mayflower, *they sighted Cape Cod and headed for harbor. The problem was, Cape Cod wasn't in Virginia, the territory in which they had contracted to settle. As word of the error made way around the ship, several of the more rugged individualists in the party made noises that they would "use their own liberty" when they came ashore, arguing that this was not the land for which they had contracted and was, therefore, no-mans land. Fearing anarchy, 41 of the ships passengers pledged allegiance to the King and formed a new colony on the basis of a single, hastily written compact. One of the writers, William Bradford, went on to govern Plymouth Colony for 31 years.*

In ye name of God, Amen. We, whose names are underwritten, the Loyal Subjects of our dread Sovereign Lord, King *James*, by the grace of God, of *Great Britain, France* and *Ireland*, King, *Defender of the Faith*, etc.

Having undertaken for the Glory of God, and advancement of the Christian Faith and Honour of our King and Country, a voyage to plant the first colony in the northern Parts of Virginia, do by these presents, solemnly and mutually in the Presence of God and one of another, covenant and combine ourselves together into a civil Body Politick, for our better Ordering and Preservation and Furtherance of the Ends aforesaid; and by virtue hereof to enact, constitute, and frame such just and equal Laws, Ordinances, Acts, Constitutions and Offices, from time to time, as shall be thought most meet and convenient for the general good of the colony, unto which we promise all due submission and obedience.

In Witness whereof we have hereunto subscribed our names at *Cape Cod* the eleventh of *November*, in the Reign of our Sovereign Lord, King *James* of *England, France* and *Ireland*, the eighteenth, and of *Scotland* the fifty-fourth.

Anno Domini, 1620.

THE DECLARATION OF INDEPENDENCE

A bold accounting of the principles on which a new nation is born

PHILADELPHIA, JULY 4, 1776— Though the Continental Congress had already announced its independence from Britain in a brief resolution a month earlier, it fell on Thomas Jefferson to explain to the world why the "United Colonies" were justified in doing so. A committee made up of John Adams, Ben Franklin, Robert Livingston, and John Sherman made 86 changes to Jefferson's original draft, which took Jefferson only three weeks to write. The last of the Declaration's 56 signatories did not affix his signature till the following August.

When in the Course of human events, it becomes necessary for one people to dissolve the political bands which have connected them with another, and to assume among the Powers of the earth, the separate and equal station to which the Laws of Nature and of Nature's God entitle them, a decent respect to the opinions of mankind requires that they should declare the causes which impel them to the separation.

We hold these truths to be self-evident, that all men are created equal, that they are endowed by their Creator with certain unalienable Rights, that among these are Life, Liberty and the pursuit of Happiness.

That to secure these rights, Governments are instituted among Men, deriving their just powers from the consent of the governed,

That whenever any Form of Government becomes destructive of these ends, it is the Right of the People to alter or to abolish it, and to institute new Government, laying its foundation on such principles and organizing its powers in such form, as to them shall seem most likely to effect their Safety and Happiness. Prudence, indeed, will dictate that Governments long established should not be changed for light and transient causes; and accordingly all experience hath shewn, that mankind are more disposed to suffer, while evils are sufferable, than to right themselves by abolishing the forms to which they are accustomed. But when a long train of abuses and usurpations, pursuing invariably the same Object evinces a design to reduce them under absolute Despotism, it is their right, it is their duty, to throw off such Government, and to provide new Guards for their future security. Such has been the patient sufferance of these Colonies; and such is now the necessity which constrains them to alter their former Systems of Government. The history of the present King of Great Britain is a history of repeated injuries and usurpations, all having in direct object the establishment of an absolute Tyranny over these States. To prove this, let Facts be submitted to a candid world.

We hold these truths to be self-evident, that all men are created equal, that they are endowed by their Creator with certain unalienable Rights, that among these are Life, Liberty and the pursuit of Happiness.

He has refused his Assent to Laws, the most wholesome and necessary for the public good.

He has forbidden his Governors to pass Laws of immediate and pressing importance, unless suspended in their operation till his Assent should be obtained; and when so suspended, he has utterly neglected to attend to them.

He has refused to pass other Laws for the accommodation of large districts of people, unless these people would relinquish the right of Representation in the Legislature, a right inestimable to them and formidable to tyrants only.

He has called together legislative bodies at places unusual, uncomfortable, and distant from the depository of their public Records, for the sole purpose of fatiguing them into compliance with his measures.

He has dissolved Representative Houses repeatedly, for opposing with manly firmness his invasions on the rights of the people.

He has refused for a long time, after such dissolutions, to cause others to be elected; whereby the Legislative powers, incapable of Annihilation, have returned to the People at large for their exercise; the State remaining in the mean time exposed to all the dangers of invasion from without, and convulsions within.

He has endeavoured to prevent the population of these States; for that purpose obstructing the Laws for Naturalization of Foreigners; refusing to pass others to encourage their migrations hither, and raising the conditions of new Appropriations of Lands.

He has obstructed the Administration of Justice, by refusing his Assent to Laws for establishing Judiciary powers.

He has made Judges dependent on his Will alone, for the tenure of their offices, and the amount and payment of their salaries.

He has erected a multitude of New Offices, and sent hither swarms of Officers to harass our people, and eat out their substance.

He has kept among us, in times of peace, Standing Armies without the Consent of our legislatures.

He has affected to render the Military independent of and superior to the Civil power.

He has combined with others to subject us to a jurisdiction foreign to our constitution, and unacknowledged by our laws; giving his Assent to their Acts of pretended Legislation:

For quartering large bodies of armed troops among us:

For protecting them, by a mock Trial, from punishment for any Murders which they should commit on the Inhabitants of these States:

For cutting off our Trade with all parts of the world:

For imposing Taxes on us without our Consent:

For depriving us in many cases, of the benefits of Trial by Jury:

For transporting us beyond Seas to be tried for pretended offences:

For abolishing the free System of English Laws in a neighbouring Province, establishing therein an Arbitrary government, and enlarging its Boundaries so as to render it at once an example and fit instrument for introducing the same absolute rule into these Colonies:

For taking away our Charters, abolishing our most valuable Laws, and altering fundamentally the Forms of our Governments:

For suspending our own Legislatures and declaring themselves invested with power to legislate for us in all cases whatsoever.

He has abdicated Government here, by declaring us out of his Protection and waging War against us.

He has plundered our seas, ravaged our Coasts, burnt our towns, and destroyed the lives of our people.

He is at this time transporting large Armies of foreign Mercenaries to compleat the works of death, desolation and tyranny, already begun with circumstances of Cruelty & Perfidy scarcely paralleled in the most barbarous ages, and totally unworthy the Head of a civilized nation.

He has constrained our fellow Citizens taken Captive on the high Seas to bear Arms against their Country, to become the executioners of their friends and Brethren, or to fall themselves by their Hands.

He has excited domestic insurrections amongst us, and has endeavoured to bring on the inhabitants of our frontiers,

The history of the present King of Great Britain is a history of repeated injuries and usurpations, all having in direct object the establishment of an absolute Tyranny over these States. To prove this, let Facts be submitted to a candid world.

the merciless Indian Savages, whose known rule of warfare, is an undistinguished destruction of all ages, sexes and conditions.

In every stage of these Oppressions We have Petitioned for Redress in the most humble terms: Our repeated Petitions have been answered only by repeated injury. A Prince, whose character is thus marked by every act which may define a Tyrant, is unfit to be the ruler of a free people.

Nor have We been wanting in attentions to our British brethren. We have warned them from time to time of attempts by their legislature to extend an unwarrantable jurisdiction over us. We have reminded them of the circumstances of our emigration and settlement here. We have appealed to their native justice and magnanimity, and we have conjured them by the ties of our common kindred to disavow these usurpations, which, would inevitably interrupt our connections and correspondence. They too have been deaf to the voice of justice and of consanguinity. We must, therefore, acquiesce in the necessity, which denounces our Separation, and hold them, as we hold the rest of mankind, Enemies in War, in Peace Friends.

We, therefore, the Representatives of the UNITED STATES OF AMERICA, in General Congress, Assembled, appealing to the Supreme Judge of the world for the rectitude of our intentions, do, in the Name, and by Authority of the good People of these Colonies, solemnly publish and declare, That these United Colonies are, and of Right ought to be Free and Independent States; that they are Absolved from all Allegiance to the British Crown, and that all political connection between them and the State of Great Britain, is and ought to be totally dissolved; and that as Free and Independent States, they have full Power to levy War, conclude Peace, contract Alliances, establish Commerce, and to do all other Acts and Things which Independent States may of right do.

And for the support of this Declaration, with a firm reliance on the protection of divine Providence, we mutually pledge to each other our Lives, our Fortunes and our sacred Honor.

THE SIGNERS OF THE DECLARATION OF INDEPENDENCE

John Adams, *Massachusetts*
Samuel Adams, *Massachusetts*
Josiah Bartlett, *New Hampshire*
Carter Braxton, *Virginia*
Chas. Carroll, *Maryland*
Samuel Chase, *Maryland*
Abraham Clark, *New Jersey*
George Clymer, *Pennsylvania*
William Ellery, *Rhode Island*
William Floyd, *New York*
Benjamin Franklin, *Pennsylvania*
Elbridge Gerry, *Massachusetts*
Button Gwinnett, *Georgia*
Lyman Hall, *Georgia*
John Hancock, *Massachusetts*
Benjamin Harrison, *Virginia*
John Hart, *New Jersey*
Joseph Hewes, *North Carolina*
Thos. Heyward, Jr., *South Carolina*
William Hooper, *North Carolina*
Stephen Hopkins, *Rhode Island*
Francis Hopkinson, *New Jersey*
Samuel Huntington, *Connecticut*
Thomas Jefferson, *Virginia*
Francis Lightfoot Lee, *Virginia*
Richard Henry Lee, *Virginia*
Francis Lewis, *New York*
Philip Livingston, *New York*
Thomas Lynch, Jr., *South Carolina*
Thomas McKean, *Delaware*
Arthur Middleton, *South Carolina*
Lewis Morris, *New York*
Robert Morris, *Pennsylvania*
John Morton, *Pennsylvania*
Thos. Nelson, Jr., *Virginia*
William Paca, *Maryland*
Robert Treat Paine, *Massachusetts*
John Penn, *North Carolina*
George Read, *Delaware*
Ceaser Rodney, *Delaware*
George Ross, *Pennsylvania*
Benjamin Rush, *Pennsylvania*
Edward Rutledge, *South Carolina*
Roger Sherman, *Connecticut*
James Smith, *Pennsylvania*
Richard Stockton, *New Jersey*
Thomas Stone, *Maryland*
George Taylor, *Pennsylvania*
Matthew Thornton, *New Hampshire*
George Walton, *Georgia*
William Whipple, *New Hampshire*
William Williams, *Connecticut*
James Wilson, *Pennsylvania*
John Witherspoon, *New Jersey*
Oliver Wolcott, *Connecticut*
George Wythe, *Virginia*

CONSTITUTION OF THE UNITED STATES

The eloquent blueprint for a continuing national experiment

*PHILADELPHIA, SEPT. 17, 1787—Only 55 of the young nation's 65 state-certified delegates arrived in the spring of 1787 to write a replacement for the flawed Articles of Confederation. After a summer of heated debate about what power should be ceded to the then exceedingly weak federal government, only 39 delegates signed it. Within four years though, the new Constitution had been ratified by every state.**

We the People of the United States, in Order to form a more perfect Union, establish Justice, insure domestic Tranquility, provide for the common defence, promote the general Welfare, and secure the Blessings of Liberty to ourselves and our Posterity, do ordain and establish this Constitution for the United States of America.

ARTICLE I

SECTION 1. All legislative Powers herein granted shall be vested in a Congress of the United States, which shall consist of a Senate and House of Representatives.

SECTION 2. The House of Representatives shall be composed of Members chosen every second Year by the People of the several States, and the Electors in each State shall have the Qualifications requisite for Electors of the most numerous Branch of the State Legislature.

No Person shall be a Representative who shall not have attained to the Age of twenty five Years, and been seven Years a Citizen of the United States, and who shall not, when elected, be an Inhabitant of that State in which he shall be chosen.

Representatives and direct Taxes shall be apportioned among the several States which may be included within this Union, according to their respective Numbers, which shall be determined by adding to the whole Number of free Persons, including those bound to Service for a Term of Years, and excluding Indians not taxed, three fifths of all other Persons. The actual Enumeration shall be made within three Years after the first Meeting of the Congress of the United States, and within every subsequent Term of ten Years, in such Manner as they shall by Law direct. The Number of Representatives shall not exceed one for every thirty Thousand, but each State shall have at Least one Representative; and until such enumeration shall be made, the State of New Hampshire shall be entitled to chuse three, Massachusetts eight, Rhode-Island and Providence Plantations one, Connecticut five, New-York six, New Jersey four, Pennsylvania eight, Delaware one, Maryland six, Virginia ten, North Carolina five, South Carolina five, and Georgia three.

When vacancies happen in the Representation from any State, the Executive Authority thereof shall issue Writs of Election to fill such Vacancies.

The House of Representatives shall chuse their Speaker and other Officers; and shall have the sole Power of Impeachment.

SECTION 3. The Senate of the United States shall be composed of two Senators from each State, chosen by the Legislature thereof, for six Years; and each Senator shall have one Vote.

Immediately after they shall be assembled in Consequence of the first Election, they shall be divided as equally as may be into three Classes. The Seats of the Senators of the first Class shall be vacated at the Expiration of the second Year, of the second Class at the Expiration of the fourth Year, and of the third Class at the Expiration of the sixth Year, so that one third may be chosen every second Year; and if Vacancies happen by Resignation, or otherwise,

*Text taken from the print issued by the U.S. Department of State and available at the Library of Congress.

during the Recess of the Legislature of any State, the Executive thereof may make temporary Appointments until the next Meeting of the Legislature, which shall then fill such Vacancies.

No Person shall be a Senator who shall not have attained to the Age of thirty Years, and been nine Years a Citizen of the United States, and who shall not, when elected, be an Inhabitant of that State for which he shall be chosen.

The Vice President of the United States shall be President of the Senate, but shall have no Vote, unless they be equally divided.

No Person shall be a Senator who shall not have attained to the Age of thirty Years, and been nine Years a Citizen of the United States, and who shall not, when elected, be an Inhabitant of that State for which he shall be chosen.

The Senate shall chuse their other Officers, and also a President pro tempore, in the Absence of the Vice President, or when he shall exercise the Office of President of the United States.

The Senate shall have the sole Power to try all Impeachments. When sitting for that Purpose, they shall be on Oath or Affirmation. When the President of the United States is tried the Chief Justice shall preside: And no Person shall be convicted without the Concurrence of two thirds of the Members present.

Judgment in Cases of Impeachment shall not extend further than to removal from Office, and disqualification to hold and enjoy any Office of honor, Trust or Profit under the United States: but the Party convicted shall nevertheless be liable and subject to Indictment, Trial, Judgment and Punishment, according to Law.

Section 4. The Times, Places and Manner of holding Elections for Senators and Representatives, shall be prescribed in each State by the Legislature thereof; but the Congress may at any time by Law make or alter such Regulations, except as to the Places of chusing Senators.

The Congress shall assemble at least once in every Year, and such Meeting shall be on the first Monday in December, unless they shall by Law appoint a different Day.

Section 5. Each House shall be the Judge of the Elections, Returns and Qualifications of its own Members, and a Majority of each shall constitute a Quorum to do Business; but a smaller Number may adjourn from day to day, and may be authorized to compel the Attendance of absent Members, in such Manner, and under such Penalties as each House may provide.

Each House may determine the Rules of its Proceedings, punish its Members for disorderly Behaviour, and, with the Concurrence of two thirds, expel a Member.

Each House shall keep a Journal of its Proceedings, and from time to time publish the same, excepting such Parts as may in their Judgment require Secrecy; and the Yeas and Nays of the Members of either House on any question shall, at the Desire of one fifth of those Present, be entered on the Journal.

Neither House, during the Session of Congress, shall, without the Consent of the other, adjourn for more than three days, nor to any other Place than that in which the two Houses shall be sitting.

Section 6. The Senators and Representatives shall receive a Compensation for their Services, to be ascertained by Law, and paid out of the Treasury of the United States. They shall in all Cases, except Treason, Felony and Breach of the Peace, be privileged from Arrest during their Attendance at the Session of their respective Houses, and in going to and returning from the same; and for any Speech or Debate in either House, they shall not be questioned in any other Place.

No Senator or Representative shall, during the Time for which he was elected, be appointed to any civil Office under the Authority of the United States, which shall have been created, or the Emoluments whereof shall have been encreased during such time; and no Person holding any Office under the United States, shall be a Member of either House during his Continuance in Office.

Section 7. All Bills for raising Revenue shall originate in the House of Representatives; but the Senate may propose or concur with Amendments as on other Bills.

Every Bill which shall have passed the House of Representatives and the Senate, shall, before it become a Law, be presented to the President of the United States; If he approve he shall sign it, but if not he shall return it, with his Objections to that House in which it shall have originated, who shall enter the Objections at large on their Journal, and proceed to reconsider it. If after such Reconsideration two thirds of that House shall agree to pass the Bill, it shall be sent, together with the Objections, to the other House, by which it shall likewise be reconsidered, and if approved by two thirds of that House, it shall become a Law. But in all such Cases the Votes of both Houses shall be determined by yeas and Nays, and the Names of the Persons voting for and against the Bill shall be entered on the Journal of each House respectively. If any Bill shall not be returned by the President within ten Days (Sundays excepted) after it shall have been presented to him, the Same shall be a Law, in like Manner as if he had signed it, unless the Congress by their Adjournment prevent its Return, in which Case it shall not be a Law.

Every Order, Resolution, or Vote to which the Concurrence of the Senate and House of Representatives may be necessary (except on a question of Adjournment) shall be presented to the President of the United States; and before the Same shall take Effect, shall be approved by him, or being disapproved by him, shall be repassed by two thirds of the Senate and House of Representatives, according to the Rules and Limitations prescribed in the Case of a Bill.

Section 8. The Congress shall have Power To lay and collect Taxes, Duties, Imposts and Excises, to pay the Debts and provide for the common Defence and general Welfare of the United States; but all Duties, Imposts and Excises shall be uniform throughout the United States;

To borrow Money on the credit of the United States;

To regulate Commerce with foreign Nations, and among the several States, and with the Indian Tribes;

To establish an uniform Rule of Naturalization, and uniform Laws on the subject of Bankruptcies throughout the United States;

To coin Money, regulate the Value thereof, and of foreign Coin, and fix the Standard of Weights and Measures;

To provide for the Punishment of counterfeiting the Securities and current Coin of the United States;

To establish Post Offices and post Roads;

To promote the Progress of Science and useful Arts, by securing for limited Times to Authors and Inventors the exclusive Right to their respective Writings and Discoveries;

To constitute Tribunals inferior to the supreme Court;

To define and punish Piracies and Felonies committed on the high Seas, and Offences against the Law of Nations;

To declare War, grant Letters of Marque and Reprisal, and make Rules concerning Captures on Land and Water;

To raise and support Armies, but no Appropriation of Money to that Use shall be for a longer Term than two Years;

To provide and maintain a Navy;

To make Rules for the Government and Regulation of the land and naval Forces;

To provide for calling forth the Militia to execute the Laws of the Union, suppress Insurrections and repel Invasions;

To provide for organizing, arming, and disciplining, the Militia, and for governing such Part of them as may be employed in the Service of the United States, reserving to the States respectively, the Appointment of the Officers, and the Authority of training the Militia according to the discipline prescribed by Congress;

To exercise exclusive Legislation in all Cases whatsoever, over such District (not exceeding ten Miles square) as may, by Cession of particular States, and the Acceptance of Congress, become the Seat of the Government of the United States, and to exercise like Authority over all Places purchased by the Consent of the Legislature of the State in which the Same shall be, for the Erection of Forts, Magazines, Arsenals, dock-Yards, and other needful Buildings;—And

To make all Laws which shall be necessary and proper for carrying into Execution the foregoing Powers, and all other Powers vested by this Constitution in the Government of the United States, or in any Department or Officer thereof.

The Privilege of the Writ of Habeas Corpus shall not be suspended, unless when in Cases of Rebellion or Invasion the public Safety may require it.

SECTION 9. The Migration or Importation of such Persons as any of the States now existing shall think proper to admit, shall not be prohibited by the Congress prior to the Year one thousand eight hundred and eight, but a Tax or duty may be imposed on such Importation, not exceeding ten dollars for each Person.

The Privilege of the Writ of Habeas Corpus shall not be suspended, unless when in Cases of Rebellion or Invasion the public Safety may require it.

No Bill of Attainder or ex post facto Law shall be passed.

No Capitation, or other direct, Tax shall be laid, unless in Proportion to the Census or Enumeration herein before directed to be taken.

No Tax or Duty shall be laid on Articles exported from any State.

No Preference shall be given by any Regulation of Commerce or Revenue to the Ports of one State over those of another: nor shall Vessels bound to, or from, one State, be obliged to enter, clear, or pay Duties in another.

No Money shall be drawn from the Treasury, but in Consequence of Appropriations made by Law; and a regular Statement and Account of the Receipts and Expenditures of all public Money shall be published from time to time.

No Title of Nobility shall be granted by the United States: And no Person holding any Office of Profit or Trust under them, shall, without the Consent of the Congress, accept of any present, Emolument, Office, or Title, of any kind whatever, from any King, Prince, or foreign State.

SECTION 10. No State shall enter into any Treaty, Alliance, or Confederation; grant Letters of Marque and Reprisal; coin Money; emit Bills of Credit; make any Thing but gold and silver Coin a Tender in Payment of Debts; pass any Bill of Attainder, ex post facto Law, or Law impairing the Obligation of Contracts, or grant any Title of Nobility.

No State shall, without the Consent of the Congress, lay any Imposts or Duties on Imports or Exports, except what may be absolutely necessary for executing it's inspection Laws: and the net Produce of all Duties and Imposts, laid by any State on Imports or Exports, shall be for the Use of the Treasury of the United States; and all such Laws shall be subject to the Revision and Control of the Congress.

No State shall, without the Consent of Congress, lay any Duty of Tonnage, keep Troops, or Ships of War in time of Peace, enter into any Agreement or Compact with another State, or with a foreign Power, or engage in War, unless actually invaded, or in such imminent Danger as will not admit of delay.

ARTICLE II

SECTION 1. The executive Power shall be vested in a President of the United States of America. He shall hold his Office during the Term of four Years, and, together with the Vice President, chosen for the same Term, be elected, as follows

Each State shall appoint, in such Manner as the Legislature thereof may direct, a Number of Electors, equal to the whole Number of Senators and Representatives to which the State may be entitled in the Congress: but no Senator or Representative, or Person holding an Office of Trust or Profit under the United States, shall be appointed an Elector.

The Electors shall meet in their respective States, and vote by Ballot for two Persons, of whom one at least shall not be an Inhabitant of the same State with themselves. And they shall make a List of all the Persons voted for, and of the Number of Votes for each; which List they shall sign and certify, and transmit sealed to the Seat of Government of the United States, directed to the President of the Senate. The President of the Senate shall, in the Presence of the Senate and House of Representatives, open all the Certificates, and the Votes shall then be counted. The Person having the greatest Number of Votes shall be the President, if such Number be a Majority of the whole Number of Electors appointed; and if there be more than one who have such Majority, and have an equal Number of Votes, then the House of Representatives shall immediately chuse by Ballot one of them for President; and if no Person have a Majority, then from the five highest on the List the said House shall in like Manner chuse the President. But in chusing the President, the Votes shall be taken by States, the Representation from each State having one Vote; A quorum for this Purpose shall consist of a Member or Members from two thirds of the States, and a Majority of all the States shall be necessary to a Choice. In every Case, after the Choice of the President, the Person having the greatest Number of Votes of the Electors shall be the Vice President. But if there should remain two or more who have equal Votes, the Senate shall chuse from them by Ballot the Vice President.

The Congress may determine the Time of chusing the Electors, and the Day on which they shall give their Votes; which Day shall be the same throughout the United States.

No Person except a natural born Citizen, or a Citizen of the United States, at the time of the Adoption of this Constitution, shall be eligible to the Office of President; neither shall any Person be eligible to that Office who shall not have attained to the Age of thirty five Years, and been fourteen Years a Resident within the United States.

"I do solemnly swear (or affirm) that I will faithfully execute the Office of President of the United States, and will to the best of my Ability, preserve, protect and defend the Constitution of the United States."

In Case of the Removal of the President from Office, or of his Death, Resignation, or Inability to discharge the Powers and Duties of the said Office, the Same shall devolve on the Vice President, and the Congress may by Law provide for the Case of Removal, Death, Resignation or Inability, both of the President and Vice President declaring what Officer shall then act as President, and such Officer shall act accordingly, until the Disability be removed, or a President shall be elected.

The President shall, at stated Times, receive for his Services, a Compensation, which shall neither be encreased nor diminished during the Period for which he shall have been elected, and he shall not receive within that Period any other Emolument from the United States, or any of them.

Before he enter on the Execution of his Office, he shall take the following Oath or Affirmation:— "I do solemnly swear (or affirm) that I will faithfully execute the Office of President of the United States, and will to the best of my Ability, preserve, protect and defend the Constitution of the United States."

SECTION 2. The President shall be Commander in Chief of the Army and Navy of the United States, and of the Militia of the several States, when called into the actual Service of the United States; he may require the Opinion, in writing, of the principal Officer in each of the executive Departments, upon any Subject relating to the Duties of their respective Offices, and he shall have Power to grant Reprieves and Pardons for Offences against the United States, except in Cases of Impeachment.

He shall have Power, by and with the

Advice and Consent of the Senate, to make Treaties, provided two thirds of the Senators present concur; and he shall nominate, and by and with the Advice and Consent of the Senate, shall appoint Ambassadors, other public Ministers and Consuls, Judges of the supreme Court, and all other Officers of the United States, whose Appointments are not herein otherwise provided for, and which shall be established by Law: but the Congress may by Law vest the Appointment of such inferior Officers, as they think proper, in the President alone, in the Courts of Law, or in the Heads of Departments.

The President shall have Power to fill up all Vacancies that may happen during the Recess of the Senate, by granting Commissions which shall expire at the End of their next Session.

Section 3. He shall from time to time give to the Congress Information of the State of the Union, and recommend to their Consideration such Measures as he shall judge necessary and expedient; he may, on extraordinary Occasions, convene both Houses, or either of them, and in Case of Disagreement between them, with Respect to the Time of Adjournment, he may adjourn them to such Time as he shall think proper; he shall receive Ambassadors and other public Ministers; he shall take Care that the Laws be faithfully executed, and shall Commission all the Officers of the United States.

Section 4. The President, Vice President and all civil Officers of the United States, shall be removed from Office on Impeachment for, and Conviction of, Treason, Bribery, or other high Crimes and Misdemeanors.

ARTICLE III

Section 1. The judicial Power of the United States, shall be vested in one supreme Court, and in such inferior Courts as the Congress may from time to time ordain and establish. The Judges, both of the supreme and inferior Courts, shall hold their Offices during good Behaviour, and shall, at stated Times, receive for their Services, a Compensation which shall not be diminished during their Continuance in Office.

Section 2. The judicial Power shall extend to all Cases, in Law and Equity, arising under this Constitution, the Laws of the United States, and Treaties made, or which shall be made, under their Authority;—to all Cases affecting Ambassadors, other public Ministers and Consuls;—to all Cases of admiralty and maritime Jurisdiction;—to Controversies to which the United States shall be a Party;—to Controversies between two or more States;—between a State and Citizens of another State;—between Citizens of different States,—between Citizens of the same State claiming Lands under Grants of different States, and between a State, or the Citizens thereof, and foreign States, Citizens or Subjects.

In all Cases affecting Ambassadors, other public Ministers and Consuls, and those in which a State shall be Party, the supreme Court shall have original Jurisdiction. In all the other Cases before mentioned, the supreme Court shall have appellate Jurisdiction, both as to Law and Fact, with such Exceptions, and under such Regulations as the Congress shall make.

The Trial of all Crimes, except in Cases of Impeachment, shall be by Jury; and such Trial shall be held in the State where the said Crimes shall have been committed; but when not committed within any State, the Trial shall be at such Place or Places as the Congress may by Law have directed.

Section 3. Treason against the United States, shall consist only in levying War against them, or in adhering to their Enemies, giving them Aid and Comfort. No Person shall be convicted of Treason unless on the Testimony of two Witnesses to the same overt Act, or on Confession in open Court.

The Congress shall have Power to declare the Punishment of Treason, but no Attainder of Treason shall work Corruption of Blood, or Forfeiture except during the Life of the Person attainted.

ARTICLE IV

Section 1. Full Faith and Credit shall be given in each State to the public Acts, Records, and judicial Proceedings of every other State. And the Congress may by general Laws prescribe the Manner in which such Acts, Records and Proceedings shall be proved, and the Effect thereof.

Section 2. The Citizens of each State shall be entitled to all Privileges and Immunities of Citizens in the several States.

A Person charged in any State with Treason, Felony, or other Crime, who shall flee from Justice, and be found in another State, shall on Demand of the executive Authority of the State from which he fled, be delivered up, to be removed to the State having Jurisdiction of the Crime.

No Person held to Service or Labour in one State, under the Laws thereof, escaping into another, shall, in Consequence of any Law or Regulation therein, be discharged from such Service or Labour, but shall be delivered up on Claim of the Party to whom such Service or Labour may be due.

Section 3. New States may be admitted by the Congress into this Union; but no new State shall be formed or erected within the Jurisdiction of any other State; nor any State be formed by the Junction of two or more States, or Parts of States, without the Consent of the Legislatures of the States concerned as well as of the Congress.

The Congress shall have Power to dispose of and make all needful Rules and Regulations respecting the Territory or other Property belonging to the United States; and nothing in this Constitution shall be so construed as to Prejudice any Claims of the United States, or of any particular State.

Section 4. The United States shall guarantee to every State in this Union a Republican Form of Government, and shall protect each of them against Invasion; and on Application of the Legislature, or of the Executive (when the Legislature cannot be convened) against domestic Violence.

ARTICLE V

The Congress, whenever two thirds of both Houses shall deem it necessary, shall propose Amendments to this Constitution, or, on the Application of the Legislatures of two thirds of the several States, shall call a Convention for proposing Amendments, which, in either Case, shall be valid to all Intents and Purposes, as Part of this Constitution, when ratified by the Legislatures of three fourths of the several States, or by Conventions in three fourths thereof, as the one or the other Mode of Ratification may be proposed by the Congress; Provided that no Amendment which may be made prior to the Year One thousand eight hundred and eight shall in any Manner affect the first and fourth Clauses in the Ninth Section of the first Article; and that no State, without its Consent, shall be deprived of its equal Suffrage in the Senate.

ARTICLE VI

All Debts contracted and Engagements entered into, before the Adoption of this Constitution, shall be as valid against the United States under this Constitution, as under the Confederation.

This Constitution, and the Laws of the United States which shall be made in Pursuance thereof; and all Treaties made or which shall be made, under the Authority of the United States, shall be the supreme Law of the Land; and the Judges in every State shall be bound thereby, any Thing in the Constitution or Laws of any State to the Contrary notwithstanding.

The Senators and Representatives before mentioned, and the Members of the several State Legislatures, and all executive and judicial Officers, both of the United States and of the several States, shall be bound by Oath or Affirmation, to support this Constitution; but no religious Test shall ever be required as a Qualification to any Office or public Trust under the United States.

ARTICLE VII

The Ratification of the Conventions of nine States, shall be sufficient for the Establishment of this Constitution between the States so ratifying the Same.

Done in Convention by the Unanimous Consent of the States present the Seventeenth Day of September in the Year of our Lord one thousand seven hundred and Eighty seven and of the Independence of the United States of America the Twelfth IN WITNESS whereof We have hereunto subscribed our Names....

THE BILL OF RIGHTS

Early additions to the Constitution to guarantee the liberty of the people

NEW YORK, SEPT. 25, 1789—The first 10 amendments were proposed to assuage fear of a strong federal government. Two other amendments were not ratified at the time; one, regarding congressional salaries, became Amendment 27 in 1992.

AMENDMENT 1

Congress shall make no law respecting an establishment of religion, or prohibiting the free exercise thereof; or abridging the freedom of speech, or of the press; or the right of the people peaceably to assemble, and to petition the Government for a redress of grievances.

AMENDMENT 2

A well regulated Militia, being necessary to the security of a free State, the right of the people to keep and bear Arms, shall not be infringed.

AMENDMENT 3

No Soldier shall, in time of peace be quartered in any house, without the consent of the Owner, nor in time of war, but in a manner to be prescribed by law.

AMENDMENT 4

The right of the people to be secure in their persons, houses, papers, and effects, against unreasonable searches and seizures, shall not be violated, and no Warrants shall issue, but upon probable cause, supported by Oath or affirmation, and particularly describing the place to be searched, and the persons or things to be seized.

AMENDMENT 5

No person shall be held to answer for a capital, or otherwise infamous crime, unless on a presentment or indictment of a Grand Jury, except in cases arising in the land or naval forces, or in the Militia, when in actual service in time of War or public danger; nor shall any person be subject for the same offence to be twice put in jeopardy of life or limb; nor shall be compelled in any criminal case to be a witness against himself, nor be deprived of life, liberty, or property, without due process of law; nor shall private property be taken for public use, without just compensation.

AMENDMENT 6

In all criminal prosecutions, the accused shall enjoy the right to a speedy and public trial, by an impartial jury of the State and district wherein the crime shall have been committed, which district shall have been previously ascertained by law, and to be informed of the nature and cause of the accusation; to be confronted with the witnesses against him; to have compulsory process for obtaining witnesses in his favor, and to have the Assistance of Counsel for his defence.

AMENDMENT 7

In Suits at common law, where the value in controversy shall exceed twenty dollars, the right of trial by jury shall be preserved, and no fact tried by a jury, shall be otherwise re-examined in any Court of the United States, than according to the rules of the common law.

AMENDMENT 8

Excessive bail shall not be required, nor excessive fines imposed, nor cruel and unusual punishments inflicted.

AMENDMENT 9

The enumeration in the Constitution, of certain rights, shall not be construed to deny or disparage others retained by the people.

AMENDMENT 10

The powers not delegated to the United States by the Constitution, nor prohibited by it to the States, are reserved to the States respectively, or to the people.

THE 17 OTHER AMENDMENTS

Constitutional additions as the needs of a growing nation evolve

The 17 additional amendments give evidence of the Constitution's continuing vitality. Some, like the 13th amendment, which abolished slavery, have strengthened the nation's civic fabric. Others have withered or even been repealed, as the 18th amendment banning alcohol was in 1933.

An amendment must go through two stages before becoming a part of the Constitution: proposal and ratification. Amendments may be proposed either by a two-thirds vote of both houses of Congress, or by a national convention summoned by Congress at the request of two-thirds of the states. (The latter method has never been used, though.) Once proposed, an amendment can be ratified either by the vote of three-fourths of the state legislatures or by Constitutional conventions in three-fourths of the states. The latter method was used only once—to pass the 21st amendment, which repealed the 18th amendment.

AMENDMENT 11

Jan. 8, 1798

The Judicial power of the United States shall not be construed to extend to any suit in law or equity, commenced or prosecuted against one of the United States by Citizens of another State, or by Citizens or Subjects of any Foreign State.

AMENDMENT 12

Sept. 25, 1804

The Electors shall meet in their respective states, and vote by ballot for President and Vice-President, one of whom, at least, shall not be an inhabitant of the same state with themselves; they shall name in their ballots the person voted for as President, and in distinct ballots the person voted for as Vice-President, and they shall make distinct lists of all persons voted for as President, and of all persons voted for as Vice-President, and of the number of votes for each, which list they shall sign and certify, and transmit sealed to the seat of the government of the United States, directed to the President of the Senate;—The President of the Senate shall, in the presence of the Senate and House of Representatives, open all the certificates and the votes shall then be counted;—The person having the greatest number of votes for President, shall be the President, if such number be a majority of the whole number of Electors appointed; and if no person have such majority, then from the persons having the highest numbers not exceeding three on the list of those voted for as President, the House of Representatives shall choose immediately, by ballot, the President. But in choosing the President, the votes shall be taken by states, the representation from each state having one vote; a quorum for this purpose shall consist of a member or members from two thirds of the states, and a majority of all the states shall be necessary to a choice. And if the House of Representatives shall not choose a President whenever the right of choice shall devolve upon them, before the fourth day of March next following, then the Vice-President shall act as President, as in the case of the death or other constitutional disability of the President.—The person having the greatest number of votes as Vice-President, shall be the Vice-President, if such number be a majority of the whole number of Electors appointed, and if no person have a majority, then from the two highest numbers on the list, the Senate shall choose the Vice-President; a quorum for the purpose shall consist of two thirds of the whole number of Senators, and a majority of the whole number shall be necessary to a choice. But no person constitutionally ineligible to the office of President shall be eligible to that of Vice-President of the United States.

AMENDMENT 13
Dec. 18, 1865

Section 1. Neither slavery nor involuntary servitude, except as a punishment for crime whereof the party shall have been duly convicted, shall exist within the United States, or any place subject to their jurisdiction.

Section 2. Congress shall have power to enforce this article by appropriate legislation.

Neither slavery nor involuntary servitude, except as a punishment for crime whereof the party shall have been duly convicted, shall exist within the United States, or any place subject to their jurisdiction.

13th Amendment

AMENDMENT 14
July 28, 1868

Section 1. All persons born or naturalized in the United States, and subject to the jurisdiction thereof, are citizens of the United States and of the State wherein they reside. No State shall make or enforce any law which shall abridge the privileges or immunities of citizens of the United States; nor shall any State deprive any person of life, liberty, or property, without due process of law; nor deny to any person within its jurisdiction the equal protection of the laws.

Section 2. Representatives shall be apportioned among the several States according to their respective numbers, counting the whole number of persons in each State, excluding Indians not taxed. But when the right to vote at any election for the choice of electors for President and Vice-President of the United States, Representatives in Congress, the Executive and Judicial officers of a State, or the members of the Legislature thereof, is denied to any of the male inhabitants of such State, being twenty-one years of age, and citizens of the United States, or in any way abridged, except for participation in rebellion, or other crime, the basis of representation therein shall be reduced in the proportion which the number of such male citizens shall bear to the whole number of male citizens twenty-one years of age in such State.

Section 3. No person shall be a Senator or Representative in Congress, or elector of President and Vice-President, or hold any office, civil or military, under the United States, or under any State, who, having previously taken an oath, as a member of Congress, or as an officer of the United States, or as a member of any State legislature, or as an executive or judicial officer of any State, to support the Constitution of the United States, shall have engaged in insurrection or rebellion against the same, or given aid or comfort to the enemies thereof. But Congress may by a vote of two thirds of each House, remove such disability.

Section 4. The validity of the public debt of the United States, authorized by law, including debts incurred for payment of pensions and bounties for services in suppressing insurrection or rebellion, shall not be questioned. But neither the United States nor any State shall assume or pay any debt or obligation incurred in aid of insurrection or rebellion against the United States, or any claim for the loss or emancipation of any slave; but all such debts, obligations and claims shall be held illegal and void.

Section 5. The Congress shall have power to enforce, by appropriate legislation, the provisions of this article.

AMENDMENT 15
March 30, 1870

Section 1. The right of citizens of the United States to vote shall not be denied or abridged by the United States or by any State on account of race, color, or previous condition of servitude—

Section 2. The Congress shall have power to enforce this article by appropriate legislation.

AMENDMENT 16
Feb. 25, 1913

The Congress shall have power to lay and collect taxes on incomes, from whatever source derived, without apportionment among the several States, and without regard to any census or enumeration.

AMENDMENT 17
May 31, 1913

The Senate of the United States shall be composed of two Senators from each State, elected by the people thereof, for six years; and each Senator shall have one vote. The electors in each State shall have the qualifications requisite for electors of the most numerous branch of the State legislatures.

When vacancies happen in the representation of any State in the Senate, the executive authority of such State shall issue writs of election to fill such vacancies: Provided, That the legislature of any State may empower the executive thereof to make temporary appointments until the people fill the vacancies by election as the legislature may direct.

This amendment shall not be so construed as to affect the election or term of any Senator chosen before it becomes valid as part of the Constitution.

AMENDMENT 18
Jan. 29, 1919 (Repealed Dec. 5, 1933)

Section 1. After one year from the ratification of this article the manufacture, sale, or transportation of intoxicating liquors within, the importation thereof into, or the exportation thereof from the United States and all territory subject to the jurisdiction thereof for beverage purposes is hereby prohibited.

Section 2. The Congress and the several States shall have concurrent power to enforce this article by appropriate legislation.

Section 3. This article shall be inoperative unless it shall have been ratified as an amendment to the Constitution by the legislatures of the several States, as provided in the Constitution, within seven years from the date of the submission hereof to the States by the Congress.

The right of citizens of the United States to vote shall not be denied or abridged by the United States or by any State on account of sex.

19th Amendment

AMENDMENT 19
Aug. 26, 1920

The right of citizens of the United States to vote shall not be denied or abridged by the United States or by any State on account of sex.

Congress shall have power to enforce this article by appropriate legislation.

AMENDMENT 20
Feb. 6, 1933

Section 1. The terms of the President and Vice-President shall end at noon on the 20th day of January, and the terms of Senators and Representatives at noon on the third day of January, of the years in which such terms would have ended if this article had not been ratified; and the terms of their successors shall then begin.

Section 2. The Congress shall assemble at least once in every year, and such meeting shall begin at noon on the third day of January, unless they shall by law appoint a different day.

Section 3. If, at the time fixed for the beginning of the term of the President, the President elect shall have died, the Vice-President elect shall become President. If a President shall not have been chosen before the time fixed for the beginning of his term, or if the President elect shall have failed to qualify, then the Vice-President elect shall act as President until a President shall have qualified; and the Congress may by law provide for the case wherein neither a President elect nor a Vice-President elect shall have qualified, declaring who shall then act as President, or the manner in which one who is to act shall be selected, and such person shall act accordingly until a President or Vice-

President shall have qualified.

Section 4. The Congress may by law provide for the case of the death of any of the persons from whom the House of Representatives may choose a President whenever the right of choice shall have devolved upon them, and for the case of the death of any of the persons from whom the Senate may choose a Vice-President whenever the right of choice shall have devolved upon them.

The right of citizens of the United States, who are eighteen years of age or older, to vote shall not be denied or abridged by the United States or any state on account of age.

26th Amendment

Section 5. Sections 1 and 2 shall take effect on the 15th day of October following the ratification of this article.

Section 6. This article shall be inoperative unless it shall have been ratified as an amendment to the Constitution by the legislatures of three fourths of the several States within seven years from the date of its submission.

AMENDMENT 21
Dec. 5, 1933

Section 1. The eighteenth article of amendment to the Constitution of the United States is hereby repealed.

Section 2. The transportation or importation into any State, Territory, or possession of the United States for delivery or use therein of intoxicating liquors, in violation of the laws thereof, is hereby prohibited.

Section 3. This article shall be inoperative unless it shall have been ratified as an amendment to the Constitution by conventions in the several States, as provided in the Constitution, within seven years from the date of the submission hereof to the States by the Congress.

AMENDMENT 22
March 1, 1951

Section 1. No person shall be elected to the office of the President more than twice, and no person who has held the office of President, or acted as President, for more than two years of a term to which some other person was elected President shall be elected to the office of the President more than once. But this Article shall not apply to any person holding the office of President when this Article was proposed by the Congress, and shall not prevent any person who may be holding the office of President, or acting as President, during the term within which this Article becomes operative from holding the office of President or acting as President during the remainder of such term.

Section 2. This article shall be inoperative unless it shall have been ratified as an amendment to the Constitution by the legislatures of three fourths of the several States within seven years from the date of its submission to the States by the Congress.

AMENDMENT 23
April 3, 1961

Section 1. The District constituting the seat of Government of the United States shall appoint in such manner as the Congress may direct:

A number of electors of President and Vice-President equal to the whole number of Senators and Representatives in Congress to which the District would be entitled if it were a State, but in no event more than the least populous State; they shall be in addition to those appointed by the States, but they shall be considered, for the purposes of the election of President and Vice-President, to be electors appointed by a State; and they shall meet in the District and perform such duties as provided by the twelfth article of amendment.

Section 2. The Congress shall have power to enforce this article by appropriate legislation.

AMENDMENT 24
Feb. 4, 1964

SECTION 1. The right of citizens of the United States to vote in any primary or other election for President or Vice-President, for electors for President or Vice-President, or for Senator or Representative in Congress, shall not be denied or abridged by the United States or any State by reason of failure to pay any poll tax or other tax.

SECTION 2. The Congress shall have power to enforce this article by appropriate legislation.

AMENDMENT 25
Feb. 10, 1967

SECTION 1. In case of the removal of the President from office or his death or resignation, the Vice-President shall become President.

SECTION 2. Whenever there is a vacancy in the office of the Vice-President, the President shall nominate a Vice-President who shall take the office upon confirmation by a majority vote of both houses of Congress.

SECTION 3. Whenever the President transmits to the President pro tempore of the Senate and the Speaker of the House of Representatives his written declaration that he is unable to discharge the powers and duties of his office, and until he transmits to them a written declaration to the contrary, such powers and duties shall be discharged by the Vice-President as Acting President.

SECTION 5. Whenever the Vice-President and a majority of either the principal officers of the executive departments, or of such other body as Congress may by law provide, transmit to the President pro tempore of the Senate and the Speaker of the House of Representatives their written declaration that the President is unable to discharge the powers and duties of his office, the Vice-President shall immediately assume the powers and duties of the office as Acting President.

Thereafter, when the President transmits to the President pro tempore of the Senate and the Speaker of the House of Representatives his written declaration that no inability exists, he shall resume the powers and duties of his office unless the Vice-President and a majority of either the principal officers of the executive department, or of such other body as Congress may by law provide, transmit within four days to the President pro tempore of the Senate and the Speaker of the House of Representatives their written declaration that the President is unable to discharge the powers and duties of his office. Thereupon Congress shall decide the issue, assembling within 48 hours for that purpose if not in session. If the Congress, within 21 days after receipt of the latter written declaration, or, if Congress is not in session, within 21 days after Congress is required to assemble, determines by two-thirds vote of both houses that the President is unable to discharge the powers and duties of his office, the Vice-President shall continue to discharge the same as Acting President; otherwise, the President shall resume the powers and duties of his office.

AMENDMENT 26
June 30, 1971

SECTION 1. The right of citizens of the United States, who are eighteen years of age or older, to vote shall not be denied or abridged by the United States or any state on account of age.

SECTION 2. The Congress shall have power to enforce this article by appropriate legislation.

AMENDMENT 27
May 7, 1992

No law, varying the compensation for the services of the Senators and Representatives, shall take effect, until an election of Representatives shall have intervened.

THE STAR-SPANGLED BANNER

PHILADELPHIA, SEPT. 17, 1812—Francis Scott Key, a lawyer and a volunteer in a light artillery company, wrote the first stanza of the "Star-Spangled Banner" on the back of an envelope as he watched the British fire some 1,500 shells on Fort McHenry in Baltimore, Md. The poem, set to the tune of "Anacreon in Heaven," was designated the national anthem by an act of Congress on March 3, 1931. The banner to which Key refers hangs today in the Smithsonian Institution.

O say, can you see, by the dawn's early light,
What so proudly we hailed at the twilight's last gleaming?
Whose broad stripes and bright stars, through the perilous fight,
O'er the ramparts we watched, were so gallantly streaming!
And the rockets' red glare, the bombs bursting in air,
Gave proof through the night that our flag was still there:
O say, does that star-spangled banner yet wave
O'er the land of the free and the home of the brave?

On the shore, dimly seen through the mists of the deep,
Where the foe's haughty host in dread silence reposes,
What is that which the breeze, o'er the towering steep,
As it fitfully blows, now conceals, now discloses?
Now it catches the gleam of the morning's first beam,
In full glory reflected now shines on the stream:
'Tis the star-spangled banner! O long may it wave
O'er the land of the free and the home of the brave!

And where is that band who so vauntingly swore
That the havoc of war and the battle's confusion
A home and a country should leave us no more?
Their blood has washed out their foul footsteps' pollution.
No refuge could save the hireling and slave
From the terror of flight, or the gloom of the grave:
And the star-spangled banner in triumph doth wave
O'er the land of the free and the home of the brave!

Oh! thus be it ever, when freemen shall stand
Between their loved homes and the war's desolation!
Blest with victory and peace, may the Heaven-rescued land
Praise the Power that hath made and preserved us a nation.
Then conquer we must, for our cause it is just,
And this be our motto: "In God is our trust."
And the star-spangled banner in triumph shall wave
O'er the land of the free and the home of the brave!

THE EMANCIPATION PROCLAMATION

A moment of clarity in a bloody war of national ideals

WASHINGTON, SEPT. 22, 1862—Lincoln long protested that he had no stand on the issue of slavery; that his only desire was to preserve the Union. But shortly after the Battle of Antietam, where 5,800 soldiers were slain, Lincoln proclaimed that slaves held in any state "in rebellion against the United States, shall be then, thenceforward, forever free," and forever changed the war from a battle for political union to a war against slavery.

A PROCLAMATION. Whereas on the 22nd day of September, A.D. 1862, a proclamation was issued by the President of the United States, containing, among other things, the following, to wit:

"That on the 1st day of January, A.D. 1863, all persons held as slaves within any State or designated part of a State the people whereof shall then be in rebellion against the United States shall be then, thenceforward, and forever free; and the executive government of the United States, including the military and naval authority thereof, will recognize and maintain the freedom of such persons and will do no act or acts to repress such persons, or any of them, in any efforts they may make for their actual freedom.

"That the executive will on the 1st day of January aforesaid, by proclamation, designate the States and parts of States, if any, in which the people thereof, respectively, shall then be in rebellion against the United States; and the fact that any State or the people thereof shall on that day be in good faith represented in the Congress of the United States by members chosen thereto at elections wherein a majority of the qualified voters of such States shall have participated shall, in the absence of strong countervailing testimony, be deemed conclusive evidence that such State and the people thereof are not then in rebellion against the United States."

. . . all persons held as slaves within any State or designated part of a State the people whereof shall then be in rebellion against the United States shall be then, thenceforward, and forever free . . .

Now, therefore, I, Abraham Lincoln, President of the United States, by virtue of the power in me vested as Commander-In-Chief of the Army and Navy of the United States in time of actual armed rebellion against the authority and government of the United States, and as a fit and necessary war measure for suppressing said rebellion, do, on this 1st day of January, A.D. 1863, and in accordance with my purpose so to do, publicly proclaimed for the full period of one hundred days from the first day above mentioned, order and designate as the States and parts of States wherein the people thereof, respectively, are this day in rebellion against the United States the following, to wit:

Arkansas, Texas, Louisiana (except the parishes of St. Bernard, Plaquemines, Jefferson, St. John, St. Charles, St. James, Ascension, Assumption, Terrebonne, Lafourche, St. Mary, St. Martin, and Orleans, including the city of New Orleans), Mississippi, Alabama, Florida, Georgia, South Carolina, North Carolina, and Virginia (except the forty-eight counties designated as West Virginia, and also the counties of Berkeley, Accomac, Northhampton, Elizabeth City,

York, Princess Anne, and Norfolk, including the cities of Norfolk and Portsmouth), and which excepted parts are for the present left precisely as if this proclamation were not issued.

And by virtue of the power and for the purpose aforesaid, I do order and declare that all persons held as slaves within said designated States and parts of States are, and henceforward shall be, free; and that the Executive Government of the United States, including the military and naval authorities thereof, will recognize and maintain the freedom of said persons.

And I hereby enjoin upon the people so declared to be free to abstain from all violence, unless in necessary self-defence; and I recommend to them that, in all cases when allowed, they labor faithfully for reasonable wages.

And I further declare and make known that such persons of suitable condition will be received into the armed service of the United States to garrison forts, positions, stations, and other places, and to man vessels of all sorts in said service.

And upon this act, sincerely believed to be an act of justice, warranted by the Constitution upon military necessity, I invoke the considerate judgment of mankind and the gracious favor of Almighty God.

THE GETTYSBURG ADDRESS

GETTYSBURG, PA., NOV. 19, 1863—Gettysburg was the only battle of the Civil War to be fought on Northern soil and the largest ever to be fought in the Western Hemisphere. More than 100,000 soldiers clashed for three days in July, leaving thousands dead and the Confederacy all but lost. The battlefield was dedicated as a national cemetery the following November. Lincoln's remarks took just under three minutes, and most newspapers of the time thought it was a failure, as did Lincoln himself.

FOUR SCORE AND SEVEN YEARS AGO OUR FATHERS BROUGHT FORTH ON THIS CONTINENT A NEW NATION, CONCEIVED IN LIBERTY, AND DEDICATED TO THE PROPOSITION THAT ALL MEN ARE CREATED EQUAL. NOW WE ARE ENGAGED IN A GREAT CIVIL WAR TESTING WHETHER THAT NATION OR ANY NATION SO CONCEIVED AND SO DEDICATED, CAN LONG ENDURE. WE ARE MET ON A GREAT BATTLE-FIELD OF THAT WAR. WE HAVE COME TO DEDICATE A PORTION OF THAT FIELD AS A FINAL RESTING PLACE FOR THOSE WHO HERE GAVE THEIR LIVES THAT THAT NATION MIGHT LIVE. IT IS ALTOGETHER FITTING AND PROPER THAT WE SHOULD DO THIS.

BUT, IN A LARGER SENSE, WE CAN NOT DEDICATE—WE CAN NOT CONSECRATE—WE CAN NOT HALLOW—THIS GROUND. THE BRAVE MEN, LIVING AND DEAD, WHO STRUGGLED HERE, HAVE CONSECRATED IT, FAR ABOVE OUR POOR POWER TO ADD OR DETRACT. THE WORLD WILL LITTLE NOTE, NOR LONG REMEMBER WHAT WE SAY HERE, BUT IT CAN NEVER FORGET WHAT THEY DID HERE. IT IS FOR US THE LIVING, RATHER, TO BE DEDICATED HERE TO THE UNFINISHED WORK WHICH THEY WHO FOUGHT HERE HAVE THUS FAR SO NOBLY ADVANCED. IT IS RATHER FOR US TO BE HERE DEDICATED TO THE GREAT TASK REMAINING BEFORE US—THAT FROM THESE HONORED DEAD WE TAKE INCREASED DEVOTION TO THAT CAUSE FOR WHICH THEY GAVE THE LAST FULL MEASURE OF DEVOTION—THAT WE HERE HIGHLY RESOLVE THAT THESE DEAD SHALL NOT HAVE DIED IN VAIN—THAT THIS NATION, UNDER GOD, SHALL HAVE A NEW BIRTH OF FREEDOM—AND THAT GOVERNMENT OF THE PEOPLE, BY THE PEOPLE, FOR THE PEOPLE, SHALL NOT PERISH FROM THE EARTH.

THE STATUE OF LIBERTY

NEW YORK, OCT. 28, 1886—"Liberty Enlightening the World," better known as the Statue of Liberty, was the gift of the people of France. Designed by Frederic Auguste Bartholdi, the copper-sheathed monument measures 151 feet from base to torch and weighs 225 tons. The sonnet by Emma Lazarus engraved on its pedestal is entitled "The New Colossus." It stood for years as a welcome to the immigrants passing through nearby Ellis Island.

NOT LIKE THE BRAZEN GIANT OF GREEK FAME,
WITH CONQUERING LIMBS ASTRIDE FROM LAND TO LAND,
HERE AT OUR SEA-WASHED, SUNSET GATES SHALL STAND
A MIGHTY WOMAN WITH A TORCH, WHOSE FLAME
IS THE IMPRISONED LIGHTNING, AND HER NAME
MOTHER OF EXILES. FROM HER BEACON-HAND
GLOWS WORLD-WIDE WELCOME; HER MILD EYES COMMAND
THE AIR-BRIDGED HARBOR THAT TWIN CITIES FRAME.
"KEEP ANCIENT LANDS, YOUR STORIED POMP!" CRIES SHE
WITH SILENT LIPS. "GIVE ME YOUR TIRED, YOUR POOR,
YOUR HUDDLED MASSES YEARNING TO BREATHE FREE,
THE WRETCHED REFUSE OF YOUR TEEMING SHORE.
SEND THESE, THE HOMELESS, TEMPEST-TOST TO ME,
I LIFT MY LAMP BESIDE THE GOLDEN DOOR!"

THE PLEDGE OF ALLEGIANCE

BOSTON, SEPT. 8, 1892—First published in the Boston boy's magazine Youth's Companion, *the authorship of the pledge is still in doubt. One of the magazine's executives, James B. Upham, originally claimed authorship, but in 1923, a former editor, Francis Bellamy, publicly proclaimed that the pledge was his own creation. The United States Flag Association in 1939 ruled that Bellamy was the author. In 1954, Congress got into the act with a vote to add "under God" to the pledge. It has remained unchanged since then.*

I PLEDGE ALLEGIANCE TO THE FLAG
OF THE UNITED STATES OF AMERICA AND TO THE REPUBLIC FOR WHICH
IT STANDS, ONE NATION UNDER GOD, INDIVISIBLE, WITH
LIBERTY AND JUSTICE FOR ALL.

KENNEDY'S INAUGURAL ADDRESS

A new decade, a new generation, and visions of Camelot

WASHINGTON, JAN. 20, 1961—The era of Eisenhower gave way reluctantly to that of the youthful John F. Kennedy, who narrowly defeated Ike's vice president, Richard Nixon. He was only 43. Kennedy spoke on the snow-covered steps of the Capitol on a bright, sunny day, preceded by poet laureate Robert Frost.

We observe today not a victory of party but a celebration of freedom—symbolizing an end as well as a beginning—signifying renewal as well as change. For I have sworn before you and Almighty God the same solemn oath our forebears prescribed nearly a century and three quarters ago.

The world is very different now. For man holds in his mortal hands the power to abolish all forms of human poverty and all forms of human life. And yet the same revolutionary beliefs for which our forebears fought are still at issue around the globe—the belief that the rights of man come not from the generosity of the state but from the hand of God.

We dare not forget today that we are the heirs of that first revolution. Let the word go forth from this time and place, to friend and foe alike, that the torch has been passed to a new generation of Americans—born in this century, tempered by war, disciplined by a hard and bitter peace, proud of our ancient heritage—and unwilling to witness or permit the slow undoing of those human rights to which this Nation has always been committed, and to which we are committed today at home and around the world.

Let every nation know, whether it wishes us well or ill, that we shall pay any price, bear any burden, meet any hardship, support any friend, oppose any foe to assure the survival and the success of liberty. This much we pledge—and more. To those old allies whose cultural and spiritual origins we share, we pledge the loyalty of faithful friends. United, there is little we cannot do in a host of cooperative ventures. Divided, there is little we can do—for we dare not meet a powerful challenge at odds and split asunder.

To those new states whom we welcome to the ranks of the free, we pledge our word that one form of colonial control shall not have passed away merely to be replaced by a far more iron tyranny. We shall not always expect to find them supporting our view. But we shall always hope to find them strongly supporting their own freedom—and to remember that, in the past, those who foolishly sought power by riding the back of the tiger ended up inside.

To those people in the huts and villages of half the globe struggling to break the bonds of mass misery, we pledge our best efforts to help them help themselves, for whatever period is required—not because the Communists may be doing it, not because we seek their votes, but because it is right. If a free society cannot help the many who are poor, it cannot save the few who are rich.

To our sister republics south of our border, we offer a special pledge—to convert our good words into good deeds—in a new alliance for progress—to assist free men and free governments in casting off the chains of poverty. But this peaceful revolution of hope cannot become the prey of hostile powers. Let all our neighbors know that we shall join with them to oppose aggression or subversion anywhere in the Americas. And let every other power know that this hemisphere intends to remain the master of its own house.

To that world assembly of sovereign states, the United Nations, our last best hope in an age where the instruments of war have far outpaced the instruments of peace, we renew our pledge of support—to prevent it from becoming merely a forum for invective—to strengthen its shield of the new and the weak—and to enlarge the area in which its writ may run.

Finally, to those nations who would make themselves our adversary, we offer not a pledge but a request: that both sides begin anew the quest for peace, before the dark powers of destruction unleashed by science engulf all humanity in planned or accidental self-destruction.

We dare not tempt them with weakness. For only when our arms are sufficient beyond doubt can we be certain beyond doubt that they will never be employed.

But neither can two great and powerful groups of nations take comfort from our present course—both sides overburdened by the cost of modern weapons, both rightly alarmed by the steady spread of the deadly atom, yet both racing to alter that uncertain balance of terror that stays the hand of mankind's final war.

So let us begin anew—remembering on both sides that civility is not a sign of weakness, and sincerity is always subject to proof. Let us never negotiate out of fear. But let us never fear to negotiate.

Let both sides explore what problems unite us instead of belaboring those problems which divide us.

Let both sides, for the first time, formulate serious and precise proposals for the inspection and control of arms—and bring the absolute power to destroy other nations under the absolute control of all nations.

Let both sides seek to invoke the wonders of science instead of its terrors. Together let us explore the stars, conquer the deserts, eradicate disease, tap the ocean depths, and encourage the arts and commerce.

Let both sides unite to heed in all corners of the earth the command of Isaiah—to "undo the heavy burdens... [and] let the oppressed go free."

And if a beachhead of cooperation may push back the jungle of suspicion, let both sides join in creating a new endeavor, not a new balance of power, but a new world of law, where the strong are just and the weak secure and the peace preserved.

All this will not be finished in the first one hundred days. Nor will it be finished in the first one thousand days, nor in the life of this administration, nor even perhaps in our lifetime on this planet. But let us begin. In your hands, my fellow citizens, more than mine, will rest the final success or failure of our course. Since this country was founded each generation of Americans has been summoned to give testimony to its national loyalty. The graves of young Americans who answered the call to service surround the globe.

Now the trumpet summons us again—not as a call to bear arms, though arms we need—not as a call to battle, though embattled we are—but a call to bear the burden of a long twilight struggle, year in and year out, "rejoicing in hope, patient in tribulation"—a struggle against the common enemies of man: tyranny, poverty, disease, and war itself.

Can we forge against these enemies a grand and global alliance, North and South, East and West, that can assure a more fruitful life for all mankind? Will you join in that historic effort?

In the long history of the world, only a few generations have been granted the role of defending freedom in its hour of maximum danger. I do not shrink from this responsibility—I welcome it. I do not believe that any of us would exchange places with any other people or any other generation. The energy, the faith, the devotion which we bring to this endeavor will light our country and all who serve it—and the glow from that fire can truly light the world.

And so, my fellow Americans: ask not what your country can do for you—ask what you can do for your country.

My fellow citizens of the world: ask not what America will do for you, but what together we can do for the freedom of man.

Finally, whether you are citizens of America or citizens of the world, ask of us here the same high standards of strength and sacrifice which we ask of you. With a good conscience our only sure reward, with history the final judge of our deeds, let us go forth to lead the land we love, asking His blessing and His help, but knowing that here on earth God's work must truly be our own.

KING'S "I HAVE A DREAM" SPEECH

A forceful vision of unity defines the civil rights movement

WASHINGTON, AUG. 28, 1963— It was on the steps of the Lincoln memorial that the Rev. Martin Luther King, Jr., before a quarter of a million people, gave the defining address of the civil rights struggle. Lamenting persisting inequalities in America, he dreamed of different days to come. He was assassinated five years later.

I am happy to join with you today in what will go down in history as the greatest demonstration for freedom in the history of our nation. Five score years ago, a great American, in whose symbolic shadow we stand today, signed the Emancipation Proclamation. This momentous decree came as a great beacon of hope to millions of slaves, who had been seared in the flames of withering injustice. It came as a joyous daybreak to end the long night of their captivity. But one hundred years later, the Negro still is not free. One hundred years later, the life of the Negro is still sadly crippled by the manacle of segregation and the chains of discrimination.

One hundred years later, the Negro lives on a lonely island of poverty in the midst of a vast ocean of material prosperity. One hundred years later, the Negro is still languishing in the corners of American society and finds himself an exile in his own land. So we have come here today to dramatize a shameful condition.

In a sense we have come to our Nation's capital to cash a check. When the architects of our republic wrote the magnificent words of the Constitution and the Declaration of Independence, they were signing a promissory note to which every American was to fall heir.

This note was a promise that all men, yes, black men as well as white men, would be guaranteed the inalienable rights of life, liberty and the pursuit of happiness.

It is obvious today that America has defaulted on this promissory note insofar as her citizens of color are concerned. Instead of honoring this sacred obligation, America has given the Negro people a bad check, a check that has come back marked "insufficient funds."

But we refuse to believe that the bank of justice is bankrupt. We refuse to believe that there are insufficient funds in the great vaults of opportunity of this nation. So we have come to cash this check, a check that will give us, upon demand, the riches of freedom and the security of justice.

We have also come to this hallowed spot to remind America of the fierce urgency of now. This is no time to engage in the luxury of cooling off or to take the tranquilizing drug of gradualism.

Now is the time to make real the promises of democracy.

Now is the time to rise from the dark and desolate valley of segregation to the sunlit path of racial justice.

Now is the time to lift our nation from the quicksands of racial injustice to the solid rock of brotherhood.

Now is the time to make justice a reality for all of God's children.

It would be fatal for the nation to overlook the urgency of the moment. This sweltering summer of the colored people's legitimate

We have also come to this hallowed spot to remind America of the fierce urgency of now. This is no time to engage in the luxury of cooling off or to take the tranquilizing drug of gradualism.

discontent will not pass until there is an invigorating autumn of freedom and equality. Nineteen sixty-three is not an end but a beginning. Those who hope that the Negro needed to blow off steam and will now be content will have a rude awakening if the nation returns to business as usual.

There will be neither rest nor tranquillity in America until the Negro is granted his citizenship rights. The whirlwinds of revolt will continue to shake the foundations of our nation until the bright day of justice emerges.

But that is something that I must say to my people who stand on the warm threshold which leads into the palace of justice. In the process of gaining our rightful place, we must not be guilty of wrongful deeds. Let us not seek to satisfy our thirst for freedom by drinking from the cup of bitterness and hatred.

We must forever conduct our struggle on the high plane of dignity and discipline. We must not allow our creative protests to dissolve into physical violence. Again and again, we must rise to the majestic heights of meeting physical force with soul force.

The marvelous new militancy which has engulfed the Negro community must not lead us to a distrust of all white people, for many of our white brothers, as evidenced by their presence here today, have come to realize that their destiny is tied up with our destiny and their freedom is inextricably bound to our freedom. We cannot walk alone.

And as we walk, we must make the pledge that we shall always march ahead. We cannot turn back. There are those who are asking the devotees of civil rights: "When will you be satisfied?" We can never be satisfied as long as the Negro is the victim of the unspeakable horrors of police brutality. We can never be satisfied as long as our bodies, heavy with the fatigue of travel, cannot gain lodging in the motels of the highways and the hotels of the cities.

We cannot be satisfied as long as the Negro's basic mobility is from a smaller ghetto to a larger one.

We can never be satisfied as long as our children are stripped of their selfhood and robbed of their dignity by signs stating "for whites only."

We cannot be satisfied as long as a Negro in Mississippi cannot vote and a Negro in New York City believes he has nothing for which to vote.

No, no we are not satisfied and we will not be satisfied until justice rolls down like water and righteousness like a mighty stream.

I am not unmindful that some of you have come here out of great trials and tribulations. Some of you have come from areas where your quest for freedom left you battered by the storms of persecutions, staggered by the winds of police brutality. You have been the veterans of creative suffering. Continue to work with the faith that unearned suffering is redemptive.

Go back to Mississippi, go back to Alabama, go back to South Carolina, go back to Georgia, go back to Louisiana, go back to the slums and ghettos of our Northern cities, knowing that somehow this situation can and will be changed. Let us not wallow in the valley of despair.

I say to you today, my friends, even though we face the difficulties of today and tomorrow, I still have a dream. It is a dream deeply rooted in the American dream.

In the process of gaining our rightful place, we must not be guilty of wrongful deeds. Let us not seek to satisfy our thirst for freedom by drinking from the cup of bitterness and hatred. We must forever conduct our struggle on the high plane of dignity and discipline. We must not allow our creative protests to dissolve into physical violence. Again and again, we must rise to the majestic heights of meeting physical force with soul force.

I have a dream that one day this nation will rise up and live out the true meaning of its creed: "We hold these truths to be self-evident that all men are created equal."

I have a dream that one day on the red hills of Georgia the sons of former slaves and the sons of former slave owners will be able to sit down together at the table of brotherhood.

I have a dream that one day even the state of Mississippi, a state sweltering with the heat of injustice, sweltering with the heat of oppression, will be transformed into an oasis of freedom and justice.

I have a dream my four little children will one day live in a nation where they will not be judged by the color of their skin but by the content of their character.

I have a dream today.

I have a dream that one day, the state of Alabama, whose vicious racists, whose governor, having his lips dripping with the words of interposition and nullification; that one day right down in Alabama, little black boys and black girls will be able to join hands with little white boys and white girls as brothers and sisters.

I have a dream today.

I have a dream that one day every valley shall be exalted, every hill shall be engulfed, and every mountain shall be made low, the rough places will be made plains and the crooked places will be made straight and the glory of the Lord shall be revealed and all flesh shall see it together.

This is our hope. This is the faith that I will go back to the South with. With this faith we will be able to hew out of the mountain of despair a stone of hope.

With this faith we will be able to transform the jangling discords of our nation into a beautiful symphony of brotherhood.

With this faith we will be able to work together, to pray together, to struggle together, to go to jail together, to stand up for freedom together, knowing that we will be free one day.

This will be the day when all of God's children will be able to sing with new meaning "My country 'tis of thee, sweet land of liberty, of thee I sing. Land where my father's died, land of the Pilgrim's pride, from every mountainside, let freedom ring!"

And if America is to be a great nation, this must become true. So let freedom ring from the prodigious hilltops of New Hampshire. From the mighty mountains of New York.

Let freedom ring from the heightening Alleghenies of Pennsylvania.

Let freedom ring from the snow-capped Rockies of Colorado.

Let freedom ring from the curvaceous slopes of California.

But not only that, let freedom ring from Stone Mountain of Georgia.

Let freedom ring from Lookout Mountain of Tennessee.

Let freedom ring from every hill and molehill of Mississippi. From every mountainside, let freedom ring.

And when it happens, when we let freedom ring, when we let it ring from every tenement and every hamlet, from every state and every city, we will be able to speed up that day when all of God's children, black men and white men, Jews and Gentiles, Protestants and Catholics, will be able to join hands and sing in the words of the old spiritual, "Free at last, free at last. Thank God Almighty, we are free at last."

And when it happens, when we let freedom ring, when we let it ring from every tenement and every hamlet, from every state and every city, we will be able to speed up that day when all of God's children, black men and white men, Jews and Gentiles, Protestants and Catholics, will be able to join hands and sing in the words of the old spiritual, "Free at last, free at last. Thank God Almighty, we are free at last."

READER'S GUIDE

WORDS THAT CHANGED THE WORLD

From Biblical times to the present, these documents have shaped our history

c. 1750 B.C.—Code of Hammurabi: One of the oldest known legal codes, it lays down the principle of "an eye for an eye."

c. 1000 B.C.—Old Testament: Written in Hebrew and Aramaic.

100—New Testament: The 27 writings, with the Jewish Old Testament, make up the Christian Bible.

313—Edict of Milan: From Roman emperors Constantine and Licinius. Grants toleration and equal rights to all religions.

c. 650—Koran (Quran): Revelations given to the prophet Muhammad by Allah instructing believers in the proper way to live.

1215—Magna Carta: Signed by English King John. The basis of constitutional government, it guarantees due process and trial by jury.

1517—Ninety-five Theses of Martin Luther: Challenged the excesses of the Roman Catholic Church and led to the Protestant Reformation.

1776—U.S. Declaration of Independence: Declares the independence of the American colonies from the rule of Great Britain.

1787—U.S. Constitution: Lays down the rules for a democratic republic.

1789—Declaration of the Rights of Man and of the Citizen: Approved by the French Assembly. It summarizes the ideals of the French Revolution.

1791—U.S. Bill of Rights: The first 10 amendments to the Constitution. Guarantees freedom of speech, religion, assembly, and press.

1804—Code Napoleon: Issued by Napoleon Bonaparte. Forms the basis of modern French civil law.

1848—Communist Manifesto: By Friedrich Engels and Karl Marx. Ending with the line "workers of the world unite," it calls for a worldwide revolution leading to a classless society.

1862—Emancipation Proclamation: President Abraham Lincoln ends slavery.

1905—Albert Einstein's Theory of Relativity: Presented in four articles. A new way of understanding motion, time, and energy. Introduces the formula $e=mc^2$.

1918—Woodrow Wilson's Fourteen Points: Stressing "open covenants of peace, openly arrived at," the document sets forth Wilson's program for world peace after World War I.

1925—Mein Kampf: Written by Adolf Hitler. Outlines the idea of creating an Aryan state for the "chosen people." Hitler's later attempt to implement his plan results in the death of 6 million Jews.

1931 Statute of Westminster: Grants autonomous government to Great Britain's former colonial possessions, creating the British Commonwealth.

1945 United Nations Charter: It created a new international organization that aimed to maintain peace and security in the world.

1948—Universal Declaration of Human Rights: Approved by the U.N. It declares freedoms and rights to be a "common standard of achievement for all peoples and all nations."

1962–5—Second Vatican Council: Modernizes Roman Catholic practice.

1973—Roe v Wade: The Supreme Court says the 14th amendment gives women the power to terminate their pregnancies.

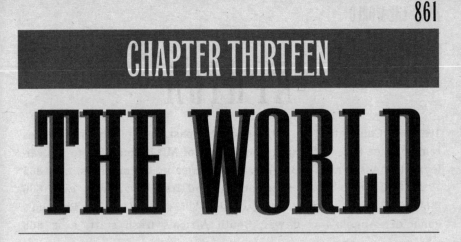

CHAPTER THIRTEEN

THE WORLD

EXPERT QUOTES

"Seek ye first the political kingdom."

—Kwame Nkrumah, first president of Ghana

Page 862

"The right of privacy... is broad enough to encompass a woman's decision to terminate her pregnancy."

—Justice Harry Blackmun, *Roe vs. Wade* majority opinion

Page 869

"The whole city and all its citizens will never forget November 9, 1989. For 28 years since the wall was built we have yearned for this day."

—Walter Momper, mayor of West Berlin

Page 890

THE YEAR AHEAD: HOPE that the genocide in Rwanda stops... **WATCH** Nigeria teeter on the verge of political and civil chaos... **APPLAUD** economic and political progress in South Africa... **EXPECT** modest reforms in Castro's Cuba... **FEAR** further repression in China... **FRET** about deepening economic woes in Japan... **ANTICIPATE** more progress toward peace in the Middle East... **WORRY** about turmoil and ethnic tensions in the former Soviet Union... **WAIT** patiently for a single European currency...

AFRICA

TIMELINE

A CONTINENT IN CRISIS

Colonialism is a relic of the past, but plenty of troubles remain

"Seek ye first the political kingdom," advised Kwame Nkrumah, who followed his own advice and became the first leader of an independent Ghana. Indeed, most of Africa followed his counsel. As Gavin Williams, a professor at Oxford University, has noted, the period from World War II to the present in Africa has been dominated by two related themes: political nationalism and economic development. With the independence of Eritrea from Ethiopia in 1993 and the election of Nelson Mandela as president of South Africa in April 1994, the African struggle for national independence reached its successful culmination.

The quest for economic development is another story altogether. At the outset of the 1990s, most African states were bankrupt. Things haven't measurably improved since. African rulers—whether military officers or civilian politicians—lost credibility, largely as a result of arbitrary or corrupt government. (Mandela remains a notable exception.) Disasters—some natural, like droughts and famines, some man-made, such as the spread of AIDS and the genocide in Rwanda—further impeded the prospects for economic progress. In the last quarter-century, Africa has changed dramatically, but it still remains a continent in crisis. Some key historical highlights:

1970—THE FINAL DAYS OF NIGERIA'S BLOODY CIVIL WAR. A civil war, which lasted over four years, ends when the Nigerian government defeats the secessionist state of Biafra. Relations improve between the Ibo, the main ethnic group in the former Biafra state, and other Nigerians. But within Ibo ranks, conflict continues between those who did and did not support secession. The year marks Nigeria's 10th anniversary of independence from Britain.

1971—IDI AMIN SEIZES POWER IN UGANDA. Amin launches a reign of terror against Ugandan opponents, torturing and killing tens of thousands—Amnesty International estimates that 300,000 may have died under his rule. Amin declares himself President for Life in 1976. He is ousted in 1979.

1974—A COUP CRUSHES ETHIOPIA'S FEUDAL SYSTEM. A revolt against Ethiopia's feudal order begins with strikes and protests by students, taxi drivers, and trade unions and ends with a bloodless coup against Ethiopian Emperor Haile Selassie I (1892-

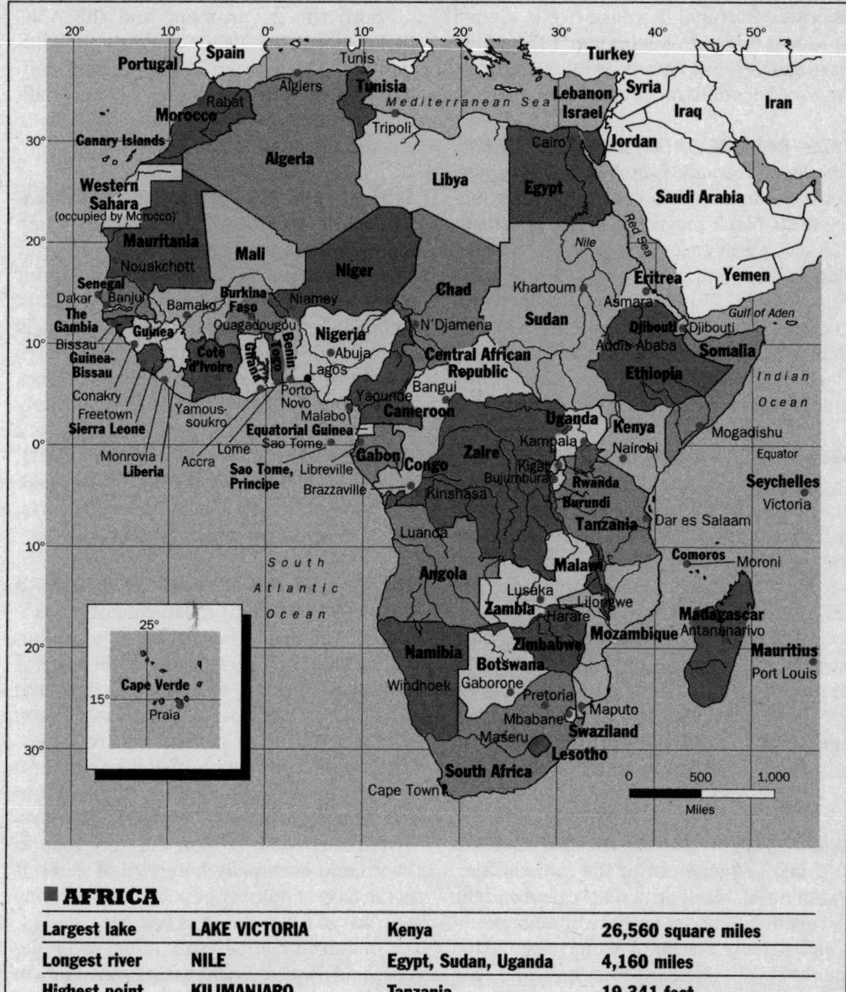

AFRICA

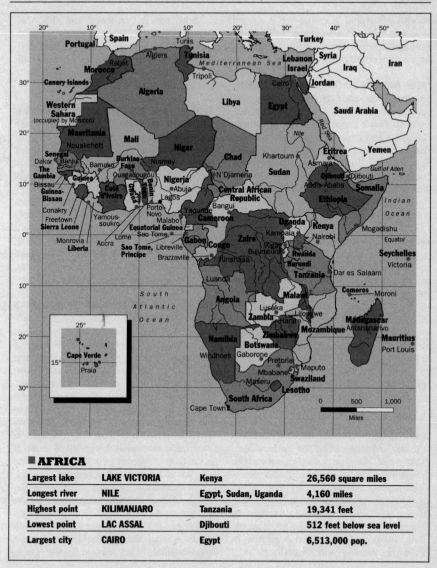

Largest lake	**LAKE VICTORIA**	**Kenya**	**26,560 square miles**
Longest river	**NILE**	**Egypt, Sudan, Uganda**	**4,160 miles**
Highest point	**KILIMANJARO**	**Tanzania**	**19,341 feet**
Lowest point	**LAC ASSAL**	**Djibouti**	**512 feet below sea level**
Largest city	**CAIRO**	**Egypt**	**6,513,000 pop.**

1975), who has ruled black Africa's oldest state since 1930. The new military regime summarily executes aristocrats and former officials and creates a nominal socialist government and nationalized economy.

1974-75—THE FALL OF PORTUGAL'S AFRICAN EMPIRE. Antonio Oliveira Salazar rules Portugal—and its African colonies, Angola and Mozambique, among others—with an iron hand from 1926 until he dies in 1970. His successor, Marcello Caetano, clings to power for four more years before being ousted by a revolution on April 25, 1974—brought down, in part, by the escalating guerrilla activity in Angola and Mozambique. (In 1973, Portugal is forced to dispatch 40,000 troops to Mozambique to fight the rebels.) The revolution not only liberates Portugal; a cease-fire is signed in Mozambique in September 1974, when Portugal agrees to grant its independence. Angola becomes independent in 1985.

1979—RHODESIA IS DEAD, LONG LIVE ZIMBABWE. Rhodesia is renamed Zimbabwe after a new constitution transfers control of the country to its black majority—in the aftermath of a seven-year civil war between the Rhodesian government and Patriotic Front guerrilla forces. Bishop Abel Muzorewa' becomes the country's first black prime minister after the new nation's first all-race election. In 1980, Zimbabwe becomes fully independent of Great Britain.

1983-85—THE DROUGHT OF THE CENTURY. The region's worst drought in 150 years threatens sub-Saharan Africa with a famine even worse than the 1973-74 disaster. Estimates put the number of people facing food shortages at 200 million. Tens of thousands are said to die from starvation.

Insect damage of Cassaba Belt (from Senegal to Mozambique) crops, outbreaks of infectious diseases in cattle, bush fires, war, and civil unrest add to the food shortage problem. Musicians around the world join for a "Live Aid" benefit, the proceeds of which go to help famine victims.

1986—SOUTH AFRICA: CRY, THE BELOVED COUNTRY. Like a scene out of the famous Alan Paton novel, black protests escalate and the government imposes a state of emergency. The African National Congress (ANC) stages school and consumer boycotts, rent strikes, and localized general strikes. In response, the South African government raids alleged ANC terrorist camps in Botswana, Zambia, and Zimbabwe.

1990—NELSON MANDELA IS FREE AT LAST. ANC leader Nelson Mandela, the world's best-known political prisoner, is freed by South African President F.W. de Klerk after 27 years in prison. A few days before his release, the government removes the ban on the ANC, the South African Communist Party, and 33 other organizations, freeing them to organize openly and recruit members.

Both the government and the ANC begin setting the stage for a new constitution and a new order. After years of delicate negotiations, South Africa holds its all-race election in April 1994. Mandela is elected president—in a landslide.

1991-93—THE RISE OF ISLAMIC FUNDAMENTALISM IN ALGERIA. The Algerian army deposes President Chadli Bendjedid after the fundamentalist Islamic Salvation Front party wins the first round of elections in December 1991. The military then cancels the second round of elections and declares a state of emergency. Government forces crack down on Islamic groups, immediately arresting 9,000 militants and interning them in Sahara camps. By October 1993, about 1,000 Islamist sympathizers are dead, 3,800 await trial by special security courts, and 240 are condemned to death.

1992-93—THE RISE OF ISLAMIC FUNDAMENTALISTS IN EGYPT. Islamic fundamentalist extremists, in an attempt to oust Egypt's secular, military-backed government, kill several Europeans traveling by cruise ship down the Nile River. Their goal is to hobble tourism, a major source of government revenues. They are successful; tourism plummets 40 percent in 1992 and another 30 percent in the first eight months of 1993. The government condemns 38 of the terrorists to death and eventually hangs 29 of them. It is the largest number of political executions at once in Egypt's recent history.

In June 1995, 14 years after his predecessor, Anwar al-Sadat, was gunned down, Egyptian president Hosni Mubarak escapes unharmed from an assassination attempt in Addis Ababa, Ethiopia. Sudanese Islamic fundamentalists are blamed for the attack.

1994—GENOCIDE IN RWANDA. Between 500,000 and 1 million Rwandans die in genocide instigated by Hutu extremists against the Tutsi minority. The Rwandan Patriotic Front, a mainly Tutsi exile force, defeats Hutu forces responsible for the massacre, resulting in a mass exodus of Hutus afraid of retaliation into Zaire, Burundi, and Tanzania. Thousands more Hutus die in refugee camps from disease.

GLOBE TROTTER'S GUIDE

VITAL STATS: AFRICA BY THE NUMBERS

From teeming Nigeria in West Africa (population: over 98 million) to the tiny Seychelles islands in the Indian Ocean (population: 72,113), Africa accounts for about 5 percent of the world's population. Life is hard: infant mortality rates are among the highest in the world; life expectancy lags far behind that of the United States; and per capita income in many countries is under $1,000 a year.

Country	Capital	Population	Life expectancy at birth (in years)	Infant mort. (deaths/1,000 live births)	Literacy (as % of pop.)	GDP/capita (in U.S. dollars)	TVs/1,000 inhabitants
UNITED STATES	Washington, D.C.	260,713,585	75.9	8.1	97	$24,700	814
NORTHERN AFRICA							
EGYPT	Cairo	60,765,028	60.79	76.4	48	$2,400	116
MOROCCO	Rabat	28,558,635	68.23	49.6	50	$2,500	74
ALGERIA	Algiers	27,895,068	67.68	52.1	57	$3,300	74
TUNISIA	Tunis	8,726,562	72.89	34.1	65	$4,000	79
LIBYA	Tripoli	5,057,392	63.88	63.4	64	$6,600	99
SUBSAHARAN AFRICA							
NIGERIA	Abuja	98,091,097	55.33	75.0	51	$1,000	33
ETHIOPIA	Addis Ababa	54,927,108	52.67	106.4	24	$400	3
SOUTH AFRICA	Pretoria	43,930,631	65.11	47.1	76	$4,000	98
ZAIRE	Kinshasa	42,684,091	47.40	110.9	72	$500	1
SUDAN	Khartoum	29,419,798	54.27	79.5	27	$750	77
KENYA	Nairobi	28,240,658	53.23	74.1	69	$1,200	10
TANZANIA	Dar Es Salaam	27,985,660	43.25	109.7	46	$600	NA
UGANDA	Kampala	19,121,934	37.46	112.2	48	$1,200	10
MOZAMBIQUE	Maputo	17,346,280	48.49	128.7	33	$600	3
GHANA	Accra	17,225,185	55.52	83.1	60	$1,500	15
CÔTE D'IVOIRE	Yamoussoukro	14,295,501	48.92	95.0	54	$1,500	59
MADAGASCAR	Antananarivo	13,427,758	53.98	89.0	80	$800	20
CAMEROON	Yaoundé	13,132,191	57.07	77.1	55	$1,500	24
ZIMBABWE	Harare	10,975,078	42.06	7.4	67	$1,400	26
BURKINA FASO	Ouagadougou	10,134,661	47.03	118.3	18	$700	5
ANGOLA	Luanda	9,803,576	45.77	145.4	42	$600	6
MALAWI	Lilongwe	9,732,409	39.73	141.1	22	$600	NA
ZAMBIA	Lusaka	9,188,190	44.18	85.0	73	$800	26
MALI	Bamako	9,112,950	45.91	106.2	17	$650	1
NIGER	Niamey	8,971,605	44.61	111.0	28	$650	5
SENEGAL	Dakar	8,730,508	56.58	75.7	38	$1,400	36
RWANDA	Kigali	8,373,963	40.25	118.7	50	$800	NA
SOMALIA	Mogadishu	6,666,873	54.75	125.8	24	$500	12
GUINEA	Conakry	6,391,536	44.13	139.2	24	$500	7
BURUNDI	Bujumbura	6,124,747	40.30	113.7	50	$700	1
CHAD	N'Djamena	5,466,771	40.79	131.8	30	$500	1
BENIN	Porto-Novo	5,341,710	51.77	110.1	23	$1,200	5
SIERRA LEONE	Freetown	4,630,037	46.40	141.9	21	$1,000	10

GLOBE TROTTER'S GUIDE

Country	Capital	Population	Life expectancy at birth (in years)	Infant mort. (deaths / 1,000 live births)	Literacy (as % of pop.)	GDP/capita (in U.S. dollars)	TVs/1,000 inhabitants
TOGO	Lome	4,255,090	56.93	88.9	43	$800	6
ERITREA	Asmara	3,782,543	NA	NA	NA	$500	NA
CENTRAL AFRICAN REP.	Bangui	3,142,182	42.54	137.2	27	$800	3
LIBERIA	Monrovia	2,972,766	57.73	113.3	40	$800	18
CONGO	Brazzaville	2,446,902	47.56	111.0	57	$2,900	5
MAURITANIA	Nouakchott	2,192,777	48.06	85.3	34	$1,050	23
LOSOTHO	Maseru	1,944,493	62.14	69.5	59	$1,500	3
NAMIBIA	Windhoek	1,595,567	61.65	61.8	38	$2,500	16
BOTSWANA	Gaborone	1,359,352	63.05	39.3	23	$4,500	12
GABON	Libreville	1,139,006	54.67	94.8	61	$4,800	36
MAURITIUS	Port Louis	1,116,923	70.54	18.4	80	$7,800	215
GUINEA-BISSAU	Bissau	1,098,231	47.44	120.0	36	$800	NA
THE GAMBIA	Banjul	959,300	50.08	123.5	27	$800	NA
SWAZILAND	Mbabane	936,369	56.39	93.2	67	$2,500	16
COMOROS	Moroni	530,136	57.81	79.6	48	$700	0
CAPE VERDE	Praia	423,120	62.59	57.7	66	$1,070	NA
DJIBOUTI	Djibouti	412,599	49.23	111.0	48	$1,200	55
EQUATORIAL GUINEA	Malabo	409,550	52.09	102.6	50	$700	9
SAO TOME, PRINCIPE	Sao Tome	136,780	63.33	63.5	57	$450	NA
SEYCHELLES	Victoria	72,113	69.67	11.7	58	$5,900	74

SOURCE: The *World Fact Book*, Central Intelligence Agency, 1994; *Statistical Yearbook*, United Nations, 1992.

TRAVELER'S GUIDE

TRAVEL WARNINGS: Within the past year or so, the U.S. State Department has issued travel warnings for Algeria, Angola, Burundi, Gambia, Lesotho, Liberia, Libya, Somalia, and Sudan. For recorded updates, call the U.S. Department of State Bureau of Consular Affairs, ☎ 202-647-5225.

VISAS: Most African countries require visas, but some waive that requirement for stays of only a few months. In lieu of visas, a few require onward or return tickets before entry. For more detailed visa information, request the U.S. Department of State's booklet, *Foreign Entry Requirements* (50¢), from the Consumer Information Center, Pueblo, CO 81009.

VACCINATIONS: Traveling directly from the United States, you'll need a yellow fever vaccination certificate to enter the following countries: Benin, Burkina Faso, Cameroon, Central African Republic, Congo, Côte d' Ivoire, Gabon, Ghana, Liberia, Mali, Mauritania (for stays of greater than two weeks), Nigeria, Rwanda, Senegal, Sao Tome and Principe (for stays of greater than two weeks), Togo, and Zaire. Other immunization certificates may be required when traveling between African countries. Malaria can be found in all African countries but Tunisia. All those except Algeria, Libya, Cape Verde, Egypt, and Morocco have malaria strains that are resistant to chloroquine, a common antimalaria prophylaxis. In these areas, the Centers for Disease Control and Prevention recommends routine prophylaxis with mefloquine. Call the CDC's automated travelers' hotline at ☎ 404-332-4559 for individual country recommendations.

WORLD WATCHER'S GUIDE

VITAL FACTS: INSIDE AFRICA TODAY

All of Africa today is independent of colonial overlords, but democracy still does not reign. Between 1958 and 1975, 41 African countries gained their independence. South Africa was the only country in white hands, and that changed in 1994 when Nelson Mandela was elected president. Some countries, such as Zaire, even though they are nominally republics, are dominated by dictatorial leaders.

COUNTRY	Date of Independence • From	**Form of Government**	*Dominant Religion*	**Official Language**	Currency
NORTHERN AFRICA					
EGYPT	Feb. 28, 1922 • UK	**Republic**	*Islam*	**Arabic**	Egytian pound
LIBYA	Dec. 24, 1951 • Italy	**Military dictatorship**	*Islam*	**Arabic**	Dinar
MOROCCO[1]	March 2, 1956 • France	**Constitutional monarchy**	*Islam*	**Arabic**	Moroccan dirham
TUNISIA	March 20, 1956 • France	**Republic**	*Islam*	**Arabic**	Tunisian dinar
ALGERIA	July 5, 1962 • France	**Republic**	*Islam*	**Arabic**	Dinar
SUBSAHARAN AFRICA					
ETHIOPIA	More than 2,000 years ago • (occupied by Italy 1935-41)	**Transitional**	*Islam*	**Amharic**	Birr
LIBERIA	July 26, 1847 • Freed American slave regime	**Republic**	*Traditional*	**English**	Liberian dollar
SOUTH AFRICA	May 31, 1910 • UK	**Republic**	*Christianity*	**Afrikaans/English, 9 others**	rand
SUDAN	Jan. 1, 1956 • Egypt & UK	**Civilian**	*Islam*	**Arabic**	Sudanese pound
GHANA	March 6, 1957 • UK	**Constitutional democracy**	*Indigenous/Islam*	**English**	new cedi
GUINEA	Oct. 2, 1958 • France	**Republic**	*Islam*	**French**	Guinean franc
CAMEROON	Jan. 1 1960 • France	**Unitary Republic**	*Indigenous*	**English/French**	CFA franc[2]
TOGO	April 27, 1960 • UN trustee, French admin.	**Republic in transition**	*Indigenous*	**French**	CFA franc[2]
MADAGASCAR	June 26, 1960 • France	**Republic**	*Indigenous/Christianity*	**French/Malagasy**	Malagasy franc
ZAIRE	June 30, 1960 • Belgium	**Republic with strong presidential system**	*Christianity*	**French**	Zaire
SOMALIA	July 1, 1960 • Italian-administered UN trusteeship	**NONE**	*Islam*	**Somali**	Somali shilling
BENIN	Aug. 1, 1960 • France	**Republic**	*Indigenous*	**French**	CFA franc[2]
NIGER	Aug. 3, 1960 • France	**Republic**	*Islam*	**French**	CFA franc[2]
BURKINA FASO	Aug. 5, 1960 • France	**Parliamentary**	*Islam/Indigenous*	**French**	CFA franc[2]
COTE D'IVOIRE	Aug. 7, 1960 • France	**Republic/multiparty presidential regime**	*Islam*	**French**	CFA franc[2]
CHAD	Aug. 11, 1960 • France	**Republic**	*Islam*	**French/Arabic**	CFA franc[2]
CENTRAL AFRICAN REPUBLIC	Aug. 13, 1960 • France	**Republic**	*Christianity/Indigenous*	**French**	CFA franc[2]
CONGO	Aug. 15, 1960 • France	**Republic**	*Christianity/Animism*	**French**	CFA franc[2]
GABON	Aug. 17, 1960 • France	**Republic/multiparty presidential regime**	*Christianity*	**French**	CFA franc[2]
SENEGAL	Aug. 20, 1960 • France	**Republic under multiparty democratic rule**	*Islam*	**French**	CFA franc[2]
MALI	Sept. 22, 1960 • France	**Republic**	*Islam*	**French**	CFA franc[2]
NIGERIA	Oct. 1, 1960• UK	**Military**	*Islam/Christianity*	**English**	naira
MAURITANIA	Nov. 28, 1960 • France	**Republic**	*Islam*	**Arabic/Wolof**	ouguiya
SIERRA LEONE	April 27, 1961 • UK	**Military**	*Islam*	**English**	leone
BURUNDI	July 1, 1962 • UN trustee, Belgian admin.	**Republic**	*Catholicism*	**Kurundi/French**	Burundi franc
RWANDA	July 1, 1962 • UN trustee, Belgian admin.	**Republic**	*Christianity*	**Kinyarwanda/French**	Rwanda franc
UGANDA	Oct. 9, 1962 • UK	**Republic**	*Christianity*	**English**	Ugandan shilling

WORLD WATCHER'S GUIDE

COUNTRY	Date of Independence • From	Form of Government	Dominant Religion	Official Language	Currency
KENYA	Dec. 12, 1963 • UK	Republic	*Christianity*	English/Swahili	Shilling
TANZANIA[3]	April 26, 1964 • UN trustee, British admin.	Republic	*Christianity*	Swahili/English	Shilling
MALAWI	July 6, 1964 • UK	Multiparty democracy	*Christianity/Islam*	English/Chichewa	Kwacha
ZAMBIA	Oct. 24, 1964 • UK	Republic	*Christianity*	English	Zambian kwacha
THE GAMBIA	Feb. 18, 1965 • UK	Republic/multiparty democracy	*Islam*	English	dalasi
BOTSWANA	Sept. 30, 1966 • UK	Republic	*Indigenous/Catholicism*	English	pula
LESOTHO	Oct. 4, 1966 • UK	Constitutional monarchy	*Christianity*	English	loti
MAURITIUS	March 12, 1968 • UK	Parliamentary	*Hindu*	English	Mauritian Rupee
SWAZILAND	Sept. 6, 1968• UK	Monarchy	*Christianity*	English/SiSwati	lilangeni
EQUATORIAL GUINEA	Oct. 12, 1968 • Spain	Republic in transition	*Catholicism*	Spanish	CFA franc[2]
GUINEA-BISSAU	Sept. 10, 1974 • Portugal	Republic/multiparty	*Indigenous*	Portuguese	G.-B. peso
MOZAMBIQUE	June 25, 1975 • Portugal	Republic	*Indigenous*	Portuguese	metical
CAPE VERDE	July 5, 1975 • Portugal	Republic	*Catholicism/Indigenous*	Portuguese/Crioulo	Escudo
COMOROS	July 6, 1975 • France	Republic	*Islam*	Arabic/French	Comoran franc
SAO TOME AND PRINCIPE	• July 12, 1975	Portugal	Republic	*Christianity*	Portuguese	dobra
ANGOLA	Nov. 11, 1975 • Portugal	Democracy, strong president	*Christianity/Indigenous*	Portuguese	new kwanza
SEYCHELLES	June 29, 1976 • UK	Republic	*Christianity/Catholicism*	English/French	Seychelles rupee
DJIBOUTI	June 27, 1977 • France	Republic	*Islam*	French/Arabic	Djiboutian franc
ZIMBABWE	April 18, 1980 • UK	Parliamentary	*Syncretic-Christian/indigenous*	English	Zimbabwe dollar
NAMIBIA	March 21, 1990 • South African mandate	Republic	*Christianity*	English	South African rand
ERITREA	May 27, 1993 • Ethiopia	Transitional	*Islam/Christianity*	Tigre/Kunama/Nora Bana/Arabic	birr

NOTES: 1. Also occupies and administers Western Sahara, but question of sovereignty is unresolved. 2. Communaute Franciere Africaine francs. 3. Its two sections gained independence in 1960 and 1963. They were united in 1964.
SOURCE: *World Fact Book*, Central Intelligence Agency, 1994.

HUMAN RIGHTS WATCH

Genocide in Rwanda • Civil war in Angola • A new start in South Africa

ANGOLA: A brutal civil war continues into its 20th year, with indiscriminate bombing by both government and rebel forces.

LIBERIA: In the midst of a civil war in which all factions are responsible for serious human rights abuses, sometimes based on ethnic affiliation, but often simply as a means of sowing terror.

NIGERIA: Moving closer to chaos, as the military government brutally suppresses pro-democracy demonstrations.

RWANDA: The country was torn asunder in 1994 by mass killings. The majority Hutus slaughtered between 500,000 and one million Tutsis.

SOUTH AFRICA: Since African National Congress leader Nelson Mandela in 1994 won the presidency in South Africa's first all-race elections, the country has moved steadily from apartheid toward democracy.

ZAIRE: Extrajudicial execution, arbitrary arrest, illegal detention, torture, rape, looting by government troops, and rampant corruption have been the hallmarks of President Mobutu Sese Seko's 30-year reign.

SOURCE: *World Report*, Human Rights Watch, 1995.

THE AMERICAS

TESTING TIME FOR A SUPERPOWER

Vietnam, Watergate, and the fall of communism have changed America

What a difference a quarter of a century makes. In 1970, the countries of the Western Hemisphere—and none more than the United States—were preoccupied with the threat of communism. Cuba, a small island nation 90 miles from Miami, was already communist and other nations in South and Central America were flirting with the idea. Castro and Cuba are perhaps in their dying days, and elsewhere the threat has not only dissipated but disappeared. Canada, Mexico, and the United States have formed a North American free trade zone (NAFTA). Chile, which in 1970 was ruled by a Marxist, is negotiating to become NAFTA's newest member and the first in South America.

NORTH AMERICA

The Vietnam War, which ended with Americans being ignominiously evacuated from the roof of the U.S. embassy in Saigon in 1975 provided one of the most excruciating tests for the world's leading superpower in the last 25 years, but it was only one of many. Richard Nixon was forced to resign, rather than face impeachment for his role in the Watergate scandal—the only American president to face such a humiliation. (Yet, when he died in 1994, he was buried at a funeral fit for a hero, not a scoundrel.) The country has struggled with the issues of abortion and affirmative action. It vanquished Iraq in the Persian Gulf War, but Saddam Hussein escaped unscathed and remains powerful within his own country. And America is still coming to grips with the meaning of the end of the Cold War. Some key events of the last 25 years:

1970—TRAGEDY AT KENT STATE. An anti-war protest at Kent State University in Ohio ends tragically with four students dead after 100 National Guardsmen fire M-1 rifles into a crowd. The event gives added fervor to an already planned Washington, D.C., demonstration protesting the U.S.-supported invasion of Cambodia. Between 60,000 and 100,000 people gather in the nation's capital for a peaceful rally.

1972—SITTING DOWN WITH THE COMMUNISTS. Richard Nixon makes the first trip to China by an incumbent president, ending 25 years of Beijing-Washington hostility. Nixon also makes the first visit by a U.S. president to the Soviet Union, where he signs the SALT I anti-ballistic missile treaty.

1972-74—THE WATERGATE SCANDAL. A 1972 break-in at the Democratic Party's Watergate headquarters launches a series of political scandals, including a White House cover-up. By 1974, the House Judiciary Committee has voted to impeach the president, and Nixon chooses to leave office voluntarily. Vice President Gerald Ford takes the presidential oath soon after and pardons Nixon for all federal crimes he may have committed.

1973—THE SUPREME COURT DECLARES ABORTION LEGAL. In *Roe vs. Wade*, the U.S. Supreme Court hands down its landmark decision extending to women the right to terminate a pregnancy. Writing for the majority, Justice Harry Blackmun says that the 14th Amendment guarantees a woman's right to choose whether or not to bear a child. The United States joins Sweden, Japan, Great Britain, and other countries where abortion is already legal.

1974-76—QUEBEC FOR THE QUEBECOIS. Separatism gains in popularity. In 1974, Quebec's provincial government votes to make French the official language of the province. Its first separatist government comes to power in 1976.

1979—A NUCLEAR DISASTER AT THREE MILE ISLAND. The United States experiences its most serious nuclear power reactor accident ever at Three Mile Island in the Susquehanna River near Harrisburg, Pa. Misinformation creates public fear that the reactor core is on the verge of meltdown, the most serious of all nuclear accidents. Although there is neither a meltdown nor a hydrogen explosion releasing radioactive material into the atmosphere, a presidential commission calls for a greater emphasis on safety and training at reactors and for better emergency planning within the government and the utility industry.

1979—AMERICA HELD HOSTAGE. Militant Islamic fundamentalist students take 63 U.S citizens hostage in the U.S. Embassy in Iran, beginning a 444-day crisis and a political furor that would ultimately, many say, lose Jimmy Carter the presidency (see "The Middle East" page 884.)

1981—PRESIDENT REAGAN IS SHOT. President Ronald Reagan, sworn in on January 20, is shot in the chest outside the Washington Hilton Hotel on March 30. Police arrest and later convict John W. Hinckley, Jr., of Evergreen, Colo., of the attack. Although Reagan recovers fully, his press secretary, James S. Brady, is critically wounded, leaving him partially paralyzed and confined to a wheelchair. Hinckley successfully pleads insanity and is confined to a mental hospital, where he remains as of 1995. Brady dedicates himself to lobbying for gun control legislation.

1986—IRANGATE SHAMES THE WHITE HOUSE. Attorney General Edwin Meese confirms that profits from U.S. arms sales to Iran have been secretly diverted to the *contras*, a U.S.-supported rebel group fighting to overthrow Nicaragua's "leftist" regime (see "Nicaragua Turns Communist" below). In 1984, Congress had passed the Boland Amendment, which banned direct or indirect U.S. military aid to the rebel group. In the most dramatic congressional hearings in decades, Lt. Col. Oliver North, a major player in the scandal, testifies before Congress, comparing the *contras* to the Founding Fathers and claiming that their cause justified his breaking the law.

1987—CANADA AND THE UNITED STATES AGREE TO FREE TRADE. The two countries reach a historic free-trade agreement after more than 16 months of negotiating. Under the agreement, all tariffs between the United States and Canada will be removed between 1989 and 1999. The issue is hotly contested in Canada by labor unions and interest groups afraid of negative effects on Canada's cultural identity.

1990-91—THE PERSIAN GULF WAR: After Iraq invades Kuwait in August, claiming the tiny oil-rich country as Iraq's 19th province, a massive U.S.-led multi-national force assembles in the region to push the Iraqis back. The U.S. and allied forces bomb Baghdad. In return, the Iraqis mount Scud missile

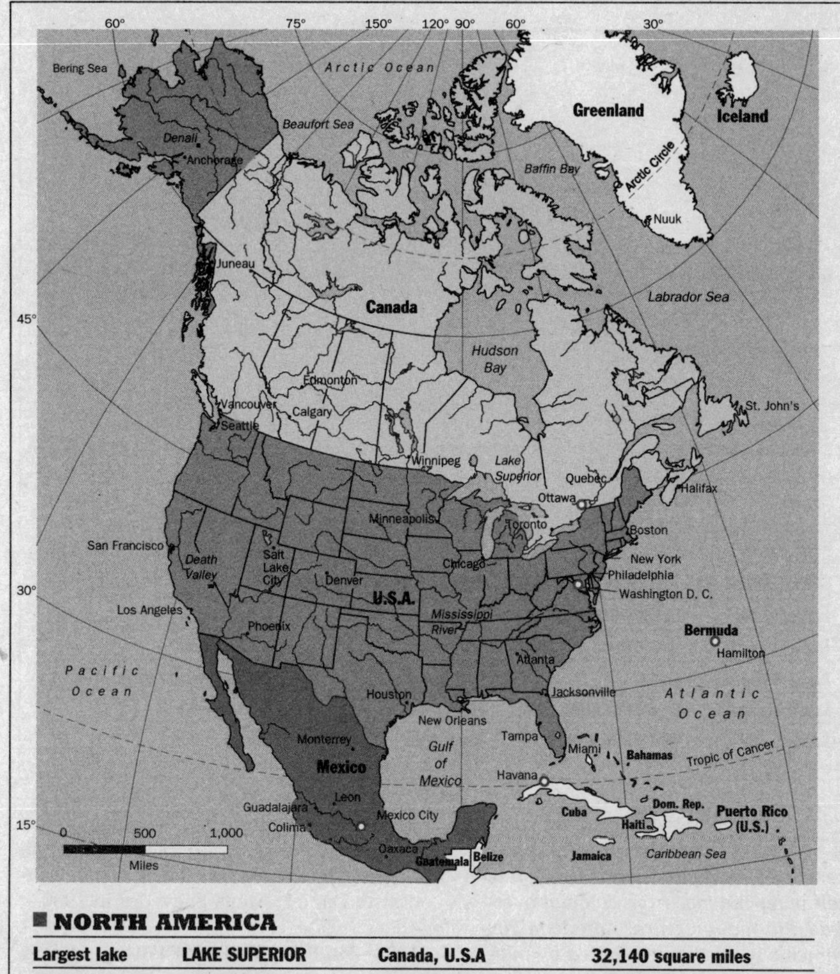

NORTH AMERICA

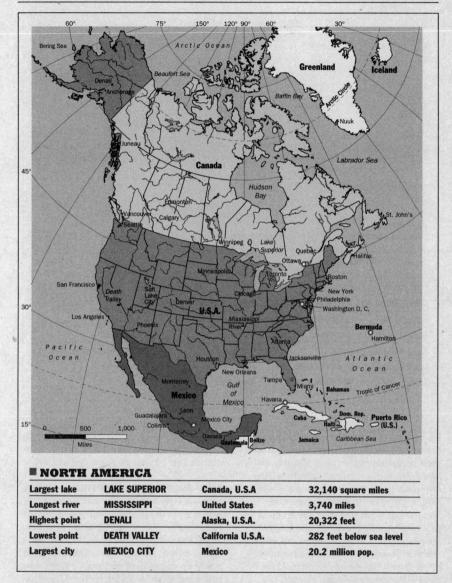

Largest lake	**LAKE SUPERIOR**	**Canada, U.S.A**	**32,140 square miles**
Longest river	**MISSISSIPPI**	**United States**	**3,740 miles**
Highest point	**DENALI**	**Alaska, U.S.A.**	**20,322 feet**
Lowest point	**DEATH VALLEY**	**California U.S.A.**	**282 feet below sea level**
Largest city	**MEXICO CITY**	**Mexico**	**20.2 million pop.**

attacks against Israel and U.S. troop facilities in Saudi Arabia. After fierce fighting, the Iraqis beat a hasty retreat. But the U.S.-led forces stop before reaching Baghdad or capturing Saddam Hussein, the Iraqi leader.

1994—REVOLT IN MEXICO. A surprise rebellion in the southern Mexican state of Chiapas breaks out on New Year's Day, just as Mexico officially enters the North American Free Trade Agreement (NAFTA). The rebels, led by the Zapatista Army of National Liberation, object to NAFTA, which, they claim, will be destructive to Mexican Indians. Government forces quickly put down the revolt. Reports circulate of government-sponsored human rights abuses against the rebels.

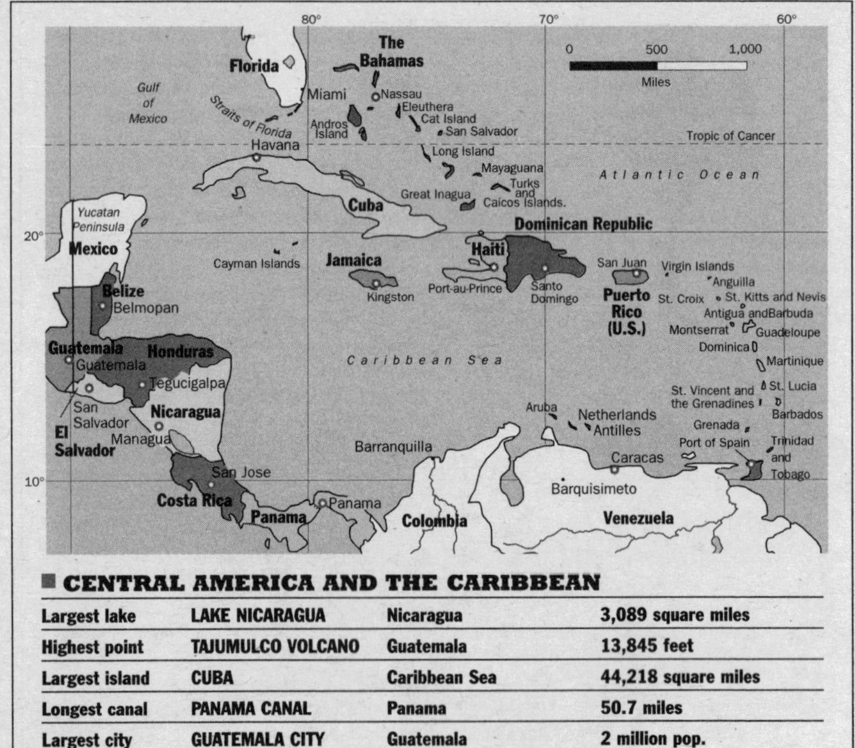

CENTRAL AMERICA AND THE CARIBBEAN

Largest lake	**LAKE NICARAGUA**	**Nicaragua**	**3,089 square miles**
Highest point	**TAJUMULCO VOLCANO**	**Guatemala**	**13,845 feet**
Largest island	**CUBA**	**Caribbean Sea**	**44,218 square miles**
Longest canal	**PANAMA CANAL**	**Panama**	**50.7 miles**
Largest city	**GUATEMALA CITY**	**Guatemala**	**2 million pop.**

CENTRAL AMERICA AND THE CARIBBEAN

By the end of the 1960s, most of the sun-drenched Caribbean islands had gained their independence from colonial overlords. But many Central American governments were still dominated by military strongmen. In Central America, Mexico has been one of the few countries to escape a military coup. The last quarter century has in many ways not been much different from years past: shaky, often dictatorial governments; just as shaky economies dominated by a wealthy few; and American intervention more than a sometime thing.

1979—NICARAGUA TURNS COMMUNIST. Sandinista guerrillas win their war against Nicaraguan dictator Anastasio Samoza and establish a communist regime. The United States throws its support to the *contra* guerrillas in their struggle to dismantle the Sandinista government. Guerrilla warfare mars the country until Violeta Barrios de Chamorro wins the presidency from Sandinista Daniel Ortega Saavedra in 1990.

1983—THE U.S. INVADES GRENADA. A military coup in Grenada sparks a U.S. invasion, which ends the island's four-year socialist experiment. About 1,200 U.S. Marines, Army Rangers, and Navy Seal commandos are involved, as well as a 300-man force made up of soldiers and police from surrounding islands. Publicly, the U.S. government justifies the invasion by citing the need to protect American students attending medical school on the island.

1989—THE U.S. INVADES PANAMA. U.S. troops invade in late December, overthrowing Panamanian ruler General Manuel Antonio Noriega in Operation "Just Cause." After Noriega nullifies May election results, initial U.S. attempts to bring about his downfall through international pressure fail, as does a coup attempt. As tensions rise and Panamanian forces kill a U.S. marine, U.S. President George Bush sends in 14,000 troops to help the 12,700 already stationed at the Panama Canal and successfully swears in a new government head. By the end of the year, the United States has 23 casualties, Panama more than 500.

1994—HAITI'S MILITARY JUNTA IS FORCED FROM POWER. A military junta seized power after the election of Jean-Bertrand Aristide in 1990 to forestall democratic reforms and proceeded to impose a reign of terror over the poorest country in the Western hemisphere. In September 1994, the threat of a U.S. invasion leads to the unopposed occupation of the country by an American-led multinational force. Within weeks, the coup leaders step down and President Aristide, who had been in exile in the United States, returns to Port-au-Prince and is restored to power.

SOUTH AMERICA

Don't cry for South America. Where there once were dictators, there now are many elected leaders publicly accountable to the voting masses. Inefficient, state-run autocracies have transformed themselves into free-market democracies. It's been a remarkable transformation in a short amount of time. Furthermore, the Yankees have, more or less, gone home. Historically, the United States has been the policeman—and sometimes the bully—in its own backyard, aiding governments it considered friendly to its interests and occasionally playing a hand in toppling those it opposed. These days, the United States is less in evidence.

1970-73—ALLENDE FALLS IN A COUP. Three years after winning the Chilean presidency, Salvador Allende dies during a successful coup led by General Augusto Pinochet in 1973. Allende, a Marxist, had nationalized industries—including U.S.-owned copper companies—and improved conditions for the poor. During the last year of Allende's regime, strikes paralyze many sectors of the economy and inflation soars to over 300 percent.

1973—THE RETURN OF JUAN PERON. Peron is elected president of Argentina. He had been ousted by a military coup in 1955, after ruling the country with an iron hand for nine years. Peron dies 10 months after his election and is succeeded by his wife Isabel who had been elected vice president and who became the first woman head of state in the Western hemisphere. In 1976, amid charges of corruption, Mrs. Peron is ousted by a military junta. A state of siege is imposed as the army battles leftists and guerrillas, killing and torturing thousands. In 1985, after a five-month trial, five former junta members are found guilty of murder and human rights abuses.

1978—MASS SUICIDE AT JONESTOWN. At the urging of their leader, the Rev. Jim Jones, 1,930 people commit suicide at their Guyana commune. Children are poisoned first, then adults drink a cyanide solution. Those who resist are reportedly injected with cyanide or shot to death. Jones had ordered the mass suicide after suspecting that authorities might soon break up the commune. He dies from a seemingly self-inflicted gunshot wound.

1982-83—WAR IN THE FALKLAND ISLANDS. British forces invade and successfully recapture the Falkland Islands, 250 miles off Argentina's coast, after Argentina briefly takes them over. Both countries had claimed sovereignty over the islands since 1833.

1985—THE COCAINE CONNECTION. Drug trafficking and related violence in Colombia, Peru, Bolivia, and Ecuador increase dramatically as the demand for cocaine in the United States rises. In 1989, the presidential candidate of Colombia's ruling party is assassinated in apparent retaliation for increased government activity against drug traffickers.

A year later, two other presidential candidates are murdered as the drug lords carry on a campaign of intimidation to stop

SOUTH AMERICA

Largest lake	**LAKE TITICACA**	**Bolivia, Peru**	**3,220 square miles**
Longest river	**AMAZON**	**Brazil**	**4.050 miles**
Highest point	**CERRO ACONCAGUA**	**Argentina**	**22,833 feet**
Lowest point	**PENINSULA VALDEZ**	**Argentina**	**131 feet below sea level**
Largest city	**SÃO PAOLO**	**Brazil**	**31,193,000 pop.**

the presidential election. The election proceeds and a strong advocate of the government's war against the drug cartel is elected. To try to stem the drug trade and bring the dealers to justice, the United States begins using an extradition treaty with Colombia, causing many dealers to go into hiding.

1989—SAVE THE AMAZON. Brazil unveils a comprehensive environmental plan for the Amazon region amid an international outcry from environmentalists and others about the ongoing destruction of the Amazonian ecosystem. The Amazon rain forest is considered a global resource because of its impact on world weather patterns.

GLOBE TROTTER'S GUIDE

VITAL STATS: THE AMERICAS BY THE NUMBERS

The United States may dominate the continent economically, but Canadians can expect to live the longest and face a lower infant mortality rate. Some Caribbean nations, like Haiti, are very much part of the Third World; others, like the Cayman Islands, are a rich man's paradise. In many places in Latin America, democracy is fragile and so is life itself. The infant mortality rate in Bolivia, for example is more than nine times that of the United States.

Country	Capital	Population	Life expectancy at birth (in years)	Infant mort. (deaths/1,000 live births)	Literacy (as % of pop.)	GDP/capita (in U.S. dollars)	TVs/1,000 inhabitants
NORTH AMERICA							
UNITED STATES	Washington, D.C.	260,713,585	75.90	8.1	97	$24,700	814
MEXICO	Mexico City	92,202,199	72.94	27.4	87	$8,200	148
CANADA	Ottawa	28,113,997	78.13	6.9	97	$22,200	639
BERMUDA	Hamilton[5]	61,158	75.03	13.2	98	$27,100	919
GREENLAND	Nuuk[1]	57,040	66.91	26.7	NA	$9,000	198
THE CARIBBEAN							
CUBA	Havana	11,064,344	76.89	10.3	94	$1,250	163
DOMINICAN REP.	Santo Domingo	7,826,075	68.35	51.5	83	$3,000	84
HAITI	Port-au-Prince	6,491,450	45.11	108.5	53	$800	5
PUERTO RICO	San Juan	3,801,977	73.95	13.8	89	$7,100	264
JAMAICA	Kingston	2,555,064	74.36	16.8	98	$3,200	131
TRINIDAD & TOBAGO	Port-of-Spain	1,328,282	70.73	16.5	95	$8,000	315
GUADELOUPE	Basse-Terre[2]	428,947	76.97	8.9	90	$8,400	263
MARTINIQUE	Fort-de-France	392,362	78.01	10.4	93	$9,500	135
THE BAHAMAS	Nassau	273,055	71.52	33.5	90	$16,500	265
BARBADOS	Bridgetown	255,827	73.83	20.3	99	$8,700	265
NETHERLANDS ANTILLES	Willemstad[3]	185,790	76.32	9.6	94	$9,700	363
SAINT LUCIA	Castries	145,090	69.36	18.5	67	$3,000	189
ST. VINCENT & THE GRENADINES	Kingstown	115,437	72.28	17.2	96	$2,000	144
U.S. VIRGIN ISLANDS	Charlotte Amalie[4]	97,564	75.29	12.5	NA	$11,000	607
GRENADA	Saint George's	94,109	70.40	12.4	98	$3,000	330
DOMINICA	Roseau	87,696	76.96	10.3	94	$2,100	72
ARUBA	Oranjestad[3]	65,545	76.43	8.4	NA	$17,400	NA
ANTIGUA & BARBUDA	Saint John's	64,762	73.11	18.5	89	$5,800	355
SAINT KITTS & NEVIS	Basseterre	40,671	66.11	19.9	98	$4,000	205
CAYMAN ISLANDS	George Town[5]	31,790	77.10	8.4	98	$23,000	197
TURKS & CAICOS IS.	Grand Turk[5]	13,552	75.34	12.7	98	$6,000	NA
BRITISH VIRGIN IS.	Road Town[5]	12,864	72.67	19.5	98	$10,600	219
MONTSERRAT	Plymouth[5]	12,701	75.73	11.6	97	$4,300	148
ANGUILLA	The Valley[5]	7,052	73.99	17.5	95	$6,800	NA
CENTRAL AMERICA							
GUATEMALA	Guatemala City	10,721,387	64.42	53.9	55	$3,000	52
EL SALVADOR	San Salvador	5,752,511	66.99	40.9	73	$2,500	92

GLOBE TROTTER'S GUIDE

Country	Capital	Population	Life expectancy at birth (in years)	Infant mort. (deaths/1,000 live births)	Literacy (as % of pop.)	GDP/capita (in U.S. dollars)	TVs/1,000 inhabitants
HONDURAS	Tegucigalpa	5,314,794	67.60	45.3	73	$1,950	73
NICARAGUA	Managua	4,096,689	64.02	52.5	57	$1,600	65
COSTA RICA	San Jose	3,342,154	77.80	11.0	93	$5,900	140
PANAMA	Panama	2,630,000	74.88	16.5	88	$4,500	166
BELIZE	Belmopan	208,949	68.08	35.6	91	$2,700	165
SOUTH AMERICA							
BRAZIL	Brasilia	158,739,257	62.25	59.5	81	$5,000	207
COLOMBIA	Bogota	35,577,556	72.10	28.3	87	$5,500	116
ARGENTINA	Buenos Aires	33,912,994	71.35	29.4	95	$5,500	220
PERU	Lima	23,650,671	65.62	54.2	85	$3,000	98
VENEZUELA	Caracas	20,562,405	73.00	27.7	88	$8,000	162
CHILE	Santiago	13,950,557	74.51	15.1	93	$7,000	209
ECUADOR	Quito	10,677,067	69.98	39.3	88	$4,000	84
BOLIVIA	La Paz	7,719,445	63.31	73.7	78	$2,100	103
PARAGUAY	Asuncion	5,213,772	73.28	25.2	90	$3,000	50
URUGUAY	Montevideo	3,198,910	74.09	17.1	96	$6,000	231
GUYANA	Georgetown	729,425	64.90	48.5	95	$1,900	39
SURINAME	Paramaribo	422,840	69.45	31.3	95	$2,800	130
FRENCH GUIANA	Cayenne[2]	139,299	75.20	15.9	82	$4,390	213
FALKLAND ISLANDS	Stanley[5]	2,261	NA	NA	NA	NA	NA

1. Part of Danish realm. 2. Overseas dept. of France. 3. Part of the Dutch realm. 4. U.S. territory. 5. UK territory.
SOURCE: *The World Fact Book*, Central Intelligence Agency, 1994; *Statistical Yearbook*, United Nations, 1992.

TRAVELER'S GUIDE

TRAVEL WARNINGS: The U.S. Department of State recently issued a travel warning for Guatemala and Colombia. Unfounded rumors that foreigners are stealing Guatemalan children to use their organs in transplants have led to threats and mob violence in several parts of the country. These incidents have not occurred in traditional tourist spots. In Colombia, U.S. citizens and institutions have been the targets of recent kidnappings and attacks. The Bureau of Consular Affairs, ☎ 202-647-5225, can provide up-to-date information.

VISAS: Proof of U.S. citizenship and a photo I.D. are required for travel to Canada and most Caribbean islands, some of which also require proof of onward/return ticket and/or sufficient funds for tourist stays. Central American country requirements range from mandatory visas in Guatemala and El Salvador to proof of U.S. citizenship, photo I.D., and sufficient funds in Mexico. In South America, only Brazil and Suriname require visas for tourist visits. Ecuador and Colombia require proof of an onward/return ticket. Since visa requirements can change unexpectedly, always check with the relevant embassies before traveling.

VACCINATIONS: No vaccines are required for travel to the Caribbean and South and Central American countries. Malaria can be a problem in rural South and Central American areas. Depending on the country, the Centers for Disease Control (CDC) recommends prophylaxis either with chloroquine or with mefloquine, due to chloroquine-resistant malaria strains in certain countries. Call the CDC's automated travelers' hotline at ☎ 404-332-4559 for individual country recommendations.

WORLD WATCHER'S GUIDE

VITAL FACTS: INSIDE THE AMERICAS TODAY

Nearly 100 years older than Canada, the United States dominates the continent both economically and politically. While in many Caribbean nations English is spoken and Christianity practiced, most retain their own cultural identity. Central and South American countries broke free of their colonial ties to Spain more than 100 years ago, but for many, independence still hasn't brought stability. Two cultural elements unify most of the region: Catholicism and the Spanish language.

COUNTRY	Date of Independence • From	**Form of Government**	*Dominant Religion*	**Official Language**	Currency
NORTH AMERICA					
UNITED STATES	July 4, 1776 • England	**Federal republic**	*Varied mix*	**English**	US dollar
MEXICO	Sept. 16, 1810 • Spain	**Federal Rep. under central gov.**	*Catholicism*	**Spanish**	Mexican peso
CANADA	July 1, 1867 • UK	**Confederation/parliamentary dem.**	*Christianity*	**English/French**	Canadian dollar
BERMUDA	none	**Territory of UK**	*Christianity*	**English**	Bermudian dollar
GREENLAND	none	**Part of Dutch realm**	*Christianity*	**Eskimo dialects/Danish**	Danish kroner
THE CARIBBEAN					
HAITI	Jan. 1, 1804 • France	**Republic**	*Catholicism (majority also practice Voodoo)*	**French**	gourde
DOMINICAN REPUBLIC	Feb. 27, 1844 • Haiti	**Republic**	*Catholicism*	**Spanish**	Dominican peso
CUBA	Dec. 10, 1898 • Spain (U.S.-admin. 1898-1902)	**Communist state**	*Catholicism*	**Spanish**	Cuban peso
JAMAICA	Aug. 6, 1962 • UK	**Parliamentary dem.**	*Christianity*	**English**	Jamaican dollar
TRINIDAD & TOBAGO	Aug. 31, 1962 • UK	**Parliamentary dem.**	*Christianity*	**English**	Trinidad & Tobago dollar
BARBADOS	Nov. 30, 1966 • UK	**Parliamentary dem.**	*Christianity*	**English**	Barbadian dollar
THE BAHAMAS	July 10, 1973 • UK	**Commonwealth**	*Christianity*	**English**	Bahamian dollar
GRENADA	Feb. 7, 1974 • UK	**Parliamentary dem.**	*Christianity*	**English**	East Caribbean dollar
DOMINICA	Nov. 3, 1978 • UK	**Parliamentary dem.**	*Catholicism*	**English**	East Caribbean dollar
SAINT LUCIA	Feb. 22, 1979 • UK	**Parliamentary dem.**	*Catholicism*	**English**	East Caribbean dollar
SAINT VINCENT & THE GRENADINES	Oct. 27, 1979 • UK	**Const. mon.**	*Christianity*	**English**	East Caribbean dollar
ANTIGUA AND BARBUDA	Nov. 1, 1981 • UK	**Parliamentary dem.**	*Christianity*	**English**	East Caribbean dollar
SAINT KITTS & NEVIS	Sept. 19, 1983 • UK	**Const. mon.**	*Christianity*	**English**	East Caribbean dollar
ANGUILLA	none	**Territory of UK**	*Christianity*	**English**	East Caribbean dollar
ARUBA	none	**Part of Dutch realm**	*Catholicism*	**Dutch**	Arubian florin
BRITISH VIRGIN ISLANDS	none	**Territory of UK**	*Christianity*	**English**	US dollar
CAYMAN ISLANDS	none	**Territory of UK**	*Christianity*	**English**	Caymanian dollar
GUADELOUPE	none	**Overseas dept. of France**	*Catholicism*	**French**	French franc
MARTINIQUE	none	**Overseas dept. of France**	*Catholicism*	**French**	French franc
MONTSERRAT	none	**Territory of UK**	*Christianity*	**English**	East Caribbean dollar
NETHERLANDS ANTILLES	none	**Part of Dutch realm**	*Christianity*	**Dutch**	Netherlands Antilles guilder
PUERTO RICO	none	**Commonwealth associated with the US**	*Catholicism*	**Spanish**	US dollar
TURKS AND CAICOS ISLANDS	none	**Territory of UK**	*Christianity*	**English**	US dollar
CENTRAL AMERICA					
COSTA RICA	Sept. 15, 1821 • Spain	**Democratic republic**	*Catholicism*	**Spanish**	Costa Rican colon
EL SALVADOR	Sept. 15, 1821 • Spain	**Republic**	*Catholicism*	**Spanish**	Salvadoran colon
GUATEMALA	Sept. 15, 1821 • Spain	**Republic**	*Christianity*	**Spanish/Indian dialects**	quetzal

WORLD WATCHER'S GUIDE

COUNTRY	Date of Independence • From	**Form of Government**	*Dominant Religion*	**Official Language**	Currency
HONDURAS	Sept. 15, 1821 • Spain	**Republic**	*Catholicism*	**Spanish**	lempira
NICARAGUA	Sept. 15, 1821 • Spain	**Republic**	*Catholicism*	**Spanish**	gold cordoba
PANAMA	Nov. 28, 1821/Nov. 3, 1903 • Spain/Colombia	**Const. republic**	*Catholicism*	**Spanish**	balboa
BELIZE	Sept. 21, 1981 • UK	**Parliamentary dem.**	*Catholicism*	**English/Spanish**	Belizean dollar
SOUTH AMERICA					
COLOMBIA	July 20, 1810 • Spain	**Republic; dominant exec. branch**	*Catholicism*	**Spanish**	Colombian peso
CHILE	Sept. 18, 1810 • Spain	**Republic**	*Catholicism*	**Spanish**	Chilean peso
PARAGUAY	May 14, 1811 • Spain	**Republic**	*Catholicism*	**Spanish**	guarani
VENEZUELA	July 5, 1811 • Spain	**Republic**	*Catholicism*	**Spanish**	bolivar
ARGENTINA	July 9, 1816 • Spain	**Republic**	*Catholicism*	**Spanish**	nuevo peso argentino
PERU	July 28, 1821 • Spain	**Republic**	*Catholicism*	**Spanish/Quechua**	nueve sol
ECUADOR	May 24, 1822 • Spain	**Republic**	*Catholicism*	**Spanish**	sucre
BRAZIL	Sept. 7, 1822 • Portugal	**Federal republic**	*Catholicism*	**Portuguese**	cruzeiro real
BOLIVIA	Aug. 6, 1825 • Spain	**Republic**	*Catholicism*	**Spanish/Quechua/Aymara**	boliviano
URUGUAY	Aug. 25, 1828 • Brazil	**Republic**	*Catholicism*	**Spanish**	Uruguayan peso
GUYANA	May 26, 1966 • UK	**Republic**	*Christianity*	**English/Amerindian dialects**	Guyanese dollar
SURINAME	Nov. 25, 1975 • Netherlands	**Republic**	*Christianity/Hinduism/Islam*	**Dutch/Sranang Tongo**	Surinamese guilder
FALKLAND ISLANDS	none	**Territory of UK**	*Christianity*	**English**	Falkland pound
FRENCH GUIANA	none	**Territory of France**	*Catholicism*	**French**	French franc

SOURCE: *World Fact Book*, Central Intelligence Agency, 1994.

HUMAN RIGHTS WATCH

Cuba's exodus • Guatemala's disappearances • Peru's self-coup

BRAZIL: People are watching anxiously to see how President Fernando Henrique Cardoso, elected by an absolute majority in 1994, will change the human rights climate. Among the abuses to be rectified are the violent attacks and murders of children who live on the streets.

COLOMBIA: President Ernesto Samper, elected in August 1994, has emphasized human rights but is haunted by his predecessor's powerful military. Elite counterinsurgency troops routinely carry out extrajudicial executions and torture.

CUBA: Dissatisfaction with the Castro regime deepened in 1994 in the face of continuing repression and economic hardship. In the last 30 years, thousands have been jailed for violating "illegal exit" laws, which forbid them to leave the country without government permission.

GUATEMALA: The government and the guerrillas made important human rights commitments with a 1994 accord—and then proceeded to flagrantly disregard it. In the last 30 years, tens of thousands of people have disappeared.

PERU: Since his 1992 "self-coup," President Alberto Fujimori has reinforced the structure that allowed human rights abuses in the 1980s. Security forces raid houses indiscriminately, raping, torturing, and carrying out extrajudicial executions in a purported crackdown on Shining Path guerrillas, but victims are often unrelated to Shining Path.

SOURCE: *World Report*, Human Rights Watch, 1995.

ASIA

THE DAWN OF THE PACIFIC CENTURY

Despite wars and turmoil, Asia emerges as an economic power

Home to more than half the world's population, Asia today is a force to be reckoned with—both economically and politically. Pacific rim nations manufacture a great deal of the world's consumer goods, and developing powerhouses like China and India are increasingly asserting their political will.

Yet, the legacy of backwardness remains. Chinese peasants still use oxen to sow the fields. The slums of Calcutta are still among the worst in the world. Primitive cultures are just a plane hop away from gleaming skyscrapers in some of Southeast Asia's most modern cities. But dynamic changes are sweeping through the region.

If the 20th century was the American Century, it looks more and more likely that the next 100 years will be dominated by the nations of the Pacific rim. Here are some of the historical highlights from the last 25 years.

NORTH, CENTRAL, AND EAST ASIA

Cultural revolution, economic miracles, assassinations, and wars continue to rock this vast region.

1970—THE AFTERMATH OF THE CULTURAL REVOLUTION. Mao Zedong formed the Red Guard in 1966 to campaign against "old ideas, old culture, old habits, and old customs." More often than not, however, the Red Guard units, dominated by youths and students, amount to uncontrolled mobs. "Class enemies," opponents of Mao's social order, are brutalized. Mass trials and executions are reported throughout the country. College admittance is based on ideology and labor experience, not academic merit.

Beginning in 1967, efforts are made to restore control. Schools, which had been closed to free students for agitation, are reopened. But the Great Proletarian Cultural Revolution was not so easily tamed. Only by about 1970 are Chinese authorities able to begin rebuilding the Communist party—and the country.

1971—INDIA WINS A WAR AGAINST PAKISTAN AND BANGLADESH IS BORN. For 25 years after gaining independence from Britain, Pakistan consists of two separate regions—East Pakistan and West Pakistan. They are united by a religion (Islam) but separated by culture and over 1,000 miles of Indian territory. The civil war changes that.

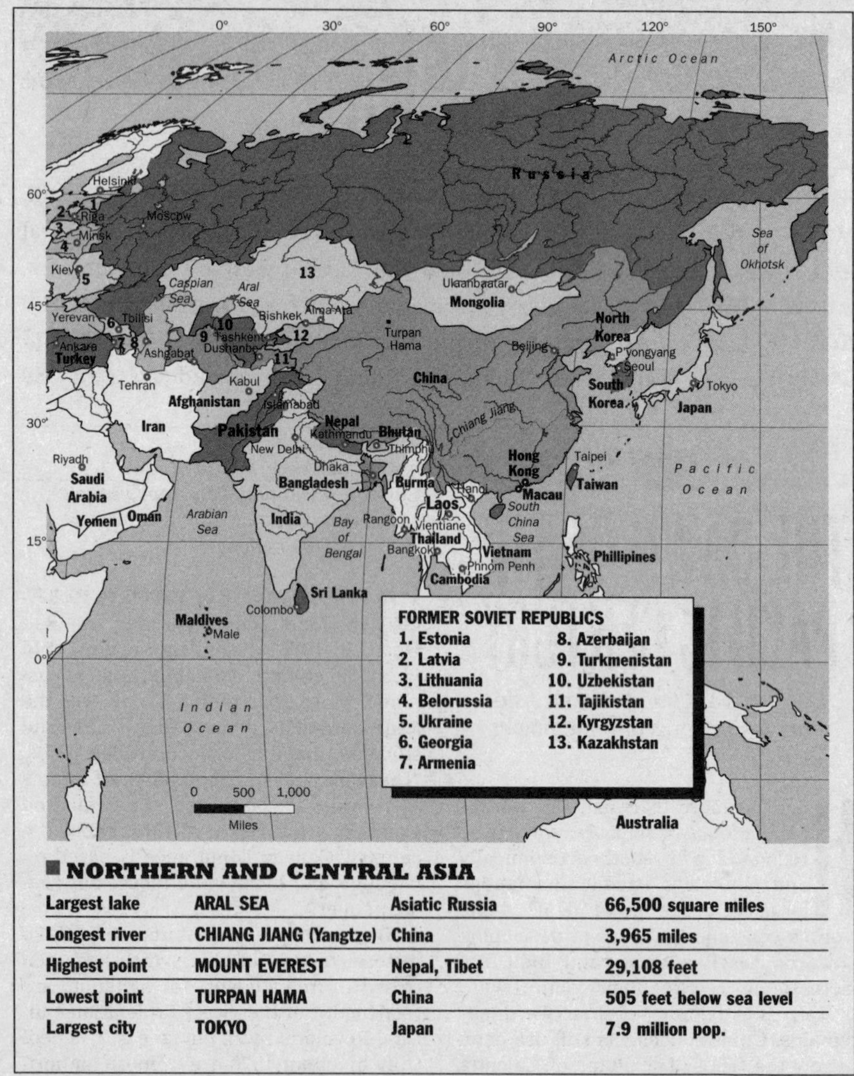

NORTHERN AND CENTRAL ASIA

Largest lake	**ARAL SEA**	**Asiatic Russia**	**66,500 square miles**
Longest river	**CHIANG JIANG (Yangtze)**	**China**	**3,965 miles**
Highest point	**MOUNT EVEREST**	**Nepal, Tibet**	**29,108 feet**
Lowest point	**TURPAN HAMA**	**China**	**505 feet below sea level**
Largest city	**TOKYO**	**Japan**	**7.9 million pop.**

The fighting begins after the 1970 election in which an East Pakistani party seeking autonomy won a majority. After riots and strikes in the East, West Pakistani troops move in. In the turmoil, an estimated 1 million Bengalis (East Pakistanis) are killed. Another 10 million or more flee to India. In part to stop the flow of refugees, India intervenes, siding with the Easterners and supporting the newly proclaimed state of Bangladesh. Before a cease-fire is declared in December, a full-scale war has broken out with fighting on both Eastern and Western fronts.

EARLY '70S—BEGINNING OF THE JAPANESE "ECONOMIC MIRACLE." By the end of the decade, Japanese exports (notably cars and electronic equipment) to the United States and other nations increase dramatically and Japan emerges as an economic superpower.

1972—NIXON GOES TO CHINA. After a secret visit to Beijing laying the groundwork by Secretary of State Henry Kissinger, President Richard Nixon meets with Chairman Mao Zedong and Zhou Enlai, the Chinese premier, to discuss the resumption of normal diplomatic relations between the two superpowers. Zhou dies in early 1976 and Mao nine months later. In January 1979, the two countries ratify a treaty that obligates the United States to cease arms sales to Taiwan.

1974—INDIA'S FIRST NUCLEAR EXPLOSION. India's first successful nuclear explosion is condemned by the international community but popular at home. Government officials claim that the experiment is research for peaceful uses of nuclear explosives, such as mining and earth moving, and assure critics that India has no plans for building nuclear weapons. In 1995, only five nations are recognized as possessing nuclear weapons—the United States, Russia, Britain, France, and China. Three others—India, Pakistan, and Israel—are assumed to have nuclear weapons or the capacity to build them but have not publicly said so.

1980—CHINA'S GANG OF FOUR GOES ON TRIAL. Chinese authorities hold trials of the Gang of Four, who were arrested following Mao's death in 1976. Charges against them include persecuting officials, plotting to murder Mao, and trying to overthrow the government. The most famous of the group, Mao's widow, receives a suspended death sentence in 1983.

1984—A CHEMICAL LEAK KILLS THOUSANDS IN BHOPAL, INDIA. As many as 2,500 people die in Bhopal, an industrial city in central India, after a lethal gas used in pesticide production escapes from a manufacturing plant tank owned by a subsidiary of Union Carbide, an American company. The gas drifts over surrounding areas, killing people in their sleep. Many others suffer eye irritation and respiratory problems. Children, who are especially vulnerable to the chemical, make up a disproportionate number of those killed.

The same year, India's prime minister, Indira Gandhi, is assassinated in New Delhi.

1989—CHINA CRUSHES THE DEMOCRACY MOVEMENT. Chinese communist party leaders order a military crackdown on a student-led democracy movement that has been growing for two years. After 1 million or more students defy a ban on demonstrations in Beijing's Tiananmen Square, authorities massacre hundreds of unarmed protesters. World opinion criticizes the move, which comes just as East European communist governments are giving way to democratic forces. The event marks a new wave of political repression in China.

SOUTHEAST ASIA

From Burma to the Philippines, Southeast Asia has had more than its share of misfortune in the last quarter century, enduring some of the most brutal governments since the Nazis ruled Germany.

1975—THE COMMUNISTS TRIUMPH IN VIETNAM. The first communists from the National Liberation Front make their way

■ SOUTHEAST ASIA

into South Vietnam in the early 1960s. By 1963, 15,000 U.S. military advisers are stationed in the country.

At the height of the Vietnam War, the United States has more than 525,000 men in Vietnam. Some 50,000 Americans and many, many more Vietnamese lose their lives in the war. A peace treaty is signed in 1973 in Paris, ending the longest military action in U.S. history (war never was formally declared). Two years later, North Vietnamese forces capture Saigon. U.S. Marine guards and U.S. civilians and dependents are evacuated by helicopter from the rooftop of the besieged U.S. embassy there. In 1994, the United States and Vietnam take the first steps toward resuming normal diplomatic relations.

1975—PHNOM PENH FALLS TO THE KHMER ROUGE. After more than five years, the war in Cambodia ends when Pol Pot leads his communist Khmer Rouge forces into the capital, Phnom Penh, where he establishes the Kampuchean People's Republic. Just days before, U.S. diplomatic staff members are evacuated by helicopter. Shortly after taking power, Khmer Rouge leaders expel the capital's entire population to the countryside. In the next two years, an estimated 2 million to 4 million Cambodians die under the brutality of the Pol Pot regime.

1986—MARCOS OUSTED. Philippines leader Ferdinand E. Marcos flees his country for exile in Hawai'i after public outcries against a fraudulent election. Political opponent Corazon C. Aquino takes over the presidency with widespread support and tries to recover an estimated $27 billion that Marcos has allegedly stolen from the national treasury.

1994—LABOR UNREST IN INDONESIA. After months of strikes, workers in Medan, North Sumatra stage a mass rally and demand higher wages and the right to organize. The demonstration later turns violent, with Chinese-owned shops primary targets, and hundreds are arrested. Labor union organizers receive the harshest penalties.

THE MIDDLE EAST

Twenty-five years ago, few would have believed that in 1995 Israeli leaders and Palestine Liberation Organization leader Yasir Arafat would be charting a program for peace. Arafat, once a brutal terrorist responsible for bombings of innocent civilians, is now regarded, albeit warily, as the legitimate representative of the Palestinian people. The City of Jericho on the West Bank and the Gaza Strip are under Palestinian control and more should follow. Many hurdles still remain, but the Arabs and Jews are closer to a comprehensive settlement of their differences than at any time since Israel became a state in 1948.

Elsewhere in the Middle East, Islam—a way of life as well as a religion—is newly resurgent. In Iran, Iraq, and other Arab states, autocratic leaders fuse Islam with government. Women are accorded few rights. Rulers go to considerable lengths to shield their citizens from "immoral" Western influences. Vast reserves of oil fuel the region's economies and keep the rest of the world responsive to Arab interests.

1967—THE SIX-DAY WAR. The third Arab-Israeli war since 1948. After Nasser imposes a blockade on Israeli shipping in the Straits of Tiran, Israel attacks Egypt, Syria, and Jordan simultaneously. When the war ends, Israel occupies the Sinai Peninsula, the Golan Heights, the Old City of Jerusalem, the Gaza Strip, and the West Bank, all of which had previously been under Egyptian or Jordanian control.

The UN Security Council unanimously adopts Resolution 242, denouncing the acquisition of territory by war but does not insist on any specific terms for the withdrawal of Israeli forces.

1969—YASIR ARAFAT TAKES OVER THE PLO. Arafat, then the leader of the al-Fatah guerrillas, is elected chairman of the Palestinian Liberation Organization's (PLO) executive committee. Former Egyptian President Gamal Abdel Nasser had led Arab leaders in creating the PLO five years earlier.

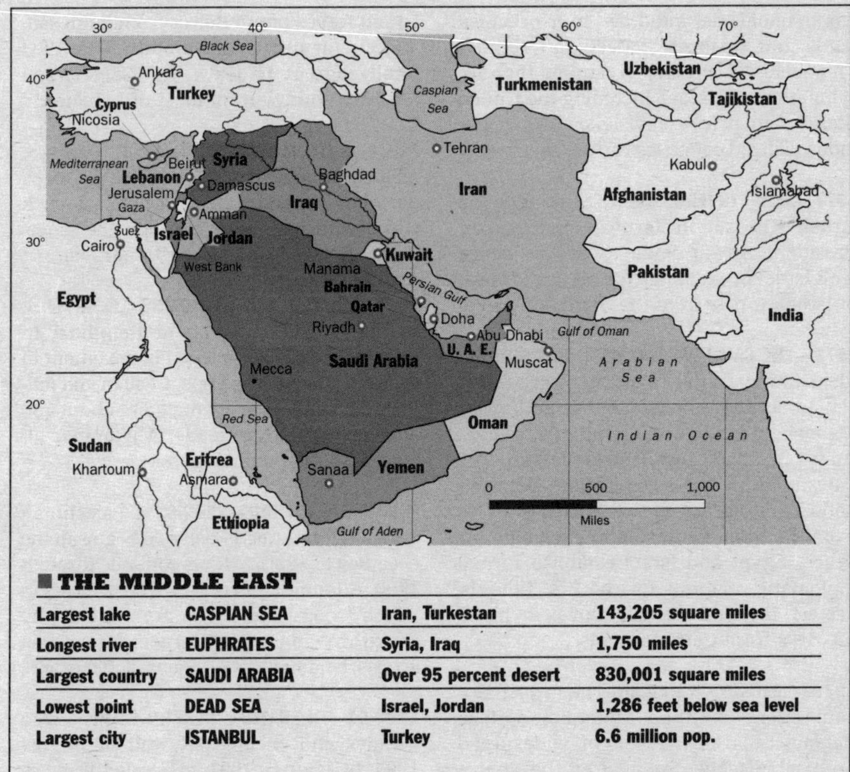

THE MIDDLE EAST

Largest lake	**CASPIAN SEA**	**Iran, Turkestan**	**143,205 square miles**
Longest river	**EUPHRATES**	**Syria, Iraq**	**1,750 miles**
Largest country	**SAUDI ARABIA**	**Over 95 percent desert**	**830,001 square miles**
Lowest point	**DEAD SEA**	**Israel, Jordan**	**1,286 feet below sea level**
Largest city	**ISTANBUL**	**Turkey**	**6.6 million pop.**

1970—THE PLO IS EXPELLED FROM JORDAN. King Hussein defeats PLO leader Yasir Arafat's guerrillas and expels the PLO from his territory. PLO headquarters move from Jordan to Lebanon.

1970—TERROR IN THE SKY. The Popular Front for the Liberation of Palestine, a radical Palestinian group, attempts to hijack four passenger planes over western Europe. The skyjacking of a New York-bound El Al plane fails, but a Pan Am plane is taken to Beirut and then Cairo. Three other flights are diverted to an unused airstrip in the Jordanian desert and demands are made for the release of Palestinians detained in Israel, West Germany, Britain, and Switzerland. The plane's passengers are released eventually, but the planes are destroyed.

1972—MURDER AT THE OLYMPICS. During the Munich Olympic games, Palestinian guerrillas capture Israeli athletes and call for release of Palestinians held by Israeli police. After promising the terrorists safe passage out of the country, West German police open fire at the Munich airport, leading the gunmen to kill all of the hostages. Israel responds with bombing raids in Lebanon.

1973—THE YOM KIPPUR WAR. The fourth Arab-Israeli war breaks out when Syria and Egypt attack Israeli forces in the Sinai and the Golan Heights on the Jewish Day of Atonement. Israel drives back enemy forces, but the initial successes of the Arab forces demonstrate that they have dramatically strengthened their military might in the six years since the previous war.

1973—THE ARAB OIL EMBARGO. Arab oil-producing countries impose an oil embargo on Israel during the Yom Kippur War and agree to cut production 5 percent each month until Israel withdraws from occupied lands and restores "Palestinian rights." They also cut exports to nations that are sympathetic to Israel, including the United States. Oil prices skyrocket and many industrialized countries restrict fuel usage.

1977—SADAT IN JERUSALEM. Speaking to the Israeli Knesset in Jerusalem, Egyptian President Anwar Sadat proposes peace with Israel in exchange for the withdrawal of Israeli forces from the Sinai Peninsula.

1978—THE CAMP DAVID ACCORDS. U.S. President Jimmy Carter finally hammers out a settlement between Israeli Prime Minister Menachem Begin and Egyptian President Anwar Sadat in which Israel recognizes the Palestinian people's right of self-determination and agrees to withdraw its forces from the Sinai Peninsula in exchange for peace. Egypt and Israel establish formal diplomatic relations for the first time. In protest, the Arab League moves its headquarters from Cairo to Tunis.

1979—REVOLUTION IN IRAN. The pro-American regime of Shah Mohammad Reza Pahlavi falls as a result of widespread political dissent. Soon after the shah's departure, the Ayatollah Ruhollah Khomeini, previously in exile, establishes an Islamic republic. Under the new constitution, final authority over all legislation and command of the armed forces are vested in the faqih, the primary theologian in the country—in this case, Khomeini.

1979-81—AMERICA HELD HOSTAGE. Muslim extremists seize the U.S. embassy in Tehran after the United States refuses to extradite the shah, who has received a death sentence from new Iranian leader Ayatollah Ruhollah Khomeini. The last 52 hostages are released on Jan. 20, 1981, after 444 days in captivity.

1981—SADAT IS ASSASSINATED. The Egyptian president is gunned down by Muslim extremists at a military parade in Cairo.

1982—ISRAEL INVADES LEBANON. To stop PLO guerrillas from mounting raids into Israel, Israeli forces bomb Beirut from land, sea, and air for nearly two months. The PLO finally agrees to leave. In 1985, Israeli troops withdraw from most of Lebanon.

1983-84—U.S. MARINES DIE IN BEIRUT. At a U.S. military compound in Beirut, 239 U.S. troops die when an Arab extremist drives a truck wired with explosives through the gates. Soon after, U.S. troops are withdrawn.

1986—UNITED STATES BOMBS LIBYA. U.S. bombers raid Tripoli and Benghazi in response to Libya's alleged involvement in terrorist attacks in Europe. Civilian and military casualties are estimated at about 130 and include Libyan leader Mu'ammar al-Qaddafi's adopted daughter.

1987—THE INTIFADA BEGINS. A Palestinian uprising protesting Israeli rule begins in the occupied territories. Riots continue through 1990. Attempting to contain the protests in which troops and police are attacked by rock-throwing mobs, Israeli forces use arrests, beatings, deportations, and curfews.

1990-91—OPERATION DESERT STORM. Iraq invades and occupies Kuwait in August 1990. In January 1991, a U.S.-led Western alliance launches Operation Desert Storm to expel the Iraqi invaders from Kuwait. More than half a million U.S. troops are involved in the action, which succeeds in expelling the Iraqis from Kuwait, but Iraqi ruler Saddam Hussein remains in power.

1993—ISRAEL AND THE PLO SIGN PACT. In Washington, D.C., Israel and the PLO sign the Declaration of Principles on Palestinian Self-Rule in the Occupied Territories. Both parties officially recognize each other.

1994—THE PLO TAKES OVER. A transfer of power from Israel to Palestinian authorities begins in the town of Jericho and much of the Gaza Strip. But violence continues, as a radical Jewish settler who opposes the peace agreement murders 29 Palestinian worshipers at a Hebron mosque with an army-issued automatic rifle. Palestinians respond with protests and random attacks against settlers.

GLOBE TROTTER'S GUIDE

VITAL STATS: ASIA & THE MIDDLE EAST BY THE NUMBERS

Asia is a continent of extremes. It includes the world's most populous nation (China) and some of the wealthiest countries in the world (Japan and the oil-rich Arab Gulf states). In Cambodia, however, per capita GDP is a mere $600 and life expectancy less than 50 years.

Country	Capital	Population	Life expectancy at birth (in years)	Infant mort. (deaths/1,000 live births)	Literacy (as % of pop.)	GDP/capita (in U.S. dollars)	TVs/1,000 inhabitants
UNITED STATES	Washington, D.C.	260,713,585	75.9	8.1	97	$24,700	814
NORTHERN AND CENTRAL ASIA							
CHINA	Beijing	1,190,431,106	67.91	52.1	78	$2,200	131
INDIA	New Delhi	919,903,056	58.58	78.4	52.11	$1,300	35
RUSSIA	Moscow	149,608,953	68.89	27.0	100	$5,190	NA
PAKISTAN	Islamabad	128,855,965	57.41	101.9	35	$1,900	18
BANGLADESH	Dhaka	125,149,469	55.08	106.9	35	$1,000	5
JAPAN	Tokyo	125,106,937	79.31	4.3	99	$20,400	613
TURKEY	Ankara	62,153,898	70.94	48.8	81	$5,100	175
SOUTH KOREA	Seoul	45,082,880	70.59	21.7	99	$9,500	208
NORTH KOREA	P'yongyang	23,066,573	69.78	27.7	99	$1,000	15
UZBEKISTAN	Tashkent	22,608,866	68.58	53.2	100	$2,430	NA
TAIWAN	Taipei	21,298,930	75.25	5.7	86	$10,600	NA
NEPAL	Kathmandu	21,041,527	52.53	83.5	26	$1,000	2
SRI LANKA	Colombo	18,129,850	71.90	21.9	88	$3,000	981
KAZAKHSTAN	Alma-Ata	17,267,554	68.04	40.9	100	$3,510	NA
AFGHANISTAN	Kabul	16,903,400	44.89	155.8	29	NA	8
AZERBAIJAN	Baku	7,684,456	70.85	34.8	100	$2,040	NA
TAJIKISTAN	Dushanbe	5,995,469	68.76	62.0	100	$1,180	NA
GEORGIA	Tbilisi	5,681,025	72.84	23.4	100	$1,390	NA
HONG KONG	Territory of UK	5,548,754	80.09	5.8	77	$21,500	278
KYRGYZSTAN	Bishkek	4,698,108	67.92	46.8	100	$2,440	NA
TURKMENISTAN	Ashgabat	3,995,122	65.14	69.9	100	$3,330	NA
ARMENIA	Yerevan	3,521,517	72.07	27.1	100	$2,040	NA
MONGOLIA	Ulaanbaatar	2,429,762	66.16	43.4	NA	$1,200	40
BHUTAN	Thimphu	716,380	50.60	121.0	NA	$700	NA
MACAU	Macau	484,557	79.75	5.5	90	$7,300	67
MALDIVES	Male	252,077	64.67	53.8	92	$620	25
SOUTHEAST ASIA							
INDONESIA	Jakarta	200,409,741	60.74	67.3	77	$2,900	59
VIETNAM	Hanoi	73,103,898	65.41	45.5	88	$1,000	41
PHILIPPINES	Manila	69,808,930	65.39	50.8	90	$2,500	44
THAILAND	Bangkok	59,510,471	68.35	37.1	93	$5,500	114
BURMA	Rangoon	44,277,014	59.98	63.7	81	$950	NA
MALAYSIA	Kuala Lumpur	19,283,157	69.15	25.6	78	$7,500	144
CAMBODIA	Phnom Penh	10,264,628	49.26	110.6	35	$600	8
LAOS	Vientiane	4,701,654	51.68	101.8	64	$900	6

GLOBE TROTTER'S GUIDE

Country	Capital	Population	Life expectancy at birth (in years)	Infant mort. (deaths/1,000 live births)	Literacy (as % of pop.)	GDP/capita (in U.S. dollars)	TVs/1,000 inhabitants
SINGAPORE		2,859,142	75.95	5.7	88	$15,000	378
BRUNEI	Bandar Seri Begawan	284,653	71.10	25.2	77	$9,000	235
THE MIDDLE EAST							
IRAN	Tehran	65,615,474	65.66	60.2	54	$4,780	63
IRAQ	Baghdad	19,889,666	65.74	67.1	60	$2,000	72
SAUDI ARABIA	Riyadh	18,196,783	67.91	52.1	62	$11,000	266
SYRIA	Damascus	14,886,672	66.46	42.5	64	$5,700	60
YEMEN	Sanaa	11,105,202	51.47	112.8	38	$800	27
ISRAEL	Jerusalem	5,050,850	77.96	8.6	92	$13,350	269
JORDAN	Amman	3,961,194	71.85	32.3	80	$3,000	80
LEBANON	Beirut	3,620,395	69.35	39.5	80	$1,720	325
UNITED ARAB EMIRATES	Abu Dhabi	2,791,141	72.26	21.7	68	$24,000	109
KUWAIT	Kuwait	1,819,322	74.99	12.5	73	$15,100	281
OMAN	Muscat	1,701,470	67.79	36.7	NA	$10,000	762
WEST BANK		1,443,790	70.39	33.8	NA	$2,050	NA
GAZA STRIP		731,296	67.78	36.9	NA	$1,275	NA
CYPRUS	Nicosia	730,084	76.22	9.0	94	G.$11,390 *T. $3,130	141
BAHRAIN	Manama	585,683	73.51	19.0	77	$12,000	402
QATAR	Doha	512,779	72.64	21.6	76	$17,500	514

* Cyprus is divided by Greek and Turkish control.

SOURCE: *World Fact Book,* Central Intelligence Agency, 1994; *Statistical Yearbook,* United Nations, 1992.

TRAVELER'S GUIDE

TRAVEL WARNINGS: Within the past year, the U.S. State Department has issued travel warnings for Afghanistan, Iran, Iraq, Lebanon, North Korea, Tajikistan, and Yemen. American citizens in Iran have been detained without charge and harassed by authorities. Call the Bureau of Consular Affairs for updates, ☎ 202-647-5225.

VISAS: Most Asian countries require visas, and some require onward/return tickets in addition to, or instead of, visas. A few also require AIDS tests for those seeking work or resident visas. U.S. passports are not valid for travel in, to, or through Iraq without State Department authorization. Check with the relevant embassies for current visa info before traveling to any country of Asia or the Middle East.

VACCINATIONS: Although no vaccines are required for travel direct from the United States, some Asian and Middle Eastern countries require yellow fever certificates when entering from infected areas. Malaria is widespread in Asia, primarily in rural areas. When traveling in Azerbaijan, Iraq, Saudi Arabia, Syria, Tajikistan, southeastern Turkey and the United Arab Emirates, prophylaxis with chloroquine should suffice. However, owing to the presence of chloroquine-resistant malaria strains, the Centers for Disease Control (CDC) recommends prophylaxis with mefloquine in Afghanistan, Bangladesh, Bhutan, Burma, Cambodia, China, India, Indonesia, Iran, Laos, Malaysia, Nepal, Oman, Pakistan, Papua New Guinea, Philippines, Sri Lanka, Thailand, Vietnam, and Yemen. Call the CDC's automated travelers' hotline at ☎ 404-332-4559 for updated country recommendations.

WORLD WATCHER'S GUIDE

VITAL FACTS: INSIDE ASIA & THE MIDDLE EAST TODAY

Many Asian countries are flirting with democracy, but heavy-handed governments are the norm. Many countries of Asia, the Middle East, and the former Soviet Union lack political and social stability. The most-spoken single language is Chinese, with more than a billion speakers of its many dialects. Asia and the Middle East have given birth to all of the worlds major religions, including Buddhism, Christianity, Hinduism, and Judaism.

COUNTRY Date of Independence • From **Form of Government** *Dominant Religion* **Official Language** Currency

NORTHERN AND CENTRAL ASIA

JAPAN 660 B.C. • Trad. founding by Emperor Jimmu **Const. monarchy** *Shintoism/Buddhism* **Japanese** yen

CHINA 221 B.C./Feb. 12, 1912/Oct. 1, 1949 • Unified under Qin Dynasty/Republic est./People's Republic est. **Communist state** *Taoism/Buddhism* **Standard Chinese/Mandarin** yuan

NEPAL 1768 • Unified by Prithvi Narayan Shah **Parliamentary democracy** *Hinduism* **Nepali** Nepalese rupee

TAIWAN Oct. 10, 1911 **Multiparty democratic regime** *Buddhism/Confucianism/Taoism* **Mandarin Chinese/Taiwanese** New Taiwan dollar

ARMENIA May 28, 1918/Sep. 23, 1991 • First Armenian Republic/Soviet Union **Republic** *Armenian Orthodox* **Armenian** dram

AFGHANISTAN Aug. 19, 1919 • UK **Transitional** *Islam* **Pashtu/Afghan Persian** afghani

MONGOLIA March 13, 1921 • China **Republic** *Tibetan Buddhism* **Khalkha Mongol** tushrik

TURKEY Oct. 29, 1923 • Successor state to the Ottoman Empire **Republican parliamentary democracy** *Islam* **Turkish** Turish lira

NORTH KOREA Aug. 15, 1945/Sep. 9, 1948 • Japan/Russia **Communist state** *Buddhism/Confucianism* **Korean** • North Korean won

SOUTH KOREA Aug. 15, 1948 • none **Republic** *Christianity/Buddhism* **Korean** South Korean won

PAKISTAN Aug. 14, 1947 • UK **Republic** *Islam* **Urdu/English** Pakistani rupee

INDIA Aug. 15, 1947 • UK **Federal republic** *Hinduism* **Hindi/Bengali/Telugu/Marathi/Tamil/Urdu/Gujarat i/Malayalam/Kannada/Oriya/Punjabi/Sindhi/Sanskrit/Assamese/Kashmiri/English** Indian rupee

SRI LANKA Feb. 4, 1948 • UK **Republic** *Buddhism* **Sinhala** Sri Lankan rupee

BHUTAN Aug. 8, 1949 • India **Monarchy; special treaty with India** *Lamaistic Buddhism* **Dzongkha** ngultrum

MALDIVES July 26, 1965 • UK **Republic** *Islam* **Divehi** rufiya

BANGLADESH Dec. 16, 1971 • Pakistan **Republic** *Islam* **Bangla** taka

GEORGIA April 9, 1991 • Soviet Union **Republic** *Georgian Orthodox* **Georgian** coupons (lari to come)

RUSSIA Aug. 24, 1991 • Soviet Union **Federation** *Russian Orthodox* **Russian** ruble

AZERBAIJAN Aug. 30, 1991 • Soviet Union **Republic** *Islam* **Azeri** manat

KYRGYZSTAN Aug. 31, 1991 • Soviet Union **Republic** *Islam* **Kirghiz** som

UZBEKISTAN Aug. 31, 1991 • Soviet Union **Republic** *Islam* **Uzbek** som

TAJIKISTAN Sep. 9, 1991 • Soviet Union **Republic** *Islam* **Tajik/Russian** ruble

TURKMENISTAN Oct. 27, 1991 • Soviet Union **Republic** *Islam* **Turkmen** manat

KAZAKHSTAN Dec. 16, 1991 • Soviet Union **Republic** *Islam/Russian Orthodox* **Kazakh/Russian** tenge

WORLD WATCHER'S GUIDE

COUNTRY	Date of Independence • From	**Form of Government**	*Dominant Religion*	**Official Language**	Currency
HONG KONG	Dependent territory of UK	**Scheduled to revert to China in 1997**	*Eclectic mixture of local religions*	**Cantonese/English**	Hong Kong dollar
MACAU	Dependent territory of Portugal	**Scheduled to revert to China in 1999**	*Buddhism*	**Portuguese/Cantonese**	pataca
SOUTHEAST ASIA					
THAILAND	1238 • Never colonized	**Const. monarchy**	*Buddhism*	**Thai**	baht
INDONESIA	Aug. 17, 1945 (proclaimed independence)/ Dec. 27, 1949 (full independence) • The Netherlands	**Republic**	*Islam*	**Bahasa Indonesia**	Indonesian rupiah
VIETNAM	Sep. 2, 1945 • France	**Communist state**	*Buddhism/Taoism/Catholicism*	**Vietnamese**	new dong
PHILIPPINES	July 4, 1946 • United States	**Republic**	*Catholicism*	**Philipino**	Philippine peso
BURMA	Jan. 4, 1948 • UK	**Military regime**	*Buddhism*	**Burmese**	kyat
LAOS	July 19, 1949 • France	**Communist state**	*Buddhism*	**Lao**	new kip
CAMBODIA	Nov. 9, 1949 • France	**Multiparty liberal democracy under a const. monarchy established in Sep. 1993**	*Buddhism*	**Khmer**	new riel
MALAYSIA	Aug. 31, 1957 • UK	**Const. monarchy**	*Islam/Buddhism/Hinduism*	**Malay**	ringgit
SINGAPORE	Aug. 9, 1965 • Malaysia	**Republic within commonwealth**	*Buddhism/Islam/Christianity/Hinduism/Sikhism/Taoism/Confucianism*	**Chinese/Malay/Tamil/English**	Singapore dollar
BRUNEI	Jan. 1, 1984 • UK	**Const. sultanate**	*Islam*	**Malay**	Bruneian dollar
THE MIDDLE EAST					
OMAN	1650 • Expulsion of Portuguese	**Monarchy**	*Islam*	**Arabic**	Omani rial
SAUDI ARABIA	Sep. 23, 1932 • Unification of the kingdom	**Monarchy**	*Islam*	**Arabic**	Saudi riyal
IRAQ	Oct. 3, 1932 • League of Nations/U.K. admin.	**Republic**	*Islam*	**Arabic/Kurdish**	Iraqi dinar
LEBANON	Nov. 22, 1943 • League of Nations/French admin.	**Republic**	*Islam*	**Arabic/French**	Lebanese pound
SYRIA	April 17, 1946 • League of Nations/French admin.	**Republic/mil. regime**	*Islam*	**Arabic**	Syrian pound
JORDAN	May 25, 1946 • League of Nations/U.K. admin.	**Const. monarchy**	*Islam*	**Arabic**	Jordanian dinar
ISRAEL	May 14, 1948 • League of Nations/U.K. admin.	**Republic**	*Judaism*	**Hebrew/Arabic**	new Israeli shekel
CYPRUS	Aug. 16, 1960 • UK	**Republic**	*Greek Orthodox*	**Greek/Turkish**	Cypriot pound
KUWAIT	June 19, 1961 • UK	**Nominal const. monarchy**	*Islam*	**Arabic**	Kuwaiti dinar
BAHRAIN	Aug. 15, 1971 • UK	**Traditional monarchy**	*Islam*	**Arabic**	Bahraini dinar
QATAR	Sep. 3, 1971 • UK	**Traditional monarchy**	*Islam*	**Arabic**	Qatari riyal
UNITED ARAB EMIRATES	Dec. 2, 1971 • UK	**Federation**	*Islam*	**Arabic**	Emirian dirham
IRAN	April 1, 1979 • Islamic Republic of Iran proclaimed	**Theocratic republic**	*Islam*	**Persian**	Iranian rial
YEMEN	May 22, 1990 • Merger of North Yemen (independent in Nov. 1918 from Ottoman Empire) and South Yemen (independent in Nov. 1967 from UK)	**Republic**	*Islam*	**Arabic**	Yemeni rial
WEST BANK & GAZA STRIP	May 4, 1994 • Cairo Agreement transferred limited powers to the Palestinian authority from Israel	**Interim self-government**	*Islam*	**Arabic**	new Israeli shekel

SOURCE: *World Fact Book*, Central Intelligence Agency, 1994.

HUMAN RIGHTS WATCH

Burma's house arrest •China's hard line • Iraq's crackdown

BURMA: Arbitrary detention and torture are common. Freedom of association, expression, and assembly are severely limited. Democratic opposition leader and Nobel Laureate Aung San Suu Kyi remains under house arrest, and many of those speaking out for her release have been arrested. Trafficking of Burmese women into sex slavery in Thailand and other Asian countries is prevalent.

CHINA: Human rights in China have been deteriorating progressively ever since President Clinton renewed China's most favored nation trading status without insisting that the Chinese show progress on human rights. Torture and beatings are common in prisons, and freedom of association, expression, assembly, and religion are severely restricted.

INDIA: Discriminatory arrests throughout the country continue unabated as security forces cite the powers granted them by the controversial Terrorists and Disruptive Activities (TADA) law. In Kashmir, Indian forces have executed detainees, killed civilians in reprisal attacks, and burned down neighborhoods and villages as punishment for suspected militants.

IRAN: Tens of thousands of Christians, Jews, and Bahais have left Iran over the past 15 years, but those who have stayed have been direct targets of government abuse. Iranian Kurds face fierce persecution and members of Kurdish opposition groups are periodically assassinated by security forces. Villages in Iraq, where Iranian Kurds had taken refuge, have been destroyed by Iranian shelling.

IRAQ: In response to rising crime, the government has established new cruel and extreme punishments, said to be founded on Islamic law. First-time convicts guilty of stealing cars and other property valued over 5,000 dinars ($15 U.S.) must have their right hands amputated and an "X" tattooed on their foreheads. Military deserters must have their earlobes amputated and their foreheads tattooed. Shi'a Muslims, which make up about 55 percent of the Iraqi population, are excluded from government by the ruling Baath party.

SAUDI ARABIA: Especially for political prisoners, arbitrary arrest, detention without trial, and torture are common. Authorities extract information from prisoners by using electric shock, falaqa (beating on the soles of the feet), and flogging with bamboo sticks. Convicted drug traffickers, almost all foreigners, are typically beheaded. Most do not get access to legal representation at trial. To rein in Islamic opposition groups who are critical of the government, a strict ban on public speaking, assembly, and association is enforced.

FORMER SOVIET REPUBLICS: Civil war and repression of political dissent are the rule. In Uzbekistan and Turkmenistan, for example, former communist leaders stifle dissent by censoring the press, prohibiting free expression and association, and keeping dissenters under constant surveillance. Armed conflict has continued in, among other areas, parts of Tajikistan and Azerbaijan.

SYRIA: A state of emergency, imposed in 1963, remains in effect, giving security forces wide powers of detention without charge. However, political dissidents have been released from prison, some having been held without charge or trial for more than 20 years. The government also has been lifting restrictions on freedom of movement for the small Jewish community by granting exit visas.

SOURCE: *World Report,* Human Rights Watch, 1995.

EUROPE

TIMELINE

CAN EUROPE GET IT TOGETHER?

With the fall of the Berlin Wall, Germany is unified. Is Europe next?

For the last quarter century, the search for European unity and the failure of communism in the Eastern Bloc nations have shaped European politics. Economically, the continent is more united than ever. The 1993 enactment of the Maastricht Treaty for European Unity was a giant step forward, making it easier to transport produce and manufactured goods across national borders.

Political union is proving more elusive, however. The fall of communism has been a boon to Eastern Bloc countries such as Poland and Hungary. But elsewhere the glue of communism has given way to chaos. The civil war ravaging the former Yugoslavia has proved a Gordian knot for European diplomats, who have been unable to agree on any plan—military or diplomatic—to stop the carnage. Commentators say that the continent's multi-ethnic, multicultural makeup makes continued factional violence almost inevitable.

1970—FOOD RIOTS PLAGUE POLAND. Price increases on meat products spur widespread unrest. Riots in Gdansk soon spread to neighboring cities. The government responds to riots in Szczecin with tanks. Ten days after the price increases are instituted, the party reshuffles its leadership and declares food prices frozen for two years.

1972-74—BRITAIN OCCUPIES NORTHERN IRELAND. Severe civil unrest leads the British government to assume direct rule over Northern Ireland and suspend the constitution. British Prime Minister Edward Heath declares that British forces will remain in Northern Ireland until innocent people are no longer terrorized by extremist Catholics or Protestants.

Increased terrorist attacks in England by the Irish Republican Army (IRA) trigger the British Parliament to pass the Prevention of Terrorism Act, which gives police added powers of arrest, detention, and expulsion. The new law also bans the IRA and forbids the wearing of any IRA symbols such as the black beret.

1977-78—ITALY BREAKS FROM VATICAN. Italian authorities and the Roman Catholic Church agree to end the classification of Roman Catholicism as the national religion. The agreement revokes the status granted the church in 1929 by Benito Mussolini.

In 1978, controversial legislation allowing free abortion on demand to women over 18 becomes law in Italy. Some Roman

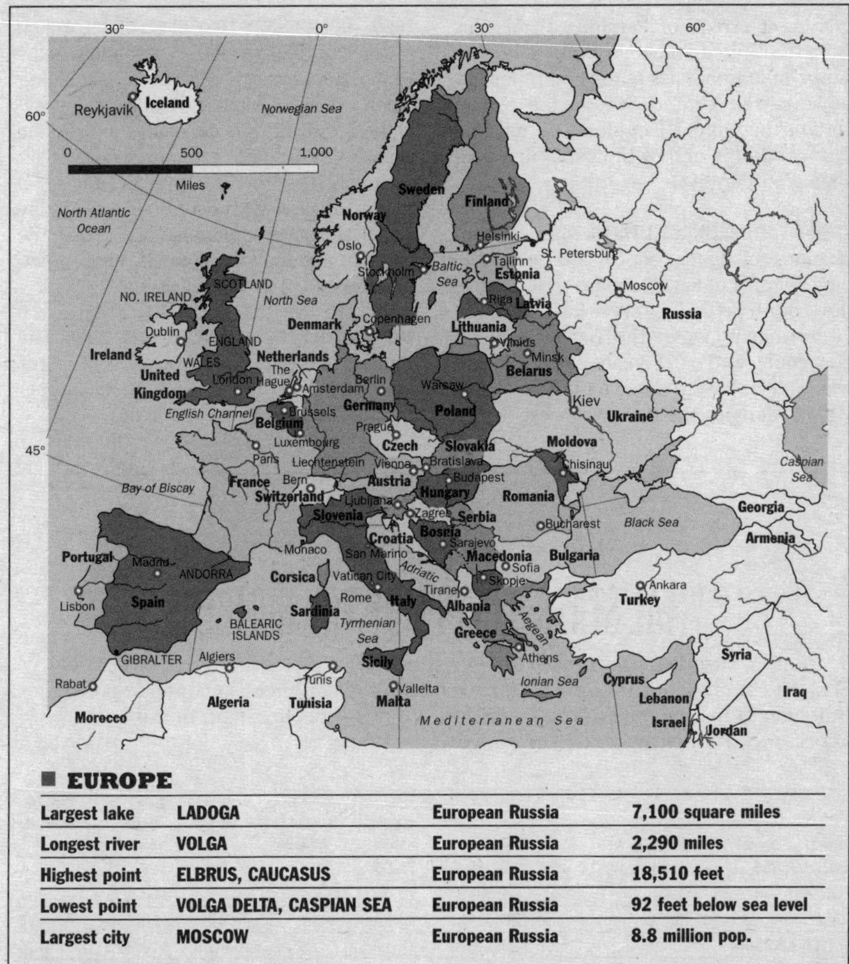

■ EUROPE

Largest lake	**LADOGA**	**European Russia**	**7,100 square miles**
Longest river	**VOLGA**	**European Russia**	**2,290 miles**
Highest point	**ELBRUS, CAUCASUS**	**European Russia**	**18,510 feet**
Lowest point	**VOLGA DELTA, CASPIAN SEA**	**European Russia**	**92 feet below sea level**
Largest city	**MOSCOW**	**European Russia**	**8.8 million pop.**

Catholic doctors take advantage of a special clause allowing them to opt out of the new plan on grounds of conscience.

1980—YUGOSLAVIA'S TITO DIES. When Yugoslavia's strong leader Marshal Tito dies in May, commentators speculate about how the multi-ethnic, autonomous communist state will survive without him. By the early 1990s, ethnic differences prove too strong, resulting in bloody wars and the break up of the country into Bosnia and Herzegovina, Croatia, Serbia and Montenegro, Slovenia, and the Former Yugoslav Republic of Macedonia.

1981—FRANCE ELECTS A SOCIALIST PRESIDENT. Marking a major turning point in French history, Francois Mitterrand becomes the nation's 21st president and the first socialist president ever to be elected by universal suffrage. During Mitterrand's first year in power, the National Assembly abolishes the death penalty, decreases the number of nuclear power plants to be built in France, and votes to nationalize major industries, private banks, and two finance companies.

1983—GREENS RALLY IN GERMANY. Antinuclear advocates stage massive demonstrations in West Germany to protest the imminent arrival of Pershing II missiles from the United States. In Bonn, a human chain links embassies of the major nuclear powers—the United States, the Soviet Union, the United Kingdom, China, and France. By the end of the year, nine missiles are operative.

1989—THE BERLIN WALL FALLS. Mass demonstrations calling for political change and the huge number of East Germans trying to flee the country finally force East German authorities to open the Berlin Wall on November 9. "For 28 years since the wall was built we have yearned for this day," says Walter Momper, the mayor of West Berlin.

1990—COMMUNISTS LOSE IN CZECHOSLOVAKIA. Following 1989's "velvet" revolution, parliamentary elections give the largest voting block to Civic Forum, the leader of the revolution, and its Slovak equivalent, Public against Violence. The communist party is left with only 47 of the Federal Assembly's 300 seats. Together with new President Vaclav Havel, the government begins planning the move to a market economy through privatization and price liberalization.

1994—WAR IN BOSNIA AND HERZEGOVINA. The gruesome war between Bosnian Muslims and Serbs continues, with Serbs perpetrating the bulk of the atrocities.

GLOBE TROTTER'S GUIDE

VITAL STATS: EUROPE BY THE NUMBERS

It's no real surprise, given the relatively short time since democracy swept over Eastern Europe, that Western Europe remains the continent's economic power. But even in the poorer eastern countries, literacy rates are high, and life expectancy hovers around 70 or above.

Country	Capital	Population	Life expectancy at birth (in years)	Infant mort. (deaths/1,000 live births)	Literacy (as % of pop.)	GDP/capita (in U.S. dollars)	TVs/1,000 inhabitants
UNITED STATES	Washington, D.C.	260,713,585	75.90	8.1	97	$24,700	814
GERMANY	Berlin	81,087,506	76.34	6.5	99	$16,500	556
ITALY	Rome	58,138,394	77.64	7.6	97	$16,700	421
UNITED KINGDOM	London	58,135,110	76.75	7.2	99	$16,900	434
FRANCE	Paris	57,840,445	78.19	6.6	99	$18,200	407
UKRAINE	Kiev	51,846,958	69.99	20.7	100	$3,960	487
SPAIN	Madrid	39,302,665	77.71	6.9	95	$12,700	400
POLAND	Warsaw	38,654,561	72.66	13.1	98	$4,680	295
ROMANIA	Bucharest	23,181,415	71.74	19.9	98	$2,700	196
NETHERLANDS	Amsterdam[1]	15,367,928	77.75	6.1	99	$17,200	485
SERBIA AND MONTENEGRO	Belgrade	10,093,314 (S) 666,583 (M)	73.39 (S) 79.44 (M)	21.4 (S) 10.8 (M)	NA	$1,000	NA
GREECE	Athens	10,564,630	77.71	8.6	93	$8,900	197
PORTUGAL	Lisbon	10,524,210	75.20	9.5	85	$8,700	187
CZECH REPUBLIC	Prague	10,408,280	73.08	9.3	NA	$7,200	476
BELARUS	Minsk	10,404,862	70.88	18.9	100	$5,890	NA
HUNGARY	Budapest	10,319,113	71.37	12.5	99	$5,500	412
BELGIUM	Brussels	10,062,836	76.96	7.2	99	$17,700	451
BULGARIA	Sofia	8,799,986	73.24	12.0	93	$3,800	252
SWEDEN	Stockholm	8,778,461	78.25	5.7	99	$17,600	468

GLOBE TROTTER'S GUIDE

Country	Capital	Population	Life expectancy at birth (in years)	Infant mort. (deaths/1,000 live births)	Literacy (as % of pop.)	GDP/capita (in U.S. dollars)	TVs/1,000 inhabitants
AUSTRIA	Vienna	7,954,974	76.65	7.1	99	$17,000	478
SWITZERLAND	Bern	7,040,119	78.17	6.5	99	$21,300	406
SLOVAKIA	Bratislava	5,403,505	72.81	10.4	NA	$5,800	NA
DENMARK	Copenhagen	5,187,821	75.81	6.9	99	$18,500	536
FINLAND	Helsinki	5,068,931	75.93	5.3	100	$16,100	501
CROATIA	Zagreb	4,697,614	73.60	8.7	NA	$4,500	221
BOSNIA AND HERZEGOVINA	Sarajevo	4,651,485	75.13	12.7	NA	NA	NA
MOLDOVA	Chisinau	4,473,033	68.07	30.3	100	$3,650	NA
NORWAY	Oslo	4,314,604	77.38	6.3	99	$20,800	423
LITHUANIA	Vilnius	3,848,389	71.24	16.7	98	$3,240	374
IRELAND	Dublin	3,539,296	75.68	7.4	98	$13,100	276
ALBANIA	Tirane	3,374,085	73.40	30.0	72	$1,100	87
LATVIA	Riga	2,749,211	69.44	21.5	100	$4,810	NA
MACEDONIA	Skopje	2,213,785	73.59	27.8	NA	$1,000	NA
SLOVENIA	Ljubljana	1,972,227	74.36	8.1	NA	$7,600	284
ESTONIA	Tallinn	1,616,882	69.96	19.1	100	$5,480	347
LUXEMBOURG	Luxembourg	401,900	76.69	6.8	100	$22,600	267
MALTA	Valletta	366,767	76.77	7.9	84	$6,600	742
ICELAND	Reykjavik	263,599	78.83	4.0	100	$16,000	319
ANDORRA	Andorra La Vella	63,930	78.37	7.9	NA	$14,000	154
GIBRALTAR	Gibraltar[2]	31,684	76.33	8.1	NA	$4,600	316
MONACO	Monaco	31,278	77.69	7.2	NA	$16,000	819
LIECHTENSTEIN	Vaduz	30,281	77.46	5.3	100	$22,300	345
SAN MARINO	San Marino	24,091	81.23	5.6	96	$16,000	351
HOLY SEE	Vatican City	821	NA	NA	NA	NA	NA

1. The Hague is seat of government. 2. Territory of UK.
SOURCE: *World Fact Book*, Central Intelligence Agency, 1994; *Statistical Yearbook*, United Nations, 1992.

TRAVELER'S GUIDE

TRAVEL WARNINGS: As this book went to press in the summer of 1995, the only U.S. State Department travel warning in effect for a European country was for Bosnia and Herzegovina because of an ongoing war there between the Bosnian Serbs and Muslims. The U.S. Embassy in Sarajevo is unable to perform consular functions except in extreme emergencies.The Bureau of Consular Affairs, ☎ 202-647-5225, can provide up-to-date information.

VISAS: European countries generally do not require American citizens to have visas for tourist or business visits of less than three months. Croatia is an exception, but visas are easily obtained at the port of entry. Nonetheless, to be sure about visa requirements call the relevant embassies before you set off on a trip.

VACCINATIONS: European countries generally require no vaccinations for entry, nor do they pose malaria risks. Portugal and Greece do require a yellow fever vaccination certificate when entering from infected areas.

Call the CDC's automated travelers' hotline at ☎ 404-332-4559 for individual country recommendations.

WORLD WATCHER'S GUIDE

VITAL FACTS: INSIDE EUROPE TODAY

The tiny state of San Marino has been indendent since 301; the Czech Republic gained its independence in 1993. A lot of history lies in between.The people of Europe speak nearly as many languages as there are countries on the continent. Christianity, the continent's dominant religion, serves as a common thread.

COUNTRY	Date of Independence • From	**Form of Government**	*Dominant Religion*	**Official Language**	Currency
SAN MARINO	301 • By tradition	**Republic**	*Catholicism*	**Italian**	Italian lire
FRANCE	486 • Unified by Clovis	**Republic**	*Catholicism*	**French**	French franc
HUNGARY	1001 • Unification by King Stephen I	**Republic**	*Catholicism*	**Hungarian**	forint
PORTUGAL	1140/Oct. 5, 1910 • By tradition/Independent republic proclaimed	**Republic**	*Catholicism*	**Portuguese**	Portuguese escudo
ANDORRA	1278 • France	**Parliamentary democracy**	*Catholicism*	**Catalan**	French franc
SWITZERLAND	Aug. 1, 1291	**Federal republic**	*Christianity*	**German/French/Italian**	Swiss franc
MONACO	1419	**Const. monarchy**	*Catholicism*	**French**	French franc
SPAIN	1492 Expulsion of Moors and unification	**Parliamentary monarchy**	*Catholicism*	**Spanish**	peseta
NETHERLANDS	1579 • Spain	**Const. monarchy**	*Christianity*	**Dutch**	Netherlands guilder
LIECHTENSTEIN	Jan. 23, 1719 • Imperial Principality est.	**Hered. const. mon.**	*Catholicism*	**German**	Swiss franc
UNITED KINGDOM	Jan. 1, 1801 • UK est.	**Const.monarchy**	*Christianity*	**English**	British pound
SWEDEN	June 6, 1809 • Const. monarchy est.	**Const. monarchy**	*Christianity*	**Swedish**	Swedish krona
GREECE	1829 • Ottoman Empire	**Presidential parliamentary**	*Greek Orthodox*	**Greek**	drachma
BELGIUM	Oct. 4, 1830 • The Netherlands	**Const. monarchy**	*Catholicism*	**Dutch/French**	Belgian franc
LUXEMBOURG	1839	**Const. monarchy**	*Catholicism*	**Luxembourgisch**	Luxembourg franc
DENMARK	1849 • Became a const. monarchy	**Const. monarchy**	*Christianity*	**Danish**	Danish krone
ITALY	March 17, 1861 • Kingdom of Italy proclaimed	**Republic**	*Catholicism*	**Italian**	Italian lira
GERMANY	Jan. 18, 1871 • German Empire unification	**Fed. Republic**	*Christianity*	**German**	deutsche mark
ROMANIA	1881 • Turkey (republic declared Dec. 30, 1947)	**Republic**	*Romanian Orthodox*	**Romanian**	leu
NORWAY	Oct. 26, 1905 • Sweden	**Const. monarchy**	*Christianity*	**Norwegian**	Norwegian krone
BULGARIA	Sept. 22, 1908 • Ottoman Empire	**Emerging democracy**	*Bulgarian Orthodox*	**Bulgarian**	leu
ALBANIA	Nov. 28, 1912 Ottoman Empire	**Nascent democracy**	*Islam*	**Albanian (Tosk dialect)**	lek
FINLAND	Dec. 6, 1917 • Soviet Union	**Republic**	*Christianity*	**Finnish/Swedish**	markka
POLAND	Nov. 11, 1918 Independent republic proclaimed	**Democratic state**	*Catholicism*	**Polish**	zloty
AUSTRIA	Nov. 12, 1918 • Austro-Hungarian Empire	**Federal republic**	*Catholicism*	**German**	Austrian schilling
IRELAND	Dec. 6, 1921 • UK	**Republic**	*Catholicism*	**English/Gaelic**	Irish pound
HOLY SEE (VATICAN CITY)	Feb. 11, 1929 • Italy	**Monarchical-sacerdotal state**	*Catholicism*	**Italian**	Vatican lira
ICELAND	June 17, 1944 • Denmark	**Republic**	*Christianity*	**Icelandic**	Icelandic krona
MALTA	Sept. 21, 1964 • UK	**Parliamentary dem.**	*Catholicism*	**Maltese/English**	Maltese lira
SLOVENIA	June 25, 1991 • Yugoslavia	**Emerging democracy**	*Catholicism*	**Slovenian**	tolar

WORLD WATCHER'S GUIDE

COUNTRY	Date of Independence • From	Form of Government	Dominant Religion	Official Language	Currency
CROATIA	June 1991 • Yugoslavia	**Parliamentary democracy**	*Catholicism*	**Serbo-Croatian**	Croatian dinar
BELARUS	Aug. 25, 1991 • Soviet Union	**Republic**	*Eastern Orthodox*	**Byelorussian**	Belarussian ruble
MOLDOVA	Aug. 27, 1991 • Soviet Union	**Republic**	*Eastern Orthodox*	**Moldovan**	leu
ESTONIA	Sept. 6, 1991 • Soviet Union	**Republic**	*Christianity*	**Estonian**	Estonian kroon
LATVIA	Sept. 6, 1991 • Soviet Union	**Republic**	*Christianity*	**Lettish**	lat
LITHUANIA	Sept. 6, 1991 • Soviet Union	**Republic**	*Christianity*	**Lithuanian**	litas
MACEDONIA	Sept. 17, 1991 • Yugoslavia	**Emerging democracy**	*Eastern Orthodox*	**Macedonian**	denar
UKRAINE	Dec. 1, 1991 • Soviet Union	**Republic**	*Ukrainian Orthodox*	**Ukrainian**	coupons
SERBIA & MONTENEGRO	April 11, 1992 • Fed. Rep. of Yugoslavia formed as self-proclaimed successor to Socialist Fed. Rep. of Yugoslavia	**Republic**	*Eastern Orthodox, Islam*	**Serbo-Croatian**	Yugoslav new dinar
BOSNIA & HERZEGOVINA	April 1992 • Yugoslavia	**Emerging dem.**	*Islam, Eastern Orthodox*	**Serbo-Croatian**	dinar
CZECH REPUBLIC	Jan. 1, 1993 • Czechoslovakia	**Parliamentary democracy**	*Christianity (40% atheist)*	**Czech/Slovak**	koruna
SLOVAKIA	Jan. 1, 1993 • Czechoslovakia	**Parliamentary democracy**	*Christianity*	**Slovak**	koruna
GIBRALTAR	NA	**Territory of UK**	*Catholicism*	**English**	Gibraltar pound

SOURCE: *World Fact Book,* Central Intelligence Agency, 1994.

HUMAN RIGHTS WATCH

Bosnia's and Croatia's ethnic civil wars • Russia's appalling prisons

ALBANIA: The country has undergone radical change since democratic reforms began in 1990. But there are still serious human rights abuses.

BOSNIA-HERZEGOVINA: Abuses against Bosnia's three ethnic groups—Muslims, Serbs, and Croats—continue but the overwhelming majority are still perpetrated by Bosnian Serbs. Most of these abuses are associated with "ethnic cleansing," whose main objective is the removal of an ethnic group from a given area through murder, population exchanges, forced displacement, and terrorization.

CROATIA: There were some human rights improvements in 1994, but the government continues to evict persons living in housing formerly owned by the Yugoslav army and to impede the functioning of a free press.

THE CZECH REPUBLIC: The human rights situation has improved dramatically, but there are still concerns about the treatment of Gypsies.

RUSSIA: Symbolic and legislative progress in 1994 was overshadowed by concerns about appalling prison conditions, abuses of military draftees, and state-sponsored ethnic and gender discrimination.

FEDERAL REPUBLIC OF YUGOSLAVIA: Human rights conditions continued to deteriorate in the remains of Yugoslavia, comprising Serbia and Montenegro. Continued oppression against Sandzak Muslims and Kosovo Albanians continued, contradicting Serbian President Slobodan Milosevic's claim that "in Serbia there is no policy of ethnic discrimination."

SOURCE: *World Report,* Human Rights Watch, 1995.

OCEANIA

ISLAND NATIONS YEARN TO BE FREE

Australia dominates a region still isolated from much of the world

The white man—not the indigenous peoples of the South Pacific islands—controls Oceania today. Although some islands have gained independence in recent decades, Australia and New Zealand, each populated primarily by descendants of European settlers, dominate the region politically and economically. Both countries have been independent for nearly a century. But for some of the younger island nations, independence remains a turbulent experiment.

1970—ANTIWAR FEVER. Public opinion condemns Australia's involvement in the Vietnam War, causing the largest antiwar protest in the nation's history. Australian Labor Party opposition members and prominent clergy urge Australian youths not to register for military service. In response to the opposition, the government declines to enforce the National Service Act, which requires young people to register.

1975—PAPUA NEW GUINEA GAINS ITS FREEDOM. Papua New Guinea's governor-general lowers the Australian flag and declares the nation an independent parliamentary state and member of the Commonwealth of Nations. Papua New Guinea's leaders pledge to maintain good relations with Australia and to reach out to China. Shortly thereafter, the new minister for defense, trade and foreign relations, Sir Maori Kiki, visits Beijing.

1978—ANTI-IMMIGRANT FEVER SWEEPS AUSTRALIA. As boatloads of poor Vietnamese refugees flood the country after the fall of Saigon to the Vietcong, Australian public opinion turns against the government's liberal immigration policy. Media reports of Vietnamese refusing to learn English, receiving preferential employment treatment, and bringing existing old rivalries and conflicts with them frighten the populace.

1983-84—TROUBLE IN HAWKE'S PARADISE. Robert Hawke establishes himself as Australia's most popular prime minister ever. Public opinion polls put his popularity at 73 percent after his first year in office. But his image tarnishes when opposition politicians declare his low inflation figures are tainted by convenient miscalculations. Later, a Hawke minister is involved in a spy scandal involving secret material leaked to a Soviet diplomat. Amid a deep recession in 1991, Hawke is ousted by Paul Keating, the first time an Australian prime minister is removed from office by his own party.

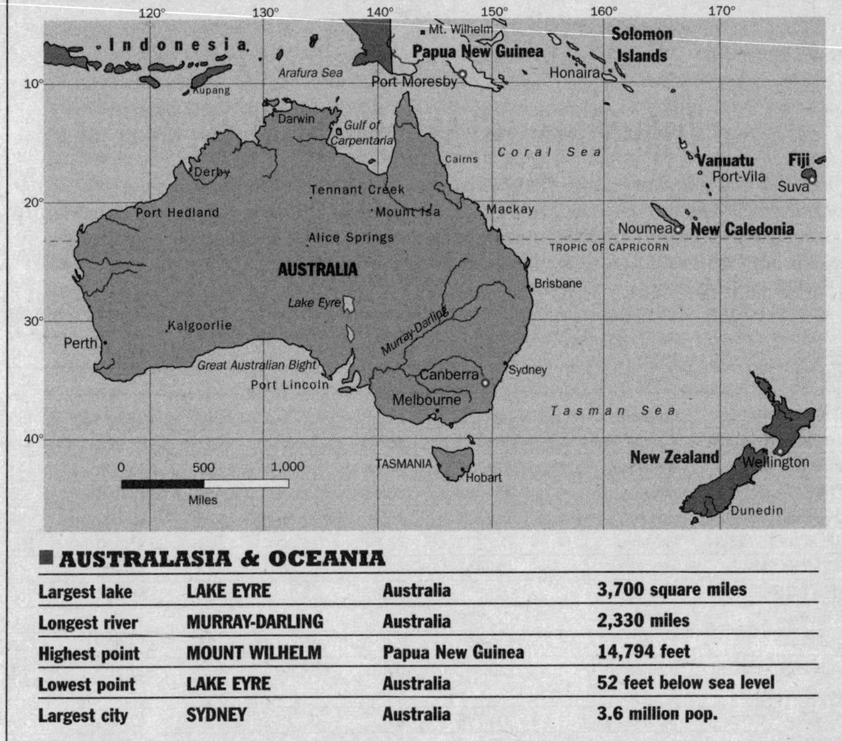

AUSTRALASIA & OCEANIA

Largest lake	**LAKE EYRE**	**Australia**	**3,700 square miles**
Longest river	**MURRAY-DARLING**	**Australia**	**2,330 miles**
Highest point	**MOUNT WILHELM**	**Papua New Guinea**	**14,794 feet**
Lowest point	**LAKE EYRE**	**Australia**	**52 feet below sea level**
Largest city	**SYDNEY**	**Australia**	**3.6 million pop.**

1985—THE RAINBOW WARRIOR BOMBED. The Rainbow Warrior, the flagship of the environment advocacy group Greenpeace, is bombed in New Zealand's Auckland Harbor. New Zealanders jail two French military agents who plead guilty to manslaughter in the incident. When France threatens to impose trade sanctions if New Zealand does not release the prisoners into French custody, both countries agree to international arbitration. In 1986, the U.N. orders the prisoners to serve their terms in French Pacific territory and demands that France formally apologize and compensate New Zealand.

1989—UNREST IN TONGA. Public dissatisfaction with the government reaches a climax when peasants' representatives stage a two-week parliamentary boycott in protest of the cabinet's refusal to boost public servant salaries. Underlying the protest is discontent with the 1875 constitution, which guarantees that the king's nominees and Tonga's nobles will dominate parliament. When they demand that more representatives be elected by popular vote, police urge citizens to respect their king, as required by law.

1991—MICRONESIA GAINS ITS INDEPENDENCE. Once known as the Caroline Islands, the Federated States of Micronesia gain independence after Fiji and 80 other countries nominate them for admission into the United Nations. Micronesia had been ruled at different times by Spain, Germany, Japan, and the United States.

1992—EXPLOSIVE BORDERS. Bougainville, legally part of Papua New Guinea but culturally part of the Solomon Islands, triggers a border dispute between the two nations when it tries to secede. When a blockade imposed on the island by Papua New Guinea is breached by the Solomon Islands, Papua New Guinean forces attack civilians across the border and destroy fuel supplies.

GLOBE TROTTER'S GUIDE

VITAL STATS: OCEANIA BY THE NUMBERS

Oceania is a checkerboard of social and economic conditions. Australia, the most populous country of the region, boasts 100 percent literacy, a low infant mortality rate, and a relatively healthy standard of living. At the same time, tiny Tuvalu has a per capita GDP lower than many African nations.

Country	Capital	Population	Life expectancy at birth (in years)	Infant mort. (deaths/1,000 live births)	Literacy (as % of pop.)	GDP/capita (in U.S. dollars)	TVs/1,000 inhabitants
UNITED STATES	Washington, D.C.	260,713,585	75.9	8.11	97	$24,700	814
AUSTRALIA	Canberra	18,077,419	77.57	7.30	100	$19,100	480
PAPUA NEW GUINEA	Port Moresby	4,196,806	56.43	63.30	52	$2,000	2
NEW ZEALAND	Wellington	3,388,737	76.38	8.90	99	$15,700	443
FIJI	Suva	764,382	65.14	18.10	86	$4,000	15
SOLOMON ISLANDS	Honiara	385,811	70.48	27.80	NA	$2,500	NA
FRENCH POLYNESIA [1]	Papeete	215,129	70.54	14.80	98	$7,000	169
WESTERN SAMOA	Apia	204,447	67.97	37.00	97	$2,000	40
NEW CALEDONIA [1]	Noumea	181,309	73.62	15.10	91	$6,000	268
VANUATU	Port-Vila	169,776	59.25	68.10	53	$1,050	9
GUAM [2]	Agana	149,620	74.29	15.17	96	$14,000	658
FEDERATED STATES OF MICRONESIA	Kolonia	120,347	67.63	37.24	90	$1,500	NA
TONGA	Nuku'alofa	104,778	67.97	20.79	57	$2,000	NA
KIRIBATI	Tarawa	77,853	54.16	98.40	NA	$525	NA
AMERICAN SAMOA [2]	Pago Pago	55,223	72.91	18.78	97	$2,600	213
MARSHALL ISLANDS	Majuro	54,031	63.13	49.30	93	$1,500	NA
N. MARIANA ISLANDS [3]	Saipan	49,799	67.43	37.96	97	$11,500	NA
PACIFIC IS. PALAU [4]	Koror	16,366	71.01	25.07	92	$2,260	NA
NAURU	Yaren district [5]	10,019	66.68	40.60	NA	$10,000	NA
TUVALU	Funafuti	9,831	63.03	27.30	NA	$700	NA

1. Overseas Department of France. 2. U.S. Territory. 3. Commonwealth in political union with U.S. 4. U.S.-administered UN trusteeship. 5. No official capital; government offices in Yaren district. SOURCE: *World Fact Book*, CIA, 1994; *Statistical Yearbook*, United Nations, 1992.

■ TRAVELER'S GUIDE

TRAVEL WARNINGS: Within the past year or so, no official travel warnings have been issued for this region. For recorded updates, call the Department of State Bureau of Consular Affairs at ☎ 202-647-5225.

VISAS: Australia and Nauru require visas and onward/return tickets. Nauru also requires sponsorship from a Nauru resident. Kiribati requires a visa only. Other countries in the region generally require no visa for tourist stays.

VACCINATIONS: Australia and many Oceania countries require yellow fever vaccination certificates when traveling from infected countries. Although malaria generally is not a problem in the region, Vanuatu and the Solomon Islands have chloroquine-resistant strains of malaria. The Centers for Disease Control (CDC) recommend prophylaxis with mefloquine in these countries.

Call the CDC's automated travelers' hotline at ☎ 404-332-4559 for updated country recommendations.

OCEANIA

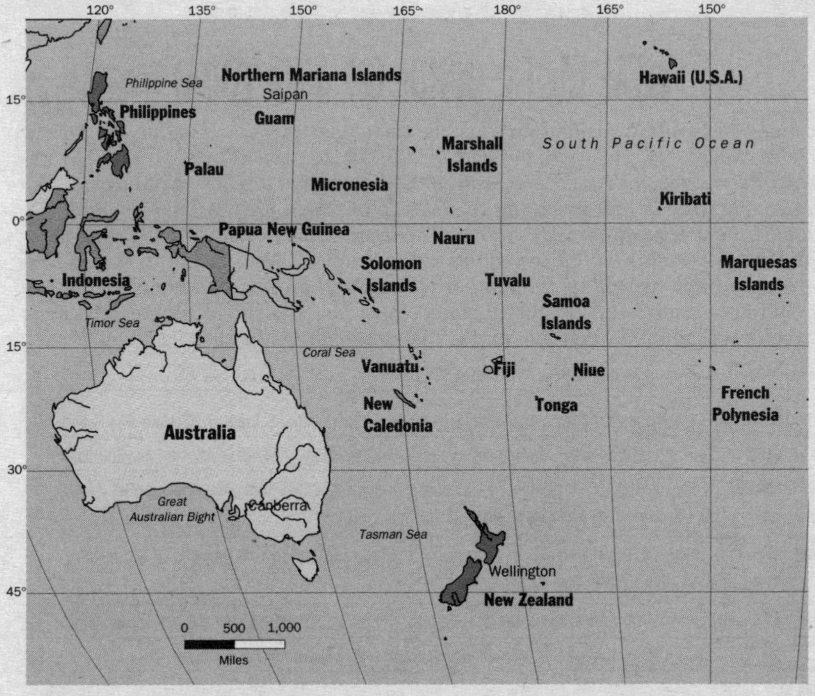

SIZING UP OCEANIA'S COUNTRIES AND TERRITORIES

Country	Area in sq. kilometers	Relative size
AUSTRALIA	7,686,850	Slightly smaller than the United States
NEW ZEALAND	268,680	About the size of Colorado
SOLOMON ISLANDS	28,450	Slightly larger than Maryland
NEW CALEDONIA	19,060	Slightly smaller than New Jersey
FIJI	18,270	Slightly smaller than New Jersey
VANUATU	14,760	Slightly larger than Connecticut
FRENCH POLYNESIA	3,941	Slightly less than one-third the size of Connecticut
WESTERN SAMOA	2,860	Slightly smaller than Rhode Island
TONGA	748	Slightly more than 4 times the size of Washington, D.C.
KIRIBATI	717	Slightly more than 4 times the size of Washington, D.C.
FEDERAL STATES OF MICRONESIA	702	Slightly less than 4 times the size of Washington, D.C.
GUAM	541.3	Slightly more than 3 times the size of Washington, D.C.
NORTHERN MARIANA ISLANDS	477	Slightly more than 2.5 times the size of Washington, D.C.
PACIFIC ISLANDS/PALAU	458	Slightly more than 2.5 times the size of Washington, D.C.
AMERICAN SAMOA	199	Slightly larger than Washington, D.C.
MARSHALL ISLANDS	181	Slightly larger than Washington, D.C.
TUVALU	26	About one-tenth the size of Washington, D.C.
NAURU	21	About one-tenth the size of Washington, D.C.

SOURCE: *World Factbook*, Central Intelligence Agency, 1994.

WORLD WATCHER'S GUIDE

VITAL FACTS: INSIDE OCEANIA TODAY

For many of Oceania's island nations, independence has come within the last two decades. Several islands remain territories, some controlled by the United States. French Polynesia and New Caledonia are still overseas territories of France. More than 25,000 islands (not including the islands of Japan, the Philippines, and Indonesia) are spread across Oceania. The area includes the world's smallest continent (Australia), and large island groups such as New Zealand, Papua New Guinea, and Fiji, as well as three other main island groups—Micronesia, Melanesia, and Polynesia. Island tribal languages and customs still exist, but English is the region's dominant language and Christianity its dominant religion.

COUNTRY	Date of Independence • From	**Form of Government**	*Dominant Religion*	**Official Language**	Currency
AUSTRALIA	Jan. 1, 1901 • UK	**Fed. parliamentary state**	*Christianity*	**English**	Australian dollar
NEW ZEALAND	Sept. 26, 1907 • UK	**Parliamentary dem.**	*Christianity*	**English**	New Zealand dollar
WESTERN SAMOA	Jan. 1, 1962 • UN trusteeship under New Zealand	**Const. monarchy under native chief**	*Christianity*	**Samoan/English**	tala
NAURU	Jan. 31, 1968 • UN trusteeship under Australia, New Zealand, and UK	**Republic**	*Christianity*	**Nauruan**	Australian dollar
TONGA	June 4, 1970 • UK	**Hereditary const. monarchy**	*Christianity*	**Tongan/English**	pa'anga
FIJI	Oct. 10, 1970 • UK	**Republic**	*Christianity/Hinduism*	**English**	Fijian dollar
PAPUA NEW GUINEA	Sept. 16, 1975 • UN trusteeship under Australia	**Parliamentary democracy**	*Christianity*	**Pidgin English**	Kina
SOLOMON ISLANDS	July 7, 1978 • UK	**Parliamentary dem.**	*Christianity*	**Melanesian**	Solomon Islands dollar
TUVALU	Oct. 1, 1978 • UK	**Democracy**	*Christianity*	**Tuvaluan/English**	Tuvaluan dollar
KIRIBATI	July 12, 1979 • UK	**Republic**	*Christianity*	**English**	Australian dollar
VANUATU	July 30, 1980 • France and UK	**Republic**	*Christianity*	**English/French**	vatu
MARSHALL ISLANDS	Oct. 21, 1986 • UN trusteeship under U.S.	**Const. government in free association with the U.S.**	*Christianity*	**English**	U.S. dollar
FEDERATED STATES OF MICRONESIA	Nov. 3, 1986 • UN trusteeship under U.S.	**Const. government in free association with the U.S.**	*Christianity*	**English**	U.S. dollar
AMERICAN SAMOA	NA	**Territory of U.S.**	*Christianity*	**Somoan/English**	U.S. dollar
FRENCH POLYNESIA	NA	**Territory of France**	*Christianity*	**French/Tahitian**	CFP franc[1]
GUAM	NA	**Territory of U.S.**	*Catholicism*	**English/Chamorro/Japanese**	U.S. dollar
NEW CALEDONIA	NA	**Overseas dept. of France**	*Catholicism*	**French**	CFP franc[1]
NORTHERN MARIANA ISLANDS	NA	**Commonwealth in political union with the U.S.**	*Catholicism*	**English/Chamorro/Carolinian**	U.S. dollar
PACIFIC ISLANDS (PALAU)	NA	**UN trusteeship under U.S.**	*Christianity*	**English/Sonsorolese/Angaur/Japanese/Tobi/Palauan**	U.S. dollar

1. Comptoirs Francais du Pacifique Franc.

SOURCE: *World Fact Book*, Central Intelligence Agency, 1994.

CHAPTER FOURTEEN

FACTS FOR LIFE

EXPERT QUOTES

"A two-day weather forecast is as accurate as a one-day forecast was 20 years ago."

—Fred Gadomski, meteorologist, Penn State University

Page 902

"A lot of people ask, 'What power is that telescope?' Actually, magnification is irrelevant."

—John Shibley, editor, *Astronomy* magazine

Page 913

"In a right triangle, the square of the hypotenuse is equal to the sum of the squares of the other two sides."

—Pythagoras, Greek philosopher and mathematician

Page 950

THE YEAR AHEAD: **EXPECT** *The Old Farmer's Almanac* weather forecast to be about as accurate as flipping a coin... **LOOK FOR** lunar eclipses on April 4 and September 27, 1996... **DO YOUR BEST** surf fishing when tidal currents are strongest... **ENJOY** an extra day for Leap Year in 1996... **DON'T** use call-waiting if you want to be polite... **START** tracing your family roots in time for your next family reunion...

WEATHER

FORECASTS

RAIN TODAY, SUN TOMORROW

Short-term predictions are much improved, say the weather pros

The days when you could claim that a flare-up of an old sports injury was a better barometer of weather changes than the forecasts provided by your local television station are fast-disappearing. Experts report that in recent years there have been significant improvements in 6- to 48-hour forecasts. "A two-day forecast is as accurate as a one-day forecast was 20 years ago," says meteorologist Fred Gadomski of Penn State University.

Meteorologists developing one- to two-day forecasts have become quite skilled at predicting whether or not storms are on the way, thanks to better short-term modeling techniques. But major errors still occur in predicting weather events that sit on the cusp between rain and snow. David Olson, Chief of the National Weather Service's Weather Forecast Branch in Camp Springs, Md., says, "We can generally narrow the rain-snow line to some tens of miles, but to say that the southern suburbs of Boston will be rain and the northern suburbs will be snow is slicing it pretty thin."

The National Weather Service's three-to-five day forecasts have also gotten better in the last decade due to improvements in meteorologists' ability to predict flow and pressure patterns in the middle part of the atmosphere. But measuring the accuracy of many types of forecasts can be very tricky. "If I say there's going to be increasing cloudiness with rain before sunset, how do you measure this forecast's accuracy?" asks Gadomski of Penn State. "It's almost impossible to put a number on publicly worded forecasts that have so much going on."

Even when forecasters predict the course of an upcoming weather event accurately, they may still have difficulty pinpointing the time of arrival. Meteorologist Walter Drag, of the National Weather Service's Taunton, Mass., branch, says that he always hesitates to recommend that people call off their plans for a Saturday afternoon picnic on the basis of a prediction made on the Tuesday before. "It may end up that the rain comes 12 hours earlier or 12 hours later," Drag says.

Even more challenging is predicting the weather months in advance. Each month, forecasters at the National Weather Service's Climate Analysis Center in Camp Springs issue a forecast of average climatic conditions for the upcoming year. The Weather Service doesn't try to predict individual storms, but does try to forecast whether the months ahead will bring above- or below-average temperature and rainfall. The suc-

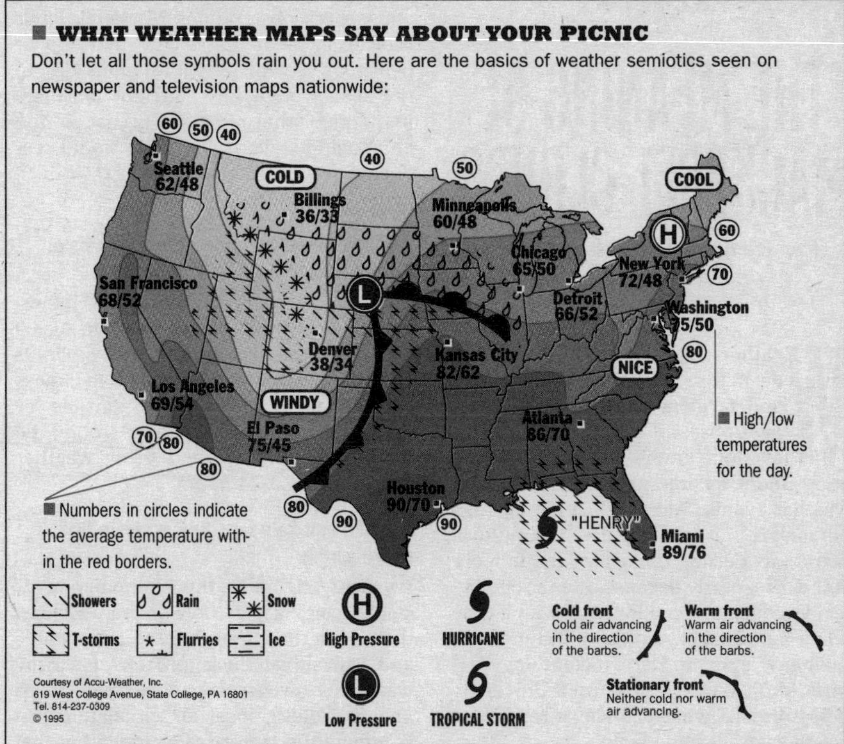

cess rates of these forecasts are just slightly better than flipping a coin, according to Kerry Emanuel, a meteorologist at the Massachusetts Institute of Technology. S. P. Huug Vandendool, chief of the Climate Analysis Center's prediction branch, estimates that the National Weather Service's temperature forecasts are correct 60 to 65 percent of the time, while its precipitation forecasts are correct 55 to 60 percent of the time.

To be more accurate would be like trying to predict the exact landing spot of a piece of paper held horizontally and then released, explains Emanuel. Not even the best aerodynamicists could accurately predict where the paper would land, he says. "It isn't because they don't understand the laws of physics, but because the results are so unbelievably sensitive to the exact position and orientation of when you let it go."

The ultimate goal of long-range weather forecasting is to provide people and governments with time to prepare for severe climatic changes. For instance, knowing that the warming of the tropical Pacific known as El Niño is on the way could prepare people on the West Coast for a tough winter of flooding and mud slides, explains Columbia University meteorologist Yves M. Tourre. Forecasters may also be able to prepare farmers for future droughts, Tourre says.

The National Weather Service would be content to be able to predict general climatic conditions up to a year in advance with 70 percent accuracy. It is counting on powerful computer models incorporating ever-more data from ocean, land, and atmosphere to bring about such progress. That would be a sea change, suggests Huug Vandendool of the Weather Service's Climate Analysis Center. Twenty years ago, he points out, most people thought the weather was driven by something in the atmosphere. Only recently have people begun to realize the oceans' influence on the weather around us.

FOLKLORE

THE MEANING OF MACKEREL CLOUDS

The science behind the farmer's and sailor's maxims

Weather folklore has been passed down through the ages by mariners and farmers who relied on their own observations of astronomical events, animal behaviors, and atmospheric changes to predict upcoming weather events. Today, while the average person's ability to observe the natural world has declined, much of the folklore still exists, partly because of a psychological yearning to keep in touch with a time when humans seemed more in tune with their environment. Here, meteorology lecturer Mark Wysocki of Cornell University helps discern what of today's remaining weather lore is still viable.

■ Red sky at night, sailors delight. Red sky in the morning, sailor take warning.

Much of the weather folklore based on observations of atmospheric phenomena is a fairly good predictor of short-range weather changes, Wysocki says. In the mid-latitude regions, the general flow of storm systems follows the jet stream from west to east. The red color at night is due to the reflection of the red colors from the sun as it lowers in the western sky. This signals that the jet stream has pushed the storm systems out of your area. If clouds appear red in the morning, this means that the sun is rising in clear skies to the east with clouds approaching from the west, indicating the storm system is to your west and moving your way.

■ Mackerel clouds in the sky, expect more wet than dry.

Wysocki cites this as another good example of accurate weather folklore based on atmospheric observations. Mackerel clouds refer to cirrocumulus clouds that appear pearly white with scaly formations akin to the scales on a fish. Ancient mariners knew that these clouds presaged the approach of a warm front that would produce rain or snow within the next 12 to 18 hours, Wysocki says.

■ When round the moon there is a halo, the weather will be cold and rough.

The halo, according to Wysocki, is generated by cirrostratus clouds 15,000 to 20,000 feet up in the atmosphere. These clouds cover large areas with a uniform thickness of ice crystals, which are responsible for many optical wonders. A halo around the moon generally means stormy weather within the next 24 hours.

■ When smoke hangs low, a storm is approaching.

Wysocki attributes the phenomenon of smoke hanging low to low-pressure systems that cause the atmosphere to be unstable and can signal the approach of stormy weather. However, sometimes near lakes and in valleys, local air circulation can dominate the larger-scale circulation that can give a false reading, he warns.

■ When hornets build their nest close to the ground, expect a hard winter.

Folklore that deals with animals and long-term weather forecasts generally is false, says Wysocki. He believes that if people observed the hornet's activities over a long period of time, they would find no correlation between the hornet's behavior and seasonal forecasts. The same is true for folklore which links a squirrel's very bushy tail or a large black band on a woolly-bear caterpillar with an upcoming severe winter.

■ If bees stay at home, rain will soon come.

Wysocki likens this folklore to stories that associate approaching storms with ants lining up to go back to their nest, cows lying down in a field, and frogs singing more than usual. He admits that these examples are difficult to prove or disprove, because scientists can't isolate what in the environment would be causing these behaviors. However, he says he would have to err on the side of bee keepers who swear by the ability of their bees to predict rain. With cows, though, he jokingly asks, "If 25 cows are lying down in a field, and 25 are standing up, does this mean there's a fifty percent chance of rain?"

■ Crickets are a poor man's thermometer.

Counting the chirps of a cricket, Wysocki asserts, is an accurate way of determining temperatures above 40 degrees Fahrenheit. Below 40 degrees, a cricket's metabolism is too slow. To get the current air temperature within one degree Fahrenheit, count the number of chirps in a 14-second period and then add 40 to this number.

■ The air smells sweet before a storm.

Science definitely has an explanation for this folklore, Wysocki says. Before a storm, lower pressure predominates, which causes plants' stomatic openings to enlarge and emit more gases, including ones that are aromatic.

■ When human hair becomes limp, rain is near.

Human hair—especially blond hair—becomes thicker and longer when exposed to increases in humidity, which sometimes mean rain is near. In fact, says Wysocki, early hygrometers designed to determine the moisture content of the air relied on measuring the changes in the length of a human hair.

■ Sinus and joint pain signals stormy weather.

This folklore, at least for arthritis sufferers, has been proved to signal rapid changes in the weather, says Wysocki. Pressure changes, the cause of the pain, signal the unstable atmospheric conditions that typically precede a storm.

FLIPPING A COIN WITH THE OLD FARMER'S ALMANAC

For centuries, farmers' almanacs have made extravagant claims for their ability to make long-term weather predictions. Not only are farmers said to plant their crops according to their favorite almanac's advice, but even city dwellers are impressed by the annual forecasts of such stalwart practitioners of the art as *The Old Farmer's Almanac*, published continuously since 1792. When *The Old Farmer's Almanac* predicted heavy snowfall in the Northeast for the winter of 1994–95, sales of snow shovels and snow tires are reported to have boomed. But how do *The Old Farmer's Almanac*'s long-term forecasts measure up to those of the National Weather Service meteorologists at the Climate Analysis Center in Camp Springs, Md.?

The almanac predicts general climatic data for each month of the year, but unlike the National Weather Service, it tries to predict specific weather events in two- to three-day time periods. The almanac's own full-time meteorologist relies on solar activity as the major indicator of future weather conditions. Its publisher, John Pierce, says, "If we believe there'll be a storm of significant magnitude, we would predict it. Otherwise we might just say rain or snow."

Pierce can't cite success rates for the almanac's forecasts, but Kerry Emanuel, of the Massachusetts Institute of Technology believes that to accurately gauge the almanac's success, one would have to track many of its forecasts over many seasons. "*The Old Farmer's Almanac* isn't showing skill by that measure," Emanuel says. "That doesn't mean that it's not occasionally right. It's right about as often as it's wrong."

A University of Illinois study supports this claim: Between November 1975 and October 1980, the almanac's temperature forecasts proved accurate 53.2 percent of the time; its precipitation forecasts were right 51.5 percent of the time.

WEATHER WATCHER'S GUIDE

SUNNY OR COLD, WINDY OR WET

W. C. Fields may have made jokes about Philadelphia, but there are a lot worse places in the United States when it comes to weather. For a coast-to-coast tour of the weather horizon, see the following breakdown of recent weather patterns in selected major American cities.

City	Average annual sunshine (%)	Mean days below freezing	AVERAGE ANNUAL TEMPERATURE (F)		Average annual rain (in.)	AVERAGE RELATIVE HUMIDITY (%)					
						Annual		January		July	
			High	Low		a.m.	p.m.	a.m.	p.m.	a.m.	p.m.
Albany, N.Y.	52	14.9	58.1	36.6	36.17	79	57	76	63	84	55
Albuquerque, N.M.	76	11.9	70.1	42.2	8.88	60	29	70	40	60	27
Atlanta, Ga.	61	5.3	71.2	51.3	50.77	77	56	74	59	85	60
Atlantic City, N.J.	56	11.0	63.2	42.8	40.29	82	56	76	58	87	57
Baltimore, Md.	57	9.7	65.0	45.2	40.70	75	54	69	57	81	53
Bismarck, N.D.	59	18.6	53.8	29.4	15.47	74	56	75	66	74	46
Boise, Idaho	64	12.4	62.8	39.1	12.11	69	43	81	70	54	21
Boston, Mass.	58	9.8	59.0	43.6	41.51	72	58	65	57	77	56
Buffalo, N.Y.	49	13.2	55.8	39.5	38.58	79	63	77	72	79	55
Burlington, Vt.	49	15.5	54.0	35.2	34.47	77	59	70	63	82	53
Charleston, W.V.	40	10.0	65.8	44.2	42.53	79	56	74	63	90	60
Charlotte, N.C.	63	6.6	70.4	49.7	43.09	76	54	72	56	83	57
Cheyenne, Wyo.	65	17.2	58.0	33.2	14.40	65	44	57	50	70	35
Chicago, Ill.	54	13.3	58.6	39.5	35.82	77	60	75	67	79	56
Cincinnati, Ohio	52	10.8	63.2	43.2	41.33	77	59	75	67	83	57
Cleveland, Ohio	49	12.3	58.7	40.5	36.63	77	62	75	69	81	57
Columbia, S.C.	64	6.0	75.1	50.9	49.91	83	51	78	54	87	54
Columbus, Ohio	49	11.9	61.2	41.6	38.09	77	59	74	67	82	56
Concord, N.H.	54	17.3	57.0	33.1	36.37	82	54	74	58	90	51
Dallas-Fort Worth, Texas	63	4.0	76.3	54.6	33.70	72	56	73	60	67	49
Denver, Colo.	70	15.7	64.2	36.2	15.40	67	40	63	49	68	34
Des Moines, Iowa	59	13.5	59.8	40.0	33.12	75	60	74	67	76	57
Detroit, Mich.	53	13.6	58.1	39.0	32.62	79	60	78	69	81	53
Duluth, Minn.	52	18.5	47.9	29.0	30.0	77	63	74	70	82	59
El Paso, Texas	84	6.5	77.5	49.0	8.81	57	28	66	35	63	30
Great Falls, Mont.	61	15.7	56.4	33.1	15.21	67	45	66	60	66	29
Hartford, Conn.	56	13.5	60.2	39.5	44.14	76	52	69	56	82	51
Honolulu, Hawai'i	69	0	84.4	70.0	22.02	76	56	81	61	73	51
Houston, Texas	56	2.1	78.6	57.3	46.07	86	60	82	64	86	58
Indianapolis, Ind.	55	11.8	62.1	42.4	39.94	80	62	78	70	84	59
Jackson, Miss.	60	5.0	76.4	52.0	55.37	87	58	84	65	90	59
Jacksonville, Fla.	63	1.5	78.9	57.1	51.32	86	56	85	57	88	58
Juneau, Alaska	30	14.1	46.9	34.1	54.31	86	73	81	77	87	70

■ WEATHER WATCHER'S GUIDE

City	Average annual sunshine (%)	Mean days below freezing	AVERAGE ANNUAL TEMPERATURE (F)		Average annual rain (in.)	AVERAGE RELATIVE HUMIDITY (%)					
						Annual		January		July	
			High	Low		a.m.	p.m.	a.m.	p.m.	a.m.	p.m.
Kansas City, Mo.	62	11.0	63.6	43.7	37.62	74	59	72	63	75	56
Little Rock, Ark.	62	6.0	72.5	51.0	50.86	79	57	76	61	83	56
Los Angeles, Calif.	73	0	70.4	55.5	12.01	79	64	70	59	86	68
Louisville, Ky.	56	8.9	66.0	46.0	44.39	76	58	72	64	81	58
Memphis, Tenn.	64	5.7	72.1	52.4	52.10	76	57	75	63	79	57
Miami, Fla.	72	0	82.8	69.0	55.91	81	61	81	59	82	63
Milwaukee, Wis.	54	14.1	54.3	37.9	32.93	78	64	75	68	80	61
Minn.-St. Paul, Minn.	58	15.6	54.3	35.3	28.32	73	60	72	67	74	54
Mobile, Ala.	59	2.2	77.4	57.4	63.96	83	57	79	61	87	60
Nashville, Tenn.	56	7.6	69.8	48.4	47.30	79	57	75	63	85	57
New Orleans, La.	59	1.3	77.6	58.5	61.88	85	63	82	66	89	66
New York, N.Y.	58	7.9	62.3	47.4	47.25	70	56	65	60	74	55
Norfolk, Va.	61	5.4	67.8	50.6	44.64	78	57	72	59	84	59
Oklahoma City, Okla.	NA	7.7	71.1	48.8	33.36	72	54	72	59	70	49
Omaha, Neb.	60	14.1	61.5	39.5	29.86	76	59	75	65	78	57
Peoria, Ill.	57	12.9	60.4	41.0	36.25	79	62	78	68	82	59
Philadelphia, Pa.	56	9.7	63.4	45.1	41.41	76	55	71	59	81	54
Phoenix, Ariz.	86	0.8	85.9	59.3	7.66	51	23	66	32	45	20
Pittsburgh, Pa.	46	12.3	59.9	40.7	36.85	75	57	73	65	80	54
Portland, Maine	57	15.7	54.9	35.8	44.34	82	59	74	60	89	59
Portland, Ore.	48	4.3	62.6	44.5	36.30	86	60	86	75	82	45
Providence, R.I.	58	11.8	59.8	41.0	45.53	76	55	69	56	83	56
Raleigh, N.C.	59	7.8	70.1	48.4	41.43	80	54	73	55	88	58
Reno, Nev.	79	17.4	66.8	34.7	7.53	70	31	79	50	63	18
Richmond, Va.	62	8.5	68.8	46.6	43.16	82	53	77	57	88	56
Sacramento, Calif.	78	1.7	73.5	48.1	17.52	82	45	90	70	76	28
Salt Lake City, Utah	66	12.5	63.6	40.3	16.18	67	43	79	69	52	22
San Diego, Calif.	68	0	70.8	57.6	9.90	76	62	70	56	82	66
San Francisco, Calif.	NA	0.2	65.2	49.0	19.70	84	62	86	66	86	59
San Juan, P.R.	66	0	86.4	74.0	52.34	83	65	82	64	84	67
Sault Ste. Marie, Mich.	47	18.1	49.6	29.8	34.23	85	67	81	75	90	61
Seattle-Tacoma, Wash.	46	3.1	59.4	44.6	37.19	83	62	81	74	82	49
Sioux Falls, S.D.	63	16.8	56.8	34.2	23.86	76	60	75	68	75	53
Spokane, Wash.	54	13.9	57.5	36.9	16.49	78	52	85	78	64	27
St. Louis, Mo.	57	10.0	65.4	46.7	37.51	76	59	77	66	77	56
Washington, D.C.	56	7.0	66.9	49.2	38.63	72	53	67	55	77	53
Wichita, Kan.	65	11.1	67.4	45.0	29.33	73	55	76	63	67	48
Wilmington, Del.	NA	10.0	63.6	44.8	40.84	78	55	73	60	83	54

SOURCE: *Statistical Abstract of the United States*, U.S. Department of Commerce, 1994.

KNOW WHICH WAY THE WIND BLOWS

Forecast the weather by gauging changes in atmospheric pressure

With a simple aneroid barometer, available at a local hardware store or marine supply center, you can make fairly accurate short-range weather predictions for $10 to $50. Generally, when the barometer is high and rising, it means high pressure is approaching. High pressure systems typically are associated with fair weather—light and variable winds, dry air, and temperatures below seasonal averages. When the barometer is low and falling, it typically means low pressure is on the way. Low pressure systems tend to bring inclement weather—strong winds, high humidity, clouds, and storm fronts.

An aneroid barometer has one pointer, similar to the hand on a clock, which measures atmospheric pressure in inches of mercury and another pointer which is used to reference pressure changes. Rising pressure causes the reading pointer to move clockwise, while falling pressure causes it to move counterclockwise.

Once or twice a day, the reference pointer should be placed to correspond with the reading pointer. Over the course of the day, you can track pressure changes by noting how the reading pointer moves in relation to the reference hand.

To ensure accurate readings, aneroid

BE YOUR OWN FORECASTER

Basic barometer reading for amateur meteorologists

Barometer reduced to sea level	Wind direction	Character of weather indicated
30.10 to 30.20 and steady	SW to NW	Fair with slight temperature changes for one to two days.
30.10 to 30.20 and rising rapidly	SW to NW	Fair followed within two days by warmer air and rain.
30.10 to 30.20 and falling slowly	SW to NW	Warmer with rain in 24 to 36 hours.
30.10 to 30.20 and falling rapidly	SW to NW	Warmer with rain in 18 to 24 hours.
30.20 and above and stationary	SW to NW	Continued fair with no decided temperature change.
30.20 and above and falling slowly	SW to NW	Slowly rising temperature and fair for two days.
30.10 to 30.20 and falling slowly	S to SE	Rain within 24 hours.
30.10 to 30.20 and falling rapidly	S to SE	Wind increasing in force with rain within 12 to 24 hours.
30.10 to 30.20 and falling slowly	SE to NE	Increasing wind with rain within 12 hours.
30.10 and above and falling slowly	E to NE	In summer with light winds, rain may not fall for several days. In winter rain within 24 hours.
30.10 and above and falling rapidly	E to NE	In summer rain probable within 12 to 24 hours. In winter rain or snow, with increasing winds will often set in.
30 or below and falling slowly	SE to NE	Rain will continue one to two days.
30 or below and falling rapidly	SE to NE	Rain with high wind, followed within 24 hours by clearing and cooler.
30 or below and rising slowly	S to SW	Clearing within a few hours, continued fair for several days.
29.80 or below and falling rapidly	S to E	Severe storm of wind and rain or snow imminent, followed within 24 hours by clearing and colder.
29.80 or below and falling rapidly	E to N	Severe northeast gales and heavy rain or snow, followed in winter by a cold wave.
29.80 or below and rising rapidly	Going to W	Clearing and colder.

barometers, and even some electronic barometers, occasionally need to be calibrated. A call to the local branch of the Weather Service or listening to the weather report on TV provides the current pressure adjusted to what it would read at sea level. Adjustments should be made on days with settled winds, which usually indicate the pressure is changing slowly.

Many amateur forecasters find useful the following chart, which bases its weather predictions on barometric changes and wind direction. However, meteorologists caution these are general rules that don't hold true for all locations and situations. For example, west winds off the Great Lakes can bring terrible lake-effect snows even when the barometer is high. Similarly, in the Northeast near the Atlantic Ocean, a sea breeze can bring cooler air, clouds, drizzle, and fog when the pressure is high.

STAYING WARM IF THE AIR IS FRIGID

Layer yourself with the new synthetics for maximum protection

Whether you're out skiing the slopes, shoveling the driveway, or just walking to work, there is a science to keeping your body warm in freezing temperatures. Heat loss is directly proportionate to the amount of body surface that you expose to the environment. Frostbite occurs when unprotected parts of the body such as your face

WHEN PUTTING A FINGER TO THE WIND WON'T DO

The Beaufort Scale of Wind Effects can help you estimate wind speed from simple observations. It also gives the basis for converting the wind descriptions used in weather reports to wind speed equivalents, and vice versa.

Wind speed (mph)	Beaufort number	Wind effect on land	Official description
Less than 1	0	Calm; smoke rises vertically.	LIGHT
1 to 3	1	Wind direction is seen in direction of smoke but is not revealed by weather vane.	LIGHT
4 to 7	2	Wind can be felt on face; leaves rustle; wind vane moves.	LIGHT
8 to 12	3	Leaves, small twigs in motion; wind extends light flag.	GENTLE
13 to 18	4	Wind raises dust, loose papers. Small branches move.	MODERATE
19 to 24	5	Small trees with leaves begin to sway; crested wavelets appear on inland waters.	FRESH
25 to 31	6	Large branches move; telegraph wires whistle; umbrellas become difficult to control.	STRONG
32 to 38	7	Whole trees sway, walking into the wind becomes difficult.	STRONG
39 to 46	8	Twigs break off trees; cars veer in roads.	GALE
47 to 54	9	Slight structural damage occurs; roof slates may blow away.	GALE
55 to 63	10	Trees are uprooted; considerable structural damage is caused.	WHOLE GALE
64 to 72	11	Widespread damage is caused.	WHOLE GALE
73 or more	12	Widespread damage is caused.	HURRICANE

or fingers freeze. As the body's temperature drops below 95 degrees Fahrenheit, some body systems are affected. Below 90 degrees Fahrenheit the body's shivering ability ceases and the body cannot warm itself without outside help. Unless you act quickly, hypothermia can set in. That's when the heart rate slows, blood pressure falls, and a person drops into a semi-comatose, then comatose state.

Dr. Warren Bowman, a physician at the Billings Clinic in Montana and a specialist in high-altitude and cold-weather care, has these tips on avoiding the problem.

■ **Wear clothing made of appropriate fabrics.** Of all the things to do, the most energy-efficient is to use proper clothing and shelter. But you have to use the right fabrics. Cotton is bad. Wool and some of the newer synthetics are better. Among your choices: polypropylene, a treated polyester; Thermax, a hollow polyester; and garments filled with a stuffing-like down such as Dacron.

FACT FILE:

FOR ACCURATE WEATHER

■ *Predicting temperature accurately is more difficult in the cool season than in the summer. That's because weather systems are stronger and move quickly in winter, leading to greater temperature variability.*

■ *In predicting precipitation, forecasts generally are less accurate when the weather is warm. Most precipitation in the warm season comes from showers and thunderstorms, which occur randomly, cover small areas, and don't last long. In winter, precipitation usually results from weather systems that cover larger areas and last many hours or days, and thus is easier to predict.*

■ **Layer your clothing.** Instead of wearing one or two thick layers, wear three, four, or five thin layers to avoid overheating. Garments lose their insulating ability when you sweat. Depending on how cold it is and what the wind chill is, an inner layer of long underwear made of wool, polypropylene, or Thermax may be a good idea. Duofold is a fabric with a cotton and a wool layer. It is good for skiing, but for any other use it's not as good as Capilene or polypropylene.

The second layer should consist of pants and a shirt made of wool or some kind of artificial fabric like acrylic. Third would be a pile jacket and pants. The fourth layer would be windproof—a Gortex parka and pants, for example. A fifth layer would include a ski jacket filled with down or synthetics and a pair of quilted pants. And your feet need a pair of boots with up to three pairs of wool socks, maybe with an inner sock of polypropylene. And don't forget a ski cap and mittens, preferably one of the three-layer systems. This should take care of you down to about 40 below zero.

■ **Fortify yourself with extra calories.** The amount of heat from a hot cup of tea is not much. An instant breakfast, powdered eggnog, or a pack of Jello makes a very nice drink and packs a lot of calories, which your body needs in cold weather.

■ **Pay special attention to children.** Babies have a large surface area compared to their volume, so they lose heat very quickly. Children also tend to lose heat faster than adults. They are not careful about keeping mittens and hats on and have to be supervised so their heads, hands, ears, and feet stay warm.

■ **In the event of hypothermia, get the victim out of the cold and to the hospital quickly.** Do not use a stove, electric blankets, or a hot tub to warm someone up. They can cause dangerous physiological changes. At the hospital, a victim can be warmed using special hypothermia blankets, warmed IV's, and humidified oxygen. In severe cases cardiopulmonary bypass or dialysis can even be used to warm the patient from the inside-out.

WEATHER HOTLINES

DIAL M FOR METEOROLOGY

Call a 900 number to get good weather information—for a fee

People planning vacations or business trips and who need accurate weather reports and forecasts for their travel destinations can turn to 900-number hotlines, the best of which are sponsored by the Weather Channel, *USA Today,* the Weather Radio Network, and Accu-Weather. All of these hotlines describe a selected city's weather conditions, including forecasts that range from three to seven days.

Both the Weather Channel and *USA Today* outdo the other services by providing the most information. Those traveling by car can find out about conditions on major highways surrounding a selected city. International travelers can use these hot lines to learn about visa requirements, tipping customs, currency exchange rates, and State Department travel advisories. Unlike *USA Today,* the Weather Channel sponsors a marine report of interest to beach-goers and boaters that includes tide information, wave heights, and water temperatures. The Weather Channel also presents slope conditions at over 400 ski areas. *USA Today*'s weather line even tries to give the traveler the chance of rain on any given date in any city.

Accu-Weather's advantage over the other hotlines is its simplicity. Callers can get good, basic weather information, and since there are fewer options, the call is shorter and so costs less money. All three services take about one and a half to two minutes on average to present a standard weather report and 36-hour forecast.

The National Radio Network is unique among weather hotlines in that it allows the caller to listen to live radio broadcasts from 85 local offices of the National Weather Service. The National Weather Service updates these weather reports every hour, which is just as often as many of the other services update their information. However, the reports become more frequent when weather conditions become particularly troublesome. Therefore, the caller can almost be guaranteed to get the most recent information on public warnings during hurricanes, floods, and tornadoes. This number provides detailed weather information, but because it is not menu driven, the caller who wants a basic weather report might have to listen to marine or road conditions before getting to the weather broadcast. On average, the calls last about 3.8 minutes.

WEATHER HOTLINES

The following hotlines can provide the current time, temperature, humidity, wind and sky conditions, and, of course, tomorrow's forecast in distant cities.

HOTLINE	Cost per minute	Number of cities	Wind chill	Barometric pressure	Dew point	Extended forecast	Driving conditions	Marine report	Ski report
Accu-Weather ☎ 900-329-2228	$.95	2,000+	Yes	No	No	3 days	No	No	No
USA Today ☎ 900-555-5555 ☎ 800-872-8632[1]	$.95	700+	Yes	Yes	No	4 days	Yes	No	No
Weather Channel ☎ 900-932-8437 ☎ 800-932-8437[1]	$.95	825+	Yes	Yes	Yes	7 days	Yes	Yes	Yes
Weather Radio Network ☎ 900-884-6622[2]	$.98	85	No	Yes	No	4 days	Yes	Yes	No

1. These services provide 800-numbers that debit credit cards at the same rate.
2. The Weather Radio Network offers discount rates of $.85 to subscribers who can access the line with an 800-number. Data may vary from radio broadcast to radio broadcast.

STARS & TIDES

STARGAZING

A MULTITUDE OF WONDERS

Every civilization has scanned the heavens for clues to the Creation

The next time you peer at the night sky and spot the North Star or the Big Dipper, think of the ancient Babylonians, Egyptians, and Mayans doing the same thing. Written records of astronomical findings and theories go back to the dawn of history.

The first students of astronomy were probably the Chinese. It is said that in 2159 B.C. two Chinese astronomers, Hi and Ho, were executed for failing to predict an eclipse. Scientists now say that the two could have been spared if the official calendar had been more accurate. By 750 B.C., the Chinese were keeping accurate records of meteors, and an astronomer named Shih Shen prepared what was probably the earliest star catalogue around 350 B.C.

The Babylonians and Assyrians knew the approximate length of the year several centuries before the birth of Christ. In pre-Christian Egypt, where the astronomers were priests, the main purpose of astronomy was to keep a calendar. Both the Egyptians and Babylonians learned to build fairly accurate sundials for timekeeping. The earliest Egyptian sundial, still preserved today, is from the eighth century, B.C.

The Greeks took their study of the heavens a step further than the Chinese and the Egyptians by trying to explain what they saw. The great Greek astronomer Thales, born in 624 B.C., introduced geometric concepts into astronomy and may have realized that the earth is a globe. His contemporary, Anaximander, may have been the first to speculate on the relative distances of the sun, the moon, and the planets. Aristotle argued against the traditional theory that the earth is flat. He recognized the changing shape of the moon during the month and considered the possibility that the earth revolves around the sun rather than the sun around the earth.

The Greek astronomer Ptolemy was the first to calculate the distance to the moon, in about 140 B.C., using a technique that is essentially the same as the one used today. The next astronomical leaps forward came from the Hindus, who developed our current system of numbers and place counting, and the Arabs, who took the Hindu number system and developed algebra. The Arab astronomer Muhammad al Battani, working in the late ninth and early 10th cen-

EXPERT TIPS

BUYING YOUR FIRST SCOPE

A telescope need not have high magnifying power or be expensive to allow you to see every planet in the solar system, It's the size of the lens aperture and the instrument's portability that count. John Shibley, an editor at Astronomy *magazine and author of that publication's annual telescope buyer's guide, has these tips on equipping yourself to scan the heavens.*

■ **Focus on a telescope's lens size.** A lot of people ask, "What power is that scope?" Actually, magnification is irrelevant. What matters is the amount of light a telescope gathers, which depends on the size of the mirror that brings light to a focus or the size of the lens itself. The bigger the mirror or the lens, the fainter the objects you'll be able to see and the better the resolution. If you don't have a large aperture, you crank up the magnification and it just ends up stretching an image that isn't any good to begin with.

■ **Start with a reflecting scope.** There are two types of telescopes: reflecting and refracting. A reflecting telescope costs about half as much as a comparable-sized refracting telescope—it is excellent for star and nebulae observations and for use in astrophotography. The refracting telescope tends to distort images less and is good for lunar and solar observation. It can distort color, though, and can be difficult to move, which may turn off beginners.

■ **Know your mounts.** A scope in the $300 to $500 range has a Dobsonian mount, which means the scope can be pivoted up and down and left and right but can't be calibrated to line up with the earth's axis so that it automatically follows the stars. More expensive scopes come with equatorial mounts—they're the ones that actually track the sky.

■ **Get several eyepieces.** Usually you want to get three eyepieces. That's because observing the moon requires a low magnification, planets a medium magnification, and the stars a high magnification. Any eyepiece with a focal length in the upper 20s to lower 30s in millimeters is considered low-powered; from the mid-teens to the lower 20s is medium-powered. Anything lower than 13 mm is high-powered. Having more than one eyepiece allows you to adjust to atmospheric changes that may make objects look blurry.

tury, A.D., predicted eclipses and compiled tables of the sun's and planets' positions.

It took Nicolaus Copernicus, a 16th-century Polish scientist, to argue scientifically that the earth and other planets revolve around the sun and not the other way around, as people before then believed. Copernicus's theory of the solar system was embraced by the Italian scientist, Galileo Galilei, who built a powerful telescope for studying the moon and the planets in the early 17th century, and figured out that gravity pulls a light object to Earth as fast as a heavy one. Galileo was followed by Isaac Newton, who built the first reflecting telescope and firmly established the role of gravity in the laws of motion. Newton also figured out that white light is a blend of all the colors of the rainbow. Knowing that, scientists today are able to study the composition of stars by analyzing the spectrum of light that they give off.

STAR GAZER'S GUIDE

THE CELESTIAL HIGHLIGHTS OF 1996

The best celestial events of the year, according to Geoff Chester, of the Albert Einstein Planetarium in the National Air and Space Museum of the Smithsonian Institution, will be the lunar eclipses on April 4 and September 27. April's eclipse will be partly visible from the eastern United States. September's can be enjoyed from anywhere in the country. Chester's recommendations for other celestial highlights in 1996 follow. Times are expressed in Universal Time (UT), an astronomy standard that is five hours ahead of Eastern Standard Time.

JANUARY 2. Mercury attains greatest eastern elongation (it reaches point in orbit farthest from the sun.)

FEBRUARY 2. Venus closest to Saturn this evening, in the southwest sky in the hour after sunset.

FEBRUARY 15. Moon near Jupiter this morning.

MARCH 14. Moon again near Jupiter this morning.

MARCH 20. Vernal equinox arrives at 8:04 UT.

MARCH 22. Moon near Venus this evening.

MARCH 31. Venus shines high in the western sky in the hour after sundown. It will be easy to spot until late May.

APRIL 4. Total lunar eclipse is partly visible in the eastern United States. Moon contacts umbra (the dense part of the earth's shadow) at 22:21 UT.

APRIL 10. Last quarter moon, 23:37 UT. Moon near Jupiter this morning.

APRIL 23. Mercury again attains greatest eastern elongation.

MAY 7. Moon near Jupiter this morning.

MAY 19. Moon near Venus this evening.

JUNE 4. Moon near Jupiter this morning.

JUNE 21. The summer solstice arrives at 2:25 UT.

JULY 1. Full moon at 3:59 UT. Moon near Jupiter this evening.

JULY 4. Jupiter at opposition (opposite side of the earth from the sun). Rising in the southeast sky at sunset, it will stand out throughout the night.

JULY 28. Moon near Jupiter this evening.

SEPTEMBER 4. Venus near Mars this morning. Check the eastern sky during the hour before sunrise.

SEPTEMBER 8. Moon near Venus and Mars this evening.

SEPTEMBER 20. Moon near Jupiter this evening.

SEPTEMBER 22. Autumnal equinox arrives 18:01 UT.

SEPTEMBER 26. Saturn at opposition. It ascends to east at sunset and is visible throughout the night.

SEPTEMBER 27. Total lunar eclipse visible from anywhere in the United States. Moon enters umbra at 1:12 UT.

OCTOBER 8. Moon near Venus this morning.

OCTOBER 18. Moon near Jupiter this evening.

NOVEMBER 8. Moon near Venus this evening.

NOVEMBER 14. Moon near Jupiter this evening.

DECEMBER 8. Moon near Venus this morning.

DECEMBER 13. Geminid meteor shower reaches climax tonight.

DECEMBER 21. Winter solstice arrives at 14:07 UT.

■ STAR GAZER'S GUIDE

■ STARS AND CONSTELLATIONS

The explosion that created the Universe gave birth to trillions of stars, but only 5,000 are visible to the naked eye. Since only half the sky can be seen at any one time, that means only 2,500 stars will be in your field of vision on the next clear night. Constellations are groups of stars whose patterns remind stargazers of familiar shapes. Today, astronomers recognize 88 such patterns. Their names and meanings:

Andromeda	Chained Maiden
Antila	Air Pump
Apus	Bird of Paradise
Aquarius	Water Bearer
Aquila	Eagle
Ara	Altar
Aries	Ram
Auriga	Charioteer
Bootes	Herdsman
Caelum	Chisel
Camelopardalis	Giraffe
Cancer	Crab
Canes Venatici	Hunting Dogs
Canis Major	Great Dog
Canis Minor	Little Dog
Capricornus	Sea-goat
Carina	Keel
Cassiopeia	Queen
Centaurus	Centaur
Cepheus	King
Cetus	Whale
Chamaeleon	Chameleon
Circinus	Compasses (art)
Columba	Dove
Coma Berenices	Bernice's Hair
Corona Australis	Southern Crown
Corona Borealis	Northern Crown
Corvus	Crow
Crater	Cup
Crux	Cross (southern)
Cygnus	Swan
Delphinus	Dolphin
Dorado	Goldfish

■ THE NIGHT SKY IN JANUARY

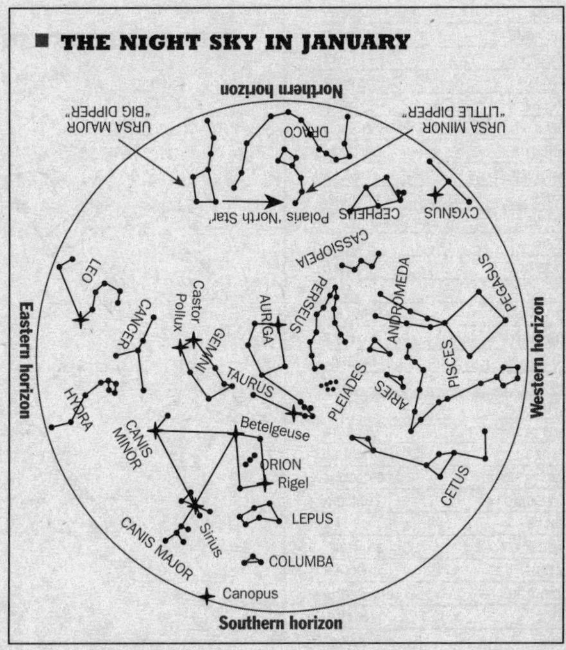

■ THE NIGHT SKY IN FEBRUARY

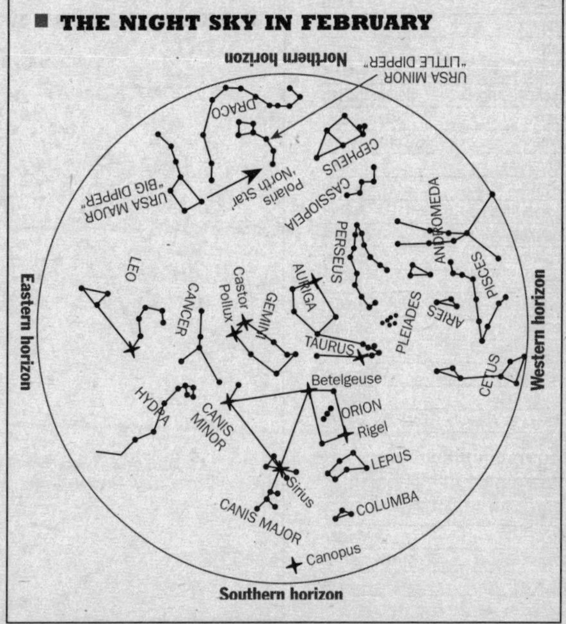

STAR GAZER'S GUIDE

Draco	Dragon
Equuieus	Little Horse
Eridanus	River
Fomax	Furnace
Gemini	Twins
Grus	Crane (bird)
Hercules	Hercules
Horologium	Clock
Hydra	Water Snake (female)
Hydrus	Water Snake (male)
Indus	Indian
Lacerta	Lizard
Leo	Lion
Leo Minor	Little Lion
Lepus	Hare
Libra	Balance
Lupus	Wolf
Lynx	Lynx
Lyra	Lyre
Mensa	Table Mountain
Microscopium	Microscope
Monoceros	Unicorn
Musca	Fly
Norma	Square (rule)
Octans	Octant
Ophiuchus	Serpent Bearer
Orion	Hunter
Pavo	Peacock
Pegasus	Flying Horse
Perseus	Hero
Phoenix	Phoenix
Pictor	Painter
Pisces	Fishes
Piscis Austrinius	Southern Fish
Puppis	Stern (deck)
Pyxis	Compass (sea)
Reticulum	Reticle
Sagitta	Arrow
Saggittarius	Archer
Scorpius	Scorpion
Sculptor	Sculptor
Scutum	Shield
Serpens	Serpent
Sextans	Sextant
Taurus	Bull
Telescopium	Telescope
Triangulum	Triangle
Triangulum Australe	Southern Triangle
Tucana	Toucan
Ursa Major	Great Bear
Ursa Minor	Little Bear
Vela	Sail
Virgo	Maiden
Volans	Flying Fish
Vulpecula	Fox

THE NIGHT SKY IN MARCH

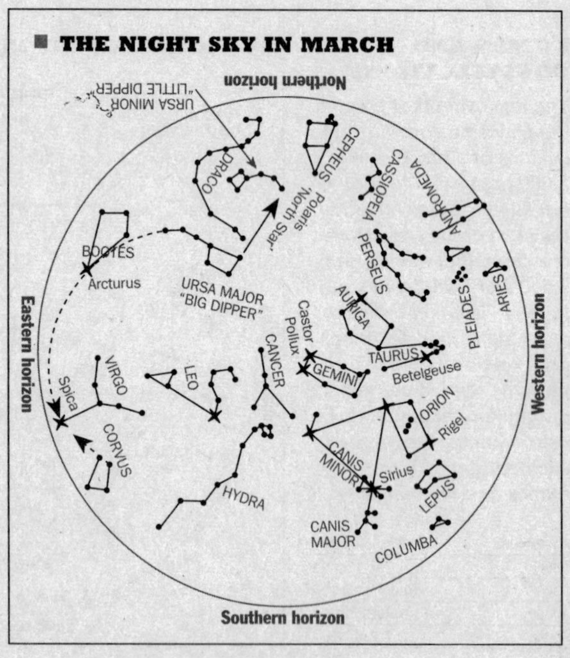

THE NIGHT SKY IN APRIL

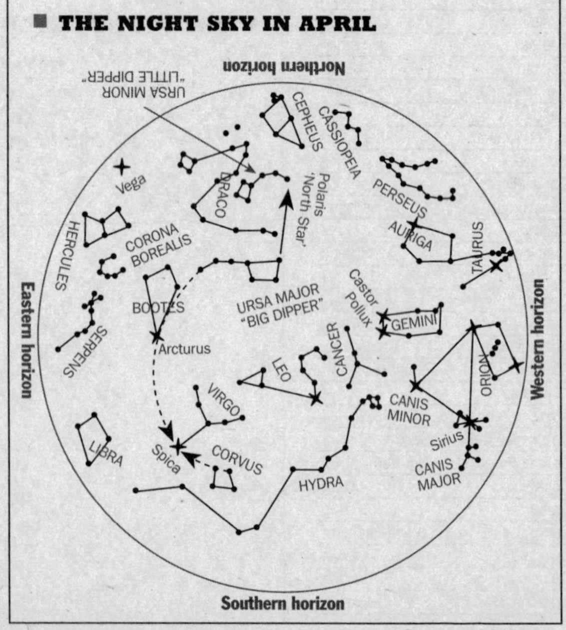

■ STAR GAZER'S GUIDE

■ THE NIGHT SKY IN MAY

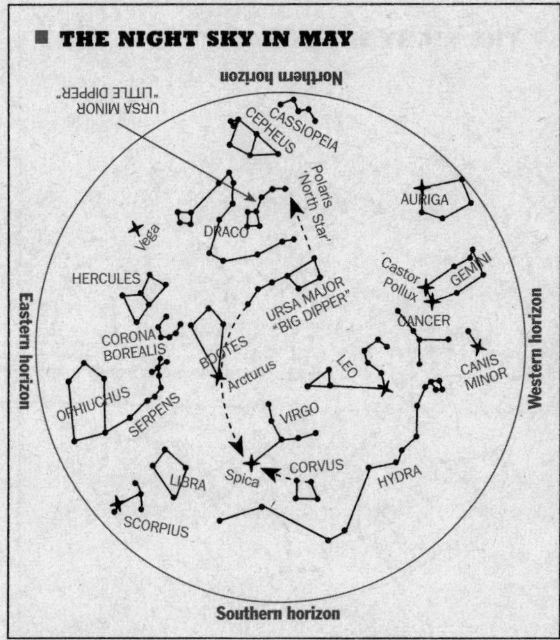

■ THE NIGHT SKY IN JUNE

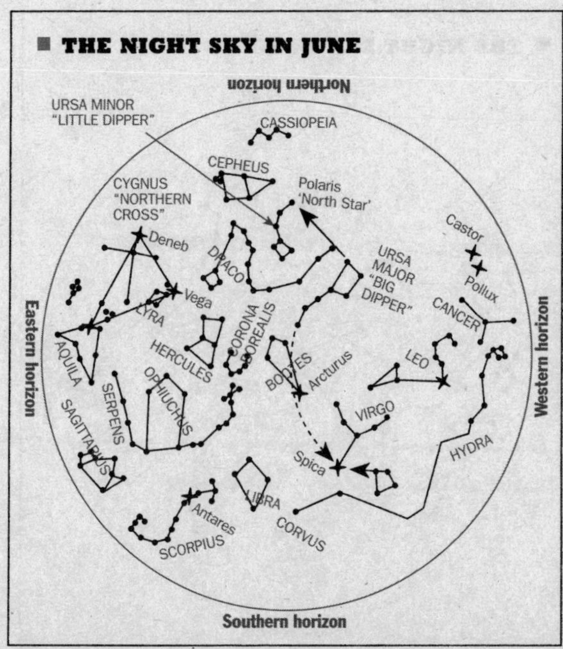

■ PLANETS

There are nine planets in the solar system, including Earth, but only four besides our own are visible to the naked eye: Venus, Mars, Jupiter, and Saturn.

■ **MERCURY:** The smallest of the planets is Mercury. Its diameter is less than half the earth's. Named for the god of the winged messenger, it is the planet closest to the sun and has no satellites. It is believed that Mercury always turns the same side toward the sun and that the sunlit part of Mercury has a temperature hotter than 600 degrees Fahrenheit. By contrast, the temperature on the side away from the sun is thought to be –460 degrees Fahrenheit.

■ **VENUS:** Named for the goddess of love and beauty, Venus is almost the same size as Earth and is often called Earth's "sister planet." The brightest of all planets, Venus is shadowed only by the sun and the moon. It is the first "star" to appear in the evening sky and the last to disappear in the morning. At its brightest, Venus may even be visible during the day. Many astronomers believe that the core of Venus is largely metallic, mostly made of iron and nickel. Because of the dense carbon dioxide clouds enveloping the planet, the surface of Venus can't be seen.

STAR GAZER'S GUIDE

EARTH: Ours is the third closest planet to the sun—they are only 93 million miles apart. Seen from space, the planet appears as a blue ocean sphere with brown and green areas marking the location of its continents. Its diameter at the equator is 7,900 miles, and its atmosphere contains 78 percent nitrogen and 21 percent oxygen, in addition to traces of water in gaseous form, carbon dioxide, and other gases. By measuring the radioactive decay of elements in the Earth's crust, scientists estimate that the planet is about 4.5 billion years old.

MARS: Like Earth, Mars has four seasons, but the diameter of Mars is just a little more than half that of Earth's, and its mass is only about a tenth of ours. Named for the god of war, Mars takes 687 days to complete one revolution of the sun. About 80 percent of the planet is carbon dioxide. The white caps that cover its poles increase in size during the Martian winter and shrink during the summer. Martian seasons are about twice as long as Earth's.

JUPITER: Next to the sun, Jupiter is the largest and most massive object in the solar system. Named for the leader of the gods, Jupiter has a mass more than twice that of all other planets combined. A body

THE NIGHT SKY IN JULY

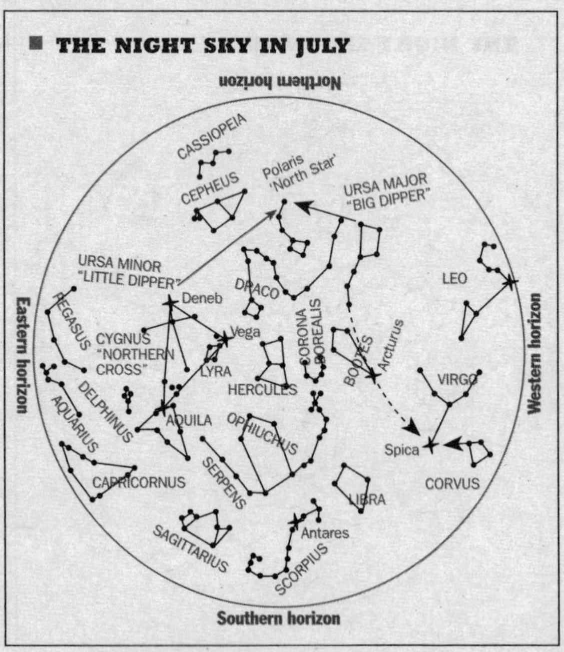

THE NIGHT SKY IN AUGUST

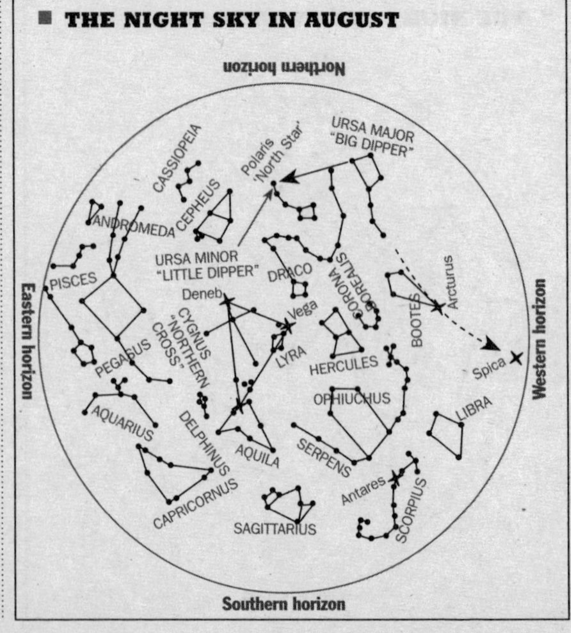

■ STAR GAZER'S GUIDE

■ THE NIGHT SKY IN SEPTEMBER

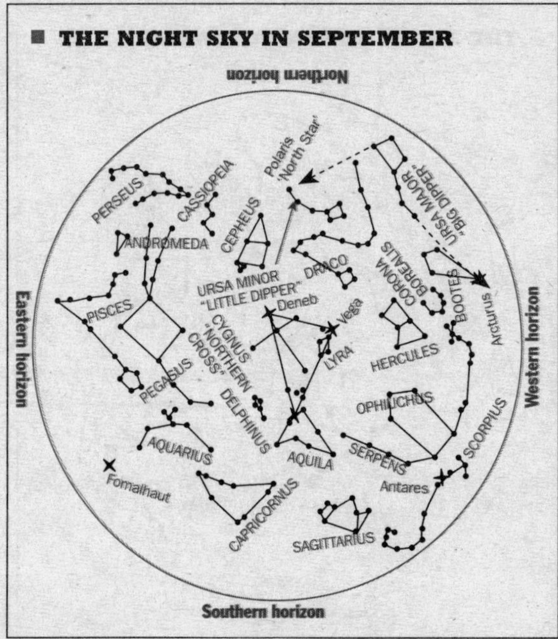

■ THE NIGHT SKY IN OCTOBER

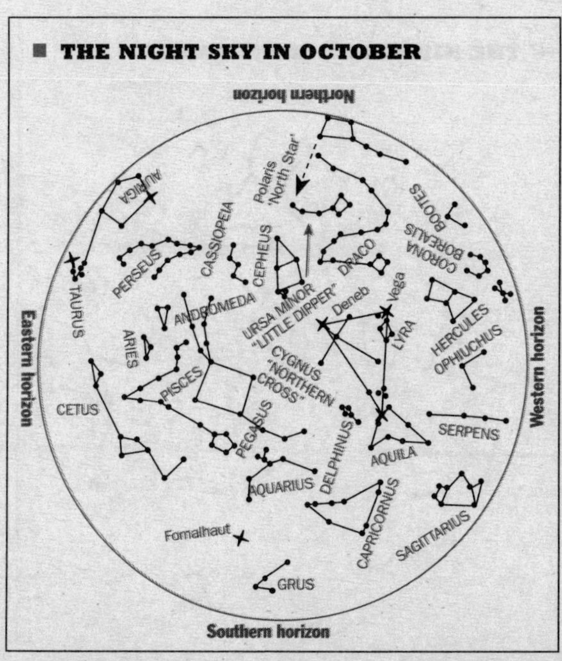

on the surface of Jupiter would weigh 2.64 times what it would weigh on Earth. Jupiter completes a revolution every 10 hours, giving it the shortest day in the solar system. It also has 12 satellites, the largest number of any planet in the solar system. It is perhaps most famous for its Great Red Spot, which scientists believe is a storm that has been going on for 300 years.

■ **SATURN:** The second largest planet in the solar system, Saturn is named for Titan, the father of Jupiter and the god of sowing. It is best known for its system of concentric rings, which are not visible to the naked eye. The rings are probably composed of debris from a shattered satellite. Saturn is the least dense of all the planets but one of the brightest.

■ **URANUS:** Visible by the naked eye on a dark, clear night, Uranus is unique because its axis of rotation lies almost in the plane of its orbit. The planet was discovered by the German-English astronomer William Herschel in 1781. Herschel proposed to name the planet Geogium Sidu, in honor of England's King George III. But in keeping with the tradition of naming planets after Greek gods, it was eventually named after the father of Titan and the grandfather of Jupiter. Uranus has five known satellites and a mass over 14 times that of Earth's. Its temperature is thought to be below –300 degrees Fahrenheit.

■ **NEPTUNE:** Named for the god of the sea, Neptune requires 165 years to complete one revolution of the sun. Its atmosphere is made of methane, hydrogen, ammonia, and helium, and its mass is about 17 times that of Earth. The planet was discovered as a result of a mathematical prediction. Two mathematicians, John Couch Adams and Urbain Le Verrier, calculated that there must be an unknown planet more distant from the sun than Uranus because they could detect the gravitational pull on Uranus.

■ **PLUTO:** There is probably little or no atmosphere on Pluto because of its extreme temperature, which is nearly –400 degrees Fahrenheit. From Pluto the sun would only appear as a bright star. While it was named for the god of the underworld, the planet's first two letters are also the initials of Percival Lowell, whose research on gravitational forces led him to predict the planet's existence around the beginning of this century. It wasn't until after Lowell's death, however, that the planet was discovered.

■ **THE NIGHT SKY IN NOVEMBER**

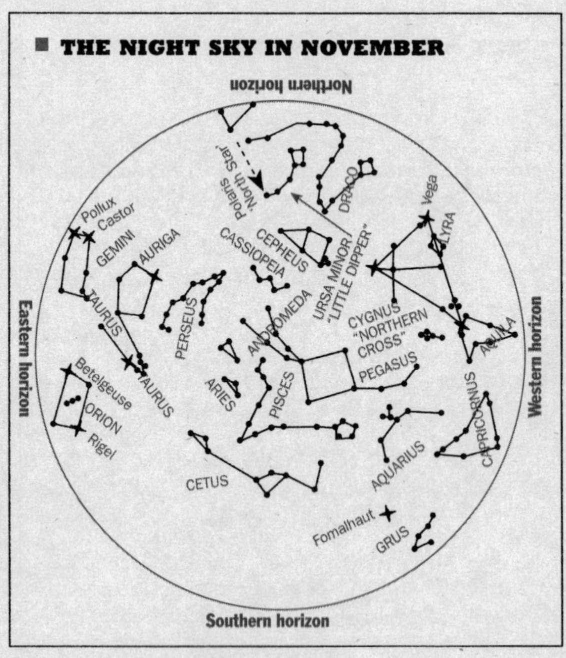

■ **THE NIGHT SKY IN DECEMBER**

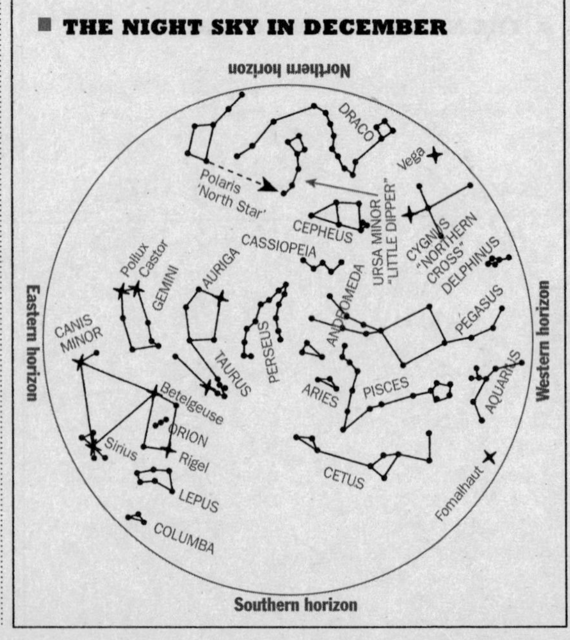

EXPERT SOURCES

MOVING BEYOND THE BIG DIPPER.

If you're curious about what beside the North Star and the Big and Little Dippers are visible in the firmament tonight, don't rush off to the bookstore just yet; sorting through the hundreds of star-gazing guides that fill the racks could leave you more confused than you were to begin. Here, Alan M. MacRobert, an amateur astronomer since age 14, provides his list of best astronomy books. MacRobert edits Sky & Telescope *magazine's "Backyard Astronomy" section and writes the* Boston Globe's *"Sky Watch" column.*

EXPLORING THE NIGHT SKY
Terence Dickinson, Camden House Publishing, 1987, $9.95
■ If you're looking for a top-quality astronomy book to start a fourth to seventh grader, this is it.

NIGHTWATCH
Terence Dickinson, Camden House Publishing, revised edition, 1989, $24.95
■ A fine all-around introduction to the basics of practical amateur astronomy. Contains beautiful naked-eye star maps.

THE STARS: A NEW WAY TO SEE THEM
H. A. Rey, Houghton-Mifflin, 1952. $10.95
■ Many guides to learning the bright stars and constellations have been published, but not many do the job successfully. This classic by the author of the *Curious George* series for children is warm, witty, and explains all the basics of how the sky works. It is recently back in print.

THE BACKYARD ASTRONOMER'S GUIDE
Terence Dickinson and Alan Dyer, Camden House Publishing, 1991, $39.95
■ A larger and more elaborate introduction to the hobby of star gazing, designed not to overlap Dickinson's book, *Nightwatch* (left). It is especially useful for understanding today's telescope market.

BINOCULAR ASTRONOMY
Craig Crossen and Wil Tirion, Willmann-Bell, Inc., 1992, $24.95
■ A big guidebook for finding over 100 interesting objects—star clusters, nebulae, galaxies, and double and variable stars—with ordinary household binoculars. Learn lots of astronomical history and science in the process. Includes the excellent sixth-magnitude Bright Star Atlas 2000.0. Assumes you already can find your way around the constellations.

BURNHAM'S CELESTIAL HANDBOOK
Robert Burnham, Jr., Dover, 1978, 3 vols., $14.95 per volume
■ A 2,138-page labor of love compiled over a 25-year period by a staff astronomer at the Lowell Observatory. In addition to the multitude of facts and descriptions for use with a star atlas at the telescope, Burnham's poetic sensibility and interest in astronomical folklore make for endless bedtime reading.

SKY ATLAS 2000.0
Wil Tirion, Sky Publishing Corp., 1981, color $44.95, bw $24.95
■ This eighth-magnitude star atlas is as essential to serious telescope users as marine charts are to boaters. Twenty-six large charts covering the whole sky plot, 43,000 stars and 2,500 other objects. Contains no text; use it with a reference such as *Burnham's Celestial Handbook*.

LUNAR SCIENCE

MOUNTAINS ON THE MOON

The man in the moon is actually a series of frozen lava fields

The moon is Earth's only natural satellite and was probably created in the same cosmic event that created the Earth. It is only 238,860 miles away, making it an object of endless human fascination—and superstition—for millennia. Although its only light is reflected from the sun, it is the brightest object in our nighttime sky. In size it is slightly more than a quarter the diameter of the Earth. Temperatures can be as high as 273 degrees Fahrenheit on the bright side and as low as –274 degrees Fahrenheit on the dark side.

There is no air, and thus no liquid water, on the lunar surface. That means the moon has no clouds, winds, rain, or snow. Without air and water to cause erosion, the moon's features are nearly permanent—they include towering mountain ranges and seas of hardened lava. The astronomer Galileo was the first to study many of these features with the telescope he built in the early 1600s.

The moon's lava fields are called maria, after the Latin word *mare* for sea, because in Galileo's time it was thought that these plains might in fact be oceans, and that there might be life on the moon. The maria look dark from Earth, suggesting to those with a vivid imagination that there is a "man in the moon."

The lunar surface has also been pitted with craters from crashing meteorites—over 30,000 can be seen from Earth. The circular depressions range in size from less than a mile to over 100 miles across. As intriguing as all of these features are, however, none of them can compare with the fact that the pull of the moon's gravity on the earth's oceans plays a huge role in creating our daily tides. (See "A Beachgoer's Guide to Tides," page 924.)

THE PHASES OF THE MOON

The moon takes slightly longer than 27 days to complete its elliptical orbit around the earth, but because the earth also moves around the sun, it takes 29 days, 12 hours, 44 minutes, and 3 seconds to go from one new moon to the next. At the start of each orbit, the moon is directly between the earth and the sun, making the moon invisible because its dark side is toward us. Gradually, a crescent appears and the moon passes through a waxing phase, in which it grows progressively more visible until it becomes full, and then a waning phase, in which its shape gradually shrinks to invisible again before repeating the cycle.

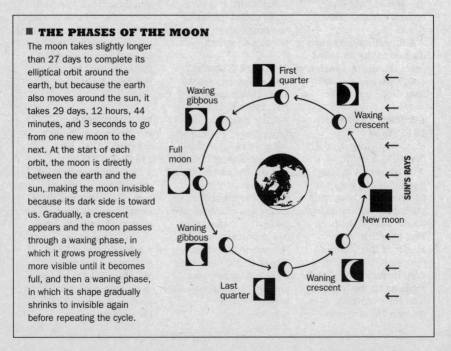

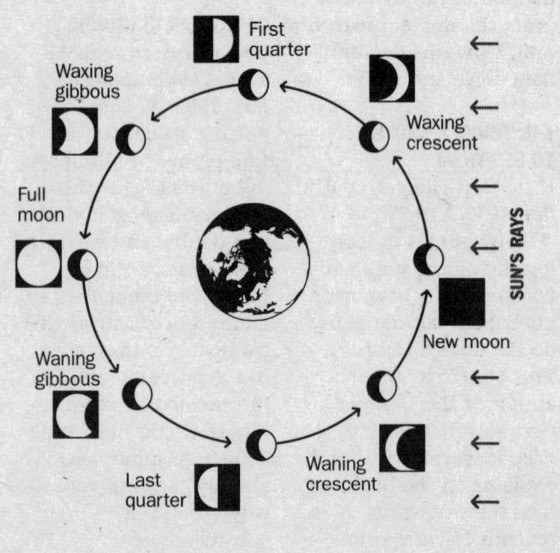

MOONLIGHT SONATA

The moon has no light of its own; it merely reflects the light of the sun. If the moon did not rotate as it revolves around the earth, we would see all its sides; as it is, we always see the same side. Here's a calendar for the moon's phases in 1996 in Universal Time (EST plus five hours):

JAN.

Fri. 5	Sat. 13	Sat. 20	Sat. 27
8:52 p.m.	8:47 p.m.	12:52 p.m.	11:13 a.m.

FEB.

Sun. 4	Mon. 12	Sun. 18	Mon. 26
3:59 p.m.	8:38 a.m.	11:32 p.m.	5:52 a.m.

MAR.

Tues. 5	Tues. 12	Tues. 19	Tues. 26
9:24 a.m.	5:16 a.m.	10:47 a.m.	1:31 a.m.

APR.

Wed. 3	Wed. 10	Wed. 17	Thurs. 25
12:09 a.m.	11:37 p.m.	10:51 p.m.	8:42 p.m.

MAY

Fri. 3	Fri. 10	Fri. 17	Sat. 25
11:50 a.m.	5:05 p.m.	11:49 a.m.	2:15 p.m.

JUNE

Sat. 1	Sat. 8	Sat. 15	Mon. 24	Sun. 30
8:49 p.m.	11:07 a.m.	1:38 a.m.	5:25 a.m.	4:00 a.m.

JULY

Sun. 7	Mon. 15	Tues. 23	Tues. 30
6:56 p.m.	4:16 p.m.	5:51 p.m.	10:37 a.m.

AUG.

Tues. 6	Wed. 14	Wed. 21	Wed. 28
5:26 p.m.	7:35 a.m.	3:38 a.m.	5:53 a.m.

SEPT.

Wed. 4	Thurs. 12	Fri. 20	Thur. 26
7:07 p.m.	11:07 p.m.	11:24 a.m.	2:51 a.m.

OCT.

Fri. 4	Sat. 12	Sat. 19	Sat. 26
12:06 p.m.	2:14 p.m.	6:10 p.m.	2:11 p.m.

NOV.

Sat. 3	Sun. 10	Sun. 17	Sun. 24
7:53 a.m.	4:16 a.m.	1:10 a.m.	4:10 a.m.

DEC.

Tues. 3	Tues. 10	Tues. 17	Tues. 24
5:08 a.m.	4:56 p.m.	9:32 a.m.	8:41 p.m.

THE SEA

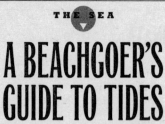

A BEACHGOER'S GUIDE TO TIDES

Skim this to know more about tidal effects than most fishermen

Some ancient myth-makers held that the earth's pulse or breathing caused the tides. The Greeks began to notice the moon's influence when they began venturing out of the relatively tideless Mediterranean. Our modern understanding of tides is based on Sir Isaac Newton's equilibrium theory of tides, which described the gravitational attractions of the sun and moon on the earth's waters. Today, tides can be predicted with astronomical precision and need no longer be a mystery. Here's what landlubbers will find when they are at the beach:

■ **If you live on the East Coast, expect the tides to be semidiurnal.** That's when high and low tides occur twice per lunar day, and the heights of both the first and second set of tides are roughly the same. A lunar day is 50 minutes longer than a day on Planet Earth, which is why in many places high and low tides occur about 50 minutes later than the corresponding tides of the previous day.

■ **If you live on the West Coast, expect mixed tides.** The tides on America's left coast rise and fall twice per lunar day, but the heights of the second set of tides differ from the first. The different tides each day are termed higher high water, lower high water, higher low water, and lower low water. Their order of occurrence varies over the course of the month and from place to place.

■ **Along the Gulf of Mexico, the tides are diurnal.** Here, high and low tides appear only once every day.

■ **About twice a month, near the time of the new and full moon, the tidal range between high and low tides is usually 20 percent above average.** These tides, known as spring tides, occur when the sun and moon are in a straight line with the earth. When the sun and moon are at right angles to each other with respect to the earth, tidal ranges between high and low tides are about 20 percent less than average. These tides, known as neap tides, occur around the time of the first and third quarters of the moon.

■ **For another big swing in height between high and low tide, wait until the moon is at perigee.** That's when the moon is at its closest point to the earth each month and is when the tidal range between high and low tide is greatest. Roughly two weeks later the moon is at apogee, which is its farthest point from the earth for the month. That's when the moon's influence is at a minimum.

■ **During the course of the month, daily inequalities between successive high or low tides also can occur.** This happens as the moon moves from about 28 degrees north of the equator to 28 degrees south. When the moon is at one of these extremes, the difference in height between morning and evening tides is greatest. When the moon is at the equator, tides are roughly equal.

■ **The tidal range also increases in January.** That's when the earth's elliptical orbit around

EXPERT SOURCE

To obtain the tide and tidal current tables for your coastal region, contact:

National Oceanic and Atmospheric Administration
Distribution Branch
6501 Lafayette Ave.
Riverdale, MD 20737
☎ 301-436-6990

THE MOON AND TIDES

The tide is the rise and fall of water throughout the earth's oceans. Occurring every 12 hours and 26 minutes, tides are created primarily by the moon's pull of gravity on the water.

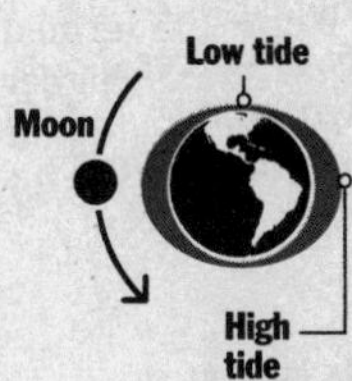

When the earth is nearer the moon, water is pulled toward the moon, producing a high tide. This happens on the opposite side of the earth at the same time.

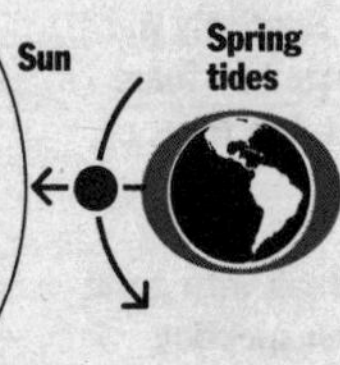

Spring tides occur when the sun and the moon are directly in line. The moon is either in front of or behind the earth. This produces a very high tide twice a month.

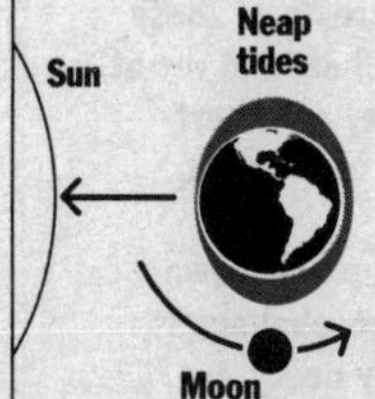

Neap tides do not rise as high as normal because the moon is at right angles to the sun. A neap tide occurs twice a month.

the sun brings the planet closest to the sun, in what astronomers call the state of perihelion. In July, when the earth is farthest away from the sun in what astronomers refer to as the state of aphelion, the tidal range decreases.

■ **The shape and depth of ocean basins change tidal ranges, too.** The smallest differences in the heights between high and low tides occur along open coasts. For example, spring tidal ranges (near the time of the new and full moon) vary from about 2 feet on the Gulf Coast to as much as 8 or 9 feet on the California coast. The largest tidal ranges are found in tidal inlets, estuaries, and salt marshes. The Bay of Fundy in Canada has the greatest difference in the world between high and low tide. There, the funnel-like opening of the bay concentrates the energy and increases the height of the incoming tide, resulting in average tidal ranges of about 45 feet.

■ **Meteorological conditions can also disrupt normal tide patterns.** While tide tables provide accurate times and heights of high and low tide, strong and persistent winds and the low atmospheric pressure associated with storm systems can alter the time and height of high or low tide. If you are planning to go clamming or to collect seashells at low tide and there is a strong onshore breeze, you may want to delay for as long as an hour after the predicted time of low tide.

■ **Horizontal water movements, known as tidal currents, are generally strongest midway between high and low tide.** When the tide rises and water flows in to fill estuaries and inlets, the water is called a flood current. When the tide goes out and water drains from these coastal areas, the flow is called an ebb current. Slack currents are found around the time of both high and low tide.

■ **Surf fishing is best done when tidal currents are strongest.** Strong flood currents force bait fish up closer to the beach and cause them to school up tighter and hide behind features such as rocks or jetties. Game fish such as bluefish or striped bass take advantage of these conditions, and so should knowledgeable surf fishermen, advises marine fisheries biologist Gregg Skomal. Game fish lie in wait for the bait fish to be swept in and out of inlets, estuaries, and bays by flood and ebb currents. Slack water is usually the worst time to fish.

■ **Boaters shouldn't rely on the tidal charts in coastal newspapers.** While most coastal newspapers list the times and heights of high and low tide, boaters need more tidal information than the newspapers provide in order to ensure safe passage over the ocean floor and to know where to anchor. They should consult the tide and tidal current tables published each year by the government.

EXPERT TIPS

SAFETY FOR SWIMMERS AND SURFERS

Lifeguards recommend swimming off sheltered beaches such as those found in coves or behind a point or peninsula. Swimming is easiest out beyond the breakwaters and away from where the biggest sets of waves are breaking. Eyeball how longshore currents are flowing by watching floating debris or swimmers, and swim with the current to limit fatigue and frustration. We asked Karl Tallman, a lifeguard for the California Department of Parks and Recreation, for some additional tips:

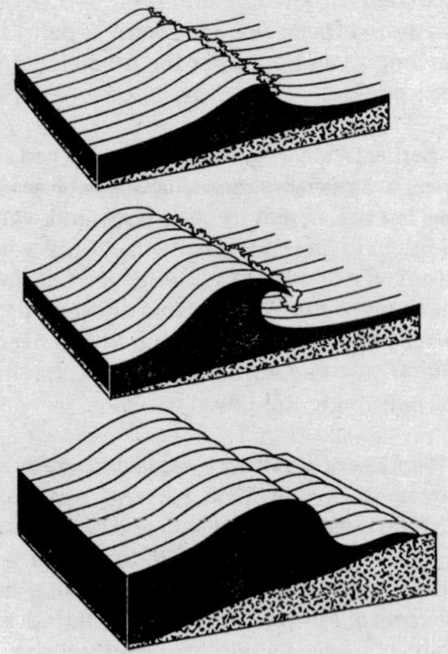

- **Spilling breakers provide body or board surfers with the longest ride. Such waves commonly occur on relatively flat beaches and are characterized by foam and bubbles that spill down the front of the wave.**

- **Plunging breakers can break with great force right on top of an unsuspecting surf swimmer. They are found on moderately steep beaches. The crests of these waves curl over a pocket of air and result in splash-up. As waves, they are short-lived and are not the best for surfing.**

- **Surging breakers slide up and down the beach creating very few challenges for the surf swimmer. They occur on steep beaches and produce little or no bubbles.**

- **Rip currents can endanger even the most experienced swimmer. Remember to swim parallel to the shore to escape the current or allow it to carry you out to where its strength diminishes.**

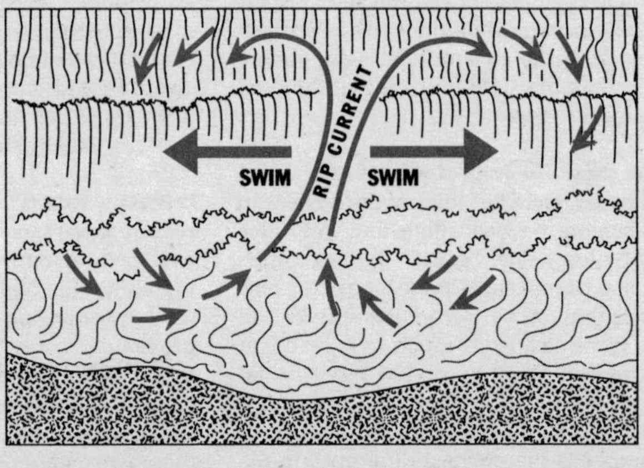

TIMES & DATES

DATES TO CELEBRATE IN '96

The stories behind the days when you can skip school or work

Merchants like holidays because they provide a good shopping opportunity. Greeting-card makers want to invent special occasions when they don't exist. The religious faithful take their Holy Days seriously. And those who need a break cheer at the prospect of a day free of the normal routines. Here is the holiday calendar for 1996:

MAJOR AMERICAN HOLIDAYS

✹NEW YEAR'S DAY, JAN. 1

Roman mythology says two-faced Janus, the god of beginnings for whom our first month is named, looked back on the old year and ahead to the new. In the United States, we ring out the old year at midnight with champagne, kisses, and a few bars of that cryptic Scottish melody, Auld Lang Syne ("The Good Old Days").

> **✹= FEDERAL HOLIDAYS**
>
> Holidays in which federal government offices nationwide, and schools, banks, and offices in Washington, D.C., are closed. In practice, most states also declare a legal holiday on these days.

✹DR. MARTIN LUTHER KING, JR., BIRTHDAY, JAN. 15

Third Monday in January

The civil rights activist, minister, and advocate of nonviolent protest was born on January 15, 1929. A bill to make his birthday a federal holiday was first introduced in 1968, the year King was assassinated. Some states added it to their calender while waiting for Congress to approve it; Ronald Reagan signed the bill in 1983.

GROUNDHOG DAY, FEB. 2

Rumor has it that if a groundhog comes out of his hole on this day and sees his shadow, winter will last for six more weeks. But if the sky is overcast and the groundhog is shadowless, mild weather is on its way. Pennsylvania's Punxsutawney Phil is the country's most famous rodent meteorologist. Since 1887, the Punxsutawney Groundhog Club has trekked up to Gobbler's Knob to watch successive generations of Phils offer their predictions.

VALENTINE'S DAY, FEB. 14

The origin of this romantic holiday is uncertain, though it may have been inspired by the martyrdom of St. Valentine in A.D. 270. The first commercial Valentine's Day cards in the United States hit the shops in the 1840s; in the early 1900s, when risqué cards were the rage, the Chicago postal service refused to deliver 25,000 valentines it deemed unfit to be mailed.

✹ PRESIDENTS' DAY, FEB. 19

Third Monday in February

Honors two of our most famous presidents, George Washington (born Feb. 22, 1732) and Abraham Lincoln (born Feb. 12, 1809), whose birthdays used to be celebrated separately. These celebrated figures stood out in the crowd even by today's standards: Washington was 6 feet tall, and lanky Lincoln was 6 feet 4 inches.

ST. PATRICK'S DAY, MARCH 17

The patron saint of Ireland was born in England around A.D. 389, and immigrants who came to America from the Emerald Isle brought his holiday with them. So many of George Washington's troops were Irish that the secret password during one Revolutionary War battle was "Saint Patrick."

VERNAL EQUINOX, MARCH 20

Day and night are equally long on this first day of spring.

APRIL FOOLS' DAY, APRIL 1

No one is sure when or why the first of April turned into a day for making friends look like fools, but the tradition dates back at least to the English, Scottish, and French practical jokers of the early 18th century. April fools are labeled "gowks" (cuckoos) in Scotland, and "gobs" or "noddies" in England; the French call April 1 pranks "poisson d'avril," or April fish.

EARTH DAY, APRIL 22

"Reduce, reuse, recycle" has become a household mantra since 1970, when the Environmental Protection Agency first asked us to "Give Earth a chance." Congress has passed laws that protect our natural resources, and curbside recycling programs are now common. But the EPA reports that the United States still produces more solid waste per person every day than any other nation—4.4 pounds.

MOTHER'S DAY, MAY 12

Second Sunday in May

Julia Ward Howe, author of the Battle Hymn of the Republic, first floated the idea of a national holiday to honor mothers in 1872. But Philadelphian Anna Jarvis, whose own mother had wanted such a day to comfort families after the Civil War, launched the campaign that made it a reality. Woodrow Wilson officially established the holiday in 1914.

✹ MEMORIAL DAY, MAY 27

Last Monday in May

The government bowed in 1868 to the campaign of a Union veterans group that wanted to honor soldiers who died in the Civil War. The holiday has evolved since then into a tribute to all fallen soldiers and deceased loved ones.

FLAG DAY, JUNE 14

The Second Continental Congress adopted the official flag design on June 14, 1777. Protocol dictates that the American flag may not touch the ground, nor may it be dipped to anyone or anything while being carried in a parade. The star-spangled banner Francis Scott Key saw by the dawn's early light was hit by 11 bullets as it flew above Baltimore's Fort McHenry; it is preserved at the Smithsonian Institution.

FATHER'S DAY, JUNE 16

Third Sunday in June

The daughter of a Civil War veteran whose wife died giving birth to their sixth child persuaded her church in Spokane, Wash., to conduct a special service in honor of fathers. That was in 1910, and though the idea soon became popular around the nation, it wasn't made an official holiday until 1966.

SUMMER SOLSTICE, JUNE 20

The first day of summer; the year's longest.

✹ INDEPENDENCE DAY, JULY 4

With many fireworks and much fanfare, Fourth of July festivities commemorate the 1776 signing of the Declaration of Independence. Two of the signers were loyal to it even in death: On July 4, 1826, John Adams, the second president, died at age

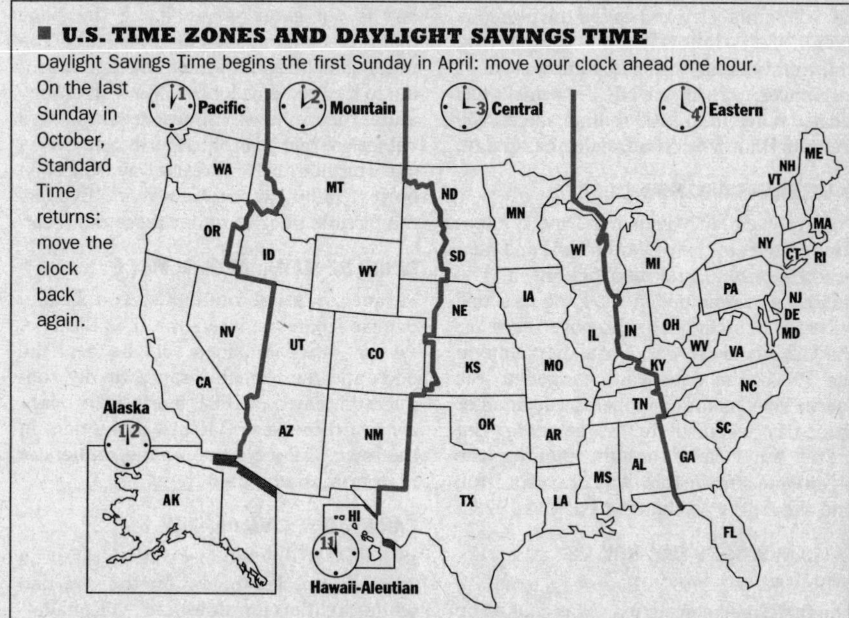

90, and Thomas Jefferson, president number three, died at age 83.

WOMEN'S EQUALITY DAY, AUG. 26

The 19th Amendment to the Constitution was passed on this day in 1920, giving women the right to vote. In Tennessee's House of Representatives, the last vote needed to ratify the amendment was cast by 24-year-old Harry Burns, who, though his district opposed the measure, promised his mother he would vote for it to break a tie.

✵ LABOR DAY, SEPT. 2

First Monday in September

During the Industrial Revolution, a bad time for laborers, union leader Peter McGuire drummed up support for a day that paid homage to America's workers. He chose early September for its pleasant weather, and because no other legal holiday broke up the stretch between Independence Day and Thanksgiving. It's always been thought of as the end of summer vacation, although many schools now resume in late August.

AUTUMNAL EQUINOX, SEPT. 22

The first day of fall.

✵ COLUMBUS DAY, OCT. 14

Christopher Columbus and his entourage first touched American soil on October 12, 1492, probably on Samana Cay in the Bahamas. At sea, Columbus kept an accurate private log of the miles traveled each day, but subtracted miles for the ship's official log. He did so to avoid mutinies caused by sailors who didn't want to be so far from home, and to make sure his directions to Asia, which turned out to be wildly inaccurate, wouldn't fall into the wrong hands.

UNITED NATIONS DAY, OCT. 24

When the United Nations was founded in 1945, it had 51 member countries. Now it has more than 150. Its six official languages are Arabic, Chinese, English, French, Russian, and Spanish.

HALLOWEEN, OCT. 31

The attendant ghouls and goblins stem from the myths of the ancient Celts, who thought witches, ghosts, and the souls of the dead wandered about on the last night of their harvest season. The name comes from the Catholic Church, which in the ninth century declared the first of November All Saints' Day and called the previous evening All Hallow Even. Candy-loving children benefit from the combination of influences, as does UNICEF, which has earned more than $100 million since 1950 from its Halloween fundraising campaign.

✸ VETERANS DAY, NOV. 11

Formerly called Armistice Day, it commemorated the end of World War I and honored those who had died fighting it. The holiday was renamed in 1954 and its scope widened to include all who have served in the U.S. armed forces. For a short time in the 1970s, the date was changed to the fourth Monday in November to add another three-day weekend to the calendar. But many Americans thought making the observance moveable was disrespectful, and the date was changed back in 1978.

✸ THANKSGIVING DAY, NOV. 28

Third Thursday in November

The first Thanksgiving feast was cooked up around 1621 when pilgrims and Native Americans sat down together to enjoy the fruits of harvest. Formerly scheduled for the last Thursday in November (which usually turns out to be the fourth), Thanksgiving was moved up in 1939—Franklin D. Roosevelt wanted to help the economy by extending the Christmas shopping season.

WINTER SOLSTICE, DEC. 21

First day of winter; shortest day of the year.

KWANZAA, DEC. 26 TO JAN. 1

The name means "first fruits" in Swahili, and the holiday is based on African harvest festivals. Brought to America in the mid-'60s by Maulana Karenga, a civil rights leader who wanted black Americans to learn about their ancestors' cultures, Kwanzaa celebrates the history and culture of African Americans.

SELECTED INTERNATIONAL HOLIDAYS

NEW YEAR, CHINA, FEB. 19

Second new moon after winter solstice

In Chinese tradition, 1996 is the year of the rat. Families gather on New Year's Eve for a sumptuous banquet (the fish dish served last is not eaten, symbolizing the hope that there will be food left at the end of the year) and children awaken the next morning to find red envelopes filled with money under their pillows. Chinese tradition says babies are one year old at birth, and everyone's birthday is New Year's Day. So a child born at 11:59 p.m. on New Year's Eve hits the terrible twos in under three minutes.

CINCO DE MAYO, MEXICO, MAY 5

Parades, parties, bullfights, and beauty pageants commemorate the 1862 Battle of Puebla, when Mexican soldiers beat the odds and the French. France finally conquered Mexico in 1864, but lost the country just three years later. A monument in the town of Puebla honors the soldiers of both armies who died there.

CANADA DAY, CANADA, JULY 1

In honor of the nation's confederation in 1867, fireworks (heavy on the red and white) light up the skies and "O Canada!" echoes through the capital city of Ottawa, which hosts an annual concert on Parliament Hill. Across the country, Canadians trot out their flags and firecrackers.

OBON FESTIVAL, JAPAN, JULY 13–15 OR AUG. 13–15 (VARIES BY REGION)

The souls of the dead are said to return for a visit during this festival, so the Japanese go to cemeteries and decorate their ancestors' graves in anticipation. Drummers and kimono-clad folk dancers perform, and lanterns and bonfires are lit to comfort the spiritual guests.

BASTILLE DAY, FRANCE, JULY 14

A Parisian mob stormed the famous fortress and prison in 1789, not satisfied to just eat cake and hell bent on releasing the political prisoners they thought were held there. They freed seven inmates, none of whom was actually a political prisoner, but the action marked the lower classes' entry into the French Revolution. Today, the Bastille is gone and the Parisians are slightly tamer: they light firecrackers, decorate their neighborhoods with paper lanterns, and waltz in the streets to accordion music.

■ INTERNATIONAL TIME ZONES

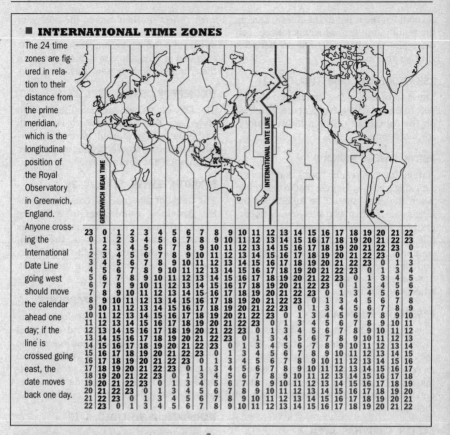

The 24 time zones are figured in relation to their distance from the prime meridian, which is the longitudinal position of the Royal Observatory in Greenwich, England. Anyone crossing the International Date Line going west should move the calendar ahead one day; if the line is crossed going east, the date moves back one day.

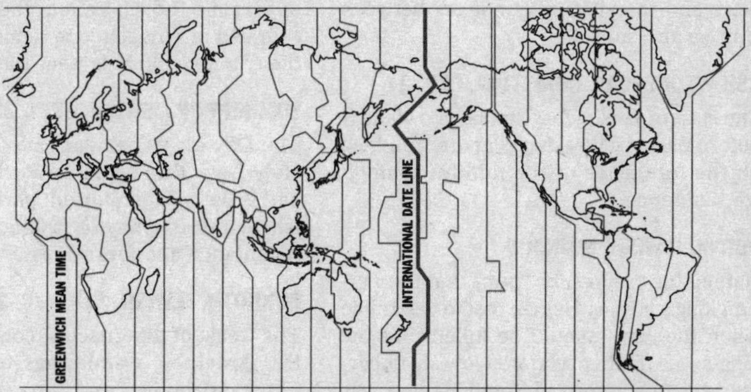

GREENWICH MEAN TIME

INTERNATIONAL DATE LINE

23	0	1	2	3	4	5	6	7	8	9	10	11	12	13	14	15	16	17	18	19	20	21	22
0	1	2	3	4	5	6	7	8	9	10	11	12	13	14	15	16	17	18	19	20	21	22	23
1	2	3	4	5	6	7	8	9	10	11	12	13	14	15	16	17	18	19	20	21	22	23	0
2	3	4	5	6	7	8	9	10	11	12	13	14	15	16	17	18	19	20	21	22	23	0	1
3	4	5	6	7	8	9	10	11	12	13	14	15	16	17	18	19	20	21	22	23	0	1	3
4	5	6	7	8	9	10	11	12	13	14	15	16	17	18	19	20	21	22	23	0	1	3	4
5	6	7	8	9	10	11	12	13	14	15	16	17	18	19	20	21	22	23	0	1	3	4	5
6	7	8	9	10	11	12	13	14	15	16	17	18	19	20	21	22	23	0	1	3	4	5	6
7	8	9	10	11	12	13	14	15	16	17	18	19	20	21	22	23	0	1	3	4	5	6	7
8	9	10	11	12	13	14	15	16	17	18	19	20	21	22	23	0	1	3	4	5	6	7	8
9	10	11	12	13	14	15	16	17	18	19	20	21	22	23	0	1	3	4	5	6	7	8	9
10	11	12	13	14	15	16	17	18	19	20	21	22	23	0	1	3	4	5	6	7	8	9	10
11	12	13	14	15	16	17	18	19	20	21	22	23	0	1	3	4	5	6	7	8	9	10	11
12	13	14	15	16	17	18	19	20	21	22	23	0	1	3	4	5	6	7	8	9	10	11	12
13	14	15	16	17	18	19	20	21	22	23	0	1	3	4	5	6	7	8	9	10	11	12	13
14	15	16	17	18	19	20	21	22	23	0	1	3	4	5	6	7	8	9	10	11	12	13	14
15	16	17	18	19	20	21	22	23	0	1	3	4	5	6	7	8	9	10	11	12	13	14	15
16	17	18	19	20	21	22	23	0	1	3	4	5	6	7	8	9	10	11	12	13	14	15	16
17	18	19	20	21	22	23	0	1	3	4	5	6	7	8	9	10	11	12	13	14	15	16	17
18	19	20	21	22	23	0	1	3	4	5	6	7	8	9	10	11	12	13	14	15	16	17	18
19	20	21	22	23	0	1	3	4	5	6	7	8	9	10	11	12	13	14	15	16	17	18	19
20	21	22	23	0	1	3	4	5	6	7	8	9	10	11	12	13	14	15	16	17	18	19	20
21	22	23	0	1	3	4	5	6	7	8	9	10	11	12	13	14	15	16	17	18	19	20	21
22	23	0	1	3	4	5	6	7	8	9	10	11	12	13	14	15	16	17	18	19	20	21	22

SINTER KLAAS, THE NETHERLANDS, DEC. 5

St. Nicholas is the patron saint of children, so the Dutch celebrate his birthday to please them. Legend says he wears a red cape, rides a white horse, and delivers presents via chimneys. Children leave their shoes out overnight (as well as carrots for the horse) and find them filled with trinkets in the morning.

SANTA LUCIA, SWEDEN, DEC. 13

St. Lucia wore a crown of candles to bring light during the darkest day of the bleak Swedish winter. At dawn in homes across the country, one girl dons a wreath topped with burning white candles (electric ones are available for wobbly Lucias) and a long white dress with a red sash. She and her white-clad siblings bring coffee and saffron bread to their parents, singing carols as they go. Students often organize "Lucia trains" and visit the homes of their teachers as well.

BOXING DAY, UNITED KINGDOM, DEC. 26

Churches used to open their collection boxes the day after Christmas and distribute the contents to the poor. Now Britons use the occasion to give gifts to the people who have helped them throughout the year—those who deliver mail, newspapers, and milk bottles are the big winners.

SELECTED RELIGIOUS HOLIDAYS

RAMADAN, ISLAM, BEGINS JAN. 21

The fourth of the five pillars of Islam is to keep the fast of Ramadan, which celebrates Muhammad's reception of the divine revelations recorded in the Koran. During the month-long fast, Muslims (except soldiers and the sick) may not eat between sunrise and sunset.

ASH WEDNESDAY, CHRISTIAN, FEB. 21

The start of Lent, a fast that begins 40 days before Easter. The ashes that are smudged on the foreheads of the faithful symbolize penitence.

PURIM, JEWISH, MARCH 5

Named for the lots, or "pur," that the Persian king's adviser Haman cast to determine when the Jews should be killed. But the king's wife, Esther, who was Jewish, uncovered his murderous plot and Haman was killed instead. During Purim, Jews dress in costumes and act out the story of Esther, and in synagogue, children with noisemakers try to drown out Haman's name whenever it is read.

PASSOVER, JEWISH, APRIL 4

The eight-day holiday reminds Jews that Moses led the Israelites from Egypt, where they had been slaves under the Pharaoh. At special dinners called seders, everyone takes part in reading the Israelites' story and tasting foods that symbolize aspects of their journey.

EASTER, CHRISTIAN, APRIL 7

The Christian religion's most important holiday, Easter, celebrates the resurrection of Jesus Christ. It is the last day of Holy Week, which includes Palm Sunday, Maundy Thursday, and Good Friday, and it marks the end of Lent. The traditional Easter eggs are thought to represent new life and immortality.

BAISAKHI, HINDU, APRIL 13

Hindus bathe in the Ganges or in other holy waters during the celebration of their new year. Charitable acts performed throughout the following month are considered especially good, so people give generously to the poor.

ROSH HASHANAH, JEWISH, SEPT. 14

The start of the Jewish new year is the first of the 10 High Holy Days, during which Jews reflect on their sins of the past year and seek forgiveness for them. A hollowed-out ram's horn, called the shofar, is sounded in synagogue to remind people of the trumpets of Judgment Day.

YOM KIPPUR, JEWISH, SEPT. 23

The Day of Atonement ends the 10 High Holy Days that begin on Rosh Hashanah and is the most important part of the Jewish year. It is a day of fasting and prayer, repentance and forgiveness.

SUKKOTH, JEWISH, SEPT. 28–29

The "feast of tabernacles" commemorates the Israelites' wanderings after fleeing Egypt. In homes and synagogues, Jews build "sukkahs," replicas of the small shelters in which the Israelites lived during their journey. It is also a celebration of harvest.

DEWALI, HINDU, LATE OCT./EARLY NOV.

The five-day festival of lights celebrates the human desire to move toward truth and light from ignorance and darkness. The streets are strewn with festive lamps and homes are decorated with flowers and colored paper. Festivities include fireworks, parties, and gift-giving.

HANUKKAH, JEWISH, DEC. 6–13

After a group of Jews led by Judah Maccabee recaptured a temple in Jerusalem that had been seized by Syrian-Greeks, they had enough oil to light the temple's lamp for a day. But the lamp burned for eight days, and Jews celebrate this miracle and the Maccabees' victory by lighting candles in the menorah (a special candelabra), adding one each night until all eight candles are lit.

CHRISTMAS DAY, CHRISTIAN, DEC. 25

Christians celebrate the birth of Jesus Christ on this day (though his birth date is a matter of much debate among theologians and historians alike), but many familiar Christmas traditions actually stem from pagan beliefs. The ancient Druids, for example, worshiped holly and mistletoe, and Norsemen burned yule logs in the winter to scare off demons.

BARGAIN HUNTER'S GUIDE

SALES MAKE THE WORLD GO 'ROUND

For every retail item, there's a season. White sales are big on Columbus Day and silverware sales flourish in the June wedding season. Here's when the following items are likely to go on sale across the United States.

JANUARY
- Holiday-related products, including wrapping paper, cards, lights, candles, holiday decorations
- Cookware
- Curtains
- Dishes
- Housewares, small appliances, including toaster ovens, blenders, food processors, coffee makers, etc.
- Rugs
- Silverware
- Toys
- White sales, including linens
- Winter apparel, including coats, furs, sweaters

FEBRUARY
- Presidents Day sales, big for the electronics industry
- Candy
- Jewelry
- Lingerie
- Stereos
- Televisions
- VCRs
- Winter clothes

MARCH
- Best time to buy winter clothes as retailers make room for spring lines
- Camping gear
- Gardening
- Spring fashion promotions

APRIL
- Bicycles
- Jewelry
- Lingerie
- Personal care products

MAY
- Furniture (bedroom sets, sofas, dining room tables)
- Gardening supplies
- Home furnishings
- Luggage
- Mattresses
- Outdoor furniture
- Refrigerators
- Spring clothing
- Stereos
- Televisions
- Tires
- VCRs
- Washer/dryers

JUNE
- Father's Day promotions
- Electronics
- Silverware (for wedding season)
- Sporting goods
- Summer recreational gear

JULY
- Bathing suits
- Bicycles
- Furniture
- Mattresses
- Refrigerators
- Tires
- Washer/dryers

AUGUST
- Back-to-school promotions for children's and junior's clothing
- Office supplies
- School supplies
- Undergarments
- Wardrobe basics

SEPTEMBER
- Labor Day "last chance" promotions on summer wear
- Air-conditioners
- Cookware
- Dishes
- Lamps
- Musical instruments (pianos, guitars, flutes, etc.)
- Recreational gear
- Stereos
- Televisions
- Tires
- VCRs

OCTOBER
- Columbus Day white sales
- Fall apparel
- Home textiles

NOVEMBER
- Curtains
- Fall apparel
- Holiday promotions
- Lamps
- Rugs
- Winter recreational gear

DECEMBER
- Consumer electronics
- Cookware
- Cosmetics
- Furniture
- Home appliances
- Jewelry
- Luggage
- Perfume
- Toys
- Washer/dryers
- Winter apparel

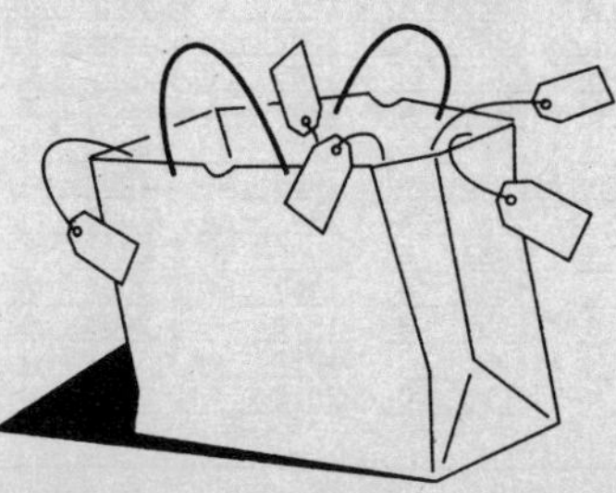

SOURCE: National Retail Federation.

THE CALENDAR

WHY 1996 IS A LEAP YEAR

We have a pope to thank for straightening out the glitch

Our calendar year has 365 days, but the earth actually takes 365 days, 5 hours, 48 minutes and 46 seconds to travel around the sun. With an extra quarter-day each year, in 120 years the calendar would be ahead by a month. New Year's Eve would arrive somewhere around Thanksgiving. Luckily, we have a built-in safeguard: the occasional February 29, which arrives again in 1996. To avoid the chaos that would ensue should our seasons fall out of sync, every fourth year an extra day is added to keep the calendar consistent with the sun.

Julius Caesar introduced the leap year in 46 B.C., but despite his admirable mathematic and administrative efforts, the calendar was 10 days ahead by 1582. Enter Pope Gregory XIII, creator of the calendar we use today. He got the months back on track by dropping 10 days from October 1582. He also rescheduled leap year to fall every fourth year except in the case of century years not evenly divisible by 400. So 2000, the next century year, will be a leap year, but 1700, 1800 and, 1900 were not.

Most of Europe adopted the Gregorian calendar right away, but England and its American colonies held out until 1752. At that point, they had accumulated 11 extra days. To make up for gained time, September 2, 1752, was followed immediately by September 14.

THE PERPETUAL CALENDAR

The letter shown for each year indicates which calendar to use. For the years 1803 to 1820, use the letters for 1983 to 2000, respectively.

Year	Letter	Year	Letter	Year	Letter	Year	Letter
1821	H	1850	I	1879	J	1908	C
1822	I	1851	J	1880	D	1909	L
1823	J	1852	D	1881	M	1910	M
1824	D	1853	M	1882	G	1911	G
1825	M	1854	G	1883	H	1912	A
1826	G	1855	H	1884	B	1913	J
1827	H	1856	B	1885	K	1914	K
1828	B	1857	K	1886	L	1915	L
1829	K	1858	L	1887	M	1916	F
1830	L	1859	M	1888	N	1917	H
1831	M	1860	N	1889	I	1918	I
1832	N	1861	I	1890	J	1919	J
1833	I	1862	J	1891	K	1920	D
1834	J	1863	K	1892	E	1921	M
1835	K	1864	E	1893	G	1922	G
1836	E	1865	G	1894	H	1923	H
1837	G	1866	H	1895	I	1924	B
1838	H	1867	I	1896	C	1925	K
1839	I	1868	C	1897	L	1926	L
1840	C	1869	L	1898	M	1927	M
1841	L	1870	M	1899	G	1928	N
1842	M	1871	G	1900	H	1929	I
1843	G	1872	A	1901	I	1930	J
1844	A	1873	J	1902	J	1931	K
1845	J	1874	K	1903	K	1932	E
1846	K	1875	L	1904	E	1933	G
1847	L	1876	F	1905	G	1934	H
1848	F	1877	H	1906	H	1935	I
1849	H	1878	I	1907	I	1936	C

Year	Letter	Year	Letter	Year	Letter	Year	Letter
1937	L	1973	H	2009	K	2045	G
1938	M	1974	I	2010	L	2046	H
1939	G	1975	J	2011	M	2047	I
1940	A	1976	D	2012	N	2048	C
1941	J	1977	M	2013	I	2049	L
1942	K	1978	G	2014	J	2050	M
1943	L	1979	H	2015	K	2051	G
1944	F	1980	B	2016	E	2052	A
1945	H	1981	K	2017	G	2053	J
1946	I	1982	L	2018	H	2054	K
1947	J	1983	M	2019	I	2055	L
1948	D	1984	N	2020	C	2056	F
1949	M	1985	I	2021	L	2057	H
1950	G	1986	J	2022	M	2058	I
1951	H	1987	K	2023	G	2059	J
1952	B	1988	E	2024	A	2060	D
1953	K	1989	G	2025	J	2061	M
1954	L	1990	H	2026	K	2062	G
1955	M	1991	I	2027	L	2063	H
1956	N	1992	C	2028	F	2064	B
1957	I	1993	L	2029	H	2065	K
1958	J	1994	M	2030	I	2066	L
1959	K	1995	G	2031	J	2067	M
1960	E	1996	A	2032	D	2068	N
1961	G	1997	J	2033	M	2069	I
1962	H	1998	K	2034	G	2070	J
1963	I	1990	L	2035	H	2071	K
1964	C	2000	F	2036	B	2072	E
1965	L	2001	H	2037	K	2073	G
1966	M	2002	I	2038	L	2074	H
1967	G	2003	J	2039	M	2075	I
1968	A	2004	D	2040	N	2076	C
1969	J	2005	M	2041	I	2077	L
1970	K	2006	G	2042	J	2078	M
1971	L	2007	H	2043	K	2079	G
1972	F	2008	B	2044	E	2080	A

A 1996

JANUARY

S	M	T	W	T	F	S
	1	2	3	4	5	6
7	8	9	10	11	12	13
14	15	16	17	18	19	20
21	22	23	24	25	26	27
28	29	30	31			

FEBRUARY

S	M	T	W	T	F	S
				1	2	3
4	5	6	7	8	9	10
11	12	13	14	15	16	17
18	19	20	21	22	23	24
25	26	27	28	29		

MARCH

S	M	T	W	T	F	S
					1	2
3	4	5	6	7	8	9
10	11	12	13	14	15	16
17	18	19	20	21	22	23
24	25	26	27	28	29	30
31						

APRIL

S	M	T	W	T	F	S
	1	2	3	4	5	6
7	8	9	10	11	12	13
14	15	16	17	18	19	20
21	22	23	24	25	26	27
28	29	30				

MAY

S	M	T	W	T	F	S
			1	2	3	4
5	6	7	8	9	10	11
12	13	14	15	16	17	18
19	20	21	22	23	24	25
26	27	28	29	30	31	

JUNE

S	M	T	W	T	F	S
						1
2	3	4	5	6	7	8
9	10	11	12	13	14	15
16	17	18	19	20	21	22
23	24	25	26	27	28	29
30						

JULY

S	M	T	W	T	F	S
	1	2	3	4	5	6
7	8	9	10	11	12	13
14	15	16	17	18	19	20
21	22	23	24	25	26	27
28	29	30	31			

AUGUST

S	M	T	W	T	F	S
				1	2	3
4	5	6	7	8	9	10
11	12	13	14	15	16	17
18	19	20	21	22	23	24
25	26	27	28	29	30	31

SEPEMBER

S	M	T	W	T	F	S
1	2	3	4	5	6	7
8	9	10	11	12	13	14
15	16	17	18	19	20	21
22	23	24	25	26	27	28
29	30					

OCTOBER

S	M	T	W	T	F	S
		1	2	3	4	5
6	7	8	9	10	11	12
13	14	15	16	17	18	19
20	21	22	23	24	25	26
27	28	29	30	31		

NOVEMBER

S	M	T	W	T	F	S
					1	2
3	4	5	6	7	8	9
10	11	12	13	14	15	16
17	18	19	20	21	22	23
24	25	26	27	28	29	30

DECEMBER

S	M	T	W	T	F	S
1	2	3	4	5	6	7
8	9	10	11	12	13	14
15	16	17	18	19	20	21
22	23	24	25	26	27	28
29	30	31				

B 1980 2008

JANUARY

S	M	T	W	T	F	S
		1	2	3	4	5
6	7	8	9	10	11	12
13	14	15	16	17	18	19
20	21	22	23	24	25	26
27	28	29	30	31		

FEBRUARY

S	M	T	W	T	F	S
					1	2
3	4	5	6	7	8	9
10	11	12	13	14	15	16
17	18	19	20	21	22	23
24	25	26	27	28	29	

MARCH

S	M	T	W	T	F	S
						1
2	3	4	5	6	7	8
9	10	11	12	13	14	15
16	17	18	19	20	21	22
23	24	25	26	27	28	29
30	31					

APRIL

S	M	T	W	T	F	S
		1	2	3	4	5
6	7	8	9	10	11	12
13	14	15	16	17	18	19
20	21	22	23	24	25	26
27	28	29	30			

MAY

S	M	T	W	T	F	S
				1	2	3
4	5	6	7	8	9	10
11	12	13	14	15	16	17
18	19	20	21	22	23	24
25	26	27	28	29	30	31

JUNE

S	M	T	W	T	F	S
1	2	3	4	5	6	7
8	9	10	11	12	13	14
15	16	17	18	19	20	21
22	23	24	25	26	27	28
29	30					

JULY

S	M	T	W	T	F	S
		1	2	3	4	5
6	7	8	9	10	11	12
13	14	15	16	17	18	19
20	21	22	23	24	25	26
27	28	29	30	31		

AUGUST

S	M	T	W	T	F	S
					1	2
3	4	5	6	7	8	9
10	11	12	13	14	15	16
17	18	19	20	21	22	23
24	25	26	27	28	29	30
31						

SEPEMBER

S	M	T	W	T	F	S
	1	2	3	4	5	6
7	8	9	10	11	12	13
14	15	16	17	18	19	20
21	22	23	24	25	26	27
28	29	30				

OCTOBER

S	M	T	W	T	F	S
			1	2	3	4
5	6	7	8	9	10	11
12	13	14	15	16	17	18
19	20	21	22	23	24	25
26	27	28	29	30	31	

NOVEMBER

S	M	T	W	T	F	S
						1
2	3	4	5	6	7	8
9	10	11	12	13	14	15
16	17	18	19	20	21	22
23	24	25	26	27	28	29
30						

DECEMBER

S	M	T	W	T	F	S
	1	2	3	4	5	6
7	8	9	10	11	12	13
14	15	16	17	18	19	20
21	22	23	24	25	26	27
28	29	30	31			

C 1992 2020

JANUARY

S	M	T	W	T	F	S
			1	2	3	4
5	6	7	8	9	10	11
12	13	14	15	16	17	18
19	20	21	22	23	24	25
26	27	28	29	30	31	

MAY

S	M	T	W	T	F	S
					1	2
3	4	5	6	7	8	9
10	11	12	13	14	15	16
17	18	19	20	21	22	23
24	25	26	27	28	29	30
31						

SEPEMBER

S	M	T	W	T	F	S
		1	2	3	4	5
6	7	8	9	10	11	12
13	14	15	16	17	18	19
20	21	22	23	24	25	26
27	28	29	30			

FEBRUARY

S	M	T	W	T	F	S
						1
2	3	4	5	6	7	8
9	10	11	12	13	14	15
16	17	18	19	20	21	22
23	24	25	26	27	28	29

JUNE

S	M	T	W	T	F	S
	1	2	3	4	5	6
7	8	9	10	11	12	13
14	15	16	17	18	19	20
21	22	23	24	25	26	27
28	29	30				

OCTOBER

S	M	T	W	T	F	S
				1	2	3
4	5	6	7	8	9	10
11	12	13	14	15	16	17
18	19	20	21	22	23	24
25	26	27	28	29	30	31

MARCH

S	M	T	W	T	F	S
1	2	3	4	5	6	7
8	9	10	11	12	13	14
15	16	17	18	19	20	21
22	23	24	25	26	27	28
29	30	31				

JULY

S	M	T	W	T	F	S
			1	2	3	4
5	6	7	8	9	10	11
12	13	14	15	16	17	18
19	20	21	22	23	24	25
26	27	28	29	30	31	

NOVEMBER

S	M	T	W	T	F	S
1	2	3	4	5	6	7
8	9	10	11	12	13	14
15	16	17	18	19	20	21
22	23	24	25	26	27	28
29	30					

APRIL

S	M	T	W	T	F	S
			1	2	3	4
5	6	7	8	9	10	11
12	13	14	15	16	17	18
19	20	21	22	23	24	25
26	27	28	29	30		

AUGUST

S	M	T	W	T	F	S
						1
2	3	4	5	6	7	8
9	10	11	12	13	14	15
16	17	18	19	20	21	22
23	24	25	26	27	28	29
30	31					

DECEMBER

S	M	T	W	T	F	S
		1	2	3	4	5
6	7	8	9	10	11	12
13	14	15	16	17	18	19
20	21	22	23	24	25	26
27	28	29	30	31		

D 2004 1976

JANUARY

S	M	T	W	T	F	S
				1	2	3
4	5	6	7	8	9	10
11	12	13	14	15	16	17
18	19	20	21	22	23	24
25	26	27	28	29	30	31

MAY

S	M	T	W	T	F	S
						1
2	3	4	5	6	7	8
9	10	11	12	13	14	15
16	17	18	19	20	21	22
23	24	25	26	27	28	29
30	31					

SEPEMBER

S	M	T	W	T	F	S
			1	2	3	4
5	6	7	8	9	10	11
12	13	14	15	16	17	18
19	20	21	22	23	24	25
26	27	28	29	30		

FEBRUARY

S	M	T	W	T	F	S
1	2	3	4	5	6	7
8	9	10	11	12	13	14
15	16	17	18	19	20	21
22	23	24	25	26	27	28
29						

JUNE

S	M	T	W	T	F	S
		1	2	3	4	5
6	7	8	9	10	11	12
13	14	15	16	17	18	19
20	21	22	23	24	25	26
27	28	29	30			

OCTOBER

S	M	T	W	T	F	S
					1	2
3	4	5	6	7	8	9
10	11	12	13	14	15	16
17	18	19	20	21	22	23
24	25	26	27	28	29	30
31						

MARCH

S	M	T	W	T	F	S
	1	2	3	4	5	6
7	8	9	10	11	12	13
14	15	16	17	18	19	20
21	22	23	24	25	26	27
28	29	30	31			

JULY

S	M	T	W	T	F	S
				1	2	3
4	5	6	7	8	9	10
11	12	13	14	15	16	17
18	19	20	21	22	23	24
25	26	27	28	29	30	31

NOVEMBER

S	M	T	W	T	F	S
	1	2	3	4	5	6
7	8	9	10	11	12	13
14	15	16	17	18	19	20
21	22	23	24	25	26	27
28	29	30				

APRIL

S	M	T	W	T	F	S
				1	2	3
4	5	6	7	8	9	10
11	12	13	14	15	16	17
18	19	20	21	22	23	24
25	26	27	28	29	30	

AUGUST

S	M	T	W	T	F	S
1	2	3	4	5	6	7
8	9	10	11	12	13	14
15	16	17	18	19	20	21
22	23	24	25	26	27	28
29	30	31				

DECEMBER

S	M	T	W	T	F	S
			1	2	3	4
5	6	7	8	9	10	11
12	13	14	15	16	17	18
19	20	21	22	23	24	25
26	27	28	29	30	31	

E — 2016 1988

JANUARY

S	M	T	W	T	F	S
					1	2
3	4	5	6	7	8	9
10	11	12	13	14	15	16
17	18	19	20	21	22	23
24	25	26	27	28	29	30
31						

FEBRUARY

S	M	T	W	T	F	S
	1	2	3	4	5	6
7	8	9	10	11	12	13
14	15	16	17	18	19	20
21	22	23	24	25	26	27
28	29					

MARCH

S	M	T	W	T	F	S
		1	2	3	4	5
6	7	8	9	10	11	12
13	14	15	16	17	18	19
20	21	22	23	24	25	26
27	28	29	30	31		

APRIL

S	M	T	W	T	F	S
					1	2
3	4	5	6	7	8	9
10	11	12	13	14	15	16
17	18	19	20	21	22	23
24	25	26	27	28	29	30

MAY

S	M	T	W	T	F	S
1	2	3	4	5	6	7
8	9	10	11	12	13	14
15	16	17	18	19	20	21
22	23	24	25	26	27	28
29	30	31				

JUNE

S	M	T	W	T	F	S
			1	2	3	4
5	66	7	8	9	10	11
12	13	14	15	16	17	18
19	20	21	22	23	24	25
26	27	28	29	30		

JULY

S	M	T	W	T	F	S
					1	2
3	4	5	6	7	8	9
10	11	12	13	14	15	16
17	18	19	20	21	22	23
24	25	26	27	28	29	30
31						

AUGUST

S	M	T	W	T	F	S
	1	2	3	4	5	6
7	8	9	10	11	12	13
14	15	16	17	18	19	20
21	22	23	24	25	26	27
28	29	30	31			

SEPEMBER

S	M	T	W	T	F	S
				1	2	3
4	5	6	7	8	9	10
11	12	13	14	15	16	17
18	19	20	21	22	23	24
25	26	27	28	29	30	

OCTOBER

S	M	T	W	T	F	S
						1
2	3	4	5	6	7	8
9	10	11	12	13	14	15
16	17	18	19	20	21	22
23	24	25	26	27	28	29
30	31					

NOVEMBER

S	M	T	W	T	F	S
		1	2	3	4	5
6	7	8	9	10	11	12
13	14	15	16	17	18	19
20	21	22	23	24	25	26
27	28	29	30			

DECEMBER

S	M	T	W	T	F	S
				1	2	3
4	5	6	7	8	9	10
11	12	13	14	15	16	17
18	19	20	21	22	23	24
25	26	27	28	29	30	31

F — 2000 1972

JANUARY

S	M	T	W	T	F	S
						1
2	3	4	5	6	7	8
9	10	11	12	13	14	15
16	17	18	19	20	21	22
23	24	25	26	27	28	29
30	31					

FEBRUARY

S	M	T	W	T	F	S
		1	2	3	4	5
6	7	8	9	10	11	12
13	14	15	16	17	18	19
20	21	22	23	24	25	26
27	28	29				

MARCH

S	M	T	W	T	F	S
			1	2	3	4
5	6	7	8	9	10	11
12	13	14	15	16	17	18
19	20	21	22	23	24	25
26	27	28	29	30	31	

APRIL

S	M	T	W	T	F	S
						1
2	3	4	5	6	7	8
9	10	11	12	13	14	15
16	17	18	19	20	21	22
23	24	25	26	27	28	29
30						

MAY

S	M	T	W	T	F	S
	1	2	3	4	5	6
7	8	9	10	11	12	13
14	15	16	17	18	19	20
21	22	23	24	25	26	27
28	29	30	31			

JUNE

S	M	T	W	T	F	S
				1	2	3
4	5	6	7	8	9	10
11	12	13	14	15	16	17
18	19	20	21	22	23	24
25	26	27	28	29	30	

JULY

S	M	T	W	T	F	S
						1
2	3	4	5	6	7	8
9	10	11	12	13	14	15
16	17	18	19	20	21	22
23	24	25	26	27	28	29
30	31					

AUGUST

S	M	T	W	T	F	S
		1	2	3	4	5
6	7	8	9	10	11	12
13	14	15	16	17	18	19
20	21	22	23	24	25	26
27	28	29	30	31		

SEPEMBER

S	M	T	W	T	F	S
					1	2
3	4	5	6	7	8	9
10	11	12	13	14	15	16
17	18	19	20	21	22	23
24	25	26	27	28	29	30

OCTOBER

S	M	T	W	T	F	S
1	2	3	4	5	6	7
8	9	10	11	12	13	14
15	16	17	18	19	20	21
22	23	24	25	26	27	28
29	30	31				

NOVEMBER

S	M	T	W	T	F	S
			1	2	3	4
5	6	7	8	9	10	11
12	13	14	15	16	17	18
19	20	21	22	23	24	25
26	27	28	29	30		

DECEMBER

S	M	T	W	T	F	S
					1	2
3	4	5	6	7	8	9
10	11	12	13	14	15	16
17	18	19	20	21	22	23
24	25	26	27	28	29	30
31						

G — 2006 1995

JANUARY

S	M	T	W	T	F	S
1	2	3	4	5	6	7
8	9	10	11	12	13	14
15	16	17	18	19	20	21
22	23	24	25	26	27	28
29	30	31				

FEBRUARY

S	M	T	W	T	F	S
			1	2	3	4
5	6	7	8	9	10	11
12	13	14	15	16	17	18
19	20	21	22	23	24	25
26	27	28				

MARCH

S	M	T	W	T	F	S
			1	2	3	4
5	6	7	8	9	10	11
12	13	14	15	16	17	18
19	20	21	22	23	24	25
26	27	28	29	30	31	

APRIL

S	M	T	W	T	F	S
						1
2	3	4	5	6	7	8
9	10	11	12	13	14	15
16	17	18	19	20	21	22
23	24	25	26	27	28	29
30						

MAY

S	M	T	W	T	F	S
	1	2	3	4	5	6
7	8	9	10	11	12	13
14	15	16	17	18	19	20
21	22	23	24	25	26	27
28	29	30	31			

JUNE

S	M	T	W	T	F	S
				1	2	3
4	5	6	7	8	9	10
11	12	13	14	15	16	17
18	19	20	21	22	23	24
25	26	27	28	29	30	

JULY

S	M	T	W	T	F	S
						1
2	3	4	5	6	7	8
9	10	11	12	13	14	15
16	17	18	19	20	21	22
23	24	25	26	27	28	29
30	31					

AUGUST

S	M	T	W	T	F	S
		1	2	3	4	5
6	7	8	9	10	11	12
13	14	15	16	17	18	19
20	21	22	23	24	25	26
27	28	29	30	31		

SEPTEMBER

S	M	T	W	T	F	S
					1	2
3	4	5	6	7	8	9
10	11	12	13	14	15	16
17	18	19	20	21	22	23
24	25	26	27	28	29	30

OCTOBER

S	M	T	W	T	F	S
1	2	3	4	5	6	7
8	9	10	11	12	13	14
15	16	17	18	19	20	21
22	23	24	25	26	27	28
29	30	31				

NOVEMBER

S	M	T	W	T	F	S
			1	2	3	4
5	6	7	8	9	10	11
12	13	14	15	16	17	18
19	20	21	22	23	24	25
26	27	28	29	30		

DECEMBER

S	M	T	W	T	F	S
					1	2
3	4	5	6	7	8	9
10	11	12	13	14	15	16
17	18	19	20	21	22	23
24	25	26	27	28	29	30
31						

H — 2001 1990

JANUARY

S	M	T	W	T	F	S
	1	2	3	4	5	6
7	8	9	10	11	12	13
14	15	16	17	18	19	20
21	22	23	24	25	26	27
28	29	30	31			

FEBRUARY

S	M	T	W	T	F	S
				1	2	3
4	5	6	7	8	9	10
11	12	13	14	15	16	17
18	19	20	21	22	23	24
25	26	27	28			

MARCH

S	M	T	W	T	F	S
				1	2	3
4	5	6	7	8	9	10
11	12	13	14	15	16	17
18	19	20	21	22	23	24
25	26	27	28	29	30	31

APRIL

S	M	T	W	T	F	S
1	2	3	4	5	6	7
8	9	10	11	12	13	14
15	16	17	18	19	20	21
22	23	24	25	26	27	28
29	30					

MAY

S	M	T	W	T	F	S
		1	2	3	4	5
6	7	8	9	10	11	12
13	14	15	16	17	18	19
20	21	22	23	24	25	26
27	28	29	30	31		

JUNE

S	M	T	W	T	F	S
					1	2
3	4	5	6	7	8	9
10	11	12	13	14	15	16
17	18	19	20	21	22	23
24	25	26	27	28	29	30

JULY

S	M	T	W	T	F	S
1	2	3	4	5	6	7
8	9	10	11	12	13	14
15	16	17	18	19	20	21
22	23	24	25	26	27	28
29	30	31				

AUGUST

S	M	T	W	T	F	S
			1	2	3	4
5	6	7	8	9	10	11
12	13	14	15	16	17	18
19	20	21	22	23	24	25
26	27	28	20	30	31	

SEPTEMBER

S	M	T	W	T	F	S
						1
2	3	4	5	6	7	8
9	10	11	12	13	14	15
16	17	18	19	20	21	22
23	24	25	26	27	28	29
30						

OCTOBER

S	M	T	W	T	F	S
	1	2	3	4	5	6
7	8	9	10	11	12	13
14	15	16	17	18	19	20
21	22	23	24	25	26	27
28	29	30	31			

NOVEMBER

S	M	T	W	T	F	S
				1	2	3
4	5	6	7	8	9	10
11	12	13	14	15	16	17
18	19	20	21	22	23	24
25	26	27	28	29	30	

DECEMBER

S	M	T	W	T	F	S
						1
2	3	4	5	6	7	8
9	10	11	12	13	14	15
16	17	18	19	20	21	22
23	24	25	26	27	28	29
30	31					

I — 2002 1991

JANUARY

S	M	T	W	T	F	S
		1	2	3	4	5
6	7	8	9	10	11	12
13	14	15	16	17	18	19
20	21	22	23	24	25	26
27	28	29	30	31		

MAY

S	M	T	W	T	F	S
			1	2	3	4
5	6	7	8	9	10	11
12	13	14	15	16	17	18
19	20	21	22	23	24	25
26	27	28	29	30	31	

SEPTEMBER

S	M	T	W	T	F	S
1	2	3	4	5	6	7
8	9	10	11	12	13	14
15	16	17	18	19	20	21
22	23	24	25	26	27	28
29	30					

FEBRUARY

S	M	T	W	T	F	S
					1	2
3	4	5	6	7	8	9
10	11	12	13	14	15	16
17	18	19	20	21	22	23
24	25	26	27	28		

JUNE

S	M	T	W	T	F	S
						1
2	3	4	5	6	7	8
9	10	11	12	13	14	15
16	17	18	19	20	21	22
23	24	26	27	27	28	29
30						

OCTOBER

S	M	T	W	T	F	S
		1	2	3	4	5
6	7	8	9	10	11	12
13	14	15	16	17	18	19
20	21	22	23	24	25	26
27	28	29	30	31		

MARCH

S	M	T	W	T	F	S
					1	2
3	4	5	6	7	8	9
10	11	12	13	14	15	16
17	18	19	20	21	22	23
24	25	26	27	28	29	30
31						

JULY

S	M	T	W	T	F	S
	1	2	3	4	5	6
7	8	9	10	11	12	13
14	15	16	17	18	19	20
21	22	23	24	25	26	27
28	29	30	31			

NOVEMBER

S	M	T	W	T	F	S
					1	2
3	4	5	6	7	8	9
10	11	12	13	14	15	16
17	18	19	20	21	22	23
24	25	26	27	28	29	30

APRIL

S	M	T	W	T	F	S
	1	2	3	4	5	6
7	8	9	10	11	12	13
14	15	16	17	18	19	20
21	22	23	24	25	26	27
28	29	30				

AUGUST

S	M	T	W	T	F	S
				1	2	3
4	5	6	7	8	9	10
11	12	13	14	15	16	17
18	19	20	21	22	23	24
25	26	27	28	29	30	31

DECEMBER

S	M	T	W	T	F	S
1	2	3	4	5	6	7
8	9	10	11	12	13	14
15	16	17	18	19	20	21
22	23	24	25	26	27	28
29	30	31				

J — 1997 1986

JANUARY

S	M	T	W	T	F	S
			1	2	3	4
5	6	7	8	9	10	11
12	13	14	15	16	17	18
19	20	21	22	23	24	25
26	27	28	29	30	31	

MAY

S	M	T	W	T	F	S
				1	2	3
4	5	6	7	8	9	10
11	12	13	14	15	16	17
18	19	20	21	22	23	24
25	26	27	28	29	30	31

SEPTEMBER

S	M	T	W	T	F	S
	1	2	3	4	5	6
7	8	9	10	11	12	13
14	15	16	17	18	19	20
21	22	23	24	25	26	27
28	29	30				

FEBRUARY

S	M	T	W	T	F	S
						1
2	3	4	5	6	7	8
9	10	11	12	13	14	15
16	17	18	19	20	21	22
23	24	25	26	27	28	

JUNE

S	M	T	W	T	F	S
1	2	3	4	5	6	7
8	9	10	11	12	13	14
15	16	17	18	19	20	21
22	23	24	25	26	27	28
29	30					

OCTOBER

S	M	T	W	T	F	S
			1	2	3	4
5	6	7	8	9	10	11
12	13	14	15	16	17	18
19	20	21	22	23	24	25
26	27	28	29	30	31	

MARCH

S	M	T	W	T	F	S
						1
2	3	4	5	6	7	8
9	10	11	12	13	14	15
16	17	18	19	20	21	22
23	24	25	26	27	28	29
30	31					

JULY

S	M	T	W	T	F	S
		1	2	3	4	5
6	7	8	9	10	11	12
13	14	15	16	17	18	19
20	21	22	23	24	25	26
27	28	29	30	31		

NOVEMBER

S	M	T	W	T	F	S
						1
2	3	4	5	6	7	8
9	10	11	12	13	14	15
16	17	18	19	20	21	22
23	24	25	26	27	28	29
30						

APRIL

S	M	T	W	T	F	S
		1	2	3	4	5
6	7	8	9	10	11	12
13	14	15	16	17	18	19
20	21	22	23	24	25	26
27	28	29	30			

AUGUST

S	M	T	W	T	F	S
					1	2
3	4	5	6	7	8	9
10	11	12	13	14	15	16
17	18	19	20	21	22	23
24	25	26	27	28	29	30
31						

DECEMBER

S	M	T	W	T	F	S
	1	2	3	4	5	6
7	8	9	10	11	12	13
14	15	16	17	18	19	20
21	22	23	24	25	26	27
28	29	30	31			

K 1998 1987

JANUARY

S	M	T	W	T	F	S
				1	2	3
4	5	6	7	8	9	10
11	12	13	14	15	16	17
18	19	20	21	22	23	24
25	26	27	28	29	30	31

FEBRUARY

S	M	T	W	T	F	S
1	2	3	4	5	6	7
8	9	10	11	12	13	14
15	16	17	18	19	20	21
22	23	24	25	26	27	28

MARCH

S	M	T	W	T	F	S
1	2	3	4	5	6	7
8	9	10	11	12	13	14
15	16	17	18	19	20	21
22	23	24	25	26	27	28
29	30	31				

APRIL

S	M	T	W	T	F	S
			1	2	3	4
5	6	7	8	9	10	11
12	13	14	15	16	17	18
19	20	21	22	23	24	25
26	27	28	29	30		

MAY

S	M	T	W	T	F	S
					1	2
3	4	5	6	7	8	9
10	11	12	13	14	15	16
17	18	19	20	21	22	23
24	25	26	27	28	29	30
31						

JUNE

S	M	T	W	T	F	S
	1	2	3	4	5	6
7	8	9	10	11	12	13
14	15	16	17	18	19	20
21	22	23	24	25	26	27
28	29	30				

JULY

S	M	T	W	T	F	S
			1	2	3	4
5	6	7	8	9	10	11
12	13	14	15	16	17	18
19	20	21	22	23	24	25
26	27	28	29	30	31	

AUGUST

S	M	T	W	T	F	S
						1
2	3	4	5	6	7	8
9	10	11	12	13	14	15
16	17	18	19	20	21	22
23	24	25	26	27	28	29
30	31					

SEPTEMBER

S	M	T	W	T	F	S
		1	2	3	4	5
6	7	8	9	10	11	12
13	14	15	16	17	18	19
20	21	22	23	24	25	26
27	28	29	30			

OCTOBER

S	M	T	W	T	F	S
				1	2	3
4	5	6	7	8	9	10
11	12	13	14	15	16	17
18	19	20	21	22	23	24
25	26	27	28	29	30	31

NOVEMBER

S	M	T	W	T	F	S
1	2	3	4	5	6	7
8	9	10	11	12	13	14
15	16	17	18	19	20	21
22	23	24	25	26	27	28
29	30					

DECEMBER

S	M	T	W	T	F	S
		1	2	3	4	5
6	7	8	9	10	11	12
13	14	15	16	17	18	19
20	21	22	23	24	25	26
27	28	29	30	31		

L 1999 1993

JANUARY

S	M	T	W	T	F	S
					1	2
3	4	5	6	7	8	9
10	11	12	13	14	15	16
17	18	19	20	21	22	23
24	25	26	27	28	29	30
31						

FEBRUARY

S	M	T	W	T	F	S
	1	2	3	4	5	6
7	8	9	10	11	12	13
14	15	16	17	18	19	20
21	22	23	24	25	26	27
28						

MARCH

S	M	T	W	T	F	S
	1	2	3	4	5	6
7	8	9	10	11	12	13
14	15	16	17	18	19	20
21	22	23	24	25	26	27
28	29	30	31			

APRIL

S	M	T	W	T	F	S
				1	2	3
4	5	6	7	8	9	10
11	12	13	14	15	16	17
18	19	20	21	22	23	24
25	26	27	28	29	30	

MAY

S	M	T	W	T	F	S
						1
2	3	4	5	6	7	8
9	10	11	12	13	14	15
16	17	18	19	20	21	22
23	24	25	26	27	28	29
30	31					

JUNE

S	M	T	W	T	F	S
		1	2	3	4	5
6	7	8	9	10	11	12
13	14	15	16	17	18	19
20	21	22	23	24	25	26
27	28	29	30			

JULY

S	M	T	W	T	F	S
				1	2	3
4	5	6	7	8	9	10
11	12	13	14	15	16	17
18	19	20	21	22	23	24
25	26	27	28	29	30	31

AUGUST

S	M	T	W	T	F	S
1	2	3	4	5	6	7
8	9	10	11	12	13	14
15	16	17	18	19	20	21
22	23	24	25	26	27	28
29	30	31				

SEPTEMBER

S	M	T	W	T	F	S
			1	2	3	4
5	6	7	8	9	10	11
12	13	14	15	16	17	18
19	20	21	22	23	24	25
26	27	28	29	30		

OCTOBER

S	M	T	W	T	F	S
					1	2
3	4	5	6	7	8	9
10	11	12	13	14	15	16
17	18	19	20	21	22	23
24	25	26	27	28	29	30
31						

NOVEMBER

S	M	T	W	T	F	S
	1	2	3	4	5	6
7	8	9	10	11	12	13
14	15	16	17	18	19	20
21	22	23	24	25	26	27
28	29	30				

DECEMBER

S	M	T	W	T	F	S
			1	2	3	4
5	6	7	8	9	10	11
12	13	14	15	16	17	18
19	20	21	22	23	24	25
26	27	28	29	30	31	

M — 2005 1994

JANUARY

S	M	T	W	T	F	S
						1
2	3	4	5	6	7	8
9	10	11	12	13	14	15
16	17	18	19	20	21	22
23	24	25	26	27	28	29
30	31					

FEBRUARY

S	M	T	W	T	F	S
		1	2	3	4	5
6	7	8	9	10	11	12
13	14	15	16	17	18	19
20	21	22	23	24	25	26
27	28					

MARCH

S	M	T	W	T	F	S
		1	2	3	4	5
6	7	8	9	10	11	12
13	14	15	16	17	18	19
20	21	22	23	24	25	26
27	28	29	30	31		

APRIL

S	M	T	W	T	F	S
					1	2
3	4	5	6	7	8	9
10	11	12	13	14	15	16
17	18	19	20	21	22	23
24	25	26	27	28	29	30

MAY

S	M	T	W	T	F	S
1	2	3	4	5	6	7
8	9	10	11	12	13	14
15	16	17	18	19	20	21
22	23	24	25	26	27	28
29	30	31				

JUNE

S	M	T	W	T	F	S
			1	2	3	4
5	6	7	8	9	10	11
12	13	14	15	16	17	18
19	20	21	22	23	24	25
26	27	28	29	30		

JULY

S	M	T	W	T	F	S
					1	2
3	4	5	6	7	8	9
10	11	12	13	14	15	16
17	18	19	20	21	22	23
24	25	26	27	28	29	30
31						

AUGUST

S	M	T	W	T	F	S
	1	2	3	4	5	6
7	8	9	10	11	12	13
14	15	16	17	18	19	20
21	22	23	24	25	26	27
28	29	30	31			

SEPTEMBER

S	M	T	W	T	F	S
				1	2	3
4	5	6	7	8	9	10
11	12	13	14	15	16	17
18	19	20	21	22	23	24
25	26	27	28	29	30	

OCTOBER

S	M	T	W	T	F	S
						1
2	3	4	5	6	7	8
9	10	11	12	13	14	15
16	17	18	19	20	21	22
23	24	25	26	27	28	29
30	31					

NOVEMBER

S	M	T	W	T	F	S
		1	2	3	4	5
6	7	8	9	10	11	12
13	14	15	16	17	18	19
20	21	22	23	24	25	26
27	28	29	30			

DECEMBER

S	M	T	W	T	F	S
				1	2	3
4	5	6	7	8	9	10
11	12	13	14	15	16	17
18	19	20	21	22	23	24
25	26	27	28	29	30	31

N — 2012 1984

JANUARY

S	M	T	W	T	F	S
1	2	3	4	5	6	7
8	9	10	11	12	13	14
15	16	17	18	19	20	21
22	23	24	25	26	27	28
29	30	31				

FEBRUARY

S	M	T	W	T	F	S
			1	2	3	4
5	6	7	8	9	10	11
12	13	14	15	16	17	18
19	20	21	22	23	24	25
26	27	28	29			

MARCH

S	M	T	W	T	F	S
				1	2	3
4	5	6	7	8	9	10
11	12	13	14	15	16	17
18	19	20	21	22	23	24
25	26	27	28	29	30	31

APRIL

S	M	T	W	T	F	S
1	2	3	4	5	6	7
8	9	10	11	12	13	14
15	16	17	18	19	20	21
22	23	24	25	26	27	28
29	30					

MAY

S	M	T	W	T	F	S
		1	2	3	4	5
6	7	8	9	10	11	12
13	14	15	16	17	18	19
20	21	22	23	24	25	26
27	28	29	30	31		

JUNE

S	M	T	W	T	F	S
					1	2
3	4	5	6	7	8	9
10	11	12	13	14	15	16
17	18	19	20	21	22	23
24	25	26	27	28	29	30

JULY

S	M	T	W	T	F	S
1	2	3	4	5	6	7
8	9	10	11	12	13	14
15	16	17	18	19	20	21
22	23	24	25	26	27	28
29	30	31				

AUGUST

S	M	T	W	T	F	S
			1	2	3	4
5	6	7	8	9	10	11
12	13	14	15	16	17	18
19	20	21	22	23	24	25
26	27	28	29	30	31	

SEPTEMBER

S	M	T	W	T	F	S
						1
2	3	4	5	6	7	8
9	10	11	12	13	14	15
16	17	18	19	20	21	22
23	24	25	26	27	28	29
30						

OCTOBER

S	M	T	W	T	F	S
	1	2	3	4	5	6
7	8	9	10	11	12	13
14	15	16	17	18	19	20
21	22	23	24	25	26	27
28	29	30	31			

NOVEMBER

S	M	T	W	T	F	S
				1	2	3
4	5	6	7	8	9	10
11	12	13	14	15	16	17
18	19	20	21	22	23	24
25	26	27	28	29	30	

DECEMBER

S	M	T	W	T	F	S
						1
2	3	4	5	6	7	8
9	10	11	12	13	14	15
16	17	18	19	20	21	22
23	24	25	26	27	28	29
30	31					

ASTROLOGY

SIGNS FOR ALL TIMES

Clues to your personality from palm-reading the heavens

Most horoscope columns are based on sun sign astrology, which is based only on one's birth date. Genethliac astrology factors in a wealth of other information, including a person's time and place of birth, the location of the sun, moon, planets, and some asteroids, and the path of the moon's orbit around the earth.

Here's a beginner's guide to what your sign may reveal about you.

ARIES

March 21–April 19 **The Ram**

Aries represents birth, and it is the first sign of the zodiac. As the first zodiac, the ram is like a baby—very self-absorbed. And like a baby, Aries puts his or her needs first. The Ram is fearless, extremely honest and direct, and very gung ho. Arians often show a ferocious temper, but after the fight, they don't hold a grudge. With all the energy they expend, you have to wonder when they relax. But they can be calm too. They find their soulmates in Sagittarius, Scorpio, and Cancer.

TAURUS

April 20–May 20 **The Bull**

Taurus is a rocky coast that's been beaten by the elements for centuries. Those born under this sign are strong and stubborn with a quiet demeanor. Taureans are steady, speak sparingly, and possess an inner strength, but don't like change. They are outstanding workers who are willing to take orders without resentment. Their hearts and pockets are open to a friend in distress, but they may have trouble expressing their own feelings. Cancer, Leo, and Capricorn will hit it off with them.

GEMINI

May 21–June 20 **The Twins**

Being born under the sign of the Twins means you never know when you might switch your looks, house, job, or spouse on an impulse. Geminis can never get enough money, fame, or love. They live by their own rules and do what they want; they have little patience for indecisive people and can be very rude, selfish, and immature. The Gemini woman has a hard time committing herself to one man at a time, and the Gemini man may shower a love interest with flowers, but he's unlikely to reveal his innermost core. Still, Gemini will be drawn to Leo, Capricorn, and Aquarius.

CANCER

June 21–July 22 **The Crab**

The Cancer person is full of laughter and loves a good joke. But at other times Cancer's moods are blacker than the darkest cavern. Yet people born under this sign also are sweet and gentle and will find a way to rise above adversity when the moon changes. Cancerans are very sentimental about their roots and their family. They have vulnerable hearts and very sensitive feelings. In love, the Cancer person can be so dependent it can border on obsession. Virgo, Leo, and Aquarius will be the most compatible.

LEO

July 23–Aug 22 **The Lion**

Leo is the leader of the jungle, a dignified, stately presence, lying luxuriously in the sun for all to see. Leos have extremely strong personalities and can be very vain. But they also are very loveable, seldom waste energy on fruitless tasks, and are good organizers. The regal ways of the Sun sign make them great hosts or hostesses. Leos like the regal treatment and spend money freely, but they'll also give money to almost anybody. They play hard, work hard, rest hard, and live hard. Leo will want to meet Pisces, Aries, and Gemini.

VIRGO

Aug 23–Sept 22 **The Virgin**

These perfectionists are dependable, industrious, practical, cool, and sincere. They are blessed with great curiosity and are very mentally alive, excelling in both the written and spoken word. The Virgo can endure and thrive on intense work longer than most others. They can also destroy relationships by being too critical, analytical, and irritable. But if you're in a jam, the Virgo will gladly roll up his or her sleeves and jump in. Capricorn, Aries, and Pisces are for Virgo.

LIBRA

Sept 23–Oct 22 **The Scales**

Being the sign of the Scales, the Libra is a natural balancer. They're excellent listeners, but they'll talk your ear off. They are extremely intelligent, but extremely naive. They love people, but hate crowds. They're gracious, caring, and calm, but when the weight of the scales change, they can be stubborn, annoying, and depressed. The Libran hates arguments, and makes an ideal mate. They will do anything to please. Gemini and Taurus stand the best chance of benefiting.

SCORPIO

Oct 23–Nov 21 **The Scorpion**

The most passionate people in the zodiac, Scorpios are nocturnal creatures. They have hypnotic intense eyes which make many people feel nervous. Scorpios have very strong emotions, but they are deeply hidden. They know what they are and what they're not and nothing anyone says will change that. They can be sarcastic, stubborn, and even cruel to those that are close to them. It is extremely hard to get to know them. They must test everyone before they show their real selves. Scorpions are fascinated with death and religion. Scorpio will appreciate Cancer and Aquarius the best.

SAGITTARIUS

Nov 22–Dec 21 **The Archer**

When you start a new job, the first person to walk up to you with a smile, shake your hand and welcome you aboard is a Sagittarius. Sagittarians mean well but are always putting a foot in their mouth. They make friends easily, are optimists, and refuse to take life seriously. But they can have violent tempers and are bad at keeping a secret. They have fantastic memories but can't remember where they left their keys. Pisces, Cancer, and Leo will be most understanding.

CAPRICORN

Dec 22–Jan 19 **The Goat**

Like the goat, the Capricorn looks and acts harmless but is tough as nails. Capricorns are steady, serious, and sensible, and never let obstacles or disappointments block the way to the top of the mountain. They are gentle and persuasive, and although they are sometimes labeled as snobbish, that's really not true. The Capricorn person is safe to trust and confide in, and they make great providers. Leo, Aries, and Virgo are Capricorn's favorites.

AQUARIUS

Jan 20–Feb 18 **The Water Bearer**

Freedom-loving Aquarians are unpredictable and secretly delight in shocking others with their erratic behavior. They are natural rebels with a dreamy look in their eyes. The Aquarian will seek the security of crowds and then demand to be alone. When it comes to friends, they seek quantity, rather than quality. Trusting people isn't natural for Aquarians, but they love to network. Sagittarius, Taurus, and Libra will be the most in sync with Aquarius.

PISCES

Feb 19–March 20 **The Fish**

Like their namesake, fish people hate to be in the same spot for too long. They are always swimming from one spot of light to another. Pisces people are the most spiritual of the signs; they are often mystical, impressionable, and intuitive. They are also creative, clever, and sarcastic, and hate to answer a direct question. Yet no sign is more sensitive to human suffering. They love to help. Pisces will find Virgo, Gemini, and Scorpio to their liking.

FIGURES & FORMULAS

WEIGHTS & MEASURES

MEASUREMENTS TO LIVE BY

Sizing up the world around you, from square pegs to round holes

Weights and measures have been a matter for pharaohs, emperors, and kings to establish and of practical men and women to follow for thousands of years. The Egyptians based their system of measurement on the human body: the little finger to the thumb tip was considered a span, and two spans were the equivalent of one cubit, which was the distance from a person's fingertips to the elbow. The mile was a Roman unit of measure: it came from the word "mille," which stood for "1,000 paces."

There are several legends to explain where the English unit of measure, the yard, came from. One is that it was the same length as King Henry I's arm. Another is that it represented the distance from the tip of Henry's nose to the end of his thumb. Yet another version suggests that it was inspired by the length of the arrows used by the King's archers. In any case, the state's role in setting standards has never been in doubt. For many centuries the weights and measures that Americans inherited from Britain were referred to as "the king's standard."

Americans have moved a fair way, however, from the Queen's English and what has come to be known as the British Imperial System of weights and measures, and in the United States today, weights and measures are usually referred to by the name "U.S. Customary System."

Most of the rest of the world, of course, follows the International (or Metric) System, which is a decimal system in which units of measurement increase by multiples of 10. First developed by ancient Hindu mathematicians and then embraced by the Arabs in the 10th century, the Metric System came into gradual use in Europe after 1100, and was officially adopted by the French in the late 1700s, about the time Louis XVI and Marie Antoinette faced the guillotine.

Led by the scientific and engineering communities, metrics are gradually winning wider acceptance in U.S. industry. But the day when the rulebook states that the proper height of a basketball hoop is 3.048 meters is still many years away.

■ LINEAR MEASURE

Use to measure lines and distances.

CUSTOMARY U.S. UNITS:

12 inches = 1 foot
3 feet = 1 yard
1,760 yards = 1 statute mile

$5\frac{1}{2}$ yards = 1 rod
40 rods = 1 furlong = 220 yards
8 furlongs = 5,280 feet = 1 statute mile

METRIC UNITS:

10 millimeters = 1 centimeter
10 centimeters = 1 decimeter
10 decimeters = 1 meter
10 meters = 1 decameter
10 decameters = 1 hectometer
10 hectometers = 1 kilometer

CUSTOMARY U.S. UNITS TO METRIC UNITS:

1 inch = 2.54 centimeters = 0.0254 meter
1 foot = 30.48 centimeters = 0.3048 meter
1 yard = 91.44 centimeters = 0.9144 meter
1 statute mile = 1,609.344 meters=
= 1.609344 kilometers

METRIC UNITS TO CUSTOMARY U.S. UNITS:

1 centimeter = 0.3937 inch
1 meter = 3.28084 feet
= 1.093613 yards
1 kilometer = 0.62137 mile

MARINERS' MEASURE

To measure distance, depth, or speed at sea.

CUSTOMARY U.S. UNITS:

6 feet = 1 fathom
1,000 fathoms (approx.) = 1 nautical mile
1 nautical mile = 1.151 statute miles
3 nautical miles = 1 league
60 nautical miles = 1 degree
1 knot = 1 nautical mile per hour

SQUARE MEASURE

Multiply length by width in units of the same denomination to find surface area.

CUSTOMARY U.S. UNITS:

144 square inches = 1 square foot
9 square feet = 1 square yard
$30\frac{1}{4}$ square yards = 2 square rods
160 square rods = 1 acre
640 acres = 1 square mile

METRIC UNITS:

100 square millimeters = 1 square centimeter
100 square centimeters = 1 square decimeter

A RULER—PLUS SOME HANDY SUBSTITUTES

A little ingenuity can go a long way when you need a measurement, albeit an approximate one, in a hurry. For example, if you need to know the dimensions of a room it might help to know that most floor tile is 9 x 9 or 12 x 12 inches. If you know the length of your tie, belt, or shoelace, you can multiply that by the number of times it covers the area to be measured.

DOLLAR BILL
$6\frac{1}{8}$ x $2\frac{5}{8}$ inches

QUARTER
approximately
1 inch diameter

PENNY
approximately
$\frac{3}{4}$ inch diameter

BUSINESS CARD
generally $3\frac{5}{8}$ x 2 inches

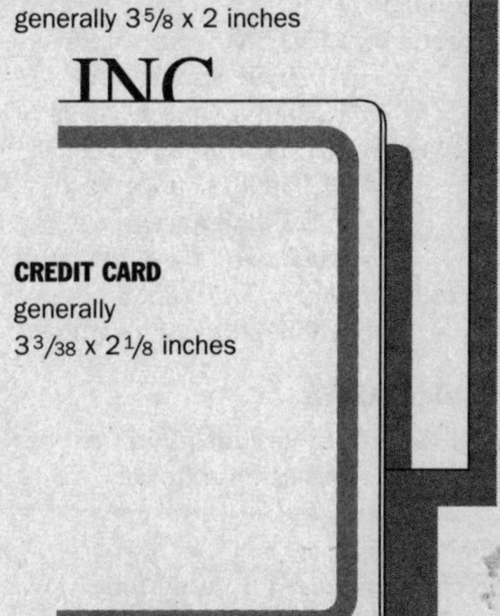

CREDIT CARD
generally
$3\frac{3}{38}$ x $2\frac{1}{8}$ inches

100 square decimeters = 1 square meter
100 square meters = 1 square decameter = 1 are
100 square decameters = 1 square hectometer
100 square hectometers = 1 square kilometer

CUSTOMARY U.S. UNITS TO METRIC UNITS:

1 square inch = 6.4516 square centimeters
1 square foot = 929.0304 square centimeters = 0.09290304 square meter
1 square yard = 8,361.2736 square centimeters = 0.83612736 square meter
1 acre = 4,046.8564 square meters = 0.40468564 square hectometer
1 square mile = 2,589,988.11 square meters = 258.998811 square hectometer = 2.58998811 square kilometers

METRIC UNITS TO CUSTOMARY U.S. UNITS:

1 square centimeter = 0.1550003 square inch
1 square meter = 1,550.003 square inches = 10.76391 square feet = 1.195990 square yards
1 hectare = 107,639.1 square feet = 11,959.90 square yards = 2.4710538 acres = 0.003861006 square mile
1 square kilometer = 247.10538 acres = 0.3861006 square miles

■ CUBIC MEASURE

Multiply length by breadth by thickness to find cubic content or volume.

CUSTOMARY U.S. UNITS:

1,728 cubic inches = 1 cubic foot
27 cubic feet = 1 cubic yard

METRIC UNITS:

1,000 cubic millimeters = 1 cubic centimeter
1,000 cubic centimeters = 1 cubic decimeter
1,000 cubic decimeters = 1 cubic meter

■ SURVEYORS' MEASURE

Use to measure the borders and dimensions of a tract of land.

CUSTOMARY U.S. UNITS:

7.92 inches = 1 link
100 links = 1 chain
1 chain = 4 rods = 66 feet
80 chains = 1 survey mile = 5,280 feet

■ SURVEYORS' SQUARE MEASURE

Multiply length by breadth to find surface area of land.

CUSTOMARY U.S. UNITS:

272 1/4 square feet = 1 square rod
16 square rods = 1 square chain
160 square rods = 10 square chains = 1 acre
640 acres = 1 square mile = 1 section
36 square miles = 36 sections = 1 township

■ LIQUID MEASURE

Use to measure a vessel's capacity to hold liquids.

CUSTOMARY U.S. UNITS:

4 gills = 2 cups = 1 pint
2 pints = 1 quart
4 quarts = 1 gallon
31 1/2 gallons = 1 barrel
2 barrels = 1 hogshead

METRIC UNITS:

10 milliliters = 1 centiliter
10 centiliters = 1 deciliter
10 deciliters = 1 liter
10 liters = 1 decaliter
10 decaliters = 1 hectoliter
10 hectoliters = 1 kiloliter

■ APOTHECARIES' FLUID MEASURE

Use in mixing medicines.

CUSTOMARY U.S. UNITS:

60 minims = 1 fluid dram
8 fluid drams = 1 fluid ounce
16 fluid ounces = 1 pint

2 pints = 1 quart
4 quarts = 1 gallon

CUSTOMARY U.S. UNITS TO METRIC UNITS:

1 fluid ounce = 29.573528 milliliters
= 0.02957 liter
1 cup = 236.588 milliliters
= 0.236588 liter
1 pint = 473.176 milliliters
= 0.473176 liter
1 quart = 946.3529 milliliters
= 0.9463529 liter
1 gallon = 3,785.41 milliliters
= 3.78541 liters

METRIC UNITS TO CUSTOMARY U.S. UNITS:

1 milliliter = 0.0338 fluid ounce
1 liter = 33.814 fluid ounces
= 4.2268 cups = 2.113 pints
= 1.0567 quarts = 0.264 gallons

DRY MEASURE

Use to measure a vessel's capacity to hold solids such as grain.

CUSTOMARY U.S. UNITS:

2 pints = 1 quart
8 quarts = 1 peck
4 pecks = 1 bushel

CUSTOMARY U.S. UNITS TO METRIC UNITS:

1 pint = 33,600 cubic inches = 0.551 liter
1 quart = 67.201 cubic inches = 1.101 liters

COOKING MEASUREMENT EQUIVALENTS

3 teaspoons = 1 tablespoon
1 tablespoon = 1/16 cup
2 tablespoons = 1/8 cup
2 tablespoons = 1/6 cup
+ 2 teaspoons
4 tablespoons = 1/4 cup
5 tablespoons = 1/3 cup
+ 1 teaspoon
6 tablespoons = 3/8 cup
8 tablespoons = 1/2 cup
10 tablespoons = 2/3 cup
+ 2 teaspoons
12 tablespoons = 3/4 cup
16 tablespoons = 1 cup
48 teaspoons = 1 cup
2 cups = 1 pint
2 pints = 1 quart
4 quarts = 1 gallon

TEMPERATURE CONVERSIONS

To convert temperatures from Fahrenheit to Celsius, subtract 32 degrees and multiply by 5, then divide by 9. To go from Celsius to Fahrenheit, multiply by 9, divide by 5, then add 32 degrees.

Celsius = Fahrenheit	Fahrenheit = Celsius
–45 = –49	–45 = –42.8
–40 = –40	–40 = –40.0
–35 = –31	–35 = –37.2
–25 = –13	–30 = –34.4
–30 = –8.5	–25 = –31.7
–20 = –4	–20 = –28.9
–15 = 5	–15 = –26.1
–10 = 14	–10 = –23.3
–5 = 23	–5 = –20.6
0 = 32	0 = –17.8
5 = 41	5 = –15.0
10 = 50	10 = –12.2
15 = 59	15 = –9.4
20 = 68	20 = –6.7
25 = 77	25 = –3.9
30 = 86	30 = –1.1
35 = 95	32 = 0.0
40 = 104	35 = 1.7
45 = 113	40 = 4.4
50 = 122	45 = 7.2
55 = 131	50 = 10.0
60 = 140	55 = 12.8
65 = 149	60 = 15.6
70 = 158	65 = 18.3
75 = 167	70 = 21.1
80 = 176	75 = 23.9
85 = 185	80 = 26.7
90 = 194	85 = 29.4
95 = 203	90 = 32.2
100 = 212	95 = 35.0
125 = 257	100 = 37.8
150 = 302	105 = 40.6
175 = 347	110 = 43.3
200 = 392	212 = 100.0
225 = 437	225 = 107.2
250 = 482	250 = 121.1
275 = 527	275 = 135.0
300 = 572	300 = 148.9
325 = 617	325 = 162.8
350 = 662	350 = 176.7
375 = 707	375 = 190.6
400 = 752	400 = 204.4
425 = 797	425 = 218.3
450 = 842	450 = 232.2
475 = 887	475 = 246.1

WOOD MEASURE

To measure the volume of a pile of wood.

CUSTOMARY U.S. UNITS:

16 cubic feet = 1 cord foot = a wood pile 4 feet high by 4 feet wide by 1 foot long
8 cord feet = 1 cord = a wood pile 8 feet long by 4 feet wide by 4 feet high

TIME MEASURE

Use to measure the passage of time.

CUSTOMARY U.S. UNITS:

60 seconds = 1 minute
60 minutes = 1 hour
24 hours = 1 day
7 days = 1 week
4 weeks (28 to 31 days) = 1 month
12 months (365 or 366 days) = 1 year
100 years = 1 century

FRACTIONS AND THEIR DECIMAL EQUIVALENTS

Rounded to the nearest four decimals

1/2	.5	4/7	.5714
1/3	.3333	4/9	.4444
1/4	.25	4/11	.3636
1/5	.2	5/6	.8333
1/6	.1667	5/7	.7143
1/7	.1429	5/8	.625
1/8	.125	5/9	.5556
1/9	.1111	5/11	.4545
1/10	.1	5/12	.4167
1/11	.0909	5/16	.3125
1/12	.0833	6/7	.8571
1/16	.0625	7/8	.875
1/32	.0313	7/9	.7778
1/64	.0156	7/10	.7
2/3	.6667	7/11	.6364
2/5	.4	7/12	.5833
2/7	.2857	7/16	.4375
2/9	.2222	8/9	.8889
2/11	.1818	8/11	.7273
3/4	.75	9/10	.9
3/5	.6	9/11	.8182
3/7	.4286	9/16	.5625
3/8	.375	10/11	.9091
3/10	.3	11/12	.9167
3/11	.2727	11/16	.6875
3/16	.1875	13/16	.8125
4/5	.8	15/16	.9375

ANGULAR AND CIRCULAR MEASURE

Use in surveying, navigating, astronomy, geography, reckoning latitude and longitude, and computing differences in time.

CUSTOMARY U.S. UNITS:

60 seconds = 1 minute
60 minutes = 1 degree
90 degrees = 1 right angle
180 degrees = 1 straight angle
360 degrees = 1 circle

The length of a degree of longitude on the earth's surface at the Equator is 69.16 miles.

TROY WEIGHT

Use in weighing gold, silver, and jewels.

CUSTOMARY U.S. UNITS:

24 grains = 1 pennyweight
20 pennyweights = 1 ounce
12 ounces = 1 pound

AVOIRDUPOIS WEIGHT

Use for weighing heavy articles such as grain and groceries.

CUSTOMARY U.S. UNITS:

27 11/32 grains = 1 dram
16 drams = 1 ounce
16 ounces = 1 pound
100 pounds = 1 short hundredweight
20 short hundredweight = 1 short ton

APOTHECARIES' WEIGHT

For weighing medicines for prescriptions.

CUSTOMARY U.S. UNITS:

20 grains = 1 scruple
3 scruples = 1 dram
8 drams = 1 ounce
12 ounces = 1 pound

METRIC WEIGHT

Use for measuring weights, distances, areas, and both dry and liquid capacities.

METRIC UNITS:

10 milligrams = 1 centigram
10 centigrams = 1 decigram
10 decigrams = 1 gram
10 grams = 1 decagram

FITTING CLOTHES TO THE TEE

Men in Europe don't have huge heads and exceptionally large feet—they just have a different system for sizing hats and shoes. A look at how clothing sizes compare:

WOMEN

BLOUSES AND SWEATERS

U.S.	**32**	**34**	**36**	**38**	**40**	**42**	**44**
British	34	36	38	40	42	44	46
Continental	40	42	44	46	48	50	52

COATS AND DRESSES

U.S.	**8**	**10**	**12**	**14**	**16**	**18**	**20**
British	30	32	34	36	38	40	42
Continental	36	38	40	42	44	46	48

SHOES						
	U.S.	**5–5½**	**6–6½**	**7–7½**	**8–8½**	**9**
	British	3½–4	4½–5	5½–6	6½–7	7½
	Continental	36	37	38	39	40

STOCKINGS							
	U.S. and British	**8**	**8½**	**9**	**9½**	**10**	**10½**
	Continental	0	1	2	3	4	5

MEN

HATS									
	U.S.	**6⅝**	**6¾**	**6⅞**	**7**	**7⅛**	**7¼**	**7⅜**	**7½**
	British	6½	6⅝	6¾	6⅞	7	7⅛	7¼	7⅜
	Continental	53	54	55	56	57	58	59	60

SHIRTS								
	U.S. and British	**14**	**14½**	**15**	**15½**	**16**	**16½**	**17**
	Continental	36	37	38	39	41	42	43

SHOES										
	U.S.	**7**	**7½**	**8**	**8½**	**9**	**9½**	**10**	**10½**	**11**
	British	6½	7	7½	8	8½	9	9½	10	10½
	Continental	39	40	41	42	43	43	44	44	45

SOCKS								
	U.S. and British	**9½**	**10**	**10½**	**11**	**11½**	**12**	**12½**
	Continental	39	40	41	42	43	44	45

SUITS AND COATS

U.S. and British	**34**	**36**	**38**	**40**	**42**	**44**	**46**
Continental	44	46	48	50	52	54	56

10 decagrams = 1 hectogram
10 hectograms = 1 kilogram
100 kilograms = 1 quintal
10 quintals = 1 ton

MASS AND WEIGHT

Though they are not the same thing, mass and weight are identical in standard conditions (sea level on Earth), meaning that grams and other metric units of mass can be used as measures of weight or converted into customary units of weight.

CUSTOMARY U.S. UNITS TO METRIC UNITS:

1 ounce = 28.3495 grams
1 pound = 453.59 grams
= 0.453569 kilogram
1 short ton = 907.18 kilograms
= 0.907 metric ton

METRIC UNITS TO CUSTOMARY U.S. UNITS:

1 milligram = 0.000035 ounce
1 gram = 0.03527 ounce
1 kilogram = 35.27 ounces
= 2.2046 pounds
1 metric ton = 2,204.6 pounds
= 1.1023 short tons

MATHEMATICS

PLACING MATH ON A TIMELINE

The study of numbers has been both practical and sublime for millennia

Without numbers it would be impossible to set a clock, keep score, or create a symphony. If numbers had not been needed, the civilizations of ancient Mesopotamia, Egypt, and China would not have felt it necessary to invent counting systems, which they then applied to their commerce and government. An early appreciation for the principles of geometry helped the Egyptians construct the pyramids and accurately record their boundaries.

By the sixth century, B.C., the Greeks took the practical math that they had learned from the Babylonians and Egyptians and ventured into more abstract investigations. The Greek philosopher Pythagoras and his disciples proposed a theorem, for instance, that showed the mathematical relationship among the three sides of a right triangle (see page 953). Another Greek, Euclid, was the first to suggest that geometry possessed a single set of logical rules. Archimedes laid the conceptual groundwork for integral calculus in the third century, B.C., and the celebrated astronomer, Ptolemy, played a leading role in developing trigonometry.

The Romans largely contented themselves with the use of math in solving practical problems, but the more ethereal inquiries into the nature of numbers championed by the Greeks were taken up by Islamic thinkers in the 9th and 10th centuries. One of them, an astronomer named Muhammad ibn Mūsā al-Khwārizmi, laid many of the foundations for algebra.

Beginning in the 11th century, Islamic advances in mathematics gradually made their way to Europe. But it was not until the Renaissance in the 15th century that Europeans contributed to the breakthroughs, with astronomers such as Nicolaus Copernicus, Galileo Galilei, and Johannes Kepler making major contributions. Working independently, Sir Isaac Newton, an Englishman, and Baron Gottfried Wilhem von Leibniz invented calculus in the 1680s, which effectively ushered in the modern age of mathematics.

Following is a ready reference to many of the most commonly used mathematical concepts and operations.

ALGEBRA

Algebra is based on five fundamental laws, which govern the operations of addition, subtraction, multiplication, and division. Each of the laws is expressed in letter variables. Where variables a, b, *and* c *are all real numbers, any number can be substituted for a variable without conflicting with the way the rule works.*

■ THE COMMUTATIVE LAW OF ADDITION

$$a + b = b + a$$

Under this law, the order in which two numbers are added has no bearing on the sum derived. Thus,
$6+7 = 7+6$, or $(-10)+(-2) = (-2)+(-10)$

■ THE ASSOCIATIVE LAW OF ADDITION

$$a + (b + c) = (a + b) + c$$

Under this law, it does not matter which combination of numbers are added first, the sum remains the same. Thus,
$1+(8+2) = (1+8)+2$

■ THE COMMUTATIVE LAW OF MULTIPLICATION

$$ab = ba$$

Under this law, it does not matter which order numbers are multiplied in, the product is the same. Thus, $6 \cdot 7 = 7 \cdot 6$

■ THE ASSOCIATIVE LAW OF MULTIPLICATION:

$$a \cdot (bc) = (ab) \cdot c$$

Under this law, numbers can be multiplied in any sequence without affecting the final product. Thus, $5 \cdot (4 \cdot 3) = (5 \cdot 4) \cdot 3$

■ THE DISTRIBUTIVE LAW OF MULTIPLICATION OVER ADDITION:

$$a(b+c) = ab+ac$$

Under this law, if a number multiplies a sum, the total is the same as the sum of the separate products of the multiplier and each of the addends represented by *b* and *c*. Thus, $3\cdot(2+9) = 3\cdot2+3\cdot9$

■ THE QUADRATIC EQUATION

Another key algebraic equation is the quadratic equation, in which the highest power to which the unknown quantity is raised is the second. Assuming *a*, *b*, and *c* are real numbers, and *a* does not equal zero, the formula is as follows:

$$\textit{If: } ax^2+bx+c = 0$$

$$\textit{Then: } x = \frac{-b \pm \sqrt{b^2-4ac}}{2a}$$

Thus, if $a = 1$, $b = 4$, and $c = 3$, and we know that $1x^2+4x+3 = 0$, then we can find the value of x as follows:

$$x = \frac{-4 \pm \sqrt{4^2-(4\cdot1\cdot3)}}{2\cdot1} = (-1,-3)$$

GEOMETRY

This branch of mathematics deals with points, lines, planes, and figures and their properties, measurement, and spatial relationships.

■ ANGLES

Angles are expressed in degrees, which are fractions of a circle. A circle has 360 degrees.

An **acute angle** is greater than zero degrees and less than 90.

A **right angle** has 90 degrees. The lines forming the angle run perpendicular to each other.

An **obtuse angle** has more than 90 degrees but less than 180 degrees.

A **straight angle** has 180 degrees and forms a straight line.

A ROMAN INNOVATION

The Roman system of recording numbers lasted considerably longer than the Roman Empire. As recently as 500 years ago, Roman numerals were still being used for addition and subtraction throughout Europe. But the Roman approach to numbers didn't translate well to higher math, and by the late 1500s Arabic numerals were being adopted in the West.

The Roman system uses only seven symbols, individually or in combination. When more than one symbol is used to form a number, the value of each symbol generally is added together, reading from left to right.

To multiply a numeral by 1,000, place a bar over the symbol like a long vowel sound. For instance, X with a bar across its top would stand for 10,000.

ROMAN NUMERALS

1	**I**	300	CCC
2	II	400	CD
3	III	500	**D**
4	IV	600	DC
5	**V**	700	DCC
6	VI	800	DCCC
7	VII	900	CM
8	VIII	1000	**M**
9	IX	1500	MD
10	**X**	1900	MCM or
15	XV		MDCCCC
20	XX	1910	MCMX
25	XXV	1940	MCMXL
30	XXX	1950	MCML
40	XL	1960	MCMLX
50	**L**	1990	MCMXC
60	LX	1996	MCMXCVI
70	LXX	2000	MM
80	LXXX	3000	MMM
90	XC	5000	$\overline{\text{V}}$
100	**C**	10,000	$\overline{\text{X}}$
150	CL	100,000	$\overline{\text{C}}$
200	CC	1,000,000	$\overline{\text{M}}$

KNOW YOUR MATH SYMBOLS

No science is more elegant when it comes to explaining the world around us than mathematics. To assist its examination of the properties, relations, and measurement of quantities, it relies on a system of mathematical signs, or directions. The most commonly used ones appear below:

- $+$ plus or positive
- $-$ minus or negative
- $\pm$ plus or minus, positive or negative
- $\cdot$ multiplied by
- $\div$ or $/$ divided by
- $=$ equal to
- $\neq$ not equal to
- $\approx$ approximately equal to
- $\sim$ of the order of or similar to
- $>$ greater than
- $<$ less than
- $\geq$ greater than or equal to
- $\leq$ less than or equal to
- $\gg$ much greater than
- $\ll$ much less than
- $\sqrt{}$ square root
- ∞ infinity
- $\propto$ proportional to
- Σ sum of
- Π product of
- Δ difference
- $\therefore$ therefore
- $\angle$ angle
- $\parallel$ parallel to
- $:$ is to (ratio)

Complementary angles exist when two angles total 90 degrees.

Supplementary angles occur when two angles add up to 180 degrees.

Conjugate angles add up to 360 degrees when combined.

TRIANGLES

The sum of the internal angles of a triangle is always 180 degrees.

An **equilateral triangle** has sides that are of equal length and internal angles that are all 60 degrees.

An **isoceles triangle** has two sides that are of equal length and two equal angles.

A **scalene triangle** has no sides and no angles of equal size.

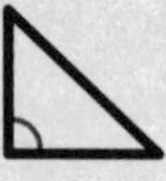

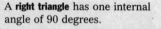

A **right triangle** has one internal angle of 90 degrees.

An **obtuse triangle** has one obtuse angle, which is an angle greater than 90 degrees but less than 180 degrees.

An **acute-angle triangle** has three acute angles, meaning that all are under 90 degrees.

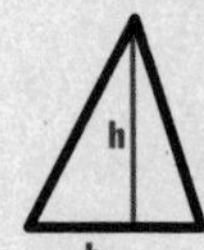

To calculate the area of a triangle, multiply the base by the height by one-half:

$$A = (1/2)bh$$

QUADRILATERALS

A quadrilateral is a four-sided polygon.

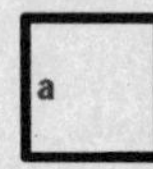

A **square** has four equal sides and four right angles. To calculate the area of a square, square the length of one side:

$$A = a^2$$

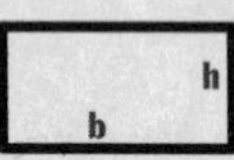

A **rectangle** has equal opposite sides and all right angles. To calculate a rectangle's area, multiply base by height:

$$A = bh$$

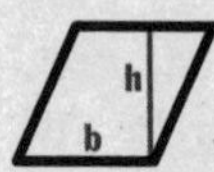

A **rhombus** has equal sides and no right angles. To calculate its area, multiply base by height:

$$A = bh$$

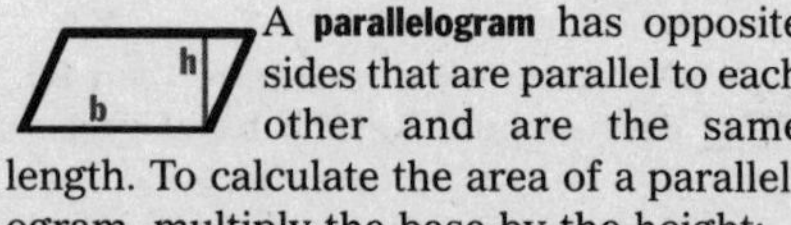

A **parallelogram** has opposite sides that are parallel to each other and are the same length. To calculate the area of a parallelogram, multiply the base by the height:

$$A = bh$$

OTHER POLYGONS

A **pentagon** is a five-sided polygon. To calculate the approximate area of a pentagon, multiply the square of the length of one side by 1.721:

$$A = 1.721a^2$$

A **hexagon** is a six-sided polygon. To calculate the approximate area of a hexagon, multiply the square of the length of one side by 2.598:

$$A = 2.598a^2$$

An **octagon** is an eight-sided polygon. To calculate the approximate area of an octagon: multiply the square of the length of one side by 4.828:

$$A = 4.828a^2$$

A **circle** is a figure in which every point on its boundary is equidistant from the center. The radius is that distance to the center. The diameter is twice the radius, or the longest distance across the circle. The circumference is the total distance around the boundary of the circle. To calculate the area of a circle, multiply the square of the radius by pi (3.1416...):

$$A = \pi r^2$$

To calculate the circumference of a circle, multiply radius of the circle by 2 and by pi (3.1416...):

$$C = 2\pi r$$

SOLIDS

Solids are three-dimensional geometric objects that exist in space.

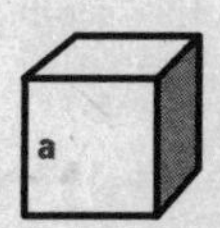

A **cube** is a solid with six equal, square sides. To calculate the surface area of a cube, multiply the square of the length of one side by 6:

$$S = 6a^2$$

To calculate the volume of a cube, cube the length of one side:

$$V = a^3$$

THE INS AND OUTS OF A RIGHT TRIANGLE

The relationships between the angles of a right triangle and its sides have been studied by mathematicians for millennia. Among the important trigonometric concepts are:

SINE: In a right triangle, the ratio of the opposite side of a given acute angle to the hypotenuse is known as the sine of that angle.

SINE OF ANGLE $A = a \div c$

COSINE: In a right triangle, the ratio of the adjacent side of an acute angle to the hypotenuse is known as the cosine of that angle.

COSINE OF ANGLE $A = b \div c$

TANGENT: In a right triangle, the ratio of the opposite to the adjacent side of an acute angle is known as the angle's tangent.

TANGENT OF $A = a \div b$

COTANGENT: In a right triangle, the ratio of the adjacent side of an acute angle to the opposite side is known as the angle's cotangent.

COTANGENT OF ANGLE $A = b \div a$

THE PYTHAGOREAN THEOREM: In a right triangle the square of the hypotenuse is equal to the sum of the square of the other two sides.

$$c^2 = a^2 + b^2$$

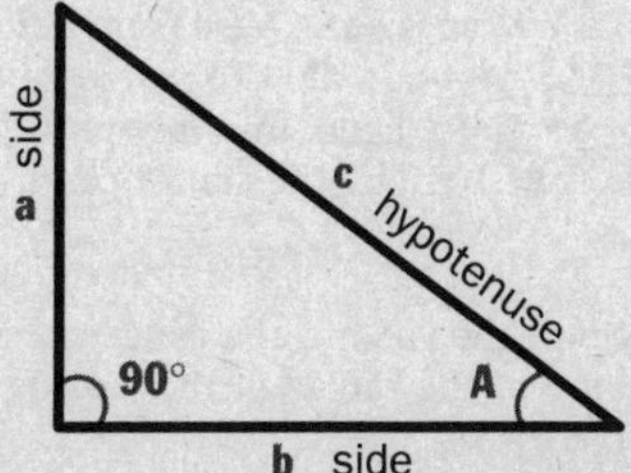

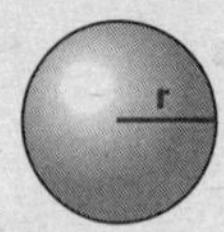

A **sphere** is a body whose surface is equally distant from the center at all points. To calculate the surface area of a sphere, multiply 4 by pi (3.1416...) by the square of the radius:

$$S = 4\pi r^2$$

To calculate the volume of a sphere, multiply the cube of the radius by pi by 4/3:

$$V = (4/3)\pi r^3$$

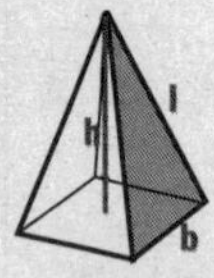

A **pyramid** is a shape with a square base and four sloping triangular sides meeting at the top. To calculate the surface area of a pyramid, multiply base by length, and multiply 2 by the base and by the height, and add the results:

$$S = bl + 2bh$$

To calculate a pyramid's volume, multiply the base's area by height and by 1/3:

$$V = (1/3)bh$$

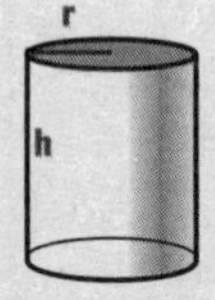

A **cylinder** is a solid described by a line that always has a point in common with a given closed curve. To calculate the surface area of a right, circular cylinder, multiply 2 by pi by radius by height:

$$S = 2\pi rh$$

To calculate the volume, multiply the square of the radius of the base by pi by height:

$$V = \pi r^2 h$$

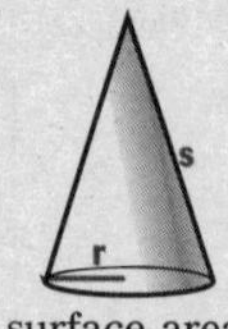

A **cone** is a flat-based, single-pointed solid formed by a rotating straight line that traces out a base from a fixed vertex point. To calculate the surface area of a cone, multiply pi by the radius of the base by the slant height (s):

$$S = \pi rs$$

To calculate the volume of a cone, multiply the square of the radius of the base by pi by height by 1/3.

$$V = (1/3)\pi r^2 h$$

BUILDING BLOCKS OF MATTER

The periodic table of elements includes them all

The periodic table of the elements was first devised in the 19th century to show the atomic weights of the elements and to group them by similar properties. The discovery of protons and electrons in atoms in the early 20th century gave rise to a new and more accurate arrangement of the elements in a periodic table. This new arrangement is based on the atomic number, which is the number of protons (positively charged particles) present in the atomic nucleus of an element.

The table lists the elements in horizontal rows (or periods), according to their atomic numbers. Each vertical column (except hydrogen in the first column) groups elements that have related properties and are likely to behave similarly in chemical reactions. Except for hydrogen, the elements on the left side of the table are metals while those in the last six columns are predominantly nonmetals. In those columns, a heavier, stepped boundary line separates the metals from the nonmetals.

Hydrogen is the lightest and simplest element in the table. It has many unique properties different from all other elements. For example, in chemical reactions, it can give up or acquire an electron from other elements, which are incapable of transferring electrons both ways.

Besides the atomic number, the periodic table also lists each element's name, chemical symbol, and atomic weight (or atomic mass). Atomic weight is the mass of an atom relative to the mass of an atom of carbon-12, which is arbitrarily assigned an atomic weight of 12 by an international convention.

THE PERIODIC TABLE OF ELEMENTS

Key: 6 — Atomic number; **C** — Chemical symbol; 12.01 — Atomic mass; Carbon — Name of element

Alkali metals (I A); Alkaline earth metals (II A); Transition metals (III B – II B); Nonmetals (III A – VII A); Noble gases (0); Other metals

	I A	II A	III B	IV B	V B	VI B	VII B	VIII	VIII	VIII	I B	II B	III A	IV A	V A	VI A	VII A	0
Period 1	1 **H** 1.01 Hydrogen																	2 **He** 4.00 Helium
Period 2	3 **Li** 6.94 Lithium	4 **Be** 9.01 Beryllium											5 **B** 10.81 Boron	6 **C** 12.01 Carbon	7 **N** 14.01 Nitrogen	8 **O** 16.00 Oxygen	9 **F** 19.00 Fluorine	10 **Ne** 20.18 Neon
Period 3	11 **Na** 23.00 Sodium	12 **Mg** 24.31 Magnesium											13 **Al** 26.98 Aluminum	14 **Si** 28.09 Silicon	15 **P** 30.97 Phosphorus	16 **S** 32.06 Sulfur	17 **Cl** 35.45 Chlorine	18 **Ar** 39.95 Argon
Period 4	19 **K** 39.10 Potassium	20 **Ca** 40.08 Calcium	21 **Sc** 44.96 Scandium	22 **Ti** 47.90 Titanium	23 **V** 50.94 Vanadium	24 **Cr** 52.00 Chromium	25 **Mn** 54.94 Manganese	26 **Fe** 55.85 Iron	27 **Co** 58.93 Cobalt	28 **Ni** 58.71 Nickel	29 **Cu** 63.55 Copper	30 **Zn** 65.37 Zinc	31 **Ga** 69.72 Gallium	32 **Ge** 72.59 Germanium	33 **As** 74.92 Arsenic	34 **Se** 78.96 Selenium	35 **Br** 79.90 Bromine	36 **Kr** 83.80 Krypton
Period 5	37 **Rb** 85.47 Rubidium	38 **Sr** 87.62 Strontium	39 **Y** 88.91 Yttrium	40 **Zr** 91.22 Zirconium	41 **Nb** 92.91 Niobium	42 **Mo** 95.94 Molybdenum	43 **Tc** 98.91 Technetium	44 **Ru** 101.07 Ruthenium	45 **Rh** 102.91 Rhodium	46 **Pd** 106.4 Palladium	47 **Ag** 107.87 Silver	48 **Cd** 112.40 Cadmium	49 **In** 114.82 Indium	50 **Sn** 118.69 Tin	51 **Sb** 121.75 Antimony	52 **Te** 127.60 Tellurium	53 **I** 126.90 Iodine	54 **Xe** 131.30 Xenon
Period 6	55 **Cs** 132.91 Cesium	56 **Ba** 137.34 Barium		72 **Hf** 178.49 Hafnium	73 **Ta** 180.95 Tantalum	74 **W** 183.85 Tungsten	75 **Re** 186.2 Rhenium	76 **Os** 190.2 Osmium	77 **Ir** 192.22 Iridium	78 **Pt** 195.09 Platinum	79 **Au** 196.97 Gold	80 **Hg** 200.59 Mercury	81 **Ti** 204.37 Thallium	82 **Pb** 207.2 Lead	83 **Bi** 208.98 Bismuth	84 **Po** (209) Polonium	85 **At** (210) Astatine	86 **Rn** (222) Radon
Period 7	87 **Fr** (223) Francium	88 **Ra** (226) Radium		104 **Rf** (261) Rutherfordium	105 **Ha** (262) Hahnium	106 (263)	107 (262)	108 (265)	109 (266)									

Rare earth elements

Lanthanide series	57 **La** 138.91 Lanthanum	58 **Ce** 140.12 Cerium	59 **Pr** 140.91 Praseodymium	60 **Nd** 144.24 Neodymium	61 **Pm** (145) Promethium	62 **Sm** 150.4 Samarium	63 **Eu** 151.96 Europium	64 **Gd** 157.25 Gadolinium	65 **Tb** 158.93 Terbium	66 **Dy** 162.50 Dysprosium	67 **Ho** 164.93 Holmium	68 **Er** 167.26 Erbium	69 **Tm** 168.93 Thulium	70 **Yb** 173.04 Ytterbium	71 **Lu** 174.97 Lutetium
Actinide series	89 **Ac** (227) Actinium	90 **Th** 232.04 Thorium	91 **Pa** 231.04 Protactinium	92 **U** 238.03 Uranium	93 **Np** 237.05 Neptunium	94 **Pu** (244) Plutonium	95 **Am** (243) Americium	96 **Cm** (247) Curium	97 **Bk** (247) Berkelium	98 **Cf** (251) Californium	99 **Es** (254) Einsteinium	100 **Fm** (257) Fermium	101 **Md** (258) Mendelevium	102 **No** (255) Nobelium	103 **Lw** (256) Lawrencium

TRADITIONS

TAKING OFF THE WHITE GLOVES

Savoir-faire today means faring with newfangled families and devices

It used to be that rules of etiquette were fairly cut and dry, and most folks followed them strictly. Married women took their husband's last name. Second marriages were rare—third marriages almost unheard of. Couples wouldn't dream of living together before they were married. There were no fax machines, beepers, or cellular phones.

But women's liberation, new technology, and the inevitable passing of time have revamped our lifestyles and created a new age of etiquette confusion. Now issues from hyphenated last names to call waiting test our good manners almost daily. For those who are just trying to keep up, here's a primer.

WOMEN'S NAMES

■ **Never-married women:** Miss is the traditional title for an unmarried woman of any age, but today it is best used when addressing girls younger than 18. "It is still used in addressing adult single women on formal invitations, but it is no longer necessary even there," notes etiquette expert Letitia Baldrige in her book *The New Manners for the '90s.* A more sophisticated (and professional) title for unmarried women: "Ms."

■ **Married women:** Traditionally, a married woman's name consists of her first name, maiden name, and husband's last name (Bridget Fox Read becomes Bridget Read Saunders when she marries). Some women prefer to keep their middle name and drop their maiden name (Bridget Fox Saunders). In either case, she should be formally addressed by using Mrs. with her husband's first name (Mrs. Richard Saunders), or Ms. with her own first name (Ms. Bridget Saunders).

Correspondence to the couple should be addressed as either "Mr. and Mrs." followed by the man's name (Mr. and Mrs. Richard Saunders), or "Mr. and Ms." followed by their first and last names (Mr. Richard Saunders and Ms. Bridget Saunders). A married woman should not be addressed as Mrs. with her own first name (Mrs. Bridget Saunders). That combination is reserved for divorced women.

Less traditional—but increasingly popular—is the practice of a married woman keeping her maiden name. In this case, the title "Ms." should precede the name she used before marriage (Ms. Bridget Fox Read). If she decides to use her maiden name in both business and social settings,

EXPERT TIPS

DINNER IS SERVED, MADAM

Tips for giving a traditional dinner party—beyond table manners

"The most important aspect of entertaining is the people," says Ellen Brown, cookbook author and food writer. "Many hosts give great thought to what they're serving rather than with whom they're breaking bread." Brown's rule for a successful dinner party is that everyone should know somebody (even if it's only the host or hostess), but no one should know everybody. "Entertaining should offer everyone the opportunity to expand their circle of friends," she says.

No matter how scintillating the guests are, a dinner party will flop if the party-giver isn't relaxed. "The point of the evening is to spend time with your guests, and not in the kitchen," says Brown.

This means selecting a menu that can be prepared almost entirely in advance. "Entertaining isn't about gourmet cooking," says the master chef. " If you feel lacking in culinary competence, you can do a wonderful party with take-out food from the supermarket, or frozen hors d'oevres. Brunches and dessert parties are a less expensive way to entertain and still accomplish the goal of the traditional dinner party."

FORMAL PLACE SETTING

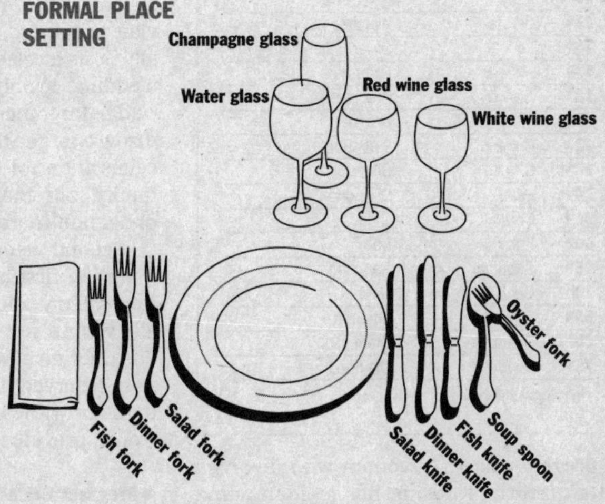

she should not be addressed as "Mrs." Correspondence to the couple should have both names (Mr. Richard Saunders and Ms. Bridget Read) on the same line.

Some married women prefer to use their maiden name at work and their husband's last name at home. In that case, the woman should be addressed as "Ms." at work (Ms. Bridget Read and either "Ms." or "Mrs." in social situations (Ms. Bridget Saunders or Mrs. Richard Saunders). Although potentially confusing, this set-up offers the best of each situation; a woman can keep her identity at work while sharing a last name with her husband and children in other settings. Business letters or invitations for the couple should follow the "work" rules (Mr. Richard Saunders and Ms. Bridget Read) while social correspondence should be addressed traditionally (Mr. and Mrs. Richard Saunders).

If a woman chooses to hyphenate her maiden name with her husband's last name, her name should be first (Bridget Read-Saunders). When addressing correspondence to the couple, both names should be used (Mr. Richard Saunders and Ms. Bridget Read-Saunders).

■ AFTER THE FIRST DIAMOND...

Wedding anniversaries and suggested gifts

Year	Traditional Gift	Modern Gift
1st	Paper	Clock
2nd	Cotton	China
3rd	Leather	Crystal or glass
4th	Fruit or flowers	Appliances
5th	Wood	Silverware
6th	Candy or ironware	Wood
7th	Copper or wool	Pens, pencils, desk sets
8th	Pottery or bronze	Linens or laces
9th	Pottery or willow	Leather
10th	Aluminum or tin	Diamond jewelry
11th	Steel	Fashion jewelry and accessories
12th	Silk or linen	Pearls or gems
13th	Lace	Textiles or furs
14th	Ivory	Gold jewelry
15th	Crystal	Watches
16th		Silver hollowware
17th		Furniture
18th		Porcelain
19th		Bronze
20th	China	Platinum
25th*	Silver	Silver
30th	Pearl	Diamond
35th	Coral	Jade
40th	Ruby	Ruby
45th	Sapphire	Sapphire
50th*	Gold	Gold
55th	Emerald	Emerald
60th*	Diamond	Diamond
75th*	Diamond	Diamond

*Indicates Jubilee anniversary.

■ **Divorced women:** A woman who divorces often returns to using her maiden name (Ms. Bridget Fox Read). But when she has children, it can be confusing for her to use a last name different from theirs. "When your family members use different surnames, for whatever reason, make sure that those who need to know are informed. A child's school should be told, as would your own office staff, for informational purposes only" advises etiquette expert Elizabeth L. Post in her book, *Emily Post's Etiquette.*

If a divorced woman has children and wants to keep their last name, she should use her first name—not her husband's (Mrs. Bridget Saunders). This way, she is easily identified as both a divorced woman and as the children's parent.

■ **Widows:** Until she remarries, a woman keeps her husband's name, and she is addressed the same way as a married woman (Mrs. Richard Saunders or Ms. Bridget Saunders). If she marries again, she can use either her former husband's last name or her maiden name as a middle name (Bridget Saunders Franklin or Bridget Read Franklin).

WEDDINGS

■ **Second Weddings:** When both the bride and groom have been married before, they usually pay for most of a simple wedding celebration themselves. (It's a wonder how appealing simplicity looks from that perspective.) If only the groom has been previously married, then the bride's family usually hosts a celebration akin to that of a first wedding. If only the bride has been married before, then the couple may decide to throw a larger-than-usual second wedding celebration for the benefit of the groom's family, but the bride's parents have no obligation to pay for it.

Second weddings usually are less formal than first ones. Brides wear a suit or dress of any color, and no veil. Grooms usually wear a suit and tie. The bride's father does not give her away, as that is a tradition reserved for first weddings. Attendants or witnesses might include children from a previous marriage, or close friends.

■ **Pregnant Brides:** Depending on how comfortable she is with her condition, a pregnant bride can choose a long wedding gown or a maternity dress in white or another light color. Traditionally, a bridal veil is a symbol of virginity, so she should opt against it. Post suggests that these weddings be simple, "so that the couple does not appear to flaunt their situation in society's face." Announcements sent by the bride's parents suggest that they support the couple in their decision.

RELATIONSHIPS

■ **Divorce:** A divorced woman does not wear her engagement ring on the fourth finger of her left hand. She may have the stone reset into a bracelet or necklace or keep it for her children's use later. A divorced couple does not return wedding gifts. A recently divorced person's friends should be supportive and sympathetic without prying for details. "If you love both people, don't take sides," suggests Baldrige. "Your job, as a friend, is to try to get each member of the couple into an affirmative, cheerful mood once again."

If children are involved, both sides of the family should be respectful of the other side's efforts to spend time with the children. Also important: one parent should not criticize the other in front of their children, even if the impulse is nearly irresistible.

■ **Living Together:** When addressing mail to an unmarried couple that lives together, each name should be on a separate line, and their names should not be joined by the word *and*.

When introducing couples who live together, most labels sound awkward (boyfriend, significant other, date), so it is best to forgo the explanation and simply introduce each person by name.

HIGH-TECH MANNERS

■ **Call waiting:** The best advice is not to succumb to this rudeness at all. But if you must and your conversation is interrupted by a beep signaling another call on your line, sound sincere in your apology to the person with whom you are talking. Switch to the other caller, and quickly explain to him or her that you'll call back. Then return to the original conversation and apologize again.

■ **Answering machines:** Keep outgoing messages clear and brief. Avoid playing elevator music or telling jokes if you don't want to be annoying. Remember that it's unnecessary to say that you can't get to the phone—that will be obvious to the caller.

A sample outgoing message: "Hello, you have reached (your name and/or phone number). Please leave your name, phone number, and message, and the date and time you called, and we'll call you back as soon as we can."

When leaving a message on an answering machine, follow the same rules: be brief and clear, and leave all the information requested in the outgoing message.

Try not to hold an extended one-way conversation unless you don't really want to talk to the person you're calling, anyway.

■ **Call forwarding:** This telephone feature allows you to send all of your calls to another phone number, usually the phone of a family or friend where you'll be for at least a few hours. It is handy for the person who has forwarded the calls, but call forwarding can be a huge inconvenience to a host, particularly one that already has to contend with the phone habits of teenagers under the same roof. If you forward your calls, be sure to ask permission from the person who will answer the line where your calls will ring. And when you receive a call at someone else's house, keep it brief.

■ **Beepers:** If you are paged, turn off your beeper immediately, and then politely excuse yourself to make the necessary phone calls. You are not required to reveal the nature of the call unless you must leave the dinner party, show, or other event.

■ **Cellular phones:** When calling a car phone or another cellular phone, remember that the person receiving the call is paying dearly for it. Keep the conversation brief and to the point. Also remember that no cellular phone conversation is completely private—your voice may be accidentally broadcast on another cellular phone, or, worse yet, purposely picked up by an ill-willed eavesdropper. And most important—don't kill anybody by having an accident while using a car phone.

GENEALOGY

TRACING YOUR FAMILY TREE

It's amazing how much you can learn about ancestors if you look

Descended from the Highlands? Ascended from the Lowlands? Are there drops of blood from Genghis Khan, Dr. Livingston, or Sor Juana de la Cruz coursing through your veins? Does that racy family secret really have any truth to it?

Whatever your reason for peering into your family's past, you need not be alone in your quest. Thanks to the growing popularity of genealogical research, there is a wealth of resources for tracing family origins, as Erma Angevine, director of The National Genealogical Society's Home Study Program, points out below. For detailed information on Angevine's references, see the Expert Sources box at the article's conclusion.

FAMILY RECORDS

Gather all the information you can from relatives and family memorabilia before delving into published sources. The more clues you have to begin with, the better. One of the first pitfalls for a genealogist can be over-eagerness. Learn early to write down, in detail, where, when, and why a search was made and the results of that search.

Remember that much of what you discover will be clues, not facts. Veteran researchers will warn you that word-of-mouth lore should be verified by consulting official records. Valuable family items include: birth, death, and marriage certificates, baptism and christening records, family bibles, diaries, old letters, newspaper clippings, photographs, school records, scrapbooks, military discharge papers, naturalization records, and passports. Pay attention to names of places, as they will be especially useful to you.

GENEALOGICAL SOCIETIES AND LIBRARIES

See what local archives might have before hitting the road in search of important documents. Certain genealogical societies and libraries have copies of records normally available only through government sources.

The Church of Jesus Christ of Latter-day Saints has the largest genealogical collection in the country. Beside maintaining a library open to the public in Salt Lake City, Utah, the church runs local family centers all over the country where one can order microfilm and copies of many types of records. These centers are open to all interested parties, regardless of religious affiliation. They can be located by calling a local Mormon organization.

The Church of the Latter-day Saints also has a Family Search CD-ROM program available both through the LDS Family Centers, the Library of Congress, and other genealogical societies and libraries. You should consult a local society or library to find out how you can access this program and what others might be available and helpful to you. The next two largest collections are maintained by the New York Public Library Research Libraries and the Library of Congress. Other noteworthy collections are those kept by the Daughters of the American Revolution and the National Genealogical Society in Washington, D.C., the Newberry Library in Chicago, the New England Historic Genealogical Society in Boston, the Bancroft Library at the University of California's Berkeley campus, the

Western Reserve Historical Society in Cleveland, and the Fort Wayne, Indiana, Public Library.

To find out whether there is a genealogical society with a good library in your vicinity, consult the Directory of Historical Societies and Agencies in the United States and Canada, published by the American Association for State and Local History.

■ LOCAL AND FAMILY HISTORIES

Consult local references early in your research. You may discover that another member of your family has investigated and documented the lineage of a certain branch of your family, saving you much time. Many local histories were either commissioned by local leaders or written with the purpose of being sold in the community; they are full of "good upstanding Americans," "hardworking farmers," and "devout Christian mothers." If you are fortunate enough to run across unusual details of your family, keep in mind that the information may not be accurate and should be verified through other sources.

To see if a history has been published of the county or locality in which your ancestors lived, consult Marion J. Kaminkow's *United States Local Histories in the Library of Congress* and P. William Filby's *A Bibliography of American County Histories*. To find out if a genealogy has been published on your family, also look in Kaminkow's *Genealogies in the Library of Congress* or in Netti Schreiner-Yantis's *Genealogical and Local History Books in Print*.

■ U.S. CENSUS

Use census records not only to pinpoint an ancestor's location in a given year, but also to glean detailed information about a person's life. Depending on the year of the census, records might include data such as birthdates for each individual in the family, number of years married for each couple, number of children, whether a residence was rented or owned, whether the residence was a home or farm, and whether it was mortgaged. For foreign-born individuals, a census may have included the year of immigration and whether the person was naturalized or not. The National Archives has microfilmed all existing census records for the period from 1790 to 1920 (conducted every 10 years). You should begin in 1920 and work backward.

To find your relatives' records, you should consult a census index if there is one. Look up your ancestor's name within the state and county in which he or she lived. If it is not indexed, you may have to search all the names in a county. Published indexes are now available for all states for censuses from 1790 to 1830 and can be found in many libraries. The 1880, 1900, 1920, and 1940 censuses are coded in a different way from earlier ones; for a full explanation of this system, you will need to consult the National Archives free booklet entitled, *Getting Started: Beginning Your Genealogical Research in the National Archives.*

Once you have figured out which census records are the most likely to bear fruit, you can obtain and use census microfilm in the following ways:

- Visit the National Archives in Washington, D.C., or one of the 12 regional archives.

EXPERT TIP

You can hire a genealogical sleuth. There are professional genealogists with an incredible array of specialties, from those who work in untranslated Spanish archives to experts in tracking indentured servants. To receive a list of certified genealogists in your area, write:

Board for Certification
of Genealogists
P.O. Box 5816
Falmouth, VA 22403

The Microfilm Reading Rooms are open to all researchers, Monday and Wednesday, 8:45 a.m. to 5:00 p.m.; Tuesday, Thursday, and Friday, 8:45 a.m. to 9:00 p.m.; and Saturday, 8:45 p.m. to 4:30 p.m.

- Rent census microfilm through your local library from the Census Microfilm Rental Program.
- Purchase microfilm from the National Archives.
- Use census microfilm at the LDS Family History Library in Salt Lake City and at its family history centers throughout the country. You do not need to belong to the Church of the Latter-day Saints to use the LDS Family History Library or its family centers.
- Census microfilm can also be found at many state libraries, state archives, and historical and genealogical society libraries.

VITAL RECORDS

Write to state agencies or county and town offices for copies of their vital records once you have learned approximate dates and places for the births, marriages, and deaths of your ancestors.

Records of births, deaths, and marriages, wills, estate settlements, and deeds are among the most useful records. Records created by the state or kept at the state level may be found in the state archives, the state vital records office, the state land office, or the state adjutant general's office. The state archives may also be the custodian of older county records. County records not transferred to the state archives are usually found in county courthouses. In certain parts of the country, vital records are kept in town halls.

For detailed information on the types of records kept and where to find them, you should consult a published guide. The National Genealogical Society suggests the following books: *Ancestry's Red Book: American State, County & Town Sources*, which contains an overview of the records in each state and the year of the earliest birth, marriage, death, land, probate, and court records in each county; *Bentley's County Courthouse Book*, which gives the address of each county courthouse in the United States; and *Kemp's International Vital Records Handbook*, which includes vital records order forms used in each state that can be photocopied.

MILITARY RECORDS

Don't overlook compiled military service records and pension application files. Compiled Military Service Records consist of rank, military unit, dates of service, presence on payrolls, and dates of discharge, desertion, or death. Pension application files are likely to include much more genealogical information, such as spouse's name, maiden name, certified vital records, birthplace, place of residence, and names and ages of children.

Indexes to these records can be viewed at the National Archives Central Reference Room in Washington, D.C., as well as at certain genealogical libraries. While the federal government stores the most military records, certain state archives and libraries hold additional records and thus should also be consulted.

PASSENGER ARRIVAL RECORDS

Search passenger arrival records to find your immigrant ancestor. Between the years of 1607 and 1920, over 30 million immigrants came to the shores of America, but Congress did not enact a law requiring ships' masters to file passenger lists until 1817. The National Archives and its regional archives have some helpful records. They include passenger and arrival records from the early 19th century through the 1950s. There are very few lists prior to 1820. All passenger arrival records and indexes have been microfilmed and are available in the Microfilm Reading Room. Depending on the year and circumstance of immigration, records may or may not exist.

The easiest way to access these records is to know the year your ancestor arrived, the port through which he or she entered this country, and the name of the ship. If you don't know this information, try consulting P. William Filby's and Mary K. Meyer's three-volume work, *Passenger and Immigration Lists Index*. While the list is not complete, their index is the largest of its kind, currently including over one million names consolidated from close to 1,000 sources.

EXPERT SOURCES

WHERE TO FIND FAMILY GHOSTS

If you're ready to track down the family history, the following archives and publications are a treasure trove of genealogical information

PUBLICATIONS

ANCESTRY'S RED BOOK: AMERICAN STATE, COUNTY & TOWN SOURCES
Alice Eichholz, ed., Ancestry Publications, 1992, $39.95

THE ARCHIVES: A GUIDE TO THE NATIONAL ARCHIVES FIELD BRANCHES
Loretto Dennis Szucks and Sandra Hargreaves Luebking, Ancestry Publications, 1988, $39.95

A BIBLIOGRAPHY OF AMERICAN COUNTY HISTORIES
P. William Filby, Genealogical Publishing Co., 1985, $24.95

COMPUTER GENEALOGY: A GUIDE TO RESEARCH THROUGH HIGH TECHNOLOGY
Richard A. Pence, ed., Ancestry, 1991, $12.95

COUNTY COURTHOUSE BOOK
Elizabeth Petty Bentley, Genealogical Publishing Co., 1990, $29.95

DIRECTORY OF GENEALOGICAL AND HISTORICAL SOCIETY PUBLICATIONS IN THE UNITED STATES AND CANADA
Dina C. Carson, Iron Gate Pub., 1994, $85

DIRECTORY OF HISTORICAL ORGANIZATIONS, AND AGENCIES IN THE UNITED STATES AND CANADA
Mary K. Meyer, AASLH, 1990, $79.95

GENEALOGICAL AND LOCAL HISTORY BOOKS IN PRINT
Netti Schreiner-Yantis, GBIP, 1981, $15

GENEALOGIES IN THE LIBRARY OF CONGRESS
Marion J. Kaminkow, Magna Carta Book Co., 1981, $95

PASSENGER AND IMMIGRATION LISTS INDEX
P. William Filby and Mary K. Meyer, Gale Research Co., 1980, 3 vols., $440

WHERE TO WRITE FOR VITAL RECORDS: BIRTHS, DEATHS, MARRIAGES, AND DIVORCES
U.S. Department of Health and Human Services, Publication PHS-93-1142, 1993, $1.75

LIBRARIES

ALLEN COUNTY LIBRARY
Fred J. Reynolds Historical Genealogical Department
900 Webster St.
Fort Wayne, IN 46802
☎ 219-424-7241

BANCROFT LIBRARY
University of California
Berkeley, CA 94720
☎ 415-642-3773

FAMILY HISTORY LIBRARY
The Church of Jesus Christ of the Latter-day Saints
35 N. Temple
Salt Lake City, UT 84150
☎ 801-240-2584

LIBRARY OF CONGRESS
Local History and Genealogy Reading Room (LJG20)
Washington, D.C. 20540
☎ 202-707-5537

NATIONAL ARCHIVES
Genealogy Division
Washington, D.C. 20408
☎ 202-501-5410

GENEALOGICAL SOCIETIES

AFRICAN AMERICAN FAMILY HISTORY ASSOCIATION
P.O. Box 115268
Atlanta, GA 30310
☎ 404-730-4001

NATIONAL SOCIETY OF THE DAUGHTERS OF THE AMERICAN REVOLUTION
1776 D St. NW
Washington, D.C. 20006
☎ 202-628-1776

NATIONAL GENEALOGICAL SOCIETY
4527 17th St. North
Arlington, VA 22207
☎ 703-525-0050

INDEX

A

B

C

D

E

F

H

J

K

L

N

P

Q

R

S

T

U

V

W

ACKNOWLEDGEMENTS

No book can go from idea stage to the printed page without the support of many patrons. *The Practical Guide* has been blessed with more than its share of believers. No one has been more constant in his encouragement of this project, or in his efforts to make it a reality than our publisher, Harold Evans at Random House. We owe him a great debt of gratitude for the faith he has shown in us. An enormous thanks, too, to our editor, Jonathan Karp, whose editorial savvy and attentiveness to this endeavor has only been matched by his sense of humor throughout. The effort that Harry and Jon and all their colleagues at Random House have made on our behalf has been remarkable.

There would be no book, of course, without the generosity of the many experts who shared their time and knowledge with us. Their commitment to explaining what they know as clearly and concisely as possible is a testament to their professionalism. Whatever mistakes that have been made are ours, of course, not theirs.

Many people assisted us in the book's creation, and we thank them all for the care and flair with which they did their work. Janice Olson, Luke Mitchell, Anna Mulrine, Jill Hockman, Rachel Englehart, and Rachel Schwartz were indispensable in the roles they played, and we thank them very much. A special bow is also due our design consultant, Rob Covey, who created the basic look of the book, and our illustrator, Steve McCracken, and chartmaker, David Merrill. Kathy Yates and her colleagues at Applied Graphics Technology were a great help, as were Michael Van Damm of Morningstar Mutual Funds, Steve Grumbacher of the American Red Cross, Dr. Dearing Johns of the University of Virginia School of Medicine, and Cindy Goldman and Joan Reinthaler of The Sidwell Friends School. Thanks, too, for the fast work and good cheer of our copy editors Patricia Abdale, Michael Burke, Vicky Macintyre, and Eva Young, our computer specialist, Mary Yee, and our indexer, Sydney Cohen and his colleagues. Our attorney, Robert Barnett, also played a pivotal role, and we benefited greatly from the professional advice of Robert Jensen and Richard Linden during the book's start-up phase.

We can't say enough for our friends and colleagues at *U.S. News & World Report,* where we are fortunate to have the support and encouragement of our editor-in-chief, Mortimer Zuckerman, and the magazine's co-editors, Merrill McLoughlin and Mike Ruby. Kathy Bushkin never fails to make everything easier. Mary Jean Hopkins and Cornelia Carter always pitch in when needed, Kathy Trimble and the *U.S. News* library staff are the best in the business, Elizabeth Gross is a great talent scout, and Susan LeClair is a paradigm of efficiency. Our friend and former colleague Edwin Taylor also contributes more than he can realize from afar.

The greatest credit—and gratitude—for seeing us through this undertaking must go to our families. Our parents, Robert and Helen Bernstein and James and Margaret Ma, deserve much of the credit for whatever common sense we may have. Our spouses, Nathalie Gilfoyle and Amy Bernstein, and our children, Olivia, Rohan, Elisabeth, Alexander, and Nicholas, more than make up for what we lack. We especially thank them for all that they have done to get us to this page of *The Practical Guide to Practically Everything.*

Christopher Ma and Peter Bernstein

READER'S QUESTIONNAIRE

From the editors

WE'D LIKE TO HEAR FROM YOU,

Please help shape the next edition of *The Practical Guide to Practically Everything*. We need to know what you liked about this book—and what you'd like to see done differently—so that we can make next year's version even more useful to you. Let us know if we've made a mistake or left out an important piece of information. And share with us your ideas for what to include next time so that *The Practical Guide* will become as much your book as ours. We look forward to your suggestions.

1. Would you like more, less, or the same amount of coverage of the following subjects?

	MORE	LESS	THE SAME
MONEY	❑	❑	❑
HEALTH	❑	❑	❑
SEXUALITY	❑	❑	❑
EDUCATION	❑	❑	❑
CAREERS	❑	❑	❑
HOUSE & GARDEN	❑	❑	❑
TRAVEL	❑	❑	❑
SPORTS	❑	❑	❑
ENTERTAINMENT	❑	❑	❑
AUTOS	❑	❑	❑
COMPUTERS	❑	❑	❑
THE U.S.A.	❑	❑	❑
THE WORLD	❑	❑	❑
FACTS FOR LIFE	❑	❑	❑

2. Should more editorial attention be paid to any of the following groups?

Teenagers ❑	Young adults ❑	People at midlife ❑
Seniors ❑	Single people ❑	Couples ❑
Families ❑	Families in which both spouses work ❑	Families with young children ❑

READER'S QUESTIONNAIRE

3. Was there any chapter or article that you particularly liked—or disliked?

4. Do you have a question that you would like to see answered, or a subject or expert that you would like to see included in next year's book? Please be as specific as possible.

5. Would you be interested in receiving updated information on the subjects included in *The Practical Guide* more often than once-a-year?

ONLINE ❑ NEWSLETTER ❑ OTHER PERIODICAL ❑

Your name (optional):

Your address (optional):

Questionnaires should be returned to:

THE PRACTICAL GUIDE, c/o Random House
201 East 50th St., New York, NY 10022

We look forward to hearing from you and thank you for your suggestions.